Encyclopedia of
American Film Comedy

Garland Reference Library of the Humanities
(Vol. 744)

Encyclopedia of
American Film Comedy

Larry Langman

Garland Publishing, Inc.
New York & London   1987

Library of Congress Cataloging-in-Publication Data

Langman, Larry.
Encyclopedia of American film comedy.

(Garland reference library of the humanities; vol. 744)
Bibliography: p.
1. Comedy films—United States—Dictionaries.
I. Title. II. Series.
PN1995.9.C55L34 1987   791.43'09'0917   87-11837
ISBN 0-8240-8496-9 (alk. paper)

Printed on acid-free, 250-year-life paper

MANUFACTURED IN THE UNITED STATES OF AMERICA

Contents

Preface

American film comedy plays a significant role in the history of film. A large portion of Hollywood's output over the past 75 years has been devoted to comedy. These films, like those in other genres, tell us much about ourselves as individuals and as a nation. But only a handful of books have dealt with American film humor or recognized the contributions made by so many talented and hard-working people. The *Encyclopedia of American Film Comedy* attempts to remedy this neglect.

This work brings together for the first time within one volume all the major American screen comedians, comediennes, comedy teams, light actors and actresses, and directors and screenwriters who have contributed substantially to silent and sound comedy films. It also includes most of the supporting and character players who have lent their unique talents to the genre.

The book also covers a variety of comedy genres such as screwball comedy, war humor, and romantic comedy. The purposes of discussing these topics are threefold: to recall how structured and repetitive were the practices of Hollywood, to summarize the major trends in the history of American film comedy, and to study their influences on contemporary comedy.

A third entry is the film critique. The selection of these comedies was based on certain criteria. They are representative of a particular comic, comedy team, or genre. Several were landmark films at the time of their release; they may have depicted Chaplin in his tramp costume for the first time or introduced a unique aspect of comedy. The films in this category were, and in many instances still are, popular with audiences. Many of them are highly acclaimed by film historians and critics. But most of all, they uniquely exemplify America's social values at the time of their release while defining the American sense of humor.

A fourth entry covers the series films such as the "Blondie" or "Andy Hardy" comedies. Many of these series were second features—low-budget films turned out by the major studios to appear on the bottom half of the double-feature program popular during the 1930s and 1940s. But they retain their own charm and are often more realistic than the general comedy fare. They usually deal with family and situation humor rather than with grotesque or absurd complications found in the films of Fields, the Marx Brothers, or Abbott and Costello.

Fictional characters in these comedy series comprise another entry. One benefit of the individual listing of these otherwise obscure characters is that the reader may remember a particular name, but can't place the films. Also, some of these fictional characters in many instances emerged as more interesting than the film itself.

The final category concerns general topics such as "animation" or "ethnic humor." The film buff and student will find these entries interesting as well as informative. They survey the topic from the earliest representative silent films to the present.

How the Book Is Arranged

Entries of performers, directors, and screenwriters begin with the dates of birth and death where possible and their principal film career. A short synopsis of their work and/or contributions follows. A filmography, labeled "selected films," concludes each entry. Filmographies are listed chronologically. Many of the above people did not work exclusively in the field of comedy. Others have appeared in hundreds of comedy films, chiefly one- or two-reelers. To keep the book within the confines of its original purposes, that of comedy and a one-volume work, only major light films and comedy shorts are listed. The only exceptions are the first and last entries in each filmography. These, which may not necessarily be comedies, are given to establish the earliest as well as the last contribution of the person.

Individual film entries contain the title, the year of release, distributing company, director, screenwriter(s), and principal players. Full-length feature films within the general text appear in italics, while short films and series titles are in quotation marks. The dates refer to the year of release.

Topic entries usually list films chronologically. Again, features are italicized while short works appear in quotation marks.

Entries of fictional characters are listed alphabetically by their last name. This is usually followed by the name of the film series, the performer who played the role, and a list of representative films.

Entries of comedy series are listed alphabetically by the first word or name; e.g., "Andy Hardy" films will appear under "A."

Cross-references appear in full CAPITALS and apply to persons, series, and topics that have their own entries elsewhere in the encyclopedia.

The author would like to thank several people who have helped in the compilation of this encyclopedia: media consultant Rita Kaikow for the use of certain materials; Little Film Society members John Kelleher, Al Boehmer, and Dr. James Mulvey for their suggestions; Helene Bell and Spencer Fisher for their editorial assistance; film collector Billy Shelley for his private showings of rare films; film researcher Paul Gold for the use of many of his film quotations; Jerry Ohlinger's Movie Material Store in New York City for assisting in the selection of the stills used in this book; and Gary Kuris for his confidence in this project.

Introduction

An anecdote tells about a much-admired veteran stage actor who is lying on his death bed. His closest friends are with him, unable to hold back their tears. The performer, wishing to alleviate their suffering, beckons them closer and whispers: "Dying is easy; comedy is difficult." In his informative book, *The Silent Clowns*, Walter Kerr states that the "business of comedy" is "to reduce pretension, to mock deep seriousness, to ask what could be so lofty about a man whose shirttail was hanging out." These functions apply no less to film comedy than to other forms of comic art. Who are the screen comics who have assumed so difficult a task? Where did they come from? To what extent have they allowed us to see another side of ourselves?

In 1893 an obscure technician assisting Thomas Edison in his many endeavors was photographed as he sneezed. This short scene, which lasts but a few seconds when projected, is known as "Fred Ott's Sneeze" or simply "The Sneeze." This crude little piece of film marks the birth of film comedy in the United States.

But American film comedy as a genre did not really develop until Mack Sennett came upon the scene in 1912. He founded Keystone studios and assembled his collection of clowns who came from vaudeville, the circus, burlesque, the stage, and English music halls. Mainstream films were concerned with dramas, westerns, romances, and a few romantic and western comedies. So the major studios left the area of slapstick comedy shorts to Sennett and a handful of others who tried to emulate his success.

By the 1920s major production companies began to turn out comedies longer than the one- or two-reelers in which Sennett chiefly specialized. Some of his stars broke away and started to appear in longer comedies for other studios, opened their own companies, or worked as second leads in major films. But Sennett, along with other producers such as Hal Roach and Al Christie, continued to grind out comedy shorts throughout the silent period.

With the advent of sound came new problems and challenges. Hollywood moguls hired top writers from Broadway and the literary scene to write comedy dialogue for the new comics, who depended more on verbal humor than on slapstick. Other genres such as sophisticated comedy and screwball comedy, which relied heavily on witty dialogue, blossomed. Comedy teams from the stage appeared first in filmed musical comedies, then in straight comedy films. Some of the brightest silent clowns found themselves relegated to second bananas or bit roles, or, at worst, out of work.

By the 1940s a new crop of comics, including Abbott and Costello and Danny Kaye, emerged while the comedy film as a genre strengthened its position. The only major silent comedian with any standing in the industry was Charlie Chaplin, but his contributions were sporadic. The comics of the 1930s, including the Marx Brothers, Will Rogers, Mae West, and W. C. Fields, either fell from favor or were gone. Some studios had always had their house comics. Paramount featured, among others, Bob Hope, W. C. Fields, and Mae West, while MGM had Red Skelton and Jimmy Durante. Other studios such as Warner Brothers rarely had comedians under contract, relying on their actors to carry the comedy.

Production of comedy films dropped during the 1950s, perhaps because audiences could see the best and the brightest in comedy at home on their television sets. The major comedy team of the 1950s was Dean Martin and Jerry Lewis. Spencer Tracy and Katharine Hepburn made up the principal romantic comedy team. Abbott and Costello, top box-office attractions in the 1940s, could not sustain their popularity in the 1950s. The major comedy directors of the past two decades, Ernst Lubitsch, Frank Capra, and Preston Sturges, were gone or were turning out mediocre films. Creative talents such as Billy Wilder took up the slack, while Judy Holliday, Marilyn Monroe, and Jack Lemmon gained a reputation as comic performers.

Comedy in the 1960s was dominated by sex or bedroom humor, as exemplified by the Doris Day–Rock Hudson films. New writers and directors began to appear on the scene. Neil Simon gave us domestic comedies, while Blake Ed-

wards returned to slapstick with his "Pink Panther" films.

In the next two decades the genre was ruled by dark or black comedy, sex, and a variation of screwball comedy. New writer–directors such as Woody Allen and Mel Brooks dominated the scene, while Simon and Edwards continued to make noteworthy contributions. Comics fresh from television began to appear in a series of offbeat comedies. Steve Martin, Bill Murray, Eddie Murphy, Richard Pryor, Chevy Chase, and Goldie Hawn became comedy stars, especially with young audiences, while traditional comic performers Jack Lemmon, Walter Matthau, and Gene Wilder maintained their popularity.

Obviously, comedy styles change with each decade or generation. It is difficult to predict what the new trends in comedy will be. The important point is that writers, directors, and comics remain free to experiment with new forms. Currently, one of the problems they seem to be facing, concerning their past black-and-white works, is that of colorization. Perhaps somewhere the spirits of former comic talents are looking down and thinking about what is happening to their output. They may want to echo what Charles Laughton said in *It Started with Eve* when he looked at himself following a serious illness: "I've been tampered with!"

Abbreviations Used in this Book

Releasing Companies

AVCO	Avco-Embassy
CIN	Cinerama
COL	Columbia
EMB	Embassy
ES	Essanay
FN	First National
KEY	Keystone
MGM	Metro-Goldwyn-Mayer
MON	Monogram
MUT	Mutual
PAR	Paramount
PAT	Pathe
RKO	RKO Studios
TCF	20th Century-Fox
U	Universal
UA	United Artists
WB	Warner Brothers

Terms

Dir.	Director
Sc.	Screenplay

Sources

Anderson, Janice. *History of Movie Comedy*. New York: Exeter Books, 1985.

Asplund, Uno. *Chaplin's Films*. New York: A.S. Barnes & Co., 1976.

Corliss, Richard. *Talking Pictures*. New York: Penguin Books, 1975.

Cowie, Peter, *Seventy Years of Cinema*. New York: Castle Books, 1969.

Dardis, Tom. *Harold Lloyd: The Man on the Clock*. New York: Penguin Books, 1984.

———. *Keaton: The Man Who Wouldn't Lie Down*. New York: Scribner's, 1979.

Dooley, Roger. *From Scarface to Scarlett: American Films in the 1930s*. New York: Harcourt Brace Jovanovich, 1979.

Eames, John Douglas. *The MGM Story*. New York: Crown Publishers, 1979.

———. *The Paramount Story*. New York: Crown Publishers, 1985.

Edelson, Edward. *Great Kids of the Movies*. Garden City, N.Y.: Doubleday, 1979.

Everson, William K. *The Films of Laurel & Hardy*. Secaucus, N.J.: Citadel, 1967.

Film Daily Year Book of Motion Pictures (annually). New York: Distributed by Arno Press, 1970.

Franklin, Joe. *Encyclopedia of Comedians*. New York: Bell Publishing, 1979.

Griffith, Richard, and Arthur Mayer. *The Movies*. New York: Simon and Schuster, 1957.

Halliwell, Leslie. *The Filmgoer's Companion*. New York: Hill and Wang, 1977.

Hirschhorn, Clive. *The Universal Story*. New York: Crown Publishers, 1983.

———. *The Warner Bros. Story*. New York: Crown Publishers, 1979.

Jewell, Richard B., and Vernon Harbin. *The RKO Story*. New York: Crown Publishers, 1982.

Kaplan, Mike, ed. *Variety Who's Who in Show Business*. New York: Garland Publishing, 1985.

Kerr, Walter. *The Silent Clowns*. New York: Alfred A. Knopf, 1975.

Knight, Arthur. *The Liveliest Art: A Panoramic History of the Movies*. New York: Macmillan, 1957.

Lahue, Kalton C. *World of Laughter: The Motion Picture Comedy Short, 1910–1930*. Norman, Okla.: University of Oklahoma Press, 1966.

———, and Terry Brewer. *Kops and Custards: The Legend of Keystone Films*. Norman, Okla.: University of Oklahoma Press, 1972.

Langman, Larry. *A Guide to American Directors: The Sound Era, 1929–1979* (2 vols.). Metuchen, N.J.: Scarecrow Press, 1981.

———. *A Guide to American Screenwriters: The Sound Era, 1929–1982* (2 vols.). New York: Garland Publishing, 1984.

Maltin, Leonard. *Movie Comedy Teams*. New York: New American Library, 1985.

McCaffrey, Donald W. *The Golden Age of Sound Comedy*. New York: A.S. Barnes, 1973.

Michael, Paul, ed. *The American Movies: A Pictorial Encyclopedia*. New York: Garland Publishing, 1969.

New York Times Film Reviews (1913–1980). New York: Quadrangle Books, Inc.

Parish, James Robert. *Hollywood Character Actors*. Carlstadt, N.J.: Rainbow Books,1979.

Quigley, Martin, Jr., and Richard Gertner. *Films in America, 1929–1969*. New York: Golden Press, 1970.

Quinlan, David. *The Illustrated Encyclopedia of Movie Character Actors*. New York: Harmony Books, 1985.

Ragan, David. *Movie Stars of the '30s*. Englewood Cliffs, N.J.: Prentice-Hall, 1985.

Schickel, Richard. *The Stars*. New York: Crown Publishers, 1962.

Sennett, Mack. *King of Comedy*. Garden City, N.Y.: Doubleday, 1954.

Smith, Ronald Lande. *The Stars of Stand-up Comedy*. New York: Garland Publishing, 1986.

Spears, Jack. *Hollywood: The Golden Era*. New York: Castle Books, 1971.

Walker, Alexander. *The Celluloid Sacrifice*. New York: Hawthorn Books, 1966.

List of Films Treated as Separate Entries*

Adam's Rib (1949)

"Adventurer, The" (1917)

African Queen, The (1951)

Airplane (1980)

American Graffiti (1973)

Animal Crackers (1930)

Annie Hall (1977)

Apartment, The (1960)

Arsenic and Old Lace (1944)

At War With the Army (1950)

Awful Truth, The (1937)

Babes in Toyland (1934)

Bachelor Mother (1939)

Ball of Fire (1941)

Bananas (1971)

Bank Dick, The (1940)

"Barney Oldfield's Race for Life" (1912)

"Battle of the Century" (1927)

"Big Business" (1929)

Blazing Saddles (1974)

Bombshell (1933)

Born Yesterday (1950)

"Brats" (1930)

Brewster's Millions (1945)

Bringing Up Baby (1938)

Broadway Danny Rose (1984)

Buck Privates (1941)

Butch Cassidy and the Sundance Kid (1969)

Cat and the Canary, The (1939)

Charley's Aunt (1941)

Check and Double Check (1930)

City Lights (1931)

Cluny Brown (1946)

Cockeyed Cavaliers (1934)

Cocoanuts, The (1929)

"Cops" (1922)

Court Jester, The (1954)

Cracked Nuts (1931)

"Cure, The" (1917)

Day at the Races, A (1937)

"Dentist, The" (1932)

Destry Rides Again (1939)

Dinner at Eight (1933)

Dr. Strangelove (1964)

Duck Soup (1933)

Easy Living (1937)

"Easy Street" (1917)

Eating Raoul (1982)

Everything You Always Wanted to Know About Sex (1972)

Farmer's Daughter, The (1947)

Father of the Bride (1950)

Fortune Cookie, The (1966)

Freshman, The (1925)

Front Page, The (1931)

Funny Thing Happened on the Way to the Forum, A (1966)

*Titles in quotation marks denote short films.

General, The (1927)

Gold Rush, The (1925)

Graduate, The (1967)

Grandma's Boy (1922)

Great Dictator, The (1940)

Great McGinty, The (1940)

Hail the Conquering Hero (1944)

Hallelujah, I'm a Bum (1933)

Hellzapoppin (1941)

Henry the Rainmaker (1949)

Here Comes Mr. Jordan (1941)

His Girl Friday (1940)

Holiday (1938)

I Married a Witch (1942)

If I Had a Million (1932)

I'm No Angel (1933)

"Immigrant, The" (1917)

International House (1933)

It Happened One Night (1934)

It's a Mad, Mad, Mad, Mad World (1963)

Kid, The (1921)

"Kid Auto Races at Venice" (1914)

Lady Eve, The (1941)

Lady for a Day (1933)

Let's Do It Again (1975)

Limelight (1952)

Long Pants (1927)

Love and Death (1975)

Love Parade, The (1929)

Loved One, The (1965)

Lovers and Other Strangers (1970)

"Making a Living" (1914)

Man Who Came to Dinner, The (1941)

M*A*S*H (1970)

Merrily We Live (1938)

Midnight (1939)

Miracle of Morgan's Creek, The (1944)

Modern Times (1936)

Monsieur Verdoux (1947)

Moon Is Blue, The (1953)

Murder, He Says (1945)

"Music Box, The" (1932)

My Favorite Year (1982)

My Little Chickadee (1940)

My Man Godfrey (1936)

Nashville (1975)

Navigator, The (1924)

Night at the Opera, A (1935)

Ninotchka (1939)

Nothing but the Truth (1941)

Nothing Sacred (1937)

Odd Couple, The (1968)

Once in a Lifetime (1932)

One, Two, Three (1961)

Paleface, The (1948)

Palm Beach Story, The (1942)

Pawnshop, The (1916)

Philadelphia Story, The (1940)

Pillow Talk (1959)

Pink Panther, The (1964)

Play It Again, Sam (1972)

Private Benjamin (1980)

Producers, The (1968)

"Putting Pants on Philip" (1927)

"Rink, The" (1933)

Roman Scandals (1933)

"Safety Last" (1923)

"Second Hundred Years, The" (1927)

She Done Him Wrong (1933)

Sherlock, Jr. (1924)

Shoulder Arms (1918)

Shriek of Araby, The (1923)

Sleeper (1973)

Some Like It Hot (1959)

Sons of the Desert (1934)

Stardust Memories (1980)

State of the Union (1948)

Strong Man, The (1926)

The
Encyclopedia

A

Abbott, Bud (1895–1974), actor. Began at the business end of show business by managing a chain of theaters which eventually failed. Having little stage experience, he bounced around as a small-time comic until he met Lou COSTELLO in 1931. He allegedly filled in as a last-minute substitute for Lou's straight man. The partnership clicked and, for the next 25 years, they were one of the most popular comedy teams in the United States, appearing in burlesque, in vaudeville, on radio, in films, and on television. After the team broke up in 1957, Abbott made a few half-hearted attempts to continue as an entertainer, appearing as a guest on various television shows and, for a short time, in a comedy act with a new partner. For filmography, see ABBOTT AND COSTELLO.

In the 1948 film *The Noose Hangs High*, Bud asks Lou: "What would you have if you had ten dollars in one pants pocket and five dollars in the other?" "Somebody else's pants on," Lou quips. ∎

Abbott and Costello. One of the most successful comedy teams of the 1940s and 1950s. Their names consistently appeared among the top ten box-office draws during the 1940s. With Bud ABBOTT as the definitive straight man (sometimes rather cruel and sadistic), and Lou COSTELLO as his lovable, child-like foil, the team excelled at fast-talking patter routines, sight gags, slapstick, low comedy, and other elements of humor they sharpened to fit their style over their many years together in vaudeville, in burlesque, and on radio.

Bud Abbott and Lou Costello

In some ways Lou emulated Oliver HARDY. He was fat, wore a derby too small for his head, and fumbled nervously with his tie. Their most memorable routine, the classic "Who's on First?," demonstrated their proficiency at precision timing and interaction. At their height during the war years, the boys could do no wrong. Panned by many film critics, they were loved by their public. They maintained a busy schedule, including their own radio show, guest appearances, and their usual hectic film commitments.

By the early 1950s their fortunes began to change. They had used up their best material; in fact, they had used these routines too frequently, and their popularity started to fade. They let John Grant, perhaps their best writer, go. Also, their static characters did not help them. They balked at defining their individual roles or adding any depth to them. Their last few films reflected only a shadow of their former greatness. Throughout their most successful period the critics were never too kind to them. They attacked the duo for their ancient routines, their shrillness, and their reliance on low comedy, the last of which particularly vexed the reviewers who believed this form of humor was not only dated but unsophisticated. By the 1950s the negative reviews, coupled with a sagging audience, took their final toll.

Compared to other movie comedy teams, they had certain shortcomings. They lacked the individual characterization and warmth of LAUREL AND HARDY or George BURNS AND Gracie ALLEN; they could not dance and sing like the RITZ BROTHERS; and they could not capture the madness and utter chaos of the MARX BROTHERS, who were also fortunate to have an exceptional array of ingenious writers. However, Bud and Lou managed to retain their popularity for sixteen years, leaving behind a filmed record of old-fashioned vaudeville and burlesque routines that would otherwise have all but disappeared from our culture. Their three dozen films contain more than a few hilarious moments. *Bud & Lou*, a biography of the team written by Bob Thomas, was published in 1977.

SELECTED FILMS: One Night in the Tropics (1940), Buck Privates, In the Navy, Hold That Ghost, Keep 'Em Flying (1941), Ride 'Em Cowboy, Rio Rita, Pardon My Sarong (1942), It Ain't Hay, Hit the Ice (1943), In Society, Lost in a Harem (1944), Here Come the Co-Eds, The Naughty Nineties (1945), Little Giant, The Time of Their Lives (1946), Buck Privates Come Home, The Wistful Widow of Wagon Gap (1947), The Noose Hangs High, A & C Meet Frankenstein, Mexican Hayride (1948), Africa Screams (1949), A & C in the Foreign Legion (1950), A & C Meet the Invisible Man, Comin' Round the Mountain (1951), Lost in Alaska, A & C Meet Captain Kidd (1952), A & C Go to Mars (1953), A & C Meet the Keystone Kops, A & C Meet the Mummy (1955), Dance With Me, Henry (1956). ■

Abel, Walter (1898–1987), actor. Appeared on stage in 1919 and entered films in 1930. He played various roles as a character actor in dramas and light films, often as an excitable and badgered professional or parent.

SELECTED FILMS: Liliom (1930), The Three Musketeers (1935), The Lady Consents, We Went to College, Second Wife (1936), Wise Girl (1937), Miracle on Main Street (1940), Skylark (1941), Glamour Boy (1941), Beyond the Blue Horizon (1942), Fired Wife (1943), Duffy's Tavern, Kiss and Tell (1945), The Kid From Brooklyn (1946), Dream Girl, That Lady in Ermine (1948), Handle With Care (1958), Quick, Let's Get Married (1966), Silent Night, Bloody Night (1974). ■

Acuff, Eddie (1908–1956), actor. Entered films in the mid-1930s as a character actor and comedian following a successful stage career. He appeared in such diversified features as *The Petrified Forest* (1936), *The Walking Dead* (1936), and *Guadalcanal Diary* (1943). He worked with some of the foremost comics of the period, including, among others, W. C. FIELDS, OLSEN AND JOHNSON, and ABBOTT AND COSTELLO. His most famous role was that of the long-suffering letter carrier in several "Blondie" movies.

SELECTED FILMS: Shipmates Forever (1935), Crash Donovan (1936), Back in Circulation, Love Is on the Air (1937), Four Daughters, She Loved a Fireman (1938), Cowboy Quarterback (1939), The Bank Dick, One Night in the Tropics (1940), Six Lessons From Madame La-Zonga, Hellzapoppin, The Great American Broadcast (1941), Pardon My Sarong (1942), It Happened Tomorrow (1944), Diamond Horseshoe (1945), Buck Privates Come Home (1947), Blondie's Big Deal (1949). ■

Adair, Jean (1873–1953), actress. Worked in vaudeville and on stage as well as in films as early as the 1920s. She appeared as a supporting player in dramas and light films, portraying matronly characters. She was especially delightful in *Arsenic and Old Lace* as one of Cary

GRANT'S spinster aunts who served poisoned wine to elderly gentlemen to help them overcome their loneliness.

SELECTED FILMS: In the Name of the Law (1922), Advice to the Lovelorn (1933), Arsenic and Old Lace (1944), Something in the Wind (1946), Living in a Big Way (1947). ■

Adams, Casey. See Max Showalter.

Adams, Claire (–1978), actress. Entered early silent films in the late 1910s as a female lead. Often playing saucy characters, she appeared in melodramas and Tom Mix westerns as well as in comedies.

SELECTED FILMS: Key to Power (1918), The Great Lover (1920), The Spenders, A Certain Rich Man (1921), Just Tony (1922), Brass Commandments, Where the North Begins, The Clean Up (1923), Daddies, The Girl in the Limousine, The Painted Flapper, The Fast Set (1924), The Kiss Barrier, Men and Women, Souls for Sables, The Big Parade (1925), The Sea Wolf (1926), Married Alive (1927). ■

Adams, Don (1926–), actor, comedian. Worked in nightclubs as a stand-up comic in the 1950s and later in television where he became a star in the 1960s in the comedy series "Get Smart." His occasional forays into films, however, have been without distinction. A short, slim comic with a distinct delivery, he has returned to live performances and television. He usually portrays pompous types who, below the boasting, reveal their true insecurity.

SELECTED FILMS: The Nude Bomb (1980), Jimmy the Kid (1983). ■

Adams, Dorothy (1910–), actress. Hollywood character actress from the late 1930s. She often appeared as a hard-working mother or career woman in both dramas and light films. She specialized in westerns, portraying the epitome of pioneer women.

SELECTED FILMS: Condemned Women (1938), Bachelor Mother, Ninotchka (1939), Whistling in the Dark, Tobacco Road (1941), Hi, Neighbor! (1942), Bathing Beauty (1944), Sitting Pretty (1948), The Jackpot (1950), The Winning Team (1952), Three for Jamie Dawn (1956), Peeper (1975). ■

Adams, Edie (1927–), singer, actress. Has appeared occasionally in films as second female lead or confidante to the heroine. After attaining recognition on her future husband's television program, "The Ernie Kovacs Show," she appeared in nightclubs and on Broadway in the 1950s. During the next two decades she appeared in a dozen films, often supporting major stars such as Rock HUDSON, Doris DAY, and Bob HOPE. Most of the films were light vehicles.

SELECTED FILMS: The Apartment (1960), Lover Come Back (1961), Call Me Bwana, It's a Mad, Mad, Mad, Mad World, Under the Yum Yum Tree (1963), The Best Man (1964), Made in Paris (1966), The Honey Pot (1967), Up in Smoke (1978), Racquet (1979), The Happy Hooker Goes to Washington (1980). ■

Adams, Ernest S. (1885–1947), actor. Worked on stage before settling in Hollywood as a supporting player in silent films. A versatile actor, he appeared in dramas, westerns, and light films during a screen career that spanned four decades.

SELECTED FILMS: A Regular Girl (1919), Curlytop (1924), The Best People, Where the Worst Begins (1925), Melting Millions (1927), So This Is Love, What a Night (1928), One Splendid Hour (1929), Hold 'Em Jail (1932), Here Comes the Groom, We're Not Dressing (1934), The Ruggles of Red Gap (1935), Cactus Makes Perfect (1942), The Perils of Pauline, Buck Privates Come Home (1947). ■

Spencer Tracy and Katharine Hepburn in
Adam's Rib (1949)

Adam's Rib (1949), MGM. *Dir.* George
Cukor; *Sc.* Garson Kanin, Ruth Gordon;
with Spencer Tracy, Judy Holliday,
Katharine Hepburn, David Wayne.

In this bright comedy Spencer Tracy
and Katharine Hepburn portray a married couple, both of whom are respected
members of the legal profession. The fun
begins when they take opposing sides on
the same court case. The stars give superb performances in this witty script by
the husband-and-wife team of Kanin and
Gordon. Judy Holliday, who makes her
film debut here, is hilarious as a feather-
brained blonde accused of shooting her
husband. Hepburn, her attorney, asks
her: "When did you suspect that you
were losing your husband's affections?"
Holliday replies, "When he stopped bat-
ting me around." Holliday is a perfect
foil character to Hepburn, whose femi-
nist views play an important role in the
film. David Wayne, Tom Ewell, and Jean
Hagen, also on screen for the first time,
give strong support, as do other members
of the cast, including veteran comedienne Polly MORAN.

Adoree, Rene (1898–1933), actress.
Immigrated to Hollywood in 1920 from
France after a brief performance with the
Folies-Bergere. She appeared in a few
dozen silent films and a handful of talkies. One of her more memorable roles
was that of a French peasant girl in *The
Big Parade*. In one especially delightful
scene American doughboy John Gilbert
tries to teach her how to chew gum. In
the 1929 musical comedy *Marianne*,
Marion DAVIES did a burlesque of
Adoree.

SELECTED FILMS: *The Strongest
(1920), Made in Heaven (1921), West of
Chicago, Honor First (1922), The Eternal
Struggle (1923), A Man's Mate (1924),
Excuse Me, Parisian Nights, Exchange of
Wives, The Big Parade (1925), The Exquisite Sinner, Blarney (1926), The
Show, Heaven on Earth, On Ze Boulevard (1927), The Michigan Kid, The Mating Call (1928), The Pagan, Tide of Empire (1929), Call of the Flesh (1930).* ∎

Adrian, Iris (1913–), actress. Played
various roles in over 100 films from 1930
to 1976, including streetwalkers, bar
girls, and waitresses. She was especially
adept as the wise-cracking, gum-chewing blonde. In *Broadway* (1942) she portrayed a brassy blonde who tells nightclub hoofer George Raft, who is playing
himself, one way to get ahead: "You've
got to get a classy name. That 'George
Raft' is too ordinary."

SELECTED FILMS: *Paramount on Parade (1930), Stage Struck, Rumba (1935),
Lady Luck (1936), Gold Diggers of 1937
(1936), Go West (1940), Road to Zanzibar
(1941), Roxie Hart, Orchestra Wives
(1942), Lady of Burlesque (1943), Swing
Hostess (1944), The Stork Club (1945),
The Paleface (1948), Always Leave
Them Laughing, The Lovable Cheat
(1949), My Favorite Spy (1951), Blue
Hawaii (1961), The Errand Boy (1962),
That Darn Cat (1965), The Odd Couple
(1968), Freaky Friday (1977).* ∎

"Adventurer, The" (1917), MUT. *Dir.*
Charlie Chaplin; *Sc.* Charlie Chaplin;
with Charlie Chaplin, Edna Purviance,
Henry Bergman, Marta Golden, Eric
Campbell.

This two-reel comedy, one of
Chaplin's famous "golden dozen" that
he made for Mutual, is an elaborate
chase movie. It clearly establishes Chaplin as a master of timing and inventiveness. His sight gags, especially those

involving the chase sequences, are so well choreographed, that they transform this humble little film into a minor comedy classic. Charlie, an escaped convict, slips through the less nimble hands of the police and ends up at a fashionable cocktail party that he turns into a shambles as the police close in on him. The chase sequences dominate the action and the comedy. Some especially precious moments include the opening scenes in which he eludes the police, the scene in which he disguises himself as a floor lamp, and the sequence in which he uses sliding parlor doors to evade his pursuers.

African Queen, The (1951), UA. *Dir.* John Huston; *Sc.* James Agee, John Huston; with Humphrey Bogart, Katharine Hepburn, Robert Morley, Peter Bull, Theodore Bikel.

This adventure-comedy, based on C. S. Forester's novel, depends more on characterization for its humor than on incident or plot. And it is precisely the two characters, Charlie Allnut and Rose Sayer, as portrayed by Bogart and Hepburn, respectively, that make this such a winning film. Rose, the spinster sister of Reverend Sayer, an English missionary, has been in Africa ten years playing the organ during services for the natives. Charlie is the gin-guzzling skipper of the beat-up *African Queen*, a 30-foot launch that chugs along the rivers of German East Africa. The film opens in 1914, World War I has broken out in Europe, and the German soldiers are burning villages along the river and rounding up the male natives as recruits. When Rose's brother dies, Charlie takes her aboard his boat to safety. But she has other plans. She is determined to use Charlie's boat to destroy the *Louisa*, a German gunboat guarding a great lake that the English must use to transport their troops. At first Charlie resists, but her stubbornness induces him to give in half-heartedly. That night he gets drunk and refuses to go on, calling her a "crazy, psalm-sing-ing old maid." While he is asleep, she dumps his case of gin overboard and refuses to speak to him until he continues the journey as he originally promised. He finally agrees and they navigate their little boat past a German fort and through treacherous rapids toward their final destination. Exhilarated with their success in surmounting these dangers, they embrace and kiss, then pause and draw back in surprise, realizing that they have fallen in love. They continue down the river, acting like two young lovers who have discovered love for the first time. After a series of new hardships, they encounter the *Louisa* and, through a set of unexpected circumstances, succeed in sinking it. Rose, who had repressed her emotions for most of her life, first begins to discover a change while riding down the dangerous rapids. "I never dreamed that any mere physical experience could be so stimulating," she confesses to Charlie. "I've only known such excitement a few times before . . . in my brother's sermons when the spirit was upon him." Later, when they are picked up by the German captain of the gunboat, she is the quintessence of English determination and pride. She admits the purpose of their journey and tells how they traversed the allegedly unnavigable river. The captain, in disbelief, exclaims, "It's impossible." Rose smiles and replies with self-satisfaction: "Nevertheless." Charlie, a shy bachelor who has spent most of his life avoiding people and getting drunk, changes under Rose's strong influence. Bogart won an Academy Award for his role.

Aherne, Brian (1902–1986), actor. Appeared on stage and in silent films in his native England before migrating to the United States in 1931 to appear on Broadway. By 1933 he began his Hollywood screen career. He usually played well-groomed, debonair gentlemen, whether in dramas or light films. His autobiography, *A Proper Job*, was published in 1969.

SELECTED FILMS: Song of Songs (1933), Beloved Enemy (1936), Merrily We Live (1938), The Lady in Question, Hired Wife (1940), Skylark (1941), My Sister Eileen (1942), A Night to Remember (1943), Smart Woman (1948), The Swan (1956), The Best of Everything (1959), Rosie! (1967). ∎

Ainslee, Mary, actress. Worked chiefly in comedy shorts during the 1940s and 1950s as a supporting player. She appeared in some of the THREE STOOGES' films.

SELECTED FILMS: Hocus Pocus (1949), He Cooked His Goose (1952). ∎

Airplane! (1980), PAR. Dir. Jim Abrahams, David Zucker, Jerry Zucker; Sc. Jim Abrahams, David Zucker, Jerry Zucker; with Robert Hays, Julie Hagerty, Robert Stack, Lloyd Bridges, Leslie Nielson, Peter Graves.

A parody of the 1957 film drama Zero Hour, which started a succession of airplane-disaster films, Airplane! is at times sophomoric and at other moments hilarious. Robert Hays is an ex-flyer who fouled up during the last war and now has a fear of flying. He follows his girl-friend, stewardess Julie Hagerty, aboard a jet to be with her, but the plane runs into trouble. With the crew unconscious from food poisoning, Hays is forced to guide the jet to its destination in Chicago. Meanwhile the trip is filled with gags and routines from the fertile imagination of the trio of writer-directors who barely miss an opportunity for a laugh. The opening shot of the film emulates the music and tension of Jaws by showing only a fin moving ominously through the clouds. The passengers include an obnoxious singing nun, a precocious child who wants to ride in the cockpit, and other oddball characters. Peter Graves, a gay pilot, receives an emergency telephone call from the Mayo Clinic, which is then interrupted by a second important call from a Mr. Ham. "All right," he says to the operator, "give

me Ham on Five and hold the Mayo." Ethnic humor runs rampant. When two black passengers speak in jive to a stewardess, English titles appear across the bottom of the screen. The front of an Israeli plane is draped with a blue and white prayer shawl. Other funny bits pop up continually, including several verbal gags that border on the outrageous. A horde of newspapermen storm the airport tower when they learn an airplane is in trouble. After a short interview with the tower crew, one reporter winds up the session with: "Okay, boys, let's get some pictures." The reporters start stripping the room of all the hanging paintings and photographs. Back on board the airplane, Hays pleads with doctor-passenger Leslie Nielson about the poisoned crew and passengers. "Surely, there's something you can do." "I'm doing everything I can," Nielson replies, then adds, "and stop calling me Surely." The comedy, rich in nostalgia, is a feast for lovers of old movies. Hays' periodic flashbacks to his days in the service include a scene in a sleazy, South-Seas-island bar, another of two lovers on a beach as the waves sweep across their bodies and the romantic music reaches a crescendo, and still another showing Hays behind the controls of his war plane during battle. Lloyd Bridges, his former commander, happens to be the ground officer called in to help Hays guide the plane to safety. The film was so successful at the box-office that a sequel, Airplane II, was released in 1982.

Alberni, Luis (1887–1962), actor. Emigrating from Spain as a young man, he appeared on stage and in silent films as well as in talkies. He specialized in portraying high-strung Latin characters. Playing broad comedy character roles, he often employed fractured English. In Easy Living (1937), for example, he is the owner of a plush metropolitan hotel who says with pride and in his best accent: "What kind of a dump do you think this is?"

SELECTED FILMS: *Little Italy (1921), Svengali, The Mad Genius (1931), Manhattan Parade, The Kid From Spain (1932), Trick for Trick (1933), the Captain Hates the Sea (1934), In Caliente, The Gay Deception (1935), Anthony Adverse (1936), I'd Give a Million (1938), The Lady Eve (1941), Babes on Broadway (1942), Captain Carey, U.S.A. (1950), What Price Glory (1952).* ∎

Albert, Eddie (1908–), actor. Worked in radio and on stage before entering films in 1938. A popular character actor, he appeared in numerous dramas and light features as an amiable friend of the leading man. He received Academy Award nominations for his roles in *Roman Holiday* (1953) and *The Heartbreak Kid* (1972).

SELECTED FILMS: *Brother Rat (1938), Four Wives, On Your Toes (1939), Brother Rat and a Baby, An Angel From Texas (1940), The Great Mr. Nobody, Treat 'Em Rough (1941), Ladies' Day (1943), The Dude Goes West (1948), The Fuller Brush Girl (1950), You're in the Navy Now (1951), The Teahouse of the August Moon (1956), Captain Newman, M.D. (1963), The Longest Yard (1974), Foolin' Around (1979).* ∎

Albertson, Frank (1909–1964), actor. Began his film career in the late 1920s as a leading man in light vehicles. He eventually developed into a popular character actor, appearing in dozens of features over three decades. One of his more memorable roles was that of a naive foil to the Marx Brothers in *Room Service.* In an attempt to get rid of young Albertson, Groucho urges him to return to his old mother sitting at her fireside crying her eyes out for him. "But we haven't got a fireside," the young innocent admits. "Then how do you listen to the President's speeches?" Groucho fires back.

SELECTED FILMS: *The Farmer's Daughter (1928), Blue Skies (1929), Born Reckless, Wild Company (1930), The Brat, Big Business Girl (1931), Rainbow Over Broadway (1933), Alice Adams,*

Ah, Wilderness! (1936), The Farmer in the Dell (1936), Room Service (1938), Father Steps Out (1941), Louisiana Purchase (1942), It's a Wonderful Life (1946), Bye Bye Birdie (1963). ∎

Albertson, Jack (1907–1981), actor. Worked in vaudeville as a dancer and straight man for comics before entering films in the 1940s. He appeared as a character player in dramas and light films, usually as a cantankerous senior citizen. He won an Oscar as Best Supporting Actor for his role in *The Subject Was Roses* (1968).

SELECTED FILMS: *The Miracle on 34th Street (1947), Top Banana (1952), The Unguarded Moment (1956), Don't Go Near the Water (1957), Teacher's Pet (1958), The Shaggy Dog (1959), Lover Come Back (1961), Son of Flubber (1963), Kissin' Cousins, The Patsy (1964), How to Murder Your Wife (1965), How to Save a Marriage—and Ruin Your Life (1967).* ∎

Albertson, Mabel (1901–), actress. Began her long film career, which spanned four decades, in the 1930s. She appeared in dramas and light films as a humorous grandmother or officious neighbor.

SELECTED FILMS: *Mutiny on the Blackhawk (1939), She's Back on Broadway (1953), Forever Darling (1956), Don't Give Up the Ship (1959), The Gazebo (1960), All in a Night's Work (1961), Period of Adjustment (1962), Barefoot in the Park (1967).* ∎

Albright, Hardie (1903–1975), actor. Worked on stage as well as in films. A versatile character player, he appeared in numerous dramas and light films, many of which were low-budget second features. He later appeared in television.

SELECTED FILMS: *Heartbreak, Hotel Continental (1931), A Successful Calamity, Cabin in the Cotton (1932), The Working Man, Three-Cornered Moon (1933), Two Heads on a Pillow (1934), Women Must Dress, Calm Yourself, La-*

dies *Love Danger, Champagne for Breakfast* (1935), *Granny Get Your Gun, Carolina Moon* (1940), *Marry the Boss's Daughter, Bachelor Daddy* (1941), *Lady in a Jam* (1942), *Captain Tugboat Annie* (1945), *Angel on My Shoulder* (1946), *The Gangster* (1947). ■

Alda, Alan (1936–), actor. Has appeared on stage, screen, and television. Best known for his role in the highly successful TV series, "M*A*S*H," he has also appeared in dramatic and comedy features and has written the screenplay for and starred in *The Seduction of Joe Tynan* (1979). He is the son of film actor Robert Alda.

In *California Suite* he and Jane FONDA played a divorced couple who spar for the custody of their daughter. "Are you going to call Jenny or shall I?" Fonda asks. "No," he replies. "No, what?" "No, sir!" he concludes.

SELECTED FILMS: *Gone Are the Days (Purlie Victorious)* (1963), *Paper Lion* (1968), *The Extraordinary Seaman* (1969), *The Moonshine War* (1970), *The Mephisto Waltz* (1971), *To Kill a Clown* (1972), *Same Time, Next Year, California Suite* (1978), *The Four Seasons* (1981). ■

Alden, Mary (1883–1946), actress. Entered early silent films in the 1910s after first appearing on the stage. She became a busy performer in both silent films and talkies, mostly as a character actress. She is best remembered for her role of Lydia, the mulatto servant to Mr. Stoneman in D. W. GRIFFITH'S classic, *Birth of a Nation* (1915). In the late 1920s she played opposite W. C. FIELDS in *The Potters* (1927) and *Fools for Luck* (1928).

SELECTED FILMS: *The Battle of the Sexes, Another Chance, The Little Country Mouse* (1914), *Birth of a Nation, Ghosts, Bred on the Bone* (1915), *The Inferior Sex, Honest Hutch* (1920), *Pleasure Mad* (1923), *The Beloved Brute* (1924), *Lovey Mary* (1926), *The Potters, The Joy Girl, Twin Flappers* (1927), *Girl Overboard* (1929), *Strange Interlude* (1932). ■

Alderson, Erville (1883–1957), actor. Began his screen career in silent films in the early 1920s. An accomplished supporting player, he appeared in dramas and light films, many of which were major productions.

SELECTED FILMS: *The Good-Bad Wife* (1921), *Isn't Life Wonderful?* (1924), *Sally of the Sawdust* (1925), *Too Many Crooks* (1931), *Cabin in the Cotton* (1932), *The County Chairman, The Virginia Judge* (1935), *Educating Father* (1936), *The Mighty Treve* (1937), *Love Finds Andy Hardy, Mr. Smith Goes to Washington* (1939), *My Favorite Blonde, The Postman Didn't Ring, Careful, Soft Shoulders* (1942), *Mr. Whitney Had a Notion* (1949), *Something to Live For* (1952). ■

Aldrich, David C. (1931–1985), child actor. Entered films as a youngster in the popular "OUR GANG" comedy shorts. He portrayed the little rich boy in the series. After graduating from the American Academy of Dramatic Arts in 1948, he appeared on Broadway in *The Philadelphia Story*, in summer stock, and on television.

Aldrich, Henry. See "Henry Aldrich" comedy series.

Aldridge, Kay (1917–), actress. Worked as a model before entering films in the late 1930s. She appeared in light comedies, westerns, and musicals for various studios, usually as a supporting player. David O. Selznick auditioned her for the Scarlett O'Hara role in *Gone With the Wind* after he saw her picture on the cover of a national magazine. She appeared with such film personalities as Nelson Eddy, Eleanor Powell, and Bob HOPE.

SELECTED FILMS: *Vogues of 1938, Rosalie* (1937), *Hotel for Women, Here I Am a Stranger* (1939), *Free, Blonde and 21, Shooting High, Sailor's Lady, Down Argentine Way* (1940), *Louisiana Pur-*

chase, Navy Blues, You're in the Army Now (1941), The Falcon's Brother (1942). ∎

Alexander, Claire (1898–1927), actress. Began her screen career in early silent comedies with producer Mack SENNETT'S KEYSTONE studios. She was one of his original "Bathing Beauties." She appeared in many of the "Jerry" comedy series.

SELECTED FILMS: *Jerry's Big Mystery, Jerry's Brilliant Scheme, Jerry's Triple Alliance, Jerry's Romance, Minding the Baby, Be Sure You're Right, The Lady Detective, Jerry's Picnic, Jerry's Finishing Touch, Jerry Joins the Army, Jerry's Master Stroke, Jerry and the Vampire* (1917), *The Fatal Sign* (1920). ∎

Alexander, Frank "Fatty" (1879–1937), actor, comic. Began his screen career with Mack SENNETT'S KEYSTONE studios and later appeared as a comic supporting player in early silent films produced by Al CHRISTIE. He worked in several of Larry SEMON'S comedy shorts.

SELECTED FILMS: *Cyclone Jones* (1923), *SOS Perils of the Sea* (1925), *Oh, What a Night!* (1926), *Play Safe* (1927). ∎

Alexander, Ross (1907–1937), actor. Worked on stage during his teen years before appearing in films during the early sound era. He played supporting roles in Warner Brothers musicals and light comedies until his career faltered and he began to get parts only in low-budget features. His death was reported as a suicide.

SELECTED FILMS: *The Wiser Sex* (1932), *Social Register, Flirtation Walk, Gentlemen Are Born* (1934), *A Midsummer Night's Dream, We're in the Money, Shipmates Forever, Going Highbrow* (1935), *Brides Are Like That, Hot Money, Here Comes Carter* (1936), *Ready, Willing and Able* (1937). ∎

Algie. Fictional comic assistant to amateur sleuth Bulldog Drummond in Paramount's detective series of the late 1930s. Algie was portrayed by English-born Reginald DENNY in such films as *Bulldog Drummond Comes Back* and *Bulldog Drummond Escapes,* both 1937, and *Bulldog Drummond's Bride* and *Bulldog Drummond's Secret Police,* both 1939.

"Alkali Ike." A series of silent comedy shorts appearing from 1911 to 1913, starring Augustus CARNEY. The comedies, produced by ESSANAY studios, exhibited a rustic quality and were heavy on slapstick. Occasionally William Todd, portraying the character "Mustang Pete," would add his support to individual entries. The "Ike" character became so popular that an "Alkali Ike" doll appeared in retail stores in 1913. E. Mason HOPPER directed virtually all the films in the series.

SELECTED FILMS: *Alkali Ike's Automobile, Mustang Pete's Love Affair* (1911), *A Western Kimono, Alkali Beats Broncho Billy, Alkali Ike Plays the Devil* (1912), *Alkali Ike's Mother-in-Law, Alkali Ike's Gal, Alkali Ike's Misfortunes, Alkali Ike and the Hypnotist* (1913). ∎

"All-Star" comedies. See Comedy All-Stars.

Allbritton, Louise (1920–1979), actress. Lively performer in many B pictures. She appeared in several major comedies during the 1940s opposite such stars as Red SKELTON and Fred MacMURRAY.

SELECTED FILMS: *Not a Ladies' Man, Who Done It?, A Date With an Angel* (1942), *Fired Wife* (1943), *San Diego, I Love You, Her Primitive Man* (1944), *Men in Her Diary* (1945), *The Egg and I* (1947), *Sitting Pretty* (1948), *The Doolans of Oklahoma* (1949). ∎

Allen, Barbara Jo. See Vera Vague.

Allen, Fred (1894–1956), actor, humorist. Had careers in vaudeville and in the theater before gaining fame as a radio comedian, especially as a biting commentator on the times. His many fans were able to see the baggy-eyed wit when he appeared in a handful of films in the 1930s and 1940s. But his screen work was never as popular or as satisfying as his radio shows. His autobiography, *Treadmill to Oblivion*, describes his experiences in radio. He made a brief attempt at television but had little impact. Radio seemed to be his forte. He wrote most of his own material.

In one of his better films, *It's in the Bag*, he poses as the president of the Jack Benny Fan Club but confesses to Benny he can't get people into the theater to see Benny's movies. "Have they tried to give away dishes?" Benny inquires. "Yes," Allen replies, "and the people threw them at the screen." "Have they tried not giving away dishes?" "Yes," Allen admits, "but the people bring their own dishes and throw them at the screen."

SELECTED FILMS: *Thanks a Million* (1935), *Sally, Irene and Mary* (1938), *Love Thy Neighbor* (1940), *It's in the Bag* (1945), *We're Not Married, O. Henry's Full House* (1952). ■

Allen, Gracie. See Burns and Allen.

Allen, Phyllis (1861–1938), actress. Began her screen career with producer Mack SENNETT. As a comedienne in numerous silent films, she appeared in more than a dozen short comedies with Charlie CHAPLIN ("Dough and Dynamite," "Tillie's Punctured Romance"), and other one- and two-reelers with Syd CHAPLIN, "Fatty" ARBUCKLE, and Mack SWAIN. A rather plump performer with an unpleasant expression, she was often cast as a shrewish wife in Sennett's KEYSTONE comedies.

SELECTED FILMS: *Caught in a Cabaret, Getting Acquainted, Fatty's Jonah Day, Ambrose's First Falsehood, The Property Man, The Rounders* (1914), *Fickle Fatty's Fall, Giddy, Gay and Ticklish, Gussle's Wayward Path, A Submarine Pirate* (1915), *A Movie Star, The Judge, No One to Guide Him* (1916), *The Adventurer* (1917), *The Kid* (1921). ■

Allen, Steve (1921–), actor, entertainer, songwriter. Worked as a disc jockey and radio show host before gaining fame as a television personality. He originated the first successful national television talk show, a genre that has since become so popular. He has also appeared in a few films, including *The Benny Goodman Story* (1956) in which he portrayed the famous bandleader. An accomplished entertainer, writer, and wit, he specializes in the ad lib. This may be why he has not been as successful in films as he has been in television. He has also written several books on a variety of subjects, including *Funny People* (1981), *Funny Men* (1956), and *More Funny People* (1982).

SELECTED FILMS: *Down Memory Lane* (1949), *I'll Get By* (1950), *The Big Circus* (1959), *College Confidential* (1960), *Warning Shot* (1967), *Where Were You When the Lights Went Out?* (1968), *The Comic* (1969), *Heart Beat* (1980). ■

Allen, Woody (1935–), actor, screenwriter, director, playwright. He began his career in the world of comedy while still in high school when he sold gags to newspaper columnists. Soon he was writing comedy material for major television personalities including Pat Boone and Sid CAESAR. Well known for his wit and comedy routines by way of recordings, print, plays, personal appearances, and films, he has been a major force in American humor since the mid-1960s. Physically unassuming and nervous, he specializes in satire, parody, understatement, self-denigration, and, at times, slapstick. He may not always provide belly laughs, but his humor often reaches levels of profundity generally lacking in his contemporaries. Each of his excursions into a new film seems to offer a fresh way of looking at ourselves and the world around us.

What's New, Pussycat? (1965) marked Allen's debut as actor and screenwriter but gave little cause for celebration. The film was panned by the critics. His next effort, *What's Up, Tiger Lily?* (1966), was the reconstruction of a blatantly bad Japanese sadistic suspense movie into a funny vehicle in which American performers inserted Woody's witty lines. A spoof of the popular James Bond series, the film concerns a quest, not for the plans of some powerful secret weapon, but for an egg salad recipe. This time the critics were kinder to the comic.

Allen appeared in *Casino Royale* (1967), another James Bond spoof. The star-studded film was an expensive failure, with Allen himself commenting: "An unredeemingly moronic enterprise."

In 1969 his play, *Don't Drink the Water*, was adapted to the screen with Jackie GLEASON and Estelle Parsons in the lead roles. It did not do well critically or commercially and did little to further Allen's reputation.

Take the Money and Run (1969), his first directorial effort, used a semi-documentary approach to unfold the life story of Virgil Starkwell (Woody), a compulsive but incompetent thief. In *Bananas* (1971) Woody, portraying Fielding Mellish, becomes embroiled in a South-American revolution when he falls for Nancy (Louise Lasser), a political activist.

In *Play It Again, Sam* (1972), based on Allen's Broadway play, movie buff Allan Felix (Woody) is obsessed with Humphrey Bogart as his sexual mentor. Divorced by his wife, Felix withdraws from the outside world. The film was not directed by Allen, as many mistakenly believe, but by Herbert Ross.

Everything You Always Wanted to Know About Sex (But Were Afraid to Ask) (1972), an episodic adaptation of David Reuben's book, explored various sexual attitudes—Allen style. *Sleeper* (1973) satirized such widely diversified topics as technology, sex, and Albert Shanker. Allen combines his verbal and visual skills to give us a winning film, almost unanimously praised by the critics.

Love and Death (1975) parodied foreign film directors such as Eisenstein and emulated such comics as CHAPLIN, Bob HOPE, and Groucho MARX. In this romp about a declared coward during the Napoleonic Wars, Allen once again touched upon some of his favorite themes—marriage, relationships, self-deprecation, and his love of films.

The Front (1976), directed by Martin Ritt, was a comedy-drama of the Hollywood blacklist period. Although the critics admired Ritt's attempt to confront the issues of the blacklist period, they gave the film little praise as a work of entertainment or art.

Annie Hall (1977) examined Allen's relationships with women and was his most successful work up to this point. It won four Academy Awards.

In *Manhattan* (1979), a story about a New York writer and his various relationships, intellectual and otherwise, he used black-and-white photography to complement the interpersonal sexual rhythms of his egocentric characters.

In *Stardust Memories** (1980) he explored the life of a successful filmmaker who finds little personal satisfaction in his achievements and sees his retinue as grotesque sycophants.

A Midsummer Night's Sex Comedy (1982), a light, romantic film, was a drastic change of environment for Allen, who eulogizes his beloved Big Apple. Like Chaplin, who had no qualms about moving from the city ("Easy Street," *Modern Times, City Lights*) to the country ("The Tramp," "Sunnyside"), Woody surprisingly makes the transition from films like *Annie Hall* and *Manhattan* to *Sex Comedy* smoothly and effectively. The setting is upstate New York, circa 1900, where a group of vacationers spend a weekend. Again, Allen deals with sexual relationships and marriage, as well as with remembrances of things past. The rustic setting does not help to assuage the frustrations of the individuals, who create their own problems.

Zelig (1983) dealt with, among others, the theme of identity, or rather the lack of it. Leonard Zelig is a chameleon-like celebrity of the 1920s and 1930s who can change his physical qualities to blend into whatever group he is with at the time. Using special effects, Allen succeeds visually, if not dramatically. Zelig conforms to different types, whether he is rubbing shoulders with American politicians or as a member of a Nazi rally. Either because of its black-and-white documentary approach or its experimental nature, the picture was not successful with the general public.

In *Broadway Danny Rose* (1984) Allen played a former mediocre comic who becomes an agent with a heart. *The Purple Rose of Cairo* (1985) is a fable set in the Depression years when millions of filmgoers flocked to the movie palaces, some to live out their fantasies, others to escape their routine lives. Mia Farrow, who has appeared consistently in Allen's later films, portrays Celia, an abused wife, and is one such patron. While watching a 1930s-type adventure yarn, she has her wildest dreams come true when the hero steps out of the screen and into her life. Allen's love of films and his explorations into illusion and reality have never been more clearly delineated than in this clever and, at times, very funny vehicle. The reviews were mixed, ranging from "blissful," "a pure enchantment," and "charming" to "slight."

Hannah and Her Sisters (1986), Allen's evolving vision of middle age, is a poignant and funny film that explores the lives and romances of three Manhattan women, played by Mia Farrow, Diane Wiest, and Barbara Hershey. Michael Caine, Max Von Sydow, and Allen portray the men who are involved with the sisters. The film was nominated for an Oscar as Best Picture while Wiest and Caine won Academy Awards as Best Supporting Actress and Actor.

Radio Days (1987), Allen's homage to oldtime radio, is set in the late 1930s and early 1940s. In this visually attractive film he explores the influence of the medium on the people's lives during the years of World War II. The characters tend to define themselves by their favorite radio shows and personalities.

Allen, through his film characters, has tended to shift from a self-effacing neurotic to a more stable, Chaplinesque "little fellow" better able to accept and cope with his environment.

Allgood, Sara (1883–1950), actress. A plump, affable, matronly character player who specialized in mother roles. Born in Ireland, she appeared in her first film in Australia. She began her Hollywood career in 1940. She acted in dramas, light musicals, and comedies.

SELECTED FILMS: That Hamilton Woman (1940), Roxie Hart, It Happened in Flatbush, Life Begins at 8:30 (1942), The Strange Affair of Uncle Harry (1945), Ivy, Mother Wore Tights (1947), The Girl From Manhattan, One Touch of Venus (1948), Cheaper by the Dozen (1950). ■

Allister, Claude (1893–1970), actor. Worked as a stock market clerk before entering films in the late 1920s. Born in England, he played in both U.S. and British films, usually as a character actor. Wearing a monocle and attired fastidiously, he epitomized an asinine figure. He appeared in dramas and light films.

SELECTED FILMS: The Trial of Mary Dugan, Bulldog Drummond (1929), Ladies Love Brutes, The Flora Dora Girl, Monte Carlo (1930), Reaching for the Moon, I Like Your Nerve, Platinum Blonde (1931), The Lady Is Willing (1934), The Awful Truth (1937), Captain Fury (1939), Lillian Russell (1940), Charley's Aunt (1941), Kiss Me Kate (1953). ■

Altman, Robert (1925–), director, screenwriter, producer. Began directing films in the late 1960s following about ten years' experience in television. His fresh style, individual wit, and satirical, often irreverent, approach to his subject matter soon made him popular with both critics and filmgoers. *M*A*S*H* (1970), an anti-war comedy set during the Korean War, is his most successful work to date. The television series based on the characters in the film became one of the most popular and longest-running shows in the history of that medium. *Brewster McCloud* (1970), the story of a young man who dreams of flying in the Houston Astrodome, is probably his most ineffable and puzzling film. In *McCabe and Mrs. Miller* (1971) he uses the western genre to satirize American big business and the free-enterprise system. In *Nashville* (1975), covered as a separate entry elsewhere in this book, he once again uses his satirical wit to explore contemporary American life and values by weaving together the lives of two dozen characters who assemble for a political rally. *Buffalo Bill and the Indians* (1976), one of the director's weakest films, debunks the almost mythical western hero, presenting him as a pretentious phony. Altman's films, although sometimes flawed and exasperating, are more often witty and provocative.

SELECTED FILMS: *The Delinquents* (1957), *Countdown* (1968), *The Long Goodbye* (1973), *Thieves Like Us, California Split* (1974), *Buffalo Bill and the Indians* (1976), *Three Women* (1977), *A Wedding* (1978), *Quintet, Health* (1979). ∎

"Ambrose" comedies. A series of comedy shorts which ran from 1914 to 1915 and starred Mack SWAIN in the title role. The comedies, produced by Mack SENNETT'S KEYSTONE studio, pictured the antics of Ambrose, a lustful rowdy sporting an oversize mustache and excessive makeup. Sometimes his antagonist would be a character called "Walrus," played by Chester CONKLIN.

SELECTED FILMS: *Ambrose's First Falsehood* (1914), *Ambrose's Sour Grapes, Ambrose's Fury, The Battle of Ambrose and Walrus, Ambrose's Little Hatchet, Love, Speed and Thrills, Ambrose's Nasty Temper, When Ambrose Dared Walrus* (1915), *Ambrose's Cup of Woe, Ambrose's Rapid Rise, Safety First Ambrose* (1916). ∎

Ameche, Don (1908–), actor. Worked in the theater and on radio before he came to Hollywood in 1936. He played in dramas and musicals as well as comedies, starring in dozens of features. With his natural good looks and his penciled mustache, he often portrayed a light-hearted playboy. His most memorable films are *The Story of Alexander Graham Bell* (1939), in which he played the title role, and *Heaven Can Wait* (1943), which showcased his potential acting capabilities. But his later films were little more than routine vehicles and failed to exploit his talents. After a respite of more than ten years, he returned to films sporadically in the 1980s. He won an Oscar for his performance in *Cocoon* (1985).

SELECTED FILMS: *Sins of Man, Ramona, Ladies in Love* (1936), *One in a Million, Love Under Fire* (1937), *Alexander's Ragtime Band* (1938), *The Three Musketeers, Midnight* (1939), *Moon Over Miami* (1941), *The Magnificent Dope* (1942), *It's in the Bag, Guest Wife* (1945), *Slightly French* (1949), *The Boatniks* (1970), *Trading Places* (1983), *Cocoon* (1985). ∎

American Graffiti (1973), U. Dir. George Lucas; Sc. George Lucas, Gloria Katz, William Huyck; with Richard Dreyfuss, Ronny Howard, Paul LeMat, Charlie Martin Smith, Cindy Williams, Candy Clark.

This painfully funny depiction of a group of teenagers' rite of passage evokes the period in which it is set—1962. Episodic in structure, the film reveals the last traces of innocence of four pals during a 12-hour period in a small California town. Richard DREYFUSS is leaving for an Eastern college the following day, as is his friend, Ronny Howard. Charlie Smith, another member of the closely knit group, consumes the night hours attempting to seduce the sexually charged Candy Clark in a borrowed car.

Paul LeMat, the oldest of the four, spends his time drag racing as he clings to his lost youth. At first fearful about leaving the town in which they were raised, Dreyfuss and Howard eventually come to terms with abandoning their youth. The use of contemporary songs, the images of chrome and neon, and the gleaming cars of the 1950s cruising the streets of the town all effectively contribute to this remarkable portrayal of a generation's "coming of age." The film catapulted Dreyfuss to stardom, helped the careers of several other players, and indirectly spawned the television series "Happy Days." Harrison Ford can be seen in a minor role. A sequel, More American Graffiti, was released in 1979, but it lacked the spirit and sense of purpose of the original.

Ames, Elsie, actress. Appeared as a female lead in several comedy shorts during the sound period. She worked in this capacity in the 1940s with Buster KEATON in his series of shorts for Columbia studios.

SELECTED FILMS: The Taming of the Snood, The Spook Speaks, His Ex Marks the Spot (1940), General Nuisance, She's Oil Mine (1941). ∎

Ames, Leon (1903–), actor. Began his acting career in 1925 in the theater. He entered films in the early 1930s and quickly became a sturdy character player in numerous dramas and light films. Distinguished-looking and sporting a trim mustache, he moved from playboy types to distraught-father roles, appearing on screen for more than 50 years. He has had a successful career in television in his later years.

SELECTED FILMS: The Murders in the Rue Morgue (1932), Alimony Madness (1933), Stowaway (1936), Bluebeard's Eighth Wife (1938), Pack Up Your Troubles (1939), East Side Kids (1940), Meet Me in St. Louis, The Thin Man Goes Home (1944), Week-End at the Waldorf (1945), The Show-Off, The Cockeyed Miracle (1946), Undercover Maisie, Song

of the Thin Man, Merton of the Movies (1947), A Date With Judy (1948), Watch the Birdie (1950), The Absent-Minded Professor (1961), Just You and Me, Kid (1979), Testament (1983). ∎

Amos 'n' Andy. The most famous comedy team in the history of radio. The black team was portrayed by white performers Freeman F. Gosden, born in 1899, and Charles V. Correll (1890–1972). They first tried their routine on radio in 1925 and it proved so successful that they were offered $250 per week. Their characters then were called Sam 'n' Henry, but when they shifted stations in 1928 they were not permitted to use those names. Thus, Amos 'n' Andy came into being. Unfortunately, the duo made only one movie in which they starred, Check and Double Check (1930). It was not a very funny film, but the popularity of the team made it one of the top box-office draws of that year. It was not until 1935 that the boys appeared in their next and last film, The Big Broadcast of 1935. But their radio show was popular until 1951. The television show, in which Gosden and Carroll did not appear, won new audiences. The social changes in America, brought about chiefly by the civil rights movement of the 1960s, took their toll on the show. The comics were considered embarrassing stereotypes and fell out of favor.

Anderson, Claire (1896–1964), actress. Appeared in early silent comedies for Mack SENNETT'S KEYSTONE studios. Mainly a supporting player, she often worked with such top slapstick comics as Chester CONKLIN and Ben TURPIN as well as with lesser-known actors of Sennett's stock company. She was one of Sennett's "Bathing Beauties."

SELECTED FILMS: Cinders of Love, The Lion and the Girl, Bath Tub Perils (1916), A Clever Dummy, The Late Lamented (1917). ∎

Anderson, Eddie "Rochester" (1905–1977), actor. Played in an all-black revue and in vaudeville during the 1920s before appearing in small parts in Hollywood films in the early 1930s. Following his success on Jack BENNY'S radio show in 1937, he began to receive larger parts in films. The wide-eyed, husky-voiced comic brightened more than 50 features over the next two decades although he was chiefly relegated to the usual stereotyped roles reserved for blacks. He remained with Benny for 21 years, retiring only after he was stricken with a heart attack.

In *Topper Returns* he played Roland Young's chauffeur who gets mixed up in a murder at an old mansion. Rochester falls into the ocean below the house and is hampered from climbing to safety by a playful seal who keeps pushing him back into the water. "You keep away from me," he finally blurts out to the persistent creature, "or you'll be a coat!"

SELECTED FILMS: *What Price Hollywood* (1932), *The Green Pastures, Three Men on a Horse* (1936), *Gold Diggers in Paris, You Can't Take It With You* (1938), *You Can't Cheat an Honest Man, Gone With the Wind* (1939), *Buck Benny Rides Again, Love Thy Neighbor* (1940), *Topper Returns, Kiss the Boys Goodbye, Birth of the Blues* (1941), *Star Spangled Rhythm* (1942), *The Meanest Man in the World, Cabin in the Sky* (1943), *Brewster's Millions* (1945), *The Sailor Takes a Wife, The Show-Off* (1946), *It's a Mad, Mad, Mad, Mad World* (1963). ∎

Anderson, Richard (1926–), actor. Began his screen career in the late 1940s, usually playing second leads. A handsome, dark-haired actor, he appeared in dramas and light films through the 1960s and then switched to television.

SELECTED FILMS: *Twelve O'Clock High* (1949), *The Magnificent Yankee* (1950), *Rich, Young and Pretty* (1951), *Just This Once, Fearless Fagan* (1952), *I Love Melvin, Dream Wife* (1953), *Give a Girl a Break* (1954), *It's a Dog's Life* (1955), *The Buster Keaton Story* (1957), *The Wackiest Ship in the Army* (1960), *The Honkers* (1972), *Rally* (1981). ∎

Anderson, Warner (1911–1976), actor. Worked in vaudeville and on stage before beginning his screen career in the early 1940s. A stern-looking, no-nonsense supporting player, he appeared in dramas as well as comedies well into the 1960s, then switched to television.

SELECTED FILMS: *Oklahoma Outlaws, This Is the Army* (1943), *Her Highness and the Bellboy, Abbott and Costello in Hollywood, Week-End at the Waldorf* (1945), *Bad Bascomb, Three Wise Fools* (1946), *Song of the Thin Man* (1947), *Tenth Avenue Angel* (1948), *The Lucky Stiff* (1949), *Rio Conchos* (1969). ∎

Andrews, Edward (1914–1985), actor. A bespectacled, round-faced character player who entered films in the mid-1950s after gaining stage experience on Broadway. He was equally at home in villainous as well as light roles.

SELECTED FILMS: *The Phenix City Story* (1955), *The Unguarded Moment* (1956), *The Absent-Minded Professor, Love in a Goldfish Bowl* (1961), *Forty Pounds of Trouble* (1962), *The Thrill of It All* (1963), *Good Neighbor Sam, Kisses for My President, Send Me No Flowers* (1964), *The Glass Bottom Boat, Birds Do It* (1966), *The Trouble With Girls* (1970), *Charlie and the Angel* (1974), *Gremlins* (1984) ∎

Andrews, Julie (1935–), actress, singer. Appeared on stage in her native England and later, in the 1950s, in the United States, before entering films in the 1960s. An attractive and very talented performer, she has appeared in musicals and other light films, including several light works directed by her husband, Blake EDWARDS. One of her more delightful roles was as a male impersonator in *Victor/Victoria*, set in pre-World War II Paris and starring Robert PRESTON as a gay entertainer and James GARNER as her lover.

SELECTED FILMS: *Mary Poppins, The Americanization of Emily* (1964), *Thoroughly Modern Millie* (1967), *10* (1979), *Little Miss Marker* (1980), *S.O.B.* (1981),

Victor/Victoria (1982), The Man Who Loved Women (1983), That's Life! (1986). ■

"Andy Hardy" series. A popular MGM domestic comedy series consisting of 15 films, beginning in the 1930s and running until 1958. *A Family Affair* (1937) introduced the Hardy family, with Lionel Barrymore as Judge Hardy giving homespun advice to his brash, wise-cracking, but obedient son, Andy, played by Mickey ROONEY. The actual series started the following year with *You're Only Young Once*, with Lewis Stone replacing Barrymore as the Judge, Fay Holden as Mrs. Hardy, Mickey continuing in the role of Andy, Cecilia Parker as Marian, Andy's sister, Sara Haden as Aunt Millie, and Ann Rutherford as Polly, the girl-next-door.

The series became a showcase for future stars. Young hopefuls on the MGM lot appeared from time to time, including Judy Garland, Lana Turner, Esther Williams, and Kathryn Grayson. The films depicted a simple life style, domestic stability, and the benefits of a virtuous life—qualities that eventually wore thin as American values changed over the years. A typical plot revolved around one of Andy's hare-brained schemes or a romantic entanglement. In the last entry, *Andy Hardy Comes Home* (1958), the chemistry of the sentimental series that had once entertained a generation of moviegoers was all but gone.

SELECTED FILMS: Judge Hardy's Children, Love Finds Andy Hardy, Out West With the Hardys (1938), The Hardys Ride High, Andy Hardy Gets Spring Fever, Judge Hardy and Son (1939), Andy Hardy Meets a Debutante, Andy Hardy's Private Secretary, Life Begins for Andy Hardy (1941), The Courtship of Andy Hardy, Andy Hardy's Double Life (1942), Andy Hardy's Blonde Trouble (1944), Love Laughs at Andy Hardy (1947). ■

Animal Crackers (1930), PAR. *Dir.* Victor Heerman; *Sc.* Morrie Ryskind; with Groucho, Harpo, Chico, Zeppo Marx, Lillian Roth, Margaret Dumont.

One of the Brothers' early Paramount entries before they switched to MGM, the film is another of their ventures into the comedy of anarchy. Groucho, an African explorer, is carried by his native bearers, Harpo busies himself in pursuit of buxom beauties, and Chico provides his customary dialect humor. This early sound comedy, which accounts for some of its staginess, has several classic moments. Groucho utters his famous line: "One morning I shot an elephant in my pajamas. How he got into my pajamas, I don't know." There is the mock-operatic number, "Hooray for Captain Spaulding." Finally, Harpo and Chico indulge in a hilarious bridge game. The Marx Brothers did funnier work in later vehicles, but this farce, their second film, in some ways has an immediacy of its own. It is based on a stage play written by George S. Kaufman and Ryskind that starred the Marx Brothers.

Animals in films. The use of animals, either as the main subject or as comic relief in films, goes back almost to the beginning of film history. Teddy, one of the first canine heroes of the screen, had the distinction of having his name appear in the title. In "Teddy at the Throttle" (1917) villainous Wallace BEERY chained Gloria SWANSON to a pair of railroad tracks. As a train roars full speed toward the defenseless heroine, Teddy leaps from a second-story window to the train in time to warn the conductor. This Mack SENNETT two-reeler aimed more for thrills than for laughs, but the film, nevertheless, is considered a comedy. Producer Hal ROACH, whose output of comedy films was second only to Sennett's (at least in quantity), saw the many possibilities of a series of all-animal films. His "DIPPY DOO-DADS" of the 1920s starred animals, chiefly chimpanzees, who mimicked the actions of humans. His studio was also responsible for for bringing us Petey, the one-eyed canine member of the "OUR GANG" comedies, who shared many of the pranks and antics of this popular group of children.

In the 1920s Rin Tin Tin made his debut. Although basically melodramatic adventures, the films which starred "the Wonder Dog," as he was called, usually contained a number of entertaining sequences that displayed his unusual skills. The Rinty films continued into the early sound era, and when he died, his offspring, Rin Tin Tin, Jr., carried on in the elder's noble tradition.

The early 1930s brought us other memorable comic-relief creatures. Cheetah, the loyal and constant playmate of Tarzan and Boy, contributed almost all the humor to the series based on Edgar Rice Burroughs' characters. Mimicking man, Cheetah, when not busy rescuing a member of the Lord of the Jungle's family, could be found trying to extricate himself from some mischief of his own invention.

The second popular pet, the adorable Asta, belonged to that kookie couple, Nick and Nora Charles. Asta appeared in all of the "THIN MAN" entries and had a difficult time competing for laughs with the tipsy sleuth and the inscrutable Nora, but he managed fairly well.

Another favorite pet, Daisy, also found stiff rivalry in vying for laughs in the long-running "BLONDIE" series; she had her own hinged panel, then an unusual feature, for entering and leaving the Bumstead residence. An obedient member of the unpredictable family, she would often join Baby Dumpling in the corner of a room when punishment was meted out. Daisy's long career began in 1938 with the first film based on Chic Young's comic strip. The series lasted well into the 1950s.

The same year introduced the solo appearance of "Baby," Katharine HEPBURN'S pet leopard, in Howard HAWKS' *Bringing Up Baby*. The following year brought us yet another single performance, that of Toto, Dorothy's affectionate dog in *The Wizard of Oz*. Along with Judy GARLAND, Toto had to suffer the threats of the Wicked Witch of the West, who promised, "I'll get you, my pretty, and your little dog, too!"

Some unusual comedies which uti-lized non-human subjects as a basis for their plots emerged during the 1940s and 1950s. In *Once Upon a Time* (1944) Cary GRANT promoted a dancing caterpillar to national prominence. Jimmy DURANTE'S trained squirrel in *The Great Rupert* (1950) uncovered hidden money. Finally, a bewildered James STEWART conjured up an invisible six-foot rabbit for his confidant in *Harvey* (1950), a screen version of the hit play.

Mr. Peabody and the Mermaid (1948) concerned William POWELL'S strange catch-of-the-day, mermaid Ann Blyth, whom he hooked while fishing.

A chimpanzee and a mule dominated animal movie comedies during the 1950s. In *Bedtime for Bonzo* (1951) the titular character stole the show from live actors, including Ronald REAGAN; the chimp repeated his hilarious antics in the sequel, *Bonzo Goes to College* (1952), this time by helping to win a football game. The most popular animal series during this otherwise tranquil decade was the "FRANCIS" comedies, in which a talking mule won most of the laughs. Appearing in seven films, the verbal creature managed to make life difficult for low-ranking West Point student Donald O'CONNOR.

The dolphin and the cat became the stars of animal films during the 1960s. *Flipper* (1963) and *Flipper's New Adventure* (1964) depicted the entertaining exploits of a dolphin befriended by a boy. Walt Disney's *That Darn Cat* (1965) unfolded the comic story of a cat who helped the FBI locate a kidnap victim.

The feature-length cartoon *Gay Purree* (1963) employed the voices of Judy Garland, Robert Goulet, Hermione GINGOLD, Red BUTTONS, Morey AMSTERDAM, and others in this sophisticated musical.

The use of animals in comedy films continued into the 1970s and 1980s. An extraordinary dog foils the plans of kidnappers to abduct two children in *Benji* (1974), a delightful family movie. The film, and the star, became so popular that an entertaining sequel, *For the Love of Benji*, was released in 1977. In the late 1970s even action star Clint Eastwood became involved in the genre by befriending an orangutan in *Every Which Way but Loose* (1978) and its sequel, *Any Which Way You Can* (1980). The mermaid theme returned with *Splash* (1984), in which Tom HANKS plunged into a romance with the water nymph. During the 1980s films like *E.T.* (1982) and *Gremlins* (1984) began a new trend when they replaced earth creatures as pets with extraterrestrials.

Animation. The history of animation begins before the invention of the motion picture camera. Peter Mark Roget's "Persistence of Vision" theory in 1824 (that held that the eye "sees" an image for a short time after the image is gone) brought forth various gadgets and devices that gave the semblance of pictures in motion, or "motion pictures." Wheels, disks, and pages, containing individually hand-drawn pictures, were spun, twirled, or flipped, so that the still drawings produced a succession of images that seemed to move.

Patented inventions applying Roget's principle abounded in the final decade of the Nineteenth Century, including one of the earliest, the Phenakistiscope, invented by Joseph-Antoine Plateau in 1832; the Zoetrope; the Stroboscope; and the Praxinoscope, which was exhibited theatrically in 1889 in its own theater named after the instrument.

By 1906 the first movie cartoon was released by Vitagraph at a special showing. J. Stuart Blackton, journalist, director, actor, and film pioneer, produced the popular "Humorous Phases of Funny Faces," utilizing for the first time the principle of stop-motion photography. He continued to make animated cartoons until 1910, at which point he turned to other film interests. Winsor McCay, a New York *Herald* cartoonist, produced "Gertie the Dinosaur" in 1909, the first animated cartoon to be presented during a regular program. "Little Nemo" followed in 1911. McCay also turned out

the first feature-length animated film, "The Sinking of the *Lusitania*" (1918). He had an uncanny genius for incorporating motion and perspective into his animation without sacrificing linear detail. McCay claimed his short films contained "10,000 drawings, each a little different from the one preceding it." Another pioneer, George McManus, who was to achieve fame with his comic strip, "Bringing Up Father," created a cartoon series called "Baby Snookums," which ran from 1912 to 1913.

John Randolph Bray, a newspaper and magazine cartoonist, produced the film short, "The Dachshund and the Sausage," in 1910 and initiated the series, "Colonel Heeza Liar," which poked fun at President Teddy Roosevelt. Some of the most famous of the animators of the 1930s and 1940s learned their craft while working for Bray, including Max and Dave Fleischer (creators of Betty Boop and Popeye), Walter Lantz (Oswald the Rabbit, Woody Woodpecker), and Paul Terry (Farmer Al Falfa). Bray's studios resembled an assembly-line animation factory, which eventually led to artistic uniformity.

The most significant advance in animation was the introduction of "cels," which were designed to replace sheets of paper. These sheets of celluloid permitted the artist to animate multiple layers of drawings against a single background.

By the 1920s the animated cartoon, whose characters were often based on familiar comic strips, became a staple feature on the American screen. One of the most popular cartoon characters of the decade was Felix the Cat, first introduced in 1914 by animator Otto Messmer and his business partner Pat Sullivan. Other successful series included "Koko the Clown," "The Katzenjammer Kids," "Mutt and Jeff," and "Krazy Kat."

George Herriman's iconoclastic comic strip, "Krazy Kat," made its appearance on the screen in 1916, again in the 1920s, and, for the final time, in the 1930s. Although much of the richness and life of the strip was missing, the main characters and the familiar mesa-like landscapes remained intact. Krazy Kat is convinced that Ignatz Mouse loves him, regardless of the number of bricks Ignatz bombards him with. Offisa Pup likes Ignatz and invariably ruins Krazy's plans. Herriman's trio has been the subject of various literary, religious, and sociological interpretations, including comparisons to Don Quixote (Krazy) and Sancho Panza (Ignatz), to Lucifer (Ignatz), and to the conflict between sentimental middle America (Krazy) and the tough, cynical, streetwise urbanites and/or immigrants (Ignatz).

The dominant figures in the world of animation during the 1920s, however, were Dave and Max Fleischer. They created a variety of cartoons, including the "Out of the Inkwell" series, featuring Koko the Clown, in which a cartoonist's hand would draw a character that would interact with its creator.

In general, these early shorts took advantage of the new technology, giving their audiences bizarre representations of a surrealistic universe in which a character was capable of removing its head and using it as a baseball. Emotions of shock by these silent, frenetic black-and-white creatures were registered by a series of exclamation marks appearing above their heads. The combination of these two limitations, monochrome and the absence of sound, prevented this genre from expanding or being considered seriously as a creative medium. The cartoons of the 1920s may have been drawn crudely, with simplistic lines against flat and bare backdrops, but the characters were spunky, unpredictable, and engaging.

With the advent of sound and color, the cartoon soon developed into an accepted and unique art form. In 1928 Walt Disney introduced the first sound cartoon, "Steamboat Willie," starring his affable rodent, Mickey Mouse. Its success prompted him to follow with others, including "The Skeleton Dance" (1929) and "The Three Little Pigs" (1933), which featured the hit song "Who's

Afraid of the Big Bad Wolf?" The tune, allegedly, became a slogan of the New Deal, which desperately sought populist symbols of optimism. Disney's artwork was more finished than that of his predecessors. His figures were more circular and rounded; his backgrounds contained more perspective and detail. Indeed, Disney and his stable of creatures, including Mickey, Donald Duck, and Pluto, dominated the world of American cartoons throughout the 1930s.

As Disney's popularity grew, his characters tended to become more complacent and conservative, losing their wild, devil-may-care charm. Their freshness dissipated in typical middle-class surroundings and plots. The only serious challenge to his throne was Max Fleischer, who, like Disney, developed his craft during the 1920s.

Fleischer, with his brother Dave, continued to produce cartoons during the Depression years. The brothers' studio was based in New York rather than in Hollywood, and their new characters reflected this difference. Their subjects were more urban but not sophisticated; they struggled for a living but were not sentimental. Popeye the Sailor was a proletarian, rough-and-tumble, swaggering gob who continually "moidered" the King's English. The "Popeye" cartoons remained popular for more than a decade, even with their crude artwork, repetitive plots, and predictable endings. Somehow Fleischer's anthropomorphic subjects seemed fresh and vibrant compared to Disney's animals. Betty Boop, another Fleischer creation during the late 1920s, brought to the screen a sexy flapper. The curvaceous, wide-eyed vamp with her short skirt and low-cut blouse proved too provocative for Hollywood's Hays Office, and the series was terminated by the censors in 1935 on grounds of "immorality." Actually, there were two Betty Boops, the more daring one drawn before the Hays Office came into being, and the more tame Betty with a longer hemline produced after the Office was created. The Fleischer brothers also experimented with longer animated films. They made *Popeye the Sailor Meets Sinbad the Sailor* in 1936. In 1939 they produced *Gulliver's Travels,* followed by *Mr. Bug Goes to Town* in 1941, their last full-length cartoon.

Disney, however, continued to reign supreme. He used sound creatively; he understood the need for vivid characterizations; he experimented with full-length animated features, producing an unprecedented series of high-quality films (including *Bambi, Snow White and the Seven Dwarfs, Fantasia, Pinocchio*); and, finally, he was able to convey his genuine love of the medium in which he worked. He was the undisputed master in the craft of animation—until the rise of the Young Turks in the 1940s.

A group of animators, dismissed by the Disney studios after a labor strike, founded a rival studio in 1943, United Productions of America, or UPA. Such talents as Stephen Bosustow, Bob Cannon, John Hubley, and Ernest Pintoff challenged the conventions of contemporary animation as practiced by Disney's factory. They added sophistication, new art styles, a fresh use of sound and color, and a gallery of unique characters. Gerald McBoing Boing, created by Bob Cannon, revolved around a boy who was able to vocalize sound effects, often with hilarious results. Mr. Magoo, created by Pete Burness and John Hubley, concerned a myopic, irascible fusspot who, oblivious to impending disaster, moves blithely along. In both characterizations the situations were often funny and highly inventive. Burness won an Academy Award for his short, "When Magoo Flew" (1953).

Some of the innovations at UPA stemmed more from economics than from artistic choice. The studio did not have the elaborate facilities and equipment of its rival; neither did it have the budget. To compensate for these shortcomings, the animators avoided unnecessary details, using a splash of color to represent a window and a form to symbolize a particular structure. Instead of

using animals as their subjects, they returned to human characters. Finally, to economize still further, they excluded the intricate, naturalistic movements of their subjects, having them instead glide or sail through a scene. These non-representational elements combined to give the Egyptian-like figures in profile a striking originality that remained in the viewer's memory long after the reel ended.

Two other major film studios, Warner Brothers and MGM, began to make serious inroads in animation during the 1940s. The Warner studio developed the popular "Bugs Bunny" series, created in part by animator Chuck Jones. Outwardly a bucolic creature, the glib, Runyonesque rabbit was more streetwise than any city slicker. The paradoxical protagonist, an early-version amalgam of Woody Allen's wise-cracking urbanite and Dirty Harry the gritty survivor, could fast-talk his way out of most predicaments. Bugs Bunny was born in 1936 but reached the height of his popularity in the 1940s. Along with Daffy Duck, Porky Pig, and a host of barnyard denizens, the studio provided a winning string of cartoons created by an unusually able group of animators, including Bob Clampett, Fritz Freleng, Norm McCabe, and Bob McKimson.

Warner Brothers also produced a series of black-and-white cartoons during World War II seldom seen by the general public. The "Private Snafu" shorts were meant to instruct our soldiers on various topics—from guarding military secrets to the importance of reading maps and field manuals—in an entertaining way. Using barracks humor, a striking visual style, and a main character who portrayed the quintessential G.I., Warner animators Chuck Jones, Fritz Freleng, and others created an interesting, although often didactic, series of cartoons.

Meanwhile, at MGM, three talented men were busy developing that studio's cartoon department. Animators Joseph Barbera and William Hanna pooled their skills with producer Fred Quimby to create the successful "Tom and Jerry" series. The adventures of the cat-and-mouse team brought their creators numerous Academy Awards, including Oscars for "Yankee Doodle Mouse" (1943), "Mouse Trouble" (1944), "Quiet, Please" (1945), "The Cat Concerto" (1946), "The Little Orphan" (1948), "The Two Mouseketeers" (1951), and "Johann Mouse" (1952).

Another creative force at MGM was Tex Avery, an animator who had started in 1930 by contributing to the "Aesop's Fables" series and later helped shape the Bugs Bunny character at Warner Brothers. Avery, a stylist who added a more violent tone to his cartoons, developed an almost anarchic approach to his material while stretching what little physical reality remained in the world of animation to the edge of abstraction. Some of his more memorable works include "Hen-Pecked Hoboes" (1941), "Swing Shift Cinderella" (1945), "Slap Happy Lion" (1947), and "The Cat That Hated People" (1949). This last cartoon exemplifies Avery in both theme and visual style. An urban cat, fed up with people treading on him, finds himself alone on the moon; but his tranquillity is soon disturbed when he is physically assailed by geometric and surrealistic objects that operate according to a logic all their own. He happily returns to earth where he accepts the orderly chaos of people trampling on him.

These inventive animators, along with others, relegated the Disney output to second place. Some individual artists even decided to go into production for themselves. The artistic surge which began in the early 1940s continued through the next two decades. John Hubley, who had worked for Disney on many of his feature-length cartoons and for UPA where in 1949 he directed the first Magoo cartoon, "Ragtime Bear," launched Storybook Productions, his own company, in 1955, producing high-quality animation. Ernest Pintoff, another graduate of UPA, opened his own studio in 1958, producing a series of superior animated featurettes.

Two other animators made significant contributions to the film cartoon. Walter Lantz, who had worked for John Bray and helped draw the "Mutt and Jeff," "Happy Hooligan," and "Krazy Kat" series during the 1920s and the 1930s, created his own characters during the 1940s, most notably Woody Woodpecker. Paul Terry, who began as a cartoonist on the Hearst newspapers, created the "Aesop's Fables" film series during the 1920s and his popular Terrytoons during the 1930s and 1940s, introducing the characters Mighty Mouse and Heckle and Jeckle.

Another widely popular animated series was the "Roadrunner," created in 1952 by Chuck Jones. The title character, a clever bird eternally pursued by a relentless coyote, represents more than the will to survive. He often metes out terrible revenge upon his foe, who never ceases in his struggle to capture the elusive bird.

The most popular animator of the 1970s was a Brooklyn boy who had worked for Terrytoons before venturing forth with a series of provocative X-rated animated features. Ralph Bakshi delighted many moviegoers—and offended others—with his *Fritz the Cat* (1972), *Heavy Traffic* (1973), and *Coonskin* (1975). Although the films received mixed reviews from the critics, they were box-office hits. His later works, such as *The Lord of the Rings* (1978), based on Tolkien's writings, and *Hey Good Lookin'* (1982), were less successful.

Aside from these occasional excursions into full-length features, theatrical animation has all but disappeared from the American screen. Any new developments in animation, either artistic or thematic, rest largely in the hands of those animators who work in television.

Ankrum, Morris (1896–1964), actor. Taught economics before entering films in the 1930s. A tall character player with a grey mustache, he was equally at home on both sides of the law. He appeared in more than 100 films, often playing villains in westerns and, later, portraying judges and law officers. He supported such screen comics as Jack BENNY, ABBOTT AND COSTELLO, and Bob HOPE.

SELECTED FILMS: *Three Texas Steers (1939), Buck Benny Rides Again (1940), Ride 'Em Cowboy (1942), Let's Face It, Dixie Dugan, The Heavenly Body (1943), Marriage Is a Private Affair, The Thin Man Goes Home (1944), The Cockeyed Miracle (1946), Undercover Maisie (1947), The Fabulous Fraud (1948), The Redhead and the Cowboy (1950), My Favorite Spy (1951), The Man With the X-Ray Eyes (1963)* ∎

Woody Allen and Diane Keaton in *Annie Hall* (1977)

Annie Hall (1977), UA. Dir. Woody Allen; *Sc.* Woody Allen, Marshall Brickman; with Woody Allen, Diane Keaton, Tony Roberts, Paul Simon, Carol Kane.

Woody Allen's Academy Award-winning comedy concerns the relationship between Alvy Singer (Allen) and Annie Hall (Diane Keaton). Allen plays a successful Jewish comedian who falls in love with Annie, a WASP, who eventually leaves him for a California record producer (Paul Simon). While the film explores their erratic relationship, we are privy to some genuinely funny moments. Waiting on line at a New York movie house, Allen soon grows weary of another patron's pontificating upon media writer Marshall McLuhan's theories. Allen suddenly presents McLuhan, who tells the prolix patron he is all wrong. Woody then faces the audience and remarks, "Why isn't life like this?" There are humorous flashbacks to Alvie's childhood and some wildly satirical moments concerning his experiences in California, but his one-liners predominate. "I would never want to belong to any club that would have someone like me as a member," Allen admits, paraphrasing Groucho Marx. After watching a World War II documentary, Annie wonders how she would stand up to torture. "The Gestapo would take away your Bloomingdales charge account," Allen replies, "and you'd tell them everything." Their apparent compatibility, however, disintegrates over their different views on sex, outside relationships, and Annie's perception of how Alvie sees her. He compares the relationship to a shark: "It has to keep moving or it dies," he concludes. "I think what we've got on our hands is a dead shark." The film won Academy Awards for Best Picture, Best Direction, Best Screenplay, and Best Actress (Keaton).

Anson, Laura (1892–1968), actress. Came to silent films in the early 1920s. She played female leads in dramas and comedies. She appeared as "Fatty" ARBUCKLE'S leading lady.

SELECTED FILMS: *The Easy Road, Crazy to Marry, The Little Clown (1921), Bluebeard, Jr., If You Believe It, It's So (1922), Skid Proof, The Silent Partner, The Way of the Transgressor (1923).* ∎

Antrum, Harry (1895–1967), actor. Began his screen career in the 1940s while he was well into his middle years following work in vaudeville and on stage. A talented supporting player, he appeared in dramas and light films for three decades as well as in television.

SELECTED FILMS: *Miracle on 34th Street (1947), The Luck of the Irish, Let's*

Live a Little (1948), *Free for All, Ma and Pa Kettle* (1949), *There's a Girl in My Heart* (1950), *Mr. Belvedere Rings the Bell, I'll See You in My Dreams* (1951), *The Solid Gold Cadillac* (1956), *Teacher's Pet* (1958), *The Monkey's Uncle* (1965). ■

Apartment, The (1960), UA. Dir. Billy Wilder; Sc. Billy Wilder, I.A.L. Diamond; with Jack Lemmon, Shirley MacLaine, Fred MacMurray, Ray Walston.

One of the director's best comedy-dramas, the film was very popular at the box-office and won several Academy Awards. The plot concerns insurance company clerk Jack Lemmon who, seeking to advance his career, lends out his apartment to his employers who use it to conduct their private love affairs. Complications set in when Lemmon becomes involved with Shirley MacLaine, the mistress of his boss, Fred MacMurray. Wilder, more bitter and cynical than usual in his comedies, gives a disturbing picture of moral behavior beneath the funny one-liners, humorous bits, and the occasional pathos. The basic story is a rather unpleasant one and contains no truly likable characters. The two principal performers manage to make their characters somewhat agreeable. Lemmon, as in his other films, is naturally funny as he gets entwined in the tangles of fate. MacLaine is charming as she begins to fall for Lemmon. MacMurray is believable as the straying married executive, but his Disney fans objected to his unsavory role and let him know it in no uncertain terms. Oscars were handed out for Best Picture, Best Director, and Best Screenplay. The film was adapted into a successful Broadway musical, *Promises, Promises.*

Apfel, Oscar (1880–1938), actor, director, producer. Began his screen career in 1911 in early silent films following some stage experience. Chiefly a supporting player, he appeared in numerous dramas, westerns, and light films. He worked in several films starring W. C. FIELDS. He later turned to directing and producing films as well as stage productions.

SELECTED FILMS: Ten Nights in a Bar Room (1922), *In Search of a Thrill* (1923), *Cheaters* (1927), *Not Quite Decent, Smiling Irish Eyes, Hurdy Gurdy* (1929), *Misbehaving Ladies, Man Trouble* (1930), *Men in Her Life, Helping Grandma, Sooky* (1931), *Hot Saturday, Business and Pleasure* (1932), *The Old-Fashioned Way* (1934), *The Nut Farm, The Man on the Flying Trapeze* (1935), *The Toast of New York* (1937). ■

Appleby, Dorothy, actress. Appeared in dramas and comedy films in the 1930s, and chiefly in shorts starring the THREE STOOGES during the 1940s. Saucy and lively, she often portrayed the comedy foil for some of the leading comedians of the period, including Andy CLYDE, the Stooges, and Buster KEATON.

SELECTED FILMS: Under Eighteen (1931), *Making the Headlines* (1938), *The Flying Irishman* (1939), *Rockin' Through the Rockies, From Nurse to Worse, Cookoo Cavaliers, Nothing but Pleasure, Pardon My Berth Marks, The Taming of the Snood, The Spook Speaks, His Ex Marks the Spot* (1940), *In the Sweet Pie and Pie, So Long, Mr. Chumps, General Nuisance* (1941), *Loco Boy Makes Good, What's the Matador* (1942). ■

Arbuckle, Macklyn (1866–1931), actor. Entered early silent films following a career in the theater. He appeared chiefly as a supporting player in light films during the 1920s.

SELECTED FILMS: The County Chairman (1915), *The Prodigal Judge, Welcome to Our City, Mr. Potter of Texas, Mr. Bingle, The Young Diana* (1922), *Broadway Broke* (1923), *Janice Meredith* (1924), *That Old Gang of Mine* (1925), *The Gilded Highway* (1926). ■

Roscoe "Fatty" Arbuckle and Mabel Normand

Arbuckle, Roscoe "Fatty" (1887–1933), actor, comedian. Appeared on stage at age 8 before starting his film career in 1908 with the Selig Company for whom he made many one-reelers. Disappointed with the direction of his career in films, he left to return to vaudeville as a comic. During this period, he met his future wife, Minta DURFEE, a fellow vaudevillian, who was also to become his leading lady in future comedy shorts. He developed into one of the most popular screen comics in Hollywood history. He worked for Mack SENNETT from 1913 until 1917, first as part of the Keystone Kops and later in his own series, turning out shorts such as "Fatty's Day Off" and "Fatty's Flirtation." The "FATTY" series continued until he left Sennett to form his own production company, Comique Films, where Buster KEATON got his start in films. His baby face, his weight, and his agility all worked in his favor and helped make him an overwhelming success. He joined Famous Players/Lasky Productions in 1920 where he made a series of feature-length comedies, but not all of these films were to be released.

His career came to an abrupt halt in 1921 when he was accused of manslaughter. The scandal, sensationalized by the press, involved a young actress who died of a ruptured bladder after being sexually assaulted, allegedly by Arbuckle. Although he was acquitted after a third trial, the first two ending in a hung jury, an outraged public who looked upon Hollywood as a sin-town forced his early retirement. His films were withdrawn from theaters, and the Hays Office, a self-regulatory agency, was hastily established to "purge" the goings-on in the film capital. He returned to the industry as a director, turning out shorts and features from 1925 to 1932, under the name of William B. Goodrich. He even acted in a half-dozen sound shorts for Vitaphone in 1932. But he never again found steady employment as a performer. Preferring acting to directing, he tried a brief tour on stage in England in 1932 but returned to the United States, disheartened and broken in spirit. He died the following year. As a comic with Sennett, he worked with many other masters of the genre, including Charlie CHAPLIN, Chester CONKLIN, Mabel NORMAND, and Ford STERLING.

Arbuckle was a master comic and a subtle director. He understood the nature of comedy better perhaps than many of his contemporaries. His "cause-and-effect" theory, that the gag must follow almost immediately after it is set up, may be seen in much of his work. He believed that if too much time lapses between these two points, e.g., a burning fuse and the explosion, the audience will begin to anticipate the result and the gag will fall flat. As rotund as he was, Arbuckle remained graceful and this added to his comedy. He maintained a boyish charm in his better comedies.

SELECTED FILMS: *Ben's Kid* (1909), *The Sanitarium* (1910), *Love and Courage, Mabel's New Hero, Mother's Boy, A Quiet Little Wedding* (1913), *A Film Johnnie, Tango Tangles, The Knockout, The Sea Nymphs* (1914), *The Little Teacher* (1915), *His Wife's Mistake, The Other Man, The Waiter's Ball* (1916), *The Butcher Boy, The Rough House, His Wedding Night* (1917), *Out West, The Bellboy, Moonshine, The Cook* (1918), *Love, A Desert Hero, Back Stage, The Hayseed* (1919), *The Life of the Party*

(1920), Brewster's Millions, Gasoline Gus (1921). ∎

Arden, Eve (1912–), actress, comedienne. Appeared in stock theater in the late 1920s at age 16, had small parts in two films a few years later, then in the Ziegfeld Follies in the mid-1930s before her re-entrance into a long film career. She usually portrayed a sharp-tongued confidante of the leading lady.

In *Stage Door*, for example, aspiring young actresses at a boarding house are elated that one of their group has finally found work in a nightclub chorus line. "She hasn't worked in so long," Arden quips, "that if she does get the job, it will practically amount to a comeback." In a later film, *Grease*, in which she played a school principal, she announces to the student body: "If you can't be an athlete, be an athletic supporter."

Equally at home in comedies, dramas, or musicals, she worked with such major stars as Cary GRANT, while holding her own with comics such as the MARX BROTHERS and Red SKELTON. She was nominated for an Academy Award as Best Supporting Actress for her role in *Mildred Pierce* (1945). Although the film was a strong drama, she managed to get off a riposte or two. She played the title role in the long-running radio and TV series, "Our Miss Brooks," the latter of which brought her an Emmy Award. After a ten-year respite, she returned to films in 1975.

SELECTED FILMS: The Song of Love (1929), Stage Door (1937), Having Wonderful Time (1938), Eternally Yours, At the Circus (1939), No, No, Nanette, Comrade X (1940), Ziegfeld Girl, Whistling in the Dark (1941), Let's Face It (1943), Cover Girl, The Doughgirls (1944), The Kid From Brooklyn, Night and Day (1946), The Voice of the Turtle (1947), One Touch of Venus (1948), Tea for Two (1950), Three Husbands (1951), We're Not Married (1952), Our Miss Brooks (1956), Anatomy of a Murder (1959), The Strongest Man in the World (1975), Grease (1978). ∎

Arkin, Alan (1934–), actor. Performed with a folk-singing group and a satirical comedy team, The Second City, in Chicago, before making his Broadway debut in 1963 in *Enter Laughing*. His major work in films has been as a comic actor although he has also played dramatic roles. An offbeat performer, he has specialized in eccentric characters.

In *Last of the Red Hot Lovers* he portrayed an innocent involved with three women. "Aren't you appalled at the promiscuity you find everywhere?" one of the objects of his desires comments. "I haven't found it anywhere," he says disappointedly.

SELECTED FILMS: The Russians Are Coming! The Russians Are Coming! (1966), Wait Until Dark (1967), Inspector Clouseau, The Heart Is a Lonely Hunter (1968), Popi (1969), Catch-22 (1970), Little Murders (1971), Last of the Red Hot Lovers (1972), Freebie and the Bean (1974), Hearts of the West (1975), The Seven-Percent Solution (1976), Fire Sale (1977), The In-Laws, Simon (1979), Bad Medicine (1985). ∎

Arling, Charles, actor. Worked in silent comedies for Mack SENNETT'S KEYSTONE studios and then switched to Fox studios in 1916 to appear in the latter's two-reelers in 1917. He starred in Fox's first short comedy entry, "Social Pirates." At Keystone, he appeared as supporting player for many of its top comics, including, among others, Syd CHAPLIN, Ford STERLING, and Mae BUSCH.

SELECTED FILMS: Court House Crooks, A Rascal in Wolfish Ways, A Favorite Fool, Crooked to the End, A Submarine Pirate (1915), An Oily Scoundrel (1916), Social Pirates (1917). ∎

Armetta, Henry (1888–1945), actor. Began his long screen career in silent films. A short, stocky figure with a neat mustache, he portrayed a variety of characters in over 100 dramas and light films from 1915 to 1945 for various Hollywood studios. Memorable for his Italian accent (he was born in Palermo, Italy), gesticulations, raised shoulder, and perplexed expression, he often attempted to bring the love interests together or comfort a child (Freddie Bartholomew in *Fisherman's Wharf*).

In *The Big Store* he complains to womanizer Harpo MARX: "Hey, pressa the grapes, no pressa my wife."

SELECTED FILMS: *The Nigger (1915), The Silent Command (1923), Street Angel (1928), Jazz Heaven, In Old Arizona (1929), The Unholy Garden (1931), Speak Easily, Hat Check Girl (1932), The Cat and the Fiddle, The Merry Widow (1934), Let's Sing Again (1936), Top of the Town (1937), Fisherman's Wharf (1939), The Big Store (1941), Anchors Aweigh, Colonel Effingham's Raid (1945).* ∎

Armstrong, Billy (1869– ?), actor. After a career in vaudeville, entered early silent films, especially as a supporting player in eleven comedy shorts starring Charlie CHAPLIN. He portrayed numerous characters, including cooks, prizefighters, hoboes, and generally shady figures.

SELECTED FILMS: *His New Job, The Champion, In the Park, By the Sea, Work, A Woman, The Bank, Shanghaied (1915), Police!, Triple Trouble, The Fireman (1916), Clancy's Kosher Wedding (1927).* ∎

Armstrong, Robert (1890–1973), actor. Worked in vaudeville and on stage before entering films in the late 1920s. A popular character actor, he appeared in numerous action and comedy films during a career that spanned five decades. His most famous role was that of Carl Denham, the showman who brought the giant ape, King Kong, to New York City in 1933.

SELECTED FILMS: *The Main Event (1927), A Girl in Every Port, Show Folks (1928), The Shady Lady (1929), Be Yourself, Dumbbells in Ermine (1930), Pan-*

ama Flo, Is My Face Red (1932), Fast Workers (1933), Palooka, She Made Her Bed, Kansas City Princess (1934), Nobody's Baby, The Girl Said No (1937), The Bride Wore Crutches (1941), It Happened in Flatbush (1942), The Paleface (1948), For Those Who Think Young (1964). ∎

Arnaz, Desi (1917–1986), actor, musician. Immigrated to the United States from his native Cuba at age 16. He formed his own band after working in others, gaining popularity as a bongo player. In 1940 he appeared in his first film and married one of his co-performers, Lucille BALL. Eventually the couple founded Desilu Productions. Their highly successful television series, "I Love Lucy," brought them great wealth. They were divorced in 1960. He appeared in comedy films and dramas, but his screen career never blossomed.

SELECTED FILMS: *Too Many Girls (1940), Father Takes a Wife (1941), The Navy Comes Through (1942), Cuban Pete (1946), Holiday in Havana (1949), The Long, Long Trailer (1954), Forever Darling (1956).* ∎

Arno, Sig (1895–1975), actor. Played in over 75 German and American films from 1923 to 1953. Best known for his comic relief in foreign-character roles, he supported such stars as ABBOTT and COSTELLO, Danny KAYE, and Bob HOPE.

SELECTED FILMS: *The Star Maker (1939), The Great Dictator (1940), This Thing Called Love, It Started With Eve (1941), The Palm Beach Story, Pardon My Sarong (1942), Taxi, Mister (1943), Up in Arms (1944), A Song to Remember (1945), The Great Lover (1949), Nancy Goes to Rio (1950), On Moonlight Bay (1951), The Great Diamond Robbery (1953).* ∎

Arnold, Cecile (–1931), actress. Worked in silent comedies for Mack SENNETT'S KEYSTONE studios in the 1910s. An attractive and spirited performer, she portrayed a range of characters, from waitresses ("Dough and Dynamite") to ingenues to cavewomen ("His Prehistoric Past"). She often appeared as supporting player for the top film comedians of· the period, including, among others, Charlie CHAPLIN (seven films), Syd CHAPLIN, and Charles MURRAY. She was one of Sennett's "Bathing Beauties."

SELECTED FILMS: The Masquerader, Such a Crook, Her Last Chance, His Talented Wife, Ambrose's First Falsehood, Those Love Pangs, Dough and Dynamite, Getting Acquainted, His Prehistoric Past, The Face on the Bar Room Floor (1914), Gussle's Day of Rest, A Game Old Knight, His Last Scent, Her Winning Luck, Hearts and Planets, A Human Hound's Triumph (1915). ■

Arnold, Edward (1890–1956), actor. On stage and in silent films by 1915, chiefly in westerns and melodramas. A portly and imposing figure, he emerged as one of Hollywood's most popular character actors during the 1930s and 1940s, and appeared in more than 100 dramas and comedies, occasionally in starring roles. He portrayed fathers, tycoons, professionals, and politicians, some of whom were quite unscrupulous. His autobiography, Lorenzo Goes to Hollywood, was published in 1940.

In Meet Nero Wolfe (1936) he portrayed Rex Stout's famous sleuth with a proclivity for beer, orchids, and thrift. His assistant, Archie (Lionel STANDER), promises a witness that some of her expenses will be paid. But when he asks his boss for a few dollars, the detective responds with laughter. "Well, why don't you pay her?" Arnold suggests. "You promised her the money."

SELECTED FILMS: When the Man Speaks (1916), Okay, America! (1932), Whistling in the Dark, Her Bodyguard, I'm No Angel, Roman Scandals (1933), Thirty Day Princess (1934), Biography of a Bachelor Girl (1935), Easy Living (1937), You Can't Take It With You (1938), Idiot's Delight, Mr. Smith Goes to Washington (1939), Slightly Honorable (1940), Meet John Doe, Nothing but the Truth (1941), The Youngest Profession (1942), Standing Room Only, Janie (1944), Three Wise Fools (1946), Dear Ruth (1947), Three Daring Daughters (1948), The Yellow Cab Man (1950), Dear Brat (1951), Living It Up (1954), The Ambassador's Daughter, Miami Expose (1956). ■

Arnold, Jessie (1877–1971), actress. Began her screen career as a supporting player in 1916 in early silent films. She appeared in dozens of dramas and light films over a period of five decades.

SELECTED FILMS: A Social Slave, He Became a Regular Fellow, The Light of Love (1916), Brothers (1930), Hot Saturday (1932), We Live Again (1934), Southern Exposure, The Four-Star Boarder (1935), Golden Girl (1951). ■

Arnold, Phil (1909–1968), actor. Appeared on stage and in vaudeville as well as in light feature films and comedy shorts. He worked with the THREE STOOGES as a supporting player in several of their later comedy shorts. He appeared occasionally in television.

SELECTED FILMS: King of the Turf (1939), Drafted in the Depot (1940), Sis Hopkins (1941), Sing a Song of Six Pants (1947), The Ghost Talks (1949), G.I. Jane, Yes Sir, Mr. Bones (1951), Pardon My Backfire (1953), The Big Chase, Money From Home (1954), It's Always Fair Weather (1955), Damn Yankees (1958), The Errand Boy (1962), The Three Stooges Go Around the World in a Daze (1963), Robin and the Seven Hoods (1964), Skidoo (1968). ■

Arnold, William R. (1883–1940), actor. Worked in vaudeville, on stage, and as a supporting player in dramas and light films beginning with the advent of sound.

SELECTED FILMS: Oh! Oh! Cleopatra, Rich Man's Folly (1931), In Love With Life, Cain and Mabel (1934), Four Days'

Wonder (1937), The Great Dictator (1940). ■

Arnt, Charles (1908–), actor. A character actor in films since the early 1930s. He often portrayed officious people, usually with a degree of mildness. He appeared in dramas, comedies, and musicals.

SELECTED FILMS: *Ladies Should Listen (1934), Two for Tonight (1935), Swing High, Swing Low (1937), Remember the Night (1940), Ball of Fire, Take a Letter, Darling (1942), Up in Arms (1944), Miss Susie Slagle's, Cinderella Jones (1946), Sitting Pretty (1948), Wabash Avenue (1950), Wild in the Country (1961), Sweet Bird of Youth (1962).* ■

Arquette, Cliff (1905–1974), actor. Worked in vaudeville, on radio, in television, and in films, usually impersonating rural types. He reached the height of his career playing Charlie Weaver on "Hollywood Squares." His appearances in mediocre films did nothing to further his career as a comic.

SELECTED FILMS: *Comin' Round the Mountain (1940), Saturday Night Bath in Apple Valley (1965), Don't Worry, We'll Think of a Title (1966).* ■

Arsenic and Old Lace (1944), WB. *Dir.* Frank Capra; *Sc.* Philip and Julius Epstein; with Cary Grant, Priscilla Lane, Raymond Massey, Peter Lorre, Josephine Hull, Jean Adair.

Capra's only black comedy, the film is based on the Broadway play about two kindly old ladies who calmly go about poisoning unsuspecting transients. Cary Grant, on the eve of his wedding, visits his two aunts and discovers a body in the window seat. It seems that the sisters only wanted to help their unhappy victims escape their misery, so they served the elderly gents poisoned elderberry wine. As if this revelation were not

Raymond Massey (left), Cary Grant (center), Jean Adair, Josephine Hull (right) in *Arsenic and Old Lace* (1944)

enough to unseat the shocked Grant, into the house come his psycho-killer brother, Raymond Massey, and his sinister underling, Peter Lorre, both of whom are hiding from the law. Massey portrays a Karloff-like character. In fact, Karloff played the role in the original Broadway production. The resulting hilarious, sometimes too frenetic, shenanigans keep the film moving. The supporting cast does more than its share to help things along. Jack Carson plays a dumb cop while John Alexander plays Grant's nutty uncle who thinks he is Teddy Roosevelt. The film was completed in 1941 but not released until three years later.

Arthur (1981), WB. *Dir.* Steve Gordon; *Sc.* Steve Gordon; with Dudley Moore, Liza Minnelli, John Gielgud, Geraldine Fitzgerald.

Reminiscent in many respects of the screwball comedies of the 1930s, *Arthur,* despite its flaws, has much going for it, particularly its two male leads. Diminutive Dudley Moore portrays a drunken millionaire playboy who will lose his inheritance unless he marries a designated heiress. Moore is personable and funny when he is drunk. When his grandmother and others condemn his irresponsible and frivolous life-style, the audience feels bound to side with him. John Gielgud, as his haughty and critical valet, is lovable as he goes about stealing one scene after another. "I think I'll take a bath," Moore announces after a night on the town. "I'll alert the media," Gielgud replies quietly and sardonically. The unique relationship between the two goes deeper than employer-employee. In one scene they reminisce about their many years together. "Remember how we would play hide-and-seek and you couldn't find me?" Moore recalls. "I couldn't find you," Gielgud confesses, "because I didn't look for you." Gielgud, the father-substitute, is not beyond rebuking his son-master for his wanton ways. Liza Minnelli, perhaps slightly too dynamic for this particular role, plays the poor working girl and aspiring actress that Moore falls in love with. In a typical screwball-comedy situation, he meets her at a plush Manhattan department store where she is shoplifting a tie. He manages to rescue her but loses his heart. Geraldine Fitzgerald plays Moore's disapproving but caring grandmother, while Jill Eikenberry portrays Moore's wealthy bride-to-be. Although writer-director Steve Gordon's attempt to recreate the zany comedy style of the Depression years resulted in too many worn-out plot contrivances, the performances of Moore and Gielgud and several very funny moments elevate this comedy above the average.

Arthur, Beatrice (1926–), actress. Has appeared on stage and in television and made her film debut in 1959. Usually portraying strong, domineering types, she has been more successful in television than on the screen, winning an Emmy Award in 1977 for her title role in "Maude."

In Mel BROOKS' *History of the World—Part I* she played an interviewer of the unemployed in ancient Rome. "Did you kill last week?" She asks brusquely, interviewing an unemployed gladiator. "Did you try to kill last week?" But her best role was in the comedy *Lovers and Other Strangers*. She confides to her daughter-in-law, Diane Keaton, about her own sex life with her husband, Frank (Richard Castellano).

"You mean you never enjoyed sex?" Keaton asks. "What's to enjoy?" Arthur questions. "Love isn't physical. Love is spiritual, like—like the great love that Ingrid Bergman had for Bing Crosby in *The Bells of St. Mary's*, when she was a nun and he was a priest and they loved each other from afar. But Frank didn't want to know from that."

SELECTED FILMS: *That Kind of Woman (1959), Lovers and Other Strangers (1970), Mame (1974), History of the World—Part I (1981).* ∎

Arthur, George K. (1899–), actor. Starred in films in his native England before immigrating to Hollywood in the early 1920s. Known mostly for his light films and comedy shorts, he occasionally appeared in more serious roles. Metro studios teamed the diminutive comic with gangling Karl DANE in a series of comedies ("Baby Mine," "Detectives," "Brotherly Love"). A lively performer, he played leads as well as supporting parts in silent and sound films.

SELECTED FILMS: *Madness of Youth, Hollywood (1923), The Salvation Hunters (1925), Irene, Kiki, The Boob, The Boy Friend, Bardelys the Magnificent (1926), Rookies, The Student Prince, Spring Fever (1927), Baby Mine, Circus Rookies, Detectives, Brotherly Love (1928), All at Sea, China Bound (1929), Chasing Rainbows (1930), Oliver Twist (1933), Vanessa: Her Love Story (1935).* ∎

Arthur, Jean (1905–), actress. Started in films in 1923 playing in westerns and two-reel comedies. She left Hollywood in 1932 for a short-lived career on the Broadway stage, then quickly returned to films. Distinguished by her raspy voice, she enlivened many films throughout the 1930s and was considered one of the decade's major comediennes by the public, the critics, and her colleagues. She was nominated for an Academy Award for her role in *The More the Merrier* (1943). She worked for such prestigious directors as John FORD, Frank CAPRA, and George Stevens. In her later years she appeared in television and taught drama at several colleges.

In *You Can't Take It With You* she played Alice, a member of the eccentric Sycamore family. She attempts to explain her parents to wide-eyed James Stewart, who has met them for the first time. "Dad makes fireworks because there's a sense of excitement about it. And Mother—know why Mother writes plays? Because eight years ago a typewriter was delivered to the house by mistake."

SELECTED FILMS: *Cameo Kirby (1923), Biff Bang Buddy, Fast and Fearless, Bringin' Home the Bacon (1924), The College Boob (1926), Husband Hunters, The Poor Nut (1927), The Whole Town's Talking, Party Wire, Diamond Jim (1935), Mr. Deeds Goes to Town (1936), The Plainsman, History Is Made at Night (1937), You Can't Take It With You (1938), Mr. Smith Goes to Washington (1939), Too Many Husbands (1940), A Foreign Affair (1948), Shane (1953).* ■

Arthur, Johnny (1883–1951), actor. Appeared in silent and sound films following a stage career of a quarter of a century. Recognizable by his short stature and complaining voice, he added his comic talents to "Our Gang" shorts as well as to feature-length comedies and dramas.

SELECTED FILMS: *The Unknown Purple (1923), Daring Love (1924), The Monster (1925), The Desert Song, Divorce Made Easy, The Aviator (1929), Cheer Up and Smile (1930), Penrod and Sam (1931), Twenty Million Sweethearts (1934), Traveling Saleslady, Doubting Thomas, Crime and Punishment (1935), The King Steps Out (1936), Pick a Star (1937), Road to Singapore (1940), The Nazty Nuisance (1943).* ■

Ashby, Hal (1936–), director. Began directing comedies and dramas in 1970 after working as an assistant editor and editor during the 1960s. He received an

Academy Award for his editing of *In the Heat of the Night* (1967).

SELECTED FILMS (as editor): *The Loved One (1965), The Russians Are Coming! The Russians Are Coming! (1966).*

SELECTED FILMS (as director): *The Landlord (1970), Harold and Maude (1971), The Last Detail (1973), Shampoo (1975), Being There (1979).* ■

Asher, Max (1880–1957), actor. Born in Oakland, California, but billed as "The funniest Dutch comedian in pictures." He began his film career with Mack SENNETT, then starred in comedy shorts for JOKER FILMS, a branch of Universal studios specializing in low-brow comedies. He frequently portrayed a light-headed Dutchman. In 1915 he co-starred with Gale Henry in a series of 11 one-reel satires, ridiculing the popular serials of the period. He also co-starred with Bobby VERNON in the comedy series, "MIKE AND JAKE." During the 1920s and into the sound era he worked as a supporting character actor in feature-length films.

SELECTED FILMS: *The Pearl of the Golden West, The Cheese Special (1913), Love and Politics, Across the Court (1914), Lady Baffles and Detective Duck (1915), Rip Van Winkle (1921), Heir-Loons (1925), We're in the Navy Now (1926), Lost at the Front, Painting the Town, Play Safe (1927), Show Boat (1929), Sweethearts on Parade (1931), Little Man, What Now? (1934).* ■

Asher, William (1919–), director. Working in films and in television, he is best known for popularizing the light, youth-oriented "beach" films of the 1960s. At times he collaborated on the film stories and screenplays.

SELECTED FILMS: *Leather Gloves (1948), Beach Party, Johnny Cool (1963), Muscle Beach Party, Bikini Beach (1964), Beach Blanket Bingo, How to Stuff a Wild Bikini (1965), Fireball 500 (1966).*

Ashton, Sylvia (1880–1940), actress. Worked on stage before entering early silent films in 1915. A supporting player, she appeared in numerous dramas and light films, retiring from the screen when sound was introduced.

SELECTED FILMS: The Nick of Time Baby (1917), Don't Change Your Husband (1919), Jenny Be Good, Conrad in Quest of His Youth (1920), The Blushing Bride, Hold Your Horses, The Love Special (1921), Our Leading Citizen, Youth to Youth (1922), Dancing Days (1926), Cheating Cheaters (1927), Bachelor's Paradise, Ladies' Night in a Turkish Bath (1928). ∎

Askin, Leon (1920–), actor. Portly character actor who frequently portrayed foreign-type roles in comedies and dramas. He often supported such popular stars as Bob HOPE, Bing CROSBY, James Cagney, and Danny KAYE.

SELECTED FILMS: Road to Bali (1953), Knock on Wood (1954), Son of Sinbad (1955), One, Two, Three (1961), Do Not Disturb (1965), What Did You Do in the War, Daddy? (1966), Double Trouble, The Perils of Pauline (1967), The Maltese Bippy (1969), Young Frankenstein (1974), Death Knocks Twice (1975). ∎

Fred Astaire and Ginger Rogers

Astaire, Fred (1899–1987), actor, dancer. Danced as a child in vaudeville with his sister Adele. They appeared on Broadway and continued to star in a string of stage successes through 1931.

After his sister married, Astaire went to Hollywood, and by 1934 he was paired with Ginger ROGERS with whom he co-starred in a series of popular musical comedies. The team was voted among the Box Office Top Ten in the years 1935–1937. But before his film success came the now famous screen test by David O. Selznick. The tough producer concluded: "I am still a little uncertain about the man, but I feel, in spite of his enormous ears and bad chin line, that his charm is so tremendous that it comes through even in this wretched test."

He later co-starred with other screen luminaries, including Rita Hayworth, Eleanor POWELL, Audrey HEPBURN, and Cyd Charisse. He ventured into drama in 1959 in On the Beach and was acclaimed by the critics. His autobiography, Steps in Time, was published in 1960.

His grace, sophistication, and expertise in the dance were influential in permanently altering the appearance of Hollywood musicals. Although his specialty was the musical, he aptly demonstrated, through his exuberance, charm, and wit, a flair for comedy, especially in his later, non-musical films. This propensity for comedy was also evident in some of his dance numbers, e.g., the hobo dance in Easter Parade (1948).

In Roberta (1935) Randolph Scott advises him: "They tell me in Paris, if you don't buy your gown from Roberta, you're not dressed at all." "I see," Astaire replies. "Nude if you don't, and nude if you do." And in Finian's Rainbow, he played the father of Petula Clark. He announces to his daughter: "Everyone in America is rich." "Are there no ill-housed and ill-clad?" she asks. "Yes," he answers, "but they're the best ill-housed and the best ill-clad in all the world."

SELECTED FILMS: Dancing Lady, Flying Down to Rio (1933), The Gay Divorcee (1934), Top Hat (1935), A Damsel in Distress (1937), You'll Never Get Rich (1941), Holiday Inn (1942), Royal Wedding (1951), The Band Wagon (1953),

Daddy Long Legs (1955), Funny Face (1957), Silk Stockings (1957), The Pleasure of His Company (1961), The Notorious Landlady (1962), The Amazing Dobermans (1977), Ghost Story (1981). ■

Astin, John (1930–), actor. Known for his comic character roles on television and in the theater. He made a handful of light films during the 1960s and 1970s.

SELECTED FILMS: West Side Story (1961), That Touch of Mink (1962), The Wheeler Dealers, Move Over, Darling (1963), The Spirit Is Willing (1967), Candy (1968), Get to Know Your Rabbit (1972), Every Little Crook and Nanny (1972), Freaky Friday (1977). ■

Astor, Gertrude (1887–1977), actress. Worked on stage while in her teens before entering films in 1914. A tall, blonde female lead and feature player, she appeared in silent and sound dramas and light films, once as Oliver HARDY'S wife in the 1931 comedy short, "Come Clean." She later played character roles and became well known for her elegance and her smart attire. Her long screen career extended over six decades.

SELECTED FILMS: Polly Redhead (1917), The Concert (1921), The Wall Flower, The Impossible Mrs. Bellew (1922), The Ne'er-Do-Well (1923), The Charmer (1925), Kiki, The Strong Man, The Cheerful Fraud (1926), The Cohens and the Kellys in Paris, Hit of the Show, The Butter and Egg Man, Stocks and Blondes (1928), Two Weeks Off, Twin Beds (1929), Dames Ahoy (1930), Misbehaving Husbands (1940), My Dear Secretary (1949), Father Makes Good (1950), All in a Night's Work (1961), The Man Who Shot Liberty Valance (1962). ■

Astor, Mary (1906–), actress. Began her long screen career in silent films at age 15. By the mid-1920s she became a star and has appeared in numerous dramas and light films over a period of five decades. A beautiful woman, she played worldly characters, her most famous role being that of Humphrey Bogart's love interest in The Maltese Falcon (1941). Her life off-screen was filled with problems, including failed marriages, scandals, and bad publicity. She has written five novels and two autobiographies, Mary Astor, My Story and A Life on Film.

In The Palm Beach Story (1942) she played a divorcee who befriends Claudette COLBERT. "We can look for husbands together," she proposes. "I'm looking for an American at the moment. It's so much more patriotic."

SELECTED FILMS: The Beggar Maid (1921), The Man Who Played God (1922), Woman Proof (1923), Beau Brummell (1924), Oh, Doctor! (1925), Forever After (1926), Two Arabian Knights (1927), Dry Martini (1928), Ladies Love Brutes (1930), The Royal Bed (1931), The Little Giant (1933), And So They Were Married (1936), Paradise for Three (1938), Midnight (1939), Turnabout (1940), Thousands Cheer (1943), This Happy Feeling (1948), Hush . . . Hush, Sweet Charlotte (1965). ■

At War With the Army (1951), PAR. Dir. Hal Walker; Sc. Fred F. Finklehoffe; with Dean Martin, Jerry Lewis, Polly Bergen, Angela Greene.

Almost every movie comedy team made at least one service feature. Wheeler and Woolsey starred in Half Shot at Sunrise (1930), Laurel and Hardy created mayhem in Pack Up Your Troubles (1932), the Marx Brothers partially engaged in war in Duck Soup (1933), the Ritz Brothers followed Stan and Ollie's advice in Pack Up Your Troubles (1939), while two years later Abbott and Costello joined up in their second film, Buck Privates. By Martin and Lewis' third film they were in the service with Jerry bungling things as usual. When Jerry, a private, is ordered about and harangued by Dean, his sergeant and long-time friend, he reminds Martin: "You were the best man at my wedding." "You're not kidding," Dean agrees.

There are some funny bits in this otherwise slow-paced comedy, including one with a soda machine and the boys doing a hilarious imitation of Bing Crosby and Barry Fitzgerald. This was their first starring film, although they had appeared in two previous comedies, *My Friend Irma* and *My Friend Irma Goes West*. The team managed to accumulate a large number of loyal fans, but never turned out an outstanding comedy such, for example, as the Marx Brothers made, although several of their films had memorable routines.

Atchley, Hooper (1887–1943), actor. Worked on stage before entering films during the early sound period. He appeared as a supporting player in dozens of dramas, westerns, and light films until his tragic suicide at age 56.

SELECTED FILMS: *Love at First Sight* (1929), *Millie, Men in Her Life* (1931), *Hot Money* (1935), *Navy Born* (1936), *A Day at the Races* (1937), *Penny's Picnic, Think First, Chicken Wagon Family, Mountain Rhythm* (1938), *In the Navy* (1941), *Rings on Her Fingers, Are Husbands Necessary?* (1942). ∎

Ates, Roscoe (1892–1962), actor. Best known for his stuttering, pop-eyed characters, he was featured in more than 100 films from 1929 to 1961, including comedies, romances, dramas, and westerns. He played Soapy, Eddie Dean's sidekick, in a series of oaters and worked with some of the leading comics of the period, including, among others, Buster KEATON, Jimmy DURANTE, and ABBOTT AND COSTELLO.

SELECTED FILMS: *South Sea Rose* (1929), *The Big House* (1930), *The Champ* (1931), *Freaks* (1932), *Alice in Wonderland* (1933), *The People's Enemy* (1935), *Gone With the Wind* (1939), *Chad Hanna* (1940), *The Palm Beach Story* (1942), *Colorado Serenade* (1946), *Abbott and Costello Meet the Keystone Kops* (1955), *The Errand Boy* (1961). ∎

Atwater, Edith (1911–1986), actress. Made her stage debut in 1929. After appearing in many productions, she entered films in 1936. A supporting actress in dramas and light films, she continued her film career into the 1970s.

SELECTED FILMS: *We Went to College* (1936), *The Gorgeous Hussy* (1936), *The Body Snatcher* (1945), *Teresa* (1951), *It Happened at the World's Fair* (1963), *Strange Bedfellows* (1965), *Pieces of Dreams* (1970), *Mackintosh & T.J.* (1975), *Family Plot* (1976). ∎

Aubrey, Jimmy, actor. Appeared in Fred KARNO'S English music hall touring company before starring in silent comedy shorts. He co-starred with Walter Kendig in the "Heinie and Louie" series in 1915 for Starlight comedies, a branch of United Film Service. In 1917 he appeared in another comedy series directed by Larry SEMON. He worked for various studios, including VITAGRAPH and Smallwood Film Company, returning to Vitagraph in 1919. Once again he starred in another successful comedy series. And again he left Vitagraph to work in a series of comedies for Standard Cinema in 1924. He continued playing supporting roles into the early sound period, appearing in LAUREL AND HARDY shorts and features.

SELECTED FILMS: *Footlights and Fakers* (1917), *Their Purple Moment* (1928), *That's My Wife* (1929), *Sons of the Desert* (1933), *Make a Million* (1935), *Abbott and Costello Meet Dr. Jekyll and Mr. Hyde* (1953). ∎

Auer, Mischa (1905–1967), actor. Migrated to the United States after the Russian Revolution. Following appearances on Broadway, he settled in Hollywood. He played in more than 100 films from 1928 to 1966, usually in the comic role of one who continually fractures the King's English. His lean frame, sad eyes, and victimized state enhanced many films. Although cast mostly in B movies, he was featured in a few major productions

Mischa Auer

such as *The Crusades* (1935), *My Man Godfrey* (1936), for which he was nominated for an Oscar as Best Supporting Actor, and *Destry Rides Again* (1939). His grandfather, Leopold Auer, was a famous violinist.

In *Seven Sinners* (1940) he portrayed a proud pickpocket who takes umbrage when he is associated with the underworld. "I'm not a thief," he protests, "I'm an artist."

SELECTED FILMS: *Something Always Happens* (1928), *Just Imagine* (1930), *The Yellow Ticket* (1931), *Sucker Money* (1933), *Viva Villa!* (1934), *The Princess Comes Across* (1936), *Sweethearts* (1938), *Unexpected Father* (1939), *Alias the Deacon, Spring Parade* (1940), *Flame of New Orleans* (1941), *Up in Mabel's Room* (1944), *A Royal Scandal* (1945), *Sentimental Journey* (1946), *The Monte Carlo Story* (1957), *Ladies First* (1963), *Arrivederci, Baby* (1966). ∎

Aunt Millie. The rigid but kindhearted maiden aunt of "ANDY HARDY" in the MGM series of that name. She was portrayed by character actress Sara HADEN in such films as *Judge Hardy's Children* (1938) and *The Hardys Ride High* (1939).

Austin, Albert (1882–1953), actor. Worked in early silent films, especially as a supporting player in 19 comedy shorts starring Charlie CHAPLIN. A versatile player, he portrayed various char-

acters, including clergymen, shop assistants, and cab drivers. Perhaps his best remembered role was that of the unfortunate customer who wants to have his alarm clock assessed by Charlie Chaplin in "The Pawnshop."

SELECTED FILMS: *The Floorwalker, The Vagabond, One A.M., The Count, The Pawnshop, Behind the Screen, The Rink* (1916), *Easy Street, The Cure, The Immigrant, The Adventurer* (1917), *A Dog's Life, Shoulder Arms* (1918), *Suds* (1920), *The Kid* (1921), *Pay Day* (1922), *City Lights* (1931). ∎

"Average Man" comedies. A series of comedy shorts produced by RKO during the 1930s and starring Edgar KENNEDY. The films depicted Kennedy as the typical American husband and breadwinner who, because of his hubris and braggadocio, became embroiled in seemingly simple chores that got out of hand. Removing a tree from his property resulted in its landing on his house. If these pressures were not enough to crush our pathetic hero, he also had to face a nagging wife and a badgering mother-in-law. His films would end with his familiar trademark—his slow burn; mortified and irate, he would slowly move his palm down from his bald head to his face.

Avery, Charles, actor, director. Began his film career in the early 1910s with Mack SENNETT'S KEYSTONE studios as one of the original KEYSTONE KOPS. He quickly advanced to director in charge of his own unit, making silent comedy shorts which starred such major comedians as Charles MURRAY, Syd CHAPLIN, and Ford STERLING. He directed nearly all of the "Hogan" comedies, a popular slapstick series starring the energetic Murray.

SELECTED FILMS: *The Telltale Light, Cohen's Outing* (1913), *Hogan's Mussy Job, Hogan the Porter, Hogan's Romance Upset, Hogan's Aristocratic Dream, Hogan Out West, Gussle's Wayward Path, Gussle Rivals Jonah* (1915), *His Lying Heart, His Last Scent* (1916). ∎

Awful Truth, The (1937), COL. *Dir.* Leo McCarey; *Sc.* Sidney Buchman, Vina Delmar; with Irene Dunne, Cary Grant, Ralph Bellamy, Cecil Cunningham.

Based on a play by Arthur Richman, this screwball comedy concerns a married couple, played by Irene Dunne and Cary Grant, who seek a divorce and then change their minds. Ralph Bellamy plays the hayseed interloper with whom Dunne becomes infatuated. Bellamy practically made a career out of playing decent but unlucky characters who never win the women of their dreams. Meanwhile, Grant becomes involved with a wealthy socialite. Each tries to foil the other's plans. The slight plot turns into high entertainment as a result of McCarey's sophisticated treatment of the complications. He won an Academy Award for his direction of the film, considered by many as the decade's definitive screwball comedy. The film was remade in 1953 as a musical and starred Ray Milland and Jane Wyman. Grant and Dunne teamed up again in 1940 for another comedy, *My Favorite Wife.*

Axelrod, George (1922–), playwright, screenwriter, director. Following his two popular stage comedies, *The Seven Year Itch* and *Will Success Spoil Rock Hunter?* (both made into films, in 1955 and 1957 respectively), he began writing screenplays. He has, at times, directed and produced films. He is equally at home with dramatic and light material. His screenwriting talents are more solidly based than his directorial capabilities, although he occasionally does show a penchant for enriching characterization and presenting a distinctly individual style of humor in his latter role. His themes, expressed in several films through fantasies and dreams, have often dealt with success, family life, and sex.

SELECTED FILMS (as screenwriter): Phffft (1954), The Seven Year Itch (1955), Bus Stop (1956), Breakfast at Tiffany's (1961), Paris When It Sizzles (1964), How to Murder Your Wife (1965), Lord Love a Duck (1966), The Secret Life of an American Wife (1968), The Lady Vanishes (1980). ∎

SELECTED FILMS (as director): Lord Love a Duck (1966), The Secret Life of an American Wife (1968). ∎

Dan Aykroyd

Aykroyd, Dan (1952–), actor, writer. Worked as writer-comic in television in his native Canada and in the United States, performed and recorded with John BELUSHI, and has appeared in light films since the late 1970s. A talented impressionist and offbeat comic actor, he specializes in satire and parody. His routines, however, tend to make his films episodic. He received an Emmy Award in 1977 as a comedy writer.

SELECTED FILMS: 1941 (1979), The Blues Brothers (1980), Neighbors (1981), It Came From Hollywood (1982), Doctor Detroit, Trading Places (1983), Ghostbusters (1984), Spies Like Us (1985). ∎

Ayres, Gordon "Freckles," child actor. A member of the "OUR GANG" comedies. He was married to Peggy Montgomery, the popular child star known as BABY PEGGY during the 1920s.

B

Babes in Toyland (1934), MGM. *Dir.* Gus Meins, Charles Rogers; *Sc.* Frank Butler, Nick Grinde; with Stan Laurel, Oliver Hardy, Charlotte Henry, Henry Brandon.

Producer Hal ROACH adapted Victor Herbert's fairy tale operetta as a framework for the talents of LAUREL AND HARDY. Containing all the major nursery rhyme characters, the film was aimed at the young audience. But enough parents accompanied their children to make the film a huge financial success. Three highlights of the comedy are the attack of the Bogeymen, the sequence with the "old woman who lives in a shoe," and the chaotic springing to life of the giant-sized wooden soldiers. The popular film, retitled *The March of the Wooden Soldiers*, is shown on television in many areas of the country during holidays. It was remade in 1961 with Ray BOLGER as the villain and Henry Calvin and Gene Sheldon trying to emulate Stan and Ollie, but the later version lacks the charm and fun of the original.

Baby DeRue (1908–), child actress. Made her screen debut in 1913 at age four in a Cecil B. DeMILLE feature. Born Carmen Faye DeRue, the little performer starred in numerous dramas and light films. When she switched to Fox studios in 1915, she specialized in playing boys' roles. Like many other child stars, she failed to capture the same popularity as an adult that she had attained as a child performer. She is considered by several film historians as the first female child star. She appeared in more than 100 films.

SELECTED FILMS: The Squaw Man (1913), Brewster's Millions, Master Mind (1914), Treasure Island (1915), Jack and the Beanstalk, Babes in the Woods, Aladdin and His Wonderful Lamp (1917), The Girl With the Champagne Eyes (1918). ■

Baby Dumpling. Fictional character in the "BLONDIE" comedy series. The child of Dagwood and Blondie Bumstead (Arthur LAKE and Penny SINGLETON), he was played by child actor Larry Simms and by the seventh film was being addressed as Alexander.

Baby Gloria, child actress. Appeared in early silent films playing orphans or mischievous types. She reached her peak in the years 1918–1919, at approximately age six, and was featured in two-reelers as well as full-length comedy-dramas. She was also known as Baby Gloria Joy.

SELECTED FILMS: No Children Wanted, The Locked Heart, Little Miss Grown-Up, Wanted, a Brother, The Fortunes of Corinne (1918), I Want to Be a Lady, Corinne, Come Here (1919). ■

Baby LeRoy (1932–), child actor. Debuted in films as a one-year-old infant. A charming little imp with slicked-down light hair and a round cherubic face, he became famous as W. C. FIELDS' nemesis in a series of films. The comic, displaying a strong dislike of children, did battle with Baby LeRoy, sometimes losing a pocket watch to the tot, other times getting in a good, swift kick to the infant's rear.

SELECTED FILMS: *A Bedtime Story, Torch Singer, Tillie and Gus, Alice in Wonderland (1933), The Old-Fashioned Way, It's a Gift, Miss Fane's Baby Is Stolen, The Lemon Drop Kid (1934), It's a Great Life (1936).* ∎

Baby Peggy (1917–), child actress. Early popular child performer who starred in many shorts and features during the 1920s. When she grew older and public interest in her waned, she entered B movies for a while under her complete name, Peggy Montgomery, and finally retired from the screen in the early 1930s.

SELECTED FILMS: *A Little Patriot (1917), Peggy Behave (1922), Hollywood, The Darling of New York (1923), Captain January (1924), The Speed Demon, Fighting Courage (1925), April Fool, Looking for Trouble (1926), Sensation Seekers, The Sonora Kid (1927), Arizona Days, Saddle Mates (1928), Eight Girls in a Boat (1934).* ∎

Baby Sandy (1938–), child actor. Charming toddler who appeared on the cover of *Life*, was voted "baby of the year," and made a series of light films during the late 1930s and early 1940s.

SELECTED FILMS: *East Side of Heaven, Little Accident (1939), Sandy Is a Lady, Sandy Gets Her Man (1940), Sandy Steps Out, Bachelor Daddy, Melody Lane (1941), Johnny Doughboy (1942).* ∎

Bacall, Lauren (1924–), actress. Worked as a model before entering films in the mid-1940s when Howard HAWKS spotted her and placed her under contract. She appeared in dramas during the 1940s with Humphrey BOGART, whom she married in 1945. Her wide

potential as an actress did not become evident until the 1950s when she began starring in comedies as well. An attractive, sensual, and intelligent performer, she has also appeared on stage and in television. Her autobiography is titled *Lauren Bacall by Myself*.

SELECTED FILMS: *To Have and Have Not (1944), Two Guys From Milwaukee (1946), How to Marry a Millionaire (1953), Woman's World (1954), Designing Woman (1957), Sex and the Single Girl (1965), Health (1979).* ∎

Bachelor Mother (1939), RKO. Dir. Garson Kanin; Sc. Norman Krasna; with Ginger Rogers, David Niven, Charles Coburn, Frank Albertson, Ernest Truex.

This entertaining film was released at the end of a decade that sparkled with romantic and screwball comedies. Ginger ROGERS, a sales clerk at a department store owned by Charles COBURN, finds an abandoned infant. Her bosses refuse to believe her disclaimers concerning the baby and demand that she keep the child if she wants to hold on to her job. She soon becomes involved with David NIVEN, the playboy son of Coburn, whom the employees suspect is the real father of the child. The succession of farcical misunderstandings is handled expertly by the game cast. The witty and scintillating dialogue helps to make this one of the better films of the decade. Rogers, who disliked the script and originally refused the role, had to be coaxed by producer Pandro S. Berman into accepting it. A gifted actress, she had done several light films before this but was never considered in the top ranks of the comic actresses of the period, including Carole LOMBARD, Jean ARTHUR, Irene DUNNE, and Barbara STANWYCK. This film proved her critics wrong. That same year she made another romantic comedy, *Fifth Avenue Girl*, released one month after *Bachelor Mother*, but it did not fare as well with audiences or critics. Niven had still not come into his own as a major star and was considered a simple co-star in this bright comedy. Garson Kanin, who directed the film, emerged as a top-flight Hollywood director. The comedy, already a remake of a 1935 Hungarian film, *Kleine Mutti*, was transformed into *Bundle of Joy* in 1956, starring Eddie FISHER, Debbie REYNOLDS, and Adolphe MENJOU in the lead roles.

Backus, Jim (1913–), actor. Worked on stage, on radio, and in vaudeville before entering films in 1949. He has appeared as a character actor in dozens of features, portraying roles both comic and dramatic. He reached a degree of fame in the 1950s as the off-screen voice of the cartoon character Mr. Magoo. His autobiography, *Rocks on the Roof*, was published in 1958, and his memoirs, *Only When I Laugh*, in 1965.

In *The Wheeler Dealers* (1963) he portrayed an owner of a Wall Street brokerage house. Living in his male-dominated world of finance, he gives his views on the opposite sex: "Women shouldn't be allowed to have lunch clubs. We've got to keep them off balance, disorganized—clawing and scratching at each other. Otherwise they might turn on us—like mad dogs."

SELECTED FILMS: *Easy Living, Father Was a Fullback* (1949), *His Kind of Woman, Bright Victory* (1951), *Deadline, USA, Pat and Mike* (1952), *Above and Beyond, Androcles and the Lion* (1953), *Rebel Without a Cause* (1955), *Meet Me in Las Vegas, The Great Man* (1956), *Boys' Night Out* (1962), *It's a Mad, Mad, Mad, Mad World* (1963), *Advance to the Rear* (1964), *Hello Down There* (1969), *Pete's Dragon* (1977), *C.H.O.M.P.S.* (1979). ∎

Bacon, Irving (1893–1965), actor. Began his long screen career in the 1910s playing leads and supporting roles in dramas and light films for a variety of producers, including Mack SENNETT. He is probably best known for his role as the beleaguered mailman in the "BLONDIE" comedies. He appeared in more than 200 films, from early silents to 1958, usually as a simple-minded or bewildered soul or a clever rural type.

SELECTED FILMS: *Anna Christie* (1923), *Million Dollar Legs* (1932), *Six of a Kind* (1934), *Diamond Jim* (1935), *You Can't Take It With You* (1938), *The Adventures of Huckleberry Finn* (1939), *The Grapes of Wrath* (1940), *Meet John Doe, Never Give a Sucker an Even Break* (1941), *Holiday Inn* (1942), *Roughly Speaking, Guest Wife* (1945), *Monsieur Verdoux* (1947), *State of the Union, Good Sam* (1948), *A Star Is Born* (1954), *Fort Massacre* (1958). ∎

Bacon, Lloyd (1890–1955), actor, director. Worked as a stage actor before appearing as a heavy in early silent screen comedies. He worked with some of the most popular comics of the period, including Lloyd HAMILTON and Charlie CHAPLIN. He appeared in 11 of Chaplin's early shorts, usually as his foil, including "The Champion," "In the Park," "The Tramp" (all 1915), "Behind the Screen," "The Rink" (both 1916), and "Easy Street" (1917). As an actor he portrayed lovers, film directors, and drug addicts. He eventually became one of the most productive screen directors. Although he specialized in musical comedies, especially those choreographed by Busby Berkeley, he also directed many better-than-average comedies and dramas.

SELECTED FILMS (as director): *Broken Hearts of Hollywood, Private Izzy Murphy* (1926), *White Flannels, A Sailor's Sweetheart* (1927), *Pay As You Enter, The Singing Fool* (1928), *Honky Tonk, So Long Letty* (1929), *She Couldn't Say No, The Office Wife* (1930), *Fifty Million Frenchmen* (1931), *You Said a Mouthful* (1932), *42nd Street* (1933), *Wonder Bar, Here Comes the Navy* (1934), *Frisco Kid* (1935), *Ever Since Eve, San Quentin* (1937), *A Slight Case of Murder* (1938), *Knute Rockne—All American* (1940), *Larceny, Inc.* (1942), *Mother Is a Freshman* (1949), *Kill the Umpire, The Good Humor Man* (1950),

The French Line, She Couldn't Say No (1954). ▪

Badger, Clarence (1880–1964), director. Began his Hollywood career with Mack SENNETT in 1915 as a continuity writer. He soon began directing two-reel comedies. By 1918 he was directing feature-length films for Sam Goldwyn and continued to make pictures through the silent and sound eras until his retirement in 1940. Most noted for his charming romantic comedies, he directed some of the most famous stars in films, including Bobby VERNON, Clara BOW, Gloria SWANSON, and Will ROGERS.

SELECTED FILMS: Gypsy Joe, His Wild Oats, A Modern Enoch Arden, Haystacks and Steeples, The Danger Girl (1916), Teddy at the Throttle, The Sultan's Wife (1917), The Floor Below, A Perfect Lady (1918), Sis Hopkins, Leave It to Susan, Jubilo (1919), Honest Hutch (1920), Doubling for Romeo (1921), Don't Get Personal, Quincy Adams Sawyer (1922), Potash and Perlmutter (1923), New Lives for Old (1925), Hands Up, Miss Brewster's Millions (1926), It, Man Power (1927), Hot News (1928), Paris (1929), No, No, Nanette (1930), The Hot Heiress, Woman Hungry, Party Husband (1931), When Strangers Marry (1933), Rangle River (1939). ▪

Baer, Buddy (1915–), prizefighter, actor. Entered films in the 1940s. A boxer-turned-character actor, he appeared in a string of chiefly light films. He worked with the comedy teams ABBOTT AND COSTELLO and the THREE STOOGES. He is the brother of prizefighter Max BAER.

SELECTED FILMS: Africa Screams (1949), Two Tickets to Broadway (1951), Jack and the Beanstalk (1952), Dream Wife (1953), Jubilee Trail (1954), Slightly Scarlet (1956), Snow White and the Three Stooges (1961). ▪

Baer, Max (1909–1959), prizefighter, actor. Popular boxer in the early 1930s who appeared sporadically in light films. In 1934 he became Heavyweight Champion of the World. He supported various screen personalities, including Myrna Loy, Abbott and Costello, and Humphrey Bogart. He was the brother of Buddy BAER, also a former prizefighter and screen actor.

SELECTED FILMS: The Prizefighter and the Lady (1933), The Navy Comes Through (1942), Ladies' Day (1943), Africa Screams, Bride for Sale (1949), Skipalong Rosenbloom (1951), The Harder They Fall (1956), Once Upon a Horse (1958). ▪

Bailey, Pearl (1918–), entertainer. Worked on Broadway, in television, and, regrettably, in only a handful of films. A personable and warm performer, she has enlivened the few films in which she has appeared.

SELECTED FILMS: Variety Girl (1947), Isn't It Romantic? (1948), That Certain Feeling (1955), St. Louis Blues (1957), The Landlord (1969). ▪

Bainter, Fay (1891–1968), actress. Began her film career in the early 1930s. Because of her naturally compassionate expression, she was often assigned to portray mothers in featured roles in both dramas and light films. She received an Academy Award as Best Supporting Actress for Jezebel (1938) and was nominated for another Oscar for her role in The Children's Hour (1962).

SELECTED FILMS: This Side of Heaven (1934), Mother Carey's Chickens, The Arkansas Traveler (1938), Our Neighbors, the Carters (1940), Babes on Broadway (1941), Woman of the Year (1942), The Heavenly Body (1943), The Kid From Brooklyn (1946), The Secret Life of Walter Mitty (1947), June Bride (1948), Bon Voyage! (1962). ▪

Baker, Art (1898–1956), actor. Worked on radio before entering films in 1937. A white-haired, pleasant character player, he appeared in dramas and light films.

He was equally comfortable on either side of the law, playing crooked politicians or sympathetic judges. But his greatest success came as master of ceremonies of a weekly television show called "You Asked for It."

SELECTED FILMS: Artists and Models (1937), Abie's Irish Rose (1946), State of the Union (1948), Easy Living (1949), Artists and Models (1955). ∎

Baker, Belle (1895–1957), comedienne, singer. Worked in vaudeville in 1909, on Broadway in 1911, and played the Palace Theater in the 1920s. She was a popular comic and song stylist through the 1920s and early 1930s. Unfortunately, her film appearances were rare: she made only two sound features. She did extensive recording for several record companies.

SELECTED FILMS: Song of Love (1929), Atlantic City (1944). ∎

Baker, Benny (1907–), actor. Worked in vaudeville, burlesque, and the theater before entering films in the early 1930s as a character actor, mostly in comic roles. He supported many major stars over the last 40 years, including, among others, Mae WEST, Fred MacMURRAY, Loretta YOUNG, and Danny KAYE.

SELECTED FILMS: The Hell Cat, Belle of the Nineties (1934), The Big Broadcast of 1936 (1935), Champagne Waltz, Hold 'Em Navy (1937), The Farmer's Daughter (1940), Up in Arms (1944), The Inspector General (1949), Papa's Delicate Condition (1963), Boy, Did I Get a Wrong Number! (1966), Jory (1973). ∎

Baker, Eddie (1897–1968), actor. Supporting actor who appeared in comedy shorts and feature-length films during the 1920s and 1930s for Hal ROACH and other studios. He worked with LAUREL AND HARDY, Charlie CHASE, and other comedians.

SELECTED FILMS: Powder and Smoke, Publicity Pays (1924), Bacon Grabbers (1929), Come Clean (1931),

Any Old Port (1932), Me and My Pal, Kickin' the Crown Around, Beauty and the Bus, Sons of the Desert (1933), Elmer and Elsie, Them Thar Hills, Babes in Toyland (1934). ∎

Baker, George D., director, screenwriter. Began his film career at Vitagraph studios in 1910 by directing comedy shorts featuring John BUNNY and Flora FINCH. He continued to direct films and write screenplays of various genres into the 1920s, mostly for Metro.

SELECTED FILMS: The New Stenographer, Captain Barnacle's Courtship (1911), Bunny All at Sea (1912), The Autocrat of Flapjack Junction (1913), Father's Flirtation, The Honeymooners (1914), A Price of Folly (1915), A Night Out (1916), Castles in the Air (1919), Heliotrope (1920), Little Eva Ascends (1922), Revelation (1924). ∎

Baldwin, Earl, screenwriter. Wrote his first screenplay in 1928 and, for the next three decades, turned out numerous scripts, alone and in collaboration, chiefly for routine melodramas and light films.

SELECTED FILMS: Brotherly Love (1928), Red Hot Rhythm (1929), Sweet Mama (1930), Naughty Flirt (1931), Central Park, The Tenderfoot (1932), Blondie Johnson, Havana Widows (1933), Here Comes the Navy, Wonder Bar (1934), The Irish in Us (1935), Ever Since Eve (1937), The Cowboy From Brooklyn, A Slight Case of Murder (1938), Off the Record (1939), Brother Orchid (1940), She Couldn't Say No (1941), Pin-Up Girl (1944), Hold That Blonde (1945), Africa Screams (1949), Juke Box Rhythm (1959). ∎

Baldwin, Walter (1896–), actor. Appeared on Broadway before entering films in 1940. A dependable character actor who specialized in rural types, he played shopkeepers and farmers in dozens of dramas and light films, many of which were second features. He worked in comedies starring ABBOTT AND COSTELLO and MARTIN AND LEWIS.

SELECTED FILMS: Angels Over Broadway (1940), Look Who's Laughing, Barnacle Bill (1941), Scattergood Rides High (1942), Always a Bridesmaid (1943), Louisiana Hayride (1944), Murder, He Says (1945), The Time of Their Lives, Claudia and David (1946), On Our Merry Way (1948), Cheaper by the Dozen (1950), Something for the Birds (1952), Living It Up (1954), You Can't Run Away From It (1956). ■

Lucille Ball

Ball, Lucille (1911–), actress, comedienne. Worked as a model and chorus girl before beginning her film career in the early 1930s as a Goldwyn Girl. She continued appearing in minor and supporting roles, usually as comic relief. Her career did not flourish until after she attained fame in television in the 1950s in the long-running "I Love Lucy" show. Together with her husband Desi AR-NAZ, whom she married in 1944, she founded Desilu Productions, which produced their series and other television shows. She worked with many of the top film stars during her 35 years in Hollywood. Vivacious and charming, she added spice to many films, even if she did not have the starring role. Charles Higham's biography, *Lucy: The Real Life of Lucille Ball*, was published in 1986.

In *Best Foot Forward*, playing herself, she accepts an invitation to a military academy prom for publicity reasons. Upon her arrival at the train depot, however, she is greeted only by a small, stray dog. "I don't mind the bands playing," she says to her manager, "but if they don't stop shoving, I'll scream!"

SELECTED FILMS: Broadway Thru a Keyhole, Roman Scandals (1933), Kid Millions, The Fugitive Lady (1934), Carnival, Top Hat (1935), Chatterbox, Follow the Fleet (1936), Stage Door (1937), Room Service (1938), Panama Lady (1939), Too Many Girls (1940), Seven Days' Leave (1942), Best Foot Forward (1943), Easy to Wed (1946), Sorrowful Jones (1949), Fancy Pants (1950), The Long, Long Trailer (1954), The Facts of Life (1960), Yours, Mine and Ours (1968), Mame (1974). ■

Ball of Fire (1941), RKO. *Dir.* Howard Hawks; *Sc.* Charles Brackett, Billy Wilder; with Gary Cooper, Barbara Stanwyck, Oscar Homolka, Dana Andrews, S.Z. Sakall.

A light reworking of the classic tale "Snow White and the Seven Dwarfs," this SCREWBALL COMEDY concerns a group of college professors who "adopt" a strip-tease dancer, played by Barbara STANWYCK, from whom they hope to learn American slang for their encyclopedia. Stanwyck, on the lam from gangsters, welcomes the opportunity to hide out for a while. Gary COOPER, a linguistics expert and leader of the scholarly but cloistered gents, falls in love with their subject. The large and competent cast adds to the comedy, especially Dana Andrews as Stanwyck's hoodlum boyfriend who wants her back and Alan JENKINS as a verbose garbage collector. The film was remade in 1948 as a musical, *A Song Is Born*, starring Danny KAYE and Virginia MAYO and was again directed by Hawks.

Ballard, Kaye (1926–), actress, comedienne, singer. Has appeared on stage, in television, and, occasionally, in light feature films.

SELECTED FILMS: *The Girl Most Likely* (1958), *A House Is Not a Home* (1964), *Which Way to the Front?* (1970), *The Ritz* (1976), *Freaky Friday* (1977), *Falling in Love Again* (1980). ∎

Bananas (1971), UA. *Dir.* Woody Allen; *Sc.* Woody Allen, Mickey Rose; with Woody Allen, Louise Lasser, Carlos Montalban, Howard Cosell.

Woody ALLEN, portraying Fielding Mellish, becomes embroiled in a South-American revolution when he falls for Nancy (Louise LASSER), a political activist. Allen's one-liners zip by as fast as the rebels' bullets. "What would you have been if you finished school?" a fellow worker asks him. "I don't know," he replies. "I was in the black studies program. By now I could have been black." At one point Lasser calls him immature. "How am I immature?" Woody asks defensively. "Emotionally, sexually, and intellectually," she delineates. "Yeah," Allen accedes, "but what other ways?" Earlier in this zany film Allen confides to her: "I love Eastern philosophy. Metaphysical and redundant—abortively pedantic." "I know just what you mean," she responds. Howard Cosell's appearances are hilarious, especially in his sportscast of Allen's marital consummation with Louise Lasser.

"Bank, The." See Charlie Chaplin.

Bank Dick, The (1940), U. *Dir.* Eddie Cline; *Sc.* W. C. Fields; with W. C. Fields, Cora Witherspoon, Una Merkel, Grady Sutton, Franklin Pangborn.

Fields portrays Egbert Souse, a small-town no-account who whiles away the hours at his favorite haunt, The Black Pussy Cat Cafe, where he regales the patrons with outlandish stories. But at home he is mistreated by his family. His shrewish wife criticizes his drinking and smoking, his mother-in-law snickers joyously each time he is caught in these acts, and his younger daughter hurls rocks at

W. C. Fields in *The Bank Dick* (1940)

him in the street. Conditions do not improve even when he unknowingly captures a bankrobber and emerges as the town hero. He is rewarded by the bank with a job as a guard. One of his first acts is the apprehension of a child with a toy pistol. "Is that gun loaded?" he questions the boy's mother. "No," she replies, "but I think you are." The comic's wit and visual gags are quite funny, and his cutting barbs on family life and other assorted topics reach their targets. An early sequence in which he substitutes for a film director shooting a picture in town is quite amusing, as is the actual event of the escaping robber tripping over Fields and being knocked unconscious. Grady SUTTON plays the dimwitted boyfriend of Fields' older daughter, while veteran comic character actor Franklin PANG-BORN portrays a bank examiner. This is one of Fields' better films. It has more sustained routines and gags than many of his other vehicles as well as a poignant ending. Fields, after being awarded a hefty contract to direct a movie, wins the respect of his now obsequious family and walks out into his garden, dressed in formal attire, with an air of pride and self-confidence.

Banks, Monty (1897–1950), actor, director. Left his native Italy and arrived in the United States in 1914. He played small parts in Roscoe ARBUCKLE'S comedies, then moved to larger roles in silent two-reelers, several of which he directed. He returned to England in 1928 to direct films. By 1940 he was back in Hollywood where he directed *Great Guns* (1941), starring LAUREL AND HARDY. He usually portrayed little chubby characters who, by some stroke of fortune, won the girl. He made one of the classic comedy shorts of the 1920s, "Play Safe," a brilliant chase film involving racing cars, trains, etc.

SELECTED FILMS: *The Geezer of Berlin* (1918), *Don't Park Here* (1920), *Racing Luck* (1924), *Keep Smiling* (1925), *Play Safe, Horse Shoes, Flying Luck* (1928), *Atlantic, Compulsory Husbands* (1930), *Weekend Wives* (1931), *Hold 'Em Jail* (1932). ∎

Barbier, George (1865–1945), actor. Worked in the silent and sound periods for more than three decades. A versatile and prolific character actor, he often played wealthy fathers. He appeared chiefly in light films with some of the leading comics of the period, including, among others, W. C. FIELDS, Harold LLOYD, and George BURNS AND Gracie ALLEN.

In *The Merry Widow* he played the King of a mythical European country. When the richest woman of the land moves to Paris, he is faced with a dilemma. Concerned about public opinion, he asks his adviser, Donald MEEK, what the average "shepherd" in the street is thinking. Meek informs Barbier that some of the shepherds are thinking of organizing. "Were they prominent shepherds?" the King asks. "A couple of East Side shepherds," Meek answers. "Intellectuals?" "Yes." "Oh," the King sighs with relief, "let them talk."

SELECTED FILMS: *Monsieur Beaucaire* (1924), *The Big Bond, The Sap From Syracuse* (1930), *The Smiling Lieutenant* (1931), *Million Dollar Legs* (1932), *Mama Loves Papa* (1933), *Many Happy Returns, Tillie and Gus, Ladies Should Listen, The Merry Widow* (1934), *Here Comes Cookie, Millions in the Air* (1935), *The Princess Comes Across* (1936), *On the Avenue, Hotel Haywire* (1937), *Little Miss Broadway, Sweethearts* (1938), *The Man Who Came to Dinner* (1941), *The Magnificent Dope* (1942), *Hello, Frisco, Hello* (1943), *Weekend Pass* (1944), *Her Lucky Night* (1945). ∎

Barclay, Don (1914–1968), actor. Worked in silent comedy shorts for Mack SENNETT'S KEYSTONE studios and in sound comedies for other studios during the 1930s. He appeared as supporting player to Mack SWAIN in the "AMBROSE" comedy series and as the principal in other slapstick shorts. In the 1930s he worked with various comedy teams, including Thelma TODD and Patsy KELLY and the THREE STOOGES. His career in film comedy ranged from silents to sound films and spanned more than four decades.

SELECTED FILMS: *Ambrose's Little Hatchet, Ambrose's Lofty Perch, A Home Breaking Hound* (1915), *Beauty and the Bus, Backs to Nature, Air Fright* (1933), *Soup and Fish, Maid in Hollywood* (1934), *Accidents Will Happen* (1938), *I'll Never Heil Again* (1941), *Sing Your Worries Away, Mexican Spitfire Sees a Ghost* (1942), *Good Morning, Judge* (1943), *Mary Poppins* (1964). ∎

Bari, Lynn (1913–), actress. Entered films in 1933 as a dancer. She appeared in numerous melodramas and light films during an extensive career that spanned four decades. She often played saucy "other women" and second lead roles.

SELECTED FILMS: *Dancing Lady* (1933), *Stand Up and Cheer* (1934), *Pigskin Parade* (1936), *Wee Willie Winkie* (1937), *I'd Give a Million, Meet the Girls* (1938), *Pack Up Your Troubles* (1939), *Free, Blonde and 21* (1940), *The Perfect Snob, Moon Over Her Shoulder* (1941), *The Night Before the Divorce, The Magnificent Dope* (1942), *Margie* (1946), *On the Loose* (1951), *Francis Joins the WACS* (1954), *Abbott and Costello Meet the Keystone Kops* (1955), *The Young Runaways* (1968). ∎

Barnes, Binnie (1905–), actress. Appeared in a series of short comedies and a handful of features in her native England before she was invited to Hollywood, where she had a long and successful career through the 1930s and 1940s. Besides starring in many films, she often played the wise-cracking supporting dame.

SELECTED FILMS: There's Always Tomorrow (1934), Small Town Girl, The Magnificent Brute (1936), Three Smart Girls, Breezing Home (1937), Three Blind Mice, Holiday (1938), Man About Town, Daytime Wife (1939), Tight Shoes, Skylark (1941), I Married an Angel (1942), Up in Mabel's Room (1944), It's in the Bag (1945), The Time of Their Lives (1946), The Trouble With Angels (1966), Forty Carats (1973). ■

Barnett, Vince (1902–1977), actor. Entered films in 1930 after a brief stage career on Broadway. Easily recognizable by his bald head, small mustache, and bemused expression, he appeared in dozens of comedies and dramas, usually as a comic character. His most famous role, perhaps, was in Scarface (1932) in which he portrayed a hood who ends an argument with a telephone by shooting it.

SELECTED FILMS: Wide Open, All Quiet on the Western Front (1930), One Heavenly Night (1931), Rackety Rax (1932), Fast Workers, Made on Broadway (1933), Madame Spy, Thirty-Day Princess (1934), Princess O'Hara (1935), A Star Is Born (1937), East Side Kids, The Ghost Creeps (1940), Thrill of a Romance (1945), The Falcon's Alibi (1946), Zebra in the Kitchen (1965), The Big Mouth (1967). ■

Barney Oldfield's Race for Life (1912), KEY. Dir. Mack Sennett; with Mabel Normand, Mack Sennett, Ford Sterling, Barney Oldfield.

This one-reel silent comedy made by the master of slapstick and thrills is a landmark film in cinema history. It was probably the first time that suspense, action, and thrills were interwoven into the plot of a comedy for purposes of enhancement and structure. Barney Oldfield, a famous racing car driver of the time, was enlisted by Sennett to do his stuff. The plot revolves around suitor Ford Sterling who is rejected by Mabel Normand and decides to seek revenge. He ties her to a railroad track and drives a locomotive toward her. Meanwhile, boyfriend Sennett and Oldfield desperately race the train in an attempt to save Mabel.

Barrat, Robert (1891–1970), actor. Appeared in dozens of action dramas and light films from the early 1930s. A versatile character player, he portrayed scoundrels as well as sympathetic types. He often represented authoritarian figures.

SELECTED FILMS: The Mayor of Hell (1933), Dames, Big-Hearted Herbert (1934), Sons o' Guns (1936), Love Is on the Air (1937), Breaking the Ice (1938), Go West (1940), Fall In (1942), Road to Utopia (1945), The Time of Their Lives (1946), Road to Rio (1947), Darling, How Could You? (1951), Tall Man Riding (1955). ■

Barrie, Wendy (1912–1978), actress. Began her screen career in England before being signed by Paramount in the early 1930s as a featured player in Hollywood. Light-haired, pretty, and vivacious, she appeared in numerous dramas and light films for almost two decades, often playing society types. Although many of her vehicles were low-budget affairs, she was always interesting to watch. When her screen career ended, she entered radio and television and was successful in both endeavors.

SELECTED FILMS: It's a Small World, The Big Broadcast of 1936 (1935), Love on a Bet, Under Your Spell (1936), A Girl With Ideas (1937), Daytime Wife (1939), The Gay Falcon (1941), It Should Happen to You (1954). ■

Barry, Wesley, juvenile actor. A famous child star who worked chiefly in silent films. Director Marshall NEILAN, who discovered the boy working in his father's grocery store, took him under his wing and featured him in several of his productions. He appeared in dramas and light films with Mary PICKFORD and other major actors. He also played in some of the "HAM AND BUD" comedy shorts.

SELECTED FILMS: *Rebecca of Sunnybrook Farm (1917), Amarilly of Clothesline Alley (1918), Daddy Long Legs (1919), Don't Ever Marry, Go and Get It, Dinty (1920), Bits of Life (1921), Penrod (1922), The Country Kid (1923), The Midshipman (1925), In Old Kentucky (1927), Top Sergeant Milligan (1928), Sunny Skies (1930), Pick a Star (1937).* ■

Barrymore, John (1882–1942), actor. The son of famous stage actors who made his stage debut in 1903 and continued with a brilliant career in the theater and highly acclaimed performances on screen. His film career began in 1913. He made a series of features, chiefly comedies, for Paramount, before portraying romantic and swashbuckling heroes from 1920 until the advent of sound. He brought an element of the grotesque and the bizarre to these films. He also added a dash of whimsy or playfulness to these dramatic roles, thereby amusing his public and demonstrating his sense of wit. Whether in silent dramas or comedies, his energy and vivacity added spark to some of these mediocre films.

When sound arrived in Hollywood, he was a declining star. The studios, however, continued to place him in various vehicles, counting on the famous Barrymore name. He portrayed bon vivants, cynical lawyers, and a gallery of other characters. His later films often were parodies of his own career, portraying him as a desperate, hard-drinking has-been yearning for a comeback. Any of his performances on film is worth watching, especially his roles in two SCREW-BALL COMEDIES of the 1930s, *Twentieth Century* and *Midnight*, in which he displays his comic genius. He was the

brother of screen stars Lionel and Ethel Barrymore.

In one of his more eccentric roles, that of Svengali in the film of the same name, two English acquaintances of the swarthy charlatan ask him when he last took a bath. "Not since I tripped and fell in the sewer," Barrymore quips. In *Midnight* he counsels Claudette COLBERT: "My dear, it's amazing how little one has to explain to a man in love." "And when he stops being in love?" she asks. "Well," he replies, "that's when the alimony begins."

SELECTED FILMS: *An American Citizen (1914), Are You a Mason?, The Incorrigible Dukane (1915), Raffles, the Amateur Cracksman (1917), Dr. Jekyll and Mr. Hyde (1920), Beau Brummel (1924), The Sea Beast, Don Juan (1926), The Beloved Rogue (1927), General Crack (1930), Svengali (1931), Grand Hotel (1932), Topaze, Reunion in Vienna, Dinner at Eight (1933), Twentieth Century (1934), Romeo and Juliet (1936), Maytime, Bulldog Drummond Comes Back (1937), Hold That Co-Ed (1938), The Great Man Votes, Midnight (1939), World Premiere, Playmates (1941).* ■

Barrymore, Lionel (1878–1954), actor. Entered silent films in 1909 after long stage experience. A versatile actor, he played a variety of roles, many for D. W. Griffith, during the silent era and occasionally directed. During the sound period he rose in prominence as a character player in numerous dramas and light films. He played Judge Hardy in *A Family Affair* (1937), the first film in the "ANDY HARDY" series, but was later replaced by veteran actor Lewis STONE in the remaining entries. After he became crippled by arthritis, he appeared in a wheelchair for the remainder of his screen career. He became one of the most beloved film personalities of his time. His screen career stretched over five decades. He was the brother of John and Ethel Barrymore, two distinguished performers who also gained popularity in films.

In *Ah Wilderness!* (1935) storekeeper Charlie GRAPEWIN stops his neighbor Barrymore to inquire about the price of his son's coat. "Five Dollars," the father replies. "You got stung . . . Serves you right. I advertise in your paper, you should buy in my store." "Well, as a matter of fact," Barrymore retorts, "that's where I did buy it."

SELECTED FILMS: *Fighting Blood* (1911), *The New York Hat* (1912), *Meddling Women* (1924), *The Lucky Lady* (1926), *Dinner at Eight, Should Ladies Behave?* (1933), *The Girl From Missouri* (1934), *The Little Colonel* (1935), *Saratoga* (1937), *You Can't Take It With You* (1938), *Lady Be Good* (1941), *It's a Wonderful Life* (1946), *Main Street to Broadway* (1953). ∎

Bartlett, Bennie, actor. Appeared in several entries of the "BOWERY BOYS" comedy series. Short and light-haired, he joined the rowdy group in 1948 as a supporting player in the role of Butch.

SELECTED FILMS: *Angels' Alley, Jinx Money, Trouble Makers* (1948), *Fighting Fools, Hold That Baby, Angels in Disguise, Master Minds* (1949), *Crazy Over Horses, Feudin' Fools* (1951), *Here Come the Marines, Hold That Line, No Holds Barred* (1952), *Clipped Wings* (1953), *Jail Busters* (1955), *Dig That Uranium* (1956). ∎

Barton, Charles (1902–), director. Worked in stock, in vaudeville, and in early films before turning his attentions to directing in 1934. During a career that has spanned four decades, he has turned out numerous low-budget action films and comedies. He has directed some of the leading comics of the period, including Joe E. BROWN, Jackie GLEASON, and ABBOTT AND COSTELLO.

SELECTED FILMS: *Wagon Wheels* (1934), *Five Little Peppers and How They Grew* (1939), *Two Latins From Manhattan* (1941), *Shut My Big Mouth, Tramp, Tramp, Tramp, Sweetheart of the Fleet, Laugh Your Blues Away* (1942), *Reveille With Beverly, Let's Have Fun, What's Buzzin', Cousin?, Is Everybody Happy?* (1943), *Beautiful but Broke, Hey Rookie, Louisiana Hayride* (1944), *The Beautiful Cheat, Men in Her Diary* (1945), *White Tie and Tails, The Time of Their Lives* (1946), *Buck Privates Come Home* (1947), *Africa Screams, Free for All* (1949), *The Milkman* (1950), *Ma and Pa Kettle at the Fair* (1952), *The Shaggy Dog* (1959), *Swingin' Along* (1962). ∎

Barton, James (1890–1962), actor. Worked in vaudeville, burlesque, musicals, and the legitimate stage before entering films. A talented character actor, he often portrayed grizzled alcoholics in both dramas and light films. His most memorable role was that of the old codger in *The Time of Your Life* (1948), starring James CAGNEY and based on William Saroyan's play.

SELECTED FILMS: *Why Women Remarry* (1923), *Captain Hurricane, His Family Tree* (1935), *The Daughter of Rosie O'Grady, Wabash Avenue* (1950), *Here Comes the Groom, Golden Girl* (1951), *The Misfits* (1961). ∎

"Baseball Bill" comedies. A series of shorts produced by Universal studios from 1916 to 1917 and starring William "Smiling Bill" MASON. The slapstick comedies, which usually concluded with a wild chase, utilized the personable talents of Mason in such films as "Baseball Bill," "The Black Nine," "Strike One!," "Flirting With Marriage," "Box of Tricks," and "Baseball Madness."

Bassett, Russell (1846–1918), actor. Worked on stage before entering early silent films in 1911. He appeared chiefly in light vehicles.

SELECTED FILMS: *The Best Man Wins* (1911), *The New Clerk* (1913), *Such a Little Queen, Those Persistent Old Maids, One of the Finest, What a Baby Did* (1914), *Jim the Penman, Little Pal, The Morals of Marcus* (1915), *A Coney Island Princess* (1916), *Broadway Jones* (1917), *Hit the Trail Holiday* (1918), *The Traveling Salesman* (1919). ∎

Bateman, Victory (1866–1926), actress. Entered films in the early 1920s following a long stage career. A veteran supporting player, she appeared in several dramas and light films during the silent era.

SELECTED FILMS: The Idle Rich, Keeping Up With Lizzie, A Trip to Paradise (1921), If I Were Queen (1922), Can a Woman Love Twice? (1923), The Turmoil (1924). ∎

Bates. Comic sidekick character of "The Falcon" in the detective-comedy series of that name. Bates was portrayed by the popular character actor Ed GARGAN.

Bates, Florence (1888–1954), actress. Worked as an attorney, career woman, and stage actress before entering films in the late 1930s. A versatile character player, she was equally at home in hideous or humorous matronly roles. She worked with some of the leading comics of the period, including Bob HOPE and Danny KAYE.

SELECTED FILMS: The Man in Blue (1937), Kitty Foyle (1940), The Devil and Miss Jones, The Chocolate Soldier (1941), We Were Dancing (1942), They Got Me Covered, His Butler's Sister (1943), Tonight and Every Night (1945), Cluny Brown, Claudia and David (1946), The Secret Life of Walter Mitty (1947), I Remember Mama (1948), On the Town (1949), Main Street to Broadway (1953). ∎

Bates, Granville (1882–1940), actor. Worked on stage before coming to films in his middle years at the beginning of the sound era. A distinguished-looking figure, he appeared as a supporting player in numerous dramas and light films. He worked with such screen luminaries as W. C. FIELDS, John BARRYMORE, and Edward G. ROBINSON.

SELECTED FILMS: Jealousy (1929), The Sap From Syracuse (1930), The Smiling Lieutenant (1934), Woman Wanted (1935), Here Comes Trouble, Poppy, Chatterbox (1936), When's Your Birthday?, Let's Get Married, It Happened in Hollywood, Waikiki Wedding, Back in Circulation (1937), Youth Takes a Fling, Mr. Chump, Go Chase Yourself (1938), The Great Man Votes, Naughty but Nice, Our Neighbors, the Carters (1939), My Favorite Wife, Brother Orchid (1940). ∎

"Bathing Beauties." A bevy of pretty young women introduced in 1915 by producer Mack SENNETT to enhance his comedy shorts and to get additional publicity for his films. Sennett believed that by surrounding his comics with a group of attractive faces and figures wearing the latest and most daring swimming fashions, his films would lure even greater audiences. He further thought that publicity pictures of the girls sent to the press would have a better chance of being printed. The idea was successful and Sennett's "Bathing Beauties" grew in popularity. Several of the girls, who were paid $12 per week to display their gifts, got their start with the "Beauties" before moving on to greater screen heights. Gloria SWANSON emerged as a major dramatic star, Marie PREVOST became a successful film comedienne, and Mary Thurman moved into westerns.

"Battle of the Century, The" (1927), MGM. Dir. Clyde Bruckman; Sc. Hal Roach; with Laurel and Hardy, Eugene Pallette, Charles Hall.

This two-reel slapstick comedy is considered one of the few classic pie-throwing films in screen history. Mack Sennett and other producers engaged in this sub-genre of comedy more than a decade before this short was made but never to the extent that it is pursued here. LAUREL portrays an inept prize fighter who hits the canvas after one blow, while HARDY plays his dispirited manager who decides to take out an insurance policy on his fighter, who is oblivious to what is happening. Somehow they become involved with a pie delivery man and total chaos breaks loose on a formerly quiet street. Pies begin to fly everywhere, involving dozens of innocent passersby who soon join the fracas. The battle forms into two camps, with Stan and Ollie, who started it all, supplying the ammunition from the back of the pie truck to both sides. The events in the film parallel several of the boys' films, which move from a simple misunderstanding to confrontation to eventual Armageddon. Of course there are those who would read more into the film, interpreting the entire pie sequence as an allegory on the behavior of nations.

Bear, Mary (–1972), actress. Worked on the stage as well as in films. She appeared chiefly as a supporting player in light films during the 1940s and 1950s.

SELECTED FILMS: *That Lady in Ermine* (1948), *Bride for Sale* (1949), *Mother Didn't Tell Me, Singing Guns, Stella* (1950). ∎

Beard, Matthew "Stymie," child actor. Member of the OUR GANG team. He joined the popular group of children after its first major change in 1929. Although blacks in films were rarely treated as the equals of whites, Stymie enjoyed the privileges (and punishments) of the white members of the gang. If they were invited to a party in a white child's home, Stymie also attended. Their classroom was integrated as well. He was one of the most popular members of the gang. However, most blacks today would feel that Stymie was stereotyped.

SELECTED FILMS: *Teacher's Pet, School's Out* (1931), *Love Business, Little Daddy* (1932), *Kid Millions* (1934), *Rainbow on the River* (1936), *Beloved Brat* (1938), *Way Down South* (1939), *The Return of Frank James* (1940). ∎

Beasley, Mr. Fictional character. He was the unfortunate mailman in the "BLONDIE" comedies who was knocked down each time Dagwood Bumstead dashed out of his house on the way to work. Beasley, whose mail became scattered over the entire lawn, was usually portrayed by supporting player Irving BACON or Eddie ACUFF.

Beatty, George (1895–1971), actor. Worked in vaudeville, on stage, and in radio before entering films in his middle years. He appeared as a supporting player in several light films. He also worked as a screenwriter.

SELECTED FILMS: *Hi' Ya, Sailor, Crazy House* (1943), *Johnny Doesn't Live Here* (1944). ∎

Beatty, May (1881–1945), actress. Migrated from New Zealand to Hollywood during the early sound period to appear as a supporting player in numerous dramas and light films.

SELECTED FILMS: *The Boudoir Diplomat* (1930), *Ex-Flame* (1931), *Horse Play* (1934), *Night Life of the Gods, Here Comes the Band, Bonnie Scotland* (1935), *Private Number* (1936), *Four Days' Wonder, She Loved a Fireman* (1937), *Eternally Yours* (1938), *Pride and Prejudice* (1940), *Forever and a Day* (1943). ∎

Beatty, Ned (1937–), actor. Worked on stage before entering films in the early 1970s. A stocky character player with a dynamic visual presence, he has an uncanny knack for dominating many scenes. He has appeared in dramas and light films. He was nominated for an Academy Award for his role in *Network* (1976).

SELECTED FILMS: *Deliverance* (1972), *The Thief Who Came to Dinner* (1974), *Nashville* (1975), *Mikey and Nicky, The Big Bus, Silver Streak* (1976), *The Great Georgia Bank Hoax* (1977), *1941* (1979), *Hopscotch* (1980), *The Incredible Shrinking Woman* (1981), *The Toy* (1982), *Stroker Ace* (1983). ∎

Beaudet, Louise (1862–1947), actress. Entered early silent films following a career in vaudeville, on stage, and in opera. She appeared as a supporting player chiefly in light comedies.

SELECTED FILMS: *Sauce for the Goose (1913), Jerry's Uncle's Namesake (1914), On Her Wedding Night (1915), The Price She Paid (1917), Her Lord and Master (1921), The Gold Diggers (1923), Sally (1925).* ∎

Beaudine, William (1892–1970), director. A veteran director of the silent era, he started as a factotum with D.W. GRIFFITH in 1909. By 1915 he was directing comedy shorts. In the 1920s he directed longer films, some of which starred Mary PICKFORD. During a career which spanned 50 years, he directed hundreds of features, most of them B films, for different studios. Although he worked in various genres, he was best known for his light films, especially the comedies of the East Side Kids and the BOWERY BOYS.

SELECTED FILMS: *Almost a King (1915), A Bad Little Good Man (1917), Watch Your Step (1922), Penrod and Sam (1923), Little Annie Rooney (1925), Sparrows (1926), Frisco Sally Levy, The Life of Riley (1927), Misbehaving Ladies (1931), Three Wise Girls (1932), The Old Fashioned Way (1934), Torchy Gets Her Man (1938), Misbehaving Husbands (1940), Detective Kitty O'Day, Crazy Knights (1944), Gas House Kids Go West (1947), Jalopy (1953), In the Money (1960), Jesse James Meets Frankenstein's Daughter (1966).* ∎

Beaumont, Harry (1888–1966), director. Appeared in stock, vaudeville, and early silent films before turning to directing. His directorial career spanned more than four decades. During the 1920s he turned out numerous shorts and some high-quality dramas. His later works, especially those of the sound era, seldom met his former standards. He directed films of different genres but is chiefly remembered for a handful of excellent silent dramas and his light features of the 1930s. He made *The Broadway Melody* (1928), the first musical.

SELECTED FILMS (as actor): *How Father Accomplished His Work, The Butler and the Maid (1912), Mother's Lazy Boy, It Wasn't Poison After All (1913), A Transplanted Prairie Flower (1914), That Heavenly Cook (1915), Putting It Over, The Grouch, His Little Wife (1916).*

SELECTED FILMS (as director): *The Call of the City (1915), Skinner's Dress Suit (1917), Wild Goose Chase, Go West Young Man (1919), The Great Accident, Dollars and Sense (1920), They Like 'Em Rough (1922), The Gold Diggers (1923), Our Dancing Daughters (1928), The Floradora Girl, Those Three French Girls (1930), Made on Broadway, When Ladies Meet (1933), When's Your Birthday? (1937), Maisie Goes to Reno (1944), Twice Blessed (1945), The Show-Off (1946), Alias a Gentleman (1948).* ∎

Beavers, Louise (1902–1962), actress. Started as a singer in a minstrel show and as a maid to actress Leatrice JOY. She entered films in the early 1920s and continued to appear in numerous features until 1960, usually in the role of a maid or housekeeper. At least two moments highlight her long film career. The first was her strong impersonation of a pancake maker in the 1934 version of *Imitation of Life.* Her second memorable film was *She Done Him Wrong* (1933), in which Mae WEST addresses her with the now-famous line: "Beulah, peel me a grape."

In *Shadow of the Thin Man* she played the maid of Mr. and Mrs. Charles (William POWELL and Myrna LOY). Mrs. Charles remarks that their child is getting to be more like his father each day. "That's true," the maid interjects. "This morning I found him playing with the corkscrew."

SELECTED FILMS: *Gold Diggers (1923), Uncle Tom's Cabin (1927), Coquette (1929), She Couldn't Say No (1930), Girls About Town (1932), Bombshell (1933), Rainbow on the River (1936), Brother Rat (1938), No Time for Comedy (1940), Shadow of the Thin Man (1941), Holiday Inn (1942), Delightfully Dangerous (1945), Lover Come Back (1946), Good Sam, Mr. Blandings Builds*

His Dream House (1948), My Blue Heaven (1950), Tammy and the Bachelor (1957), The Facts of Life (1960). ∎

Beckett, Scotty (1929–1968), actor. Began his film career as a member of the "OUR GANG" team. After making eight comedy shorts for Hal ROACH'S popular "Gang" series, he advanced to feature films, often portraying the son of lead characters. For example, he played Spencer TRACY'S boy in *Dante's Inferno* (1935), and Fredric MARCH'S youngster in *Anthony Adverse* (1936). A personable and charming performer, both as a child actor and later as an adolescent, he appeared in more than 80 films. Although his career lasted longer than those of most other former child actors, he never attained the stardom of some ex-child performers like Donald O'CONNOR.

SELECTED FILMS: Gallant Lady (1933), Stand Up and Cheer (1934), Our Gang Follies of 1936, Old Hutch (1936), Life Begins With Love (1937), You're Only Young Once (1938), Our Neighbors, the Carters, Mickey the Kid, The Flying Irishman (1939), The Blue Bird, My Favorite Wife, Gold Rush Maisie (1940), It Happened in Flatbush (1942), Junior Miss (1945), The Jolson Story (1946), A Date With Judy (1948), Nancy Goes to Rio (1950), Corky of Gasoline Alley (1951), Three for Jamie Dawn (1956). ∎

Beddoe, Don (1888–), actor. Worked on Broadway before entering films in the late 1930s. A character player who appeared chiefly in comedies, he has been in more than 100 films, both comedy shorts and features, often portraying policemen, sheriffs, or reporters.

SELECTED FILMS: There's That Woman Again (1938), Blondie Meets the Boss (1939), Sing for Your Supper (1941), The Talk of the Town (1942), The Farmer's Daughter, Buck Privates Come Home, The Bachelor and the Bobby-Soxer (1947), The Lady Gambles (1949), Dear Wife, The Great Rupert (1950), *Stop, You're Killing Me (1952), The Clown (1953), Pillow Talk (1959), Saintly Sinners (1962), How Do I Love Thee? (1970).* ∎

Bedroom farce. See Sex comedy.

Beery, Noah, Jr. (1913–), actor. Began his long screen career as a child actor in silent films. An amiable performer during the sound era, he played light roles as a supporting actor, often as sidekicks in serials and westerns. He never attained the status that his father, Noah, or his uncle, Wallace BEERY, had.

SELECTED FILMS: The Mark of Zorro (1920), Penrod (1923), Penrod and Sam (1929), Some Blondes Are Dangerous (1937), A Little Bit of Heaven (1940), Tanks a Million (1941), Dudes Are Pretty People (1942), Calaboose, What a Woman! (1943), See My Lawyer (1944), Her Lucky Night (1945), The Best Little Whorehouse in Texas (1982), Waltz Across Texas (1983). ∎

Wallace Beery (right) and Jackie Cooper

Beery, Wallace (1885–1949), actor. Worked as an elephant trainer, singer, and actor before entering films in 1913. He made a series of short comedies for Essanay studios in which he portrayed Sweedie, a muscular Swedish maid. It was at this studio that he met Gloria SWANSON, whom he married in 1916. He then moved to Keystone and Universal studios, again making comedy shorts. He graduated to feature films, playing heavies and comedy roles throughout the 1920s. He joined Paramount studios where he co-starred with Raymond HATTON in a series of silent comedies.

He reached the zenith of his career during the Depression years while at MGM, becoming everyone's favorite likable, ugly hero. His brawny physique, gravelly voice, and tough but gentle character often found him cast in action and comedy-action features. He won the Academy Award as Best Actor for his portrayal in *The Champ* (1931). He made a string of memorable films, including *Grand Hotel* (1932) and *Dinner at Eight* (1933). One of his most endearing roles was in *Bad Bascomb* (1946), in which child star Margaret O'Brien keeps spelling out her thoughts to him, but, as an uneducated outlaw, he can't understand what she's saying.

SELECTED FILMS: Sweedie the Swatter (1914), The Slim Princess (1915), A Dash of Courage (1916), Cactus Nell (1917), Robin Hood (1922), We're in the Navy Now (1926), Casey at the Bat (1927), The Big House, Min and Bill (1930), Tugboat Annie, The Bowery (1933), Viva Villa!, Treasure Island (1934), Ah, Wilderness! (1935), A Message to Garcia (1936), Stablemates (1938), Barnacle Bill (1941), This Man's Navy (1945), The Mighty McGurk (1947), A Date With Judy (1948), Big Jack (1949). ■

Beggs, Lee (1871–1943), actor. Worked on stage as well as in early silent films, getting his start with the pioneer Solax studios. He later turned to directing. He appeared as a supporting player in numerous light films throughout the silent period.

SELECTED FILMS: His Musical Soul (1911), The Gold Brick, Father and the Boys, Canned Harmony, Billy's Shoes, Saved by a Cat, Mickey's Pal, The Wooing of Alice, The Detective Dog (1912), Eats, Father's Timepiece, The Egyptian Mummy (1914), Forcing Dad's Consent, A Mix-Up in Dress-Suit Cases (1915), *Playing for Desire (1924), Stepping Along (1926).* ■

Belasco, Jay, actor. Appeared in early silent comedy shorts for Mutual studios. He co-starred with Billie Rhodes in a series of one-reel comedies under the Strand banner, a subsidiary of Mutual. As the series progressed, the films improved in quality. Although the comedies emphasized traditional slapstick, including the obligatory chase, touches of polite comedy were introduced.

SELECTED FILMS: Her Hero, A Two Cylinder Courtship (1917), The Woman Accused (1933). ■

Belasco, Leon (1902–), actor. Began his screen career in silent films in the 1920s. He played character parts in over 50 Hollywood films, especially in comical roles portraying easily agitated Slavic types, including balletmasters and headwaiters. He appeared in features as well as comedy shorts with some of the leading comics of the period, including, among others, W. C. FIELDS, Bob HOPE, and the THREE STOOGES.

SELECTED FILMS: The Best People (1926), Topper Takes a Trip (1939), Comrade X (1940), Nothing but the Truth, Never Give a Sucker an Even Break, Where Did You Get That Girl? (1941), Pin-Up Girl, Road to Morocco (1944), Swing Parade of 1946 (1946), Nancy Goes to Rio (1950), Call Me Madam (1953), Can-Can (1960), The Art of Love (1965), Superdad (1974). ■

Bell, Hank (1892–1950), actor. Began his film career in the 1920s, chiefly as a character player in westerns. Slim and mustached, he originally played outlaws. Later, as his mustache grew larger and more distinctive, he went straight and played old-timers, including sidekicks and sheriffs.

SELECTED FILMS: Beyond the Rockies, Fiddlin' Buckaroo, Young Blood (1933), Comin' Round the Mountain,

Disorder in the Court, Three Troubledoers (1936), Goofs and Saddles, The Man From Music Mountain (1937), Spoilers of the Range, Teacher's Pest (1939). ■

Bell, Rex (1905–1962), actor. Entered films in the late 1920s as a supporting player in a series of romantic comedies. Dark-haired and good-looking, he continued in this capacity into the early 1930s, occasionally playing leads. But his eventual popularity was a result of his western features of the 1930s. He became lieutenant governor of Nevada in 1954.

SELECTED FILMS: The Girl-Shy Cowboy, The Cowboy Kid, Wild West Romance (1928), Salute, They Had to See Paris, Happy Days (1929), Harmony at Home, True to the Navy, Lightnin' (1930), From Broadway to Cheyenne, Crashin' Broadway (1932), Lone Star (1952), The Misfits (1961). ■

Bell, Rodney (1916–1968), actor. Began his screen career in the 1940s as a supporting player. He appeared in numerous comedy shorts as well as light films.

SELECTED FILMS: The Strange Affair of Uncle Harry, An Angel Comes to Brooklyn (1945), Meet Me After the Show, So You Want to Be a Handyman, So You Want to Be a Paperhanger, So You Want to Be a Plumber (1951), Something for the Birds, So You Want to Get It Wholesale, So You're Going to the Dentist (1952), So You Want a Television Set (1953), So You're Having Neighbor Trouble, So You Want to Be Your Own Boss (1954), The Missouri Traveler (1958), Go Naked in the World (1961). ■

Bellamy, Ralph (1904–), actor. Worked in the theater in various capacities, including actor, director, and producer. After appearing on Broadway in the late 1920s, he entered films in 1931. He starred in numerous low-budget films, including the title role in the "Ellery Queen" detective series, until the late '30s when he was featured as the "other man" in a succession of comedies. In these films he lost the leading lady to the male star because of his own incompetence, dullness, or arrogance. A versatile actor, he was equally comfortable in villainous or light roles. He received an Academy Award nomination as Best Supporting Actor for his part in *The Awful Truth* (1937).

In *Lady on a Train* (1945) he played a nephew who, upon the reading of his uncle's will, learns that the deceased has left him one dollar. "Aren't you disappointed?" he is asked. "On the contrary," he rejoins, "he once threatened to cut me out of his will entirely."

SELECTED FILMS: The Secret Six (1931), Rebecca of Sunnybrook Farm (1932), Second Hand Wife (1933), Spitfire (1934), Hands Across the Table (1935), Let's Get Married (1937), Fools for Scandal, Boy Meets Girl, Carefree (1938), Trade Winds (1939), His Girl Friday, Brother Orchid (1940), Affectionately Yours (1941), Lady in a Jam (1942), Delightfully Dangerous (1945), Cancel My Reservation (1972), Oh, God! (1977). ■

Bellaver, Harry (1905–), actor. A sturdy character player in the Runyonesque style who began his screen career in the late 1930s. Moon-faced with a serious expression, he appeared in dramas and light films. He portrayed detectives, cabbies, and saloon patrons.

SELECTED FILMS: Another Thin Man (1939), Perfect Strangers (1950), The Lemon Drop Kid (1951), The Birds and the Bees (1956), A Fine Madness (1966), The Hot Rock (1972), God Told Me To (1976), Hero at Large (1979). ■

Belmont, Joseph, actor. Began his acting career in the theater in 1897. He made his film debut at Crystal studios where he developed the "Baldy" Belmont comedy films, a series he wrote, directed, and starred in. By 1916 he was with Mack SENNETT'S KEYSTONE studios. Teamed with Ora CAREW, another stage veteran, he made a series of delightful and popular short comedies.

SELECTED FILMS: *Better Late Than Never, Wife and Auto Trouble, Wings and Wheels, A la Cabaret, Dollars and Sense, Love Comet* (1916), *Her Circus Knight, Oriental Love, Skidding Hearts* (1917). ■

Belmore, Daisy (1874–1954), actress. Entered films during the late silent period following a career on stage. She appeared as a supporting player in dramas as well as in light films.

SELECTED FILMS: *We Americans* (1928), *Seven Days' Leave, Alias French Gertie, Way for a Sailor* (1930), *Fifty Million Frenchmen, My Past, Born to Love* (1931). ■

Belmore, Lionel (1867–1953), actor. Appeared on stage in his native England before settling in Hollywood. He began his screen career in silent films in the early 1920s and for two decades appeared in numerous dramas and light comedies.

SELECTED FILMS: *Jes' Call Me Jim* (1920), *A Shocking Night, Midnight Follies, Two Minutes to Go* (1921), *Head Over Heels* (1922), *Jazzmania* (1923), *Try and Get It* (1924), *Madame Behave* (1925), *Stop, Look and Listen* (1926), *The Wife's Relations* (1928), *The Love Parade* (1929), *Monte Carlo, The Boudoir Diplomat* (1930), *The Constant Wife* (1933), *Bonnie Scotland* (1935), *It's Love I'm After* (1937), *Diamond Frontier* (1940). ■

Beloin, Edmund (1910–), screenwriter. Comedy writer for such stars as Bob HOPE and Jerry LEWIS in the 1950s. He began by working on screenplays for Jack BENNY films in the early 1940s. He had previously written for the Jack Benny radio shows.

SELECTED FILMS: *Buck Benny Rides Again* (1940), *Love Thy Neighbor* (1941), *The Harvey Girls* (1946), *My Favorite*

Brunette, *Road to Rio* (1947), *A Connecticut Yankee in King Arthur's Court, The Great Lover* (1949), *The Lemon Drop Kid* (1951), *The Sad Sack* (1957), *Don't Give Up the Ship* (1959), *Visit to a Small Planet* (1959), *G.I. Blues* (1960), *All in a Night's Work* (1961). ■

John Belushi

Belushi, John (1949–1982), actor. Appeared in television where he gained a large following on the "Saturday Night Live" comedy show before entering films in the late 1970s. A highly popular television comedian, he brought his loyal fans with him to his films. He was a close friend of comic actor Dan AYKROYD, with whom he made several films. Stockily built and with a flair for the offbeat and crazy comedy with which he is closely associated, he played slobs well but lovers with varying degrees of success. Just as he was emerging as a major screen comic, his career was cut short by his untimely and tragic drug-related death. The news shocked his fans and the public at large.

SELECTED FILMS: *National Lampoon's Animal House, Goin' South* (1978), *Old Boyfriends, 1941* (1979), *The Blues Brothers* (1980), *Neighbors, Continental Divide* (1981). ■

Benchley, Robert (1889–1945), actor, critic, humorist, screenwriter. Worked as a magazine editor, drama editor, and entertainer in a Broadway revue in 1923. He began his career in Hollywood writing and appearing in a series of one-reel comedies, ostensibly as a lecturer on sundry topics. One of these, "How to Sleep," won an Academy Award as Best Comedy Short of 1935. He often portrayed serious-minded, middle-class homeowners or husbands whose mundane activities would result in embarrassment or frustration. His subtle humor usually revealed people's foibles. On occasion he appeared in feature films, sometimes as a good-natured intruder.

In *China Seas* (1935), for example, he played an author who is intoxicated during an entire voyage. The ship has experienced a typhoon and a pirate attack, but he has remained unperturbed and unharmed. When the vessel reaches Singapore, its destination, he falls off the gangplank and lands in the water. "These streets are in deplorable condition," he remarks, still plastered. In *The Major and the Minor* he offers Ginger ROGERS a drink: "No matter what the weather, I always say, 'Why don't you get out of your wet clothes and into a dry martini?'"

SELECTED FILMS: The Treasurer's Report, The Sex Life of the Polyp (1928), Stewed, Fried and Broiled (1929), Your Technocracy and Mine (1933), How to Behave, How to Vote (1936), The Romance of Digestion, A Night at the Movies (1937), How to Figure Income Tax (1938), How to Sub-Let, How to Eat (1939), Hired Wife (1940), I Married a Witch (1942), See Here, Private Hargrove (1944), Weekend at the Waldorf (1945), Road to Utopia, The Bride Wore Boots, Janie Gets Married (1946). ∎

Bendix, William (1906–1964), actor. Appeared in films as a child actor before beginning his adult screen career in 1942. He usually played dumb, brawny cops or toughs, but often with a heart; his roots—Brooklyn or New Jersey; his favorite team—the Dodgers or, as they are known more affectionately, the "Bums." In *Where There's Life*, for instance, he portrayed a New York cop suspicious of

his sister's boyfriend. When he asks her what he did when they were alone, she replies, "It was no different than when you go out with a girl." "I'll kill him!" Bendix shouts furiously. He appeared in dramatic roles, such as the title character in *The Hairy Ape* and a wounded sailor in Alfred Hitchcock's *Lifeboat* (both 1944), in dramatic films as the comic relief, and in comedies. He starred in the successful radio series of the 1940s, "The Life of Riley." His father, Max Bendix, was conductor of the Metropolitan Opera Orchestra.

SELECTED FILMS: Woman of the Year, Who Done It? (1942), Taxi, Mister (1943), Abroad With Two Yanks (1944), It's in the Bag, Don Juan Quilligan (1945), Where There's Life (1947), The Time of Your Life, The Babe Ruth Story (1948), The Life of Riley (1949), Kill the Umpire (1950), Detective Story (1951), Boys' Night Out (1962), Young Fury (1965). ∎

Benedict, Billy (1917–), actor. Perennial office boy, newsboy, or Western Union messenger. He joined the "BOWERY BOYS" comedy series in the late 1930s in the role of Whitey. He played in more than 100 films and serials from 1935 to 1976. Later in his screen career he graduated from juvenile occupations to cabbie and bartender roles.

In *Libeled Lady* (1936) he played a copy boy for a big-city newspaper managed by Spencer TRACY. Tracy, intending to use a phony story planted in his paper as a ploy, hands the bogus page to Benedict and orders: "Tell Douglas to print up one copy of the evening edition." "One copy?" Benedict questions. "That's what I said." "Gosh," the bewildered copy boy mumbles, "our circulation is certainly falling off."

SELECTED FILMS: Ten Dollar Raise, College Scandal (1935), Ramona (1936), Laughing at Trouble (1937), My Little Chickadee, Call a Messenger (1940), Road to Utopia (1945), The Kid From Brooklyn (1946), Bowery Battalion (1951), Lover Come Back (1961), The Hallelujah Trail (1965), The Sting

(1973), Won Ton Ton, the Dog Who Saved Hollywood (1976). ∎

Benedict, Brooks (–1968), actor. Worked on the stage as well as in both silent and sound films for three decades. He appeared as a supporting player in dramas and light films. He worked with some of the leading comics of the period, including, among others, Buster KEATON, Harry LANGDON, and LAUREL AND HARDY.

SELECTED FILMS: Cupid's Fireman (1923), The Freshman, His Master's Voice, Shoes (1925), College Days, Tramp, Tramp, Tramp, Why Girls Go Back Home (1926), The Kid Sister, Back at the Front, Three's a Crowd (1927), The Sophomore, The Garden of Eatin' (1929), Girl Crazy (1932), Sons of the Desert (1933), Belle of the Nineties (1934), Follow the Fleet (1936), Pick a Star (1937), Hi' Ya, Chum (1943), Three on a Ticket (1947). ∎

Benedict, Jean (1876–1943), actress. Worked on the stage as well as on screen. She appeared occasionally as a supporting player in films, chiefly light comedies.

SELECTED FILMS: A Slight Case of Murder, Blondes at Work, Little Miss Thoroughbred (1938). ∎

Benge, Wilson (1875–1955), actor. Worked on stage in his native England before immigrating to Hollywood during the silent era. He appeared as a supporting player in dramas and light films through the early sound period. He was also a theatrical producer.

SELECTED FILMS: Robin Hood (1922), Anybody Here Seen Kelly?, A Gentleman Preferred (1928), A Most Immoral Lady, This Thing Called Love (1929), Raffles, Her Wedding Night, Charley's Aunt (1930), Men in Her Life (1931), Big Executive, By Appointment Only (1933), Twin Husbands (1934), Dancing Feet (1936), Easy Living, Mr. Boggs Steps Out (1937), Trade Winds (1938). ∎

Benham, Harry (1886–1969), actor. Began his screen career in 1911 in early silent films. He appeared as a supporting player in several dramas and numerous light films. He was the father of screen actress Dorothy Benham (1910–1956) and actor Leland Benham.

SELECTED FILMS: Their Burglar, The Tomboy (1911), When a Count Counted (1912), Louie the Life Saver (1913), Henry's Waterloo (1914), A Freight Car Honeymoon (1915), Her Wonderful Secret, Mischief Makers (1916), Polly With a Past (1920), Your Best Friend (1922). ∎

Benjamin, Richard (1938–), actor. Worked mostly in stock, on Broadway, and in television before becoming a major film actor in the late 1960s and 1970s. He specializes in comedy, usually with a contemporary theme. One of his more memorable, and thankless, roles was that of the exasperated nephew of Walter Matthau in Neil SIMON'S film version of the *The Sunshine Boys*. He has also done some directing, namely *My Favorite Year* and *Racing With the Moon*.

SELECTED FILMS: Thunder Over the Plains (1953), Crime Wave (1954), Goodbye, Columbus (1969), Diary of a Mad Housewife, Catch-22 (1970), The Marriage of a Young Stockbroker (1971), Portnoy's Complaint (1972), The Last of Sheila, Westworld (1973), The Sunshine Boys (1975), House Calls (1978), Love at First Bite (1979), The Last Married Couple in America, How to Beat the High Cost of Living (1980), City Heat (1984). ∎

Bennett, Alma (1904–1958), actress. Began her screen career in silent films in the early 1920s. She appeared as a supporting player in dramas and light films, continuing into the early sound period.

SELECTED FILMS: Flaming Hearts (1922), Three Jumps Ahead (1923), Don Juan's Three Nights (1926), Long Pants, Orchids and Ermine (1927), Painted Faces, Two Men and a Maid, Girl Crazy, Midnight Daddies (1929), Hail the Princess (1930). ∎

Bennett, Belle (1891–1932), actress. Worked in vaudeville and on stage before entering films during the early silent era. She appeared as a supporting player in numerous dramas and light comedies in a screen career that spanned three decades.

SELECTED FILMS: Sweet Kitty Bellairs (1916), Your Best Friend (1922), In Hollywood With Potash and Perlmutter (1924), His Supreme Moment (1925), Reckless Lady, The Amateur Gentleman (1926), Wild Geese (1927), Battle of the Sexes (1928), Molly and Me (1929), Night Work, One Romantic Night (1930), The Big Shot (1932). ■

Bennett, Constance (1904–1965), actress. Began her film career in 1922, at age 17, appearing in silent features. She retired from the screen in 1926, only to return in 1929 to star in sophisticated comedies. Known for her deep voice and her wisecracks, she also played in many dramas. One of her most popular roles was that of the fun-loving ghost of Marion Kirby in Topper. She was the daughter of actor Richard Bennett and sister of Joan and Barbara Bennett.

SELECTED FILMS: Reckless Youth, What's Wrong With the Women? (1922), The Goose Hangs High, The Goose Woman (1925), Married? (1926), This Thing Called Love (1929), Rich People, Sin Takes a Holiday (1930), The Easiest Way, Born to Love (1931), What Price Hollywood, Rockabye (1932), Our Betters, After Tonight (1933), After Office Hours (1935), Topper (1937), Merrily We Live (1938), Two-Faced Woman (1941), Madame Spy (1942), Centennial Summer (1946), It Should Happen to You (1954), Madame X (1966). ■

Bennett, Enid (1895–1969), actress. Began her long screen career in 1917 following stage experience in her native Australia. She appeared as the female lead and later as a supporting player in numerous dramas and light films, chiefly for Paramount.

SELECTED FILMS: Princess in the Dark (1917), The Biggest Show on Earth, Fuss and Feathers, The Vamp, When Do We Eat? (1918), Happy Though Married, The Haunted Bedroom, Partners Three, Stepping Out (1919), Hairpins, Silk Hosiery, The Woman in the Suitcase (1920), Keeping Up With Lizzie (1921), The Wrong Mr. Wright (1927), Good Medicine (1929), Skippy, Sooky (1931), Strike Up the Band (1940). ■

Bennett, Joan (1910–), actress. Appeared on stage before embarking on a Hollywood career in 1928. After one minor film role she became a star the following year. She made numerous dramas and light films, appearing in her early works as a blonde and switching to a brunette in 1938. She continued her long film career into the 1970s. She is the sister of Barbara and Constance BENNETT and the daughter of actor Richard Bennett.

In Father's Little Dividend (1951) she played the wife of Spencer TRACY who returns home to find his grandson chewing on his favorite silk scarf. He removes it to the cries and tears of the infant. "Honey," she demands, "what are you doing?" "He was eating my scarf," he explains. "That's all right," she replies with complete disregard for her husband's expensive and cherished scarf. "It's clean."

SELECTED FILMS: Power (1928), Three Live Ghosts (1929), Puttin' on the Ritz (1930), She Wanted a Millionaire (1932), The Pursuit of Happiness (1934), She Couldn't Take It (1935), Wedding Present (1936), Artists and Models Abroad (1938), The Housekeeper's Daughter (1939), Wild Geese Calling (1941), Twin Beds (1942), Colonel Effingham's Raid (1946), The Reckless Moment (1949), Father of the Bride (1950), We're No Angels (1955), House of Dark Shadows (1970). ■

Bennett, Marjorie (1895–1982), actress. Emigrated from Australia to the United States and appeared on stage, on screen, and in television. She entered films during the sound era as a supporting player in dramas and light films. She was the sister of actress Enid BENNETT, who encouraged her to come to Hollywood. She appeared in several television shows, including "Dobie Gillis" and "The Eve Arden Show."

SELECTED FILMS: Monsieur Verdoux (1947), June Bride (1948), Perfect Strangers (1950), Young at Heart, Sabrina (1954), The Rat Race (1960), Promises! Promises! (1963), Mary Poppins (1964), The Family Jewels (1965), Charley Varrick (1973). ∎

Bennett, Mickey (1915–1950), actor. Began his screen career as a child in silent films in the early 1920s. He appeared as a supporting player in dramas and light films into the early sound period. He occasionally worked as an assistant director.

SELECTED FILMS: The Man Who Played God (1922), The New School Teacher, Second Youth (1924), The Cohens and the Kellys, Grabbing Grabbers, It's the Old Army Game, There Ain't No Santa Claus (1926), Babe Comes Home (1927), Tillie's Punctured Romance, United States Smith (1928), The Dummy, Footlights and Fools (1929), Strictly Modern, Swing High (1930), The Mayor of Hell (1933). ∎

Benny, Jack (1894–1974), actor, comedian, aspiring violinist. Began his show business career as a violinist, then switched to vaudeville comedy, and finally appeared in Broadway musicals. Although Benny, whose real name was Benjamin Kubelsky, made his film debut in 1929, he achieved his popularity from his radio show, the format of which he eventually brought to television. The characters he portrayed in films were often based on the one he created for radio—a vain, miserly entertainer. The comedy was that of self-deprecation. Known mostly for his excellent timing, his unique type of comedy revolved

around his character; this gave the punch lines to his troupe of players rather than to him. But he was never as funny on screen as he was on radio or in television. Like other major radio comedians who failed in films, including AMOS 'N' ANDY and his friend Fred ALLEN, Benny somehow failed to bring his numerous radio listeners out of their homes and into the movie houses. The screen was not his forte, although some of his vehicles have some very entertaining moments. His films eventually became the butt of his gags on his radio and television shows.

In Artists and Models Abroad (1938) he portrayed the manager of a penniless troupe of entertainers. Trying to register in a Parisian hotel, he is told: "We must collect in advance. You're strangers." "We're not strangers," he protests. "I've known these boys for years, haven't I, fellers?" And in George Washington Slept Here (1942) he criticizes his maid (Hattie McDANIEL): "It wouldn't surprise me if she turned out to be a foreign agent. All she does around here anyway is to come in and rearrange the dust."

SELECTED FILMS: Hollywood Revue of 1929 (1929), Chasing Rainbows (1930), Transatlantic Merry-Go-Round, It's in the Air (1935), College Holiday, Artists and Models (1937), Man About Town (1939), Buck Benny Rides Again (1940), Charley's Aunt (1941), To Be or Not to Be (1942), The Meanest Man in the World (1943), The Horn Blows at Midnight, It's in the Bag (1945), A Guide for the Married Man (1967). ∎

Bergen, Edgar (1903–1978), ventriloquist. Appeared in vaudeville, in nightclubs, and on radio with his dummy, Charlie McCarthy, and finally worked his way to Hollywood. His films, however, whether shorts or features, never permitted him to attain the popularity he had gained on radio. It is difficult to discuss Bergen without mentioning his most famous creation. He had also given us Mortimer Snerd, the hayseed with the homespun common sense, but it is

Charlie who dominates every situation. The lovable Charlie, with his top hat, monocle, and tails, could be vulnerable, wisecracking, sophisticated, and cynical. Sometimes his radio audiences forgot that Charlie was only a dummy. But that was the gift of its creator.

In *Stage Door Canteen* Bergen portrayed a swami. "Do you know what I see when I look into that?" he asks Charlie while gazing into his crystal ball. "Goldfish?" Charlie asks. In the same film Charlie recalls one of his classmates. "Good old Bessie. She sat in front of me in history class." "Did you learn much about history?" Bergen asks. "Not as much as I learned about Bessie," Charlie replies. In *You Can't Cheat an Honest Man* (1939) Bergen and Mortimer Snerd sail through the air in a balloon. He tries to explain the principle of balloon flight to Mortimer, who listens carefully and concludes: "I don't think it'll work." Later in his career Bergen occasionally worked with Charlie in nightclubs and appeared in films without his famous dummies. He retired in 1978 and within two weeks he died. He was the father of Candice Bergen.

SELECTED FILMS: The Goldwyn Follies (1938), Charlie McCarthy, Detective (1939), Look Who's Laughing (1941), Here We Go Again (1942), Stage Door Canteen (1943), Song of the Open Road (1944), Fun and Fancy Free (1947), I Remember Mama (1948), One-Way Wahine (1965), Don't Make Waves (1967), The Muppet Movie (1979). ∎

Bergman, Henry (1870–1946), actor, assistant director. Worked in early silent films beginning in 1914 after leaving his home in Sweden. He was a supporting player in 20 comedy shorts starring Charlie CHAPLIN, often playing a villain. A large-framed, versatile performer, he portrayed an array of characters, including film directors, pawnbrokers, anarchists, and masseurs. In addition to playing heavies in Chaplin's films, he was frequently given the thankless task of impersonating irate and abused ma-

tronly women. He often worked as Chaplin's assistant director, a relationship that lasted over the years until Bergman's death.

SELECTED FILMS: Almost a Scandal (1915), The Pawnshop, Behind the Screen, The Rink (1916), Easy Street, The Cure, The Immigrant, The Adventurer (1917), A Dog's Life, Shoulder Arms (1918), Sunnyside, A Day's Pleasure (1919), The Kid, The Idle Class (1921), Pay Day (1922), The Pilgrim, A Woman of Paris (1923), The Gold Rush (1925), The Circus (1928), City Lights (1931), Modern Times (1936). ∎

Berkeley, Busby (1895–1976), choreographer, director. On stage at age five, on Broadway following military service in World War I, and by the late 1920s a noted dance director. He came to Hollywood as a choreographer in 1930 and within a few years he began to turn out for Warner Brothers studios dazzling musical numbers using scores of dancers in symmetrical patterns which were shot from a variety of angles. Soon he was directing his own musical and comedy films. He was forced into retirement when the film musical declined in the early 1960s. His earlier works have been the focus of attention at festivals and revivals, where new generations have found them fresh and entertaining.

SELECTED FILMS (as director): She Had to Say Yes (1933), Gold Diggers of 1935, I Live for Love (1935), The Go-Getter, Hollywood Hotel (1937), Men Are Such Fools, Garden of the Moon (1938), Babes in Arms (1939), Forty Little Mothers (1940), Blonde Inspiration, Babes on Broadway (1941), The Gang's All Here (1943), Cinderella Jones (1946), Take Me Out to the Ballgame (1949). ∎

Berle, Milton (1908–), comedian, actor. Appeared in vaudeville, on stage, and started in films in 1937. His greatest success, however, was in television, especially the years from 1948 through the mid-1950s, when he was aptly nicknamed "Mr. Television," the medium's

Milton Berle (left)

first superstar. The new medium which brought him into millions of homes each week gave him a chance to endear himself to his audience. Most of his 20 films were light comedies, giving him an opportunity to wisecrack his way through the thin plots. But, like his contemporary, Lucille BALL, his films were never as popular as his television show was. He has appeared occasionally as a guest on various radio and television shows, regaling audiences with his show business stories. He has also starred in television dramas.

SELECTED FILMS: *New Faces of 1937 (1937), Tall, Dark and Handsome, Sun Valley Serenade (1941), Over My Dead Body (1943), Always Leave Them Laughing (1949), The Bellboy, Let's Make Love (1960), It's a Mad, Mad, Mad, Mad World (1963), The Oscar (1966), Who's Minding the Mint? (1967), Lepke (1975).* ■

Berman, Shelley (1924–), comedian, actor. Worked with an improvisational group on stage, in nightclubs as a stand-up comic, and has turned out comedy records. Rather shy-looking with a worried expression, he has focused his routines on pet peeves that have caused him frustration and rage. He has appeared in relatively few films with little success; his comic style is perhaps more in tune with live audiences. His comedy records have sold in the millions, attesting to his talent as a comedian. He is famous for his "telephone" routines.

SELECTED FILMS: *The Wheeler Dealers (1963), The Best Man (1964), Divorce, American Style (1967), Think Dirty (1970).* ■

Bernard, Harry, actor. A leading figure in early silent screen comedy. He worked for Mack SENNETT'S KEYSTONE studios in the mid-1910s, usually as supporting player for such luminaries as Ford STERLING, Louise FAZENDA, and Mack SWAIN. With the advent of sound films, he appeared in many comedy shorts and features, often with LAUREL AND HARDY. He appeared in the "BOY FRIENDS" comedy series in the early 1930s with Grady SUTTON and Gertrude MESSINGER.

SELECTED FILMS: *Our Daredevil Chief, Crossed Love and Swords, Dirty Work in a Laundry, The Battle of Ambrose and the Walrus (1915), Two Tars (1928), Liberty, Wrong Again, That's My Wife, Men O' War, A Perfect Day (1929), Knight Owls, Blotto, Another Fine Mess (1930), Laughing Gravy, High Gear, Let's Do Things, Call a Cop, Mama Loves Papa (1931), Love Pains, The Knockout, Any Old Port (1932), Sons of the Desert, Sneak Easily, Maids à la Mode (1933), The Live Ghost (1934), The Bohemian Girl, On the Wrong Trek (1936), Way Out West (1937), Saps at Sea (1940).* ■

Bernard, Sam, actor. Appeared on stage before working in early silent comedies for Mack SENNETT'S KEYSTONE-Triangle studios. A portly, relatively obscure performer decorated with a wax mustache, he managed to earn $1,000 per week. He made shorts such as "Because He Loved Her" and "The Great Pearl Tangle" (1916). In the former, a bizarre comedy, a pie that he has prepared with poison and destined for an adversary is served by mistake to a little girl! Fortunately, there is a last-minute rescue.

SELECTED FILMS: *Wanted by the Police (1938), The Vicious Circle, When My Baby Smiles at Me (1948).* ■

Bernds, Edward (1911–), director. Began his film career in Hollywood in the early 1930s as a sound man for Frank CAPRA before turning to directing. Working for various studios and especially on B pictures, he directed many of the "BLONDIE" and "BOWERY BOYS" comedies. He also turned out 25 comedy shorts and three features starring the THREE STOOGES at Columbia studios. The genres that best suited his craft were the crime and comedy films.

SELECTED FILMS: *Micro-Phonies* (1945), *The Three Troubledoers, Monkey Businessmen, Three Little Pirates* (1946), *Fright Night, Out West, Brideless Groom* (1947), *Blondie's Secret* (1948), *Blondie's Big Deal, Feudin' Rhythm* (1949), *Gasoline Alley, Gold Raiders* (1951), *Loose in London, Hot News, Private Eyes* (1953), *Navy Wife, Calling Homicide* (1956), *Reform School Girls* (1957), *Return of the Fly* (1959), *The Three Stooges in Orbit* (1962). ∎

Bernoudy, Jane, actress. Appeared as a supporting player in early silent comedy shorts for Universal and other studios. She played in several of Eileen SEDGWICK'S early comedies.

SELECTED FILMS: *Hired, Tired and Fired, Some Heroes, I'll Get Her Yet, Ain't He Grand?, Room Rent and Romance* (1916). ∎

Besser, Joe (1907–), actor. Worked as a magician in vaudeville, comedian in vaudeville and burlesque, and appeared in several hundred comedy shorts before becoming a member of the THREE STOOGES in 1956 after Shemp HOWARD died. Having previously contracted for a full-length film, he left the team in 1958. He appeared in features without the other members of the team, including *Africa Screams* (1949), which starred ABBOTT AND COSTELLO, and *Say One for Me* (1959). His autobiography, *Not Just a Stooge*, contains numerous photographs and a filmography.

SELECTED FILMS: *Hoofs and Goofs, Muscle Up a Little Closer, A Merry Mix Up, Space Ship Sappy, Guns a Poppin', Horsing Around, Rusty Romeos, Outer Space Jitters* (1957), *Quiz Whiz, Fifi Blows Her Top, Pies and Guys, Sweet and Hot, Flying Saucer Daffy, Oil's Well That Ends Well* (1958), *Triple Crossed, Sappy Bullfighters* (1959). ∎

Best, Willie (1913–1962), actor. Featured in more than 75 films, usually as the black stereotype of a wide-eyed, shuffling, slow-witted servant. From 1930 to 1935 he was billed as Sleep 'n' Eat. He probably appeared in more "ghost" movies than any other actor. He later joined the Charlie Chan troupe as Chatanooga Brown and played in a few "SCATTERGOOD BAINES" comedies. Possibly one of his funniest roles was in *The Body Disappears*. He accidentally sits on a hypodermic needle whose contents turn people invisible. In *The Shanghai Chest* (1948), a Charlie Chan mystery, the detective's chauffeur, Mantan MORELAND, discovers Best in a jail cell and says, "Maybe I can get you out. I got an 'in' around here." "I don't need no 'in,'" Willie replies, "I'm already in. I want to get out." "What are you in for?" "Oh, just loitering." "Where?" "In a bank." "When?" Moreland asks. "Around midnight," Best replies.

SELECTED FILMS: *Feet First* (1930), *The Monster Walks* (1932), *Little Miss Marker* (1934), *The Littlest Rebel* (1935), *Thank You, Jeeves, Mummy's Boys* (1936), *Blondie* (1938), *The Ghost Breakers* (1940), *High Sierra, The Body Disappears, The Smiling Ghost* (1941), *Whispering Ghosts, A-Haunting We Will Go* (1942), *Cabin in the Sky* (1943), *Pillow to Post* (1945), *The Bride Wore Boots* (1946), *South of Caliente* (1951). ∎

Bevan, Billy (1887–1957), actor. Began his prolific film career in 1917 in the United States after migrating from his native Australia. He appeared at first as a supporting player in comedy shorts for L-KO studios. Working for Mack SEN-

NETT, he made dozens of two-reel comedies during the 1920s, a period in which he reached the height of his popularity. Short in stature and often sporting a mustache that fitted like a brush, he specialized in slapstick. On more than one occasion his films contained sexual innuendoes that even today are capable of raising a few eyebrows. His success was due in part to his excellent supporting players, including such talents as Madeleine HURLOCK and Andy CLYDE, and accomplished directors, including Del LORD and Roy DEL RUTH. During the sound era he became a competent comic character actor in full-length features.

SELECTED FILMS: Let 'Er Go, The Quack Doctor, Love, Honor and Behave (1920), Be Reasonable (1921), The Duck Hunter, Oh, Daddy, Ma and Pa (1922), Nip and Tuck, Inbad the Sailor (1923), One Spooky Night (1924), Honeymoon Hardships, Butter Fingers (1925), Hoboken to Hollywood, A Sea Dog's Tale (1926), The Bull Fighter (1927), Hubby's Latest Alibi (1928), Foolish Husbands (1929), Deferred (1932), The Girl of the Golden West (1938), Cluny Brown (1946), Fortunes of Captain Blood (1950). ∎

Bevans, Clem (1880–1963), actor. Tall, bewhiskered ex-vaudevillian and character actor who often played ill-natured old prospectors and crotchety senior citizens. He appeared in more than 90 films from 1935 to 1956, including B westerns and major productions.

SELECTED FILMS: Way Down East (1935), Come and Get It (1936), Maisie, Idiot's Delight (1939), Abe Lincoln in Illinois (1940), Sergeant York (1941), Saboteur (1942), The Human Comedy (1943), The Yearling (1946), Mourning Becomes Electra (1947), The Paleface (1948), Harvey (1950), Davy Crockett and the River Pirates (1956). ∎

Biberman, Abner (1909–1977), actor. Worked as a journalist before switching to acting. He migrated to Hollywood in the late 1930s where he specialized in playing sinister roles. Squat and Oriental in appearance, he appeared chiefly in dramas but occasionally performed in light films. In the 1950s he turned to directing films for Universal studios.

In His Girl Friday he played a shady character who worked for Cary GRANT. Grant, to prevent his ex-wife, Rosalind RUSSELL, from remarrying, hires Biberman to interfere. But Russell catches on to his ploy. "What'd you pull on Mrs. Baldwin this time, you and that albino of yours?" Russell asks Biberman. "You talkin' about Angelina," he replies in a wounded voice as he protects his girlfriend. "She ain't no albino. She was born in this country."

SELECTED FILMS (as actor): Soak the Rich (1936), Another Thin Man, Panama Lady (1939), His Girl Friday, The Girl From Havana (1940), The Gay Vagabond (1941), Beyond the Blue Horizon, Whispering Ghosts (1942), Knock on Wood, The Golden Mistress (1954). ∎

"Big Business" (1919), MGM. Dir. James Horne; Sc. Not listed; with Laurel and Hardy, James Finlayson, Tiny Sanford.

This two-reeler was among the last of the silents for Laurel and Hardy. It is also one of their funniest. Many consider it one of the two or three best films they ever made. The boys are Christmas tree salesmen in California, and they are meeting with stiff resistance. When they get to James FINLAYSON'S house, a dispute arises between the duo and the homeowner, with Finlayson breaking Ollie's watch while Ollie damages his antagonist's doorway. The confrontation escalates as Finlayson systematically dissects their car and the boys wreak havoc on the house. Passersby gather in disbelief to watch the madness. Finally, a policeman arrives, but he just observes and takes notes. Once again in a Laurel and Hardy film, a small disagreement leads to utter destruction. At the end, after the house is in shambles and the boys' car is wrecked and their trees destroyed, both sides make up and Hardy offers Finlayson a cigar that explodes in his face as the boys, smiling, dash away with the officer hot in pursuit. This well-constructed little film holds up rather well today although current audiences seem perplexed at the policeman's hesitation to stop the fracas sooner.

Big city comedy. See Urban comedy.

"Billy" films. A series of comedy shorts starring debonair Billy QUIRK, and which were produced by Vitagraph from 1912 to 1915.

SELECTED FILMS: *Billy Fools Dad, Billy's Troubles (1913), Billy's Wager, Billy, the Bear Tamer (1915).* ■

Bing, Herman (1889–1947), actor. Heavy-set, thick-accented comic relief character. He migrated from Germany in the 1920s to work with F. W. Murnau on *Sunrise.* He appeared in more than 75 films during the 1930s and 1940s, including comedies, musicals, and dramas, often playing excitable restaurant and cafe managers, bureaucrats, etc. He worked for most of the major studios and with many top stars. He committed suicide when he could no longer find work in Hollywood.

SELECTED FILMS: *Sunrise (1927), A Song of Kentucky (1929), Married in Hollywood (1930), The Great Lover (1931), Flesh (1932), Dinner at Eight, The Bowery, Footlight Parade (1933), Manhattan Love Song, The Merry Widow, Twentieth Century (1934), Rose Marie, Dimples, The King Steps Out (1936), Maytime (1937), Sweethearts, Bluebeard's Eighth Wife (1938), The Devil With Hitler (1942), Night and Day (1946).* ■

Binney, Constance, actress. Worked in early silent films as the female lead or second lead. She appeared in dramas and light films, especially for Paramount studios.

SELECTED FILMS: *Sporting Life (1918), First Love, Such a Little Queen (1921), The Sleep Walker (1922).* ■

Binyon, Claude (1905–1978), screenwriter, director. Worked as a writer for periodicals before switching his career in the early 1930s to a Hollywood screenwriter, chiefly for Paramount. He was best known for his sophisticated comedies. In the late '40s he began directing films, but after a few years he returned to the craft he knew best— screenwriting.

SELECTED FILMS: *If I Had a Million (1932), The Gilded Lily, Mississippi, The Bride Comes Home (1935), I Met Him in Paris (1937), Sing, You Sinners (1938), Too Many Husbands (1940), Take a Letter, Darling, Holiday Inn (1942), This Is the Army (1943), The Well-Groomed Bride (1946), The Saxon Charm (1948), Woman's World (1954), Rally 'Round the Flag, Boys! (1958), Kisses for My President (1964).* ■

Biograph. A film company founded in 1896 to sell a peep-show device called the Mutoscope to penny arcades and a combination camera and projector, the Biograph. Hence, the official name of the company, the American Mutoscope and Biograph Company. The founders, W. K. L. Dickson, H. N. Marvin, and H. Casler, began to produce films in 1897 on the roof of a Manhattan office building. The company's 14th Street studio began operations in 1906 with D. W. Griffith one of their pioneer directors. By 1910 the company opened a branch in California, following the trend of other film producers. Many early screen stars worked for Biograph, including, among others, Mary PICKFORD, Lillian and Dorothy GISH, Mae MARSH, and Florence Lawrence. Producer-director Mack SENNETT got his start in the New York studio before moving to California to organize KEYSTONE studios. Biograph went out of business in 1915, two years after Griffith left to work for Mutual.

Birmingham. Fictional comic-relief chauffeur, played by Mantan MORE-LAND, in the popular "Charlie Chan" detective series.

Bishop, Joey (1918–), actor, entertainer. Worked as a nightclub comic before the Second World War and was then drafted. Returning from the service, he continued as a stand-up comic, sometimes earning as much as $1,000 per week, and moved on to television as a performer and, finally, talk show host in the late 1960s. He has appeared occasionally in films, including those starring his friend, Frank SINATRA, and other members of the once-famous "Rat Pack." He usually plays the role of a comic character on screen but has never gained popularity or recognition in this medium. He works steadily in clubs and has appeared regularly in television. His style of humor includes the anecdote and the one-liner, which he delivers almost grudgingly.

SELECTED FILMS: *The Deep Six, The Naked and the Dead, Onionhead (1958), Ocean's Eleven, Pepe (1960), Sergeants Three (1962), Johnny Cool (1963), Texas Across the River (1966), A Guide for the Married Man, Who's Minding the Mint?, Valley of the Dolls (1967).* ∎

Bishop, Julie (1914–), actress. Starting her career as Jacqueline Wells in silent films, she joined the Hal ROACH studios in the early 1930s and appeared in a series of comedy shorts. She then moved on to feature-length westerns and other B movies. In 1941 she changed her name to Julie Bishop. Signing with Warner Bros. studios, she started a new and more successful phase in her career.

SELECTED FILMS: *Maytime, Bluebeard's Eighth Wife (1923), The Home Maker (1925), Tillie and Gus, Alice in Wonderland (1933), The Bohemian Girl (1936), Spring Madness (1938), Princess O'Rourke (1943), Rhapsody in Blue (1945), Cinderella Jones (1946), High Tide (1947), The Big Land (1957).* ∎

Bissell, Whit (1919–1981), actor. Appeared on Broadway before entering films in the 1940s as a character actor, frequently in querulous, petty roles ranging from parking attendants to lawyers. He often portrayed weak or cowardly characters.

SELECTED FILMS: *Holy Matrimony (1943), A Double Life (1947), That Lady in Ermine (1948), When Willie Comes Marching Home (1950), Skirts Ahoy! (1952), It Should Happen to You (1953), I Was a Teenage Frankenstein (1958), Advance to the Rear (1963), The Hallelujah Trail (1965), Five Card Stud (1968), Pete 'n' Tillie (1972), Casey's Shadow (1978).* ∎

Black comedy. Treating serious and morbid subjects, such as illness, death, and war, lightly. Known also as gallows humor, dark comedy, or sick humor, black comedy probably dates back to Roman satire. Surely the gravediggers in Shakespeare's *Hamlet* reveal strong elements of this kind of humor as they go about their digging tasks while they joke about suicide and gallowsmakers. Discounting the innumerable comedies about ghosts that Hollywood released during the silent and sound periods, a substantial number of "realistic" comedies contain elements of black comedy.

One of the earliest sound films, *The Front Page* (1931), is a good example. Based on the famous play by Ben HECHT and Charles MacARTHUR, who were writing from personal experience, the film has a group of cynical, hard-nosed reporters cracking jokes about an impending hanging and playing cards in a press room at a local jail. The two other screen versions that followed tended to play down this type of comedy, focusing rather on the stars and their personal problems. Sometimes a dramatic film will have brief moments of dark humor, such as in *Condemned* (1929), a story about the convicts on Devil's Island. One such prisoner, Louis Wolheim, has a tattoo of a dotted line around his neck. When a guard asks the significance of the markings, Wolheim replies: "When you are ready, just cut on the dotted line." In 1936 Robert MONTGOMERY and Rosalind RUSSELL starred in the unusual comedy *Trouble for Two*, a story about the pair joining a London Suicide Club. Another full-length black comedy during the 1930s was *A Slight Case of Murder* (1938), starring Edward G. ROBINSON. He played a rehabilitated gangster who takes a vacation in a summer house only to discover a roomful of corpses. The film deals with how he and his cronies attempt to get rid of the bodies. Based on a play by Damon Runyon and Howard Lindsay, the comedy was remade years later as *Stop, You're Killing Me* (1952), starring Broderick CRAWFORD.

The 1940s had its share of black comedies. Ernst LUBITSCH directed *To Be or Not to Be* (1942), a comedy starring Jack BENNY and Carole LOMBARD as the principal players of a Polish theatrical troupe during World War II. The film at the time of its release was considered tasteless by several critics. How could the director joke about a country that was invaded by Nazis? Forty years later Mel BROOKS decided to do a remake of the film. *Arsenic and Old Lace* (1944) was perhaps the best of the genre during the decade. Who would imagine that two sweet old ladies could commit such horrible crimes! They poisoned their victims and buried them in their cellar. Cary GRANT played their nephew who discovers their little secret. Again, it was based on a successful Broadway play. Perhaps the bleakest film of the post-war years was CHAPLIN'S *Monsieur Verdoux* (1947). He played a Bluebeard-type character who murders rich widows for their money. Audiences and critics found the film more uncomfortable than funny.

The 1940s also presented several popular fantasy-comedies, such as *Here Comes Mr. Jordan* (1941) and *Angel on My Shoulder* (1946). The former, starring Robert MONTGOMERY and James GLEASON, concerns a boxer who is summoned to heaven before his time. Meanwhile, his body is cremated. The remainder of the film is taken up with his search for another body. *Angel*, starring Paul Muni, centers on a gangster sent to earth by the devil to replace a judge. Muni does battle with the devil in this entertaining fantasy.

The 1950s made its contributions to the genre. Dean MARTIN and Jerry LEWIS starred in *Living It Up* (1954), a remake of *Nothing Sacred* (1937), which originally starred Fredric MARCH and Carole LOMBARD. Jerry played an alleged victim of radiation poisoning who is brought to New York as a publicity stunt, with hilarious results. The following year director Alfred Hitchcock, in a rare display of comedy, turned out *The Trouble With Harry*, starring Shirley MacLAINE and John Forsythe. A corpse seems to be creating a problem for otherwise peaceful citizens of a New England town. With the advent of nuclear weapons and the continuation of the Cold War, someone was bound to give us a film like *Dr. Strangelove* (1964). Made in England but directed by Stanley Kubrick and starring predominantly American actors, this quintessential satirical black comedy gives a devastating picture of the madmen at the controls of "the bomb," including politicians, the military, and the scientists. That same year Hollywood released a much lighter film, *Send Me No Flowers*, starring Rock HUDSON, Doris DAY, and Tony RANDALL. Hudson believes he hasn't long to live and arranges for a new husband for his wife. Meanwhile, Paul LYNDE tries to sell him a cemetery plot. In 1965 we were treated to *The Loved One*, another quintessential black comedy. The film concerned California's funeral business and its unusual cemeteries. The following year, 1966, Tony Curtis starred in *Arrivederci, Baby*, another comedy about a Bluebeard-type who murders women for their money.

The next decade continued the tradition of the black comedy. *M*A*S*H* (1970) satirized the stupidity and absurdity of war. During the Korean conflict, members of an American hospital unit find ways to divert their attentions from the horrors of war. The following year we are back to the Bluebeard theme as Walter MATTHAU plans to marry and then murder Elaine MAY for her money in *A New Leaf*. In 1973 Hollywood offered two entries. *Arnold* is scattered with multiple deaths and a marriage between beautiful Stella Stevens and a corpse! In *Paper Moon* a father-daughter team (played by real-life father Ryan O'NEAL and his daughter Tatum O'NEAL), after checking the obituary pages, sells Bibles to recent widows. In *The Fortune* (1975) Jack Nicholson teams up with Warren BEATTY to kill a rich heiress for her money in this comedy set in the 1920s. *Mother, Jugs & Speed* (1976), starring Bill COSBY and Raquel Welch, concerns a rag-tag ambulance service that offers little care to its patients. In *The End* (1978) Burt REYNOLDS learns that he doesn't have long to live. The comedy has an all-star cast, including, among others, Sally FIELD, Dom DeLUISE, Joanne Woodward, and Carl REINER.

In *S.O.B.* (1981) director Blake EDWARDS helped to launch the next decade's dark comedies. His comedy, besides dealing satirically with Hollywood and success and failure, mixes in suicide and corpses being transported about. In *Eating Raoul* (1982) Paul Bartel and Mary Woronov portrayed a very conventional couple who end up inviting "yuppies" and oddballs to their apartment, then killing them to help support their plans for a special restaurant. Jonathan Demme's *Something Wild* (1986) depicts the transformation of a naive tax consultant from his conservative existence to a world of absurdity and violence.

Whatever the reasons for Hollywood's, and ultimately the American public's, fascination with black comedy, the genre appears to be thriving. To blame the horrors of World War II would be too simple; this type of film has been with us from the early 1930s. To attribute the interest to our contemporary society with its dehumanization and self-centered, inner directedness may also be too simplistic. Perhaps we experience a sense of release and escape in seeing others suffering instead of us or in temporarily laughing at subjects that we know we will have to face inevitably.

Blackmer, Sidney (1894–1973), actor. Entered Hollywood films playing in serials during the silent era, but it was not until the sound period that he established himself as a steady actor. Sophisticated and business-like, he portrayed lawyers, executives, and other professional types on either side of the law in more than 100 dramas and light films. He never attained star status but remained a reliable, familiar minor actor.

SELECTED FILMS: The Perils of Pauline (1914), Strictly Modern (1930), One Heavenly Night (1931), Down to Their Last Yacht (1934), The Little Colonel (1935), Early to Bed (1936), Girl Overboard (1937), Straight, Place and Show (1938), It's a Wonderful World (1939), Love Crazy (1941), Broadway Rhythm (1944), A Song Is Born (1948), High Society (1956), Tammy and the Bachelor (1957), Rosemary's Baby (1968). ∎

Blaine, Vivian (1921–), actress, singer. Worked as a band vocalist and nightclub singer before entering films in the early 1940s. She often portrayed vivacious leads in light comedies and musicals. In *Jitterbugs* (1943) she holds her own against co-stars Laurel and Hardy.

SELECTED FILMS: Thru Different Eyes, Girl Trouble (1942), He Hired the Boss, Jitterbugs (1943), Greenwich Village, Something for the Boys (1944), State Fair, Doll Face (1945), If I'm Lucky, Three Little Girls in Blue (1946), Skirts Ahoy! (1952), Main Street to Broadway (1953), Guys and Dolls (1955), Public Pigeon No. 1 (1957), The Dark (1978). ∎

Blair, Janet (1921–), actress, singer. Worked as a band vocalist before entering films in 1941. A spirited leading lady, she appeared in many comedies as well as musicals, especially second features, during the 1940s.

SELECTED FILMS: *Three Girls About Town (1941), Blondie Goes to College, Broadway, My Sister Eileen (1942), Something to Shout About (1943), Once Upon a Time (1944), Tonight and Every Night (1945), Tars and Spars (1946), The Fabulous Dorseys (1947), I Love Trouble, The Fuller Brush Man (1948), Boys' Night Out (1962), The One and Only Genuine Original Family Band (1968).* ∎

Blake, Madge (1900–1969), actress. Began her screen career in her late 40s as a character player with MGM. Short and plump, she played matronly roles through the 1940s and 1950s before turning her attentions to television. One of her more noteworthy performances was as Spencer TRACY'S mother in *Adam's Rib.*

SELECTED FILMS: *Adam's Rib (1949), An American in Paris (1951), Singin' in the Rain (1952), Rhapsody (1954), The Solid Gold Cadillac (1956).* ∎

Blake, Marie (1896–1978), actress. After a career in vaudeville and stock, she came to Hollywood in the late 1930s to make a handful of films, usually portraying an officious busybody or a confidante to the leading lady. Her younger sister was the famous Jeanette MacDONALD.

SELECTED FILMS: *Mannequin (1937), Everybody Sing!, Love Finds Andy Hardy (1938), The Women (1939), Caught in the Draft (1941), The Major and the Minor (1942), Pillow to Post (1945), The Girl From Manhattan (1948), The Second Time Around (1961), The Best Man (1964).* ∎

Blanc, Mel (1908–), actor, voice specialist, musician. Began a career as a musician, but by 1937 he provided the off-screen voices for various Warner Bros. cartoon characters, including Bugs Bunny, Porky Pig, and Daffy Duck. He has, on occasion, appeared in films. He has also had a successful radio career on "The Jack BENNY Show" as a character actor portraying different voices and sound effects.

SELECTED FILMS: *Neptune's Daughter (1949), Kiss Me, Stupid (1964).* ∎

Blandick, Clara (1880–1962), actress. Began as a stage actress in 1908. She appeared in numerous films, especially during the 1930s and 1940s, as a character player. She often portrayed down-to-earth servants and aunts in dramas and light films.

SELECTED FILMS: *The Girl Said No (1930), Huckleberry Finn (1931), One Sunday Afternoon (1933), Broadway Bill (1934), Straight From the Heart (1935), The Gorgeous Hussy, Make Way for a Lady (1936), Her Husband's Secretary (1937), The Wizard of Oz (1939), It Started With Eve (1941), Can't Help Singing (1944), People Are Funny (1946), Life With Father (1947), The Bride Goes Wild (1948), Love That Brute (1950).* ∎

Blane, Sally (1910–), actress. Began her career in films as a child extra. During the 1930s she played female leads in numerous low-budget second features, including light films. Born Elizabeth Jane Young, she never attained the status that her sister, Loretta YOUNG, achieved.

SELECTED FILMS: *Sirens of the Sea (1917), Rolled Stockings, Casey at the Bat (1927), Fools for Luck (1928), The Vagabond Lover, Half Marriage, Tanned Legs (1929), Little Accident (1930), Annabelle's Affairs, Women Men Marry (1931), Hello Everybody (1933), No More Women (1934), This Is the Life (1935), Way Down South (1939).* ∎

Blatty, William Peter (1916–), novelist, screenwriter. Although he is best known for his successful supernatural novel, *The Exorcist*, he had previously written screenplays for a handful of film comedies before doing the script for the film version of the above novel.

SELECTED FILMS: The Man From the Diners Club (1963), A Shot in the Dark (1964), John Goldfarb, Please Come Home (1965), Promise Her Anything, What Did You Do in the War, Daddy? (1966), The Great Bank Robbery (1969), The Exorcist (1973). ■

Blazing Saddles (1974), WB. *Dir.* Mel Brooks; *Sc.* Mel Brooks, Norman Steinberg, Andrew Bergman, Richard Pryor, Alan Uger; with Cleavon Little, Gene Wilder, Harvey Korman, Madeline Kahn, Slim Pickens.

This western spoof was the director's biggest hit up to this date, both commercially and critically, although a minority of critics found it unfunny. Cleavon Little plays a black hipster sheriff who struggles to overcome racism and political corruption to save a town. Gene WILDER portrays the Waco Kid, an alcoholic gunslinger, who teams up with Sheriff Little. Madeline KAHN impersonates a Dietrich-like barroom entertainer, and Harvey KORMAN plays the principal villain, Hedley Lamarr. Brooks' chaotic film is an amalgam of western cliches, verbal gags, visual humor, and satire, some of which work while other routines fall flat. But the public flocked to see it. Highlights include Kahn's parody of Marlene Dietrich, the sequence with the black railroad workers, and Dom DeLUISE as a contemporary film director whose set is invaded by the out-of-control cast of *Blazing Saddles*. Some viewers found portions of the film tasteless, vulgar, and even scatological, while others accepted the crudities as fresh and original.

Bletcher, Billy (1894–1979), actor. Entered early silent films in 1913 as a supporting player. He assisted the famous comic John BUNNY. Working for Mack SENNETT, he appeared in a group of two-reel comedies. By the 1920s he was the featured comic in his own series. In the 1930s he co-starred with Billy GILBERT in a comedy series, then played in many of the "OUR GANG" and THREE STOOGES shorts.

SELECTED FILMS: Dry and Thirsty (1920), Billy Jim (1922), The Dude Cowboy (1926), Better Days (1927), The Cowboy Kid (1928), Dancing Sweeties (1930), Diplomaniacs (1933), Babes in Toyland (1934), High, Wide and Handsome (1937), Destry Rides Again (1939), Chatterbox (1943), The Patsy (1964), Hello, Dolly! (1969). ■

Blonde Bombshell. See *Bombshell*.

Blondell, Joan (1909–1979), actress. Appeared in vaudeville, in stock, and on Broadway before she was invited to Hollywood to star in *Sinner's Holiday*, a film version of *Penny Arcade* in which she was currently appearing. She played in more than 75 dramas and light films, either as the star or as the second lead, often portraying gum-chewing, sardonic characters, including golddiggers and reporters. Her popularity reached its peak in the 1930s. Her autobiographical novel, *Center Door Fancy*, was published in 1972.

In *Topper Returns* (1941) she played a wise-cracking friend of Carole LANDIS. They travel to an eerie old mansion to claim Landis' inheritance. "How long have you been here?" Blondell asks an ancient housekeeper. "Twenty years," the woman replies. "It might turn out to be a steady job," Joan cracks. Later, the same housekeeper opens their bedroom windows, letting in the sound of the ocean waves. When Landis asks what that noise is, the woman announces ominously: "It's the waves, angry waves. Day after day, night after night, they beat with savage fury against the black rocks below. For 20 years they've been calling, calling, calling someone who never answers." "Just like the 'Pot of Gold' program," Blondell quips.

SELECTED FILMS: The Office Wife, Sinners' Holiday (1930), God's Gift to Women, Public Enemy, Blonde Crazy (1931), The Greeks Had a Word for Them, Three on a Match (1932), Gold Diggers of 1933, Havana Widows (1933), Dames, Kansas City Princess (1934), Traveling Saleslady, We're in the Money (1935), Three Men on a Horse (1936), Back in Circulation (1937), Good Girls Go to Paris (1939), Model Wife (1941), For Heaven's Sake (1950), The Opposite Sex (1956), The Champ, The Woman Inside (1979). ■

"Blondie" series. Based on Chic Young's popular comic strip characters, the 28 "Blondie" films spanned a period of 13 years (1938–1951). The cast remained basically unchanged. Penny SINGLETON played the title character; Arthur LAKE portrayed Dagwood Bumstead, Blondie's bungling, often bewildered husband; Larry Simms, Baby Dumpling; Jonathan Hale, Mr. Dithers, Dagwood's boss; and Irving BACON and Eddie ACUFF had the thankless role of Mr. Beasley, the tormented mailman. Most of the films were directed by Frank L. Strayer or Abby Berlin.

The domestic tranquillity of the Bumstead family and its dog, Daisy, was usually disturbed by some grand scheme of Blondie's or Dagwood's, which caused havoc and laughs until all was resolved. The later entries became more predictable and less humorous, especially when lower production values were introduced. Recurring memorable bits include Daisy's special entrance to the household, Dagwood's obligatory collisions with the letter carrier, and J. C. Dithers' frustrations with Dagwood's bungling of some real estate deal.

Aside from the usual preposterous hare-brained schemes concocted by Dagwood and other plot contrivances, the series did offer a semblance of reality. Baby Dumpling grows up and attends school, a daughter, Cookie, is born in the eleventh entry, and Daisy eventually has a family of her own. Often the humor seems to emanate from real-life

situations. In Blondie Takes a Vacation (1939), Blondie takes one look at Baby Dumpling's disheveled appearance and cries, "Oh, look at your child!" Dagwood squints and ripostes, "Whenever he looks like that, he's my child!" In Blondie for Victory (1942) she invites a group of women to her home for a meeting, nervously introducing them to Dagwood. "These are the Housewives of America," she announces. Her befuddled husband scans the group and inquires, "All of them?" But these elements were not enough to sustain the series, which was finally relegated to late-night television.

Columbia was having financial problems at the time it released its first "Blondie" entry. The film cost $85,000 to make and grossed $9 million, leading to its many sequels. From time to time, familiar stars appeared in individual films, including Glenn Ford, Rita Hayworth, Larry Parks, and Anita Louise.

SELECTED FILMS: Blondie (1938), Blondie Meets the Boss, Blondie Brings Up Baby, Blondie Takes a Vacation (1939), Blondie on a Budget, Blondie Plays Cupid, Blondie Has Servant Trouble (1940), Blondie in Society, Blondie Goes Latin (1941), The Boss Said No, A Bundle of Trouble, Blondie for Victory, Blondie Goes to College, Blondie's Blessed Event (1942), It's a Great Life (1943), Blondie Knows Best, Henpecked, Blondie's Lucky Day (1946), Blondie in the Dough, Blondie's Anniversary, Blondie's Big Moment, Blondie's Holiday (1947), Blondie's Reward, Blondie's Secret (1948), Blondie Hits the Jackpot, Blondie's Big Deal (1949), Blondie's Hero (1950). ■

"Bloom Center" comedies. A series of one- and two-reel comedy shorts with a rural setting initiated in 1915 by Selig studios. The film company apparently conceived the idea to compete with SENNETT'S successful "SNAKEVILLE" series. The comedies, whose formal title was "The Chronicles of Bloom Center," starred, among others, Irene Wallace and

Harold Howard. Several directors worked on the series, including Burton King and Marshall NEILAN, the latter having directed such entries as "Landing the Hose Reel," "The Come-Back of Percy," and "Spooks."

Blore, Eric (1887–1959), actor. Appeared on stage in his native England before migrating to Hollywood. Starting in silent films, he played in more than 75 features, usually as an irascible hotel manager or fretful butler but more often as a gentleman's gentleman, a role which he embellished with a sharp tongue, a raised eyebrow, and acerbic wit.

In the musical comedy *Top Hat*, for example, he exhibits a touch of drollery when he presents himself to his prospective employer. "Allow us to introduce ourselves, sir," he announces to Fred Astaire. "We are Bates." He joined the Lone Wolf detective film series in the 1940s as Jamison, Warren William's butler.

SELECTED FILMS: *The Great Gatsby* (1926), *Laughter* (1930), *Top Hat* (1935), *Swing Time* (1936), *Shall We Dance* (1937), *Swiss Miss* (1938), *The Lone Wolf Strikes* (1940), *The Lady Eve* (1941), *Holy Matrimony* (1943), *San Diego, I Love You* (1944), *Kitty* (1945), *Abie's Irish Rose* (1946), *Love Happy* (1949), *Fancy Pants* (1950), *Bowery to Bagdad* (1954). ■

Blue, Ben (1900–1975), actor, comedian, dancer. Appeared in vaudeville and Broadway musicals before entering films in 1926. At one period during the 1920s, he, together with a partner, owned a chain of dancing schools. Slight of build with a rubber face, he made numerous short films for various studios. Later, he appeared in full-length features as a somber-faced character actor, enlivening many films. He co-starred briefly with the veteran film comic Billy GILBERT in a series of comedy shorts called "The TAXI BOYS." In all, he starred or was featured in more than 150

films. In the 1950s he appeared often as a guest on different television shows.

In *My Wild Irish Rose* he played a bellhop who is berated by hotel owner George TOBIAS: "You don't have the brains of a two-year-old child!" "I know," Blue explains, "look at the difference in our ages."

SELECTED FILMS: *College Rhythm* (1934), *Follow Your Heart, College Holiday* (1936), *Top of the Town, High, Wide and Handsome* (1937), *College Swing, Cocoanut Grove* (1938), *Paris Honeymoon* (1939), *Panama Hattie, For Me and My Gal* (1942), *Thousands Cheer* (1943), *Two Girls and a Sailor* (1944), *Two Sisters From Boston* (1946), *My Wild Irish Rose* (1947), *One Sunday Afternoon* (1948), *It's a Mad, Mad, Mad, Mad World* (1963), *The Russians Are Coming! The Russians Are Coming!* (1966), *The Busy Body* (1967), *Where Were You When the Lights Went Out?* (1968). ■

Blue, Monte (1890–1963), actor. Worked in a circus before entering silent films as a stuntman for the legendary director, D. W. Griffith. His good looks and screen presence soon catapulted him to popularity as a leading man in romantic dramas and light films through the silent era and early sound period. Later, he was successful as a character player. He appeared in hundreds of films during a career that spanned five decades.

SELECTED FILMS: *The Birth of a Nation* (1915), *Wild and Woolly, Hands Up!* (1917), *M'Liss* (1918), *The Affairs of Anatol* (1921), *Broadway Rose* (1922), *The Marriage Circle* (1924), *So This Is Paris* (1926), *College Rhythm* (1934), *The Big Broadcast of 1938* (1938), *Road to Singapore* (1940), *Sullivan's Travels* (1941), *The Palm Beach Story* (1942), *Thousands Cheer* (1943), *The Horn Blows at Midnight* (1945), *Two Sisters From Boston* (1946), *Life With Father* (1947), *Apache* (1954). ■

Blystone, John G. (1892–1938), director. Began his career in the motion picture industry in 1916 as a property man. As a director, he worked with Buster KEATON and LAUREL AND HARDY in the 1920s and 1930s. Most of his directorial work was with comedies.

SELECTED FILMS: *Friendly Husband, Our Hospitality* (1923), *Ladies to Board, The Last Man on Earth* (1924), *The Lucky Horseshoe, The Best Bad Man* (1925), *Hard Boiled, The Family Upstairs* (1926), *Ankles Preferred, Pajamas* (1927), *Mother Knows Best* (1928), *The Big Party, So This Is London* (1930), *Mr. Lemon of Orange, The Young Sinners* (1931), *She Wanted a Millionaire, Too Busy to Work* (1932), *Hot Pepper, Shanghai Madness* (1933), *Coming Out Party* (1934), *The County Chairman* (1935), *Little Miss Nobody, The Magnificent Brute* (1936), *Great Guy, Woman Chases Man* (1937), *Swiss Miss, Block-Heads* (1938). ∎

Blystone, Stanley (–1956), actor. Worked chiefly in comedy shorts during the 1930s, 1940s, and 1950s as a supporting player. He appeared in many of the THREE STOOGES' films as well as those of other leading comics of the period, including LAUREL AND HARDY, WHEELER AND WOOLSEY, the MARX BROTHERS, and ABBOTT AND COSTELLO.

SELECTED FILMS: *Hold 'Em Jail* (1932), *Sons of the Desert* (1933), *Hips Hips Hooray, We're Not Dressing* (1934), *Restless Knights, A Night at the Opera* (1935), *Half-Shot Shooters, False Alarms* (1936), *Goofs and Saddles* (1937), *Room Service* (1939), *A Chump at Oxford* (1940), *Buck Privates* (1941), *Even as I.O.U.* (1942), *Spook Louder, Back From the Front, Crash Goes the Hash* (1943), *Fright Night, Out West* (1947), *Shivering Sherlocks, Pardon My Clutch* (1948), *A Missed Fortune* (1952), *Pals and Gals* (1954), *Of Cash and Hash* (1955). ∎

Blythe, Betty (1893–1972), actress. Entered silent films in the 1920s. She appeared in dramas and light films during a career that extended into the sound era and spanned five decades. During the 1920s she played female leads; with the advent of sound, she turned to supporting roles.

SELECTED FILMS: *Nomads of the North* (1920), *In Hollywood With Potash and Perlmutter* (1924), *Chu Chin Chow* (1925), *The Girl From Gay Paree* (1927), *Glorious Betsy* (1928), *Only Yesterday* (1933), *Ever Since Eve* (1934), *The Gorgeous Hussy* (1936), *Top Sergeant Mulligan* (1941), *Jiggs and Maggie in Society* (1947), *My Fair Lady* (1964). ∎

"Boat, The." See Buster Keaton.

Bogart, Humphrey (1899–1957), actor. Worked as theater office boy and stage manager before turning to acting in the 1920s. He began his film career in 1930, playing second leads in minor films. In 1935, while appearing on Broadway, he attracted critical attention for his portrayal of the gangster Duke Mantee in *The Petrified Forest*. Hollywood took notice and his roles improved. Known more for the tough, cynical characters he portrayed on screen, he appeared also in a handful of light films. In fact, his only Academy Award was won for his portrayal of the hard-drinking skipper in the adventure comedy, *The African Queen*. His name is still magic in the world of films, and some of his features have become classics.

Some of his best lines may be found in *Casablanca*. Bogart plays Rick, an American expatriate and cafe owner in Vichy-controlled Casablanca during World War II. When his friend, Claude Rains, the prefect of police, asks him why he came to Casablanca, Bogart says, "For the waters." "But there are no waters in Casablanca," Rains reminds him. "Then I was misinformed," the elusive Bogart replies. In another scene a suspicious Nazi officer questions the American. "What's your nationality?" "I'm a drunkard," Bogart quips.

SELECTED FILMS: Broadway's Like That, A Devil With Women (1930), Women of All Nations (1931), Love Affair (1932), Stand-In (1937), Swing Your Lady (1938), All Through the Night (1942), Thank Your Lucky Stars (1943), Two Guys From Milwaukee (1946), It's a Great Feeling (1949), The African Queen, Road to Bali (1952), Love Lottery (1953), Beat the Devil, Sabrina (1954), We're No Angels (1955), The Harder They Fall (1956). ■

Boland, Eddie (1883–1935), actor. Starred in early silent comedy shorts. In 1915 he was an established comic working for Universal's "Joker Comedies" unit. By 1920 he was turning out one-reel comedies for producer Hal ROACH. He appeared in several feature-length films in the 1920s and 1930s.

SELECTED FILMS: Within the Law, Long Live the King (1923), Little Robinson Crusoe (1924), The Kid Brother (1927), Vanity Street (1932), I Have Lived (1933). ■

Boland, Mary (1880–1965), actress. She began her acting career as a teenager on stage and in silent films playing in tragedies. But she achieved more fame for her comic roles in films during the 1930s. Her roles often consisted of the scatterbrained wife or mother, which she played with delight and charm. In *Nothing but Trouble* (1944), the matronly Boland shares the spotlight with Laurel and Hardy whom she unfortunately hires as servants. Her memorable roles include that of Effie Froud, Charles RUGGLES' husband in *Ruggles of Red Gap*, and that of Mrs. Bennet, the harassed mother of five unmarried daughters in *Pride and Prejudice*. In the former she portrayed the social-climbing wife of a rich rancher who has won an English butler (Charles LAUGHTON) in a poker game. When she hears Laughton say "indubitably," she is so impressed that she exclaims: "What beautiful French you speak, Ruggles!"

In *Early to Bed* she played Charles Ruggles' sweetheart for 20 years, always hoping he would pop the question. Visiting her on their anniversary, he says romantically: "You know, you haven't changed one little bit." "No, I haven't," she replies. "I was single then and I'm still single."

SELECTED FILMS: The Edge of the Abyss (1915), His Temporary Wife (1919), Secrets of a Secretary (1931), Trouble in Paradise, If I Had a Million (1932), Mama Loves Papa (1933), Six of a Kind, Down to Their Last Yacht (1934), Ruggles of Red Gap (1935), Early to Bed, College Holiday (1936), Marry the Girl (1937), Artists and Models Abroad (1938), The Magnificent Fraud, The Women (1939), He Married His Wife, Pride and Prejudice (1940), Julia Misbehaves (1948), Guilty Bystander (1950). ■

Bolger, Ray (1904–1987), actor, dancer. Appeared in vaudeville and on Broadway before entering films in 1936. Although his full range of talents was underutilized by Hollywood studios, he became widely known for his role of the sorrowful scarecrow in *The Wizard of Oz* (1939). One of his better roles occurred in *April in Paris*, in which he portrayed a petty Washington bureaucrat. In one especially memorable moment he is haggling with a New York cabbie over a tip. "I believe your rates are set by the Interstate Commerce Commission," Bolger pronounces, "and I'm sure you receive a living wage." The frustrated taxi driver retorts, "Would you like to marry me for my money?"

SELECTED FILMS: The Great Ziegfeld (1936), Rosalie (1937), Sweethearts (1938), Sunny (1941), Four Jacks and a Jill (1942), Stage Door Canteen (1943), Four Jacks and a Jill (1944), The Harvey Girls (1946), Look for the Silver Lining, Make Mine Laughs (1949), Where's Charley? (1952), April in Paris (1953), Babes in Toyland (1961), The Daydreamer (1966), The Entertainer (1975), The Runner Stumbles (1979). ■

Bologna, Joseph (1936–), actor. Has worked on stage and in television as well as in films. He has appeared chiefly in light films since his screen debut in the early 1970s. He is the husband of actress and playwright Renee TAYLOR.

In *Chapter Two* he sends off his just-married brother with the following advice: "Here's your plane ticket and complete honeymoon instructions. Come out of your room at least once a week. Food is very important."

SELECTED FILMS: Lovers and Other Strangers (1970), Made for Each Other (1971), Cops and Robbers (1973), Mixed Company (1974), The Big Bus (1976), Chapter Two (1979), My Favorite Year (1982), Blame It on Rio, The Woman in Red (1984), Transylvania 6–5000 (1985). ∎

Bolton, Guy (1885–1979), playwright, screenwriter, novelist. Wrote many musicals and light plays as well as screenplays, some in collaboration. His stage plays and stories have often been adapted for the screen, including *Sally*, both the 1925 silent and the 1929 sound versions; *Lady Be Good* (1928); *Rio Rita* (1929); *Girl Crazy* (1932); *Words and Music* (1948); and *Anything Goes* (1956). His screenwriting career spanned more than 20 years.

SELECTED FILMS: Grounds for Divorce (1925), The Love Doctor (1929), The Love Parade (1930), The Lady Refuses, Delicious (1931), Careless Lady, The Woman in Room 13 (1932), Pleasure Cruise (1933), The Lady Is Willing (1934), The Morals of Marcus (1935). ∎

Bombshell (1933), MGM. Dir. Victor Fleming; Sc. John Lee Mahin, Jules Furthman; with Jean Harlow, Lee Tracy, Franchot Tone, Frank Morgan, Una Merkel.

This wise-cracking, satirical comedy about Hollywood was Jean HARLOW'S thirteenth feature film. By now she had established herself as something more than a blonde sexpot. Critics lauded her acting ability, her exuberance, and her gift for comedy. In 1932 she had switched to MGM whose mentors were adept at creating stars. This, for the most part, is the subject of the film. Harlow portrayed a film star whose public and private life is exploited and manipulated by her studio and her ruthless publicity agent, played to the hilt by Lee TRACY. When she protests about a series of scandalous stories he's been feeding the press, Tracy enlightens her on her importance. "Strong men take one look at your picture and go home and kiss their wives for the first time in ten years. You're an international tonic. You're a boon to repopulation in a world thinned out by war and famine!" Franchot TONE, whom she meets at a dude ranch, hilariously tries to make love to her with such lines as: "Your hair is like a field of daisies. I should like to run barefoot through your hair." Other players who helped make this fast-paced comedy a success include Frank MORGAN, Una MERKEL, Pat O'BRIEN as a flippant director, and Louise BEAVERS as Harlow's maid. The film is sometimes listed under its alternate title, *Blonde Bombshell*.

Bonavona, Fortunio (1893–1969), actor, singer, writer. Studied law in his native Spain before appearing on stage. As a singer, he toured Europe and appeared as a baritone with the Paris Opera; he debuted on Broadway in 1930, acting in *Dishonored Lady*. He entered Hollywood films in 1932, often playing comic foreign types, especially excitable characters. His most notable role was that of the exasperated singing coach to Kane's future wife, Susan Alexander, in *Citizen Kane* (1941).

SELECTED FILMS: Careless Lady (1932), Tropic Holiday (1938), That Night in Rio (1941), Larceny, Inc. (1942), Going My Way (1944), Monsieur Beaucaire (1946), Fiesta (1947), Adventures of Don Juan (1948), Nancy Goes to Rio (1950), The Moon Is Blue (1953), The Running Man (1963), Million Dollar Collar (1969). ∎

Bond, Lillian (1910–), actress. Performed on stage as a teenager in her native England before coming to Hollywood in the mid-1920s. She appeared in a string of comedy shorts and moved on to dramatic and light features in a career that spanned more than four decades. She portrayed "other woman" roles into the early sound era, eventually maturing into a fine character actress.

SELECTED FILMS: Lost and Found (1927), Just a Gigolo (1931), Fireman, Save My Child, Beauty and the Boss, Man About Town, Hot Saturday (1932), Hot Pepper, When Strangers Marry, Double Harness, Her Splendid Folly (1933), Affairs of a Gentleman, Hell Bent for Love (1934), The Bishop Misbehaves (1935), The Housekeeper's Daughter (1939), Pirates of Tripoli (1955). ■

Bond, Tommy (1927–), actor. Although he appeared in various feature-length films during the 1930s and 1940s, he is mostly remembered for his role as "Butch," the tough bully who often terrorized Spanky and Alfalfa in the "Our Gang" shorts of the 1930s. He appeared occasionally in features, some of which starred such popular comics of the period as Eddie CANTOR and LAUREL AND HARDY.

SELECTED FILMS: Beauty and the Bus (1933), Kid Millions (1934), Silly Billies (1936), Block-Heads, City Streets (1938), A Little Bit of Heaven, Five Little Peppers at Home (1940), Adventure in Washington (1941), Man From Frisco (1944), Call Me Mister (1951). ■

Bond, Ward (1903–1960), actor. Appeared in films from the early sound period and continued in character roles through the 1950s. A personal friend of John FORD, he was featured in many of the director's films. His big, brawny physique (he had been a football star at USC) and blustery voice permitted him to play heavies as well as good-natured tough guys, sheriffs, and confidants of the leads in dramas and comedies. In Joan of Arc (1948) he played a French general, one of his most unusual roles. "There must be no swearing in the army," Joan (Ingrid Bergman) demands of her generals. "You want our army to be dumb?" Bond asks, balking at the order.

SELECTED FILMS: The Big Trail (1930), Rackety Rax (1932), When Strangers Marry (1933), Broadway Bill (1934), Little Big Shot, Muss 'Em Up (1935), Crash Donovan (1936), 23 1/2 Hours' Leave (1937), Hawaii Calls, Professor Beware (1938), Made for Each Other (1939), Tobacco Road (1941), Hello, Frisco, Hello, Slightly Dangerous (1943), The Time of Your Life (1948), Riding High (1950), The Quiet Man (1952), Mister Roberts (1955), Rio Bravo (1959). ■

Bondi, Beulah (1888–1981), actress. Enjoyed an extremely successful stage career before settling in Hollywood in the early 1930s. She rapidly proved to be a highly talented character player, continuing in this role for four decades. With sharp, distinct features and piercing eyes, she usually portrayed matronly types such as mothers, widows, and dowagers in dramas and light films. She was nominated twice for a Best Supporting Oscar.

SELECTED FILMS: Street Scene (1931), Christopher Bean (1933), Ready for Love (1934), The Gorgeous Hussy (1936), Vivacious Lady (1938), The Under-Pup (1939), The Captain Is a Lady (1940), Our Hearts Were Young and Gay (1944), Breakfast in Hollywood (1945), The Life of Riley (1949), Latin Lovers (1953), Tammy, Tell Me True (1962), Tammy and the Doctor (1963). ■

Boniface, Symona, actress. Began her Hollywood career in silent films. From the 1940s she appeared chiefly in comedy shorts starring the THREE STOOGES. She played elegant and dignified figures, in the manner of Margaret DUMONT, thereby creating the perfect foil for the wild, low-comedy antics of Larry, Moe, and Curley.

SELECTED FILMS: A-Plumbing We Will Go, No Census No Feeling (1940), All the World's a Stooge, An Ache in Every Stake, In the Sweet Pie and Pie (1941), Spook Louder (1943), Micro Phonies (1945), G.I. Wanna Go Home (1946), Half-Wits Holiday (1947), The Pest Man Wins (1951), Bedlam in Paradise (1955), Scheming Schemers (1956). ∎

Booker, Harry (1850–1924), actor. Worked in early silent comedy shorts in Mack SENNETT'S KEYSTONE studios. Although he appeared as supporting player to many of the top comedians of the period, including Louise FAZENDA and Ford STERLING, he performed most frequently in the comedies starring Charles MURRAY.

SELECTED FILMS: A Game Old Knight, Her Painted Hero, The Great Vacuum Robbery (1915), His Hereafter, The Judge, A Love Riot, Pills of Peril (1916), Maggie's First False Step, Her Fame and Shame, Her Torpedoed Love (1917). ∎

Bordoni, Irene (1894–1953), actress, singer. Emigrated from her native Corsica to the United States in 1912 to appear on Broadway and in vaudeville after scoring successfully in French vaudeville. Lively and personable, she delighted theater audiences for years in musical comedies. She made her screen debut in the late 1920s, and appeared in several comedy shorts and light features during the early sound era. Twenty years later she was still performing, in a revival of South Pacific.

SELECTED FILMS: Paris, The Show of Shows (1929), Louisiana Purchase (1941). ∎

Borg, Veda Ann (1915–1973), actress. Worked as a model before entering films in 1936. She appeared as the lead or supporting player in scores of routine melodramas and light films, usually as a tough blonde waitress, unfaithful wife, or gun moll who was down on her luck. She was a brunette until 1939.

In The Bachelor and the Bobby-Soxer (1947) she becomes infatuated with Cary GRANT. "Now there's a guy who never goes out of a girl's mind," she coos. "He just stays there like a heavy meal."

SELECTED FILMS: Three Cheers for Love (1936), The Singing Marine (1937), She Loved a Fireman (1938), Glamour for Sale (1940), The Pittsburgh Kid (1941), About Face, Two Yanks in Trinidad, She's in the Army (1942), Something to Shout About (1943), Detective Kitty O'Day, The Big Noise (1944), What a Blonde!, Scared Stiff, Life With Blondie (1945), Wife Wanted (1946), Mother Wore Tights (1947), Julia Misbehaves (1948), One Last Fling (1949), Aaron Slick From Punkin Crick (1952), Three Sailors and a Girl (1953), Guys and Dolls (1955), The Alamo (1960). ∎

Born Yesterday (1950), COL. Dir. George Cukor; Sc. Albert Mannheimer; with Judy Holliday, Broderick Crawford, William Holden.

This highly entertaining film comedy, based on Garson Kanin's Broadway success, brought Judy Holliday an Oscar for Best Actress and catapulted her to stardom. She had played the role on stage after Jean Arthur left before the Broadway opening. Broderick CRAWFORD, a millionaire junk dealer, hires newspaper reporter William HOLDEN to teach Holliday, his mistress, some of the social graces. One memorable scene is the card game between Holliday and Crawford. But Judy doesn't get all the funny lines. At one point she calls Crawford a Fascist. "I was born in Plainfield, New Jersey," he protests to his lawyer. "She knows that!" In spite of the vast experience of the two male stars, Judy makes the picture hers. After she is transformed, she stands up to her crooked junk dealer. "This country and its institutions," she pronounces, "belong to the people who inhibit it." Unfortunately, she continued to be typecast as the beautiful-but-dumb blonde in subsequent films. The Washington, D.C., setting allows for some slight didacticism to slip in, but Cukor's fluid direction keeps the film on target and the comedy predominates.

Borzage, Frank (1893–1962), director. Worked in silent films in 1912 as an actor in westerns and comedies. He began directing films in 1916. Known more for dramas which were heavily embellished with sentimentalism and romanticism, he turned out a handful of light films as well. The latter, however, never attained the popularity of his dramatic works.

SELECTED FILMS: *That Gal of Burke's* (1916), *Wee Lady Betty* (1917), *Get-Rich-Quick Wallingford* (1921), *Daddy's Gone A-Hunting, Lazybones* (1925), *Early to Wed* (1926), *They Had to See Paris* (1929), *Young As You Feel* (1931), *Flirtation Walk* (1934), *Living on Velvet, Shipmates Forever* (1935), *Stage Door Canteen, His Butler's Sister* (1943), *The Big Fisherman* (1959). ∎

Bosley, Tom (1927–), actor. Portly comic actor who has appeared on Broadway as well as in television and films, mostly in light features.

SELECTED FILMS: *Love With the Proper Stranger* (1963), *The World of Henry Orient* (1964), *Divorce, American Style* (1967), *The Secret War of Harry Frigg, Yours, Mine and Ours* (1968), *To Find a Man* (1972), *Mixed Company* (1974), *Gus* (1976), *O'Hara's Wife* (1982). ∎

Boteler, Wade (1891–1943), actor. Worked on stage as well as in silent films from 1919. He appeared as a supporting player in hundreds of dramas and light films during a screen career that touched four decades. The majority of his output was in the area of comedy, particularly two-reelers. He also wrote screenplays. He worked with some of the leading comics of the period, including, among others, the MARX BROTHERS, Mae WEST, W. C. FIELDS, and ABBOTT AND COSTELLO.

SELECTED FILMS: *23 1/2 Hours Late, An Old Fashioned Boy* (1919), *Ducks and Drakes* (1921), *Second Hand Rose* (1922), *Going Up* (1923), *Hold That Lion* (1926), *Soft Cushions* (1927), *Just Married* (1928), *Fainting Lover* (1931), *For the Love of Ludwig* (1932), *Duck Soup* (1933), *Belle of the Nineties* (1934), *Goin' to Town* (1935), *The Country Gentleman* (1936), *Peck's Bad Boy With the Circus* (1938), *Dog Daze* (1939), *My Little Chickadee* (1940), *Ride 'Em Cowboy* (1942), *Hit the Ice* (1943), *The Last Ride* (1944). ∎

Bothwell, John F. (1921–1967), child actor. Appeared as a member of "OUR GANG" in several of the comedy shorts. He was known as "Freckles."

Bouchey, Willis (1895–1977), actor. Appeared on Broadway for years before settling in Hollywood in 1951, late in his career. A sturdily built character actor, he usually portrayed bankers, leading citizens, and sheriffs.

SELECTED FILMS: *Elopement* (1951), *Just for You, Million Dollar Mermaid* (1952), *The 'I Don't Care' Girl* (1953), *Fireman, Save My Child* (1954), *Forever Darling* (1956), *McHale's Navy Joins the Air Force* (1964), *Follow Me, Boys!* (1966), *Support Your Local Sheriff* (1969), *Support Your Local Gunfighter* (1971). ∎

"Bowery Boys." A series of low-budget films which ran from 1946 to 1957, concerning the comic antics of a gang of young ruffians. The origins of the group can be traced to William Wyler's *Dead End* (1937), a highly rated film based on Sidney Kingsley's realistic Broadway play about a gang of slum kids surrounded by poverty and crime. But the similarity ends there. The early film singles out environment as the fundamental cause of crime and condemns society's indifference. The later films shun thematic issues and the harsh realities of the boys' lives, dwelling only on low comedy, mainly slapstick and hackneyed sight gags. Led by Leo GORCEY and Huntz HALL, the gang becomes embroiled in a variety of improbable situations. Some of the members include Gabriel DELL, Billy BENEDICT, Billy Halop, and Bobby JORDAN. Others drift in and out of the series. As with many film series, the earlier entries were the best, while the later films suffered from low production values and repetition. The films, 48 in all, were generally ignored by the critics but were relatively popular at the box-office. They seem to gain new audiences each time they appear on television.

SELECTED FILMS: Smart Alecks, Bowery at Midnight, 'Neath Brooklyn Bridge (1942), Kid Dynamite (1943), Block Busters (1944), Mr. Muggs Rides Again (1945), Bowery Buckaroos, News Hounds (1947), Master Minds (1949), Ghost Chasers (1951), No Holds Barred (1952), Jalopy (1953), The Bowery Boys Meet the Monsters (1954), Bowery to Bagdad (1955). ∎

"Boy Friends, The." A comedy series of two-reelers which ran from 1930 to 1932. The shorts starred two former "OUR GANG" members, Mickey DANIELS and Mary KORNMAN, as well as character actor Grady SUTTON and actor-stuntman David SHARPE. The directors included comic actor Edgar KENNEDY, Robert McGOWAN, James Horne, and George STEVENS. Hal ROACH produced the series.

SELECTED FILMS: Doctor's Orders, Ladies Last (1930), Blood and Thunder, High Gear, Air Tight, Call a Cop, Mama Loves Papa, The Kickoff (1931), The Knockout, Too Many Women (1932). ∎

Bracken, Eddie (1920–), actor. Appeared on stage as a child, in vaudeville, in nightclubs, and in some film comedy shorts, including the "OUR GANG" series in the 1930s. His feature film debut occurred in 1940. Displaying a bewildered expression, naive manner, and shy appearance, he emerged as one of the most popular comic actors of the 1940s, especially in the comedy films he made

at Paramount for director Preston STURGES.

In The Miracle of Morgan's Creek he confesses: "I knew a girl once who told me to jump in the lake and when I came back she was gone."

SELECTED FILMS: Too Many Girls (1940), Life With Henry, Caught in the Draft (1941), The Fleet's In, Sweater Girl (1942), Young and Willing, Happy Go Lucky (1943), The Miracle of Morgan's Creek, Hail the Conquering Hero (1944), Bring On the Girls, Duffy's Tavern, Hold That Blonde (1945), Ladies' Man (1947), The Girl From Jones Beach (1949), Summer Stock (1950), Two Tickets to Broadway (1951), About Face, We're Not Married (1952), A Slight Case of Larceny (1953), National Lampoon's Vacation (1983). ∎

Brackett, Charles (1892–1969), screenwriter, producer. Began his screenwriting career at Paramount in 1935, eventually leading him into collaboration with Billy WILDER. Together, they penned some of the most sparkling screenplays to come out of Hollywood. Their screenplay of Clifford Goldsmith's Broadway comedy, What a Life (1938), generated the "HENRY ALDRICH" comedy series. Brackett and Wilder won Academy Awards for The Lost Weekend (1945) and Sunset Boulevard (1950).

Brackett was so overshadowed by the strong personality of his colleague that their collaborative efforts became known as "Wilder" films. Brackett's contributions tended toward the warm, sentimental, light side of human nature, while Wilder, the worldly European, provided the cynical, sarcastic, hard-edged elements to their films. Brackett worked at various times with other writers, including Richard BREEN and Walter REISCH.

SELECTED FILMS: Enter Madame, College Scandal (1935), Live, Love and Learn (1937), Bluebeard's Eighth Wife (1938), Midnight, What a Life, Ninotchka (1939), Ball of Fire (1942), A Foreign Affair (1948), The Mating Season (1951),

The Model and the Marriage Broker (1952), *Niagara* (1953).* ■

Bradley, Mr. Fictional character in the "HENRY ALDRICH" comedy series. He was Henry's (Jackie COOPER in the first two films, Jimmy LYDON in the remaining entries) glowering high school principal. He was portrayed with gusto by character actor Vaughan GLASER.

Brady, Alice (1892–1939), actress. Starred on stage before entering early silent films. Daughter of Broadway and film producer William A. Brady, she left films for a while and returned to the stage where she was rediscovered in the early 1930s. Back in Hollywood, she was often cast as society matrons and mothers in dramas and light films. She played in SCREWBALL COMEDIES during the 1930s and was nominated for Best Supporting Actress for her role as the confused mother of Carole Lombard in *My Man Godfrey* (1936). She won the Best Supporting Actress award for her part as Mrs. O'Leary in *In Old Chicago* (1938).

In *The Gay Divorcee* she says to Ginger ROGERS: "I do adore Paris. It's so much like Chicago. It's such a relief when you travel to feel that you've never left home at all." In *My Man Godfrey* she played the dizzy mother of a wealthy family of spoiled children. When her husband (Eugene PALLETTE) announces that the family fortune has been lost, butler William POWELL announces that he "sold short" in the stock market and rescued the family funds. "I don't understand," the confused mother interjects. "You sold short? You mean gentlemen's underwear?"

SELECTED FILMS: *As Ye Sow* (1914), *Tangled Fates* (1916), *Maternity* (1917), *The Leopardess* (1923), *When Ladies Meet, Broadway to Hollywood* (1933), *The Gay Divorcee* (1934), *Gold Diggers of 1935, Lady Tubbs, Metropolitan* (1935), *My Man Godfrey, Go West, Young Man* (1936), *Three Smart Girls, Mama Steps Out* (1937), *Joy of Living,*

Goodbye Broadway (1938), *Zenobia, Young Mr. Lincoln* (1939). ■

Brady, Pat (1914–1972), actor. Started in Hollywood in 1937 as a member of The Sons of the Pioneers, a popular western singing group. He appeared in more than 75 films, chiefly westerns. His most memorable role, however, was as cowboy star Roy Rogers' amusing sidekick, Sparrow Biffle. His jeep in the series, "Nellie Bell," became popular.

SELECTED FILMS: *West of Cheyenne* (1938), *The Durango Kid, Two-Fisted Rangers* (1940), *Son of Texas* (1943), *The Gay Ranchero* (1948), *The Golden Stallion, Down Dakota Way* (1949), *Twilight in the Sierras* (1950). ■

Brandenberg, Ed, actor. Worked as supporting actor in silent and sound comedies. He was a supporting player chiefly for LAUREL AND HARDY shorts and features.

SELECTED FILMS: *Love 'Em and Weep, Sailors, Beware!, The Battle of the Century* (1927), *Their Purple Moment* (1928), *Liberty, Double Whoopee, The Hoose-Gow* (1929), *Any Old Port* (1932), *Thicker Than Water* (1935), *Our Relations* (1936), *Swiss Miss, Block-Heads* (1938). ■

Brandon, Harry (1912–), actor. Began his Hollywood screen career in the early 1930s portraying sinister types and continued in that characterization for almost four decades. He appeared as a character player in dramas, serials, and light films. He supported some of the leading comedians, including, among others, LAUREL AND HARDY, Bob HOPE, Danny KAYE, and Mel BROOKS.

SELECTED FILMS: *Babes in Toyland* (1934), *Big Brown Eyes, Poker Faces* (1936), *Two in a Taxi* (1941), *The Paleface* (1948), *Scared Stiff* (1953), *Knock on Wood* (1954), *Auntie Mame* (1958), *To Be or Not to Be* (1983). ■

"Brats" (1930), MGM. Dir. James Parrott; Sc. Leo McCarey; with Laurel and Hardy.

By the year this two-reeler was made, LAUREL AND HARDY had turned out more than three dozen shorts. They had established themselves as a formidable comedy team and had made a successful transition to sound. This clever little comedy provided the pair with the opportunity to play dual roles—as parents and as their own little sons! Stan and Ollie volunteer to babysit while their wives take an evening off. Meanwhile, little Stan and Ollie get into all kinds of mischief and squabbles upstairs in their bedroom. The boys are quite convincing and funny in their portrayals of younger versions of themselves, with Stan causing problems for Ollie and the latter snitching on Stan. The large-sized sets built to show the pair as tiny tots are effective and add to the good humor of this unusual film. The bathroom scenes, in particular, underscore the infantile nature of the Laurel and Hardy relationship.

Breakston, George (1922–1973), actor. French-born actor who appeared in juvenile roles in dramas and light films during the early sound period. He later produced his own action and adventure films.

SELECTED FILMS: Great Expectations, Mrs. Wiggs of the Cabbage Patch (1934), Second Wife (1936), Love Finds Andy Hardy (1938), Andy Hardy Gets Spring Fever (1939), Judge Hardy and Son (1940), The Courtship of Andy Hardy (1942). ∎

Brecher, Irving S. (1914–), director, screenwriter. Worked as a writer of comedy material for various radio stars, including Al Jolson and Milton BERLE, before turning to screenwriting in 1937. He concentrated mostly on comedy films and musicals.

SELECTED FILMS: New Faces of 1937 (1937), Fools for Scandal (1938), At the Circus (1939), Go West (1940), Shadow of the Thin Man (1941), DuBarry Was a Lady (1943), Meet Me in St. Louis (1944),

The Life of Riley (1949), Cry for Happy (1961), Sail a Crooked Ship (1962), Bye, Bye Birdie (1963). ∎

Breen, Richard L. (1919–1967), screenwriter. Wrote screenplays for many comedies, sometimes collaborating with Billy WILDER and Charles BRACKETT. His style of humor is light and good-natured and is readily apparent in such films as *Captain Newman, M.D.* His collaborations in such films as *A Foreign Affair* resulted in works of a more satirical tone, strongly reflecting the handiwork of his co-writers, especially Wilder.

SELECTED FILMS: A Foreign Affair, Isn't It Romantic?, Miss Tatlock's Millions (1948), Top o' the Morning (1949), The Mating Season (1951), Wake Me When It's Over (1960), State Fair (1962), Mary, Mary (1963), Captain Newman, M.D. (1964), Do Not Disturb (1965), A Man Could Get Killed (1966), Tony Rome (1967). ∎

Brendel, El (1890–1964), actor. Began his show business career in 1913 in vaudeville, appeared in Broadway musicals, and finally in Hollywood in 1926. He was most noted for his comic characters, especially those with a Swedish accent, and for his expression, "Yumpin' Yiminy." Actually he was born and raised in Philadelphia. In the late 1930s he starred in a series of comedy shorts which usually portrayed him as a simple-minded yokel. These two-reelers carried him into the early 1940s. However, he more often appeared as a supporting player in more than 100 films during a screen career that spanned three decades.

Two films in which he appeared are worth noting. In Raoul Walsh's *The Cock-Eyed World* (1929), a World War I comedy, an army officer studying the local maps of a French province bellows the now-famous order, "Bring me the lay of the land," and it is Brendel who responds by presenting the local prostitute. The second film, *Just Imagine* (1930), is a science fiction musical comedy which travels into the world of the future, specifically, the year 1980.

SELECTED FILMS: *You Never Know Women, The Campus Flirt (1926), Rolled Stockings, Wings, Too Many Crooks (1927), Sunny Side Up, Hot for Paris (1929), Happy Days (1930), Mr. Lemon of Orange (1931), Disorderly Conduct (1932), Hot Pepper, Olsen's Big Moment (1933), Little Miss Broadway (1938), Risky Business (1939), If I Had My Way (1940), I'm From Arkansas (1944), The Beautiful Blonde From Bashful Bend (1949), Paris Model (1953), The She-Creature (1956).* ■

Brennan, Eileen (1937–), actress. Began her screen career in 1967 after extensive appearances in stock, off-Broadway, and in television. Usually assigned to supporting roles in dramas and light films, she proved her comedic talents in *Private Benjamin*, starring Goldie Hawn, in which she played Hawn's spit-and-polish superior and for which she was nominated for an Oscar.

SELECTED FILMS: *Divorce, American Style (1967), The Sting (1973), Hustle (1975), Murder by Death, The Great Smokey Roadblock (1976), The Cheap Detective (1978), Private Benjamin (1980), The Funny Farm (1982), Clue (1985).* ■

Brennan, Walter (1894–1974), actor. Worked for a short time in vaudeville and at other odd jobs before entering silent films. Having lost his teeth during World War I (other sources attribute this loss to his work as a stuntman), he was typecast early in his career as elderly types, often as crotchety old-timers. He won Best Supporting Actor three times: *Come and Get It* (1936), *Kentucky* (1938), and *The Westerner* (1940). In addition, he was nominated for his portrayal of the pastor in *Sergeant York* (1941). He had featured roles in more than 100 films, many of them for major studios.

Brennan brought more to a role than that expected of a typical character player. Whether interpreting comic sidekicks or villains, he embellished each role with individual traits and a sense of reality without stepping out of character. In *Red River* (1948), for example, he played John Wayne's humorous wagon driver, but when Wayne undeservedly disaffected his hired help, Brennan turned serious and was quick to criticize his boss. In *My Darling Clementine* (1946) he played the whip-wielding, tyrannical father of a clan of murderous sons with such complexity and conviction that Freudians could have written a complete case study on the character.

SELECTED FILMS: *Tearin' Into Trouble, The Ridin' Rowdy (1927), The Shannons of Broadway (1929), Neck and Neck (1931), The All-American (1932), Sing, Sinner, Sing (1933), Half a Sinner (1934), The Wedding Night (1935), Banjo on My Knee (1936), She's Dangerous, The Affair of Cappy Ricks (1937), Mother Carey's Chickens, The Cowboy and the Lady (1938), Joe and Ethel Turp Call on the President (1939), Meet John Doe (1941), To Have and Have Not, The Princess and the Pirate (1944), Red River (1948), The Far Country (1955), Tammy and the Bachelor (1957), Rio Bravo (1959), Support Your Local Sheriff (1969).* ■

Brent, Lynton, actor. Worked chiefly in comedy shorts during the 1930s and 1940s as a supporting player. He appeared in many of the THREE STOOGES' films.

SELECTED FILMS: *Restless Knights (1935), Three Dumb Clucks (1937), A-Ducking They Did Go, We Want Our Mummy, Yes, We Have No Bonanza (1939), Nutty but Nice, From Nurse to Worse, Cookoo Cavaliers, Boobs in Arms (1940), In the Sweet Pie and Pie (1941), Loco Boy Makes Good, Three Smart Saps (1942), Dizzy Detectives (1943), Gents With Cents (1944), Micro-Phonies (1945).* ■

Bressart, Felix (1880–1949), actor. Forced to leave Nazi Germany in the 1930s, where he had appeared in many films. He immigrated to Hollywood and continued his career, often portraying likable, eccentric characters chiefly in light films. Appearing with disheveled hair and sad eyes, he offered wit and philosophy to a host of stars.

Some of his more famous roles include those of a defecting Russian emissary in *Ninotchka* (1939) and a Jewish actor in Nazi-occupied Poland in *To Be or Not to Be* (1942). In the former, he enters a posh Parisian hotel with his Russian colleagues. "I'm afraid our rates are too high," the hotel manager warns the three Bolsheviks. "Why should you be afraid?" Bressart asks.

In *Comrade X* he had the honor of delivering the last line. An avowed anti-Communist, he escapes from Russia and immigrates to the United States where his daughter Hedy Lamarr and son-in-law Clark GABLE take him to his first baseball game. Awakened suddenly by the cheering crowds, he asks: "What happened?" "The Dodgers are murdering the Reds!" Lamarr shouts with joy. "Aha!" proclaims Bressart, "the counter-revolution!"

SELECTED FILMS: *Three Smart Girls Grow Up, Bridal Suite (1939), It All Came True, Comrade X (1940), Ziegfeld Girl, Married Bachelor (1941), Cross-roads (1942), Above Suspicion (1943), Greenwich Village, Blonde Fever (1944), Without Love, Ding Dong Williams (1945), The Thrill of Brazil (1946), A Song Is Born (1948), Take One False Step (1949).* ■

Brewster's Millions (1945), UA. Dir. Allan Dwan; Sc. Sig Herzig, Wilkie Mahoney, Charles Rogers; with Dennis O'Keefe, Helen Walker, Eddie "Rochester" Anderson, June Havoc.

A landmark comedy in terms of the number of times it has been filmed, the story is based on a novel by George McCutcheon that was converted into a play by Winchell Smith and Byron Ongley. Dennis O'KEEFE plays the heir to a vast fortune with one stipulation. O'Keefe has to spend one million dollars, secretly, in 24 hours to inherit the entire estate. The comedy aspect involves his almost unsuccessful attempts to spend the money. None of the seven versions is completely satisfying, but this 1945 adaptation comes closest. The first filming was in 1914. That was followed by a 1921 version with Fatty Arbuckle playing the lead. In 1926 Bebe DANIELS starred in the female version, titled *Miss Brewster's Millions*. In 1935, in the first sound version, English actor Jack Buchanan portrayed the frantic heir. The title was again changed in 1961 to *Three on a Spree* with Jack Watling. Finally, Richard Pryor starred in a lackluster production of the story in 1985.

Brice, Fanny (1891–1951), singer, comedienne. Appeared in vaudeville, burlesque, many Ziegfeld Follies from 1910 to 1923, and on radio. She appeared in her first film in 1928, making only occasional features over the next two decades. Her attempts at straight comedy, either on stage or in films, were not as successful as her roles in musical comedy. Three films were based on her life: *Rose of Washington Square* (1938), a fanciful retelling of her love affair with gambler Nicky Arnstein, *Funny Girl* (1968), and *Funny Lady* (1975), in which she was played by Barbra Streisand. Not a very pretty entertainer, she nevertheless was able to captivate her audiences with her comic and musical talent and her personality.

SELECTED FILMS: *My Man, Night Club (1928), Be Yourself!, The Man From Blankley's (1930), The Great Ziegfeld (1936), Everybody Sing (1938), Ziegfeld Follies (1946).* ■

Brickman, Marshall, screenwriter. Comedy writer who collaborated with Woody Allen on two of his films. He also worked as a comic in television.

SELECTED FILMS: *Annie Hall (1977), Manhattan (1979), Simon (1980).* ■

Bridge, Al (1891–1957), actor. Appeared as a character actor during the 1940s. Known for his rough voice, he was part of director-writer Preston STURGES' stock company of comic eccentrics.

SELECTED FILMS: The Lawless Nineties (1936), Woman Chases Man (1937), Christmas in July (1940), Sullivan's Travels (1942), The Miracle of Morgan's Creek, Hail the Conquering Hero (1944), Cross My Heart (1946), Unfaithfully Yours (1948), The Beautiful Blonde From Bashful Bend (1949), Mad Wednesday (1951), We're Not Married (1952). ∎

Bringing Up Baby (1938), RKO. Dir. Howard Hawks; Sc. Dudley Nichols, Hagar Wilde; with Cary Grant, Katharine Hepburn, Charles Ruggles, Barry Fitzgerald, May Robson.

One of the last of the 1930s screwball comedies and a box-office problem for Howard Hawks, this hilarious romp concerns members of the upper class pursuing a hyperactive dog, a missing, priceless dinosaur bone, and a leopard. Cary Grant, as a serious-minded paleontologist, has his sedate life-style turned upside-down by wealthy heiress Katharine Hepburn and "Baby," her pet leopard. The richly derived characters play an intricate part in this zany story, especially Charles Ruggles, who portrays a pretentious big-game hunter skilled in loon calls. In fact, practically all the major characters are crazy to some degree. When Grant arrives at erratic Hepburn's apartment and discovers her pet leopard, he shouts frantically: "You've got to get out of this apartment!" "But David," she replies, "I can't. I have a lease." The film is more popular with audiences today than it was in 1938. When the studio realized that it had lost money on the film and that Hawks had gone over the budget, it canceled his contract. Hepburn fared no better although this comedy proved that she was adept at madcap farce. Already a poor box-office draw, she was let go by RKO

and did not make a strong comeback until she starred in MGM's The Philadelphia Story in 1940. Peter Bogdanovich borrowed heavily from the plot for his comedy, What's Up Doc? (1972), starring Barbra Streisand and Ryan O'Neal.

Bringing Up Father. See Jiggs and Maggie.

Broadway Danny Rose (1984), UA. Dir. Woody Allen; Sc. Woody Allen; with Woody Allen, Mia Farrow, Nick Apollo Forte, Sandy Baron.

In this black-and-white comedy Allen plays a former mediocre comic who becomes an agent with a heart. Betrayed by his clients as soon as they achieve success and hunted by vindictive hoodlums, Danny survives more by luck than by his wits. In typical Allen fashion, the film affords him the opportunity to interject an abundance of gags, both visual and verbal. Mia Farrow tells him that her gangster husband got shot in the eyes. "Is he blind?" Allen asks. "He's dead," Mia replies. "That's right," he concludes, "bullets go right through." In a flashback Allen, doing his comedy act, asks an aged woman how old she is. "Eighty-one," she answers. "You don't look a day over 80," he says. Mia Farrow expresses her modus vivendi to Woody: "You know what my philosophy of life is? It's over quick so have a good time. You see what you want, go for it. Don't pay any attention to anybody else. And do it to the other guy first, 'cause if you don't, he'll do it to you." Allen, in disbelief and shock, questions: "This is a philosophy of life? It sounds like the screenplay of Murder, Incorporated." Although the pathetic character, Danny Rose, is original and interesting and the film contains some funny material, it remains an uneven work.

Broderick, Helen (1891–1959), actress. Had a successful career in vaudeville and on Broadway before settling in

Hollywood in the early 1930s. A talented comedienne with wide eyes and a cracked voice, she appeared in a string of light comedies. She brightened more than 25 films with her acerbic wit, including some Fred Astaire-Ginger Rogers musicals.

Her comedic contributions are especially noticeable in Olsen and Johnson's *Fifty Million Frenchmen*, in which she confides to them that she has come to Paris to be "dishonored." In *The Rage of Paris* she confides to Danielle Darrieux, who has regrets about misleading a desirable bachelor: "All women are dishonest. If they weren't, the world would be divided into two classes of people: old maids and bachelors." She was the mother of actor Broderick Crawford.

SELECTED FILMS: *High Speed (1924), Fifty Million Frenchmen (1931), Top Hat (1935), Love on a Bet, Swing Time (1936), Meet the Missus, The Life of the Party (1937), Radio City Revels, The Rage of Paris (1938), Naughty but Nice (1939), No, No, Nanette (1940), Virginia, Nice Girl? (1941), Three Is a Family (1944), Love, Honor and Goodbye (1945), Because of Him (1946).* ∎

Brodney, Oscar (1907–), screenwriter. Had become a practicing attorney before his desire to write comedy led him to Hollywood where he wrote light screenplays alone or in collaboration.

SELECTED FILMS: *Moonlight in Havana (1942), When Johnny Comes Marching Home (1943), On Stage Everybody (1945), She Wrote the Book (1946), If You Knew Susie, Mexican Hayride (1948), Yes Sir, That's My Baby (1949), Harvey (1950), Francis Goes to the Races (1951), Lady Godiva (1955), Tammy and the Bachelor (1957), I'd Rather Be Rich (1964), The Sword of Ali Baba (1965).* ∎

Bronson, Betty (1906–1971), actress. Appeared in minor roles in silent films before achieving success in the 1924 film version of James Barrie's *Peter Pan*. Groomed by her studio to follow in the footsteps of "America's Sweetheart,"

Mary Pickford, she was given similar parts. However, what Paramount failed to realize at the time was that the tastes of the audiences were changing; there was more demand for contemporary stories and themes and less for these fantasy-comedies. Her pixie-like charm lost its luster and, despite her genuine acting abilities, including those of subtlety and grace, her popularity fell in a very short time. She continued to make films into the early sound era, abandoning her career in 1932. She made brief, half-hearted attempts at returning to the screen in 1937 and the 1960s and early 1970s. Although her fame was short-lived, she starred in some bright and entertaining comedies.

SELECTED FILMS: *Anna Ascends (1922), Are Parents People? Not So Long Ago, The Golden Princess (1925), A Kiss for Cinderella, Paradise, Everybody's Acting, The Cat's Pajamas (1926), Paradise for Two, Ritzy, Brass Knuckles (1927), The Singing Fool (1928), Sonny Boy, A Modern Sappho, One Stolen Night (1929), The Medicine Man (1930), Lover Come Back (1931), The Yodelin' Kid From Pine Ridge (1937), Pocketful of Miracles (1961), The Naked Kiss (1964), Evel Knievel (1971).* ∎

Brooke, Hillary (1914–), actress. Worked as a model and on stage before entering films in the late 1930s. An attractive blonde, she appeared in dramas and light films as lead or supporting player. In addition to playing the female lead in a handful of Sherlock Holmes mysteries, she was featured in films with some of the leading comedians of the period, including Bob HOPE, Red SKELTON, and ABBOTT AND COSTELLO.

SELECTED FILMS: *New Faces of 1937 (1937), The Philadelphia Story (1940), Lady in the Dark, Standing Room Only (1944), Road to Utopia, Monsieur Beaucaire (1946), The Fuller Brush Man (1948), Africa Screams (1949), The Admiral Was a Lady, Beauty on Parade (1950), Abbott and Costello Meet Captain Kidd, Never Wave at a WAC (1952),*

The Lady Wants Mink (1953), Spoilers of the Forest (1957). ∎

Brooke, Van Dyke, actor, director. Began his Hollywood career in 1909 with Kalem studios, eventually directing many films in which he also appeared. He directed many of comedian John BUNNY'S films. By 1915 he gave up directing but continued to act until 1921.

SELECTED FILMS: The Artist's Revenge (1909), A Dixie Mother (1910), Her Hero (1911), Billy's Burglar (1912), Just Show People, Cupid Through a Keyhole, The Honorable Algernon, O'Hara Helps Cupid, Father's Hatband, Fanny's Conspiracy (1913), Cupid Versus Money, Sunshine and Shadows (1914), Rags and the Girl (1915). ∎

Brooks, Albert (1947–), director, writer, actor. Worked in television as an actor and writer, particularly with the popular "Saturday Night Live" comedy show. An offbeat director who specializes in quirky characters, he began writing and turning out films in 1969. His father, PARKYAKARKUS (Harry Einstein), was a famous radio and film comic.

SELECTED FILMS (as writer-director and actor): Real Life (1979), Modern Romance (1981).
SELECTED FILMS (as actor only): Private Benjamin (1980), Unfaithfully Yours (1983). ∎

Brooks, Louise (1906–1985), actress. Began her show business career as a dancer, appeared in Ziegfeld Follies, and was invited to Hollywood in 1925. After appearing in many comedies depicting the "flapper age," she portrayed more serious characters in major productions during the 1920s in the United States and in Germany where she worked with director G. W. Pabst. An unusually beautiful and gifted performer, easily recognized by her bobbed, brunette hair, she was never really allowed to develop to her full potential in Hollywood. By the 1930s, upon her return from Europe where she was permitted to demonstrate her dramatic abilities, she was offered only minor roles in low-budget Hollywood productions. Disenchanted with the direction in which her career was drifting, she retired from the screen in 1931. She made a half-hearted but unsuccessful attempt at a comeback in 1936. She has been particularly revered in Europe where her films are continually revived. Her autobiography, *Lulu,* received critical acclaim. A biographical study, *Louise Brooks: Portrait of an Anti-Star,* edited by Roland Jaccard, was published in 1986. In her later years she gave several interviews in which she revealed her distaste for Hollywood life.

SELECTED FILMS: The Street of Forgotten Men (1925), The American Venus, A Social Celebrity, The Show-Off, Love 'Em and Leave 'Em (1926), Evening Clothes, Rolled Stockings, The City Gone Wild (1927), A Girl in Every Port, Beggars of Life (1928), Windy Riley Goes to Hollywood (1930), It Pays to Advertise, God's Gift to Women (1931), When You're in Love, Overland Stage Raiders (1938). ∎

Brooks, Mel (1926–), comedian, screenwriter, director. After performing comic routines in nightclubs, on television, and on records, he began making farcical, hilarious films, some of which have been considered tasteless and offensive. Brooks' first film, *The Producers* (1968), is an irreverent comedy about a down-and-out producer, Max Bialystock (Zero Mostel), who intentionally oversells shares in a doomed show so that he can pocket the remaining funds.

The Twelve Chairs (1970), Brooks' next film, revolves around a dining room chair containing a fortune in jewels hidden in its seat. The chair becomes the object of a frantic and madcap search by an indigent Russian aristocrat (Ron Moody) and his principal rival (Dom DeLUISE). Although the critics in general found Brooks funny, they felt the film was rather bland compared to his first effort.

Blazing Saddles (1974), a spoof on the western genre, was Brooks' most successful feature thus far, both commercially and critically. His next entry, the popular *Young Frankenstein* (1974), was a black-and-white burlesque of the mad-monster movies of the 1930s and starred Gene Wilder. Gene portrays the mad scientist assisted by his loyal underling, Igor, played by Marty Feldman.

Silent Movie (1976) has Brooks portraying a movie producer attempting a comeback. The film contains numerous slapstick variations, of which only a few result in any success. Despite its large cast, which included, among others, Marty Feldman, Sid CAESAR, Dom DeLUISE, Bernadette Peters, Burt REYNOLDS, Paul NEWMAN, Liza MINNELLI, and Anne Bancroft, the film was generally disappointing to Brooks' fans.

His next attempt, *High Anxiety* (1977), a warm homage to director Alfred Hitchcock, received better reviews and a warmer response from the public although it left some wondering whether the master of suspense, witty in his own right, was a proper subject for spoofing. Brooks again plays the main character, this time a psychiatrist who takes over the reins of a sanitarium. Movie buffs will delight in the many humorous allusions to Hitchcock's works, but the film is uneven.

In *History of the World—Part 1* (1981), Brooks continues his use of crude comedy with a vengeance, offering something offensive to everyone. The episodic comedy covers many epochs, including the Stone Age, the Roman Empire, and the French Revolution. Bad jokes and old routines abound. As Moses (Brooks) descends from the mountain, carrying the cherished tablets, he says over his shoulder, "Yes, Lord, I will pass unto thy people your fifteen—" a tablet falls and shatters, "—er, your Ten Commandments." In the role of the waiter at the Last Supper, Brooks asks, "Separate checks?" Gumchewing Empress Nympho (Madeline KAHN), in a reclining position, holds out her wine cup. "Say when," her steward inquires. "Eight-thirty," she replies. While some scenes are genuinely riotous, others fall flat.

In an unusual move for Brooks, he starred in a remake of a film that was already acknowledged as a minor classic, Ernst LUBITSCH'S 1942 BLACK COMEDY, *To Be or Not to Be*, which featured Jack BENNY and Carole LOMBARD. Brooks and his wife, Anne Bancroft, played the lead roles, Polish actors during the Nazi occupation of their country. Admittedly, the 1983 version, directed by Alan Johnson, in some ways was funnier than the original, although it lacked Lubitsch's style and substance. Mel Brooks' originality stems from his outrageousness, his willingness to seek humor in every sacrosanct topic, and his readiness to break with traditional comedy techniques and styles. His directorial efforts may not be consistently successful in their attempts at comedy; indeed, they can often be labeled gross, lacking in subtlety, even at times vulgar. But he should be commended for his thrusts into new areas of comedy, whether or not they offend. There is much to enjoy in any one of his works, including his clever musical numbers, stylized routines, and exceptional lyrics that contain genuine parody. These qualities should be enough to list him as one of the major forces in film comedy.

Brooks, Phyllis (1914–), actress. Worked as a model before entering films in the mid-1930s. An attractive blonde, she appeared as lead or supporting actress chiefly in routine B films. She played in numerous light vehicles, including a few Shirley TEMPLE features. She retired from the screen in the mid-1940s.

SELECTED FILMS: *I've Been Around (1934), Lady Tubbs, To Beat the Band (1935), You Can't Have Everything (1937), Rebecca of Sunnybrook Farm, Little Miss Broadway, Straight, Place and Show (1938), Slightly Honorable (1940), No Place for a Lady (1943), Lady in the Dark (1944), Dangerous Passage (1945).* ∎

Brooks, Roy, actor. Worked in silent films during the 1920s, especially as a supporting actor in many of Harold LLOYD'S comedies. A tall, well-educated, and witty performer, he sometimes portrayed Lloyd's pal, but more often he was cast as his rival.

SELECTED FILMS: *High and Dizzy, Number Please, Never Weaken (1920).* ∎

Brophy, Edward (1895–1960), actor. Appeared in more than 100 silent and sound films, often as a tough but kind hoodlum. His short, stocky frame and wisecracks in Brooklynese graced many a B movie, especially the popular Falcon detective series in which he played the title character's servant, Goldie Locke.

In *The Falcon in San Francisco* (1945) he once again played the title character's sidekick. On board a train he finds a little girl's lost dog. "You've got Diogenes," the child says in relief, seeing him with her pet. "What, me?" he questions. "I ain't never been sick a day in my life."

SELECTED FILMS: *Yes or No (1920), West Point (1927), Free and Easy (1930), The Champ (1931), The Thin Man (1934), Strike Me Pink (1936), The Hit Parade (1937), You Can't Cheat an Honest Man (1939), Calling Philo Vance (1940), The Bride Came C.O.D., The Gay Falcon (1941), All Through the Night, Larceny, Inc. (1942), It Happened Tomorrow (1944), Wonder Man (1945), It Happened on Fifth Avenue (1947), The Last Hurrah (1958).* ∎

Brown, Chattanooga. Fictional comic-relief black chauffeur in several "Charlie Chan" films. Played by veteran comic character actor Willie BEST, he alternated with BIRMINGHAM, portrayed by

Mantan MORELAND, in the series. Best appeared as Chattanooga, a typical Hollywood stereotype, in *Red Dragon* (1945), *Dangerous Money* (1946), and *The Shanghai Chest* (1948), all produced as second features by Monogram.

Joe E. Brown

Brown, Joe E. (1892–1973), actor. Appeared in circuses as a child acrobat, in vaudeville, in burlesque, and on Broadway in the early 1920s. Before all his theatrical experience, he had played professional baseball. He began his film career in 1928 and remained popular into the 1940s. An affable comedian known for his wide mouth, he appeared mostly in low-budget features, enlivening them with his rubbery face and slapstick antics. He appeared among the Box Office Top Ten in the years 1932, 1935, and 1936. Following the loss of one of his sons during World War II, he became very active as an entertainer of American soldiers, often performing close to the front lines. His autobiography, *Laughter Is a Wonderful Thing*, was published in 1959.

In *Flirting With Fate* (1938) he decides to commit suicide by drinking from a jug marked "Ant Poison." However, someone had replaced the contents with liquor. Totally pie-eyed, he staggers around his hotel room. "Boy," he concludes, "ants certainly have a beautiful death."

After his retirement, he occasionally returned to the screen for guest appearances, most notably as Captain Andy in *Show Boat* and as a raffish millionaire in *Some Like It Hot* (1959). It was in the latter film that he uttered his immortal line. In love with Jack LEMMON, who has appeared in drag throughout the film, he proposes marriage. "I'm terrible," Lemmon confesses in an attempt to dissuade Brown. "For three years I've lived with a saxophone player." "I forgive you." "We can never have children," Lemmon persists. "We can adopt some." "You don't understand," Lemmon finally declares, whipping off his wig. "I'm a man." "Well, nobody's perfect," replies Brown.

SELECTED FILMS: Crooks Can't Win, Hit the Show (1928), Molly and Me, My Lady's Past (1929), Hold Everything, Going Wild (1930), Sit Tight, Broad Minded (1931), The Tenderfoot, You Said a Mouthful (1932), Elmer the Great, Son of a Sailor (1933), The Circus Clown (1934), Alibi Ike, A Midsummer Night's Dream (1935), Sons o' Guns (1936), Riding the Air (1937), Wide Open Faces, The Gladiator (1938), Beware, Spooks! (1939), So You Won't Talk? (1940), Shut My Big Mouth (1942), Chatterbox (1943), Pin Up Girl (1944), Show Boat (1951), It's a Mad, Mad, Mad, Mad World, The Comedy of Terrors (1963). ∎

Brown, Wally (1898–1961), comedian, actor. Worked in vaudeville as a comic before entering films. As a fast-talking straight man, he was teamed with fellow comedian Alan CARNEY in the 1940s to compete in style and content with the popular ABBOTT AND COSTELLO.

SELECTED FILMS: Around the World (1943), Adventures of a Rookie, Rookies in Burma, Seven Days Ashore, Step Lively (1944), Zombies on Broadway, Genius at Work (1945), As Young As You Feel (1951), The Absent-Minded Professor (1961). ∎

Brownlee, Frank (–1948), actor. Worked chiefly as a character player in silent films and continued in minor roles

into the sound era. He worked occasionally with LAUREL AND HARDY.

SELECTED FILMS: With Love and Hisses (1927), Pack Up Your Troubles (1932), The Midnight Patrol (1933). ∎

Bruce, Nigel (1895–1953), actor. Appeared on stage in England and the United States during the 1920s, in British films, and in 1934 debuted on the American screen. Often cast in aristocratic roles, sometimes as a bungling, absent-minded fussbudget, he is best known for his portrayal of Dr. Watson in the Sherlock Holmes series in which he co-starred with Basil Rathbone.

In *The Adventures of Sherlock Holmes* (1939) he complains to his famous detective friend about a rabbit's foot. "I've always thought those things in very poor taste," he huffs. "Fancy going about with a dead animal's foot dangling from your pocket."

SELECTED FILMS: Coming-Out Party, Springtime for Henry, The Lady Is Willing (1934), Becky Sharp, The Man Who Broke the Bank at Monte Carlo (1935), Follow Your Heart, Make Way for a Lady (1936), The Baroness and the Butler (1938), The Hound of the Baskervilles (1939), The Chocolate Soldier, Free and Easy (1941), This Above All, Journey for Margaret (1942), Follow the Boys, The Pearl of Death (1944), Son of Lassie, The Corn Is Green (1945), Terror by Night, Dressed to Kill (1946), The Exile (1947), Julia Misbehaves (1948), Bwana Devil, Limelight (1952), World for Ransom (1954). ∎

Bruce, Virginia (1910–1982), actress. Appeared on Broadway before entering films. A blue-eyed blonde, she began her Hollywood career in the late 1920s playing minor roles in early sound films. During the 1930s she started to get lead roles in low-budget, second features but never quite rose to stardom. She appeared in dramas and light films. She worked with some of the top comics of the period, including, among others, Eddie CANTOR and ABBOTT AND COSTELLO.

SELECTED FILMS: Fugitives, The Love Parade (1929), Slightly Scarlet, Whoopie! (1930), Times Square Lady (1935), Born to Dance (1936), Wife, Doctor and Nurse (1937), There Goes My Heart (1938), Hired Wife (1940), Pardon My Sarong, Careful, Soft Shoulders (1942), Brazil (1944), Love, Honor and Goodbye (1945), Two Grooms to a Bride (1957), Strangers When We Meet (1960). ■

Bruckman, Clyde (1894–1955), director, screenwriter. Worked as a journalist before entering films as a writer for silent film comic Monty BANKS. During the 1920s and 1930s he worked with many other film comedians, including, among others, BUSTER KEATON (as his chief collaborator and gagman) and W. C. FIELDS, Harold LLOYD, and LAUREL AND HARDY (as director). One of his more famous shorts as director is "The Battle of the Century," which contains the ultimate pie-throwing sequence involving dozens of characters and hundreds of custard pies.

Bruckman was a skilled director and screenwriter who had an uncanny ability to adapt to the individual comedian with whom he was working. This talent for cutting a scene at just the right moment and finding the proper rhythm for each personality resulted in some of the best work by Laurel and Hardy, Keaton, and Lloyd. In fact, some of the comics depended upon him to an inordinate degree.

By the mid-1930s, however, with the major funnymen facing their own decline brought on by the talkies and changing public taste, Bruckman found it difficult to obtain steady work. For the next 20 years he was never able to reestablish himself as a major director. Already facing a drinking problem and personal troubles, he shot himself with a pistol he had borrowed from Keaton.

SELECTED FILMS: Rouged Lips, Our Hospitality (1923), Sherlock, Jr., The Navigator (1924), Seven Chances (1925), For Heaven's Sake (1926), Call of the Cuckoos, Putting Pants on Philip, The Battle of the Century (1927), Leave 'Em Laughing, The Finishing Touch, A Perfect Gentleman (1928), Welcome Danger (1929), Feet First (1930), Everything's Rosie (1931), Movie Crazy (1932), The Fatal Glass of Beer (1933), The Man on the Flying Trapeze (1935), Professor Beware (1938), She Gets Her Man (1945). ■

Bryant, Nana (1888–1955), actress. Appeared on Broadway before entering films in the mid-1930s in character roles. She usually portrayed dignified matrons in dramas and light films.

SELECTED FILMS: Guard That Girl, A Feather in Her Hat (1935), Theodora Goes Wild, The King Steps Out (1936), Mad About Music (1938), Nice Girl? (1941), Bathing Beauty (1944), Brewster's Millions (1945), Weekend at the Waldorf (1945), The Lady Gambles (1949), Harvey (1950), Geraldine (1953), The Private War of Major Benson (1955). ■

Buchanan, Edgar (1902–1979), actor. Practiced dentistry before embarking on a full-time Hollywood career in the late 1930s. Round-faced and stocky, he became a well-known character actor, often portraying sheriffs and disheveled old-timers in westerns where he worked both sides of the law. He appeared in dramas and light films as well.

In Ride the High Country (1962) he played a preacher at a mining camp. During a wedding ceremony he sermonizes: "A good marriage is like a rare animal—it's hard to find and almost impossible to keep."

SELECTED FILMS: My Son Is Guilty (1939), Three Cheers for the Irish, Too Many Husbands, The Doctor Takes a Wife (1940), Her First Beau (1941), Bride by Mistake (1944), Cheaper by the Dozen (1950), It Happens Every Thursday, She Couldn't Say No (1953), Chartroose Caboose (1960), Tammy Tell Me True (1961), Move Over, Darling (1963), Benji (1974). ■

Buchman, Sidney (1902–1975), screenwriter, producer. Worked as assistant stage manager in England, then came to Hollywood as a screenwriter. He is most remembered for his sophisticated comedies, especially those which he wrote for Columbia studios. He was blacklisted during the McCarthy era until the early 1960s.

Buchman's light scripts range from SCREWBALL COMEDY to fantasy to musical biography, but they invariably contain a level of humanity that underlines his populist beliefs. His comic characters are charming and warm, zany and compassionate. Veteran character player James GLEASON, Robert MONTGOMERY'S comic sidekick and fight manager in *Here Comes Mr. Jordan*, can bring us to tears as he mourns for his lost pal. He comes across as more than just a business partner. Ludwig Donath, who plays the mammy singer's cantor-father in *The Jolson Story* (1946), is both humorous and very human as he boastfully and incorrectly attempts to explain show business to his bewildered wife.

SELECTED FILMS: If I Had a Million (1932), Broadway Bill (1934), She Married Her Boss (1935), The King Steps Out, Theodora Goes Wild (1936), The Awful Truth, Lost Horizon (1937), Holiday (1938), Mr. Smith Goes to Washington (1939), Here Comes Mr. Jordan (1941), The Talk of the Town (1942), Over 21 (1945), The Group (1966). ∎

Buck Privates (1941), U. *Dir.* Arthur Lubin; *Sc.* Arthur T. Horman; with Bud Abbott, Lou Costello, Lee Bowman, Alan Curtis, The Andrews Sisters.

Abbott and Costello had appeared in *One Night in the Tropics* in 1940 before making this army comedy, but they were not the leads. Perhaps their most popular film, *Buck Privates* shows the duo at their most hilarious, vibrant, and fresh in contrast to their later work, which was heavily derivative and repetitious. Although Bud and Lou are strongly supported by a love plot and musical numbers supplied by the talented Andrews Sisters ("Boogie Woogie Bugle Boy," "I'll Be With You in Apple Blossom Time"), the film remains their vehicle.

Abbott plays the quintessential straight man to cherub-faced Costello. The dice game scene in which Lou asks to be taught this "new" recreation is especially amusing. Handed this golden opportunity, Bud obliges to instruct the alleged novice, who soon begins calling out phrases like "Let it ride" and "Fade that," and finally winning. The drill scene is another memorable moment in the film. After Lou continues to foul up various instructions, the drill instructor appoints Abbott to give his buddy extra help. He orders: "Throw out your chest!" "I'm not through with it yet!" Lou shouts back. The comedy helps demonstrate why the pair became the most popular comedy team in Hollywood during the 1940s.

"Bunny" films. See John Bunny.

Bunny, John (1863–1915), actor. Worked in minstrel shows and in the theater as actor and manager before he signed with Vitagraph studios in 1910. Rotund and weighing 300 pounds, he exploited his weight and shape to his advantage in many of his plots. Other techniques that he employed in his farce comedies included FEMALE IMPERSONATION, flirting, extramarital pursuits, and bouts with alcohol, all in the style of polished pantomime. In the marital farce "Polishing Up," for example, after he is caught flirting with two young sweet things, he patches things up with his wife and toasts: "Here's to our wives and sweethearts—may they never meet."

He appeared in more than 200 one- and two-reel comedies in his short, five-year film career, becoming the first star comedian of the American screen. On a trip to England he made a series of films based on Charles Dickens' *Pickwick Papers* and a few other shorts. Although these side excursions into dramatic acting underscored his histrionic abilities, it was for his comic talents that he was best loved.

He also starred in his own popular series, the "Bunny" films, often co-starring with comedienne Flora FINCH, which included "Bunny's Suicide," "Bunny All at Sea," "Bunny at the Derby" (1912), "Bunny Blarneyed," "Bunny as a Reporter," "Bunny for the Cause," "Bunny's Dilemma," "Bunny's Honeymoon" (1913), "Bunny Buys a Harem," "Bunny's Birthday," "Bunny's Mistake" (1914), "Bunny in Bunnyland" (1915).

SELECTED FILMS: In Neighboring Kingdoms (1910), Her Crowning Glory, Her Hero, Vanity Fair, The Politician's Dream (1911), Ida's Christmas, Stenographers Wanted, Chumps, Freckles, A Cure for Pokeritis (1912), And His Wife Came Back, The Autocrat of Flapjack Junction (1913), Father's Flirtation, Pigs Is Pigs, Love's Old Dream, Love, Luck and Gasoline, Polishing Up (1914). ∎

Buono, Victor (1938–1982), actor. Began his screen career in the early 1960s. A corpulent and imposing figure, he appeared in dramas and light films. He was a talented character actor who could play suave villains as well as sympathetic types with equal conviction. He was nominated for an Academy Award for his role in What Ever Happened to Baby Jane? (1962), his first screen appearance. He had done much work in television before his untimely death.

In The Silencers (1966), a James Bond-type film starring Dean MARTIN, Buono played a delightful villain. "The explosion," he informs his adversary, "will raise a cloud of radioactive dust that will settle over vast areas in the southwest . . . Beautiful!"

SELECTED FILMS: Four for Texas, My Six Loves (1963), Robin and the Seven Hoods (1964), Who's Minding the Mint? (1966), Arnold (1973), The Man With Bogart's Face (1979). ∎

Burke, Billie (1885–1970), actress. Appeared on stage in comedies and musicals in England in 1903, in New York in 1907, and in silent films for Thomas INCE in 1915, with her husband, Florenz Ziegfeld, as her manager. She starred in more than a dozen films in the late 1910s and early 1920s. She returned to the theater in 1921 and was back in films in 1931. Her most memorable roles were those of dizzy, timorous, light-headed women. She played Cosmo Topper's (Roland Young) confused wife in the short-lived "Topper" series.

In Topper Returns (1941) she reflects: "My, isn't it strange how it's cold in the winter and warm in summer, isn't it?" Her autobiographies are With a Feather on My Nose (1949) and With Powder on My Nose (1959).

SELECTED FILMS: Peggy (1916), Arms and the Girl (1917), Let's Get a Divorce (1918), The Frisky Mrs. Johnson (1920), Dinner at Eight (1933), We're Rich Again (1934), A Feather in Her Hat (1935), Topper (1937), Zenobia, The Wizard of Oz (1939), The Captain Is a Lady (1940), The Man Who Came to Dinner, Girl Trouble (1942), Gildersleeve on Broadway (1943), The Bachelor's Daughters (1946), And Baby Makes Three (1949), Father of the Bride (1950), Father's Little Dividend (1951), Pepe (1960). ∎

Burke, James (1886–1968), actor. After a long career in vaudeville and the theater, he switched to films in the 1930s, appearing in more than 150 features, many of which were light comedies. He played a variety of character parts, specializing in confused New York cops. A familiar face among character actors, he worked with some of the leading comics of the period, including W. C. FIELDS, Mae WEST, and the MARX BROTHERS.

SELECTED FILMS: College Humor (1933), Six of a Kind, Little Miss Marker (1934), It's a Gift, Ruggles of Red Gap (1935), Klondike Annie (1936), At the Circus, Beau Geste (1939), All Through the Night (1942), Anchors Aweigh, The Horn Blows at Midnight (1945), Down to Earth (1947), June Bride (1948), You're Never Too Young (1955), The Hallelujah Trail (1965). ∎

Burnett, Carol (1933–), comedienne, actress. Has appeared on television, on Broadway in 1959, in nightclubs, and, sporadically, in films. Her humorous facial expressions, warm personality, and slapstick style have endeared her to her large public. The klutzy, sympathetic characters she portrays seem to work better for her in her television shows than they do on the big screen, where she has not attained the same attention she has gotten in other areas of show business. However, she is always entertaining and a delight to watch. Her memoirs, *One More Time*, were published in 1986.

In *Annie* she played an evil orphanage supervisor. Holding Annie (Aileen Quinn) by the collar of her dress, Burnett muses: "Why anyone would want to be an orphan is beyond me."

SELECTED FILMS: *Who's Been Sleeping in My Bed?* (1963), *Pete 'n' Tillie* (1972), *The Front Page* (1974), *A Wedding* (1978), *Health* (1979), *Chu Chu and the Philly Flash*, *The Four Seasons* (1981), *Annie* (1982). ∎

Burnette, Smiley (1911–1967), actor, songwriter. After appearing on radio and in vaudeville, he began his film career in 1934 as the amusing sidekick of his long-time friend, Gene Autry, with whom he made more than 80 westerns. He later repeated his comic-relief role with other western stars, including Sunset Carson, Allan Lane, and Charles Starrett. His total output reached approximately 200 films. Slightly pudgy in appearance, he displayed a warm and cheerful disposition that endeared him to his many fans.

SELECTED FILMS: *Border Patrolman* (1936), *Boots and Saddles*, *Manhattan Merry-Go-Round* (1937), *Under Western Skies* (1938). ∎

Burns, Bob (1893–1956), actor. Appeared in vaudeville, in nightclubs, and on radio as a comic. He entered films in 1913 in a minor role but returned to the stage after this solo attempt. He returned to the screen in 1931, often playing country bumpkins with more than a dash of horse sense. In real life, however, he was well educated. One of his claims to fame was his invention of the "bazooka," a musical instrument derived from two gas pipes and a whiskey funnel.

SELECTED FILMS: *Quick Millions* (1931), *The Singing Vagabond* (1935), *Rhythm on the Range*, *The Big Broadcast of 1937* (1936), *Mountain Music*, *Waikiki Wedding* (1937), *The Arkansas Traveler*, *Tropic Holiday*, *Radio City Revels* (1938), *I'm From Missouri*, *Our Leading Citizen* (1939), *Alias the Deacon*, *Comin' Round the Mountain* (1940), *Belle of the Yukon* (1944). ∎

Burns, David (1902–1971), actor. Worked on stage and in films in both England and the United States. Although his major work was in the theater, he began to appear in the 1950s as a supporting player in several light films and dramas. He also worked in television.

SELECTED FILMS: *Knock on Wood* (1954), *It's Always Fair Weather* (1955), *Once Upon a Horse* (1958), *Let's Make Love* (1960), *The Tiger Makes Out* (1967), *Move* (1970). ∎

Burns, George. See Burns and Allen.

Burns, Jack (1933–), comedian. Joined George Carlin in a comedy act (1959–1962), then teamed with Avery Schreiber for television appearances, comedy record albums, and personal appearances. The team split up in 1974 and Burns went on to write and produce *The Muppet Movie* (1978).

Burns, Neal (–1969), actor. Appeared on stage before entering films in 1915. He worked in comedy films for Nestor studios, supervised in part by Al CHRISTIE in the 1910s. When Christie left the company in 1916, Burns joined him, continuing his career as a comedian in early silent comedy shorts. In 1924 he made a series of comedies for Educational studios. His popularity continued into the late 1920s, at which time he made ten films for Christie during the 1926–27 season and twelve more the next year.

SELECTED FILMS: Cupid's Uppercut (1917), Mary's Ankle (1920), That Son of a Sheik (1922), Sob Sister (1931), Men in Black, Six of a Kind (1934). ∎

Burns, Sammy, actor. Worked as a comedian in his native England before entering films in the United States in the 1910s. Featured chiefly in early silent comedy shorts, he starred in his own series, "Kuku Comedies." He frequently appeared with comedienne Dot FARLEY, of the same studio, in various farces. In 1919 he was featured in a series of comedies for Nestor studios which were released through Universal.

SELECTED FILMS: Sammy's Scandalous Schemes (1915), Sammy vs. Cupid (1916). ∎

George Burns and Gracie Allen

Burns and Allen. A popular husband-and-wife comedy team of stage, radio, and films during the 1930s and 1940s. George Burns (1896–) appeared in vaudeville, on radio, and in films. He teamed up in 1925 with Gracie Allen whom he met backstage while he was performing at a New Jersey theater. She

had left show business and had enrolled for a secretarial course. A friend had brought her backstage and Burns invited her to become his stage partner. They were married the following year. Gracie (1906–1964) began her long show business career in vaudeville at age 14 portraying an ingenuous Irish character. The brogue had become so ingrained in her that she had difficulty dropping it. Often with cigar in hand, George was the straight man of the comedy team, feeding Gracie the cues she needed for her feather-brained replies. The partnership lasted for 35 years. Although their fame extended from vaudeville to radio and films, their screen endeavors were never as successful as their vaudeville and radio appearances. Later in their career they had a successful television show for several years. After her death in 1964, he retired from show business but returned for a successful comeback in films, winning an Academy Award for his role in The Sunshine Boys (1975).

Perhaps in less capable hands, Gracie's zany ripostes would have been pure corn. But this lovable duo made it all sound believable and funny. In The Big Broadcast Gracie announces: "My brother goes to San Quentin." "He goes to San Quentin?" George asks. "He's working his way through," she explains. And in Damsel in Distress Gracie, as George's befuddled secretary, answers his telephone and astutely announces: "It's a Hawaiian." "A Hawaiian?" he questions. "Well, he must be," she affirms. "He said he's Brown from the Morning Sun." Another typical Gracie Allen line: "My name is Grace, but everybody calls me Gracie for short."

SELECTED FILMS: The Big Broadcast (1932), International House (1933), Six of a Kind, We're Not Dressing, Many Happy Returns (1934), Big Broadcast of 1936, Here Comes Cookie (1935), College Holiday (1936), A Damsel in Distress (1937), College Swing (1938), Honolulu (1939).

SELECTED FILMS (Gracie Allen alone): The Gracie Allen Murder Case

(1939), Mr. and Mrs. North (1941), Two Girls and a Sailor (1944).

SELECTED FILMS (George Burns alone): Oh, God! (1977), Sergeant Pepper's Lonely Hearts Club Band (1978), Just You and Me, Kid, Going in Style (1979), Oh, God! Book II (1980), Oh, God! You Devil (1984). ∎

Burstyn, Ellen (1932–), actress. Began her show-business career as a fashion model, then switched to dancing, and finally acting. An attractive and highly talented actress, she has appeared on stage and in films in both dramas and light films. She won an Academy Award as Best Actress for her role in Alice Doesn't Live Here Anymore (1974).

In Same Time Next Year (1978) she played a married woman who meets annually with her long-time lover, Alan ALDA. "What's your pleasure," she asks Alda, "a walk by the ocean, or a good book, or me?" "You," he replies. "Oh," she says, "I thought you would never ask."

SELECTED FILMS: Goodbye Charlie, For Those Who Think Young (1964), Alex in Wonderland (1970), Harry and Tonto (1974). ∎

Busch, Mae (1897–1946), actress. Began her film career in 1912, working for Mack SENNETT'S KEYSTONE studios, for whom she made comedy shorts, both as principal player and support for some of the major comedians of the period, including Chester CONKLIN and Charley CHASE. She starred in many silent comedies and dramas during the 1920s, and by 1930 she appeared in many Laurel and Hardy shorts and feature-length films, sometimes as Ollie's wife. In "Chickens Come Home" (1931) she plays Oliver's old sweetheart whom she tries to blackmail. In a similar role in "Come Clean" (1931), after the boys save her from drowning, she attempts to blackmail them!

SELECTED FILMS: The Agitator (1912), A One Night Stand, Settled on the Seaside, The Rent Jumpers, A Rascal in Wolfish Ways, The Best of Enemies (1915), A Bath House Blunder (1916), A Parisian Scandal (1921), Foolish Wives (1922), Married Flirts (1924), Fools for Fashion (1926), Their First Mistake (1932), Sons of the Desert (1933), The Live Ghost (1934), The Bohemian Girl (1936), Masquerade in Mexico (1946). ∎

Bushman, Francis X. (1883–1966), actor. Appeared in stock before entering early silent films in 1911. A good-looking young actor, he rose to stardom playing romantic roles in numerous dramas. He became one of the most highly paid and popular stars in silent screen history. In his earlier career in films, however, he was featured in comedy shorts for ESSANAY studios. Occasionally, he supported comics like John Steppling; at other times he co-starred with his wife, Beverly Bayne, in his own comedy series. His popularity declined in the 1930s, and he was relegated to minor roles. His screen career spanned six decades.

SELECTED FILMS: His Friend's Wife, Fate's Funny Frolic (1911), The Mail Order Bride, A Good Catch, Neptune's Daughter (1912), The Farmer's Daughter, Tony the Fiddler (1913), A Million a Minute (1916), Cyclone Higgins, D.D., A Pair of Cupids (1918), Say It With Sables (1928), The Dude Wrangler, Once a Gentleman (1930), Sabrina (1954), The Ghost in the Invisible Bikini (1966). ∎

"Buster Brown" comedies. A popular comic strip character created in 1902 by Richard F. Outcalt. The cartoonist had already created the first modern comic strip, "The Yellow Kid," in 1896. Buster first came to the screen as a cartoon series in 1914 by animator Charles H. France for the Edison studios. In 1925 Universal studios resurrected Buster in a series of two-reel comedies starring Arthur Trimble.

Butch Cassidy and the Sundance Kid (1969), TCF. Dir. George Roy Hill; Sc. William Goldman; with Paul Newman, Robert Redford, Katherine Ross, Strother Martin.

This entertaining western parody has outlaws Newman and Redford in the title roles trying to evade a pursuing posse led by a relentless marshal. The co-stars provide plenty of action and laughs as they head for South America, taking along Katherine Ross, a schoolteacher. Here they continue to ply their trade of bankrobbing but with hilarious results when they fail because of a language barrier. They finally get hired as payroll guards in the employ of impish Strother Martin, who happily says, "I'm what is known as a colorful character." Before a fierce gun battle with bandits, Newman admits that he has never killed a man before. There are many memorable scenes, including a train robbery with a determined clerk bent on protecting the payroll, a farcical fight at the hideout of the Hole-in-the-Wall gang, and a literal cliff-hanger. The two anti-heroes are surrounded by a posse and Newman insists that they jump into the river below. Redford finally confesses why he will not jump. "I can't swim!" he shouts at his partner. "That's all right," Newman returns. "The fall will probably kill you anyway." Goldman's original and literate script works on two levels. He pokes fun at the overblown myths of the westerns while simultaneously glorifying the special breed of men who originated them. The anachronistic song, "Raindrops Keep Falling on My Head," became a popular hit.

Butler, David (1894–1979), director. Began as a stage and screen actor in the 1910s and 1920s. He started his directing career in 1927, specializing mainly in comedies and light musicals. He directed many of the Shirley Temple films of the 1930s as well as features for comedians Eddie CANTOR and Bob HOPE. He also directed the unique science-fiction musical comedy starring El BRENDEL, *Just Imagine*.

SELECTED FILMS: *High School Hero (1927), Win That Girl, Prep and Pep (1928), Sunny Side Up (1929), Just Imag-*

ine (1930), A Connecticut Yankee (1931), Business and Pleasure, Handle With Care (1932), Bottoms Up, Bright Eyes (1934), The Little Colonel (1935), Pigskin Parade (1936), Ali Baba Goes to Town (1937), Kentucky (1938), Caught in the Draft (1941), They Got Me Covered (1943), Two Guy From Milwaukee (1946), Tea for Two (1950), Where's Charley? (1952), Let's Live a Little (1967). ∎

Butler, Frank (1890–1967), screenwriter. Appeared on the stage in England and in silent films in the United States in the 1920s before turning to screenwriting in 1927. Although he wrote screenplays for dramas and musicals, he was best known for his comedies, especially the "Road" movies of HOPE and CROSBY and the LAUREL AND HARDY films.

SELECTED FILMS: *No Man's Law (1927), Just Married (1928), Those Three French Girls (1930), This Modern Age (1931), College Humor (1933), Babes in Toyland (1934), Bonnie Scotland (1935), Strike Me Pink (1936), Champagne Waltz (1937), Tropic Holiday (1938), Paris Honeymoon (1939), Road to Singapore (1940), Road to Zanzibar (1941), My Favorite Blonde (1942), Going My Way (1944), Incendiary Blonde (1945), The Kid From Brooklyn (1946), Golden Earrings (1947), Road to Bali (1953), The Miracle (1959).* ∎

Butterworth, Charles (1896–1946), actor. Worked as a reporter and acted on stage before entering films in 1930. A slim, balding figure, he specialized in shy, nervous, and sad-looking souls. He appeared in almost 50 films in a period of 15 years, often portraying a timid butler, clerk, or effete millionaire bachelor who couldn't make up his mind.

In *Second Chorus*, for example, he laments to Paulette GODDARD: "I said 'music' and Father said 'bottlecaps.' Father won." He died in an auto accident.

SELECTED FILMS: *The Life of the Party (1930), Side Show (1931), Love Me Tonight (1932), My Weakness (1933),*

Charles Butterworth

The Cat and the Fiddle (1934), *Ruggles of Red Gap* (1935), *Rainbow on the River* (1936), *Every Day's a Holiday* (1937), *Thanks for the Memory* (1938), *Second Chorus* (1940), *Sis Hopkins* (1941), *What's Cooking?* (1942), *This Is the Army* (1943), *Follow the Boys* (1944). ■

Buttons, Red (1919–), comedian, actor. Worked in burlesque, on Broadway, and in television before entering films in 1957 although he appeared on screen in a bit part in *Winged Victory* in 1944. His appearances on stage led to a television portrayal of comedian Joe E. Lewis, which, in turn, gave him his own show for two seasons. Although his television show was canceled, it gave his career enough momentum to make him a sought-after comedian in nightclubs and films. He has projected warmth and sincerity in his film roles. But his limited range of humor, consisting chiefly of facial expressions, one-liners, and some slapstick, has prevented him from furthering his screen career as a major comic. He appears occasionally in television.

In *Winged Victory*, Buttons, as a G.I. at an Air Force base, describes the facilities to some new cadets: "To the right, gentlemen, is Pneumonia Gulch. That is where we sleep. You fry by day and you freeze by night. To the left, just a little ways, about a mile and a half, is Ptomaine Tavern. That is where we eat. The wheatcakes we leave are used by the Navy—as depth bombs."

Buttons won an Oscar for Best Supporting Actor for his role in *Sayonara*.

SELECTED FILMS: Sayonara (1957), *Imitation General* (1958), *The Big Circus* (1959), *One, Two, Three* (1961), *A Ticklish Affair* (1963), *Harlow* (1965), *Who Killed Mary What's Her Name?* (1971), *Gable and Lombard* (1976), *Pete's Dragon* (1977), *The Day the World Ended* (1979). ■

Buzzell, Edward (1897–1985), director. Began in show business as an actor on Broadway and in films in the 1920s. At Columbia he directed and appeared in a group of short comedies. Later, he became a full-fledged director of features, chiefly comedies, including two Marx Brothers films, *At the Circus* and *Go West*.

SELECTED FILMS: The Big Timer, Hollywood Speaks (1932), *Love, Honor and Oh, Baby!* (1933), *Cross Country Cruise* (1934), *The Girl Friend* (1935), *Three Married Men* (1936), *Paradise for Three, Fast Company* (1938), *At the Circus* (1939), *Go West* (1940), *Best Foot Forward* (1943), *Easy to Wed* (1946), *Song of the Thin Man* (1947), *Neptune's Daughter* (1949), *Emergency Wedding* (1950), *Ain't Misbehavin'* (1955). ■

Byington, Spring (1893–1971), actress. Appeared in plays on Broadway before entering films. Often playing warm mothers, scatterbrained wives, or silly matrons, she appeared in more than 100 films. The perennial mother, she portrayed Mrs. Jones in the popular "JONES FAMILY" film series. She played Mrs. Hardy in the first "ANDY HARDY" movie. She was nominated for an Oscar as Best Supporting Actress for her portrayal of Penny Sycamore in *You Can't Take It With You* (1938).

SELECTED FILMS: Little Women (1933), *Way Down East* (1935), *Dodsworth* (1936), *A Family Affair* (1937), *Jezebel* (1938), *Too Busy to Work* (1939), *Meet John Doe* (1941), *In the Good Old Summertime* (1949), *Angels in the Outfield* (1951), *Please Don't Eat the Daisies* (1960). ■

C

Cabanne, Christy (1888–1950), director. Began his film career as an actor in early silents, then switched to directing in 1913. He turned out numerous features in a variety of genres during a career that stretched across four decades. His best work occurred in the 1920s, after which he was relegated to low-budget vehicles. He directed many of the "SCATTER-GOOD BAINES" films of the 1940s.

SELECTED FILMS: The Adopted Brother (1913), The Lamb, Double Trouble (1915), Reggie Mixes In (1916), The Pest (1919), What's a Wife Worth? (1921), The Spitfire (1924), Don't Tell the Wife, The Outcasts of Poker Flat (1937), Everybody's Doing It, This Marriage Business (1938), Scattergood Baines (1941), Top Sergeant (1942), Keep 'Em Slugging (1943), Dixie Jamboree (1944), Silver Trails (1948). ∎

Caesar, Sid (1922–), comedian, actor. Studied saxophone and clarinet at Juilliard before appearing as a comic in nightclubs, on Broadway, and in television. A beefy figure with a husky voice, he started out as a stand-up comic doing sound effects and other routines. By the time he appeared in television, he had mastered the art of pantomime. One of his techniques was to take a simple gag and, usually assisted by his co-star Imogene COCA, push it to its absurd limits. He has made occasional films, chiefly portraying comic characters. Some of his hilarious routines that made him famous on the popular TV series, "Your Show of Shows," have been compiled into a feature-length film, *Ten From Your Show of Shows* (1973). His personal problems kept him from contributing more fully to comedy in the 1960s and 1970s.

In *Over the Brooklyn Bridge* he played a successful manufacturer in New York's garment center. His nephew, Elliott GOULD, visits Caesar's suburban home one rainy night, but Caesar's wife doesn't let the dripping nephew sit in the living room. "What are you worried about?" he complains to his wife as she escorts the two men to the bathroom. "Everything's covered with plastic! A battleship couldn't do any damage in here!" He then confides in Gould: "Did you ever see anyone polish plastic before? I haven't sat in that room since my son was born. I keep slipping off everything."

SELECTED FILMS: Tars and Spars (1946), The Guilt of Janet Ames (1947), It's a Mad, Mad, Mad, Mad World (1963), A Guide for the Married Man, The Busy Body, The Spirit Is Willing (1967), Airport 1975 (1974), Silent Movie (1976), Fire Sale (1977), The Cheap Detective, Grease (1978), Over the Brooklyn Bridge (1984). ∎

Cagney, James (1899–1986), actor. Worked on Broadway in a chorus line, in vaudeville, and on the Broadway stage before making his film debut in 1930. Although he is best remembered for his action and gangster roles, he also brought his exuberance and warmth to a handful of light comedies and musicals. His overpowering presence in a scene that featured his staccato speech and distinct facial mannerisms proved just as effective in these farces and musicals, earning him an Academy Award as Best Actor in his role of George M. COHAN in *Yankee Doodle Dandy* (1942). The films of the early 1930s in which he appeared established his comic style, including his high energy, dialect humor, body language, and wise-cracking repartee. His autobiography, *Cagney on Cagney*, was published in 1976.

In *The Bride Came C.O.D.* he portrayed a flyer who is hired by Bette Davis' father to kidnap his heiress-daughter, thereby preventing her from marrying inept Jack CARSON. On board Cagney's plane, the haughty millionairess wants to know what exorbitant sum he is being paid for kidnapping her. "Just carrying charges," Cagney retorts.

SELECTED FILMS: *Sinners' Holiday* (1930), *Blonde Crazy* (1931), *Taxi* (1932), *Hard to Handle, Footlight Parade* (1933), *Jimmy the Gent, Here Comes the Navy* (1934), *The Irish in Us, A Midsummer Night's Dream* (1935), *Great Guy* (1936), *Something to Sing About* (1937), *Boy Meets Girl* (1938), *The Bride Came C.O.D.* (1941), *The Time of Your Life* (1948), *What Price Glory* (1952), *Mr. Roberts* (1955), *One, Two, Three* (1961), *Ragtime* (1981). ■

"Calamity Anne" films. A successful series of western comedy shorts starring Louise Lester, directed by Allan Dwan, and produced sporadically by the American Film Company from 1912 to 1914. Lillian Christy added support as a young innocent. The films were above average both technically and artistically.

SELECTED FILMS: *Calamity Anne's Ward* (1912), *Calamity Anne, Detective* (1913). ■

Calhern, Louis (1895–1956), actor. Began his long screen career playing romantic leads in silent films during the early 1920s. Tall and distinguished-looking, he made a smooth transition to the sound era portraying both sympathetic

and roguish characters in dramas and light films. He was the unlucky victim of Chico and Harpo MARX's antics in *Duck Soup* (1933).

SELECTED FILMS: *The Blot, Too Wise Wives* (1921), *Blonde Crazy* (1931), *Night After Night* (1932), *Strictly Personal, Diplomaniacs* (1933), *Sweet Adeline* (1935), *The Gorgeous Hussy* (1936), *Charlie McCarthy, Detective* (1939), *Nobody's Darling* (1943), *Up in Arms* (1944), *Nancy Goes to Rio* (1950), *We're Not Married* (1952), *Remains to Be Seen* (1953), *Forever, Darling* (1956). ■

Callahan, Robert (–1938), actor. Appeared chiefly as a supporting player in comedy shorts during the 1930s, including those of LAUREL AND HARDY. He also worked with Curly of the THREE STOOGES team.

SELECTED FILMS: *Helpmates* (1931), *Roast Beef and Movies* (1934). ■

Callas, Charlie, comedian, actor. Has appeared in television, in nightclubs, and occasionally in films. Thin and nervous in appearance, he began his show business career as a band drummer. He drifted into comedy by doing impressions of objects and people. He later added gags and one-liners. Although he has had supporting roles in several light films, he is more effective as a stand-up performer.

SELECTED FILMS: *The Big Mouth* (1967), *Pete's Dragon* (voice only), *High Anxiety* (1977), *History of the World— Part 1* (1981). ■

Cambridge, Godfrey (1933–1976), actor. Appeared in off-Broadway plays before entering films in 1959. He was known for his broad comedy and his expressive face and voice. His incisive humor, which frequently included racial issues, reflected the social upheaval of the 1960s. He appeared in light comedies as well as in comedies that dealt with racism. Perhaps his best role was in *Watermelon Man*, a comedy-drama in which he portrayed a prejudiced suburban white man who turns black overnight and has to cope with this Kafkaesque nightmare.

Cambridge was one of the first black comedians in the 1960s to shed the stereotypical role of the stupid, grinning, servile black who was always ready with a song or dance. Along with other comics like Dick Gregory, he became a vocal participant in the civil rights movement, employing his humor to inspire the main body of activists during this volatile period.

In *Gone Are the Days* he played the servant of a bigoted southern landowner who misses the days of the Old South. "How hard it is to find those old-fashioned Uncle Tom Negroes today," the old man laments. "By the grace of God," Cambridge intones as he simulates fond remembrances of things past, "there are still a few of us left."

SELECTED FILMS: *The Last Angry Man (1959), Gone Are the Days (1963), The Troublemaker (1964), The Busy Body, The President's Analyst (1967), The Biggest Bundle of Them All, Bye, Bye Braverman (1968), Watermelon Man, Cotton Comes to Harlem (1970), The Biscuit Eater, Come Back, Charleston Blue (1972), Whiffs, Friday Foster (1975), Scott Joplin (1976).* ∎

Camp. Art carried to an excess or extravagance, resulting in bad taste and unintentional ironic humor. In films, camp may be found in silents and talkies, in dramas and musicals, in American and foreign works; it may be the work of a director, a screenwriter, a choreographer, or a performer. Camp crosses over into the various elements that make up a film; e.g., costumes, plot, atmosphere, sets, props, characterization.

The 1930s and 1940s comprise the Golden Age of Camp. Such directors as Cecil B. DeMille and Josef von Sternberg, such choreographers as Busby Berkeley, and such art directors as Hans Dreier reached new heights of absurdity and craziness during these two decades.

Much in DeMille's works can be considered pure camp. His *Cleopatra* (1934) contains the classic seduction scene of the Queen of the Nile (Claudette COLBERT) luring Caesar to her palace-size barge festooned with lattices of flowers, falling petals, and dancing maidens—while a half-naked slave drums out a cadence to guide an army of oarsmen. The mighty Caesar joins the voluptuous Queen on her bed as the vessel sails up the Nile into the night.

During the Depression years, von Sternberg directed Marlene Dietrich, the Queen of Camp, through a string of ludicrous sequences, if not entire films. In *Morocco* (1930) she rejects wealthy Adolphe Menjou and, dressed in high heels and a flowing gown, follows her legionnaire lover (Gary Cooper) into the desert. In *Blonde Venus* (1932) she appears on stage in a gorilla suit which she removes to sing the sultry "Hot Voodoo." In Sternberg's *Scarlet Empress* (1934) he surrounds Catherine the Great (Dietrich) with a myriad of lighted candles and a horde of life-size gargoyles.

If Marlene Dietrich was the Queen of Camp in the 1930s, then Busby Berkeley was the undisputed King. His lavish musical production numbers, consisting of geometric patterns constructed of dozens of dancers, overhead shots, colossal sets, and imaginative costumes, dominated the Warner Brothers musicals of the 1930s. The lengthy "Shanghai Lil" sequence from *Footlight Parade* (1933) moves from a sleazy Oriental waterfront bar to an opium den, then to dockside where American sailors march aboard their ship and, in the process, smuggle James Cagney's reformed mistress aboard. In the same film another song, "By a Waterfall," produces an endless number of female swimmers who glide in perfect unison amid phallic images and suggestive actions, including squirming between each others' legs, opening zipper-like formations of swimmers, and sensuously cascading down gently curving falls; the culmination of which leads the bathers to the steps of a mammoth spurting fountain. In *Gold Diggers of 1935* a production number built around the song "Lullaby of Broadway" depicts a nightmare-induced sequence fraught with Freudian symbolism. A battery of uniformly clad tap dancers close in on Wini Shaw and force her off a skyscraper balcony from which she plunges to the sidewalk below. Berkeley continued to project his surrealistic-erotic visions into the 1940s with *The Gang's All Here* (1943). The Carmen Miranda number, "The Lady With the Tutti Frutti Hat," may be the epitome of eroticism as dozens of chorines hold enormous bananas horizontally erect as the Brazilian Bombshell promenades down a corridor of strawberries with a fruit-filled hat that extends beyond the top of the screen.

The Depression years generated other camp vehicles as well, mainly from the "poverty row" studios. In *The Great Gabbo* (1929) ventriloquist Erich von Stroheim can't seem to get along with his dummy, while on stage performers clad as flies and spiders climb around an enormous web to the strains of "Caught in the Web of Love." *Dante's Inferno* (1935) is set in a carnival where Spencer Tracy runs an attraction which portrays the Italian poet's netherworld, replete with writhing half-naked humans, sulfuric smoke and flames, and sweaty cavernous walls. Perhaps the highlight of 1930s camp emerging from low-budget studios is the unintentionally hilarious *Reefer Madness* (1936). Meant as a cautionary tale, this badly dated film has become a cult classic in its depiction of high school students who commit murder, suicide, and other depravities after a few puffs of marijuana.

Camp may be divided into low and high camp. All the above, for the most part, are examples of high camp—unconscious exaggeration with a degree of class or panache—terrible films, or parts, but highly entertaining. Low camp refers to conscious efforts at comedy. Mae West and her mocking of contemporary sexual taboos are an example of low camp. So are many of the serials of the 1930s and 1940s. In the first *Flash Gordon* cliffhanger (1936) our titular hero (Larry Buster Crabbe) parachutes from a doomed airplane on a stormy night and lands in a jungle in the middle of nowhere. Suddenly Dr. Zarkoff steps out from behind a bush, identifies himself, and invites Flash to join him on a journey to Mars. Of course our drenched but undaunted hero accepts the offer and they leave together. The popularity of this serial led to two "Gordon" sequels and one *Buck Rogers* serial. *Ace Drummond* (1936), another popular serial, depicts the pilot-hero singing a rousing flying song to enthusiastic passengers aboard a clipper plane, after which he parachutes out to follow a suspicious airplane that has passed the clipper.

The 1940s presented a new set of camp performers. One of the leading exponents was Maria Montez. Often scantily attired in pseudo-Arabian-exotic costumes, she fulfilled some of her audience's wildest fantasies during the war years. The highlight of her camp films was *Cobra Woman* (1944), in which she portrayed the dual role of two sisters, one an evil empress who is oppressing her people on Cobra Island, and the other, the good sister who seeks to bring democracy to the island. The throne which the sarong-covered empress embraces consists of a gold replica of a huge cobra, coiled at the base and rising ten feet into the air, its threatening fangs poised to strike.

The 1950s found a new home in which camp could dwell—the post-nuclear, pseudo-science-fiction films in which prehistoric creatures and other mutant monsters were resurrected as the result of underground testing. Some low-camp entries include *Attack of the Crab Monsters* (1957), *Attack of the 50 Foot Woman* (1958), and *Attack of the Giant Leeches* (1959). One of the high, or low, points in this sub-genre was *Attack of* the *Killer Tomatoes* (1980), a film perhaps more in the realm of parody than of camp, in which giant tomatoes devour innocent citizens. These films have more than their titles in common. They are ludicrous in their execution and laughable in their special effects.

Low and high camp can be found in each genre and in every decade. Camp depends on the extent and type of the excesses inherent in the production and the degree to which the public's tastes change. Today's award-winners, therefore, may result in tomorrow's camp.

Eric Campbell (right) and Charlie Chaplin

Campbell, Eric (1870–1917), actor. Immigrated to the United States from his native Scotland. He entered films in 1916 at CHAPLIN'S invitation after appearing with Fred KARNO'S English troupe. His large size and menacing look made him the ideal foil for the diminutive Chaplin. He appeared in eleven of Charlie's Keystone comedies. His most memorable roles are those of Chaplin's adversary in "The Rink" and the local bully whom Charlie the cop overcomes with a gas lamp in "Easy Street." His untimely death in an auto accident in 1917 brought to an end a short-lived career (two years) in films by a talented actor who will be remembered as one of the screen's most unsympathetic heavies.

SELECTED FILMS: *The Floorwalker, The Fireman, The Vagabond, The Count, The Pawnshop, Behind the Screen, The Rink (1916), Easy Street, The Cure, The Immigrant, The Adventurer (1917).* ■

Campus comedy. Light films with a college background that originated during the early silent period, peaked in the 1930s, showed some signs of life following World War II, and, except for isolated entries, almost drifted into oblivion as a genre until they were resurrected in the 1970s.

One of the earliest entries, a one-reel farce titled "College Chums" (1908), concerned a student who convinces his best pal to disguise himself as his sister to convince his sweetheart that the girl she saw him with was not just another flirtation. Another early entry was a crude slapstick short, "Those College Girls" (1915), produced by Mack SENNETT. Surprisingly, the King of Comedy turned out very few college comedies among his hundreds of one- and two-reelers. *One Touch of Nature* (1917), a comedy-drama produced by Thomas Edison's studio, concerned a Yale college student who is a star player on the school baseball team.

During the 1920s major screen comedians appeared in campus films. Harold LLOYD'S *The Freshman* (1925) told the story of an obscure college student with so little football ability that the coach assigned him to waterboy. However, he proves his worth by making the key touchdown in one of the funniest football sequences in film history. Universal studios produced "THE COLLEGIANS," a series of silent comedy-drama shorts which ran from 1926 through 1929. The films depicted the deeds of a young innocent who wins an athletic scholarship. Actor George LEWIS portrayed the hayseed who experiences the rites of passage on the college campus in such shorts as "Benson at Calford" and "Around the Bases," both 1926. In 1927 Buster KEATON starred in *College*, another comedy about a klutzy student. Keaton, to win the girl of his dreams who is infatuated with the star campus athlete, decides to try out for each sport—

with disastrous results. Although a very small number of America's young people attended college in the 1920s, the genre was very popular for two reasons. The campus became an idyllic setting for youth-oriented fantasies of physical achievement through sports, academic attainment, and romantic fulfillment. Secondly, many Americans followed college football and most of the films focused on this sport.

By the time sound became a permanent fixture in movie houses, Hollywood was ready with a host of campus comedies and light musicals. Jack OAKIE and Helen KANE starred in *Sweetie*, while Elliott Nugent appeared in *So This Is College*, both 1929. Joe E. BROWN starred in *Local Boy Makes Good* (1931) and later appeared in another college comedy, *The Gladiator* (1938). The four MARX BROTHERS cause mayhem at Huxley College with Groucho as president in *Horse Feathers* (1932). By 1933 Bing CROSBY, George BURNS, and Gracie ALLEN enrolled in *College Humor* and Jimmy DURANTE and Jack PEARL joined Cuddle College in *Meet the Baron*. That same year Victor McLAGLEN appeared in a college satire, *Rackety Rax*, concerning crooked football teams. A stable of comic character actors took over *Hold 'Em Yale* (1935), including William FRAWLEY, Andy DEVINE, and Warren HYMER. In 1936 Jack Oakie graduated to dean of a girls' school in *Collegiate*, co-starring Joe PENNER. Jack BENNY appeared that same year in *College Holiday* with Burns and Allen and Martha RAYE, while Hugh HERBERT appeared as a professor in *We Went to College*, a spoof on reunions. The RITZ BROTHERS were featured in *Life Begins in College* in 1937. Jimmy Durante returned to campus in 1937 with Charles Starrett in *Start Cheering*. The following year John BARRYMORE starred in *Hold That Co-Ed*.

LAUREL AND HARDY ushered in the next decade with *A Chump at Oxford* (1940). Following the Second World War and countless war comedies, both the G.I.'s and Hollywood returned to the classroom. In 1945 ABBOTT AND COSTELLO starred in *Here Come the Co-Eds*. On the run from the law, they took jobs as caretakers at Bixby College, an all-girls' school, creating chaos on the campus. In *Apartment for Peggy* (1948) newlyweds Jeanne Crain and William Holden try to adjust to campus life as veteran Holden furthers his education. Clifton WEBB starred in *Mr. Belvedere Goes to College*, Fred MacMURRAY made *Father Was a Fullback*, and Loretta Young cracked the books in *Mother Is a Freshman*, all released in 1949.

Except for generally weak entries like *Bonzo Goes to College* (1952), *How to Be Very, Very Popular* (1955) with Betty GRABLE hiding out in a college fraternity, and *Getting Straight* (1970) with Elliott GOULD as a harassed graduate student, the next few decades offered little campus cheer until John BELUSHI appeared in *National Lampoon's Animal House* (1978). Generally dismissed by the critics as a weak comedy, it became very successful at the box office and initiated a rash of campus farces. One of the better entries was the funny *Back to School* (1986), starring Rodney DANGERFIELD as a father who returns to college to encourage his son to continue his studies.

Candy, John (1950–), actor, writer. Worked in television before entering films in his native Canada in 1978. Stocky in appearance, he has portrayed oddball characters in leads or supporting roles. By virtue of his size, Candy follows in a long and honorable tradition of rotund comedians, including John BUNNY, Roscoe ARBUCKLE, Oliver HARDY, and Lou COSTELLO. As yet he has not established a distinct screen character such as Arbuckle's grace and boyish charm or Hardy's potentially destructive pretentiousness. But his popularity attests to his winning personality, while his timing and dedication to comedy suggest the possibilities for his professional growth.

In *Splash* he played Tom HANKS' brother. Hanks, whose girlfriend is a mermaid, is the object of his fellow workers' curiosity at the fruit market where he works. "What are you looking at?" Candy yells at them. "You never saw a guy that slept with a fish before?"

SELECTED FILMS: *Silent Partner* (1978), *Stripes* (1981), *Going Berserk* (1983), *Splash* (1984), *Volunteers* (1985), *Armed and Dangerous*, *Little Shop of Horrors* (1986). ■

Army, *Joan of Ozark* (1942), *Chatterbox* (1943), *Louisiana Hayride* (1944), *Hit the Hay* (1945), *Singing in the Corn* (1946), *Honeychile* (1951), *Oklahoma Annie* (1952), *Untamed Heiress* (1954), *Lay That Rifle Down* (1955), *The Adventures of Huckleberry Finn* (1960), *Cannonball* (1976). ■

Eddie Cantor (left), Alan Mowbray (center), and Edward Arnold (right)

Judy Canova

Canova, Judy (1916–1983), comedienne, singer. Appeared in vaudeville, on radio at age 12, and on Broadway in 1934 before entering films in 1935. Known chiefly for her hillbilly comedies, she also co-starred with other comics, including Jack BENNY and ABBOTT AND COSTELLO, in many features, most of which were B films. Between her assignments in her two dozen films, she made numerous appearances on radio and in television and appeared in two shows on Broadway. She hosted her own radio show for a decade.

In *Artists and Models* (1937) Ben BLUE portrayed a rainmaker who is attracted to Judy who, in turn, finds him repulsive. "I'm Jupiter Plubius the Second," he announces, introducing himself to the girl of his dreams. "Don't tell me there are two of you!" she cries.

SELECTED FILMS: *In Caliente*, *Going Highbrow* (1935), *Thrill of a Lifetime* (1937), *Scatterbrain* (1940), *Sis Hopkins* (1941), *Sleepytime Gal*, *True to the*

Cantor, Eddie (1892–1964), comedian, singer. Worked as a singing waiter, starred in vaudeville and burlesque, in Ziegfeld Follies, on Broadway through the 1920s, and on radio in the 1930s and 1940s. A wide-eyed, vivacious, and personable entertainer, he began appearing in films in 1926 but did not reach his peak as a screen star until the 1930s. For decades he was a headliner in each phase of show business that he entered. After leaving the Follies, he starred successfully in Broadway musical comedies in the 1920s. He was a hit in a series of light films in the early 1930s. His radio show during this decade and into the 1940s was one of the top-rated programs.

His stage experience helped him to develop his excellent sense of timing and comic presence. In the Goldwyn comedy *Roman Scandals* (1933) he portrayed a grocery clerk who dreams he is living in ancient Rome. Offered as a slave at public auction, he announces his own attributes: "I can cook a little, I can take care of the children. If there are no children, I can take care of that." Later, when a slatternly old woman bids for him, he tries to discourage her. "I'm weak. I can't do any work." "I'm not buying you for that," she says seductively. "Just what I was afraid of," Cantor utters. Affectionately called "Banjo Eyes" because of his big eyes, he often joked about his having five daughters. He wrote several autobiographies, the last of which, *As I Remember Them*, was published in 1962.

SELECTED FILMS: *Kid Boots* (1926), *Special Delivery* (1927), *Glorifying the American Girl* (1929), *Whoopee!* (1930), *Palmy Days* (1931), *The Kid From Spain* (1932), *Roman Scandals* (1933), *Kid Millions* (1934), *Strike Me Pink* (1936), *Ali Baba Goes to Town* (1937), *Forty Little Mothers* (1940), *Thank Your Lucky Stars* (1943), *Show Business, Hollywood Canteen* (1944), *If You Knew Susie* (1948), *The Story of Will Rogers* (1952). ∎

Caper comedy. A light film whose plot revolves around the execution of a crime or scam. Larceny has always been a popular film theme with movie audiences. Caper comedy films have their origins in the silent period. One of the earliest works in this genre was Mack SENNETT'S 1912 comedy short, "The Great Vacuum Robbery" in which Edgar KENNEDY and Louise FAZENDA decide to empty a bank of its contents using a vacuum cleaner. Another early example of the genre was *The Confidence Man*, a 1925 Paramount release starring Thomas Meighan and Virginia Valli.

In the delightful *Topaze*, one of the best films released in 1933, an honest school teacher who is duped by some unscrupulous members of the business establishment turns these methods to his advantage. The film, starring John BARRYMORE and Myrna LOY, was based on Pagnol's satirical play.

In Warner's 1942 funny gangster spoof, *Larceny, Inc.*, Edward G. Robinson portrayed a small-time hoodlum just released from prison who opens a luggage shop next to a bank with the intentions of drilling through the wall to get to the bank's money. He was ably assisted by a host of comic character actors including Ed BROPHY.

The 1960s blossomed with caper comedies. *Ocean's Eleven* (1960) starred the famous "Rat Pack," which included Frank Sinatra, Dean Martin, Sammy Davis, Jr., and Peter Lawford. An eleven-man hit-team plotted to rob five Las Vegas casinos, with an unpredictable ending. The following year Columbia released *Sail a Crooked Ship*, a crime comedy starring con artist Robert Wagner, Ernie Kovacs, and Dolores Hart. The film was based on a novel by Nathaniel Benchley. In 1964 *Topkapi* scored a success at the box-office while Peter Ustinov won an Oscar for his performance as one of a group of incompetents trying to rob the Istanbul Museum. Using actual locales, the film, based on a novel by Eric Ambler, was a visual treat as well as a delightful comedy. One of the most popular caper comedies that led to its own series was *THE PINK PANTHER* (1964), starring David NIVEN and Robert WAGNER as jewel thieves and Peter SELLERS as the bungling French Inspector Clouseau. Director Blake EDWARDS turned out a successful group of sequels starring Sellers. In 1967 *Who's Minding the Mint?* had a rag-tag crew of incompetents trying to enter the United States Mint in an attempt to assist Robert Hutton. The cast included Milton BERLE, Joey BISHOP, Walter BRENNAN, and Victor BUONO. The underground sequence with Buono as the captain of a sorry vessel and a pitiful crew was hilarious. The following year, 1968, gave us the Mel BROOKS classic, *The Producers*. Theatrical producer Zero MOSTEL and his accomplice, neurotic accountant Gene WILDER, plotted to bilk a group of oversubscribed investors out of their money by producing a flop musical. The only problem was that the show became a smash hit. Comic actor Dick SHAWN was perfect as an aging hippie who played Hitler in the fateful production.

The film *Skin Game* (1971) successfully took the caper comedy back to the Civil War era as con men James GARNER and Lou Gossett postured as white master and black slave. The biggest caper comedy hit of the 1970s, however, was *The Sting* (1973), starring Paul NEWMAN, Robert REDFORD, and Robert Shaw. Newman and Redford sought revenge on Shaw for their buddy's death. They concocted an intricate "sting" operation that was both suspenseful and entertaining. The theme music of the film re-introduced the public to the ragtime tunes of Scott Joplin. In the same year Ryan O'NEAL played a computer pro who turned jewel thief in the unsuccessful *The Thief Who Came to Dinner*. In 1979 Albert Brooks, writer-director-comic, in his spoof of social realism contrives to make a documentary of a typical American family in his unsuccessful *Real Life*.

French director Louis Malle attempted his version of a comedy caper in *Crackers* (1984), a film about con men in San Francisco. It starred Donald SUTHERLAND and Jack WARDEN and was based on the Italian feature, *Big Deal on Madonna Street*. The caper comedy is an attractive genre for writers and directors since it contains built-in suspense. But if the comedy is not sustained, the film can fail just as easily as entries of other genres.

Capra, Frank (1897–), director. Came to California from Sicily at age six and later studied chemical engineering. He worked as film editor, as gagman for Hal ROACH studios, as comedy writer for Mack SENNETT'S star comic, Harry LANGDON, as director for First National studios and a major director for Columbia Pictures. At First National he directed some of Langdon's best comedies, including "Tramp, Tramp, Tramp," "The Strong Man," and "Long Pants." But it was at Columbia that he was to achieve his greatest success and acclaim. Capra's major features are sometimes affectionately labeled "Capra-corn" because of their excessive sentimentalism. But his genuine feelings for the common man, his belief that good will always triumph, and a perceptive comedic sense endeared his sentimental comedies to the public and won him three Academy Awards.

In the early 1930s he joined forces with screenwriter Robert RISKIN to form one of the most successful director-writer comedy teams in Hollywood. Together they turned out a string of popular films, including *Platinum Blonde* starring Jean Harlow, *American Madness*, *Lady for a Day*, and the now classic *It Happened One Night*.

His first Oscar was for *It Happened One Night* (1934), a story about a rebellious heiress (Claudette Colbert) who flees from her wealthy father. She meets a conceited newspaperman (Clark Gable) who joins her on her journey, resulting in some witty incidents. In *Mr. Deeds Goes to Town* (1936), Longfellow Deeds (Gary Cooper), who has inherited twenty million dollars, is accused of insanity for wanting to give the money away. *You Can't Take It With You* (1938), for which Capra received his third Oscar, was based on the Broadway play by George S. Kaufman and Moss Hart. The comedy concerns an eccentric patriarch and his zany family and household of free souls whose individuality comes into conflict with the powers of big business.

His autobiography, *Frank Capra: The Name Above the Title*, was published in 1971.

SELECTED FILMS: *Fisher's Boarding House* (1922), *The Strong Man, Tramp, Tramp, Tramp* (1926), *For the Love of Mike* (1927), *That Certain Feeling* (1928), *The Younger Generation* (1929), *Ladies of Leisure* (1930), *Platinum Blonde* (1931), *American Madness* (1932), *Lady for a Day* (1933), *Broadway Bill* (1934), *Lost Horizon* (1937), *Mr. Smith Goes to Washington* (1939), *Meet John Doe* (1941), *Arsenic and Old Lace* (1944), *It's a Wonderful Life* (1946), *State of the Union* (1948), *Riding High* (1950), *Here Comes the Groom* (1951), *A Hole in* the Head (1959), Pocketful of Miracles (1961). ∎

Carew, Ora (1893–1955), actress. Began her acting career in 1900 in the theater, followed by vaudeville and musical comedy. She then joined Mack SENNETT'S KEYSTONE studios in 1915. She was teamed with Joseph BELMONT, another stage veteran, with whom she made a successful series of silent comedy shorts. Later, she starred in many silent comedies as well as other genres.

SELECTED FILMS: The Martyrs of the Alamo, Saved by Wireless (1915), Wings and Wheels, A la Cabaret, Dollars and Sense, Love Comet (1916), Oriental Love, Her Circus Knight, Skidding Hearts (1917), Go West, Young Man, Too Many Millions (1918), After Your Own Heart, Ladyfingers (1921), Smiles Are Trumps, Sherlock Brown, Smudge (1922), Waterfront Wolves, Getting Her Man (1924), Cold Fury (1925). ∎

Carey, Harry (1878–1947), actor. Entered early silent films in 1909 working under D.W. Griffith. He soon emerged as a popular western star. A handsome and likable performer, he played in more than 300 dramas and comedies, which were often directed by his friend John FORD. With the advent of sound he developed into a reliable and talented character player. His belated Broadway stage debut did not come until after more than 30 years in films. He was the father of actor Harry Carey, Jr.

SELECTED FILMS: Bill Sharkley's Last Game (1909), As It Happened (1915), Bucking Broadway, The Fighting Gringo (1917), Wild Women, A Woman's Fool (1918), Roped, A Gun-Fighting Gentleman (1919), Mr. Smith Goes to Washington (1939), The Great Moment (1944), So Dear to My Heart (1948). ∎

Carle, Richard (1871–1941), actor. Appeared on stage for three decades before entering silent films in the early 1920s. A

resourceful character actor, he portrayed a variety of roles during a career that spanned almost four decades. He often played wealthy characters in both dramas and light films.

SELECTED FILMS: It Can Be Done (1921), Eve's Leaves (1926), Soft Cushions (1927), The Fleet's In (1928), The Grand Parade (1930), The Old-Fashioned Way (1934), The Ghost Walks (1935), Anything Goes (1936), Top of the Town, True Confession (1937), It's a Wonderful World, Maisie, Ninotchka (1939), The Great McGinty, Seven Sinners (1940), That Uncertain Feeling, The Devil and Miss Jones (1941). ∎

Carlisle, Mary (1912–), actress. Starred in numerous second-feature melodramas and light films through the 1930s. A blonde, blue-eyed ingenue, she played opposite such popular comics as Jimmy DURANTE and Joe E. BROWN as well as crooner Bing CROSBY. She was the stepdaughter of industrial magnate Henry J. Kaiser.

SELECTED FILMS: This Reckless Age (1932), College Humor, Ladies Must Love, The Sweetheart of Sigma Chi (1933), Palooka, Girl of My Dreams (1934), Grand Old Girl, It's in the Air (1935), Lady Be Careful (1936), Hotel Haywire, Double or Nothing (1937), Dr. Rhythm (1938), Beware Spooks! (1939), Call a Messenger (1940), Rags to Riches (1941), Dead Men Walk (1943). ∎

Carlson, California. Fictional comic sidekick in several Hopalong Cassidy westerns produced by United Artists. He was portrayed by screen comedian Andy CLYDE in such films as Hoppy Serves a Writ and Bar 20, both 1943, and Hoppy's Birthday and Dangerous Venture, both 1948.

Carlson, June (1924–), actress. Appeared as teenager in light films during the late 1930s. She played in many of the "JONES FAMILY" features as well as other films through the 1940s and 1950s.

SELECTED FILMS: *Every Saturday Night, Educating Father, Back to Nature (1936), Off to the Races, Big Business, Hot Water (1937), Love on a Budget, Safety in Numbers (1938), Too Busy to Work (1939), Young As You Feel (1940), A Very Young Lady (1941), Come Out Fighting (1945), Mom and Dad (1957).* ■

Carmel, Roger C. (1932–), actor. Has worked on Broadway, in television, and occasionally in films. Chiefly a character actor, he has appeared in dramas as well as light films.

SELECTED FILMS: *The Greatest Show on Earth (1952), Goodbye Charlie (1964), Hardly Working (1981).* ■

Carney, Alan (1911–1973), actor. Long-time vaudevillian who turned character actor in the 1940s. He appeared chiefly in light films as part of the team of BROWN AND CARNEY. RKO teamed him with comic Wally Brown to compete with the popular ABBOTT AND COSTELLO. But by 1946 the studio did not renew their contract. Carney continued to appear alone in films and on television.

SELECTED FILMS: *Mr. Lucky, Around the World (1943), Seven Days Ashore, Step Lively (1944), Zombies on Broadway (1945), The Pretender (1947), Li'l Abner (1959), It's a Mad, Mad, Mad, Mad World (1963), The Love Bug Rides Again (1973).* ■

Carney, Art (1918–), actor. Worked as a singer and mimic on various radio shows before World War II. When he returned from military service, he continued to appear on radio as a comic with Fred ALLEN, Edgar BERGEN, and Bert LAHR. He appeared on Broadway in the late 1950s while simultaneously doing several television shows. He did not win nationwide attention until he immortalized the role of Ed Norton, Jackie GLEASON'S pal, on the popular television comedy series, "The Honeymoon-

ers." Except for a minor role in *Pot o' Gold* (1941), he did not enter films until 1964. He is one of those rare personalities, in the tradition of Jimmy DURANTE and Jack LEMMON, who are naturally funny in the sense that their personalities can often surmount weak comic material and whom audiences can warm up to very quickly. He won an Academy Award as Best Actor for his role in *Harry and Tonto* (1974).

SELECTED FILMS: *The Yellow Rolls Royce (1964), A Guide for the Married Man (1967), Harry and Tonto (1974), W.W. and the Dixie Dance Kings (1975), Won Ton Ton—The Dog That Saved Hollywood (1976), The Late Show, Scott Joplin (1977), House Calls, Movie Movie (1978), Steel, Sunburn (1979).* ■

Carney, Augustus, comic actor. Appearing first in vaudeville, he became a popular silent screen comedian during the 1910s. He appeared in a series of short comedies in 1910 called "Hank and Lank." Another popular series, the "Snakeville" comedies, which he made for ESSANAY studios, dealt with home-spun humor and raised his status as a top silent film comedian. He reached his greatest heights in another series, the "Alkali Ike" comedies of 1911–1913, which he made for the same studio. He was best known for his slapstick humor.

SELECTED FILMS: *Alkali Ike's Auto (1911), Alkali Ike's Love Affair (1912), Alkali Ike and the Hypnotist (1913).* ■

Carr, Alexander (1878–1946), actor. Worked in the circus, burlesque, and the theater before appearing occasionally in comedy films. He was best known for his portrayal of Perlmutter in the "POTASH AND PERLMUTTER" comedy series in the 1920s.

SELECTED FILMS: *Potash and Perlmutter (1923), In Hollywood With Potash and Perlmutter (1924), Partners Again, The Beautiful Cheat, April Fool (1926), Uptown New York, Hypnotized*

(1932), *Out All Night (1933), Christmas in July (1940).* ∎

Carr, Mary (1874–1973), actress. Worked as a character player during the silent period. She appeared in numerous comedy shorts for producer Hal ROACH, including films starring Charley CHASE and LAUREL AND HARDY. She often portrayed genial grandma types.

SELECTED FILMS: The Beloved Rogue (1918), The Custard Cup, Broadway Broke (1923), Drusilla With a Million, The Wizard of Oz (1926), Special Delivery, On Your Toes (1927), Lights of New York (1928), Hot Curves, The Midnight Special (1930), Pack Up Your Troubles (1932), Friendly Persuasion (1956). ∎

Carradine, John (1906–), actor. Began his long screen career in the early 1930s as a feature player following stage experience that included appearances with a Shakespearean stock company. A tall, angular figure with an excellent speaking voice, he drew several good roles during his first 20 years in Hollywood. One of his most famous portrayals was that of Preacher Casey in John FORD'S *The Grapes of Wrath* (1940). Later, he developed into a prolific character actor and appeared in low-budget features, often playing self-parodies in exploitation horror films. During his five decades as an actor, he has appeared in more than 100 dramas and light films. He has been in so many B horror films that it is easy to overlook his support of some of the leading screen comics of the period, including, among others, Eddie CANTOR, the RITZ BROTHERS, Fred ALLEN, Bob HOPE, and Danny KAYE. His three sons, David, Keith, and Robert, have had successful film careers.

SELECTED FILMS: Tol'able David (1930), The Meanest Gal in Town (1934), She Gets Her Man (1935), Anything Goes, Captain January, Dimples (1936), Ali Baba Goes to Town (1937), Kentucky Moonshine (1938), The Three Musketeers (1939), It's in the Bag (1945), Casanova's Big Night (1953), The Court

Jester (1956), The Patsy (1964), The Trouble With Girls (1969), Zorro the Gay Blade (1981), The Tomb (1985). ∎

Carrillo, Leo (1881–1961), actor. Worked as a dialect comedian in vaudeville before appearing in more than 75 films. He was equally competent in serious as well as comedy roles. He began as a lead player but soon became a character actor. His comedy consisted of mutilating the King's English, usually with a Spanish accent, playing oddball characters, and portraying friendly but talkative Latins.

In *Too Hot to Handle* (1938) he played newsreel cameraman Clark GABLE'S comic-relief assistant. In a South American jungle they come across a fierce tribe of natives who practice human sacrifice. "What are you shivering about?" Gable asks. "I'm just thinking about how cold I'm going to be when they take off my skin and I sit around in my bones," Carrillo replies.

SELECTED FILMS: The Dove (1928), Hell Bound (1931), Moonlight and Pretzels (1933), Viva Villa! (1934), In Caliente, Love Me Forever (1935), The Gay Desperado (1936), Manhattan Merry-Go-Round, History Is Made at Night (1937), Girl of the Golden West (1938), Fisherman's Wharf, Rio (1939), Twenty-Mule Team (1940), One Night in the Tropics (1940), Barnacle Bill (1942), Top Sergeant, Crazy House, The Phantom of the Opera (1943), Ghost Catchers (1944), Under Western Skies (1945), Pancho Villa Returns (1952). ∎

Carroll, Madeleine (1902–), actress. Appeared on the stage and in films in her native England before immigrating to Hollywood in the mid-1930s. She had co-starred in two Alfred Hitchcock thrillers. A blue-eyed blonde beauty (who had naturally dark hair), she became one of the most highly paid American screen stars during her brief career (1936–1942), bringing style and grace to a handful of dramas and light comedies. She returned to England during World War II to help on the civilian front. After the war, she returned to the United States to star on Broadway and make occasional films.

SELECTED FILMS: *The Case Against Mrs. Ames (1936), On the Avenue, It's All Yours (1937), Cafe Society, Honeymoon in Bali (1939), Virginia, One Night in Lisbon (1941), My Favorite Blonde (1942), An Innocent Affair (1948), The Fan (1949).* ∎

Carroll, Nancy (1904–1965), actress. Appeared in vaudeville and on Broadway through the 1920s before entering films in 1927. After a few minor roles, she was given leads and soon became a major actress. She starred in many features, especially musical comedies. However, she was equally adept in dramatic roles as well, receiving a nomination for an Academy Award for her role in *Devil's Holiday* (1930). Movie audiences in 1930 rated her the most popular actress in films. By the late 1930s her career began to falter, so she retired from the screen and switched to radio. She later appeared in television and on Broadway.

SELECTED FILMS: *Ladies Must Dress (1927), Abie's Irish Rose, Manhattan Cocktail (1928), The Shopworn Angel, Sweetie (1929), Honey, Laughter (1930), The Night Angel, Personal Maid (1931), Hot Saturday (1932), Child of Manhattan, I Love That Man (1933), Springtime for Henry, Transatlantic Merry-Go-Round (1934), Atlantic Adventure (1935), There Goes My Heart, That Certain Age (1938).* ∎

Carson, Jack (1910–1963), actor. Appeared in vaudeville before entering movies in 1937. He was capable of playing a wide range of roles, from clowns to treacherous cowards. A beefy figure who often employed his famous double-take, he is probably best remembered for his roles as the humorous friend of the main character. He supported a host of stars, including Cary GRANT, Katharine HEPBURN, James CAGNEY, James STEWART, and especially Dennis MORGAN, with whom he made a series of musical comedies. He began to appear in televi-

sion during the early 1950s and later worked in theatrical productions.

SELECTED FILMS: *Stage Door, You Only Live Once (1937), Vivacious Lady, Bringing Up Baby (1938), Mr. Smith Goes to Washington, Destry Rides Again (1939), I Take This Woman, Lucky Partners (1940), Love Crazy (1941), The Male Animal, Larceny, Inc. (1942), Arsenic and Old Lace, Make Your Own Bed, Roughly Speaking (1944), Two Guys From Milwaukee (1946), Love and Learn (1947), Two Guys From Texas (1948), It's a Great Feeling (1949), The Good Humor Man (1950), The Groom Wore Spurs (1951), Dangerous When Wet (1954), Ain't Misbehavin' (1955), Rally 'Round the Flag, Boys! (1958), King of the Roaring Twenties (1961).* ∎

Carter, Jack (1923–), comedian, actor. On radio, on stage, and in television as a comic before entering films. An all-around performer, he is a dynamic entertainer filled with nervous energy. His act consists of songs, gags, and impressions. Unfortunately, the films in which he has appeared, usually as a supporting player, have not helped to further his career.

SELECTED FILMS: *The Horizontal Lieutenant (1962), Viva Las Vegas (1964), The Extraordinary Seaman (1969), The Happy Hooker Goes to Washington (1980), History of the World—Part 1, Heartbeeps (voice only) (1981), The Funny Farm (1982), Hambone and Hillie (1984).* ∎

Carter, Nancy. See Minna Gombell.

Caruso, Anthony (1915–), actor. Worked as a singer before entering Hollywood films in the early 1940s. Tall, dark, and heavy-set, he appeared chiefly as a character actor and was usually assigned to criminal roles in dramas and light films.

SELECTED FILMS: *Johnny Apollo (1940), Tall, Dark and Handsome, The Bride Came C.O.D. (1941), Always in My Heart (1942), The Ghost and the Guest*

(1943), Don Juan Quilligan (1945), Monsieur Beaucaire (1946), My Favorite Brunette (1947), Never a Dull Moment (1967), The Zebra Force (1976). ∎

Carver, Louise (1898–1956), actress. Began her screen career in the early 1920s in silent comedies. She quickly gained prominence as one of the decade's most popular comediennes. With the advent of sound films, she switched to character roles.

SELECTED FILMS: *The Extra Girl (1923), Shameful Behavior (1926), The Fortune Hunter (1927), The Man From Blankley's (1930), Side Show (1931), Hallelujah, I'm a Bum (1933), Every Night at Eight (1935).* ∎

Cass, Maurice (1884–1954), actor. Began on Broadway in 1906, in films from 1935. He usually played in light comedies as a monocled, affable gentleman.

SELECTED FILMS: *Two for Tonight (1935), Champagne Waltz, Life Begins in College, Ali Baba Goes to Town (1937), The Baroness and the Butler, Gold Diggers in Paris (1938), Second Fiddle (1939), Charley's Aunt (1941), Up in Arms (1944), Easy to Look At (1945), Angel on My Shoulder (1946), We're Not Married (1952).* ∎

Cass, Peggy (1924–), actress. Appeared on Broadway and in television, and sporadically in feature films, usually in comedy roles.

SELECTED FILMS: *The Marrying Kind (1952), Auntie Mame (1958), Gidget Goes Hawaiian (1961), If It's Tuesday, This Must Be Belgium (1969).* ∎

Castle, Irene (1893–1969), dancer, actress. Appeared on stage and in silent films with her husband. She was part of the famous dance team of Vernon and Irene Castle until her husband was killed in a World War I plane crash in 1918. She starred in dramas and light films through the 1920s. Fred ASTAIRE and Ginger ROGERS starred in a 1939 film biography, *The Story of Vernon and Irene Castle.*

SELECTED FILMS: *The Whirl of Life (1915), The Girl From Bohemia (1918), The Firing Line (1919), The Amateur Wife (1920), The Broadway Bride (1921), French Heels, No Trespassing, Slim Shoulders (1922), Broadway After Dark (1924).* ∎

Cat and the Canary, The (1939), PAR. Dir. Elliott Nugent; Sc. Walter DeLeon, Lynn Starling; with Bob Hope, Paulette Goddard, Gale Sondergaard, John Beal.

This mystery-comedy is one of four versions of the classic tale concerning an heiress who is threatened out of her inheritance and the sinister goings-on in a haunted house. This adaptation, which emphasized the comic element, helped to propel Bob HOPE into the front ranks of screen comedians. Before he made this film, he was featured in minor, routine comedies. Hope plays a role he will repeat numerous times in future comedies, that of a semi-cowardly ham actor who wisecracks his way through the creaky plot as he half-heartedly protects Paulette GODDARD against a crazed murderer. In the haunted mansion Nydia Westman asks Hope: "Don't big empty houses scare you?" "Not me," he replies. "I used to be in vaudeville." Hope provides plenty of laughs, including several political barbs, another of his trademarks. "Do you believe in reincarnation?" Westman asks Hope. "You know, that dead people come back?" "You mean like Republicans?" he questions. The first version of *Canary*, a 1927 silent thriller, starred Laura La Plante and Tully Marshall. The 1930 sound film was retitled *The Cat Creeps* and starred Helen TWELVETREES, while the latest remake, a 1978 British production, featuring Honor Blackman and Michael Callan, blended a dash of sex, some spoofing, and a few chills. Hope and Goddard appeared in a sequel, *The Ghost Breakers,* the following year.

Catlett, Walter (1889–1960), actor. Began his screen career in silent films in the early 1920s. Appearing in well over 100 silent and sound films, he frequently portrayed addle-brained, nervous characters easily upset by the slightest problem. He worked for many of the major studios until the late 1940s, after which he co-starred with Raymond WALBURN in a series of B movies for Monogram studios. See "HENRY" entry.

SELECTED FILMS: *Second Youth* (1924), *Why Leave Home?* (1929), *The Front Page* (1931), *Rain* (1932), *Mama Loves Papa, Only Yesterday* (1933), *The Captain Hates the Sea* (1934), *Mr. Deeds Goes to Town* (1936), *Wake Up and Live* (1937), *Bringing Up Baby* (1938), *Maisie Gets Her Man, Yankee Doodle Dandy* (1942), *They Got Me Covered* (1943), *Up in Arms, Ghost Catchers* (1944), *The Boy With Green Hair* (1948), *Henry the Rainmaker, The Inspector General* (1949), *Friendly Persuasion* (1956), *Beau James* (1957). ■

Cavanaugh, Hobart (1886–1950), actor. Entered movies in the 1920s following a brief stage career. He appeared in more than 300 features, often as an unassuming, meek little clerk, henpecked husband, or nervous subordinate.

One of his funniest portrayals was that of a drunken heckler in *Rose of Washington Square* (1938) who is brazen under the influence but meek when sober. Al JOLSON, playing a blackface singer making his stage debut, is continually interrupted by a voice from a box seat. "What's going on behind the curtain?" the inebriated heckler (Cavanaugh) insists on knowing. "Nothing is going on backstage," the nervous Jolson insists, trying to reassure the pest while the audience roars with laughter. Each time Jolson tries to return to his act, the intruder intervenes. "Something must be going on behind the curtain," Cavanaugh

concludes, "because nothing is going on in front of it."

SELECTED FILMS: *San Francisco Nights* (1928), *The Kennel Murder Case, Gold Diggers of 1933, Wonder Bar* (1933), *Harold Teen* (1934), *Bordertown* (1935), *Stage Struck* (1936), *Three Smart Girls* (1937), *Idiot's Delight* (1939), *Hired Wife* (1940), *Skylark* (1941), *My Favorite Spy* (1942), *The Human Comedy* (1943), *Margie* (1946), *A Letter to Three Wives* (1948), *Stella* (1950). ■

Cavanna, Elise (1902–1963), actress. Worked on stage before entering films as a supporting player during the silent period. She appeared in comedy shorts during the early sound era, especially those produced by Mack SENNETT. Her most memorable role was that of W. C. FIELDS' patient in his now classic short, "The Dentist." While she is seated in his dentist's chair, she wraps her legs around him as he attempts to ply his profession. The scene has been considered risque for many decades and is often cut from television versions.

SELECTED FILMS: *Love 'Em and Leave 'Em, It's the Old Army Game* (1926), *A Melon-Drama* (1931), *The Dentist* (1932), *The Pharmacist, The Barber Shop* (1933), *You're Telling Me* (1934), *Everybody Sing* (1938), *Ziegfeld Follies* (1944). ■

Cavender, Glen (1884–1962), actor, director. Began his film career as actor in silent film comedies. He worked for Mack SENNETT'S KEYSTONE studios in the mid-1910s and was soon recognized as one of the leading screen comedians of his period. By 1916 he had been promoted to director, supervising his own unit for Sennett. Much of his film work was in collaboration with "Fatty" ARBUCKLE. He was one of the original Keystone Kops. His screen career spanned four decades.

SELECTED FILMS: *A Submarine Pirate, Fickle Fatty's Fall* (1915), *Fatty and Mabel Adrift, Because He Loved Her,*

The Surf Girl (1916), The Pawnbroker's Heart (1917), Skirts, Straight From the Shoulder (1921), Iron to Gold (1922), Keep Smiling, Manhattan Madness (1925), The General (1927), Penrod's Double Trouble (1938), Yankee Doodle Dandy (1942). ∎

Cawthorn, Joseph (1868–1949), actor. Worked on stage in the United States and in England before entering Hollywood films in 1926. He was allegedly President Wilson's favorite stage comic. Bald and fatherly, he appeared in light silent and sound films, chiefly as a character player. He worked with such stars as Douglas FAIRBANKS and Al JOLSON.

SELECTED FILMS: Very Confidential, Two Girls Wanted (1927), Silk Legs (1928), Jazz Heaven, The Taming of the Shrew (1929), Dixiana (1930), Kiki, A Tailor Made Man (1931), Love Me Tonight (1932), Whistling in the Dark (1933), Housewife, The Last Gentleman (1934), Go Into Your Dance, Naughty Marietta (1935), The Postman Didn't Ring (1942). ∎

Cecil, Nora (–1954), actress. Appeared chiefly as a character player in early sound comedies, especially those produced by Hal ROACH. A homely looking figure, she was often cast as a disagreeable old spinster. She worked with some of the leading comics of the period, including, among others, LAUREL AND HARDY, Charley CHASE, and W. C. FIELDS.

SELECTED FILMS: Pack Up Your Troubles, Girl Grief (1932), The Bank Dick (1940). ∎

Cedar, Ralph, director. Began directing during the silent era, chiefly comedy shorts starring Snub POLLARD and Stan LAUREL (in films he made before he teamed up with Oliver HARDY). Cedar continued to direct light features during the 1930s and up to 1940.

SELECTED FILMS (with Pollard): Down and Out, Pardon Me, The Bow Wows, Hot Off the Press, The Anvil Chorus, Jump Your Job, Kill the Nerve, Some Baby (1922), Do Your Duty (1926).
SELECTED FILMS (with Laurel): Roughest Africa, The Soilers, Mother's Joy (1923), Zeb vs. Paprika, Brothers Under the Chin, Near Dublin (1924).
SELECTED FILMS (general): A Fool's Advice (1933), She Had to Choose (1934), Meet the Mayor (1938), West of Abilene (1940). ∎

Chan, Charlie. Famous fictional oriental detective based in Hawaii. Created by writer Earl Derr Biggers, who did none of the screenplays, the detective appeared as the chief character in numerous films dating back to 1926 when George Kuwa portrayed him in a serial. The most popular actors to play the sleuth in the black-and-white series were Warner Oland during the 1930s (16 films), Sidney TOLER in the 1940s (22 entries), and finally Roland Winters (six films), who stayed with the series until its demise in 1952. Comic relief was supplied by Mantan MORELAND, who usually played Chan's chauffeur, and by a variety of actors who played one of the detective's sons. The films were low-budget B vehicles which appeared in movie theaters on the bottom half of a double bill.

Chan's witty sayings ultimately became an integral part of each entry. From Charlie Chan's Chance (1932): "This is unexpected as squirt from aggressive grapefruit," from Charlie Chan's Courage (1934): "Hen squats with caution on thin egg," and from Charlie Chan at the Race Track (1936) when his inept but enthusiastic son rushes in with a new clue after Chan has solved the case: "Too late. Save for next case, please."

Occasionally, other actors have portrayed the detective, but the films generated little or no interest. Peter USTINOV's comic version, Charlie Chan and the Curse of the Dragon Queen (1981), fell flat despite its all-star cast. Veteran character actor J. Carroll NAISH portrayed him in a 1957 television series. In 1972 the luckless sleuth was relegated to a television cartoon series, "Charlie Chan and the Chan Clan."

Chandler, Chic (1905–), actor. Appeared in vaudeville and on the stage before entering films during the silent period. He continued performing on screen into the sound era, especially in comic relief roles as well as lead parts which usually involved slapstick and wisecracks. Not a creative comedian, he depended less on his comic talents than on scripts, which were, for the most part, routine. In the second-rate mystery *Mr. Moto Takes a Chance* (1938), for example, he plays an assistant newsreel cameraman assigned to an island in the South Pacific. At a native feast he tries his hand at some sleight of hand and accidentally swallows a lighted cigarette. "Boy," he announces to the other guests, "am I hot tonight!" His material rarely rose above this level of comedy.

SELECTED FILMS: *Red Love* (1925), *Melody Cruise* (1933), *The Party's Over* (1934), *Tango, Three of a Kind* (1936), *Time Out for Romance* (1937), *Time Out for Murder* (1938), *Hollywood Cavalcade* (1939), *Free, Blonde and 21* (1940), *The Bride Came C.O.D.* (1941), *The Magnificent Dope* (1942), *He Hired the Boss* (1943), *Irish Eyes Are Smiling* (1944), *Mother Wore Tights* (1947), *Family Honeymoon* (1949), *The Girl Who Knew Too Much* (1969). ∎

Chandler, George (1902–1985), actor. After a stint in vaudeville as "The Musical Nut," he worked in Hollywood for most of the major studios and appeared in more than 150 films. He was generally cast as a delivery man, newsman, or energetic comic.

SELECTED FILMS: *The Kid's Clever* (1929), *Only Saps Work* (1930), *Blessed Event* (1932), *Hi, Nellie!* (1934), *Stars Over Broadway* (1935), *The Princess Comes Across* (1936), *Nothing Sacred* (1937), *Jesse James* (1939), *Roxie Hart* (1942), *It Happened Tomorrow* (1944), *This Man's Navy* (1945), *The Secret Life of Walter Mitty* (1947), *Pretty Baby* (1950), *Dead Ringer* (1964), *Escape to Witch Mountain* (1975). ∎

Chaney, Norman "Chubby" (1918–1936), child actor. Appeared in early "OUR GANG" comedies. A tubby youngster with a broad smile and an abundance of personality, he rapidly became a popular member of the gang. In 1928, a large shift in the "Our Gang" cast occurred. As the result of a nationwide contest, Chaney was chosen to replace the personable but maturing Joe COBB as the fat boy of the gang. He appeared in numerous entries through the 1930s, including those which featured Jackie COOPER, "Stymie" BEARD, and Bobby "Wheezer" HUTCHINS.

SELECTED FILMS: *Teacher's Pet, School's Out* (1930), *Love Business, Little Daddy* (1931). ∎

Channing, Carol (1921–), actress, comedienne. Appeared on stage, in nightclubs, in television, and, sporadically, in films. A personable entertainer with a unique, raspish voice, she is remembered most for her rendition of the song, "Diamonds Are a Girl's Best Friend," which she performed in the play version of *Gentlemen Prefer Blondes*. She received an Academy Award nomination as Best Supporting Actress for her role in *Thoroughly Modern Millie*.

SELECTED FILMS: *Paid in Full* (1950), *The First Traveling Saleslady* (1956), *Thoroughly Modern Millie* (1967), *Skidoo* (1968), *Shinbone Alley* (1971). ∎

Channing, Stockard (1944–), actress. Appeared on stage and in television before performing in films. Her talent and personality have helped make her a popular performer, especially in comedy roles.

SELECTED FILMS: *The Hospital* (1971), *Up the Sandbox* (1972), *The For-*

tune (1975) *Sweet Revenge, The Big Bus (1976), The Cheap Detective, Grease (1978), Silent Victory, The Fish That Saved Pittsburgh (1979).* ■

Charlie Chaplin and Jackie Coogan (right)

Chaplin, Charlie (1889–1977), actor, comedian, director, screenwriter. Born Charles Spencer Chaplin in London, he was the son of music hall performers. He appeared at age nine in a traveling dance act, in vaudeville, and, by his mid-teens, in Fred Karno's pantomime troupe (1906–1913) in his native England. Touring with the company throughout Europe and the United States, he decided to try his fortune in America during his second trip. In 1913 the KEYSTONE Film Company invited him to join Mack SENNETT at its West Coast studios at $150 a week. The 24-year-old "English music hall" comic made his first film for the studio in 1914.

"Making a Living," an inauspicious beginning for Chaplin, has him playing an impoverished Englishman sporting a frock coat, monocle, and walrus mustache. His famous "tramp" character had not yet emerged, but his inventiveness and his subtlety can be seen. His second film, "Kid Auto Races at Venice," shows him in his tramp outfit for the first time. By his third film for Sennett, a one-reel comedy called "Mabel's Strange Predicament," his costume and much of his style were established; little nuances,

such as his tripping over a cuspidor followed by his tipping his hat in apology, added originality and humor to his newly created character. At the same time, his more conventional visual gags such as getting entangled in a dog's leash or causing confusion at a hotel reception desk are present as well in this early comedy co-starring Mabel NORMAND.

The remainder of the Keystone films, including many with comedienne Normand, afforded him the opportunity to develop other well-known bits: his convulsive hops while running, his absurd bouts with inanimate objects (swinging doors, a mannequin), his nimble acrobatics, his exit by shrugging his problems away before continuing on the "road of life," his female impersonations, his use of sentimentality, and his use of dream sequences.

His stay with Keystone also inhibited him from reaching his full potential. Sennett's emphasis on tempo, slapstick, and the final chase conflicted with Chaplin's concepts, which included slower pacing, more characterization for his tramp, and pathos. His switch to ESSANAY was to offer him, at least in part, an opportunity to fulfill some of these ideas. Still, Keystone provided him with a large degree of spontaneity, a chance to work with an exceptional group of actors, and, most of all, invaluable experience as a director.

After completing 35 one- and two-reel comedies for Sennett, he signed with Essanay in 1915 at $1,250 per week, many times his old salary. The first few of the 14 two-reelers he was to make for his new studio were similar to the shorts he turned out for Keystone; they contained the conventional slapstick, a rapid pace, and a final madcap pursuit. But in "The Tramp" he gave full dimension for the first time to his quintessential down-and-out vagabond, the pathetic loner who surrenders the girl he loves, fails at work, and returns to the open road. The tramp is a sympathetic and pitiful creature who, despite his shabby garments and his disappointments, maintains a dignified gentleness and an abundance of hope that tomorrow promises a better day. Another film made at Essanay which depicted Charlie at his height was "The Bank," a well-plotted two-reeler that combined comedy with sentiment. Charlie, in love with a bank teller (Edna Purviance), proves his worth by foiling a bank robber. But it is all a dream. When he awakens, he sees the love of his life with her beau. Chaplin was given more freedom and spent additional time on each of the films he made for Essanay, which came to be known as his "transitional period."

His next move was to Mutual, where he made 12 two-reelers (1916–1917), a series of outstanding comedies which presented him at his peak, and which many call his "golden dozen." His new contract paid him $670,000 a year with a $150,000 starting bonus. To help him along at the new studio, he induced many of his co-actors to join him, including his leading lady, Edna PURVIANCE. He spent even more time on each film than he had at Essanay. He made better use of sets and integrated his highly inventive sight gags with the plot lines. He introduced social elements along with satire, romance, and pathos. Lyrical films like "The Vagabond" continued in the vein of "The Tramp."

In "One A.M." Charlie, the only actor in the film, portrays a playboy who returns home slightly soused and does battle with sundry inanimate objects, including a bear rug, a clock pendulum, and a bed. His solo performance through a succession of visual gags established him as an expert pantomimist as well as comic.

"The Pawnshop" contains the classic comedy scene in which he disembowels an alarm clock in front of its owner and then rejects it as unworthy of pawning. But he does more with this simple inanimate object: he almost transforms it into something alive and human. "The Rink" displayed Charlie's expertise with roller skates. The socially conscious "Easy Street" finds him joining the police force and hilariously cleaning up a terrorized

slum street. In "The Cure" he returned to slapstick. Again playing the drunk, but without his tramp costume, he checks into a fashionable spa. "The Adventurer," an elaborate chase movie, showed off his timing and inventiveness. "The Immigrant" was his last film for Mutual. In it he combines slapstick and pathos, comedy and character development, as he befriends Edna Purviance, another newcomer to these shores.

His contract with Mutual completed, he moved to First National (1918–1922), where he would receive one million dollars for making eight films. Once again, he was given artistic freedom, which he used to explore longer films. Three-reel works like "A Dog's Life" (1918) and "Shoulder Arms" (1918) contained social and satirical elements. The former is a strong comedy-drama set realistically among wretched social conditions as Charlie tries to survive in a yard containing his makeshift dwelling with only a stray dog, which symbolizes his own existence, for his friend. "Shoulder Arms," a fantasy-comedy set during World War I and considered his best film to date, contains much satire as well as comedy. "Sunnyside" (1919), a rural comedy with a dream sequence, and "A Day's Pleasure" (1919), a domestic comedy containing several misadventures and much repetition, were not very successful at the box office or with the critics.

In the full-length feature *The Kid* (1921), treated more fully elsewhere in this work, Charlie regained his former standing. His tramp character finds an abandoned baby and raises it, eventually returning the boy (Jackie COOGAN) to his natural mother. The film has been criticized for its sentimentality, which Chaplin not only controlled, but exploited to support the comedy.

"The Pilgrim" (1923), his last film for First National, was a four-reeler that cast Chaplin as an escaped convict who impersonates a minister—with some hilarious moments, especially the now famous scene in which he pantomimes the story of David and Goliath.

Free from any studio obligations after "The Pilgrim," Chaplin was at liberty to pursue his own concepts through United Artists, a company formed in 1919 by Douglas FAIRBANKS, Mary PICKFORD, D. W. Griffith, and Chaplin. He had previously been unable to produce through UA since he had been under commitment to First National.

His first film for the pioneering studio, A Woman of Paris (1923), was a sophisticated drama which he directed but in which he did not appear. In 1925 he made The Gold Rush, covered elsewhere in this work. Many critics consider this his greatest film. Charlie tackles the Yukon and several other unexpected problems in this EPIC COMEDY.

In The Circus (1928), for which he won a special Oscar, he tried his hand at lion-taming and tightrope walking, with humorous results. His next feature was the satirical and ironic Modern Times (1936), in which he satirizes the machine age in general and the assembly line in particular.

The remainder of his work consisted of all-talking films. They ranged from brilliant to forgettable. In the comedy The Great Dictator (1940) Charlie portrays a Jewish barber who impersonates his look-alike, Adenoid Hynkel, dictator of Tomania. Unfortunately, Chaplin ends the film with an anticlimactic, didactic speech which dismayed many of his fans. This was the last appearance of Charlie's beloved little tramp. After two world wars and one Great Depression, Chaplin felt it was incongruous to resurrect his vagabond, the simple soul who could kick up his heels at adversity and look forward to a better tomorrow. The world had changed too drastically. Instead, Chaplin turned to BLACK COMEDY. In Monsieur Verdoux (1947) he portrayed the dual-natured loving husband and murderer of rich widows. Limelight (1952) unfolds the bitter-sweet story of the last days of Calvero, a music-hall entertainer. Both films are treated elsewhere in this work.

Controversy surrounded him early in his career. During World War I he was attacked for not returning to England to enlist. His penchant for teen-age wives brought down the wrath of another segment of the public. He was involved in a paternity suit in which the court declared him the father of the child. Another element assailed him for never becoming an American citizen, while conservatives criticized his left-wing themes in films like Modern Times. Following World War II he was accused of having Communist leanings; there were outcries to deport him. When he left the country in 1952, the immigration service was ordered not to readmit him unless he agreed to an inquiry. His last two films were produced in England. A King in New York (1957), in which an embittered Chaplin starred, and A Countess From Hong Kong (1967), a bedroom comedy in which he made only a cameo appearance as a ship's steward, are slight works, revealing little of the genius that was once Chaplin. In 1972 he returned briefly to the United States to a triumphant reception where he received an Oscar for his contributions to the film industry. His memoirs were published in My Autobiography in 1964.

SELECTED FILMS (at Keystone): Between Showers, A Film Johnnie, Tango Tangles, His Favorite Pastime, Cruel, Cruel Love, The Star Boarder, Mabel at the Wheel, Twenty Minutes of Love, The Knockout, Tillie's Punctured Romance, Caught in a Cabaret, Caught in the Rain, A Busy Day, The Fatal Mallet, Her Friend the Bandit, Laughing Gas, The Face on the Barroom Floor, The Masquerader, His New Profession, The Rounders, The New Janitor, Dough and Dynamite, His Trysting Place, His Prehistoric Past (1914).

SELECTED FILMS (at Essanay): His New Job, A Night Out, The Champion, In the Park, A Jitney Elopement, By the Sea, Work, Shanghaied, A Night in the Show (1915), Carmen, Police (1916).

SELECTED FILMS (at Mutual): The Floorwalker, The Fireman, The Vagabond, *One A.M., The Count, The Pawn-shop, Behind the Screen, The Rink (1916), Easy Street, The Cure, The Immigrant, The Adventurer (1917).*

SELECTED FILMS (at First National): A Dog's Life, Shoulder Arms (1918), Sunnyside, A Day's Pleasure (1919), The Kid, The Idle Class (1921), Pay Day (1922), The Pilgrim (1923).

SELECTED FILMS (at United Artists): The Gold Rush (1925), The Circus (1928), City Lights (1931), Modern Times (1936), The Great Dictator (1940), Monsieur Verdoux (1947), Limelight (1952).

SELECTED FILMS (at Universal): A King in New York (1957), A Countess From Hong Kong (1967). ▪

Chaplin, Sydney (1885–1965), actor. Appeared on stage, then in Fred KARNO'S troupe of performers in England. In 1914 he was in the United States making comedy shorts for Mack SENNETT'S KEYSTONE studios. He made a series of shorts in which he portrayed "Gussle," an impetuous and brazen character. He never became as popular as his half-brother, Charlie; he never developed a personal style or character as did the top comics of the silents although his tempo was faster than that of his more famous brother. His specialty was slapstick, which he often blended with thinly disguised off-color material. He gave up his film career in 1916 to manage his brother's affairs, appearing only occasionally in Charlie's films as well as other comedies.

SELECTED FILMS: Fatty's Wine Party, Gussle the Golfer (1914), Hushing the Scandal, Giddy, Gay and Ticklish, That Springtime Feeling, Gussle's Day of Rest (1915), No One to Guide Him (1916), A Dog's Life, Shoulder Arms (1918), Pay Day (1922), The Pilgrim, The Rendezvous (1923), The Perfect Flapper (1924), Charley's Aunt (1925), The Fortune Hunter (1927). ▪

Charley's Aunt. This old stage farce probably saw more film versions than any other theatrical comedy. No fewer than seven features sprouted from the 1896 play by Brandon Thomas. (*Brewster's Millions*, another stage farce, also produced seven screen versions.) Sydney CHAPLIN, Charlie's half-brother, starred as the university student who impersonates a maiden aunt in the first adaptation in 1925, a popular silent comedy produced by Al Christie. The film helped to revive the comic's moribund film career. The next version was a talkie made in 1931 and starred Charles RUGGLES. England produced the second sound remake in 1940 starring Arthur Askey. This was followed by Jack Benny's interpretation in 1941. Broadway turned the tiresome play into a stage musical and retitled it *Where's Charley?* which Hollywood then borrowed as a 1952 vehicle for the versatile star of the play, Ray Bolger. Two other countries attempted to breathe new life into the comedy. Germany released its version in 1954 with Heinz Ruhmann playing the lead, while Australia in 1963 released its entry with Peter Alexander as the student. Some critics wonder whether the Thomas play was worth all the trouble, but the timeless plot of two college students needing a chaperon for a party and convincing a third to impersonate an aunt allows for many hilarious situations, and female impersonation usually does brisk box-office business.

Charters, Spencer (1878–1943), actor. Began his screen career in silent films in the early 1920s. For the next three decades he was a busy character player. He often portrayed shrewd hayseeds who outfoxed the city slickers. He appeared in dramas and light films, working with some of the foremost comics of the period, including, among others, Eddie CANTOR and W. C. FIELDS.

SELECTED FILMS: Little Old New York (1923), Whoopee! (1930), The Front

Page, Palmy Days (1931), The Tender-foot (1932), Female (1933), Wake Up and Dream, It's a Gift, The Ghost Walks (1934), The Nut Farm (1936), Banjo on My Knee (1936), Professor Beware!, Top-per Takes a Trip (1938), He Married His Wife (1940), Tobacco Road (1941), The Remarkable Andrew, Juke Girl (1942). ■

Chase, Charley (1893–1940), actor, screenwriter, director. Appeared in vaudeville where he did Irish dialect humor, sang, and danced; he also appeared in musicals, then in films in 1914. Sporting a thin mustache and twitching nose, he was an affable comic whose precision had much to do with the success of his films. He worked in the Billy WEST comedies early in his career. He started with producer Mack SENNETT as a supporting comic, developing his craft and studying the techniques of his fellow comedians. He left Sennett's "Fun Factory" which emphasized slapstick and signed with Hal ROACH, where he gained fame and his own starring roles in the 1920s.

Although his early shorts were similar in style to those made at Sennett's studios, he gradually began to develop his own characterization while relying less on slapstick. He usually portrayed either a shy character or a youthful, aggressive bon vivant similar in manner to that of Harold LLOYD. Specializing in fast-paced farce and the "comedy of embarrassment," he appeared in hundreds of comedy shorts. Many of them contain a good deal of sexual innuendo. While with Roach, he occasionally alternated between acting in and directing two-reelers. But his real love was performing before the cameras.

Part of Chase's style was having his character besieged by objects and situations which he was incapable of handling. His attempts at coping often led to greater problems. In "All Wet" (1924), for instance, he accidentally drives his car into a large mudhole while rushing to meet a train. His attempts to get the vehicle out lead only to his getting splashed with mud. Aid from a local gas station is to no avail as his car sinks deeper into the mud. Finally, in frustration, he dives into the abyss and attaches the tow hook to the vehicle's axle, which is all that is salvaged by the tow truck. He finally decides to walk to the depot where he literally loses his pants to a caged lion. The world of simple objects and conditions is transformed into a nightmare of bafflement and defeat to our hapless hero.

In 1937 he returned to directing comedy shorts, this time starring different comics, including the THREE STOOGES and Andy CLYDE. Marital troubles and his drinking problem began to take their toll on his health and his career. He died at age 47.

SELECTED FILMS: The Knockout, Til-lie's Punctured Romance (1914), Hello, Trouble (1918), Ship Ahoy! (1919), All Wet (1924), Bad Boy, His Wooden Wedding (1925), Dog Shy, Mighty Like a Moose (1926), What Women Did for Me, The Way of All Pants, Never the Dames Shall Meet (1927), Limousine Love (1928), Movie Night, Crazy Feet (1929), The Real McCoy (1930), Rough Seas (1931), Sons of the Desert, Fallen Arches (1933), Nurse to You (1935), Kelly the Second (1936), The Wrong Miss Wright (1937), Rattling Romeo (1939), South of the Boudoir (1940). ■

Chase, Chevy (1943–), actor. Worked as actor-writer in television during the 1970s, winning several Emmys, before entering films in the late 1970s. One of the original performers on the popular "Saturday Night Live" show, he often regaled television audiences with his Gerald Ford pratfalls. He has relied on some of his old routines for laughs, such as his trademark of impersonating klutzes, and has embraced new material as well. An appealing and, at times, irreverent comedian, he has had mixed results in his film career. Some of his films are flat, uninspired, and at worst unfunny, despite his charm and natural ease, while others are quite hilarious.

In *Spies Like Us* he and Dan AYKROYD played American undercover agents. During their rigorous training for the position, they grow discouraged and decide to call it quits. "We'd like to go home now," Chase informs their tough superior officer. "Thanks for the bruises, and you can keep the stool samples."

SELECTED FILMS: *Foul Play* (1978), *Oh, Heavenly Dog!, Caddyshack, Seems Like Old Times* (1980), *Under the Rainbow, Modern Problems* (1981), *National Lampoon's Vacation, Deal of the Century* (1983), *Spies Like Us, Fletch* (1985), *Three Amigos!* (1986). ∎

Chase, Ilka (1903–1978), actress, writer. Worked on Broadway in the early 1920s and in films in the latter part of the decade. A supporting actress, she appeared chiefly in light films during the 1930s and occasionally in the following decades. She was more famous for her novels and her columns than for her screen roles.

In *No Time for Love* she played the sister of photographer Claudette COLBERT. "Did you ever see an exciting photograph of an egg?" she asks Ilka. "The only time an egg excites me," she replies, "is when I'm hungry."

SELECTED FILMS: *Paris Bound, Why Leave Home?, Red Hot Rhythm, South Sea Rose* (1929), *Let's Go Places, The Floradora Girl, On Your Back, Fast and Loose* (1930), *The Gay Diplomat* (1931), *The Animal Kingdom* (1932), *Soak the Rich, The Lady Consents* (1936), *No Time for Love* (1943), *Miss Tatlock's Millions* (1948), *It Should Happen to You* (1954), *Ocean's Eleven* (1960). ∎

Chase as comedy, The. One of the more widely used comic techniques in film. Pioneer filmmakers applied the chase as a laugh-getter early in the history of film comedy. It had already become one of the ploys of melodrama, beginning with the 1903 classic, "The Great Train Robbery." Model Ts, trains, motorcycles—with or without sidecars—airplanes, boats, and any other available vehicles were employed in creative ways. Mack SENNETT'S KEYSTONE KOPS made an art of stumbling into and tumbling out of their police wagon. Every silent comic engaged in some form of chase sequence. Whether it was CHAPLIN in "The Adventurer" being chased by the law or Buster KEATON in "Cops" also being pursued by armies of police officers, the chase was always good for laughs. It played a very important role in Harold LLOYD'S silent and sound comedies. Sometimes the chase is reversed, and the hero becomes the hunter, as in Keaton's classic, *The General*, in which he, almost singlehandedly, goes after a group of Union spies who have stolen his train.

The advent of sound did nothing to slow down the numerous variations of the chase, whether it occupied a major portion of the feature and included a large star-studded cast as in Stanley Kramer's *It's a Mad, Mad, Mad, Mad World*, or a minor segment as in Woody ALLEN'S *Broadway Danny Rose*, in which he is hunted by two hoodlums across New Jersey marshes. The SCREWBALL COMEDIES of the 1930s and 1940s, such as *It Happened One Night* and *Sullivan's Travels*, were not exempt from relying on chase sequences. The chase has become an integral element of most comedy films since it lends itself to suspense, excitement, and visual movement, the last of which provides the necessary comic situations.

Check and Double Check (1930), RKO. *Dir.* Melville Brown; *Sc.* J. Walter Ruben; with Freeman S. Gosden, Charles V. Correll, Sue Carroll, Charles Morton.

AMOS 'N' ANDY were the most famous characters on radio during the 1930s. Millions of Americans would stop whatever they were doing and tune into the radio show starring two white actors, Freeman Gosden and Charles Correll, portraying two blacks. The actors created the pair, at first called Sam 'n' Henry, in 1925. By 1928 they had changed the names to Amos 'n' Andy for their new national radio show. This film, their screen debut, is their only starring one, and not a very good comedy, but their radio fame pushed it to one of the top box-office hits of the year. The studio, unfortunately, supplied them with a script that was so weak and dull that even their vivid characterizations could not improve the film. They also appeared in *The Big Broadcast of 1936* (1935).

the screen in a string of films popular with young audiences.

SELECTED FILMS: Up in Smoke (1978), Cheech and Chong's Next Movie (1980), Cheech and Chong's Nice Dreams (1981), Things Are Tough All Over, It Came From Hollywood (1982), Still Smokin', Yellowbeard (1983), Cheech and Chong's the Corsican Brothers (1984). ■

Cherrill, Virginia (1908–), actress. Had no acting experience when she was chosen by CHAPLIN to play the blind girl with whom he falls in love in *City Lights* (1931). She appeared in a handful of light films during the 1930s before settling in England.

SELECTED FILMS: Girls Demand Excitement, The Brat, Delicious (1931), Fast Workers, The Nuisance, Ladies Must Love, He Couldn't Take It (1933), White Heat (1934). ■

Cheech and Chong

Maurice Chevalier

Cheech and Chong. Irreverent comedy team of the 1970s and 1980s. Richard "Cheech" Marin, born in 1946, and Tommy Chong, born in 1939, first teamed up as a comedy act in the 1960s. Since then they have performed in coffee houses, accompanied rock groups, cut albums, and played concerts. Using burlesque, satire, improvisation, and their particular style of "stoned" comedy, they have brought their offbeat humor to

Chevalier, Maurice (1888–1972), singer, actor. Worked as an acrobat, cafe singer, Folies Bergere entertainer at age 21, and silent film actor in his native France. He became a Hollywood film star during the 1930s. He played debonair, sometimes roguish characters in a string of light films that were always filled with his optimism. Easily recognized by his straw hat, bowtie, and personable smile, the charming and vibrant entertainer gained international success. He returned to the screen occasionally in his later years to charm new generations of moviegoers. He wrote three autobiographies, the last of which, I Remember It Well, was published in 1972.

In The Merry Widow he played a lieutenant in a mythical European kingdom who woos almost every female within reach. In one scene the King catches him with the Queen in her bedroom. "This must be kept out of history," the King says. "Not a soul must know." "Nobody," the Queen quickly responds, "not a soul." Then Chevalier attempts to reassure the King. "We were planning not even to tell your Majesty."

SELECTED FILMS: Innocents of Paris, The Love Parade (1929), The Big Pond, Playboy of Paris (1930), The Smiling Lieutenant (1931), One Hour With You, Love Me Tonight (1932), A Bedtime Story, The Way to Love (1933), The Merry Widow (1934), Gigi (1958), A Breath of Scandal (1960), Fanny (1961), I'd Rather Be Rich (1964), Monkeys, Go Home! (1967). ■

Child comedy stars. Children as main characters have been popular in American films since the early silent days. One of the first and most famous was Mary PICKFORD, who started in films in 1909 at age 16, following her stage appearances. Within a few years she became "America's Sweetheart" and an international celebrity. A charming performer, she starred in hundreds of shorts and features through the 1920s in her long screen career playing youthful roles. BABY GLORIA JOY, another popular child star of the pre-1920s, appeared in a succession of light films, including "No Children Wanted" at about age six, "The Locked Heart," and Little Miss Grown-Up, all released in 1918. She continued to make heartwarming comedies into 1919 and then her career ended abruptly. Another successful child star of the 1920s was BABY PEGGY, who began her screen career in 1917, the same year she was

born, in "A Little Patriot." By the early 1920s the little trouper was a film star in such films as "Peggy Behave" and "Captain January." Another extremely popular little performer was Jackie COOGAN. A discovery of Charlie CHAPLIN, he co-starred with Chaplin in the comedy-drama, The Kid, in 1921, and became an immediate success. Coogan continued to star in films into the early sound period.

The golden age of child comedy stars was the 1930s. The decade provided such notables as the talented Shirley TEMPLE, boisterous Mickey ROONEY, lovable Jackie COOPER, feisty Anne SHIRLEY, the "OUR GANG" members, mischievous Jane WITHERS, impish Virginia WEIDLER, and innocent little BABY LEROY, who vexed W. C. FIELDS in several comedies. Junior Durkin, who began his show business career on stage in the 1920s, appeared in several early sound films in juvenile roles until his untimely death in a car accident in 1935 at age 20.

The 1940s began with the continued career of Mickey Rooney starring in the "ANDY HARDY" comedies for MGM. Another MGM child who brought joy to any film in which he appeared was freckle-faced Jackie "Butch" JENKINS. He almost stole the film The Human Comedy (1943) from Rooney. He was forced to retire from his short screen career of six years when he developed a speech problem. Donald O'CONNOR, like Rooney, appeared in several light films in the late 1930s and continued without interruption into the 1950s. BABY SANDY, who was born in 1938, began her screen career in the late 1930s and had a successful career through the early 1940s in such films as Sandy Is a Lady and Sandy Steps Out.

With the break-up of the studio system, fewer child stars emerged during the next few decades. Some exceptions were Tatum O'NEAL, actor Ryan O'NEAL'S daughter, who captured the hearts of audiences in Paper Moon (1973) and also walked off with an

Academy Award for her role. The only true child star of the 1980s is little Gary COLEMAN, who gained a world of experience during his years in television. But the films in which he starred were mediocre and did little to further his career.

American audiences, always ready to catapult a charming and talented youngster to fame, will have to look elsewhere rather than to Hollywood for the next star. The most likely medium, of course, is television.

Christie, Al (1886–1951), director, producer. Began his film career in 1909 performing various tasks for a film company. His talents in the field of comedy emerged when he directed shorts starring Betty COMPSON and other comics. He then formed his own production company, competing with the two giants in comedy production, Mack SENNETT and Hal ROACH. Although his product did not match the quality of that of his rivals—the sets were shoddier, the performers often rejects of his competitors—his films, which he continued to turn out into the 1930s, were consistently popular at the box office.

While Sennett controlled many of the top comics and Roach had the remaining major and second-string clowns under his roof, Christie had his troop of funnymen. They included Larry SEMON, Lupino LANE, Lloyd HAMILTON, Eddie LYONS, Lee MORAN, Neal BURNS, and Louise FAZENDA during the silent period, and Shemp HOWARD, Billy GILBERT, Marie DRESSLER, Andy CLYDE, and Buster KEATON churning out two-reel comedy shorts during the sound era of the 1930s.

SELECTED FILMS: When the Mummy Cried for Help, All Aboard (1915), Wanted: a Husband, Seminary Scandal (1916), Five Little Widows, Who's Looney Now? (1917), Wedding Blues, The Reckless Sex (1920), See My Lawyer (1921), One Stormy Knight (1922), The Chaste Bride (1923), Love, Bright Lights (1924), Hot Doggie (1925), Meet the Folks (1927), Divorce Made Easy (1929). ∎

Christine, Virginia (1917–), actress. Began her Hollywood screen career in the early 1940s. A spirited blonde actress who never advanced to major roles, she played leads and second leads, often as working-girl types, in numerous minor dramas and light films.

SELECTED FILMS: Women at War (1942), Idea Girl (1946), Never Wave at a WAC, The First Time (1952), Good Morning, Miss Dove (1955), Four for Texas (1963), Guess Who's Coming to Dinner (1967), Hail, Hero! (1969). ∎

Christy, Dorothy (1906–), actress. Appeared in many light films and dramas in the 1930s and 1940s, often as a character performer. Although she played in many B movies, she also supported many comics as well as other major stars, some of whom include LAUREL AND HARDY, Maurice CHEVALIER, and Shirley TEMPLE.

SELECTED FILMS: So This Is London, Playboy of Paris (1930), Parlor, Bedroom and Bath, Caught Cheating (1931), Union Depot (1932), Only Yesterday (1933), Sons of the Desert, Bright Eyes (1934), The Daring Young Man (1935), Woman Against Woman (1938), Junior Miss (1945), The Magnificent Rogue (1946), Fighting Back (1948), So Big (1953). ∎

Churchill, Berton (1876–1940), actor. Worked on stage in his native Canada and on Broadway before settling in Hollywood. A prolific character actor with a heavy-set frame and an uncompromising expression, he was often cast as a strict father or hard-nosed businessman. He appeared in more than a hundred dramas and light films during the silent period and the 1930s.

SELECTED FILMS: Six Cylinder Love (1923), Nothing but the Truth (1929), Cabin in the Cotton, The Rich Are Al-

ways With Us, If I Had a Million (1932), The Little Giant (1933), Dames, Kid Millions (1934), Steamboat 'Round the Bend (1935), Dimples (1936), The Singing Marine (1937), Sweethearts (1938), The Way of All Flesh, Turnabout (1940). ■

City Lights (1931), UA. *Dir.* Charlie Chaplin; *Sc.* Charlie Chaplin; with Charlie Chaplin, Virginia Cherrill, Florence Lee, Harry Myers, Hank Mann, Henry Bergman.

Although made during the sound era, the comedy was basically a silent film with a few sound effects. To make the story of mutual romance involving Charlie the Tramp more plausible, Chaplin arranged for the object of his affection to be a blind flower girl. The situation had been used previously with another comic. Harry Langdon, in *The Strong Man* (1926), played a World War I soldier who comes home to look for his pen-pal love whom he doesn't know is blind. But Chaplin's version develops its emotional and pathetic aspects more fully, to the last tearful scene when the girl's eyesight is restored and she sees him for the first time. The comedy contains numerous classic scenes, including Charlie asleep on a statue about to be unveiled; a rich companion who, only when he is drunk, acknowledges the Tramp; Charlie at a gala party where he swallows a whistle (one of his several scenes utilizing the creative use of sound); and his misadventures as a challenger in a boxing match. With this entry, one of his best films, Chaplin proved that silent films, with controlled and creative sound effects, could compete with the new talkies. He had trouble with his female lead during the shooting. He discovered Cherrill, who had no acting experience. But he thought she was a natural for the role. However, she was unable to respond appropriately during sensitive and emotional scenes. Chaplin dismissed her, but was forced to re-hire her when production fell behind schedule while expenses mounted. Re-released in the 1950s in major theaters around the country, the film drew large crowds as a new generation was able to appreciate the remarkable talents of one of the greatest screen comedians of all time.

Claire, Ina (1892–1985), actress. A vaudeville and musical comedy performer since 1909. She appeared briefly in films in 1915 before returning to the stage. In 1929 she again appeared on screen in comedy feature films, plying her comedic talents.

SELECTED FILMS: Wild Goose Chase, The Puppet Crown (1915), Polly With a Past (1920), The Awful Truth (1929), The Royal Family of Broadway, Rebound (1931), The Greeks Had a Word for Them (1932), Ninotchka (1939), Stage Door Canteen, Claudia (1943). ■

Clark, Bobby. See Clark and McCullough.

Clark, Eddie (1879–1954), actor. Worked on stage before entering silent films in the 1920s. He appeared as a supporting player in dramas and light films, including comedy shorts, during a screen career that spanned four decades. He was also a television performer and a screenwriter.

SELECTED FILMS (as actor): Millionaires, Private Izzy Murphy (1926), The Gay Old Bird, Sally in Our Alley, Hills of Kentucky (1927), Marriage by Contract (1928), Silks and Saddles (1929), Bitter Friends (1930), Oh, You Beautiful Doll (1949), Dancing in the Dark, Pretty Girl (1950), Little Egypt, Bedtime for Bonzo, Mr. Belvedere Rings the Bell, Rhubarb (1951), It Happens Every Thursday (1953), Crashout (1955). ■

Clark, Fred (1914–1968), actor. A versatile character player who was effective in serious and comic roles. Easily recognized by his baldness, he was often

Gary Crosby (left), Fred Clark (center), and
Larry Blyden (right)

cast as an underworld character or hyperactive executive. He appeared in over 50 films, at times as the suspicious and explosive father attempting to protect his daughter from unworthy beaux.

SELECTED FILMS: *Ride the Pink Horse* (1947), *Mr. Peabody and the Mermaid* (1948), *The Lady Takes a Sailor* (1949), *Sunset Boulevard* (1950), *The Lemon Drop Kid* (1951), *Three for Bedroom C, Dreamboat* (1952), *The Caddy* (1953), *Living It Up* (1954), *Daddy Long Legs* (1955), *The Solid Gold Cadillac* (1956), *Don't Go Near the Water* (1957), *Auntie Mame* (1958), *The Mating Game* (1959), *Visit to a Small Planet* (1960), *Move Over, Darling* (1963), *Eve* (1969). ■

Clark, Harvey (1886–1938), actor. Came to films in 1916 following a vaudeville and stage career. He appeared chiefly as a supporting player in dramas and light films for three decades. He worked with several major comedians, including, among others, LAUREL AND HARDY and WHEELER AND WOOLSEY.

SELECTED FILMS: *The Innocence of Lizette, The Voice of Love* (1916), *New York Luck, Snap Judgment* (1917), *High Gear Jeffrey, Her Face Value* (1921), *Alias Julius Caesar, Elope If You Must* (1922), *The Roughnecks* (1924), *The Arizona Romeo* (1925), *Putting Pants on Phillip* (1927), *Ladies' Night in a Turkish Bath, Beautiful but Dumb* (1928), *His Lucky Day* (1929), *What a Man* (1930), *Cracked Nuts* (1931), *Peck's Bad Boy*

(1934), *It's Love I'm After* (1937), *Mother Carey's Chickens* (1938). ■

Clark, Johnny (1916–1967), actor. Worked on stage before entering films as a supporting player in the early 1940s. He appeared in dramas and light films and continued his acting career in television.

SELECTED FILMS: *Las Vegas Nights* (1941), *Jive Junction* (1943), *Hey Rookie, Weekend Pass, The Sultan's Daughter, Irish Eyes Are Smiling* (1944), *The Locket* (1947). ■

Clark, Marguerite (1883–1940), actress. Entered early silent films in 1914 following a brief stage career. A diminutive, pretty actress with dark hair, she starred in numerous light films, particularly romantic comedies. She signed a five-year contract with Famous Players in 1914 for $1,000 per week, but by the last year was earning more than five times that amount. Her role in *Snow White* was so natural and effective that Walt Disney, many years later, used her interpretation as the basis for his animated color version, *Snow White and the Seven Dwarfs* (1937). Like her competitor, Mary PICKFORD, she played youthful roles for years and although quite popular, never attained the success of her rival. She retired from the screen in 1921.

SELECTED FILMS: *Wildflower* (1914), *The Goose Girl* (1915), *Mice and Men, Molly Make Believe, Silk and Satins, Miss George Washington, Snow White* (1916), *The Fortunes of Fifi, The Valentine Girl, Bab's Diary, Bab's Matinee Idol* (1917), *Rich Man, Poor Man, Little Miss Hoover* (1918), *Three Men and a Girl, Come Out of the Kitchen* (1919), *Easy to Get, All of a Sudden Peggy* (1920), *Scrambled Wives* (1921). ■

Clark, Wallis (1889–1961), actor. Worked as a supporting player in Hollywood from the early 1930s. Originally from England, he appeared in numerous dramas and light films.

SELECTED FILMS: *Okay America, My Pal the King, The Night Mayor (1932), Double Harness, Lady for a Day, They Just Had to Get Married, The Working Man (1933), It Happened One Night, The Life of Vergie Winters, I'll Fix It (1934), It Happened in New York (1935), The Unguarded Hour, Come Closer Folks, Easy Money (1936), The Last of Mrs. Cheyney, Big Business, She Had to Eat (1937), The Higgins Family (1938), Blondie Meets the Boss (1939).* ∎

Clark and McCullough. A popular vaudeville and movie comedy team of the 1930s. Bobby Clark (1888–1960) teamed up with his childhood buddy Paul McCullough (1884–1936) in 1900. They worked at odd jobs in a traveling minstrel show, a circus, as comedians in vaudeville in 1912, in burlesque in 1917, and in musical comedy revues in 1922.

By 1928 they were invited to Hollywood by Fox studios where they adapted their comedy routines for a series of one-reelers. Clark continued the use of his trademark, painted-on horn-rimmed glasses. Other props were also utilized. Clark carried a cane and wore oversized clothes, while his partner often wore a fur coat and a derby. Dissatisfied with their Hollywood experience, they returned to Broadway. But by 1931 they were back in films, this time starring in two-reelers for RKO. Saturated with slapstick, sight gags, rapid-fire dialogue, and the duo's lunatic antics, the series, which ran until 1935, was generally successful. Much of their comedy is reminiscent of those of other teams. Clark's use of insult humor, his rapid delivery, and his duck-like walk remind the viewer of the style of Groucho MARX. McCullough's puns are not unlike those of Chico. At other times they are similar to LAUREL AND HARDY, at least in visual appearance: Clark is thin and his partner is fleshy; McCullough, like Hardy, wears a derby and a small mustache.

The team was doing fairly well by the mid-1930s, but McCullough, nervous and distraught, committed suicide in 1936. Clark returned to the stage following a few months' seclusion and made only one more film, *The Goldwyn Follies* (1938).

One of their RKO shorts, "Love and Hisses" (1934), is a good example of their comedy style. Asleep on their employer's desk, they are awakened when their boss hits them across their feet with a cane. "Just because we're working for you," the indignant Clark remarks, "doesn't mean you can trifle with my sole." Later in the film Clark wonders out loud: "What causes the water in watermelon?" McCullough is quick to reply. "They plant the seeds in the spring."

SELECTED FILMS: *Clark and McCullough in the Honor System (1928), The Bath Between, The Diplomats (1929), False Roomers, Scratch as Scratch Can (1931), The Iceman's Ball, The Millionaire Cat, Jitters the Butler, The Gay Nighties (1932), The Druggist's Dilemma, Snug in the Jug (1933), Hey Nanny Nanny, Bedlam of Beards, Love and Hisses, Odor in the Court (1934), Flying Down to Zero, Alibi Bye Bye (1935).* ∎

Clarke, Mae (1907–), actress. Appeared as a cabaret dancer while still a teenager and in musical comedies and dramas before entering films in 1929. A saucy performer, she played leads in dramas and light films through the 1930s. She had the dubious distinction of being part of a classic film scene. She played the hapless mistress of James CAGNEY who slaps her in the face with half a grapefruit in *Public Enemy* (1931). After appearing in a string of B pictures, she was relegated chiefly to minor roles.

SELECTED FILMS: *Big Time, Nix on Dames (1929), The Front Page, The Good Bad Girl (1931), The Impatient Maiden (1932), Made on Broadway (1933), Let's Talk It Over (1934), The Daring Young Man (1935), Here Come the Waves*

(1944), Annie Get Your Gun (1950), Singin' in the Rain (1952), Ask Any Girl (1959), A Big Hand for the Little Lady (1966), Thoroughly Modern Millie (1967), Watermelon Man (1970).

Clayton, Ethel (1884–1966), actress. Began her long career in films in 1910, appearing in one-reel comedies for Essanay studios. She reached stardom in the 1920s, playing in melodramas, and continued working into the 1930s as a character player.

SELECTED FILMS: Art and Honor, When the Earth Trembled (1913), The Lion and the Mouse (1914), The College Widow, Mazie Puts One Over (1915), Husband and Wife (1916), Easy Money, Whims of Society (1918), Maggie Pepper (1919), Sunny Side Up, His New York Wife (1926), The Princess From Hoboken (1927), Hit the Deck, The Call of the Circus (1930), Artists and Models (1937), Ambush (1939). ■

Clemens, William B. (1905–), director. Began his career in films in the 1930s as an editor before switching his talents to directing. He turned out many low-budget light films, although his forte lay in the mystery and detective genre, including the "Torchy Blane" and "Falcon" series. Even these crime vehicles suggested his flair for comedy.

SELECTED FILMS: Man Hunt, Down the Stretch, Here Comes Carter! (1936), The Footloose Heiress (1937), Accidents Will Happen, Mr. Chump (1938), The Dead End Kids on Dress Parade (1939), She Couldn't Say No (1941), A Night in New Orleans, Sweater Girl (1942), Lady Bodyguard (1943), The Thirteenth Hour (1947). ■

Clements, Stanley (1926–1981), actor. Began his Hollywood screen career in the early 1940s in youthful roles and continued in that capacity for several years. He played young toughs, bullies, and other assorted adolescent types. He appeared in some of the "BOWERY BOYS" comedies, eventually replacing Leo GORCEY in the series.

SELECTED FILMS: Accent on Love (1941), Smart Alecks, On the Sunny Side, 'Neath Brooklyn Bridge, They Got Me Covered (1942), The More the Merrier, Ghosts on the Loose, Thank Your Lucky Stars (1943), Cover Girl (1944), See My Lawyer (1945), Army Bound, Off Limits (1952), Hot Shots, Hold That Hypnotist (1956), Spook Chasers (1957), Tammy and the Doctor (1963), The Timber Tramp (1973). ■

Cleveland, George (1883–1957), actor. Had a busy career on the stage before entering films in the early 1930s. He made well over 100 features, many of which were westerns, as well as serials (e.g., Flash Gordon). A reliable character actor with a twinkle in his eye and a grey mustache, he usually portrayed crotchety but basically amiable fathers, grandfathers, or old-timers.

SELECTED FILMS: Girl o' My Dreams (1934), His Night Out (1935), Don't Get Personal (1936), Swing It Professor! (1937), Rose of the Rio Grande (1938), Streets of New York (1939), Chasing Trouble (1940), Playmates (1941), My Favorite Spy (1942), Klondike Kate, Cowboy in Manhattan (1943), Abroad With Two Yanks (1944), It's in the Bag (1945), Angel on My Shoulder (1946), The Wistful Widow of Wagon Gap (1947), A Date With Judy (1948), Walking My Baby Back Home (1953), Racing Blood (1954). ■

Cline, Eddie (1892–1961), director. Began his long career in films as a Keystone Kop for SENNETT. He soon was directing comedies for Sennett as well as for other studios, both two-reelers and features. He worked with some of the greatest comedians of the silent and sound periods, including, among others, Buster KEATON, Andy CLYDE, Ben TURPIN, Mae WEST, and W. C. FIELDS.

His contributions as Keaton's director on more than a dozen films may not have been that extensive. Cline was an easygoing soul who got along very well with the comic, and this close relationship may have been responsible for some of the shortcomings in the comedies. Others close to Keaton believe he needed a firmer director, especially in his early period. Cline's work with Fields, however, was another story. He was strongly in control of the comedian's films and was responsible to a great extent for their success.

SELECTED FILMS: The Winning Punch, His Busted Trust (1916), A Bedroom Blunder, That Night (1917), The Kitchen Lady, Hide and Seek Detective (1918), Cupid's Day Off (1919), One Week, Neighbors (1920), Hard Luck, The Boat (1921), The Paleface, Cops, The Frozen North (1922), The Balloonatic (1923), Along Came Ruth (1924), The Rag Man, Old Clothes (1925), A Harem Knight, A Blonde's Revenge (1926), Soft Cushions (1927), Man Crazy (1928), The Forward Pass (1929), Sweet Mama (1930), Cracked Nuts (1931), Million Dollar Legs (1932), Peck's Bad Boy (1934), My Little Chickadee, The Bank Dick (1940), Never Give a Sucker an Even Break (1941), Private Buckaroo (1942), Crazy House (1943), Bringing Up Father (1946). ■

Cluny Brown (1946), TCF. Dir. Ernst Lubitsch; Sc. Samuel Hoffenstein, Elizabeth Reinhardt; with Charles Boyer, Jennifer Jones, Peter Lawford, Helen Walker, Reginald Gardiner.

This was LUBITSCH'S last complete work before his death the following year. That Lady in Ermine (1948) lists him as its director, but Otto PREMINGER completed the film. Cluny Brown is a fitting tribute to the great director, for it carries his stamp of quality, wit, and mischief. He managed to slip some sexual innuendos related to plumbing into the script and past the Code office. Jennifer Jones plays the title character, who is a plumber, in this satirical romantic com-

edy set in pre-World War II rural England. Charles Boyer, as an anti-fascist European who has fled the continent to escape assassination, encourages Cluny to defy social customs. There are delightful performances by a host of talented comic character players. Richard HAYDN portrays a prissy, overbearing druggist dominated by his mother, played by Una O'Connor. Lubitsch entertainingly satirizes English snobbery as he depicts the prejudices of each social class, including labor and several foolish liberals, while Cluny the plumber refuses to "know her place." The film was based on a novel by Margery Sharp.

Clute, Chester (1891–1956), actor. Began his film career in the 1930s in two-reel comedies. A pint-sized character actor sporting a surprised expression and a small mustache, he specialized in portraying petty, crotchety fussbudgets or abused husbands.

SELECTED FILMS: Exclusive (1937), Annabel Takes a Tour, Rascals (1938), Hired Wife (1940), She Couldn't Say No, Sun Valley Serenade (1941), The Man Who Came to Dinner, My Favorite Spy (1942), Chatterbox, Crazy House (1943), Rationing, Arsenic and Old Lace (1944), Anchors Aweigh, Mildred Pierce (1945), Cinderella Jones (1946), Winner Take All (1948), Kentucky Jubilee (1951), Colorado Sundown (1952). ■

Clyde, Andy (1892–1967), actor. Appeared in more than 100 two-reelers and feature-length films, especially westerns, often portraying crusty oldtimers. He worked in silent films assisting comic Billy BEVAN and made many shorts for Mack SENNETT. He later played California Carlson, Hoppy's sidekick, in a few Hopalong Cassidy films.

SELECTED FILMS: His New Mama (1924), Should a Girl Marry? (1928), Midnight Daddies (1930), Million Dollar Legs (1932), The Little Minister (1934), Annie Oakley (1935), Straight From the Shoulder (1936), It's a Wonderful World

Andy Clyde (right) and William Boyd

(1939), *Abe Lincoln in Illinois* (1940), *This Above All* (1942), *Roughly Speaking* (1945), *The Green Years* (1946), *Abilene Trail* (1951), *Gunslingers* (1950), *The Road to Denver* (1955). ∎

Coates, Phyllis (1927–), actress. Entered films in the late 1940s as a supporting player in a series of comedy shorts, "JOE McDOAKES," directed by her first husband, Richard L. Bare. She then moved to low-budget comedies and westerns while still appearing in shorts. She eventually found her forte in serials such as *Jungle Drums of Africa* (1952) as this genre entered its final years. She is considered the "last of the serial queens." She has also had a successful television career.

SELECTED FILMS: So You Want to Be in Politics (1948), *So You're Having In-Law Trouble* (1949), *Blues Busters* (1950), *So You Want to Be a Cowboy, So You Want to Buy a Used Car, So You Want to Be a Bachelor, So You Want to Be a Plumber* (1951), *So You Want to Get It Wholesale, So You're Going to a Convention, So You Want to Wear the Pants* (1952), *So Your Wife Wants to Work* (1956). ∎

Cobb, Irwin S. (1876–1944), humorous writer, actor. Worked as reporter, editor, and contributor to magazines. Some of his plays and novels, especially his Judge Priest stories, were adapted for the screen. He appeared occasionally as a character actor in silent and sound films, and was often thought of as another Will ROGERS.

SELECTED FILMS (as actor): The Arab (1915), *Pardon My French* (1921), *The Five Dollar Baby* (1922), *The Great White Way* (1924), *Turkish Delight* (1927), *Steamboat 'Round the Bend* (1935), *Everybody's Old Man, Pepper* (1936), *Hawaii Calls, The Young in Heart, The Arkansas Traveler* (1938). ∎

Cobb, Joe. One of the members of the popular "OUR GANG" comedy series produced by Hal ROACH. The fat, personable Cobb was not one of the original kids who appeared in the first comedy short, called "Our Gang," but was introduced in the second "wave." During another major change in 1929, Cobb, who outgrew the role, was replaced by Norman "Chubby" CHANEY. Cobb appeared in other roles with some of the leading performers of the period, including Charley CHASE.

SELECTED FILMS: The Champeen, The Big Show, A Pleasant Journey, Dogs of War (1923), *The Trouble, Big Business, The Buccaneers, Seein' Things, The Fraidy Cat, Young Oldfield, Girl Shy* (1924), *The Big Town, Circus Fever, Dog Days, The Love Bug* (1925), *Shivering Spooks, The Fourth Alarm* (1926), *Where Did You Get That Girl?* (1941). ∎

Coburn, Charles (1877–1961), actor. Appeared on Broadway as early as 1901 but did not come to films until the 1930s. Sporting his trademark, a monocle, he usually played tough businessmen with soft hearts. He portrayed both comic and ruthless characters. He won an Oscar as Best Supporting Actor for his role in *The More the Merrier* (1943).

In *The Lady Eve* he played a sophisticated con man. He reminds his daughter (Barbara Stanwyck) that standards must be maintained: "Let us be crooked but never common."

SELECTED FILMS: Boss Tweed (1933), *The People's Enemy* (1935), *Vivacious*

Lady (1938), *Idiot's Delight, Bachelor Mother, In Name Only* (1939), *Road to Singapore, The Captain Is a Lady* (1940), *The Lady Eve, The Devil and Miss Jones* (1941), *Kings Row, George Washington Slept Here* (1942), *The Constant Nymph* (1943), *Knickerbocker Holiday* (1944), *A Royal Scandal* (1945), *Colonel Effingham's Raid* (1946), *Everybody Does It* (1949), *Peggy* (1950), *Monkey Business* (1952), *Gentlemen Prefer Blondes* (1953), *How to Murder a Rich Uncle* (1957), *Pepe* (1960). ∎

Coburn, Dorothy, actress. Worked as supporting actress for Hal ROACH'S studios. She appeared in silent comedy shorts during the late 1920s, especially in LAUREL AND HARDY films.

SELECTED FILMS: *Do Detectives Think?, Flying Elephants, Sailor, Beware!, Sugar Daddies, The Second Hundred Years, Hats Off, Putting Pants on Philip, The Battle of the Century* (1927), *Leave 'Em Laughing, The Finishing Touch, From Soup to Nuts, Should Men Go Home?* (1928). ∎

Coca, Imogene (1908–), comedienne, actress. Worked in a Broadway chorus at age 15, and as a comedienne in the 1930s in the revue, *New Faces of 1934.* She appeared in several musical comedies and other revues, but her greatest success came as Sid CAESAR'S co-star in the television series, "Your Show of Shows." A diminutive and zany performer, she equaled his antics and got as many laughs as he did. Although she has appeared in a few films and has had her own television show, she has not been able to recapture the fame she knew when she accompanied Caesar.

SELECTED FILMS: *Under the Yum Yum Tree* (1963), *Rabbit Test* (1978), *National Lampoon's Vacation* (1983), *Nothing Lasts Forever* (1985). ∎

Cockeyed Cavaliers (1934), RKO. Dir. Mark Sandrich; Sc. Edward Kaufman, Ben Holmes; with Bert Wheeler,

Robert Woolsey, Thelma Todd, Dorothy Lee, Noah Beery.

Wheeler and Woolsey were a minor but popular comedy team in a medium dominated by such giants as LAUREL AND HARDY, the MARX BROTHERS, and BURNS AND ALLEN. Probably their best feature comedy, this film gives the duo an opportunity to display their comic talent in a 17th-century English setting. Wheeler, who plays a kleptomaniac, continually causes problems for his buddy as well as for himself. Finally, Woolsey suggests, "Take something for it!" "I've already taken everything," replies Wheeler. Mistaken for the King's physicians, they crash into society and cause their usual brand of havoc. The boys look good in costume and provide plenty of laughs. One especially witty scene parodies Greta Garbo in her male-impersonation sequence from *Queen Christina.* Several veteran comedians, including Billy GILBERT, Snub POLLARD, and Franklin PANGBORN, give ample support to this entertaining comedy.

Coco, James (1929–1987), actor. Worked on the stage since 1957 and made his film debut in 1964. A roly-poly character actor, he usually portrayed humorous and eccentric types.

SELECTED FILMS: *Ensign Pulver* (1964), *Generation* (1969), *The Strawberry Statement, Tell Me That You Love Me, Junie Moon* (1970), *A New Leaf, Such Good Friends* (1971), *Man of La Mancha* (1972), *The Wild Party* (1975), *Murder by Death* (1976), *Bye, Bye Monkey, The Cheap Detective, Charleston* (1978). ∎

Cocoanuts, The (1929), PAR. Dir. Robert Florey, Joseph Santley; Sc. George S. Kaufman; with Groucho, Harpo, Chico, Zeppo Marx, Mary Eaton, Kay Francis, Margaret Dumont.

The MARX BROTHERS had been playing on Broadway in their successful *Animal Crackers* when Paramount invited them to film their previous stage hit, *The Cocoanuts*, at its Astoria studio in Long Island. Only minutes from Times Square, the studio afforded many Broadway stars an opportunity to appear in silent films during the 1920s. Although the film, the Brothers' first screen appearance, simply looks stagey, the boys succeeded in bringing their unique brand of chaotic comedy to the screen. As in all their features to follow, Groucho provides the wisecracks and insults, Harpo supplies the offbeat pantomime, and Chico does his Italian dialect comedy. Zeppo, always awkward within the comic framework involving his brothers, plays straight man to them. The film contains several of their famous routines, including the viaduct, auction, and Kay Francis-bedroom scenes. The dependable pillar of society, Margaret DUMONT, plays foil to Groucho's eccentric courtship. "Just think," Groucho coos to Dumont, "tonight, tonight when the moon is sneaking around the clouds, I'll be sneaking around you. I'll meet you tonight under the moon. Oh, I can see you now—you and the moon. You wear a necktie so I'll know you." Unfortunately, the musical interludes intrude upon the antics of the madcap brothers.

Codee, Ann (1890–1961), actress. Worked in vaudeville before entering films in the early 1930s. She co-starred with her husband, Frank ORTH, in a series of comedy shorts and then moved on to feature-length films, chiefly light vehicles.

SELECTED FILMS: *Under the Pampas Moon* (1935), *Hi, Gaucho!* (1936), *Expensive Husbands* (1938), *Come Live With Me* (1941), *Bathing Beauty* (1944), *Holiday in Mexico* (1946), *That Midnight Kiss* (1949), *Mr. Imperium, On the Riviera, The Lady Pays Off* (1951), *Kiss Me Kate* (1953), *Daddy Long Legs* (1955), *Can-Can* (1960). ∎

Cogley, Nick (1869–1936), actor, director. Worked in early silent comedies for Mack SENNETT'S KEYSTONE stu-

dios. He appeared as a principal player in one- or two-reelers and as supporting player to many of the top comics of the period, including, among others, Mabel NORMAND, "Fatty" ARBUCKLE, and Chester CONKLIN.

SELECTED FILMS: *Mabel's Heroes, The Speed Queen, Mother's Day* (1913), *Peanuts and Bullets, A Lucky Leap, Saved by Wireless, Dizzy Heights and Daring Hearts* (1915), *A la Cabaret, Dollars and Sense* (1916), *Her Circus Knight* (1917), *Toby's Bow* (1919), *Jes' Call Me Jim* (1920), *In Old Kentucky* (1927), *Abie's Irish Rose* (1928), *The Cohens and Kellys in Africa* (1930), *Cross-Fire* (1933). ∎

Cohan, George M. (1878–1942), actor, singer, playwright, producer, etc. A famous Broadway talent and personality who appeared occasionally in light films as early as the 1910s. A few of his plays have been adapted for the screen and he has written several screenplays. He was portrayed on screen by James Cagney in *Yankee Doodle Dandy* in 1942.

SELECTED FILMS: *Broadway Jones, Seven Keys to Baldpate* (1917), *Hit-the-Trail Haliday* (1918), *The Phantom President* (1932), *Gambling* (1934). ∎

"Cohen comedies." A series of early silent shorts produced by Mack SENNETT'S KEYSTONE studios. The comedies starred Ford STERLING as the title character and were supported by such comics from Sennett's stock players as Fred MACE. The films alternated between a half-reel and one reel in length and usually portrayed Cohen as a coward who somehow manages to survive unfavorable circumstances. The comedies, often crudely executed and heavily reliant upon slapstick, stereotyped the main character.

SELECTED FILMS: *Cohen Collects a Debt* (1912), *Cohen's Outing, Cohen Saves the Flag* (1913). ∎

"Cohens and the Kellys." A popular comedy series about a Jew and an Irishman starring George SIDNEY as Cohen and Charlie MURRAY as Kelly. These domestic farces were produced by Universal studios. The first entry, *The Cohens and the Kellys* (1926), a silent feature, was so successful that several sequels followed right into the sound era. The films specialized in low comedy and sentimentalism as the title characters and their families became entangled in nonsensical brawls. The role of Kelly was played by various actors.

SELECTED FILMS: *The Cohens and the Kellys in Paris* (1928), *The Cohens and the Kellys in Atlantic City* (1929), *The Cohens and the Kellys in Scotland, The Cohens and the Kellys in Africa* (1930), *The Cohens and the Kellys in Hollywood* (1932), *The Cohens and the Kellys in Trouble* (1933). ∎

Colbert, Claudette (1905–), actress. Appeared on stage in 1923 and in films in 1927. Born in Paris, she was sent to the United States at age nine to be educated. A pretty actress with a sparkling personality, she specialized in sophisticated comedy after playing various roles in the early 1930s. Her performance in *The Smiling Lieutenant* (1931), starring Maurice CHEVALIER, was highly lauded by the critics and the public and helped to propel her to stardom. Her popularity extended into the 1950s, after which she occasionally returned to the stage. She played the attractive, strong-willed, but vulnerable heroine, co-starring with some of the top actors. Fred MacMURRAY often played her leading man. She won an Academy Award as Best Actress for her portrayal of the runaway heiress in *It Happened One Night* (1934).

In *The Palm Beach Story* she enlightens her husband, Joel McCrea, who considers himself a financial failure: "Men don't get smarter as they grow older. They just lose their hair."

SELECTED FILMS: *For the Love of Mike* (1927), *The Lady Lies* (1929), *Man-slaughter* (1930), *Honor Among Lovers, The Smiling Lieutenant* (1931), *The Wiser Sex, The Misleading Lady* (1932), *Tonight Is Ours* (1933), *Cleopatra, Imitation of Life* (1934), *The Gilded Lily, The Bride Comes Home* (1935), *I Met Him in Paris, Tovarich* (1937), *Bluebeard's Eighth Wife* (1938), *Midnight* (1939), *The Palm Beach Story* (1942), *Guest Wife* (1945), *Without Reservations* (1946), *The Egg and I* (1947), *Family Honeymoon* (1949), *Let's Make It Legal* (1951), *Texas Lady* (1955), *Parrish* (1961). ∎

Coleman, Charles (1885–1951), actor. Migrated from Australia to Hollywood to appear in silent and sound films as the perennial butler. A plump character player, he appeared chiefly in light films which starred some of the leading comics of the period, including Leon ERROL, W. C. FIELDS, and MARTIN AND LEWIS.

SELECTED FILMS: *Big Dan* (1923), *That's My Daddy* (1928), *Bachelor Apartment* (1931), *The Heart of New York* (1932), *Diplomaniacs* (1933), *Down to Their Last Yacht* (1934), *The Poor Little Rich Girl* (1936), *Three Smart Girls* (1937), *First Love, Mexican Spitfire, You Can't Cheat an Honest Man* (1939), *It Started With Eve* (1941), *Design for Scandal* (1942), *Kitty, Cluny Brown* (1946), *Trouble Makers* (1948), *My Friend Irma* (1949). ∎

Coleman, Dabney (1932–), actor. Talented character actor, usually in light films, who worked his way up from bit roles in the 1960s to second leads. He played a romantic part in *How to Beat the High Cost of Living* and a dual role in *Cloak and Dagger*. He specializes in neurotic characters. Perhaps his strongest and most hilarious role was as the antifeminist employer in *9 to 5*.

SELECTED FILMS: *The Slender Thread* (1965), *This Property Is Condemned* (1966), *The Trouble With Girls* (1969), *I Love My Wife* (1970), *North Dallas Forty* (1979), *Nothing Personal, How to Beat the High Cost of Living,*

Melvin and Howard, 9 to 5 (1980), Modern Problems (1981), Tootsie (1982), Cloak and Dagger, The Muppets Take Manhattan (1984), The Man With One Red Shoe (1985). ■

Coleman, Frank J., actor. Worked in early silent films, especially as a supporting player in fourteen comedy shorts starring Charlie CHAPLIN, ten of which were produced by Mutual studios. A versatile performer, he portrayed various characters, including gypsies, policemen, and restaurant owners.

SELECTED FILMS: The Bank (1915), Carmen, Police!, The Fireman, The Count, The Pawnshop, Behind the Screen, The Rink (1916), Easy Street, The Cure, The Immigrant, The Adventurer (1917). ■

Coleman, Gary (1968–), child actor. Pint-sized precocious young actor with vast experience in television. A charming little performer, he made his film debut in 1981 with little fanfare. He has not been as successful in films as he has been in television.

SELECTED FILMS: On the Right Track (1981), Jimmy the Kid (1983). ■

College. See Buster Keaton.

College humor. See Campus comedy.

"Collegians, The." A series of silent comedy-drama shorts produced by Universal studios depicting the deeds of a young innocent who wins an athletic scholarship. Actor George LEWIS portrayed the hayseed who experiences the rites of passage on the college campus. Pretty Dorothy GULLIVER played his girl friend who happens to be the dean's daughter, while Edward Phillips, as the hero's foil, was the "wise-guy" who gets his come-uppance.

The series, which began in 1926 with "Benson at Calford" and ran through 1929, was directed by some of the best comedy directors of the time, including, among others, Wesley RUGGLES and Harry EDWARDS. Edwards turned out some of the finest shorts of Harry LANGDON, Ben TURPIN, and Billy BEVAN. "Around the Bases," another 1926 entry in the series, concerns college baseball.

Collier, Constance (1878–1955), actress. Appeared on stage in her native England before entering silent films in the United States in 1916. She turned to supporting roles in the 1930s and 1940s. She portrayed stately matrons, frequently with a sharp tongue, in both comedies and dramas.

SELECTED FILMS: Intolerance, Macbeth (1916), Dinner at Eight (1933), Shadow of Doubt (1935), Girls' Dormitory, Little Lord Fauntleroy (1936), Wee Willie Winkie, Stage Door, A Damsel in Distress, She Got What She Wanted (1937), Half a Sinner (1940), Kitty, Week-End at the Waldorf (1945), Monsieur Beaucaire (1946), The Perils of Pauline (1947), The Girl From Manhattan (1948), Whirlpool (1949). ■

Collier, William (1866–1944), actor, writer. Appeared in many stage comedies, becoming a Broadway star by 1890. He made his film debut in Mack SENNETT'S comedy shorts. He continued to work in sound features as a light character actor. He wrote several plays that were eventually adapted to the screen.

SELECTED FILMS: Fatty and the Broadway Stars (1915), Plain Jane (1916), The Servant Question (1920), Free and Easy, Up the River (1930), Mr. Lemon of Orange (1931), Hot Saturday (1932), The Bride Comes Home (1935), Love on a Bet, Cain and Mabel (1936), Thanks for the Memory (1938), Invitation to Happiness (1939), The Hard-Boiled Canary (1941). ■

Collins, Eddie (1884–1940), actor. Appeared in vaudeville before his film debut in 1938. Short in stature, with a very expressive face, he played character parts in a handful of features. He is probably best remembered for his portrayal of Shirley TEMPLE'S dog, Tylo, in The Blue Bird (1940).

SELECTED FILMS: In Old Chicago, Sally, Irene and Mary, Penrod and His Twin Brother, Alexander's Ragtime Band, Always in Trouble, Kentucky Moonshine (1938), Charlie Chan in Reno, Young Mr. Lincoln, Stop, Look and Love, Quick Millions, Hollywood Cavalcade, Drums Along the Mohawk (1939), The Return of Frank James (1940). ■

Collins, Monty (–1951), actor. A versatile supporting actor from the early sound period through the 1940s. A tall, slender foil character, he appeared in numerous comedy shorts and features with some of the leading comics and comedy teams of the period, including the THREE STOOGES, CLARK AND McCULLOUGH, WHEELER AND WOOLSEY, and the two-reelers of Thelma TODD. He often wrote comedy material for the above stars.

The comedy short, "Love and Hisses" (1934), starring Clark and McCullough, offers a prime example of how he was used as the butt of the duo's humor. When Collins, as a dapper butler, answers the door to let Clark in, Clark pins the "Welcome" doormat on the rear of Collins' uniform; later, the uninvited guest quips, "Don't sit down or you'll wear out your welcome."

SELECTED FILMS: Peach O'Reno (1931), Girl Crazy, Hold 'Em Jail, Hollywood Handicap, Show Business, The Gay Nighties (1932), I'm No Angel (1933), Love and Hisses (1934), Three Missing Links (1938), The Gracie Allen Murder Case (1939), A-Plumbing We Will Go (1940), Some More of Samoa (1941), Cactus Makes Perfect, Matri-Phony (1942). ■

Collins, Ray (1885–1965), actor. Began his Hollywood screen career in 1940, in his middle years. A thick-set and imposing figure, he had been a regular member of Orson Welles' Mercury Theater. In films he played politicians and executives who showed a streak of sympathy. He portrayed Boss Getty, Welles' nemesis, in Citizen Kane (1941) and later appeared in several "Ma and Pa Kettle" comedies.

SELECTED FILMS: The Grapes of Wrath (1940), Slightly Dangerous, Whistling in Brooklyn (1943), See Here, Private Hargrove, Can't Help Singing (1944), Up Goes Maisie (1945), Three Wise Fools (1946), The Bachelor and the Bobby-Soxer, The Senator Was Indiscreet (1947), Good Sam (1948), It Happens Every Spring (1949), Francis, Kill the Umpire (1950), Ma and Pa Kettle on the Farm (1951), Dreamboat (1952), The Solid Gold Cadillac (1956), I'll Give My Life (1961). ■

Collyer, June (1907–1968), actress. Appeared in light films during the late 1920s and 1930s. She was often cast as an aristocratic leading lady, sometimes co-starring with her husband, Stuart ERWIN.

SELECTED FILMS: East Side West Side (1927), Woman Wise (1928), Not Quite Decent, The Love Doctor (1929), Sweet Kitty Bellairs, Charley's Aunt (1930), Honeymoon Lane, Dude Ranch, The Brat (1931), Before Midnight (1933), Cheaters (1934), The Ghost Walks (1935). ■

Colman, Ronald (1891–1958), actor. Worked on the stage and in films in minor roles in his native England before immigrating to the United States. After several obscure stage and film appearances, he finally gained recognition in 1923 when he co-starred with Lillian Gish in The White Sister. Soft-spoken and elegant, he made a smooth transition from silent to sound films as a heroic character. He was very successful in romantic and costume dramas but turned out several entertaining light films as well. He received an Oscar for his role in *A Double Life* (1948). He starred with his wife Benita Hume in an early television comedy series, "The Halls of Ivy," one of the few intelligent shows to grace the medium. A biography, *Ronald Colman— A Very Private Person*, penned by his daughter Juliet Benita Colman, was published in 1975.

In *The Late George Apley* (1947) he played one of the traditional pillars of Boston society. When he learns that his son is receiving letters from a love-interest outside of Boston, he exclaims: "Oh, good heavens! It's postmarked Worcester! The girl's a foreigner!"

SELECTED FILMS: *Handcuffs or Kisses* (1921), *The White Sister* (1923), *$20 a Week, His Night of Romance* (1924), *His Supreme Moment, The Sporting Venus, Her Sister From Paris, Lady Windermere's Fan* (1925), *Kiki* (1927), *Raffles, Handsome Gigolo, Poor Gigolo* (1930), *The Man Who Broke the Bank at Monte Carlo* (1935), *Lucky Partners* (1940), *My Life With Caroline* (1941), *Champagne for Caesar* (1950), *The Story of Mankind* (1957). ∎

Colonna, Jerry (1904–1986), comedian, actor. Appeared in nightclubs, in musical revues, on radio, and in films as comic characters. Memorable for his rolling eyes, his wide mustache, and his unusual vocal chords, he appeared as a guest comic in several light films, quite often as foil to Bob HOPE. He also appeared as a regular on Hope's radio shows and several television programs, contributing his own brand of zaniness and getting many laughs.

In *Star Spangled Rhythm* he appeared in a skit with Hope and William Bendix. Bendix suspects his wife of having affairs with other men, but Hope convinces him otherwise. "Can you ever forgive me?" Bendix pleads. "It's not for me to forgive you," Hope says, "but for this little flower whom you have wronged." "I didn't realize—" Bendix

continues regretfully. "Of course you didn't realize," Hope interjects. "You don't know women. But if there's one thing Bob Hope knows, it's women. Goodbye, and remember that little wife of yours is as honest as the day is long." As Hope is about to leave, he opens the closet door by mistake and out steps Colonna, who quips: "Short day, wasn't it?"

SELECTED FILMS: *52nd Street, Rosalie* (1937), *College Swing* (1938), *Naughty but Nice* (1939), *Road to Singapore* (1940), *Sis Hopkins* (1941), *True to the Army, Star Spangled Rhythm* (1942), *Atlantic City* (1944), *It's in the Bag* (1945), *Road to Rio* (1947), *Kentucky Jubilee* (1951), *Meet Me in Las Vegas* (1956), *Andy Hardy Comes Home* (1958), *Road to Hong Kong* (1961). ∎

"Comedy All-Stars, The." A series of silent two-reel comedies produced by Hal Roach during the mid-1920s. The performers were made up of Roach's stock company of comics, including, among others, James FINLAYSON, Edgar KENNEDY, Noah YOUNG, Eugene PALLETTE, Clyde COOK, Max DAVIDSON, Mae BUSCH, Anita GARVIN, Stan LAUREL, and Oliver HARDY. One of the purposes of this hodge-podge cast was to find some latent genius, some talent that the producer could eventually single out and build up as star quality. It was through their performances and the interaction between them in the All-Star Comedies that the individuals Laurel and Hardy were thought of as a possible team.

SELECTED FILMS: *Forty-Five Minutes From Hollywood* (1926), *Duck Soup, Slipping Wives, Leave 'Em and Weep, Why Girls Love Sailors, Sailors Beware, Do Detectives Think?, Sugar Daddies, The Call of the Cuckoo* (1927). ∎

Comedy-drama. A film that blends serious themes and dramatic elements with comic characters, situations, and dialogue. Hollywood, always seeking new material and genres to feed its voracious appetite, turned out numerous comedy-dramas beginning in the silent period. Hoping to capture both audiences, those who preferred comedies and those who liked a good drama, the studios probably succeeded as often as they failed to meet this goal.

The genre was popular as early as the pre-World War I years, as can be seen by the numerous releases from the major and minor film studios. Such popular stars as Carter and Flora de Haven, J. Walter KERRIGAN, and Franklyn FARNUM starred in *The College Orphan* (1915), *Langdon's Legacy* (1915), and *A Stranger From Somewhere* (1916), respectively. Irene Fenwick and Owen Moore starred in *Coney Island Princess*, while Jack Pickford, Mary's brother, co-starred with Louise Huff in *Seventeen*, both 1916. In 1917 Broadway personality George M. Cohan starred in *Broadway Jones*, based on his play, while actor-director Donald Crisp turned out a succession of comedy-dramas, including, among others, *The Cook of Canyon Camp* and *His Sweetheart*. Even the great opera singer Enrico Caruso was enticed to star in a comedy-drama in 1918 titled *My Cousin*.

The comedy-drama continued to flourish during the 1920s. *The Man From Home*, a 1922 Paramount release starring James Kirkwood and Anna Q. Nilsson, mixed blackmail and murder with comedy. MGM's *Cheaper to Marry* (1924) contrasted two law partners, Conrad NAGEL, who found romance and financial success through marriage, and Lewis STONE, who was almost driven to financial ruin and suicide because of his affair with his mistress. Charles RAY, a popular star of the 1920s, appeared in numerous comedy-dramas.

The 1930s supplied an almost unending succession of comedy-dramas. Clara BOW, the "It" girl of the 1920s, starred in *Call Her Savage* (1932), an entertaining film that moved gracefully from comedy to drama, thanks to its talented cast, including Thelma TODD and Gilbert Roland. In the following year Lee

TRACY exploited a lonelyhearts newspaper column by turning it into a profitable enterprise. The film was based on Nathanael West's short novel, *Miss Lonelyhearts*, which was later made into a depressing and realistic film starring Montgomery Clift, Robert Ryan, and Maureen STAPLETON and retitled *Lonelyhearts* (1958). Comedian Joe E. BROWN, who usually did straight slapstick comedy, played a circus headliner whose father vehemently disapproved of his career in *Circus Clown* (1934). That same year Carole LOMBARD appeared in *The Gay Bride*, a film that tried unsuccessfully to blend comedy and drama. She played a girl who wanted to strike it rich regardless of her reputation. Her ambition led her to liaisons with numerous underworld characters. *Riffraff* (1935) combined the fishing business with crime, while its stars, Jean HARLOW and Spencer TRACY, tried to solve their marital problems. In *Love Affair* (1939) a romance aboard a ship between Irene DUNNE and Charles Boyer met with difficulties on shore.

In *The Great Mike* (1944) a popular comic actor of the 1930s, Stuart Erwin, played a charming con artist who trained a horse to win the big race. That same year *The Great Moment*, one of Preston Sturges' great mistakes, was released. An offbeat film, it dealt with the life of the inventor of anesthesia. Fred MacMURRAY had his hands full in *Pardon My Past* (1945), a tale of mistaken identity. MacMurray was confused with a reckless playboy whom he closely resembled, resulting in several comical situations. Rosalind RUSSELL and Jack CARSON starred as a married couple in *Roughly Speaking* in 1945, a strong film in which Russell devoted herself to raising her family while her husband was off on one of his wild schemes trying unsuccessfully to hit the jackpot.

In the interesting *People Will Talk* (1951) doctor Cary GRANT married Jeanne Crain, one of his patients. In one of Marilyn MONROE'S best dramatic films, *Bus Stop* (1956), she played a saloon singer with whom naive cowboy Don Murray falls in love.

One of the best comedy-dramas of the 1960s, Billy WILDER'S *The Apartment* (1960), told the sordid story of Jack LEMMON who lent out his flat to his superiors for their extramarital affairs to guarantee his employment. The film also starred Shirley MacLAINE and Fred MacMurray. Another film set in New York City that year was *The Rat Race* in which Tony CURTIS, as a musician, and Debbie REYNOLDS, an aspiring dancer, came to the Big Apple, shared an apartment, and eventually fell in love. Another interesting 1960s entry was *Captain Newman, M.D.* (1963), about a psychiatrist and his mental patients at a military hospital. Tony Curtis was hilarious as a roguish attendant who was bent on helping the doctor, played by Gregory Peck. Carl REINER'S *The Comic* (1969) gave a poignant picture of the life of a self-destructive silent-screen comedian. Dick VAN DYKE, Michele Lee, and Mickey ROONEY were excellent in this flawed but true-to-life portrayal of several of the old comics.

In 1972 Leonard Gershe's Broadway play, *Butterflies Are Free*, was brought to the screen with Goldie HAWN portraying the zany neighbor of the blind Edward Albert who falls in love with her. Eileen Heckart won an Oscar for her portrayal of Albert's domineering mother. Elliott GOULD teamed up with Robert Blake to play unconventional Los Angeles vice-cops in *Busting* (1974), a film that angered gay groups for its caricatures of homosexuals in particular scenes. *Claudine* (1974) attempted to depict the real world in which blacks lived by telling the story of ghetto mother Diahann Carroll and garbageman James Earl Jones who fell in love with her. In *Corvette Summer* (1978) high school student Mark Hamill searched for a stolen sports car in Las Vegas and ended up falling in love with Annie Potts, who wanted to make the big time by becoming a prostitute. The bittersweet *Same Time, Next Year* (1978) revealed as much about evolving American values as it did about the illicit love affair between Alan ALDA and Ellen Burstyn, who met secretly once a year for 26 years. Neil SIMON'S successful Broadway play, *Chapter Two*, about a widower unprepared for a new love affair, was adapted to the screen in 1979 with James Caan and Marsha Mason in the lead roles. The film lacked the punch of the original.

The decade of the 1980s has had its share of comedy-dramas. In *Some Kind of Hero* (1982) Richard PRYOR portrayed a Vietnam veteran and former POW who returned home to a less-than-happy life. In *48 Hours* (1982) police officer Nick NOLTE enlisted the talents of convict Eddie MURPHY to hunt down a murderer, while in *Beverly Hills Cop* (1984) Murphy switched to the right side of the law as he played a cop searching for a friend's killer.

Often, combining comedy with drama confuses the audience, as it did in Martin Ritt's *The Front* (1976), starring Woody Allen, resulting in an unsatisfying film. At other times, it succeeds, as in *Nothing in Common* (1986), starring Tom HANKS and Jackie GLEASON, a film in which a son re-established his relationship with his distant father. Comedy-drama requires a very delicate balance that must take into account comedy that for the most part is natural, whether verbal or visual; concern for the characters; and a plausible story.

Comedy of manners. See Sophisticated comedy.

Comedy teams. The concept of combining the talents of two or more comics in one film dates back almost to the first days of movies. Early American silent comedy teams came about in the same ways as did the teams of the sound era. Some had their origins in burlesque or vaudeville while others were created by the different film studios. Still others emerged accidentally. And, like their counterparts of the sound era, early teams had their triumphs and failures.

One of the earliest comedy teams in American film was that of "HANK AND LANK," played by Victor POTEL and Augustus CARNEY. The series, initiated in 1910, was produced by ESSANAY studios. Released weekly, the films generally were one-reelers and proved popular with the public. Potel and Carney had not been an established comedy team; they emerged from a troupe of comedians at Essanay and just happened to stumble upon these humorous characters. In fact, each continued to appear in separate comedy series while turning out the Hank and Lank shorts. In 1911 Ham Fisher's famed comic strip, "Mutt and Jeff," was adapted to the screen in a series of comedy shorts, but the actors who portrayed the odd-sized duo were never listed.

The following year, 1912, introduced to audiences the most popular comedy team of this period, John BUNNY and Flora FINCH. Bunny had made the transition to films from the legitimate stage to become a genuine film star. Miss Finch had already established herself as an accomplished screen comedienne. Bunny usually played the philandering husband while Finch portrayed the betrayed wife who eventually learned of her husband's antics. VITAGRAPH turned out a series of Bunny and Finch comedy shorts, affectionately called "Bunnyfinches," all to the delight of movie audiences. Another popular team of this period was Mr. and Mrs. Sidney DREW, whose comedy explored various aspects of married life. The series, also produced by Vitagraph, reached its peak in 1915, with at least one short released each week. Drew's death in 1919 ended these entertaining comedies. In 1914 film actors William Wadsworth and Arthur HOUSEMAN combined their comic abilities and appeared in the short-lived series, "Waddy and Arty," with Waddy sporting a walrus mustache and glasses.

The year 1915 saw a succession of comedy teams introduced to the silent world of films. Lloyd HAMILTON and Bud DUNCAN, two talented comics under contract to Kalem studios, began a long series of "HAM AND BUD" comedies for their studio. They continued to star in these shorts for several years. Another commercially successful team that emerged the same year blended the talents of Eddie LYONS and Lee MORAN, two film comedians who had had separate careers. Their series ran for two years. The renowned vaudeville team, WEBER AND FIELDS, made their film debut in 1915 in the two-reeler, "The Best of Enemies," produced by Mack SENNETT for KEYSTONE studios. Sennett also turned out numerous "Ambrose and Walrus" comedies with large-framed Mack SWAIN and a frail Chester CONKLIN. Each had earned a reputation as a notorious scene-stealer, and pitting them against each other led to comical results. Finally, the year offered the minor comedies of "Heinie and Louie," played by Jimmy Aubrey and Walter Kendig. They were unable to match the talents of their competition and, after several entries, the series was dropped.

Other minor comedy teams appeared from time to time before the 1920s rolled in. Harry MYERS, a talented actor who continued to appear in films into the 1930s, joined Rosemary Theby in 1916 to portray a married couple beset with typical humorous problems. Myers later had a featured role as a drunken millionaire in CHAPLIN'S *City Lights* (1931). The same year brought forth Bobbie Burns and Walter Stull in the "Pokes and Jabbs" comedies. Oliver HARDY, who was later to co-star in the most successful comedy team ever, linked up in 1918 with Billy Ruge, a minor comedian, to make the "Plump and Runt" comedies. But fame was to elude Hardy for several more years.

The early 1920s contributed little to the formation of new and successful comedy teams. Not until the middle and latter parts of the decade did new teams sprout. But only one, LAUREL AND HARDY, was to achieve fame and immortality in both silent and sound features. However, the 1920s did bring about some changes in comedy. In addition to better photography and direction, more elaborate sets, and less emphasis on knockabout comedy, the appearance of the comics themselves changed. The exaggerated walrus and handlebar mustaches disappeared, and, for the most part, their attire seemed more realistic.

Although movie audiences tired of dramas about World War I, King Vidor's box-office hit, the dramatic *The Big Parade* (1925), and Raoul Walsh's *What Price Glory* (1926) brought renewed interest in the Great War, and Hollywood responded with a string of war comedies. In fact, the latter film spawned several spin-offs with Captain Flagg (Victor McLAGLEN) and Sergeant Quirt (Edmund LOWE) continuing their amorous misadventures. Produced before censorship became entrenched, the films contained several sexual innuendos. Paramount responded to this lighter approach to the war by combining the abilities of two veteran comedians, Wallace BEERY and Raymond HATTON, in a series of mediocre military comedies beginning with *Behind the Front* (1926). Metro studios released *Rookies* (1927), the first in a series of comedies co-starring the lanky Karl DANE and the diminutive George K. ARTHUR. Universal, not to be outdone, brought out *Lost at the Front* (1927), starring George SIDNEY and Charlie MURRAY, who temporarily discarded their "Cohen and Kelly" roles of the previous year to don the uniform of the doughboy. They were to return to the ethnic comedy genre during the early 1930s.

Except perhaps for Sidney and Murray, whose comedy series was steeped in slapstick and low comedy, none of these teams survived the advent of sound. In the late 1920s one team did emerge from the Hal ROACH studios and made a very smooth transition to the talkies. Stan LAUREL and Oliver HARDY had each been making silent comedy shorts for years as minor comics, but it was their work as a team that brought them their greatest popularity.

The introduction of sound made it possible for studios and the comics to add new dimensions to the art of comedy. Sound effects could be added directly to the audio track of the film. Dialect comics like El BRENDEL and Chico MARX could demonstrate their talents. Comedy teams like BURNS AND ALLEN who relied heavily on verbal routines could now enter the screen world. Hollywood met the challenge by recruiting comedy teams from radio and the stage, but for many the transition was not an easy one. Performing before the cameras was not the same as working before live audiences: the timing was different; reliable comedy material that normally would last for years was used up in one film; there was a higher dependence on studio writers, many of them, unfortunately, hacks who did not understand the nuances of a particular team; and, finally, the comics had to rely on film directors and producers who selected the scripts and worked within tight budgets and structured schedules.

Bobby CLARK and Paul McCULLOUGH were one of the first teams to enter sound films after their appearances on Broadway. They began with one-reelers for Fox studios based on their stage routines, then moved to RKO where they made two- and three-reel comedies. Their output exceeded three dozen shorts from 1928 to 1935, all of which demonstrated their offbeat and eccentric skills with sight gags and slapstick. Another team that started on the stage and in vaudeville was WHEELER AND WOOLSEY, but their transition was not a smooth one. Although they were gifted and experienced comedians, they were not always handed quality material. However, there are enough hilarious moments in their 25 feature films to showcase their talents. The unique comedy of BURNS AND ALLEN, who had come from vaudeville, transferred very well to the screen, although the duo received strong support from other stars. George Burns played straight man to the zany world of Gracie, all to the delight of their many fans. OLSEN AND JOHNSON, another team that came out of the vaudeville tradition, brought their crazy antics to the screen in 1930, adding inventive visual gags to a string of otherwise uneven films that ran until 1945. A survey of the 1930s would not be complete without the mention of the THREE STOOGES. Regardless of the attacks by critics and highbrows, the low comedy, slapstick, knockabout style of the trio spanned 25 years of shorts and features, longer than any other comedy team. Their acceptance by an approving public can be seen by the continual revivals on television.

Two "brother" teams emerged during the early talkies. The RITZ BROTHERS first appeared on the screen in 1934 and, for the next decade, joked, danced, and sang their way through a succession of chiefly low-budget features. Their material and combined talents never matched the brilliance of the MARX BROTHERS, under whose shadow they were destined to linger for much of their career. The Marx Brothers had appeared in vaudeville and on Broadway before entering films in 1929. Each brother contributed his unique gifts to the act. Groucho delivered a steady stream of irreverent insults, Chico punned shamelessly, and Harpo lusted after every pretty face within his range. These talents, combined with their anarchistic humor, satirical wit, and eccentric costumes and props, have made their films as funny to watch today as they were when first released.

Other comedy teams surfaced for a short time during the early sound period. The legendary vaudevillians, SMITH AND DALE, renowned for their "Dr. Kronkite" routine, appeared sporadically in films, but they never attained the acceptance they did on stage. FIBBER McGEE AND MOLLY, the fa-

mous radio comedy couple, met with a similar fate after a few minor screen appearances. MORAN AND MACK, affectionately known as "the Two Black Crows," were a successful blackface vaudeville comedy act before they entered films. However, after just a few features their popularity declined and the handful of shorts they made in the early 1930s were judged mediocre. In 1934 Charlie Mack was killed in a car crash. George Moran continued his career in show business as a minor comic until his death in 1949.

Some comedy teams came about by combining the individual talents of two recognized performers, such as Laurel and Hardy. MGM attempted such an arrangement by bringing together the former silent screen giant, Buster KEATON, with vaudeville and stage comic Jimmy DURANTE. They made two films together in 1932 (*The Passionate Plumber* and *Speak Easily*) and one in 1933 (*What! No Beer?*), but the results proved harmful to Keaton's career. The subtle style of the Great Stoneface was no match for the dynamics and verbal assaults of Durante. Nor did they get along personally. As a result, Keaton was relegated to working for minor studios in routine two-reel comedies. Universal tried a similar tactic with Slim SUMMERVILLE and ZaSu PITTS, two experienced comics of the silents. They made a handful of feature comedies for Universal, but the scripts were generally mediocre and the films faded into oblivion.

The dominant comedy team of the 1940s was ABBOTT AND COSTELLO. Following years of experience in burlesque and vaudeville, they exploded upon the big screen in 1940 and were instant successes, making more than 30 features in a span of about 15 years. The dapper, and sometimes cruel, Bud played straight man to the very funny and lovable Lou. Comedian Bob HOPE and crooner Bing CROSBY joined forces during this decade to make their famous "ROAD" films, with both performers competing for the affection of sexy Dorothy LAMOUR. Like Bud and Lou, their films reached the peak of popularity during the 1940s. But unlike their counterparts, Bob and Bing did not work together as a team on stage or on the radio. Each continued to pursue his separate career between "Road" assignments at Paramount.

If the 1940s belonged to Abbott and Costello, the 1950s were commanded by the offbeat style of an unlikely pair. Singer Dean MARTIN and comic Jerry LEWIS brought their brand of humor to the screen in 1949 and quickly became the leading comedy duo in films and on stage for the next 17 years.

The idea of movie comedy teams declined during the 1960s. Some, like ROWAN AND MARTIN and the SMOTHERS BROTHERS, who have had success in television, have tried to revitalize the concept, but the movie public was unreceptive. CHEECH AND CHONG, with their streetwise, drug-oriented humor, have attempted to fill the gap, but their handful of films seem to be aimed at a younger audience. The beginning of the 1980s offered the promising start of a new team. John BELUSHI and Dan AYKROYD appeared in the 1980 film, *The Blues Brothers*, but Belushi's tragic death ended that prospect. Another possibility for a comedy team occurred when Gene WILDER was paired with Richard PRYOR in *Stir Crazy* (1980). They had worked together in an earlier comedy, *Silver Streak* (1976). But the two comics have since gone their own ways.

Comic hero. In films, the main character who displays certain characteristics or traits that evoke amusement or laughter, the essential element that distinguishes the comic hero from the chief character in drama or the tragic hero in tragedy. One quality is his apparent cowardice in the face of danger. Bob HOPE tended to specialize in the cowardly hero in films such as *The Cat and the Canary* and his spy comedies. Other film comedians, including Danny KAYE, Lou COSTELLO, and Eddie CANTOR, have portrayed temporary cowards in several of their vehicles. However, this comic cowardice should not lead to the point where harm comes to the heroine or that the forces of villainy triumph. The comic hero ultimately overcomes this weakness, bringing the plot to a happy conclusion.

Another characteristic of the comic hero is his ability to bilk society, especially those members who are pompous, corrupt, or self-serving. Just as Hope is the quintessential comic coward, Groucho MARX is the expert con man. He fleeces his perennial foil, Margaret DUMONT, who is usually seeking to buy her way into society or to lure him into marriage. He assails the pompous (Sig RUMANN, the impresario in *A Night at the Opera*) or the corrupt (Douglass DUMBRILLE, who is trying to cheat the heroine out of her inheritance in *A Day at the Races*). But the comic hero usually does not profit directly from his deceit. It results in either a worthy character's benefiting or the comic hero's getting caught in his own deception.

The comic hero often possesses a child-like spirit, which makes him both vulnerable in an indifferent world and innocent in a society of those less pure. Silent screen comedians such as Buster KEATON and Harry LANGDON exemplify this trait. In the short film, "Cops," Keaton's innocence causes him a heap of trouble. In one instance he is riding his horse and wagon of furniture past a parade of policemen when suddenly an anarchist positioned on a roof tosses a bomb at the representatives of law and order. Instead, it lands next to Keaton, who innocently uses it to light his cigarette. When he tosses it away, it explodes and disrupts the ceremony, causing an army of police to pursue him. Langdon, on the other hand, has his sexual innocence assaulted by designing women, as is the case in *The Strong Man*. Stan LAUREL faces a similar problem in *Way Out West* when the mistress of a saloon owner traps him in her bedroom and tries to undress him to retrieve a map. He undergoes the same treatment in the short, "Putting Pants on Philip," when he arrives from Scotland and his relatives try to strip him of his kilts. Jerry LEWIS often takes on this child-like innocence, only to be exploited by his partner, Dean MARTIN. Our sympathies in these situations are invariably with Jerry. Other comics have adopted this trait from time to time. One of the best examples occurs in *Modern Times* when Charlie CHAPLIN sees the red "warning" flag fall off the rear of a truck. He picks it up and tries to follow the truck to return the flag. Meanwhile, a throng of discontent workers march behind him, leading to his arrest as a "red" agitator.

The comic hero may also have more than a streak of mischief. In this category Chaplin is the foremost exponent. In "The Cure" he causes a guest with his leg in a cast untold pain as his foot is caught in a revolving door. Later, Chaplin causes his victim other hardships. In "The Rink" he is a waiter who collides with a fellow worker and puts a scrub brush on the unsuspecting waiter's tray. During his lunch break he visits a roller-skating rink and uses his cane to trip those he dislikes. Harpo MARX engages in this practice as well. In *Duck Soup* he deliberately cuts the tails off pompous Louis Calhern's tuxedo, tears up his mail, and puts sticky fly paper on his chair. In the same film he destroys vendor Edgar KENNEDY'S lemonade and peanut stand. He enjoys creating havoc and chaos wherever he goes.

The comic hero should not be too smug or self-satisfied. In *City Lights* Chaplin, after helping a blind girl home, expresses joy and a heightened sense of exhilaration. All of a sudden he is hit on the head with a flower pot. In *Modern Times* he shows off his skating ability to Paulette GODDARD by skating blindfolded. She saves him in the nick of time by stopping him as he is about to skate off a landing. When Oliver HARDY criticizes his partner on some point and then pompously takes over the situation, we know he is headed for trouble. When he addresses someone harshly, he gets punched. When he demands of Stan that he, Oliver, be permitted to go first, we know he is headed for a pratfall.

The comic hero faces certain restrictions. He must never be handsome or even good-looking. In other words, he must not be a physical threat or competition to the males in the audience. This, of course, holds true for comediennes as well. They should never appear prettier or more alluring than their female counterparts in the audience. The comic hero must never appear more intelligent than his audience. The viewer must feel superior to the stupidity of the comic's actions. His blundering and pomposity make us in the audience feel superior. But he should have just enough resolve, courage, and wits to bring the film to a happy conclusion. Finally, the comic hero sometimes displays other vices. He may be lazy (Stepin FETCHIT), clumsy (Danny KAYE, Red SKELTON), stupid (LAUREL AND HARDY, the THREE STOOGES), or overly romantic (Eddie BRACKEN, Charlie CHAPLIN).

Comic strips. The daily and Sunday comic strips have supplied comedy material to the film industry almost from its first flickerings. The strips were popular and had a built-in audience. The comic-strip plots moved rapidly, one of the essential elements of film. The strips took different forms in their transformations to the screen: ANIMATION, one- or two-reel silent shorts, and feature-length films with extensive budgets.

Winsor McCay's "Gertie the Dinosaur" (1909) was a landmark film—the first commercially successful animated short and the first film to be based on a comic strip. Cartoonist Sidney Smith saw two of his creations adapted to the screen. "Old Doc Yak" was made into an animated cartoon in 1913, while "The Gumps" emerged as a series of two-reel comedies which ran from 1923 to 1928. George McManus, another popular cartoonist, contributed the animated "Snookums" (1913), which was resurrected in 1927 in the form of two-reel comedies and renamed "The Newlyweds"; "Let George Do It," which also became a series of comedy shorts in 1926; and "BRINGING UP FATHER," his most popular strip, made into a feature-length series in the 1940s. Richard Outcault's popular character Buster Brown, which originated as a comic strip in 1902, was made into a cartoon series in 1914 and a comedy series in 1925.

Other well-known comic strips converted to the screen in animated form from the 1910s through the 1940s include, among others, Rudolph Dirk's "The Katzenjammer Kids," which premiered in 1917 and returned in 1938 as MGM's "The Captain and the Kids"; George Herriman's "Krazy Kat" (1916–1918, 1926–1928, 1930-1938); Bill Nolan's "Happy Hooligan" (1913–1917); Bud Fisher's "Mutt and Jeff" (c. 1910s), later brought back to the screen in 1930; Bill DeBeck's "Barney Google," which was adapted to live comedy shorts from 1928 to 1929; E. C. Segar's "Popeye" (1933), which was made into a feature-length film directed by Robert Altman and starred Robin Williams in the title role and Shelley Duvall as Olive Oyl; Otto Soglow's "The Little King" (1933–1934); Marge's "Little Lulu" (c. 1940s); and Ernie Bushmiller's "Nancy" (1942).

Many favorite cartoon series were adapted to live comedies. George McManus' BRINGING UP FATHER was made into a feature-length movie in 1928 and into a series in the 1940s. Rube Goldberg had the honor of seeing his characters, "Ike and Mike," come alive in 1928. "Winnie Winkle," starring Ethlyn Gibson, was turned into a series. Fox's tough little "Mickey McGuire," sporting a derby and a cigar, appeared as a series of comedy shorts in 1927, starring Mickey ROONEY, who continued in the role until 1933, when he outgrew the part. He appeared in about 50 of the shorts, using the name of the title character. In 1926 the talented actress Colleen Moore portrayed "Ella Cinders," which was based on a strip created by Bill Counselman and Charley Plumb. Carl Ed's comic strip, "Harold Teen," came to the movie screen in 1928 and starred Arthur LAKE, who was to appear later as Dagwood Bumstead in the BLONDIE series. Office girl "Tillie the Toiler," created by Russ Westover in 1921, was portrayed by Marion Davies in 1927 and Kay Hughes in 1942. Percy Crosby's lovable tot, "Skippy," starring Jackie Cooper, appeared in 1930 and won for its director, Norman Taurog, an Academy Award, plus two additional nominations, for best picture and best actor. In 1938 a cartoon series based on the "Skippy" strip appeared but failed to win audience support. "Little Orphan Annie," drawn by Harold Gray, saw three versions. In 1932 David O. Selznick's production starred Mitzi Green as Annie; in 1938 Ann Gillis portrayed the spirited foundling; and in 1982 John Huston directed Annie, an adaptation of the Broadway musical, which starred Albert Finney as Daddy Warbucks, Carol Burnett, and Aileen Quinn as Annie. Ham Fisher's handsome pugilist, "Joe Palooka," also had more than one rendering. In 1934 Stu ERWIN played the fighter and Jimmy DURANTE co-starred as his excitable manager, Knobby Walsh, in a feature titled Palooka. In 1936 Warner Brothers presented an unsuccessful series of comedy shorts based on the character; it was discontinued in 1937. In 1947 the strip was once again revived, with Joe Kirkwood in the title role and Leon ERROL as his manager. James GLEASON continued as Walsh after Errol's death. Chic Young's popular comic strip, "Blondie," was perhaps the most successful of all. The BLONDIE series, which began in 1938, lasted into the 1950s, with Penny SINGLETON in the title role and Arthur Lake as the confounded Dagwood.

The comic strips continued to function as a source of comedy material for films through the 1940s and 1950s. Al Capp's "Li'l Abner" was made into a feature-length film in 1940. Starring Granville Owen as Abner and Buster KEATON as Lonesome Polecat, the film steered clear of the social and political satire that was part of the charm of the original strip. Aside from Keaton, several other silent screen stars appeared in the production, including Edgar KENNEDY, Billy BEVAN, and Chester CONKLIN. In 1959 the characters of Dogpatch returned to the screen, this time in an adaptation of the Broadway musical, *Li'l Abner*. Frank King's "Gasoline Alley," a realistic but slow-moving strip, saw the production of two features in 1951: *Gasoline Alley* and *Corky of Gasoline Alley*. But the series made no impact on the movie audiences and was discontinued. With the advent of television, the comic strips found a new medium in which to parade their characters, with occasional exceptions such as the previously mentioned *Popeye* and *Annie* and the successful "Superman" series.

Comingore, Dorothy (1918–1971), actress. Worked in stock before entering films in the 1930s. She appeared in several short comedies, including one with the THREE STOOGES ("Rockin' in the Rockies," 1940). In 1941 she co-starred with Orson Welles in his classic, *Citizen Kane*, portraying Susan Alexander, Kane's second wife.

SELECTED FILMS: *Prison Train, Comet Over Broadway* (1938), *Trade Winds, Blondie Meets the Boss, Mr. Smith Goes to Washington, Cafe Hostess* (1939), *Pioneers of the Frontier* (1940), *Any Number Can Play* (1949), *The Big Night* (1951). ∎

Compilation comedy. A feature-length film composed of excerpts or complete one- and two-reelers starring one or more screen comedians. From time to time a producer, studio, or comic would assemble a film based on past works of a solo performer (Harold LLOYD), a team (LAUREL AND HARDY), or a period (the silents). The 1930s produced at least three important compilations of CHAPLIN'S works—*The Charlie Chaplin Carnival, Charlie Chaplin Cavalcade,* and *Charlie Chaplin Festival*, all released in 1938. During the late 1940s comedian Steve ALLEN narrated *Down Memory Lane*. Ten years later Robert YOUNGSON produced a successful series drawn from the silent days, including *The Golden Age of Comedy* (1958), *When Comedy Was King* (1960), and *Days of Thrills and Laughter* (1961). Other similar films include *30 Years of Fun* (1963), *Laurel and Hardy's Laughing Twenties* (1965), *The Crazy World of Laurel and Hardy* (1966), and *Four Clowns* (1969). Then came MGM's *Big Parade of Comedy* and *Harold Lloyd's World of Comedy*. *The Great Chase* (1963) was another popular film in the series. Two exceptionally successful films released in the 1970s that combined comedy and musical excerpts were *That's Entertainment* (1974), which drew from nearly 100 MGM films, and its sequel, *That's Entertainment Part 2* (1976).

Compson, Betty (1897–1974), actress. Entered silent films in 1915 after appearing first in vaudeville. She worked for a few years in a series of two-reel comedies produced by Al CHRISTIE, then went on to star in major silent features through the 1920s. She became a supporting actress during the 1930s and 1940s.

SELECTED FILMS: *Wanted: A Leading Lady* (1915), *His at Six O'Clock* (1916), *A Bold Bad Night* (1917), *Betty Makes Up* (1918), *Ladies Must Live* (1921), *Kick In* (1922), *The Rustle of Silk, Hollywood* (1923), *Miami, The Enemy Sex, The Fast Set* (1924), *The Wise Guy* (1925), *Cheating Cheaters* (1927), *Docks of New York* (1928), *On With the Show, The Time, the Place and the Girl* (1929), *The Boudoir Diplomat* (1930), *The Lady Refuses* (1931), *A Slight Case of Murder* (1938),

Second Chance (1947), Here Comes Trouble (1948). ∎

Compton, Joyce (1907–), actress. Began in films in 1925 and appeared in many two-reel comedies and features. She often played feather-brained blondes. Sometimes she was the only spark in an otherwise weak comedy, as in her role of the dumb-blonde secretary in OLSEN AND JOHNSON'S Country Gentlemen (1937). She appeared in more than 100 features and comedy shorts during a career that spanned four decades.

SELECTED FILMS: What Fools Men, Broadway Lady (1925), Ankles Preferred (1927), Soft Living (1928), Wild Party, Dangerous Curves (1929), The Three Sisters, High Society Blues (1930), Up Pops the Devil (1931), Only Yesterday (1933), The White Parade (1934), Love Before Breakfast (1936), Kid Galahad, The Awful Truth (1937), Spring Madness (1938), Reno (1939), Bedtime Story, Scattergood Meets Broadway (1941), Let's Face It (1943), Roughly Speaking (1945), A Southern Yankee (1948), Girl in the Woods (1958). ∎

Condon, Jackie, child actor. One of the original members of the OUR GANG series. He appeared in the first of Hal ROACH'S film shorts, "Our Gang," in 1922, along with Peggy Cartwright, Winston Doty, and Ernie "Sunshine Sammy" MORRISON. He also appeared in a few Harold LLOYD comedies during the 1920s.

SELECTED FILMS: Young Sherlocks, Doctor Jack (1922), The Champeen, The Cobbler, The Big Show, A Pleasant Journey, Dogs of War (1923), The Trouble, Big Business, The Buccaneers, Seein' Things, Girl Shy (1924), The Big Town, Circus Fever, Dog Days, The Love Bug (1925), Shivering Spooks, The Fourth Alarm (1926). ∎

Conklin, Charles "Heinie" (1880–1959), actor. Came from vaudeville and the theater to films in 1915. He appeared

in many short comedies for producer Mack SENNETT and others. He became a supporting player in numerous features throughout the 1920s and 1930s, frequently in comedy roles. He had a small part in All Quiet on the Western Front (1930), in which he portrayed the character Hammacher, and appeared in two ABBOTT AND COSTELLO films toward the end of his film career.

SELECTED FILMS: Battle Royal (1918), East Lynne With Variations (1919), You Wouldn't Believe It (1920), George Washington, Jr. (1924), Hogan's Alley (1925), The Sap, Hard Boiled (1926), Silk Stockings, Ham and Eggs at the Front (1927), Beau Broadway (1928), The Show of Shows, Tiger Rose (1929), Little Miss Broadway (1938), Hollywood Cavalcade (1939), Lost in a Harem (1944), Abbott and Costello Meet the Keystone Kops (1955).∎

Conklin, Chester (1888–1971), actor. Worked in vaudeville doing a solo Dutch comedy act and in the circus as a clown before entering films in 1913. He began as one of the KEYSTONE KOPS for producer Mack SENNETT and as a supporting comic for Charlie CHAPLIN in many of his 1914 films. Sporting a walrus-type mustache, he co-starred in the "Ambrose-Walrus" series with another Keystone comic, Mack SWAIN. He also made a series of short films for Fox's "Sunshine Comedies." Although his salary at Fox was higher than what he was getting at Keystone, he was destined to remain a second-string comedian throughout the 1920s, often supporting other comics. During his entire silent screen career he was always overshadowed by other, more popular comedians like Chaplin, Buster KEATON, and Harold LLOYD.

He worked as a featured and supporting player in several films until 1950. One of his more memorable roles was as Chaplin's senior worker in Modern Times, in which he gets entangled in the complex mechanism of a giant machine, with only his head protruding. Charlie nonchalantly proceeds to feed him his lunch, with hilarious results.

SELECTED FILMS: Making a Living, Dough and Dynamite, Tillie's Punctured Romance (1914), Ambrose's Sour Grapes (1915), A Tugboat Romeo (1916), A Clever Dummy (1917), Ladies First, The Village Chestnut (1918), Yankee Doodle in Berlin (1919), Skirts (1921), Greed (1924), The Nervous Wreck (1926), Two Flaming Youths, Tell It to Sweeney (1927), The Big Noise, The Haunted House (1928), Swing High (1930), Hallelujah, I'm a Bum (1933), Modern Times (1936), Every Day's a Holiday (1938), The Great Dictator (1940), Hail the Conquering Hero (1944), A Big Hand for the Little Lady (1966). ■

Conley, Lige (1899–1937), comic actor. Appeared in several of Mack SENNETT'S two-reelers at Keystone studios before switching to Fox and then to Educational studios. Here he became a featured performer in Jack White's "Mermaid Comedies" during the 1921–1922 season. In 1924 he starred in another series. He specialized in sight gags and slapstick.

SELECTED FILMS: Air Pockets (1924), Fast and Furious (1927), The Charge of the Gauchos (1928). ■

Conlin, Jimmy (1884–1962), actor. Began his show business career as a vaudeville comic before entering films in 1928. He appeared in many features as a comic character actor, especially as a member of Preston STURGES' stock company of comedians.

SELECTED FILMS: Sharps and Flats, Lights of New York (1928), College Humor (1933), The Great McGinty, Second Chorus (1940), The Lady Eve, Sullivan's Travels (1941), The Remarkable Andrew, The Palm Beach Story (1942), The Miracle of Morgan's Creek, Hail the Conquering Hero (1944), Bring on the Girls (1945), Mad Wednesday, The Hucksters (1947), The Great Rupert (1950), Anatomy of a Murder (1959). ■

Walter Connolly (right) and Lee Tracy

Connolly, Walter (1887–1940), actor. Appeared on Broadway before entering films in 1932. He played both principal and supporting roles in more than 40 comedies and dramas, often portraying disgruntled fathers, irascible editors, and nervous businessmen. His portly frame and chins would shake when he grew excited.

"I'm a firm believer in democracy," he says to Francis Compton in Soak the Rich, "provided that it lets me alone." And in Nothing Sacred he portrays a heartless newspaper editor who witnesses the fainting of a young girl at a nightclub. Suspecting her collapse may be fatal, he says to the doctor: "I want to know the worst. I don't want you to spare our feelings. We go to press in 15 minutes."

SELECTED FILMS: Washington Merry-Go-Round, Man Against Woman, No More Orchids (1932), Lady for a Day, Man's Castle (1933), It Happened One Night, Twentieth Century, Lady by Choice, The Captain Hates the Sea (1934), She Couldn't Take It (1935), Soak the Rich, Libeled Lady (1936), Let's Get Married, Nothing Sacred (1937), Four's a Crowd, Too Hot to Handle (1938), Bridal Suite, Good Girls Go to Paris, The Great Victor Herbert, Fifth Avenue Girl (1939). ■

Conried, Hans (1917–1982), actor. Performed on radio before entering films. He played principal as well as supporting roles in more than 70 films, often as an oddball clerk, waiter, etc. He frequently portrayed Nazi officers during World War II. He was generally known for his animated and peculiar behavior. He worked with several popular comedians of the period, including OLSEN AND JOHNSON and MARTIN AND LEWIS.

In *Siren of Bagdad* (1953) he asks a guard: "I beg your pardon. I realize they haven't been invented yet, but do you have a match?"

SELECTED FILMS: *Dramatic School* (1938), *It's a Wonderful World* (1939), *Maisie Was a Lady, The Gay Falcon* (1941), *The Wife Takes a Flyer, Blondie's Blessed Event* (1942), *A Lady Takes a Chance, Crazy House* (1943), *The Senator Was Indiscreet* (1947), *My Friend Irma, Nancy Goes to Rio* (1950), *Behave Yourself!* (1951), *The Affairs of Dobie Gillis* (1953), *Bus Stop* (1956), *Rock-a-Bye Baby* (1958), *The Patsy* (1964), *The Shaggy D.A.* (1976), *The Cat From Outer Space* (1978). ∎

Conway, Jack (1887–1952), director. Worked as an actor on stage and in early silent films before turning his talents toward directing in 1913. He turned out numerous silent and sound films, chiefly action vehicles, although he directed a handful of competent romantic comedies beginning with his early silent period. At MGM for many years, he worked with some of the foremost screen personalities of the period, including, among others, Clark GABLE, Jean HARLOW, and Spencer TRACY.

SELECTED FILMS: *The Old Armchair* (1913), *Polly Redhead* (1917), *The Rage of Paris* (1921), *Another Man's Shoes* (1922), *What Wives Want* (1923), *Bringing Up Father* (1928), *They Learned About Women* (1930), *The Easiest Way* (1931), *Red Headed Woman* (1932), *The Nuisance* (1933), *The Gay Bride* (1934), *One New York Night* (1935), *Libeled Lady* (1936), *Saratoga* (1937), *Love Crazy* (1941), *The Hucksters* (1947), *Julia Misbehaves* (1948). ∎

Conway, Tim (1933–), actor. Worked in television as a writer, director, and comedian before entering films in 1964 as a comedy performer. He often portrays light-hearted, good-natured bunglers, more silly than comical, especially in films for the younger market.

SELECTED FILMS: *McHale's Navy* (1964), *The World's Greatest Athlete* (1973), *The Apple Dumpling Gang* (1975), *Gus, The Shaggy D.A.* (1976), *The Billion Dollar Hobo, They Went That-Away and That-Away* (1978), *The Apple Dumpling Gang Rides Again, The Prize Fighter* (1979), *The Private Eyes* (1980). ∎

Coogan, Jackie (1914–1984), child actor. Appeared in a revue when he was four years old. Charlie CHAPLIN hired him for a comedy short and as his co-star in the 1923 classic film, *The Kid*, the latter making the child an overnight star. Jackie's phenomenal success brought him international fame and a million-dollar contract from Metro. Armed with his trademarks—a cap turned to one side, baggy pants, and a worn-out sweater—he proved to be a talented little trouper in a string of sentimental dramas and light comedies. He often portrayed troublesome brats and pitiful orphans. But whatever the role, he always gave an effective performance, and once he opened those wide eyes, the audience succumbed. As he grew older, his popularity abated. By 1927 he appeared in his final part as a juvenile star. He attempted to revive his screen popularity in the early 1930s, but within a few years he was relegated to supporting roles in obscure B films.

SELECTED FILMS: *Skinner's Baby* (1917), *A Day's Pleasure* (1919), *Peck's Bad Boy* (1921), *My Boy, Oliver Twist* (1922), *Daddy, Circus Days* (1923), *Little Robinson Crusoe, A Boy of Flanders* (1924), *The Rag Man* (1925), *The Bugle Call, Buttons* (1927), *Tom Sawyer* (1930), *Huckleberry Finn* (1931), *Home on the Range* (1935), *College Swing*

(1938), Million Dollar Legs (1939), Kilroy Was Here (1947), Skipalong Rosenbloom (1951), Sex Kittens Go to College (1960), A Fine Madness (1966), Marlowe (1969), Human Experiments (1979). ∎

Cook, Clyde (1891–1984), actor. Began his show business career as a circus clown before entering films in 1915 as a comic for Mack SENNETT'S comedy shorts. The Australian acrobat soon proved his talent and was labeled "The Kangaroo Boy." He later signed with Fox studios (1920), appearing in the "Sunshine Comedies." In the late 1920s he joined the Hal ROACH stock company of comics and was teamed with Franklin PANGBORN as one of a pair of incompetent cabbies in a series called "THE TAXI BOYS," an attempt to emulate the success of LAUREL AND HARDY. He also co-starred with veteran comedienne Louise FAZENDA in 1927 and 1928 in a group of feature-length films dominated by slapstick.

SELECTED FILMS: The Show Down (1917), Soldiers of Fortune (1919), Don't Tickle (1920), Skirts (1921), The Eskimo (1922), He Who Gets Slapped (1924), The Winning of Barbara Worth (1926), Simple Sis, The Bush Leaguer, Good Time Charley (1927), Domestic Troubles, Beware of Bachelors (1928), Masquerade, Taming of the Shrew (1929), The Dude Wrangler, Sunny (1930), Blondie of the Follies (1932), Wee Willie Winkie (1937), The Little Princess (1939), The Man From Down Under (1943), Pride of Maryland (1951), Loose in London (1953). ∎

Cook, Elisha, Jr. (1906–), actor. Worked in vaudeville, on stage, and appeared in more than 75 films, beginning in 1929. More generally known for his dramatic roles, often as a neurotic underworld character or a fall guy, he has also played light-headed collegiates and other roles in frothy comedies. His most memorable roles, no doubt, were as the gunsel in *The Maltese Falcon* (1941) and as Marie Windsor's jealous husband in

The Killing (1956). "Keep on ridin' me," he warns Bogart in *The Maltese Falcon*, "they're gonna be pickin' iron out of your liver." This line has often been used in recent films as an almost parodic reference to his former roles.

SELECTED FILMS: Her Unborn Child (1929), Two in a Crowd, Pigskin Parade (1936), Breezing Home, Danger—Love at Work, Life Begins in College (1937), My Lucky Star, Three Blind Mice (1938), He Married His Wife (1940), Love Crazy, Ball of Fire (1941), Sleepytime Gal, A-Haunting We Will Go (1942), Phantom Lady, Up in Arms (1944), Joe Palooka—Champ (1946), The Fall Guy (1947), Behave Yourself! (1951), Shane (1953), Papa's Delicate Condition (1963), The Black Bird (1975), St. Ives (1976). ∎

Cook, Joe (1890–1959), comedian, actor. Worked as a juggler at age 14, in vaudeville with his half-brother doing a musical comedy act, and on Broadway in 1919. Through the 1920s and 1930s he performed in various stage revues. With his winning smile and gift for making his audiences laugh, he finally entered films in the 1930s, appearing in a series of comedy shorts. He later had featured roles on radio before retiring in 1942.

SELECTED FILMS: Rain or Shine (1930), Hold Your Horses (1933), The Sound of Laughter (1964 documentary). ∎

Cooke, Baldwin (–1953), actor. Appeared in late silent and early sound comedy shorts, especially for producer Hal ROACH, since he was a member of Roach's stock company of comic character players. He worked as a lead comic as well as a supporting actor with some of the leading comedians of the period, including, among others, Charley CHASE and LAUREL AND HARDY.

SELECTED FILMS: A Perfect Day (1929), Twice Two (1933). ∎

Cookie. Fictional character in the "BLONDIE" comedy series. The infant daughter of Dagwood and Blondie Bumstead (Arthur LAKE and Penny SINGLETON), she did not appear in the films until the eleventh entry. Her brother, Baby Dumpling, by this time was being addressed as Alexander. Cookie was portrayed by Marjorie Kent.

Coolidge, Philip (1909–1967), actor. Worked on Broadway before entering films as a character player. Bald and worried-looking, he appeared in a variety of roles in dramas and light films, alternating his time between the stage and screen.

SELECTED FILMS: *The Mating Game, It Happened to Jane* (1959), *The Russians Are Coming, the Russians Are Coming* (1966), *Never a Dull Moment* (1968). ■

Cooper, Gary (1901–1961), actor. Began his film career as a cowboy extra, getting his big opportunity in 1926 as a featured player in *The Winning of Barbara Worth,* starring Ronald COLMAN. His first sound film, *The Virginian* (1929), made him a star. It was in this film that Cooper had the dubious distinction of uttering the immortal line, "When you say that, smile." For the next 30 years he starred in numerous features, playing both dramatic and comedy roles. Although his acting capabilities were limited, he brought more than a degree of force and intelligence to such diverse roles as Hemingway's heroes in *A Farewell to Arms* (1932) and *For Whom the Bell Tolls* (1943), the hilarious White Knight who keeps falling off his horse in *Alice in Wonderland,* and the naive drifter in *Meet John Doe.*

He won two Academy Awards as Best Actor for his roles in *Sergeant York* (1941) and *High Noon* (1952). His quiet demeanor, shy behavior, and resolute manner won him both male and female admirers. He was particularly adept in comedy, whether a sophisticated film by director Ernst LUBITSCH or a social comedy by Frank CAPRA. His flair for humor may even be demonstrated in one of Cecil B. DeMille's outdoor adventure spectacles, *Northwest Mounted Police.* An officer in the Mounties observes with curiosity that Texas Ranger Cooper, who has journeyed north to hunt down an outlaw, has two holstered guns. "Why do you carry two guns?" the officer asks. "One doesn't shoot far enough," Cooper quips. In the same film he says to Madeleine Carroll: "I've always held that a bachelor is a feller who never made the same mistake once."

SELECTED FILMS: *It, Children of Divorce, Wings* (1927), *Half a Bride, Lilac Time* (1928), *Seven Days Leave, Morocco* (1930), *I Take This Woman* (1931), *If I Had a Million* (1932), *Design for Living, Alice in Wonderland* (1933), *Mr. Deeds Goes to Town* (1936), *Bluebeard's Eighth Wife, The Cowboy and the Lady* (1938), *Meet John Doe* (1941), *Ball of Fire, The Pride of the Yankees* (1942), *Casanova Brown* (1944), *Along Came Jones* (1945), *Good Sam* (1948), *Friendly Persuasion* (1956), *Love in the Afternoon* (1957), *The Wreck of the Mary Deare* (1959). ■

Cooper, Gladys (1881–1971), actress. Starred on stage in her native England before journeying to Hollywood. A light-haired, distinguished performer, she enhanced numerous dramas and light films with her grace. She usually portrayed members of the aristocracy. She received three nominations for Academy Awards.

SELECTED FILMS: *The Eleventh Commandment* (1913), *Kitty Foyle* (1940), *Mr. Lucky, Princess O'Rourke* (1943), *The Cockeyed Miracle* (1946), *The Bishop's Wife* (1947), *The Pirate* (1948), *The Man Who Loved Redheads* (1955), *My Fair Lady* (1964), *The Happiest Millionaire* (1967), *A Nice Girl Like Me* (1969). ■

Cooper, Jackie (1921–), actor. Began his film career at age three in two-reel comedies with Bobby CLARK and Lloyd HAMILTON. He appeared also in "OUR

GANG" comedies in the early 1930s. He developed into one of the most famous child stars during the 1930s, especially following his portrayal of the title character in *Skippy* (1930), which brought him an Academy Award nomination as Best Actor. His popularity steadily diminished during the 1940s, and he found himself appearing in B films. He switched to Broadway where he appeared in a series of comedies and eventually went into television. In 1972 he turned to directing films and soon became one of the most successful television film directors. His autobiography, *Please Don't Shoot My Dog*, was published in 1981. The title derives from director Norman Taurog's (his uncle) remark during the filming of *Skippy*. To get nine-year-old Jackie to cry during a particular scene, Taurog threatened to shoot the boy's dog.

SELECTED FILMS: *Fox Movietone Follies, Sunny Side Up* (1929), *Teacher's Pet, School's Out* (1930), *Donovan's Kid, The Champ, Sooky* (1931), *When a Feller Needs a Friend* (1932), *The Bowery* (1933), *Peck's Bad Boy* (1934), *Dinky* (1935), *That Certain Age* (1938), *Two Bright Boys, What a Life* (1939), *Seventeen* (1940), *Life With Henry, Her First Beau, Glamour Boy* (1941), *The Navy Comes Through* (1942), *Stork Bites Man, Kilroy Was Here* (1947), *French Leave* (1948), *Everything's Ducky* (1961), *The Love Machine* (1971), *Superman* (1978). ■

Cooper, Melville (1896–1973), actor. Appeared on stage in England in 1914 and in films in 1934. He began his American film career in 1936 in *The Gorgeous Hussy*. His drooping eyes and stocky frame helped him portray haughty and droll buffoons. His most memorable role perhaps was as Greer Garson's suitor in *Pride and Prejudice* (1940). He appeared in more than 50 features.

SELECTED FILMS: *The Last of Mrs. Cheyney, Thin Ice, Tovarich* (1937), *The Adventures of Robin Hood, Comet Over Broadway* (1938), *I'm From Missouri*

Melville Cooper

(1939), *Too Many Husbands* (1940), *The Lady Eve* (1941), *Life Begins at 8:30* (1942), *My Kingdom for a Cook* (1943), *Love Happy* (1949), *Father of the Bride* (1950), *Bundle of Joy* (1956), *From the Earth to the Moon* (1958). ■

Coote, Robert (1909–1982), actor. Appeared in films in his native England before coming to Hollywood in the early 1930s. A chubby and cheerful character player, he portrayed basically uppercrust English types in dramas and light films. He played the sergeant to whom Victor McLaglen and Douglas Fairbanks, Jr., administer the elephant tonic in *Gunga Din* (1939).

SELECTED FILMS: *Sally in Our Alley* (1931), *The Sheik Steps Out* (1937), *The Girl Downstairs* (1938), *You Can't Fool Your Wife* (1940), *The Ghost and Mrs. Muir* (1947), *Soldiers Three* (1951), *The Merry Widow* (1952), *Merry Andrew* (1958), *A Man Could Get Killed* (1966). ■

"Cops" (1922), FN. *Dir.* Buster Keaton, Eddie Cline; *Sc.* Buster Keaton, Eddie Cline; with Buster Keaton, Virginia Fox, Joe Roberts, Eddie Cline.

One of KEATON'S most famous shorts, this two-reeler is a composite of pathos, highly inventive gags, and an unforgettable climactic chase. The opening shot shows a close-up of Keaton framed by what appear to be prison bars—until the camera moves back to display the gates of a manor house. His sweetheart, who lives there, rejects him, insisting he succeed in business. Following a series of misadventures, he winds up with a horse and wagon and what he believes is his first business deal—the purchase of a load of furniture, which in reality belongs to a police officer who is in the process of moving. Keaton calmly guides his horse and wagon through the city streets and soon finds himself in the center of a policemen's parade. Suddenly an anarchist hurls a bomb which lands next to our hero. He picks it up to light his cigarette from the fuse and casually tosses it in the midst of a reviewing stand where it explodes. Almost instantly, hundreds of police begin to pursue the luckless Keaton. The chase, the highlight of the film, leads Buster to a ladder leaning on a fence. He quickly climbs it to get to safety, but some officers begin to tug at one end as others pull at the other, leaving Keaton in the middle. Finally, he is catapulted through the air to relative safety. Near the end of the pursuit he leads the hordes of cops into a large building, which turns out to be a station house, from which he alone emerges. He locks the door and discards the keys in a nearby bin. He then happily notices his sweetheart passing by. But she rejects him with a finality that even he cannot mistake. So he recovers the keys, unlocks the door, and allows himself to be scooped up by officers. The film exemplifies Keaton's underlying pessimism which appears in much of his work and which some viewers find more disturbing than funny.

Corey, Irwin (1912–), comedian, actor. Began his show business career in the early 1940s as a nightclub entertainer, moved on to television, and has appeared in a handful of films since the late 1970s. Known professionally as "Professor Irwin Corey," he has become proficient at the art of doubletalk, the basis for the bulk of his humor. A thin figure with a disheveled appearance, he has also been featured in several Broadway shows. Unfortunately, his film forays as a comic supporting player have done little to advance his comedy image or career.

SELECTED FILMS: *Car Wash* (1976), *Thieves* (1977), *How to Commit Marriage* (1969), *The Comeback Trail* (1974), *Crackers* (1984). ∎

Corrado, Gino (–1983), actor. Appeared as a minor character actor in comedy shorts during the 1940s. He usually portrayed emotional characters and drunks. He worked with several popular comics, including Buster KEATON and the THREE STOOGES.

SELECTED FILMS: *Pest From the West*, *Saved by the Belle* (1939), *An Ache in Every Stake* (1941), *Micro Phonies* (1945). ∎

Correll, Charles V. See Amos 'n' Andy.

Corrigan, Lloyd (1900–1969), actor, screenwriter, director. Began his film career as an actor in the 1920s. He later tried his hand at writing film scripts and directed a few features in the 1930s. He returned to acting in the 1940s, usually in light films. Short and portly, he often portrayed affable as well as uneasy characters.

In *Lucky Jordan* (1943) he played draftee Alan Ladd's lawyer. Ladd castigates him for not making the right connections to restore him to civilian life. "You can't fix Washington," Corrigan parries. "For one thing, you can't find out who's in charge."

SELECTED FILMS: *The Splendid Crime* (1925), *The Ghost Breakers*, *The Lady in Question* (1940), *Kathleen* (1941), *The Great Man's Lady* (1942), *The Thin Man Goes Home* (1945), *The Ghost Goes Wild* (1947), *A Date With Judy, The Bride Goes Wild* (1948), *Dancing in the Dark* (1949), *Cyrano de Bergerac* (1950), *Son of Paleface* (1952), *The Bowery Boys Meet the Monsters* (1954), *It's a Mad, Mad, Mad, Mad World* (1963). ∎

Cosby, Bill (1937–), comedian, actor. Received a Ph.D. in Education, worked as a nightclub comic and television performer, and made several successful comedy recordings before appearing in films. Working in small clubs during the 1960s, he was spotted doing his stand-up comedy act by television executives and was hired to co-star with Robert Culp in the series, "I Spy." This made him the first black to star in a dramatic television series. He continued to star in different shows in television through the 1960s, 1970s, and 1980s. He has also had success in films, usually starring or co-starring in light comedies. He has won several television Emmy Awards (his show was voted the best comedy series of the 1985–1986 season) as well as Grammy Awards for his comedy recordings.

SELECTED FILMS: Man and Boy, Hickey and Boggs (1972), Uptown Saturday Night (1974), Let's Do It Again (1975), Mother Juggs & Speed (1976), A Piece of the Action (1977), California Suite (1978), The Devil and Max Devlin (1981). ∎

Cossart, Ernest (1876–1951), actor. On stage in his native England before coming to the United States and Broadway. A portly and dapper figure, he appeared in several silent films and, with the advent of sound, became a steady character actor in numerous dramas and light films. He usually played snobbish butlers.

In Lady of the Tropics (1939) he played a missionary, Father Antoine, in pre-World War II Saigon. "Don't the French accept the half-castes?" an American tourist asks. "No," says Cossart, "they only create them."

SELECTED FILMS: The Strange Case of Mary Page (1916), Accent on Youth (1935), Champagne Waltz (1936), Three Smart Girls, Angel (1937), Letter of Introduction (1938), The Magnificent Fraud (1939), Kitty Foyle (1940), Charley's Aunt, Skylark (1941), Casanova Brown (1944), Tonight and Every Night (1945), Cluny Brown (1946), John Loves Mary (1949). ∎

Costello, Anthony "Pat," actor. Worked as a supporting player in several ABBOTT AND COSTELLO comedies. He appeared in other light films for low-budget studios. The brother of comedian Lou Costello, he later produced the boys' television series.

SELECTED FILMS: Little Giant (1946), Mexican Hayride (1948). ∎

Costello, Lou (1906–1959), comedian, actor. Worked in vaudeville and burlesque before settling in Hollywood as a major film comic. A short, pudgy figure with a bubbling personality, he joined Bud ABBOTT in 1931, and they became one of the most popular comedy teams in films during the 1940s. The pair separated in 1957, and Lou made one solo film, The 30-Foot Bride of Candy Rock (1959). He died of a heart attack at age 53. See also ABBOTT AND COSTELLO.

Court Jester, The (1956), PAR. Dir. Norman Panama, Melvin Frank; Sc. Norman Panama, Melvin Frank; with Danny Kaye, Glynis Johns, Basil Rathbone, Angela Lansbury, Cecil Parker.

One of the greatest comedy routines in film history emerged from this costume farce starring Danny Kaye. Equally hilarious, if not as well known, as Abbott and Costello's "Who's on First" is the bit in which Kaye is informed about the placement of a poison. "The pellet with the poison is in the vessel with the pestle; the chalice from the palace has the brew that is true," he is told. After he finally memorizes this complicated mnemonic, the poison is switched, and he is told to forget the previous message and learn the new, more complex one. There are other funny bits in this classic comedy that entangles him in romance, intrigue, and mortal combat, including his sword fight with Basil Rathbone. This is probably Kaye's best film.

Courtney, Inez (1908–1975), actress. Worked in vaudeville and in the theater before her debut in films in 1930. Her specialty was portraying wise-cracking dames in light comedies as well as dramas.

SELECTED FILMS: *Spring Is Here, Bright Lights, Sunny (1930), Loose Ankles, The Hot Heiress (1931), Big City Blues (1932), Cheating Blondes (1933), Broadway Bill (1934), Ship Cafe (1935), Magnificent Obsession, Suzy (1936), The Hit Parade (1937), Having Wonderful Time (1938), Blondie Meets the Boss (1939), The Shop Around the Corner (1940).* ∎

Courtot, Marguerite (1897–1986), actress. Worked as a fashion model before entering films with Kalem studios in 1912 at age fifteen. An auburn-haired beauty, she starred in numerous dramas, serials, and light films. She appeared frequently with Tom Moore as her leading man. Shortly after her marriage to another co-star, Raymond McKee, in the early 1920s, she gave up her screen career.

SELECTED FILMS: *Breaking Into the Big League (1913), The Adventures of Briarcliff, The Girl and the Bachelor (1915), The Kiss, The Tricksters (1916), The Perfect Lover (1919), Pirate Gold (1920), The Cradle Buster (1922).* ∎

Cowan, Jerome (1897–1972), actor. Appeared in vaudeville and on Broadway before making his film debut in 1936 as the Irish patriot in *Beloved Enemy*. He played a variety of roles, including the dapper, happy-go-lucky "other man," either in lead or character parts, in almost 150 films. He appeared in several "Blondie" films. His most famous role was as Miles Archer, Humphrey Bogart's short-lived partner, in *The Maltese Falcon* (1941).

SELECTED FILMS: *Shall We Dance (1937), The Goldwyn Follies (1938), Torrid Zone (1940), Kiss the Boys Goodbye (1941), Getting Gertie's Garter (1945), The Kid From Brooklyn (1946), June Bride (1948), Blondie's Secret (1949), The Fuller Brush Girl (1950), Visit to a Small Planet (1960), Pocketful of Miracles (1961), The Patsy (1964), The Comic (1969).* ∎

Cox, Wally (1924–1973), actor. Began in show business in the late 1940s as a nightclub comic, then gained popularity on television as the shy, wistful "Mr. Peepers." In 1952 he was voted television's "Most Promising Male Star." When the show was canceled, thousands of protest letters from his fans helped to return the program to television. Bespectacled and unassuming, he brought his humorous character to the screen for the first time in 1962.

SELECTED FILMS: *State Fair (1962), Spencer's Mountain (1963), The Yellow Rolls Royce (1964), A Guide for the Married Man (1967), The Cockeyed Cowboys of Calico County (1970), The Barefoot Executive (1971).* ∎

Cracked Nuts (1931), RKO. Dir. Edward Cline; Sc. Al Boasberg, Richard Spence; with Bert Wheeler, Robert Woolsey, Dorothy Lee, Edna May Oliver, Stanley Fields, Boris Karloff, Ben Turpin.

WHEELER AND WOOLSEY, a popular comedy team of the 1930s, had starred in vaudeville and in the Ziegfeld Follies before bringing their stage routines and puns to the screen. In this satire of political and military arrogance, Woolsey wins the kingship of the mythical Eldorania in a crap game. But the boys have to contend with political corruption, represented by Boris Karloff, and a vindictive military, exemplified by Stanley FIELDS who plays General Bogardus. Wheeler falls for Dorothy LEE, who appeared as the female lead in several of the team's comedies. Meanwhile, her aunt, the stalwart Edna May OLIVER, opposes the affair. Veteran silent screen comedian Ben TURPIN portrays a cross-eyed precision bomber in the employ of the villainous Karloff. Wheeler and Woolsey's verbal and visual gags succeed for the most part, including several of their puns. "It's impossible to ford the river here," Woolsey says, referring to a map. "Why?" inquires Wheeler. "For divers reasons." One clever routine concerning two towns named What and Which predates ABBOTT AND COSTELLO'S "Who's on First" classic. The film also predates other comedies which dealt with similar subject matter, namely *Million Dollar Legs* (1932) with W. C. FIELDS and Jack OAKIE and *Duck Soup* (1933) starring the MARX BROTHERS. Although their later films suffered from repetitive gags, mediocre scripts, and lower production costs, Wheeler and Woolsey continued to appear in RKO films until Woolsey's death in 1938.

Craig, Alec (1885–1945), actor. Prolific character actor who proved competent in both dramatic and humorous roles. He appeared in more than 75 features within a 12-year period. Craggy-faced and slim of stature, he often portrayed frugal characters for many of the major Hollywood studios.

SELECTED FILMS: The Little Minister (1934), Sweepstakes Annie (1935), That Girl From Paris (1936), Meet the Missus (1937), She's Got Everything, Crashing Hollywood, Vivacious Lady (1938), Charlie McCarthy, Detective (1939), Three Cheers for the Irish (1940), Barnacle Bill, A Date With the Falcon (1941), To Be or Not to Be, Her Cardboard Lover (1942), Holy Matrimony (1943), Ghost Catchers (1944), Tonight and Every Night (1945), Girl on the Spot, Three Strangers (1946). ∎

Craig, Nell (1891–1965), actress. Made her debut in films in the late 1910s as a silent screen actress for Essanay studios. She portrayed various characters into the 1940s, with her role as the contentious

Nurse Parker in the "Dr. Kildare" series perhaps her most memorable.

SELECTED FILMS: The Return of Richard Neal (1915), The Triflers (1920), The Flirt, Remembrance (1922), The Abysmal Brute (1923), Cimarron (1931), Palm Springs (1936), Calling Dr. Kildare (1939), Calling Dr. Gillespie (1942), Three Men in White (1944), Between Two Women (1945), Our Hearts Were Growing Up (1946), Dark Delusion (1947). ∎

Cramer, Richard (1889–1960), actor. Worked for two decades in the theater before he began a new career in films in 1929. He specialized in villainous roles. His rough features and large, threatening frame made him the quintessential heavy. He appeared in dramas as well as light films, including several comedies starring LAUREL AND HARDY.

SELECTED FILMS: Kid Gloves (1929), Sweet Mama (1930), An American Tragedy (1931), The Tenderfoot, Scram, Pack Up Your Troubles (1932), Woman Chases Man, Turn Off the Moon (1937), Saps at Sea (1940), Double Trouble (1941), Song of Old Wyoming (1945), Law of the Lash (1947). ∎

Crane, Phyllis, actress. Worked chiefly in comedy shorts and features during the 1930s as a supporting player. She had the thankless task of appearing as foil to the THREE STOOGES in several of their films.

SELECTED FILMS: So This Is College, The Forward Pass, The Girl Said No (1930), Men in Black, Three Little Pigskins (1934), Pop Goes the Easel, Uncivil Warriors, Hoi Poloi (1935), Ants in the Pantry, A Pain in the Pullman (1936). ∎

Cravat, Nick (1911–), actor. Worked as an acrobat before joining his friend from their circus days, Burt Lancaster, in two light adventure films in the 1950s. Diminutive in stature, he added exciting and entertaining stunts as well as comic relief to many of the features in which he appeared. He retired from his screen career in 1977.

SELECTED FILMS: The Flame and the Arrow (1950), The Crimson Pirate (1952), Veils of Bagdad (1953), King Richard and the Crusades (1954), Run Silent, Run Deep (1958), The Way West (1967), The Scalphunters (1968), Valdez Is Coming (1971), Ulzana's Raid (1972), The Midnight Man (1974), The Island of Dr. Moreau (1977). ■

Craven, Frank (1875–1945), actor. A playwright who switched to acting in films in the late 1920s. An affable character player, he appeared in dramas and light films chiefly in fatherly and other mature roles that permitted him to offer words of wisdom. He occasionally had leads in low-budget family features.

SELECTED FILMS: We Americans (1928), The Very Idea (1929), State Fair (1933), That's Gratitude, He Was Her Man (1934), Small Town Girl (1936), Penrod and Sam, Blossoms on Broadway (1937), You're Only Young Once (1938), Our Neighbors, the Carters (1939), Harrigan's Kid (1943), My Best Gal (1944), Colonel Effingham's Raid (1945). ■

Crawford, Broderick (1911–1986), actor. Worked in vaudeville, in radio, and on stage. He made his Hollywood debut in the mid-1930s as a supporting player in unimportant films. He was frequently assigned roles as large, somewhat stupid but often powerful figures. Finally, in 1949, he was given the chance to play the truculent Willie Stark in All the King's Men. His dynamic portrayal won him an Academy Award as Best Actor and wide recognition of his talents. He was as gifted at portraying comic characters as he was at playing dramatic roles. He was the son of stage and screen actress Helen BRODERICK.

In Slightly Honorable law partners Pat O'BRIEN and Crawford contemplate a baffling series of murders. Crawford laughs at his partner's confidence that he will solve the case. "All right," O'Brien

says, "they laughed at Marconi, too." "I don't know why," Crawford retorts. "I didn't think his stuff was funny." His most memorable comic role was his portrayal of a tycoon junk dealer in Born Yesterday (1950). Judy HOLLIDAY, as his mistress, calls him a fascist. "I was born in Plainfield, New Jersey," he protests to his lawyer, "she knows that!"

SELECTED FILMS: Woman Chases Man (1937), Ambush, Beau Geste, The Real Glory, Eternally Yours (1939), Slightly Honorable, Seven Sinners, Tight Shoes (1941), Larceny, Inc., Butch Minds the Baby (1942), The Time of Your Life (1948), Born Yesterday (1950), Stop, You're Killing Me (1952), Convicts Four (1962), A Little Romance (1979). ■

Crisp, Donald (1880–1974), actor, director. Entered early silent films in 1908 as an actor following some brief experience. He acted in several films for D. W. Griffith and by 1914 turned to directing. He continued in this capacity until the advent of sound, at which time he returned to acting. His screen career spanned more than 50 years. Although remembered more for his acting, especially in dramas, he also directed many light films and comedy-dramas during the silent era.

SELECTED FILMS (as director): The Cook of Canyon Camp, The Clever Mrs. Carfax, Countess Charming, His Sweetheart, Lost in Transit, A Roadside Impresario (1917), Believe Me, Xantippe, The Goat (1918), Johnny Get Your Gun, Something to Do, Under the Top, Venus in the East, A Very Good Young Man, Why Smith Left Home (1919), Too Much Johnson (1920). ■

Crosby, Bing (1904–1977), singer, actor. Began his show business career as a singer, eventually working for the famous Paul Whiteman and his band in 1926. He entered films in 1930 with the band. He then signed with Mack SENNETT in 1931 and made a handful of short comedy films. He began making recordings and started a radio program. He was soon recognized as one of the most popular singers of the 1930s. His offhand, loose manner became his trademark, along with his song, "Where the Blue of the Night." He starred in numerous light musicals and comedies for Paramount, such as *Going Hollywood* and *We're Not Dressing*, usually enhancing them with his affability and charm. In 1940 he teamed up with Bob HOPE to make a series of lucrative "ROAD" comedies, also for Paramount. Occasionally he played dramatic roles, one of which, *Going My Way* (1944), brought him an Academy Award as Best Actor for his role of a crooning priest. Probably only an exceptional talent like Crosby's could have made this sentimental tale work.

SELECTED FILMS: *King of Jazz* (1930), *The Big Broadcast* (1932), *College Humor, Going Hollywood* (1933), *We're Not Dressing* (1934), *Mississippi, Two for Tonight* (1935), *Anything Goes, Pennies From Heaven* (1936), *Waikiki Wedding, Double or Nothing* (1937), *East Side of Heaven, The Star Maker* (1939), *Road to Singapore* (1940), *Birth of the Blues* (1941), *Holiday Inn, Road to Morocco* (1942), *Dixie* (1943), *The Bells of St. Mary's* (1945), *Blue Skies* (1946), *Road to Rio* (1947), *The Emperor Waltz* (1948), *A Connecticut Yankee in King Arthur's Court* (1949), *Riding High* (1950), *White Christmas, The Country Girl* (1954), *High Society* (1956), *Stagecoach* (1966). ∎

Crosland, Alan (1894–1936), director. Worked in the theater from 1909 as an actor and stage manager before entering films. Employed by the Edison Film Company in 1912, he began to direct film shorts two years later. By 1925 he was directing for Warner Brothers, turning out major productions including *The Jazz Singer* (1927), the first talking feature. He directed dramas and comedies during the 1930s until his untimely death in an automobile accident. More a

skilled craftsman than an innovator, he turned out several entertaining films.

SELECTED FILMS: *Kidnapped, The Apple Tree Girl* (1917), *The Flapper* (1920), *Room and Board* (1921), *Slim Shoulders, The Snitching Hour* (1922), *Three Weeks, Miami* (1924), *Bobbed Hair* (1925), *The Beloved Rogue* (1927), *Glorious Betsy* (1928), *On With the Show* (1929), *Big Boy, Viennese Nights* (1930), *Week Ends Only* (1932), *It Happened in New York, Mr. Dynamite, Lady Tubbs, King Solomon of Broadway, The Great Impersonation* (1935). ∎

Crosley, Mr. Fictional faculty member of Centerville High in several "HENRY ALDRICH" comedies starring Jimmy LYDON. Veteran comic character actor Lucien LITTLEFIELD played the easily vexed Crosley in *What a Life* (1939), *Henry Aldrich for President* (1941), and *Henry Aldrich Haunts a House* (1943), all produced by Paramount.

Crosman, Henrietta (1861–1944), actress. Worked in the theater as a leading lady before making her screen debut in 1914. She appeared in early silent films from the mid-1910s and in sound features through most of the 1930s. As a character actress during the latter part of her film career, she often portrayed bubbling characters, whether in dramas or light comedies. One of her more memorable, offbeat roles was as the dying Grand Old Dame of the theater in *The Royal Family of Broadway* (1930).

SELECTED FILMS: *The Unwelcome Mrs. Hatch* (1914), *How Molly Made Good* (1915), *Broadway Broke* (1923), *Three on a Honeymoon, Carolina, Such Women Are Dangerous* (1934), *Hitchhike to Heaven, Charlie Chan's Secret, The Moon's Our Home, Girl of the Ozarks, Follow Your Heart* (1936), *Personal Property* (1937). ∎

Crosthwaite, Ivy, supporting player. Worked occasionally in early silent comedy shorts for Mack SENNETT'S KEY-

STONE studios. She appeared with some of the leading screen comics of the period, including, among others, "Fatty" ARBUCKLE, Mack SWAIN, and Polly MORAN.

SELECTED FILMS: Fatty and the Broadway Stars (1915), By Stork Delivery (1916). ∎

Crowley, Pat (1933–), actress. Worked as a child model before entering films. She has appeared as a leading lady and in supporting roles, chiefly in light films.

SELECTED FILMS: Forever Female, Money From Home, Red Garters (1954), There's Always Tomorrow, Hollywood or Bust (1956), The Wheeler Dealers (1963), To Trap a Spy (1966), The Biscuit Eater (1972). ∎

Cruze, James (1884–1942), director, actor. Worked as an actor in road shows, in stock, and on Broadway before entering silent films in 1908. By 1918 he switched to directing, a profession that carried him through the silent period and well into the 1930s. He turned out a variety of films, both dramas and comedies, working with some of the foremost screen personalities of the period, including, among others, "Fatty" ARBUCKLE, W. C. FIELDS, and Will ROGERS. An efficient and talented craftsman, he directed vigorously if not creatively. Many of his films are routine fare, but others, such as The Covered Wagon (1923), an influential western, and I Cover the Waterfront (1933), a somber and cynical crime drama, show traces of originality.

SELECTED FILMS: Too Many Millions (1918), The Lottery Man (1919), Food for Scandal, A Full House, Mrs. Temple's Telegram, The Six Best Cellars, What Happened to Jones (1920), Crazy to Marry, The Dollar-a-Year Man, Gasoline Gus (1921), One Glorious Day (1922), Ruggles of Red Gap (1923), The Fighting Coward (1924), Beggar on Horseback, Marry Me (1925), If I Had a Million

(1932), Sailor Be Good (1933), David Harum (1934), Come On Leathernecks (1938). ∎

Cukor, George (1899–1984), director. Worked as stage manager in 1919, director in 1920. He entered films in 1930 as dialogue director for Paramount studios, then full-fledged director a few years later. He moved to RKO and finally settled in at MGM where he and his friend, producer David O. Selznick, combined their talents to create a string of distinguished films.

He has been labeled by critics and others as a "woman's director," but this was only one of his gifts. His contributions to the cinema were far greater. Although he did get exceptional performances from such stars as Katharine HEPBURN, Greta Garbo, and Judy HOLLIDAY, he did as well by his male leads. Fredric MARCH, Charles Boyer, James Mason, and Anthony Quinn were nominated for Academy Awards, while James STEWART, Ronald COLMAN, and Rex Harrison won Oscars. His films reflected his discernment and style, his ability to extract character and set mood and tone. His style might have been subjective, but his camera was unobtrusive. He won an Academy Award in 1964 for his direction of My Fair Lady. Although he was not an auteur director (he did not write his own scripts), he has, nevertheless, left behind more than 50 films, a body of work that any of his contemporaries would have been proud to have claimed as their own.

SELECTED FILMS: Grumpy, The Royal Family of Broadway (1930), Tarnished Lady (1931), Girls About Town, A Bill of Divorcement (1932), Dinner at Eight (1933), Sylvia Scarlett (1936), Holiday (1938), The Philadelphia Story (1940), Two-Faced Woman (1941), Keeper of the Flame (1943), Gaslight (1944), Adam's Rib (1949), Born Yesterday (1950), The Model and the Marriage Broker, The Marrying Kind, Pat and Mike (1952), It Should Happen to You

(1954), Travels With My Aunt (1972), The Blue Bird (1976). ■

Cummings, Constance (1910–), actress. Worked in stock and on Broadway in the late 1920s as a chorine before making her Hollywood debut in 1931. A pretty actress with an abundance of talent, she played leads in dramas and light films until the mid-1930s when she abandoned Hollywood for the British stage and screen.

SELECTED FILMS: The Criminal Code, Traveling Husbands, Lover Come Back (1931), The Big Timer, Movie Crazy, Night After Night, Washington Merry-Go-Round (1932), The Charming Deceiver (1933), Glamour (1934), Remember Last Night (1935). ■

Cummings, Irving (1888–1959), actor, director. Worked on stage with Lillian Russell before turning his talents toward silent films in 1909. After playing leads into the 1920s, he switched to directing, showing a penchant for comedy, even in his melodramas. A dependable, if not very creative director, he made a smooth transition into the sound era, specializing in light features starring some of the leading screen personalities of the period, including Shirley TEMPLE, Bob HOPE, and Betty GRABLE.

SELECTED FILMS (as actor): Camille (1912), The Saleslady, The Gilded Cage (1916), A Royal Romance (1917), Don't Change Your Husband (1919), The Saphead (1921).
SELECTED FILMS (as director): East Side—West Side (1923), The Dancing Cheat, The Rose of Paris (1924), Bertha the Sewing Machine Girl (1926), Not Quite Decent (1929), On the Level (1930), Man Against Woman (1932), The White Parade (1934), It's a Small World, Curly Top (1935), The Poor Little Rich Girl (1936), Little Miss Broadway (1938), Hollywood Cavalcade (1939), Down Argentine Way (1940), Louisiana Purchase (1941), What a Woman! (1943), The Dolly Sisters (1945), Double Dynamite (1951). ■

Cummings, Robert (1908–), actor. Appeared on Broadway in 1931 before making his film debut in 1935. A good-looking, amiable, and charming actor, he was very popular in light comedies during the 1930s and 1940s. He would occasionally appear in dramatic roles, most notably in *Kings Row* (1942) and in Hitchcock's *Saboteur* (1942). He began a successful second career in television in his middle years.

SELECTED FILMS: Virginia Judge, So Red the Rose (1935), Arizona Mahoney (1936), Sophie Lang Goes West (1937), College Swing, Touchdown Army (1938), Everything Happens at Night, Charlie McCarthy, Detective (1939), One Night in the Tropics (1940), The Devil and Miss Jones, It Started With Eve (1941), You Came Along (1945), Heaven Only Knows (1947), The Petty Girl (1950), The First Time (1952), My Geisha (1962), Five Golden Dragons (1967). ■

Cunningham, Cecil (1888–1959), actress. Worked in the theater before making her debut in films in 1929. She appeared in more than 75 features over two decades, almost invariably as a supporting player. She was as deft at straight roles as she was at lighter ones, often portraying wise-cracking confidantes, career women, or facetious secretaries.

In *Blossoms in the Dust* (1941), for example, she confides to Greer Garson: "My husband and I have decided to give the advantage of our home to one of your foundlings. . . . Of course, we wouldn't want one that cries."

SELECTED FILMS: Their Own Desire (1929), Anybody's Woman, Playboy of Paris (1930), Monkey Business (1931), The Impatient Maiden, If I Had a Million (1932), Baby Face (1933), Manhattan Love Song (1934), Mr. Deeds Goes to Town (1936), Artists and Models (1937), College Swing (1938), Laugh It Off (1939), Kitty Foyle (1940), I Married an Angel (1942), DuBarry Was a Lady (1943), Wonder Man, The Horn Blows at Midnight (1945), The Bride Goes Wild (1948). ■

"Cure, The" (1917), MUT. *Dir.* Charlie Chaplin; *Sc.* Charlie Chaplin; with Charlie Chaplin, Edna Purviance, Eric Campbell, Henry Bergman, Albert Austin.

In "The Cure," one of Chaplin's famous "golden dozen" he made at Mutual studios, he returned to Mack Sennett's world of slapstick. Again playing the drunk—but without his tramp costume—Charlie checks into a fashionable spa. Dressed in a white suit and straw hat and swinging his cane, he soon causes havoc at the once tranquil establishment. He has come here to cure himself of his drinking problem. His luggage, however, is stacked with bottles of liquor. When his supply is accidentally dumped into the mineral water at the hotel, all the guests become inebriated. Eric CAMPBELL, Charlie's perpetual foil at Mutual, is a guest at the spa and has a bandaged foot. But this doesn't stop Charlie from attacking him, including pushing his wheelchair with such force that Campbell plunges head first into the pool of mineral water. Charlie's encounters with revolving doors and a massage parlor where he transforms a massage into a wrestling match also liven things up in this well-paced classic comedy rich in sight gags and slapstick.

Curtis, Alan (1909–1953), actor. Began his screen career in the mid-1930s. Dark and handsome, he chiefly played leads or second leads in low-budget romances, action films, and light comedies. He worked with several comics, including ABBOTT AND COSTELLO and OLSEN AND JOHNSON.

SELECTED FILMS: *The Smartest Girl in Town, Walking on Air (1936), Don't Tell the Wife (1937), Shopworn Angel (1938), Good Girls Go to Paris (1939), Come Live With Me, Buck Privates (1941), Crazy House (1943), Follow the Boys (1944), Frisco Sal, Shady Lady, The Naughty Nineties, See My Lawyer (1945), The Masked Pirate (1950).* ∎

Curtis, Allen, director. Worked in early silent films turning out chiefly one-reel comedies for studios such as Victor, Universal, and Nestor. He directed many of Eileen SEDGWICK'S early comedies.

SELECTED FILMS: *It's Cheaper to Be Married, A Bare Living, Good Morning, Nurse, A Woman in the Case, His Family Tree, Swearing Off, Flat Harmony, Making Monkey Business, Not Too Thin to Fight, The Paperhanger's Revenge (1917), A Kitchen Hero, Passing the Bomb, The Butler's Blunder, Oh, Man! (1918).* ∎

Curtis, Dick (1902–1952), actor. Began his screen career in 1918 as an extra before specializing as a character player in sound films, often as a heavy in westerns. He appeared in comedy shorts and features with some of the leading comics of the period, including the THREE STOOGES.

SELECTED FILMS: *Girl Crazy (1932), Time Out for Trouble, Flat Foot Stooges (1938), We Want Our Mummy, Yes, We Have No Bonanza (1939), Rockin' Through the Rockies (1940), Two Yanks in Trinidad (1942), Pardon My Gun, Higher Than a Kite (1943), Spook Town, Crash Goes the Hash (1944), Three Troubleshooters (1946), Three Arabian Nuts, Don't Throw That Knife (1951), My Six Convicts (1952).* ∎

Curtis, Jack (1880–1956), actor. Began his screen career in early silent films. He appeared as a supporting player in dramas and light films, specializing in action vehicles, through the silent period and into the early part of the sound era.

SELECTED FILMS: *Her Great Part, The Romance of Billy Goat Hill, It Happened in Honolulu (1916), A Prairie Romeo (1917), My Husband's Friend (1918), The Pest (1919), Reno (1923), The Show of Shows (1929), The Love Racket, Hold Everything (1930), Westward Ho (1935), Spook Town (1944), My Six Convicts (1952).* ∎

Tony Curtis

Curtis, Tony (1925–), actor. Worked in stock and off-Broadway after his discharge from the Navy, making his film debut in 1949. By 1951 Curtis, born Bernard Schwartz, became firmly established as a popular and successful film personality. At first the studios exploited his looks and appeal to young females by placing him in costume adventures. His talent as a more than competent actor, however, was soon to emerge in films like *Sweet Smell of Success* (1957), in which he portrayed a sleazy, immoral publicity hound, and *Some Like It Hot* (1959), in which he hilariously impersonated a female musician. The latter film demonstrated his flair for comedy. He has displayed both control and electricity in his roles.

In *Captain Newman, M.D.*, he portrayed a hypochondriac corporal who is assigned to a military mental ward under the supervision of Capt. Newman (Gregory Peck). Querulous and disrespectful, Curtis enters his superior's office. "I believe that it's customary for a soldier to address an officer as 'sir,'" Peck announces. "Sir," Curtis says grudgingly, and then continues, "Well, it's customary for a soldier, but it's tough for a civilian." "But you're not a civilian," Peck counters. "I feel like a civilian," Curtis insists. Peck tries to allay the corporal's fears about working with mental patients. "Patients are not allowed to have matches or razors or sharp objects of any kind." "But teeth they've got," Curtis adds.

SELECTED FILMS: *Criss Cross, City Across the River* (1949), *Francis* (1950), *No Room for the Groom* (1952), *So This Is Paris* (1955), *The Perfect Furlough, Operation Petticoat* (1959), *Spartacus* (1960), *Forty Pounds of Trouble* (1963), *Captain Newman, M.D., Goodbye Charlie, Paris When It Sizzles* (1964), *The Great Race* (1965), *Don't Make Waves* (1967), *The Bad News Bears Go to Japan* (1978). ■

Cutting, Richard H. (1912–1972), actor. Began his screen career in the early 1950s as a supporting player in westerns. He later widened his roles by appearing in dramas and light films but near the end of his career reverted to westerns.

SELECTED FILMS: *War Paint* (1953), *The Vagabond King, The Private War of Major Benson, You're Never Too Young* (1955), *You Can't Run Away From It* (1956), *Top Secret Affair, Rock All Night, Teenage Doll* (1957), *South Pacific* (1958), *Rally 'Round the Flag, Boys, A Nice Little Bank That Should Be Robbed* (1959), *The Ride to Hangman's Tree* (1967). ■

D

Dale, Charles. See Smith and Dale.

Dale, Esther (1885–1961), actress. Worked as a singer and stage actress before coming to Hollywood. As a character player in more than 75 films, including dramas, musicals, and light comedies, she brought a business-like quality to her parts, which often consisted of domineering mothers, straitlaced menials, and officious matrons. She appeared as Mrs. Hicks in the MA AND PA KETTLE comedy series.

SELECTED FILMS: Crime Without Passion (1934), I Dream Too Much, Curly Top (1935), The Farmer in the Dell (1936), Easy Living, The Awful Truth (1937), Broadway Serenade (1939), Blondie Has Servant Trouble (1940), Mr. and Mrs. Smith (1941), I Married an Angel, Maisie Gets Her Man (1942), Swing Your Partner (1943), Bedside Manner (1945), Margie (1946), The Egg and I (1947), A Song Is Born (1948), Holiday Affair (1949), Too Young to Kiss (1951), Ma and Pa Kettle at the Fair (1952), The Oklahoman (1957). ■

Daley, Cass (1915–1975), singer, comedienne, actress. Began her show business career as a singer, then switched to comedienne in nightclubs and radio. A lively performer, she appeared in the Ziegfeld Follies of 1936 and made her debut in films in 1942. Known for her buck teeth and her shrill-like singing, she brightened many musicals and light films with her voice and comedy during the 1940s and 1950s. One of her more zany roles was in *Crazy House*, in which she matched wits with comics OLSEN AND JOHNSON.

SELECTED FILMS: The Fleet's In, Star Spangled Rhythm (1942), Crazy House, Riding High (1943), Out of This World, Duffy's Tavern (1945), Ladies' Man, Variety Girl (1947), Here Comes the Groom (1951), Red Garters (1954), The Spirit Is Willing (1967), Norwood (1970). ■

Dalio, Marcel (1900–1985), actor. Worked in films in his native France from 1933 before immigrating to Hollywood during World War II. Although he gained fame for his dramatic roles at home, including the classic, *Grand Illusion* (1938), he played well-dressed comic characters during his American stay. After the war he returned to Europe, acting in films on both sides of the Atlantic.

SELECTED FILMS: Unholy Partners (1941), The Pied Piper (1942), The Constant Nymph, Paris After Dark, The Desert Song (1943), Pin-Up Girl (1944), On the Riviera, Rich, Young and Pretty (1951), The Happy Time (1952), Gentlemen Prefer Blondes (1953), Anything Goes (1956), The Perfect Furlough (1958), Pillow Talk (1959), Made in Paris, How to Steal a Million (1966), How Sweet It Is! (1968), Catch-22 (1970). ■

Dalton, Dorothy, actress. Entered early silent films in the 1910s. She played female leads in dramas and comedies, chiefly for Paramount studios.

SELECTED FILMS: Flare-Up Sal (1918), Hard-Boiled, The Home Breaker (1919), A Romantic Adventuress (1920). ▪

Damita, Lili (1901–), actress. Appeared on stage and in films in her native France before coming to Hollywood where she made a succession of light films. She appeared also in films produced in other countries before retiring from the screen following her marriage to actor Errol Flynn.

SELECTED FILMS: The Rescue, The Cock-Eyed World (1929), The Woman Between, Friends and Lovers (1931), This Is the Night, The Match King (1932), Goldie Gets Along (1933), Brewster's Millions (1935), The Devil on Horseback (1936). ▪

Dana, Viola (1897–), actress. Appeared on stage before entering early silent films in 1914. She played female leads in numerous dramas and light films. With John Collins, her first husband, directing, she starred in a series of pre-1920 features before switching to MGM studios in the 1920s. She retired from the screen when sound was introduced.

SELECTED FILMS: Molly the Drummer Boy (1914), Rosie O'Grady (1917), Please Get Married, Some Bride (1919), Parlor, Bedroom and Bath (1920), The Match-Breaker (1921), June Madness, The Five Dollar Baby (1922), Rouged Lips (1923), Open All Night, Merton of the Movies (1924), Forty Winks (1925), Kosher Kitty Kelly (1926), Naughty Nanette, Salvation Jane (1927), That Certain Thing (1928), One Splendid Hour, The Show of Shows (1929). ▪

Dane, Karl (1886–1934), actor. Appeared on stage in Copenhagen before immigrating to Hollywood during World War I. His first big break came in 1925 as a supporting player in The Big Parade. His portrayal of a tall, awkward, happy-go-lucky doughboy who could, among

other feats, extinguish a candle with a mouthful of tobacco juice brought him offers to play comic roles in silent shorts and features. Metro studios teamed him with English-born George K. ARTHUR in a series of comedies ("Baby Mine," "Detectives," "Brotherly Love"). He also appeared occasionally in dramatic films, including, among others, The Big House and Billy the Kid, both released in 1930, and in the serial Whispering Shadows (1933). Burdened with a heavy Danish accent, he had difficulty finding film work in sound films and, for a time, did carpentry work on the MGM lot. He committed suicide at age 48.

SELECTED FILMS: My Four Years in Germany, To Hell With the Kaiser (1918), The Everlasting Whisper, Lights of Old Broadway (1925), The Son of the Sheik, Mardelys the Magnificent, Monte Carlo, War Paint (1926), The Red Mill, Slide, Kelly, Slide, Rookies (1927), Baby Mine, Alias Jimmy Valentine, Detectives, Brotherly Love (1928), The Duke Steps Out, Speedway, All at Sea, China Bound, Navy Blues (1929), Montana Moon, Free and Easy (1930). ▪

Dangerfield, Rodney (1921–), actor, comedian. Began his show business career as a small-time comedian. To supplement his meager income, he sold jokes to several major comics. It wasn't until he reached middle-age that he gained recognition as a stand-up comic in nightclubs and television. He has made several comedy records, receiving a Grammy for one in 1980. His film appearances have been sporadic and uneventful, but by the mid-1980s he joined the ranks of the top screen comics. Stocky and sad-faced, he has built his comic career around self-deprecation, epitomized by his famous line: "I don't get no respect."

In Back to School he played a millionaire who is separated from his wife and who goes to college to help his son stay in school. The film offered him a golden opportunity to demonstrate his skill with one-liners. "Do I think you're extravagant?" he says to his avaricious wife. "Of course not. Everybody goes to Switzerland to have their watches fixed." In another scene he announces to a society matron attired in a green evening gown: "If that dress had pockets, you'd look like a pool table."

SELECTED FILMS: The Projectionist (1971), Caddyshack (1980), Easy Money (1983), Back to School (1986). ∎

Daniell, Henry (1894–1963), actor. Appeared on stage in his native England and on Broadway before seeking a career in Hollywood films in the late 1920s. A serious figure with a cold stare, he was used chiefly in villainous roles. But he made his share of light films as a character actor and, at times, lead player during a screen career that spanned four decades.

SELECTED FILMS: Jealousy, The Awful Truth (1929), The Unguarded Hour (1936), The Firefly (1937), Holiday (1938), The Great Dictator, The Philadelphia Story (1940), Four Jacks and a Jill, The Feminine Touch (1941), Diane (1955), Around the World in 80 Days (1956), Les Girls (1957), The Notorious Landlady (1962), My Fair Lady (1964). ∎

Daniels, Bebe (1901–1971), actress. Began her acting career with her father's theater company. She first appeared in films at age nine, gradually moving into more adult parts, especially with the Hal ROACH studios. By the time she was eighteen she had already appeared in hundreds of comedy shorts with, among others, Snub POLLARD and Harold LLOYD. She co-starred with Lloyd in many of his "LONESOME LUKE" comedy shorts. A spirited comedienne, she was frequently called upon to play the role of a tomboy. During the 1920s, the height of her popularity, she made many feature films for Paramount studios.

When sound arrived, the studio dismissed her and she switched to RKO. When her popularity began to fade in the 1930s, she and her husband, actor Ben Lyons, moved to England, where she continued to act in films. One of her more memorable roles was as the testy Broadway star in 42nd Street. Guy Kibbee, her lover and financial backer of her show, becomes disenchanted with her and threatens to pull out. "I've got half a mind—" he begins. "You're telling me!" she retorts.

SELECTED FILMS: The Common Enemy (1910), An Awful Romance, Luke's Society Mixup (1917), The Lamb, Here Come the Girls, Nothing but Trouble (1918), Young Mr. Jazz, The Marathon, Be My Wife, Everywoman (1919), Why Change Your Wife, You Never Can Tell (1920), The Affairs of Anatol, The Speed Queen (1921), Nancy From Nowhere (1922), The World's Applause, Her Children's Children (1923), Daring Youth, Sinner's Heaven (1924), Miss Bluebeard, Wild, Wild Susan (1925), Miss Brewster's Millions, The Palm Beach Girl (1926), Senorita (1927), Hot News, Take Me Home (1928), Rio Rita (1929), Alias French Gertie, Dixiana (1930), Reaching for the Moon, The Maltese Falcon (1931), Silver Dollar (1932), Cocktail Hour (1933), Registered Nurse (1934), Music Is Magic (1935). ∎

Daniels, Mickey, child actor. Freckle-faced member of Hal ROACH'S early "OUR GANG" comedies of the 1920s. He often portrayed a tough but cute juvenile. He was featured in a few of Harold LLOYD'S comedies in the early 1920s, and later appeared in another series for Hal Roach, "The Boy Friends," which concerned the antics of teenagers.

SELECTED FILMS: Doctor Jack (1922), Safety Last (1923), Girl Shy, The Fraidy Cat (1924), Let's Do Things (1931), At the Circus (1939). ∎

Daniels, William (1927–), actor. Worked on stage and in television. He made his film debut in 1949. Known for his character portrayals, he has appeared in dramas, comedies, and musicals.

SELECTED FILMS: Family Honeymoon (1949), Ladybug, Ladybug (1963), A Thousand Clowns (1965), The President's Analyst, The Graduate, Two for the Road (1967), Marlowe (1969), 1776 (1972), The Parallax View (1974), Oh, God! (1977), The One and Only (1978), Sunburn (1979). ∎

Darden, Severn (1937–), actor. Has appeared on stage with the original Second City troupe and on screen as a character actor in dramas and light films during the 1960s and 1970s, chiefly in comic roles.

SELECTED FILMS: Dead Heat on a Merry-Go-Round, The President's Analyst (1967), Luv (1968), Pussycat, Pussycat, I Love You (1970), Cisco Pike (1971), The War Between Men and Women (1972), Who Fears the Devil (1974). ∎

Darling, Jean, child actress. Cute member of Hal ROACH'S popular "OUR GANG" comedies. She functioned as the love interest, replacing Mary KORNMAN, who, in turn, had replaced Peggy Cartwright, one of the original members of the gang.

Darmond, Grace (1898–1963), actress. Worked on stage before entering early silent films in 1914. Within four years she rose to stardom while at Vitagraph studios. An attractive performer with dark eyes, she appeared in dramas, serials, and comedies for a variety of studios. She abandoned her screen career when sound arrived.

SELECTED FILMS: When the Clock Went Wrong, Your Girl and Mine (1914), A Texas Steer (1915), An American Ace (1919), Even as Eve, So Long Letty (1920), See My Lawyer, White and Unmarried, The Beautiful Gambler (1921), I Can Explain (1922), Daytime Wives (1923), Discontented Husband, The Gaiety Girl (1924), Flattery, The Painted Flapper (1925), Her Big Adventure, Her Man O' War (1926), Wide Open (1927). ∎

Darro, Frankie (1917–1976), actor. Began in silent films as a child performer, chiefly playing tough little kids from the wrong side of the tracks, and continued in these roles into the 1930s and the sound era. Later in his career he was relegated to minor roles in low-budget films. Pint-sized with dark hair, he appeared in scores of films in his 50-year screen career, including dramas, serials, action features, and comedies.

SELECTED FILMS: Judgment of the Storm (1923), Memory Lane, Confessions of a Queen (1925), Kiki, Hearts and Spangles (1926), Long Pants, Her Father Said No (1927), The Circus Kid (1928), Amateur Daddy (1932), Tugboat Annie (1933), The Merry Frinks (1934), Three Kids and a Queen (1935), Mind Your Own Business (1936), Irish Luck (1939), Up in the Air (1940), The Gang's All Here (1941), Freddie Steps Out (1946), Sarge Goes to College (1947), Hold That Baby (1948), Riding High (1950), Operation Petticoat (1960), Hook, Line and Sinker (1969). ∎

Darwell, Jane (1879–1967), actress. Appeared on stage and in silent films before establishing herself as a major character player during the sound era. A plump figure with a moon-shaped, sympathetic face, she played strong matronly roles in numerous dramas and light films, most memorably as Ma Joad in The Grapes of Wrath (1940). She appeared in over 100 films.

SELECTED FILMS: The Capture of Aquinaldo (1913), Brewster's Millions (1914), Good Housewrecking, Design for Living, He Couldn't Take It (1933), Let's Talk It Over, Blind Date, Embarrassing Moments (1934), Curly Top (1935), Captain January, Poor Little Rich Girl (1936), The Singing Marine (1937), Little Miss Broadway (1938), Unexpected Father (1939), Small Town Deb (1941), It Happened in Flatbush (1942), Gildersleeve's Bad Day (1943), Captain Tugboat Annie (1945), Father's Wild Game (1950), Mary Poppins (1964). ∎

Davenport, Alice (1864–), actress. Worked in early silent comedies for Mack SENNETT'S KEYSTONE studios. She was one of the original group of supporting players for the studio when it began operations on the West Coast in 1912. A matronly, broad-shouldered actress, she portrayed shrewish wives and other similar roles. She appeared in numerous films with many of the leading comics of the period, including, among others, Charlie CHAPLIN (nine films), Mabel NORMAND, "Fatty" ARBUCKLE, and Mack SWAIN. She was married for a time to actor Harry DAVENPORT and was the mother of actress Dorothy Davenport.

SELECTED FILMS: The Best Man Wins (1911), Mabel's Lovers, Drummer's Vacation (1912), Just Brown's Luck, The Telltale Light, Cohen's Outing (1913), Making a Living, Mabel's Strange Predicament, The Star Boarder, Caught in a Cabaret, Caught in the Rain, Mabel's New Job, Tillie's Punctured Romance (1914), The Home Breakers, Ambrose's Fury, My Valet, Fickle Fatty's Fall, Stolen Magic (1915), Wife and Auto Trouble, His Last Scent (1916), Secrets of a Beauty Parlor (1917), Skirts (1921), The Legend of Hollywood (1924), The Dude Wrangler (1930). ∎

Davenport, Harry (1866–1949), actor. Began film career in minor silents. During the 1930s and 1940s he played character roles in more than 100 features, dramas as well as light films, often as a gracious old man dispensing understanding and wisdom. He portrayed Grandpa in the comedy series, "THE HIGGINS FAMILY," starring the GLEASON family. He was the husband of actress Alice DAVENPORT and father of actress Dorothy Davenport.

In The Bride Came C.O.D. (1941) he played a kindly old recluse whose privacy is invaded when James CAGNEY is hired by Bette DAVIS' tycoon father to kidnap her to prevent her upcoming marriage. "Ain't much difference between kidnapping and marriage," Davenport philosophizes. "You get snatched from your parents. But in marriage, nobody offers a reward."

SELECTED FILMS: Father and the Boy (1915), One Night (1916), The False Friend (1917), A Girl at Bay, The Unknown Quantity (1919), Her Unborn Child (1930), Get That Venus (1933), Three Men on a Horse (1936), Her Husband's Secretary (1937), You Can't Take It With You, The Higgins Family (1938), Gone With the Wind (1939), That Uncertain Feeling (1941), Larceny, Inc. (1942), Gangway for Tomorrow (1943), Meet Me in St. Louis, The Thin Man Goes Home (1944), Too Young to Know (1945), Claudia and David (1946), The Farmer's Daughter, The Bachelor and the Bobby-Soxer (1947), Three Daring Daughters (1948), Tell It to the Judge (1949), Riding High (1950). ∎

Davidson, Max (1875–1950), actor. Worked in early silent comedies for Mack SENNETT'S KEYSTONE studios. During the 1920s he appeared in comedy shorts for producer Hal ROACH. Davidson was one of numerous screen comics of this period who were not naturally funny, depending more on comical situations or physical surroundings for their laughs. Neither did he have a distinct screen personality as did several of his contemporaries, such as CHAPLIN, Harold LLOYD, KEATON, or Harry LANGDON. He was destined to remain a minor screen comic. However, in the spring of 1908 he suggested to his friend D. W. Griffith that he try to sell some of his stories to film studios or possibly take a job as a screen actor. Griffith promptly followed his friend's advice.

During the sound period he was employed as a supporting actor by various studios, appearing in comedy shorts. He worked with some of the major film comedians of the period, including, among others, "Fatty" ARBUCKLE, Fred MACE, Charley CHASE, LAUREL AND HARDY, and CLARK AND McCULLOUGH.

SELECTED FILMS: Love in Armor (1915), The Village Vampire (1916), The

Darling of New York (1924), Old Clothes, Hogan's Alley (1925), Call of the Cuckoos, Hats Off (1927), So This Is College (1929), Oh! Oh! Cleopatra (1931), Hokus Focus (1933), The Girl Said No (1937), No Census, No Feeling (1940), The Great Commandment (1942). ∎

Davies, Marion (1897–1961), actress. Appeared on stage and worked as a model before entering films in 1917 for Famous Players, which was later to be known as Paramount studios. Both talented and attractive, she made numerous dramatic and light films during the silent era as well as in the 1930s. Newspaper publisher William Randolph Hearst took an interest in her career and invested in a studio to showcase her talents. He tried to steer her toward more dramatic roles, which, some critics believe, may have hindered her career since her best performances tended to be in light features. In Show People (1928), one of her better silent comedies, she satirized a movie queen. In the World War I musical comedy Marianne (1929), one of her more memorable roles, she did a clever burlesque of the then popular screen star Renee ADOREE. She played the love-sick ex-school teacher who follows Bing CROSBY to the film capital in Going Hollywood. Her popularity declined by the mid-1930s, at which time she retired from acting. She was not the untalented performer thrust into stardom depicted as the character Susan Alexander in Orson Welles' Citizen Kane (1941).

SELECTED FILMS: Runaway Romany (1917), Cecilia of the Pink Roses (1918), Getting Mary Married (1919), April Folly (1920), The Bride's Play (1921), When Knighthood Was in Flower (1922), Adam and Eva (1923), Janice Meredith (1924), Tillie the Toiler (1927), The Patsy, Show People (1928), Not So Dumb (1930), Five and Ten (1931), Polly of the Circus, Blondie of the Follies (1932), Peg o' My Heart, Going Hollywood (1933), Page Miss Glory (1935), Cain and Mabel (1936), Ever Since Eve (1937). ∎

Davis, Bette (1908–), actress. Worked in stock and on Broadway in 1929 before entering films. The young performer, who was soon to become one of the greatest actresses of the screen, appeared in routine roles in minor films. Eventually, Warner Brothers signed her to a contract and her fortune began to change, but not without conflicts with studio heads. She battled constantly for better parts and the right to work for other studios. She starred in numerous dramas, receiving multiple Academy Awards and the American Film Institute's Life Achievement Award in 1977. Remembered chiefly for her strong portrayals of liberated, independent females in a male-dominated world, she starred as well in several appealing light films that showcased her talent for comedy. Her autobiography, The Lonely Life, was published in 1962.

In The Man Who Came to Dinner (1941) she portrayed a personal secretary with a mind of her own. Cheering up newspaperman Richard Travis, who has dreams of marriage, she says: "I suppose some poor girl could fall for you—if you came with a set of dishes."

SELECTED FILMS: Bad Sister (1931), Way Back Home, The Dark Horse, Cabin in the Cotton (1932), Ex-Lady (1933), Jimmy the Gent, Housewife (1934), The Girl From 10th Avenue (1935), Kid Galahad, That Certain Woman, It's Love I'm After (1937), The Bride Came C.O.D. (1941), Thank Your Lucky Stars (1943), Hollywood Canteen (1944), June Bride (1948), All About Eve (1950), Pocketful of Miracles (1961), The Anniversary (1968). ∎

Davis, Boyd (1885–1963), actor. Appeared in stock, on stage in London (1912) and on Broadway, and in several silent films during the 1920s. Following a successful return to the stage during the 1930s, he once again turned his acting talents to the screen in the early 1940s. Mature and imposing, at times stern and authoritarian, he played character roles in dramas and light films.

SELECTED FILMS: Smiling Faces (1932), You'll Never Get Rich, Two Latins From Manhattan (1941), Harvard, Here I Come, Star Spangled Rhythm (1942), Colonel Effingham's Raid (1945), The Senator Was Indiscreet (1947), A Foreign Affair (1948), Ma and Pa Kettle (1949), At Sword's Point (1952). ▪

Davis, Edwards (1871–1936), actor. Worked in vaudeville and on stage before entering early silent films in the 1910s. Working for studios such as Universal and First National, he appeared as a supporting player in numerous dramas and light films.

SELECTED FILMS: The Plaything of Broadway (1921), The Good Bad Boy (1924), The Best People, Flattery, Part Time Wife, Her Husband's Secret, My Neighbor's Wife (1925), The Amateur Gentleman, High Steppers, Tramp, Tramp, Tramp (1926), The Life of Riley, Face Value, Singed (1927), The Sporting Age, Happiness Ahead (1928), A Song of Kentucky (1929), The Love Racket, Love in the Rough (1930), Hello, Everybody! (1933). ▪

Davis, George (1889–1965), actor. Entered silent films in the 1920s following a career in vaudeville. He appeared as a supporting player in dramas and light films, especially comedy shorts. He also appeared in a variety of European films. He worked with some of the foremost comedians of the period, including, among others, Buster KEATON, Charlie CHAPLIN, and Danny KAYE.

SELECTED FILMS: Sherlock, Jr. (1924), The Circus (1928), Devil May Care (1929), Not So Dumb (1930), Parlor, Bedroom and Bath, Laugh and Get Rich (1931), Love Me Tonight (1932), The Good Fairy (1935), I Met Him in Paris, Thin Ice (1937), The Baroness and the Butler (1938), Topper Takes a Trip (1939), See My Lawyer (1945), The Kid From Brooklyn (1946), On the Riviera (1951), Gentlemen Prefer Blondes (1953). ▪

Davis, Jack (–1968), actor. Began his screen career in the 1940s. He appeared as a supporting player chiefly in low-budget dramas and light films.

SELECTED FILMS: Up Goes Maisie, Talk About a Lady (1946), Blondie's Big Moment (1947), Crowded Paradise (1956), The Gnome-Mobile (1967). ▪

Davis, James G. (1874–1937), actor. Worked on stage in his native England before immmigrating to Hollywood in the early 1920s. He appeared chiefly in supporting roles in dramas and light films, and continued his screen career into the early sound era.

SELECTED FILMS: A Certain Rich Man (1921), Chastity (1923), Jealous Husbands, The Trouble Shooter (1924), His Lucky Horseshoe (1925), Twinkle Toes, The Notorious Lady (1927), A Melon Drama (1931), The Bride of Frankenstein (1935). ▪

Joan Davis, Evelyn Ankers, Lou Costello, Bud Abbott

Davis, Joan (1907–1961), actress, comedienne. Appeared on stage as a child performer, in vaudeville with husband Sy Wills, and in films in the early 1930s. Performing in two-reel comedies for producer Mack SENNETT at first, she employed much physical humor, which included hitting herself in the jaw. She co-starred with many famous comics, including ABBOTT AND COSTELLO and Eddie CANTOR. She was chosen Best Comedienne of the Year in 1938 by the New York Film Critics. In Hold That Ghost (1941), starring Bud and Lou, she played a professional radio screamer. She had marked success in radio during the 1940s and in television in the 1950s.

One of her better vehicles was *Show Business* (1944) in which she and Eddie CANTOR played small-time vaudevillians. Friction between the two causes her to announce: "Now that I've met you again, I feel that I've led a full life. I think I'll go home and kill myself."

SELECTED FILMS: *Millions in the Air* (1935), *On the Avenue, Life Begins in College, Love and Hisses* (1937), *Hold That Co-Ed* (1938), *Daytime Wife* (1939), *Two Latins From Manhattan* (1941), *Yokel Boy* (1942), *Around the World* (1943), *Show Business* (1944), *She Gets Her Man* (1945), *She Wrote the Book* (1946), *If You Knew Susie* (1948), *Make Mine Laughs* (1949), *Traveling Saleswoman* (1950), *The Groom Wore Spurs* (1951), *Harem Girl* (1952). ◼

Davis, Mildred (1900–1969), actress. Began her relatively short screen career in early silent comedies in the 1910s. Sweet and innocent-looking, she co-starred in several of Harold LLOYD'S short comedies and made four feature-length films with him. When she decided to sign with another studio where she would play straight roles, Lloyd married her and she retired from acting.

SELECTED FILMS: *Marriage à la Carte* (1916), *His Royal Slyness, From Hand to Mouth* (1919), *High and Dizzy* (1920), *Among Those Present, Sailor-Made Man, Grandma's Boy, Doctor Jack* (1922), *Safety Last, Why Worry?, Temporary Marriage* (1923), *Too Many Crooks* (1927). ◼

Davis, Sammy, Jr. (1925–), actor, dancer, singer. As a child, performed as part of the Will Mastin Trio, his uncle's act, which also included Sammy's father. His talents extended to playing musical instruments, joke-telling, and mimicry, while the trio received bookings in better nightclubs and theaters after World War II. He began appearing in films in 1956, many of them come-

dies. A gifted and versatile performer, he has been rated one of the most popular entertainers of his period.

SELECTED FILMS: *The Benny Goodman Story* (1956), *Anna Lucasta* (1958), *Porgy and Bess* (1959), *Ocean's 11, Pepe* (1960), *Sergeants 3, Convicts 4* (1962), *Johnny Cool* (1963), *Robin and the Seven Hoods* (1964), *Stop the World—I Want to Get Off* (1966), *Sweet Charity* (1969), *One More Time* (1970), *Gone With the West* (1975). ◼

Daw, Marjorie (1902–1979), actress. Began her screen career in the 1910s in early silent films following some training as a singer. She appeared as a female lead in dramas, romances, and light films, frequently playing opposite Douglas FAIRBANKS. She abandoned her career when sound came to motion pictures.

SELECTED FILMS: *The Warrens of Virginia* (1915), *Rebecca of Sunnybrook Farm, A Modern Musketeer* (1917), *He Comes Up Smiling, Say, Young Fellow* (1918), *The Knickerbocker Buckaroo* (1919), *Don't Ever Marry, Dinty* (1920), *Penrod* (1922), *Going Up, The Barefoot Boy* (1923), *His Master's Voice* (1925), *Redheads Preferred* (1926), *Spoilers of the West* (1927). ◼

Dawley, J. Searle (–1950), director. Worked as a stage actor and producer before entering early silent films in 1907 as assistant to movie pioneer Edwin S. Porter. He later joined Paramount studios, known then as Famous Players, where he turned out numerous dramas and light films, both shorts and features. In all, he directed several hundred films before retiring from his screen career in the 1920s. Many of his films were based on literary classics, such as "Frankenstein" and "A Christmas Carol," both released in 1910.

SELECTED FILMS: *Hansel and Gretel* (1909), *One in a Million* (1914), *Always in the Way, Miss George Washington, Snow White* (1916), *Bab's Daughter, Bab's Diary, Bab's Matinee Idol, The*

Mysterious Miss Terry, The Seven Swans, Rich Man, Poor Man (1918), *The Phantom Honeymoon, Everybody's Business* (1919), *Broadway Broke* (1923). ∎

Rock Hudson and Doris Day

Day, Doris (1924–), actress, singer. Started show business career as a singer on radio, in nightclubs, and with bands. She made her film debut in 1948, following which she starred in musicals and dramas. After portraying numerous blonde-haired, freckle-faced girl-next-door and tomboy roles, which made her the country's number one female star as well as the highest paid performer, she switched to romantic comedies in the late 1950s. With co-stars such as Rock HUDSON and Cary GRANT she made a string of popular sex comedies that dealt with "bedroom problems."

In *Pillow Talk*, for instance, she struggles to ward off the seductive charms of Rock Hudson. "At least my bedroom problems can be solved in one bedroom," she charges; "you couldn't solve yours in a thousand bedrooms." She criticizes Hudson for his loose life-style. "So I have sown a few wild oats," he admits. "A few?" she repeats. "You could qualify for a farm loan!" However great the temptations were in these films, she managed to remain virginal and innocent to the end in spite of the rapidly changing morality of the decade.

SELECTED FILMS: *Romance on the High Seas* (1948), *My Dream Is Yours* (1949), *Tea for Two* (1950), *Lullaby of Broadway, On Moonlight Bay* (1951), *April in Paris* (1952), *By the Light of the Silvery Moon* (1953), *Young at Heart* (1955), *The Pajama Game* (1957), *Teacher's Pet, Tunnel of Love* (1958), *Pillow Talk* (1959), *Lover Come Back, That Touch of Mink* (1962), *The Thrill of It All, Move Over, Darling* (1963), *Send Me No Flowers* (1964), *Do Not Disturb* (1965), *The Glass-Bottom Boat* (1966), *Caprice* (1967), *With Six You Get Eggroll* (1968). ∎

Day, Marceline (1907–), actress. Worked in late silent and early sound films, many of which were light comedies. She played lead parts in features which co-starred many of the major comedians of the period, including, among others, Harry LANGDON, Charlie CHASE, and Buster KEATON. She appeared with Karl DANE and George K. ARTHUR in two entries of their comedy series. With the advent of sound, her popularity slowly diminished. She dropped out of films after appearing in a handful of unimportant B films.

SELECTED FILMS: *The Taming of the West, The Splendid Road* (1925), *That Model From Paris, College Days, The Boy Friend, The Gay Deceiver, Fools for Fashion* (1926), *The Beloved Rogue, Rookies* (1927), *The Cameraman, Detectives* (1928), *The Jazz Age, The Wild Party, The One Woman Idea, A Single Man* (1929), *Paradise Island, Sunny Skies* (1930), *The Mad Parade* (1931), *The Fighting Fool* (1932), *Damaged Lives* (1933). ∎

Day at the Races, A (1937), MGM. Dir. Sam Wood; Sc. Robert Pirosh, George Seaton; with Groucho, Harpo, Chico Marx, Maureen O'Sullivan, Allan Jones, Margaret Dumont, Sig Rumann.

MGM producer Irving Thalberg, who had successfully guided the ailing Marx Brothers' career at the studio, died before this film was completed. He had been responsible for their highly popular and critically acclaimed *A Night at the Opera*. He sent part of the cast on the road to test out the various routines before live audiences; he employed the same director; he kept several of the key cast, including Dumont and Jones; all in an effort to make *Races* as successful as *Opera* had been. Perhaps he would have eliminated some of the musical numbers that tend to slow the pace of an otherwise hilarious comedy. The film contains the classic scenes of horsedoctor Groucho and his brothers examining Margaret Dumont, Chico touting racing manuals to Groucho, and Harpo's attempts to delay the final race.

"Day's Pleasure, A." See Charlie Chaplin.

Deacon, Richard (1922–1984), actor. Appeared as a comic character player, chiefly in light films. Easily distinguished by his baldness and spectacles, he frequently portrayed humorous meddlers.

SELECTED FILMS: *My Sister Eileen, Abbott and Costello Meet the Mummy (1955), Francis in the Haunted House, The Solid Gold Cadillac (1956), Spring Reunion (1957), A Nice Little Bank That Should Be Robbed, The Remarkable Mr. Pennypacker, Blackbeard's Ghost (1958), John Goldfarb, Please Come Home (1965), The Gnome-Mobile, Enter Laughing (1967), The One and Only Genuine Original Family Band (1968).* ∎

Dead End Kids. See Bowery Boys.

Dean, Priscilla (1896–), actress. Performed on stage since early childhood and began her film career in 1910 at age fourteen. By 1911 she was portraying coquettish and frivolous characters for Universal studios in comedies starring Eddie LYONS and Lee MORAN. Six years later she became a popular screen star, appearing mainly in dramas. Her career in films ended in 1932, following her appearance in a few routine films

and a few years after the advent of sound.

SELECTED FILMS: *Love, Dynamite and Baseball (1916), Even As You and I, Beloved Jim (1917), The Brazen Beauty, Kiss or Kill, She Hired a Husband, Wildcat of Paris (1918), The Wicked Darling, The Exquisite Thief, Silk Lined Burglar (1919), Wild Honey (1922), Drifting (1923), The Siren of Seville, A Cafe in Cairo (1924), West of Broadway, The Speeding Venus, The Danger Girl (1926), The Dice Woman (1927), Behind Stone Walls (1932).* ∎

DeCamp, Rosemary (1914–), actress. Worked on stage and radio before entering films in the early 1940s. Chiefly a character player, she appeared in numerous dramas and light films, frequently as a friend to the female lead or in mother roles. She has appeared regularly in television comedies.

SELECTED FILMS: *Cheers for Miss Bishop (1941), Yankee Doodle Dandy (1942), This Is the Army (1943), The Merry Monahans, Bowery to Broadway (1944), Practically Yours, Weekend at the Waldorf (1945), Two Guys From Milwaukee (1946), On Moonlight Bay (1951), So This Is Love (1953), Thirteen Ghosts (1960).* ∎

Dee, Frances (1907–), actress. Began her screen career in 1929 as an extra and by the following year was co-starring in dramas and light films. An unusually pretty actress, she played leads and second leads for 25 years, often cast as virtuous women. She retired in 1954. She appeared in several films with her husband, Joel McCrea.

SELECTED FILMS: *Words and Music (1929), Playboy of Paris, Along Came Youth (1930), June Moon (1931), If I Had a Million (1932), Coming Out Party (1934), The Gay Deception (1935), Meet the Stewarts (1942), Happy Land (1943), Patrick the Great (1945), Because of You (1952), Mr. Scoutmaster (1953), Gypsy Colt (1954).* ∎

Dee, Sandra (1942–), actress. Worked as a model and in television before she began appearing in films in 1957. Charming and attractive, she starred in teenage romantic comedies that were highly successful with youthful audiences. She made the first, and best, of the "Gidget" films in 1959, co-starring with James Darren.

SELECTED FILMS: Until They Sail (1957), The Reluctant Debutante, The Restless Years (1958), Gidget, A Summer Place (1959), Romanoff and Juliet, Tammy Tell Me True (1961), If a Man Answers (1962), Tammy and the Doctor, Take Her, She's Mine (1963), I'd Rather Be Rich (1964), That Funny Feeling (1965), A Man Could Get Killed (1966), Rosie! (1968), The Dunwich Horror (1970). ▪

Defore, Don (1917–), actor. Worked in stock and on Broadway before making his screen debut in 1941. He appeared frequently as a grinning, ingenuous character in light comedies, either as the lead or as a supporting actor.

SELECTED FILMS: We Go Fast (1941), The Male Animal (1942), The Human Comedy (1943), The Affairs of Susan, The Stork Club (1945), Without Reservations (1946), It Happened on Fifth Avenue (1947), Romance on the High Seas, One Sunday Afternoon (1948), My Friend Irma (1949), A Girl in Every Port, No Room for the Groom, Jumping Jacks (1952), The Facts of Life (1960). ▪

DeHaven, Carter (1896–1977), actor, director. Worked in vaudeville and in the theater before making his film debut as an actor in the mid-1910s. He appeared principally in silent films, usually in light two-reelers, embracing a comedic mode similar to that of the popular Sidney DREW. In 1916 he appeared in a series of two-reel comedies as "Timothy Dobbs," which he made for Universal. The National Film Corporation signed him in 1919, and he starred in thirteen comedies for the company. By 1920 he was working for Paramount,

making a series of ten two-reel comedies with his wife, Flora Parker. While employed by R-C Pictures in 1923, he created a comedy series that followed the misadventures of a newly married couple. He occasionally worked with Charlie CHAPLIN (as an actor in The Great Dictator and his assistant in Modern Times, 1936).

SELECTED FILMS: The College Orphan (1915), Get the Boy, From Broadway to a Throne (1916), Close to Nature, Why Divorce? (1919), Beating Cheaters, Twin Beds, Hoodooed (1920), Marry the Poor Girl, My Lady Friends (1922), Their First Vacation, A Ring for Dad (1923), The Great Dictator (1940), The Notorious Landlady (1962). ▪

Dehner, John (1915–), actor. Began his screen career in the 1940s. A dark-haired character player often seen with a thin, dark mustache, he has chiefly played sinister roles. He has appeared in scores of dramas, westerns, and light films.

SELECTED FILMS: Lake Placid Serenade (1944), State Fair, Christmas in Connecticut, Club Havana, She Went to the Races (1945), Dream Girl (1947), Let's Live a Little (1948), Corky of Gasoline Alley (1951), The Bowery Boys Meet the Monsters (1954), Critic's Choice (1963), Support Your Local Gunfighter (1971), Fun With Dick and Jane (1976), Jagged Edge (1985). ▪

Dell, Gabriel (1919–), actor. Appeared as a supporting player in several films, reaching the peak of his screen career in the 1940s as one of the "BOWERY BOYS" in the comedy series of that name. He played characters with names like "T.B.," "Bingo," and "String." Not as hyperactive as Huntz HALL or as verbal as Leo GORCEY, he nevertheless contributed his share to the hijinks. A tall, dark-haired performer, he also worked on stage and in television.

SELECTED FILMS: Little Tough Guy (1938), You're Not So Tough, Give Us Wings (1940), Hit the Road, Mob Town

(1941), *Tough As They Come, Mug Town, Let's Get Tough, Smart Alecks, 'Neath Brooklyn Bridge* (1942), *Keep 'Em Slugging, Kid Dynamite, Million Dollar Kid* (1943), *Block Busters* (1944), *Come Out Fighting* (1945). ∎

Del Ruth, Roy (1895–1961), director. Worked as a journalist before joining Mack SENNETT in 1915 as a gagman and screenwriter. By 1917 he was directing two-reel comedies starring some of the leading silent screen comics of the period, including, among others, Ben TURPIN and Harry LANGDON. By the mid-1920s he switched to feature-length comedies and dramas, and, by the 1930s, he began directing musicals as well as light films. He worked in the 1930s with such popular performers as Bing CROSBY, Dick POWELL, and Eddie CANTOR.

SELECTED FILMS: *Eve's Lover, Hogan's Alley* (1925), *Three Weeks in Paris, The Little Irish Girl, Footloose Widows* (1926), *Wolf's Clothing, If I Were Single, Ham and Eggs at the Front* (1927), *Powder My Back, Beware of Bachelors* (1928), *The Hottentot* (1929), *Hold Everything, Life of the Party* (1930), *Divorce Among Friends, Blonde Crazy* (1931), *Taxi, Blessed Event* (1932), *Little Giant, Lady Killer* (1933), *Kid Millions* (1934), *Thanks a Million* (1935), *It Had to Happen* (1936), *On the Avenue* (1937), *Happy Landing, My Lucky Star* (1938), *Tail Spin, The Star Maker* (1939), *He Married His Wife* (1940), *Topper Returns, The Chocolate Soldier* (1941), *Maisie Gets Her Man* (1942), *DuBarry Was a Lady* (1943), *Broadway Rhythm* (1944), *It Happened on Fifth Avenue* (1947), *Always Leave Them Laughing* (1949), *On Moonlight Bay* (1951), *About Face, Stop, You're Killing Me* (1952), *Three Sailors and a Girl* (1953), *The Alligator People* (1959). ∎

DeLuise, Dom (1933–), actor. Worked on stage, in television, and on Broadway. He made his screen debut in the 1960s. Portly and baby-faced, sometimes sporting a beard, he often portrays eccentric

and zany characters in light films, participating frequently in Mel BROOKS' irreverent comedies. He has also co-starred sporadically with Gene WILDER.

In *The Last Married Man in America* (1978) he played an unemployed actor who is practicing roller skating at a rink for an upcoming role in a porno film called *Roller Bang*. He meets his old buddy George SEGAL and confesses: "I'm divorced—third time. But I just got married again, though. I need to be in love. I can't live without the aggravation."

SELECTED FILMS: *Fail Safe* (1964), *The Glass-Bottom Boat* (1966), *The Busy Body* (1967), *What's So Bad About Feeling Good?* (1968), *Norwood, The Twelve Chairs* (1970), *Every Little Crook and Nanny* (1972), *Blazing Saddles* (1974), *The Adventures of Sherlock Holmes' Smarter Brother* (1975), *Silent Movie* (1976), *The World's Greatest Lover* (1977), *Sextette, The End, The Cheap Detective* (1978), *Fatso* (1980), *The Cannonball Run, History of the World—Part I* (1981), *The Best Little Whorehouse in Texas* (1982), *Johnny Dangerously* (1985). ∎

William Demarest (foreground center)

Demarest, William (1892–1983), actor. Veteran comic actor for almost 50 years, appearing in almost 150 films. He worked in vaudeville, in carnivals, and on stage before entering films in 1927, mainly in supporting roles as a sharp-talking, comical hustler or good-natured friend. He was part of Preston STURGES' stock company, appearing in many of the director's best satirical films. He supported many of the top comic stars of the 1940s, including ABBOTT AND COSTELLO, Bob HOPE, Eddie BRACKEN, and Betty HUTTON. He was nominated for an Academy Award as Best Supporting Actor for his portrayal of Al Jolson's friend and business manager in *The Jolson Story* (1946).

In *Rebecca of Sunnybrook Farm* (1938) he's confronted with plucky Shirley Temple, who overhears his conversation and questions: "What's stage-fright?" He hesitates for a moment and then quips: "Well, that's something *you'll* never have to worry about."

SELECTED FILMS: *When the Wife's Away* (1926), *Finger Prints, The Jazz Singer* (1927), *A Girl in Every Port* (1928), *Broadway Melody* (1929), *Many Happy Returns* (1934), *Hands Across the Table* (1935), *Mind Your Own Business* (1936), *Easy Living* (1937), *Mr. Smith Goes to Washington* (1939), *The Farmer's Daughter, The Great McGinty* (1940), *The Lady Eve, Sullivan's Travels, The Devil and Miss Jones* (1941), *My Favorite Spy, Pardon My Sarong* (1942), *True to Life* (1943), *Hail the Conquering Hero, The Miracle of Morgan's Creek* (1944), *Duffy's Tavern* (1945), *Pardon My Past* (1946), *The Perils of Pauline* (1947), *On Our Merry Way* (1948), *Sorrowful Jones* (1949), *Riding High* (1950), *Behave Yourself* (1951), *The Lady Wants Mink* (1953), *It's a Mad, Mad, Mad, Mad World* (1963), *Viva Las Vegas* (1964), *That Darn Cat* (1965), *The Wild McCullochs* (1975). ■

Dennehy, Brian (1940–), actor. Began his film career in the late 1970s. A light-haired, husky figure, he has appeared as a character player in dramas and light films. He was the bartender at the island resort where Dudley MOORE registered to be near his dream girl, Bo Derek, in the comedy film *10.*

SELECTED FILMS: Semi-Tough *(1977),* Foul Play *(1978),* 10 *(1979), Little Miss Marker (1980), Finders Keepers (1984), Cocoon (1985).* ■

Denny, Reginald (1891–1967), actor. Appeared on the stage in his native England from the age of eight. He began his Hollywood screen career in 1912 and, for the next fifty years, appeared in approximately 200 films. His initial roles were those of clean-cut, well-dressed, energetic characters, much in the mold of Harold LLOYD. He starred in two unique film series during the silent era. In "The Leather Pushers" series of two-reelers he portrayed a man of action; he also starred in a group of adventure comedies playing a character not unlike that of the then popular Douglas FAIRBANKS. His comic talents ranged from zany antics (*California Straight Ahead*) to the comedy of manners (*Skinner's Dress Suit*).

During the sound era he became a supporting player, sometimes portraying dull-witted Englishmen. In the popular Bulldog Drummond detective series he played Algy, the title character's humorous sidekick. He worked with many of the leading film comedians, including Bob HOPE, Danny KAYE, and ABBOTT AND COSTELLO.

SELECTED FILMS: *The Melting Pot* (1912), *Bringing Up Betty* (1919), *Footlights, Tropical Love* (1921), *The Kentucky Derby* (1922), *The Abysmal Brute* (1923), *The Fast Worker* (1924), *Oh, Doctor!, California Straight Ahead, Where Was I?* (1925), *Skinner's Dress Suit, The Cheerful Fraud* (1926), *Out All Night* (1927), *His Lucky Day* (1929), *Embarrassing Moments* (1930), *Kiki, Stepping Out* (1931), *Only Yesterday* (1933), *We're Rich Again* (1934), *No More Ladies* (1935), *Bulldog Drummond Comes Back* (1938), *Seven Sinners* (1940), *My Favorite Brunette* (1947), *Cat Ballou* (1965), *Batman* (1966). ■

Dent, Vernon (1895–1963), actor. Played in numerous two-reel silent and sound comedies. A stocky supporting player with a gruff countenance, he worked with many comics of the period. His most memorable roles were those as second banana in many Harry LANGDON comedy shorts and supporting actor to the THREE STOOGES. He appeared with the trio from 1936 to 1954 in 68 of their shorts for Columbia Pictures. He portrayed professionals, public officials, laborers, and even royalty (appeared as a king four times).

SELECTED FILMS: All Night Long, Saturday Afternoon (1926), Slippery Silks (1936), Dizzy Doctors, Back to the Woods (1937), Wee Wee Monsieur, Tassels in the Air, Mutts to You (1938), Three Little Sew and Sews, A-Ducking They Do Go, Yes We Have No Bananas (1939), From Nurse to Worse, Nutty but Nice, How High Is Up, No Census No Feeling (1940), So Long, Mr. Chumps, Dutiful But Dumb, I'll Never Heil Again, An Ache to Every Stake (1941), Loco Boy Makes Good (1942), Punchy Cowpunchers (1950). ■

"Dentist, The" (1932), PAR. Dir. Leslie Pearce; Sc. W. C. Fields; with W. C. Fields, Babe Kane, Zedna Farley, Elise Cavanna, Bud Jamison, Dorothy Granger, Bobby Dunn, Billy Bletcher.

W. C. Fields made four two-reel comedies for Mack SENNETT in the early 1930s between his feature contracts for Paramount. Sennett, once the king of comedy during the silent period, was having trouble adjusting to the sound era. His major comics had left him for features and the big studios, and the demand for short films was declining. He had hoped to re-establish some of his former greatness partly through these four films. "The Dentist" is the best of the quartet. Fields, in the title role, practices his profession on the main floor of his private home. His friend calls to play a game of golf and off he goes. After some misadventures on the course where he hits another player with one of his golf balls and throws his caddy into a lake, he returns to his practice. His first patient, a pretty young woman with an excellent figure, bends over with her rear facing Fields as she shows him where a dachshund has bitten her. "You're rather fortunate it wasn't a Newfoundland dog that bit you," he says. His second patient, another woman,

squirms in pain as he goes for her bad tooth. She wraps her legs around him as he walks around the room with her holding tightly to him. Some of the more prudish members of the audience found these scenes too suggestive. In fact, in the 1950s they were cut for television viewing. His next patient is a diminutive man with a massive beard that covers his face. Fields has trouble locating his mouth. As he brushes the man's beard, several birds fly out and Fields goes for his rifle and hunting cap. The skit is based on a vaudeville routine Fields once did in Earl Carroll's Vanities.

Denver, Bob (1935–), actor. Worked as a comedian in television ("Gilligan's Island") before entering films. He has appeared in light vehicles, chiefly in the 1960s.

SELECTED FILMS: A Private's Affair (1959), Take Her, She's Mine (1963), For Those Who Think Young (1964), Who's Minding the Mint?, The Sweet Ride (1967), Did You Hear the One About the Traveling Saleslady? (1968). ■

Depp, Henry (1886–1957), actor. Appeared in early silent comedy shorts for MUTUAL studios. Working under the Strand banner, a subsidiary of Mutual, he co-starred with Elinor FIELD in a series of bright comedies involving domestic entanglements and the complexities of modern technology as symbolized by the automobile.

SELECTED FILMS: Honest Thieves, A Male Governess (1916), The Book Worm Turns (1917), What Will Father Say? (1918), 'Twas Henry's Fault (1919), His Last Race, Nobody's Money (1923), When the Wife's Away (1926), Swing It, Professor (1937), The Magnificent Dope (1942), Black Magic (1944). ■

DeRita, Joe (1909–), actor. Worked as a dancer in a family act in vaudeville, as a comedian in vaudeville, and as a top banana in Minsky's burlesque before entering films in the 1930s. He appeared in comedy shorts at Columbia studios before joining the THREE STOOGES in 1958 after Joe BESSER bowed out. The roly-poly DeRita, who resembled Curly, remained with the team until 1969, the year the trio disbanded. Most of his work with the group was in feature-length comedies.

SELECTED FILMS: *Have Rocket, Will Travel* (1959), *The Three Stooges Meet Hercules, The Three Stooges in Orbit* (1962), *The Three Stooges Go Around the World in a Daze* (1963), *The Outlaws Is Coming* (1965). ∎

Destry Rides Again (1939), U. Dir. George Marshall; Sc. Felix Jackson, Gertrude Purcell, Henry Myers; with Marlene Dietrich, James Stewart, Charles Winninger, Brian Donlevy.

Max Brand's western novel has been filmed several times, but this 1939 version converted the conventional story of law and order arriving in the West into a satirical comedy-drama bursting with energy. The film marked a comeback for Marlene's waning career. She had become box-office poison, but *Destry* revived her importance as a major screen personality. James STEWART, as the sheriff's deputy who is gun-shy, proved that he could do more than play simple romantic roles. The two stars are responsible for most of the success of this rowdy, brawling, entertaining western. Unforgettable are the fight between Una MERKEL and Dietrich over Mischa AUER'S pants and Dietrich's rendition of "See What the Boys in the Backroom Will Have." Several veteran comic character actors, including Auer, Billy GILBERT, Warren HYMER, and Allen JENKINS, add to the mayhem. Tom Mix starred in the 1932 version. A 1950 adaptation retitled *Frenchy* starred Shelley WINTERS. Finally, World War II hero Audie Murphy appeared as the title character in 1954 in a remake titled *Destry*.

Devine, Andy (1905–1977), actor. Began his Hollywood career in the mid-1920s in small parts in silent films, gradually moving up to supporting roles, often as a hayseed, in light features. With the arrival of sound, he developed into one of Hollywood's most popular comic-relief performers. Best known as a portly character actor with a raspy, high-pitched voice, he usually portrayed the comical sidekick of western heroes in numerous B films. One of his better roles was that of Buck, the affable stagecoach driver, in John FORD'S 1939 western classic, *Stagecoach*.

In *The Flame of New Orleans* (1941) he played a seaman aboard a ship about to be visited by the glamorous "Flame," Marlene Dietrich. Captain Bruce Cabot, dissatisfied with conditions, barks: "This boat looks like a pig pen. You want her to think we live like this?" "Well," Andy interjects, "don't we?"

SELECTED FILMS: *We Americans, Red Lips* (1928), *Hot Stuff* (1929), *Impatient Maiden* (1932), *Doctor Bull, Saturday's Millions* (1933), *Wake Up and Dream* (1934), *The Farmer Takes a Wife* (1935), *Romeo and Juliet* (1936), *You're a Sweetheart, Double or Nothing* (1937), *Dr. Rhythm* (1938), *Never Say Die* (1939), *Buck Benny Rides Again* (1940), *Top Sergeant* (1942), *Crazy House* (1943), *Follow the Boys, Babes on Swing Street* (1944), *That's the Spirit* (1945), *Never a Dull Moment* (1950), *Around the World in 80 Days* (1956), *It's a Mad, Mad, Mad, Mad World* (1963), *Zebra in the Kitchen* (1965), *A Whale of a Tale* (1977). ∎

DeVito, Danny (1944–), actor. Pint-sized character actor who has enlivened both dramas and comedies since the 1970s. Although he scored a success in his film debut in 1975, he did not receive any substantial roles until the mid-1980s, when his comedy career on film was revitalized.

SELECTED FILMS: *One Flew Over the Cuckoo's Nest* (1975), *The Van* (1976), *The World's Greatest Lover* (1977), *Goin' South* (1978), *Going Ape!* (1981), *Terms of Endearment (1983), Romancing the Stone (1984), Ruthless People (1986).* ∎

Devore, Dorothy (1899–1976), actress. Worked on stage, in nightclubs, and in vaudeville. She made her film debut in 1916 and, within a short time, scored a hit with her audiences in a succession of simplistic but popular two-reel comedies for producer-director Al CHRISTIE. One of the leading comedy figures of the silent era, she left the movie business with the advent of talkies.

SELECTED FILMS: *Mile-a-Minute Mary, Hazel From Hollywood, String Beans (1918), The Girl Dodger (1919), Movie Mad (1920), The Magnificent Brute (1921), When Odds Are Even (1923), Hold Your Breath, The Tomboy (1924), A Broadway Butterfly, His Majesty, Bunker Bean (1925), Money to Burn (1926), The First Night, Better Days (1927), Cutie, No Babies Wanted (1928), Auntie's Mistake (1929), Take the Heir (1930).* ∎

De Wolfe, Billy (1907–1974), actor. Worked in vaudeville and nightclubs as a comedian and dancer. He made his film debut in 1943. Usually appearing as a dapper gentleman with a neatly trimmed mustache, he gained wide popularity as a supporting player in light comedies and musicals.

In *Blue Skies* he and Olga SAN JUAN visit a maternity ward and watch a nurse as she gently feeds a newborn baby. "Look," Olga exclaims ecstatically, eyeing her beau, "doesn't that sort of make you yearn for something?" "Yeah, dinner," Billy replies. "I'm starving."

SELECTED FILMS: *Dixie (1943), Duffy's Tavern (1945), Miss Susie Slagle's, Our Hearts Were Growing Up, Blue Skies (1946), Dear Ruth, Variety Girl, The Perils of Pauline (1947), Isn't It Romantic? (1948), Dear Wife, Tea for Two (1949), Lullaby of Broadway, Dear Brat (1951), Call Me Madam (1953), Billie (1965), The World's Greatest Athlete (1973).* ∎

Diamond, I.A.L. (1920–), screenwriter, associate producer. Began his Hollywood career writing inconsequential scripts for Columbia studios after finishing college. He later worked for MGM, Paramount, and other studios, finally teaming up with Billy WILDER, with whom he wrote a series of biting and witty satires. Their 1960 film, *The Apartment,* won them an Academy Award for Best Picture.

Assessing Diamond's contributions as a comedy writer is difficult since he collaborated chiefly with such a dominating figure as Wilder. To what extent did each contribute to the wit, satire, or style of each film? Was Diamond, as at least one film critic, Richard Corliss, suggests, simply a "typist" or English translator for the European genius who felt uncomfortable in his adopted language? Diamond's screenplays, written either alone or with others, provide some clues. *Two Guys From Milwaukee,* which he wrote with Charles Hoffman, *Two Guys From Texas,* with Allen Boretz, *Let's Make It Legal,* with F. Hugh Herbert, and other comedies of the calibre of the above films are entertaining and well-paced diversions, but lack the satirical punch of the films he penned with Wilder. Most of his earlier work pales next to comedies like *Some Like It Hot, The Apartment, One, Two, Three,* and *The Fortune Cookie,* all written with Wilder.

SELECTED FILMS: *Murder in the Blue Room (1944), Two Guys From Milwaukee (1946), Love and Learn (1947), Two Guys From Texas (1948), The Girl From Jones Beach (1949), Let's Make It Legal (1951), Monkey Business, Something for the Birds (1952), That Certain Feeling (1956), Love in the Afternoon (1957), Merry Andrew (1958), Some Like It Hot (1959), The Apartment (1960), One, Two, Three (1961), Irma La Douce (1963), Kiss Me, Stupid (1964), The Fortune Cookie (1966), Cactus Flower (1969), Avanti! (1972), The Front Page (1974), Buddy Buddy (1981).* ∎

Dickerson, Dudley (–1968), actor. Appeared as a character player in several films of the 1940s and 1950s. One of the few black comics to work with the leading comedy teams, he supported the THREE STOOGES in some of their comedy shorts.

SELECTED FILMS: A-Plumbing We Will Go, From Nurse to Worse (1940), Sock-a-Bye Baby (1942), They Stooge to Conga, A Gem of a Jam (1943), Hold That Lion (1947), Who Done It? (1949), Scheming Schemers (1956). ■

Dillaway, Donald (1904–1982), actor. Began his screen career in the 1930s as a minor supporting player. A thin, dark-haired, clean-cut type, he appeared in several comedy shorts for producer Al CHRISTIE and in a few feature-length films. But he never achieved any prominence in films.

SELECTED FILMS: Pack Up Your Troubles (1932), The Little Giant (1933), The Circus Clown (1934), The People Against O'Hara (1951). ■

Diller, Phyllis (1917–), actress, comedienne. Worked in nightclubs in the mid-1950s and television before making her film debut in 1961. A housewife and mother of five, she began her comedy career at age 37. Known for her outlandish outfits, self-mocking humor, and frantic delivery, she became an almost immediate success as a stand-up comedienne. During the 1960s she appeared sporadically in films, most of which were routine vehicles that failed to exploit her full talent. In recent years she has undergone a facelift and changed her attire in search of a new image.

SELECTED FILMS: Splendor in the Grass (1961), Boy, Did I Get a Wrong Number, The Fat Spy (1966), Eight on the Lam (1967), The Private Navy of Sgt. O'Farrell, Did You Hear the One About the Traveling Saleslady? (1968), The Adding Machine (1969), The Sunshine Boys (1975). ■

Dillon, John Francis (1887–1934), director. Began his film career in Hollywood as an actor, and, by 1914, moved to directing short comedies. He was soon directing feature-length silents. During the 1920s he turned out a string of successful comedies as well as dramas. With the advent of sound he was relegated to directing routine films. The bulk of his output displayed a workmanlike, but unexceptional, quality.

SELECTED FILMS: Almost a Widow, Anita's Butterfly, Almost a King (1915), Indiscreet Corrine (1917), Betty Takes a Hand, Nancy Comes Home, She Hired a Husband, Beans (1918), The Plaything of Broadway (1921), The Self-Made Wife (1923), The Perfect Flapper, Flirting With Love (1924), Chickie, The Half-Way Girl, We Moderns (1925), Too Much Money (1926), Smile, Brother, Smile (1927), The Heart of a Follies Girl (1928), Spring Is Here, One Night at Susie's (1930), Millie (1931), The Cohens and the Kellys in Hollywood (1932), The Big Shakedown (1934). ■

Dilson, John (1891–1944), actor. Appeared on stage since 1909. He managed two theatrical companies before settling in Hollywood in the early 1930s. Bald and bespectacled, he became a busy character actor playing professional types and clerks in dramas and light films.

SELECTED FILMS: The Westerner (1934), Hitch Hike to Heaven (1936), Johnny Apollo (1940), Andy Hardy's Private Secretary, Father Steps Out, Cyclone on Horseback (1941). ■

Dinehart, Alan (1889–1944), actor. A prolific character player throughout the 1930s. He appeared in more than 75 films in 15 years. He often portrayed nervous businessmen in dramas and light comedies, supporting some of the leading comedians and stars of the period, including Eddie CANTOR, Shirley TEMPLE, Eleanor Powell, Dick POWELL, and James CAGNEY.

SELECTED FILMS: *The Brat* (1931), *Disorderly Conduct* (1932), *No Marriage Ties, Her Bodyguard* (1933), *Jimmy the Gent, Baby Take a Bow* (1934), *Redheads on Parade, Thanks a Million* (1935), *Everybody's Old Man* (1936), *Woman Wise, Step Lively, Jeeves* (1937), *Rebecca of Sunnybrook Farm* (1938), *Fast and Loose, Slightly Honorable* (1939), *Girl Trouble* (1942), *Sweet Rosie O'Grady, Fired Wife, The Heat's On* (1943), *Seven Days Ashore, Oh, What a Night* (1944). ∎

Jean Hersholt, John Barrymore, and Lee Tracy in *Dinner at Eight* (1933)

Dinner at Eight (1933), MGM. *Dir.* George Cukor; *Sc.* Herman Mankiewicz, Frances Marion, Donald Ogden Stewart; with Marie Dressler, John Barrymore, Wallace Beery, Jean Harlow, Lionel Barrymore, Lee Tracy, Billie Burke.

Before this star-studded production, *Grand Hotel* headed the list of films containing the most top stars of the period. MGM decided to outdo itself with this entertaining comedy. Based on a successful stage play by George S. Kaufman and Edna Ferber, the film is concerned with a dinner given by a socialite for visiting royalty. Fluttery Billie BURKE plays the hostess, while her husband, Lionel BARRYMORE, faces financial ruin of his shipping lines. Stage and screen veteran Marie DRESSLER plays an out-of-work actress. John BARRYMORE portrays a washed-up, alcoholic matinee idol whose agent,

Lee TRACY, confronts him with the truth about himself. Wallace BEERY, a hard-nosed businessman, and his unrefined, social-climbing wife, played wonderfully by Jean HARLOW, also are guests at the dinner. Among other gems, the film contains Dressler's immortal reply to Harlow. Harlow says that she read where machines will replace all occupations. "Oh, my dear," Dressler comforts her, "that is something *you* need never worry about."

"Dippy Doo-Dads, The." A series of silent comedy shorts produced by Hal ROACH in 1924 that featured monkeys in the starring roles. Roach, one of the earliest pioneers in ANIMAL HUMOR, engaged his subjects in slight story lines which emulated the affairs of humans, often resulting in highly original and humorous situations.

SELECTED FILMS: *Handle 'Em Rough* (1924). ∎

Dishy, Bob, actor. Has appeared on stage, in films, and in television. A dark-haired performer often cast as a contemporary urban type, he has played supporting roles chiefly in light films.

SELECTED FILMS: *Lovers and Other Strangers* (1970), *The Big Bus* (1976), *The Last Married Couple in America, First Family* (1980), *Author! Author!* (1982), *Brighton Beach Memoirs* (1986). ∎

Dithers, J.C. The fictional boss of BLONDIE'S confused husband, Dagwood Bumstead, in the long-running comedy series produced by Columbia studios. The easily flustered employer was portrayed by character actor Jonathan HALE in such films as *Blondie* (1938), *Blondie Meets the Boss* (1939), and *Blondie Has Servant Trouble* (1940). He was later replaced by Mr. Radcliffe, played by Jerome COWAN.

Dixon, Jean (1896–1981), actress. Worked in the theater before appearing in films in 1929. A character player in many early sound films, she often portrayed the comical confidante to the female lead. She played alongside many popular stars of the period, including Melvyn DOUGLAS, Claudette COLBERT, Cary GRANT, Katharine HEPBURN, and William POWELL.

SELECTED FILMS: The Lady Lies (1929), The Kiss Before the Mirror (1933), Mr. Dynamite, She Married Her Boss (1935), My Man Godfrey, The Magnificent Brute (1936), Swing High, Swing Low (1937), Joy of Living, Holiday (1938). ■

Dizzy. Fictional character in the "HENRY ALDRICH" comedy series starring Jimmy LYDON. Portrayed by Charles Smith, Dizzy was Henry's high school pal and confidant. Comic actor Eddie BRACKEN played the role in the first two entries, in which Jackie COOPER starred as Henry.

Dr. Strangelove, or: How I Learned to Stop Worrying and Love the Bomb (1964), COL. Dir. Stanley Kubrick; Sc. Stanley Kubrick, Terry Southern, Peter George; with Peter Sellers, George C. Scott, Sterling Hayden, Keenan Wynn.

Dr. Strangelove is not only one of the most highly praised films of the 1960s, it is one of the best satirical films ever made. Kubrick's scathing anti-war movie stars Peter Sellers playing three roles, United States President Muffley, an upper-crust R.A.F. captain, and Strangelove, the mad inventor of the Bomb; Sterling Hayden as General Jack D. Ripper, a paranoid right-winger who believes that the Communists plan to "sap and impurify all our precious bodily fluids" by fluoridating our drinking water; George C. Scott as General Turgidson, who is willing to gamble on total war; and Keenan WYNN as Major Bat

Guano. Strangelove, a scientist and former Nazi now confined to a wheelchair, has trouble controlling a trick arm that occasionally extends out into a Nazi salute. When a group of bombers on its way to bomb Russia cannot be recalled, he suggests that a few thousand carefully selected politicians, military advisers, and scientists could survive by living in a deep mine shaft, proposing ten women for each man. Turgidson, obsessed by Russian threats, warns: "We must not allow a mine shaft gap!" The savage humor continues when an American general grapples with the Soviet ambassador. "Gentlemen," the President intervenes, "you can't fight in here. This is the War Room." When the R.A.F. captain orders Guano to shoot open a vending machine to get a coin for a vital telephone call to the President, he is reproached. "That's private property," Guano announces. "You'll have to answer to the Coca Cola company." The film may be frightening and controversial in its portrayal of madmen at the helm, but it is also entertaining and quite funny.

Dodd, Claire (1908–1973), actress. Worked as a chorine in the Ziegfeld Follies before entering films in the early 1930s. She appeared in leading and supporting roles in many Warner Brothers dramas and light films. She often portrayed the wealthy socialite who lures the leading man away from the female lead, as in Ring LARDNER'S baseball comedy Elmer the Great, in which she attempts to snatch naive Joe E. BROWN from his true love, Patricia ELLIS.

SELECTED FILMS: Our Blushing Brides (1930), Up Pops the Devil, The Road to Reno, Girls About Town (1931), Man Wanted, This Is the Night, Dancers in the Dark (1932), Hard to Handle, Ex-Lady, Elmer the Great, Footlight Parade (1933), The Singing Kid, Navy Born (1936), Three Loves Has Nancy (1938), If I Had My Way, Slightly Honorable (1940), In the Navy (1941), The Mad Doctor of Market Street (1942). ■

Dodd, Jimmie (1913–1964), actor. Began his screen career in the early 1940s as a supporting player in low-budget light films and westerns. Eternally youthful and wide-eyed, he appeared in several "Snuffy Smith" comedy films and as comic relief characters in B westerns. A minor Hollywood actor, he finally gained recognition in television as the emcee and leader of Disney's "Mickey Mouse Club." He also composed hundreds of songs.

SELECTED FILMS: Hillbilly Blitzkrieg (1942), Riders of the Rio Grande, Thundering Trails (1943), Moon Over Las Vegas (1944), Buck Privates Come Home (1947), Song of My Heart (1948), The Winning Team (1952). ■

"Dog's Life, A." See Charlie Chaplin.

Domestic comedy. A film concerned chiefly with a middle-class family and its daily problems, the humor of which stems from the characters and their personal complications. The main characters, especially in the low-budget and series films of this genre, were predictable and stereotyped. The husband-wife relationship was often a play on Don Quixote and Sancho Panza: the bungling husband would concoct a get-rich-quick scheme or a crackpot invention, which he dreamed would shower wealth upon the family; in turn, his more down-to-earth spouse would frown upon his fantasies. They often had an older daughter ready to take the marriage vows. A younger son or daughter, usually bratty or precocious or both, completed the immediate family. Sometimes a cantankerous maiden aunt or bachelor uncle or grandparent resided within the household, as did an outspoken, wise-cracking maid or cook.

The first traces of domestic comedy can be found in the early silent shorts of comedian John BUNNY. The rotund comic co-starred with the gawky comedienne Flora FINCH in films like "A Cure for Pokeritis" (1912), in which she organizes a group of wives to raid a club where their husbands, supposedly at some innocent activity, are actually playing poker. In "Love, Luck, and Gasoline" (1914) Bunny tries to prevent his daughter from eloping. He appeared in hundreds of comedies before his untimely death in 1915. Sidney and Lucille DREW made a series of domestic comedies centered around flirtations, the management of finances, and jealous spouses, with titles like "Jerry's Uncle's Namesake" (1914), "Too Many Husbands" (1914), and "A Safe Investment" (1915). Carter and Flora DeHAVEN, another husband-and-wife comedy team, co-starred in a series of domestic comedies in the 1910s and 1920s. Comic Charlie MURRAY starred in several domestic comedies in which he played a henpecked husband with a roving eye. In "A Bedroom Blunder" (1917) he is absorbed with the female bathers at a resort, much to his wife's objections. In "Watch Your Neighbor," also released in 1917, undertaker Murray, employing some very funny gags, steals his partner's wife.

By the late 1920s the popular stage comedy Abie's Irish Rose, which ran for six years on Broadway, had been made into a film with Buddy ROGERS and Nancy CARROLL as the Jewish-Irish lovers who cause complications for the two protesting families. There followed a stream of light films based on Irish-Jewish stereotypes, including the "COHENS AND THE KELLYS" series, starring George SIDNEY and others, which continued into the sound period.

By the early 1930s the genre was firmly entrenched. In the Money (1934) concerned a widower-scientist and his screwball family. That same year Hugh HERBERT and Aline McMAHON starred in The Merry Frinks, another comedy about an eccentric family. Sometimes the families in these films were from the upper class but had fallen on hard times as in The Poor Rich, We're Rich Again, and Down to Their Last Yacht, all released in 1934. Typically, these families, who had lost their fortunes, recouped their losses by marrying off their daughter to a wealthy suitor or by some other convenient device.

Some of the more famous participants in domestic comedy were W. C. FIELDS and Will ROGERS. In several of Fields' films he was encumbered with a family and a troublesome mother-in-law, including *It's a Gift* (1934), *The Man on the Flying Trapeze* (1935), and *The Bank Dick* (1940). Stage and screen comedian Will Rogers starred in a series of family comedies, sometimes referred to as folksy comedies, beginning in 1929 with *They Had to See Paris*. *So This Is London* (1930), *Young As You Feel* (1931), and *Down to Earth* (1932) followed. In the last, he teaches his frivolous and spendthrift family a lesson when he announces that he is broke. He also starred in *Handy Andy* (1934) and *Life Begins at Forty* (1935).

Film comediennes as well contributed substantially to the genre. Marie DRESSLER, popular with film audiences in the 1930s, won an Academy Award for her role as the owner of a boarding house in *Min and Bill* (1931), which co-starred Wallace BEERY. The two stars, who had been in silent comedies, were teamed up again in *Tugboat Annie* (1933), with Dressler as the captain of the "Narcissus" and Beery as her rum-soaked husband. May ROBSON, another mature actress, made a series of domestic comedies. As a widow in *Strangers All* (1935), she raises four spoiled children. Mary BOLAND brought her matronly talents to the genre when she teamed up with comic actor Charles RUGGLES in a succession of family comedies. *Mama Loves Papa* (1933) concerns an ambitious wife who competes with a temptress. *People Will Talk* (1935) is about a young married woman returning home without her husband. In *Early to Bed* (1936) a sleepwalking husband causes trouble for his wife when he gets mixed up with gangsters. In *Wives Never Know* (1936) a middle-aged couple try to ignite their lost love by making each other

jealous. *Night Work* (1939) concerns an apartment house manager who gets involved in comical complications with tenants and his own family. Spring BYINGTON was another actress who specialized in the genre, invariably playing wives and mothers.

Other screen personalities of all ages joined the steady flow of domestic comedies. Former silent comic Edgar KENNEDY, famous for his "slow burn," made comedy shorts during the Depression years known as the "AVERAGE MAN" series. He played an inept husband who was easily overwhelmed by some relatively mundane household task which soon swelled into a major problem. Judy GARLAND and Freddie Bartholomew in *Listen, Darling* (1938) attempt to find a husband for their widowed mother, Mary ASTOR. In the same year the most eccentric and famous family of the decade made their way from the stage to the screen in *You Can't Take It With You*. The Sycamores, who lived in New York City and paid no taxes, believed that each member of the household should "do his or her own thing." The film starred, among others, Jean ARTHUR, Lionel BARRYMORE, James STEWART, and Edward ARNOLD.

By the late 1930s the studios were transforming the domestic comedy into series. The "JONES FAMILY" began the trend in 1936 with *Every Saturday Night*, starring Jed PROUTY and Spring Byington. Florence Roberts was featured as Granny. The "ANDY HARDY" films, starring Mickey ROONEY as the eternal teenager, began in 1937 with *A Family Affair*, from MGM. Lewis STONE and Fay HOLDEN portrayed his parents in the series, replacing Lionel Barrymore and Spring Byington, who appeared in the initial film. Another series, starring James, Lucille, and Russell GLEASON, was introduced in 1938 from Republic studios, called *The HIGGINS FAMILY*. Character actor Harry DAVENPORT played Grandpa. Perhaps the Hardy films were the most popular series of the genre, but the longest-running was

BLONDIE. From its inception in 1938, the lead players, Penny SINGLETON in the title role and Arthur LAKE as her husband, Dagwood Bumstead, seemed perfect as the young couple. Indeed, minor performers before they appeared in the films, they quickly emerged as stars.

While many of the series persevered into the 1940s, other single entries, many now in Technicolor, continued to be released. *There's One Born Every Minute* (1942) starred Hugh HERBERT as the head of a daffy family. Young Elizabeth Taylor made her film debut as one of his children. In *San Diego, I Love You* (1944), the eccentric members of father Edward Everett HORTON'S family journey to the California city to help promote his invention. The classic stage comedy by Howard Lindsay and Russell Crouse, *Life With Father*, came to the screen in 1947, starring William POWELL and Irene DUNNE. In *Mother Wore Tights* (1947) Betty GRABLE and Dan DAILEY starred as a vaudeville couple trying to raise a family while continuing their show-business careers. Loretta YOUNG has a different problem in *Mother Is a Freshman* (1949). She attends college with her daughter Betty Lynn, both of whom compete for the attention of Van JOHNSON.

The 1950s and 1960s showed no decline in domestic comedies. *Father Is a Bachelor*, *Cheaper by the Dozen*, and *The Goldbergs* were released in 1950. These were followed by, among others, *Mr. Hobbes Takes a Vacation* (1952), *The Seven Little Foys* (1955), *Please Don't Eat the Daisies* (1960), *Bon Voyage* (1962), *Take Her, She's Mine*, *The Courtship of Eddie's Father*, and *For Love or Money*, all 1963, *Never Too Late* (1965), and *With Six You Get Eggroll* (1968).

The genre continued into the 1970s and 1980s with *Charley and the Angel* (1972), *Mixed Company* (1974), *Casey's Shadow* (1978), and *Author! Author!* (1982), starring Al Pacino as a writer whose wife walks out on him and leaves him saddled with the children. Although the Walt Disney studios tend to specialize in the family comedy, other studios occasionally produce films that are comical and original in this genre that refuses to quit in spite of the popularity and dominance of R-rated movies.

Donen, Stanley (1924–), director. Appeared as a dancer on Broadway in 1940 and worked as associate choreographer in the theater and in Hollywood. He began his directing career as Gene KELLY'S collaborator on the 1949 musical *On the Town*. After working with Kelly on a series of popular MGM musicals, he struck off on his own or in collaboration with George Abbott to direct light comedies as well as other musicals both in Hollywood and abroad. His collaborations with Kelly revolutionized the Hollywood musical by integrating the music and the choreography with the story line. In his later works he experimented with suspense and sophisticated comedies as well as with social comedies.

SELECTED FILMS: Royal Wedding (1951), *Singin' in the Rain*, *Fearless Fagan* (1952), *Give a Girl a Break* (1953), *Seven Brides for Seven Brothers* (1954), *Funny Face*, *The Pajama Game* (1957), *Indiscreet*, *Damn Yankees* (1958), *Once More With Feeling*, *Surprise Package*, *The Grass Is Greener* (1960), *Charade* (1963), *Arabesque* (1966), *Two for the Road*, *Bedazzled* (1967), *Staircase* (1969), *The Little Prince* (1974), *Lucky Lady* (1975), *Movie Movie* (1978). ■

Donlevy, Brian (1899–1972), actor. Worked as a model in the 1920s and in bit parts on Broadway and in early 1930s films. By the mid-1930s he became established as one of Hollywood's major villains. A stocky actor with good features and a neat mustache, he played leads and supporting roles into the next decade when writer-director Preston STURGES and Paramount exploited his comic potential. In the broadly satirical *The Great McGinty*, perhaps his best role, he played a dull-witted tramp who, with the help of racketeer Akim TAMIROFF, rises to the governorship of the state. In several other comedies, such as *Destry Rides Again*, he played more villainous roles, particularly as a foil to the lead character.

SELECTED FILMS: *Damaged Hearts* (1924), *School for Wives* (1925), *Mother's Boy* (1929), *Strike Me Pink* (1936), *Destry Rides Again* (1939), *The Great McGinty* (1940), *The Remarkable Andrew*, *Two Yanks in Trinidad*, *A Gentleman After Dark* (1942), *The Miracle of Morgan's Creek*, *An American Romance* (1944), *Our Hearts Were Growing Up* (1946), *Heaven Only Knows* (1947), *A Southern Yankee* (1948), *The Lucky Stiff* (1949), *The Errand Boy* (1961), *Pit Stop* (1969). ∎

Donnell, Jeff (1921–), actress. Appeared in numerous light films of the 1940s as a saucy friend of the female lead. A red-haired, cheerful performer, she played teenagers early in her career, and eventually moved to matronly roles.

SELECTED FILMS: *My Sister Eileen* (1942), *A Night to Remember* (1943), *Once Upon a Time* (1944), *He's My Guy*, *Over 21* (1945), *The Fuller Brush Girl* (1950), *So This Is Love* (1953), *My Man Godfrey* (1957), *Gidget Goes Hawaiian* (1961), *The Comic* (1969), *Stand Up and Be Counted* (1972). ∎

Donnelly, Leo (1878–1935), actor. Worked in vaudeville, on stage, and in films from the early 1920s. He appeared chiefly as a supporting player in light films, including several shorts during the early sound era.

SELECTED FILMS: *Potash and Perlmutter* (1923), *Roadhouse Nights*, *Stepping Out*, *The Music Racket* (1930). ∎

Donnelly, Ruth (1896–1982), actress. Worked as a chorus girl in 1913, in Broadway productions, and in films beginning in 1927. She appeared in almost 100 films in over three decades, many of which were light comedies. She usually played supporting parts as a wise-cracking friend of the female lead, a self-sufficient woman, or a nagging spouse. She worked with many of the leading stars of the period, including Al JOLSON, James STEWART, Gary COOPER, Edward G. ROBINSON, Mae WEST, and W. C. Fields. In the late 1940s and 1950s she appeared in a handful of dramatic films, including *The Snake Pit* (1948) and *Autumn Leaves* (1956).

SELECTED FILMS: *Rubber Heels* (1927), *Transatlantic* (1931), *Blessed Event* (1932), *Hard to Handle*, *Female* (1933), *Wonderbar*, *Housewife* (1934), *Metropolitan*, *Hands Across the Table* (1935), *Mr. Deeds Goes to Town* (1936), *A Slight Case of Murder* (1938), *Mr. Smith Goes to Washington* (1939), *My Little Chickadee* (1940), *Model Wife*, *Rise and Shine* (1941), *Johnny Doughboy* (1942), *Sleepy Lagoon* (1943), *Pillow to Post* (1945), *Cinderella Jones* (1946), *Little Miss Broadway*, *The Ghost Goes Wild* (1947), *The Way to the Gold* (1957). ∎

Dooley, Billy (1893–1938), comedian. Worked in silent two-reel comedies during the 1920s. He was a minor supporting comic who capitalized on the scarcity of comedians available for comedy shorts when many of the major clowns moved into longer films. He starred in six two-reelers for Al CHRISTIE in 1926 and made another eight the following year, often in a sailor outfit. His chief attribute, besides portraying a dull-witted character, as he did in the "Goofy Gob" series of the 1920s, was his ability to curl his mouth into the shape of the number "eight."

SELECTED FILMS: *Anything Goes* (1936), *Call of the Yukon*, *The Marines Are Here* (1938). ∎

Dooley, Paul (1928–), actor. Worked as a television comedy writer before entering films in the late 1960s. A stocky, round-faced performer, he has appeared as a character actor as well as a lead in dramas and light films.

In *Breaking Away* he gave a hilarious performance as the father of the young bicycle rider, Dennis Christopher, who has taken a year off between school and a full-time job. Dooley, who has worked hard all his life, resents his son's carefree life. "He's never tired. He's never miserable," he complains to his wife. "He's young," she explains. "When I was young," the father continues, "I was tired and miserable."

SELECTED FILMS: *What's So Bad About Feeling Good?* (1968), *The Out-of-Towners* (1969), *Up the Sandbox* (1972), *Slap Shot* (1976), *A Perfect Couple, Rich Kids, Breaking Away* (1979), *Popeye* (1980), *Paternity* (1981), *Kiss Me Goodbye* (1982), *Sixteen Candles* (1984). ■

Doran, Ann (1911–), actress. Entered films in the early 1930s and appeared in numerous dramas and light films. A prolific character player, she frequently portrayed a friend of the female lead. She worked in Columbia comedy shorts with some of the leading comics of the period, including, among others, the THREE STOOGES, Charley CHASE, Buster KEATON, and Harry LANGDON.

SELECTED FILMS: *Charlie Chan in London* (1934), *Palm Springs* (1936), *You Can't Take It With You, Blondie* (1938), *Mr. Smith Goes to Washington* (1939), *My Sister Eileen, Yankee Doodle Dandy* (1942), *My Favorite Brunette* (1947), *Never a Dull Moment, Riding High* (1950), *Love Is Better Than Ever* (1952), *Captain Newman, M.D.* (1963), *Rosie* (1967), *The Hired Hand* (1971). ■

Dorety, Charles R. (1898–1957), actor. Worked in the circus and in vaudeville before turning to Hollywood. He appeared in several early sound comedies, most of which were shorts starring the THREE STOOGES. He also directed and produced films.

SELECTED FILMS: *Men in Black, Three Little Pigskins* (1934), *Uncivil War-*

riors, *I'm a Father, Sawbones* (1935), *Ants in the Pantry, Movie Maniacs* (1936). ■

D'Orsay, Fifi (1904–1984), actress. Worked as a chorus girl and performer in vaudeville with GALLAGHER AND SHEAN before entering films in 1929. Although she was ballyhooed by her studio as a Parisian sexpot, she had never been to France. She played supporting and lead roles in light comedies, mainly in the 1930s, often as a dumb, amoral character.

SELECTED FILMS: *They Had to See Paris, Hot for Paris* (1929), *Women Everywhere, Those Three French Girls* (1930), *Mr. Lemon of Orange, Women of All Nations, Young As You Feel* (1931), *Girl From Calgary* (1932), *Going Hollywood* (1933), *Wonderbar* (1934), *Accent on Youth* (1935), *Three Legionnaires* (1937), *The Gangster* (1947), *What a Way to Go!* (1964), *The Art of Love* (1965), *Assignment to Kill* (1968). ■

Doty, Weston and Winston (1915–1934), child actors. Twin brothers who appeared sporadically in silent films. They were in several entries of producer Hal ROACH'S "OUR GANG" comedy shorts. They both drowned at age 19.

SELECTED FILMS: *Peter Pan* (1925). ■

Doucet, Catherine (1875–1958), actress. Entered films in the early 1930s following a long stage career. An accomplished actress, she played minor character roles in dramas and light films into the 1940s. She was married to actor M. Paul DOUCET.

SELECTED FILMS: *Rendezvous at Midnight* (1933), *As Husbands Go, Wake Up and Dream, Servant's Entrance* (1934), *Millions in the Air* (1935), *Poppy, The Luckiest Girl in the World* (1936), *When You're in Love, Oh, Doctor!* (1937), *Nothing but the Truth, It Started With Eve* (1941), *Family Honeymoon* (1949). ■

Doucet, M. Paul (1886–1928), actor. Worked on stage in his native France before entering silent films in the United States in the early 1920s. He appeared as a supporting player in dramas and light films until his untimely death at age 42. He was married to actress Catherine DOUCET.

SELECTED FILMS: Tropical Love (1921), Polly of the Follies (1922), Heart of a Siren, The Little French Girl (1925), The Broadway Drifter (1927). ▪

Douglas, Gordon (1909–), director. Began his directorial career in Hollywood in the mid-1930s. He has turned out comedies and action and war features for a variety of studios. He directed radio comedy actor Hal PEARY in the low-budget "Gildersleeve" comedy series. His career has spanned five decades during which time he has worked with several of the leading comics of the period, including, among others, LAUREL AND HARDY, Eddie CANTOR, and Bob HOPE.

SELECTED FILMS: General Spanky (1936), Zenobia (1939), Saps at Sea (1940), Road Show (1941), The Great Gildersleeve (1942), Girl Rush (1944), If You Knew Susie (1948), Mr. Soft Touch (1949), She's Back on Broadway (1953), Young at Heart (1954), Follow That Dream (1962), Call Me Bwana (1963), Robin and the Seven Hoods (1964), Way . . . Way Out (1966), Viva Knievel! (1977). ▪

Douglas, Melvyn (1901–1981), actor. Appeared in stock and on Broadway before making his Hollywood debut in 1931. Born Melvyn Edouard Hesselberg, he emerged as a popular actor of the 1930s and 1940s, portraying suave, debonair leading men in numerous romantic comedies. He co-starred with some of the most glamorous actresses of the period. His acting appearances fluctuated between Broadway and Hollywood and, in the 1960s, he turned to character roles in such films as Billy Budd (1962). He won an Oscar as Best Supporting Actor for his portrayal of the ethical, uncompromising patriarch in Hud (1963) and another for his role in Being There (1979). His autobiography, See You at the Movies, was published in 1986.

In Ninotchka Commissar Greta Garbo, who arrives in Paris straight from Russia, stops playboy Douglas at an intersection. "I'm looking for the Eiffel Tower," she inquires in a businesslike manner. "Good heavens," he replies glibly, "is that thing lost again?" Later in the film she questions Douglas about his frivolous life. "What do you do for mankind?" "For mankind, not so much," he replies, "but for womankind, my record is not so bleak."

SELECTED FILMS: Tonight or Never, The Wiser Sex (1931), As You Desire Me (1932), She Married Her Boss (1935), And So They Were Married, Theodora Goes Wild (1936), I Met Him in Paris, I'll Take Romance (1937), There's Always a Woman, That Certain Age, The Shining Hour (1938), Good Girls Go to Paris, Ninotchka (1939), Too Many Husbands, Third Finger, Left Hand (1940), Our Wife, Two-Faced Woman (1941), We Were Dancing, They All Kissed the Bride (1942), Three Hearts for Julia (1943), Mr. Blandings Builds His Dream House (1948), On the Loose (1951), The Americanization of Emily (1964), Being There (1979). ▪

Douglas, Paul (1907–1959), actor. Had careers as professional football player, radio sportscaster, and Broadway actor before entering films in 1948. Although he appeared in many dramatic roles, his forte was portraying rough but amiable characters in light comedies.

SELECTED FILMS: A Letter to Three Wives (1948), It Happens Every Spring, Everybody Does It (1949), Love That Brute (1950), Angels in the Outfield (1951), When in Rome, We're Not Married (1952), Never Wave at a Wac (1953), Forever Female (1954), The Solid Gold Cadillac (1956), This Could Be the Night, Beau James (1957), The Mating Game (1959). ▪

Dove, Billie (1900–), actress. Worked as a model and Broadway performer before her screen debut in 1921. Considered one of the prettiest stars of silent films, she appeared in dramatic roles as well as comedies. She successfully made the transition to sound but retired after appearing in a few talkies. She returned to films in 1962 for a small role in a Charlton Heston film.

SELECTED FILMS: Get-Rich-Quick Wallingford, At the Stage Door (1921), Polly of the Follies, Beyond the Rainbow (1922), Soft Boiled, The Thrill Chaser (1923), Yankee Madness, Try and Get It (1924), The Marriage Clause, Kid Boots, The Lone Wolf Returns (1926), Sensation Seekers, The Tender Hour, American Beauty, The Love Mart (1927), The Heart of a Follies Girl (1928), Her Private Life (1929), A Notorious Affair, Sweethearts and Wives, One Night at Susie's (1930), The Lady Who Dared (1931), Cock of the Air, Blondie of the Follies (1932), Diamond Head (1962). ■

Downs, Johnny (1913–), actor. Began in films as a child actor in silent comedies, then appeared in vaudeville and on Broadway, only to return to Hollywood in the 1930s. He was a member of Hal ROACH'S "OUR GANG" family during the 1920s. For the next 20 years he appeared mainly in undistinguished light films and routine musicals, several of which were CAMPUS COMEDIES. He once again turned to Broadway in the 1940s after his film career faltered.

SELECTED FILMS: Your Own Back Yard, Better Movies, One Wild Ride (1925), Thundering Fleas, Shivering Spooks, The Fourth Alarm (1926), Outlaws of Red River (1927), Babes in Toyland (1934), College Scandal, The Virginia Judge (1935), Everybody's Old Man, The First Baby, Pigskin Parade (1936), Turn Off the Moon, Blonde Trouble (1937), Hold That Co-Ed, Swing, Sister, Swing (1938), Hawaiian Nights, Laugh It Off (1939), Melody and Moonlight, Slightly Tempted (1940), Honeymoon for Three, Moonlight in Hawaii (1941), Behind the Eight Ball (1942),

Campus Rhythm (1943), What a Man! (1944), The Kid From Brooklyn (1946), Cruisin' Down the River (1953). ■

Drake, Charles (1914–), actor. Began his screen career in the late 1930s. A tall figure with light hair, he appeared chiefly as a minor player during the 1940s, eventually moving up to second leads. Often burdened with bland roles, he has found it difficult to assert his full potential in films.

SELECTED FILMS: Career (1939), Affectionately Yours, You're in the Army Now, The Man Who Came to Dinner (1941), The Male Animal, The Gay Sisters, Larceny, Inc. (1942), A Night in Casablanca (1946), Peggy, Harvey (1950), You Never Can Tell (1951), Bonzo Goes to College (1952), Tammy Tell Me True (1961), The Lively Set (1964), Hail, Hero! (1969). ■

Drake, Tom (1918–1982), actor. Appeared on stage and on Broadway by age 20 before entering films in 1940. A handsome performer with an affable personality, he played lead roles in several MGM light films and dramas until his contract expired. During the 1950s he was relegated to minor roles in routine films and by the 1970s all but disappeared from the screen.

SELECTED FILMS: The Howards of Virginia (1940), Two Girls and a Sailor, Maisie Goes to Reno, Meet Me in St. Louis (1944), This Man's Navy (1945), Faithful in My Fashion (1946), Words and Music (1948), Mr. Belvedere Goes to College (1949), The Singing Nun (1966). ■

Dreifuss, Arthur (1908–), director. Emigrated from his native Germany in the 1930s and began his directorial career in Hollywood in the early 1940s. For three decades he turned out chiefly low-budget light films which appeared on the bottom half of dual-feature programs. He worked for a variety of studios, including Monogram, Columbia, and MGM.

SELECTED FILMS: *Mystery in Swing* (1940), *Reg'lar Fellers* (1941), *Sarong Girl, Melody Parade, Campus Rhythm, Nearly Eighteen* (1943), *Ever Since Venus* (1944), *Eadie Was a Lady, The Gay Senorita* (1945), *Junior Prom, Freddie Steps Out* (1946), *Vacation Days, Betty Co-Ed, Little Miss Broadway, Two Blondes and a Redhead* (1947), *Glamour Girl, I Surrender, Dear* (1948), *An Old-Fashioned Girl* (1949), *Life Begins at 17* (1958), *Juke Box Rhythm* (1959), *The Young Runaways* (1968). ∎

Dressler, Marie (1869–1934), actress. Worked in stock in 1873, on the stage, and on Broadway in 1892. After a stint in vaudeville as a headliner, the Canadian-born comedienne entered films in 1914 in *Tillie's Punctured Romance* co-starring Charlie CHAPLIN and Mabel NORMAND, and continued to appear in silent comedies. She returned to the stage for a few years, became actively involved in union activities in the theater, then reappeared in films in 1927. She made a series of successful comedies with fellow comedienne Polly MORAN. She became so popular with her audiences that in 1930 alone she appeared in ten films. With the coming of sound, her popularity climbed, unlike that of many other leading silent performers who found the transition difficult. She won an Academy Award for Best Actress in 1930 as Wallace BEERY'S foil in *Min and Bill*. A rather plain-looking actress with a bulldog expression, she often appeared in supporting roles as gruff, elderly characters. In 1933 trade periodicals considered her the top box-office draw.

Although she is known for more than one notable role, she is best remembered for her famous reply to Jean HARLOW in *Dinner at Eight*. Attempting to emulate a person of intelligence and culture, the sultry "Blonde Bombshell" comments to Dressler as they go in to dinner: "Do you know, machinery is going to take the place of every profession?" "Oh, my dear," the veteran Broadway star observes, "that is something *you* need never worry about." Her autobiography was titled *The Life Story of an Ugly Duckling*.

SELECTED FILMS: *Tillie's Tomato Surprise* (1915), *Tillie Wakes Up, The Scrub Lady* (1917), *The Cross Red Nurse, The Agonies of Agnes* (1918), *The Joy Girl, Breakfast at Sunrise* (1927), *Bringing Up Father, The Patsy* (1928), *The Divine Lady* (1929), *Chasing Rainbows, Anna Christie, Caught Short, Let Us Be Gay* (1930), *Reducing, Politics* (1931), *Emma, Prosperity* (1932), *Tugboat Annie, Dinner at Eight, Christopher Bean* (1933). ∎

Drew, Ellen (1915–), actress. Came to Hollywood after winning a regional beauty contest. A lively performer with hazel eyes, she appeared at first as a bit player in dozens of films before advancing to leads in melodramas and comedies during a career that spanned three decades. She worked with some of the leading comics of the period, including Jack BENNY, Gracie ALLEN, and Bob HOPE.

SELECTED FILMS: *College Holiday, Rhythm on the Range* (1936), *Bluebeard's Eighth Wife* (1938), *The Lady's From Kentucky, The Gracie Allen Murder Case* (1939), *Buck Benny Rides Again, French Without Tears, Christmas in July* (1940), *Our Wife* (1941), *My Favorite Spy* (1942), *Man Alive* (1945), *Outlaw's Son* (1957). ∎

Drew, Sidney (1864–1919), actor. Appeared in silent comedy shorts in the early 1910s. With his attractive second wife, he made DOMESTIC COMEDIES in the style of vaudeville sketches, that is, material which required limited props and single sets, such as a businessman's or doctor's office. In general, his comedies, like those of his predecessor, John BUNNY, avoided the coarseness and unwieldiness of the typical fare of the period. The subject matter of the two comics, however, differed. Bunny was eternally trying to flee from some termagant, while Drew and his spouse epitomized the typical couple's struggles with the daily shortcomings of married life. Drew also shunned the heavy makeup, drooping mustache, or exaggerated eyebrows commonly used by many of his contemporaries. When the successful couple moved to Metro studios in 1916, they received a contract for $90,000 a year for a projected series of 52 one-reelers annually.

SELECTED FILMS: When Two Hearts Are Won (1911), The Professional Patient (1912), Jerry's Uncle's Namesake, Too Many Husbands (1914), Wanted, a Nurse, The Story of a Glove, A Safe Investment, Miss Sticky-Moufie-Kiss (1915), At the Count of Ten (1916), The Hypochondriac (1917), His First Love, A Youthful Affair (1918), The Amateur Liar, Romance and Rings, A Sisterly Scheme (1919). ■

Dreyfuss, Richard (1948–), actor. Worked on and off Broadway and in television before entering films in 1968. Short and stocky in appearance, he starred in dramas as well as comedies. He won an Academy Award as Best Actor for his role in *The Goodbye Girl* (1977). His flair for comedy may be best demonstrated in *American Graffiti* (1973) and the Canadian film *The Apprenticeship of Duddy Kravitz* (1974).

SELECTED FILMS: The Young Runaways (1968), Hello Down There (1969), Dillinger (1973), The Second Coming of Suzanne (1974), Jaws (1975), Inserts (1976), Close Encounters of the Third Kind (1977), The Big Fix (1978), All That Jazz (1979), The Competition (1980), Down and Out in Beverly Hills (1986). ■

Driscoll, Marian. See Fibber McGee and Molly.

Duck Soup (1933), PAR. Dir. Leo McCarey; Sc. Bert Kalmar, Harry Ruby, Nat Perrin, Arthur Sheekman; with Groucho, Harpo, Chico, Zeppo Marx, Margaret Dumont, Louis Calhern.

The film was the Marx Brothers' last at Paramount and it flopped at the theaters. But it has since been elevated to classic status by loyal followers and general audiences as well. The boys attack almost everything, including politics, patriotism, and war. Groucho, as President of the mythical Freedonia, leads the country into utter chaos. As the country prepares for war, Groucho invokes the image of Margaret DUMONT to stir his troops to victory. "Remember," he announces, "we're fighting for this woman's honor, which is probably more than she ever did." In an earlier scene the unpredictable Groucho attempts to woo Dumont. "What are you thinking of?" she asks romantically as he snuggles up to her. "All the years I wasted collecting stamps," he replies. The satirical film abounds in famous moments, which include Harpo and Chico's encounter with Louis Calhern, the mirror scene in which Harpo imitates Groucho, the incident with vendor Edgar KENNEDY and Harpo, and the final battle sequences. The film shows the brothers at their funniest, unhampered by musical interludes or romantic sub-plots. Zeppo, who usually played straight man, left the team when the boys moved to MGM.

Duffy, Jack (1882–1939), actor. Began his Hollywood career during the silent era as a comic character player following a career in vaudeville and on stage. He worked for producer Al CHRISTIE in several comedy shorts and continued into the early sound period in the same capacity. He appeared in a few comedies with the THREE STOOGES.

SELECTED FILMS: Neighbors (1920), The Brass Bowl, Reckless Romance (1924), Madame Behave, Stop Flirting (1925), Ella Cinders (1926), Harold Teen (1928), Loose Change, Hot Scotch, Divorce Made Easy, Sally (1929), The Skin Game (1930), Heaven on Earth (1931), Alice in Wonderland (1933), Restless Knights, Pop Goes the Easel, Ants in the Pantry (1935). ■

Dugan, Tom (1889–1955), actor. Supporting player who began his film career in the late 1920s. He frequently portrayed an Irish policeman, chiefly in light films. He worked with some of the foremost comedians of the period, including Bob HOPE, Jimmy DURANTE, Jack BENNY, and Danny KAYE.

SELECTED FILMS: Sharp Shooters (1927), Sonny Boy (1929), Bright Lights (1930), Palooka (1934), Princess O'Hara (1935), Pick a Star (1936), The Housekeeper's Daughter (1939), The Ghost Breakers (1940), To Be or Not to Be (1942), Up in Arms (1944), Bringing Up Father (1946), Good News (1947), The Lemon Drop Kid (1951). ■

Dumbrille, Douglass (1888–1974), actor. Worked in stock and the theater before making his Hollywood debut in 1931. He was a prolific character actor for over thirty years with a list of approximately 100 films to his credit. A mustached, strait-laced, commanding figure, he often played corrupt figures in numerous melodramas and light films, especially in the latter as foil to such comics as Joe E. BROWN, the MARX BROTHERS, the RITZ BROTHERS, ABBOTT AND COSTELLO, and Bob HOPE.

SELECTED FILMS: His Woman (1931), Blondie of the Follies (1932), Elmer the Great (1933), Harold Teen (1934), Naughty Marietta (1935), The Lone Wolf

Returns, The Princess Comes Across (1936), A Day at the Races (1937), Kentucky (1938), The Three Musketeers (1939), Slightly Honorable (1940), The Big Store (1941), Ride 'Em Cowboy (1942), DuBarry Was a Lady (1943), Lost in a Harem (1944), Road to Utopia (1945), Spook Busters (1946), It's a Joke, Son! (1947), Tell It to the Judge (1949), Riding High (1950), Son of Paleface (1952), What a Way to Go! (1964). ■

Dumke, Ralph (1899–1964), actor. Appeared in vaudeville, on stage, and on the radio before entering films as a supporting player in the late 1940s. Thickset with a receding hairline and mustache, he often portrayed corrupt politicians and businessmen in dramas and light films.

SELECTED FILMS: All the King's Men (1949), We're Not Married (1952), She Couldn't Say Yes (1954), Daddy Long Legs, Artists and Models (1955), Francis in the Haunted House, Forever Darling, The Solid Gold Cadillac (1956), The Buster Keaton Story (1957), Wake Me When It's Over (1960), All in a Night's Work (1961). ■

Dumont, Margaret (1889–1965), actress. Began her show business career as a singer, appeared on the Broadway stage in 1907, and with the MARX BROTHERS in their 1928 stage success Cocoanuts. Often described as the perfect comic foil, she proceeded to make seven films with the zany comedy team. She usually portrayed a wealthy dowager of propriety and dignity who had to withstand the continuous insults and advances of the lecherous and scheming Groucho. In Duck Soup, for example, Groucho studies her for a moment and says: "Say, you cover a lot of ground. . . . You better beat it, lady, or they're gonna tear you down and put up an office building where you're standing." Moments later he asks, "Where is your husband?" "Why, he's dead," she replies sadly. "I bet he's just using that as an excuse." "I was with him till the very end." "No wonder he passed away." "I held him in my arms and kissed him," she continues. "Oh, I see," Groucho concludes, "so it was murder."

She was also memorable in the role of the exasperated home owner who has her carpet ruined by Lou COSTELLO as a vacuum cleaner salesman in *Little Giant* (1946). Other famous comedians with whom she worked include Jack BENNY, Danny KAYE, W. C. FIELDS, and LAUREL AND HARDY.

SELECTED FILMS: The Cocoanuts (1929), Animal Crackers (1930), The Girl Habit (1931), Duck Soup (1933), A Night at the Opera (1935), Anything Goes (1936), A Day at the Races, High Flyers, Wise Girl (1937), At the Circus (1939), The Big Store, Never Give a Sucker an Even Break (1941), The Dancing Masters (1943), Up in Arms, Bathing Beauty (1944), The Horn Blows at Midnight (1945), Stop, You're Killing Me (1952), Auntie Mame (1958), Zotz! (1962), What a Way to Go! (1964). ■

Duncan, Bud (–1960), actor. Worked in early silent comedy shorts for various pioneer Hollywood studios, reaching his peak of popularity in the "HAM AND BUD" comedy series, co-starring Lloyd HAMILTON and, at times, Ruth ROLAND. Short in stature, he was often attired in oversized clothes for comical effect. One of his major contributions to this series of knockabout comedies included his agility as well as his comic abilities, for he was often tossed out windows and down staircases. When the team split up, Duncan pooled his talents with those of Dot FARLEY and Kewpie Morgan, two popular fellow comics, to make a series of slapstick films called "Clover Comedies" for the National Film Corporation. He also joined Fred MACE, an ambitious and well-known comedian in these early pre-war years, turning out a handful of comedies for Apollo Films. In the 1940s he portrayed Snuffy Smith in Monogram's inadequate attempt to bring the comic strip to the screen.

SELECTED FILMS: The Tattered Duke, Don't Monkey With the Buzz Saw, Si's Wonderful Mineral Spring, Ham and the Villain Factory (1914), Private Snuffy Smith, Hillbilly Blitzkrieg (1942). ■

Dunn, Bobby (–1937), actor, comic. Worked in early silent comedy shorts for Mack SENNETT'S KEYSTONE studios. A cross-eyed comic, he portrayed one of the original KEYSTONE KOPS in the popular series. Although he was often cast as a minor supporting player, he appeared with some of the leading screen comedians of the period, including, among others, Ford STERLING, Mack SWAIN, Polly MORAN, Hank MANN, and Slim SUMMERVILLE. In the early 1920s he was featured in a series of comedy shorts called the Mirthquake comedies, which he made for Arrow Film Corporation. With the advent of sound, he continued in the role of supporting player in many of LAUREL AND HARDY'S comedy shorts and features.

SELECTED FILMS: His Pride and Shame, His Auto Ruination, By Stork Delivery, His Bread and Butter, Bubbles of Trouble, The Winning Punch (1916), Villa of the Movies, Secrets of a Beauty Parlor (1917), Why Girls Love Sailors (1927), Bacon Grabbers (1929), Pardon Us (1931), Me and My Pal (1933), Them Thar Hills (1934), Tit for Tat (1934), The Fixer-Uppers (1935), The Bohemian Girl, Our Relations (1936), Way Out West (1937). ■

Dunn, Eddie (1896–1951), actor. Appeared in many comedy shorts for Hal ROACH'S studios during the 1930s and in feature-length films for other studios. He worked as a supporting player for various comedians, including LAUREL AND HARDY, CLARK AND McCULLOUGH, and ABBOTT AND COSTELLO.

SELECTED FILMS: Another Fine Mess (1930), A Melon-Drama, The Pajama Party, Pardon Us, False Roomers (1931), Me and My Pal, The Midnight Patrol,

Asleep in the Feet (1933), Here Comes Cookie (1935), Go West, Young Man, The Big Broadcast of 1937 (1936), One Night in the Tropics (1940), In the Navy (1941), Hit the Ice (1943), Nothing but Trouble, Lost in a Harem (1944), See My Lawyer, Here Come the Co-eds (1945), Buck Privates Come Home (1947). ∎

Dunn, James (1905–1967), actor. Appeared on stage and on Broadway before entering films in the early 1930s. A good-looking actor with a pleasant personality, he played leads in several routine light films and dramas for two decades and appeared a few times with Shirley TEMPLE. He earned an Oscar as Best Supporting Actor for his role in A Tree Grows in Brooklyn (1945). However, he never became a major Hollywood star.

SELECTED FILMS: Bad Girl, Over the Hill (1931), Handle With Care (1932), Sailor's Luck, Arizona to Broadway (1933), Stand Up and Cheer, Baby Take a Bow, Bright Eyes (1934), The Daring Young Man (1935), We Have Our Moments, Living on Love (1937), Hold That Woman (1940), The Living Ghost (1942), Leave It to the Irish (1944), The Oscar (1966). ∎

Dunn, Josephine (1906–), actress. Made her Broadway debut in 1921 as a chorus girl and by 1926 was in Hollywood making films for Paramount. An attractive, blonde-haired actress, she appeared as the lead player in light films as well as in dramas. But during the sound era, when she was given subordinate roles, she chose to retire from the screen.

SELECTED FILMS: Fascinating Youth (1926), Swim, Girl, Swim, Fireman, Save My Child, She's a Sheik, Get Your Man (1927), We Americans, The Singing Fool, Excess Baggage (1928), Melody Lane, Big Time, Our Modern Maidens (1929), Safety in Numbers (1930), One Hour With You, The Fighting Gentleman (1932), Mr. Broadway (1933). ∎

Dunne, Irene (1898–), actress. Began her career as a singer, appeared on Broadway in Show Boat (1929), and entered films in 1930. She starred in SCREWBALL COMEDIES as well as melodramas but is perhaps best remembered for her portrayals of elegant, stylish leading ladies in romantic comedies. Along with comic actresses Jean ARTHUR, Claudette COLBERT, and Carole LOMBARD, she helped to elevate the stature of 1930s comedies. By the late 1940s, during the latter part of her career, she played more mature, but memorable, roles with grace and dignity. She was nominated for the Academy Award as Best Actress for Cimarron (1931), Theodora Goes Wild (1936), The Awful Truth (1937), Love Affair (1939), and I Remember Mama (1948).

In Love Affair she sidestepped a compromising situation with Charles Boyer. "It's not that I'm prudish," she says warily. "It's just that my mother told me never to enter any man's room in months ending in 'R.'"

SELECTED FILMS: Leathernecking (1930), Bachelor Apartment, Consolation Marriage (1931), If I Were Free (1933), The Age of Innocence (1934), Sweet Adeline, Roberta (1935), Show Boat (1936), High, Wide and Handsome (1937), Joy of Living (1938), Invitation to Happiness (1939), My Favorite Wife (1940), Unfinished Business (1941), Lady in a Jam (1942), Over 21 (1945), Anna and the King of Siam (1946), Life With Father (1947), Never a Dull Moment, The Mudlark (1950), It Grows on Trees (1952). ∎

Durant, Jack. See Mitchell and Durant.

Durante, Jimmy (1893–1980), entertainer, comedian, actor. Worked as a piano player in Bowery nightclubs and as an entertainer in vaudeville and on Broadway (with partners Lou Clayton and Eddie Jackson). He began his long career in films in 1930. He was teamed for a while with Buster KEATON, but the

Jimmy Durante (right)

comedy material they were forced to work with was below either of their talents. Later, MGM used him in supporting roles in romantic comedies and musicals. As a character actor, he enlivened many comedies and musicals with his clowning, singing, and exceptionally warm personality. But he was given few opportunities to star in his own vehicles. He was one of the most lovable comedians ever to appear on the stage, in films, and in television.

Some of his more memorable roles include that of the irascible Knobby Walsh, Joe Palooka's fight manager, in *Palooka* (1934) and an excitable and frenetic Bowery club entertainer in *Two Sisters From Boston* (1946). In the former film he is knocked down by a bruiser of a prize fighter who demands, "Are you gonna give me that money?" Rising, Durante replies, "I'm givin' you a slight curl of my lip." He is knocked down again, but remains undaunted. "What's brawn against brains?" he questions. "Mentally, I got you licked!" A biography, *Schnozzola*, by Gene Fowler, was published in 1951, and another, *Goodnight Mrs. Calabash*, by William Cahn, appeared in 1963.

SELECTED FILMS: *Roadhouse Nights* (1930), *The Cuban Love Song* (1931), *The Passionate Plumber, The Wet Parade, Speak Easily, The Phantom President* (1932), *Broadway to Hollywood, Meet the Baron* (1933), *Hollywood Party, Strictly Dynamite* (1934), *Carnival* (1935), *Little Miss Broadway* (1938), *Melody Ranch* (1940), *You're in the Army Now* (1941), *The Man Who Came to Dinner* (1942), *Two Girls and a Sailor* (1944), *Music for Millions* (1945), *It Happened in Brooklyn* (1947), *On an Island With You* (1948), *The Great Rupert, The Milkman* (1950), *Pepe* (1960), *Jumbo* (1962), *It's a Mad, Mad, Mad, Mad World* (1963). ∎

Durfee, Minta (1897–1975), actress. Worked as a chorus girl before she and her husband, Roscoe "Fatty" AR-BUCKLE, joined Mack SENNETT'S KEY-STONE studios. She appeared in numerous silent comedy shorts, alone and with her husband, and soon became one of the leading comic performers of the screen. An attractive soubrette, she enlivened many of Sennett's farces. She co-starred with some of the major comedians of the period, including Charlie CHAPLIN (eleven films), Ford STERLING, and Mack SWAIN. She continued to appear on screen during the sound era but only in bit roles. She later made occasional appearances on television.

SELECTED FILMS: *Fatty's Day Off, Fatty at San Diego* (1913), *Making a Living, A Film Johnnie, Twenty Minutes of Love, Caught in a Cabaret, The Knockout, Tillie's Punctured Romance, Fatty and the Heiress, Fatty's Debut* (1914), *Ambrose's Fury, Hearts and Planets, The Home Breakers, Fatty's Reckless Fling, Dirty Work in a Laundry, A Village Scandal* (1915), *The Great Pearl Tangle, Bright Lights, His Wife's Mistake* (1916), *Mickey* (1918), *Naughty Marietta* (1935), *The Unsinkable Molly Brown* (1964). ∎

Durning, Charles (1933–), actor. Appeared on stage before entering films in 1965. A stout character actor with a cherubic expression, he usually plays light roles although he can use these same features to portray cold, unsympathetic characters. He became prominent in the 1970s after getting a succession of good roles which he embellished with his particular uniqueness.

SELECTED FILMS: Harvey Middle-man—Fireman (1965), Dealing (1972), The Sting (1973), The Front Page (1974), Dog Day Afternoon (1975), Harry and Walter Go to New York (1976), The Choirboys (1977), Starting Over (1979), The Best Little Whorehouse in Texas, Tootsie (1982), To Be or Not to Be, Two of a Kind (1983), Mass Appeal (1984), The Man With One Red Shoe (1985), Tough Guys (1986). ∎

Duvall, Shelley (1950–), actress. Entered films with no previous acting experience when director Robert ALTMAN met her and signed her for a role in *Brewster McCloud.* An angular performer with prominent teeth, she has proved to be a talented player in both light films and dramas, appearing in several of Altman's films.

SELECTED FILMS: Brewster McCloud (1970), Nashville (1975), Annie Hall (1977), Popeye (1980), Time Bandits (1981). ∎

Dvorak, Ann (1912–1979), actress. Began her screen career as a child performer in a 1920s silent film. In 1929 she played a chorus girl in an early sound film. A sultry, energetic, dark-haired actress, she starred in dramas as well as light films, gaining recognition in two early sound films, *Sky Devils* co-starring Spencer Tracy and *Scarface* with Paul Muni, both 1932 productions.

SELECTED FILMS: The Hollywood Revue of 1929 (1929), Free and Easy (1930), The Guardsman (1931), Love Is a Racket, Three on a Match (1932), College Coach (1933), Housewife (1934), Sweet Music, Thanks a Million (1935), Racing Lady, *Manhattan Merry-Go-Round (1937), Merrily We Live (1938), Masquerade in Mexico (1945), The Secret of Convict Lake (1951).* ∎

Dwan, Allan (1885–1982), director. Began his prolific Hollywood career in 1909 as a writer for ESSANAY studios, and soon began directing silent comedies, westerns, and dramas for various studios, including American Film Company, Universal, Famous Players, Triangle, Artcraft, Fox, First National, United Artists, and Republic. His unobtrusive directorial style has left critics still undecided where to place him in the hierarchy of filmmakers. Some call him the "last of the old masters," while director Peter Bogdanovich titled his work on Dwan *The Last Pioneer.* Whatever the final evaluation, his more than 400 films still entertain and delight their audiences.

SELECTED FILMS: Brandishing a Bad Man, The Yiddisher Cowboy (1911), The Animal Within, Calamity Anne's Ward (1912), Calamity Anne, Detective, Cupid Throws a Brick (1913), David Harum (1915), Betty of Greystone, Manhattan Madness (1916), Mr. Fix-It (1918), Cheating Cheaters (1919), The Luck of the Irish (1920), Robin Hood (1922), Summer Bachelors (1926), French Dressing (1927), What a Widow! (1930), Navy Wife (1935), Heidi (1937), Rebecca of Sunnybrook Farm (1938), The Three Musketeers, The Gorilla (1939), Sailor's Lady (1940), Look Who's Laughing (1941), Friendly Enemies (1942), Abroad With Two Yanks (1944), Brewster's Millions, Getting Gertie's Garter (1945), I Dream of Jeanie (1952), Tennessee's Partner (1955), Slightly Scarlet (1956), Most Dangerous Man Alive (1961). ∎

E

East Side Kids. See Bowery Boys.

Easy Living (1937), PAR. *Dir.* Mitchell Leisen; *Sc.* Preston Sturges; with Jean Arthur, Edward Arnold, Ray Milland, Franklin Pangborn, William Demarest.

The charming and feisty Jean ARTHUR had appeared in a string of routine films before 1935 when she appeared in *The Whole Town's Talking*, where she demonstrated a definite penchant for comedy. After several more good roles in light films, especially as a reporter in *Mr. Deeds Goes to Town* (1936), she joined the ranks of the top screen comediennes of the period, which included Claudette COLBERT, Myrna LOY, Carole LOMBARD, and Irene DUNNE. In *Easy Living* she gets a fur coat dumped on her while she is riding in the open deck of a Fifth Avenue bus. It had been tossed out of a window by furious tycoon Edward ARNOLD, "the Bull of Wall Street," when he learns the price of the item from his wife. When Arthur attempts to return it, the millionaire banker gives it to her with his blessing. The remainder of this romantic, SCREWBALL COMEDY depends upon misunderstandings, especially when others conclude that she is Arnold's mistress. Luis ALBERNI, the desperate owner of a swank hotel, gives her a plush suite, thinking that she will attract the society crowd to his establishment. Other circumstances bring her into contact with Ray MILLAND, Arnold's rich and spoiled son, who soon falls for her. This completes the Cinderella yarn that was practically a Hollywood staple in the 1930s. A penniless working girl, Jean Arthur gets an expensive sable coat, has a chance to live in a luxurious suite, and wins her Prince Charming. This was an important fantasy for millions of similarly situated young women during the dark, jobless Depression years. The film not only spoofs this myth, but also satirizes those who seek to profit from their knowledge of this "illicit" affair. Some shower Arthur with presents in an effort to influence the tycoon, while others relocate to the hotel to be "where the action is." This lampooning of the greedy extends down to the common masses in a chaotic scene at an Automat. When someone releases a key lever which opens all the little windows containing dishes of food, crowds storm the place, grabbing everything in sight and fighting for each other's trays in a spectacle of avarice. Preston STURGES, who wrote the screenplay, was to emerge as a major writer-director of comedies in the 1940s. The lush sets and generally decorative good looks of the comedy can be largely attributed to director Mitchell LEISEN'S special gifts. He had been a successful art director before he switched to directing. Unfortunately, the film was forced to compete with another, more successful screwball comedy with wittier dialogue released the same year—*Nothing Sacred*, starring Carole Lombard and Fredric MARCH. *Easy Living*, for all its charm and spirit, has continued to live in the shadow of its competitor.

"Easy Street" (1917), MUT. *Dir.* Charlie Chaplin; *Sc.* Charlie Chaplin; with Charlie Chaplin, Edna Purviance, Albert Austin, Eric Campbell, Henry Bergman.

One of Chaplin's best and most famous comedy shorts, the film blends farce with social commentary. The main setting is a slum street, no doubt typical of innumerable streets of the period, an environment where bullies terrorize the inhabitants, drug addiction flourishes, and decent but indigent women are forced to steal. Charlie joins a city police force and is assigned to the toughest street in the precinct, a block controlled by a brutal bully played by Eric CAMPBELL. Charlie's encounter with the bully seems almost hopeless. His nightstick has no effect upon the skull of the troublemaker, who is able to bend lampposts with his bare hands. However, our hero finds time to romance Edna Purviance, poke a little fun at the Salvation Army, and subdue the villain in one of the funniest scenes ever recorded on film. The film is one of the "golden dozen" Chaplin made at Mutual.

Eating Raoul (1982), TCF. *Dir.* Paul Bartel; *Sc.* Paul Bartel, Richard Blackburn; with Paul Bartel, Mary Woronov, Robert Beltran, Buck Henry.

A contemporary black comedy about the Blands, a conventional couple who dream of opening a chic restaurant. Opportunity comes to their door, almost literally, as they attract rich swingers to their apartment where they murder their victims. They rationalize their acts as an aid to the community by ridding it of undesirable elements and gaining support for their restaurant. One of the highlights of this offbeat comedy is the scene in a hot tub. The unique plot provides plenty of satirical fun.

Ebsen, Buddy (1908–), actor. Worked in vaudeville and on Broadway as a dancer before making his film debut in 1935. He has appeared chiefly in light films, often with rural settings, during the Depression years and in various genres following World War II. He has since attained greater success in television than he has from his performances on film. His most popular show was "The Beverly Hillbillies," a comedy series during the 1960s.

In *Born to Dance* (1936), a musical comedy in which he demonstrated his comedic and dancing talents, he played a sailor on shore leave who befriends a waitress. "I'm crossing parrots with carrier pigeons," he confesses to her. "What for?" she inquires. "So you can send verbal messages," he explains.

SELECTED FILMS: Broadway Melody of 1936 (1935), Captain January, Born to Dance, Banjo on My Knee (1936), My Lucky Star (1938), Four Girls in White (1939), Sing Your Worries Away (1942), Under Mexicali Stars (1950), Red Garters (1954), Mail Order Bride (1964), The One and Only Genuine Original Family Band (1968). ■

Eburne, Maude (1875–1960), actress. Appeared as a character actress in almost 100 films over a period of 25 years, mainly in elderly spinster roles. Although of slight frame, she was able to express a tough countenance when required and a sharp tongue when one was called for. She portrayed Mrs. Hastings, Dr. Christian's housekeeper, in a half-dozen entries in that series. She enlivened many light films, westerns, and dramas with her various antics.

SELECTED FILMS: The Bat Whispers, Blonde Crazy (1931), Under 18, Panama Flo (1932), Havana Widows (1933), Here Comes the Navy (1934), Don't Bet on Blondes (1935), Doughnuts and Society, Poppy (1936), Champagne Waltz (1937), My Wife's Relatives (1939), The Courageous Dr. Christian (1940), Melody for Three (1941), To Be or Not to Be (1942), Reveille With Beverly (1943), Up in Arms (1944), Leave It to Blondie (1945), Mother Wore Tights (1947), The Prince of Peace (1951). ■

Eddy, Helen Jerome, actress. Began her long Hollywood career in early silent films. She was a feature player in Mary PICKFORD'S 1917 version of *Rebecca of Sunnybrook Farm*. She continued to appear as a character actress in light films and dramas through 1940.

SELECTED FILMS: *The Turn in the Road* (1919), *Pollyanna* (1920), *The Ten-Dollar Raise* (1921), *The Flirt* (1922), *The Country Kid, To the Ladies* (1923), *Marry Me* (1925), *Reaching for the Moon* (1930), *Girls Demand Excitement* (1931), *Skippy, Sooky* (1932), *Frisco Jenny, Strictly Personal* (1933), *The Girl From 10th Avenue* (1935), *Klondike Annie, Stowaway* (1936), *Strike Up the Band* (1940). ∎

Edelman, Herb (1930–), actor. A character player who has appeared in films since the 1960s. A tall, bald actor almost always cast in comic roles, he has worked with some of the leading film comedians of the period, including Walter MATTHAU and Jack LEMMON.

SELECTED FILMS: *In Like Flint, Barefoot in the Park* (1967), *The Odd Couple* (1968), *The Front Page* (1974), *The Yakuza* (1975). ∎

"Edgar" comedies. A series of feature-length films produced during the early 1920s and based on Booth Tarkington's writings about a boy's adventures in and around a small town. E. Mason HOPPER directed the comedies and young Johnny Jones starred as the title character. The films were generally well received by the critics, who described the rural comedies as good-natured entertainment for the younger audiences.

SELECTED FILMS: *Edgar and the Teacher's Pet, Edgar's Hamlet, Edgar's Little Saw* (1920), *Edgar, the Explorer* (1921). ∎

Edwards, Blake (1922–), director, screenwriter. Began his film career as a minor actor in the 1940s, radio writer, and highly successful television script writer. Born William Blake McEdwards and the son of a theater director, he occasionally wrote screenplays, including, among others, *Rainbow Round My Shoulder* (1950), *All Ashore* (1953), *My Sister Eileen* (1955), and *Operation Mad Ball* (1957). In 1955 he was given the opportunity to direct his first film, *Bring Your Smile Along*. His next few films were popular successes, but his directorial career faltered as a result of a few uneven films. Although his characters display a degree of restraint and, like most of his films, are frivolous, his direction hints at no constraints. His style is often broad and flashy, filled with visual exaggerations. He is more than capable of handling dramatic material, such as his highly acclaimed *Days of Wine and Roses* (1962). His largest commercial successes, however, have been his series of "PINK PANTHER" comedies.

These popular comedy features starred Peter SELLERS as the inept Inspector Clouseau. Herbert Lom and Burt Kwouk, both of whom joined the series with the first sequel, played Clouseau's volatile boss and his Oriental valet, respectively. The films originated with *The Pink Panther* (1963), the title referring to a rare jewel. But in subsequent entries the title pertained to Clouseau's archrival, an international jewel thief. Edwards is married to actress Julie ANDREWS, who has starred in many of his films.

SELECTED FILMS: *He Laughed Last* (1956), *Mister Cory* (1957), *This Happy Feeling* (1958), *The Perfect Furlough, Operation Petticoat* (1959), *High Time* (1960), *Breakfast at Tiffany's* (1961), *A Shot in the Dark, The Pink Panther* (1964), *The Great Race* (1965), *What Did You Do in the War, Daddy?* (1966), *The Return of the Pink Panther* (1975), *The Pink Panther Strikes Again* (1976), *Revenge of the Pink Panther* (1978), *10* (1979), *S.O.B.* (1981), *Victor/Victoria* (1982), *A Fine Mess, That's Life!* (1986). ∎

Edwards, Cliff (1895–1971), actor, singer. Fondly known as "Ukulele Ike," he began his show business career strumming his uke and singing in bars, in vaudeville, and on Broadway during the 1920s. He made his film debut with the advent of sound in light musicals, eventually settling in to character roles, mainly as comic relief. Warm and personable, he enlivened numerous films of various genres, including comedies, westerns and action features. He was famous for introducing two hit songs, "Charley My Boy" and "Singin' in the Rain."

In *His Girl Friday* he played a cynical reporter who, along with other newspapermen, is covering a hanging at the city jail. The mayor storms into the newsroom looking for the sheriff whom everyone knows is corrupt. "Have you seen Sheriff Hartwell?" the mayor shouts. "Well, it's so hard to tell," Edwards replies, "there are so many cockroaches around here."

SELECTED FILMS: *The Hollywood Revue of 1929, So This Is College (1929), Lord Byron of Broadway, Way Out West, Good News, Dough Boys (1930), Parlor, Bedroom and Bath (1931), Fast Life (1932), Take a Chance (1933), George White's Scandals (1934), Maisie, Gone With the Wind (1939), His Girl Friday (1940), The Monster and the Girl (1941), The Falcon Strikes Back (1943).* ∎

Edwards, Harry (1888–), director. Began his film career as a prop boy before advancing to director of silent comedy shorts for Mack SENNETT'S KEYSTONE studios in the early 1910s. He left the company in 1914 to direct films for Lehrman-Knockout Comedies. Some of his most important work occurred in the 1920s, involving his collaboration with screenwriter Frank CAPRA on vehicles for Harry LANGDON. In this capacity he turned out two dozen shorts, many of them of high quality. He and Capra were assigned the task of trying to define an individual style for the baby-faced comic. Most of his directorial ef-

forts involved comedy shorts, especially those featuring Billy BEVAN, Carole LOMBARD, and Ben TURPIN. Considered one of the best comedy directors of silent films, he has left behind a body of work that holds up very well, even by today's standards.

SELECTED FILMS: *The First Hundred Years, The Luck of the Foolish, The Hansom Cabman, Feet of Mud (1924), The Sea Squawk, Boobs in the Woods, His Magic Wow, Plain Clothes, Lucky Stars (1925), Saturday Afternoon, Soldier Man, Tramp, Tramp, Tramp (1926), The Golf Nut, Gold Digger of Weepah, A Hollywood Hero, Daddy Boy (1927), The Beach Club, The Best Man, His Unlucky Night (1928), Calling Hubby's Bluff (1929).* ∎

Edwards, Neely (1889–1965), actor. Worked in vaudeville and on stage before entering silent films in the early 1920s. He worked chiefly in light films and was featured in several entries of the "HALL ROOM BOYS" comedy shorts.

SELECTED FILMS: *Brewster's Millions, The Little Clown (1921), I'll Show You the Town (1925), Footloose Widows (1926), The Princess of Broadway (1927), Excess Baggage, Sunny California (1928), Gold Diggers of Broadway (1929), Her Relatives, The Window Cleaners, The Milky Way (1930), The Hangover (1931), Junior, The Weekend (1932), Diplomaniacs, Love, Honor and Oh, Baby! (1933), Mr. Moto in Danger Island (1939).* ∎

Edwards, Penny (1919–), actress. Appeared as female lead in light films during the 1940s and in various genres in the next decade. Her screen career consisted chiefly of low-budget features.

SELECTED FILMS: *Let's Face It (1943), That Hagen Girl (1947), Two Guys From Texas (1948), Powder River (1953).* ∎

Edwards, Sarah (1883–1965), actress. Appeared as a supporting actress, chiefly in light films, during the 1930s and 1940s. A dark-haired, matronly figure, she portrayed various characters in routine as well as major productions. She had roles in several Frank CAPRA comedies.

SELECTED FILMS: Glorifying the American Girl (1930), Ruggles of Red Gap (1935), Early to Bed (1936), We're on the Jury, It's Love I'm After (1937), Women Are Like That, Touchdown Army (1938), Strike Up the Band (1940), Calaboose (1943), The Big Noise (1944), Abbott and Costello in Hollywood (1945), It's a Wonderful Life (1946), The Bishop's Wife (1947), The Petty Girl, The Glass Menagerie (1950). ■

Edwards, Snitz (1862–1937), actor. Worked on stage before entering silent films in the early 1920s. He appeared as a character actor in numerous dramas and light films, including several sound features. He worked in several of Buster KEATON'S silent comedies.

SELECTED FILMS: The City of Masks (1920), The Charm School, Ladies Must Live, The Love Special (1921), The Ghost Breaker, June Madness (1922), Modern Matrimony, Teak With a Kick (1923), Hill Billy, Inez From Hollywood (1924), Seven Chances, Heir-Loons, Old Shoes (1925), Battling Butler, April Fool, The Lady of the Harem (1926), College, Night Life (1927), Sit Tight, Public Enemy (1931). ■

Edwards, Vivian, actress. Worked in early silent comedy shorts for Mack SENNETT'S KEYSTONE studios. As a supporting player, she appeared in films with some of the leading screen comics of the period, including Charlie CHAPLIN, Mack SWAIN, Charlie MURRAY, and Hank MANN.

SELECTED FILMS: The Masquerader, Dough and Dynamite (1914), From Patches to Plenty, Only a Farmer's Daughter, A One Night Stand, When Ambrose Dared Walrus, A Human Hound's Triumph (1915), The Village Blacksmith, His Lying Heart (1916). ■

Eggenton, Joseph (1870–1946), actor. Entered films in the 1940s following a long career on stage. He appeared as a supporting player in several light films.

SELECTED FILMS: The Doctor Takes a Wife, You'll Find Out (1940). ■

Eilers, Sally (1908–1978), actress. Made her film debut in the 1920s playing ingenues in comedy shorts for Mack SENNETT. Although she appeared in numerous dramas, westerns, and light films throughout the 1930s and much of the 1940s, many of them were routine vehicles, doing little for her career. During the latter part of her film career she was relegated to minor roles. An attractive blonde with a sense of humor, she displayed a flair for comedy in one of her first full-length features, The Goodbye Kiss (1928), a World War I farce about a shy doughboy. Unfortunately, her comedic talents remained underutilized.

SELECTED FILMS: Slightly Used, Sunrise (1927), Dry Martini (1928), Sailor's Holiday, Trial Marriage, Broadway Babies (1929), She Couldn't Say No, Let Us Be Gay, Dough Boys (1930), Reducing, Quick Millions, Bad Girl (1931), Disorderly Conduct (1932), Sailor's Luck, Made on Broadway (1933), Three on a Honeymoon (1934), Strike Me Pink (1936), Lady Behave (1938), They Made Her a Spy (1939), Stage to Tucson (1951). ■

Elam, Jack (1916–), actor. Began his screen career as a supporting player in the late 1940s. A tall, menacing figure with dark hair and only one good eye (his right one), he has chiefly played treacherous outlaws in westerns. More recently, he has appeared in light films, sometimes even as a congenial character or as a self-parody of his more sinister roles. He has also appeared in television.

SELECTED FILMS: Trailin' West (1949), Love That Brute (1950), Artists and Models (1955), Pardners (1956), Pocketful of Miracles (1961), Four for Texas (1963), Never a Dull Moment

(1967), Support Your Local Sheriff (1968), The Cockeyed Cowboys of Calico County (1969), Support Your Local Gunfighter (1971), The Apple Dumpling Gang Rides Again (1979), The Cannonball Run (1981), Jinxed! (1982), Cannonball Run II (1983). ■

Ellis, Patricia (1916–1970), actress. Worked in the theater before appearing in films during the early 1930s. A tall and attractive blonde, she played leading and supporting roles in many light comedies featuring some of the leading performers of the period, including Joan BLONDELL, Joe E. BROWN, Bette DAVIS, and LAUREL AND HARDY.

SELECTED FILMS: *Three on a Match, Central Park (1932), The King's Vacation, Elmer the Great, 42nd Street (1933), Easy to Love, Here Comes the Groom, The Circus Clown, Let's Be Ritzy (1934), Hold 'Em, Yale, A Night at the Ritz, Bright Lights (1935), Love Begins at 20 (1936), Step Lively, Jeeves (1937), Block-Heads (1938), Fugitive at Large (1939).* ■

Ellison, James (1910–), actor. Worked in stock and in a Hollywood studio film laboratory before getting his chance to appear on screen in the early 1930s. A handsome and personable actor, he played leads and second leads in dramas, westerns, and romantic comedies for two decades. He was Hopalong Cassidy's young sidekick in several entries of the popular western series. Appearing chiefly in low-budget features, he never developed into a major star.

SELECTED FILMS: *Play Girl (1932), Reckless (1935), Annapolis Salute (1937), Vivacious Lady, Next Time I Marry (1938), Zenobia, Fifth Avenue Girl (1939), You Can't Fool Your Wife, Anne of Windy Poplars (1940), Charley's Aunt (1941), Careful, Soft Shoulder (1942), Dixie Dugan, The Gang's All Here (1943), The Ghost Goes Wild, Calendar Girl (1947), Dead Man's Trail (1952).* ■

Elsom, Isobel (1893–1981), actress. Worked in her native England as star of stage and screen from 1915 before her American film debut in 1941. Appearing in more than 75 films as lead or supporting player, she added glamour and class to her roles. She often played officious, pompous matrons in dramas, light films, and musicals. She was a wonderful foil to Jerry Lewis in a few of his comedies.

SELECTED FILMS: *Ladies in Retirement (1941), You Were Never Lovelier (1942), My Kingdom for a Cook (1943), Casanova Brown (1944), Two Sisters From Boston (1946), Ivy (1947), Smart Woman (1948), Her Wonderful Lie (1950), Love Is a Many Splendored Thing (1955), Rock-a-Bye Baby (1958), The Bellboy (1960), The Second Time Around (1961), The Errand Boy (1962), Who's Minding the Store? (1963), My Fair Lady, The Pleasure Seekers (1964).* ■

Emerson, Hope (1897–1960), actress. Large-framed, masculine-looking supporting player who appeared in both dramas and light films in the 1940s and 1950s. In more serious roles she could appear very sinister, as in *Caged* (1950); in comedies she played foil to actors like Spencer TRACY (*Adam's Rib*) and Jerry LEWIS (*Rock-a-Bye Baby*).

SELECTED FILMS: *Smiling Faces (1932), Cry of the City, That Wonderful Urge (1948), Adam's Rib, Dancing in the Dark (1949), Double Crossbones, Belle La Grande (1951), The Lady Wants Mink, Champ for a Day (1953), Casanova's Big Night (1954), The Day They Gave Babies Away (1956), Rock-a-Bye Baby (1958).* ■

Emery, Gilbert (1875–1945), actor. Appeared in films in his native England and Australia before coming to Hollywood during the early sound period. A tall, sophisticated supporting actor with a thin mustache, he portrayed a variety of roles in dramas and light films.

SELECTED FILMS: *Let Us Be Gay, The Royal Bed (1930), The Lady Refuses, Ladies' Man (1931), Gallant Lady, Coming-Out Party (1934), Goin' to Town,*

Harmony Lane, Let's Live Tonight, Ladies Crave Excitement (1935), Wife vs. Secretary (1936), Double or Nothing (1937), The Lady From Kentucky (1939), The Remarkable Andrew (1942), The Brighton Strangler (1945). ■

Emery, John (1905–1964), actor. Entered films in the 1930s following some stage experience. He played supporting roles in dramas and light films during a screen career that spanned four decades. He also appeared in television.

SELECTED FILMS: The Road Back (1937), Here Comes Mr. Jordan (1941), Two Yanks in Trinidad, Ship Ahoy, George Washington Slept Here (1942), Mademoiselle Fifi (1944), The Voice of the Turtle (1947), Let's Live Again (1948), Forever Darling, The Girl Can't Help It (1956), Youngblood Hawke (1964). ■

Emhardt, Robert (1901–), actor. Worked on Broadway in 1940 before making his film debut in 1952 as a character actor. Portly in shape and fatherly in manner, he has portrayed comic characters as well as heavies. He has appeared in both light films and dramas while working in stock and television. One of his more memorable roles was that of the eccentric father in *The Group.*

SELECTED FILMS: The Iron Mistress (1952), Wake Me When It's Over (1960), Kid Galahad (1962), The Group (1966), Where Were You When the Lights Went Out? (1968), Rascal, Change of Habit (1969), Suppose They Gave a War and Nobody Came? (1971), Alex and the Gypsy (1976), Fraternity Row (1977). ■

Emmett, Fern (1896–1946), actress. Entered films during the early sound period following some stage experience. She appeared as a supporting player in numerous dramas, westerns, and light films, including several comedy shorts.

SELECTED FILMS: Bar L Ranch, Second Honeymoon, Skip the Maloo! (1930), *A Fool About Women, Boy Oh Boy, Anybody's Goat, Bridge Wives, Mother's Holiday (1932), His Weak Moment, Frozen Assets, Hello Everybody! (1933), An Old Gypsy Custom (1934), Southern Exposure (1935), Three on a Limb (1936), Glamour Boy, Scattergood Baines, Love Crazy (1941), Henry Aldrich, Editor (1942), The Kid From Brooklyn (1946).* ■

Emory, May, actress. Worked in early silent comedy shorts for Mack SENNETT'S KEYSTONE studios. A supporting player, she appeared in films with some of the leading comedians of the period, including "Fatty" ARBUCKLE and Mack SWAIN.

SELECTED FILMS: Fickle Fatty's Fall, The Hunt, Fido's Fate (1915), By Stork Delivery, Madcap Ambrose, Vampire Ambrose, Ambrose's Cup of Woe (1916), Stars and Bars, Thirst (1917). ■

Engle, Billy (1889–1966), actor. Appeared as a comic supporting player in light features and comedy shorts during the silent and sound periods. He worked with minor and major comedians, including, among others, Jack DUFFY, Buster KEATON, and W. C. FIELDS.

SELECTED FILMS: Red Hot Leather, Chicken Feathers (1926), The Cat and the Canary (1927), Knight Duty (1933), The Gold Ghost (1934), I'm a Father, Uncivil Warriors, It's a Gift (1935), Wedding Present (1936), Our Neighbors, the Carters (1940), Glamour Boy (1941), The Wistful Widow of Wagon Gap (1947). ■

Englund, Ken (1911–), screenwriter. Worked as a writer for periodicals, vaudeville, radio, and musical theater before penning scripts for films. He wrote screenplays, mainly for light films, from the late 1930s to the late 1960s. Although the quality of his work may be uneven, his adaptations (G. B. Shaw, Thurber) have generally been lively and sometimes creative.

SELECTED FILMS: The Big Broadcast of 1938, Artists and Models Abroad (1938), Good Girls Go to Paris (1939), Slightly Honorable, The Doctor Takes a Wife, No, No, Nanette (1940), This Thing Called Love, Nothing but the Truth (1941), Rings on Her Fingers (1942), Sweet Rosie O'Grady (1943), Here Come the Waves (1944), The Secret Life of Walter Mitty (1947), Good Sam (1948), A Millionaire for Christy (1951), Androcles and the Lion, The Caddy (1953), The Wicked Dreams of Paula Schultz (1968). ∎

Enright, Ray (1896–1965), director. Worked in early silent comedies as gagman and editor for Mack SENNETT. After being employed by various studios, he started his directorial career in 1927. For the next 25 years he directed numerous dramas, westerns, musicals, and light comedies. Many of his works were undistinguished, but some of his later westerns were tough and hard-hitting.

SELECTED FILMS: Tracked by the Police, The Girl From Chicago (1927), Domestic Troubles (1928), The Little Wildcat, Skin Deep (1929), Dancing Sweeties (1930), Play Girl, The Tenderfoot (1932), Blondie Johnson, Havana Widows (1933), The Circus Clown, Dames (1934), Traveling Saleslady, Alibi Ike, Miss Pacific Fleet (1935), Ready, Willing and Able, Back in Circulation (1937), Swing Your Lady, Hard to Get (1938), Naughty but Nice, On Your Toes (1939), Brother Rat and a Baby (1940), Good Luck, Mr. Yates (1943), The Man From Cairo (1953). ∎

Ephron, Henry (1912–) **and Phoebe** (1914–1971), screenwriters. Began their writing careers in the 1930s scripting light Broadway plays. By the 1940s the husband-and-wife team was writing screenplays for comedies and musicals. He was also the producer of a handful of films, including Desk Set and A Certain Smile. They wrote sparkling and delightful films for various stars, including Danny KAYE, Ethel MERMAN, Donald

O'CONNOR, Marilyn MONROE, and Fred ASTAIRE. Henry's memoir, We Thought We Could Do Anything, was published in 1977.

SELECTED FILMS: Bride by Mistake (1944), Always Together (1947), Wallflower (1948), John Loves Mary (1949), The Jackpot (1950), On the Riviera (1951), There's No Business Like Show Business (1954), Daddy Long Legs (1955), Desk Set (1957), Captain Newman, M.D. (1964). ∎

Epic comedy. A light film that embodies many of the traits of the literary epic, either oral or written. These include the addition of fictional characters into historical scenes, the depiction of a hero's deeds, an exaggeration of minor events for comic effect, and a general blending of fact and fiction. The term "epic comedy" has occasionally been applied to films that contain few of the above elements but are epic in size or spirit, such as It's a Mad, Mad, Mad, Mad World. Other comedies like Mel BROOKS' History of the World, Part 1 simply satirize the epic film. One of the earliest major films to be considered an epic was CHAPLIN'S Shoulder Arms (1918). Charlie portrayed a doughboy on the Western Front during the Great War. Through circumstances not of his own making, he winds up in enemy territory and, in true heroic fashion, manages to capture the Kaiser. Chaplin perfected the epic comedy in The Gold Rush (1925), setting his Little Tramp in the Yukon amid prospectors, murderers, and dancehall girls.

Mark Twain's popular social satire, A Connecticut Yankee in King Arthur's Court, was filmed three times, in 1921 starring Harry MYERS, in 1931 with comedian-humorist Will ROGERS in the title role, and finally in 1949 starring Bing CROSBY. Buster KEATON'S silent comedy, The General (1927), takes place during the Civil War. Keaton, a railroad man, is rejected by the Army because of his importance in keeping the trains running. Like Chaplin, he manages to perform his heroic deed by chasing and capturing a group of spies after a long and hilarious train chase through the countryside. The film, like all true epics, was based on a real incident.

Comic Red SKELTON starred in a similar vehicle in 1948, *A Southern Yankee*, in which he portrayed an inept Northern spy in Dixieland. Of course, he emerges as a hero. Keaton was said to have written many of the star's routines. Another epic comedy of the 1940s but in a minor vein was Republic's *Captain Tugboat Annie* (1945), starring Jane Darwell as the title character and Edgar Kennedy. The most memorable epic comedy of the 1950s was the Academy Award-winning *Around the World in 80 Days* (1956), based on Jules Verne's classic novel. The story was first adapted to the screen by Richard Oswald in Germany in 1919. Douglas FAIRBANKS starred in a humorous parody of the book in his 1931 production, *Around the World in 80 Minutes*.

Producer-director Stanley Kramer entered the genre with his *It's a Mad, Mad, Mad, Mad World* (1963), which boasted a cast of comedians unrivaled by any other film. In this sprawling comedy, a tribute to the slapstick humor of Mack SENNETT and the silent days, a variety of characters race across the country in search of hidden bank money—with many hilarious moments. Another epic comedy during the 1960s was Blake EDWARDS' lavish production, *The Great Race* (1965), starring Tony CURTIS, Natalie Wood, Jack LEMMON, Peter FALK, and Keenan WYNN. The plot was concerned with a turn-of-the-century car race from New York to Paris. The following year *A Funny Thing Happened on the Way to the Forum* was released. Based on Menander and early Roman comedy and more directly on the Broadway musical of the same name, the film starred Zero MOSTEL, Phil SILVERS, Buster KEATON, and Jack GILFORD. Mostel portrayed a shrewd slave in ancient Rome. The music was written by Stephen Sondheim.

The 1970s offered little in epic comedy. One exception was Arthur Penn's *Little Big Man* (1970), a sprawling western comedy-drama in which the hero, played by Dustin Hoffman, encounters real-life legends Wild Bill Hickok and General Custer. Another entry was Woody ALLEN'S satirical farce, *Love and Death* (1975). Allen played a coward during the Napoleonic wars, goaded on by his co-star Diane Keaton to assassinate the emperor. The film affords Allen an opportunity to satirize several works of Russian literature as well as foreign films.

Other silent and sound comedies have elements of epic comedy and can be included if one stretches the definition. Features like Bob HOPE'S *The Princess and the Pirate* (1944) and *Monsieur Beaucaire* (1946) are strong candidates, as are Eddie CANTOR'S *Roman Scandals* (1933), WHEELER AND WOOLSEY'S *Cockeyed Cavaliers* (1934), and the Ritz Brothers' *The Three Musketeers* (1939). But each of the above lacks some characteristic, such as an actual historical event or a true heroic element.

Epstein, Julius J. (1909–), screenwriter. Worked in radio and, briefly, as a playwright before writing for films. Collaborating with his brother Philip, he turned out high-quality scripts for numerous films, including the classic *Casablanca* (1943), for which they received an Academy Award. The brothers often enhanced their scripts with witty dialogue and sympathetic characterizations. He has occasionally produced comedies, including *Plaza Suite* (1971), based on the play by Neil SIMON.

SELECTED FILMS: The Big Broadcast of 1936, Living on Velvet, Broadway Gondolier (1935), Sons o' Guns (1936), No Time for Comedy (1940), The Bride Came C.O.D. (1941), The Man Who Came to Dinner, The Male Animal (1942), Arsenic and Old Lace (1944), Born Yesterday (1950), Forever Female (1953), Young at Heart (1955), Tall Story (1960), Send Me No Flowers (1964), Pete 'n' Tillie (1972), House Calls (1978). ∎

Erdman, Richard (1925–), actor. Began his screen career in the 1940s portraying self-assertive young men. A cheerful-looking supporting actor with a shock of light hair, he appeared chiefly in light films in affable roles. He worked in several films with Dean MARTIN and Jerry LEWIS. Later in his career he occasionally tried his hand at directing.

SELECTED FILMS: Hollywood Canteen, Janie (1944), Too Young to Know (1945), Janie Gets Married (1946), That Way With Women (1947), Easy Living, Four Days' Leave (1949), The Admiral Was a Lady, USS Teakettle (1950), The Stooge (1951), The Happy Time, Jumping Jacks (1952), Francis in the Navy (1955), Anything Goes (1956), Bernardine (1957), Tomboy (1985). ■

Errol, Leon (1881–1951), actor. Worked in burlesque, in vaudeville, and on Broadway before entering the movie business in 1924. The Australian-born comic actor appeared in numerous silent and sound shorts and features, either as a lead or supporting player. He was particularly memorable as a sensitive waiter in Sally (1925), in which he co-starred with Colleen MOORE. Short, bald, and bow-legged, he made dozens of comedy shorts during the 1930s as well as the feature-length comedy series, "MEXICAN SPITFIRE." In the 1940s he portrayed Knobby Walsh, Joe Palooka's manager, in a series of Monogram low-budget films based on Ham Fisher's popular comic strip character. He specialized in broad, fast-paced humor, including slapstick, pratfalls, and mistaken identities. He often played the abused husband dominated by a suspicious wife.

SELECTED FILMS: Yolanda (1924), Clothes Make the Pirate (1925), The Lunatic at Large (1927), Only Saps Work (1930), Finn and Hattie (1931), Alice in Wonderland (1933), We're Not Dressing (1934), Make a Wish (1937), Mexican Spitfire (1939), Never Give a Sucker an Even Break (1941), Higher and Higher (1943), Babes on Swing Street (1944),

What a Blonde!, Mama Loves Papa (1945), Joe Palooka, Champ (1946), The Noose Hangs High (1948), Footlight Varieties (1951). ■

Stuart Erwin

Erwin, Stuart (1902–1967), actor. Worked in stock and as a stage manager before making his film debut in 1928. Often portraying a naive, wide-eyed country bumpkin who eventually gets the girl, he appeared as lead or supporting player in more than 100 films. His screen career spanned five decades, the most popular period being the 1930s. He was nominated for an Academy Award as Best Supporting Actor for his role in Pigskin Parade. Although his acting range was rather narrow, his folksy charm and innocence reminded his audiences of another time, another place. In his later years he occasionally returned to the stage and had a successful television show. He was married to actress June Collyer.

SELECTED FILMS: Mother Knows Best (1928), Dangerous Curves, The Cock-Eyed World (1929), Happy Days, Only Saps Work (1930), No Limit, Dude Ranch (1931), The Misleading Lady, The Big Broadcast (1932), International House, Going Hollywood (1933), Palooka (1934), After Office Hours (1935), All American Chump, Pigskin Parade (1936), Small Town Boy, Second Honeymoon (1937), Three Blind Mice (1938), It Could Happen to You (1939), Our Town (1940), The Bride Came C.O.D. (1941),

He Hired the Boss (1943), Pillow to Post (1945), Killer Dill (1947), Strike It Rich (1948), Father Is a Bachelor (1950), Son of Flubber (1963), The Adventures of Merlin Jones (1964). ■

Essanay. Film company founded by George Spoor and Gilbert M. Anderson in 1907. Essanay had branches in various European countries. The name stemmed from the initials of the two founders. The company was famous for its "Broncho Billy" westerns starring Anderson, of which 376 were produced. In 1914 the company, which had already been experimenting with two-reel comedies, had a host of comics under contract. Ben TURPIN, Augustus CARNEY, and Wallace BEERY were churning out numerous two-reelers for the hungry market. Other stars under contract were Francis X. Bushman and Max LINDER. However, the company decided to add Charlie CHAPLIN, who had just left SENNETT'S KEYSTONE company. In all, Chaplin made 15 films for Essanay over one year, with Edna PURVIANCE as his leading lady. He left in 1916, and the company was reorganized, combined with Edison's studios, and renamed Perfection Pictures. The year that Chaplin was under contract was the studio's most profitable. With the Tramp's departure, the studio produced little of note and, by 1917, dissolved.

Ethnic humor. Film comedy based on nationality, religion, or race is as old as the industry itself. The history of Hollywood reveals that in at least one area the studios were nondiscriminatory—every minority group was open to ridicule and stereotyping. The blacks, however, often received the worst treatment and suffered for the longest period of time in contrast to other groups. The portrayal of the black on screen varied slightly from the way white authors envisioned him. The conventional black stereotypes such as the "contented slave," the "local color black," and the "exotic primitive"

spilled over occasionally from the written word to the silver screen. The most predominant black image that Hollywood exploited, however, was that of the "comic black." To what extent this affected American race relations as well as the blacks' own self-image during the first half of this century may never be known.

In one early silent comedy, "The Nigger in the Woodpile," a white farmer suspects that someone is stealing his firewood. He fills one log with gunpowder. Later that night a lone black steals some of the wood, returns home, and places it into his stove. All of a sudden, his shack explodes. By the 1920s the blacks became the object of visual and verbal humor (via title cards). In D. W. Griffith's "The White Rose" (1923), a film which casts whites in blackface, the director has blacks attacked by alligators for comic relief. In "His Darker Self" (1924), a Lloyd HAMILTON comedy short, a black character is called "Smokes." During the same year the film "Fools in the Dark" showed a scared black named "Diploma," who says, "Feet, don't fail me now." This type of comedy would be repeated numerous times in the films of the 1930s and 1940s.

During the Depression years the blacks were the acknowledged second-class citizens of the screen, stereotyped as entertainers, maids, chauffeurs, and other domestics. American audiences laughed at the lazy, shuffling antics of Stepin FETCHIT and the wide-eyed mugging of Mantan MORELAND, who frequently played Charlie Chan's chauffeur. Several black actors faced further degradation in the names assigned to them by their studios or to characters in the films. Comic actor Willie BEST was often listed in the screen credits as "Sleep 'n' Eat," while moon-faced Fred TOONES, in films such as The Palm Beach Story (1942), was listed as "Snowflake" in the credits. Mae WEST in I'm No Angel (1933) addresses her maid as "Shadow." Not until after World War II, with the return of black and other minority servicemen, did the blacks and other ethnic groups feel a sense of outrage at the way they were portrayed by Hollywood. Films like *Body and Soul* (1947), in which Canada Lee throws intended bribe money back into the face of a white hoodlum, brought the blacks a new spirit of liberation—at least on film.

The portrayal of Jews on the American screen paralleled that of the blacks, despite the disproportionate number of Jewish producers, writers, and other contributors to the fledgling industry. If the blacks were domestics, the Jews were, more often than not, tailors, pawnshop owners, or delicatessen store proprietors. Where the blacks were depicted as lazy and easily frightened, the Jews were portrayed as evil shysters and clowns. One major difference in the film industry's treatment of these two minorities was that the Jews figured more prominently as major comic characters and in the titles. As early as 1903 comedy shorts with such titles as "Levi and Cohen: the Irish Comedians" began to appear, followed shortly by "Cohen's Advertising Scheme" (1904) and "Cohen's Fire Sale" (1907). Other films included "Old Isaacs, the Pawnbroker" (1908), "Such a Business" (1914), "Mike and Jake in Society" (1913), and "Cupid at the Cohens" (1916). At about this period producer Mack SENNETT turned out a series of crude "COHEN COMEDIES," starring Ford STERLING in the title role. During the 1920s the trend was to mix the Jews with the Irish, no doubt as a result of the successful Broadway play *Abie's Irish Rose*, which saw several adaptations over the years, the first appearing in 1928. Other hybrid Irish-Jewish comedies included *Kosher Kitty Kelly* (1926), *Private Izzy Murphy* (1926), *Clancy's Kosher Wedding* (1927), and the "COHENS AND THE KELLYS" series starring George SIDNEY and Charlie MURRAY, which spilled over into the sound era.

One curious little comedy released in 1913, "Levinsky's Holiday," has the dubious distinction of deriding both Jews and blacks. Levinsky, a salesman, tries to sneak into the circus as a bearded lady. Unsuccessful at this attempt at beating the admission price, he volunteers as the object for the "Hit the Nigger" booth. As with the blacks, the Jews saw an end to the more blatant depictions of anti-semitism following World War II. Films such as *Crossfire* and *Gentleman's Agreement* (1947) made noble attempts to attack bigotry.

The American Indians for almost five decades suffered from the results of Hollywood's negative depiction of them in silent and sound western dramas. But the film studios did not neglect the native Americans in film comedies. Douglas FAIRBANKS, in his western spoof, *Wild and Woolly* (1917), pictured them as cowards and buffoons. As late as 1940 in *Go West*, a MARX BROTHERS comedy, and in *My Little Chickadee*, starring Mae WEST and W. C. FIELDS, the Indian was treated mockingly. He fared no better in Mel Brooks' *Blazing Saddles* (1974).

Hollywood's stereotypes continued into other ethnic groups. The Italian-Americans and Irish-Americans often were the targets of ridicule. The former rarely spoke good English, never played a lead role, owned Italian restaurants or did menial labor, and were usually portrayed by comic character actors such as J. Carroll NAISH and Henry ARMETTA, performers who were meant to elicit laughter. The Irish-Americans were portrayed as dumb cops or belligerent oafs. But they were the subjects of an almost unending chain of light comedies, including *Irish Eyes* (1918), *The Irish in Us* (1935), *Irish Eyes Are Smiling* (1944), and *The Luck of the Irish* (1920, 1936, 1948). Perennial Irish characters were played by William BENDIX, Mary GORDON, Barry FITZGERALD, Ed GARGAN, and many other famous and obscure players.

Contemporary films generally have grown up, but occasional lapses quickly evoke outcries from ethnic groups about their treatment in individual features. The very funny *Lovers and Other Strangers* (1970), with Bea ARTHUR, Gig YOUNG, and the unforgettable Richard

"So What's the Story?" CASTELLANO, may have offended some Italian-Americans, while such comedies as *Goodbye Columbus* (1969) and *Over the Brooklyn Bridge* (1984) may be insulting to some members of the Jewish faith. Similarly, *Uptown Saturday Night* (1974) and *Soul Man* (1986) may be offensive to blacks.

Evans, Gene (1922–), actor. Worked in stock before entering films in the late 1940s. A heavy-set, red-haired versatile character player with a rough voice, he appeared in action films and comedies, often playing tough characters. Occasionally, he was given lead roles.

SELECTED FILMS: *Under Colorado Skies* (1947), *Mother Is a Freshman, It Happens Every Spring* (1949), *Never a Dull Moment* (1950), *The Sad Sack* (1957), *Operation Petticoat* (1959), *Support Your Local Sheriff* (1968), *Support Your Local Gunfighter* (1971). ∎

Evans, Madge (1909–1981), actress. Worked as a child model and performer in silent films, starred on Broadway at age 15, and returned to Hollywood films in the early 1930s at age 23. A beautiful and charming blonde, she became a popular performer almost overnight. In 1933 alone she had leading roles in ten features. She played leads in dramas and light films, working with some of the leading screen personalities of the period, including Al JOLSON, Shirley TEMPLE, James CAGNEY, and Fred MacMURRAY. She retired from films in 1938, after which she occasionally appeared on Broadway. She was married to playwright Sidney Kingsley.

SELECTED FILMS: *Alias Jimmy Valentine, Zaza* (1915), *Seventeen, Husband and Wife* (1916), *Little Duchess* (1917), *The Greeks Had a Word for Them* (1932), *Hallelujah, I'm a Bum, The Nuisance, Made on Broadway, Dinner at Eight* (1933), *The Show-Off, Stand Up and Cheer, Stand Up and Cheer* (1934), *Piccadilly Jim,*

Pennies From Heaven (1936), *Sinners in Paradise, Army Girl* (1938). ∎

Everything You Always Wanted to Know About Sex (But Were Afraid to Ask) (1972), UA. Dir. Woody Allen; Sc. Woody Allen; with Woody Allen, John Carradine, Lou Jacobi, Louise Lasser, Lynn Redgrave, Tony Randall, Burt Reynolds.

An episodic adaptation of David Reuben's book, this comedy explores various sexual attitudes—Allen style. In the first satirical sketch, Woody, a court jester, attempts to seduce the voluptuous queen (Lynn Redgrave). Visiting the local sorcerer for an aphrodisiac, Allen observes a simmering, steaming cauldron and says, "Your eggs are boiling over." Later, in the same sequence, Woody is stymied by the queen's chastity belt. "I better do something quickly," he announces, "or before we know it, the Renaissance will be here and we'll all be painting." Much of the film contains sight gags and other one-liners. The final, imaginative sketch, one of the most visually hilarious scenes ever put on film, shows what occurs internally when a man has sex. It pictures a type of mission-control center with the brain sending signals to, among other areas, the sex organs, with Woody portraying an apprehensive sperm. As in most episodic films, some segments are better than others. However, this is Allen's most visually satisfying comedy.

Ewell, Tom (1909–), Worked on stage for many years before appearing in films in 1949. His forte, on Broadway and on screen, was comedy, especially in his characterizations of the frailties of the average man. He gave an amusing portrayal of a World War II G.I. in *Up Front*, based on Bill Mauldin's popular cartoon series. He was also quite funny in *The Seven Year Itch* as the bungling husband who becomes infatuated with neighbor

Marilyn MONROE while his family is on vacation.

SELECTED FILMS: *Adam's Rib* (1949), *A Life of Her Own, Mr. Music* (1950), *Up Front* (1951), *Finders Keepers, Lost in Alaska* (1952), *The Seven Year Itch* (1955), *The Lieutenant Wore Skirts, The Girl Can't Help It* (1956), *State Fair* (1962), *Suppose They Gave a War and Nobody Came?* (1970), *To Find a Man* (1972), *The Great Gatsby* (1974). ■

F

Fabray, Nanette (1920–), actress. Appeared in "OUR GANG" silent comedy shorts when she was seven years old. A Broadway musical comedy star, she appeared sporadically in films.

SELECTED FILMS: A Child Is Born (1940), The Band Wagon (1953), The Happy Ending (1969), The Cockeyed Cowboys of Calico County (1970), Harper Valley P.T.A. (1978). ∎

Fairbanks, Douglas (1883–1939), actor. Made his film debut in 1915 after a successful career on stage. Born Douglas Elton Ulman in Denver, Colorado, he starred in light satirical comedies for Triangle studios before initiating his own production company. His early films established those qualities which were to make him one of the greatest screen stars of the '20s—his exuberance, his optimism, and his acrobatic abilities. These light, sometimes satirical, films spoke to every male in the audience, promising him the same success attained by the Fairbanks characters if he stopped fretting and began confronting his life with a smile. An inordinate optimist as well as an extraordinary athlete, he infected virtually all of his light films with his upbeat philosophy. In 1919 he joined CHAPLIN, D.W. Griffith, and Mary PICKFORD to form United Artists, the studio through which he released his major action spectacles. He married Mary Pickford in 1920. His productions were known for their lavish sets, straightforward plots, and abounding

wit. His career faltered with the coming of sound and he retired in 1934.

SELECTED FILMS: The Lamb, Double Trouble (1915), The Habit of Happiness, The Good Bad Man, Reggie Mixes In, Flirting With Fate, Manhattan Madness, American Aristocracy, The Matrimaniac, The Americano (1916), In Again, Out Again, Wild and Woolly, Down to Earth, Reaching for the Moon (1917), A Modern Musketeer, Headin' South, Mr. Fix-It, Young Fellow, Bound in Morocco, He Comes Up Smiling (1918), His Majesty the American, Till the Clouds Roll By (1919), The Mark of Zorro (1920), The Nut, The Three Musketeers (1921), Robin Hood (1922), The Thief of Bagdad (1924), Don Q, Son of Zorro (1925), The Black Pirate (1926), The Iron Mask (1928), The Taming of the Shrew (1929), Around the World in 80 Minutes (1931), Mr. Robinson Crusoe (1932). ∎

Fairbanks, Douglas, Jr. (1909–), actor. Began his long screen career at age 13 in silent films and played leads in another two dozen features before sound arrived in Hollywood. Possessing an excellent speaking voice, charm, and good looks, he made more than a successful transition into sound films, rising to stardom in dramas, historical vehicles, and light films. A versatile performer, he played and seemed to enjoy a variety of roles ranging from swashbuckling heroes to personable villains. During World War II he served in the United States Navy as a lieutenant commander and participated in and led many military engagements for which he received several medals and decorations. He has spent a good portion of his later life in England, appearing occasionally on stage on both sides of the Atlantic. He had some success in early television. His father was the famous stage and screen personality, Douglas FAIRBANKS.

SELECTED FILMS: *Stephen Steps Out (1923), Women Love Diamonds, Is Zat So? (1927), The Barker, A Woman of Affairs (1928), Fast Life, The Show of Shows (1929), Loose Ankles, Little Accident, One Night at Susie's (1930), I Like Your Nerve (1931), It's Tough to Be Famous, Love Is a Racket (1932), Joy of Living, The Rage of Paris, Having Wonderful Time, The Young in Heart (1938), Angels Over Broadway (1940), That Lady in Ermine (1948), Mister Drake's Duck (1951).* ■

Falk, Peter (1927–), actor. Appeared off-Broadway before entering films in melodramas and light comedies. A short, squinty-eyed, fast-talking actor, he has been cast often as a Runyonesque character. His performances in *Murder, Inc.* (1960) and *Pocketful of Miracles* (1961) led to two Academy Award nominations for Best Supporting Actor.

SELECTED FILMS: *Wind Across the Everglades (1958), It's a Mad, Mad, Mad, Mad World (1963), Robin and the Seven Hoods (1964), The Great Race (1965), Penelope (1966), Luv (1967), Murder by Death, Mikey and Nicky (1976), The Brink's Job (1978), The In-Laws (1979).* ■

Falkenburg, Jinx (1919–), actress. Worked as a model before entering films in the 1940s. She appeared in light films without much success.

SELECTED FILMS: *Two Latins From Manhattan, Sing for Your Supper (1942), Two Senoritas From Chicago, Lucky Legs (1943), Cover Girl, Tahiti Nights (1944), Talk About a Lady (1946).* ■

Family comedy. See Domestic comedy.

Fantasy comedy. A type of film whose humor depends upon unrealistic or imaginary events, such as ghosts, spirits, time travel, etc. The use of fantasy as film entertainment began in France with Georges Meliès (1861–1938), a magician who witnessed an early demonstration of motion pictures and saw in them the potential for a "new kind of magic." By 1896 he had produced "The Vanishing Lady," "The Haunted House," and "A Nightmare," short films using a variety of special effects. He manipulated his subjects so that they seemed to appear and vanish as if by miracle. He employed double exposure, superimposition, and elaborately designed sets to achieve his striking results. Working in England during the same period were two pioneer filmmakers, James Williamson and George A. Smith, who were turning out comedies while occasionally experimenting in fantasy. In "The Clown Barber" (1899), for example, the title character slices off a customer's head, shaves it, and replaces it onto the torso of the patron.

American filmmakers were slow to incorporate fantasy as a comedy theme, preferring instead to rely upon slapstick and pseudo-realism among their methods for evoking laughter. Edwin S. Porter, the pioneer director-producer, was one of the first in the United States to imitate the style of Meliès in several of his early comedy shorts, including "How Jones Lost His Roll" (1905) and "The Dream of a Rarebit Fiend" (1906), a film which contains a humorous yet disturbing dream sequence of a floating bed with its owner holding on for dear life. Eventually, other studios began exploring fantasy as a suitable film subject. A version of "Cinderella" was made as early as 1914.

By the 1920s fantasy comedy had established a foothold in Hollywood, especially in light films based upon literature. Mark Twain's satirical fantasy, *A Connecticut Yankee in King Arthur's Court* was released in 1921, J. M. Barrie's *Peter Pan* and L. Frank Baum's *Wizard of Oz*, both in 1925, and Lewis Carroll's *Alice in Wonderland* in 1926.

The Depression years produced several interesting fantasies, including *Just Imagine* (1930), a science-fiction musical comedy anticipating Woody ALLEN'S *Sleeper*. The main character (El BRENDEL), who had died in 1930, is resurrected in 1980 and is introduced to the wonders of the futuristic society. In *It's Great to Be Alive* (1933), a musical comedy, a lone man surviving an epidemic is hounded by women and governments. The following year LAUREL AND HARDY starred in Victor Herbert's operetta, *Babes in Toyland*. Thorne Smith's satirical novel, *The Night Life of the Gods*, was adapted to the screen in 1935 and featured Alan MOWBRAY who invents a ray that transforms people into statues as well as performing the reverse. Smith's other fantasies were to be adapted to the screen within the next few years. In 1936 *The Green Pastures* was released with an all-black cast, including Rex Ingram as "de Lawd." Based on dramatist Marc Connelly's work, the film highlighted several stories from the Bible. Thorne Smith's novel, *Topper*, was made into a popular series of light fantasies by producer Hal ROACH. The first entry, released in 1937, starred Roland YOUNG as the repressed banker whose quiet life is turned upside-down by the light-hearted ghosts of the Kerbys, a happy-go-lucky couple, played by Cary GRANT and Constance BENNETT, who perished in a car crash. They return to Young to teach him the true meaning of happiness, thereby performing their one good deed required of them before their spirits can find peace. *Topper* was the epitome of adult fantasy comedy in the 1930s. By the end of the decade, fantasy once again combined with musical comedy in the now classic version of *The Wizard of Oz* (1939), starring Judy GARLAND, Bert LAHR, Ray BOLGER, and Jack HALEY. Judy's song from the film, "Over the Rainbow," was to be associated with her throughout her entire career.

Fantasy comedy reached its peak in the 1940s. No longer was the genre relegated only to low-budget films and second-rate directors. Spearheaded by the earlier "Topper" series, the films incorporated a large degree of sophisticated comedy. In an attempt to duplicate the success of MGM's *Wizard*, Fox produced the extravagant color production, *The Bluebird* (1940), starring Shirley TEMPLE. But the film was a resounding failure. The following year proved more successful for fantasy with the release of the warm and charming *Here Comes Mr. Jordan*, starring Robert MONTGOMERY and Claude Rains. The film was remade in 1978 as *Heaven Can Wait*, starring Warren Beatty and Julie Christie. In 1942 movie audiences were treated to two "marital" fantasies. In *I Married an Angel* Nelson Eddy portrayed a playboy who dreams that he weds angel Jeanette MacDONALD. By far the better of these two films was René Clair's *I Married a Witch*, starring Fredric MARCH and Veronica LAKE. She played an early American witch burned by March's ancestors who returns to seek revenge on him. Her father, played by veteran character actor Cecil KELLAWAY, almost steals the film from the stars with his mischievous antics. The following year, 1943, Vincente MINNELLI, in his first directing assignment, made *Cabin in the Sky*, a musical comedy fantasy starring Eddie "Rochester" ANDERSON and an all-black cast. Ernst LUBITSCH directed *Heaven Can Wait* the same year. The fantasy is a satire on the pruderies of the 1890s, with Don AMECHE portraying a deceased rakish gent who explains to a trustee of Hades why he should reside there instead of in heaven. The remainder is a charming and witty flashback to his earlier life and loves. In 1944 Dick POWELL, the singing star of a succession of Warner Brothers musicals in the 1930s, portrayed a reporter in *It Happened Tomorrow*, an absorbing comedy in which he gains access to newspapers 24 hours in advance. The next year Jack OAKIE, portraying a long-dead dancer, returned to earth to help his daughter with her show-business career in *That's the Spirit*. *Wonder Man* was produced the same year and starred Danny KAYE in a dual role. His twin brother's ghost returns to convince the live Kaye to take the place of the dead brother, leading to hilarious situations. One of the best-loved films of the decade was Frank CAPRA'S *It's a Wonderful Life* (1946), starring James STEWART as a clerk who feels his life is a failure until the whimsical angel, Clarence, convinces him otherwise. Clarence shows him what the life of the town and his loved ones would have been like without Stewart's presence. In the entertaining *The Bishop's Wife* (1947) Cary Grant played an angel who comes to earth to assist despondent bishop David NIVEN and his wife, Loretta YOUNG, with their efforts to raise church funds. In the same year and with a similar theme but a western setting, Robert CUMMINGS starred in *Heaven Only Knows*. He played an angel who tries to save the soul of miscreant Brian DONLEVY. Also released in 1947 was *Miracle on 34th Street*, which starred Edmund GWENN as Santa Claus. Gwenn won an Oscar for his role. *Down to Earth*, also released in 1947, starred Rita Hayworth as Terpsichore, the Goddess of Dance, who appears on earth to assist Larry Parks in his staging of an extravagant musical. In *The Luck of the Irish* (1948) Cecil Kellaway portrayed a lively leprechaun who works on the conscience of reporter Tyrone Power. In the slight comedy *Mr. Peabody and the Mermaid*, released the same year, William POWELL hooks mermaid Ann Blyth while fishing and has trouble ridding himself of her presence. The film anticipates *Splash* (1984).

The next two decades witnessed a decline in the number and quality of fantasy comedies. In *For Heaven's Sake* (1950) Clifton WEBB and Edmund Gwenn portrayed angels who return to earth to help with the arrival of a couple's baby. Heavenly messengers also descend to help the Pittsburgh Pirates in

Angels in the Outfield (1951), starring Paul DOUGLAS, Janet LEIGH, and Keenan WYNN. ABBOTT AND COSTELLO starred in several fantasies, including *Abbott and Costello Meet the Invisible Man*, also released in 1951, in which they played detectives trying to help prizefighter Arthur Franz. The most sophisticated fantasy comedy of the 1950s was *Bell, Book and Candle* (1958), in which publisher James STEWART comes under the spell of witch Kim Novak, while her light-headed warlock brother, Jack LEMMON, uses his powers to get into mischief.

By the 1970s a half-hearted attempt was made to revive the genre. Harry Belafonte portrayed a black angel named Levine who decides to help Zero MOSTEL in *The Angel Levine* (1970). Veteran comedian George BURNS starred in a series of "Oh, God" comedies, beginning with *Oh, God!* (1977) in which he played the title character.

The 1980s saw several entries of fantasy comedies. Elliott GOULD, who is restored to life in *The Devil and Max Devlin* (1981), attempts to sign up several innocents for the devil, played by Bill COSBY. In 1982 James Caan played the ghost of Sally Field's dead husband who returns to visit her before her marriage to Jeff Bridges in *Kiss Me Goodbye*, a remake of a Brazilian comedy. Tom HANKS falls in love with a mermaid (Daryl Hannah) in *Splash* (1984). Time travel has become a popular theme in the films of the 1980s. *Back to the Future* (1985) and *Peggy Sue Got Married* (1986) both deal with this topic. In the latter film Kathleen TURNER returns to the 1960s to relive one week in her life as a high school senior.

Whichever technique is employed in the making of fantasy comedies, the results often strongly reflect the values of the times. Marriage, war, politics, love, relationships, and family ties have all been subjects handled comically and satirically in fantasy films. Although the genre has fallen in and out of favor through the years, writers and directors will inevitably return to it to explore fresh modes of comedy as well as to poke fun at human foibles, intentions that are both healthy and optimistic.

Farce. Farce involves the use of ridiculous or incongruous situations, low and physical comedy, and generally unsubtle humor to provoke laughter. Farces do not usually contain serious themes. Because of the strictures of the medium, most early silent comedies emphasized plot situations over characterization. Early film critics referred to these films as "farces." Virtually all of the major silent screen comics (as well as many comics of the sound era) appeared in farces.

One of the earliest and most successful farces was *Tillie's Punctured Romance* (1914), which featured an all-star cast including Charlie CHAPLIN, Marie DRESSLER, Mack SWAIN, Mabel NORMAND, Charlie CHASE, and Chester CONKLIN. Others include "Moonshine" (1918) with "Fatty" ARBUCKLE, "Here Comes the Bride" (1919) with John BARRYMORE, *Good Gracious, Annabelle* (1919) with Billie BURKE, and *Leave It to Susan* (1919) with Madge KENNEDY, who is captured by bandits and ends up taming them.

The popularity of the farce continued into the 1920s with such films as *His Royal Slyness* (1920) starring Harold LLOYD, *Twin Beds* (1920), *Don't Tell Everything* (1921) with Wallace REID, *Is Matrimony a Failure?* (1922), *The Hottentot* (1923), *Her Temporary Husband* (1924), *Miss Bluebeard* (1925), and *Charley's Aunt* (1925), as well as its many subsequent adaptations.

With the advent of sound, farce comedies did not decline. Instead, many stage farces were adapted to the screen. Also, the new crop of comics, moving from the stage and vaudeville, brought new life to the film farce with their verbal gags and outrageous skits. Mae WEST, W. C. FIELDS, the MARX BROTHERS, Eddie CANTOR, the RITZ BROTHERS, Joe E. BROWN, and Jimmy DURANTE, to name but a few, made significant contributions during the 1930s. Many of the more sophisticated comedies of the 1930s, including the SCREWBALL COMEDY, contained farcical elements.

The decade of the 1940s continued the trend. OLSEN AND JOHNSON starred in *Hellzapoppin* (1942), while ABBOTT AND COSTELLO, Red SKELTON, and Danny KAYE became popular practitioners of the genre, as did writer-directors like Preston STURGES. The most popular comedy team of the 1950s, Dean MARTIN and Jerry LEWIS, carried on the tradition. In the 1970s and 1980s well-known screen personalities such as Goldie HAWN, Gene WILDER, Eddie MURPHY, Steve MARTIN, Lily TOMLIN, and a host of other talented performers appeared or starred in farces.

Farina. See Allen Clayton Hoskins.

Farley, Dot (–1971), actress. Appeared in early silent comedy shorts for Mack SENNETT'S KEYSTONE and other studios. A homely, buck toothed comedienne, she starred in film comedies as early as 1910 for the American Film Manufacturing Company. By 1915 the diminutive and slender comedienne starred in a series of comedy shorts for United Film Service. Under Sennett's aegis, she was featured in his "Sennett Girl" comedies of 1927–1928, along with Daphne Pollard and his famous "Bathing Beauties." As a leading and supporting player, she worked with some of the major comics of the period, including Ford STERLING and well-known English comedian Sammy Burns.

SELECTED FILMS: Romantic Redskins (1910), *A Wife Wanted, A Life in the Balance* (1913), *Sammy's Scandalous Schemes* (1915), *Sammy vs. Cupid* (1916), *The Crossroads of New York* (1922), *The Enemy Sex* (1924), *The Grand Duchess and the Waiter, The Little Irish Girl* (1926), *All Abroad* (1927), *Lady Be Good* (1928), *Marquis Preferred*

(1929), Little Accident (1930), The Road to Reno (1938). ∎

Farmer's Daughter, The (1947), RKO. *Dir.* H.C. Potter; *Sc.* Allen Rivkin, Laura Kerr; with Loretta Young, Joseph Cotten, Ethel Barrymore, Charles Bickford.

Loretta Young walked off with an Oscar for her warm and touching portrayal of the title character in this light political comedy. A headstrong Swedish girl just off a Minnesota farm, she takes a job in the household of sophisticated congressman Joseph Cotten. Although a romance blossoms between them, they have different political views. After gaining enough political savvy, she runs against him, eventually winning a seat of her own. Other cast members provide considerable support to this charming Capralike film. Veteran actress Ethel Barrymore plays Cotten's politically wise mother. Charles Bickford portrays the family butler. The film, based on a Swedish play, has no connection with a 1940 Paramount feature bearing the same title.

Farnum, Franklyn (1876–1961), actor. Entered early silent films in 1914 following experience in vaudeville and on stage. He appeared in numerous dramas, westerns, and light films, at first in starring roles and later as a supporting player. His screen career spanned more than four decades.

SELECTED FILMS: Love Never Dies (1914), A Stranger From Somewhere (1916), Anything Goes, The Man Who Took a Chance, The Clean-Up, Bringing Home Father (1917), Fast Company, The Fighting Grin, The Rough Lover (1918). ∎

Farrell, Charles (1901–), actor. Appeared on stage before entering silent films in the early 1920s as a minor player. A handsome and charming actor, he became a star in 1927 playing opposite Janet Gaynor in *Seventh Heaven*. They were teamed as screen lovers in a succession of films which audiences flocked to see. He starred in dramas and comedies, making a smooth transition to sound films. By the mid-1930s Farrell fell out of favor with the movie public. In 1940, following several more appearances in routine films in England and Hollywood, he retired. He enjoyed success in two television shows, "My Little Margie" and "The Charlie Farrell Show." He was the mayor of Palm Springs for several years.

SELECTED FILMS: The Cheat, Rosita (1923), The Freshman, The Love Hour (1925), Sandy (1926), Lucky Star, Sunny Side Up (1929), Happy Days, High Society Blues, The Princess and the Plumber (1930), Delicious (1931), Wild Girl (1932), Girl Without a Room (1933), Falling in Love (1934), The Flying Doctor (1937), Just Around the Corner (1938), The Deadly Game (1941). ∎

Farrell, Glenda (1904–1971), actress. Worked in stock and on Broadway before beginning her long career in Hollywood, where she appeared in more than 100 films. After portraying gangsters' molls in several crime films in the early 1930s, she played the gum-chewing, wise-cracking blonde, often co-starring with Joan BLONDELL, in light feature films. In 1937 she starred in her own series as Torchy Blane, staunch reporter-sleuth. Following a short absence from the screen, she reappeared in character roles. It was in *The Gold Diggers of 1937* that she uttered the oft-quoted line: "It's so hard to be good under the capitalistic system."

SELECTED FILMS: Little Caesar (1931), Life Begins, Three on a Match, I Am a Fugitive From a Chain Gang (1932), Grand Slam, Lady for a Day (1933), Hi, Nellie!, The Personality Kid (1934), Gold Diggers of 1935, Traveling Saleslady, Little Big Shot (1935), Nobody's Fool (1936), Smart Blonde, Fly Away, Baby, Torchy Blane the Adventurous Blonde (1937), Hollywood Hotel, Stolen Heaven (1938), Torchy Blane in Chinatown (1939), I Love Trouble (1947), Lulu Belle (1948), Susan

Slept Here (1954), The Girl in the Red Velvet Swing (1955), Kissin' Cousins, The Disorderly Orderly (1964), Tiger by the Tail (1970). ∎

Farrow, Mia (1945–), actress. Appeared on stage, in films, and in television. A frail figure with delicate features, she had been a sickly child. After playing various dramatic roles in British, French, and American features through the 1960s and 1970s, she switched to light films in the early 1980s, demonstrating a flair for comedy. She has co-starred frequently with Woody ALLEN. Her father was the noted film director John Farrow and her mother the famous screen star Maureen O'Sullivan.

SELECTED FILMS: Guns at Batasi (1964), A Wedding (1978), A Midsummer Night's Sex Comedy (1982), Zelig (1983), Broadway Danny Rose (1984), The Purple Rose of Cairo (1985), Radio Days (1987). ∎

Father of the Bride (1950), MGM. Dir. Vincente Minnelli; Sc. Frances Goodrich, Albert Hackett; with Spencer Tracy, Joan Bennett, Elizabeth Taylor, Don Taylor.

Based on Edward Streeter's book, this domestic comedy satirically examines all the rituals of marrying off a daughter, including, among others, the engagement party, announcements, rehearsals, and the caterers. Spencer Tracy gives one of his finest and funniest performances as the frustrated father who is caught up in all these wedding rites. Elizabeth Taylor, who looks more beautiful than ever, plays the bride. Joan BENNETT portrays Taylor's mother who attempts to keep a lid on things. The film was so popular that a sequel, Father's Little Dividend, was released the following year.

Fay, Frank (1894–1961), actor. Worked in vaudeville and on Broadway at age 8, returned to vaudeville at 15, and in musical comedy in 1918. By the 1920s he became famous as an emcee, the first comedian to use this term. He was one of the first comics to deliver his material without costumes or pratfalls. He made his debut in films in the late 1920s, usually appearing in comic roles in light films. His screen career, however, remained grounded in routine features. He also starred on Broadway in the original Harvey.

SELECTED FILMS: The Show of Shows (1929), Under a Texas Moon, The Matrimonial Bed (1930), God's Gift to Women, Bright Lights (1931), Stars Over Broadway (1935), Nothing Sacred (1937), They Knew What They Wanted (1940), Spotlight Scandals (1943), Love Nest (1951). ∎

Fay, Hugh, actor. Worked as a supporting player in early silent comedy shorts for Mack SENNETT'S KEYSTONE studios. He appeared with some of the leading comedians of the period, including Fred MACE and Ford STERLING.

SELECTED FILMS: Crooked to the End, An Oily Scoundrel, Bath Tub Perils, She Loved a Sailor (1915), Stars and Bars, Secrets of a Beauty Parlor (1917), Little Annie Rooney (1929). ∎

Faye, Alice (1912–), actress. Worked as a professional dancer at age 13, as a chorine on Broadway, and as a singer in Rudy VALLEE'S band before entering films in 1934. An attractive blonde with a pleasant singing voice and a gift for bringing warmth to her screen characters, she specialized in musical comedies and light films throughout the 1930s and 1940s, during which time she was a major star. A popular performer with movie audiences, she appeared as one of the Box Office Top Ten in 1938 and 1939. Although she retired from the screen in 1945, she occasionally returned to films and the Broadway stage.

SELECTED FILMS: George White's Scandals, She Learned About Sailors (1934), Every Night at Eight (1935), Poor

Little Rich Girl, Sing Baby Sing (1936), Wake Up and Live, You Can't Have Everything, You're a Sweetheart (1937), Sally, Irene and Mary (1938), Little Old New York, Tin Pan Alley (1940), That Night in Rio, Weekend in Havana (1941), The Gang's All Here (1943), State Fair (1962), Every Girl Should Have One, The Magic of Lassie (1978). ■

Faye, Herbie (1899–1980), comic, character actor. Appeared in more than 100 films and television series. He worked with some of the leading personalities of the screen, including Jack LEMMON, Walter MATTHAU, and Frank SINATRA.

SELECTED FILMS: Top Banana (1954), Come Blow Your Horn (1963), The Fortune Cookie (1966), Thoroughly Modern Millie (1967), The Night They Raided Minsky's (1968). ■

Faye, Julia (1896–1966), actress. Began her screen career in 1916 with D. W. Griffith and then worked in early silent comedy shorts for Mack SENNETT'S KEYSTONE studios, appearing as one of his original "Bathing Beauties." Within a few years she joined Cecil B. DeMille for whom she made many features, usually in supporting roles.

SELECTED FILMS: As in Days of Old (1915), His Last Laugh (1916), Old Wives for New, Don't Change Your Husband (1918), Male and Female (1919), The Life of the Party, Something to Think About (1920), The Snob, Fool's Paradise (1921), Nice People (1922), Adam's Rib (1923), Meet the Prince, The Volga Boatman (1926), Turkish Delight (1927), Not So Dumb (1930), Only Yesterday (1933), The Buccaneer (1958). ■

Faylen, Frank (1909–), actor. Made his film debut in 1935 following his experience as a clown. He has appeared in more than 75 films, both dramas and light comedies, often as a blue-collar

worker, cabbie, or bartender, and occasionally as a villain.

SELECTED FILMS: Thanks a Million (1935), Down the Stretch (1936), Wine, Women and Horses (1937), It's a Wonderful World (1939), No Time for Comedy (1940), Father Steps Out, Top Sergeant Mulligan (1941), Fall In (1942), Taxi, Mister, Good Morning, Judge, Yanks Ahoy (1943), And the Angels Sing, The Canterville Ghost (1944), Bring On the Girls (1945), It's a Wonderful Life (1946), Road to Rio (1947), Francis (1949), Red Garters (1954), Funny Girl (1968). ■

Fazenda, Louise (1895–1962), actress. Began her film career in 1913 as a comedienne, then signed with Mack SENNETT'S KEYSTONE studios in 1915 where she rose to stardom as one of the most popular silent screen comics. She co-starred with some of the leading comedians of the period, including Mack SWAIN, Charlie MURRAY, Slim SUMMERVILLE, Edgar KENNEDY, and W. C. FIELDS. Specializing in rural character roles, she continued her film career as a character actress in feature-length films during the 1920s and into the sound era.

SELECTED FILMS: Almost an Actress, Mike and Jake at the Beach (1913), Traffic in Soles (1914), The Great Vacuum Robbery, Ambrose's Fury, Stark Mad, A Versatile Villain (1915), Summer Girl, Bombs and Brides, The Judge (1916), Her Torpedoed Love (1917), Her Screen Idol (1918), Hearts and Flowers (1919), It's a Boy (1920), Quincy Adams Sawyer (1921), The Gold Diggers (1923), Being Respectable (1924), Grounds for Divorce, Bobbed Hair, Hogan's Alley (1925), Footloose Widows, The Lady of the Harem (1926), A Sailor's Sweetheart (1927), Tillie's Punctured Romance (1928), No, No, Nanette, Leathernecking, Loose Ankles (1930), Misbehaving Ladies (1931), Alice in Wonderland (1933), Wonder Bar (1934), Broadway Gondolier (1935), Colleen (1936), Swing Your Lady (1938), The Old Maid (1939). ■

Feist, Felix E. (1906–1965), director. Began his film career in film sales and as a newsreel cameraman. He began directing in 1933, specializing in short subjects such as the comedy series, the "Pete Smith Specialties." He returned to directing feature-length films in 1943, many of which were of B quality. He specialized in light vehicles, few of which ever achieved the wit and sparkle of the "Pete Smith" shorts.

SELECTED FILMS: *The Deluge (1933), All by Myself, You're a Lucky Fellow, Mr. Smith (1943), This Is the Life, Pardon My Rhythm, Reckless Age (1944), George White's Scandals (1945), The Devil Thumbs a Ride (1947), The Man Who Cheated Himself (1950), This Woman Is Dangerous (1952), Pirates of Tripoli (1955).* ■

Feld, Fritz (1900–), actor. Worked in the theater and in films in Germany. He came to the United States in the mid-1920s and has appeared in more than 100 light comedies and musicals as a character player. A dapper comedian, he portrayed excitable, eccentric foreigners as well as haughty waiters and crackpot psychiatrists, often as foil to some of the leading comedians of the period, including, among others, Danny KAYE, Eddie CANTOR, ABBOTT AND COSTELLO, Jack BENNY, and Jerry LEWIS.

SELECTED FILMS: *The Last Command (1928), Broadway, One Hysterical Night (1929), I Met Him in Paris, Tovarich (1937), Hollywood Hotel, Bringing Up Baby, Gold Diggers in Paris (1938), Idiot's Delight, At the Circus (1939), It's a Date (1940), Maisie Gets Her Man (1942), Knickerbocker Holiday (1944), The Secret Life of Walter Mitty (1947), If You Knew Susie, Mexican Hayride (1948), Riding High (1950), Call Me Madam (1953), The Errand Boy (1961), Promises! Promises! (1963), The Patsy (1964), Silent Movie (1976), The World's Greatest Lover (1977).* ■

Feldman, Marty (1938–1982), actor, comedian. Worked in variety shows in his native England, in television, and in films from 1969. Known for his zany, eccentric humor and his bulging eyes, he became popular in the United States for his portrayal of Gene Wilder's assistant in Mel Brooks' *Young Frankenstein* (1974).

SELECTED FILMS: *The Adventure of Sherlock Holmes' Smarter Brother (1975), Silent Movie (1976), The Last Remake of Beau Geste (1977).* ■

Feldon, Barbara (1941–), actress. Worked as a fashion model before scoring a success in television, especially in the 1960s as Don ADAMS' assistant in the comedy series, *Get Smart*. A talented performer, she has appeared on Broadway and in light films. Her occasional screen appearances, however, have not brought her additional status as an actress or a potential star. She was reunited with Adams, her television co-star, in *No Deposit, No Return*. Although both were good in their roles in this Disney comedy, it did nothing to further their careers.

SELECTED FILMS: *Fitzwilly (1967), Smile (1975), No Deposit, No Return (1976).* ■

Fell, Norman (1924–), actor. Worked in summer stock and television before beginning his screen career in the late 1950s as a supporting player. Light-haired with a perpetually fretful look, he has appeared in dramas as well as in light films.

SELECTED FILMS: *Pork Chop Hill (1959), The Rat Race, Ocean's Eleven (1960), It's a Mad, Mad, Mad, Mad World (1963), Quick, Before It Melts (1964), The Secret War of Harry Frigg, Fitzwilly, The Graduate (1967), If It's Tuesday, This Must Be Belgium (1969), Rabbit Test, The Boatniks (1970), The End (1978), Paternity (1981).* ■

Female impersonation. The concept of a male dressing and acting like a member of the opposite sex for comic effect has its roots in the birth of the theater. Almost as soon as films began to tell stories, comic actors began impersonating women. In American films, one of the earliest comedians was John BUNNY (1863–1915). Starring in silent comedy shorts as early as 1910, he occasionally did female impersonations as part of his bag of comical routines. Roscoe "Fatty" ARBUCKLE posed as a female to evade his wife in "Fatty at Coney Island" (1917). Sitting on a bench with dress, wig, and parasol, he becomes the love interest of a passerby, until a fishhook gets caught in his hair and he is exposed. The film short co-starred Buster KEATON. Julian Eltinge, a comic screen actor of the pre-1920s, specialized in female impersonation. He starred in *The Clever Mrs. Carfax*, *Countess Charming* (both 1917), and *The Widow's Might* (1918). He reappeared decades later as a supporting player in *If I Had My Way*, a 1940 musical starring Bing CROSBY. Even the superstar Charlie CHAPLIN was not above engaging in this frivolity in several shorts. His first appearance as a female occurred in "A Busy Day" (1914) in which he played a shrewish wife who becomes incensed when "her" husband takes an interest in another woman. The remainder of the short film consists of a series of slapstick situations that show Charlie knocking people about, including policemen and "her" rival. In 1915 he made "A Woman," a two-reel comedy in which he again dresses up as a young woman so that he can get closer to the one he loves (Edna Purviance).

Other major and minor silent screen comics indulged in the art of female impersonation. Like Chaplin, Harold LLOYD in his early silent period also played a female. The film was a 1915 short, "Spit Ball Sadie," in which he impersonated a female pitcher on an all-women's baseball team. Comic Charlie MURRAY portrayed a detective disguised as a female in a popular 1915 Mack SENNETT comedy, "The Great Vacuum Robbery," which had an all-star cast of film comics, including Edgar KENNEDY, Louise FAZENDA, and Slim SUMMERVILLE. In "A Seminary Scandal" (1916) comedienne Billie RHODES' boy friend accompanies her to a girls' boarding school, dressed as a female. Sydney CHAPLIN, Charlie's half-brother, starred in the first of several film versions of the stage farce, *Charley's Aunt* in 1925. He portrayed the maiden aunt with gusto, as did actor-comedian Charles RUGGLES in 1931, in the first sound adaptation. Jack BENNY portrayed the role in 1941 and Ray BOLGER starred in the stage and film musical version of the story, *Where's Charley?* (1952).

The 1930s had its share of female impersonators. Bert Wheeler, of the comedy team of WHEELER AND WOOLSEY, donned feminine garments in their film *Peach O'Reno* in 1931. He portrayed a correspondent in a divorce suit. A wilder impersonation was that of comic character actor George "Gabby" Hayes in a B western, *The Lucky Texan* (1934). He played John Wayne's sidekick who dresses in drag as a disguise so that he can enter a courtroom as a witness without the outlaws suspecting him. Around the same period another fine character player, Grady SUTTON, who often portrayed slow-witted types, dressed as a female in the comedy short, "Wigwam."

The earliest example in the 1940s was the distinguished character actor Charles COBURN'S portrayal of an old woman in *The Captain Is a Lady* (1940). He disguises himself in this slight comedy so that he can accompany his wife, played by Beulah BONDI, who is going into a home for elderly women. The following year the debonair William POWELL, of "The THIN MAN" fame, impersonated a middle-aged spinster in *Love Crazy* to prevent a divorce. In the same year, 1941, Jimmy DURANTE, co-starring with Phil SILVERS in *You're in the Army Now*, disguised himself as a female dancer to avoid his sergeant, Joe SAW-YER. Cary GRANT, as a French army officer in *I Was a Male War Bride* (1949), dresses in drag to accompany his American wife to the United States.

In the 1950s the THREE STOOGES played their own leading ladies in "Self-Made Maids" (1950). *At War With the Army* (1950) was Dean MARTIN and Jerry LEWIS' first big hit. Jerry appears in drag in one bar scene in which he flirts with several soldiers. But the most popular comedy of the decade involving female impersonation was Billy WILDER'S *Some Like It Hot* (1959), starring Tony CURTIS and Jack LEMMON. After they witness a Valentine's Day rubout, the stars dress in drag and hide out among an all-female orchestra to escape from the killers. Eccentric millionaire Joe E. BROWN becomes infatuated with Jack LEMMON and wants to marry "her," creating several hilarious situations. Meanwhile, Curtis makes a play for Marilyn MONROE, another member of the orchestra.

One of the more notable films of this genre in more recent times was director Sydney Pollack's comedy, *Tootsie* (1982), starring Dustin Hoffman. Frustrated at not being able to land an acting job, Hoffman, portraying the out-of-work thespian, decides to impersonate a female and becomes an overnight sensation in a television soap opera. The film also starred Jessica Lange, who is strangely attracted to the new actress. She won an Oscar as Best Supporting Actress for her role. Pollack, besides directing the film, played Hoffman's agent.

Fennelly, Parker, actor. Worked in stock, on Broadway in the 1920s, and on radio before entering films. Gaunt and elderly in appearance, he has chiefly played rural types, especially New Englanders, in several light films. He is perhaps more widely known for his bread commercials in television.

SELECTED FILMS: Lost Boundaries, Ma and Pa Kettle (1949), *It Happened to*

Jane (1959), *Angel in My Pocket* (1969), *How to Frame a Frigg* (1971). ∎

Ferguson, Frank (1899–1978), actor. Began his Hollywood screen career in the early 1940s. Sad-looking and sporting a grey mustache, he appeared as a character player in numerous films. He was frequently cast in comic roles in genres ranging from drama to comedy, supporting such personalities as ABBOTT AND COSTELLO and Mickey ROONEY. He switched to television in the 1960s.

SELECTED FILMS: Father Is a Prince (1940), *This Gun for Hire* (1942), *Little Miss Big* (1946), *Variety Girl* (1947), *Abbott and Costello Meet Frankenstein, The Walls of Jericho, That Wonderful Urge* (1948), *Slightly French* (1949), *The Good Humor Man, He's a Cockeyed Wonder* (1950), *Elopement* (1951), *Million Dollar Mermaid* (1952), *Andy Hardy Comes Home* (1958), *Raymie* (1960), *Pocketful of Miracles* (1961), *Hush . . . Hush, Sweet Charlotte* (1965). ∎

Fetchit, Stepin (1902–1985), actor. Worked in vaudeville before making his film debut in the late 1920s. He was soon to become Hollywood's first widely known black actor. He appeared as a character actor in dozens of films, portraying a lazy, slow-moving, but lovable character, a role later criticized by some as demeaning to other blacks. He was at the peak of his popularity during the 1930s, accompanying such stars as Shirley TEMPLE, Janet Gaynor, and Will ROGERS.

It has been estimated that he earned several million dollars, but by 1947 he filed for bankruptcy. Although he was criticized for his portrayals of idle, easily frightened, shuffling blacks, he claimed in interviews that he opened the doors for future black performers by being the first black actor to receive feature billing in American mainstream films. He was honored with the American Classic Screen Award in 1981 by the National Film Society. The 79-year-old veteran comedian, on crutches at the time, responded at the ceremonies by doing his famous shuffle.

SELECTED FILMS: In Old Kentucky (1927), The Ghost Talks, Hearts in Dixie, Show Boat, Salute (1929), The Big Fight, Cameo Kirby, Swing High (1930), The Prodigal (1931), Carolina, David Harum, Stand Up and Cheer, Judge Priest (1934), The County Chairman, Charlie Chan in Egypt, Steamboat 'Round the Bend (1935), Dimples (1936), On the Avenue, Love Is News (1937), Zenobia (1939), Miracle in Harlem (1947), Bend of the River (1952), The Sun Shines Bright (1953), Amazing Grace (1974). ■

Fibber McGee and Molly. A popular radio comedy team whose show ran from 1935 to 1956. In 1941 the program was voted the Number One show on the air. James Edward Jordan (1897–) portrayed Fibber, the mendacious husband who was always trying to extricate himself from one of his stories. Marian Driscoll (1898–1961) played Molly, his long-suffering wife. Together, they entertained millions of their fans who found the show required listening each week. They made a handful of films that were never as successful as the radio show itself. The highlight of each show was the famous closet scene in which every possible item would tumble out each time Fibber opened the door.

SELECTED FILMS: This Way Please (1938), Look Who's Laughing (1941), Here We Go Again (1942), Heavenly Days (1944). ■

Fiedler, John (1925–), actor. Appeared in stock and television in the 1950s as a character player before beginning his film career. Bald and bespectacled, he has played hard-nosed clerks and small-town citizens in several dramas and light films.

SELECTED FILMS: Twelve Angry Men (1957), That Touch of Mink (1962), The World of Henry Orient (1964), Kiss Me, Stupid (1964), A Fine Madness (1966), Fitzwilly (1967), The Odd Couple (1968), Rascal (1969), Making It (1971). ■

Field, Elinor (1901–), actress. Worked in stock for one season before entering the comedy film world at age seventeen. She co-starred in early silent comedy shorts with Henry DEPP for the Strand company, a subsidiary of MUTUAL studios. Directed by Scott Sidney, these films were bright comedies dealing with the misadventures of young marrieds and the complexities of their modern technological world as represented by the automobile. By the early 1920s she had featured roles in westerns opposite such popular cowboy stars as Jack Hoxie and Hoot GIBSON.

SELECTED FILMS: What Will Father Say? (1918), 'Twas Henry's Fault (1919). ■

Field, Sally (1946–), actress. Established her reputation as an actress in television, especially in comedy shows like "Gidget" and "The Flying Nun." She received an Emmy Award in 1977. She entered films in 1967 as a minor character in a western, but it was not until the next decade that she was able to obtain lead roles in comedies and dramas. She has won Oscars for her roles in Norma Rae (1979) and Places in the Heart (1984).

In Smokey and the Bandit she played a hitchhiker who says to trucker Burt REYNOLDS: "You got a nice profile—especially from the side."

SELECTED FILMS: The Way West (1967), Stay Hungry (1976), Smokey and the Bandit, Heroes (1977), The End (1978), Smokey and the Bandit II (1980), Kiss Me Goodbye (1982). ■

Fields, Herbert (1897–1958), screenwriter, playwright. Appeared on stage as an actor, directed and choreographed shows, and began writing plays in 1925. He settled in Hollywood during the 1930s, turning his attention to writing screenplays chiefly for comedies. Many of his stage productions, some of which he wrote in collaboration with his sister Dorothy Fields, were adapted for the screen. He was the son of vaudevillian Lew Fields of the famous comedy team of WEBER AND FIELDS and the brother of writer Joseph FIELDS.

SELECTED FILMS (as screenwriter): The Hot Heiress (1931), Let's Fall in Love, Down to Their Last Yacht (1934), Mississippi, People Will Talk, Hands Across the Table (1935), Love Before Breakfast, The Luckiest Girl in the World (1936), Fools for Scandal (1938), Honolulu (1939), Father Takes a Wife (1941).

SELECTED FILMS (from his plays): Panama Hattie (1942), Let's Face It, DuBarry Was a Lady (1943), Something for the Boys (1944), Up in Central Park (1948), Annie Get Your Gun (1950), Hit the Deck! (1955). ∎

Fields, Joseph (1895–1966), screenwriter, playwright. Worked as a writer for periodicals and shows before entering films in the same capacity. He collaborated with Jerome Chodorov, Anita Loos, and others on many light films. He was a successful playwright of musicals and comedies, many of which he adapted for the screen. His father was the famous comedian Lew Fields from the comedy team of WEBER AND FIELDS.

SELECTED FILMS: The Big Shot (1931), When Love Is Young (1937), Fools for Scandal, Rich Man Poor Girl (1938), The Girl From Mexico (1939), Mexican Spitfire, Two Girls on Broadway (1940), Louisiana Purchase, My Sister Eileen (1942), A Night in Casablanca (1946), Lost Honeymoon (1947), The Farmer Takes a Wife (1953), The Tunnel of Love (1958), Happy Anniversary (1959), Flower Drum Song (1961). ∎

Fields, Lew. See Weber and Fields.

Fields, Stanley (1883–1941), actor. Former boxer and vaudeville performer. He made his film debut in 1930 and appeared in more than 75 films, often as a gangster. His most striking performance was that of Edward G. Robinson's rival in Little Caesar (1930). He also played the tough guy in many light films opposite some of the leading comedians of the 1930s, including Eddie CANTOR, Jimmy DURANTE, Joe E. BROWN, and LAUREL AND HARDY.

SELECTED FILMS: Street of Chance (1930), Cracked Nuts (1931), The Kid From Spain (1932), He Couldn't Take It (1933), Palooka (1934), Show Boat, The King Steps Out (1936), Ali Baba Goes to Town (1937), Wide Open Faces (1938), Pack Up Your Troubles (1939), The Lady From Cheyenne (1941). ∎

Fields, W. C. (1879–1946), actor, comedian, screenwriter. Worked as a tramp clown and comic juggler in vaudeville and musical comedy before embarking on a film career in the 1920s. Throughout his stage career and all of his film appearances until Million Dollar Legs (1932), he wore a clip-on mustache. He then discarded this trademark for no apparent reason. Although he portrayed different characters, their range was not that widely diverse. For the most part, he played carnival charlatans, charming, fast-talking rapscallions or rogues, or browbeaten, middle-class husbands. Much of the material for his films derived from his old vaudeville routines or from his many years with the Ziegfeld Follies.

He had an excellent sense of timing and, in the sound era, displayed effective control over his delivery. His verbal attacks against such hallowed subjects as children, marriage, animals, and banks were not only refreshing but endeared him to his audiences. Four of his comedy shorts which he made for Mack SENNETT have become classics: "The Dentist" (1932), "The Fatal Glass of Beer," "The Pharmacist," and "The Barber

Shop" (1933). He wrote many of his own screenplays under various pseudonyms, including Charles Bogle and Mahatma Kane Jeeves. His one-liners and retorts have often been quoted. *The Art of W. C. Fields*, a study of the comedian's work by William K. Everson, was published in 1967.

In *Poppy*, for example, the destitute Fields orders hot dogs for himself and his daughter but returns the half-eaten franks to the vendor who wants cash, not promises of payment. The angry vendor complains: "How am I going to sell these again?" The shocked Fields replies with indignation. "First you insult me, then you ask my advice concerning salesmanship! You are a dunce!" In *It's a Gift* an irate businessman, exasperated after fruitless haggling with Fields, exclaims: "You're drunk!" "Yeah, and you're crazy," retorts the wily Fields. "I'll be sober tomorrow, and you'll be crazy the rest of your life."

SELECTED FILMS: Pool Sharks (1915), Sally of the Sawdust (1925), It's the Old Army Game, So's Your Old Man (1926), The Potters, Running Wild (1927), Tillie's Punctured Romance (1928), Her Majesty Love (1931), Million Dollar Legs, If I Had a Million (1932), International House, Tillie and Gus (1933), Six of a Kind, The Old-Fashioned Way, Mrs. Wiggs of the Cabbage Patch, It's a Gift (1934), David Copperfield, The Man on the Flying Trapeze (1935), Poppy (1936), You Can't Cheat an Honest Man (1939), My Little Chickadee, The Bank Dick (1940), Never Give a Sucker an Even Break (1941), Follow the Boys, Song of the Open Road, Sensations of 1945 (1944). ■

Film biographies. Hollywood has occasionally depicted the lives of film comedians. One of the earliest sound films of an entertainer's life was *The Jazz Singer* (1927), the fictionalized biography of singer-comedian Al JOLSON. Two other versions were produced, one in 1953 starring Danny THOMAS and another in 1980 with Neil Diamond. The

later adaptations, however, have little to do with any real-life comic. In 1946 Columbia released *The Jolson Story*, a slightly more accurate portrayal of the blackface singer, starring Larry Parks. A sequel, *Jolson Sings Again*, in which Parks repeated his portrayal of Jolson, followed in 1949.

In 1939 20th Century-Fox released *Hollywood Cavalcade*, a romanticized version of the history of Hollywood moviemaking. The film suggests broadly fictionalized biographies of two major forces in silent comedy, producer Mack SENNETT and comedienne Mabel NORMAND. Don AMECHE starred as a pioneer director, a combination of D. W. Griffith and Sennett, who is overly concerned with camera techniques and pie-throwing, while Alice FAYE, reminiscent of Normand in her heyday, played a new slapstick queen who co-stars with Buster KEATON in a knockabout comedy. James Cagney won an Academy Award for his performance as the celebrated song-and-dance man George M. COHAN in *Yankee Doodle Dandy* in 1942. He repeated his Cohan impersonation in 1955 in *The Seven Little Foys*. Will Rogers, Jr., gave a faithful depiction of his humorist-father in *The Story of Will Rogers* (1952). The banjo-eyed comedian-singer, Eddie CANTOR, was played by Keefe Brasselle in *The Eddie Cantor Story* in 1953 with Jackie Barnett as Jimmy DURANTE.

Bob HOPE delivered a buoyant impersonation of the famous vaudeville comic Eddie FOY in *The Seven Little Foys* (1955). Eddie Foy, Jr., depicted his father on screen more accurately in such films as *Yankee Doodle Dandy* (1942), *Bowery to Broadway* (1944), and *Wilson* (1944). In 1957 Donald O'CONNOR portrayed the renowned "stoneface" comedian in *The Buster Keaton Story*, which offered more fiction than fact and more private matter than funny on-screen moments.

The famous Broadway and radio comedienne Fanny BRICE had four films based on her colorful life: *Broadway Thru a Keyhole* (1933); *Rose of Washing-*

ton Square (1938) starring Alice FAYE; and *Funny Girl* (1968) and *Funny Lady* (1975), both of which starred Barbra STREISAND as the Ziegfeld star.

Errol Flynn portrayed the tragic life of stage and screen actor John BAR-RYMORE in *Too Much, Too Soon* (1958). Jean HARLOW, the sexy and sensational "blonde bombshell" of the 1930s, had two screen biographies devoted to her escapades, one starring Carroll Baker and a second starring Carol Lynley. Both were released in 1965. Carl REINER directed the 1967 film version of his hit Broadway play *Enter Laughing*, a semi-autobiographical account of his early years as a struggling actor. *The Sunshine Boys* (1975), starring George BURNS and Walter MATTHAU, adapted from Neil SIMON'S funny Broadway play, was based in part on the careers of the legendary vaudeville comedy team of SMITH AND DALE. The lives of two giants of the screen, Clark GABLE and Carole LOMBARD, were given mediocre treatment in *Gable and Lombard* (1976), starring James Brolin and Jill Clayburgh in the title roles. Finally, Rod Steiger starred in the entertaining, but highly fictionalized, *W. C. Fields and Me* in 1976.

Finch, Flora (1869–1940), actress. Worked in the theater in England before making her United States film debut in 1909. She became popular as the skinny, unattractive foil to rotund John BUNNY in a string of comedy shorts popularly known as "Bunnyfinches" or "Bunnygraphs." After Bunny's untimely death in 1915, her studio tried to salvage her career by starring her in her own series. The experiment failed at the box office and for the next two years she was given minor roles. She then established the Flora Finch Film Company in 1917, producing numerous slapstick shorts. But her popularity soon declined as a major comedienne, although she continued to appear in films as a character player during the sound era.

SELECTED FILMS: Mrs. Jones Entertains, Jones and the Lady Book Agent (1909), All on the Account of the Milk (1910), The New Stenographer (1911), Bunny and the Twins, Bunny's Suicide, Pandora's Box (1912), And His Wife Came Back, Bunny's Mistake (1913), Love's Old Dream, Father's Flirtation, Bunny Buys a Harem (1914), The Starring of Flora Finchurch (1915), Prudence the Pirate (1916), War Prides (1917), His Better Half, Unwelcome Guest (1919), When Knighthood Was in Flower (1922), Monsieur Beaucaire (1924), Fifth Avenue, Oh, Baby! (1926), Five and Ten Cent Annie (1928), Come Across (1929), Show Boat (1936), The Women (1939). ∎

Fine, Larry (1902–1975), actor. Worked as a musician in vaudeville before joining Ted HEALY'S Stooges in 1925. Along with Moe and Curly, he was one of the original THREE STOOGES who appeared in films beginning in 1934. As the brillo-haired middleman of the trio, he didn't get as many funny lines or key routines as were bestowed upon Curly, but neither did he receive as much bodily mistreatment from Moe. In "No Census, No Feeling" (1940) Moe asks a society matron her age. "How old do I look?" she responds. "Oh," Moe replies, obviously impressed with the woman, "you look like a million." "Naah," Larry interjects, "she can't be that old." Larry stayed with the act through 1969, the year the boys split up. See The Three Stooges for selected films.

Finklehoffe, Fred F. (1910–1977), screenwriter, playwright. Began his writing career as a playwright (*Brother Rat*) before entering films as a screenwriter. He wrote, alone or in collaboration, a group of light, witty comedies and some of MGM's more sparkling, charming musicals.

SELECTED FILMS: Brother Rat and a Baby, Strike Up the Band (1940), Babes on Broadway, For Me and My Gal (1942),

Best Foot Forward, Girl Crazy (1943), Meet Me in St. Louis (1944), Mr. Ace (1946), The Egg and I (1947), Words and Music (1948), At War With the Army (1951), The Stooge (1953). ■

Finlayson, James (1887–1953), actor. Worked in the theater in Scotland and, while on tour in the United States in 1916, decided to enter films. After appearing in comedy shorts for different studios, he signed with Mack SENNETT for whom he made features. He switched to Hal ROACH'S studios in 1923, taking lead roles as well as supporting parts in a series of comedies. Distinguished by several distinct features, his bald head, mustache, omnipresent squint, and apoplectic rage, he often played the foil to LAUREL AND HARDY in their comedy shorts as well as their feature-length films. In "Big Business" (1929), one of their most famous shorts, the boys are Christmas tree salesmen who play havoc with Finlayson's house while he, in turn, demolishes their automobile.

SELECTED FILMS: Married Life (1920), A Small Town Idol (1921), Homemade Movies (1922), Welcome Home (1925), Do Detectives Think?, Sugar Daddies, No Man's Law, The Second Hundred Years (1927), Ladies' Night in a Turkish Bath, Bachelor's Paradise (1928), Two Weeks Off, Men o' War, Hoosegow, Wall Street (1929), Chickens Come Home, The Dawn Patrol (1930), Our Wife, Pardon Us (1931), Pack Up Your Troubles (1932), Bonnie Scotland (1935), The Bohemian Girl, Our Relations (1936), Way Out West (1937), Block-Heads (1938), The Flying Deuces (1939), A Chump at Oxford, Saps at Sea (1940), To Be or Not to Be (1942), The Perils of Pauline (1947), Royal Wedding (1951). ■

Fiske, Richard (–1944), actor. Worked as a comic supporting player, chiefly in sound comedy shorts starring the THREE STOOGES, for whom he was often the foil. He also appeared in several shorts in

the 1940s starring Buster KEATON. He was killed in World War II.

SELECTED FILMS: Boobs in Arms, Nothing but Pleasure, Pardon My Berth Marks, The Taming of the Snood (1940), All the World's a Stooge, In the Sweet Pie and Pie (1941), Dizzy Pilots (1943). ■

Fitzgerald, Barry (1888–1961), actor. Acted at Dublin's Abbey Theatre and in Alfred Hitchcock's film, Juno and the Paycock (1930), before coming to Hollywood in 1936. He appeared in dozens of films, establishing himself as one of America's best-loved character actors. A talented performer, he proved he could also play dramatic roles with his part in And Then There Were None (1945). He specialized in heavily accented Irish roles which he played with caprice and warmth. He received an Academy Award as Best Supporting Actor for his portrayal of Father Fitzgibbon in Leo McCAREY'S Going My Way (1944). In the same film he confides to Bing CROSBY: "The joy of giving is indeed a pleasure—especially when you get rid of something you don't want." He was the brother of actor Arthur SHIELDS.

SELECTED FILMS: The Plough and the Stars (1937), Bringing Up Baby, Four Men and a Prayer (1938), The Saint Strikes Back, Full Confession (1939), I Love a Soldier (1944), Incendiary Blonde, Duffy's Tavern, The Stork Club (1945), Easy Come, Easy Go, Welcome Stranger, Variety Girl (1947), Miss Tatlock's Millions (1948), Top o' the Morning (1949), The Quiet Man (1952), The Catered Affair (1956). ■

Flagg, Captain. Fictional World War I officer based on the character from the Broadway play What Price Glory? by Maxwell Anderson and Laurence Stallings. The fast-talking Flagg, played by Edmund LOWE, and the slow-witted Sergeant Quirt (Victor McLAGLEN), two feuding buddies in the 1926 film version of the drama, continued their brawling comedy in The Cockeyed World (1929),

Women of All Nations (1931), and *Hot Pepper* (1933).

Flavin, James, actor. Appeared as a supporting actor in several films from the mid-1930s to the 1950s. He played minor character roles in both dramas and comedies, including three ABBOTT AND COSTELLO vehicles.

SELECTED FILMS: *My Man Godfrey* (1936), *Buck Privates* (1941), *Ride 'Em Cowboy* (1942), *It Ain't Hay* (1943), *Easy to Wed* (1946), *One Touch of Venus, The Velvet Touch* (1948), *South Sea Sinner* (1950). ■

Flippen, Jay C. (1898–1971), actor. Worked as a minstrel and comic before entering films. After making several comedy shorts in the early sound period, he settled down in Hollywood for a long screen career as a reliable and versatile character actor. Husky in stature with a rugged face, he chiefly portrayed sympathetic types in dramas and light films.

SELECTED FILMS: *The Ham What Am* (1928), *The Home Edition* (1929), *Oh, You Beautiful Doll* (1949), *The Yellow Cab Man, Love That Brute* (1950), *The Lemon Drop Kid, The Model and the Marriage Broker* (1951), *Carnival Story* (1954), *It's Always Fair Weather* (1955), *Public Pigeon Number One* (1957), *Where the Boys Are* (1960), *Cat Ballou* (1965), *The Spirit Is Willing* (1967). ■

Flowers, Bess (1900–), actress. Worked chiefly as a supporting player in comedy shorts from the early 1920s to the 1940s and in features until the early 1960s. She appeared in hundreds of films, including many of the THREE STOOGES' comedies as well as those of other comedians, including LAUREL AND HARDY. She was affectionately known as "the queen of the Hollywood extras."

SELECTED FILMS: *We Faw Down* (1928), *Twin Triplets* (1935), *Termites of*

1938, *Tassels in the Air, Mutts to You* (1938), *Honolulu* (1939), *A-Plumbing We Will Go* (1940), *An Ache in Every Stake* (1941), *Ghost Catchers* (1944), *Micro-Phonies* (1945), *The Noose Hangs High* (1948). ■

Flynn, Errol (1909–1959), actor. Began his screen career at age 24 in an Australian film, *In the Wake of the Bounty*, following miscellaneous occupations as a prospector and sailor. After a small part in *Murder at Monte Carlo*, a British film, Flynn, born Errol Leslie Flynn in Tasmania, was signed by Warners. His first big hit was *Captain Blood* (1935), a swashbuckler that was to influence his future roles. Charming, athletic, handsome, and at times impudent, he starred in numerous adventure and war films and a handful of comedies. He remained a popular performer for two decades, but his hard drinking and carefree life-style took their tolls.

His later films revealed his physical deterioration. He tried to re-establish his acting career in European film ventures but only succeeded in increasing his mounting debts. He returned to Hollywood in the mid-1950s and appeared as an alcoholic in several films. Although he received adequate reviews, the downward slide of his career became irreversible. He died of a heart attack. His son, Sean, who appeared in a few mediocre films, disappeared in Viet Nam after being captured in 1971. Flynn's autobiography, *My Wicked, Wicked Ways*, was published posthumously in 1959.

In the adventure-comedy *The Adventures of Don Juan* (1948) he played the title character who persuades himself about his own powers as a lover. "Since there is a little of Don Juan in every man, there must be more of it in me."

SELECTED FILMS: *The Perfect Specimen* (1937), *Four's a Crowd* (1938), *Thank Your Lucky Stars* (1943), *Never Say Goodbye* (1946), *The Adventures of Don Juan* (1948), *It's a Great Feeling* (1949). ■

Flynn, Joe (1924–1974), actor, comic. Worked in television and films, making his Hollywood debut in 1956. Usually wearing glasses, he enlivened many films with his comic antics.

SELECTED FILMS: The Boss (1956), Portland Expose (1957), This Happy Feeling (1958), Cry for Happy (1961), Lover Come Back (1962), McHale's Navy (1964), Divorce, American Style (1967), The Love Bug (1969), The Computer Wore Tennis Shoes (1970), The Barefoot Executive (1971), Superdad (1974), The Strongest Man in the World (1975). ∎

Fonda, Henry (1905–1982), actor. Worked in stock and on Broadway from 1929 to 1934 prior to his screen debut in 1935. Specializing in shy, "American-type" characters, he soon became a major star of dramas and light films. Regardless of the role he played, he conveyed the homespun virtues of honesty and sincerity. He is known chiefly for his realistic portrayals in social dramas, but he has also starred in some of the best comedies to come out of Hollywood, bringing to such films as The Lady Eve (1941) the same virtues as those mentioned above. Even in his later years he brought a salty performance to films like Mister Roberts (1955), in which he repeated his stage role as a cargo ship officer who prefers being on a fighting ship.

He was nominated for an Oscar for his starring role as Tom Joad in The Grapes of Wrath (1940), but had not won an Academy Award as Best Actor until On Golden Pond (1981). That same year he was presented with a special award for his contributions to the art of motion pictures. A biography, Fonda: My Life, written by Howard Teichmann, was published in 1981.

In The Mad Miss Manton he proposes to socialite Barbara Stanwyck and suggests honeymooning in South America. "Can you afford it?" she asks. "No, but you can." "Isn't there a drop of red blood in your veins? I wanted to live on your

income." "That's foolish," he returns. "Who's going to live on yours?"

SELECTED FILMS: The Farmer Takes a Wife (1935), I Dream Too Much, The Moon's Our Home (1936), Slim, That Certain Woman (1937), The Mad Miss Manton (1938), The Lady Eve (1941), The Male Animal, Rings on Her Fingers, The Magnificent Dope (1942), On Our Merry Way (1948), Mister Roberts (1955), Sex and the Single Girl (1964), Yours, Mine and Ours (1969), On Golden Pond (1981). ∎

Fonda, Jane (1937–), actress. Worked as a model and as an actress on Broadway. A talented and intelligent performer, she achieved almost immediate acclaim in her first few films in the early 1960s. She soon began to immerse herself in political and social causes, thereby prompting much public criticism and outcry. A strong activist against the Vietnam War and an outspoken supporter of certain controversial radical groups at home, she ran afoul of several government agencies. Meanwhile, she became involved with several documentary films and, by 1971, had won two New York Film Critics Awards and one Oscar. By the end of the decade she had returned to commercial films and added another Academy Award to her growing collection. She has starred in dramas and comedies with equal success. She is the daughter of Henry FONDA.

In Barefoot in the Park she played the wife of lawyer Robert REDFORD. Referring to his last case, he admits: "We were awarded six cents." "How much of that do we get?" she asks.

SELECTED FILMS: Tall Story (1960), Sunday in New York (1964), Cat Ballou (1965), Any Wednesday (1966), Barefoot in the Park (1967), Fun With Dick and Jane (1977), California Suite (1978), 9 to 5 (1980), Rollover (1981). ∎

Foran, Dick (1910–1979), actor. Worked as a singer on radio and in a band before entering films in the mid-1930s. He starred in a wide range of genres, from low-budget westerns to slapstick comedies. H ' was a popular leading man in the 1930s and 1940s and continued to appear in films through the 1960s. He frequently played the nice guy who lost the girl to the male lead.

SELECTED FILMS: Stand Up and Cheer, Gentlemen Are Born (1934), The Perfect Specimen, She Loved a Fireman (1937), Cowboy From Brooklyn, Boy Meets Girl (1938), My Little Chickadee (1940), Four Mothers, In the Navy (1941), Butch Minds the Baby, Ride 'Em Cowboy (1942), He's My Guy (1943), Guest Wife (1945), Brighty of Grand Canyon (1967). ∎

Ford, Glenn (1916–), actor. Worked in stock before entering films in the late 1930s. A handsome performer displaying a quiet charm, he began to emerge as a serious actor of some stature in the early 1940s until World War II forced his career to be postponed. Following the war, he developed into one of the major talents of the 1940s and 1950s, displaying his versatility by starring in dramas and light films with equal effectiveness.

SELECTED FILMS: Heaven With a Barbed Wire Fence (1939), Blondie Plays Cupid, The Lady in Question (1940), Go West Young Lady (1941), The Mating of Millie (1948), The Doctor and the Girl (1949), The Redhead and the Cowboy (1951), The Teahouse of the August Moon (1956), Don't Go Near the Water (1957), It Started With a Kiss (1959), Advance to the Rear (1964), Superman (1978). ∎

Ford, Harrison (1894–1957), actor. Began his long screen career in the 1910s in light films. A good-looking male lead, he appeared as a supporting player in features, light films, and comedy shorts. One of his early leading ladies was the popular comic actress Wanda HAWLEY. Others include Gloria SWANSON, Marion DAVIES, and Marie PREVOST. He also had a successful stage career. There is no connection between him and the popular actor of the 1970s–1980s who bears the same name.

SELECTED FILMS: The Mysterious Mrs. M (1916), A Pair of Silk Stockings, Such a Little Pirate (1918), Hawthorne of the U.S.A., The Third Kiss (1919), Find the Woman, The Primitive Lover (1922), Maytime (1923), The Average Woman (1924), Lovers in Quarantine (1925), Up in Mabel's Room, That Royal Girl, Almost a Lady, The Nervous Wreck (1926), The Girl in the Pullman, The Night Bride (1927), Let 'Er Go Gallagher, Golf Widows, The Rush Hour, Three Week Ends (1928), The Flattering Word (1929), Love in High Gear (1932). ∎

Ford, John (1895–1973), director. Began directing silent films in 1917 after handling various studio jobs. Although he soon became a major Hollywood director known for his westerns and dramas, many of which have since become film classics, he turned out a series of light comedies during the silent era starring Harry CAREY, a life-long friend. He would occasionally return to comedy, as he did in several films during the 1930s and again in the 1950s, using top stars such as Will ROGERS and John Wayne. A talented director with a special eye for detail and a strong belief in tradition, he earned the respect of critics and his fellow artists.

SELECTED FILMS: Bucking Broadway (1917), Wild Women, A Woman's Fool (1918), A Gun-Fighting Gentleman, Roped (1919), The Prince of Avenue A (1920), Jackie (1921), Thank You (1925), Riley the Cop (1928), The Brat (1931), Steamboat 'Round the Bend (1935), Tobacco Road (1941), The Quiet Man (1952). ∎

Ford, Paul (1901–1976), actor. Worked in radio in the 1940s and on Broadway by 1944. He entered films in 1945 as a character actor and appeared occasionally on stage as well as in television in a long-running series with comedian Phil SILVERS. Often portraying an easily harassed character with a lugubrious expression, he reached the height of popularity in films when he appeared in the screen version of his stage success *Never Too Late* (1965). In the film middle-aged Maureen O'Sullivan and Paul Ford react to impending parenthood. "I thought everybody would be so happy," she says. "There's all kinds of happiness," Ford explains. "This is the happiness that everybody isn't too happy about."

SELECTED FILMS: *The House on 92nd Street* (1945), *Perfect Strangers* (1950), *The Teahouse of the August Moon* (1956), *The Missouri Traveler*, *The Matchmaker* (1958), *The Music Man*, *Who's Got the Action?* (1962), *It's a Mad, Mad, Mad, Mad World* (1963), *The Russians Are Coming, the Russians Are Coming*, *A Big Hand for the Little Lady*, *The Spy With a Cold Nose* (1966), *The Comedians* (1967), *Lola* (1973). ■

Ford, Wallace (1897–1966), actor. Worked on Broadway before entering films in 1930. A light-haired, stocky figure, he played generally sympathetic roles, although at times he was found on the wrong side of the law. He appeared as a supporting player in dramas and light films. During the 1930s he was occasionally cast as the lead. One of his more famous roles was that of Frankie McPhillip, the Irish patriot betrayed by Victor McLAGLEN in *The Informer* (1935).

SELECTED FILMS: *Absent-Minded*, *Fore!*, *The Swellhead* (1930), *Goodbye Again*, *She Had to Say Yes* (1933), *I Hate Women* (1934), *The Nut Farm*, *She Couldn't Take It* (1935), *Swing It, Sailor* (1937), *Love, Honor and Oh! Baby* (1940), *Scattergood Survives a Murder* (1942), *Rendezvous With Annie* (1946), *Magic Town* (1947), *Harvey* (1950), *She Couldn't Say No* (1953), *A Patch of Blue* (1965). ■

Forde, Eugenie (–1940), actress. Entered early silent films following experience on stage. She appeared as a supporting player in dramas and light films throughout the silent period. Her daughter, Victoria FORDE, was also a screen actress in silent films.

SELECTED FILMS: *A Pair of Jacks* (1912), *The Doughnut Vendor*, *Polishing Up Polly*, *Curly* (1915), *The Gentle Intruder*, *Annie-for-Spite* (1917), *Fair Enough* (1918), *Strictly Confidential*, *Sis Hopkins*, *The Man Who Turned White* (1919), *The Virgin of Stamboul* (1920), *Blow Your Own Horn* (1923), *Memory Lane*, *That's My Baby* (1926), *Wilful Youth* (1927). ■

Forde, Victoria (1897–1964), actress. Began her short but active screen career in early silent films. She appeared as a leading lady and supporting player in numerous dramas, westerns, and light films, often co-starring with her husband, Tom Mix, whom she later divorced. She was the daughter of stage and screen actress Eugenie FORDE.

SELECTED FILMS: *Lottery Ticket*, *Uncle Bill*, *A Pair of Jacks*, *Settled Out of Court*, *The Everlasting Judy* (1912), *Those Persistent Old Maids*, *Cupid Pulls a Tooth*, *He Never Said a Word*, *His Strenuous Honeymoon*, *When the Girls Joined the Force*, *Sophie of the Films* (1914), *When the Spirit Moved*, *Lizzie's Dizzy Career*, *When the Mummy Cried for Help*, *The Mixup at Maxim's*, *Eddie's Awful Predicament* (1915), *An Angelic Attitude*, *A Western Masquerade* (1916), *Please Be My Wife* (1917). ■

Fortune Cookie, The (1966), UA. Dir. Billy Wilder; Sc. Billy Wilder, I.A.L. Diamond; with Jack Lemmon, Walter Matthau, Ron Rich, Cliff Osmond, Judi West.

Director Billy Wilder's comedy takes a satirical look at the small world of chiselers and vultures and their distorted view of the American Dream. When television cameraman Jack LEMMON is hurt by a football player during a game, Lemmon's brother-in-law, ambulance-chasing lawyer Walter MATTHAU, overstates the damage for insurance purposes. Attempting to convince the reluctant Lemmon, Matthau explains: "What's wrong? Insurance companies have so much money, they have to microfilm it!" While in a hospital, Lemmon opens a fortune cookie and reads the contents to Matthau: "You can fool some of the people all of the time, all of the people some of the time—." The shyster lawyer snatches the message, reads it, and concludes: "Those Chinese—what do they know!" The smell of money attracts Lemmon's ex-wife, who now snuggles up to him, pleading with him to sue. His own mother, played by Lurene Tuttle, gets into the act, sensing a windfall. But the ultimate comic villain is the squinting, lip-smacking Matthau, whose monomaniacal obsession with the case leads to his almost total disregard of his family. While he is at home on the telephone, his two children are causing a racket with their roller skates. "Why don't you kids go play on the freeway!" he shouts at them. His hilarious performance in the film won him an Academy Award.

Foster, Lewis R. (1900–1974), director, screenwriter. Worked as a gagman in the early 1920s for Hal ROACH; directed silent comedy shorts, including some with LAUREL AND HARDY (1929); and advanced to directing full-length films in the mid-1930s. He wrote the screenplay for many light films (many of which he directed), eventually winning an Oscar for his original story of Frank CAPRA'S *Mr. Smith Goes to Washington* (1939). Some of his more popular screenplays include *The Magnificent Brute* (1936), *Some Like It Hot* (1939), *The Farmer's Daughter* (1940), *The More the Merrier* (1943), and *Never Say Goodbye* (1946).

SELECTED FILMS (as director): Double Whoopie, Unaccustomed As We Are, Berth Marks, Men o' War, Bacon Grabbers, Angora Love (1929), Love Letters of a Star (1936), She's Dangerous, The Man Who Cried Wolf (1937), The Lucky Stiff, Manhandled (1949), Those Redheads From Seattle (1953), The Sign of Zorro (1960).

Foster, Norman (1900–1976), actor, director. Worked in stock and on Broadway before appearing in light comedies during the 1930s. Many were insignificant routine features, although he co-starred with some of the leading actresses of the period, including Loretta YOUNG. Eventually, he turned to directing films, ranging from comedies to adventures.

SELECTED FILMS (as actor): Gentlemen of the Press (1929), Love at First Sight (1930), It Pays to Advertise, Up Pops the Devil, Reckless Living (1931), Play Girl, Week-End Marriage, Smilin' Through, Under Eighteen (1932), State Fair, Professional Sweetheart (1933), Strictly Dynamite (1934), Fatal Lady (1936). ■

Foster, Preston (1902–1970), actor. Worked on stage as a singer and on Broadway as an actor in the late 1920s before entering films in the early 1930s. Tall and well-proportioned, he was featured in numerous action features as well as light films. He appeared in approximately 100 films during a screen career that spanned four decades.

SELECTED FILMS: Follow the Leader (1930), Hoopla (1933), We're Only Human (1935), Love Before Breakfast (1936), You Can't Beat Love, First Lady (1937), Moon Over Burma (1940), My Friend Flicka (1943), Twice Blessed (1945), The Harvey Girls (1946), Chubasco (1968). ■

Foulger, Byron (1900–1970), actor. Began his prolific screen career in the 1930s as a prissy fusspot, a role he invariably played for many years. Mean-faced and bespectacled, he often portrayed hard-hearted bureaucrats, storekeepers, and other petty types in dramas and light films. Besides supporting comedians such as the MARX BROTHERS and Danny KAYE, he was part of Preston STURGES' stock company of comic character players. He appeared in hundreds of features during a career that spanned more than four decades.

SELECTED FILMS: True Confession, The Duke Comes Back, A Day at the Races, The Awful Truth (1937), You Can't Take It With You (1938), At the Circus (1939), The Great McGinty (1940), Sullivan's Travels (1941), The Palm Beach Story (1942), What a Woman! (1943), The Miracle of Morgan's Creek (1944), Wonder Man (1945), The Show-Off (1946), Hard-Boiled Mahoney (1947), A Southern Yankee (1948), The Inspector General (1949), My Six Convicts (1952), Onionhead (1958), Who's Minding the Store? (1964), There Was a Crooked Man (1970). ■

Fowley, Douglas (1911–), actor. Prolific character player who has appeared in hundreds of films, chiefly as an uneasy hoodlum or comic villain. His long screen career, which began in 1934, has spanned five decades.

SELECTED FILMS: I Hate Women, Let's Talk It Over (1934), Two for Tonight (1935), On the Avenue (1937), Lucky Night (1939), Tanks a Million (1941), The Devil With Hitler (1942), Jitterbugs (1943), One Body Too Many, See Here, Private Hargrove (1944), Don't Fence Me In (1945), Merton of the Movies (1947), If You Knew Susie (1948), Singin' in the Rain (1952), The White Buffalo (1977). ■

Fox, Virginia, actress. Appeared as a female lead in several silent comedies during the 1920s. She co-starred with Buster KEATON in several of his early shorts.

SELECTED FILMS: Neighbors (1920), The Haunted House, Hard Luck, The Goat, The Play House (1921), Cops, The Blacksmith, The Electric House (1922), The Love Nest (1923). ■

Fox, Wallace (1895–1958), director. Worked in minstrels and vaudeville before entering films during the silent era, mainly as assistant director. He directed

his first film in 1927 and continued directing into the sound period, mainly turning out low-budget films. He directed many of the "BOWERY BOYS" comedies of the 1940s, as well as action and western films.

SELECTED FILMS: The Bandit's Son (1927), Come and Get It, Laughing at Death (1929), Racing Lady (1937), Bowery Blitzkrieg, Spooks Run Wild (1941), The Corpse Vanishes, Smart Alecks (1942), Kid Dynamite, Career Girl (1943), Men on Her Mind, Block Busters, Million Dollar Kid (1944), Mr. Muggs Rides Again (1945), Docks of New York (1948). ■

Foy, Bryan (1896–1977), director, producer. Worked in vaudeville with his famous father, Eddie Foy, as one of the Seven Little Foys. He began directing silent comedy shorts in 1918, wrote gags and screenplays for major comics, and finally directed some of the very first full-length sound features for Warner Brothers studios. He collaborated with some of the leading comics of the period, including Buster KEATON and the RITZ BROTHERS.

SELECTED FILMS: Lights of New York, The Home Towners (1928), Queen of the Night Clubs, The Royal Box (1929), The Gorilla (1931). ■

Foy, Eddie (1854–1928), comedian, actor. Famous vaudeville comic who appeared sporadically in films. He was impersonated by his son, Eddie FOY, Jr., in various FILM BIOGRAPHIES.

SELECTED FILMS: A Favorite Fool (1915). ■

Foy, Eddie, Jr. (1905–1983), actor. Worked in vaudeville with his famous father, Eddie FOY, as one of the Seven Little Foys; on Broadway in 1929; and in sound films as a supporting actor. He appeared in light features and musicals, often depicting his celebrated father.

SELECTED FILMS: Queen of the Night Clubs (1929), Leathernecking (1930),

Broadway Thru a Keyhole (1933), Turn Off the Moon (1937), The Cowboy Quarterback (1939), Lillian Russell (1940), Yankee Doodle Dandy, Moonlight Masquerade (1942), Dixie (1943), And the Angels Sing (1944), The Farmer Takes a Wife (1953), Lucky Me (1954), The Pajama Game (1957), Bells Are Ringing (1960), Gidget Goes Hawaiian (1961). ∎

Francis, Connie (1938–), actress, singer. Worked as a singer and recording star as well as an actress in light films during the 1960s. She gained popularity as a lead player in youth-oriented features. Her autobiography, *Who's Sorry Now?*, contains photographs and a discography.

SELECTED FILMS: *Where the Boys Are (1960), Follow the Boys (1963), Looking for Love (1964), Where the Boys Meet the Girls (1965).* ∎

Francis, Kay (1903–1968), actress. Worked in stock and on Broadway before making her film debut in 1929. A pretty brunette with a husky voice, she quickly became a popular star of the 1930s and 1940s. She often played urbane women in numerous romantic and light films. After having been reduced to low-budget features, she returned to the stage for several seasons and finally retired from acting in the early 1950s. She had appeared in more than 60 films during a career that spanned four decades.

SELECTED FILMS: *Gentlemen of the Press, The Cocoanuts, Dangerous Curves, The Marriage Playground (1929), Raffles, Let's Go Native (1930), Ladies' Man, Girls About Town (1931), Trouble in Paradise (1932), Wonder Bar (1934), Living on Velvet, The Goose and the Gander (1935), First Lady (1937), It's a Date (1940), Charley's Aunt (1941), Between Us Girls (1942), Four Jills in a Jeep (1944), Wife Wanted (1946).* ∎

Francis the Mule. A comedy series produced during the 1950s starring Donald O'CONNOR and a talking mule wiser than many humans. More popular with younger audiences, the moderately humorous but inane series was a box-office success, providing a total of seven entries over as many years. Arthur LUBIN directed all the films except *Francis in the Haunted House* (1956), which was made by Charles Lamont. O'Connor appeared in the first six entries and Mickey ROONEY starred in the final one. The series was used by the studio, Universal, as a showcase for its rising stars, including Piper Laurie and Julie Adams. Other popular stars who appeared from time to time included Clint Eastwood, Tony CURTIS, ZaSu PITTS, and David Janssen. The voice of Francis was that of Allan Lane.

SELECTED FILMS: *Francis (1950), Francis Goes to the Races (1951), Francis Goes to West Point (1952), Francis Covers the Big Town (1953), Francis Joins the Wacs (1954), Francis in the Navy (1955).* ∎

Franey, Billy (–1940), actor. Appeared as a comic in several silent comedy shorts during the 1920s.

Frank, Melvin (1913–), director, screenwriter, producer. Worked as writer for radio shows before turning out scripts in collaboration with Norman PANAMA for Hollywood films. Together they wrote and often directed many humorous films during the 1940s and 1950s. By the 1960s the team split up, with Frank moving to England where he continued his career as writer-director-producer. They wrote many of the better vehicles for Bob HOPE and Danny KAYE. The films below represent their work as screenwriters.

SELECTED FILMS: *Happy Go Lucky, Thank Your Lucky Stars (1943), And the Angels Sing (1944), Duffy's Tavern, Road to Utopia (1945), Monsieur Beau-*

caire, *Our Hearts Were Growing Up* (1946), *Mr. Blandings Builds His Dream House* (1948), *The Reformer and the Redhead* (1950), *Strictly Dishonorable* (1951), *Knock on Wood, White Christmas* (1954), *The Court Jester, That Certain Feeling* (1956), *Li'l Abner* (1959), *The Facts of Life* (1960), *The Road to Hong Kong* (1962), *A Funny Thing Happened on the Way to the Forum* (1966), *Buona Sera, Mrs. Campbell* (1968), *A Touch of Class* (1973), *Lost and Found* (1979). ∎

William Frawley, Arline Judge, Richard Arlen, Arthur Hunnicutt

Franklin, Sidney (1893–1972), director, producer. Began his Hollywood career in 1913 as an actor and cameraman in early silent films following an assortment of jobs. He began directing comedy shorts in 1914 and feature-length films a year later, many of which he made with his brother Chester M. Franklin. He turned out a series of respectable dramas and comedies starring some of the most famous screen personalities of the period, including, among others, Greta GARBO, Mary PICKFORD, the TALMADGE sisters, and Jennifer Jones. He worked for several major studios, among them Warner Brothers and MGM.

A talented craftsman, he directed many prestigious productions during the silent and early sound periods, handling his stars, especially actresses, with such sensitivity that he earned the appellation "woman's director." Except for one film that he made in England in 1957, he gave up directing in 1937 and focused his attentions on producing films.

SELECTED FILMS: Let Katy Do It, Martha's Vindication (1915), *The Little Schoolma'am, Gretchen the Greenhorn, Sister of Six* (1916), *Babes in the Woods* (1917), *Fan Fan, Six Shooter Andy* (1918), *Two Weeks* (1920), *The Primitive Lover, East Is West* (1922), *Her Night of Romance* (1924), *Her Sister From Paris* (1925), *The Duchess of Buffalo* (1926), *The Last of Mrs. Cheyney* (1929), *Reunion in Vienna* (1933), *The Good Earth* (1937), *The Barretts of Wimpole Street* (1957). ∎

Frawley, William (1887–1966), actor. Worked in vaudeville before entering films. Bald and short of stature, he appeared in more than 100 features, mainly as a supporting player, but occasionally as the lead. He usually portrayed coarse, cigar-chewing, but likable characters in both dramas and light films, supporting many leading personalities, including Bob HOPE, Harold LLOYD, Bing CROSBY, James CAGNEY, and Gary COOPER. He was best known for his portrayal of Fred Mertz in the "I Love Lucy" television show.

In *The Bride Came C.O.D.* he played a gruff sheriff trying to get information from ghost-town hermit Harry DAVENPORT. "I ain't been out of this town in 40 years," the old recluse confesses. "I ain't never seen a movie." "Never seen a movie!" Frawley repeats in disbelief. "Well, it sounds un-American to me!"

SELECTED FILMS: Surrender (1931), *Moonlight and Pretzels* (1933), *The Lemon Drop Kid* (1934), *Hold 'Em, Yale!* (1935), *Strike Me Pink, Desire, The Princess Comes Across* (1936), *High, Wide and Handsome, Something to Sing About* (1937), *Professor Beware, Sons of the Legion* (1938), *Rose of Washington Square, Stop, Look and Love* (1939), *The Bride Came C.O.D.* (1941), *Going My Way* (1944), *Monsieur Verdoux, Mother Wore Tights* (1947), *Good Sam* (1949), *Pretty Baby* (1950), *The Lemon Drop Kid, Rhubarb* (1951), *Safe at Home!* (1962). ∎

Frazee, E.A., director. Directed early silent comedy shorts for Mack SENNETT'S KEYSTONE studios. Sometimes he worked in collaboration with others directing such silent comics as Polly MORAN and Fred MACE. He directed the famous vaudeville comedian Eddie FOY and the Seven Little Foys in one of their rare film appearances.

SELECTED FILMS: A Favorite Fool, Crooked to the End (1915). ■

Frazee, Jane (1918–), actress. Sang and danced professionally as a child in vaudeville and on radio before entering films. She appeared in numerous light films throughout the 1940s, chiefly low-budget features. She retired from her short screen career in the early 1950s.

SELECTED FILMS: Melody and Moonlight (1940), Buck Privates, Moonlight in Hawaii, Hellzapoppin (1941), What's Cookin', Almost Married, Get Hep to Love (1942), Hi 'Ya Chum (1943), Kansas City Kitty (1944), The Big Bonanza, Practically Yours (1945), Calendar Girl (1947), Rhythm Inn (1951). ■

Frederick, Pauline (1883–1938), actress. On stage as a chorus girl at age 19 and within a few years emerged as a Broadway star. She made her screen debut in 1915, appearing in dramas and comedies. She played leads and later supporting roles into the sound period.

SELECTED FILMS: The Eternal City (1915), Mistress of Shenstone, Salvage (1921), Three Women, Married Flirts (1924), Her Honor the Governor (1926), This Modern Age (1931), Social Register (1934), Thank You, Mr. Moto (1937). ■

Freeland, Thornton (1898–), director. Appeared as stage actor before entering the film world via Vitagraph as cameraman, cutter, and director. He directed light films as well as musicals and melodramas, working with many of the leading performers of the period, including Eddie CANTOR, Humphrey BOGART,

Ginger ROGERS, and Fred ASTAIRE. He settled in England for a time where he continued to direct films.

SELECTED FILMS: Three Live Ghosts (1929), Be Yourself, Whoopee! (1930), Six Cylinder Love (1931), Week-end Marriage, The Unexpected Father, Love Affair (1932), Flying Down to Rio (1933), George White's Scandals (1934), Marry the Boss's Daughter, Too Many Blondes (1941). ■

Freeman, Devery (1913–), screenwriter. Wrote many light screenplays, alone and in collaboration, for such leading personalities of the period as Red SKELTON, Jane Powell, ABBOTT AND COSTELLO, Lucille BALL, Ginger ROGERS, and Donald O'CONNOR. His brother, Everett FREEMAN, was also a screenwriter.

SELECTED FILMS: The Thrill of Brazil (1946), The Fuller Brush Man (1948), Miss Grant Takes Richmond (1949), Watch the Birdie, The Yellow Cab Man (1950), Dear Brat (1951), Three Sailors and a Girl (1953), Francis Joins the Wacs (1954), Ain't Misbehavin' (1955), Dance With Me Henry, The First Traveling Saleslady (1956), The Girl Most Likely (1957). ■

Freeman, Everett (1911–), screenwriter. Worked as a short story writer and radio producer before turning his skills to films in the 1930s. He wrote screenplays, alone or in collaboration, for many light films, including those which starred such popular comedians as W. C. FIELDS, Jack BENNY, Bob HOPE, and Danny KAYE. He is the brother of Devery FREEMAN.

SELECTED FILMS: Married Before Breakfast (1937), The Chaser (1938), You Can't Cheat an Honest Man (1939), George Washington Slept Here, Larceny, Inc. (1942), The Princess and the Pirate (1944), It Happened on Fifth Avenue, The Secret Life of Walter Mitty (1947), Lulu Belle (1948), The Lady Takes a Sailor (1949), Pretty Baby (1950), Million Dollar Mermaid (1952), My Man

Godfrey (1957), The Maltese Bippy (1969), How Do I Love Thee (1970). ■

Freeman, Howard (1899–1967), actor. Worked on stage before entering films in 1943. A rotund character actor, he frequently portrayed cranky businessmen or outspoken fathers. He appeared with some of the leading comedians of the period, including, among others, LAUREL AND HARDY, Red SKELTON, and Bob HOPE.

SELECTED FILMS: Margin for Error, Slightly Dangerous, Air Raid Wardens, Girl Crazy (1943), Whistling in Brooklyn, Once Upon a Time (1944), Monsieur Beaucaire (1946), The Perfect Marriage, My Brother Talks to Horses (1947), If You Knew Susie, Up in Central Park, The Time of Your Life (1948), Double Dynamite (1951), Dear Brigitte (1965). ■

Freeman, Kathleen (1919–), actress. Began her film career in the 1940s. She has appeared as a comic character player in melodramas and light films.

SELECTED FILMS: The Naked City (1947), Bonzo Goes to College (1952), The Ladies' Man (1961), The Disorderly Orderly (1965), Three on a Couch (1966), Support Your Local Gunfighter (1971), Stand Up and Be Counted (1972). ■

Freeman, Mona (1926–), actress. Worked as a model while still in her teens before making her screen debut in the early 1940s. Appearing chiefly in light films, she attained a certain degree of success as a spunky teenager or ingenue in her early features but was less effective in adult roles. She decided to abandon the big screen in the late 1950s after having been relegated to unrewarding roles in low-budget films. She continued her acting career, however, in television.

SELECTED FILMS: National Velvet, Our Hearts Were Young and Gay, Here Come the Waves (1944), Junior Miss (1945), That Brennan Girl (1946), Dear Ruth, Mother Wore Tights (1947), Isn't It Romantic? (1948), Dear Wife (1950), Dear Brat, Darling, How Could You! (1951), Jumping Jacks (1952), The World Was His Jury (1958). ■

Freshman, The (1925), PAT. Dir. Sam Taylor, Fred Newmeyer; Sc. Sam Taylor, John Grey, Ted Wilde, Tim Whelan, Clyde Bruckman; with Harold Lloyd, Jobyna Ralston, Brooks Benedict, James Anderson.

Life on the college campus was a popular subject in the United States during the 1920s and the target of Harold Lloyd's successful satirical comedy. A work of many collaborators, some credited, others uncredited, it centers on collegiate Harold "Speedy" Lamb, who tries practically anything to gain popularity, including acting as a live tackle dummy for the school football team. He is oblivious to the fact that everyone is laughing at him. But he eventually proves his worth by helping to win the big football game. Several comic highlights help to make this a memorable film, including the football game at the finale and the college dance. At the latter affair Lloyd, attired in a tuxedo that is only temporarily stitched together, must continually dance by a curtain behind which his tailor tries to finish his work. During the evening festivities, the inevitable occurs. The stitches start to fall apart and the garment starts to separate. Lloyd had effectively used a suit of clothes for the purpose of comedy embarrassment in an earlier comedy, *Grandma's Boy* (1922). *The Freshman* grossed millions, helping to account for Lloyd's accumulation of 15 million dollars by the time the silent era drew to a close.

Fries, Otto (1887–1938), actor. Appeared as a supporting player in silent comedy shorts during the late 1920s and sound films during the 1930s. A rather heavy-set comic performer, he worked with some of the leading comics and comedy teams of the period, including LAUREL AND HARDY, the MARX BROTHERS, and film shorts starring Thelma TODD.

In one of his rare starring roles, he played the lead in "Car Shy," a late silent short produced by Al CHRISTIE. This almost entirely forgotten but clever and original comedy depicts various ways that car thieves operate. In one particularly hilarious scene, the car owner perches himself with a shotgun atop his vehicle while his wife shops at a local store. When she returns, her spouse is still sitting on a platform, gun in hand, but the vehicle, to his surprise, has disappeared from under him.

SELECTED FILMS: The Second Hundred Years, Call of the Cuckoos, Hotel Imperial (1927), Riley, the Cop, Leave 'Em Laughing, From Soup to Nuts (1928), Pardon Us, On the Loose, Monkey Business (1931), The Old Bull (1932), Pick a Star (1937), Every Day's a Holiday (1937), Expensive Husbands (1938). ∎

Frisco, Joe (1890–1958), comedian, actor. In vaudeville before World War I with various partners doing a comedy-dance routine, on Broadway in the 1920s as a solo comic, and in silent and early sound films sporadically. Wearing a derby and chewing on a cigar, he amused his audiences with his famous stuttering delivery. He was a popular comic for four decades, beloved by his fellow entertainers who honored him with a plaque that read: "America's Greatest Wit."

SELECTED FILMS: The Gorilla (1930). ∎

Front, The. See Woody Allen.

Front Page, The (1931), UA. *Dir.* Lewis Milestone; *Sc.* Bartlett Cormack; with Adolphe Menjou, Pat O'Brien, Mary Brian, Edward Everett Horton.

Ben HECHT and Charles MacARTHUR'S hit Broadway comedy about cynical and hard-nosed Chicago report-

ers and editors was filmed three times. In this first version Adolphe MENJOU plays the conniving editor trying to hold on to his best reporter. This was a change of pace for Menjou, who had previously played dapper, urbane men-about-town. Pat O'BRIEN, in his film debut, portrays the distrustful reporter who hides an escaped murderer. Director Milestone, fresh from his award-winning antiwar drama, *All Quiet on the Western Front*, keeps the camera fluid and the plot moving in this dialogue-heavy drama. The 1940 remake, directed by Howard HAWKS and retitled *His Girl Friday*, switched the sex of the reporter. Rosalind RUSSELL played O'Brien's role while Cary GRANT enacted the scheming editor. The original film caused a rash of newsroom dramas, chiefly produced by Warner Brothers. The third and weakest version of the play was directed by Billy WILDER and released in 1974. Jack LEMMON starred as the reporter and Walter MATTHAU portrayed the editor.

Funicello, Annette (1942–), actress. Began her screen career in the 1950s as a lead or second lead in lightweight Walt Disney productions. An attractive and personable young performer, she moved up to starring roles in a series of "beach" films aimed at youthful audiences.

SELECTED FILMS: The Shaggy Dog (1959), Babes in Toyland (1961), Beach Party (1963), The Misadventures of Merlin Jones, Pajama Party, Bikini Beach (1964), How to Stuff a Wild Bikini, The Monkey's Uncle (1965), Fireball 500 (1966). ∎

Funny Thing Happened on the Way to the Forum, A (1966), UA. *Dir.* Richard Lester; *Sc.* Melvin Frank, Michael Pertwee; with Zero Mostel, Phil Silvers, Buster Keaton, Jack Gilford.

An imperfect farce based on the stock characters of Roman comedy, the film displays the exceptional talents of three lovable clowns. And it's a delight to watch Zero MOSTEL, Phil SILVERS, and Buster KEATON in action in this broad burlesque set in ancient Rome. Mostel portrays a conniving Roman slave plotting his freedom. There is plenty of old-fashioned fun in the mistaken-identity plot contrivances and the Sennett-like chases. At a slave market prospective buyer Mostel examines luscious twin slaves. "I don't suppose you'd break up a set," he impishly inquires. Puns and anachronisms flow like old wine. Mostel examines a jug of wine and, with an air of a connoisseur, inquires: "Was 1 a good year?" A Roman prepares to ignite a bier on which allegedly lies a dead virgin. "Wait!" Mostel cries. "The gods will be angry if you send up a smoked virgin." He chides an innocent, impetuous young Roman for falling in love with a courtesan. "Is that shameful?" the youth asks. "It's hardly an achievement," Mostel replies. Phil Silvers, the owner of a house of pleasure, says to his women: "I'll be back to lead you in noon-day prayers." Stephen Sondheim's music adds to the festivities. The madcap film is based on the Broadway musical.

Furthman, Jules (1888–1960), screenwriter. Began his Hollywood writing career, which was to span five decades, in 1915 furnishing stories for silent films following work on newspapers and periodicals. By 1918 he was writing screenplays for dramas, adventures, and comedies. Considered by several film critics and historians as a major screenwriter, he has turned out alone or in collaboration some of the most entertaining films to come out of the film capital. His most popular works have been dramas, including *Morocco* (1930), *Mutiny on the Bounty* (1935), *To Have and Have Not* (1944), and *The Big Sleep* (1946). Unfortunately, many of his silent films have been lost. His brother, Charles, also wrote screenplays.

SELECTED FILMS: *The Camouflage Kiss, More Trouble, Hobbs in a Hurry (1918), Some Liar, This Hero Stuff (1919), Leave It to Me (1920), The Blushing Bride (1921), The Ragged Heiress (1922), Try and Get It (1924), You'd Be Surprised (1926), Casey at the Bat (1927), Abie's Irish Rose (1929), Merely Mary Ann (1931), Bombshell (1933), Pretty Baby (1950), Rio Bravo (1959).* ■

G

Gable, Clark (1901–1960), actor. Worked at odd jobs before appearing on stage where he was eventually spotted by Hollywood talent scouts. At first rejected by producer Darryl F. Zanuck ("his ears are too big"), MGM finally put him under contract. In 1931 alone he played supporting roles in a dozen features. A handsome, masculine figure who exuded earthy warmth, he soon rose to stardom in the early 1930s, winning an Academy Award as Best Actor for his role as the swaggering newspaperman in *It Happened One Night.* Dubbed "The King" in the 1930s by his admiring audiences and fellow actors alike, he turned up on the Box Office Top Ten list of screen favorites from 1932 to 1943, 1947 to 1949, and in 1955. Although overage, he enlisted in the Armed Forces during the Second World War. Following the conflict, he returned to Hollywood in triumph. He starred in dramas and light films for more than 25 years.

SELECTED FILMS: *The Painted Desert, Laughing Sinners* (1931), *Polly of the Circus, Red Dust, No Man of Her Own* (1932), *Hold Your Man, Dancing Lady* (1933), *It Happened One Night* (1934), *Wife vs. Secretary, Cain and Mabel, Love on the Run* (1936), *Saratoga* (1937), *Idiot's Delight* (1939), *Any Number Can Play* (1949), *To Please a Lady* (1950), *Teacher's Pet* (1958), *But Not for Me* (1959), *It Started in Naples* (1960), *The Misfits* (1961). ■

Gabor, Zsa Zsa (1920–), actress. Appeared on stage in Vienna in the mid-1930s before immigrating to the United States from her native Hungary. More of a show business personality than a serious performer, she has decorated a handful of films, stage plays, and television shows with her glamour. She has been married several times, including once to actor George SANDERS. Her sister, Eva, has also appeared in several films. Her autobiography is titled *Zsa Zsa Gabor: My Story* (1960).

SELECTED FILMS: *Lovely to Look At* (1952), *Lili* (1953), *Three Ring Circus* (1954), *The Girl in the Kremlin* (1957), *Pepe* (1960), *Boys' Night Out* (1962), *Arrivederci, Baby* (1966), *Every Girl Should Have One* (1978). ■

Gagman. A term used mainly during the silent era depicting the role of an idea man or a writer who developed or originated a comedy routine, situation, or piece of business either on location or in advance. Some of our major directors, screenwriters, and comics, including, among others, Clyde BRUCKMAN, Frank CAPRA, Leo McCAREY, Roy DEL RUTH, George STEVENS, Mervyn LeRoy, George MARSHALL, Raymond GRIFFITH, and Tay GARNETT, began their film careers as gagmen working for Mack SENNETT, Hal ROACH, or other comedy producers.

Gallagher, Richard "Skeets" (1891–1955), actor. Worked in vaudeville as a song-and-dance man before entering films in the early 1920s. He was a supporting player as well as occasional lead actor in dozens of light films, both silent and sound. He also appeared in many shorts.

SELECTED FILMS: The Daring Years (1923), The Potters, For the Love of Mike (1927), Alex the Great, Stocks and Blondes (1928), Pointed Heels (1929), Honey, Love Among the Millionaires, Let's Go Native, Her Wedding Night (1930), It Pays to Advertise (1931), The Night Club Lady (1932), Easy Millions, Too Much Harmony, Alice in Wonderland (1933), The Meanest Gal in Town (1934), Yours for the Asking (1936), Idiot's Delight (1939), Three for Bedroom C (1952). ■

Gallagher and Shean. A famous vaudeville comedy team that dates back to the early 1900s. The duo starred in a few early sound shorts. Their comedy songs and routines usually included their memorable: "Absolutely, Mr. Gallagher?" "Positively, Mr. Shean." Although their act and their famous song became legends in show business, they actually worked together as partners very little—1910–1912 and 1922–1926. They appeared in Broadway shows and at the famous Palace Theater during the 1920s. When Gallagher died, Al Shean (1868–1949) appeared as a character actor in several films.

SELECTED FILMS (Shean alone): Music in the Air (1934), Traveling Saleslady (1935), 52nd Street, Live, Love and Learn (1937), The Great Waltz (1938), Broadway Serenade (1939), The Blue Bird (1940), Ziegfeld Girl (1941), Tish (1942), Atlantic City (1944). ■

Gambino, Papa. Fictional head of a family in a series of action films. Veteran comic character actor Henry ARMETTA played the humorous, wildly gesticulating, and explosive Papa in such second features as Speed to Burn (1938), Road Demon (1938), and Winner Take All (1939), all produced by 20th Century-Fox.

Garbo, Greta (1905–), actress. Appeared in films in her native Sweden and in Germany before accompanying her director, Mauritz Stiller, to America. Stiller, who had been signed by Louis B. Mayer, convinced the movie mogul to place his actress under contract as well. Chiefly a dramatic star in such films as The Temptress, Flesh and the Devil (both 1927), and Love (1928), she portrayed characters whose unconventional love lives resulted in tragedy. She did not attempt comedy until well into the sound era, when she made the now classic Ninotchka (1939), starring Melvyn DOUGLAS. Her second light film, Two-Faced Woman (1941), was a box-office failure and she retired from the screen.

Her real-life shyness and capacity to avoid incursions into her private life led to her reputation as a woman of mystery, a distinction her studio did not discourage. She was known for her sensuality and beauty, which became even more evident in screen close-ups. These two qualities have made her films as popular today as they were when they were first released.

SELECTED FILMS: The Torrent (1926), Ninotchka (1939), Two-Faced Woman (1941). ■

Gardenia, Vincent (1922–), actor. Worked in the theater and in television before making his debut in films in 1958. A short, stocky character player, he has appeared in both dramas and light films, often as a gruff but amicable character. He was nominated for an Academy Award for his role in Bang the Drum Slowly (1973).

SELECTED FILMS: Cop Hater (1958), Jenny, Where's Poppa? (1970), Cold Turkey, Little Murders (1971), Hickey and Boggs (1972), The Front Page (1974), The Manchu Eagle Murder Caper Mystery (1975), Fire Sale, Greased Lightning (1977), Heaven Can Wait (1978), Home Movies (1979), The Last Flight of Noah's Ark (1980), Movers and Shakers (1985), Little Shop of Horrors (1986). ■

Gardiner, Reginald (1903–1980), actor. Worked in his native England as an actor and entertainer on stage, in revues, and in films before making his Hollywood debut in 1936. He appeared as a supporting player in dozens of films, often as a polished and pretentious snob. He worked with some of the leading comics of the period, including George BURNS and Gracie ALLEN, LAUREL AND HARDY, and Jack BENNY.

SELECTED FILMS: Born to Dance (1936), A Damsel in Distress (1937), Sweethearts (1938), The Flying Deuces (1939), The Great Dictator (1940), The Man Who Came to Dinner (1942), The Horn Blows at Midnight, Molly and Me, The Dolly Sisters (1945), Cluny Brown (1946), That Lady in Ermine (1948), The Birds and the Bees (1956), Mr. Hobbs Takes a Vacation (1962), What a Way to Go! (1964), Do Not Disturb, Sergeant Deadhead (1965). ■

Garfield, Allen (1939–), actor. A former boxer and journalist who began his screen career in the late 1960s, originally billed as Allen Goorwitz. A stocky character player with a moon-shaped face, he has often played sleazy types. In the second half of his film career, however, he advanced to executive-type roles in which the characters exhibit a degree of uneasiness. He has appeared in dramas and light films.

SELECTED FILMS: Greetings (1968), Putney Swope (1969), The Owl and the Pussycat (1970), Bananas (1971), Get to Know Your Rabbit (1972), Busting (1973), The Front Page (1974), Nashville (1975), The Brink's Job (1978), Continental Divide (1981), Teachers, Irreconcilable Differences (1984), Desert Bloom (1985). ■

Gargan, Ed (1902–1964), actor. Tall character player with a puzzled expression who appeared in more than 150 films, chiefly light comedies. He often portrayed dim-witted but sympathetic cops, as well as other Runyonesque urban types. He played Bates, the Falcon's sidekick and man-servant, in a few of the en-tries of the popular detective-comedy series. As a supporting and character actor, he worked with some of the leading screen personalities of the period, including, among others, William POWELL, Claudette COLBERT, John BARRYMORE, and Carole LOMBARD. In Hands Across the Table (1935) he says to vivacious Carole Lombard: "You'll sperl your dinner if you keep on eatin' them nuts."

SELECTED FILMS: The Girl in 419 (1933), Twentieth Century, The Lemon Drop Kid (1934), The Bride Comes Home, Here Comes Cookie (1935), Anything Goes, My Man Godfrey (1936), A Girl With Ideas (1937), The Rage of Paris (1938), Pack Up Your Troubles (1939), Tugboat Annie Sails Again (1940), Tight Shoes (1941), Lady in a Jam (1942), Hit the Ice (1943), The Thin Man Goes Home (1944), Life With Blondie (1945), Little Giant (1946), Little Miss Broadway (1947), The Dude Goes West (1948), Love Happy (1949), Triple Trouble (1950), Abbott and Costello Meet the Invisible Man (1951). ■

Garland, Judy (1922–1969), singer, actress. Began her show-business career as a child-singer with her sisters in vaudeville. MGM placed her under contract at age 13, but was slow to exploit her talents. By 1938 she started to get better roles and the following year she reached stardom in The Wizard of Oz. She made a succession of hit musical comedies for MGM, some of which were directed by her second husband, Vincente MINNELLI.

Stardom and the rigors of the Hollywood star system soon took their toll on the young Garland, who relied on pills for her weight problem and her nerves. Faced with many personal problems and ill-equipped to handle them, she became an undependable performer and had to be replaced by others several times. She began to give successful stage concerts on both sides of the Atlantic, remaining in the theater for several years. She appeared sporadically in films, but never regained her former popularity. An overdose of sleeping pills ended her life. Her daughter, Liza MINNELLI, has inherited many of her mother's show-business talents. *Judy* (1986), a biography by T.J. Watson and B. Chapman, contains numerous photographs.

SELECTED FILMS: *Pigskin Parade (1936), Broadway Melody of 1938, Thoroughbreds Don't Cry (1937), Love Finds Andy Hardy, Listen Darling (1938), Babes in Arms (1939), Andy Hardy Meets a Debutante, Little Nellie Kelly (1940), Life Begins for Andy Hardy (1941), Babes on Broadway (1942), Presenting Lily Mars, Girl Crazy (1943), Meet Me in St. Louis (1944), The Harvey Girls (1946), The Pirate, Easter Parade (1948), In the Good Old Summertime (1949), Summer Stock (1950), I Could Go On Singing (1963).* ∎

Garner, James (1928–), actor. Worked in television before his film debut. His popularity as a TV performer, combined with his charm and his good looks, brought him almost instant fame in films. Although he has starred in dramas as well as in light films, it is the latter in which he has been the more successful.

In *The Pink Jungle* (1968), for example, he portrays a C.I.A. agent working in a remote area of South America. When his assignment is completed and he has won the heart of voluptuous Eva Renzi, he radios back to his chief that he will be staying on for a week. "No, it's not official," he says slyly, with Eva on his mind. "But you may call it undercover activity."

SELECTED FILMS: *Toward the Unknown, The Girl He Left Behind (1956), Sayonara (1957), Boys' Night Out (1962), The Thrill of It All, The Wheeler Dealers, Move Over Darling (1963), The Americanization of Emily (1964), The Art of Love (1965), A Man Could Get Killed, Mister Buddwing, Grand Prix (1966), How Sweet It Is (1968), Support Your Local Sheriff (1969), Support Your Local Gunfighter, Skin Game (1971), The Castaway Cowboy (1974), Health (1979), Victor/Victoria (1982), Tank (1983).* ∎

Garner, Peggy Ann (1931–1984), actress. Worked as a child in summer stock and as a model before becoming a Hollywood child star in the 1940s, appearing in dramas and comedies. After a bright start, her screen career declined by the 1950s although she appeared in several Broadway plays and in television. She later worked as a real estate broker and automobile sales manager. In 1945 she received an Oscar as the "outstanding child performer" of that year.

SELECTED FILMS: *Little Miss Thoroughbred (1938), In Name Only (1939), The Pied Piper (1942), Junior Miss (1945), Home Sweet Homicide (1946), A Wedding (1978).* ∎

Garnett, Tay (1894–1977), director, screenwriter. Began his film career in silent films as a GAGMAN and screenwriter for Mack SENNETT and Hal ROACH. He began directing in the late 1920s, turning out films for different studios. The quality of his work varied from above average to mediocre, while the subject matter ranged from drama to adventure to light films. His comedies were notable for their rowdiness as well as for their use of a fluid camera. He wrote the screenplays for many of the films he directed.

SELECTED FILMS: *Celebrity (1928), The Flying Fool, Oh Yeah! (1929), Officer O'Brien, Her Man (1930), Okay America (1932), She Couldn't Take It (1935), Professional Soldier (1936), Love Is News, Stand-In (1937), Joy of Living (1938), Eternally Yours, Slightly Honorable, Seven Sinners (1940), Cheers for Miss Bishop (1941), My Favorite Spy (1942), A Connecticut Yankee in King Arthur's Court (1949), Soldiers Three (1951), Main Street to Broadway (1953), Timber Tramp (1973).* ∎

Garr, Teri (1949–), actress. A ballet dancer at age 13, in television, and in films since the late 1960s. She has appeared in dramas and light films as a supporting player and female lead.

In *Young Frankenstein* Gene WILDER, standing in front of his father's castle and carrying buxom Teri Garr, says of the two huge appurtenances hanging from the door: "What a pair of knockers!" "Thank you," she says.

SELECTED FILMS: *Head* (1968), *Young Frankenstein* (1974), *Won Ton Ton, the Dog Who Saved Hollywood* (1976), *Oh, God!* (1977), *Tootsie* (1982), *The Sting II, Mr. Mom* (1983). ■

Garrett, Betty (1919–), actress, entertainer. Worked as an actress and dancer on stage and as a nightclub singer before she made her film debut in 1948. Her success as a scintillating and buoyant musical comedy performer was short-lived when the studios hesitated to hire her after her husband, Larry Parks, confessed to his past ties to the Communist party. She made a slight comeback in the 1950s.

SELECTED FILMS: *Big City, Words and Music* (1948), *Take Me Out to the Ball Game, Neptune's Daughter, On the Town* (1949), *My Sister Eileen* (1955), *The Shadow on the Window* (1957). ■

Garvin, Anita, actress. A member of the Hal ROACH stock company of screen comics during the 1920s and 1930s. She was a gifted comedienne whose expert sense of timing and flexible face enlivened many comedy shorts. She often co-starred with LAUREL AND HARDY, Edgar KENNEDY, and other comedians, mainly in comedy shorts. She appeared in two comedy classics, "The Battle of the Century" with Laurel and Hardy and "A Pair of Tights" with Edgar Kennedy and Stuart ERWIN. One of her best and most hilarious roles was in "From Soup to Nuts," a LAUREL AND HARDY short. A social climber desperately seeking to elevate her standing in society, she hires Stan and Ollie as servants for her dinner party—with the predictable chaotic results.

SELECTED FILMS: *Sailors Beware, The Battle of the Century, Bertha, the Sewing Machine Girl* (1927), *The Play Girl, From Soup to Nuts, A Pair of Tights, Their Purple Moment* (1928), *All Steamed Up* (1929), *So Big, Blotto* (1930), *The Millionaire Cat, Hollywood Handicap* (1932), *Swiss Miss, A Chump at Oxford* (1938), *Cookoo Cavaliers* (1940). ■

Gateson, Marjorie (1891–1977), actress. Appeared in vaudeville and on Broadway before making her debut in Hollywood films in 1931. As a character actress in more than 75 films, she often portrayed rich society wives and mothers. She supported such screen personalities as Mae WEST, Red SKELTON, Jean HARLOW, Fred ASTAIRE, and Dean MARTIN and Jerry LEWIS.

SELECTED FILMS: *The Beloved Bachelor* (1931), *Society Girl* (1932), *The King's Vacation, Employees' Entrance, Cocktail Hour, Melody Cruise* (1933), *Hi, Nellie!* (1934), *Goin' to Town* (1935), *Turn Off the Moon, First Lady* (1937), *Spring Madness, The Duke of West Point* (1938), *Too Busy to Work* (1939), *You'll Never Get Rich* (1941), *Rings on Her Fingers* (1942), *I Dood It, No Time for Love* (1943), *Seven Days Ashore* (1944), *One More Tomorrow* (1946), *The Caddy* (1953). ■

Gaxton, William (1893–1963), actor. Worked on stage before entering films in the 1930s. He appeared occasionally in light features, but never attained the popularity he had won while on the stage.

SELECTED FILMS: *It's the Old Army Game* (1926), *Fifty Million Frenchmen* (1931), *Their Big Moment* (1934), *Something to Shout About* (1942), *Best Foot Forward, The Heat's On* (1943), *Tropicana* (1944), *Diamond Horseshoe* (1945). ■

Gaye, Gregory (1900–), actor. Began his career on the screen in the late 1920s. He appeared as a character player in numerous dramas and light films, chiefly during the 1930s and '40s. He worked in several films with Will ROGERS.

SELECTED FILMS: They Had to See Paris (1929), High Society Blues, What a Widow (1930), Once in a Lifetime (1932), Affairs of a Gentleman, Handy Andy (1934), That Girl From Paris, Tovarich (1937), Love, Honor and Behave (1938), Ninotchka (1939), Down Argentine Way (1940), The Bachelor and the Bobby Soxer (1947), Bailout at 43,000 (1957). ∎

Gaynor, Janet (1906–1984), actress. Worked at odd jobs before beginning her Hollywood career as an extra in silent films. She quickly rose to stardom in both silent and sound films. Displaying innocence and charm, she starred in dramas and light films through the 1930s, often with her co-star Charles FARRELL. She appeared on the Box Office Top Ten list of screen personalities from 1932 to 1934. It was in her latter films that she revealed a carefree and joyous approach to her roles. She won the first Academy Award for Best Actress for her performances in Sunrise and Seventh Heaven (1927) and was nominated for an Oscar for her performance in A Star Is Born (1937). She retired from her screen career in 1939 but returned to appear in one more film after a 20-year absence.

SELECTED FILMS: The Johnstown Flood, The Shamrock Handicap, The Midnight Kiss (1926), Two Girls Wanted (1927), Lucky Star, Sunny Side Up (1929), Happy Days, High Society Blues (1930), Daddy Long Legs, Merely Mary Ann, Delicious (1931), State Fair, Adorable, Paddy, the Next Best Thing (1933), Carolina, Change of Heart, Servants' Entrance (1934), The Farmer Takes a Wife (1935), Small Town Girl, Ladies in Love (1936), Three Loves Has Nancy, The Young in Heart (1938), Bernardine (1957). ∎

Gaynor, Mitzi (1930–), actress. Appeared in ballet as a child before entering films in 1950. A lively and captivating performer, she enhanced several light films during the 1950s and 1960s. Disappointed with the direction of her screen career, she returned to the stage and appeared in television.

In Les Girls she played a chorine who comments on the love-life of her dancing partner, Gene Kelly: "Barry fell in love with himself the first time he looked in the mirror and he's been faithful ever since."

SELECTED FILMS: My Blue Heaven (1950), Take Care of My Little Girl, Golden Girl (1951), We're Not Married, Bloodhounds of Broadway (1952), The I Don't Care Girl (1953), Anything Goes, The Birds and the Bees (1956), The Joker Is Wild, Les Girls (1957), South Pacific (1958), Happy Anniversary (1959), Surprise Package (1960), For Love or Money (1963). ∎

Gear, Luella (1900–1980), actress. Appeared on the stage and on Broadway before making her screen debut in silent films. As a comedienne, she enlivened many films, including talkies, with her vivacious wit. She worked with many major stars for more than four decades, including Ginger ROGERS, Fred ASTAIRE, Judy HOLLIDAY, and Jack LEMMON.

SELECTED FILMS: Adam and Eva (1923), The Confidence Man (1924), Carefree (1938), The Perfect Marriage (1947), Jigsaw (1949), Phffft! (1954). ∎

General, The (1927), UA. Dir. Buster Keaton, Clyde Bruckman; Sc. Clyde Bruckman; with Buster Keaton, Marion Mack, Glen Cavender, Jim Farley.

Buster Keaton's famous Civil War comedy has a train, The General, as his co-hero. The plot is based on an actual incident that occurred during the Civil War in which Union soldiers, dressed as civilians, stole the General, a locomotive. In Keaton's version, he plays Johnny Gray, railroad man, who tries to impress his girl by enlisting in the army. But they reject him. However, when he learns that his train has been stolen, he springs into action. Our Southern hero saves his sweetheart, rescues the train, and helps to capture the spies. The film has been noted for the superb timing of its sight gags, especially the scene involving the loaded cannon aimed at Keaton and the one in which he has to remove railroad ties scattered on the tracks before him. In the former scene the ignited cannon, originally aimed high and situated on a railway car in front of him, begins to drop because of the movement of the train until the mouth of the weapon stares him in the face. But the train turns in time and the cannonball barely misses him. The railroad ties strewn across the tracks before his moving train comprise another obstacle. He removes all but the last one, which he dislodges by dropping another he is holding on the edge of the first. Both ties fall harmlessly out of the way. The marvel of the scene is in the split-second timing by Keaton. The comedy has also been singled out for its pace and pictorial beauty. Considered by many to be Keaton's best work, the film contains the longest chase sequence in the history of film comedy.

George, Gladys (1900–1954), actress. Had extensive show business experience, including vaudeville, stock, and Broadway, before settling in Hollywood as female lead and, later, character actress. A handsome actress who evoked an impression of worldliness, she appeared in both dramas and light films during a career stretching across four decades, but she reached her peak during the 1930s and 1940s.

SELECTED FILMS: *Red Hot Dollars* (1919), *Home Spun Folks* (1920), *Chickens* (1921), *Love Is a Headache* (1938), *I'm From Missouri* (1939), *Hit the Road* (1941), *Nobody's Darling*, *The Crystal Ball* (1943), *Christmas Holiday*, *Minstrel Man* (1944), *Steppin' in Society* (1945), *Millie's Daughter* (1947), *Alias a Gentleman* (1948), *Lullaby of Broadway* (1951), *It Happens Every Thursday* (1953). ■

Geray, Steven (1899–1973), actor. Worked on the stage in Hungary and in films in England before moving to Hollywood in 1940. A short figure with a receding hairline, he quickly became a familiar character player to American audiences. He often appeared in mousy roles in dramas and light films although he was just as apt to pop up as a sympathetic type. He worked with some of the leading comics of the period, including, among others, Red SKELTON, Bob HOPE, Danny KAYE, and Dean MARTIN and Jerry LEWIS.

SELECTED FILMS: *The Wife Takes a Flyer* (1942), *Henry Aldrich Swings It*, *Whistling in Brooklyn* (1943), *Meet the People*, *In Society* (1944), *Blondie Knows Best* (1946), *Once More, My Darling* (1949), *My Favorite Spy* (1951), *Call Me Madam*, *Gentlemen Prefer Blondes* (1953), *Knock on Wood* (1954), *Artists and Models* (1955), *Count Your Blessings* (1959), *The Swinger* (1966). ■

Ghost comedies. The use of apparitions as a popular comic device in films emerged almost simultaneously with the birth of movies. During the first decade of this century Georges Meliès, a French magician, experimented with trick photography and double exposures, turning out dozens of short fantasies and films involving spirits. American filmmakers within a few years began to incorporate his techniques into their own, more conventional films. The ghost comedy differs from fantasy in that the former relies more on slapstick and low humor. Its conventions include the obligatory spooky house, one or more suspicious-looking servants, trap doors, secret rooms, a hero or heroine about to come into an inheritance and whose life is therefore in danger, and a fair number of scary incidents.

The first attempts in the genre came from Mack SENNETT'S KEYSTONE studios. A half-reel comedy titled "Brown's Seance" (1912) starred comedienne Mabel NORMAND. In 1914 Cecil B. De MILLE directed *The Ghost Breaker*, a comedy drama which was remade in 1922, 1940, 1945, and again in 1953. Comic Fred MACE made "The Village Vampire" (1916), and Mack SWAIN and Polly MORAN appeared in "Vampire Ambrose" (1916), both Keystone releases. Selig studios the same year released the comedy short "Spooks." *The Ghost House*, an early ghost comedy of 1917, starred Jack Pickford and Louise Huff, while *The Ghost of Old Morro* appeared the same year. The following year offered *The Ghost of Rosy Taylor* with Mary Miles MINTER and *The Ghost of the Rancho*.

By the 1920s the genre had established itself. Producer Hal ROACH turned out "Haunted Spooks" with Harold LLOYD in 1920. *The Ghost in the Garret*, a haunted house comedy starring Dorothy GISH, appeared in 1921. That same year Buster KEATON appeared in "The Haunted House" in which he was pursued by a horde of ghosts. *One Exciting Night* (1922), starring Carol Dempster and Henry HULL, initiated the pattern for the "old dark house" comedy thrillers that were soon to follow.

By the next decade ghost comedies benefited from the advent of sound. Not only was the exposition of the story easier to handle, but sound encouraged verbal humor. One good example is *The Gorilla* (1930), first filmed in 1927 as a straight melodrama. Now director Bryan Foy unleashed the comic talents of Joe Frisco and Harry GRIBBON. The film was remade once more, in 1939, as a showcase for the comedy of the RITZ BROTHERS, the same year that Bob HOPE appeared in a comic remake of *The Cat and the Canary*. *The Ghost Talks* appeared in 1929, and *The Ghost Walks* in 1935. And by the next year the ubiquitous apparition decided to travel in *The Ghost Goes West*, starring Robert Donat and Eugene PALLETTE, a British comedy in which an entire castle and its resident ghost is moved to America. The comic character actor Willie BEST appeared perhaps in more ghost comedies than any other Hollywood player. These

include *The Monster Walks* (1932), *The Ghost Breakers* (1940), *The Smiling Ghost*, *The Body Disappears* (both 1941), *Whispering Ghosts*, and *A-Haunting We Will Go* (both 1942).

If it seemed as if the genre had deteriorated in the 1930s, it was to suffer further in the 1940s in the hands of the BOWERY BOYS (*Spooks Run Wild, Ghosts on the Loose, Spook Busters*) and the THREE STOOGES ("If a Body Meets a Body" released in 1945 and "The Ghost Talks" in 1949). ABBOTT AND COSTELLO starred in two fairly funny entries, *Hold That Ghost* (1941) and *The Time of Their Lives* (1946), LAUREL AND HARDY made *A-Haunting We Will Go* in 1942, and another comedy team, OLSEN AND JOHNSON, appeared in *Ghost Catchers* in 1944. Other entries included *The Ghost Comes Home* (1940), *The Ghost and the Guest* (1943), *The Ghost Steps Out* (1946), *The Ghost and Mrs. Muir* and *The Ghost Goes Wild* (1947). One film that transcended the genre was *The Canterville Ghost* (1944), a charming film starring Charles LAUGHTON as a cowardly spirit.

MARTIN AND LEWIS made their contribution in the 1950s with *Scared Stiff* (1953), while the Bowery Boys continued with *Ghost Chasers* (1951) and *Spook Chasers* (1957). William CASTLE directed the gimmicky *Thirteen Ghosts* which appeared in 3-D in 1960 and *The Spirit Is Willing* in 1967, a weak haunted house comedy starring Sid CAESAR. The final "Beach Party" comedy, *Ghost in the Invisible Bikini* (1966), failed to save the teenage series, despite its large cast. New life was breathed into the genre in the 1980s. Sally FIELD, James Caan, and Jeff Bridges starred in *Kiss Me Goodbye* (1982), about the ghost of a young woman's first husband interfering with her upcoming second marriage. The most popular ghost comedy of the period, however, was *Ghostbusters* (1984), starring Bill MURRAY, Dan AYKROYD, Harold RAMIS, and Sigourney WEAVER in a multi-million-dollar production about meddlesome spirits in Manhattan.

Gibson, Hoot (1892–1962), actor. Worked with the circus as a teenager, joined a rodeo, then came to films in 1910 as a stunt rider. He soon began to appear in westerns and rapidly became very popular. Many of his westerns had a slightly different slant in that they were humorous, although this was not entirely unique. Harry CAREY, under several directors including John FORD (with whom Gibson got his start), as well as cowboy star Tom Mix turned out western comedies. However, Gibson seemed just right for the role and appeared at home in this genre for the next 20 years. He often carried no gun in his films, and if he did, it was either tucked in his belt or in his boot and not in the usual gun-belt holster.

SELECTED FILMS: *His Only Son* (1912), *Shotgun Jones* (1914), *The Galloping Kid, The Lone Hand* (1922), *Blinky, The Gentleman From America, Out of Luck* (1923), *Broadway or Bust, 40-Horse Hawkins, Hit and Run* (1924), *Chip of the Flying U, The Texas Streak* (1926), *Galloping Fury, Hey! Hey! Cowboy* (1927), *The Horse Soldiers* (1959). ∎

Gibson, Wynne (1905–), actress. Worked in vaudeville, in the theater, and on Broadway before settling in Hollywood as a leading player and supporting actress during the early years of the sound era. She specialized in portraying good-natured gun molls and floozies in dozens of melodramas and light comedies. She retired from the screen in 1943.

SELECTED FILMS: *Nothing but the Truth* (1929), *The Fall Guy* (1930), *June Moon, Man of the World, Kick In, Ladies of the Big House* (1931), *Lady and Gent, Night After Night, If I Had a Million* (1932), *Her Bodyguard, Aggie Appleby—Maker of Men* (1933), *The Captain Hates the Sea* (1934), *Cafe Hostess* (1940), *The Falcon Strikes Back, Mystery Broadcast* (1943). ∎

"Gidget" comedies. A popular series of films about a spirited teenager and her romantic misadventures. Aimed at young audiences, the films spawned television features and an animated version, as well as a weekly series with Sally FIELD playing the title role. The first film, *Gidget* (1959), starred Sandra DEE; the second, *Gidget Goes Hawaiian* (1961), showcased Deborah Walley; and in the last theatrical release, *Gidget Goes to Rome* (1963), Cindy Carol portrayed the spunky teenager.

Gifford, Frances (1920–), actress. Began her screen career in 1937, playing leads and secondary roles in dramas and light films for various studios. An attractive and personable actress, she never became a major star. However, she attained some dubious distinction in 1941 as Nyoka, the lead in the serial *Jungle Girl*.

SELECTED FILMS: *Woman Chases Man* (1937), *Mr. Smith Goes to Washington* (1939), *Hold That Woman* (1940), *The Reluctant Dragon, Louisiana Purchase* (1941), *The Remarkable Andrew, Beyond the Blue Horizon* (1942), *Marriage Is a Private Affair* (1944), *Thrill of a Romance, She Went to the Races* (1945), *Little Mr. Jim* (1947), *Luxury Liner* (1948), *Riding High* (1950), *Sky Commando* (1953). ∎

Billy Gilbert (standing), Frank Sinatra (left), Kathryn Grayson, and Gene Kelly

Gilbert, Billy (1894–1971), actor. Worked in vaudeville and burlesque before making his debut in silent films in the early 1920s. Large-framed and stout in appearance, he appeared in more than two hundred comedy shorts and features which spanned five decades. He played leads, supporting roles, and comic relief characters. One of his more memorable roles was that of the voice of Sneezy in Walt Disney's *Snow White and the Seven Dwarfs* (1938). Chiefly a visual comic, he proved to be a very capable performer in sound films as well as silents. Even in small, independent productions such as the offbeat *Paradise Alley* (1961), directed by Hugo Haas, he evoked much warmth and good-natured humor. Petulant neighbor Margaret HAMILTON shouts at him: "If you were my husband, I'd give you poison!" "If I were your husband," he retorts, "I'd take it!" Gags like this were the stuff of vaudeville, but veteran funnymen like Gilbert made them seem fresh. He appeared as supporting player in many LAUREL AND HARDY and THREE STOOGES films, portraying menacing but easily frustrated adversaries.

SELECTED FILMS: *Dynamic Allen* (1921), *Noisy Neighbors* (1929), *The Music Box*, *Million Dollar Legs*, *Pack Up Your Troubles* (1931), *Them Thar Hills* (1934), *On the Avenue*, *Rosalie* (1937), *Happy Landing*, *Joy of Living* (1938), *The Under-Pup*, *Rio* (1939), *His Girl Friday*, *The Great Dictator*, *Seven Sinners* (1940), *Model Wife*, *Week-End in Havana* (1941), *Arabian Nights* (1942), *Crazy House* (1945), *The Kissing Bandit* (1948), *Down Among the Sheltering Palms* (1953), *Five Weeks in a Balloon* (1962). ∎

Gilchrist, Connie (1901–), actress. Worked with various repertory groups and on Broadway before making her film debut in 1940. She appeared as a character actress in more than 75 dramatic and light films, often as a sharp-tongued maid, lively matron, or similar role. Memorable roles included the soused mother in *A Letter to Three Wives* (1948) and the outspoken Christina in *A Woman's Face* (1941).

SELECTED FILMS: *Hullabaloo* (1940), *Barnacle Bill*, *Two-Faced Woman* (1941), *We Were Dancing*, *Tortilla Flat* (1942), *Thousands Cheer*, *Presenting Lily Mars* (1943), *Music for Millions* (1944), *Junior Miss* (1945), *Merton of the Movies* (1946), *The Hucksters*, *Song of the Thin Man*, *Good News* (1947), *Peggy*, *Louisa* (1950), *Here Comes the Groom* (1951), *It Should Happen to You* (1954), *Auntie Mame* (1958), *A House Is Not a Home* (1964), *The Monkey's Uncle*, *Tickle Me* (1965), *Some Kind of a Nut* (1969). ∎

Gildersleeve. A pompous character created by actor Harold PEARY on radio originally as part of the "Fibber McGee and Molly" show, then as the star of his own show, and finally in a series of low-budget light comedies produced during the 1940s. He usually became embroiled in some innocuous situation until he extricated himself from it with the help of his two adopted children.

Gilford, Jack (1907–), actor. Worked in vaudeville and revues as a comic before making his film debut in 1944. He specialized as a comic relief and character actor, often supporting other leading actors and comics, including Milton BERLE, Phil SILVERS, George C. SCOTT, and Elliott GOULD.

In *Who's Minding the Mint?* he played a hard-of-hearing safecracker who is hired by Robert Hutton to steal the plates from the United States Treasury. But Gilford has lost his hearing aid and can't hear the safe tumblers. "Try to think," Hutton says frantically. "Where did you lose your hearing aid?" "You'll have to talk louder," replies Gilford. "I lost my hearing aid."

SELECTED FILMS: *Hey Rookie* (1944), *Main Street to Broadway* (1953), *The Daydreamer*, *Mr. Buddwing*, *A Funny Thing Happened on the Way to the Forum* (1966), *Enter Laughing*, *Who's*

Minding the Mint? (1969), *Catch-22* (1970), *They Might Be Giants* (1971), *Harry and Walter Go to New York* (1976). ■

Gillingwater, Claude (1870–1939), actor. Began his Hollywood career in silent films. He appeared in more than 75 dramas and light comedies, usually as a hard-hearted, complaining old man. Tall and bald-headed, he enlivened many films as a fusspot and grouch. He gave a forceful performance in 1921 as the cold grandfather of Little Lord Fauntleroy. Later, in the sound era, he portrayed similar roles in Shirley Temple films, but she, like the little Lord, was able to teach him all about tenderness.

SELECTED FILMS: My Boy (1921), *Fools First* (1922), *Alice Adams* (1923), *Daddies* (1924), *That's My Baby* (1926), *Oh, Kay!* (1928), *Smiling Irish Eyes* (1929), *Dumbbells in Ermine* (1930), *Daddy Long Legs* (1931), *Before Midnight* (1933), *The Show-Off* (1934), *Calm Yourself* (1935), *Poor Little Rich Girl* (1936), *Top of the Town* (1937), *Little Miss Broadway* (1938), *Cafe Society, There Goes My Heart* (1939). ■

Gillmore, Margalo (1897–1986), actress. Appeared in films following a long stage career that began in 1917. She worked chiefly as a supporting player in light films during the 1950s.

SELECTED FILMS: The Happy Years (1950), *Elopement* (1951), *High Society* (1956), *The Trouble With Angels* (1966). ■

Gilmore, Helen (1900–1947), actress. Worked in silent films as a supporting player. She appeared occasionally in some of Harold LLOYD'S early comedy shorts. She portrayed landladies and mothers and other matronly characters.

SELECTED FILMS: Bumping Into Broadway, Captain Kidd's Kids (1919). ■

Gingold, Hermione (1897–1987), actress. Worked on stage and in revues in her native London and in the United States. She became a popular comedienne on both sides of the Atlantic, appearing sporadically in light films as a character player. One of her more memorable roles was as a delightful and charming matriarchal witch in *Bell, Book and Candle.*

SELECTED FILMS: Around the World in 80 Days (1956), *Gigi, Bell, Book and Candle* (1958), *The Music Man* (1962), *I'd Rather Be Rich* (1964), *Harvey Middleman—Fireman* (1965), *Munster, Go Home!, Promise Her Anything* (1966), *A Little Night Music* (1978), *Garbo Talks!* (1984). ■

Girardot, Etienne (1856–1939), actor. Worked in silent film shorts as well as sound features. He appeared in more than 40 films, both dramas and light comedies, as a character actor. His roles varied from efficient, fussy public servants to meek eccentrics. His most notable and hilarious appearance was in *Twentieth Century* (1934), in which he portrayed a religious zealot who wanders through train cars plastering stickers everywhere and signing bogus checks.

SELECTED FILMS: The Violin of Monsieur (1912), *The Belle of New York* (1919), *The Kennel Murder Case* (1933), *The Whole Town's Talking, Curly Top* (1935), *College Holiday, Go West, Young Man* (1936), *Breakfast for Two* (1937), *Professor Beware* (1938), *Fast and Loose, For Love or Money, Little Accident, Hawaiian Nights, The Hunchback of Notre Dame* (1939), *Isle of Destiny* (1940). ■

Gish, Dorothy (1898–1968), actress. Appeared on stage as a child actor before joining D. W. Griffith with whom she made her film debut in 1912 in "The Unseen Enemy." Her first feature-length starring role was in *Old Heidelberg* (1915), in which she played a tavern waitress. Although she did not reach the level of popularity which her celebrated sister, Lillian, achieved, she became famous in her own right, especially in light films in which she demonstrated a flair for pantomime and mimicry. She often appeared with her sister and, later, when their careers separated them, they still retained a close relationship. During the 1930s she abandoned her waning film career for the New York stage, returning to films only sporadically. Unfortunately, many of her films are lost while others are rarely shown. Only about six of her seventeen features of the 1920s are known to exist.

SELECTED FILMS: The New York Hat, My Hero (1912), The Lady and the Mouse, Almost a Wild Man (1913), Liberty Belles, The City Beautiful (1914), An Old-Fashioned Girl, How Hazel Got Even (1915), Susan Rocks the Boat, Gretchen the Greenhorn (1916), The Little Yank, Her Official Fathers (1917), Battling Jane (1918), Boots, Peppy Polly, I'll Get Him Yet, Nugget Nell (1919), Mary Ellen Comes to Town, Remodeling Her Husband, Little Miss Rebellion, Flying Pat (1920), The Country Flapper (1922), Night Life of New York, Clothes Make the Pirate (1925), Our Hearts Were Young and Gay (1944), Centennial Summer (1946), The Cardinal (1963). ∎

Glaser, Vaughan (1872–1958), actor. Entered films in the 1930s in his middle years following a long stage career. He appeared as a character player chiefly in light comedies. His most memorable role was that of the stern high school principal, Mr. Bradley, in the "HENRY ALDRICH" comedy series of the late 1930s and 1940s.

SELECTED FILMS: What a Life (1938), Those Were the Days (1940), Adventure in Washington, Henry Aldrich for President (1941), Henry Aldrich, Editor, Henry and Dizzy, My Favorite Spy (1942), Henry Aldrich Gets Glamour, Henry Aldrich Haunts a House (1943), Arsenic and Old Lace, Henry Aldrich Plays Cupid (1944). ∎

Glass, Everett (1891–1966), actor. Began his screen career in the 1940s. He appeared as a supporting player in dramas and light films.

SELECTED FILMS: The Undercover Man, Easy Living (1949), Mother Didn't Tell Me, Father Makes Good, The Petty Girl (1950), Dreamboat (1952), Three Sailors and a Girl (1953), Friendly Persuasion (1956), The Marriage-Go-Round (1960). ∎

Glass, Gaston (1898–1965), actor. Entered early silent films in the late 1910s. He appeared in dramas, action films, and comedies during a screen career that spanned three decades. He also worked as a stage actor, assistant film director, and television production manager.

SELECTED FILMS: Open Your Eyes (1919), The World and His Wife (1920), Her Winning Way (1921), Little Miss Smiles (1922), Mothers-in-Law (1923), The Mad Marriage, Parisian Nights (1925), Subway Sadie, Sweet Sadie, Sweet Daddies (1926), A Gentleman Preferred, Obey Your Husband, The Wife's Relations (1928), She Got What She Wanted, The South Seas Pearl (1930), The Princess Comes Across (1936), Espionage (1937). ∎

Glazer, Benjamin (1887–1958), screenwriter, producer. Practiced law, worked as a journalist, wrote stage plays and adaptations (denoted by *), before he began his 35-year career in films. He wrote screenplays and adaptations, alone or in collaboration, and produced numerous films, many of them delightful comedies. He produced films for Paramount during the 1930s.

SELECTED FILMS: A Trip to Paradise* (1921), The Merry Widow, Fine Clothes (1925), Memory Lane, The Gay Deceiver, You Never Know Women, Everybody's Acting (1926), The Lady in Ermine, A Gentleman of Paris*, The Love Mart (1927), Happiness Ahead (1928), The Boudoir Diplomat (1930), A Bedtime Story* (1933), We're Not Dressing* (1934), *Tortilla Flat* (1942), *Song of My Heart* (1948), *Carousel** (1956). ∎

Jackie Gleason

Gleason, Jackie (1916–1987), actor, comic, writer, composer. Worked in vaudeville and nightclubs before appearing in films in the early 1940s. A portly and convivial character actor, he was chiefly confined to minor roles at Warner Brothers. After his inauspicious entrance into films, he returned to New York where he appeared in several shows during the mid-1940s. His successes on Broadway led to a television contract. He starred in various revues and situation comedies, ultimately portraying his most famous character, Ralph Kramden, in "The Honeymooners." It was not until the 1960s, after a successful television career, that he obtained starring roles in dramas and comedies. He played the exasperated sheriff in the "Smokey and the Bandit" series. J. Bacon's biography, *How Sweet It Is: The Jackie Gleason Story* (1985), includes photographs and a filmography.

In *Nothing in Common* he played an embittered old-time salesman whose wife has left him after 34 years of marriage and whose son, Tom HANKS, is preoccupied with his own advertising career. Gleason telephones his son, who is in bed with one of his girlfriends, to tell him about his marital breakup. "This is Max Basner, your father," he announces. "You heard of me?"

SELECTED FILMS: *Navy Blues* (1941), *Larceny, Inc., Orchestra Wives, All Through the Night* (1942), *The Hustler* (1961), *Gigot, Requiem for a Heavyweight* (1962), *Papa's Delicate Condition, Soldier in the Rain* (1963), *Skidoo* (1968), *How to Commit Marriage, Don't Drink the Water* (1969), *Smokey and the Bandit* (1977), *Smokey and the Bandit II* (1980), *The Sting II* (1983), *Nothing in Common* (1986). ∎

James Gleason

Gleason, James (1886–1959), actor, playwright, screenwriter. Worked in stock and on Broadway, wrote plays, and made his screen debut as an actor in 1922. With the advent of sound, he became one of the most popular character actors of the 1930s and 1940s, appearing in more than 100 films, both dramas and comedies, either as lead or supporting player. He portrayed exasperated policemen, street-wise hoodlums, wise-cracking city slickers, and other urban characters who were outwardly pugnacious and irascible but basically soft-hearted and sentimental. In the mid-1930s he played the simple-minded police inspector Oscar Piper in a series of crime films that co-starred the indomitable Edna May OLIVER as a competing sleuth. He also starred in "THE HIGGINS FAMILY," a comedy series for Republic studios. He was nominated for an Oscar as Best Supporting Actor for his role in *Here Comes Mr. Jordan*.

In *Once Upon a Time* (1941) he played Cary GRANT'S crony. Grant, about to lose his theater, is pulled through by his pal. "I got a hot poker game tonight," Gleason announces. "I better go home and mark some cards. One of us has got to make a living."

SELECTED FILMS: *Polly of the Follies* (1922), *The Count of Ten* (1928), *The Flying Fool, The Shannons of Broadway* (1929), *The Swellhead, Puttin' on the Ritz, Her Man, Big Money* (1930), *Sweepstakes* (1931), *Blondie of the Follies* (1932), *Hoopla* (1933), *Helldorado* (1935), *The Plot Thickens* (1936), *Forty Naughty Girls* (1937), *On Your Toes* (1939), *Money to Burn* (1940), *Meet John Doe, Here Comes Mr. Jordan* (1941), *Babes on Broadway* (1942), *Arsenic and Old Lace* (1944), *The Hoodlum Saint* (1946), *The Bishop's Wife* (1947), *The Life of Riley* (1949), *The Yellow Cab Man, Riding High* (1950), *We're Not Married* (1952), *Spring Reunion* (1957), *The Last Hurrah* (1958). ∎

Gleason, Lucille (1886–1947), actress. Appeared in light films during the 1930s and 1940s as a character player. She often co-starred with her husband, James GLEASON, especially in "THE HIGGINS FAMILY" comedy series. She was the mother of actor Russell GLEASON.

SELECTED FILMS: *The Shannons of Broadway* (1929), *Girls About Town* (1931), *Nice Women* (1932), *Don't Bet on Love, Love, Honor and Oh, Baby!* (1933), *I Like It That Way* (1934), *Klondike Annie* (1936), *First Lady* (1937), *Beloved Brat, Nurse From Brooklyn, The Higgins Family* (1938), *Lucky Partners* (1940), *The Clock* (1945). ∎

Gleason, Russell (1908–1945), juvenile actor. Appeared in dramas and light films during the 1930s and 1940s, including "THE HIGGINS FAMILY" comedy series co-starring his real-life parents, James and Lucille GLEASON. His career was cut short by a fatal fall from a hotel window.

SELECTED FILMS: *Strange Cargo, The Shady Lady* (1929), *Laugh and Get Rich* (1931), *Nice Women* (1932), *Private Jones* (1933), *Off to the Races, Big Business, Hot Water* (1937), *A Trip to Paris, The Higgins Family* (1938), *Unexpected Uncle* (1941), *Salute to the Marines* (1943), *The Adventures of Mark Twain* (1944). ∎

Gobel, George (1920–), comedian, actor. Worked as a singer on radio and in nightclubs before turning to comedy. He starred chiefly in television comedy shows during the 1950s and '60s before appearing occasionally in films. A short comic with a crew-cut, he usually portrayed easily intimidated characters while specializing in a slow-paced comedy style. He failed to generate the excitement on the large screen that he did on the television tube.

SELECTED FILMS: *The Birds and the Bees* (1956), *I Married a Woman* (1957), *Rabbit Test* (1978). ∎

Goddard, Paulette (1911–), actress. Worked in musical theater before entering films in 1929. A spirited brunette, she obtained bit parts in various features and joined Hal ROACH'S film troupe. In 1932 she met Charlie CHAPLIN who married her and made her his co-star in *Modern Times* (1936). She became a popular actress in the late 1930s and 1940s, starring in dramas as well as light films, the latter of which showcased her flair for zany comedy. She was nominated for an Academy Award as Best Supporting Actress for her role in *So Proudly We Hail* (1943).

SELECTED FILMS: *Berth Marks* (1929), *The Kid From Spain* (1932), *The Young in Heart* (1938), *The Ghost Breakers, The Great Dictator* (1940), *Second Chorus, Nothing but the Truth* (1941), *The Lady Has Plans* (1942), *Standing Room Only* (1944), *Kitty, The Diary of a Chambermaid* (1946), *Suddenly It's Spring* (1947), *Babes in Bagdad* (1952), *Paris Model* (1953). ∎

Goff, Norris. See Lum and Abner.

Gold Rush, The (1925), UA. *Dir.* Charlie Chaplin; *Sc.* Charlie Chaplin; with Charlie Chaplin, Mack Swain, Tom Murray, Georgia Hale, Henry Bergman.

Many consider this silent comedy Chaplin's greatest work. It pits Charlie against the harsh Klondike elements and the even harsher greed of men. This epic comedy, which contains sharp satirical implications, provides several classic scenes. Charlie, facing starvation, eats his cooked shoe and delights in its spaghetti-like shoelace, all to the puzzlement of his cabin partner, Mack SWAIN; he performs a dance with two dinner rolls; and he battles against death in a cabin that has settled on the edge of a precipice. In the epilogue we find the two prospectors, now millionaires, on board ship where Charlie unexpectedly finds Georgia Hale, the girl of his dreams. The film, in part a testament to man's dreams and frustrations, succeeds because of Chaplin's carefully executed pantomime and tender story. Originally, the feminine lead was to go to Lita Grey, Chaplin's latest love interest, but the 16-year-old actress could not carry the role. She became Mrs. Chaplin instead. The marriage ended several years later.

Goldblum, Jeff (1953–), actor. Began his screen career in 1974. A thin, dark figure, he has appeared as a supporting player in dramas as well as light films. He has played sympathetic as well as treacherous roles. *Silverado* (1985) is an example of the latter.

SELECTED FILMS: *Death Wish, California Split* (1974), *Nashville, Next Stop, Greenwich Village* (1975), *Special Delivery* (1976), *Annie Hall* (1977), *Thank God It's Friday* (1978), *The Big Chill* (1982), *The Adventures of Buckaroo Banzai* (1984), *Transylvania 6-5000* (1985). ∎

Gombell, Minna (1893–1973), actress. Made her film debut in 1929, eventually appearing in more than 75 dramas, melodramas, and light comedies. An attractive blonde character actress, she usually portrayed ex-wives, floozies, or sharp-tongued women who have been around. She appeared also under the names Winifred Lee and Nancy Carter.

SELECTED FILMS: *The Great Power* (1929), *Sob Sister* (1931), *Bachelor's Affairs* (1932), *Pleasure Cruise* (1933), *The Thin Man, Strictly Dynamite* (1934), *Miss Pacific Fleet* (1935), *Banjo on My Knee* (1936), *Blockheads* (1938), *Stop, Look and Love* (1939), *Boom Town* (1940), *Mexican Spitfire Sees a Ghost* (1942), *Night Club Girl* (1945), *Mr. Reckless* (1948), *Here Comes the Groom* (1951). ∎

Goodrich, Frances (1891–1984), screenwriter, playwright. Worked as an actress before turning her attention to writing for the screen and stage. She wrote numerous screenplays over a period of four decades, in collaboration with her husband, Albert Hackett, for many high-quality dramas and light films. She was responsible for several of the better "THIN MAN" scripts. The play, *The Diary of Anne Frank*, which she co-wrote with her husband, received a Pulitzer Prize and was adapted for the screen in 1959.

SELECTED FILMS: *Penthouse* (1933), *The Thin Man* (1934), *Naughty Marietta, Ah! Wilderness* (1935), *Rose Marie, After the Thin Man* (1936), *The Firefly* (1937), *Lady in the Dark* (1944), *It's a Wonderful Life* (1946), *The Pirate, Easter Parade* (1948), *In the Good Old Summertime* (1949), *Father of the Bride* (1950), *Father's Little Dividend* (1951), *Seven Brides for Seven Brothers* (1954), *Gaby* (1956), *A Certain Smile* (1958), *Five Finger Exercise* (1962). ∎

Goodwin, Bill (1910–1958), actor. Worked as a radio announcer for some of the top comedians, including Eddie CANTOR, Bob HOPE, and Edgar BER-

GEN, before appearing in films in the early 1940s. An attractive character actor, he usually played amiable roles in light films as well as dramas. He portrayed Al Jolson's stage acquaintance in *The Jolson Story*.

SELECTED FILMS: *Let's Make Music* (1941), *No Time for Love, Riding High* (1943), *Bathing Beauty* (1944), *Incendiary Blonde* (1945), *The Jolson Story* (1946), *Mickey, So This Is New York* (1948), *The Life of Riley, It's a Great Feeling* (1949), *Tea for Two* (1950), *The Atomic Kid, Lucky Me* (1954), *The Opposite Sex* (1956), *The Big Beat* (1958). ■

Goodwin, Harold, actor. Appeared as a supporting player in comedy shorts during the sound period. He worked in several films starring Buster KEATON.

SELECTED FILMS: *One-Run Elmer* (1935), *Three on a Limb, Grand Slam Opera* (1936), *Jail Bait, Ditto* (1937). ■

Goodwins, Fred, actor. Worked in early silent films, especially as a supporting player in a handful of comedy shorts made by ESSANAY studios and starring Charlie CHAPLIN. A versatile performer, he portrayed a variety of characters, including fathers, preachers, and farmers.

SELECTED FILMS: *The Jitney Elopement, The Tramp, The Bank, Shanghaied, A Night in the Show* (1915), *Police!* (1916). ■

Goodwins, Leslie (1899–1969), director. Worked in Hollywood from the early 1930s, mainly as a director of B films. He turned out dozens of melodramas and light comedies. His most popular films were the zany "MEXICAN SPITFIRE" slapstick comedies of the 1940s starring Leon ERROL and Lupe VELEZ.

SELECTED FILMS: *With Love and Kisses* (1936), *Anything for a Thrill, Young Dynamite* (1937), *Mr. Doodle Kicks Off* (1938), *The Day the Bookies Wept* (1939), *Mexican Spitfire, Million-*

aire Playboy, Pop Always Pays (1940), Let's Make Music, They Met in Argentina (1941), The Adventures of a Rookie, Rookies in Burma (1943), Goin' to Town, Hi Beautiful! (1944), What a Blonde! An Angel Comes to Brooklyn (1945), Genius at Work, Vacation in Reno (1946), The Lone Wolf in London (1947), Fireman, Save My Child (1954), Tammy and the Millionaire (1967). ■

Gorcey, Bernard (1888–1955), actor. Worked in vaudeville and on stage before entering films in the late 1920s. A diminutive character player with a large head, he appeared in dramas and light films, often with his sons Leo and David GORCEY in the "BOWERY BOYS" comedy series. He portrayed Louie, the owner of the Sweet Shop.

SELECTED FILMS: *Abie's Irish Rose* (1928), *The Great Dictator* (1940), *No Minor Vices, Master Minds* (1949), *Ghost Chasers* (1951), *No Holds Barred* (1952), *Jalopy* (1953), *The Bowery Boys Meet the Monsters* (1954). ■

Gorcey, David (1918–), actor. Appeared on stage in the original cast of *Dead End* before entering films in the late 1930s. The son of veteran stage actor David GORCEY and the brother of comic actor Leo GORCEY, he became an occasional member of the "BOWERY BOYS" comedy series. He was not as verbal as his brother, playing a rather more subdued character with names like "Sniper" and "Yap."

SELECTED FILMS: *Little Tough Guy, Little Tough Guys in Society* (1938), *Code of the Streets, Call a Messenger* (1939), *You're Not So Tough, Boys of the City, That Gang of Mine, Pride of the Bowery* (1940), *Flying Wild* (1941), *In Fast Company* (1946), *Hard Boiled Mahoney* (1947). ■

Gorcey, Leo (1915–1969), actor. Began his acting career portraying the young delinquent Spit in Sidney Kingsley's play, *Dead End*, a role he repeated in the

1937 film version. The "gang" from the film appealed to the public and the "Dead End Kids" appeared in a series of crime features. Gorcey, with his Brooklyn accent and nasal voice, continued in the youthful role as leader of the "East Side Kids," a spin-off of the previous gang when some members moved to Monogram studios.

Later, another low-budget series of knockabout films continued the misadventures of Gorcey and his gang, this time named the "BOWERY BOYS." Each new series lowered the quality of the films as repetition set in and stale, low-comedy routines took their toll. Gorcey's autobiography is titled *Dead End Yells, Wedding Bells, Cockle Shells, and Dizzy Spells.*

SELECTED FILMS: *Dead End* (1937), *Mannequin, Crime School* (1938), *The Ghost Creeps, Pride of the Bowery* (1940), *Road to Zanzibar, Flying Wild, Spooks Run Wild* (1941), *Mr. Wise Guy* (1942), *Docks of New York* (1945), *So This Is New York* (1948), *Ghost Chasers* (1951), *Paris Playboys* (1954), *Crashing Las Vegas* (1956), *It's a Mad, Mad, Mad, Mad World* (1963), *The Phynx* (1970). ■

Gordon, Bert (1898–1974), actor, comedian. Worked in vaudeville with different partners, on Broadway in the 1920s, and in radio during the 1930s. For the remainder of his show business career he specialized as a comic character on radio, but appeared occasionally in light films. He was best known as "the Mad Russian," a popular comic character on Eddie CANTOR'S radio show.

SELECTED FILMS: *New Faces of 1937* (1937), *Outside of Paradise* (1938), *Sing for Your Supper* (1941). ■

Gordon, Gale (1906–), actor. Has appeared occasionally in light films in comedy roles. Portraying fleshy fussbudgets, he is better known for his television roles than for those in films.

SELECTED FILMS: *Here We Go Again* (1942), *A Woman of Distinction* (1950), *Rally 'Round the Flag, Boys!* (1958), *Don't Give Up the Ship* (1959), *Visit to a Small Planet* (1960), *All in a Night's Work, All Hands on Deck* (1961), *Sergeant Deadhead* (1965), *Speedway* (1968). ■

Gordon, Mary (1882–1963), actress. A Scottish-born matronly character player who often portrayed Irish women and mothers in Hollywood films. She appeared in more than 100 dramas and light comedies during her 25 years in movies. Rather short and heavy-set, she enlivened many films with her charm and blarney. She played Mrs. Hudson, Sherlock Holmes' housekeeper, and Leo Gorcey's mother in several of the "BOWERY BOYS" films.

SELECTED FILMS: *The Home Maker* (1925), *Clancy's Kosher Wedding* (1927), *Subway Express* (1931), *Almost Married* (1932), *The Little Minister* (1934), *The Irish in Us* (1935), *Way Out West* (1936), *A Damsel in Distress* (1937), *She Married a Cop* (1939), *Kitty Foyle* (1940), *It Started With Eve* (1941), *It Happened in Flatbush* (1942), *Sweet Rosie O'Grady* (1943), *Ever Since Venus* (1944), *See My Lawyer, Kitty* (1945), *The Secret Life of Walter Mitty* (1947), *West of Wyoming* (1950). ■

Gordon, Maude Turner (1868–1940), actress. Began her screen career during the silent period and continued into sound films as a supporting actress. She appeared in numerous light features during both periods.

SELECTED FILMS: *Homeward Bound* (1923), *Little French Girl* (1925), *Cheating Cheaters, Home Made* (1927), *Sporting Goods, Just Married* (1928), *The Glad Rag Doll, The Marriage Playground, Sally* (1929), *The Floradora Girl* (1930), *Ladies' Man* (1931), *She Loves Me Not* (1934), *Living on Velvet* (1935). ■

Gordon, Michael (1909–), director. Worked on stage as actor and director before coming to film in the early 1940s. He began directing routine crime films, advanced to dramas, and, after a few years' absence because of being blacklisted, returned to direct several fairly good light films. One of his better directorial efforts was *Pillow Talk* starring Doris DAY and Rock HUDSON, the first entry of a contemporary genre known as bedroom or SEX COMEDIES. The film, loaded with double entendres and sexual innuendos, started a new trend. Among his more notable serious films was *Cyrano de Bergerac* (1950), although even this screen adaptation of Rostand's romantic play did not lack wit and humor.

SELECTED FILMS: *Boston Blackie Goes Hollywood* (1942), *The Lady Gambles* (1949), *Pillow Talk* (1959), *Boys' Night Out* (1962), *For Love or Money, Move Over, Darling* (1963), *A Very Special Favor* (1965), *Texas Across the River* (1966), *The Impossible Years* (1968), *How Do I Love Thee?* (1970). ■

Gordon, Ruth (1896–1985), actress, screenwriter, playwright. Appeared in minor roles in silent films and on stage in dramas and comedies. She wrote screenplays alone or in collaboration with her husband, Garson KANIN. Her screen performances, mostly in dramatic roles, although sporadic, were forceful. It was in her writing that she made her greatest contributions to film comedy. However, she gave a memorable performance as a member of a witches' coven in *Rosemary's Baby* (1968), a role that won her an Oscar as Best Supporting Actress.

SELECTED FILMS (as screenwriter): *Adam's Rib* (1949), *The Marrying Kind, Pat and Mike* (1952), *The Actress* (1953). ■

SELECTED FILMS (as actress): *Camille* (1918), *Two-Faced Woman* (1941), *Lord Love a Duck* (1966), *Harold and Maude* (1972), *Every Which Way but Loose* (1978), *Any Which Way You Can, My Bodyguard, Smokey and the Bandit*

II (1980), *Jimmy the Kid* (1982), *Trouble With Spys* (1985). ■

Gorshin, Frank (1935–), impressionist, actor. Worked in television as a minor actor, in small nightclubs as a comic impressionist, and finally in major television shows where he gained national exposure. This led to Hollywood contracts for a variety of roles. He has played comic characters and straight supporting parts. His impressions of famous Hollywood personalities are uncannily realistic, not only in voice but in facial expressions and physical movements as well.

SELECTED FILMS: *The True Story of Jesse James* (1957), *Where the Boys Are* (1960), *The George Raft Story, The Great Impostor* (1961), *Sail a Crooked Ship* (1962). ■

Gosden, Freeman F. See Amos 'n' Andy.

Elliott Gould (right)

Gould, Elliott (1938–), actor. Worked in television and in musicals before making his film debut in 1968. Within a short time he became one of the busiest and most popular actors on the American screen. Unlike the glamorous film stars of the past, he is not extraordinarily handsome or conspicuous. But to his young audiences he has represented the urban generation replete with its anxieties and frustrations.

In *Getting Straight* he played a graduate student and former activist who is still called upon to lend his support to new causes. He turns down a black leader and acquaintance who half-sarcastically call out to the departing Gould, "I don't want to marry your sister!" "You marry my sister!" Gould fires back. "I will arrange it for you! Man, with the analyst and the astrologist and the two neurotic kids and the payments on the pool and the bill for the hysterectomy—you can be husband number four she wipes out!"

SELECTED FILMS: The Night They Raided Minsky's (1968), Bob & Carol & Ted & Alice (1969), M*A*S*H, Getting Straight, Move, I Love My Wife (1970), Little Murders (1971), Busting, S*P*Y*S, California Split (1974), Who?, Nashville, Whiffs (1975), Harry and Walter Go to New York (1976), Matilda (1978), Escape to Athens (1979), Over the Brooklyn Bridge (1984). ■

Goulding, Alfred J. (1896–1972), director. Worked chiefly in the 1910s and 1920s turning out silent comedy shorts starring Harold LLOYD. Unfortunately, many of the "LONESOME LUKE" entries featuring Lloyd went uncredited, so it is difficult to determine which specific shorts were directed by Goulding. He directed two full-length features during the sound era, one of which starred LAUREL AND HARDY.

SELECTED FILMS: From Hand to Mouth, Haunted Spooks (1920), Excuse Me (1925), All at Sea (1929), A Chump at Oxford (1940). ■

Grable, Betty (1916–1973), actress. Began her film career in chorus lines during the early sound period. By the mid-1930s she was appearing in low-budget comedies and musicals, but it was not until the early 1940s that she reached stardom as a female lead in major light musicals and occasional dramas. Famous for her legs, she was voted by American servicemen during World War II as their Number One "Pin-Up Girl." By the 1950s the pretty blonde singer-dancer's popularity began to decline. Just a few years earlier she had become one of the highest-paid performers. Spero Pastos wrote an informative biography titled Pin-Up: The Tragedy of Betty Grable (1986).

SELECTED FILMS: Happy Days, Let's Go Places (1930), Palmy Days (1931), The Greeks Had a Word for Them, The Kid From Spain (1932), Melody Cruise (1933), The Gay Divorcee (1934), The Nitwits (1935), Pigskin Parade (1936), Thrill of a Lifetime (1937), Give Me a Sailor (1938), Million Dollar Legs (1939), Moon Over Miami (1941), Coney Island (1943), Pin-Up Girl (1944), That Lady in Ermine (1948), The Farmer Takes a Wife, How to Marry a Millionaire (1953), How to Be Very, Very Popular (1955). ■

Anne Bancroft and Dustin Hoffman in The Graduate (1967)

Graduate, The (1967), EMB. Dir. Mike Nichols; Sc. Buck Henry, Calder Willingham; with Dustin Hoffman, Anne Bancroft, Katharine Ross, Murray Hamilton.

Shortly after it was released, The Graduate became one of the top-grossing films of all time. Mike Nichols' irreverent comedy, based on the novel by Charles Webb, must have touched a particular spot in the American public. Whether he triggered the social-protest element of the country's youth or the latent romance in the more mature audiences, the film emerged as a 1960s phenomenon. Dustin HOFFMAN portrays Benjamin, the title character, who is disillusioned with the older generation's conservatism and vacuous life-style. Anne Bancroft, as a friend of his parents and a restless wife who longs for youth, seduces him. Katharine Ross, her daughter, falls in love with Benjamin, but is forced to marry someone else. From these characters the director has stylishly fashioned a satirically funny and poignant work that has become a watershed film in its questioning of morals and values. The film made instant stars of Hoffman and Ross, while Bancroft finally got the recognition she should have received years before.

Grandma's Boy (1922), PAT. *Dir.* Fred Newmeyer; *Sc.* Hal Roach, Sam Taylor, Jean Havez; with Harold Lloyd, Mildred Davis, Anna Townsend, Charles Stevenson, Dick Sutherland.

This comedy of a coward who overcomes his weakness was Harold LLOYD'S first major success and first feature-length film, but when it was first shown to audiences it drew poor responses. Producer Hal ROACH convinced Lloyd to add more comic routines, which he did. The film required many additional months of reworking before it reached its final, and more appealing, form. Lloyd plays the small-town milksop whose cowardice can be traced back to his school days. He is in love with Mildred DAVIS, but his rival, Charles Stevenson, has tossed him down a well. His grandmother, determined to help the disheartened Lloyd, invokes the family tradition of honor by telling a story about his once- cowardly grandfather who became a Civil War hero. Encouraged by the tale and handed a magical amulet, Lloyd proceeds to capture a local miscreant and even the score with his rival. Many of Lloyd's contemporaries were impressed with the film, including Charlie CHAPLIN, who admired its structure. Its success was more important to Lloyd because it was his first work that blended gags within a well-plotted story, a winning combination

that was to serve him well for the remainder of the silent period.

Granger, Dorothy, actress. Supporting actress for Hal ROACH studios during the early sound era. A pretty brunette, she appeared in many comedy shorts with some of the leading comedians of the period, including the comedy teams of LAUREL AND HARDY and CLARK AND McCULLOUGH. She played the wife of Leon ERROLL for years in his comedy series.

SELECTED FILMS: Hog Wild, The Laurel-Hardy Murder Case (1930), One Good Turn (1931), Jitters the Butler (1932), The Gay Nineties (1933), In the Devil's Doghouse, Kentucky Kernels, Punch Drunks (1934), Alibi Bye Bye (1935), Termites of 1938 (1938). ■

Grant, Cary (1904–1986), actor. Worked as song-and-dance man in his native England and in the United States, on Broadway, and in operetta. Born Archibald Leach, he began his Hollywood career in the early 1930s in straight romantic roles, appearing with such stars as Marlene Dietrich and Mae WEST. By the late 1930s he was portraying carefree, sophisticated playboys in a series of films, including *Holiday* and *Bringing Up Baby* (both 1938) and *In Name Only* (1939), that displayed his propensity for SCREWBALL COMEDY. This screen personality made him popular with his audiences for the next three decades.

Grant was a talented comic actor who brought a high degree of professionalism to his roles. He made nonchalance, wit, and sophistication appear natural on screen in such diverse films as *The Philadelphia Story* and *Operation Petticoat*. Even in less humorous roles, as in the films he made for Alfred Hitchcock (*Suspicion, Notorious, To Catch a Thief,* and *North by Northwest*), he brought a degree of wit and innocent charm. In 1969 he was presented with a special Academy

Award for his contributions to the world of movies.

In *Once Upon a Honeymoon* he reveals to pretty Ginger ROGERS his first impressions of her: "If a gnat had broken into your pool of knowledge, it would have broken its neck."

SELECTED FILMS: *This Is the Night, Blonde Venus, Madame Butterfly (1932), She Done Him Wrong, I'm No Angel (1933), Kiss and Make-Up, Ladies Should Listen (1934), Enter Madame (1935), Sylvia Scarlett, Suzy, Wedding Present (1936), Topper, The Awful Truth (1937), Bringing Up Baby, Holiday (1938), Gunga Din, In Name Only (1939), His Girl Friday, My Favorite Wife (1940), The Philadelphia Story (1941), Once Upon a Honeymoon (1942), Mr. Lucky (1943), Arsenic and Old Lace (1944), The Bachelor and the Bobby-Soxer, The Bishop's Wife (1947), Mr. Blandings Builds His Dream House (1948), I Was a Male War Bride (1949), People Will Talk (1951), Room for One More, Monkey Business (1952), Dream Wife (1953), Kiss Them for Me (1957), Houseboat (1958), North by Northwest, Operation Petticoat (1959), That Touch of Mink (1962), Charade (1963), Father Goose (1964), Walk, Don't Run (1966).* ∎

Grant, John, screenwriter. Began writing screenplays in 1941, alone or in collaboration, for ABBOTT AND COSTELLO. Occasionally he would adapt material for other comedy teams such as Dean MARTIN and Jerry LEWIS.

SELECTED FILMS: *Hold That Ghost, In the Navy (1941), Ride 'Em Cowboy, Pardon My Sarong (1942), Hit the Ice, It Ain't Hay (1943), In Society, Lost in a Harem (1944), Here Come the Co-Eds, The Naughty Nineties, Ten Cents a Dance (1945), Buck Privates Come Home (1947), Mexican Hayride (1948), Abbott and Costello Meet the Killer Boris Karloff (1949), Abbott and Costello in the Foreign Legion (1950), Abbott and Costello Meet the Invisible Man (1951), Ma and Pa Kettle at the Fair (1952), Abbott and Costello Go to Mars (1953), Abbott and Costello Meet the Mummy (1955).* ∎

Grapewin, Charles (1875–1956), actor. Worked in vaudeville and in the theater before making his film debut as a character actor in 1929. Often portraying contentious but amicable old timers, he appeared in more than 100 dramas and light films. Some of his most famous roles included those of Gramp Maple in *The Petrified Forest* (1936), Grampa Joad in *The Grapes of Wrath* (1940), and Jeeter Lester in *Tobacco Road* (1941). He also played Ralph BELLAMY'S police-inspector father in the Ellery Queen detective films of the early 1940s.

In *They Died With Their Boots On* (1941) he explains to Errol Flynn, who played General Custer: "My business is shootin', not salutin'."

SELECTED FILMS: *The Shannons of Broadway (1929), Only Saps Work (1930), Gold Dust Gertie (1931), Lady and Gent (1932), Don't Bet on Love (1933), The Quitter, Judge Priest, The President Vanishes (1934), Alice Adams, Ah! Wilderness (1935), Libeled Lady (1936), A Family Affair (1937), Artists and Models Abroad (1938), The Wizard of Oz (1939), Ellery Queen—Master Detective (1940), Follow the Boys, The Impatient Years (1944), When I Grow Old (1951).* ∎

Gray, Lawrence (1898–1970), actor. Starred in silent and early sound films, both dramas and light comedies, as vigorous heroes opposite many leading actresses of the period. In the comedy farce *Oh Kay* (1928), for example, he played a penniless hero pursued by titled English lady Colleen MOORE, disguised as a housemaid.

SELECTED FILMS: *The Dressmaker From Paris, Are Parents People?, Stage Struck (1925), The American Venus, The Untamed Lady, Kid Boots, Love 'Em and Leave 'Em (1926), Ankles Preferred, The Callahans and the Murphys, Pajamas, Ladies Must Dress (1927), Love Hungry, The Patsy, Marriage by Contract (1928), Marianne, The Gay Nineties (1929), The Floradora Girl, Children of Pleasure, Spring Is Here, Sunny (1930), Going*

Wild, She-Wolf (1931), *Here Comes the Groom* (1934), *Timber War* (1936). ∎

Great Dictator, The (1940), UA. Dir. Charlie Chaplin; Sc. Charlie Chaplin; with Charlie Chaplin, Paulette Goddard, Jack Oakie, Reginald Gardiner, Billy Gilbert, Henry Daniell.

A flawed work, chiefly because of its didacticism, Chaplin's first all-talking film and the last to employ the character of the tramp nevertheless offers several rewards. After its preachy opening—"This is a story of a period between two World Wars—an interim in which Insanity cut loose, Liberty took a nose dive and Humanity was kicked around somewhat"—we find Charlie comically struggling with a cannon in the midst of battle during World War I. Eventually, he is wounded and suffers from amnesia. The war ends and Charlie, a barber, returns to his little shop. From this point on, Chaplin begins his attack on fascism. He satirizes Hitler in the form of Adenoid Hynckel, a Hitler-like dictator, also played by Chaplin, who has taken over the country of Tomania. The plot allows for the barber to exchange places with Hynckel and take over the government. Chaplin performs his famous ballet scene in which, as the power-crazed dictator, he dances with a globe of the world. Jack Oakie does a brilliant parody of Mussolini. Chaplin's comic inventiveness appears throughout this devastating satire, but the last scene, in which he abandons the barber character to present a speech on how to better the world situation, is totally out of place and weakens the impact of the work.

Great Gildersleeve, The. See Harold Peary.

Great McGinty, The (1940), PAR. Dir. Preston Sturges; Sc. Preston Sturges; with Brian Donlevy, Akim Tamiroff, William Demarest, Muriel Angelus, Thurston Hall.

This political satire was Sturges' first directorial effort, a reward Paramount bestowed upon their successful screenwriter. It was the beginning of the director's brief but highly successful career during the 1940s. Brian DONLEVY portrays a slow-witted down-and-outer who is elevated to the state governorship with more than a little help from the Boss, a crooked power broker played by Akim Tamiroff. Sturges pokes fun at big-city politics in this fast-paced comedy. Donlevy begins his rise when he learns he can vote multiple times for the same candidate. And soon he is on his crooked way up the ladder. Ironically, he falls only when he decides to go straight. In one particularly humorous scene Tamiroff invites the lowly Donlevy into his bullet-proof limousine and, in a nostalgic mood, begins to reminisce about his humble beginnings. "Where I come from is very poor, see—" "What makes this bus so quiet?" Donlevy interjects. "It's the armor," the boss answers, annoyed; he then continues: "All the richness is gone a long time ago—" "Armored for what?" Donlevy interrupts again. "So people shouldn't interrupt me!" Tamiroff exclaims. Sturges won an Oscar for Best Original Screenplay.

Green, Alfred E. (1889–1960), director. Began his film career in 1912 as an actor before he started directing comedy shorts and, eventually, feature-length films by 1917. His long and active career as director included films of various genres, with light comedies his specialty. His works featured many of the leading personalities of the period. In the 1920s, for instance, he directed Mary PICKFORD and Colleen MOORE in some of their most popular pictures.

SELECTED FILMS: *The Princess of Patches* (1917), *The Double-Dyed Deceiver* (1920), *Just Out of College, Little Lord Fauntleroy* (1921), *Our Leading Citizen, The Bachelor Daddy* (1922), *The Ne'er-Do-Well* (1923), *Pied Piper Malone* (1924), *Irene, Ella Cinders, Ladies at*

Play (1926), It's Tough to Be Famous (1932), Baby Face (1933), The Merry Frinks (1934), They Met in a Taxi, More Than a Secretary (1936), Let's Get Married (1937), The Gracie Allen Murder Case (1939), Mr. Winkle Goes to War (1944), The Jolson Story (1946), The Girl From Manhattan (1948), Two Gals and a Guy (1951), Paris Model (1953), Top Banana (1954). ∎

Green, Harry (1892–1958), comedian, actor. Worked chiefly on stage as a comic, appearing only occasionally in films during the 1930s. He played supporting roles in several films in England, including Charlie CHAPLIN'S *A King in New York* (1957). He had been a lawyer at one time.

SELECTED FILMS: Close Harmony, Why Bring That Up?, The Kibitzer (1929), Be Yourself, Honey (1930), Too Much Harmony (1933), Bottoms Up, She Learned About Sailors (1934), The Cisco Kid and the Lady (1937), Star Dust (1940), An Alligator Named Daisy (1957), Next to No Time (1958). ∎

Green, Mitzi (1920–1969), actress. Worked in vaudeville in her parents' act before becoming a child star of early sound films. A winsome and charming youngster, she appeared chiefly in light films. In 1932 she had the lead in the first adaptation of Harold Green's popular comic strip, "Little Orphan Annie." In 1934, with her popularity declining, she retired from films, but made a slight comeback in 1940 in routine comedies.

SELECTED FILMS: The Marriage Playground (1929), Honey, Love Among the Millionaires, Tom Sawyer (1930), Finn and Hattie, Skippy, Dude Ranch, Newly Rich, Huckleberry Finn (1931), Girl Crazy, Little Orphan Annie (1932), Transatlantic Merry-Go-Round (1934), Walk With Music (1940), Lost in Alaska, Bloodhounds of Broadway (1952). ∎

Greene, Harrison (1884–1945), actor. Worked in vaudeville in a husband-and-wife act and with several famous comics including WEBER AND FIELDS before settling in Hollywood in the late 1920s. Thick-set and dark-haired, he played character roles in many light films.

SELECTED FILMS: International House (1933), The Singing Cowboy (1936), A Bride for Henry (1937), Mr. Boggs Steps Out (1938), The Honeymoon's Over (1939), You Can't Fool Your Wife (1940), Between Two Women (1944). ∎

Greenwood, Charlotte (1893–1978), actress, comedienne. Worked in nightclubs as a comic, sporadically in silent films, and on Broadway before settling in Hollywood. Tall and thin with long legs, she exploited her physical awkwardness and developed into one of the most popular comediennes of her time. She appeared in sound comedies and musicals, applying her vivacious and unique style of comedy and eccentric dancing to many otherwise mediocre films. Some of her best work was with Eddie CANTOR, Don AMECHE, and Betty GRABLE. She played opposite Buster KEATON in *Parlor, Bedroom and Bath* in 1931.

In *Springtime in the Rockies* (1942), for instance, she played a man-hungry confidante to Grable. "Where have you been?" Betty inquires. "Fishing," her friend replies. "Any luck?" "No," Charlotte admits, "but you should have seen the one that got away." In the same film she does a delightful and graceful solo dance while apparently inebriated.

SELECTED FILMS: Jane (1915), Baby Mine (1928), So Long Letty (1930), Parlor, Bedroom and Bath, Palmy Days, Stepping Out (1931), Cheaters at Play (1932), Down Argentine Way (1940), Tall, Dark and Handsome, Moon Over Miami (1941), Dixie Dugan, The Gang's All Here (1943), Up in Mabel's Room (1944), Wake Up and Dream (1946), The Great Dan Patch (1949), Peggy (1950), Dangerous When Wet (1953), Oklahoma! (1955), The Opposite Sex (1956). ∎

Greig, Robert (1880–1958), actor. Worked as a Hollywood character actor for almost two decades. He began his career in films during the early sound era. A portly actor who was born in Melbourne, Australia, he appeared in more than 100 features, usually playing prissy hotel managers or haughty butlers. In *Peg o' My Heart*, for example, he announces: "I beg your pardon, Sir Gerald. There's an unkempt sort of an individual outside to see you." He worked with some of the leading comedy directors of the period, including Ernst LUBITSCH and Preston STURGES.

SELECTED FILMS: *Animal Crackers, Paramount on Parade (1930), Tonight or Never (1931), Horse Feathers, Love Me Tonight, Trouble in Paradise (1932), Peg o' My Heart (1933), Cockeyed Cavaliers (1934), The Bishop Misbehaves (1935), Theodora Goes Wild (1936), Easy Living (1937), Way Down South (1939), No Time for Comedy (1940), The Lady Eve (1941), Sullivan's Travels, I Married a Witch, The Palm Beach Story (1942), Million Dollar Kid (1944), The Cheaters (1945), Mad Wednesday (1947), Unfaithfully Yours (1948), Bride of Vengeance (1949).* ■

Grey, Virginia (1917–), actress. Began her film career at age 9 in silent films. By the time she was 16, she appeared as a chorus girl in early sound films at Warner Brothers studios. Eventually, she was assigned lead roles, playing floozies and comical heroines in low-budget features. A beautiful blonde, she had a long screen career that stretched across six decades. She worked with some of the leading comics of the period, including, among others, the MARX BROTHERS, Red SKELTON, and ABBOTT AND COSTELLO. Retiring from the screen in 1970, she has appeared occasionally on stage.

SELECTED FILMS: *Uncle Tom's Cabin (1927), Misbehaving Ladies (1931), Dames (1934), Gold Diggers of 1935 (1935), Shopworn Angel (1938), Idiot's Delight, The Hardys Ride High, Another Thin Man (1939), Three Cheers for the Irish, Hullabaloo (1940), The Big Store, Whistling in the Dark (1941), Sweet Rosie O'Grady (1943), So This Is New York, Mexican Hayride (1948), Tammy Tell Me True, Bachelor in Paradise (1961), Rosie! (1967), Airport (1970).* ■

Gribbon, Eddie (1890–1965), actor. Worked as a comic character player for various studios, including producer Mack SENNETT, Monogram, and RKO. Large-framed and rough-looking, he frequently played boisterous characters. In fact, in one of his earliest appearances (*The Victor*) and in a series of "Joe Palooka" films more than 25 years later, he played similar types—men involved with prizefighting. He accompanied some of the leading comedians of the period. His brother, Harry GRIBBON, was a film comedian in silent and sound films.

SELECTED FILMS: *The Victor (1923), Stop That Man (1928), Two Weeks Off, Twin Beds, Honeymoon, Two Men and a Maid (1929), Dames Ahoy (1930), Mr. Lemon of Orange (1931), Everything's Ducky (1934), Flying Down to Zero (1935), Love on a Bet (1936), The Big Shot (1937), Maid's Night Out (1938), The Great Dictator (1940), To Heir Is Human (1944), Joe Palooka in the Counterpunch (1949).* ■

Gribbon, Harry (1886–1961), actor. Worked in early silent comedy shorts for Mack SENNETT'S KEYSTONE studios. He appeared as a supporting player for some of the leading screen comics of the period, including "Fatty" ARBUCKLE, Mabel NORMAND, Mack SWAIN, and Ford STERLING. His screen career spanned three decades, taking him into the sound era in which he continued to play supporting roles. His brother, Eddie GRIBBON, was a comic character actor in silent and sound films.

SELECTED FILMS: *Mabel, Fatty and the Law, Ye Olden Grafter, Ambrose's Sour Grapes, A Janitor's Wife's Temptation (1915), The Great Pearl Tangle, Perils of the Park, Love Will Conquer (1916), Stars and Bars, Two Crooks (1917), A*

Pullman Blunder (1918), Self-Made Man (1922), The Extra Girl (1923), The Tomboy (1924), On With the Show (1929), Snug in the Jug (1933), Sleepless Hollow (1936), Arsenic and Old Lace (1944). ∎

Griffin, Carlton Elliott (1893–1940), actor. Worked in vaudeville in an act called "Magic Glasses" before entering silent films in the early 1920s. He appeared as a supporting player in light features and numerous comedy shorts.

SELECTED FILMS: *At the Stage Door (1921), Girl Shy, The Painted Flapper (1924), The Great Jewel Robbery (1925), Her Big Adventure, Tramp, Tramp, Tramp (1926), Shivering Shakespeare, High C's (1930), The Pip From Pittsburgh, Rough Seas (1931), First in War (1932), Nature in the Wrong, Arabian Tights (1933), Maid in Hollywood, Another Wild Idea (1934), Southern Exposure, Nurse to You, Slightly Static (1935).* ∎

Griffith, Andy (1926–), actor. Appeared on Broadway before making his film debut in 1957. He starred in light comedies, often playing hayseeds and other innocents. But his film career never really took off after his initial success in his first two or three endeavors. He moved on to his own television shows, which became very popular. He is best remembered for his portrayal of the country bumpkin in *No Time for Sergeants.*

SELECTED FILMS: *A Face in the Crowd (1957), No Time for Sergeants, Onionhead (1958), The Second Time Around (1961), Angel in My Pocket (1969), Hearts of the West (1975).* ∎

Griffith, Corinne (1896–1979), actress. Made her film debut in 1916 after being put under contract by Vitagraph studios. She then moved to First National studios. She starred in dramas as well as light comedies, retaining her hold on stardom for 14 years. She retired from the screen in the early 1930s a

wealthy woman after appearing in a few films during the sound era. She made a brief return to films in 1961 in the offbeat *Paradise Alley,* directed by Hugo Haas, in which she played a hard-working wife and mother dreaming of a career in movies. Possessing an exceptional beauty, she was billed as "The Orchid Lady" of the silent screen. Because of her loveliness and her popularity, several film historians and critics have paralleled her career with that of Hedy Lamarr's in the 1940s.

SELECTED FILMS: *The Last Man (1916), The Love Doctor (1917), Miss Ambition, The Girl of Today (1918), Thin Ice (1919), The Garter Girl (1920), Divorce Coupons (1922), Single Wives (1924), The Marriage Whirl (1925), Mademoiselle Modiste, Syncopating Sue (1926), The Lady in Ermine (1927), The Garden of Eden (1928), Back Pay (1930), Paradise Alley (1961).* ∎

Griffith, Edward H. (1894–), director. Appeared on stage before beginning a long career in films in 1915 as an actor-writer. Within two years he turned to directing and worked steadily in this capacity through the 1940s, specializing in light films of routine quality.

SELECTED FILMS: *Law of the North (1917), The Garter Girl (1920), Scrambled Wives (1921), Atta Boy (1926), Hold 'Em, Yale (1928), Paris Bound, The Shady Lady (1929), Holiday (1930), The Animal Kingdom, Lady With a Past (1932), Biography of a Bachelor Girl, No More Ladies (1935), I'll Take Romance (1937), Honeymoon in Bali (1939), One Night in Lisbon (1941), Young and Willing, The Sky's the Limit (1943), Perilous Holiday (1946).* ∎

Griffith, Gordon (1907–1958), child actor, director. Appeared in early silent comedy shorts for Mack SENNETT'S KEYSTONE studios in the 1910s. He occasionally worked as a supporting player in films starring some of the leading screen comics of the period, including Charlie CHAPLIN, Mabel NOR-

MAND, and Chester CONKLIN. Finally, he turned his attentions to directing.

SELECTED FILMS (as actor): Kid Auto Races at Venice, The Star Boarder, Twenty Minutes of Love, Caught in a Cabaret, Tillie's Punctured Romance (1914), Huckleberry Finn (1920), That Something (1921), Catch My Smoke, Penrod, The Village Blacksmith (1922), Little Annie Rooney (1925), The Cat's Pajamas (1926), The Crusades (1935). ■

Griffith, James (1919–), actor. Began his long screen career in the mid-1940s. A thin, dark-haired supporting player, he has appeared in a variety of roles in dramas and light films, specializing in westerns.

SELECTED FILMS: Pardon My Rhythm (1944), Every Girl Should Be Married (1948), Oh, You Beautiful Doll! (1949), As Young As You Feel, The Lady Pays Off (1951), Ma and Pa Kettle at the Fair (1952), Anything Goes (1956), Advance to the Rear (1963), A Big Hand for the Little Lady (1966), The Main Event (1979). ■

Griffith, Raymond (1890–1957), actor, screenwriter. Spent his childhood in the theater as the son of show people. A dapper performer, he worked for Mack SENNETT in minor roles and, by 1923, became a gagman for actor-producer Douglas MacLEAN. That same year he returned to acting, appearing as a supporting or lead player in comic as well as straight roles throughout the silent period. His most memorable part was as the dying Belgian soldier in the trench with Lew Ayers in All Quiet on the Western Front. During the 1930s he turned to producing.

Some critics, including Walter Kerr, consider him an underrated comedian and place him just below the four giants of the silent era: CHAPLIN, LLOYD, KEATON, and LANGDON. It is difficult to assess Griffith's work, however, since few of his films are available to the public for viewing or study.

SELECTED FILMS: A Scoundrel's Toll (1916), The Follies Girl (1918), The Crossroads of New York, Fools First (1922), Red Lights, The Eternal Three (1923), Changing Husbands, Lily of the Dust, Open All Night (1924), Forty Winks, The Night Club, Paths to Paradise, A Regular Fellow, When Winter Went, Fine Clothes (1925), Hands Up, Wet Paint, You'd Be Surprised (1926), Wedding Bells, Time to Love (1927), Trent's Last Case (1929), All Quiet on the Western Front (1930), The Great Profile (1940). ■

Griffith, William M. (1897–1960), actor. Entered films in the 1930s following a career on stage. He appeared as a supporting player in dramas and light films.

SELECTED FILMS: Time Out for Romance (1937), Everybody Does It (1949).■

Grodin, Charles (1935–), actor. Made his New York stage debut in 1962 before entering films in the latter part of the decade. A good-looking lead player, he has appeared in dramas and light films, his screen career peaking in the 1970s. He has continued his stage career, between film assignments.

SELECTED FILMS: Rosemary's Baby (1968), Sex and the College Girl, Catch-22 (1970), The Heartbreak Kid (1972), Heaven Can Wait (1978), Sunburn, Real Life (1979), It's My Turn, Seems Like Old Times (1980), The Incredible Shrinking Woman, The Great Muppet Caper (1981), The Lonely Guy, The Woman in Red (1984), Movers & Shakers (1985). ■

Guilfoyle, Paul (1902–1961), actor. Appeared in more than 50 films, often as a hoodlum or treacherous punk. A sinister-looking character actor, he showed up as an urban type or Runyonesque figure in melodramas and light films during a career that extended from the mid-1930s to 1960. He occasionally tried his hand at directing.

SELECTED FILMS: *Special Agent* (1935), *You Can't Beat Luck* (1937), *I'm From the City, The Mad Miss Manton* (1938), *Unexpected Father* (1939), *Brother Orchid* (1940), *Petticoat Larceny* (1943), *It Happened Tomorrow* (1944), *Miss Mink of 1949, There's a Girl in My Heart, Trouble Preferred* (1949), *When I Grow Up* (1951), *The Boy and the Pirates* (1960). ■

Guiol, Fred (1898–), director. Worked for Hal Roach studios in the late silent period as a director of comedy shorts, mainly starring comedians LAUREL AND HARDY and Charley CHASE. With the advent of sound, he directed full-length features, chiefly low-budget comedies.

SELECTED FILMS: *Slipping Wives, Love 'Em and Weep, Why Girls Love Sailors, With Love and Hisses, Do Detectives Think?, Sugar Daddies, The Second Hundred Years* (1927), *What's Your Racket?* (1934), *The Rainmakers* (1935), *Silly Billies, Mummy's Boys* (1936), *Tanks a Million, Miss Polly* (1941), *Hay Foot* (1942), *Here Comes Trouble* (1946), *As You Were* (1951). ■

Gulliver, Dorothy, actress. Appeared in silent films during the late 1920s. She played the female lead in a series of comedy shorts produced by Universal studios titled "THE COLLEGIANS," co-starring George LEWIS.

SELECTED FILMS: *Benson at Calford, Around the Bases* (1926), *Shield of Honor* (1927), *Good Morning, Judge* (1928), *College Love* (1929), *Cheating Blondes* (1933), *Faces* (1968). ■

"Gumps, The." A series of two-reel comedies produced by Universal studios from 1923 to 1928. The films, heavily laden in slapstick, were based on the popular comic strip created by Sidney Smith. Joe MURPHY played Andy

Gump, to whom he bore an uncanny resemblance; Fay TINCHER portrayed Min; and Jackie Morgan took the role of Chester. Several famous directors got their experience working on this series, including Erle C. KENTON and Norman TAUROG.

"Gussle" comedies. A series of one- and two-reel shorts produced by Mack SENNETT'S KEYSTONE studios starring Sydney CHAPLIN, Charlie's half-brother. Sydney portrayed the brash and impetuous "Gussle" in these crude slapstick comedies made from 1914 to 1915. The series was directed by Charles AVERY.

SELECTED FILMS: *Gussle, the Golfer* (1914), *Gussle's Day of Rest, Gussle's Wayward Path, Gussle Rivals Jonah, Gussle's Backward Way, Gussle Tied to Trouble* (1915). ■

Guttenberg, Steve (1958–), actor. Worked in television before entering films in the late 1970s. He has appeared chiefly in off-beat comedies, although he has done some competent work in dramas as well. His lighter films, although popular at the box-office, have been generally panned by the critics. One exception is *Cocoon,* a film in which he did not have a featured role.

SELECTED FILMS: *The Chicken Chronicles* (1978), *Players* (1979), *Police Academy* (1984), *Police Academy 2, Cocoon, Bad Medicine* (1985). ■

Gwenn, Edmund (1875–1959), actor. Appeared on stage in his native England at the turn of the century and on Broadway. Although he made films in England as early as 1916, his popularity as a character actor grew chiefly with his Hollywood films. Short and balding, he portrayed elderly characters, sometimes charmingly mischievous, almost always kind. He won an Oscar as Best Supporting Actor for his role in *Miracle on 34th Street.*

SELECTED FILMS: *The Bishop Misbehaves* (1935), *Sylvia Scarlett* (1936), *The Earl of Chicago, The Doctor Takes a*

Wife, Pride and Prejudice (1940), Cheers for Miss Bishop, The Devil and Miss Jones, Charley's Aunt (1941), A Yank at Eton (1942), The Meanest Man in the World (1943), She Went to the Races (1945), Miracle on 34th Street, Life With Father (1947), Apartment for Peggy (1948), Pretty Baby, Mister 880 (1950), Bonzo Goes to College (1952), Mister Scoutmaster, The Bigamist (1953), The Trouble With Harry, It's a Dog's Life (1955). ∎

Gwynne, Ann (1918–), actress. Worked as a model and on stage before entering films in the late 1930s. Born Marguerite Gwynne Trice, she played female leads and supporting roles in numerous routine melodramas and light films.

SELECTED FILMS: Unexpected Father (1939), Spring Parade, Honeymoon Deferred, Sandy Is a Lady (1940), Tight Shoes (1941), Jail House Blues, Ride 'Em Cowboy (1942), South of Dixie, Moon Over Las Vegas (1944), The Ghost Goes Wild, Killer Dill (1947), Breakdown (1952). ∎

H

Haade, William (1903–1966), actor. Began his screen career in the late 1930s as a supporting player, a station he maintained for the next two decades. Tall, fair-haired, and rough-looking, he appeared in scores of dramas, westerns, and light films. He was comfortable on either side of the law. He worked with some of the leading comics of the period, including, among others, Gracie ALLEN, Bob HOPE, ABBOTT AND COSTELLO, and LAUREL AND HARDY.

SELECTED FILMS: Kid Galahad, He Couldn't Say No (1937), Boy Meets Girl, Down on the Farm (1938), The Gracie Allen Murder Case (1939), Rise and Shine, You're in the Army Now (1941), I Married a Witch (1942), The Dancing Masters (1943), Here Come the Waves (1944), Honeymoon Ahead (1945), The Well Groomed Bride (1946), Where There's Life, Buck Privates Come Home (1947), Good Sam (1948), Skirts Ahoy! (1952), Abbott and Costello Meet the Keystone Kops (1955), Spoilers of the Forest (1957). ■

Hackett, Albert (1900–), screenwriter. See Frances Goodrich.

Hackett, Buddy (1924–), actor, comic. Began his show business career as a waiter-entertainer in resort hotels. Short and dumpy in appearance, but with an abundance of charm, he found work as a comedian in small local nightclubs. Much of his comedy is based on his personal experiences and observations in the military service, in his father's upholstery business, etc. He effectively integrates his rubber face and body motions into his verbal delivery. Interested in trying other branches of show business, he worked as a comic actor on stage in the 1950s and in films in the 1950s and 1960s. These ventures led to television assignments in which he starred as a general entertainer. He has appeared sporadically in light films, adding his charm and wit to any part he portrays.

In Everything's Ducky (1961) he was in charge of a talking duck that also had athletic pretensions. Buddy has to talk his charge out of playing tennis. "You'd look so stupid jumping over the net with those short legs."

SELECTED FILMS: Walking My Baby Back Home (1953), God's Little Acre (1958), All Hands on Deck, Everything's Ducky (1961), The Wonderful World of the Brothers Grimm, The Music Man (1962), It's a Mad, Mad, Mad, Mad World (1963), Muscle Beach Party (1964), The Love Bug, The Good Guys and the Bad Guys (1969). ■

Haden, Sara (1897–1981), actress. Worked as a child actress and appeared on Broadway and in films since the early 1930s. As a character player, she appeared in many films, especially in the roles of spinster and office worker. Her most popular portrayal was that of ANDY HARDY'S sweet Aunt Milly in the MGM comedy series.

SELECTED FILMS: Spitfire, The White Parade (1934), Captain January, Little Miss Nobody (1936), A Family Affair

(1937), Out West With the Hardys (1938), The Hardys Ride High (1939), Love Crazy (1941), Woman of the Year (1942), The Youngest Profession, Thousands Cheer (1943), Bathing Beauty (1944), Mr. Ace (1946), The Bishop's Wife (1947), Rachel and the Stranger (1948), The Great Rupert (1950), Andy Hardy Comes Home (1958). ■

Hagart, Dorothy, actress. Appeared in early silent comedy shorts in supporting roles for Mack SENNETT'S KEYSTONE studios. She worked with some of the leading screen comics of the period, including Ford STERLING, Polly MORAN, and Bobby VERNON.

SELECTED FILMS: A Home Breaking Hound, The Hunt (1915), Black Eyes and Blue (1916). ■

Hagen, Jean (1923–1977), actress. Appeared on radio and on Broadway before making her film debut in 1949 in *Adam's Rib.* Perhaps her most memorable role was her hilarious caricature of the dumb silent movie star with a shrill voice in *Singin' in the Rain.* A gifted actress and comedienne, she was, for the most part, never given the opportunity to reach her full potential.

SELECTED FILMS: Adam's Rib (1949), A Life of Her Own (1950), No Questions Asked (1951), Singin' in the Rain (1952), Arena, Latin Lovers, Half a Hero (1953), Spring Reunion (1957), The Shaggy Dog (1959), Dead Ringer (1964). ■

Hagman, Larry (1930–), actor. Has appeared on stage and sporadically in light films, chiefly in comedy roles. His major success, however, has been in television, especially "Dallas."

SELECTED FILMS: Ensign Pulver (1964), Up in the Cellar (1970), Harry and Tonto (1974), Mother, Jugs and Speed, The Big Bus (1976). ■

Hail the Conquering Hero (1944), PAR. Dir. Preston Sturges; Sc. Preston Sturges; with Eddie Bracken, Ella Raines, Raymond Walburn, William Demarest.

One of the most enjoyable of the director's satirical comedies, the film pokes gentle fun at several institutions of American life. Army reject Eddie BRACKEN, reluctant to face his family and friends, is encouraged by a group of compassionate marines to temporarily play the role of a homecoming hero. The conspiracy gets out of hand as Bracken is compelled to challenge the incumbent mayor. Finally, the bogus hero confesses all and is forgiven and accepted by his neighbors. Beneath the warm humor lurks the director's trenchant attacks on politics, heroism, small-town life, and the military. Events are helped considerably by an excellent supporting cast of comic character actors, a familiar Sturges trademark. William DEMAREST plays a sympathetic marine, while Franklin PANGBORN portrays a prissy emcee who tries to organize the homecoming ceremonies for Bracken. STURGES was at his peak when he made this film, but his career and popularity came to an abrupt end within the next few years.

Haines, William (1900–1973), actor. Worked in a Wall Street office before winning a Hollywood "new faces" contest. He made his film debut in 1922 and gained popularity in a series of light romances and comedies. He specialized in the roles of brash youths or conceited college boys who had to reform before they won the love of the leading ladies. He played this type of part as well as the "eternal youth" for many years. He retired from the screen in the mid-1930s.

SELECTED FILMS: Brothers Under the Skin (1922), Three Wise Fools (1923), Three Weeks, True as Steel, The Midnight Express (1924), Little Annie Rooney, Sally, Irene and Mary (1925), The Thrill Hunter, Mike, Lovey Mary, Tell It to the Marines (1926), Slide, Kelly,

Slide, Spring Fever (1927), The Smart Set, Excess Baggage, Show People, Alias Jimmy Valentine (1928), The Duke Steps Out, Navy Blues (1929), Free and Easy, Way Out West (1930), A Tailor-Made Man (1931), Fast Life (1932), Young and Beautiful, The Marines Are Coming (1934). ■

Errol Flynn, Alan Hale, Ronald Reagan

Hale, Alan (1892–1950), actor, director. Attempted a career in opera, then became a silent screen actor in 1911 in D. W. Griffith's films of the Biograph period. During the 1920s Hale, born Rufus Alan McKahan, directed a handful of films for Cecil B. DeMille, appeared as a lead actor in films, then settled into character parts during the silent era. He emerged as one of the most popular character actors in Hollywood, often in the role of comic relief and confidant to Errol Flynn, and appeared in hundreds of films. Large-framed and brawny, he usually played oafish but comical roles in action films. He had the distinction of portraying Little John in the 1922 and 1938 film versions of the Robin Hood legend, the former starring Douglas FAIRBANKS and the latter, Errol FLYNN.

In Strawberry Blonde (1941) he played the ebullient father of a dentist during the Gay Nineties. Learning that his son has just been fired and has trouble holding a job, Hale tries to console him: "I wasn't cut out to be a street cleaner, and it's no use reaching for the stars."

SELECTED FILMS: The Cowboy and the Lady (1911), The Price She Paid (1917), One Glorious Day, Robin Hood (1922), Cameo Kirby (1923), Sal of Singapore, Sailor's Holiday (1929), She Got What She Wanted (1930), Rebecca of Sunnybrook Farm (1932), It Happened One Night (1934), Grand Old Girl (1935), Our Relations (1936), Thin Ice (1937), Dodge City, The Man in the Iron Mask (1939), Tugboat Annie Sails Again (1940), The Smiling Ghost (1941), Desperate Journey (1942), This Is the Army (1943), Make Your Own Bed (1944), Roughly Speaking (1945), My Wild Irish Rose (1947), Adventures of Don Juan (1948), The Inspector General (1949), Rogues of Sherwood Forest (1950). ■

Hale, Alan, Jr. (1918–), actor. Began his screen career in the early 1930s. A brawny, cheerful character player who occasionally got leads, he followed in his father's footsteps portraying affable, happy-go-lucky types in dramas and light films. He never attained the status that Hale, Sr., had achieved but carved a solid place for himself in television with several successful series, especially "Gilligan's Island."

SELECTED FILMS: Wild Boys of the Road (1933), All-American Co-Ed (1941), Monsieur Beaucaire (1946), Sarge Goes to College (1947), It Happens Every Spring (1949), Kill the Umpire! (1950), Honeychile (1951), The Lady Takes a Flyer (1957), Advance to the Rear (1963), The North Avenue Irregulars (1978), Hambone and Hillie (1983), The Red Fury (1985). ■

Hale, Creighton (1882–1965), actor. Appeared on stage in his native Ireland before coming to Hollywood. Born Patrick Fitzgerald, he played in featured roles from 1914 and in supporting parts well into the sound era. Besides appearing in serials and numerous dramas, he also performed in light films, often as docile characters.

SELECTED FILMS: The Million Dollar Mystery (1914), Mary of the Movies, Three Wise Fools (1923), The Marriage Circle (1924), Seven Days (1925), Oh, Baby! (1926), Thumbs Down (1927), Holiday (1930), The Masquerader (1933), Larceny, Inc. (1942), The Perils of Pauline (1947), Beyond the Forest (1949). ■

Hale, Jonathan (1891–1966), actor. Appeared as a character actor in more than 200 films. He often portrayed an easily annoyed businessman in dramas and light films. His most famous role was that of Mr. Dithers in the BLONDIE comedies in which he appeared from 1937 to 1946.

In Blondie for Victory (1942) he delivered what was probably his best line. He visits Dagwood's home, only to learn that Blondie is on voluntary patrol as a fire watcher at a local dam. The sexist Dithers strongly disapproves. "It's up to you," he orders Dagwood, "to convince Blondie a woman's place is in the home, not by a dam site."

SELECTED FILMS: Lightning Strikes Twice (1934), Alice Adams (1935), Charlie Chan at the Race Track (1936), You Only Live Once (1937), Judge Hardy's Children, Blondie (1938), In Name Only (1939), The Saint Takes Over (1940), Blondie Goes Latin (1941), Calling Dr. Gillespie (1942), Sweet Rosie O'Grady (1943), My Buddy (1944), Leave It to Blondie (1945), Easy to Wed (1946), The Ghost Goes Wild (1947), Three Husbands (1950), My Pal Gus (1952), She Couldn't Say No (1954), Jaguar (1956). ■

Hale, Louise Closser (1872–1933), actress. Appeared on Broadway before entering films at the beginning of the sound era. She frequently portrayed domineering women in both dramas and comedies during her short Hollywood career.

SELECTED FILMS: The Hole in the Wall, Paris (1929), Dangerous Nan McGrew, Big Boy, The Princess and the Plumber (1930), Daddy Long Legs, Platinum Blonde (1931), Movie Crazy, No

More Orchids (1932), The Barbarian, Another Language, Dinner at Eight (1933). ■

Haley, Jack (1899–1979), actor. Worked in vaudeville and on Broadway in the early 1920s before making his film debut in 1927. He appeared chiefly in light films as a lead or supporting actor. After making a film in 1930, he returned to the stage for a few seasons and then came back to Hollywood in 1933. His most famous role was that of the Tin Man in the film classic The Wizard of Oz (1939). He also co-starred with Shirley TEMPLE and other popular screen personalities during the 1930s and 1940s. He did some radio work between Hollywood assignments. He retired from films in 1949.

SELECTED FILMS: Broadway Madness (1927), Follow Thru (1930), Sitting Pretty (1933), Here Comes the Groom (1934), The Girl Friend (1935), The Poor Little Rich Girl, Pigskin Parade (1936), She Had to Eat (1937), Rebecca of Sunnybrook Farm, Hold That Co-Ed (1938), Moon Over Miami (1941), Higher and Higher (1943), One Body Too Many (1944), People Are Funny, Vacation in Reno (1946), Make Mine Laughs (1949), Norwood (1970). ■

Hall, Alexander (1894–1968), director. Worked in the theater as a child actor and entered films before World War I as an actor. By the 1920s he became a director. He turned out many light films, including fantasies such as Here Comes Mr. Jordan (1941). He directed many of the leading stars of the period, including Shirley TEMPLE, Mae WEST, and Bob HOPE. He was the husband of actress Lola Lane.

SELECTED FILMS: Sinners in the Sun, Madame Racketeer (1932), The Girl in 419 (1933), Little Miss Marker (1934), Goin' to Town (1935), There's Always a Woman (1938), Good Girls Go to Paris (1939), He Stayed for Breakfast (1940), Bedtime Story (1941), My Sister Eileen (1942), The Heavenly Body (1944), She

Wouldn't Say Yes (1945), Down to Earth (1947), The Great Lover (1949), Up Front (1951), Let's Do It Again (1953), Forever Darling (1956). ■

Hall, Charlie (1890–1959), actor. Performed in music halls in his native England and in theaters in the United States before entering Hollywood films in 1927. He was a prolific supporting actor, often appearing as the heavy in LAUREL AND HARDY film shorts as well as features. He appeared with Stan and Ollie in at least two acknowledged classics: the two-reeler "Battle of the Century" with its definitive pie-throwing sequence, and the award-winning "The Music Box." He remained active into the 1950s.

SELECTED FILMS: Love 'Em and Weep, The Battle of the Century (1927), Leave 'Em Laughing, You're Darn Tootin', Two Tars (1928), Wrong Again, That's My Wife, Double Whoopie, Berth Marks, Men O' War, They Go Boom, Bacon Grabbers, Angora Love (1929), Below Zero (1930), Laughing Gravy, Pardon Us, Come Clean, Scratch as Scratch Can (1931), Any Old Port, The Music Box (1932), Twice Two, Me and My Pal, Sons of the Desert, Sneak Easily (1933), The Live Ghost, Tit for Tat, Kentucky Kernels, Babes in the Goods (1934), Thicker Than Water (1935), Our Relations (1936), Pick a Star (1937), Saps at Sea (1940), Top Sergeant Mulligan (1941), The Vicious Years (1951). ■

Hall, Huntz (1920–), actor. Appeared on radio before making his film debut in *Dead End* (1937) as a member of the gang of delinquents. He stayed with the gang, wise-cracking and mugging his way through a series of low-budget comedy spin-offs from the film. He portrayed the dumb gangmember, Dippy, usually the catalyst for the low-comedy routines which saturated the series as the gang's name changed from the "Dead End Kids" to the "East Side Kids" and, finally, to the BOWERY BOYS. He made a few attempts at acting in major produc-

tions, especially after the series was abandoned.

SELECTED FILMS: Spooks Run Wild (1941), Wonder Man (1945), A Walk in the Sun (1946), The Gentle Giant (1967), Herbie Rides Again (1974), The Manchu Murder Caper Mystery (1975). ■

Hall, James (1900–1940), actor. Worked on stage before entering films during the silent period. A good-looking male lead, he appeared in numerous dramas and light films in a career that carried him into sound features.

SELECTED FILMS: The Man Alone (1923), The Campus Flirt, Stranded in Paris (1926), Ritzy, Rolled Stockings, Silk Legs (1927), Just Married, The Fleet's In (1928), Smiling Irish Eyes (1929), Let's Go Native, Divorce Among Friends (1930), Millie, The Good Bad Girl (1931), Manhattan Tower (1932). ■

Hall, Porter (1888–1953), actor. Worked on stage before entering films in the mid-1930s. A short figure with a dark mustache, he specialized in sly, craven types. He was not averse to double-dealing or shooting someone in the back (Gary Cooper in *The Plainsman*). He appeared as a character actor in numerous dramas and light films and was a member of Preston STURGES' stock company of comic supporting players.

SELECTED FILMS: The Thin Man (1934), The Princess Comes Across (1936), This Way Please, Hotel Haywire (1937), Dangerous to Know, The Arkansas Traveler (1938), Mr. Smith Goes to Washington (1939), His Girl Friday (1940), Sullivan's Travels (1941), Butch Minds the Baby (1942), The Great Moment (1943), The Miracle of Morgan's Creek (1944), Murder, He Says (1945), Mad Wednesday (1947), Vice Squad (1953). ■

Hall, Thurston (1883–1958), actor. Worked on stage before entering films during the silent era as a leading player and returned during the sound era in character roles. Rather stocky and silver-haired, he appeared in over 150 films as a character actor, chiefly as an easily annoyed, crooked businessman.

SELECTED FILMS: Idle Hands (1921), Fair Lady (1922), The Girl Friend (1935), Theodora Goes Wild (1936), Don't Tell the Wife (1937), Little Miss Roughneck, Professor Beware (1938), Million Dollar Legs, Jeepers Creepers (1939), The Great McGinty (1940), She Knew All the Answers (1941), The Great Gildersleeve (1942), I Dood It (1943), In Society (1944), Brewster's Millions (1945), She Wrote the Book (1946), The Farmer's Daughter (1947), Up in Central Park (1948), Blondie's Secret (1949), One Too Many (1950), Skirts Ahoy (1952), Affair in Reno (1957). ▪

"Hall Room Boys" comedies. A series of two-reelers produced by Harry Cohn and his brother Jack and released through Federated Film Exchange. The comedy shorts, made between 1919 and 1923, starred several former vaudevillians as well as screen comics, including Neely EDWARDS, Ed Flanagan, Sidney Smith, Harry McCoy, and George Monberg. When McCoy left, he was replaced by comic Jimmie Adams. A variety of directors were involved with the comedies, including Al Santell, Archer McMackin, Arthur Hotaling, Harry Williams, Henry Kerman, Noel Mason Smith, and Herman Raymaker. The series, consisting of more than 70 shorts, was based on the comic strip created by H. A. McGill. These comedy shorts helped the brothers Cohn build up their company in 1924 into the famous Columbia Pictures Corporation.

SELECTED FILMS: Taming the West (1919), A Close Shave (1920), We'll Get You Yet, Beach Nuts, Two Faces West, Whoa, Henry! (1921), Still Going Strong, A Tailor-Made Chauffeur, High Flyers (1922). ▪

Hallelujah, I'm a Bum (1933), UA. Dir. Lewis Milestone; Sc. S. N. Behrman, Ben Hecht; with Al Jolson, Madge Evans,

Frank Morgan, Harry Langdon, Chester Conklin, Edgar Connor.

In this unique romantic comedy set in the Depression, Al JOLSON portrays the hobo Bumper, a sort of unofficial mayor of Central Park, where he resides with his friends Egghead (LANGDON) and Acorn (Connor). The plot involves Bumper's meeting Madge Evans, who is suffering from amnesia, and falling in love with her. When she regains her memory, Bumper learns that she is the fiancee of his old acquaintance, the mayor of the city, played by Frank MORGAN. The film is unusual in several respects. Jolson wears no blackface and much of the dialogue is in rhyming couplets. The title song and others, including "You Are Too Beautiful," all of which Jolson handles effectively, are by Rodgers and Hart. The film evokes a rich tone and feel of a Hollywood Depression movie, replete with its sentimentality and charming romanticism.

Halliday, John (1880–1947), actor. Worked as a mining engineer and acted on stage before entering films during the silent era. Urbane and distinguished-looking with a neatly trimmed mustache, he appeared in numerous silent and sound dramas and light films as a male lead or character actor. One of his more important roles was as Katharine Hepburn's father in The Philadelphia Story.

SELECTED FILMS: The Woman Gives (1920), East Side Sadie (1929), Millie, Fifty Million Frenchmen, Captain Applejack, Consolation Marriage (1931), The Impatient Maiden (1932), Housewife, Happiness Ahead (1934), Three Cheers for Love (1936), Hotel for Women, That Certain Age (1939), The Philadelphia Story (1940), Lydia (1941). ▪

Hallor, Ray (1900–1944), actor. Began his screen career in early silent films. He appeared chiefly as a supporting player in dramas and light films, working until the advent of sound. He was killed suddenly in a car accident at age 44.

SELECTED FILMS: *An Amateur Orphan (1917), Dream Street (1921), The Circus Cowboy, Inez From Hollywood (1924), Learning to Love, Sally (1925), The High Flyer, It Must Be Love (1926), Quarantined Rivals (1927), Man Crazy, Manhattan Knights, Tropical Nights (1928), Fast Life, Noisy Neighbors (1929), The Truth About Youth (1930).* ■

Halton, Charles (1876–1959), actor. Began his screen career in the early 1930s as a supporting player and continued in this capacity for well over 100 dramas and light films. Small and bespectacled and with a dark mustache, he emerged as one of the most prolific and easily recognizable character actors in Hollywood. He often portrayed petty bureaucrats and hard-hearted businessmen who were especially rough on the unfortunate in society.

SELECTED FILMS: *The Strange Case, Honor Among Lovers (1931), Twenty Million Sweethearts (1934), Penrod and Sam, Pick a Star (1937), Penrod's Double Trouble, Bluebeard's Eighth Wife (1938), I'm From Missouri (1939), Tugboat Annie Sails Again (1940), Meet the Chump (1941), To Be or Not to Be (1942), My Kingdom for a Cook (1943), Up in Arms (1944), Mama Loves Papa (1945), It's a Wonderful Life (1946), The Bachelor and the Bobby-Soxer (1947), Here Comes the Groom (1951), Friendly Persuasion (1956).* ■

Ham, Harry (1891–1943), actor. Began his screen career in early silent comedy shorts. He appeared chiefly as a supporting player to some of the leading film comics of the period.

SELECTED FILMS: *A Seminary Scandal (1916), Tramp, Tramp, Tramp, A Gay Deceiver, His Wedded Wife, Kidding Sister, He Fell on the Beach, Down by the Sea, Crazy by Proxy, The Honeymooners, Skirts (1917), His Pajama Girl (1921), A Spanish Jade (1922).* ■

"Ham and Bud" comedies. A series of one-reel silent slapstick comedies produced by KALEM studios starring Lloyd HAMILTON and Bud DUNCAN. The approximately 200 film shorts, made prior to World War I, featured the antics of two tramps—the large-framed, bushy eyebrowed, heavily mustached Hamilton and Duncan, his diminutive foil. One of the many supporting players in the series was Marin SAIS, a popular comedienne and dramatic actress, who went on to star in serials and feature-length films. Two other players who occasionally joined the comedy team as the romantic interest were Ruth Roland, the future serial queen, and Marshall NEILAN, who directed many of the shorts.

SELECTED FILMS: *Ham the Lineman, Ham the Piano Mover, Ham and the Villain Factory, Ham the Iceman, The Tattered Duke, Don't Monkey With the Buzz Saw, Si's Wonderful Mineral Spring (1914), Ham and the Jitney Bus, Ham Among the Redskins, Ham the Detective, Ham in the Harem, Ham at the Garbage Gentlemen's Ball, Ham at the Beach, Blundering Blacksmiths (1915).* ■

Hamilton, Hale (1880–1942), actor. Appeared on stage before entering early silent comedy shorts. He worked as a lead comic as well as a supporting player throughout the silent era and one decade into the sound period, accompanying some of the leading screen personalities of the period.

SELECTED FILMS: *Her Painted Hero (1915), The Winning of Beatrice (1918), That's Good (1919), The Manicure Girl (1925), Summer Bachelor (1926), Listen, Lady (1929), Good Intentions (1930), A Tailor-Made Man, Strangers May Kiss, New Adventures of Get-Rich-Quick Wallingford, Oh! Oh! Cleopatra (1931), Call Her Savage (1932), Employees' Entrance, Sitting Pretty (1933), Big-Hearted Herbert, Heartburn (1934), The Nitwits, Hold 'Em Yale, Calm Yourself, Three Kids and a Queen (1935), Meet the Mayor (1938).* ■

Hamilton, Jack "Shorty" (1879–1925), actor. Appeared as a supporting player in early silent comedy shorts for Mack SENNETT'S KEYSTONE studios. He also starred in a series of comedies for Triangle studios, each listed as "a Shorty Hamilton Kay Bee Comedy." He worked with several of the leading silent comedians of the period, including, among others, Chester CONKLIN and Slim SUMMERVILLE. His career was cut short by a fatal car accident. He was 46 years old.

SELECTED FILMS: Shorty in the Clutches of the Cannibals, Shorty's Troubled Sleep, Shorty Turns Actor (1915), Gypsy Joe, Bucking Society, A Rough Knight, She Loved a Sailor, His Busted Trust (1916), Adventures of Shorty Hamilton (1917), Denny From Ireland (1918). ∎

Hamilton, John (1887–1958), actor. Worked on stage, in vaudeville, and as a comic supporting player in comedy shorts and features from the 1920s. He appeared with some of the most popular comedians of the period, including, among others, ABBOTT AND COSTELLO, the BOWERY BOYS, and the THREE STOOGES.

SELECTED FILMS: Rainbow Riley (1926), Dangerous Nan McGrew, Heads Up (1930), Two Wise Maids (1937), Dr. Rhythm (1938), Pound Foolish (1940), The Girl Who Dared, Meet Miss Bobby Socks, I'm From Arkansas, Crazy Knights (1944), Wife Wanted (1946), Her Wonderful Lie (1950), Listen, Judge (1952). ∎

Hamilton, Lillian (1896–), actress. Worked on stage as a juvenile before appearing in films in 1914. An attractive and talented performer in both comedies and dramas, she co-starred as the female lead in many of Ben TURPIN'S comedy shorts for Vogue studios. She worked for various studios, including Universal, Premier, and Vogue. She appeared also in films for the notable comedy producer Al CHRISTIE.

SELECTED FILMS: The Delinquent Bridegroom, For Ten Thousand Bucks, Some Liars, Poultry a la Mode, Ducking a Discord, He Did and He Didn't, Jealous Jolts (1916), Frightened Flirts, Masked Mirth (1917). ∎

Hamilton, Lloyd (1891–1935), actor. Worked in burlesque and in the theater before making his screen debut in 1914. He co-starred with Bud DUNCAN in a series of silent comedy shorts for KALEM studios known as HAM AND BUD comedies. He switched to Fox studios where he became a popular comedian. He eventually began his own company and starred in a string of successful comedy shorts. The two-reelers were released through Educational Pictures, where, unfortunately, a major fire destroyed much of the work of the comedian. The funny characters he portrayed on screen changed dramatically from the gruff, self-assured Ham to the more effeminate roles he assumed later in his career.

Hamilton never advanced beyond a second-string comic, but he was one of the better minor clowns. Several of his own contemporaries, especially Buster KEATON and Charley CHASE, appreciated his comic style and singled him out as a formidable talent. Various factors might have hampered him. He did not really develop a distinct screen personality as the above two comics or as CHAPLIN and Harry LANGDON had done. He fared better than some other comedians in that he was naturally funny and talented, but often his material was weak. This may have been due to his studio's tight budget and its relatively minor writers. Producer Al CHRISTIE, who turned out many comical shorts and helped many careers to blossom, was nevertheless the third-ranking contributor to the world of film comedy. Mack SENNETT was the real genius, followed closely by Hal ROACH, who superseded Sennett in the 1920s.

Christie ran a distant third. These two components, which have hampered many other screen clowns, were certainly enough to relegate this once funny comic to relative obscurity today.

SELECTED FILMS: *Ham the Lineman* (1914), *A Twilight Baby* (1918), *His Darker Self, A Self-Made Failure* (1924), *Rolling Stones* (1925), *The Rainmaker* (1926), *Robinson Crusoe Ltd.* (1928), *Black Waters, Tanned Legs, The Show of Shows* (1929), *Are You There?* (1931), *False Impressions* (1932), *Too Many Highballs* (1933). ▪

Margaret Hamilton and W. C. Fields

Hamilton, Margaret (1902–1985), actress. Worked on stage before making her film debut in 1933. Appearing as a character actress in numerous dramas and light films, she often portrayed an officious maid or neighbor, a busybody, or, as she herself characterized her roles, "women with a heart of gold and a corset of steel." Her most unforgettable role was that of the Wicked Witch of the West in *The Wizard of Oz* (1939) in which she threatens Judy Garland with the following: "I'll get you, my dearie, and your little dog, too!" And in *Stablemates* (1938) she informs Wallace BEERY: "I look the same—wet or dry."

SELECTED FILMS: *Another Language* (1933), *Broadway Bill* (1934), *The Farmer Takes a Wife* (1935), *Chatterbox* (1936), *Nothing Sacred* (1937), *A Slight Case of Murder* (1938), *Babes in Arms* (1939), *My Little Chickadee* (1940), *Play Girl* (1941), *Meet the Stewarts* (1942), *Johnny Come Lately* (1943), *Janie Gets Married* (1946), *Mad Wednesday* (1947), *State of the Union* (1948), *Riding High* (1950), *Comin' Round the Mountain* (1951), *13 Ghosts* (1960), *The Daydreamer* (1966), *Rosie!* (1967), *Angel in My Pocket* (1969), *Journey Back to Oz* (1974). ▪

Hamilton, Murray (1923–1986), actor. Worked in films and television for more than three decades. A talented character player, he appeared in dramas and light films, making his screen debut in the early 1950s.

SELECTED FILMS: *Bright Victory* (1951), *Houseboat, No Time for Sergeants* (1958), *The Graduate* (1967), *1941* (1979), *Hysterical* (1983). ▪

Hampton, Hope (1899–1982), actress. Appeared in light silent films during the 1920s, usually as a female lead.

SELECTED FILMS: *The Bait* (1921), *Star Dust* (1922), *The Gold Diggers, Hollywood, Lawful Larceny* (1923), *The Price of a Party, The Truth About Women* (1924), *Lover's Island* (1925), *The Unfair Sex* (1926), *The Road to Reno* (1938). ▪

"Hank and Lank" comedies. A series of one-reel comedy shorts produced in 1910 starring Augustus CARNEY and Victor POTEL. The first of the series, "Joyriding," was so popular that the studio, ESSANAY, followed with a series for weekly release. The co-stars slowly developed two distinct rural characters whom the audiences identified with and delighted in. The short-lived series ended when Carney moved on to create his ALKALI IKE character in 1911, forcing his partner, Potel, to find a new role, that of "Slippery Slim."

Hanks, Tom (1956–), actor. Worked in television before entering films. He has made a few successful comedies during the 1980s and is popular with youthful audiences. He has portrayed suave, wise-cracking but charming characters.

In *Nothing in Common* he played a wise-cracking super-salesman on his way up. The opening scene finds him on board an airplane under a blanket with a pretty stewardess. "I'm a frequent flier," he says to another passenger. "They give me a bonus." Later, he observes horses mating. "Afterwards, what do they do," he asks, "go back to the barn for a cigarette?"

SELECTED FILMS: *Bachelor Party, Splash (1984), Volunteers, The Man With One Red Shoe (1985), The Money Pit, Nothing in Common (1986).* ∎

Harding, Ann (1901–1981), actress. Appeared in stock and on Broadway during the 1920s as a female lead before entering early sound films. Born Dorothy Walton Gatley, she rapidly rose to stardom in dramas and light films. A talented and confident actress of unusual beauty, she received an Academy Award nomination for her role in *Holiday* (1930). She left Hollywood temporarily in the late 1930s to star on Broadway, returning to the screen in 1942 as a character player. She retired from films in 1956, appearing occasionally on stage.

SELECTED FILMS: *Paris Bound, Her Private Affair (1929), The Animal Kingdom (1932), When Ladies Meet, Double Harness (1933), Biography of a Bachelor Girl (1935), The Lady Consents (1936), Janie, Nine Girls (1944), Those Endearing Young Charms (1945), Janie Gets Married (1946), It Happened on Fifth Avenue (1947), Strange Intruder (1956).* ∎

Hardy, Oliver (1892–1957), actor, comic. Worked as a child performer in minstrel shows and later on stage. Born in Harlem, Georgia, he began his film career in 1913 in "Outwitting Dad." Be-

cause of his large frame, he was often cast as a "heavy" in silent comedies, supporting many leading comedians. Occasionally he appeared in feature-length films. He developed his comic style during his early years in film from a comic strip character called Helpful Henry.

He was destined to remain a minor comic in Hal ROACH'S stable of comics until, in 1926, he was teamed with Stan LAUREL, the thin, bemused comic from England who was also appearing solo in silent shorts. "Putting Pants on Philip" (1926) is generally considered their first "official" LAUREL AND HARDY film. Hardy's childlike expressions, blinking eyelashes, florid gestures, and double chins all worked together to attest that his self-assuredness would usually result in some disaster; his pretentious assertiveness, as when he repeatedly announces to Stan: "Let me do it" or "I'll go first," continuously betrayed him. Several film historians have written that Laurel was the creative half of the famous team, but any observer knows that Ollie certainly contributed his share. The films below represent Hardy's work without Laurel. For their films as a team, see LAUREL AND HARDY.

SELECTED FILMS: *Spaghetti and Lottery, Charley's Aunt, Mixed Flats (1915), Dreamy Knights, The Serenade, Aunt Bill, Love and Duty (1916), The Handyman, The Chef, Hello Trouble, Playmates (1918), Mules and Mortgages (1919), Married to Order (1920), Little Wildcat, Fortune's Mask (1922), The Three Ages (1923), The Wizard of Oz (1925), Stop, Look and Listen, The Perfect Clown (1926), No Man's Law, Fluttering Hearts (1927), Zenobia (1939), The Fighting Kentuckian (1949), Riding High (1950).* ∎

Hardy, Sam (1883–1935), actor. Began his screen career in early silent films and continued into the 1930s as a supporting actor. He appeared in numerous dramas and light films.

SELECTED FILMS: *A Woman's Experience* (1918), *Get-Rich-Quick Wallingford* (1921), *Little Old New York* (1923), *Bluebeard's Seven Wives* (1925), *The Perfect Sap, Orchids and Ermine, The Life of Riley* (1927), *The Big Noise, The Butter and Egg Man* (1928), *The Floradora Girl* (1930), *Annabelle's Affairs, Peach O'Reno* (1931), *Goldie Gets Along* (1933), *Little Miss Marker* (1934), *Hooray for Love* (1935), *Powdersmoke Range* (1936). ∎

Harlam, Macey (–1923), actress. Worked on stage before beginning her short career in silent films in the early 1920s. She appeared as a supporting player in several dramas and light films.

SELECTED FILMS: *The Woman and the Puppet* (1920), *The Plaything of Broadway, You Find It Everywhere* (1921), *Always the Woman, Beyond the Rainbow, Fair Lady, When Knighthood Was in Flower* (1922), *Broadway Broke, Bella Donna* (1923). ∎

Harlan, Kenneth (1895–1967), actor. Appeared on stage and in vaudeville as a hoofer before entering silent films in 1917. A dark-haired, handsome actor, he played leading roles through the 1920s and, with the advent of sound, became a supporting player in dramas and light films. He was relegated generally to low-budget vehicles, including those starring the BOWERY BOYS.

SELECTED FILMS: *A Black Sheep* (1915), *Betsy's Burglar* (1917), *Finders Keepers, Mama's Affair, Lessons in Love* (1921), *The Married Flapper* (1922), *Temporary Marriage* (1923), *Bobbed Hair* (1925), *The Sap, Twinkletoes* (1926), *Cheating Cheaters* (1927), *Cappy Ricks Returns* (1936), *Penrod and Sam* (1937), *The Headleys at Home* (1938), *Slightly Honorable, A Little Bit of Heaven, The Under-Dog* (1940), *Pride of the Bowery* (1941). ∎

Harlan, Otis (1865–1940), actor. Began his film career in silents after extensive vaudeville and stage experience. A portly character actor, he appeared in many light films well into the 1930s. He played Cap'n Andy in the 1929 version of *Show Boat*. He was the uncle of actor Kenneth HARLAN.

SELECTED FILMS: *Diamonds Adrift, Keeping Up With Lizzie* (1921), *The Girl in the Taxi* (1922), *The Barefoot Boy* (1923), *What Happened to Jones?, Fine Clothes, Lightnin'* (1925), *The Cheerful Fraud, Silk Stockings* (1927), *Girl Overboard, Barnum Was Right* (1929), *Dames Ahoy!, Loose Ankles* (1930), *Man to Man* (1931), *That's My Boy* (1932), *Marriage on Approval* (1933), *The Old Fashioned Way, Married in Haste* (1934), *A Midsummer Night's Dream* (1935), *Mr. Boggs Steps Out* (1938). ∎

Jean Harlow

Harlow, Jean (1911–1937), actress. Began her film career as an extra, then as supporting player in Hal ROACH'S comedy shorts in the last years of silent films. With the advent of sound, her career took a turn for the better when Howard Hughes signed her for his aviation epic *Hell's Angels* (1930). It was in this film that she uttered her famous line. Dressed in an open-backed, low-cut evening gown, she moves toward her bedroom and asks suggestively of her guest, Ben Lyon: "Would you be shocked if I put on something more comfortable?" In 1932 she moved to MGM and within a short time became a superstar. Exploiting her platinum-blonde hair and her sexuality, she wise-cracked her way through films co-starring Clark GABLE and other leading men. Harlow, born Harlean Carpenter in Kansas City, became a major sex symbol of the 1930s. In *Red Dust* she portrayed a good-bad floozie who winds up at an Indochina rubber plantation run by Gable. When she is told that the climate makes it difficult to sleep, she replies, "Guess I'm not used to sleeping nights anyway." Films like *Red Dust*, *Bombshell*, and *Libeled Lady* demonstrated her flair for comedy. Her glamorous and sparkling career was cut short when, during the filming of *Saratoga*, she became ill and died at the age of 26. Irving Shulman's biography, *Harlow*, was published in 1964.

SELECTED FILMS: *Moran of the Marines* (1928), *The Saturday Night Kid* (1929), *The Secret Six*, *The Iron Man*, *The Public Enemy*, *Goldie*, *Platinum Blonde* (1931), *Three Wise Girls*, *Red-Headed Woman*, *Red Dust* (1932), *Hold Your Man*, *Bombshell*, *Dinner at Eight* (1933), *The Girl From Missouri* (1934), *Reckless*, *China Seas* (1935), *Riffraff*, *Wife vs. Secretary*, *Suzy*, *Libeled Lady* (1936), *Personal Property*, *Saratoga* (1937). ■

"Harold Teen." A popular comic strip created by Carl Ed and made into two feature films. The first version of this perennial favorite (it ran in numerous newspapers for more than three decades) was a 1928 silent starring Arthur LAKE, who was to gain popularity ten years later for his portrayal of another comic strip character, Dagwood Bumstead of BLONDIE fame. The second filming of *Harold Teen*, a musical starring Hal LeRoy, was released in 1934.

Harper, Valerie (1940–), actress. Has appeared in numerous television shows for which she won several Emmy Awards, on stage, and in light films, making her screen debut in the late 1970s. Her slight appearances thus far

show a flair for comedy, especially in terms of male-female relationships.

In *Chapter Two* she confides to her friend Marsha MASON that she has been told recently that she has character in her face, but somehow she doesn't feel complimented. "Why is life going so fast?" she questions. "First I was pretty. Now I'm interesting with character. Soon I'll be handsome, followed by stately; and then, worst of all, finally, remarkable for her age."

SELECTED FILMS: *Chapter Two* (1979), *The Last Married Couple in America* (1980), *Blame It on Rio* (1984). ■

Harris, Barbara (1937–), actress. Worked on stage before making her film debut in 1965. She has appeared chiefly in light comedies.

SELECTED FILMS: *A Thousand Clowns* (1965), *Oh, Dad, Poor Dad— Mama's Hung You in the Closet and I'm Feeling So Sad* (1967), *Plaza Suite* (1971), *The War Between Men and Women* (1972), *Mixed Company* (1974), *The Manchu Eagle Murder Caper Mystery*, *Nashville* (1975), *Family Plot* (1976), *Freaky Friday* (1977), *North Avenue Irregulars*, *Movie Movie* (1978), *The Hamster of Happiness*, *The Senator* (1979). ■

Harris, Mildred (1901–1944), actress. Worked in vaudeville, burlesque, and in the theater as well as in silent and sound films. She appeared as the leading lady in many light features and, later in her career, turned to supporting roles. She was only 13 when she portrayed Dorothy in the 1914–15 *Wizard of Oz* series. She was Charlie CHAPLIN'S first wife.

SELECTED FILMS: *Enoch Arden* (1915), *Hoodoo Ann*, *Old Folks at Home* (1916), *Bad Boy* (1917), *For Husbands Only*, *Borrowed Clothes* (1918), *Home* (1919), *The Inferior Sex* (1920), *Old Dad*, *Habit*, *Fool's Paradise* (1921), *The First Woman* (1922), *The Daring Years* (1923), *The Dressmaker From Paris*, *My Neighbor's Wife* (1925), *The Girl From Rio*,

The Show Girl (1927), *Lingerie, The Heart of a Follies Girl, Melody of Love* (1928), *No, No, Nanette* (1930), *Lady Tubbs, Never Too Late* (1935), *Movie Maniacs* (1936), *The Story of Dr. Wassell* (1944). ■

Harris, Phil (1906–1985), actor, musician. Worked as a drummer, bandleader, radio personality, and in films as a bandleader and comic. He was popular for his southern accent and his drinking, both of which became the target of much of his humor.

SELECTED FILMS: *Melody Cruise* (1933), *Turn Off the Moon* (1937), *Man About Town* (1939), *Buck Benny Rides Again* (1940), *I Love a Bandleader* (1945), *Here Comes the Groom* (1951), *Anything Goes* (1956), *The Wheeler Dealers* (1963), *The Patsy* (1964), *The Cool Ones* (1967). ■

Harris, Robert H. (1909–), actor. Has appeared as a character actor in dramas and light films, usually in haughty roles.

SELECTED FILMS: *How He Lied to Her Husband* (1931), *For Them That Trespass* (1950), *Laughing Anne* (1954), *Bundle of Joy* (1956), *The Fuzzy Pink Nightgown* (1957), *How to Make a Monster* (1958), *Valley of the Dolls* (1967). ■

Harrison, June, actress. A minor supporting player whose most popular appearances were in the 1940s series of "JIGGS AND MAGGIE" comedies produced by Monogram studios. A pretty actress, she played Nora, the zany couple's marriageable daughter, in the series based on the characters from George McManus' famous comic strip.

SELECTED FILMS: *Bringing Up Father* (1946), *Jiggs and Maggie in Court, Jiggs and Maggie in Society* (1948), *Jiggs and Maggie in Jackpot Jitters* (1949), *Jiggs and Maggie Out West* (1950). ■

Harrison, Rex (1908–), actor. Worked on stage as a teenager, in films in his native England, and on Broadway in 1936 before making his Hollywood debut in 1946. A dapper and personable performer for five decades, he has delighted audiences on both sides of the Atlantic, particularly as Professor Higgins in both the stage and film versions of *My Fair Lady*. He was exceptionally witty and devious as the avenging husband in Preston STURGES' *Unfaithfully Yours*.

SELECTED FILMS: *Anna and the King of Siam* (1946), *The Ghost and Mrs. Muir* (1947), *Unfaithfully Yours* (1948), *The Four Poster* (1952), *Main Street to Broadway* (1953), *The Reluctant Debutante* (1958), *The Happy Thieves* (1962), *My Fair Lady* (1964), *The Honey Pot* (1967), *The Fifth Musketeer* (1979). ■

Hartman, Don (1900–1958), screenwriter, director. Worked as a stage actor, writer for musicals and radio performers, and lyricist in Hollywood in 1930. By 1935 he became a full-time screenwriter of light features, occasionally producing and directing his own scripts. His writing resulted in frothy, romantic stories for some of the leading personalities of the period, including Carole LOMBARD, Fred MacMURRAY, Bing CROSBY, Bob HOPE, and Danny KAYE.

SELECTED FILMS: *The Gay Deception* (1935), *The Princess Comes Across* (1936), *Champagne Waltz, Waikiki Wedding* (1937), *Tropic Holiday* (1938), *Paris Honeymoon, The Star Maker* (1939), *Road to Singapore* (1940), *Road to Zanzibar, Nothing but the Truth* (1941), *My Favorite Blonde, Road to Morocco* (1942), *True to Life* (1943), *Up in Arms, The Princess and the Pirate* (1944), *Wonder Man* (1945), *The Kid From Brooklyn* (1946), *Down to Earth* (1947), *Every Girl Should Be Married* (1948), *Mr. Imperium* (1951). ■

Hartman, Paul (1904–1973), actor. Worked as a dancer-comic-entertainer in vaudeville, in nightclubs, and on Broadway in the 1940s. His most popular act was a comedy-ballroom dancing routine which he performed with his wife, Grace. Except for an isolated appearance in the late 1940s, it was not until the early 1950s that Hollywood invited him to act in films. He played various character roles, chiefly in light films, and then switched to television.

SELECTED FILMS: *Forty-Five Fathers* (1947), *Soldier in the Rain* (1963), *Those Callaways* (1965), *How to Succeed in Business Without Really Trying* (1967). ∎

Hartmann, Edmund L. (1911–), screenwriter. Worked as a songwriter before switching to writing scripts for Hollywood. He turned out many light comedies as well as scripts for other genres, sometimes in collaboration. He wrote for various comedians, including ABBOTT AND COSTELLO, Dean MARTIN and Jerry LEWIS, and Bob HOPE.

SELECTED FILMS: *Helldorado* (1934), *Without Orders* (1936), *The Feminine Touch* (1941), *In Society* (1944), *See My Lawyer, The Naughty Nineties* (1945), *Variety Girl* (1947), *The Paleface* (1948), *Sorrowful Jones* (1949), *Fancy Pants* (1950), *The Lemon Drop Kid* (1951), *The Caddy* (1953), *Casanova's Big Night* (1954), *The Shakiest Gun in the West* (1968). ∎

Harvey, Paul (1883–1953), actor. Made his film debut in the late 1920s as a character player, appearing in more than 150 dramas and light films. A tall, commanding figure at home in serious or humorous roles, he often portrayed nervous businessmen or friends of the family. He worked with such popular screen comics as Eddie CANTOR, Mae WEST, the RITZ BROTHERS, and Jack BENNY.

SELECTED FILMS: *The Awful Truth* (1929), *The Wiser Sex* (1932), *Kid Millions* (1934), *Goin' to Town* (1935), *Three Men on a Horse* (1936), *The Higgins Family* (1938), *The Gorilla* (1939), *Brother Rat and a Baby* (1940), *Great Guns* (1941), *Larceny, Inc.* (1942), *Henry*

Aldrich Plays Cupid (1944), *The Horn Blows at Midnight* (1945), *Up Goes Maisie* (1946), *Perils of Pauline* (1947), *Blondie's Reward* (1948), *The Yellow Cab Man* (1949), *The Milkman* (1950), *Let's Go Navy* (1951), *Three for the Show* (1955). ∎

Hatton, Raymond (1887–1971), actor. Worked in vaudeville and on stage before making his film debut in 1912. A versatile actor who appeared in hundreds of shorts and features, he began playing villains and light roles in early silent films. During the 1920s he teamed up with Wallace BEERY in a series of military comedies. He also joined comic Victor MOORE in the "Chimmie McFadden" comedy films. With the advent of sound, he portrayed the comic sidekick of various cowboy stars.

SELECTED FILMS: *The Circus Man* (1914), *The Wild Goose Chase, Armstrong's Wife* (1915), *The Little American* (1917), *For Better for Worse, You're Fired, Male and Female* (1919), *Jes' Call Me Jim* (1920), *Peck's Bad Boy, Doubling for Romeo* (1921), *The Hottentot* (1922), *Behind the Front, We're in the Navy Now* (1926), *Wife Savers* (1928), *The Office Scandal* (1929), *Woman Hungry* (1931), *Polly of the Circus* (1932), *Alice in Wonderland* (1933), *Steamboat 'Round the Bend* (1935), *Torchy Blane* (1937), *Love Finds Andy Hardy* (1938), *Paris Honeymoon* (1939), *In Cold Blood* (1967). ∎

Haver, Phyllis (1899–1960), actress. Began her film career as one of Mack SENNETT'S "Bathing Beauties" in silent comedy shorts. She co-starred with some of the leading comedians of the period, including, among others, Ben TURPIN and Buster KEATON. Tall, blonde, and pretty, she moved to feature films in a short time, playing dramatic as well as light roles throughout the 1920s.

SELECTED FILMS: *A Bedroom Blunder, The Pullman Bride* (1917), *Ladies First* (1918), *The Foolish Age, Hearts and Flowers, Yankee Doodle in Berlin*

(1919), Love, Honor and Behave, Married Life (1920), Home Talent (1921), The Perfect Flapper (1924), Hard Boiled, Up in Mabel's Room, Three Bad Men, The Nervous Wreck (1926), Nobody's Widow, The Little Adventuress (1927), Tenth Avenue, The Battle of the Sexes (1928), Sal of Singapore, The Shady Lady, The Office Scandal, Thunder (1929). ∎

Hawks, Howard (1896–1977), director, screenwriter, producer. Began his long film career in the property department of Mary PICKFORD'S film company. He advanced to the cutting room, to scriptwriter, and finally to director in 1926. A versatile director, he worked for more than four decades in many genres with equal success, including those of crime, adventure, war, MUSICAL COMEDY, and SCREWBALL COMEDY. It was in this last category that he is perhaps best remembered, giving his audiences hilarious films that were fast-paced, visually economical, and generally well-crafted. He was able to successfully blend elements of the chase and slapstick with bright dialogue and zany characters, the chief ingredients of the "screwball" genre. Robin Wood's study of the director, titled *Howard Hawks*, was published in 1968.

SELECTED FILMS: The Road to Glory (1926), The Cradle Snatchers (1927), A Girl in Every Port (1928), Today We Live (1933), Twentieth Century (1934), Bringing Up Baby (1938), His Girl Friday (1940), Ball of Fire (1942), A Song Is Born (1948), I Was a Male War Bride (1949), Monkey Business (1952), Gentlemen Prefer Blondes (1953), Man's Favorite Sport? (1964), Rio Lobo (1970). ∎

Hawley, Wanda (1897–1963), actress. Began her screen career in early silent films in the 1910s. An attractive blonde, she played female leads in numerous dramas and light films, chiefly for Paramount studios. She co-starred with some of the most popular actors of the period, including, among others, Douglas FAIR-

BANKS, Wallace REID, and Harrison FORD. Her forte was romantic comedy. She abandoned her screen career with the arrival of sound.

SELECTED FILMS: The Derelict (1917), Mr. Fix-It (1918), Greased Lightning, The Lottery Man, You're Fired (1919), Double Speed, Fool for Scandal, Her Beloved Villain, Her First Elopement, Miss Hobbs, Mrs. Temple's Telegram, The Six Best Cellars (1920), Her Sturdy Oak, The House That Jazz Built, A Kiss in Time, The Love Charm, The Outside Woman, The Snob (1921), Bobbed Hair, Thirty Days, Too Much Wife (1922), Pirates of the Sky (1927). ∎

Goldie Hawn

Hawn, Goldie (1945–), actress. Appeared on stage while in her teens and then gained national popularity in the "Laugh In" series on television. Her first major film role, a supporting part in *Cactus Flower*, brought her an Oscar. Often stereotyped as the dumb, giggly, kookie blonde, in the tradition of Judy HOLLIDAY and Marilyn MONROE, she has developed her characters so that they demonstrate more charm and humor than the original material contained. She has emerged as one of the leading comediennes of her time, embracing the traits of those memorable performers mentioned above as well as those characteristics of the more "classy" female comics such as Katharine HEPBURN and Claudette COLBERT.

Not only is she visually funny, but her delivery and timing are first-rate. In *Private Benjamin*, one of her more memorable roles, she portrays a spoiled little rich girl who enlists in the army and is shocked by the army attire and conditions of the barracks. "Excuse me," she politely inquires when issued her uniform, "is green the only color these come in?" Later, she complains to her sergeant about the sleeping quarters. "Look at this place," she says in disgust. "The army couldn't afford drapes?"

SELECTED FILMS: *Cactus Flower (1969), There's a Girl in My Soup (1970), $ (1971), Butterflies Are Free (1972), The Sugarland Express, The Girl From Petrovka (1974), Shampoo (1975), The Duchess and the Dirtwater Fox (1976), Foul Play (1978), Travels With Anita (1979), Seems Like Old Times, Private Benjamin (1980), Best Friends (1982), Protocol, Swing Shift (1984), Wild Cats (1986).* ∎

Haydn, Richard (1905–1985), actor. Worked in revues in his native England before making his Hollywood film debut in 1941. A talented character actor, he usually portrayed haughty fusspots, eccentric busybodies, and nervous types. In *And Then There Were None* (1945) he portrayed a butler on an island where guests are mysteriously murdered one at a time. As the remaining guests huddle together in fear, Haydn enters and calmly inquires: "How many of you will be for dinner tonight?"

SELECTED FILMS: *Charley's Aunt (1941), Ball of Fire (1942), Cluny Brown (1946), The Late George Apley (1947), Sitting Pretty, The Emperor Waltz, Miss Tatlock's Millions (1948), Mr. Music (1950), Money From Home, Her Twelve Men (1954), Jupiter's Darling (1955), Please Don't Eat the Daisies (1960), The Sound of Music, Clarence, the Cross-Eyed Lion (1965), Young Frankenstein (1974).* ∎

Hayes, Frank (1875–1923), actor. Appeared in early silent comedy shorts for Mack SENNETT'S KEYSTONE studios. As a supporting actor, he worked with some of the leading comedians of the period, including, among others, Mabel NORMAND, "Fatty" ARBUCKLE, Polly MORAN, and Mack SWAIN.

SELECTED FILMS: *Mabel, Fatty and the Law (1915), Stolen Magic, Fatty and Mabel Adrift, Fido's Fate, A Bathhouse Blunder, Her Marble Heart, Madcap Ambrose (1916), His Uncle Dudley (1917).* ∎

George "Gabby" Hayes

Hayes, George "Gabby" (1885–1969), actor. Worked in vaudeville before entering films in the 1920s. He portrayed both heavies and comic relief characters, the former chiefly in silents and the latter in sound features, mainly westerns. A prolific, bewhiskered character player, he appeared in more than 200 films, usually as roguish, toothless, outspoken old-timers or humorous sidekicks to various cowboy stars. He played "Windy," William Boyd's comical sidekick in 19 Hopalong Cassidy entries.

In *Tall in the Saddle* (1944) he enlightens newcomer John Wayne that the town has no sheriff. "Don't you believe in law and order?" Wayne inquires. "It depends who's dishing it out," Hayes replies. In *Trail Street* (1947) he helps Randolph

Scott to establish law and order. "Larkin," he addresses a local outlaw, "you're gonna get 30 days for that killin'. Then we're gonna hang you."

SELECTED FILMS: Why Women Re-Marry (1923), The Rainbow Man (1929), Rose of the Rio Grande (1931), Love Me Tonight (1932), Beggars in Ermine (1934), Hopalong Cassidy (1935), Mr. Deeds Goes to Town (1936), Gold Is Where You Find It (1938), Colorado (1940), In Old Oklahoma (1943), The Big Bonanza, Don't Fence Me In (1945), El Paso (1949), The Cariboo Trail (1950), Pals of the Golden West (1951). ∎

Hays, Robert (1947–), actor. Appeared in television before entering films in the early 1980s. His biggest successes were in the "Airplane" comedies; otherwise his screen career has not advanced. A pleasant and talented performer capable of carrying lead roles, he might need better scripts to further his screen career.

SELECTED FILMS: Airplane! (1980), Take This Job and Shove It (1981), Airplane II: the Sequel (1982), Trenchcoat, Utilities (1983), Scandalous (1984). ∎

Healy, Ted (1896–1937), actor, comic. Worked as a stand-up comedian in burlesque and vaudeville in the 1920s before entering films during the early sound period. His stage act, which he began in 1925 and called "Ted Healy and His Stooges," helped launch the careers of several comics, including the THREE STOOGES. The routine, a rather violent one, consisted of his getting the boys into an altercation, at which point he would step aside and become a spectator.

It was Healy who was instrumental in much of the success of the film Stooges. He suggested their hair styles and devised some of their slapstick routines while they worked for him on stage. His brief screen appearances never brought him the popularity or success he had experienced with his stage act.

SELECTED FILMS: Soup to Nuts (1930), Meet the Baron, Dancing Lady, Hollywood on Parade, Nertsery Rhymes, Beer and Pretzels, Hello Pop!, Plane Nuts (1933), The Big Idea, Myrt and Marge, Fugitive Lovers, The Band Plays On (1934), The Winning Ticket, It's in the Air (1935), Sing, Baby, Sing (1936), Love Is a Headache, The Good Old Soak, Hollywood Hotel (1937). ∎

Hecht, Ben (1893–1964), screenwriter, director, playwright, producer, novelist. Worked as a Chicago reporter, World War I correspondent, and columnist before joining Paramount studios in the late 1920s as a writer. One of the most talented and respected screenwriters to have ever worked in Hollywood, he wrote well over 75 screenplays, alone or in collaboration with his close friend Charles MacARTHUR or others. Many of his scripts became classic films. Some of his screenplays captured various awards. The plays he co-wrote with MacArthur were often successfully adapted to films, including *The Front Page*. Tired of Hollywood in the mid-1930s, he and MacArthur produced and directed several films at the New York Astoria studios, including *The Scoundrel* starring Noel Coward.

A versatile writer, he worked in several genres, turning out crime, historical, adventure, and comedy films. Hecht, whose career in films spanned 40 years, was often called upon to revise screenplays of other writers, for which he received no screen credit. His strengths included his ability to tell a good story and develop realistic characters, two qualities he imbued with his robust and action-packed style. He won the first Best Original Story Oscar in 1927 for *Underworld*. His autobiography, *A Child of the Century*, was published in 1954.

SELECTED FILMS: The Unholy Garden (1931), Hallelujah, I'm a Bum, Design for Living (1933), Twentieth Century (1934), Once in a Blue Moon, Soak the Rich (1936), Nothing Sacred (1937), The Goldwyn Follies, Gunga Din, It's a

Wonderful World (1939), Angels Over Broadway, Comrade X (1940), Her Husband's Affairs (1947), Actors and Sin, Monkey Business (1952), Circus World (1964). ∎

Heckart, Eileen (1919–), actress. Appeared on Broadway before entering films in the mid-1950s. Thin and dark-haired, she has alternated between stage and screen. A talented supporting actress, she has portrayed characters who enjoy dominating others in dramas and light films. She won an Academy Award as Best Supporting Actress for her role in *Butterflies Are Free.*

SELECTED FILMS: *Miracle in the Rain, Bus Stop (1956), Hot Spell (1958), Heller in Pink Tights (1960), My Six Loves (1963), No Way to Treat a Lady (1967), Butterflies Are Free (1972), Fifty Fifty (1984).* ∎

Heggie, O.P. (1879–1936), actor. Began his screen career in the late 1920s. Balding and serious-looking, he appeared as a character player in dramas and light films. Perhaps his most memorable role was that of the blind hermit in *The Bride of Frankenstein* (1935). His film career was cut short when he succumbed to pneumonia at age 56.

SELECTED FILMS: *The Actress (1928), The Vagabond King, One Romantic Night, Playboy of Paris, Sunny, Broken Dishes (1930), Too Young to Marry (1931), The King's Vacation (1933), Midnight, Peck's Bad Boy, Anne of Green Gables (1934), Chasing Yesterday, Ginger (1935), The Prisoner of Shark Island (1936).* ∎

Hellman, Sam, screenwriter. Wrote several comedy screenplays during the 1930s and 1940s. Except for a few above-average dramas, most of his output consisted of routine films.

SELECTED FILMS: *The County Chairman, In Old Kentucky (1935), Captain January, The Poor Little Rich Girl (1936), The Baroness and the Butler, We're Go-*

ing to Be Rich (1938), The Three Musketeers (1939), He Married His Wife (1940), The Doughgirls (1944), The Horn Blows at Midnight (1945), The Runaround (1946), Pirates of Monterey (1947). ∎

Hellzapoppin (1941), U. Dir. H.C. Potter; Sc. Nat Perrin, Warren Wilson; with Ole Olsen, Chic Johnson, Martha Raye, Robert Paige, Jane Frazee.

OLSEN AND JOHNSON brought their successful stage comedy to the screen, but the conventions of Hollywood put strictures on the production. The duo's mad routines, audience participation, and some help from influential columnists helped keep the show on Broadway for more than one thousand performances, despite poor reviews from the drama critics. The film version, unfortunately, does not follow the freewheeling style of the play. Instead, it adds an insipid love triangle that interrupts the pace of the comedy. However, there are enough sight gags and one-liners to give the filmgoer a good sample of the particular uniqueness of a comedy team that was very popular in its time. Several veteran comic character actors, including Hugh HERBERT, Mischa AUER, and Shemp HOWARD, add to the fun.

Helton, Percy (1894–1971), actor. Began his screen career in silent films and continued into the sound era. A soft-spoken, portly comic supporting player, he appeared chiefly in light features. His forte was expressing astonishment.

SELECTED FILMS: *Silver Wings (1921), Miracle on 34th Street (1947), My Friend Irma, Chicken Every Sunday (1949), A Girl in Every Port, Call Me Madam (1952), How to Marry a Millionaire (1953), Butch Cassidy and the Sundance Kid (1969).* ∎

Henderson, Dell (1883–1956), director, actor. Worked as an actor on stage and in silent films (1909) and as a free-lance writer, selling occasional stories to

BIOGRAPH, before becoming a director in early silent comedy shorts for Mack SENNETT'S KEYSTONE studios. Later, he began directing feature-length films.

With the advent of sound, he returned to acting, appearing as a supporting player in such films as *The Champ* (1931), *It's a Gift* (1934), and *Our Relations* (1936), which starred, respectively, Wallace BEERY, W. C. FIELDS, and LAUREL AND HARDY. He directed, alone or in collaboration, some of the leading comedians of the period, including, among others, Charlie MURRAY, Polly MORAN, and Eddie FOY.

SELECTED FILMS (as director): *As It Might Have Been, Ambrose's First Falsehood* (1914), *A Favorite Fool, A Janitor's Wife's Temptation* (1915), *The Great Pearl Tangle, Perils of the Park, Wife and Auto Trouble, A Bathhouse Blunder, A Coney Island Princess* (1916), *A Girl Like That, The Outcast, Please Help Emily* (1917), *Her Second Husband, By Hook or Crook* (1918), *Love in a Hurry* (1919), *The Shark* (1920), *Quick Change* (1925), *The Pay-Off* (1926).

SELECTED FILMS (as actor): *Getting Gertie's Garter* (1927), *The Patsy* (1928), *Wrong Again* (1929), *The Laurel-Hardy Murder Case* (1930), *The Old Fashioned Way, Men in Black* (1934), *Slightly Static, Here Comes Cookie* (1935), *Our Relations* (1936), *You Can't Fool Your Wife* (1940), *Nothing but Trouble* (1944), *Abbott and Costello in Hollywood* (1945). ∎

Henry, Buck (1930–), screenwriter, actor. Worked in the theater and with a comedy group before relocating in Hollywood where he began writing comedy material for television. Born Buck Henry Zuckerman, he soon began writing for films, gaining wide recognition for his collaboration on *The Graduate* in 1967. He has occasionally tried directing. His work, while at times uneven, is often fresh and offbeat. He is the son of silent screen actress Ruth TAYLOR.

SELECTED FILMS (as screenwriter): *The Troublemaker* (1964), *Candy* (1968), *Catch-22, The Owl and the Pussycat* (1970), *What's Up, Doc?* (1972), *The Day of the Dolphin* (1973), *Protocol* (1984).

SELECTED FILMS (as actor): *The Troublemaker* (1964), *The Secret War of Harry Frigg* (1968), *Catch-22, The Owl and the Pussycat* (1970), *Taking Off, Is There Sex After Death?* (1971), *Heaven Can Wait* (1978), *Old Boyfriends* (1979). ∎

Henry, Gale (–1972), actress. Began her screen career in the 1910s as a comedienne in silent comedies. She continued to appear in films as a supporting player during the 1920s. She worked with various popular comedians, including Charley CHASE.

SELECTED FILMS: *The Big Squawk* (1929), *Skip the Maloo!* (1931), *Now We'll Tell One, Mr. Bride* (1932), *Luncheon at Twelve* (1933). ∎

"Henry Aldrich" comedies. A popular film series of the 1940s based on Clifford Goldsmith's 1938 Broadway play *What a Life.* Paramount in 1939 adapted the play into a warm and charming little film starring Jackie COOPER as Henry and Eddie BRACKEN as his pal Dizzy. The screenwriters were the famous team of Billy WILDER and Charles BRACKETT. Two years later the two boys repeated their roles in a sequel, *Life With Henry.*

The official series, however, did not begin until Jimmy LYDON replaced Cooper in the title role. Other changes included Charles SMITH as Dizzy, John LITEL as the uncompromising Mr. Aldrich, Olive BLAKENEY as Henry's understanding mother, and Vaughan GLASER as the scowling principal, Mr. Bradley. The troupe turned out nine entries, all directed by Hugh Bennett. Although they were not as successful as the "ANDY HARDY" films, they provided enough laughs and entertainment as accident-prone Henry attempted to extricate himself from complex difficulties brought on by his own machinations.

SELECTED FILMS: *Henry Aldrich for President* (1941), *Henry and Dizzy, Henry Aldrich, Editor* (1942), *Henry*

Aldrich Gets Glamour, Henry AldrichSwings It, Henry Aldrich Haunts a House (1943), Henry Aldrich, Boy Scout, Henry Aldrich Plays Cupid, Henry Aldrich's Little Secret (1944). ∎

Henry the Rainmaker (1949), MON. Dir. Jean Yarbrough; Sc. Lane Beauchamp; with Raymond Walburn, Walter Catlett, William Tracy, Mary Stuart.

One of the entries in a short-lived comedy series, the film tells the unstartling story of how the title character, played by the wide-eyed, eccentric character actor Raymond WALBURN, discovers a scientific method for making rain. The low-budget films, produced by Monogram, a second-string studio, were used as second features and usually contained several funny moments. Dependable comic character players such as William TRACY, Walter CATLETT, and Roscoe ATES helped to provide laughs, while minor but competent directors kept the plots moving. The stories were set in a small town where Henry (Walburn) would usually get upset at some small injustice and take things into his own hands. In *Leave It to Henry* (1949), also directed by YARBROUGH, he destroys a toll bridge when his son, the toll collector, is dismissed. In *Father Makes Good* (1950), another Yarbrough effort, Henry buys his own cow as a protest against the new milk tax. He decides to hunt for his own food in defiance of the high cost of meat in *Father's Wild Game* (1950), directed by Herbert I. LEEDS. In *Father Takes the Air* (1951), directed by Frank McDONALD, Henry gets mixed up with a flying school and apprehends a thief. With wide stage experience and 20 years of film acting behind him, Walburn was more than capable of carrying the lead in these pleasant little diversions.

Hepburn, Audrey (1929–), actress. Belgian-born talented stage and screen star who appeared in English films before making her debut in Hollywood. Exhibiting elegance, charm, and femininity, she has starred in dramas and light films and has won an Oscar for her role in *Roman Holiday* (1953) and earned four other Academy Award nominations. *Audrey Hepburn*, a biography written by Ian Woodward, was published in 1984.

In *Charade* she played a widow whom Cary GRANT assists in recovering her husband's fortune. "Won't you come in for a minute?" she says to Grant. "I don't bite, you know, unless it's called for."

SELECTED FILMS: *Sabrina* (1954), *Funny Face* (1957), *Breakfast at Tiffany's* (1961), *Charade* (1963), *Paris When It Sizzles, My Fair Lady* (1964), *How to Steal a Million* (1966), *Two for the Road* (1967), *Bloodline* (1979). ∎

Hepburn, Katharine (1909–), actress. Worked in stock and on Broadway in 1929 before making her film debut in *A Bill of Divorcement* in 1932, co-starring with John Barrymore. By the following year she won her first Oscar, for her performance in her second film, *Morning Glory*. She was to attain two more Academy Awards and eight nominations over the years. Despite such an illustrious beginning, her career faltered because of audience disinterest and her headstrong resistance to studio heads who attempted to shape her professionally as they saw fit. After a few years, however, she proved she was much more than a competent actress, diplaying a flair for comedy as well as drama—and her audiences grew larger. In the 1930s she made three delightful comedies with Cary GRANT, but it was during the next two decades with Spencer TRACY, with whom she had a special rapport and a personal relationship, that she achieved her greatest success. From their almost-failed marriage in *State of the Union* to their professional competition as opposing attorneys in *Adam's Rib* to their battle of the sexes in *Pat and Mike*, they brought warmth and laughter to their audiences.

She demonstrated her staying power by bringing her talents and her professionalism to more mature roles, for example, in her portrayal of the inexperienced spinster in *The African Queen* or in her Oscar-winning role as Eleanor of Aquitaine in *The Lion in Winter*, while winning new audiences.

SELECTED FILMS: *Little Women* (1933), *Spitfire, The Little Minister* (1934), *Alice Adams* (1935), *Sylvia Scarlett, A Woman Rebels* (1936), *Stage Door* (1937), *Bringing Up Baby, Holiday* (1938), *The Philadelphia Story* (1940), *Woman of the Year* (1942), *State of the Union* (1948), *Adam's Rib* (1949), *The African Queen* (1951), *Pat and Mike* (1952), *Desk Set* (1957), *The Lion in Winter* (1968), *Rooster Cogburn* (1976), *Olly Olly Oxen Free* (1978). ■

Herbert, F. Hugh (1897–1958), screenwriter. Wrote numerous film scripts for silent and sound films as well as stage plays and stories. He specialized in light comedies, one of which (*The Moon Is Blue*) caused much controversy during the early 1950s because of its frank language for its time ("pregnant," "virgin"). He occasionally collaborated on screenplays.

SELECTED FILMS: *The Waning Sex* (1926), *The Demi-Bride, Tea for Three* (1927), *Baby Mine, The Cardboard Lover* (1928), *A Single Man* (1929), *Single Wife, He Knew Women* (1930), *The Constant Woman* (1933), *Traveling Saleslady* (1935), *As Good as Married* (1937), *Kiss and Tell* (1945), *Home Sweet Homicide, Margie* (1946), *Sitting Pretty* (1948), *Let's Make It Legal* (1951), *The Moon Is Blue* (1953), *The Little Hut* (1957). ■

Herbert, Holmes (1883–1956), actor. Appeared on stage in his native England before migrating to Hollywood during the silent period. He soon emerged as a popular leading man. During the sound era he was relegated to supporting roles. Tall and distinguished-looking, he often portrayed uncompromising characters in numerous dramas and light films during a career that spanned five decades.

SELECTED FILMS: *A Doll's House* (1917), *My Lady's Garter* (1920), *Daddy's Gone A-Hunting* (1925), *Honeymoon Express* (1926), *Gentlemen Prefer Blondes* (1928), *The Hot Heiress* (1931), *The Girl Said No* (1937), *The Little Princess* (1939), *Angel From Texas* (1940), *Lady in a Jam* (1942), *Our Hearts Were Young and Gay* (1944), *The Law and the Lady* (1951), *The Brigand* (1952). ■

Hugh Herbert and Fernand Gravet

Herbert, Hugh (1887–1952), actor. Worked in vaudeville and on stage before making his film debut in the late 1920s. A familiar comic-relief supporting actor who occasionally played leads, he appeared in more than 100 light comedies and musicals. With rolling eyes and fluttering fingers, two of his trademarks, he often portrayed kind-hearted but fidgety businessmen or hen-pecked husbands.

In *Gold Diggers of 1935* he quips to Glenda FARRELL: "Snuff is not to be sneezed at."

SELECTED FILMS: *Husbands for Rent, Lights of New York* (1928), *Hook, Line and Sinker* (1930), *Laugh and Get Rich* (1931), *Million Dollar Legs* (1932), *Footlight Parade, College Coach* (1933), *Wonder Bar, Dames* (1934), *A Midsummer Night's Dream* (1935), *That Man Is Here Again, Marry the Girl, Sh! the Octopus* (1937), *Four's a Crowd* (1938), *The Family Next Door, Little Accident* (1939), *La Conga Nights, Slightly*

Tempted (1940), Meet the Champ, Hellzapoppin (1941), A Miracle Can Happen (1948), The Beautiful Blonde From Bashful Bend (1949), Havana Rose (1951). ∎

Herbert, Thomas F. (1888–1946), actor. Entered films in the early 1930s following a career in vaudeville and on stage. He appeared as a supporting player chiefly in light films, working with such famous screen comics as Mae WEST and Harold LLOYD. He was the brother of the popular comic character actor Hugh HERBERT.

SELECTED FILMS: Traveling Husbands (1931), Bed of Roses (1933), Belle of the Nineties (1934), Topper, Banjo on My Knee, Stars Over Arizona (1937), Professor Beware (1938), Remedy for Riches (1940), Tennessee Johnson (1942). ∎

Herbie. The name of the independent-minded Volkswagen that starred in four slapstick comedy films produced by the Disney studios. The entries usually employed the talents of several top screen personalities, including, among others, Cloris Leachman, Buddy HACKETT, Don KNOTTS, Helen Hayes, Keenan WYNN, and Dean Jones.

SELECTED FILMS: The Love Bug (1969), Herbie Rides Again (1974), Herbie Goes to Monte Carlo (1977), Herbie Goes Bananas (1980). ∎

Here Comes Mr. Jordan (1941), COL. Dir. Alexander Hall; Sc. Sidney Buchman, Seton I. Miller; with Robert Montgomery, Claude Rains, Evelyn Keyes, James Gleason, Edward Everett Horton.

One of the first FANTASY COMEDIES to come out of Hollywood (Topper appeared in 1937), the film helped to set the pattern for a succession of similar features. But none of the imitators matched its freshness and charm. Prizefighter Robert Montgomery is killed in an airplane crash and his spirit is removed too hastily by inept angels while his body is cremated. When he arrives in heaven, Mr. Jordan, who is in charge of celestial affairs of this nature, arranges for him to enter a new body. And so the search for a body commences. The highly imaginative story, appearing while war clouds gathered around the real world, was questioned by some at the time. Treating life and death comically, they warned, seemed in poor taste. But the audiences did not object. In fact, they made it into a hit. Claude Rains as Mr. Jordan is witty and affable as he accompanies Montgomery to Earth in his quest. The venerable James GLEASON, one of the great comic character players, portrays Montgomery's manager who can't comprehend his fighter's spirit returning in search of a body. Evelyn Keyes plays the woman who falls in love with the spirit of Montgomery, then meets him in his new body. This last scene is both poignant and human, qualities which set the film above other fantasy comedies. Several of the characters reappeared in the musical Down to Earth (1947) with Rita Hayworth and Larry Parks, while a remake, Heaven Can Wait, appeared in 1978 starring Warren Beatty.

Herman, Al (1896–1967), actor. Began his long screen career in the early 1920s. He appeared as a supporting player in dramas and light films during a career that spanned four decades.

SELECTED FILMS: Captain Blood (1924), The Assassin of Grief (1928), Bad Company (1931), Harmony Lane (1935), Hollywood Cowboy, Torchy Blane, the Adventurous Blonde, Manhattan Merry-Go-Round, Headin' East (1937), Dream Boat (1952). ∎

Hernandez, Anna (1867–1945), actress. Entered early silent films following a long career on stage. She appeared in dramas and light films. She was married to actor George F. Hernandez (1863–1922).

SELECTED FILMS: The Rosary (1915), Battling Jane (1918), Leave It to Susan (1919), Darling Mine, Burglar Proof, An Amateur Devil (1920), Molly O', The Rowdy (1921), The Kentucky Derby (1922), The Extra Girl (1923), Fainting Lover, The Cannonball (1931), Speed in the Gay Nineties (1932). ∎

Hersholt, Jean (1886–1956), actor. On stage in his native Denmark before settling in Hollywood in 1915. Following appearances in several of Thomas Ince's films, he emerged as a major screen actor during the 1920s. When sound arrived, his foreign accent relegated him to lesser roles in dramas and light films, often playing genial elderly men. He starred in a low-budget series of "Dr. Christian" films. He received a special Oscar in 1939 for his humanitarian achievements. After his death the Motion Picture Academy founded the annual Jean Hersholt Humanitarian Award.

SELECTED FILMS: The Disciple (1915), Jazzmania (1923), Her Night of Romance (1924), The Old Soak (1926), The Wrong Mr. Wright (1927), Abie's Irish Rose, The Battle of the Sexes (1928), Viennese Nights (1930), Dinner at Eight (1933), One in a Million, Heidi (1937), I'll Give a Million (1938), Remedy for Riches (1940), Melody for Three (1941), Dancing in the Dark (1949), Run for Cover (1955). ∎

Hervey, Irene (1910–), actress. Appeared in films during the 1930s and 1940s, initially as a female lead, then in supporting roles. Her attractive looks enhanced many second-rate films, several of which were light features.

In Mr. Peabody and the Mermaid she played the wife of William POWELL, who is worried about turning 50 years old, while she takes the birthday in stride. "A wife doesn't feel safe," she explains, "until her husband turns the 'fifty' corner."

SELECTED FILMS: The Stranger's Return (1933), Let's Try It Again (1934), His Night Out (1935), Absolute Quiet, Along Came Love (1936), The Girl Said No (1937), Say It in French (1938), Destry Rides Again (1939), Three Cheers for the Irish, The Boys From Syracuse (1940), Mr. Dynamite (1941), Frisco Lil (1942), He's My Guy (1943), Mr. Peabody and the Mermaid (1948), The Lucky Stiff (1949), Cactus Flower (1969), Play Misty for Me (1971). ∎

Hickman, Howard (1880–1949), actor. Appeared on stage in 1903 before entering early silent films in 1914. He directed several silent films but returned to acting. A grey-haired character player, he appeared in numerous dramas and light films playing hard-nosed newspapermen and executives during a screen career that spanned four decades.

SELECTED FILMS: Jimmy the Gent (1934), Libeled Lady (1936), Start Cheering (1938), It All Came True (1940), Cheers for Miss Bishop (1941). ∎

Hicks, Mrs. A fictional character from Betty MacDonald's novel, The Egg and I. She appeared in several entries of the "MA AND PA KETTLE" comedies. An exasperating busybody, she was portrayed by veteran comic character actress Esther DALE in The Egg and I (1947), Ma and Pa Kettle (1949), Ma and Pa Kettle at the Fair (1952), and Ma and Pa Kettle at Waikiki (1955).

Hicks, Russell (1895–1957), actor. Began his prolific Hollywood career in the early 1920s as a casting director. Following some stage experience, he turned to acting during the sound era, appearing as a character player in hundreds of dramas and light films, including comedies starring some of the leading funnymen of the period (ABBOTT AND COSTELLO, the

RITZ BROTHERS, and W. C. FIELDS). He frequently played businessmen.

SELECTED FILMS: *Happiness Ahead* (1934), *Living on Velvet*, *Lady Tubbs* (1934), *Follow the Fleet* (1936), *Hold That Co-Ed*, *Kentucky* (1938), *The Three Musketeers* (1939), *The Bank Dick*, *No, No Nanette* (1940), *The Big Store*, *Hold That Ghost*, *Great Guns* (1941), *Air Raid Wardens* (1943), *The Seventh Cavalry* (1956). ■

Hiers, Walter (1893–1933), actor. Entered early silent films in 1915 working for D. W. Griffith. He appeared chiefly as a supporting player in light films.

SELECTED FILMS: *Jimmy* (1915), *It Pays to Advertise*, *Leave It to Susan* (1919), *A Kiss in Time*, *The Snob*, *Two Weeks With Pay* (1921), *The Ghost Breaker* (1922), *Mr. Billings Spends His Dime* (1923), *Fair Week*, *Hold Your Breath* (1924), *Excuse Me*, *Good Spirits*, *Tender Feet*, *Off His Beat*, *Hot Doggies* (1925), *Hold That Lion* (1926), *Beware of Widows*, *Naughty*, *Hot Lemonade*, *The Girl From Gay Paree*, *The Wrong Mr. Wright*, *Husband Hunters* (1927), *Dancers in the Dark* (1932). ■

Higby, Wilbur (1866–1934), actor. Began his screen career in the early 1910s. He appeared as a supporting player chiefly in light films.

SELECTED FILMS: *Nugget Nell* (1919), *Live Wires*, *Play Square*, *Girls Don't Gamble* (1921), *Do and Dare*, *My Dad*, *The Ladder Jinx* (1922), *The Love Trap* (1923), *Hat, Coat and Glove*, *The Mighty Barnum* (1934). ■

"Higgins Family, The." A domestic comedy series launched in 1938 starring the real-life family of James and Lucille GLEASON and their son, juvenile actor Russell GLEASON. There were five entries in this low-budget, low-comedy series produced by Universal studios.

SELECTED FILMS: *The Higgins Family* (1938), *My Wife's Relatives*, *Should*

Husbands Work? (1939), *Money to Burn*, *Grandpa Goes to Town* (1940). ■

High Anxiety. See Mel Brooks.

Hill, Hallene (1876–1966), actress. Appeared occasionally as a supporting player in several dramas and light films during a sporadic screen career that spanned four decades.

SELECTED FILMS: *One Hour Late* (1935), *Remedy for Riches* (1940), *Tramp, Tramp, Tramp*, *Wedding Blitz* (1942), *Forty Pounds of Trouble* (1963), *Cat Ballou* (1965). ■

Hill, Jack (1900–1972), actor. Worked as a supporting player in silent films during the late 1920s and in sound films during the 1930s. He appeared in numerous comedy shorts and features starring some of the foremost comedians of the period, including LAUREL AND HARDY and Charley CHASE.

SELECTED FILMS: *Leave 'Em Laughing*, *Their Purple Moment*, *Should Married Men Go Home?*, *Two Tars* (1928), *Liberty*, *Wrong Again* (1929), *Blotto*, *Below Zero* (1930), *Be Big*, *Pardon Us*, *Beau Hunks*, *On the Loose* (1931), *Any Old Port*, *The Chimp* (1932), *The Devil's Brother*, *Busy Bodies* (1933), *Babes in Toyland* (1934), *Bonnie Scotland*, *The Bohemian Girl* (1935), *Our Relations* (1936), *Way Out West*, *Pick a Star* (1937), *Swiss Miss*, *Block-Heads* (1938), *Saps at Sea* (1940). ■

Hill, Thelma (1906–1938), actress. Began her brief screen career in the late 1920s working for producer Mack SENNETT. She appeared as a supporting player in a handful of comedies before her untimely death at age 32.

SELECTED FILMS: *The Fair Co-ed* (1927), *The Chorus Kid*, *The Play Girl* (1928), *The Old Barn*, *The Bee's Buzz*, *The Big Palooka*, *Girl Crazy*, *The Barber's Daughter*, *The Constable*, *The Lunkhead* (1929), *The Plus Fours* (1930),

The Miracle Woman (1931), Sunkissed Sweeties (1932). ∎

Hiller, Arthur (1923–), director. Worked as a television director before entering films in the 1950s. He has turned out both dramas and comedies, some of which were not only very successful at the box office, but showed the director's artistic abilities in the film medium. His comedy style has ranged from slapstick to contemporary themes to satire, the last of which seems to be his most promising. During the 1980s his work in comedy suffered chiefly from weak scripts until he turned out the critically successful *Outrageous Fortune* starring Bette MIDLER and Shelley LONG.

SELECTED FILMS: *The Careless Years (1957), The Wheeler Dealers (1963), The Americanization of Emily (1964), Promise Her Anything, Penelope (1966), The Tiger Makes Out (1967), The Out-of-Towners (1970), Plaza Suite, The Hospital (1971), The Crazy World of Julius Vrooder (1974), W. C. Fields and Me, Silver Streak (1976), The In-Laws, Nightwing (1979), Author! Author! (1982), Romantic Comedy (1983), The Lonely Guy, Teachers (1984), Outrageous Fortune (1987).* ∎

Hilliard, Ernest (1890–1947), actor. Began his long screen career in 1912. He appeared chiefly as a supporting player in romances, dramas, and light films during a career that spanned four decades.

SELECTED FILMS: *Annabel Lee (1921), Married People (1922), Man and Wife, Modern Marriage (1923), Trouping With Ellen (1924), Broadway Lady (1925), A Broadway Cinderella, Let It Rain, Smile, Brother, Smile (1926), Lady Raffles, The Big Hop (1928), Red Hot Rhythm, The Awful Truth (1929), Second Honeymoon (1931), Life of the Party (1937), The Magnificent Dope (1942), Deadline for Murder (1946).* ∎

Hilliard, Harriet (1914–), actress, singer. Began her show business career as a band vocalist. She switched to films in the mid-1930s, appearing in routine romantic comedies and musicals. Her screen career diminished in the 1940s, but by the 1950s she scored a hit with her husband, Ozzie Nelson, in a successful television series.

SELECTED FILMS: *Follow the Fleet (1936), The Life of the Party (1937), She's My Everything, Cocoanut Grove (1938), Sweetheart of the Campus (1941), Juke Box Jenny (1942), Honeymoon Lodge, Gals, Inc. (1943), Swingtime Johnny (1944), Here Come the Nelsons (1952).* ∎

Hinds, Samuel S. (1875–1948), actor. Acted on stage before entering films in his later years. A prolific character player, he appeared as a kindly father figure in numerous roles in more than 100 dramas and light films. He played in several ABBOTT AND COSTELLO features.

SELECTED FILMS: *Shore Leave (1925), The Nuisance, Bed of Roses (1933), The Women in His Life, Hat, Coat and Glove, Have a Heart (1934), Living on Velvet (1935), Rhythm on the Range (1936), Top of the Town, Double or Nothing (1937), The Rage of Paris, You Can't Take It With You (1938), Charlie McCarthy, Detective (1939), Buck Privates (1941), Ride 'Em Cowboy (1942), It Ain't Hay (1943), Uncle Harry (1945), It's a Wonderful Life (1946), The Egg and I (1947), The Return of October (1949).* ∎

Hines, Johnny (1895–), actor. Worked on stage before appearing in early silent comedy shorts beginning in 1915. He starred in the "Torchy" comedy series, first released in 1920. The main character, an office boy, was based on a character adapted from the short stories of Sewell Ford. Pretty Dorothy MACKAILL co-starred with Hines. After the success of this series, he moved to feature-length comedy films and, with First National studios, became a top box office draw by the mid-1920s. He sported a flashing smile that blended well with his brash and energetic personality.

SELECTED FILMS: *Burn 'Em Up Barnes (1921), Little Johnny Jones (1923), The Speed Spook (1924), The Crackerjack (1925), The Brown Derby (1926), All Aboard, Home Made (1927), The Runaround (1931), Whistling in the Dark (1932), The Girl in 419, Her Bodyguard (1933), Too Hot to Handle (1938).* ∎

His Girl Friday (1940), COL. *Dir.* Howard Hawks; *Sc.* Charles Lederer; with Cary Grant, Rosalind Russell, Ralph Bellamy, John Qualen, Helen Mack.

Based on the popular Broadway play, *The Front Page* by Ben HECHT and Charles MacARTHUR, the film converts the character of reporter Hildy Johnson from male to female, thereby transforming the work into a romantic comedy. Cary GRANT plays Walter Burns, the manipulating editor who is trying to win back his ex-wife, Hildy, played admirably by Rosalind RUSSELL. But she plans to marry a dull insurance salesman (Ralph BELLAMY) and settle in upstate New York. The film continues the tradition of the SCREWBALL COMEDIES of the 1930s. The pace is hectic. A convicted murderer about to be executed escapes. Bellamy's elderly mother is kidnapped while he is wrongfully arrested, the result of Grant's design to keep Russell from leaving. The witty repartee and sardonic banter monopolize the plot. "I sort of like him," Bellamy says naively of Grant. "He's got a lot of charm." "He comes by it naturally," explains Russell. "His grandfather was a snake." A host of comic characters help to enliven things. Abner BIBERMAN is hilarious as a small-time hood working for Grant. The play was adapted to the screen on two other occasions, once in 1931 with Adolphe MENJOU and Pat O'BRIEN and again in 1974 starring Jack LEMMON and Walter MATTHAU.

History of the World—Part 1. See Mel Brooks.

Hively, Jack (1907–), director. Turned out routine dramas and light comedies during the 1930s and 1940s. He directed several entries in the popular "Saint" detective series.

SELECTED FILMS: *They Made Her a Spy, Panama Lady, Two Thoroughbreds (1939), Anne of Windy Poplars, Laddie (1940), They Met in Argentina, Father Takes a Wife (1941), Four Jacks and a Jill (1941), Are You With It? (1948).* ∎

Hobart, Rose (1906–), actress. Came to Hollywood in the early 1930s following a successful Broadway stage career. An attractive performer born Rose Kefer, she often played sympathetic heroines during this period. By the 1940s she was relegated to supporting roles, usually as revengeful women.

SELECTED FILMS: *Liliom, A Lady Surrenders (1930), Lady Be Good, Ziegfeld Girl, Nothing but the Truth (1941), A Gentleman at Heart (1942), Swing Shift Maisie (1943), Song of the Open Road (1944), Claudia and David (1946), The Farmer's Daughter, The Trouble With Women (1948), Mickey (1948), Bride of Vengeance (1949).* ∎

Hobbes, Halliwell (1877–1962), actor. Appeared on stage in his native England before migrating to Hollywood during the silent period although he did not make any films until 1929. Bald and gentle-mannered with a penchant toward comedy, he portrayed various characters in dramas and light films but tended to specialize in butler roles.

SELECTED FILMS: *Jealousy, Lucky in Love (1929), Grumpy, Charley's Aunt (1930), Bachelor Father (1931), Lady for a Day (1933), Millions in the Air (1935), Here Comes Trouble (1936), Fit for a King (1937), You Can't Take It With You (1938), The Hardys Ride High (1939), Here Comes Mr. Jordan (1941), To Be or Not to Be (1942), You Gotta Stay Happy (1948), Miracle in the Rain (1956).* ∎

"Hogan" comedies. A series of silent shorts produced for Mack SENNETT'S KEYSTONE studio and starring the popular comic Charlie MURRAY. Curiously, there was nothing exceptional about this particular screen character, except that many screen comedians at the time had their own series. Mack SWAIN portrayed a character named Ambrose, CHAPLIN created the Tramp, ARBUCKLE played the Fat Boy, Stan LAUREL was Hickory Hiram, etc. Murray, however, endowed his fictional character with his own inimitable personality. The films, which ranged in length from one-half to two reels each, were all directed by one of Sennett's key assistants, Charles AVERY.

SELECTED FILMS: *Hogan's Wild Oats, Hogan's Mussy Job, Hogan the Porter, Hogan's Romance Upset, Hogan's Aristocratic Dream, Hogan Out West* (1915). ∎

Holden, Fay (1895–1973), actress. Worked in the theater in her native England before making her film debut in the United States in the mid-1930s. Born Dorothy Fay Hammerton, she appeared as a supporting actress in many dramas and light films, gaining some popularity as the patient mother of ANDY HARDY in the successful comedy series starring Mickey ROONEY.

SELECTED FILMS: *I Married a Doctor, Polo Joe* (1936), *Double or Nothing* (1937), *You're Only Young Once, Love Is a Headache, Judge Hardy's Children, Hold That Kiss, Sweethearts* (1938), *Sergeant Madden* (1939), *Bitter Sweet* (1940), *Ziegfeld Girl* (1941), *Andy Hardy's Blonde Trouble* (1944), *Andy Hardy Comes Home* (1958). ∎

Holiday (1938), COL. Dir. George Cukor; Sc. Sidney Buchman, Donald Ogden Stewart; with Katharine Hepburn, Cary Grant, Doris Nolan, Lew Ayres, Edward Everett Horton.

Philip Barry's 1928 sophisticated comedy was adapted to the screen in 1930 and starred Ann Harding and Mary As-

tor. But somehow this film, which had received fairly good reviews, is rarely revived in movie houses or seen on television. Perhaps it has been overshadowed by the 1938 version and the vivacity of its stars, Katharine HEPBURN and Cary GRANT. Grant visits the luxurious home of his fiance, Julia Seton (Doris Nolan), only to learn that her rigid beliefs concerning money, social restraints, and ambition conflict strongly with his own nonconforming ideas about a more free-wheeling, individualistic outlook on life. Instead of marrying her, he falls in love with her rebellious sister, Linda (Hepburn). Considered by many today as one of the best social comedies to come out of the 1930s, it did poorly at the box office when it was originally released. Perhaps a plot about a family troubled by too much money did not impress an audience whose problems during the Depression were the result of not enough money. The film contained several interesting ties to the original stage and film versions. Hepburn had understudied her film role in the 1928 play; Edward Everett HORTON, who played Grant's eccentric professor-friend, Nick Potter, portrayed the same character in the earlier film; and screenwriter Stewart played the role of Potter in the play.

Judy Holliday and Jack Lemmon

Holliday, Judy (1922–1965), actress. Appeared in Broadway revues before making her film debut in 1944 in a minor role. Back on Broadway, she scored a hit as Billie Dawn in *Born Yesterday*. She repeated her role in the 1950 film version and walked off with the Academy Award for Best Actress. Although she continued to delight her audiences with her singular roles depicting dumb-blonde innocence, her full potential was never realized in films. She was a gifted comedienne who had an excellent sense of timing, a whining voice, and an abundance of charm, the last of which won her the affection of the public.

Typical of the characters she played on screen was the part-time actress she portrayed in *The Solid Gold Cadillac*, co-starring Paul DOUGLAS. Relating her stage experiences to Douglas, especially a stint with the Young Shakespeareans, she asks: "Do you like Shakespeare?" "Well," he replies, "I've read a lot of it." "Well, take my advice," Judy suggests, "don't play it. It's so tiring. They never let you sit down unless you're a king." An intelligent and vivacious comedienne, she died of cancer at age 43.

SELECTED FILMS: *Greenwich Village, Something for the Boys, Winged Victory* (1944), *Adam's Rib* (1949), *Born Yesterday* (1950), *The Marrying Kind* (1952), *It Should Happen to You* (1954), *The Solid Gold Cadillac, Full of Life* (1956), *Bells Are Ringing* (1960). ■

Holliday, Windy. Fictional comic sidekick to Hopalong Cassidy in the popular Paramount western series. Windy was played by the prolific character actor George "Gabby" HAYES, the perennial old-timer, in such films as *Bar 20 Rides Again* (1935), *Three on the Trail* (1936), *Hopalong Rides Again* (1937), and *Bar 20 Justice* (1938).

Holloway, Sterling (1905–), actor. Worked on stage as a comedian and singer before entering films in the late 1920s. A thin, slow-talking character actor with disheveled hair, he appeared in approximately 100 films, many of which were light comedies. He usually portrayed young hayseeds, country bump-

kins, or minor clerks. He worked with some of the leading comics of the period, including Joe E. BROWN, Harold LLOYD, and ABBOTT AND COSTELLO. He has continued to remain active in different areas of show business. He has occasionally appeared in stock and in television and has made several children's records, for which he earned a Grammy Award in 1974.

SELECTED FILMS: *Casey at the Bat* (1927), *Elmer the Great, Alice in Wonderland* (1933), *Strictly Dynamite* (1934), *Life Begins at 40* (1935), *Palm Springs* (1936), *Varsity Show* (1937), *Professor Beware, Spring Madness* (1938), *The Blue Bird, Little Men* (1940), *Top Sergeant Mulligan* (1941), *The Lady Is Willing* (1942), *Sioux City Sue* (1946), *The Beautiful Blonde From Bashful Bend* (1949), *Her Wonderful Lie* (1950), *The Adventures of Huckleberry Finn* (1960), *It's a Mad, Mad, Mad, Mad World* (1963), *Thunder on the Highway* (1977). ■

Holm, Celeste (1919–), actress. Worked in stock and on Broadway before entering films in 1946. A clever and quick-witted actress, she appeared as a supporting player and lead in dramas and light films. She won an Academy Award as Best Supporting Actress for her role in *Gentleman's Agreement* (1947) and distinguished herself as the compassionate friend in *All About Eve* and as Frank Sinatra's assistant in *High Society*.

SELECTED FILMS: *Three Little Girls in Blue* (1946), *Carnival in Costa Rica* (1947), *Chicken Every Sunday, Come to the Stable, Everybody Does It* (1949), *Champagne for Caesar, All About Eve* (1950), *The Tender Trap* (1955), *High Society* (1956), *Bachelor Flat* (1961), *Doctor, You've Got to Be Kidding!* (1967), *The Private Files of J. Edgar Hoover* (1978). ■

Holmes, Stuart (1887–1971), actor. Appeared on stage before entering early silent films in 1911. He starred in a long string of dramas and comedies, usually playing urbane, sophisticated roles. With the advent of sound, he was well entrenched as a versatile character actor. His long screen career spanned six decades.

SELECTED FILMS: How Mrs. Murray Saved the Army (1911), In the Stretch (1914), The Other Man's Wife (1919), Tea—With a Kick (1923), Good and Naughty, My Official Wife (1926), Your Wife and Mine, Polly of the Movies (1927), Belle of the Nineties (1934), Her Husband's Secretary (1937), A Letter to Three Wives (1948), The Man Who Shot Liberty Valance (1962). ∎

Holmes, Taylor (1872–1959), actor. Worked on stage before starting a long screen career that covered five decades. A dark-haired, handsome actor, he played romantic leads before being relegated to character roles during the sound era. He specialized in playing likable rogues and hustlers although he worked on both sides of the law.

SELECTED FILMS: Efficiency Edgar's Courtship (1917), Ruggles of Red Gap (1918), Taxi (1919), $20 a Week (1924), One Hour of Love (1928), Dinner at Eight (1933), Make Way for a Lady, The First Baby (1936), The Egg and I (1947), That Wonderful Urge (1948), Mr. Belvedere Goes to College (1949), Father of the Bride (1950), Rhubarb (1951), Gentlemen Prefer Blondes (1953), The Maverick Queen (1956). ∎

Homolka, Oscar (1898–1978), actor. Appeared on stage and in silent and sound films in Germany and England before migrating to the United States in the mid-1930s. A stocky figure with dark hair and shifty eyes, he worked on Broadway and in dramatic and light films, giving strong performances as a character actor. He was nominated for an Academy Award as Best Supporting Actor for his portrayal of Uncle Chris in I Remember Mama (1948). In Comrade X he played a ruthless Communist police chief who curtails the foreign press in Russia. Several of the reporters demand

to speak with the head of the press department. "The former head of the press department was a victim last night of a traffic accident," he informs the journalists. "He apparently, shall we say, did not watch his step."

SELECTED FILMS: Comrade X (1940), Ball of Fire (1941), I Remember Mama (1948), The Seven Year Itch (1955), Boys' Night Out (1962), Joy in the Morning (1965). ∎

Hood, Darla (1931–1979), child actress. Appeared in 132 "OUR GANG" comedy shorts. She began her ten-year association with Hal ROACH'S famous children's group in 1935. As the gang's "leading lady," she often supplied the singing and romantic interest. She occasionally appeared in feature-length films.

SELECTED FILMS: The Bohemian Girl, Our Relations (1936), Born to Sing (1942). ∎

Bing Crosby, Dorothy Lamour, and Bob Hope

Hope, Bob (1903–), actor. Worked in musical comedies and revues before appearing in films in 1934. His screen debut consisted of a series of comedy shorts. By 1938 he was starring in feature-length comedies and musicals. His success as a film comedian was strengthened with his appearance in the highly popular The Cat and the Canary (1939) and when he teamed with crooner Bing CROSBY in the popular "ROAD" series. He developed a screen character that was a blundering, weak coward who wise-cracked his way through assorted dangers while half-heartedly protecting the heroine. During the 1940s he was consistently on the list of top ten box-office draws.

Hope's movie humor, like that of other comedians of the period, was strongly influenced by radio. Rarely did the lusty, visual gags and routines from vaudeville and burlesque dominate the loosely conceived scripts; instead, a more quiet, informal, and more personal delivery pervaded the films of the late 1930s and 1940s. While his films with Crosby gained wide acceptance, he emerged a stronger comic and entertainer when he starred sans the crooner. His solo films are consistently funnier and are paced better. His film career as a popular comic has spanned five decades. His autobiography, *The Road to Hollywood*, was published in 1977.

For five decades he entertained his audiences with his quips and gags. In *The Ghost Breakers* Richard Carlson describes to Paulette GODDARD and Bob Hope the zombies they would encounter on a Cuban island: "You see them sometimes walking around blindly with dead eyes, following orders, not knowing what they do—not caring—" "You mean like Democrats?" Hope asks. In *Casanova's Big Night* (1954) he impersonated the title character, taking to the gondola to serenade his women who soon fall prey to his charms. "I'm getting to the age where I can only work a canal a day," he sighs. In *The Great Lover* (1949) pretty Rhonda Fleming volunteers to get him out of a jam; as she departs, she gives him a passionate kiss. Stunned, Hope says to himself: "I'm not worth it. But if I'm not, who is?" And in *My Favorite Brunette* (1947) attractive Dorothy Lamour desperately confesses to Hope that she's in trouble, while showing him a photograph. "What's the wheelchair for?" Hope asks. "My husband is an invalid," she explains. "He hasn't been out of that chair in seven years." "You're in trouble," he agrees.

See the "Road" movies entry for titles with Crosby.

SELECTED FILMS: The Big Broadcast of 1938, College Swing, Give Me a Sailor, Thanks for the Memory (1938), Some Like It Hot, The Cat and the Canary (1939), The Ghost Breakers (1940), Caught in the Draft, Louisiana Purchase (1941), My Favorite Blonde (1942), They Got Me Covered, Let's Face It (1943), The Princess and the Pirate (1944), Monsieur Beaucaire (1946), Where There's Life (1947), The Paleface (1948), Sorrowful Jones, Fancy Pants (1950), The Lemon Drop Kid, My Favorite Spy (1951), Off Limits, Here Come the Girls (1953), The Seven Little Foys (1955), That Certain Feeling (1956), Beau James (1957), The Facts of Life (1960), Call Me Bwana (1963), How to Commit Marriage (1969), Cancel My Reservation (1972). ■

Hopkins, Miriam (1902–1972), actress. Worked as a chorus girl in the early 1920s, switched to dramatic roles within a few years and appeared on Broadway, and in 1930 signed a Hollywood contract. A fascinating and temperamental blonde performer, she was almost an overnight success in films at Paramount. She starred in dramas and light films through the 1930s, several of which were bright, sophisticated comedies directed by Ernst LUBITSCH. In *The Smiling Lieutenant* she plays a naive princess trying to ensnare Maurice CHEVALIER; in *Trouble in Paradise* she portrays a jewel thief who falls in love with her partner, Herbert Marshall; and in *Design for Living* she abandons impoverished suitors Gary COOPER and Fredric MARCH for wealthy Edward Everett HORTON. By the end of the decade her popularity slipped and within the next few years she retired from the screen. She returned to the stage, occasionally appearing in films in her later years as a character player.

In *Design for Living* her new husband, Edward Everett Horton, asks: "Do you love me?" "People should not ask that question on their wedding night," she replies. "It's either too late or too early."

SELECTED FILMS: Fast and Loose (1930), The Smiling Lieutenant (1931), Dancers in the Dark, Trouble in Paradise (1932), Design for Living (1933), All of Me, She Loves Me Not, The Richest Girl in the World (1934), Woman Chases Man, Wise Girl (1937), A Gentleman After Dark (1942), The Mating Season (1951), The Chase (1966). ▪

Hopper, E. Mason (1885–1966), director. Acted in vaudeville and the theater, worked as a cartoonist, and directed plays before entering films in 1911 as a director. For the next two decades he turned out light comedies as well as dramas.

SELECTED FILMS: Mr. Wise—Investigator (1911), Alkali Ike in Jayville (1913), Tar Heel Warrior (1917), Her American Husband, The Love Brokers (1918), Edgar and the Teacher's Pet (1920), Hold Your Horses (1921), Up in Mabel's Room (1926), Getting Gertie's Garter, The Night Bride, The Wise Wife, The Rush Hour (1927), A Blonde for a Night (1928), The Carnation Kid (1929), Her Mad Night (1932), Curtain at Eight (1934). ▪

Hopper, Hedda (1890–1966), actress, gossip columnist. Began her long show business career as a Broadway chorus girl before moving to Hollywood in 1915 with her celebrated actor-husband DeWolf Hopper. While her husband starred in silent dramas, she began to appear in vamp roles and, later, as a supporting player. In the late 1930s she introduced her Hollywood gossip column and became one of the most influential columnists in the movie capital. Her collection of hats became the butt of many good-natured jokes. During the sound era she appeared as a character actress or as herself in numerous romances and light films. She wrote two autobiographies, From Under My Hat (1952) and The Whole Truth and Nothing But (1963).

SELECTED FILMS: Battle of Hearts (1916), Her Excellency the Governor (1917), Miami, The Snob (1924), Raffles, the Amateur Cracksman (1925), Orchids and Ermine (1927), Harold Teen (1928), His Glorious Night (1929), Holiday, Let Us Be Gay (1930), Speak Easily (1932), Lady Tubbs, Alice Adams (1935), Artists and Models, Topper (1937), Thanks for the Memory (1938), Midnight, What a Life (1939), Life With Henry (1941), Breakfast in Hollywood (1946), Pepe (1960), The Oscar (1966). ▪

Hopper, William (DeWolf) (1915–1970), actor. Began his screen career in the mid-1930s in minor roles. A tall, dark performer, he worked on the stage after serving in World War II. When he returned to films, he received larger and better parts. He appeared in dramas and light films for Warner Brothers and 20th Century-Fox before turning his career toward television. His mother was the famous Hollywood columnist Hedda HOPPER and his father, the popular stage actor DeWolf Hopper.

SELECTED FILMS: Sissy, The Big Broadcast of 1937 (1936), Mr. Dodd Takes the Air, Footloose Heiress (1937), Brother Orchid (1940), Affectionately Yours, The Bride Came C.O.D., Here Comes Happiness (1941), Larceny, Inc., The Male Animal (1942), Myra Breckinridge (1970). ▪

Horne, James W. (1880–1942), director. Worked as a stage actor and director before signing with Kalem studios in 1911 to direct serials. He also turned out many comedy shorts for Hal ROACH, starring some of the leading comedians of the period, including Charley CHASE, Buster KEATON, and LAUREL AND HARDY. His career spanned four decades, the last of which he spent churning out action-packed serials.

SELECTED FILMS: The Accomplice, The Barnstormers (1915), Social Pirates (1916), Occasionally Yours (1920), Don't Doubt Your Wife, The Hottentot (1922), Blow Your Own Horn (1923), Stepping Lively, Laughing at Danger (1924), Kosher Kitty Kelly (1926), College (1927),

Big Business (1929), Laughing Gravy, Our Wife, Beau Chumps (1931), Bonnie Scotland (1935), The Bohemian Girl (1936), Way Out West, All Over Town (1937), Captain Midnight, Perils of the Royal Mounted (1942). ∎

Horne, Victoria (1920–), actress, comedienne. Appeared as a comic character player in a handful of films during the 1940s and 1950s.

SELECTED FILMS: The Scarlet Claw (1944), She Wrote the Book, Blue Skies (1946), Suddenly It's Spring, The Ghost and Mrs. Muir (1947), The Life of Riley, Abbott and Costello Meet the Killer (1949), Harvey (1950), Affair With a Stranger (1953). ∎

Horton, Edward Everett (1886–1970), actor. Worked as a chorus boy and actor on Broadway in the 1910s, toured the country in a variety of productions, and in the early 1920s directed stage plays. He entered films in the 1920s and continued into the sound period. He was best known for his supporting roles in light films, often as prissy, flustered characters. He worked in several films directed by Ernst LUBITSCH and accompanied some of the leading screen personalities of the period, including, among others, Harold LLOYD and Douglas FAIRBANKS. In a career that spanned more than five decades, perhaps his best moments were those of the mid-1930s in which he portrayed Fred ASTAIRE'S companion in a series of light musical comedies. In Springtime in the Rockies (1942) he played an eccentric well-to-do scholar whose fortune was derived from toothpaste. Another tycoon, a flabby, rotund man, recognizes him and says, "You're toothpaste, aren't you? I'm gelatin." "Really?" Horton replies, perusing the fleshy speaker. "I believe it."

SELECTED FILMS: Too Much Business, The Ladder Jinx (1922), Ruggles of Red Gap, To the Ladies (1923), Flapper Wives (1924), Marry Me (1925), Poker

Faces (1926), The Hottentot, The Sap (1929), Take the Heir (1930), The Front Page (1931), Trouble in Paradise (1932), Design for Living, Alice in Wonderland (1933), The Gay Divorcee (1934), Top Hat (1935), Shall We Dance (1937), Bluebeard's Eighth Wife, Holiday (1938), Here Comes Mr. Jordan (1941), Arsenic and Old Lace (1944), Down to Earth (1947), Pocketful of Miracles (1961), It's a Mad, Mad, Mad, Mad World (1963), Cold Turkey (1971). ∎

Hoskins, Allen Clayton ("Farina") (1921–1980), child actor. One of the original "OUR GANG" members. Another of producer Hal ROACH'S discoveries, he made his debut into the famous gang in the 1920s. He appeared in over 300 comedy shorts.

SELECTED FILMS: Young Sherlocks (1922), The Champeen, The Cobbler, The Big Show, A Pleasant Journey, Dogs of War (1923), The Trouble, Big Business, The Buccaneers, Seein' Things (1924), The Big Town, Circus Fever, Dog Days, The Love Bug (1925), Shivering Spooks, The Fourth Alarm (1926), Teacher's Pet, School's Out (1930), Love Business, Little Daddy (1931). ∎

Hotely, May (1872–1954), actress. Appeared in early silent comedy shorts for the Lubin studios. She starred in "The Gay Time" series of comedies, directed by Arthur Hotaling. The films seemed more like documentaries as the audience was transported to different scenic locations where the cast performed its antics. Although the series failed, Hotely continued to appear in Hotaling's new half-reel comedies, produced during the 1913–14 season.

SELECTED FILMS: A Question of Modesty, The Wise Detective, A Stage Door Flirtation, Business and Love (1911), Nora, the Cook (1912), Fixing Auntie Up, A Masked Mix-Up, Kate the Cop, The Widow's Wiles, Her Wooden Leg, The Engaging Kid, Giving Bill a Rest, She Must Elope (1913), A Lucky Strike, The Twin Sister, Price of Pies,

Think of the Money, Playing Horse, His Bodyguard, The New Butler (1915), Girls Who Dare (1929). ∎

Housman, Arthur (1888–1942), actor. Worked in silent and sound films as a supporting player. He appeared as a drunk in several films, including two of Harold LLOYD'S sound comedies of the 1930s. He also worked in several films with LAUREL AND HARDY. He made scores of films in his twenty years in Hollywood, and no doubt would have continued if he had not succumbed to pneumonia at age 53.

SELECTED FILMS: *The Fighter, The Way of a Maid (1921), Under the Red Robe (1923), Manhandled (1924), Fools for Luck (1928), Feet First (1930), Five and Ten, Caught Plastered (1931), Movie Crazy, Scram! (1932), She Done Him Wrong (1933), Punch Drunks, The Live Ghost, Babes in the Goods, Done in Oil (1934), The Fixer-Uppers, Treasure Blues, Sing, Sister, Sing, Here Comes Cookie (1935), Our Relations (1936), Step Lively, Jeeves (1937), Go West (1940).* ∎

Howard, Jerry "Curly" (1903–1952), actor. Worked as a comedy band conductor in vaudeville and stand-up comedian before joining the THREE STOOGES act in 1932. The rotund simpleton and patsy of the trio, whose trademark consisted of a shaved head, was the most popular member of the team. He appeared to be naturally funny, especially in his body movements and his grunts and squeals, including his often imitated "woo-woo-woo." Joan H. Maurer's biography, *Curly* (1985), contains hundreds of photographs and complete credits of the comic's work.

The trio was not known for their witty lines. As poor as the one-liners were, Curly usually got the best ones. In "Slippery Silks" (1936) he overhears a plump woman remark: "I think I'd look stunning in that riding habit." He turns to Larry and Moe and quips: "I think I'd have trouble figuring out which one is

the horse." And in "Booby Dupes" (1945), when Moe asks him the name of a certain song, Curly replies: "Don't Chop the Wood, Mother—Father's Coming Home With a Load." He was forced to leave the act in 1946 because of a stroke. Many critics believe that the shorts with Curly are generally the best in the series. See the Three Stooges for selected films.

Howard, Kathleen (–1956), actress. Began her screen career in the early 1930s as a supporting player. She appeared in several of W.C. Fields' films in which she played his stern and self-righteous shrewish wife.

SELECTED FILMS: *It's a Gift (1934), The Man on the Flying Trapeze (1935).* ∎

Howard, Moe (1897–1975), actor. Worked as a child actor in silent films, as a dramatic actor in stock, and as a vaudeville comedian before becoming "first stooge" of the THREE STOOGES team in 1925. He guided the trio in films through three decades of popularity, finally retiring from the act in 1969, the year the group disbanded. His dark hair combed down in front in bangs became his trademark. In a sense, he often played the straight man to the blunders of Larry and the madcap antics of Curly. But once in a while he interjected a typical Stooges one-liner. For example, in "Violent Is the Word for Curly" (1938) a matronly college official says to Moe: "We have a lovely student body." "Yours wouldn't be too bad, either," he retorts, "if you took off about 20 pounds." He made solo appearances occasionally as a bit player in feature films. See the Three Stooges for selected films.

Howard, Samuel (Shemp) (1895–1955), actor. Began his career in show business as a vaudeville comedian before joining Ted HEALY'S Stooges in 1925 as an original member of the team.

He then brought in his brother Moe HOWARD and Larry FINE. Seeking a solo career, he left the comedy team in 1932 and was replaced by his second brother "Curly" HOWARD. After starring in comedy shorts, he returned to the group in 1946 when Curly dropped out because of illness. Unfortunately, he was faced with the monumental task of replacing the much-loved Curly, a role that almost no comic would wish upon himself. Without the chubby third stooge's shenanigans, the act seemed to suffer. A hard-working, professional comic, Shemp stayed with the Stooges until his death in 1955, appearing in 77 shorts. Comic Joe BESSER replaced him in 1956. Shemp made several feature films without the team, including *The Bank Dick* (1940) starring W.C. FIELDS and *Africa Screams* (1949) starring ABBOTT AND COSTELLO.

SELECTED FILMS: *Fright Night, Out West, All Gummed Up (1947), Shivering Sherlocks, Fiddlers Three (1948), The Ghost Talks, Who Done It?, Malice in the Palace (1949), Punchy Cowpunchers, Love at First Bite, Three Hams on Rye (1950), Don't Throw That Knife, The Tooth Will Out, Pest Man Wins (1951), A Missed Fortune, Gents in a Jam, Three Dark Horses (1952), Booty and the Beast, Loose Loot, Spooks (1953), Musty Musketeers, Knutzy Knights Scotched in the Frontier (1954), Bedlam in Paradise, Hot Ice, Blunder Boys (1955), Husbands Beware, Creeps, Commotion on the Ocean (1956).* ■

Howard, Tom (1886–1955), actor. Entered films in the early 1930s following careers in burlesque, in vaudeville, and on stage. He appeared as a supporting player in light features and shorts.

SELECTED FILMS: *Rain or Shine (1930), The Mouse Trapper, The Acid Test, The Vest With a Tale (1932), A Drug on the Market, The Great Hokum Mystery (1933), Static, The Big Meow, A Good Scout (1934), Easy Money, An Ear for Music, Grooms in Gloom, Time Out, The Magic Word, Stylish Scouts, He's a*

Prince (1935), Where Is Wall Street? (1936). ■

Howard, Willie (1886–1949), comedian, actor. Popular comic of vaudeville during the 1920s and 1930s. He worked in an act with his brother Eugene for ten years before he reached Broadway. He occasionally appeared in films during the 1930s but never came close to the success he attained on stage. His best material was heavily ethnic. He had the distinction of being one of the first performers to be recorded on sound film in 1926 and was also a pioneer in early television, having performed in this medium in the 1930s.

SELECTED FILMS: *A Theatrical Manager's Office, Between the Acts of the Opera, Pals (1927), The Music Maker (1929), The Thirteenth Prisoner (1930), Millions in the Air (1935), Rose of the Rancho (1936), Broadway Melody of 1938 (1937).* ■

Howe, Wallace, actor. Worked in early silent comedies as a supporting player, often portraying uncles, fathers, and valets. He appeared in a few Harold LLOYD comedies during the 1920s as part of the comedian's stock company.

SELECTED FILMS: *Haunted Spooks, High and Dizzy (1920), Grandma's Boy (1922), Why Worry? (1923), $20 a Week (1924), Tundra (1926).* ■

Howell, Alice (–1961), actress. Worked in early silent comedies for Mack SENNETT'S KEYSTONE studios as a supporting player and occasional lead. She appeared with some of the leading comics of the period, including, among others, Charlie CHAPLIN, Mabel NORMAND, and Mack SWAIN.

SELECTED FILMS: *Caught in a Cabaret, The Knock-out, Mabel's Married Life, Laughing Gas, Shot in the Afternoon, Shot in the Excitement, His Musical Career, Cursed by His Beauty (1914), Wandering Daughters (1923).* ■

Howes, Reed (1900–1964), actor. Entered silent films in the early 1920s. He appeared as a supporting player in numerous dramas and light films during a career that spanned five decades. He also maintained a stage career.

SELECTED FILMS: High Speed Lee (1923), Bobbed Hair (1925), The Night Owl, The High Flyer (1926), Rough House Rosie, Catch as Catch Can (1927), Ladies' Night in a Turkish Bath (1928), Clancy in Wall Street (1929), Sweethearts of the Navy (1937), Mexican Hayride (1948), Rich, Young and Pretty (1951), The Sinister Urge (1961). ■

Howland, Jobyna (1881–1836), actress. Entered early silent films following some stage experience. She appeared as female leads and in supporting roles chiefly in light films. She was the sister of actor Olin HOWLIN.

SELECTED FILMS: The Way of a Woman (1919), Second Youth (1924), A Lady's Morals, Soul Kiss, Honey, Dixiana, Hook, Line and Sinker, The Cuckoos (1930), Big City Blues, Silver Dollar, Once in a Lifetime, Rockabye, Stepping Sisters (1932), Topaze, Cohens and Kellys in Trouble (1933), Ye Old Saw Mill (1935). ■

Howlin, Olin (1896–1959), actor. Began his film career in early silent comedy shorts following experience in vaudeville and on stage. He appeared as a character player in numerous light films during a screen career that spanned five decades. He was the brother of actress Jobyna HOWLAND. He worked with many of the leading comics of the period, including ABBOTT AND COSTELLO and Bob HOPE.

SELECTED FILMS: Independence B'Gosh (1918), The Great White Way (1924), Cheaters at Play (1932), Behold My Wife (1935), The Big Noise (1936), Marry the Girl (1937), The Mad Miss Manton (1938), Blondie Brings Up Baby (1939), Comin' Round the Mountain (1940), Almost Married, Henry and Dizzy (1942), Lady Bodyguard (1943),

Nothing but Trouble (1944), The Wistful Widow of Wagon Gap (1947), The Paleface (1948), Father Makes Good (1950), The Blob (1958). ■

Hoyt, Arthur (1873–1953), actor. Began his film career with Universal studios working in early silents. A short, balding character actor, he portrayed executives, professors, and prominent society figures in well over 150 films, many of which were light or domestic comedies. Late in his career, which spanned four decades, he became a permanent fixture in Preston STURGES' troupe, appearing in many of the director's social comedies.

SELECTED FILMS: Love Never Dies (1916), Bringing Home Father (1917), Don't Neglect Your Wife (1921), Too Much Wife (1922), Eve's Leaves (1926), Tillie the Toiler (1927), Home James (1928), Dumbbells in Ermine (1930), Gold Dust Gertie (1931), Goldie Gets Along (1933), Springtime for Henry (1934), Mr. Deeds Goes to Town (1936), Ever Since Eve (1937), The Cowboy and the Lady (1938), The Great McGinty (1940), The Lady Eve (1941), The Palm Beach Story (1942), The Miracle of Morgan's Creek, Hail the Conquering Hero (1944), My Favorite Brunette, Brute Force (1947). ■

Hubbard, John (1914–), actor. Appeared in films since the 1930s. He played male leads in a string of comedies produced by Hal ROACH as well as supporting roles in other routine films.

SELECTED FILMS: The Housekeeper's Daughter (1939), Turnabout (1940), Road Show, She Knew All the Answers, Our Wife, You'll Never Get Rich (1941), Chatterbox, What's Buzzin', Cousin? (1943), Up in Mabel's Room (1944), Mexican Hayride (1949), Herbie Rides Again (1973). ■

Huber, Harold (1904–1959), actor. Practiced law before entering films in 1932. A character player in more than 75

melodramas and light films, he worked both sides of the law, sometimes as a sly villain and other times as a bungling detective. He appeared in various series, including those of "Charlie Chan" and "Mr. Moto." In *Mr. Moto's Gamble* (1938) he played a detective who, in a relaxed moment, confesses to the Japanese sleuth: "Yes, sir, I'd still be single if I hadn't gone to the policemen's ball one year in a tiger skin."

SELECTED FILMS: *The Match King (1932), Frisco Jenny, Midnight Mary, The Bowery (1933), No More Women, A Very Honorable Guy, The Thin Man (1934), Klondike Annie, Muss 'Em Up, Kelly the Second (1936), A Trip to Paris, Little Tough Guys in Society (1938), Charlie McCarthy, Detective (1939), Country Fair, Down Mexico Way (1941), Sleepytime Gal (1942), My Friend Irma Goes West, Let's Dance (1950).* ■

Hudson, Rock (1925–1985), actor. Began his film career in 1948 in minor roles. Within a few years his popularity increased and he became a major box-office attraction. He won an Oscar nomination for his role in *Giant* (1956), which further enhanced his standing. By the 1960s he switched from romantic dramas to bedroom or sex comedies, often co-starring with Doris DAY. The films were very successful and, if they did not create this new genre, the Hollywood sex comedy, they certainly urged it forward. The films contained situations and dialogue rife with sexual innuendos.

For example, bachelor Hudson in *A Very Special Favor* watches as the girl who has just made him breakfast leaves his apartment hugging a skillet. "She says my eggs will touch no pan but hers," he sighs. In the 1970s, as his popularity with movie audiences diminished, he turned to television. When he was fatally stricken with AIDS in 1985, the entire nation was shocked. Two biographies were published in 1986 following his death: *Rock Hudson: His Story* by Rock Hudson and Sara

Davidson and *Idol: Rock Hudson* by Jerry Oppenheimer and Jack Vitek.

SELECTED FILMS: *Fighter Squadron (1948), Peggy (1950), Here Come the Nelsons, Has Anybody Seen My Gal? (1952), Pillow Talk (1959), Lover Come Back (1962), Man's Favorite Sport?, Send Me No Flowers (1964), Strange Bedfellows, A Very Special Favor (1965), Darling Lili (1970), Avalanche (1978).* ■

Huff, Louise, actress. Entered early silent films in the 1910s. She appeared as a leading lady or supporting player chiefly in light films for Paramount studios.

SELECTED FILMS: *Seventeen (1916), Freckles, The Ghost House, The Varmint, What Money Can't Buy, Tom Sawyer (1917), His Majesty Bunker Bean, Mile-a-Minute Kendall, Sandy (1918), Oh, You Women! (1919).* ■

Hughes, Carol, actress. Appeared chiefly in comedy films during the 1930s and 1940s, of which almost all were routine, low-budget productions. She returned to the screen in the early 1950s as a character actress.

SELECTED FILMS: *The Golden Arrow, Polo Joe, Three Men on a Horse (1936), Ready, Willing and Able, Ever Since Eve, Marry the Girl (1937), The Day the Bookies Wept (1939), Married and in Love (1940), Scattergood Baines, Top Sergeant Mulligan (1941), Pillow to Post (1945), The Bachelor and the Bobby Soxer (1947), Scaramouche (1952).* ■

Hull, Henry (1890–1977), actor. Appeared on stage in the 1910s before entering silent films during the same decade. After playing leads in silents, he was relegated, for the most part, to character roles during the sound era. A versatile actor who continued his stage appearances while maintaining a full screen career, he turned in numerous remarkable performances in serious and comic relief roles. Of the 75 or more films in which he appeared, only a handful were comedies, but several of the dramas cast him in comedy relief roles.

In *Jesse James* (1939), for example, he played an emotional publisher of a frontier-town newspaper. Each time another element of society irritated him—politicians, businessmen, lawmen—he would change his editorial. Concerning his latest peeve, he dictates his next editorial to an assistant: "If we are ever to have law and order in the West, the first thing we've got to do is to take out all the lawyers and shoot 'em down like dogs!"

SELECTED FILMS: *The Volunteer (1918), One Exciting Night (1922), A Bride for a Knight (1923), Transient Lady (1935), Paradise for Three (1938), Babes in Arms, Judge Hardy and Son (1939), What a Man (1943), Goodnight, Sweetheart (1944), The Walls of Jericho (1948), Covenant With Death (1967).* ∎

Hull, Josephine (1884–1957), actress.
Worked on stage before appearing sporadically in films as a character actress. She won an Oscar as Best Supporting Actress for her role in *Harvey*.

SELECTED FILMS: *After Tomorrow, Careless Lady (1932), Arsenic and Old Lace (1944), Harvey (1950), The Lady From Texas (1951).* ∎

Humberstone, H. Bruce (1903–1984),
director. Turned out numerous feature films in a variety of genres, including dramas and light comedies for several major studios. His most productive years were the 1930s-1940s. He worked with several screen comics, including the RITZ BROTHERS and Danny KAYE.

SELECTED FILMS: *If I Had a Million (1932), The Merry Wives of Reno (1934), Ladies Love Danger, Three Live Ghosts (1935), Checkers (1937), Pack Up Your Troubles (1939), The Quarterback (1940), Hello, Frisco, Hello (1943), Pin-Up Girl (1944), Wonder Man (1945), Three Little Girls in Blue (1946), She's Working Her Way Through College (1952), Madison Avenue (1962).* ∎

Hunnicut, Arthur (1911–1979), actor.
Worked on stage before appearing in films in the 1940s as a character actor. He specialized in portraying wizened old-timers and other rustic types, chiefly in western films and light comedies. He was nominated for an Academy Award for his role in *The Big Sky* (1952).

SELECTED FILMS: *Wildcat, Hayfoot, Fall In (1942), Pardon My Gun (1943), Abroad With Two Yanks (1944), She Couldn't Say No (1953), The French Line (1954), The Kettles in the Ozarks (1956), Cat Ballou (1965), Million Dollar Duck (1971), Harry and Tonto, The Spikes Gang, Moonrunners (1974), Winter Hawk (1975).* ∎

Hurlock, Madeleine (1905–), actress.
Worked as one of Mack SENNETT'S "BATHING BEAUTIES" and in many early silent comedy shorts. She appeared with some of the leading comedians of the period, including, among others, Billy BEVAN, Harry LANGDON, and Ben TURPIN. She was considered one of the prettiest of Sennett's troupe of young women. When sound arrived, she decided to leave films.

SELECTED FILMS: *Pitfalls of a Big City, Inbad the Sailor (1923), The Halfback of Notre Dame, Smile Please, His New Mama, Bull and Sand (1924), The Wild Goose Chaser, The Marriage Circus (1925), Don Juan's Three Nights, Whispering Whiskers, When a Man's a Prince, A Sea Dog's Tale, Flirty Four-Flushers (1926), The Best of Friends, The Bull Fighter, Love in a Police Station (1927), The Beach Club, Love at First Sight (1928).* ∎

Hurst, Paul (1888–1953), actor.
Worked as writer and actor in early silent westerns and occasionally directed features and serials. With the advent of sound he became a full-time supporting actor in dramas, musicals, and light comedies, playing both heavies and likable guys. A prolific performer with a rough-

hewn face and a distinctive voice, he appeared in more than 200 films.

SELECTED FILMS: The Tragedy of Bear Mountain, The Girl Detective (1915), Buttons (1927), Oh, Yeah! (1929), Hot Curves (1930), Panama Flo (1932), Tugboat Annie (1933), Mississippi (1935), It Had to Happen (1936), Ali Baba Goes to Town (1937), Topper Takes a Trip (1938), Gone With the Wind, On Your Toes (1939), Star Dust (1940), Caught in the Draft (1941), Pardon My Stripes (1942), Coney Island (1943), Something for the Boys (1944), The Big Showoff (1945), On Our Merry Way (1948), The Sun Shines Bright (1953). ∎

Hussey, Ruth (1914–), actress. Worked in radio, as a fashion model, and on Broadway before entering films in 1937. A versatile brunette performer born Ruth Carol O'Rourke, she has appeared in dramas and light films, sometimes as the wise-cracking female lead but more often cast in wife roles. She received an Academy Award nomination for her supporting role as a magazine photographer in The Philadelphia Story (1940). In the film her co-worker, writer James STEWART, complains about their new assignment in which they have to cover a frivolous society wedding. "It's degrading! It's undignified!" he protests. "So is an empty stomach," she returns.

SELECTED FILMS: The Big City, Madame X (1937), Judge Hardy's Children, Rich Man, Poor Girl, Spring Madness (1938), Honolulu, Maisie, Another Thin Man (1939), Free and Easy, Our Wife, Married Bachelor, H. M. Pulham, Esq. (1941), Pierre of the Plains (1942), Bedside Manner (1945), Mr. Music (1950), That's My Boy (1951), The Lady Wants Mink (1953), Facts of Life (1960). ∎

Hutchins, Bobby "Wheezer," child actor. Appeared in numerous "OUR GANG" comedies in the early 1930s, along with some of the early members,

including Jackie COOPER and "Chubby" CHANEY.

SELECTED FILMS: Teacher's Pet, School's Out (1931), Love Business, Little Daddy (1932). ∎

Hutton, Betty (1921–), actress. Worked as a band vocalist and on Broadway before making her film debut in 1942. Pretty, vivacious, and talented, Hutton, born Betty June Thornburg, deserved the appellation thrust upon her, the "Blonde Bombshell." She proved to be a more than able comedienne in her early roles and, with the chance to play the lead in Annie Get Your Gun, she established herself as a musical comedy star. In the early 1950s, following a dispute with Paramount, she left films at the height of her career, appearing only sporadically in minor productions over the years. Having earned $10 million, she was discovered penniless in the 1970s in a New England Catholic rectory.

SELECTED FILMS: The Fleet's In, Star Spangled Rhythm (1942), Happy Go Lucky, Let's Face It (1943), The Miracle of Morgan's Creek, And the Angels Sing, Here Come the Waves (1944), Incendiary Blonde, Duffy's Tavern, The Stork Club (1945), Cross My Heart (1946), The Perils of Pauline (1947), Dream Girl (1948), Red, Hot and Blue (1949), Annie Get Your Gun (1950), The Greatest Show on Earth, Somebody Loves Me (1952), Spring Reunion (1957). ∎

Hutton, Jim (1933–1979), actor. Worked on stage while in the military service before appearing in films. He played leads in dramas and light comedies, the latter being his specialty. Tall, good-looking, and charming, he graced the roles he portrayed until his untimely death at age 46. Actor Timothy Hutton is his son.

In Where the Boys Are he portrayed a college student in financial straits. Rich student George Hamilton, in a discussion with Hutton concerning girls and marriage, says: "They don't realize what a risk marriage is for a man." "Not for you," Hutton adds. "You can afford to be wrong. I can't even afford to be right."

SELECTED FILMS: A Time to Love and a Time to Die (1958), Where the Boys Are (1960), The Honeymoon Machine, Bachelor in Paradise (1961), The Horizontal Lieutenant, Period of Adjustment (1962), Looking for Love (1964), The Hallelujah Trail, Never Too Late (1965), The Trouble With Angels (1966), Who's Minding the Mint? (1967), Psychic Killer (1975). ■

Hymer, Warren (1906–1948), actor. Familiar character actor during the 1930s and 1940s who appeared in more than 100 features, often as a half-witted hood, punch-drunk fighter, or dumb police officer. He began his career in films with the advent of sound (1929), playing tough-guy roles in straight melodramas as well as comedy-relief characters in light films.

Also known for his mangling of the English language, he could always be counted on for a few good laughs. In Kid Millions (1934) he plays a con man who informs his moll that an ex-boyfriend of hers has died and left a large fortune— with no known heir. "Seventy-seven million?" she says. "Where is it?" "In Eggipt," he replies. "Eggipt?" she questions. "E-G-Y-P-T," he spells out and then repeats, "Eggipt!" And in You Only Live Once (1937) he confides to ex-cellmate Henry Fonda: "Gee, Eddie, the old cell won't seem the same without you."

During his last few years in films he became unreliable because of his heavy drinking. He was last seen in Los Angeles' Skid Row before his untimely death at age 42.

SELECTED FILMS: Fox Movietone Follies of 1929 (1929), Oh, for a Man! (1930), Goldie (1931), Hold 'Em Jail (1932), Her First Mate (1933), The Gilded Lily (1935), Mr. Deeds Goes to Town (1936), Married Before Breakfast (1937), Bluebeard's Eighth Wife (1938), Destry Rides Again (1939), Love, Honor, and Oh, Baby! (1940), Meet John Doe (1941), Henry and Dizzy (1942), Danger— Women at Work (1943), Three Is a Family (1944), Gentleman Joe Palooka (1946). ■

I

I Married a Witch (1942), UA. *Dir.* René Clair; *Sc.* Marc Connelly, Robert Pirosh; with Fredric March, Veronica Lake, Robert Benchley, Susan Hayward, Cecil Kellaway.

This fantasy-comedy is considered French director René Clair's best American film. When Veronica Lake, a Salem witch in Puritan New England, and her father, Cecil KELLAWAY, are burned, she vows vengeance on the descendants of her persecutor, Fredric MARCH. Centuries later, March, portraying the latest member of the family and engaged to Susan Hayward, is running for governor. Meanwhile, Lake returns to make life uncomfortable for him. She is delightful as the mischievous spirit who eventually falls in love with her intended victim. Kellaway is hilarious as an impish sorcerer who, when drunk, forgets the magical words to make him disappear and ends up behind bars; he almost steals the film from its two stars. Robert BENCHLEY is as witty as ever as March's friend. The excellent cast and the high production values, including the clever special effects, elevate the film into a very entertaining comedy. Clair had directed another fantasy-comedy in England in 1936, *The Ghost Goes West*, written by Robert E. Sherwood.

If I Had a Million (1932), PAR. *Dir.* James Cruze, H. Bruce Humberstone, Stephen Roberts, William A. Seiter, Ernst Lubitsch, Norman Taurog, Norman Z. McLeod; *Sc.* Claude Binyon, Sidney Buchman, Lester Cole, Isabel Dawn, Grover Jones, M. Boylan, Jack Bright, Walter DeLeon, B. DeGaw, Otis Garrett, Harvey Gates, Ernst Lubitsch, L. Mackall, Joseph Mankiewicz, Seton Miller, William McNutt, Tiffany Thayer; with Gary Cooper, George Raft, Mary Boland, Charles Laughton, W. C. Fields, Charles Ruggles, Alison Skipworth, Jack Oakie.

Hollywood's first collection of humorous short stories on film, this unique comedy centers on how different people react when faced with a windfall of one million dollars. A dying tycoon selects the recipients randomly from a telephone book and personally presents each with a check. Each of the eight tales has its own director and cast. Some of the more memorable episodes include the one in which Charles LAUGHTON, playing a lowly clerk, gives his employer a Bronx cheer; Charles RUGGLES, a salesperson in a fancy shop, smashes all the china; and W. C. FIELDS and Alison SKIPWORTH, who, after their car was wrecked, buy a fleet of autos and go on a wild but purposeful joyride to punish all roadhogs by totaling their cars. May ROBSON, in the final and most poignant segment, uses the money to purchase a home for elderly women in which the members, previously under the control of a tyrannical matron, can now drink, smoke, and socialize with their male friends. There are some ironic tales as well, as in the cases of criminals for whom the money comes too late, or with Gary COOPER, who thinks the check is a prank and practically gives it away. A similar idea, this time using a dress tailcoat as the motivating force, was used in *Tales of Manhattan* (1942), with Laughton again as one of the principal characters. A television series, "The Millionaire," was based on the film.

"Ike and Mike." A series of silent comedy shorts released during the 1927–28 season based on Rube Goldberg's comic strip characters. Universal studios produced the films, which starred Charley Dorety.

I'm No Angel (1933), PAR. *Dir.* Wesley Ruggles; *Sc.* Mae West; with Mae West, Cary Grant, Gregory Ratoff, Edward Arnold, Ralf Harolde, Kent Taylor, Gertrude Michael.

Cary Grant and Mae West in *I'm No Angel* (1933)

Any vintage Mae WEST comedy offers rewards to its viewers, and this film is one of her best. Mae West was an actress, a star, a famous show business personality, and, most important of all, a woman. In the Hollywood of the 1930s, when almost all of the major comics were male, West managed to squirm her way into the top echelon of screen greats. The characters she played were usually independent women able to cope with the society around them, often on their own terms. West's life, in these respects, paralleled that of her characters. For her

third screen appearance she adapted a good script by Lowell Brentano to fit her character and loaded it with numerous one-liners and clever dialogue, chiefly aimed at satirizing sex, the essence of her comedy. To her maid, she orders the immortal line: "Beulah, peel me a grape." When a circus mystic looks into his crystal ball and says, "I see a man in your life," she quips: "What, only one?" He then adds, "I see a change . . . a change of position." "Sitting or standing?" West asks. An admirer inquires: "Do you mind if I get personal?" "I don't mind if you get familiar," she replies. A female critic comments: "You haven't a streak of decency in you." "I don't show my good points to strangers," West returns. She also sings several of her suggestive songs during the course of the film. The plot revolves around a small-time circus where West works as a sideshow star. During one of her acts she meets and falls in love with playboy Cary GRANT. The film is not only entertaining but is an excellent example of the comedy and style of one of Hollywood's greatest comediennes.

Imhof, Roger (1875–1958), actor. Appeared as a character player in numerous dramas and light films during the 1930s and 1940s. He worked for various studios but chiefly for 20th Century-Fox. He worked in several films starring Will ROGERS.

SELECTED FILMS: Paddy the Next Best Thing, Hoopla (1933), *David Harum, Ever Since Eve, Handy Andy, Judge Priest, Music in the Air* (1934), *The Farmer Takes a Wife, Steamboat Round the Bend* (1935), *There Goes the Groom* (1937), *Every Day's a Holiday* (1938), *It Happened in Flatbush* (1942). ∎

Immigrant, The (1917), MUT. *Dir.* Charlie Chaplin; *Sc.* Charlie Chaplin; with Charlie Chaplin, Edna Purviance,

Kitty Bradbury, Albert Austin, Henry Bergman, Eric Campbell.

Charlie first meets Edna PURVIANCE aboard a ship of immigrants heading for the United States. Following some inventive comedy business, they arrive in the land of their dreams, with Charlie penniless and hungry. A restaurant scene follows in which the little tramp has difficulty in paying the bill. By coincidence, Edna happens to be at another table. After several humorous incidents involving an intimidating waiter played by Eric CAMPBELL, the couple meet an artist, Henry BERGMAN, who wants to paint Edna. Things finally begin to look up for the two immigrants, and the film ends with a marriage. "The Immigrant," one of Chaplin's famous "golden dozen" made at Mutual, was his last film for the studio. With its social implications and autobiographical overtones, it reminded many urban dwellers of the harsh realities they had undergone in search of a new home and a fresh beginning. The film was one of his darkest of this period.

IMP. A motion picture company founded by Carl Laemmle in 1909. IMP (Independent Motion Picture Company) was one of the early leaders in producing comedy-dramas. Their major contributions to straight comedy came in 1912–13 in the form of split-reel comedies or comic material approximately one-half reel in length with a drama, western, or other genre completing the reel. Some of the directors handling comedy films during these years included Fred MACE, himself an accomplished comedian, and Edward Le Saint. By this time (1912), the company was absorbed by Universal.

Inescort, Frieda (1901–1976), actress. Worked in the theater before appearing in films in the mid-1930s in leading as well as supporting roles. Often portray-

ing elegant and stately characters, she appeared in dramas and light comedies.

SELECTED FILMS: The Dark Angel (1935), The King Steps Out (1936), The Great O'Malley, Call It a Day (1937), Beauty for the Asking, A Woman Is the Judge (1939), Pride and Prejudice (1940), You'll Never Get Rich (1941), The Courtship of Andy Hardy (1942), Heavenly Days (1944), The Judge Steps Out (1949), Never Wave at a WAC (1953), Casanova's Big Night (1954), The Crowded Sky (1960). ∎

Ingels, Marty (1936–), actor, comedian. Worked on stage and in television and nightclubs before appearing sporadically in light films during the 1960s and 1970s. His inability to establish a strong and unique screen character and a lack of good comedy material prevented him from developing into a major film comedian.

SELECTED FILMS: The Ladies' Man (1961), The Horizontal Lieutenant (1962), Wild and Wonderful (1964), A Guide for the Married Man, The Busy Body (1967), For Singles Only (1968), If It's Tuesday, This Must Be Belgium (1969), How to Succeed With Sex (1970), How to Seduce a Woman (1974). ∎

Insley, Charles, actor. Appeared in early silent comedy shorts, mainly for ESSANAY'S Charlie CHAPLIN entries. As a supporting player, he worked with other leading comedians of the period, including Ben TURPIN, Gloria SWANSON, and Edna PURVIANCE.

SELECTED FILMS: His New Job, Work, A Woman, The Bank, A Night in the Show (1915). ∎

International House (1933), PAR. Dir. A. Edward Sutherland; Sc. Walter DeLeon, Francis Martin, Lou Heifetz, Neil Brant; with W. C. Fields, Peggy Hopkins Joyce, Stuart Erwin, George Burns, Gracie Allen, Bela Lugosi, Rudy

Vallee, Cab Calloway, Colonel Stoopnagel.

Paramount specialized in putting together all-star productions during the early 1930s, hoping to offer something for everyone, thereby filling the movie houses during the dark Depression years. Most of these features were musical revues such as *Paramount on Parade* (1930). But *International House* differs in that it is pure comedy with only a few musical interludes, and even these, especially Cab Calloway's "Reefer Man," are highly entertaining. Comics W. C. FIELDS and BURNS AND ALLEN are at their peak in this zany story of a television invention to be sold at a hotel in China. Fields literally drops in by helicopter, and when informed that he may be lost, he counters: "Kansas City is lost. I am here." When an attractive blonde discovers a litter of kittens, she ponders: "I wonder what their parents were?" "Careless, my little nutcake," Fields ripostes, "careless." Later, when she invites him to join her in a glass of wine, he quips, "You go in first. I'll join you if there's enough room." In his hotel room Fields rings for room service and orders: "Bring me a drink." "Water, sir?" the bellboy asks. "A little on the side," he replies, "very little." Burns and Allen get in their fair share of humor. Burns portrays the hotel physician while Gracie is his usual dizzy nurse. "Have you seen my stethoscope?" he inquires. "Not now, doctor," she replies. "I'll look at it later." There are some very funny routines in the film, including Fields' encounter with prissy hotel clerk Franklin PANGBORN. Surprisingly, the comic material holds up rather well after so many years. This is one of Fields' best vehicles. Ironically, several Paramount executives at first refused to hire him because his last two features had done poorly at the box office. Director SUTHERLAND convinced them otherwise and the film became a critical and commercial success.

Irving, Margaret, actress. Appeared as a supporting player during the 1930s and 1940s. She played in dramas and light films, working with some of the leading comics of the period, including, among others, the MARX BROTHERS and ABBOTT AND COSTELLO.

SELECTED FILMS: Animal Crackers (1930), Thanks a Million (1935), Wife vs. Secretary, Follow Your Heart, Three Men on a Horse (1936), The Outcasts of Poker Flat, Sh! The Octopus (1937), The Baroness and the Butler, Love, Honor and Behave (1938), In Society (1944). ■

Clark Gable and Claudette Colbert in *It Happened One Night* (1934)

It Happened One Night (1934), COL. Dir. Frank Capra; Sc. Robert Riskin; with Clark Gable, Claudette Colbert, Walter Connolly, Roscoe Karns.

This early screwball comedy seems slightly dated today, but in its time it was very popular and was the first film to capture all the major Academy Awards, including Best Picture, Best Actor, Best Actress, Best Director, and Best Screenplay. Clark GABLE portrays the brash, self-confident reporter who hunts down a runaway heiress (Claudette COLBERT), a perennial 1930s film character. Walter CONNOLLY, her rich father, is willing to pay a small fortune to get her back. Gable finds her at a bus depot and, keeping his identity secret, joins her on her journey. As Colbert and Gable are about to settle down for the night in a motel with a makeshift blanket separating them, she asks him who he is. "Why, I'm the whippoorwill that cries in the night. I'm the soft morning breeze that caresses your face," he replies evasively. "You've got a name, haven't you?" she inquires, unimpressed. Director CAPRA'S love of characters is displayed on board the bus as all the passengers warble "The Man on the Flying Trapeze." There is the delightful scene in which the cocky Gable tries to teach Colbert the art of hitchhiking. When his erudite methods fail, she approaches the side of the road, exposes her leg, and brings the first passing car to a screeching halt. The "Walls of Jericho" scene, in which Gable expounds upon the way a man removes his clothes, has been pointed out in Philip Wylie's *Generation of Vipers*. The author notes that Gable's lack of an undershirt resulted in a drastic reduction in that garment's sales in the following years. Capra, referring to the motel scene in a 1986 interview in the *New York Times*, stated that the sexual attraction between Gable and Colbert, although merely hinted at, was in many ways more erotic than in many modern films. The work generally remains entertaining.

It's a Mad, Mad, Mad, Mad World

(1963), UA. *Dir.* Stanley Kramer; *Sc.* William and Tania Rose; with Spencer Tracy, Milton Berle, Sid Caesar, Buddy Hackett, Ethel Merman, Mickey Rooney, Dick Shawn, Phil Silvers, Terry-Thomas, Jonathan Winters.

Never have so many comics been assembled to ply their trade in one frenetic, crazy, and funny movie. If Kramer's purpose was to pay homage to Mack SENNETT, the master of slapstick and chase comedies, he has succeeded; if his purpose was to produce an epic comedy, here too he has prevailed. The incident that leads to all the wild antics is a dying motorist in the desert who reveals the clue to where a small fortune is stashed away. The chase is on, as each character in the film races toward the money. An allegorical overtone of human greed creeps in, but the fun predominates. Some of the highlights include Buddy HACKETT and Mickey ROONEY in an airplane, Jonathan WINTERS and his revenge on a garage, and Edie Adams and Sid CAESAR'S attempts to escape from a hardware basement. There are literally dozens of veteran and contemporary comedians popping in and out of this unique comedy. Stanley Kramer, whose films include *On the Beach* (1959) and *Judgment at Nuremberg* (1961), was not known as a comedy director; his films usually dealt with topical themes or social messages.

J

Jackson, Anne (1926–), actress. Has appeared on stage and occasionally in films, chiefly in light comedies. The themes of her films often deal with domestic situations and male-female relationships. She is married to actor Eli WALLACH.

SELECTED FILMS: So Young So Bad (1950), Tall Story (1960), The Tiger Makes Out (1967), How to Save a Marriage and Ruin Your Life, The Secret Life of an American Wife (1968), Zigzag, The Angel Levine, Lovers and Other Strangers (1970), The Bell Jar (1979). ■

Jackson, Eugene "Pineapple," child actor. Appeared as a member of the early silent "OUR GANG" comedies produced by Hal ROACH. He later went on to play in feature-length silent and sound films.

SELECTED FILMS: The Big Town, Circus Fever, Dog Days, The Love Bug, Little Annie Rooney (1925), Hearts in Dixie (1929), Dixiana (1930), Sporting Blood, Sporting Chance (1931), The Lady's From Kentucky (1939). ■

Jackson, Glenda (1936–), actress. Appeared on stage and in films in her native England before starring in several American films. Famous chiefly for her dramatic portrayals, she has successfully drifted toward comedy in her later films. She won an Oscar for her performance in A Touch of Class.

SELECTED FILMS: A Touch of Class (1973), Nasty Habits (1977), House Calls (1978), Lost and Found, Health (1979). ■

Jackson, Mary Ann, child actor. Part of the "second wave" of children featured in Hal ROACH'S popular "OUR GANG" series. She appeared in the early sound comedy shorts, along with Jackie COOPER, "Stymie" BEARD, and Bobby "Wheezer" Hutchins.

SELECTED FILMS: Teacher's Pet, School's Out (1930), Love Business, Little Daddy (1931). ■

Jackson, Thomas E. (1886–1967), actor. Worked on Broadway stage before coming to Hollywood in 1929. He appeared as a character player in numerous dramas and light films over a period of more than twenty years. He frequently portrayed policemen.

SELECTED FILMS: Broadway (1929), Good News (1930), Sweepstakes, Women Go On Forever (1931), Strictly Personal (1933), Myrt and Marge, The Personality Kid (1934), Gold Diggers of 1935, The Irish in Us (1935), It Had to Happen (1936), She's No Lady (1938), Free, Blonde and 21 (1940), Shady Lady (1945), Here Comes Trouble (1948), Phone Call From a Stranger (1952). ■

Jacobi, Lou (1913–), actor. Worked on stage in his native Canada and on Broadway before appearing as a character actor in films. He was equally at home in dramas as well as comedies. His most notable comedy role was in Woody Allen's Everything You Always Wanted to Know About Sex . . . But Were Afraid to

Ask (1972). He often portrays New York Jewish figures.

SELECTED FILMS: The Diary of Anne Frank (1959), Irma La Douce (1963), The Last of the Secret Agents?, Penelope (1966), Cotton Comes to Harlem (1970), Little Murders (1971), Next Stop Greenwich Village (1976), Roseland (1977), My Favorite Year (1982). ∎

Jacobs, Paul (1910–), child actor. Began his Hollywood career in 1913 as a child actor in silent comedy shorts for KEYSTONE studios. Comedy actor-director Henry LEHRMAN discovered the three-year-old child while searching for a youngster he needed for one of his films. By 1914 little Paul was starring in his own series, the "Little Billy" comedies. He appeared with some of the leading comics of the period, including, among others, Mack SWAIN, Ford STERLING, and Polly MORAN.

SELECTED FILMS: Little Billy's Triumph, Little Billy's Strategy, Little Billy's Cousin, A Back Yard Theater (1914), Ambrose's Cup of Woe, His Lying Heart (1916), Cactus Nell, Thirst, Lost—a Comic (1917). ∎

Jameson, Joyce (1932–), actress. Made her film debut in the early 1950s. A well-proportioned blonde, she has appeared in dramas and comedies, often playing comical, low-class women. She has alternated between films and television.

SELECTED FILMS: The Strip, Show Boat (1951), The French Line (1953), Phffft! (1954), The Apartment (1960), Comedy of Terrors (1963), Good Neighbor Sam (1964), Boy, Did I Get a Wrong Number! (1966), Scorchy (1976), Every Which Way but Loose (1978), Leo and Loree (1979). ∎

Jamison. Fictional butler character in the "Lone Wolf" detective series of the 1940s starring Warren WILLIAM in the title role. That wonderful comic charac-

ter actor, Eric BLORE, played Jamison, William's butler, in such films as The Lone Wolf Meets a Lady (1940), The Lone Wolf Takes a Chance (1941), and The Lone Wolf Keeps a Date (1941).

Jamison, Bud (1894–1944), actor. Worked in stock and vaudeville before entering films in 1914. A versatile supporting player who began his prolific Hollywood career in early silent comedy shorts, especially in the thirteen films produced by ESSANAY studios starring Charlie CHAPLIN. He portrayed a variety of characters, including headwaiters, prizefighters, and an assortment of villains. He worked with some of the leading comedians of the period, including Harold LLOYD, LAUREL AND HARDY, the THREE STOOGES, and W. C. FIELDS. He appeared with the Stooges in 36 of their shorts from 1934 to 1944 in various roles, including butlers, cops, businessmen, and public officials. With all his experience in silent and sound comedies, he never starred in his own series or played leading roles.

SELECTED FILMS: His New Job, A Night Out, The Champion, By the Sea, The Bank (1915), Carmen (1916), A Dog's Life (1918), Strictly Unreliable, The Soilers, The Dentist (1932), In the Devil's Doghouse, In a Pig's Eye (1934), Flying Down to Zero, Uncivil Warriors, Three Little Beers (1935), Disorder in the Court (1936), Dizzy Doctors, Back to the Woods (1937), Termites of 1938, Violent Is the Word for Curly (1938), We Want Our Mummy (1939), I'll Never Heil Again (1941), Loco Boy Makes Good (1942), Phony Express (1943), Crash Goes the Hash (1944). ∎

Janis, Conrad (1926–), actor. Began his screen career in teen-age roles during the 1940s. He appeared in dramas and light films.

SELECTED FILMS: Snafu (1945), Margie (1946), That Hagen Girl (1947), Beyond Glory (1948), Keep It Cool (1958).

Janis, Elsie (1889–1956), actress, singer. Famous Broadway musical comedy star of the 1910s and 1920s who made occasional light silent films and one sound feature.

SELECTED FILMS: Betsy in Search of a Thrill, A Regular Girl (1919), Women in War (1940). ∎

"Jarr Family, The." A short series of silent film comedies produced in 1915 starring Harry DAVENPORT and Rose TAPLEY in the title roles. Davenport, who developed into a popular character player during the 1930s and 1940s, also directed the films.

SELECTED FILMS: The Jarr Family Visits Harlem, The Jarrs Visit Arcadia (1915). ∎

Jason, Leigh (1904–1979), director. Began his long association with Hollywood as an electrician, then became a screenwriter in 1926 following a brief stint as college instructor. By 1928 he switched to directing films, a career that spanned four decades. His output consisted chiefly of low-budget melodramas and light films.

SELECTED FILMS: The Price of Fear (1928), Love on a Bet, The Bride Walks Out, That Girl From Paris (1936), Wise Girl (1937), The Mad Miss Manton (1938), The Flying Irishman (1939), Model Wife, Three Girls About Town (1941), Lady for a Night (1942), Carolina Blues (1944), Out of the Blue (1947), Okinawa (1952). ∎

Jean, Gloria (1926–), singer, actress. Sang on stage and radio as a child before entering films at age 13. A pretty teenager with plenty of charm and a pleasant voice, she was very popular in the 1940s. Her career faltered, however, when she tried to move to more mature roles.

In Never Give a Sucker an Even Break (1941) she played the niece of W. C. FIELDS, who depresses her by announcing she will soon be returning to school.

"Don't you want to be smart?" he asks. "No," she returns, "I want to be like you."

SELECTED FILMS: The Under-Pup (1939), If I Had My Way (1940), What's Cookin', Get Hep to Love (1942), It Comes Up Love (1943), Follow the Boys, Ghost Catchers (1944), Easy to Look At (1945), Copacabana (1947), An Old-Fashioned Girl (1949), The Ladies' Man (1961), The Madcaps (1963). ∎

Jeans, Isabel (1891–1985), actress. Appeared on stage and in films in her native England before making her Hollywood film debut in the 1930s. She portrayed cultivated and dignified women in lead and supporting roles in light films on both sides of the Atlantic.

SELECTED FILMS: Tovarich (1937), Fools for Scandal, Garden of the Moon, Youth Takes a Fling, Hard to Get (1938), Good Girls Go to Paris, Man About Town (1939), Gigi (1958), A Breath of Scandal (1960). ∎

Jeeves. A fictional butler based on the writings of P. G. Wodehouse and portrayed in a projected comedy series by one of Hollywood's perennial servants, Arthur TREACHER. The first entry, Thank You, Jeeves (1936), starred David NIVEN as Bertie Wooster, Jeeves' master, while the second and final film in the series, Step Lively, Jeeves (1937), featured Treacher alone.

Jeffreys, Anne (1923–), actress. Appeared in opera, stock, and on Broadway before entering films in the early 1940s. She was cast as the female lead in numerous low-budget melodramas and light films during her 25-year screen career. She is married to actor Robert Sterling.

SELECTED FILMS: X Marks the Spot, I Married an Angel (1942), Chatterbox, Step Lively (1944), Zombies on Broadway (1945), Genius at Work (1946), Boys'

Night Out (1962), Panic in the City (1968). ∎

Allen Jenkins (center) and Ed Brophy (right)

Jenkins, Allen (1900–1974), actor. Worked on Broadway stage before making his film debut in 1931. A prolific character actor who appeared in over 150 features and the son of performers, he usually portrayed petty hoods, cabbies, chauffeurs, and other assorted Runyonesque figures in light films as well as crime dramas.

In *A Date With the Falcon* (1941) he played the title character's assistant. As they are leaving a police station after wrapping up a complex murder, Jenkins, addressing the cops, declares: "You're on your own now. What a break for crime!"

SELECTED FILMS: The Girl Habit (1931), Blessed Event, Three on a Match (1932), Hard to Handle, 42nd Street (1933), Jimmy the Gent (1934), Three Men on a Horse (1936), Ever Since Eve (1937), A Slight Case of Murder, Fools for Scandal (1938), Brother Orchid, Tin Pan Alley (1940), Ball of Fire, They All Kissed the Bride (1942), Wonder Man (1945), The Senator Was Indiscreet (1947), Behave Yourself (1951), Pillow Talk (1959), Doctor, You've Got to Be Kidding (1967), The Front Page (1974). ∎

Jenkins, Jackie "Butch" (1937–), child actor. Popular, freckle-faced player who appeared in many light films during the 1940s. His most memorable performance, perhaps, was that of Ulysses in MGM's version of William Saroyan's novel, *The Human Comedy* (1943).

SELECTED FILMS: An American Romance (1944), Abbott and Costello in Hollywood, Our Vines Have Tender Grapes (1945), Little Mr. Jim (1946), My Brother Talks to Horses (1947), Big City, Summer Holiday, The Bride Goes Wild (1948). ∎

Jenks, Frank (1902–1962), actor. Worked in vaudeville before entering Hollywood films in the early 1930s. A talented and prolific character actor, he appeared in dozens of light features and dramas over a period of three decades, often portraying small-time crooks, comic-relief characters, and sidekicks to the leads.

SELECTED FILMS: College Humor (1933), Follow the Fleet (1936), Goodbye Broadway, Youth Takes a Fling (1938), The Under-Pup (1939), His Girl Friday, Three Cheers for the Irish (1940), Thousands Cheer, His Butler's Sister (1943), Two Girls and a Sailor, Follow the Boys (1944), Zombies on Broadway (1945), Family Honeymoon (1948), The Petty Girl, To Please a Lady (1950), Artists and Models (1956), The Amazing Colossal Man (1957). ∎

Jergens, Adele (1917–), actress. Worked on stage as a chorus girl and as a model before making her film debut in the 1940s. An attractive blonde, she appeared in approximately 50 features, many of them light comedies. She usually portrayed cynical, wise-cracking chorines or gangsters' molls in lead or supporting roles.

SELECTED FILMS: A Thousand and One Nights, She Wouldn't Say Yes (1945), The Corpse Came C.O.D., Down to Earth (1947), The Fuller Brush Man (1948), Slightly French (1949), Show Boat, Abbott and Costello Meet the Invisible Man (1951), Aaron Slick From Punkin Crick, Somebody Loves Me (1952), The Lonesome Trail (1958). ∎

Jeske, George (1891–1951), director. Worked chiefly during the 1920s as a director of silent comedy shorts. He turned out many films for Hal ROACH'S studios, especially those starring Snub POLLARD and Stan LAUREL in his comedies before he teamed up with Oliver HARDY. Jeske directed one film during the sound era, *Flaming Signal* (1933), in collaboration with C. E. Roberts.

SELECTED FILMS (with Laurel): White Wings (1922), *Noon Whistle, Under Two Jags, Pick and Shovel, Collars and Cuffs, Oranges and Lemons* (1923).

SELECTED FILMS (with Pollard): The Walkout, Join the Circus, Fully Insured, It's a Boy (1923), *The Smithy, Postage Due, Wide Open Spaces, Short Kilts, The Big Idea* (1924), *The Old Warhorse* (1926). ∎

Jessel, George (1898–1981), actor, singer, producer. Worked in vaudeville, on Broadway, in films, on radio, and in television. He was in the original stage production of *The Jazz Singer* that Warner Bros. purchased as a vehicle for Al JOLSON in 1927. He has also written several books. He appeared on stage as a child performer and entertainer before making his film debut in silent comedies. A sentimental and humorous raconteur, he made relatively few films, devoting much of his professional time to nightclubs and other media. Later in his career, he became a producer for 20th Century-Fox studios. He was awarded the Jean Hersholt Humanitarian Award. His third autobiography, *The World I Live In*, was published in 1975.

SELECTED FILMS: Widow at the Races (1911), *The Other Man's Wife* (1919), *Private Izzy Murphy* (1926), *Sailor Izzy Murphy, Ginsberg the Great* (1927), *George Washington Cohen* (1928), *Lucky Boy, Love, Live and Laugh* (1929), *Happy Days* (1930), *Stage Door Canteen* (1943), *Four Jills in a Jeep* (1944), *The Busy Body* (1967), *The Phynx* (1970). ∎

Jewell, Isabel (1909–1972), actress. Appeared on Broadway before moving to Hollywood in the early 1930s. A platinum blonde, she had minor roles in dramas and comedies through the Depression years. She later played hard-hearted broads who have been around. Her film career never fulfilled the promise that her early stage success seemed to suggest.

SELECTED FILMS: Blessed Event (1932), *Bombshell, Design for Living, Advice to the Lovelorn* (1933), *She Had to Choose, Here Comes the Groom, Let's Be Ritzy* (1934), *Small Town Girl, Big Brown Eyes, Go West Young Man* (1936), *Swing It, Sailor* (1937), *Love on Toast* (1938), *Scatterbrain* (1940), *The Merry Monaghans* (1944), *Steppin' in Society* (1945), *Unfaithfully Yours* (1948), *Bernardine* (1957). ∎

Jewison, Norman (1926–), director. Worked as a television actor, writer, and director in his native Canada and in the United States before becoming a film director. He has made light comedies as well as musicals and dramas, often popular with both the critics and the public. He produced musical specials for CBS.

SELECTED FILMS: Forty Pounds of Trouble, The Thrill of It All (1963), *Send Me No Flowers* (1964), *The Art of Love, The Cincinnati Kid* (1965), *The Russians Are Coming, the Russians Are Coming* (1966), *Gaily Gaily* (1969), *Fiddler on the Roof* (1971), *. . . And Justice for All* (1979). ∎

"Jiggs and Maggie." Characters based on the comic strip, "Bringing Up Father," created in 1913 by artist George McManus (1884–1954). The strip has been the subject of various screen interpretations. Jiggs, who has recently come into money, and his socially aspiring wife, Maggie, made their film debut in 1916 in cartoon form, drawn by animator Frank Moser for International Film Service. Following the Great War, the couple reappeared in a series of two-reel comedies by Pathe studios. A well-known comedian, Johnny Ray, starred as Jiggs in such titles as "Jiggs and the Social Lion." MGM in 1928 produced an overly sentimental feature-length version of the strip, starring J. Farrell MacDONALD as Jiggs and Marie DRESSLER as Maggie.

In the 1940s the popular characters were once again resurrected, this time by Monogram studios in a low-budget series starring Joe YULE, Mickey ROONEY'S father, as Jiggs and Renie RIANO as Maggie. Their daughter Nora was played by June Harrison. Although the two chief performers physically resembled their comic strip counterparts and did a workmanlike job in their portrayals, the series suffered from low production budgets. Joe Yule's death in 1950 brought the series to an end.

McManus' famous couple appeared also in a successful stage play in 1921 called *Bringing Up Father at the Seashore* and as a weekly radio show in 1941 starring Neil O'Malley and Agnes Moorehead.

SELECTED FILMS: *Bringing Up Father* (1946), *Jiggs and Maggie in Court, Jiggs and Maggie in Society* (1948), *Jiggs and Maggie in Jackpot Jitters* (1949), *Jiggs and Maggie Out West* (1950). ∎

"Joe McDoakes" comedies. A series of one-reelers produced by Warner Brothers from the late 1940s through the 1950s. Each entry was usually titled "So You Want . . . " or "So You're Going . . ." and dealt with some domestic or contemporary situation such as buying a used car, going to a convention, etc. George O'HANLON starred in the series, Phyllis COATES appeared often as his wife, and Richard L. Bare directed. Other veteran comic character players showed up from time to time, including Fred KELSEY, Chester CLUTE, Rodney BELL, and Phil VAN ZANDT. The last entry, "So Your Wife Wants to Work," was released in 1956.

SELECTED FILMS: *So You Want to Be in Politics* (1948), *So You're Having In-Law Trouble* (1949), *So You Want to Be a Cowboy, So You Want to Buy a Used Car, So You Want to Be a Bachelor, So You Want to Be a Plumber* (1951), *So You Want to Get It Wholesale, So You're Going to a Convention, So You Want to Wear the Pants* (1952), *So You Want to Be a Television Star* (1953), *So You're Having Neighbor Trouble* (1954), *So Your Wife Wants to Work* (1956). ∎

Johnson, Arte, actor. Has appeared in television and occasionally in films since the 1950s. An accomplished comedian usually bespectacled, he has played light characters.

In *Love at First Bite* he played the man-servant of Dracula, portrayed by George Hamilton. Johnson suggests to his boss: "If you're hungry, master, we can ring for the night maid."

SELECTED FILMS: *Miracle in the Rain* (1956), *The Subterraneans* (1960), *The Third Day* (1965), *The President's Analyst* (1967), *Love at First Bite* (1979). ∎

Johnson, Chic. See Olsen and Johnson.

Johnson, Nunnally (1897–1977), screenwriter, director, producer. Worked as a journalist and short-story writer before moving to Hollywood in the early 1930s to become one of its most prolific screenwriters. He adapted major works for the screen and wrote original dramas and comedies. Later in his career he ventured into directing. It was as a screenwriter that he made his greatest contributions to an impressive list of comedies and superior dramas, several of which were historical films. He was especially adept at witty and romantic dialogue.

In *Holy Matrimony* unpretentious Gracie Fields, rooted deeply in the middle class, studies the esoteric menu of an exclusive French restaurant. "What is that?" she asks a waiter, pointing to an obscure selection on the menu. "That, madam," he answers scornfully, "is the name of the selection the orchestra is playing." "Well," the spirited Fields parries, "there's not much nourishment in that."

SELECTED FILMS: Kid Millions (1934), Thanks a Million (1935), Banjo on My Knee (1936), Wife, Husband and Friend, Rose of Washington Square (1939), The Pied Piper, Life Begins at 8:30 (1942), Holy Matrimony (1943), Casanova Brown (1944), Mr. Peabody and the Mermaid (1948), Everybody Does It (1949), We're Not Married (1952), How to Marry a Millionaire (1953), How to Be Very Very Popular (1955), The Man Who Understood Women (1959), Mr. Hobbs Takes a Vacation (1962), Take Her, She's Mine (1963), The World of Henry Orient (1964), The Dirty Dozen (1967). ■

Johnson, Rita (1912–1965), actress. Appeared on radio, in stock, and, finally, on Broadway in the mid-1930s before entering films in 1937. She played the female lead in numerous second features for various studios, including MGM. Her films ranged from dramas to light comedies.

SELECTED FILMS: London by Night (1937), Rich Man, Poor Girl (1938), Broadway Serenade, They All Came Out (1939), Congo Maisie, Forty Little Mothers (1940), Here Comes Mr. Jordan (1941), The Major and the Minor (1942), The Affairs of Susan, The Naughty Nineties (1945), Pardon My Past (1946), The Perfect Marriage (1947), An Innocent Affair (1948), Family Honeymoon (1949), Susan Slept Here (1954), All Mine to Give (1957). ■

Johnson, Tor (1903–1971), actor. A former Swedish wrestler who began his Hollywood screen career in the early 1930s. Giant-sized and bald-headed, he brought his imposing and terrifying appearance to dramas, horror films, and comedies. He intimidated several leading comics of the period, including Eddie CANTOR, W. C. FIELDS, Bob HOPE, and ABBOTT AND COSTELLO.

SELECTED FILMS: Kid Millions (1934), Man on the Flying Trapeze (1935), Swing Out the Blues (1943), Lost in a Harem, Ghost Catchers (1944), Road to Rio (1947), State of the Union (1948), Abbott and Costello in the Foreign Legion (1950), Dear Brat, The Lemon Drop Kid (1951), The Beast of Yucca Flats (1961). ■

Johnson, Van (1916–), actor. Appeared on Broadway in choruses before entering films in the early 1940s. His good looks, charm, and innocence rapidly moved him into the front ranks of stardom. Specializing in romantic comedies while under contract to MGM where he played leading men with a sense of boyishness, he occasionally tried dramatic roles for that studio and others. He reached the peak of his popularity during the war years but continued as a major actor into the 1950s.

In A Guy Named Joe (1943) he played a World War II air force pilot who returns from a mission to the arms of Irene DUNNE. "You're the prettiest girl I ever saw!" he exclaims. "You're prettier than a P-38!"

SELECTED FILMS: Too Many Girls (1942), Two Girls and a Sailor (1944), Between Two Women, Thrill of a Romance, Weekend at the Waldorf (1945), Easy to Wed (1946), State of the Union, The Bride Goes Wild (1948), Mother Is a Freshman (1949), Grounds for Marriage, Too Young to Kiss (1951), When in Rome (1952), Confidentially Connie, Remains to Be Seen, Easy to Love (1953), Divorce, American Style (1967), Yours, Mine and Ours, Where Angels Go . . . Trouble Follows (1968). ■

Joker Comedies. A film production unit or branch of Universal studios devoted strictly to comedy shorts during the early silent period. The company was formed in 1913 by Carl Laemmle, who headed Universal, to compete with KEYSTONE, which was highly successful in the field of comedy. Various comics would often star in their own series under this brand. For instance, Max ASHER, a popular comedian of the period, appeared in a string of comedy shorts in which he portrayed a Dutch character. Later, he co-starred with Harry McCOY in another profitable series, "Mike and Jake." Other performers who appeared in the company's films included Louise FAZENDA and Bobby VERNON. The first film released under the Joker banner was "The Cheese Special." The contents and style of the shorts were far from tasteful, more often bordering on the gross. The films were made quickly and economically, and frequently betrayed their lack of production values. The company closed its doors in 1918.

Jolson, Al (1886–1950), singer, entertainer. Performed as a black-faced singer, chiefly on stage, starred in his own successful radio show for years, and appeared in a handful of films. Born Asa Yoelson in St. Petersburg, Russia, he came to the United States as a child and for a time sang in a synagogue where his father was the cantor. He appeared in the first sound feature, *The Jazz Singer* in 1927. Although intended basically as a silent feature with a few Jolson songs inserted periodically, the film became the first "talkie" when the star, sitting at a piano in his parents' home, jokes with his mother. He continued to star in other Warner Brothers musicals, but he never gained the popularity in films that he had attained on stage or as a recording artist.

His declining career sprang back to life when Columbia studios released *The Jolson Story* in 1946. He provided the dubbed songs which actor Larry Parks mimicked on screen. Chiefly a singer, he demonstrated his extensive comic talents in many of his films. *Jolson*, a biography by Michael Freedland, was published in 1973.

SELECTED FILMS: *The Singing Fool (1928), Sonny Boy, Say It With Songs (1929), Mammy, Big Boy (1930), Halle-*
lujah, I'm a Bum (1933), Wonder Bar (1934), Go Into Your Dance (1935), The Singing Kid (1936), Alexander's Ragtime Band (1938), Rose of Washington Square (1939), Swanee River (1940), Rhapsody in Blue (1945), Jolson Sings Again (1949). ■

Jones, Allan (1905–), singer, actor. Sang in concerts and opera companies across the United States and on Broadway after his voice training in Europe. Seen and heard in New York, he was quickly signed for Hollywood films, his first major hit being *The Firefly* (1937), starring Jeanette MacDONALD, in which he sang his big solo, "The Donkey Serenade." A handsome tenor, he went on to play leads in a succession of entertaining light films, including two MARX BROTHERS vehicles in which he provided the romantic interest. He worked with other popular comedians of the period, including ABBOTT AND COSTELLO and OLSEN AND JOHNSON. He is the father of singer Jack Jones.

SELECTED FILMS: *Reckless, A Night at the Opera (1935), Rose Marie, Show Boat (1936), A Day at the Races (1937), Honeymoon in Bali (1939), The Boys From Syracuse, One Night in the Tropics (1940), Moonlight in Havana, True to the Army (1942), Crazy House (1943), The Singing Sheriff (1944), The Senorita From the West, Honeymoon Ahead (1945), A Swingin' Summer (1965).* ■

Jones, Carolyn (1929–1983), actress. Worked in radio and on stage before entering films in the early 1950s. A versatile but offbeat actress, she appeared in dramas and light films, often as the female lead. She was nominated for an Academy Award as Best Supporting Actress for her role in *The Bachelor Party* (1957). She also did much television work.

SELECTED FILMS: *The Turning Point, Road to Bali (1952), Off Limits (1953), The Seven Year Itch, The Tender Trap (1955), The Opposite Sex (1956), A Hole* in the Head (1959), Sail a Crooked Ship (1961), A Ticklish Affair (1963), Eaten Alive (1977). ∎

Jones, F. Richard (1890–), director. Directed numerous silent comedy shorts for Mack SENNETT and, later, made feature-length films. He worked with some of the leading comics of the period, including, among others, Billy BEVAN, Chester CONKLIN, Ben TURPIN, Polly MORAN, and Charles MURRAY. He directed one of Harry LANGDON'S better films, "The First Hundred Years" (1924).

SELECTED FILMS: A Game Old Knight, Her Painted Hero, The Great Vacuum Robbery (1915), A Love Riot (1916), It Pays to Exercise, Saucy Madeline, The Battle Royal, Sleuths (1918), The Foolish Age, Love's False Faces, The Speakeasy, Yankee Doodle in Berlin (1919), Gee Whiz!, Love, Honor and Behave (1920), The Ghost in the Garret (1921), The Country Flapper (1922), The Shriek of Araby, The Extra Girl (1923), Little Robinson Corkscrew (1924), Someone to Love (1928), Bulldog Drummond (1929). ∎

Jones, Henry (1912–), actor. Appeared on stage and in television before entering films in the early 1950s, usually as a character player in dramas and light films. A versatile performer, he portrayed both light and portentous characters with equal conviction.

SELECTED FILMS: The Lady Says No (1951), The Girl Can't Help It (1956), Will Success Spoil Rock Hunter? (1957), Never Too Late (1965), Stay Away, Joe (1968), Support Your Local Sheriff, Butch Cassidy and the Sundance Kid (1969), Support Your Local Gunfighter (1971), Pete 'n' Tillie (1972), The Outfit (1974), 9 to 5 (1980). ∎

Jones, James Earl (1931–), actor. Appeared on Broadway in the late 1950s before entering films in 1964. He attracted much attention for his Shakespearean roles on the New York stage

but has generally not been given suitable screen material to match his talent. A strong actor with a commanding voice, he has appeared in dramas and light films.

SELECTED FILMS: Dr. Strangelove (1964), Claudine (1974), The Bingo Long Traveling All-Stars and Motor Kings, Swashbuckler (1976), The Last Remake of Beau Geste, A Piece of the Action (1977), Soul Man (1986). ∎

Jones, Marcia Mae (1924–), actress. Began her film career in 1926 while only a two-year-old child. During the Depression years she portrayed children's roles, and in the 1940s she played young innocents. She appeared in dramas as well as light films, giving generally competent performances, but she never caught the public's attention as did other young performers of her period.

SELECTED FILMS: Mannequin (1926), The Champ (1931), Heidi (1937), Mad About Music (1938), The Little Princess, First Love (1939), Tomboy (1940), Let's Go Collegiate (1941), The Youngest Profession, Top Man (1943), Snafu (1944), The Way We Were (1973). ∎

Jones, Shirley (1934–), actress, singer. A popular star of musical comedies, she appeared in dramas as well as light films. She frequently played virtuous and pleasant leads. She won an Oscar for Best Supporting Actress as the vindictive prostitute in Elmer Gantry (1960).

SELECTED FILMS: Oklahoma! (1955), April Love (1957), Bobbikins (1960), The Music Man (1962), A Ticklish Affair (1963), Bedtime Story (1964), Fluffy, The Secret of My Success (1965), The Happy Ending (1969), The Cheyenne Social Club (1970), Tank (1984). ∎

Jones, Spike (1911–1964), songwriter, bandleader. Worked as a teenager in the 1920s on radio, as a band drummer in the 1930s, and as a bandleader for NBC radio shows. Jones and his zany band came to national prominence for their comic renditions of popular songs, which they recorded for Bluebird. Spike Jones and His City Slickers earned their own radio show, appeared in a series of routine comedy films in the 1940s, and were featured on several television shows during the 1950s. Jones usually wore outrageous suits as he led his talented band. Some of the group's more popular numbers included "Der Fuehrer's Face," "Cocktails for Two," and "Chloe." J.R. Young's biography, *Spike Jones and His City Slickers* (1984), includes numerous photographs, a discography, and a filmography.

SELECTED FILMS: *Thank Your Lucky Stars* (1943), *Meet the People* (1944), *Bring on the Girls* (1945), *Variety Girl* (1947), *Fireman, Save My Child* (1954). ■

"Jones Family, The." A popular series of domestic comedies, based on the fiction of Katharine Kavanaugh, about the shenanigans of a small town family. Jed PROUTY played Pa Jones and Spring BYINGTON co-starred as Ma. Character actress Florence ROBERTS portrayed Granny. The initial feature, *Every Saturday Night* (1936), launched seventeen entries, virtually all of which were low-budget films.

SELECTED FILMS: *Educating Father, Back to Nature* (1936), *Off to the Races, Big Business, Hot Water, Borrowing Trouble* (1937), *Love on a Budget, A Trip to Paris, Safety in Numbers* (1938), *The Jones Family in Hollywood, Everybody's Baby, Quick Millions, Too Busy to Work* (1939). ■

Jordan, Bobby (1923–1965), actor. Appeared on Broadway stage in the original production of Sidney Kingsley's *Dead End* before settling in Hollywood where he recreated his role as a member of the juvenile gang. Except for occasional excursions into melodramas, he appeared chiefly in the low-comedy, low-budget series, "THE BOWERY BOYS." Perhaps his best comedy role was in *A Slight Case of Murder* (1938), a hilarious farce in which he played a tough, streetwise orphan who is treated to a vacation at the country estate of ex-mobster Edward G. ROBINSON.

SELECTED FILMS: *Dead End* (1937), *That Gang of Mine* (1940), *Spooks Run Wild, Pride of the Bowery* (1941), *Let's Get Tough* (1942), *Clancy Street Boys* (1943), *Bowery Champs* (1944), *Bowery Bombshell* (1946), *Hard Boiled Mahoney* (1947), *This Man Is Armed* (1956). ■

Jordan, Dorothy (1908–), actress. Worked in Broadway musicals before entering early sound films. She appeared in dramas and light films in both lead and secondary roles but stardom eluded her.

SELECTED FILMS: *Words and Music, The Taming of the Shrew, Devil-May-Care* (1929), *In Gay Madrid, Love in the Rough, Min and Bill* (1930), *A Tailor-Made Man, Shipmates, The Beloved Bachelor* (1931), *Down to Earth, That's My Boy* (1932), *Strictly Personal* (1933), *The Wings of Eagles* (1957). ■

Jordan, Glenn (1936–), director. Had long experience in television, including an Emmy Award, and in the theater before entering films in 1981. His screen work has chiefly concerned light themes. He has directed some of the major film personalities, including Richard DREYFUSS and Jack LEMMON.

SELECTED FILMS: *Only When I Laugh* (1981), *The Buddy System* (1984), *Mass Appeal* (1985). ■

Jordan, Jim. See Fibber McGee and Molly.

Jordan, Will comedian, actor. Has worked extensively as a comic and impressionist in television and appeared in the Broadway production of *Bye Bye Birdie*. He gained recognition for his uncanny look-alike impersonation of the late Ed Sullivan. His screen appearances, usually as a comic actor, have been relatively few, while his television spots have numbered in the hundreds.

SELECTED FILMS: The Buddy Holly Story, I Wanna Hold Your Hand (1978), Broadway Danny Rose (1984). ∎

Joslin, Rusty. Fictional comic sidekick in "The Three Mesquiteers" western series. He was portrayed by veteran silent screen actor Raymond HATTON, who replaced screen comedian and ventriloquist Max TERHUNE in the role.

Joslyn, Allyn (1901–1981), actor. Worked on Broadway in light comedies before making his film debut in the mid-1930s. Tall and slim with a thin mustache, he appeared in numerous light films and dramas portraying a variety of characters, including stuffy suitors, upper-class snobs, and other pompous types.

SELECTED FILMS: They Won't Forget (1937), Hollywood Hotel, Sweethearts (1938), Cafe Society (1939), The Great McGinty, No Time for Comedy (1940), This Thing Called Love, Bedtime Story (1941), My Sister Eileen (1942), The Horn Blows at Midnight, Junior Miss (1945), It Shouldn't Happen to a Dog (1946), The Shocking Miss Pilgrim (1947), If You Knew Susie (1948), As Young As You Feel (1951), I Love Melvin (1953), The Brothers O'Toole (1973). ∎

Jourdan, Louis (1919–), actor. Made his film debut in 1939 in his native France but returned to the stage. He returned to films on a steady basis in 1943. After World War II he was invited to Hollywood where he continued to appear in romantic comedies, the genre which first brought him recognition. He starred in several dramas and light films, working on both sides of the Atlantic. Urbane and handsome, he was popular with American audiences. But these assets eventually hindered him by limiting his roles and he fell out of favor. He occasionally appeared in minor films during the 1970s and 1980s.

In Letter From an Unknown Woman (1948) he played a pianist who has been challenged to a duel but has no intention of keeping the appointment. "I don't mind so much being killed," he quips, "but you know how hard it is for me to get up in the morning."

SELECTED FILMS: The Paradine Case, No Minor Vices (1948), The Happy Time (1952), Decameron Nights (1953), Three Coins in the Fountain (1954), Julie (1956), Gigi (1958), The Best of Everything (1959), Can-Can (1960), Made in Paris (1966), A Flea in Her Ear (1968), Silver Bears (1977), Octopussy (1983). ∎

Joy, Leatrice (1896–1984), actress. Began her Hollywood film career as an extra in 1915. Three years later she was playing the female lead in comedies starring Billy WEST (the first of which was titled "The Slave") and Oliver HARDY. She later appeared in many of Cecil B. DeMILLE'S silent features. Whether portraying career women in or out of men's suits or spoiled society females in elegant gowns, she symbolized a free and independent spirit during the 1920s, a unique and popular heroine who charmed her audiences with her vivacity and talent.

SELECTED FILMS: The Folly of Revenge (1916), The Man Hunter, The Water Lily (1919), Just a Wife, Blind Youth, Smiling All the Way (1920), Bunty Pulls the Strings, Ladies Must Live, The Poverty of Riches (1921), Saturday Night, The Bachelor Daddy, Minnie (1922), You Can't Fool Your Wife (1923), Changing Husbands (1924), The Dressmaker From Paris (1925), Eve's Leaves, For Alimony Only (1926), Nobody's Widow, The Angel of Broadway (1927), Tropic Madness (1928), Strong Boy, A Most Immoral Lady (1929), The Love Trader (1930), Love Nest (1951). ∎

Joy, Nicholas (1884–1964), actor. Appeared on stage in London in 1910 and on Broadway in 1912. Tall and sophisticated, he appeared for years in stage productions, specializing in comic roles. With the advent of sound, he became a character player in dramas and light films, including several which starred some of the leading comics of the period.

SELECTED FILMS: Daisy Kenyon (1947), The Fuller Brush Man (1948), Song of Surrender, Abbott and Costello Meet the Killer (1949), Here Comes the Groom (1951), Desk Set (1957). ∎

Joyce, Brenda (1915–), actress. Blonde, athletic female lead of the 1940s who specialized in innocent types. She appeared in dramas and light films. She portrayed Jane in several entries of the "Tarzan" series. She abandoned her screen career in 1949.

SELECTED FILMS: The Rains Came (1939), Little Old New York, Public Deb No. 1 (1940), Marry the Boss's Daughter (1941), The Postman Didn't Ring, Whispering Ghosts (1942), Little Giant (1946), Shaggy (1948), Tarzan's Magic Fountain (1949). ∎

Judels, Charles (1882–1969), actor. Appeared in supporting roles in early sound comedies, especially in several of OLSEN AND JOHNSON'S features of the early 1930s. He also worked with WHEELER AND WOOLSEY in High Flyers, their last film.

SELECTED FILMS: The Life of the Party, Captain Thunder, Oh Sailor Behave! (1930), Fifty Million Frenchmen, Gold Dust Gertie (1931), High Pressure (1932), Enchanted April (1935), When's Your Birthday?, The Life of the Party, High Flyers (1937), The Villain Still Pursued Her (1940), Her Adventurous Night (1946). ∎

Judge, Arline (1912–1974), actress, dancer. Worked as a dancer on Broadway in the 1920s. While in George White's Scandals she proved to be an adept comedienne as well. She made her film debut in 1931 under the guidance of director Wesley RUGGLES, whom she married, and quickly achieved stardom. An attractive performer, she played leads in numerous light films and dramas during the 1930s and 1940s. She appeared with some of the leading stars of the period, including, among others, Spencer TRACY, Constance Cummings, Jack OAKIE, Fred MacMURRAY, and Marlene DIETRICH.

SELECTED FILMS: Bachelor Apartment (1931), Girl Crazy, Love Starved (1932), Looking for Trouble, Shoot the Works, Sensation Hunters (1934), Million Dollar Baby (1935), King of Burlesque, It Had to Happen, Star for a Night, Pigskin Parade (1936), One in a Million (1937), The Lady Is Willing, Wildcat (1942), Song of Texas (1943), Mad Wednesday (1947), Two Knights in Brooklyn (1949). ∎

K

Kahn, Madeline (1942–), actress. Trained as an opera singer and worked on stage and in nightclubs before appearing in films during the 1970s. Her comic talents brought her two Oscar nominations as Best Supporting Actress for her roles in *Paper Moon* (1973) and *Blazing Saddles* (1974).

In *High Anxiety* she receives a telephone call from Mel BROOKS. But before he can speak to her, an intruder enters his booth and attempts to strangle him with the phone wire. Meanwhile, Madeline overhears his gasps and other choking sounds. "Listen, mister, I don't go for this sort of thing," she says. "I know a lot of other girls are turned on to kinky phone calls, but I don't go in for this. . . ."

SELECTED FILMS: *What's Up, Doc?* (1972), *Young Frankenstein* (1974), *At Long Last Love, The Adventure of Sherlock Holmes' Smarter Brother* (1975), *Won Ton Ton, the Dog Who Saved Hollywood* (1976), *High Anxiety* (1977), *The Cheap Detective* (1978), *Simon* (1979), *Wholly Moses, First Family* (1980), *History of the World—Part I* (1981), *Slapstick of Another Kind* (1984). ■

Kalmar, Bert (1884–1947), screenwriter, songwriter. Appeared in vaudeville before coming to Hollywood during the early sound period to write screenplays and songs. He worked alone and in collaboration, usually with Harry RUBY, turning out comedy material for some of the major performers of the period, including, among others, the MARX BROTHERS and Eddie CANTOR.

SELECTED FILMS: *Check and Double Check* (1930), *Broad-Minded* (1931), *The Kid From Spain, Horse Feathers* (1932), *Duck Soup* (1933), *Hips, Hips, Hooray, Kentucky Kernels* (1934), *Bright Lights* (1935), *Walking on Air* (1936), *The Life of the Party* (1937). ■

Kane, "Babe." See Helen Kane.

Kane, Carol (1952–), actress. Worked on stage as a teenager and in minor roles in films before playing leads beginning in the mid-1970s. She received an Academy Award nomination for her role in *Hester Street* (1975). A small, lively performer, she has been featured in dramas and light films with some of the leading comics of the period, including, among others, Woody ALLEN and Gene WILDER. She has won several Emmys for her television appearances.

SELECTED FILMS: *Is This Trip Really Necessary?* (1970), *Desperate Characters* (1971), *The Last Detail* (1973), *Harry and Walter Go to New York* (1976), *Annie Hall, The World's Greatest Lover* (1977), *Norman Loves Rose* (1982), *Over the Brooklyn Bridge* (1984). ■

Kane, Eddie (–1969), actor. Worked as a character player for some of the leading producers of comedy films, including Mack SENNETT and Al CHRISTIE. He appeared in shorts and light features with several of the leading comics of the period, including, among others, Al JOLSON, LAUREL AND HARDY, Danny KAYE, and ABBOTT AND COSTELLO.

SELECTED FILMS: Lights of New York (1928), Why Bring That Up? (1929), The Cohens and the Kellys in Africa (1930), Stolen Jools, Goldie (1931), Once in a Lifetime, Love Is a Racket, The Slippery Pearls (1932), Autobuyography, Fixing a Stew, Wonder Bar (1934), Million Dollar Baby (1935), Pick a Star (1937), Swiss Miss (1938), Some Like It Hot (1939), Interior Decorator (1942), Up in Arms (1944), The Big Beef (1945), Mexican Hayride (1948), The Ten Commandments (1956). ■

Kane, Helen (1904–1966), singer, actress. Appeared as a singer in vaudeville and in Broadway revues in the mid-1920s with little fanfare until 1928. While singing "I Wanna Be Loved by You" in a show, she added her now famous expression, "Boop-boop-a-doo," and became an almost immediate star. She appeared in several light feature films and shorts. The comic strip and movie cartoon, "Betty Boop," were based on this unique singer-comedienne. Debbie REYNOLDS portrayed her in the film Three Little Words (1950), but when it came to the above tune, Kane sang it off screen. She appeared in several comedy shorts with W. C. FIELDS.

SELECTED FILMS: Nothing but the Truth, Sweetie, Pointed Heels (1929), Paramount on Parade, Dangerous Nan McGrew, Heads Up (1930), The Dentist, The Spot on the Rug (1932), The Pharmacist (1933), Counsel on the Fence (1934). ■

Kanin, Fay, screenwriter, playwright. Has written light comedies and dramas for the stage, screen, and television, alone or in collaboration. She has often collaborated with her husband, screenwriter Michael KANIN.

SELECTED FILMS: Sunday Punch (1942), My Pal Gus (1952), Rhapsody (1954), The Opposite Sex (1956), Teach-

er's Pet (1958), The Right Approach (1961), The Outrage (1964). ■

Kanin, Garson (1912–), director, screenwriter. Worked as a musician, vaudeville comic, and stage actor and director before going to Hollywood in the late 1930s. He directed a handful of light comedies until the beginning of World War II, at which time he turned out documentaries for the war effort. In 1946 he scored a hit with his play Born Yesterday, which was adapted into a successful film in 1950. Collaborating with his wife, Ruth GORDON, he wrote some of the most endearing film comedies for director George CUKOR, including Adam's Rib, The Marrying Kind, and Pat and Mike.

SELECTED FILMS (as director): A Man to Remember, Next Time I Marry (1938), The Great Man Votes, Bachelor Mother (1939), My Favorite Wife, They Knew What They Wanted (1940), Tom, Dick and Harry (1941), Where It's At, Some Kind of a Nut (1969).

SELECTED FILMS (as screenwriter): The More the Merrier (1943), Adam's Rib (1949), The Marrying Kind (1951), Pat and Mike (1952), It Should Happen to You (1954), The Rat Race (1960), Where It's At, Some Kind of a Nut (1969). ■

Kanin, Michael (1910–), screenwriter. Worked as an artist and musician before turning to screenwriting in the 1930s. Specializing in light comedies, he won an Oscar for Woman of the Year (1942), a film which he wrote in collaboration with Ring Lardner, Jr. He has written many of his screenplays in collaboration with his wife, Fay KANIN. He is the brother of director-screenwriter Garson KANIN.

SELECTED FILMS: They Made Her a Spy (1939), Anne of the Windy Poplars (1940), Sunday Punch (1942), Centennial Summer (1946), Honeymoon (1947), My Pal Gus (1952), Rhapsody (1954), The Opposite Sex (1956), Teacher's Pet

(1958), The Right Approach (1961), How to Commit Marriage (1969). ∎

Kannon, Jackie (1919–1974), comedian, actor. Popular stand-up comic in nightclubs and television. He appeared sporadically in films.

SELECTED FILMS: Diary of a Bachelor (1964). ∎

Kanter, Hal (1918–), screenwriter. Wrote light screenplays for some of the most popular film stars, especially those of the 1950s, including, among others, Bob HOPE, Eddie BRACKEN, Doris DAY, and James GARNER. Although his output consisted chiefly of humorous material, he occasionally wrote dramas as well.

SELECTED FILMS: Two Tickets to Broadway (1951), Road to Bali, Off Limits (1953), Money From Home, Casanova's Big Night, About Mrs. Leslie (1954), Artists and Models (1956), Once Upon a Horse (1958), Bachelor in Paradise, Pocketful of Miracles, Blue Hawaii (1961), Move Over, Darling (1963), Dear Brigitte (1965). ∎

Kaplan, Gabe (1946–), comedian, actor. Worked as a stand-up comic in small clubs, appeared as a guest in the early 1970s on different television programs, and recorded a comedy album. Many of his early routines, including those on the album, dealt with the rowdy humor of teenagers in a school setting. It was this motif that stirred television executives a few years later to star him in his own comedy show. By the late 1970s he began appearing in films. Although several of his films did well at the box office, he was not as successful on the big screen as he had been in television. He has continued to perform in nightclubs and television.

SELECTED FILMS: Fast Break (1979), Nobody's Perfekt, Tulips (1981). ∎

Kaplan, Marvin (1924–), actor. Appeared in light films and dramas, chiefly in the 1950s and 1960s. An owlish-looking, bespectacled character player, he is best known for his comedy roles.

SELECTED FILMS: The Reformer and the Redhead (1950), Angels in the Outfield (1951), Behave Yourself (1951), Wake Me When It's Over (1960), It's a Mad, Mad, Mad, Mad World (1963), The Great Race (1965). ∎

Karlin, Bo-Peep (–1969), actress. Entered films in the late 1920s. She appeared as a character player in occasional light films. She also appeared on a variety of television shows. She was married to actor Gaston GLASS.

SELECTED FILMS: Happy Days (1929), Just Imagine (1930), Bye Bye Birdie (1963). ∎

Karno, Fred (1866–1941), famous British music hall director known for his pantomime troupe. He toured the United States in 1910 with his show, *A Night in an English Music Hall*, based on his British production, *Mumming Birds*. His second tour, in 1913, introduced two new comic talents to American audiences. Charlie CHAPLIN and Stan LAUREL had their American debuts as a result of this tour. Other silent film comedians and performers who got their start with Karno's troupe included Eric CAMPBELL, Jimmy Aubrey, and Billy Reeves. Some film historians credit Karno with the earliest introduction of slapstick into American film comedy, rather than placing this distinction with Mack SENNETT, whose creativity made it into a popular art form.

Karns, Roscoe (1893–1970), actor. Began his acting career on stage before appearing in Hollywood films during the silent era. A prolific character actor and comedian, especially during the 1930s, he often portrayed sourish, crabby characters in scores of features, ranging from 1920 to the 1960s. He appeared with some of the leading stars of the period, including, among others, Clark GABLE, Claudette COLBERT, John BARRYMORE, John Garfield, Bette DAVIS, Katharine HEPBURN, and Spencer TRACY.

SELECTED FILMS: The Life of the Party (1920), Too Much Married (1921), Conquering the Woman (1922), Dollar Down (1925), Ritzy (1927), Moran of the Marines (1928), Laughing Sinners (1931), If I Had a Million (1932), Alice in Wonderland (1933), It Happened One Night, Twentieth Century (1934), Alibi Ike (1935), Cain and Mabel (1936), Clarence (1937), Thanks for the Memory (1938), Everything's on Ice (1939), His Girl Friday (1940), Woman of the Year (1942), It's a Wonderful Life (1946), Onionhead (1958), Man's Favorite Sport? (1964). ■

Kascier, Johnny, actor. Worked chiefly in comedy shorts during the 1930s, 1940s, and 1950s as a supporting player. He appeared in many of the THREE STOOGES' films.

SELECTED FILMS: Three Little Pigskins (1934), Horses' Collars, Pardon My Scotch (1935), Half-Shot Shooters (1936), Nutty but Nice, From Nurse to Worse, Boobs in Arms (1940), I'll Never Heil Again, In the Sweet Pie and Pie (1941), Back From the Front (1943), Crash Goes the Hash (1944), Uncivil Warbirds (1946), Brideless Groom, Sing a Song of Six Pants (1947), Blunder Boys (1955), Pies and Guys (1955).■

Kasznar, Kurt (1913–1979), actor. On stage in his native Austria and in the United States in the 1930s before entering films in the 1950s. A stout, moon-faced character actor, he appeared in dramas and light films, often in lively and whimsical roles.

SELECTED FILMS: The Light Touch (1951), Anything Can Happen, Lovely to Look At, The Happy Time (1952), Lili, Kiss Me Kate (1953), My Sister Eileen

(1955), Anything Goes (1956), For the First Time (1959), The Thrill of It All (1963), Casino Royale, The Perils of Pauline, The Ambushers (1967), Suddenly, Love (1968). ■

Kaufman, George S. (1889–1961), playwright. Wrote numerous comedies, often in collaboration with Moss Hart, many of which were adapted by other writers for the screen. Because of his aversion to Hollywood, he repeatedly rejected offers from various studios to become a full-time screenwriter. He did, however, make sporadic attempts at applying his talents to film comedy. He wrote the story for Roman Scandals (1933), an Eddie CANTOR vehicle, and did the screenplay for A Night at the Opera (1935), which starred the MARX BROTHERS. Still unhappy with the way writers were treated, he left Hollywood. His next and last association with films was as the director of The Senator Was Indiscreet (1947), but he found the experience unrewarding.

SELECTED FILMS (from his plays): Dulcy (1923), Merton of the Movies (1924), The Cocoanuts (1929), Animal Crackers, The Royal Family of Broadway (1930), Once in a Lifetime (1932), Dinner at Eight (1933), You Can't Take It With You (1938), The Man Who Came to Dinner (1941), George Washington Slept Here (1942), The Solid Gold Cadillac (1956). ■

Kaye, Danny (1913–1987), actor, comedian. Entertained in vaudeville, in nightclubs, and on Broadway before making his feature film debut in 1944 in Up in Arms. Born Daniel David Kaminsky, he had appeared in several two-reel comedies in the late 1930s but did not gain any recognition until he starred in feature-length vehicles. A talented singer-comic-entertainer, he starred in a series of popular musical comedies during the 1940s and 1950s. His humorous style, which ranged from satire to pathos to facial distortions, was

Danny Kaye and Mai Zetterling

highlighted by his "scat" routines, creative word-play musical numbers. When the style of film comedy changed in the 1950s, he began to fall out of favor with movie audiences. He received a special Oscar in 1954 for his singular talents in particular and his contributions to film art in general.

His screen characterization was similar to that of silent-screen star Charley CHASE. Kaye was usually a well-attired buoyant figure who never gave up. But his screen character was more inept than the one created by Chase. On the other hand, he was more versatile; he could sing and dance. And he had the advantages of better production values from his studios: color, larger casts, and lavish sets. His comedy style was quite different from that of his contemporaries. He didn't rattle off one-liners in the style of Bob HOPE and he didn't generally engage in slapstick as did Lou COSTELLO or Jerry LEWIS. Instead, he employed double-talk, engaged in comic musical numbers, and depended for laughs on characterization and situation. His comic spirit was more akin to that of another contemporary, Red SKELTON—that of a warm, sympathetic soul often overwhelmed by circumstances not of his making. He appeared in fewer feature films than did his fellow comedians—only 17 in his 25-year screen career. But the best of these demonstrate his tremendous vitality, his unique comic gifts, and his general talents as an all-around entertainer. M. Freedland's biography, *The Secret*

Life of Danny Kaye, adequately covers the entertainer's life.

In *Me and the Colonel* (1959) he played a chauffeur for Nazi officer Curt Jurgens, who romantically delivers to a bevy of European women his charmer line: "In the cathedral of my heart a candle will always burn for you." Kaye quips: "That must be the best lit cathedral in Europe."

SELECTED FILMS: *Wonder Man* (1945), *The Kid From Brooklyn* (1946), *The Secret Life of Walter Mitty* (1947), *A Song Is Born* (1948), *The Inspector General* (1949), *On the Riviera* (1951), *Hans Christian Andersen* (1952), *Knock on Wood, White Christmas* (1954), *The Court Jester* (1956), *Merry Andrew* (1958), *The Five Pennies* (1959), *On the Double* (1961), *The Man From the Diners' Club* (1963), *The Madwoman of Chaillot* (1969). ∎

Kaye, Stubby (1918–1987), actor. Worked in vaudeville and on Broadway before appearing in a handful of films beginning in 1953. A portly supporting actor, he clowned his way through light comedies and musicals after his successful portrayal of Nicely-Nicely in the Broadway production and the 1955 film version of *Guys and Dolls*.

SELECTED FILMS: *Taxi* (1953), *Li'l Abner* (1959), *40 Pounds of Trouble* (1963), *Sex and the Single Girl* (1964), *Cat Ballou* (1965), *The Way West* (1967), *Sweet Charity* (1969), *The Cockeyed Cowboys of Calico County* (1970), *The Dirtiest Girl I Ever Met* (1973), *Six Pack Annie* (1975). ∎

Keane, Robert Emmett (1883–1981), actor. Came to films in the early 1930s as a character player. Sporting a small mustache, he appeared in numerous dramas and light films for various studios. He worked with some of the leading comics of the period, including LAUREL AND HARDY and OLSEN AND JOHNSON.

SELECTED FILMS: *Laugh and Get Rich, Men Call It Love* (1931), *The Big*

Noise (1936), The Chaser (1938), Fifth
Avenue Girl, Hawaiian Nights, Pack
Up Your Troubles (1939), We're in the
Army Now (1940), The Devil and Miss
Jones (1941), A-Haunting We Will Go
(1942), Jitterbugs, Crazy House (1943),
Casanova Brown (1944), Everybody
Does It (1949), When My Baby Smiles at
Me (1950). ∎

Keating, Larry (1896–1963), actor. Appeared in several dramas and light films
as a character player. He often portrayed
administrators and haughty characters.
He switched to television in the 1950s.

SELECTED FILMS: Song of the Sarong
(1945), Mr. 880 (1950), The Mating Season, Too Young to Kiss (1951), Monkey
Business, About Face, Something for the
Birds (1952), She's Back on Broadway
(1953), Daddy Long Legs (1955), The
Buster Keaton Story (1957), Who Was
That Lady? (1960), Boys' Night Out
(1962), The Incredible Mr. Limpet
(1964). ∎

Keaton, Buster (1895–1966), actor, director. Appeared in his parents' acrobatic comedy act at age 3. Known as
"The Human Mop," he was tossed about
by his father as part of the skit. When the
act split up in 1917, Buster entered silent
films. He quickly made friends with
"Fatty" ARBUCKLE and became in-
trigued with the technical aspects of
filmmaking. His years of knockabout
comedy experience made the transition
to film comedy easy for him. In "The
Butcher Boy" (1917), his first film, his
efficient style contrasted sharply with
that of the other comics.

By 1920 producer Joseph Schenck provided him with his own company to turn
out two-reel comedies. In a remarkable
series of shorts he experimented with
and refined his ideas, which were to
coalesce into his major theme in his
feature-length films: a solitary soul struggling against a world of uncontrollable
forces, finally succeeding through resourcefulness, boldness, and utter surprise. In "The Boat" (1921) he calmly

meets with a chain of calamities as he
tries to sail his home-made vessel while
his family looks on in disbelief. The
family pleasure boat sinks with an air of
nobility on its maiden launching. Keaton
encounters similar results in his other
films of this period.

He left the world of short films in
1923. In The Three Ages (1923), a
parody of Griffith's Intolerance, he sets
his story in three different periods of
history, with some highly inventive
humor. That same year he turned out
Our Hospitality, a creative full-length
comedy replete with elaborate settings
as well as the physical dangers of a river
and impending disasters with a canoe.
Keaton travels to the Shenandoah Valley
estate that was willed to him. He finds
himself in the midst of a murderous
blood feud. He is treated with honor and
respect when he is indoors, reflecting
the region's southern hospitality. But
whenever he steps out, he becomes a
proper target for the local residents. In
Sherlock, Jr. (1924) he employs a dream
sequence and trick camera work. In The
Navigator (1924), which some consider
his greatest film if not one of the
funniest ever made, Keaton portrays a
dissolute millionaire who is set adrift on
an abandoned ocean liner with only his
helpless girlfriend to aid him. Go West
(1925), Battling Butler (1925), and Seven
Chances (1926) were not up to his high
standards although they were quite
entertaining. The General (1927), another acknowledged masterpiece of
comedy, is based on a true incident that
occurred during the Civil War when
Union soldiers, dressed as civilians,
stole the General, a locomotive. The film
has been noted for the superb timing
of its sight gags, pace, and pictorial
beauty.

College (1927) has Keaton as a student
involved in some funny athletic stunts to
impress his girlfriend. More interested in
books than in brawn, he fails at every
sport he tries out for. Some highlights are
the decathlon when he throws himself
instead of the hammer and the climax

when he overcomes every obstacle as he races to his true love's rescue.

In *Steamboat Bill, Jr.* (1928) he portrays the son of a rough and tough steamboat captain and has to prove his manhood to his disappointed father. Keaton shows up dressed like a dandy. He sports a flashy tie and a beret and carries a ukulele. His father looks on with disgust. The hilarious cyclone sequence is the highlight of the film and includes the famous bit in which a two-ton wall comes down on Keaton, who is saved miraculously by an open window in the structure.

His next two major works, *The Cameraman* (1928) and *Spite Marriage* (1929), were made for MGM, which supervised the entire production. Previously, Keaton worked independently, his works only being released by the studio. But he gave up control of his films and his artistic freedom, to work under the strictures of the studio. The results proved that he still could be inventive and funny, but in the years that followed, MGM relegated him to supporting roles in a string of inferior sound features. For the next three decades he continued to appear in shorts and features both in the United States and in Europe, but the "Great Stoneface" never regained his former reputation. He, along with Charlie CHAPLIN, Harold LLOYD, and Harry LANGDON, was one of the four true geniuses of silent comedy. His autobiography, *My Wonderful World of Slapstick*, was published in 1960.

SELECTED FILMS: *A Reckless Romeo, The Rough House* (1917), *Out West, The Bellboy* (1918), *The Hayseed* (1919), *One Week, The Saphead* (1920), *The Paleface* (1921), *Cops, My Wife's Relations, The Frozen North* (1922), *The Balloonatic* (1923), *What! No Beer?* (1933), *Streamlined Swing* (1938), *Hollywood Cavalcade* (1939), *Li'l Abner* (1940), *That's the Spirit* (1945), *In the Good Old Summertime* (1949), *Sunset Boulevard* (1950), *Limelight* (1952), *Around the World in 80 Days* (1956), *The Adventures of Huckleberry Finn* (1960), *It's a Mad,* *Mad, Mad, Mad World* (1963), *A Funny Thing Happened on the Way to the Forum* (1966). ■

Keaton, Diane (1946–), actress. Worked in summer stock and on Broadway before making her film debut in 1970. An attractive, sometimes unconventional actress, she has frequently appeared in Woody ALLEN'S films. She has had leading roles in dramas as well as light films. She played Al Pacino's girlfriend in *The Godfather* (1972), giving a straight, almost bland, performance. On the other hand, in *Sleeper* she is delightful as Woody Allen's dumb girl who helps him escape from the law. She also gives a funny imitation of the character, Stanley, from *A Streetcar Named Desire*, while Allen impersonates Blanche Dubois. She won an Academy Award for Best Actress for her portrayal of the title role in *Annie Hall* (1977).

SELECTED FILMS: *Lovers and Other Strangers* (1970), *Play It Again, Sam* (1972), *Sleeper* (1973), *Love and Death* (1975), *I Will, I Will . . . for Now, Harry and Walter Go to New York* (1976), *Manhattan* (1979), *Crimes of the Heart* (1986), *Radio Days* (1987). ■

Keaton, Michael (1951–), actor. Worked as a stand-up comic and in television before entering films in the early 1980s. He is a talented performer with a good screen presence. A product of late-night television comedy, he has developed a zany but amicable style. Aside from his successful screen debut in *Night Shift*, his other films, however, have not thus far thrust him into the realm of stardom.

SELECTED FILMS: *Night Shift* (1982), *Mr. Mom* (1983), *Johnny Dangerously* (1984), *Touch and Go* (1987). ■

Keighley, William (1889–1984), director. Began his show business career as a stage actor and director before immigrating to Hollywood during the early years of the sound era. In a short time he began directing films for Warner Brothers, specializing in crime and adventure films. A versatile and talented craftsman, he also made a series of first-rate light comedies that ranged from sentimental (*Four Mothers*) to SCREWBALL (*The Bride Came C.O.D.*) to sophisticated (*The Man Who Came to Dinner*). Keighley was not a stylist. Instead he applied the Warner Brothers' hard-boiled approach to his comedies, giving them a surface toughness, a spark of cynicism, and a fast pace. Several of his films were adaptations of Broadway plays.

SELECTED FILMS: *The Match King, Ladies They Talk About* (1933), *Easy to Love, Kansas City Princess, Big Hearted Herbert* (1934), *Stars Over Broadway, Mary Jane's Pa* (1935), *The Green Pastures* (1936), *Varsity Show* (1937), *Brother Rat* (1938), *Yes, My Darling Daughter* (1939), *Torrid Zone, No Time for Comedy* (1940), *Four Mothers, The Bride Came C.O.D.* (1941), *The Man Who Came to Dinner, George Washington Slept Here* (1942), *Honeymoon* (1947), *Close to My Heart* (1951). ∎

Kellaway, Cecil (1893–1973), actor. Worked in the theater and films in Australia before making his Hollywood film debut in the mid-1930s. Slightly on the chubby side and possessing a devilish gleam in his eye, Kellaway, born in Capetown, South Africa, often portrayed mischievous but likable characters. His warm and jolly presence graced more than 100 films over a career that spanned four decades. He was nominated for an Oscar as Best Supporting Actor for his role in *Luck of the Irish* (1948) and again for *Guess Who's Coming to Dinner* (1967).

In *I Married a Witch* (1942) he portrayed the playful warlock-father of Veronica Lake, an early American witch who puts a curse on all the male descendants of Fredric MARCH. When he asks his daughter what the curse entails, she explains that they will marry the wrong women. "Every man who marries, marries the wrong woman," he quips.

SELECTED FILMS: *It Isn't Done* (1937), *Brother Orchid* (1940), *Appointment for Love* (1941), *My Heart Belongs to Daddy, Are Husbands Necessary?* (1942), *The Good Fellows* (1943), *Practically Yours* (1944), *Kitty* (1945), *The Cockeyed Miracle* (1946), *The Luck of the Irish* (1948), *Harvey* (1950), *The Shaggy Dog* (1959), *Fitzwilly, Guess Who's Coming to Dinner* (1967), *Getting Straight* (1970). ∎

Kellerman, Sally (1938–), actress. Worked in television and had minor roles in films before scoring a major success as the prudish Major "Hot Lips" Houlihan in *M*A*S*H* (1970). A tall, velvet-voiced performer, she has appeared in dramatic as well as light films; the latter best demonstrate her singular comedic talents.

In *M*A*S*H* she played an uptight army officer in Korea who finds more than solace in a religious army doctor. "God meant us to have each other," he declares. Opening her bathrobe, she intones, "His will be done!"

SELECTED FILMS: *Reform School Girl* (1959), *The April Fools* (1969), *Last of the Red Hot Lovers* (1972), *Rafferty and the Gold Dust Twins* (1975), *The Big Bus* (1976), *Welcome to L.A.* (1977), *She'll Be Sweet* (1978), *A Little Romance* (1979), *Foxes, Serial, Loving Couples* (1980), *Moving Violations* (1984), *That's Life!* (1986). ∎

Kelley, Barry (1908–), actor. Worked on stage during the Depression years before settling in Hollywood in 1947. A thick-set and imposing character player, he often portrayed judges, executives, and law officers in dramas and light films although he could be found on either side of the law. One of his specialties was the corrupt head of a syndicate.

SELECTED FILMS: *Boomerang!* (1947), *Mr. Belvedere Goes to College, Red, Hot and Blue, Ma and Pa Kettle* (1949), *Love That Brute, Wabash Avenue*

(1950), Francis Goes to the Races (1951), Back at the Front (1952), Remains to Be Seen (1953), The Police Dog Story (1960), The Clown and the Kid (1961), The Love Bug (1968). ∎

Kelly, Dorothy "Dot" (1894–1966), actress. Entered early silent comedy shorts in the 1910s. She appeared in numerous films as the female lead or supporting player.

SELECTED FILMS: All for a Girl, Suing Susan (1912), Playing the Pipers, Bunny's Honeymoon, Disciplining Daisy, The Flirt, The Tables Turned (1913), In the Old Attic, Regan's Daughter, A Double Error (1914), Four Grains of Rice, The Man, the Mission and the Maid, A Madcap Adventure (1915), The Money Mill (1917). ∎

Kelly, Emmett (1898–1979), circus clown, actor. Began his show business career as a circus trapeze artist in the 1920s, then switched to a clown in the early 1930s. In 1942 he joined the famous Ringling Brothers Barnum and Bailey Circus. His act consisted of portraying the character "Weary Willie," an unhappy soul who is forever searching for a little dignity. He was considered by many to be the greatest clown. He appeared on Broadway and in several films. His autobiography, *Clown*, was published in 1954.

SELECTED FILMS: The Fat Man (1950), The Greatest Show on Earth (1952), Wind Across the Everglades (1958). ∎

Kelly, Gene (1912–), dancer, actor, director. Worked at odd jobs including dance instructor before appearing in the chorus of a Broadway show in 1938. Following several assignments as a choreographer he entered films in 1942 as Judy GARLAND'S lead in *For Me and My Gal*. His individual dancing style and congenial personality catapulted him to stardom in a string of superior musical

comedies, especially those directed by Vincente MINNELLI. His dancing was more informal and casual than that of Fred ASTAIRE, the reigning Hollywood dancer of the period. Kelly later began directing films in which he occasionally starred. His acting attempts in straight dramas were less successful. As a choreographer and entertainer in light films he has demonstrated an abundance of wit and intelligence and received a special Oscar in 1951 for his many talents and achievements in film.

SELECTED FILMS (as actor): For Me and My Gal (1942), Du Barry Was a Lady, Thousands Cheer (1943), Cover Girl, Christmas Holiday (1944), Anchors Aweigh (1945), The Pirate, Words and Music (1948), Take Me Out to the Ball Game, On the Town (1949), Summer Stock (1950), An American in Paris (1951), Singin' in the Rain (1952), Les Girls (1957), What a Way to Go! (1964), 40 Carats (1973), Viva Knievel! (1977).

SELECTED FILMS (as director only): Tunnel of Love (1958), Gigot (1962), A Guide for the Married Man (1967), Hello Dolly! (1969), The Cheyenne Social Club (1970). ∎

Kelly, James T., actor. Worked chiefly in early silent films, especially as a supporting player in comedy shorts starring Charlie CHAPLIN. He portrayed various characters, including drunks, gypsies, and, when the occasion required it, females. He appeared in 14 Chaplin films, ten of which were made by Mutual studios.

SELECTED FILMS: A Night in the Show (1915), Police!, Triple Trouble, The Floorwalker, The Fireman, The Vagabond, The Pawnshop, Behind the Screen, The Rink (1916), The Cure, The Immigrant (1917), A Dog's Life (1918). ∎

Kelly, John (1901–1947), actor. Entered films in the 1920s. He appeared as a supporting player in dramas and light films during a screen career that spanned three decades. He worked with some of the leading comics of the period, including, among others, W. C. FIELDS, Eddie CANTOR, and Bob HOPE.

SELECTED FILMS: After Midnight (1927), Subway Express (1931), Hold 'Em Jail (1932), Three-Cornered Moon (1933), Little Miss Marker, Many Happy Returns, The Old Fashioned Way, Kid Millions (1934), Poor Little Rich Girl (1936), Bringing Up Baby (1938), Road to Singapore (1940), My Gal Sal (1942), Blonde From Brooklyn (1945), Sofia (1948). ■

Kelly, Kitty (1902–1968), actress. Began her screen career in the 1920s in silent films as second female lead, but her career faltered and she was relegated to supporting player. She continued in that role through the 1930s and 1940s. She appeared in dramas and light films.

SELECTED FILMS: A Kiss in the Dark (1925), The Head Man (1930), Behind Office Doors, Bachelor Apartment, White Shoulders (1931), Girl Crazy (1932), Too Much Harmony (1933), All of Me, The Lemon Drop Kid (1934), The Farmer Takes a Wife (1935), Blossoms on Broadway (1937), The Lady Is Willing (1942), So Proudly We Hail (1943). ■

Kelly, Lew (1879–1944), actor, comedian. Appeared as a stand-up comic in vaudeville, in burlesque, and on Broadway before settling in Hollywood in 1929, the beginning of the sound era. He became famous in the 1920s for his stage comedy, especially playing a sympathetic character who innocently falls under the influence of drugs. In films he was relegated to character roles, supporting other comics, including Joe E. BROWN.

SELECTED FILMS: Strange People (1933), Six of a Kind (1934), Man From Music Mountain, Flirting With Fate (1938), Taxi, Mister (1942), Lady of Burlesque (1943). ■

Kelly, Patsy (1910–1981), actress, comedienne. Appeared on Broadway as a chorus girl and then featured comedienne before making her Hollywood debut in 1933. One of the great comics of the screen, she began her film career co-starring in a series of comedy shorts with Thelma TODD and, later, with Lyda ROBERTI. Eventually she would portray the leading lady's confidante or servant, wisecracking her way through numerous light comedies and musicals, chiefly during the 1930s and 1940s. By 1943 her screen career came to a sudden halt, allegedly due in part to a drinking problem. However, she continued to appear on radio, in television, and on stage.

SELECTED FILMS: Going Hollywood (1933), The Girl From Missouri (1934), Every Night at Eight, Thanks a Million (1935), Sing, Baby, Sing, Kelly the Second, Pigskin Parade (1936), Wake Up and Live, Pick a Star, Ever Since Eve (1937), Merrily We Live, The Cowboy and the Lady (1938), The Gorilla (1939), Topper Returns, Playmates (1941), Ladies' Day (1943), The Naked Kiss (1964), The Ghost in the Invisible Bikini (1966), Freaky Friday (1977), North Avenue Irregulars (1979). ■

Kelly, Walter C. (1873–1939), actor, comedian. Worked in vaudeville for years as a dialect comic. But his greatest recognition came in the 1920s with his creation of the Virginia Judge. He appeared in a handful of light films during the 1930s.

SELECTED FILMS: McFadden's Flats, The Virginia Judge (1935), Laughing Irish Eyes (1936). ■

Kelsey, Fred (1884–1961), actor. Appeared as a supporting actor in numerous silent and sound comedy shorts and features, especially those starring OLSEN AND JOHNSON and the THREE STOOGES during the 1930s and 1940s. He also worked with comediennes Thelma TODD and Patsy KELLY in some of their comedy shorts during the early 1930s.

SELECTED FILMS: *Paths of Paradise (1925), That's My Baby (1926), The Gorilla (1927), Naughty Baby (1929), She Got What She Wanted (1930), If I Had a Million (1932), I'll Be Suing You (1934), Horse Collars, Hot Money (1935), At Sea Ashore (1936), All Over Town (1937), The Invisible Ghost (1941), Busy Buddies (1944), If a Body Meets a Body, Micro Phonies (1945), Monkey Businessmen, Bringing Up Father (1946), Hans Christian Andersen (1952), Racing Blood (1964).* ∎

Kelton, Pert (1907–1968), actress. Worked in vaudeville and on Broadway before making her film debut in 1929. A charming and comical lead and supporting actress, she often portrayed loose women in dramas as well as light films. She worked for producer Hal ROACH in the mid-1930s and made a few films with comedienne Patsy KELLY. In fact, Roach tried to team them in a series of comedy shorts, but the chemistry was not there. After one film, "Pan Handlers," he replaced Miss Kelton with Lyda ROBERTI.

SELECTED FILMS: *Sally (1929), Hot Curves (1930), Bed of Roses, The Bowery (1933), The Meanest Gal in Town, Bachelor Bait (1934), Hooray for Love, Annie Oakley (1935), Kelly the Second, Cain and Mabel, Pan Handlers (1936), The Hit Parade (1937), The Music Man (1962), Love and Kisses (1965), The Comic (1969).* ∎

Kennedy, Edgar (1890–1948), actor. Worked in vaudeville and on stage before entering films in 1914. Joining Mack SENNETT'S KEYSTONE studios, he became a supporting player in numerous silent comedy shorts starring some of the leading comics of the period, including Charlie CHAPLIN (ten films with Keystone studios), Charles MURRAY, Louise FAZENDA, and Slim SUMMERVILLE.

By the 1920s he appeared as a comic supporting character in features as well as shorts. A bald second banana with an expressive face, he was best known for his trademark, the slow burn, which he developed while working with LAUREL AND HARDY and while under contract to Hal ROACH in the late 1920s. He also appeared in several "OUR GANG" comedies and, by 1931, starred in his own comedy series entitled "The AVERAGE MAN." Whether portraying a lemonade vendor, an irate motorist, or a frustrated policeman, he brought laughter to his audiences during a career that spanned four decades.

SELECTED FILMS: *The Star Boarder, The Knockout, Tillie's Punctured Romance (1914), The Great Vacuum Robbery (1915), His Hereafter, His Bitter Pill (1916), Oriental Love (1917), Skirts (1921), The Battling Fool (1924), Going Crooked (1926), Finger Prints (1927), Two Tars, A Pair of Tights (1928), Night Owls (1930), Bad Company (1931), Tillie and Gus, Duck Soup (1933), Twentieth Century, Kid Millions (1934), The Bride Comes Home (1935), Three Men on a Horse (1936), Kennedy's Castle (1938), Air Raid Wardens, Crazy House (1943), It Happened Tomorrow (1944), Anchors Aweigh (1945), Mad Wednesday, Unfaithfully Yours (1948), My Dream Is Yours (1949).* ∎

Edgar Kennedy

Kennedy, Madge (1892–), actress. Worked on Broadway stage before making her film debut in silent films in 1917. She starred in both dramas and light films. She abandoned her film career during the 1930s and 1940s but returned to the screen in the 1950s as a character actress.

SELECTED FILMS: Baby Mine, Nearly Married (1917), The Fair Pretender, Friendly Husband, A Perfect Lady (1918), Day Dreams, Leave It to Susan (1919), The Blooming Angel, Dollars and Sense (1920), Oh, Mary Be Careful, The Girl With a Jazz Heart (1921), Oh, Baby! (1926), The Marrying Kind (1952), Three Bad Sisters, The Catered Affair (1956), Let's Make Love (1960), The Baby Maker (1970), The Day of the Locust (1975). ∎

Kennedy, Merna (1908–1944), actress. Appeared on stage during the 1920s, where she was observed by Charlie CHAPLIN. He quickly signed her for his 1928 film The Circus. She continued to star in dramas and light comedies during the 1930s. She abandoned her film career in 1934 to marry director-choreographer Busby Berkeley.

SELECTED FILMS: The Circus (1928), Broadway, Barnum Was Right, Skinner Steps Out (1929), Embarrassing Moments, The Midnight Special (1930), Stepping Out (1931), Lady With a Past, The Gay Buckaroo, The All American, Red-Haired Alibi (1932), Laughter in Hell, Don't Bet on Love (1933), Wonder Bar, I Like It That Way (1934). ∎

Kennedy, Tom (1884–1965), actor. Began his career in films as supporting player in Mack SENNETT'S KEYSTONE films following a stint as an amateur boxer. A versatile character actor, he appeared in more than 100 silent and sound films during a career which spanned nearly a half-century, portraying everything from villains to incompetent policemen. He worked with some of the leading comics of the period, including W. C. FIELDS, LAUREL AND HARDY, the MARX BROTHERS, Mae

WEST, and Bob HOPE. He appeared in a few "TORCHY" comedies of the 1930s. He never attained the recognition that his brother, Edgar KENNEDY, received.

SELECTED FILMS: The Village Blacksmith (1916), Skirts (1921), The Flirt (1922), The Yankee Senor, We're in the Navy Now (1926), The Cop (1928), The Cohens and Kellys in Atlantic City, The Shannons of Broadway (1929), See America Thirst (1930), Monkey Business (1931), Pack Up Your Troubles (1932), She Done Him Wrong (1933), Poppy (1936), Torchy Blane in Panama (1938), Ladies' Day (1943), The Princess and the Pirate (1945), The Paleface (1948), It's a Mad, Mad, Mad, Mad World (1963), The Bounty Killer (1965). ∎

Kent, Barbara (1906–), actress. Worked in silent and sound films as a lead, often co-starring with some of the major personalities of the period, including Reginald DENNY and Harold LLOYD.

SELECTED FILMS: Prowlers of the Night (1926), The Drop Kick, The Small Bachelor (1927), That's My Daddy, Modern Mothers (1928), Welcome Danger (1929), Dumbbells in Ermine, Feet First (1930), Emma (1932), Marriage on Approval (1933), Old Man Rhythm, Swell Head (1935), Under Age (1941). ∎

Kenton, Erle C. (1896–1980), director. Began his film career in 1914 working for Mack SENNETT as an actor and factotum. Within five years he was directing comedy shorts. By 1920 he was turning out full-length films. His career spanned four decades, during which time he directed scores of horror films, romances, action films, and light comedies. He directed a handful of ABBOTT AND COSTELLO comedies. The quality of his work, like that of many other directors with his background and productivity, was uneven. Under contract to studios with tight budgets, his films often reflected these limited production values.

SELECTED FILMS: Down on the Farm, Love, Honor and Behave (1920), Tea With a Kick (1923), Red Hot Tires (1925), The Sap (1926), Wedding Bills (1927), Bare Knees, Golf Widows, Nothing to Wear (1928), Mexicali Rose (1929), Lover Come Back, Leftover Ladies (1931), Big Executive (1933), You're Telling Me (1934), Best Man Wins, Party Wire (1935), She Asked for It (1937), The Lady Objects, Little Tough Guys in Society (1938), Everything's on Ice (1939), Remedy for Riches (1940), Petticoat Politics (1941), Frisco Lil, Pardon My Sarong (1942), Always a Bridesmaid (1943), She Gets Her Man (1945), Little Miss Big (1946), Bob and Sally (1948), One Too Many (1950). ∎

Kerrigan, J. M. (1887–1964), actor. Appeared on stage and in films in his native Ireland before migrating to Hollywood in 1917. A short, stocky figure with a round face, he became a popular character player both on the screen and on Broadway, often portraying Irishmen. He played in both dramas and light films.

One of his more memorable roles was that of Terry, Victor McLAGLEN'S fairweather friend in The Informer (1935). Kerrigan joins McLaglen at a brothel, sponging drinks from him. Suddenly McLaglen is taken away to be tried as an informer and Terry is stuck with the bill. "I have a queer feeling there's going to be a strange face in heaven in the morning," he says to himself.

SELECTED FILMS: Little Old New York (1923), Lucky in Love (1929), Lightnin' (1930), Merely Mary Ann (1931), Colleen, Laughing Irish Eyes (1936), The Great Man Votes, The Flying Irishman (1939), Three Cheers for the Irish, No Time for Comedy (1940), Abie's Irish Rose (1946), The Luck of the Irish (1948), The Fastest Gun Alive (1956). ∎

Kerry, Norman (1889–1956), actor. Began his long screen career in early silent films. Born Arnold Kaiser, he often played male leads in light films and

dramas, reaching the height of his popularity in the 1920s. He later appeared in character roles, continuing in films into the early 1940s.

SELECTED FILMS: Manhattan Madness (1916), The Wild Goose, Get-Rich-Quick Wallingford (1921), Three Live Ghosts, Brothers Under the Skin, Find the Woman (1922), Merry-Go-Round (1923), Between Friends (1924), Fifth Avenue Models (1925), Mlle. Modiste, The Love Thief (1926), The Irresistible Lover (1927), Man, Woman and Wife (1928), Trial Marriage (1929), Bachelor Apartment (1931), Tanks a Million (1941). ∎

Kershner, Irvin (1923–), director. Made film and television documentaries before turning his talents to directing feature films in the late 1950s for Roger Corman. His earlier films dealt with serious human and social themes, which he handled with great sensitivity. His later films generally have dealt with lighter material, ranging from satirical comedy to fantasy.

SELECTED FILMS: Stakeout on Dope Street (1958), A Fine Madness (1966), The Flim-Flam Man (1967), Up the Sandbox (1972), S*P*Y*S (1974), The Empire Strikes Back (1980), Never Say Never Again (1983). ∎

Keyes, Evelyn (1919–), actress. Appeared as a dancer in nightclubs before entering films in the late 1930s. She rose from supporting roles to leads in a variety of genres, including dramas, musicals, and comedies. She played Al JOLSON'S wife in the musical biography of the Jazz singer, The Jolson Story (1946). Another important role was as the female lead in Here Comes Mr. Jordan. Her autobiography, Scarlett O'Hara's Younger Sister, was published in 1977.

SELECTED FILMS: The Buccaneer, Artists and Models Abroad (1938), Slightly Honorable (1939), The Lady in Question (1940), Here Comes Mr. Jordan, *Ladies in Retirement* (1941), *Dangerous Blondes* (1943), *A Thousand and One Nights* (1945), *The Thrill of Brazil* (1946), *The Mating of Millie* (1948), *Mr. Soft Touch, Mrs. Mike* (1949), *The Seven Year Itch* (1955), *Around the World in 80 Days* (1956). ∎

Keystone Film Company. An American production company founded by Charles Baumann and Adam Kessel in 1912. Mack SENNETT, who had been directing at Biograph, became its first director, with stars Mabel NORMAND, Fred MACE, and Ford STERLING featured in the early films. The purpose was to supply comedies for the parent company, MUTUAL. With Sennett at the helm, the studio soon established itself in the forefront of film comedy, its trademarks consisting of the chase, a frantic pace, absurd plots, more absurd-looking comics, and, above all, plenty of slapstick.

Keystone was able to entice most of the major comedians to enter its "Fun Factory," including "Fatty" ARBUCKLE, his wife, Minta DURFEE, Chester CONKLIN, Charlie CHASE, Hank MANN, Charles MURRAY, Slim SUMMERVILLE, Edgar KENNEDY, Mack SWAIN, Syd CHAPLIN, Eddie CLINE, and, for one year and more than 35 films, Charlie CHAPLIN. In 1915 Keystone split from Mutual, joined Triangle studios, and added to its already formidable list of talents, including Wallace BEERY, Harold LLOYD for a brief period, and Frank CAPRA. Sennett, who had created the successful KEYSTONE KOPS in 1913, gave his audiences another first, the "BATHING BEAUTIES," who perhaps contributed more to visual appeal than to action or comedy. By 1917 he sold his share of the company and with a few loyal players and craftsmen, started independent production. Although many of his comics stayed on with Keystone, the films released by the company without the King of Comedy's supervision suffered in quality and the studio soon collapsed.

In its five years of producing films under the supervision of Sennett, the company turned out about five hundred comedies, films that reflected the best in comedy and the comic talent of numerous men and women. These works, however, owed a large part of their existence to one man—Sennett—whose madcap genius and boundless energy inspired an air of creativity at Keystone that was rarely found at other studios.

Keystone Kops

Keystone Kops. A group of bungling, incompetent police officers created by Mack SENNETT around 1913 for KEYSTONE studios. Although many film performers through the years have traced their humble beginnings to the now legendary Keystone ensemble, Sennett himself confirmed that there were but seven original Kops: Charles AVERY, Bobby DUNN, George JESKY, Edgar KENNEDY, Hank MANN, Mack Riley, and Slim SUMMERVILLE.

Some historians list "The Bangville Police," a one-reel comedy made in 1913, as the first in the series. This short film has a handful of grossly unfit members of the local constabulary coming to the rescue of a damsel who suspects burglars lurking near her rural home. By 1914 the Kops were firmly entrenched in their madcap misadventures. They were led by their chief, Ford STERLING, sporting a rectangular beard. Their uniforms and their anarchy had been established. In one of their shorts, "In the Clutches of a Gang" (1914), a typical entry, their patrol wagon swerves out of control and crashes while the officers' bodies are strewn across the California landscape.

Sennett would give new comic hopefuls a chance to show their stamina as well as craft by giving them parts in these films. If they were able to survive the chases, acrobatics, and frantic pace of these films, they could probably fit into his stock company. Although the comedy displayed by these stalwart performers was frowned upon by many critics—they described it derogatorily as "knockabout comedy"—the film series remained extremely popular with the public. The players, composed mainly of experienced acrobats and tumblers, deserve a permanent place in the annals of film comedy. By late 1914, only one year from their official inception, the Keystone Kops slowly began to lose their luster. Although they no longer played a prominent part in Sennett's comedies, the slapstick troupe continued its frantic chases and slapstick comedy until 1920.

including lustful Broadway angels; small town lawyers, judges, and doctors; and beleaguered fathers and husbands. Although he added a light, comical touch to his many characters, he could be deceptively humorous with more than a streak of meanness or corruptibility. But his jocund manner predominated, as displayed in *Joy of Living* (1938), when he confides to Alice Brady: "I've been drinking over 40 years, and I haven't acquired the habit yet." He starred in the "SCATTERGOOD BAINES" series during the 1940s. He appeared in more than 100 dramas, musicals, and light comedies.

SELECTED FILMS: *Stolen Heaven, Blonde Crazy (1931), Taxi!, Weekend Marriage (1932), 42nd Street, Gold Diggers of 1933, Lady for a Day, Footlight Parade (1933), Dames, Big-Hearted Herbert, Harold Teen, Babbitt (1934), Mary Jane's Pa, Don't Bet on Blondes (1935), The Big Noise, Captain January (1936), Don't Tell the Wife (1937), Babes in Arms (1939), Henry Goes to Arizona (1940), Scattergood Baines (1941), Whistling in Dixie (1942), Girl Crazy (1943), The Horn Blows at Midnight (1945), Lone Star Moonlight (1946), Three Godfathers (1948).* ∎

Guy Kibbee and Shirley Temple

Kibbee, Guy (1882–1956), actor. Began his acting career on stage before entering films in 1931. A bald, rotund, smiling character actor during the 1930s and 1940s, he portrayed a variety of roles,

Kibbee, Roland (1914–), screenwriter. Wrote for some of radio's top comics, including Fred ALLEN, Fanny BRICE, and Groucho MARX before turning his talents to films in the 1940s. He penned both melodramatic and light screenplays, which he wrote alone or in collaboration. He later switched to writing for television, receiving an Emmy Award for one of his shows.

SELECTED FILMS: *A Night in Casablanca, Angel on My Shoulder (1946), Painting the Clouds With Sunshine, Pardon My French (1951), The Desert Song, Three Sailors and a Girl (1953), Top Secret Affair (1957), The Devil's Disciple (1959), The Midnight Man (1974).* ∎

Kid, The (1921), FN. *Dir.* Charlie Chaplin; *Sc.* Charlie Chaplin; with Charlie Chaplin, Edna Purviance, Jackie Coogan, Carl Miller, Tom Wilson, Henry Bergman, Albert Austin.

This was Chaplin's first actual feature-length film. Charlie, playing his customary tramp role, meanders into an alley and finds an abandoned baby whom he assumes was thrown out of a window along with the garbage that had just struck him. He takes the infant to his squalid quarters and raises it as his own, giving it love and care. A few years later, the boy, played winningly by Jackie COOGAN, becomes the tramp's constant companion and apprentice at Charlie's new vocation, window repairman. The tot appears first, smashes a window by hurling an object at it, then Charlie strolls by to replace it. However, complications set in when the child and the mother are reunited. But the film, amid the tears, ends happily for all. A sequence in a flophouse with Charlie trying to hide the child is one of the many hilarious moments in this delightful film. It is one of Chaplin's most critically acclaimed and most successful works. Some dissenters found the story too sentimental.

"Kid Auto Races at Venice" (1914), KEY. *Dir.* Henry Lehrman; *Sc.* not listed; with Charlie Chaplin, Henry Lehrman.

Charlie Chaplin's second film shows him in his tramp outfit for the first time. He borrowed the oversized trousers from "Fatty" ARBUCKLE and the shoes from Ford STERLING. Mack SWAIN provided the mustache. The cane was his own inspiration; it gave an air of ironic dignity to the character of the tramp. The crude film is no more than an improvisation at an actual event, a children's boxcar race at which Chaplin does some mugging, interferes with cameramen who are trying to film the event, and makes himself a general nuisance to the spectators. Early film companies often sent their camera crews and several actors to special events or catastrophes such as fires in the hope of attaining interesting footage for future use or as background for on-the-scene improvisations.

Kilbride, Percy (1888–1964), actor. Worked in stock before entering films in 1933. He attained a degree of fame with his portrayal of Pa Kettle, a waspish farmer in *The Egg and I* (1947), a part that led to the popular "MA AND PA KETTLE" series co-starring Marjorie MAIN. He often played a knavish hayseed always ready to outsmart some city slicker.

SELECTED FILMS: *White Woman* (1933), *Soak the Rich* (1936), *George Washington Slept Here* (1942), *Crazy House* (1943), *Knickerbocker Holiday* (1944), *State Fair, She Wouldn't Say Yes* (1945), *The Well-Groomed Bride* (1946), *Welcome Stranger* (1947), *You Gotta Stay Happy* (1948), *Ma and Pa Kettle* (1949), *Riding High* (1950), *Ma and Pa Kettle Back on the Farm* (1951), *Ma and Pa Kettle at Waikiki* (1955). ■

Kilian, Victor (1891–1979), actor. Worked in vaudeville, in stock, and on Broadway before entering films in the late 1920s. A physically imposing character actor, he often played villains. He appeared in more than 100 light films and dramas.

SELECTED FILMS: *Gentlemen of the Press* (1929), *The Wiser Sex* (1932), *The Girl Friend, Riffraff* (1935), *Banjo on My Knee* (1936), *Tovarich* (1937), *Gold Diggers in Paris* (1938), *Paris Honeymoon* (1939), *My Favorite Wife, Barnyard Follies, Gold Rush Maisie, Tugboat Annie Sails Again* (1940), *Little Giant* (1946), *The Tall Target* (1951). ■

King, Alan (1927–), comedian, actor, producer. Worked as a musician, then as a comic at resort hotels, nightclubs, and in television, gaining recognition by the 1950s as a major stand-up comedian. A stocky figure attired in a vested suit and brandishing a cigar, he has appeared on screen occasionally, usually in light films. On stage King, who was born Alan Kinberg, specializes in monologues that poke fun at suburban living and explore the frustrations of the average middle-class family.

SELECTED FILMS: Hit the Deck (1955), Miracle in the Rain, The Girl He Left Behind (1956), Operation Snafu (1965), Bye Bye Braverman (1968), Just Tell Me What You Want (1979), Cattle Annie and Little Britches (1980), Author! Author! (1982), Lovesick (1983). ∎

King, Henry (1888–1982), director. Appeared in vaudeville, in burlesque, on stage, and in films by 1912. Within three years he was alternating between acting and directing. By 1919 he became a successful director, a career that was to extend through the next fifty years. A skilled and prolific director, he turned out numerous features in a variety of genres including period pieces (Lloyds of London), westerns (The Gunfighter), biographies (Stanley and Livingstone), contemporary dramas (Over the Hill), and swashbucklers (The Black Swan). But he often returned to his favorite subjects—American history and rural life. One of his earliest successes was Tol'able David (1921) starring Richard Barthelmess. His particular style—his unobtrusive use of the camera, unhurried pace, and preference for outdoor scenes—may be found in his comedies as well as his more serious films. He was the brother of Louis King.

SELECTED FILMS: Who Pays? (1915), Twin Kiddies (1917), The Ghost of Rosy Taylor, Hobbs in a Hurry (1918), Brass Buttons, Some Liar, 23 1/2 Hours Leave (1919), Help Wanted—Male (1920), Sonny (1922), She Goes to War (1929), Merely Mary Ann (1931), State Fair (1933), Margie (1946), Tender Is the Night (1962). ∎

Kingsford, Walter (1882–1958), actor. Appeared on stage in his native England and on Broadway before entering Hollywood films in 1934. A dapper character actor, he played sympathetic gentlemen in more than 100 dramas and light films during a screen career of 25 years.

SELECTED FILMS: Pursuit of Happiness (1934), Naughty Marietta (1935), Trouble for Two, Mad Holiday (1936), Double or Nothing (1937), There's Always a Woman, Say It in French (1938), Kitty Foyle (1940), The Devil and Miss Jones, Hit the Road (1941), My Favorite Blonde (1942), Hi Diddle Diddle (1943), Ghost Catchers (1944), Two Dollar Bettor (1951), Loose in London (1953), Around the World in 80 Days (1956), Merry Andrew (1958). ∎

Kingsley, Dorothy (1909–), screenwriter. Worked as a comedy writer for Bob HOPE on radio before turning to screenwriting in the mid-1940s. She turned out dozens of light comedies and musicals alone or in collaboration for such stars as Red SKELTON, Esther WILLIAMS, George MURPHY, and Frank SINATRA.

SELECTED FILMS: Broadway Rhythm, Bathing Beauty (1944), Easy to Wed (1946), A Date With Judy (1948), Neptune's Daughter (1949), Two Weeks With Love (1950), Angels in the Outfield (1951), Dangerous When Wet, Kiss Me Kate (1953), Seven Brides for Seven Brothers (1954), Pal Joey, Don't Go Near the Water (1957), Can-Can, Pepe (1960), Half a Sixpence (1967). ∎

Kingston, Natalie (1905–), actress. Worked on Broadway before entering films. She appeared in early silent comedy shorts for Mack SENNETT, often as female leads to some of the leading comics of the period, including, among others, Ben TURPIN and Harry LANGDON. By the mid-1920s the pretty, dark-haired actress moved to feature-length films, continuing into the early 1930s before giving up her screen career.

SELECTED FILMS: The Daredevil (1923), Black Oxfords, Romeo and Juliet, The Reel Virginian (1924), Boobs in the Woods, His Marriage Wow, Remember When?, Lucky Stars (1925), Wet Paint, Kid Boots, The Silent Lover (1926), Figures Don't Lie, His First Flame, Framed (1927), A Girl in Every Port, Painted Post (1928), River of Romance (1929), Her Wedding Night (1930), His Private Secretary (1933). ∎

Kinskey, Leonid (1903–), actor. Worked on stage in Europe and South America before appearing in American films during the early sound period. Born in St. Petersburg, Russia, he was often seen in continental roles as a supporting player. He enlivened his characters with buoyancy and humor. Perhaps his most famous part was that of Humphrey BOGART'S loyal and slightly lecherous bartender in *Casablanca* (1942). He produced industrial films in later years.

SELECTED FILMS: Trouble in Paradise (1932), Duck Soup, Girl Without a Room (1933), Rhythm on the Range (1936), Cafe Metropole, Make a Wish (1937), Three Blind Mice, Professor Beware (1938), On Your Toes, Daytime Wife (1939), He Stayed for Breakfast, Down Argentine Way (1940), That Night in Rio, Week-End in Havana (1941), Ball of Fire, I Married an Angel, The Talk of the Town (1942), Presenting Lily Mars (1943), Can't Help Singing (1944), Monsieur Beaucaire (1946), Glory (1956). ∎

Kirk, Joe (–1975), actor. Appeared as a supporting player in several films starring ABBOTT AND COSTELLO. He was Lou's brother-in-law. He also worked with the boys in their television series.

SELECTED FILMS: Here Come the Co-Eds (1945), Lost in Alaska (1952), Abbott and Costello Go to Mars (1953). ∎

Kirk, Tommy (1941–), juvenile actor. Starred as a child in several Walt Disney features before moving on to light teenage films in the 1960s.

SELECTED FILMS: Old Yeller (1957), The Shaggy Dog (1959), The Absent-Minded Professor, Babes in Toyland (1961), Bon Voyage! (1962), Son of Flubber (1963), The Misadventures of Merlin Jones (1964), The Monkey's Uncle (1965), The Ghost in the Invisible Bikini (1966), My Name Is Legend (1976). ∎

Kirtley, Virginia, actress. Appeared in early silent comedies as a supporting player. Some of her earliest work was in one-reel comedies released by IMP studios during 1912–1913. She later joined the KEYSTONE stock company under the direction of Mack SENNETT, for whom she made several comedy shorts starring Charlie CHAPLIN. She worked with some of the leading film comics of the period, including "Fatty" ARBUCKLE and the KEYSTONE KOPS.

SELECTED FILMS: Making a Living, A Film Johnnie (1914). ∎

Klein, Robert (1942–), comedian, actor. Worked as an actor in off-Broadway productions, as a comic in small nightclubs and on Broadway, in television, and in films. A youngish, good-looking comedian, he delivers routines on a variety of topics ranging from the mundane to the counterculture. His screen appearances have generally gone unnoticed, with virtually no effect on his career.

SELECTED FILMS: The Landlord (1970), The Owl and the Pussycat, Pursuit of Happiness (1971), Rivals (1972), Hooper (1978), Nobody's Perfekt (1981). ∎

Klugman, Jack (1922–), actor. Began his sporadic screen career in the mid-1950s as a serious dramatic performer. Finding little advancement for himself in films, he switched to television where he became a popular light actor. He has occasionally returned to films.

SELECTED FILMS: *Timetable* (1955), *I Could Go On Singing* (1962), *The Yellow Canary, Act One* (1963), *Goodbye Columbus* (1969), *Two-Minute Warning* (1976). ■

Knapp, Evalyn (1908–), actress. Worked in the theater before entering Hollywood films in the early 1930s. A pretty blonde, she appeared in many B dramas and light comedies as a leading and supporting player. She worked with several leading personalities of the period, including, among others, James CAGNEY, Joan BLONDELL, and OLSEN AND JOHNSON.

SELECTED FILMS: *Sinners' Holiday* (1930), *Fifty Million Frenchmen, The Millionaire, The Bargain, Side Show* (1931), *Fireman, Save My Child, A Successful Calamity, This Sporting Age, The Night Mayor* (1932), *His Private Secretary, Dance, Girl, Dance* (1933), *Ladies Crave Excitement, Confidential* (1935), *Laughing Irish Eyes, Three of a Kind* (1936), *The Lone Wolf Takes a Chance* (1941), *Two Weeks to Live* (1943). ■

Knight, Fuzzy (1901–1976), actor. Worked in nightclubs, in vaudeville, and on stage, chiefly in some area of music, before entering films. After appearing in musical shorts, he found his niche portraying comic relief characters in over 200 westerns. He was the sidekick to some of the most popular cowboy stars of the 1930s, including, among others, Johnny Mack Brown and Tex Ritter. He appeared as well in light comedies and dramas.

In *She Done Him Wrong* he played a piano player in a run-down saloon. "Ever since I sang that song, it's been haunting me," a saloon singer confesses to him. "It should," he returns. "You murdered it."

SELECTED FILMS: *Hell's Highway* (1932), *She Done Him Wrong* (1933), *Moulin Rouge, Music in the Air* (1934),

Home on the Range, Wanderer of the Wasteland (1935), The Plainsman (1936), The Cowboy and the Lady (1938), My Little Chickadee (1940), The Singing Sheriff (1944), Frisco Sal (1945), The Egg and I (1947), Topeka (1954), Hostile Guns (1967). ■

Knotts, Don (1924–), actor. Worked in nightclubs, on radio, on Broadway, and in television before entering films in 1958. A gifted comedian with bulging eyes and a frenetic style of humor, he never achieved the popularity in films that he did in his Emmy-winning television performances. He usually portrays timid and nervous types with a gift for fouling up a speech.

In *The Shakiest Gun in the West* he played a Philadelphia dentist out west who comments on his bachelorhood: "I always thought I was a little too thin for marriage."

SELECTED FILMS: *No Time for Sergeants* (1958), *Wake Me When It's Over* (1960), *The Last Time I Saw Archie* (1961), *It's a Mad, Mad, Mad, Mad World, Move Over, Darling* (1963), *The Incredible Mr. Limpet* (1964), *The Ghost and Mr. Chicken* (1966), *The Reluctant Astronaut* (1967), *The Shakiest Gun in the West* (1968), *How to Frame a Figg* (1971), *The Apple Dumpling Gang* (1975), *No Deposit, No Return* (1976), *Herbie Goes to Monte Carlo* (1977), *Hot Head and Cold Feet* (1978). ■

Knowles, Patric (1911–), actor. Worked on stage and in films in Ireland and his native England before immigrating to Hollywood in the mid-1930s. Tall, good-looking, and charming, he played leads and second leads in dramas and light films. During the Second World War he served as a flight instructor in both England and the United States. He never achieved major stardom as did his long-time friend, Errol FLYNN, with whom he appeared in several features. He worked with some of the leading comedians of the period, including, among others, ABBOTT AND

COSTELLO, OLSEN AND JOHNSON, and Bob HOPE.

SELECTED FILMS: Give Me Your Heart (1936), It's Love I'm After, Expensive Husbands (1937), Four's a Crowd (1938), Beauty for the Asking, Another Thin Man (1939), Married and in Love (1940), Lady in a Jam, Who Done It? (1942), Hit the Ice, Crazy House (1943), This Is the Life, Pardon My Rhythm (1944), Masquerade in Mexico (1945), The Bride Wore Boots, Monsieur Beaucaire (1946), Dream Girl, Isn't It Romantic? (1948), Auntie Mame (1958), Arnold (1973). ■

Kolb, Clarence (1875–1964), actor. Worked in vaudeville before appearing in silent film comedies. He made one full-length feature with Max Dill, his theater partner, and a group of two-reel comedies during the 1916–1917 season before returning to the stage. He reappeared in films in the late 1930s, often portraying affluent but short-tempered characters.

In Beware, Spooks! (1939) he portrayed a police commissioner who reprimands several of his officers whom he catches in the act of pulling a prank on a fellow policeman. "Isn't the police department enough of a joke without making a spectacle of it?" he pronounces.

SELECTED FILMS: Glory (1917), The Toast of New York (1937), Merrily We Live, Carefree (1938), Honolulu, It Could Happen to You, Our Leading Citizen (1939), His Girl Friday, No Time for Comedy (1940), Caught in the Draft, Hellzapoppin (1941), Bedtime Story (1942), Standing Room Only, Irish Eyes Are Smiling (1944), The Kid From Brooklyn (1946), Christmas Eve (1947), Adam's Rib (1949), Man of a Thousand Faces (1957). ■

Korman, Harvey (1927–), actor. Worked on stage and in television before entering films in the early 1960s. He has appeared in light features, usually insup-

porting roles. He has worked in several of Mel BROOKS' films.

SELECTED FILMS: Living Venus (1961), Gypsy (1962), Lord Love a Duck (1966), Three Bites of the Apple (1967), Don't Just Stand There! (1968), The April Fools (1969), Blazing Saddles, Huckleberry Finn (1974), High Anxiety (1977), Americathon (1979), Curse of the Pink Panther (1983). ■

Kornman, Mary (1917–1973), child actress. Appeared in early silent "OUR GANG" comedy shorts during the 1920s. She remained with Hal ROACH'S young troupe for four years, then toured in vaudeville. She appeared in several B movies and eventually drifted out of show business. She co-starred with other "Our Gang" regulars during the silent period, including Farina HOSKINS, Mickey DANIELS, Johnny Downs, Jackie Condon, Joe COBB, and Jay R. Smith.

SELECTED FILMS: Young Sherlocks (1922), The Champeen, The Cobbler, The Big Show, A Pleasant Journey, Dogs of War (1923), The Trouble, Big Business, The Buccaneers, Seein' Things (1924), The Big Town, Circus Fever, Dog Days, The Love Bug (1925), Shivering Spooks, The Fourth Alarm (1926), Doctor's Orders, Bigger and Better (1930), Blood and Thunder, High Gear, Are These Our Children? (1931), Love Pains, The Knockout (1932), Flying Down to Rio, College Humor (1933), The Quitter (1934), King of the Newsboys (1938). ■

Koster, Henry (1905–), director. Worked as a cartoonist, journalist, film critic, and film director in his native Germany before immigrating to France and, in 1936, to the United States. A skilled director with a strong visual sense, and whose career spanned four decades, he made both dramatic and light features. However, he demonstrated a natural proclivity for the latter.

SELECTED FILMS: Three Smart Girls (1936), 100 Men and a Girl (1937), The Rage of Paris (1938), First Love (1939),

Spring Parade (1940), It Started With Eve (1941), Between Us Girls (1942), Two Sisters From Boston (1946), The Bishop's Wife (1947), The Luck of the Irish (1948), Come to the Stable, The Inspector General (1949), Harvey (1950), Mr. Belvedere Rings the Bell (1951), My Cousin Rachel (1953), Good Morning Miss Dove (1955), My Man Godfrey (1957), Flower Drum Song (1961), Mr. Hobbs Takes a Vacation, Take Her, She's Mine (1963), Dear Brigitte (1965), The Singing Nun (1966). ∎

Kovacs, Ernie (1919–1962), actor. Worked in radio as a disc jockey and in television as host comic of his own network show before entering the film world in 1957 as an eccentric and whimsical comic. Easily recognized by his familiar trademarks, his mustache and cigar, he was considered by many of his peers to be the first true creative genius in television. He explored and utilized visual and sound techniques in the relatively new medium in his comedy routines. His promising career was cut short by a fateful car accident.

In Bell, Book and Candle publisher James STEWART rejects his scholarly and well-researched manuscript about witchcraft in New York City, calling it "trash, garbage" and a "spoof." The stunned Kovacs pauses for a moment and, as he leaves Stewart's office, suggests: "I don't suppose you'd be interested in a sequel I have in mind about the islands in the Caribbean, Voodoo Among the Virgins?"

SELECTED FILMS: Operation Mad Ball (1957), Bell, Book and Candle (1958), It Happened to Jane (1959), Our Man in Havana, Pepe, Wake Me When It's Over (1960), Five Golden Hours (1961), Sail a Crooked Ship (1962). ∎

Krasna, Norman (1909–1984), screenwriter, playwright, director. Worked as a newspaper film critic, Hollywood publicity director, and playwright before writing stories for Hollywood features during the 1930s. Specializing in light films, for which he displayed a distinct penchant, he turned out some of the best and most charming comedies of the Depression and war years, including Hands Across the Table, Bachelor Mother, and It Started With Eve. Often using the ploy of deception or mistaken identity in his own romantic farces of the 1930s (as well as in several dramas), he greatly enriched this already grand decade of dialogue comedies. He has also directed and produced several films. His later work lacked the spark and freshness of his earlier comedies.

SELECTED FILMS (as screenwriter): Hollywood Speaks, That's My Boy (1932), So This Is Africa, Meet the Baron, Love, Honor and Oh, Baby! (1933), The Richest Girl in the World, Romance in Manhattan (1934), Hands Across the Table (1935), Wife vs. Secretary (1936), The King and the Chorus Girl, As Good As Married, The Big City (1937), Bachelor Mother (1939), It's a Date (1940), The Devil and Miss Jones, It Started With Eve (1941), Princess O'Rourke (1943), Practically Yours (1945), Dear Ruth (1947), Bundle of Joy (1956), Indiscreet (1958), Let's Make Love (1960), My Geisha (1962), Sunday in New York (1963), I'd Rather Be Rich (1964). ∎

Kruger, Alma (1871–1960), actress. Appeared on stage and radio in her long theatrical career that included Shakespearean plays and repertory companies. In films chiefly during the 1930s and 1940s, she played character roles in dramas and comedies. Her most popular portrayal was that of Molly Byrd, the unyielding nurse in the "Dr. Kildare" film series with Lionel Barrymore.

SELECTED FILMS: Craig's Wife (1936), The Great Waltz (1938), The Secret of Dr. Kildare (1939), Our Hearts Were Young and Gay (1944), A Scandal in Paris (1946). ∎

Kruger, Otto (1885–1974), actor. Had a long career on stage before settling in Hollywood during the silent period. Thin-faced and urbane, he developed into a versatile and popular character player portraying lawyers, executives, and other sophisticated types in dramas and light films. He was equally comfortable on either side of the law. During the 1930s he appeared in several British films. He played in scores of features during a screen career that spanned six decades.

SELECTED FILMS: When the Call Came (1915), The Home Girl (1928), Ever in My Heart, The Prizefighter and the Lady, The Women in His Life (1933), Springtime for Henry (1934), Glamourous Night (1937), Another Thin Man (1939), Seventeen (1940), The Men in Her Life (1941), Stage Door Canteen (1943), Cover Girl, Knickerbocker Holiday (1944), On Stage, Everybody!, Wonder Man (1945), Love and Learn (1947), Lulu Belle (1948), Sex and the Single Girl (1964). ■

Kulky, Henry (1911–1965), actor. A former boxer and wrestler who came to films as a character player in the 1940s to portray tough guys or good-natured slobs. Thick-set and dark-haired, he could be menacing or happy-go-lucky. He appeared in dozens of dramas and light films.

SELECTED FILMS: Call Northside 777, A Likely Story (1947), Jackpot Jitters, Jiggs and Maggie Out West (1950), Chinatown Chump, You Can Never Tell (1951), Gobs and Gals (1952), Fireman, Save My Child (1954), Abbott and Costello Meet the Keystone Kops (1955), The Girl Can't Help It (1965), A Global Affair (1963). ■

Kurnitz, Harry (1909–1968), screenwriter. Worked as a reporter before settling in Hollywood to write dramatic and light screenplays either alone or in collaboration. He penned vehicles for some of the leading comics of the period, including Bob HOPE and Danny KAYE. He was also the author of several novels.

SELECTED FILMS: Fast Company (1938), I Love You Again (1940), Shadow of the Thin Man (1941), They Got Me Covered, The Heavenly Body (1943), See Here, Private Hargrove (1944), One Touch of Venus (1948), The Inspector General, A Kiss in the Dark (1949), Pretty Baby (1950), Tonight We Sing (1953), Once More, With Feeling, Surprise Package (1960), Goodbye Charlie (1964), How to Steal a Million (1966). ■

L

La Cava, Gregory (1892–1952), director. Worked as a cartoonist and animator with Walter Lang before writing and directing comedy shorts. By 1922 he began directing full-length features, a career which carried over well into the sound era. Known for his delicate touch in guiding many light films to the screen, he was capable of working in various forms of comedy, including satire, sophisticated comedy, screwball comedy, and comedy-drama. He worked with most of the major comediennes of the period, including, among others, Claudette COLBERT, Irene DUNNE, Carole LOMBARD, Katharine HEPBURN, and Ginger ROGERS. The New York Film Critics Circle cited him for his direction of *Stage Door* (1936).

SELECTED FILMS: *His Nibs* (1922), *The New School Teacher* (1924), *Womanhandled* (1925), *Let's Get Married, So's Your Old Man* (1926), *Tell It to Sweeney* (1927), *Half a Bride* (1928), *Laugh and Get Rich* (1931), *The Half-Naked Truth* (1932), *Gabriel Over the White House* (1933), *The Affairs of Cellini, What Every Woman Knows* (1934), *She Married Her Boss* (1935), *My Man Godfrey* (1936), *Fifth Avenue Girl* (1939), *Unfinished Business* (1941), *Lady in a Jam* (1942), *Living in a Big Way* (1947). ∎

La Plante, Laura (1904–), actress. Worked in early silent comedy shorts for Al CHRISTIE. A film star during the 1920s, she appeared in westerns, melodramas, and comedies. She retired from the screen in the early 1930s after mak-ing a few sound films, occasionally returning before the cameras in minor roles.

SELECTED FILMS: *The Great Gamble* (1919), *The Old Swimmin' Hole* (1922), *Out of Luck* (1923), *Sporting Youth, Excitement, The Dangerous Blonde* (1924), *The Teaser* (1925), *The Beautiful Cheat, Skinner's Dress Suit, Poker Faces, Her Big Night, Butterflies in the Rain* (1926), *Beware of Widows, Silk Stockings* (1927), *Thanks for the Buggy Ride, Finders Keepers* (1928), *Scandal, Show Boat, Hold Your Man* (1929), *The King of Jazz* (1930), *Lonely Wives, God's Gift to Women* (1931), *Little Mister Jim* (1946), *Spring Reunion* (1957). ∎

La Rocque, Rod (1896–1969), actor. Began his acting career as a child performer and appeared on Broadway. Born Roderick La Roque de La Rour, he made his screen debut in early silent films produced in Fort Lee, New Jersey, before journeying to Hollywood. Although still relatively young, he portrayed villains and minor characters in a string of two-reelers and features for ESSANAY studios. He became a silent screen star during the 1920s, especially in social comedies directed by Cecil B. DeMille. Tall and handsome, he became extremely popular with the women in the audience. With the advent of sound, he continued in leading, then minor, roles for the next decade, retiring in the 1940s.

SELECTED FILMS: *The Alster Case* (1915), *Efficiency Edgar's Courtship* (1917), *The Venus Model* (1918), *Easy to Get, The Discarded Woman* (1920), *Pay-*

ing the Piper, Suspicious Wives (1921), Slim Shoulders, What's Wrong With Women? (1922), Jazzmania, The French Doll (1923), A Society Scandal (1924), The Golden Bed, Night Life of New York, The Coming of Amos, Wild Wild Susan, Braveheart (1925), Bachelor Brides, Gigolo (1926), Hold 'Em, Yale, Captain Swagger, Love Over Night (1928), The One Woman Idea, The Delightful Rogue (1929), Beau Bandit, One Romantic Night, Let Us Be Gay (1930), Taming the Wild (1938), Meet John Doe (1941). ∎

Lachman, Harry (1886–1975), director. Worked as an illustrator in Chicago, established himself in the 1920s as an artist and a film set designer in France, and, in 1928, turned to directing films in England. He returned to the United States in 1933 and began directing dramas and comedies in Hollywood. Although his vehicles were chiefly low-budget affairs, he occasionally imbued his dramatic films with his own visual style. He abandoned his directorial career in the early 1940s and went back to painting.

SELECTED FILMS: Face in the Sky, Paddy, the Next Best Thing (1933), George White's Scandals, I Like It That Way, Baby Take a Bow (1934), Dressed to Thrill (1935), Our Relations (1936), It Happened in Hollywood (1937), No Time to Marry (1938), Dr. Renault's Secret (1942). ∎

Lady Eve, The (1941), PAR. Dir. Preston Sturges; Sc. Preston Sturges; with Barbara Stanwyck, Henry Fonda, Charles Coburn, Eugene Pallette, William Demarest.

Sturges was one of the few directors capable of successfully blending sophisticated comedy with slapstick. In this film, his third as director, he has alluring con artist Barbara STANWYCK chase rich, bashful Henry FONDA with humorous results. When he gets the best of her, she seeks revenge, but all ends well for both in this charming comedy. The supporting players, as in all of Sturges'

works, contribute immeasurably to the goings-on. Charles COBURN plays a likable cardsharp who enlightens Stanwyck about their standards: "Let us be crooked, but never common." Eugene PALLETTE portrays a capitalist while William DEMAREST, one of the director's reliable character actors, plays a bodyguard. Eric BLORE, the perennial servant, plays a con man this time around. Paramount showed its confidence in Sturges by giving him this big-budget picture after his two previous successes, The Great McGinty and Christmas in July. Stanwyck commanded a high price while 20th Century-Fox had to be paid for the services of Fonda. A weak remake appeared in 1956 titled The Birds and the Bees starring George GOBEL, Mitzi GAYNOR, and David NIVEN.

Lady for a Day (1933), COL. Dir. Frank Capra; Sc. Robert Riskin; with Warren William, May Robson, Guy Kibbee, Glenda Farrell, Walter Connolly, Ned Sparks.

Damon Runyon's tales and his offbeat urban characters were a constant source of material for the major Hollywood studios, including, among others, MGM, Paramount, 20th Century-Fox, RKO, and Universal. This film, based on his short story, "Madame La Gimpe," concerns a tattered street vendor, played by May ROBSON, who is helped by a good-natured underworld character portrayed by Warren WILLIAM. Robson wants her visiting daughter to think she is doing well, so William transforms her into a model woman and mother. The skillful direction by CAPRA and strong performances by the able cast result in a charming and entertaining fable. A sequel, Lady by Choice, appeared the following year starring Carole LOMBARD and May Robson. The original was remade in 1961 as Pocketful of Miracles, again directed by Capra with Bette DAVIS and Glenn FORD in the starring roles, but it lacked the impact of the first version.

Lahr, Bert (1895–1967), actor, entertainer. Worked in burlesque, in vaudeville, and on Broadway. Born Irving Lahrheim, he began appearing in films with the advent of sound in the early 1930s, chiefly in supporting roles in musicals and light comedies. Except for his notable portrayal of the Cowardly Lion in *The Wizard of Oz* (1939), he was not as well known for his screen appearances as he was for those on the stage. A warm and lovable performer, he specialized in pathos and charm in his wide range of characterizations. *Notes on a Cowardly Lion*, a biography written by his son, John Lahr, was published in 1969.

In *The Wizard of Oz* he played the Cowardly Lion. When Dorothy is captured by the Wicked Witch, he screws up all his courage to enter the witch's castle to save the child. "There's only one thing I want you fellers to do," he says to the Tinman and the Scarecrow. "What's that?" they ask. "Talk me out of it."

SELECTED FILMS: *Flying High* (1931), *Mr. Broadway* (1933), *Merry-Go-Round of 1938*, *Love and Hisses* (1937), *Josette*, *Just Around the Corner* (1938), *Zaza* (1939), *Sing Your Worries Away*, *Ship Ahoy* (1942), *Meet the People* (1944), *Always Leave Them Laughing* (1949), *Mr. Universe* (1951), *Rose Marie* (1954), *The Second Greatest Sex* (1955), *The Night They Raided Minsky's* (1968). ∎

Lahti, Christine (1950–), actress. Has appeared on stage and in television as well as in films, usually portraying professional characters in comedy-dramas. She has played attorneys, doctors, and television reporters. A tall, attractive performer, she was nominated for an Academy Award as Best Supporting Actress for her role as Hazel in *Swing Shift*.

SELECTED FILMS: *. . . And Justice for All* (1979), *Whose Life Is It Anyway?* (1981), *Swing Shift* (1984), *Just Between Friends* (1986). ∎

Lake, Alice (1896–1967), actress. Worked in early silent films at Vitagraph studios and in comedy shorts for Mack SENNETT'S KEYSTONE studios. An attractive brunette supporting actress, she appeared in films with some of the leading comics of the period, including, among others, "Fatty" ARBUCKLE (who discovered her in New York and invited her to join Keystone on the West Coast), Al ST. JOHN, and Marie PREVOST. By 1920, she became a featured player for Metro studios. With the advent of sound, she was relegated to minor roles and films.

SELECTED FILMS: *Her Picture Idol* (1912), *The Moonshiners*, *The Waiter's Ball*, *A Creampuff Romance* (1916), *Her Nature Dance* (1917), *The Sheriff* (1918), *Cupid's Day Off*, *Should a Woman Tell?* (1919), *Shore Acres*, *The Misfit Wife*, *Body and Soul* (1920), *The Infamous Miss Revell* (1921), *The Marriage Market* (1923), *The Dancing Cheat*, *The Virgin* (1924), *The Angel of Broadway* (1927), *Obey Your Husband*, *Women Men Like* (1928), *Twin Beds* (1929), *Wharf Angel*, *Glamour* (1934). ∎

Lake, Arthur (1905–1987), actor. Worked as a child performer in vaudeville and early silent films. Born Arthur Silverlake, he was cast in juvenile roles for years and starred in *Harold Teen* (1928), an adaptation of the famous comic strip created by Carl Ed. He starred in a series of comedy shorts for Universal studios and appeared in supporting roles in features, including *Topper* (1937). He finally attained wide popularity in 1938, again in the role of a comic strip character. He portrayed Chic Young's flustered husband, Dagwood Bumstead, in the "BLONDIE" series, costarring Penny SINGLETON as his wife. Squeaky-voiced and befuddled, he did justice to the character but hampered his own career by becoming identified with the part. Although he appeared in other comedies in the early 1940s, he always returned to the series. He also portrayed Dagwood on radio from 1939 to 1950 and in the television series in 1957. He was the brother of actress Florence LAKE.

SELECTED FILMS: Jack and the Beanstalk (1917), Where Was I? (1925), Skinner's Dress Suit (1926), The Cradle Snatchers, The Irresistible Lover (1927), The Count of Ten, Stop That Man (1928), On With the Show, Tanned Legs (1929), Cheer Up and Smile, She's My Weakness (1930), Indiscreet (1931), Midshipman Jack (1933), The Silver Streak (1934), Orchids to You (1935), Topper (1937), Blondie Meets the Boss (1939), Footlight Glamour (1943), Sailor's Holiday, The Ghost That Walks Alone (1944), Sixteen Fathoms Deep (1948), Beware of Blondie (1950). ∎

Lake, Florence (1905–1980), actress. Worked in early silent and sound films, chiefly as a supporting player. An attractive blonde, she will perhaps be remembered best for her co-starring role as Edgar KENNEDY'S wife in his comedy shorts. Her brother, Arthur LAKE, was famous for his portrayal of BLONDIE'S confused husband, Dagwood Bumstead.

SELECTED FILMS: Thru Different Eyes (1929), The Rogue Song (1930), Ladies of the Jury (1932), The Sweetheart of Sigma Chi, Midshipman Jack (1933), To Mary, With Love (1936), I Met My Love Again (1938), San Diego, I Love You (1944). ∎

Lake, Veronica (1919–1973), actress. Popular diminutive actress who hit her peak in the 1940s. Born Constance Frances Marie Ockelman, she became one of the most glamorous screen figures in her time. She was famous for her long blonde hair that draped over one eye and her tough-girl roles, especially in those films in which she appeared opposite Alan Ladd. She was equally adept in comedy and dramatic vehicles. Her biography, Veronica, was published in 1971.

SELECTED FILMS: All Women Have Secrets (1939), Young As You Feel, 40 Little Mothers (1940), Sullivan's Travels (1941), I Married a Witch (1942), Star Spangled Rhythm (1943), Bring On the Girls, Out of This World, Duffy's Tavern, Hold That Blonde (1945), Miss Susie Slagle's (1946), Isn't It Romantic? (1948), Flesh Feast (1970). ∎

Lamarr, Hedy (1913–), actress. Appeared in films in her native Austria and worked for Max Reinhardt. Born Hedwig Eva Maria Kiesler, she gained notoriety when she appeared in the nude in Ecstasy, a 1933 Czech film. She migrated to Hollywood in the late 1930s where she was promoted as the world's most beautiful woman. She starred in dramas and light films through the 1940s. At the peak of her career during this decade, she emerged as an international celebrity. By the 1950s, however, her popularity had declined sharply.

In Comrade X, a satirical comedy about Russian Communism, she portrayed a devoted Communist. Her father, however, convinces Clark GABLE, an American reporter, to take her to America. Believing that she will be spreading propaganda for Mother Russia, she agrees to go, but they must first be married so that she can get a passport. On their wedding night, she explains to Gable the Russian view of marriage. "It is like going into partnership with somebody. It's like opening a store. If business is bad, you close the store."

SELECTED FILMS: Algiers (1938), I Take This Woman, Comrade X (1940), Come Live With Me, Ziegfeld Girl (1941), Tortilla Flat (1942), The Heavenly Body (1944), Her Highness and the Bellboy (1945), Let's Live a Little (1948), My Favorite Spy (1951), The Female Animal (1958). ∎

Lamas, Fernando (1915–1982), actor. Starred in films in his native Argentina before appearing in American light features. He usually portrayed Latin lovers in MGM films during the 1950s.

SELECTED FILMS: The Avengers (1950), Rich, Young and Pretty, The Law and the Lady (1951), The Merry Widow (1952), The Girl Who Had Everything,

Dangerous When Wet (1953), Rose Marie (1954), The Girl Rush (1955), The Cheap Detective (1978). ■

Lamb, Gil (1906–), dancer, comedian. Appeared in vaudeville and on Broadway before entering films in 1942. His rubber-legged dancing style provided comic relief to several musicals during the war years and after.

SELECTED FILMS: *The Fleet's In, Star Spangled Rhythm (1942), Riding High (1943), Rainbow Island, Practically Yours (1944), Make Mine Laughs (1949), Her Wonderful Lie, Humphrey Takes a Chance (1950), Bye, Bye Birdie (1963), The Gnome-Mobile, Blackbeard's Ghost (1967), The Love Bug (1969).* ■

Lamont, Charles (1898–), director. Appeared on stage and in silent films before beginning a long career as a director in 1922. He made numerous comedy shorts for Mack SENNETT, Al CHRISTIE, and other studios. With the advent of sound he began to turn out feature-length vehicles, chiefly low comedies for Universal studios. He directed many of the ABBOTT AND COSTELLO and MA AND PA KETTLE films, as well as pedestrian adventures and westerns. Other screen comics he worked with include Jack OAKIE, Donald O'CONNOR, and Joan DAVIS.

SELECTED FILMS: *The Curtain Falls (1934), The Girl Who Came Back, Happiness, C.O.D. (1935), Ring Around the Moon, August Week-End (1936), Wallaby Jim of the Islands (1937), Unexpected Father, Little Accident (1939), Oh Johnny, How You Can Love!, Sandy Is a Lady, Love, Honor and Oh, Baby! (1940), San Antonio Rose, Moonlight in Hawaii, Melody Lane (1941), Don't Get Personal, You're Telling Me!, Almost Married (1942), It Comes Up Love, Hit the Ice, Fired Wife (1943), Chip off the Old Block, Her Primitive Man, Bowery to Broadway (1944), That's the Spirit (1945), She Wrote the Book (1946), Ma and Pa Kettle (1949), Abbott and Costello in the Foreign Legion (1950),*

Untamed Heiress (1954), Lay That Rifle Down (1955), Francis in the Haunted House (1956). ■

Lamour, Dorothy (1914–), actress. Worked as a singer and radio performer before making her film debut in 1936. A shapely, pleasant performer, she appeared in musicals and light comedies, especially in the "ROAD COMEDIES," in which she co-starred with Bob HOPE and Bing CROSBY. Throughout the series both men competed for her affections, with straight-man Crosby usually winning. Often attired in a sarong, she enhanced many films during the 1930s and 1940s and became one of the most popular stars of the period. Her screen career spanned three decades.

SELECTED FILMS: *The Jungle Princess (1936), Swing High, Swing Low, College Holiday, Thrill of a Lifetime (1937), Her Jungle Love, Tropic Holiday (1938), St. Louis Blues, Man About Town (1939), Road to Singapore, Moon Over Burma (1940), Caught in the Draft (1941), The Fleet's In, Beyond the Blue Horizon (1942), They Got Me Covered, Dixie, Riding High (1943), And the Angels Sing, Rainbow Island (1944), A Medal for Benny, Duffy's Tavern (1945), My Favorite Brunette (1947), Lulu Belle, The Girl From Manhattan (1948), Slightly French, Manhandled, The Lucky Stiff (1949), Road to Bali (1953), Pajama Party (1964), The Phynx (1970).* ■

Lanchester, Elsa (1902–1986), actress. Appeared on stage and in films in her native England before migrating to Hollywood in the mid-1930s. A charming and offbeat character actress, she played a variety of roles in dramas and light films. She was married to Charles Laughton. Her autobiography, *Charles Laughton and I*, was published in 1938.

SELECTED FILMS: *Naughty Marietta (1935), Ladies in Retirement (1941), Thumbs Up (1943), The Bishop's Wife (1947), Come to the Stable, The Inspector General (1949), Dreamboat (1952),*

Bell, Book and Candle (1958), Mary Poppins (1964), That Darn Cat (1965), Easy Come, Easy Go (1967), Murder by Death (1976). ∎

Landers, Lew (1901–1962), director. Began his directing career in the 1930s, turning out chiefly second features. He worked in all genres, specializing in westerns. But he also directed a handful of entertaining light comedies during a career that spanned four decades.

SELECTED FILMS: The Raven (1935), They Wanted to Marry (1937), Crashing Hollywood, Annabel Takes a Tour (1938), Honeymoon Deferred, La Conga Nights, Girl From Havana (1940), The Stork Pays Off (1941), Harvard, Here I Come (1942), Redhead From Manhattan, Doughboys in Ireland (1943), I'm From Arkansas (1944), Beauty on Parade (1950), Terrified (1963). ∎

Landis, Carole (1919–1948), actress. Worked as singer- dancer before entering Hollywood films in 1937 at age 18. A pretty blonde, she became a star by 1940 in pedestrian features. She played a wide range of characters, eventually finding her niche in light comedies, especially those produced by Hal ROACH. In the late 1940s, just before her suicide, she starred in a handful of films produced in England.

SELECTED FILMS: A Star Is Born, A Day at the Races (1937), Four's a Crowd (1938), Turnabout (1940), Road Show, Topper Returns, Moon Over Miami, Dance Hall, Cadet Girl (1941), It Happened in Flatbush, My Gal Sal (1942), Four Jills in a Jeep (1944), Having Wonderful Crime (1945), It Shouldn't Happen to a Dog, A Scandal in Paris (1946), Out of the Blue (1947), The Noose (1948). ∎

Landis, Cullen (1895–1975), actor. Appeared on stage before entering silent films in 1917. He starred in scores of romances, melodramas, light comedies, and action features, including the first all-talking film, Lights of New York (1928). Although rather short for a leading man (5′ 6″), he attained some success and popularity during the 1920s, abandoning his acting career shortly after the advent of sound.

SELECTED FILMS: Beware of Blondes (1918), Almost a Husband, The Outcasts of Poker Flat, The Girl From Outside (1919), It's a Great Life (1920), Bunty Pulls the String, The Old Nest (1921), Watch Your Step, Gay and Devilish, Love in the Dark (1922), Born Rich, Cheap Kisses (1924), Easy Money, A Broadway Butterfly, Peacock Feathers (1925), The Dixie Flyer, Sweet Rosie O'Grady (1926), We're All Gamblers (1927), On to Reno, The Little Wild Girl (1928), The Convict's Code (1930). ∎

Landis, Jessie Royce (1904–1972), actress. Worked on the stage for most of her professional life, appearing occasionally on screen over a period which spanned four decades. She usually portrayed matronly members of the upper class in light features.

SELECTED FILMS: Derelict (1930), Mr. Belvedere Goes to College, It Happens Every Spring (1949), Mother Didn't Tell Me (1950), To Catch a Thief (1955), The Swan, The Girl He Left Behind (1956), My Man Godfrey (1957), I Married a Woman (1958), North by Northwest (1959), Boys' Night Out (1962), Critic's Choice, Gidget Goes to Rome (1963), Airport (1970). ∎

Landis, John (1951–), director. Worked in television before entering films. Turning out chiefly light, offbeat films, he has established a name for himself, especially among young audiences. He has worked closely with today's new crop of comedians, including Dan AYKROYD, Eddie MURPHY, and the late John BELUSHI. His films, although generally commercial successes, have been criticized in part for their absence of subtlety and their lack of tight structure.

SELECTED FILMS: *Schlock* (1971), *The Kentucky Fried Movie* (1977), *National Lampoon's Animal House* (1978), *The Blues Brothers* (1980), *An American Werewolf in London* (1981), *Trading Places* (1983), *Three Amigos!* (1986). ■

Lane, Charles (1899–), actor. Appeared as a character player in the 1930s, chiefly in comedy roles. Portraying petty clerks and prying characters in a succession of light films, he supported numerous screen personalities including, among others, Eddie CANTOR, Harold LLOYD, James STEWART, Bing CROSBY, Cary GRANT, and ABBOTT AND COSTELLO.

SELECTED FILMS: *Without Limit* (1921), *The Music Master, Service for Ladies* (1927), *Two for Tonight* (1935), *The Milky Way, Mr. Deeds Goes to Town* (1936), *Ali Baba Goes to Town* (1937), *You Can't Take It With You* (1938), *The Cat and the Canary* (1939), *You Can't Fool Your Wife* (1940), *Hot Spot* (1941), *Ball of Fire* (1942), *Arsenic and Old Lace* (1944), *State of the Union* (1948), *Teacher's Pet* (1958), *The Gnome-Mobile* (1967), *What's So Bad About Feeling Good?* (1968). ■

Lane, Lupino (1892–1959), actor. Worked in music halls and in comedy shorts as early as 1915 in his native England before making his debut in Hollywood in the 1920s. He was a member of an outstanding family of music hall and stage talents which include Ida Lupino, a second cousin. An oval-eyed, youthful-looking comic with acrobatic prowess, he was capable of performing almost extraordinary feats with his rubbery body. Despite these gimmicks and a degree of popularity, he was unable to develop an individual screen character of any lasting interest that might have brought him the greatness that some of his contemporaries achieved; e.g., Buster KEATON or Harry LANGDON.

Although he had the same type of training as two of his fellow countrymen, CHAPLIN and Stan LAUREL, his music hall experience (without the gift of comic genius or a distinct personality mentioned above) was not enough to enlist him as a comic in the highest echelons. He starred in two-reel comedies as well as some feature-length films. With the advent of sound, he returned to England where he continued working in films for another ten years.

SELECTED FILMS: *The Reporter* (1922), *A Friendly Husband, Wrong Way Willie* (1923), *Isn't Life Wonderful?* (1924), *Sword's Point, The Fighting Dude* (1925), *Movieland, Monty of the Mounted* (1927), *Hectic Days* (1928), *The Love Parade, The Show of Shows* (1929), *Bride of the Regiment, Golden Dawn, The Yellow Mask* (1930). ■

Lane, Priscilla (1917–), actress. Worked as a singer with Fred Waring's radio show before entering films in 1937. A pretty, blue-eyed blonde, she soon began to get major roles in dramas and light comedies, occasionally co-starring with her sisters Lola (1909–1981) and Rosemary (1914–1974) in films like *Four Daughters* (1938). Priscilla, however, was the most successful of the sisters.

SELECTED FILMS: *Varsity Show* (1937), *Love, Honor and Behave, Men Are Such Fools, Cowboy From Brooklyn, Brother Rat* (1938), *Yes, My Darling Daughter, Daughters Courageous, Four Wives* (1939), *Brother Rat and a Baby, Three Cheers for the Irish, Ladies Must Live* (1940), *Million Dollar Baby* (1941), *The Meanest Man in the World* (1943), *Arsenic and Old Lace* (1944), *Fun on a Weekend* (1947), *Bodyguard* (1948). ■

Lane, Richard (1900–1982), actor. Worked as a sports announcer before entering films in the late 1930s. A versatile supporting player, he frequently portrayed policemen, reporters, or flustered executives in numerous dramas and light films. He worked with some of the leading comedians of the period, including, among others, ABBOTT AND COSTELLO, OLSEN AND JOHNSON,

Danny KAYE, and LAUREL AND HARDY.

SELECTED FILMS: *The Outcasts of Poker Flat, The Life of the Party (1937), Go Chase Yourself, Mr. Doodle Kicks Off (1938), Unexpected Father, The Day the Bookies Wept (1939), Hired Wife (1940), The Bride Wore Crutches, Tight Shoes (1941), Ride 'Em Cowboy, Butch Minds the Baby (1942), It Ain't Hay, Fired Wife, Crazy House (1943), Bowery to Broadway (1944), The Bullfighters, Wonder Man (1945), Take Me Out to the Ball Game (1949), The Admiral Was a Lady (1950), I Can Get It for You Wholesale (1951).* ■

Lanfield, Sidney (1898–1972), director. Appeared in vaudeville and worked as a jazz musician before coming to Hollywood where he was employed as a GAGMAN. He began directing films in 1930, turning out romantic films and light comedies for the next 20 years. Mainly a director of routine vehicles, he often managed to overcome weak scripts and low budgets to bring his audiences many entertaining films. He worked with some of the leading comics of the period, including the RITZ BROTHERS, Joan DAVIS, Bob HOPE, and Jack BENNY.

SELECTED FILMS: *Cheer Up and Smile (1930), Three Girls Lost (1931), Society Girl, Hat Check Girl (1932), The Last Gentleman (1933), Hold 'Em, Yale (1935), King of Burlesque, Sing, Baby, Sing (1936), One in a Million, Thin Ice, Love and Hisses (1937), Second Honeymoon, Swanee River (1939), You'll Never Get Rich (1941), My Favorite Blonde (1942), The Meanest Man in the World (1943), Standing Room Only (1944), Bring On the Girls (1945), The Well Groomed Bride (1946), The Trouble With Women, Where There's Life (1947), Sorrowful Jones (1949), Skirts Ahoy! (1952).* ■

Lang, June (1915–), actress. Worked as a dancer before entering films in the early 1930s. Born Winifred June Vlasek,

she played leads and supporting roles in dozens of dramas and light films through the 1940s. Although she was under contract to Fox, a major studio, she never attained stardom in major productions.

SELECTED FILMS: *Young Sinners (1931), Music in the Air (1934), Bonnie Scotland (1935), Captain January (1936), Wee Willie Winkie, Ali Baba Goes to Town (1937), One Wild Night, Meet the Girls (1938), Zenobia (1939), Redhead (1941), Footlight Serenade (1942), Lighthouse (1947).* ■

Lang, Walter (1898–1972), director. Worked as a stage actor and produced and directed plays before entering films. He began directing silent films by the mid-1920s and continued in this capacity until the early 1960s. He directed for various studios, finally settling in with 20th Century-Fox, where he made some of his brightest musicals and comedies. He worked with many leading screen comics and entertainers of the period, including, among others, Danny KAYE, Shirley TEMPLE, Carole LOMBARD, Betty GRABLE, Phil SILVERS, Ethel MERMAN, and Donald O'CONNOR. In general, his style is both modest and proficient.

SELECTED FILMS: *Red Kimono (1925), Money to Burn (1926), Sally in Our Alley (1927), The Spirit of Youth (1929), Hello, Sister, Cock o' the Walk (1930), Women Go On Forever (1931), Meet the Baron (1933), Carnival (1935), Love Before Breakfast (1936), Second Honeymoon (1937), The Baroness and the Butler (1938), The Little Princess (1939), Tin Pan Alley (1940), Moon Over Miami (1941), Coney Island (1943), Sitting Pretty (1947), Cheaper by the Dozen (1950), On the Riviera (1951), Call Me Madam (1953), The King and I (1956), Desk Set (1957), The Marriage-Go-Round, Snow White and the Three Stooges (1961).* ■

Langdon, Harry (1884–1944), actor. Worked in vaudeville, carnivals, and musical comedies before appearing in

Harry Langdon

early silent comedy shorts for Mack SENNETT in 1924. With just 23 films he established himself as a comedian of high stature, an artist in a medium that recognized few true geniuses. He became the fourth member of the quartet of comic greats of the silent period, along with Charlie CHAPLIN, Buster KEATON, and Harold LLOYD.

The screen character that he created was unique among those that were popular at the time. Portraying a shy, child-like soul in a bewildering and indifferent world, he managed to survive through faith and luck. His sad face and large eyes suggested a boyish sincerity, while his quick hand gestures epitomized his perpetual state of confusion. His early two-reelers reflected little of this innocence. Instead, they depended heavily on mechanical props, stunts, and thrills. His first important short, "Picking Peaches" (1924), showed signs of his superior comic talents.

Langdon's art was a fragile one, needing expert scripts. Fortunately, he had writers such as Frank CAPRA and directors like Harry EDWARDS who understood his screen character. They were more than instrumental in aiding him as he moved from shorts to longer films. All those who worked closely with him while he developed into a star comic knew this, except Langdon himself. When he decided to write and direct his own films, his fortunes turned. His own works showed a steady deterioration in quality and laughs, and by 1928 his releasing company failed to renew his contract.

The sound era was even more unkind to this gentle comic. Hal ROACH signed him for a series of sound comedies that Langdon hoped would restore him to the top echelons of the world of comedy. However, this was not to be. The films failed to generate any excitement. He continued to accept any roles that were offered to him and, in the late 1930s, he resorted to writing comedy material for others. Finally, he was signed by Universal studios in the early 1940s to star in another group of comedy shorts, but the results were disappointing. He continued to appear in routine series comedies, such as the "BOWERY BOYS" films, playing bit parts that gave almost no hint of the unusual talents that were once present in the actor. He died of a cerebral hemorrhage in 1944 at the age of 60, never realizing his dream of a comeback. A study of the comedian's work appears in both Donald W. McCaffrey's *Four Great Comedians: Chaplin, Lloyd, Keaton, Langdon,* published in 1968, and Walter Kerr's *The Silent Clowns,* published in 1975.

SELECTED FILMS: *Picking Peaches, Smile Please, The Cat's Meow, The First Hundred Years, All Night Long, Feet of Mud* (1924), *The Sea Squawk, Boobs in the Woods, Lucky Stars, There He Goes* (1925), *Saturday Afternoon, Fiddlesticks, The Soldier Man, Tramp, Tramp, Tramp, The Strong Man* (1926), *Long Pants, Three's a Crowd* (1927), *The Chaser, Heart Trouble* (1928), *Hotter Than Hot, The Fighting Parson, The Sky Boy, Skirt Shy* (1929), *See America Thirst* (1930), *The King* (1932), *Hallelujah, I'm a Bum, My Weakness* (1933), *Atlantic Adventure* (1935), *There Goes My Heart* (1938), *Zenobia* (1939), *Misbehaving Husbands* (1940), *Double Trouble* (1941), *House of Errors* (1942), *Block Busters, Hot Rhythm* (1944), *Swingin' on a Rainbow* (1945). ∎

Langdon, Sue Anne (1940–), actress. Has appeared on television and in films during the 1960s and 1970s. An effective comedienne, she has had lead roles in several big productions.

SELECTED FILMS: *The Rounders (1965), A Fine Madness (1966), A Guide for the Married Man (1967), The Cheyenne Social Club (1970), Without Warning (1980), Zapped! (1982).* ■

Lange, Hope (1931–), actress. Worked in stock, on Broadway, and in television before entering films in 1956. A pretty blonde and talented comedienne, she has played leads in dramas as well as light films. She has continued to appear on Broadway and in television.

SELECTED FILMS: *Bus Stop (1956), The Best of Everything (1959), Wild in the Country, Pocketful of Miracles (1961), Love Is a Ball (1963), Jigsaw (1968), I Am the Cheese (1983).* ■

Langford, Frances (1914–), actress, singer. Appeared in numerous musicals and comedies during the 1930s and 1940s. An attractive, pert lead and supporting actress who made her film debut in 1935, she has played in major Hollywood productions as well as in routine light films. She had a successful radio career during the 1940s.

In *Born to Dance* (1936) she played a waitress who catches the roving eye of sailor Buddy EBSEN. "I have an inventive mind," he says in an attempt to impress her. "Well," she quips, "most sailors do."

SELECTED FILMS: *Every Night at Eight (1935), Collegiate, Palm Springs (1936), The Hit Parade (1937), Hollywood Hotel (1938), Too Many Girls, Dreaming Out Loud (1940), All-American Co-Ed (1941), Yankee Doodle Dandy (1942), Cowboy in Manhattan, Never a Dull Moment (1943), The Girl Rush (1944), The Bamboo Blonde (1946), Beat the Band (1947), Make Mine Laughs (1949), The Glenn Miller Story (1954).* ■

Lansing, Joi (1928–1972), actress. Worked as a singer before settling in Hollywood in the late 1940s as a supporting player. An attractive, well-proportioned blonde, she appeared in dramas and light films, including several comedy shorts. A second-string sexpot, she played wisecracking blondes, appearing occasionally as the female lead in minor films.

SELECTED FILMS: *Julia Misbehaves, Easter Parade (1948), The Girl From Jones Beach, Neptune's Daughter (1949), On the Riviera, Two Tickets to Broadway (1951), Singin' in the Rain (1952), The French Line (1953), A Hole in the Head, It Started With a Kiss, Who Was That Lady? (1959), Marriage on the Rocks (1965), Hillbillys in a Haunted House (1967), Bigfoot (1969).* ■

Lardner, Ring, Jr. (1915–), screenwriter. Worked as a newspaper reporter and publicity writer before trying his hand at screenwriting. Turning out both dramatic and comic scripts, he won an Oscar in 1942 for his collaboration on *Woman of the Year.* In the late 1940s he received a one-year prison sentence for contempt of Congress when he refused to testify for the House Un-American Activities Committee. Although he continued to submit screenplays, he had to use pseudonyms because of the blacklist imposed by the studios against many artists and craftsmen, including the Hollywood Ten of which he was one. He is the son of the famous humorist.

SELECTED FILMS: *A Star Is Born, Nothing Sacred (1937), Meet Dr. Christian (1939), Arkansas Judge (1941), Marriage Is a Private Affair (1944), Virgin Island (1959), A Breath of Scandal (1960), M*A*S*H (1970), The Greatest (1977).* ■

Lasser, Louise (1941–), actress. Worked in revues and on Broadway before appearing in films with Woody ALLEN, to whom she was married for a brief time. An eccentric comedienne, she works best in broad farce or satire. Unfortunately, some of the films in which she has appeared have her in such minor roles that her capabilities are restricted. She starred in the television series, "Mary Hartman, Mary Hartman."

SELECTED FILMS: What's New, Pussycat? (1965), What's Up, Tiger Lily? (1966), Bananas, Such Good Friends (1971), Everything You Always Wanted to Know About Sex but Were Afraid to Ask (1972), Slither (1973), In God We Trust (1979), Stardust Memories (1980). ∎

Lauck, Chester. See Lum and Abner.

Laughton, Charles (1899–1962), actor. Appeared on stage and in two-reel silent comedies in his native England before entering feature-length films. In 1932 he made his film debut in the United States. His long career as stage and screen actor took him back and forth across the Atlantic many times. Although he was primarily a dramatic actor capable of handling complex roles, his wide range of talent allowed him to portray successfully and poignantly a variety of humorous characters in light films. One of his most hilarious and critically acclaimed roles was that of the English butler, Ruggles, won by an American in a card game. He was married to actress Elsa LANCHESTER.

In It Started With Eve he played an eccentric millionaire who has just recovered from a serious illness. Noticing his loss of weight, he comments: "I've been tampered with."

SELECTED FILMS: Devil and the Deep, If I Had a Million (1932), Ruggles of Red Gap (1935), They Knew What They Wanted (1940), It Started With Eve (1941), The Tuttles of Tahiti, Tales of Manhattan (1942), The Canterville Ghost (1944), Captain Kidd (1945), The Girl From Manhattan (1948), Abbott and Costello Meet Captain Kidd (1952), Advise and Consent (1962). ∎

Laughton, Eddie (1903–1952), actor. Worked chiefly in comedy shorts during the 1930s and 1940s as a supporting player. He appeared in a variety of roles in many of the THREE STOOGES' films.

SELECTED FILMS: Three Little Beers (1935), Movie Maniacs, Half-Shot Shooters, Disorder in the Court, A Pain in the Pullman, False Alarms, Whoops I'm an Indian, Slippery Silks (1936), Three Dumb Clucks, Goofs and Saddles, Cash and Carry (1937), We Want Our Mummy, Oily to Bed, Oily to Rise, Three Sappy People (1939), You Nazty Spy, A-Plumbing We Will Go, Boobs in Arms (1940), So Long, Mr. Chumps, Dutiful but Dumb, In the Sweet Pie and Pie (1941), Loco Boy Makes Good, Cactus Makes Perfect (1942), They Stooge to Conga (1943), Busy Buddies, Idle Roomers (1944). ∎

Laurel, Stan (1890–1965), actor, comic. Performed in plays and in music halls in his native England from age 16. Born Arthur Stanley Jefferson, he joined the Fred KARNO troupe in 1910, appearing in sketches with other members, including Charlie CHAPLIN. He toured the United States with the Karno company, then signed on with different American vaudeville circuits. He was hired by Universal in 1917 to star as HICKORY HIRAM in a series of comedy shorts. When the studio failed to renew his contract, he returned to vaudeville for a brief time. Eventually, he found himself back in silent films, working for various studios. He appeared in comedy spoofs of popular features, often writing his own material and sometimes directing. A talented pantomimist with an uncanny ability to improvise, he nevertheless became bogged down in routine comic roles similar to those of dozens of other comics. As a solo funnyman, he was not advancing his career as rapidly as other comedians around him. After signing a contract with Hal ROACH in 1926 to work as a gagman and occasional director, Stan drifted back into acting, appearing in comedies with Oliver HARDY, although they were not yet a formal team. With shorts like "Slipping Wives" and "Love 'Em and Weep," the legendary pair had each developed his individual character and interplay that were to make them one of the most successful comedy teams in film history. For films with Oliver HARDY, see LAUREL AND HARDY.

SELECTED FILMS: Nuts in May (1917), Hickory Hiram, Huns and Hyphens, Frauds and Frenzies, It's Great to Be Crazy (1918), Hoot Man, Lucky Dog, Scars and Stripes (1919), Make It Snappy (1921), Week End Party, Mud and Sand, The Pest (1922), Under Two Jags, Collars and Cuffs, Kill or Cure, Man About Town, Roughest Africa, The Soilers, Searching Sands (1923), The Smithy, Rupert of Hee-Haw, Wide Open Spaces, West of Hot Dog (1924), Twins, Snow Hawk, Dr. Pickle and Mr. Pride (1925), On the Front Page (1926). ∎

Stan Laurel and Oliver Hardy

Laurel and Hardy. One of the most popular comedy teams in film history. Stan LAUREL and Oliver HARDY each appeared in early silent films. In fact, they appeared in the same comedy short, "Lucky Dog," in 1919, but not as a team. That fateful match was to come years later when both were employed by Hal ROACH. Always on the lookout for potential stars as well as for new and funny

combinations, Roach introduced a series of films called the "Comedy All Stars." Each short would feature a number of comics from his troupe, including Stan and Ollie. After a few entries, the boys started to interact favorably with each other, and, by 1927, with the film "Putting Pants on Philip," they became a bona fide team, according to many film historians.

Their first films together were remarkable for their overall quality. Just as Chaplin made his famous "Golden Dozen" for the Mutual studio, L&H turned out a string of 23 consistently funny two-reelers for Roach during the 1928–1929 season. The boys were at their peak. Their characters were firmly established. Ollie played the pretentious surrogate father, well-bred and civil. Imagining himself the more intelligent member of the team, he would take control of a situation. His failure, therefore, was all the more hilarious because of his misguided arrogance. He demonstrated his frustration to the audience through two of his most popular characteristics—by his playing nervously with his tie and his stare into the camera lens. Complementing him was the mischievous, child-like Stan; rash and unreliable, unable to cope with everyday problems, he quickly resorted to whimpering and to his famous trademark, scratching his head. Their many fans were quick to laugh at the antics of these half-wits, feeling they were infinitely smarter than the pair of bunglers on the screen. Using simple plots, L&H proceeded to expand a solitary idea into a funny gag. Incidents dominated over plot structure, and visuals prevailed over dialogue. Relatively harmless situations swelled into near disaster as the duo tried to set things right.

They made a smooth transition into sound films, starring in their first feature-length work, Pardon Us, in 1931. After leaving Roach in 1940, they had problems adjusting to other studios that required rigid schedules, formal scripts, and exact directions. They had come from an environment that afforded them relatively more freedom; they were able to improvise when necessary and to shoot their films in sequence. The quality of their later work reflected these new restraints.

In the 1950s Roach offered the team a chance to make a filmed series for television, but Hardy died in 1957. Laurel lived long enough to witness a revival of the L&H films and a new generation of admirers. He died in 1965. The team had made more than 100 films together, of which 27 were features. Their short, "The Music Box" (1932), won them an Academy Award. William K. Everson's study of the team, *The Films of Laurel and Hardy*, was published in 1967, followed by Charles Barr's *Laurel and Hardy* in 1968.

SELECTED FILMS: *Duck Soup, With Love and Hisses, Sailors Beware!, Do Detectives Think?, Sugar Daddies, The Battle of the Century (1927), From Soup to Nuts, Two Tars (1928), Big Business (1929), Brats, Another Fine Mess (1930), Laughing Gravy, Our Wife (1931), County Hospital, Pack Up Your Troubles (1932), Busy Bodies, Dirty Work, Sons of the Desert (1933), Them Thar Hills, Babes in Toyland (1934), Tit for Tat (1935), Our Relations (1936), Way Out West (1937), Swiss Miss, Block-Heads (1938), The Flying Deuces (1939), A Chump at Oxford, Saps at Sea (1940), Great Guns (1941), A-Haunting We Will Go (1942), Air Raid Wardens, Jitterbugs, The Dancing Masters (1943), The Big Noise (1944), Nothing but Trouble, The Bullfighters (1945), Atoll K (1950).* ∎

Lawford, Peter (1923–1984), actor. Appeared sporadically in films from the age of eight. His Hollywood career as a popular actor began in the 1940s when he began appearing in light romantic films and musicals at MGM. Blessed with a charming personality and good looks, he co-starred in many films with some of the leading actors and actresses of the 1940s and 1950s. He was a member of the famous "rat pack," which in-

cluded, among other Hollywood personalities, Frank SINATRA, Sammy DAVIS, Jr., and Joey BISHOP.

In *Buona Sera, Mrs. Campbell* he portrayed a World War II veteran who returns with his wife to the Italian town in which he had spent part of the war. Moments after they exit from the bus, his wife experiences her first brush with Italian customs. "Oh!" she exclaims. "I just had my bottom pinched!" "Welcome to Southern Italy," says Lawford jokingly. "Do I acknowledge it in any way?" she asks. "Just turn the other cheek," he replies.

SELECTED FILMS: *Lord Jeff (1938), Girl Crazy (1943), The Canterville Ghost (1944), Cluny Brown, Two Sisters From Boston (1946), It Happened in Brooklyn, My Brother Talks to Horses, Good News (1947), Easter Parade, Julia Misbehaves (1948), Please Believe Me (1950), Just This Once (1952), It Should Happen to You (1954), Pepe (1960), Skidoo (1968), Buona Sera, Mrs. Campbell, Hook, Line and Sinker, The April Fools (1969), One More Time (1970), Seven From Heaven (1979).* ∎

Lawrence, Barbara (1928–), actress. Worked as a child model before entering films. Although she has appeared chiefly as a supporting player in light comedies and musicals, she has at times played leads. She frequently portrayed wisecracking confidantes of leading actresses.

SELECTED FILMS: *Diamond Horseshoe (1945), Margie (1946), You Were Meant for Me, Give My Regards to Broadway, Unfaithfully Yours (1948), Mother Is a Freshman (1949), Peggy (1950), Two Tickets to Broadway (1951), Her Twelve Men (1954), Oklahoma! (1955), Man in the Shadow (1957).* ∎

Lawrence, Florence (1886–1938), actress. Worked in early silent films for the BIOGRAPH studios. One of D. W. Griffith's earliest stars, she appeared in dramas and light films, moving to the IMP studio in 1910. She was known as "The

Biograph Girl" and, later, as "The IMP Girl." Traditionally, early film companies refrained from releasing the names of their stars for fear of having to pay out more money. However, Florence Lawrence was the first actress to be known to her audiences by her name. Her popularity declined sharply by the mid-1920s. With the advent of sound, she was relegated to minor roles.

SELECTED FILMS: *Romeo and Juliette, A Smoked Husband, The Taming of the Shrew* (1908), *Mrs. Jones Entertains, The Joneses Have Amateur Theatricals, At the Altar* (1909), *A Good Turn, The Slavey's Affinity* (1911), *After All, All for Love, The Advent of Jane, Flo's Discipline* (1912), *A Singular Cynic* (1914), *The Satin Girl* (1923), *Gambling Wives* (1924). ∎

Lawrence, Marc (1910–), actor. Appeared on stage before he decided to settle in Hollywood. Dark-complexioned and sinister-looking, he was soon typecast as an underworld character, a role that he repeated in numerous films and that he is best identified with. Later in his film career, however, he self-parodied the part in several comedies, especially those starring Bob HOPE and ABBOTT AND COSTELLO. He continued playing character roles through the 1970s.

SELECTED FILMS: *White Woman* (1933), *Beware, Spooks, The Housekeeper's Daughter* (1939), *Hold That Ghost* (1941), *Calaboose, Hit the Ice* (1943), *Rainbow Island, The Princess and the Pirate* (1944), *Abbott and Costello in the Foreign Legion* (1950), *My Favorite Spy* (1951), *Frazier—the Sensuous Lion* (1973), *A Piece of the Action* (1977), *Foul Play, Goin' Coconuts* (1978), *Swap Meet* (1979). ∎

Leachman, Cloris (1926–), actress. Worked in television before entering films in the mid-1950s. An attractive blonde-haired performer brimming with talent, she has appeared in dramas and light films with equal success. She won an Oscar for her role in *The Last Picture Show* (1971).

SELECTED FILMS: *Kiss Me Deadly* (1955), *Butch Cassidy and the Sundance Kid* (1969), *Lovers and Other Strangers* (1970), *The Steagle* (1971), *Young Frankenstein* (1974), *High Anxiety* (1977), *The Muppet Movie, The North Avenue Irregulars* (1978), *Herbie Goes Bananas* (1980), *History of the World—Part 1* (1981). ∎

Lear, Norman (1922–), screenwriter, producer. Worked in early television as a comedy writer before entering films as a screenwriter and occasional producer. He collaborated with director Bud YORKIN on a series of light comedies. His films, which often dealt with contemporary social themes, were not as popular as his television shows, which, ironically, touched upon similar subject matter.

SELECTED FILMS: *Come Blow Your Horn* (1963), *Divorce, American Style* (1967), *Cold Turkey* (1971). ∎

Lebedoff, Ivan (1895–1953), actor. Appeared in films in Germany and France during the 1920s after emigrating from Russia. Settling in Hollywood in 1925, he played character roles in numerous dramas and light films, frequently as foreign gigolos or reprobates. He occasionally wrote screenplays and in 1940 published a novel, *Legion of Dishonor*. His screen career spanned four decades.

SELECTED FILMS: *The Sorrows of Satan* (1926), *Angel of Broadway* (1927), *Let 'Er Go Gallagher* (1928), *The One Woman Idea, They Had to See Paris* (1929), *The Cuckoos* (1930), *Bachelor Apartment, The Gay Diplomat* (1931), *Made on Broadway, Laughing at Life, Bombshell* (1933), *Kansas City Princess* (1934), *Goin' to Town* (1935), *Pepper* (1936), *Straight, Place and Show* (1938), *You Can't Cheat an Honest Man* (1939), *Public Deb No. 1* (1940), *The Snows of Kilimanjaro* (1952). ∎

Lederer, Charles (1910–1976), screenwriter. Worked as a journalist before turning to screenwriting in 1931. Writing alone or in collaboration (often with his close friend, Ben HECHT), he specialized in light comedies and musicals. One of his recurrent themes was cutting the pompous down to size, whether through the use of witty repartee or inventive spitefulness, e.g., Cary Grant's treatment of Ralph Bellamy in *His Girl Friday*.

SELECTED FILMS: *The Front Page* (1931), *Cock of the Air* (1932), *Topaze* (1933), *Mountain Music, Double or Nothing* (1937), *Broadway Serenade* (1939), *His Girl Friday, I Love You Again, Comrade X* (1940), *Love Crazy* (1941), *Slightly Dangerous, The Youngest Profession* (1943), *Her Husband's Affairs* (1947), *I Was a Male War Bride* (1949), *Wabash Avenue* (1950), *Fearless Fagan, Monkey Business* (1952), *Gentlemen Prefer Blondes* (1953), *Kismet* (1955), *Gaby* (1956), *It Started With a Kiss* (1959), *Can-Can, Ocean's 11* (1960), *Follow That Dream* (1962), *A Global Affair* (1964). ∎

Lee, Doris, actress. Entered early silent films in the 1910s. She appeared as the female lead in dramas and light films, chiefly for Paramount.

SELECTED FILMS: *His Mother's Boy* (1917), *The Hired Man* (1918), *The Girl Dodger, Hay Foot, Straw Foot* (1919). ∎

Lee, Dorothy (1911–), actress. Began her film career while still in her teens, appearing in early sound comedies. A lively and pretty actress with plenty of charm but little acting experience and a flat speaking voice, she appeared as ingenue, foil, and love interest in many of WHEELER AND WOOLSEY'S madcap romps.

SELECTED FILMS: *Rio Rita* (1929), *The Cuckoos, Dixiana, Half Shot at Sunrise, Hook, Line and Sinker* (1930), *Cracked Nuts, Caught Plastered, Peach O'Reno* (1931), *Girl Crazy* (1932), *Take a Chance* (1933), *Hips, Hips, Hooray!, Cockeyed Cavaliers* (1934), *The Rainmakers* (1935), *Silly Billies* (1936), *Twelve Crowded Hours* (1937). ∎

Lee, Gwen (1904–1961), actress. Appeared in silent and early sound films as a supporting actress, chiefly in light films. A buoyant blonde and natural performer, she added spice to several features from 1925 to 1933.

SELECTED FILMS: *His Secretary* (1925), *Upstage* (1926), *Orchids and Ermine* (1927), *Sharp Shooters, Her Wild Oat, Show Girl* (1928), *Lucky Boy, The Man and the Moment* (1929), *Lord Byron of Broadway, Free and Easy, Extravagance* (1930), *Inspiration, Traveling Husbands* (1931), *Corruption* (1933). ∎

Lee, Gypsy Rose (1913–1970), stripper, entertainer, actress. Appeared in vaudeville and as burlesque queen in the 1930s before entering films. She played in light vehicles which gave only a hint of her true talents. Her autobiography, *Gypsy*, was published in 1957 and became the basis for the Broadway musical and film (1962) of the same name.

SELECTED FILMS: *You Can't Have Everything, Ali Baba Goes to Town* (1937), *Sally, Irene and Mary, The Battle of Broadway, My Lucky Star* (1938), *Stage Door Canteen* (1943), *Babes in Bagdad* (1952), *The Trouble With Angels* (1966). ∎

Lee, Lila (1901–1973), actress. Worked in vaudeville as a child before entering silent films at age 17. A talented performer who became extremely popular in the 1920s, she made a smooth transition into sound features, continuing well into the 1930s. She appeared in dramas as well as light films, often portraying prudish characters. She worked with some of the leading screen stars of the period, including such diverse personalities as Rudolph Valentino and OLSEN AND JOHNSON. She left Hollywood in 1937 to appear on stage.

SELECTED FILMS: The Cruise of the Make-Believe, Such a Little Pirate (1918), The Lottery Man, Puppy Love (1919), Midsummer Madness (1920), The Charm School, Crazy to Marry, Gasoline Gus (1921), One Glorious Day (1922), The Ne'er-Do-Well, Woman-Proof (1923), Just Married, The Adorable Cheat, The Little Wild Girl (1928), Love, Live and Laugh (1929), Misbehaving Ladies (1931), In Love With Life (1934), Country Gentlemen, Two Wise Maids (1937). ∎

Lee, Pinky (1916–), comedian, actor. Worked in stage revues, burlesque, nightclubs, and television in the early 1950s. A zany, wide-eyed comic with a lisp, he appeared in several films as well. His stage and television popularity did not follow him to the screen. In the late 1960s he was back on stage, touring with a show.

SELECTED FILMS: Earl Carroll's Vanities (1945). ∎

Lee, Winifred. See Minna Gombel.

Leeds, Herbert I. (1900–1954), director. Began his film career as an editor in the 1930s. By 1917 he began directing dramas and comedies. Although his output consisted chiefly of B films, he crafted them with skill and care, making them highly entertaining.

SELECTED FILMS: Love on a Budget, Keep Smiling, Five of a Kind (1938), Chicken Wagon Family (1939), Blue, White and Perfect (1941), Just Off Broadway (1942), It Shouldn't Happen to a Dog (1946), Let's Live Again (1948), Father's Wild Game (1950). ∎

Lees, Robert, screenwriter. Wrote screenplays, chiefly in collaboration, during the 1940s and 1950s. He specialized in comedy, contributing scripts for some of the foremost comedy teams of the period, including OLSEN AND JOHNSON, ABBOTT AND COSTELLO, and MARTIN AND LEWIS.

SELECTED FILMS: Street of Memories (1940), Bachelor Daddy, Hold That Ghost (1941), Juke Box Jenny (1942), Crazy House, Hit the Ice (1943), Buck Privates Come Home (1947), Abbott and Costello Meet Frankenstein (1948), Holiday in Mexico (1949), Abbott and Costello Meet the Invisible Man, Comin' Round the Mountain (1951), Jumping Jacks (1952). ∎

Lehman, Gladys, screenwriter. Wrote screenplays for Hollywood films from the late silent period until the early 1950s. Writing alone and in collaboration, she turned out dozens of dramas and light films. She was equally adept at farce and sophisticated comedy and at low-brow material.

SELECTED FILMS: Out All Night (1927), Broadway Hoofer, The Fall of Eve (1929), A Lady Surrenders, The Little Accident, Embarrassing Moments (1930), Strictly Dishonorable (1931), They Just Had to Get Married (1932), Enter Madame, Little Miss Marker (1934), The County Chairman (1935), Captain January (1936), The Lady Objects (1938), Good Girls Go to Paris (1939), Hired Wife (1940), Her Highness and the Bellboy (1945), Golden Girl (1951). ∎

Lehrman, Henry (1886–1946), director. Began his career in films in 1909 as an actor for BIOGRAPH studios. He quickly demonstrated an affinity for comedy and was assigned to Mack SENNETT'S unit. When Sennett left Biograph in 1912 to produce comedies for KEYSTONE studios, Lehrman joined him, acting in and directing many comedy shorts. When Ford STERLING, a popular comic in Sennett's stable of clowns, left Keystone over a salary dispute and signed with Universal, Lehrman went with him. But the venture proved unsuccessful, and Sterling returned to his old studio. Lehrman then opened his own studio, L-KO, where he made comedies much in the style of his former employer. His Lehrman Knock-

Out Comedies continued until 1917, at which time he joined the Fox studio to direct the Sunshine Comedies. He directed films well into the 1920s, and, with the advent of sound, tried his hand at screenwriting, the results of which include *The Poor Millionaire* (1930), *Moulin Rouge* (1934), and *Show Them No Mercy* (1935). He decided to leave the world of films in the mid-1930s. During his career in the frenetic surroundings of film comedy, he was privileged to have taken part in some historic moments. He directed the first four films of Charlie CHAPLIN, and he worked with some of the true pioneers of American comedy.

SELECTED FILMS: *Algy the Watchman* (1912), *Cupid in a Dental Parlor, The Peddler, Just Kids, Fatty at San Diego, The Champion* (1913), *Making a Living, Kid Auto Races at Venice, Mabel's Strange Predicament* (1915), *Who's Your Father?, The Fatal Marriage* (1918), *Double Dealing* (1923), *On Time* (1924), *For Ladies Only, Private Izzy Murphy* (1927), *Husbands for Rent, Why Sailors Go Wrong, Chicken a la King, Homesick* (1928), *New Year's Eve* (1929). ∎

Leibman, Ron (1937–), actor. Worked on stage and in television before entering films during the 1970s. Often portraying unconventional characters, he has appeared in dramas and light films, the latter of which seem to be his specialty. He has played leads and supporting roles.

SELECTED FILMS: *Where's Poppa?* (1970), *The Hot Rock, Slaughterhouse-Five* (1972), *Your Three Minutes Are Up* (1973), *The Super Cops* (1974), *Won Ton Ton, the Dog Who Saved Hollywood* (1976), *Norma Rae* (1979), *Up the Academy* (1980), *Zorro, the Gay Blade* (1981), *Romantic Comedy* (1983), *Door to Door, Rhinestone* (1984). ∎

Leigh, Janet (1927–), actress. First appeared in films in the late 1940s in ingenue roles. As she developed her acting talents, she received better parts and

more critical acclaim. She has been featured in dramas and light films, but her forte seems to be comedy. Her most famous role was that of Norman Bates' victim in *Psycho* (1960). Her autobiography, *There Really Was a Hollywood*, was published in 1984.

SELECTED FILMS: *The Romance of Rosy Ridge* (1947), *Words and Music* (1948), *The Doctor and the Girl, Holiday Affair* (1949), *Strictly Dishonorable, Angels in the Outfield, Two Tickets to Broadway* (1951), *Just This Once, Fearless Fagan* (1952), *Confidentially Connie* (1953), *Living It Up* (1954), *My Sister Eileen* (1955), *The Perfect Furlough* (1959), *Who Was That Lady?, Pepe* (1960), *Bye, Bye Birdie* (1963), *Three on a Couch* (1966), *The Fog* (1979). ∎

Leisen, Mitchell (1898–1972), director. Began his film career during the early silent years in Hollywood as a costume designer for C. B. DeMille and other important directors. By the mid-1920s he advanced to art director, designing sets for some of DeMille's major productions. With the advent of sound he turned to directing, embellishing the sets of his films with his own singular style. Such films as *Death Takes a Holiday* (1934) with its ornate mansion, *Easy Living* (1937) with its posh hotel suites, *Midnight* (1939) with its lavish country estate, and *Remember the Night* (1940) reflected his artistic bent in turning out works that were both entertaining and visually radiant.

Employed chiefly by Paramount studios, he was forced to compete against such distinguished directors as Ernst LUBITSCH, Preston STURGES, and Billy WILDER. Unfortunately, he often lost out to his colleagues and was handed scripts of lower quality. It was to his credit and because of his gift for pictorial style that many of these secondary works contain the charm and sparkle they do.

SELECTED FILMS: *Cradle Song* (1933), *Behold My Wife, Hands Across the Table* (1935), *Artists and Models Abroad* (1938), *The Lady Is Willing,*

Take a Letter, Darling (1942), No Time for Love (1943), Lady in the Dark, Practically Yours (1944), Kitty, Masquerade in Mexico (1945), Dream Girl (1948), Captain Carey, USA (1950), The Mating Season, Darling, How Could You!, Young Man With Ideas (1951), The Girl Most Likely (1957), Spree (1967). ■

Lembeck, Harvey (1923–1982), actor. Worked on stage and in television as well as in films. Scoring a hit in the stage version of *Stalag 17*, he went to Hollywood to repeat his role as comic relief in the film version (1953). He appeared chiefly as a light character actor in comedies and war dramas.

SELECTED FILMS: You're in the Navy Now, The Frogmen (1951), Willie and Joe Back Up Front (1952), Mission Over Korea (1953), Sail a Crooked Ship (1961), Beach Party (1963), Bikini Beach, The Unsinkable Molly Brown (1964), Beach Blanket Bingo (1965), Ghost in the Invisible Bikini (1966). ■

Jack Lemmon and Walter Matthau

Lemmon, Jack (1925–), actor. Began his show business career playing piano, acting on radio, on the stage, and in television. He appeared on Broadway before entering films, and, with his Oscar-winning role as the lecherous Ensign Pulver in *Mister Roberts* (1955), he emerged as one of Hollywood's leading comic actors. He won another Academy Award as Best Actor for his role in *Save the Tiger* (1973).

His acting talents have allowed him to successfully portray a wide gamut of roles in serious dramas as well as a wide range of comedic styles. In *Bell, Book and Candle*, for example, he played an impish warlock who enjoys switching traffic lights and turning off street lamps. In *The Apartment* he portrayed an office employee who allows his flat to be used by his superiors for their illicit romances. In *The Fortune Cookie* he was an accident victim who is exploited by his brother-in-law (Walter Matthau), a shyster lawyer. And in *The Out-of-Towners* he and Sandy Dennis played two unfortunates in New York City who face a variety of misfortunes.

His comedies often cast him as a sincere, self-effacing middle-class character caught up in an unsympathetic, dehumanized society—a role he effectively underplays. He can portray a character in pain, which produces a certain tension in his comic roles. His style may appear natural, but this is the result of his craft. His association with director Billy WILDER has been a fortuitous one for both parties, resulting in seven highly entertaining and very popular comedies. He has often been teamed with Walter MATTHAU. M. Freedland wrote a biography titled *Lemmon* (1985).

In *Some Like It Hot* he watches Marilyn Monroe's sensual movements as she walks past him to board a train. "Look how she moves," he remarks. "That's just like jello with springs."

SELECTED FILMS: It Should Happen to You, Phffft (1954), Three for the Show, My Sister Eileen (1955), You Can't Run Away From It (1956), Operation Mad Ball (1957), Bell, Book and Candle, Some Like It Hot, It Happened to Jane (1959), The Apartment, Pepe, The Wackiest Ship in the Army (1960), The Notorious Landlady (1962), Irma La Douce, Under the Yum Yum Tree (1963), Good Neighbor Sam (1964), How to Murder Your Wife, The Great Race (1965), The Fortune Cookie (1966), Luv (1967), The Odd Couple (1968), The April Fools (1969), The Out-of-Towners (1970), The

War Between Men and Women, Avanti! (1972), The Front Page (1974), The Prisoner of Second Avenue (1975), The Entertainer, Alex and the Gypsy (1976), Buddy Buddy (1981), Mass Appeal (1985), That's Life! (1986). ■

Lennart, Isobel (1915–1971), screenwriter. Began her Hollywood writing career in the 1940s. She specialized in light romantic comedies and musicals, some of which she wrote in collaboration. She adapted her successful Broadway musical, Funny Girl (1964), into a hit movie in 1968. Her films starred many of the leading personalities of the period, including, among others, Frank SINATRA, Walter Pidgeon, Jane POWELL, Kathryn Grayson, Jimmy DURANTE, Janet LEIGH, Jane FONDA, and Danny KAYE. Her scripts ranged from fast-paced slapstick (This Could Be the Night) to heartwarming comedy (Period of Adjustment).

SELECTED FILMS: Once Upon a Thursday (1942), Anchors Aweigh (1945), Holiday in Mexico (1946), It Happened in Brooklyn (1947), The Kissing Bandit (1948), Holiday Affair (1949), A Life of Her Own (1950), Skirts Ahoy! (1952), Latin Lovers (1953), Meet Me in Las Vegas (1956), This Could Be the Night (1957), Merry Andrew, The Inn of the Sixth Happiness (1958), Please Don't Eat the Daisies (1960), Period of Adjustment, Two for the Seesaw (1962), Fitzwilly (1967). ■

Lenz, Rick (1939–), actor. Began his film career in 1970 as a supporting actor. He has appeared chiefly in light films, occasionally with some of the leading comedy performers of the period, including Walter MATTHAU and Goldie HAWN.

SELECTED FILMS: Cactus Flower (1970), Where Does It Hurt? (1972), The Little Dragons, Melvin and Howard (1980). ■

Leonard, Gus (1856–1939), actor. Worked in early silent comedy shorts as a supporting player. He appeared in a few Harold LLOYD comedies. His relatively short screen career spanned the years 1915–1932.

SELECTED FILMS: Bumping Into Broadway (1919), His Royal Slyness (1920), Grandma's Boy (1922), The Girl I Loved, When a Feller Needs a Friend (1932). ■

Leonard, Jack E. (1911–1975), comedian, actor. Worked in vaudeville, toured as a comic with big bands, and appeared as a guest on numerous major television shows. A corpulent figure with horn-rimmed glasses, he appeared in several films. But his forte was stand-up comedy with a live audience whose members he insulted at random, thereby paving the way for other comics like Don RICKLES. He depended on the wisecrack and one-liners.

SELECTED FILMS: Three Sailors and a Girl (1953), The Disorderly Orderly (1964). ■

Leonard, Robert Z. (1889–1968), director. Appeared on stage and in silent films before turning his attentions to directing in 1914. For more than 40 years he turned out a wide range of films, from dramas to musicals. An expert at his craft with no pretenses at art, he directed well-constructed, pleasing films for different studios. His early work at Universal during the World War I period included several comedies. He produced several of his own films.

SELECTED FILMS: The Master Key (1914), The Love Girl, Little Eve Edgarton (1916), Danger Go Slow (1918), The Delicious Little Devil (1919), The Gilded Lily (1921), Broadway Rose (1922), Cheaper to Marry (1925), Tea for Three (1927), Marianne (1929), In Gay Madrid (1930), The Bachelor Father (1931), Piccadilly Jim (1936), Broadway Serenade (1939), Pride and Prejudice, Third Finger, Left Hand (1940), When

Ladies Meet (1941), Marriage Is a Private Affair (1944), Weekend at the Waldorf (1945), Nancy Goes to Rio, Duchess of Idaho, Grounds for Marriage (1950), The Clown (1953), Her Twelve Men (1954), Kelly and Me (1956). ∎

Leonard, Sheldon (1907–), actor. Worked in the theater before entering films in 1939, chiefly as a character actor in melodramas and comedy-mysteries. Portraying underworld characters in the Runyon style, he was blessed with names like Lefty, Louie, Slip, Jinx, and Harry the Horse. He enhanced more than 50 melodramas and light films, many of which were B movies, with his tough talk from the side of his mouth, his Brooklyn accent, and his sinister countenance. His self-parodies were more entertaining than his serious attempts at tough-guy roles. In Lucky Jordan (1942) he prepares to rub out Alan Ladd. "I'm going to do you one favor, just for old times' sake," he quips sardonically. "Where do you want it—in the front or in the back?"

SELECTED FILMS: Another Thin Man (1939), Week-End in Havana, Rise and Shine (1941), Pierre of the Plains (1942), Klondike Kate, Hit the Ice (1943), The Falcon in Hollywood, To Have and Have Not (1944), Why Girls Leave Home, Zombies on Broadway (1945), The Gentleman Misbehaves, It's a Wonderful Life, Rainbow Over Texas (1946), Sinbad the Sailor (1947), If You Knew Susie, Jinx Money (1948), My Dream Is Yours (1949), Abbott and Costello Meet the Invisible Man, Behave Yourself! (1951), Stop, You're Killing Me (1952), Money From Home (1953), Guys and Dolls (1955), Pocketful of Miracles (1961). ∎

LeRoy, Mervyn (1900–), director. Worked in vaudeville, as an assistant cameraman in Hollywood, and as a minor actor before turning his attentions to directing in 1927. He rapidly emerged as one of the major directors of the 1930s, especially at Warner Brothers where he turned out worthy social dramas. But he was also gifted in comedy and directed several entertaining films for different studios. Although a flawed director in some respects—his characterizations are often weak while his serious films frequently betray a lack of substance—he has produced several works that rank among the best to come out of Hollywood.

SELECTED FILMS: No Place to Go (1927), Flying Romeos, Harold Teen, Oh, Kay! (1928), Naughty Baby, Hot Stuff, Broadway Babies (1929), Playing Around (1930), Too Young to Marry, Broad Minded, Tonight or Never (1931), Elmer the Great, Gold Diggers of 1933, Tugboat Annie (1933), Hi, Nellie! (1934), Three Men on a Horse (1936), The King and the Chorus Girl (1937), Fools for Scandal (1938), Without Reservations (1946), Million Dollar Mermaid (1952), No Time for Sergeants (1958), A Majority of One, Gypsy (1962), Mary, Mary (1963), Moment to Moment (1965). ∎

Let's Do It Again (1975), WB. Dir. Sidney Poitier; Sc. Richard Wesley; with Sidney Poitier, Bill Cosby, Jimmie Walker, Calvin Lockhart.

Combining elements of the boxing and gambling worlds and hypnotism, director Sidney POITIER put together a sequel to Uptown Saturday Night (1974), also directed by Poitier, that is funnier than the original. Poitier and Bill Cosby return as the personable, ne'er-do-well lodge brothers who hypnotize the underweight Jimmie Walker in an effort to transform him into a champion prizefighter. Underworld hoods John Amos and Calvin Lockhart intervene for a piece of the action. In the 1970s a succession of black films emerged from Hollywood. They emulated the popular genres but employed black actors and directors, including Gordon Parks, Ossie Davis, and Poitier. Richard Roundtree starred in the three "Shaft" entries about the action-packed adventures of a private detective; William Marshall portrayed the title character in Blacula (1972), a black version of Dracula;

Godfrey Cambridge and Raymond St. Jacques starred as two cops in the 1970 comedy-drama *Cotton Comes to Harlem;* and Sidney Poitier and Harry Belafonte were featured in *Buck and the Preacher* (1972), a western comedy.

Levant, Oscar (1906–1972), pianist, actor. Taught piano, played at clubs and with dance bands while studying music, appeared on radio, toured in concerts, and made several recordings. Both scholarly and musically gifted, he entertained his radio audiences with his knowledge of classical music. He entered films as a bit player and contributed musical film scores, eventually working under George Gershwin. His witty radio personality landed him supporting roles in a series of light films in which he played waspish, humorous, and neurotic characters. His neuroses, however, were real and led him to psychoanalysis, which helped little. Whenever he appeared in person, his nervousness and anxieties were apparent.

SELECTED FILMS: *The Dance of Life* (1929), *Rhythm on the River* (1940), *Kiss the Boys Goodbye* (1941), *You Were Meant for Me, Romance on the High Seas* (1948), *The Barkleys of Broadway* (1949), *An American in Paris* (1951), *O. Henry's Full House* (1952), *The I Don't Care Girl, The Band Wagon* (1953), *The Cobweb* (1955). ∎

Levene, Sam (1907–1980), actor. Worked in theater before entering films in the mid-1930s. As a supporting actor, he often portrayed hard-boiled urban characters with a heart. He appeared in light films as well as melodramas, almost invariably in sympathetic roles or as comic relief.

In *Shadow of the Thin Man* he played a wise-cracking detective, one of his typical roles. He arrives at the scene of a murder and finds a suspect, a gun, and a corpse in the same room. About to book the suspect for murder, the man objects that the gun has not been fired. "So it hasn't been fired," Levene remarks, sniffing the barrel of the weapon. "It must be using a new perfume—black powder."

SELECTED FILMS: *Three Men on a Horse, After the Thin Man* (1936), *The Shopworn Angel, The Mad Miss Manton* (1938), *Shadow of the Thin Man, The Big Street* (1942), *I Dood It* (1943), *Whistling in Brooklyn* (1944), *Three Sailors and a Girl* (1953), *The Opposite Sex* (1956), *Designing Woman* (1957), *Such Good Friends* (1971), *God Told Me To* (1976), *. . . And Justice for All* (1979). ∎

Levin, Henry (1909–1980), director. Began his career as a Hollywood director in the 1940s. He turned out numerous light films over a period of four decades, many of which were quite entertaining and highly successful at the box office.

SELECTED FILMS: *Sergeant Mike* (1944), *Dancing in Manhattan, I Love a Mystery* (1945), *The Mating of Millie* (1948), *Mr. Soft Touch* (1949), *And Baby Makes Three, The Petty Girl* (1950), *Belles on Their Toes* (1952), *The President's Lady, The Farmer Takes a Wife, Mister Scoutmaster* (1953), *The Remarkable Mr. Pennypacker* (1959), *Where the Boys Are* (1960), *Come Fly With Me* (1963), *Honeymoon Hotel* (1964), *Run for the Roses* (1978). ∎

Lewin, Albert (1894–1968), director, screenwriter. Taught college English, worked as a film and drama critic, and served as a script reader for several studios and directors before becoming a screenwriter in the mid-1920s for MGM, turning out chiefly comedies. He continued in this capacity into the 1960s, alternating occasionally at producing and directing dramatic films for which he also wrote the scripts.

SELECTED FILMS (as screenwriter): *Bread* (1924), *The Fate of a Flirt* (1925), *Blarney, Tin Hats* (1926), *Spring Fever* (1927), *Call Me Mister, Alice in Wonderland* (1951), *Down Among the Sheltering Palms* (1953), *Boy, Did I Get a Wrong Number!* (1966), *The Wicked Dreams of Paula Schultz* (1968). ∎

Lewis, George, actor. Appeared in silent film comedies, especially during the 1920s. He reached the peak of his movie career as the star of a series of college comedy-dramas initiated in 1926 by Universal studios. Titled "The Collegians," the shorts, which co-starred Dorothy GULLIVER, revolved around Lewis' portrayal of a rural innocent winning a college scholarship and discovering the various activities of campus life. He stayed with the series until its completion in 1929. He later played character roles during the sound era.

SELECTED FILMS: *Proud Heart* (1925), *Benson at Calford, Around the Bases* (1926), *The Fourflusher, We Americans, Give and Take* (1928), *College Love* (1929), *Lazy River* (1934), *Lulu Belle, When My Baby Smiles at Me* (1948), *Captain Carey, USA* (1950), *Drum Beat* (1954). ∎

Lewis, Jerry (1926–), actor, director. Worked as a child entertainer with his show business parents and as a solo comic at summer resorts. Born Joseph Levitch, he teamed up in 1946 with another struggling performer, singer Dean MARTIN. The act was a hit almost from its inception, reaching its peak in the late 1940s. Paramount signed them to a contract in 1949 and they made 18 films together before they dissolved their partnership in 1956 after their last film, *Hollywood or Bust.*

Lewis continued to star in films, which were all but ignored by American critics but highly praised in France by influential film journals. His film career as a comic, spanning more than three decades, has continued into the 1980s, regardless of generally poor reviews. Lewis' comedy consists of more than just mugging and slapstick, two elements some of his critics feel he engages in to excess (others compare him favorably to the great silent screen comedians). He has many attributes as a comic: he just happens to look funny; his childlike simplicity and penchant for mischief have resulted in many hilarious sight gags; at times he can create sympathetic characters who evoke both sadness and laughter. But, too often, he engages in sentimentality; he aims for effect rather than content, thereby weakening the overall story. This becomes more evident in the films he wrote and directed, comedies geared more for juvenile audiences. A tireless worker, he spends much of his time raising funds for charities. See also MARTIN AND LEWIS.

SELECTED FILMS (without Martin): *The Delicate Delinquent, The Sad Sack* (1957), *Rock-a-bye Baby, The Geisha Boy* (1958), *Don't Give Up the Ship* (1959), *Visit to a Small Planet, The Bellboy, Cinderfella* (1960), *The Ladies' Man, The Errand Boy* (1961), *It's Only Money* (1962), *The Nutty Professor, Who's Minding the Store?* (1963), *The Patsy, The Disorderly Orderly* (1964), *The Family Jewels, Boeing Boeing* (1965), *Three on a Couch, Way . . . Way Out* (1966), *The Big Mouth* (1967), *Don't Raise the Bridge—Lower the River* (1968), *Hook, Line and Sinker* (1969), *Which Way to the Front?* (1970), *Hardly Working* (1979), *The King of Comedy* (1983). ∎

Lewis, Robert Q. (1924–), comedian, emcee, actor. Worked in radio as a disc jockey, in nightclubs as a comic, and in television in his own show and also as a guest on other shows. Good-looking and bespectacled, he appeared in a handful of light films, but never gained any popularity in that medium.

SELECTED FILMS: *An Affair to Remember* (1957), *Good Neighbor Sam* (1964), *How to Succeed in Business Without Really Trying* (1967), *CHOMPS* (1979). ∎

Libeled Lady (1936), MGM. *Dir.* Jack Conway; *Sc.* Maurine Watkins, Howard Emmett Rogers, George Oppenheimer; with William Powell, Myrna Loy, Spencer Tracy, Jean Harlow, Walter Connolly.

This SCREWBALL COMEDY is blessed with more than just a good script with a brisk plot and wisecracking dialogue. It also showcases the comedic talents of four of MGM's brightest stars. Myrna LOY, portraying an heiress, sues Spencer TRACY'S newspaper for libel. Tracy, a hard-nosed editor, then hires smooth William POWELL, whom he had fired several months previously, to get the heiress in a compromising position so she will be forced to drop the five-million-dollar suit. But Powell, who is actually broke, plays cat-and-mouse with Tracy until he worms a lucrative contract from the editor. Meanwhile, Tracy convinces Jean HARLOW, his tough, shrill-voiced bride-to-be, to marry Powell for just a few weeks to strengthen his position and to act as the wronged wife. The fast-paced plot allows for a number of clever deceptions and double-dealings and several hilarious scenes. Powell, to gain a foothold with Loy's father, played admirably by veteran character actor Walter CONNOLLY, poses as an expert angler. The fishing trip proves hilarious as the bewildered Powell blunders his way downstream, pulled by one of his accidental catches. Other supporting players who contribute to the fun include E. E. Clive as a fay fishing instructor and Billy BENEDICT as a copy boy.

Lightner, Winnie (1899–1971), actress. Worked in vaudeville and musicals as a comedienne before entering films in the early sound era. She gave up her movie career in 1934 after a few years of making a handful of films. Working chiefly for Warner Brothers studios, she appeared as the lead or supporting actress in both light comedies and musicals with some of the leading comedians of the period, including, among others, OLSEN AND JOHNSON and Joe E. BROWN.

SELECTED FILMS: *The Gold Diggers of Broadway, The Show of Shows* (1929), *She Couldn't Say No, Hold Everything, The Life of the Party* (1930), *Gold Dust Gertie, Sit Tight, Side Show* (1931), *Manhattan Parade, Play Girl* (1932), *She Had to Say Yes, Dancing Lady* (1933), *I'll Fix It* (1934). ∎

"Li'l Abner." A popular comic strip created by Al Capp and adapted into several film versions. The first, produced in 1940, was a curious film in which the characters wore masks and bizarre makeup. Granville Owen, who resembled the title character, was miscast. Martha O'Driscoll portrayed Daisy Mae and Buster KEATON did a more than competent job in playing the Indian, Lonesome Polecat. The cast included other film comedians of the silent era, including Billy BEVAN, Chester CONKLIN, and Edgar KENNEDY. The film failed to capture the social and political satire of the original strip, depending rather on low comedy for its humor.

The second film version to depict rural life in and around Dogpatch, released in 1959, was based on a successful musical comedy. Peter Palmer, another unknown actor who resembled Abner, repeated his stage role. The one memorable performance in this lavishly produced film was Stubby KAYE'S portrayal of Marryin' Sam. The only other attribute of this otherwise lackluster film was some of the music. Again, Al Capp's charming and clever lampoon of American society, which he brought the nation for a quarter of a century, eluded the filmmakers.

Lilley, Edward C. (1896–1974), director. Worked in theater as an actor and director before entering films in the 1940s. Although he directed many musical comedies for Universal studios with a degree of professional craftsmanship, the pedestrian scripts and low budgets predominated. He never developed into a top-ranking comedy director.

SELECTED FILMS: *Cross Your Fingers, Never a Dull Moment* (1942), *Honeymoon Lodge, Larceny With Music, Moonlight in Vermont* (1943), *Allergic to Love, Babes on Swing Street, Hi, Good*

Lookin', My Gal Loves Music, Sing a Jingle (1944), Her Lucky Night, Swing Out, Sister (1945). ∎

Lillie, Beatrice (1898–), actress. Appeared in British and American revues and plays and on radio. She made her Broadway debut in 1924 before beginning a sporadic film career in 1926. A popular and very talented stage comedienne on both sides of the Atlantic, she never achieved the same success on the screen. *Every Other Inch a Lady*, her autobiography, was published in 1972.

SELECTED FILMS: *Exit Smiling* (1926), *The Show of Shows* (1929), *Are You There?* (1930), *Dr. Rhythm* (1938), *Around the World in 80 Days* (1956), *Thoroughly Modern Millie* (1967). ∎

Limelight (1952), UA. *Dir.* Charlie Chaplin; *Sc.* Charlie Chaplin; with Charlie Chaplin, Claire Bloom, Sydney Chaplin, Nigel Bruce, Buster Keaton.

Limelight unfolds the bittersweet story of the last days of Calvero, a music-hall entertainer. Calvero, like Chaplin, expressed his love for his art and his camaraderie with fellow performers. As his career fades from the limelight, he helps a gifted young ballet dancer, played by Claire Bloom, attain stardom. Chaplin's genius, even at this relatively late stage of his career, permeates the work. He directed, wrote the screenplay for, starred in, and composed the music for the film. He proved his acting ability in the many dramatic scenes as well as in the comic ones, including a funny routine with veteran comedian Buster KEATON. In this bit Calvero attempts a comeback in a dual bill with one of his fellow performers of former days (Keaton). They score a hit, and the audience beckons for an encore. The excitement, however, is too great for the old clown, and he suffers a heart attack. The theme song, "Eternally," gained wide popularity. But the film did not do well at the box office. Following its completion, and 37 years after making his first

silent short in the United States, Chaplin left the country. In fact, while he was on tour with the film in Europe, the United States immigration office made it difficult for him to return. The political, moral, and tax controversies that dogged him for years became too much of a burden, so he settled in Europe.

Linder, Max (1883–1925), actor. Appeared on stage in his native France in secondary parts before entering films in 1905. Signing with Pathe studios, he starred in a series of silent comedy shorts. He created the character of Max, the bewildered bachelor dandy. Advancing to the principal comic of the studio, he began turning out one film each week. His comedies continued to depict the exploits of Max as he pursued pretty women along the boulevards of Paris. When he became ill in 1911 and stopped making his popular comedies, his public demanded an explanation. He produced a documentary explaining why he left films and, shortly after, returned to the screen. His films and his personal appearances around Europe made him internationally famous by 1914.

He journeyed to the United States in 1916, after having served for a time in the trenches where he was wounded. He had signed a contract with ESSANAY to star in eight films. But illness forced him to complete only three before he returned home. He returned to Hollywood in the early 1920s and made three more comedies. After his journey back to France, his health deteriorated and he committed suicide. He was soon forgotten, and it was not until the 1960s, when his films were uncovered, that his genius and his influence were recognized. Historians, critics, and actors, including Charlie CHAPLIN, whom Linder strongly influenced, have acknowledged his contributions to the development of film comedy. His slapstick style predated Mack SENNETT and Chaplin.

SELECTED FILMS: *Max Comes Across, Max Wants a Divorce, Max in a Taxi* (1917), *Be My Wife, Seven Years Bad Luck* (1921), *The Three Must-Get-There's* (1922). ∎

Lindsay, Margaret (1910–1981), actress. Worked on stage before entering films. In 1933 Warner Brothers put her under contract. An attractive, personable brunette, she played leads in more than 50 dramas and light films during the 1930s and 1940s. She portrayed Ellery Queen's secretary in several entries of that series. After 1948 she appeared only occasionally on screen.

SELECTED FILMS: *Okay America!* (1932), *Baby Face* (1933), *Gentlemen Are Born* (1934), *The Frisco Kid* (1935), *The Lady Consents, Sinner Take All* (1936), *Slim, Back in Circulation* (1937), *Garden of the Moon* (1938), *The Under-Pup* (1938), *Club Havana* (1945), *Please Don't Eat the Daisies* (1960), *Tammy and the Doctor* (1963). ∎

Lipson, Jack "Tiny" (–1947), actor. Appeared in several film comedies, especially as a heavy. He worked with the THREE STOOGES and other comics as well.

SELECTED FILMS: *Punch Drunks* (1934), *Three Little Beers* (1935), *Slippery Silks* (1936), *Playing the Ponies* (1937), *I'll Never Heil Again* (1941), *Back From the Front* (1943). ∎

Lithgow, John (1946–), actor. Came to films in the early 1970s as a supporting player. On the chubby side with intense, deep-set eyes, he has appeared in dramas and light films, giving expert portrayals of various characters. He has twice received nominations for Academy Awards, one for his role in *The World According to Garp*, and another for *Terms of Endearment* (1983).

SELECTED FILMS: *Dealing* (1971), *The Big Fix* (1978), *Rich Kids* (1979), *The World According to Garp* (1982), *Footloose, The Adventures of Buckaroo Banzai* (1984), *Mesmerized, Santa Claus the Movie* (1985), *Harry and the Hendersons* (1987). ∎

Little, Cleavon (1939–), actor. Appeared on stage before entering films. He has played both lead and supporting roles, chiefly in comedies. His biggest success has been as the black sheriff in *Blazing Saddles*.

SELECTED FILMS: *What's So Bad About Feeling Good?* (1968), *Cotton Comes to Harlem* (1970), *Blazing Saddles* (1974), *FM* (1978), *Scavenger Hunt* (1979), *High Risk* (1981), *Jimmy the Kid, Surf II* (1984). ∎

"Little Orphan Annie." A popular comic strip created in the 1920s by Harold Gray and concerned with the adventures of a resourceful foundling. Hollywood produced three versions of the spunky red-haired child and her dog, Sandy. In 1932 David O. Selznick starred Mitzi GREEN in an inept adaptation of Gray's strip. The child actress had scored some success in earlier films but was unable to capture the vivacity of the "Annie" character.

In 1938 Paramount brought out its version, starring Ann Gillis in the title role, but again the film did not succeed. The spirit of the original characters seemed to elude the young actress and the remainder of the cast.

The third attempt, released in 1982, was an adaptation of the popular musical, *Annie*, based on the characters in Gray's strip. Directed by John Huston with an all-star cast including Albert Finney as Daddy Warbucks, Carol Burnett, and Bernadette Peters, the film featured Aileen Quinn as the famous orphan. Despite some good acting, a hit song ("Tomorrow"), and high production values, the film, like its predecessors, did not arouse much enthusiasm.

Littlefield, Lucien (1895–1960), actor. Worked in early silent melodramas and comedies as a supporting actor. Appearing in more than 200 silent and sound films in a career that spanned five decades, he portrayed numerous submissive as well as irascible characters in low-budget and major productions. One of his more memorable roles was that of the easily vexed Mr. Crosley in several "HENRY ALDRICH" films. He accompanied some of the leading film comics of the period, including, among others, W. C. FIELDS, Jack OAKIE, Joe E. BROWN, and Red SKELTON. He occasionally collaborated on film scripts.

In *Wide Open Faces* (1938), starring Joe E. Brown, he played the owner of a drug store with Brown, as his soda jerk, thinking of becoming a detective like William POWELL in *The Thin Man*. But Littlefield pooh-poohs the idea. "What's William Powell got that I haven't got?" Brown asks. "Myrna Loy," his boss replies.

SELECTED FILMS: *The Ghost Breaker* (1914), *A Gentleman of Leisure* (1915), *The Wild Goose Chase* (1919), *Why Change Your Wife?* (1920), *The Little Clown* (1921), *Tillie* (1922), *Three Wise Fools* (1923), *Babbitt* (1924), *Charley's Aunt* (1925), *Harold Teen* (1928), *No, No, Nanette* (1930), *Misbehaving Ladies* (1931), *If I Had a Million* (1932), *Stand Up and Cheer* (1934), *Ruggles of Red Gap* (1935), *Hotel Haywire* (1937), *Wide Open Faces* (1938), *What a Life* (1939), *Whistling in Dixie* (1942), *One Body Too Many* (1944), *Rendezvous With Annie* (1946), *Casanova's Big Night* (1954), *The High Cost of Loving* (1958). ∎

Livingston, Margaret (1900–), actress. Began her Hollywood career in early silent films. A lively lead player and supporting actress, she appeared in numerous dramas and light films into the early sound era. She usually played "the other woman" roles. She accompanied such leading performers as Colleen MOORE and George O'Brien.

SELECTED FILMS: *Within the Cup* (1917), *The Busher* (1919), *What's Your Husband Doing?* (1920), *The Home Stretch, Colorado Pluck* (1921), *Her Marriage Vow, The Chorus Lady* (1924), *The Best People* (1925), *Womanpower* (1926), *Married Alive* (1927), *Say It With Sables, His Private Life, Beware of Bachelors* (1928), *Innocents of Paris* (1929), *For the Love o' Lil, What a Widow!* (1930), *Kiki, God's Gift to Women* (1931), *Call Her Savage* (1932), *Social Register* (1934). ∎

Lloyd, Doris (1900–1968), actress. Appeared on stage in her native England before entering films in the mid-1920s. A talented supporting player for more than 40 years, she frequently portrayed characters of social position in numerous dramas and light films.

SELECTED FILMS: *The Lady* (1925), *Exit Smiling* (1926), *Is Zat So?* (1927), *Charley's Aunt* (1930), *The Bachelor Father* (1931), *Looking Forward* (1933), *She Was a Lady* (1934), *Don't Get Personal* (1936), *Tovarich* (1937), *I'm From Missouri* (1939), *The Constant Nymph* (1943), *Molly and Me* (1945), *The Secret Life of Walter Mitty* (1947), *Kind Lady* (1951), *The Notorious Landlady* (1962), *Rosie* (1967). ∎

Harold Lloyd

Lloyd, Harold (1893–1971), actor. Appeared on stage from the age of four. After appearing in a minor part in an early Edison film, he met Hal ROACH in Hollywood while both were working as extras. When Roach started his own film company to produce comedy shorts, Lloyd went to work for him. It was here that he created the character of "Willie Work." He left his friend's employ and joined KEYSTONE studios but quickly returned to Roach, following a lucrative offer to star in one-reel comedies.

The two men agreed that another character was needed, so in 1915 "LONESOME LUKE," a country bumpkin blended with a Chaplin imitation, was born. Luke performed more slapstick and was more violent than Chaplin's Keystone persona. By 1917 Lloyd tired of this character and introduced a new one, a dapper young man with horn-rimmed glasses who brimmed with an All-American personality and charm. This was the one which would catapult the comic to worldwide fame throughout the silent era and into the early talkies. Lloyd was now on his way to film success. But a freak accident was to set the comic's career back for a brief time. A small explosion during the taking of studio publicity stills caused Lloyd to lose the thumb and forefinger of his right hand. Following the accident, Lloyd wore a special glove to hide the bad hand, favoring the other in shots.

His new character firmly established by the 1920s, he starred in a series of high-quality comedies that displayed a rare combination of creative energy, comic invention, and expert stunting. The basic plots were similar: a wholesome young American who is having trouble advancing his career or winning the girl of his dreams eventually attains both through sheer optimism, determination, and luck. The audiences accepted Lloyd's concept, making him the most popular film comedian as well as the highest paid.

Lloyd has long been associated with the "thrill" comedy, e.g., "Safety Last," which contains the famous scene of the comic dangling from a skyscraper's clock. The entire sequence has entered the annals of film history along with other great screen moments, such as CHAPLIN'S ballet with a globe in The Great Dictator, KEATON'S race down a hill as myriads of boulders come tum-

bling after him in Seven Chances, and LAUREL AND HARDY'S struggle to move a piano up an endless stairway in "The Music Box." Actually, Lloyd, who did much of the stunt work himself, appeared in relatively few of these thrill comedies, alternating them with character comedies.

Although he made the transition to sound easily, his popularity began to slip as his style of comedy became dated. His talkies, Welcome Danger (1929), Feet First (1930), Movie Crazy (1932), The Cat's Paw (1934), The Milky Way (1936), and Professor Beware (1938), still provided plenty of laughs for the audiences. He relied heavily on visual gags, several of which were variations of earlier material from his silent days. This prompted some critics to describe his films as essentially silent comedies. Lloyd even attempted to adapt to the sound comedy practice of utilizing various comic character players to increase the comic effect. Although his films showed a profit at the box office, his influence as a major screen comic declined. He retired from the screen in 1947.

As a comedian, he differed from the giants of his period. CHAPLIN, Buster KEATON, and Harry LANGDON could easily fall back on their naturally funny selves, but Lloyd had to depend heavily upon his material. His scripts relied on a fast tempo and suspenseful comedy. However, if money is one yardstick of success, then he did very well by having amassed more than 15 million dollars by the close of the silent era. Harold Lloyd: The Man on the Clock, a biography by Tom Dardis, was published in 1983.

SELECTED FILMS: Algy on the Force (1913), Willie, Willie's Haircut (1914), Once Every Ten Minutes, Spitball Sadie (1915), An Awful Romance, Unfriendly Fruit (1916), Over the Fence, Pinched (1917), The Big Idea, The Lamb (1918), Ask Father, Next Aisle Over (1919), Haunted Spooks, High and Dizzy (1920), Now or Never, A Sailor-Made Man (1921), Grandma's Boy, Dr. Jack (1922), Safety Last, Why Worry? (1923),

Girl Shy, *Hot Water* (1924), *The Freshman* (1925), *For Heaven's Sake* (1926), *The Kid Brother* (1927), *Speedy* (1928), *Welcome Danger* (1929), *Feet First* (1930), *Movie Crazy* (1932), *The Cat's Paw* (1934), *The Milky Way* (1936), *Professor Beware* (1938), *Mad Wednesday* (1947). ∎

Locke, Goldie. Comic sidekick character of the debonair amateur sleuth, "The Falcon." He appeared in several entries of the popular detective-comedy series of the same name. Goldie was portrayed by character actor Ed BROPHY.

Lockhart, Gene (1891–1957), actor. Began his professional career as a child performer, advanced to Gilbert and Sullivan productions, and acted on Broadway before entering films in 1922. One of the most easily recognized character actors on the screen, he appeared in more than one hundred silent and sound dramas and light films over a period spanning four decades. Short and rotund in appearance, he was often cast as the heavy in both sympathetic (*The Sea Wolf*) and unsympathetic (*Geronimo*) roles. To his credit, he was always convincing, especially in portraying nasty, treacherous, and disloyal characters. He was the husband of Kathleen and the father of June Lockhart.

He was particularly effective as the insensitive, ironically named Mayor Lovett in *Meet John Doe* (1941) when he learns of Gary COOPER'S plans. "What about me?" he complains over the telephone. "It's my building he's jumping off of—and I'm up for re-election too."

SELECTED FILMS: *Smilin' Through* (1922), *The Gay Bride* (1934), *Ah, Wilderness!* (1935), *Brides Are Like That, Mind Your Own Business* (1936), *Mama Steps Out* (1937), *Penrod's Double Trouble, Blondie* (1938), *I'm From Missouri* (1939), *His Girl Friday* (1940), *That's the Spirit* (1945), *Miracle on 34th Street, Her Husband's Affairs* (1947), *That Wonderful Urge* (1948), *The Inspector General* (1949), *Riding High* (1950), *A Girl in*

Every Port, Bonzo Goes to College (1952), *Francis Covers the Big Town* (1953), *Jeanne Eagels* (1957). ∎

Lockhart, Kathleen (1881–1978), actress. Appeared as a supporting player from the mid-1930s to the 1950s. She portrayed various types in dramas and light films. She had minor roles in the initial film entries of two comedy series, "BLONDIE" and "HENRY ALDRICH." She was the wife of actor Gene LOCKHART.

SELECTED FILMS: *Brides Are Like That* (1936), *Something to Sing About* (1937), *Men Are Such Fools, Give Me a Sailor, Blondie* (1938), *Our Leading Citizen, What a Life* (1939), *Roughly Speaking* (1945), *Mother Wore Tights* (1947), *Walking My Baby Back Home, The Glenn Miller Story* (1954). ∎

Logan, Jacqueline (1901–), actress. Appeared on Broadway and in the Ziegfeld Follies during the early 1920s before entering silent films. She became a popular actress in many dramas and light comedies. When sound films arrived, her career began to falter and in 1932 she abandoned films.

SELECTED FILMS: *A Perfect Crime, Molly O, A Fool's Paradise* (1921), *Salomy Jane* (1923), *Manhattan* (1924), *Peacock Feathers, Wages for Wives* (1925), *White Mice, Tony Runs Wild, Footloose Widows* (1926), *For Ladies Only, The Wise Wife* (1927), *Stocks and Blondes, The Cop, Nothing to Wear* (1928), *Bachelor Girl* (1929), *General Crack* (1930), *Strictly Business* (1932). ∎

Loggia, Róbert (1930–), actor. Has appeared in television, on stage, and sporadically in films. Tall and handsome with wavy hair, he has never been given important roles or achieved major recognition as an actor although his performances are often more than competent. Recently, he has appeared rather steadily in several comedies directed by Blake EDWARDS.

SELECTED FILMS: Somebody Up There Likes Me (1956), Revenge of the Pink Panther (1978), S.O.B. (1981), Trail of the Pink Panther (1982), Curse of the Pink Panther (1983), Prizzi's Honor (1985), That's Life! (1986). ∎

Edgar Kennedy and Carole Lombard

Lombard, Carole (1908–1942), actress. Began her screen career as a child in the silent film A Perfect Crime (1921). In the late 1920s she appeared in a handful of Mack SENNETT'S comedy shorts before starring in feature-length comedies during the 1930s. Following a few routine films, she attained stardom as a comedienne, especially in the genre known as SCREWBALL COMEDY. A glamorous and talented actress, she portrayed temperamental performers, socialites, and ingenues in farces as well as social and sophisticated comedies. She worked alongside such famous silent comics as Billy BEVAN, Chester CONKLIN, and Mack SWAIN. In sound films she co-starred with such personalities as John BARRYMORE, Fredric MARCH, and Jack BENNY.

In the wild and hilarious Twentieth Century, stage director John BARRYMORE threatens to slash his throat if she doesn't return to him. "If you did," she quips, wise to his histrionics, "greasepaint would run out of it." Co-starring with March in Nothing Sacred, a screwball comedy that offered her one of her best roles, she portrayed Hazel Flagg, a young woman who purportedly is dy-

ing of radium poisoning. Reporter March, seeking to exploit her condition in a series of human interest stories, is nauseated at the overwhelming sentiment of the public. "For good clean fun," he comments sardonically, "there's nothing like a wake." "Oh, please, please," she retorts, "let's not talk shop." Lombard's highly successful career was cut short when she was killed in a plane crash in 1942 while on a tour to sell war bonds.

SELECTED FILMS: Marriage in Transit (1925), The Divine Sinner, Show Folks (1928), Safety in Numbers, Fast and Loose (1930), It Pays to Advertise, Ladies' Man (1931), No More Orchids, No Man of Her Own (1932), We're Not Dressing, Twentieth Century (1934), Hands Across the Table (1935), Love Before Breakfast, The Princess Comes Across, My Man Godfrey (1936), Nothing Sacred, True Confession (1937), Fools for Scandal (1938), In Name Only (1939), They Knew What They Wanted (1940), Mr. and Mrs. Smith (1941), To Be or Not to Be (1942). ∎

"Lonesome Luke" comedies. A series of silent shorts produced from 1915 to 1917 by Hal ROACH that starred Harold LLOYD as a ne'er-do-well hayseed whose character and attire were reminiscent of CHAPLIN'S—with variations. Like the Tramp, Lloyd employed trousers that were short and tight, as was the vest, and he wore a derby and mustache; even the sight gags and situations were pure Chaplin. Knockabout comic Snub POLLARD supported Lloyd in the series.

In chiefly formula films containing much knockabout comedy, the Luke character would get into predictable situations with police, a variety of attractive females, fathers, and other customary foils. The poorly made comedies at first were greeted with a lack of enthusiasm. But they soon became moderately successful at the box office, and the releasing company, Pathe, called for at least three one- or two-reel shorts per month. Lloyd, however, grew tired of the character and, after about 50 entries, he created the "glasses" character that was to skyrocket him to fame.

SELECTED FILMS: Just Nuts, Lonesome Luke, Spit-Ball Sadie, Soaking the Clothes, Lonesome Luke, Social Gangster (1915), Luke Lugs Luggage, Luke Foils the Villain, Luke and the Rural Roughnecks, Luke's Double, Luke and the Mermaids, Luke the Chauffeur, Luke, the Gladiator, Luke Locates the Loot (1916), Luke's Lost Liberty, Lonesome Luke on Tin Can Alley, Lonesome Luke's Wild Women, Lonesome Luke in We Never Sleep (1917). ∎

Long, Shelley (1949–), actress. Has appeared in television and on the stage, appearances in the former bringing her an Emmy Award in 1983. A supporting player in several undistinguished film comedies in the early 1980s, she received little attention until she co-starred with Bette MIDLER in the critically successful *Outrageous Fortune.*

SELECTED FILMS: A Small Circle of Friends (1980), Caveman (1981), Night Shift (1982), Losin' It (1983), Outrageous Fortune (1987). ∎

Long, Walter (1879–1952), actor. Began his long screen career in 1915 in early silent films. Thick-set and mean-looking, he played villains for almost 40 years in dramas and light films. Perhaps his most famous role was that of Gus, the mulatto renegade, in Griffith's *Birth of a Nation,* in which he hounds "Little Sister," forcing her to choose between his lust and suicide. He appeared as foil to LAUREL AND HARDY in several of their comedy shorts.

SELECTED FILMS: The Birth of a Nation (1915), Bobbed Hair, Raffles, the Amateur Cracksman (1925), Eve's Leaves (1926), Pardon Us, Taxi Troubles (1931), Any Old Port (1932), Six of a Kind, Three Little Pigskins, The Live Ghost, Going Bye Bye (1934), Pick a Star (1937), No More Relatives (1948), Wabash Avenue (1950). ∎

Long Pants (1927), FN. *Dir.* Frank Capra; *Sc.* Frank Capra; with Harry Langdon, Alma Bennett, Priscilla Bonner.

The last comedy in Harry LANGDON'S trilogy of great films—the other two being *Tramp, Tramp, Tramp* (1926) and *The Strong Man* (1926)—has been rated as his best by some critics while others are equally divided between the other two. Langdon portrays an overgrown country boy competing with city slickers. He daydreams that he is a great lover but is kept in knee pants by his parents. When he finally gets long pants, he becomes innocently involved with Bebe, a gun moll, played by Alma Bennett, at the expense of his true love, portrayed by Priscilla Bonner. The entanglement leads to many hilarious scenes, including his thoughts of killing Bonner. Alone in the woods with her, he is deterred by a sign that reads: "No Shooting." Meanwhile, he battles barbed wire and a bear trap. Later, his involvement with Bebe embroils the naive Langdon in her one-woman crime spree. This was his last film to be directed by either Frank CAPRA or Harry EDWARDS, two of his closest confidants who understood his screen character and helped to guide his career so successfully. He decided to direct his own films. Thereafter he also added more pathos to his comedies, against Capra's advice. Film historians differ as to which of the decisions was the major cause of his downfall within the next two years.

Loos, Anita (1893–1986), screenwriter, playwright. Appeared as stage actress before turning to writing. She contributed scenarios to D.W. Griffith and wrote sardonic and humorous screenplays for some of Douglas FAIRBANKS' silent films. She wrote many light comedies alone or in collaboration, some of which contained rather witty dialogue. Her novel, *Gentlemen Prefer Blondes,* became a successful stage musical and film.

SELECTED FILMS: The New York Hat (1912), The Power of the Camera, The Hicksville Epicure (1913), The Wall Flower, A Flurry in Art (1914), Symphony Sal (1915), The Social Secretary (1916), Reaching for the Moon (1917), Let's Get a Divorce (1918), Getting Mary Married (1919), Mama's Affair (1921), Polly of the Follies (1922), Gentlemen Prefer Blondes (1928), Red-Headed Woman (1932), Hold Your Man (1933), The Biography of a Bachelor Girl (1935), Mama Steps Out (1937), When Ladies Meet (1941), I Married an Angel (1942). ■

Lord, Del (1895–1960?), director. Worked as a stunt driver for Mack SENNETT during the silent era before switching to directing. He turned out many two-reelers starring several leading comics of the silent and sound period, including Billy BEVAN, El BRENDEL, Charlie CHASE, Ben TURPIN, and Andy CLYDE. He directed 39 shorts starring the THREE STOOGES, beginning in 1935. Under his guidance, the trio turned out some of their best work for their studio, Columbia Pictures, where he remained until 1949.

SELECTED FILMS: The Daredevil (1923), Lizzies of the Field, The Cannon Ball Express (1924), Giddap, The Lion's Whiskers (1925), Wandering Willies, A Sea Dog's Tale (1926), Pop Goes the Easel, Uncivil Warriors, Pardon My Scotch, Hoi Poloi, Three Little Beers (1935), Movie Maniacs, False Alarms, Whoops, I'm an Indian (1936), Dizzy Doctors, Cash and Carry (1937), Termites of 1938, Wee Wee Monsieur (1938), Three Little Sew and Sews, We Want Our Mummy (1939), How High Is Up?, No Census, No Feeling (1940), Dutiful but Dumb, Some More of Samoa (1941), Rough, Tough and Ready (1945). ■

Lord, Robert (1902–1976), screenwriter. Worked as a journalist before entering films during the 1920s. He wrote many light and dramatic screenplays over a period of four decades. Working chiefly for Warner Brothers, he turned out films with some of the leading stars of that studio, including, among others, Dick POWELL and Edward G. ROBINSON. One of Lord's most humorous scripts, the very entertaining The Little Giant, depicted Robinson as a culture-hungry mobster who decides to go straight.

SELECTED FILMS: The Johnstown Flood (1926), For Ladies Only, The Swell-Head, A Reno Divorce (1927), Five and Ten Cent Annie, Detectives, Beware of Bachelors (1928), Hardboiled Rose, The Time, the Place and the Girl, Gold Diggers of Broadway, So Long Letty, The Sap (1929), Hold Everything (1930), Fireman, Save My Child (1932), The Little Giant (1933), Dames (1934), Page Miss Glory (1935). ■

Lorne, Marion (1886–1968), actress. Appeared on stage for years before coming to films as a character player in the early 1950s. She usually played eccentric, confused, matronly women in occasional films. She enjoyed a long run in television as a dizzy member of the cast of the "Mr. Peepers" comedy show starring Wally COX.

SELECTED FILMS: Strangers on a Train (1951), The Girl Rush (1955), The Graduate (1968). ■

Louise, Anita (1915–1970), actress. Appeared on stage and in silent films at age eight. By the 1930s she had developed into an attractive and talented actress. She was featured in numerous dramas and light films until the 1950s when she left films and started a new career in television. She was considered by her contemporaries as one of the best dressed and most beautiful women in Hollywood.

SELECTED FILMS: The Sixth Commandment (1924), Square Shoulders, The Marriage Playground (1929), The Floradora Girl (1930), Millie, Everything's Rosie (1931), Judge Priest (1934), Lady Tubbs, A Midsummer Night's Dream (1935), Brides Are Like That

(1936), Call It a Day, Tovarich (1937), Going Places (1938), The Gorilla, These Glamour Girls (1939), The Villain Still Pursued Her (1940), Casanova Brown (1944), Retreat Hell! (1952). ■

Love, Bessie (1898–1986), actress. Began her screen career in early silent films appearing with such major personalities as William S. Hart and Douglas FAIRBANKS. A comely and versatile actress who was born Juanita Horton, she starred in dramas, westerns, and light comedies. She received an Academy Award nomination for her leading role in *The Broadway Melody* (1929), the first all-talking musical. Burdened with lines like "It's cream in the can," she had to overcome the staginess of the film as well as its crude attempts at comedy.

She left American films after the advent of sound but continued her acting career in England where she appeared in the theater and, sporadically, in films. Although she was a popular and gifted actress and gave some striking performances, stardom, for some unknown reason, seemed to elude her. Critics often singled her performance out as the only worthwhile part of an otherwise routine film.

SELECTED FILMS: The Flying Torpedo, Reggie Mixes In (1916), How Could You, Caroline? (1918), Yankee Princess, The Little Boss (1919), Pegeen, Bonny May (1920), The King of Main Street (1925), Song and Dance Man, Lovey Mary, Young April, Going Crooked (1926), Dress Parade (1927), Anybody Here Seen Kelly? (1928), The Idle Rich, The Girl in the Show (1929), Chasing Rainbows, Good News, See America Thirst (1930), The Ritz (1976). ■

Love, Montagu (1877–1943), actor. Worked as a newspaper cartoonist before migrating to Hollywood from his native England to act in early silent films. A heavy-set, imposing figure, he appeared as a character actor in scores of dramas and light films. He was often cast as a villain, but during the sound era he played less menacing roles. His screen career spanned four decades.

SELECTED FILMS: The Suicide Club (1914), The Grouch (1918), The Mad Marriage (1925), Good Time Charley (1927), Charming Sinners (1929), His Double Life (1933), Hi Gaucho (1935), Sing, Baby, Sing (1936), Tovarich (1937), Professor Beware! (1938), Private Affairs (1940), The Devil and Miss Jones, Lady for a Night (1941), Holy Matrimony (1943), Thieves' Holiday (1946). ■

Love and Death (1975), UA. Dir. Woody Allen; Sc. Woody Allen; with Woody Allen, Diane Keaton, Harold Gould, Alfred Lutter, Olga Georges-Picot.

Woody ALLEN'S epic comedy parodies foreign film directors like Eisenstein and emulates such comics as CHAPLIN, Bob HOPE, and Groucho MARX. In this romp about a declared coward during the Napoleonic Wars, Allen once again touches upon some of his favorite themes—marriage, relationships, self-deprecation, and his love of films. In bed at night, Allen reaches out to his wife. "No, not here," she says. In another scene a woman asks Allen, "It must be lonely at the front. How long has it been since you made love to a woman?" "What's today?" Allen ponders, "Monday, Tuesday? Two years." Later, the same woman admits, "You're the greatest lover I ever had." "Well," explains Allen, "I practice a lot when I'm alone." "Sex without love is an empty experience," Diane KEATON says. "Yes," Allen replies, "but as empty experiences go, it's one of the best." Woody also has a chance to direct his lines to the audience. "Some men are heterosexual; some men are bisexual; some men don't think about sex at all—they become lawyers." "There are worse things than death. If you've ever spent an evening with an insurance salesman, you know exactly what I mean." And: "If it turns out there is a God, I don't think He's evil. The worst thing you can say about Him is that He's basically an underachiever."

Allen seems to have problems with his period comedies. This film and his uneven *A Midsummer Night's Sex Comedy* (1982), each of which contains isolated hilarious scenes, are not among his best works.

and the music. It was to set the standard for similar productions for years to come.

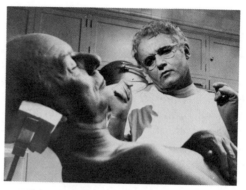

John Gielgud and Rod Steiger in *The Loved One* (1965)

Jeanette MacDonald and Maurice Chevalier in *The Love Parade* (1929)

Love Parade, The (1929), PAR. *Dir.*
Ernst Lubitsch; *Sc.* Guy Bolton; with Maurice Chevalier, Jeanette MacDonald, Lillian Roth, Lupino Lane, Lionel Belmore, Ben Turpin.

Based on the play, *The Prince Consort*, by Leon Xanrof, this early sound comedy helped to establish the careers of many of its participants. The director displayed his famous "Lubitsch touch"—a perceptive, subjective camera and the use of gestures and glances to mean more than appears on the surface. French singer Maurice CHEVALIER, in his second American feature, won the approval of the public with his personality and his voice. Also, Jeanette MacDONALD made her film debut. The supporting players, especially the delightful Lillian Roth and former silent comics Lupino LANE and Ben TURPIN, added immeasurably to the light tone. A frothy, sophisticated film, its slight story of romance among royalty was enriched not only by the cast and director but also by the elaborate sets by art director Hans Dreier

Loved One, The (1965), MGM. *Dir.*
Tony Richardson; *Sc.* Terry Southern, Christopher Isherwood; with Robert Morse, Jonathan Winters, Rod Steiger, Dana Andrews, Milton Berle, James Coburn, John Gielgud, Tab Hunter, Margaret Leighton.

Evelyn Waugh's biting novel was adapted into an entertaining BLACK COMEDY in the mid-1960s. English director Tony Richardson deserves credit for his effort, if not for his success, in irreverently exploring the funeral rites and customs of various Californians. He ended up with a flawed but humorous, offbeat film. When a Hollywood actor, played by John Gielgud, hangs himself, his English nephew, Robert MORSE, arranges for the funeral. The film contains several hilarious moments and memorable characterizations, including that of Mr. Joyboy and Reverend Glensworthy, supervisor of Whispering Glades cemetery. The latter is played by Jonathan Winters. Several critics, however, panned it as a weak and sophomoric interpretation of Waugh's satirical work. The film, at times pretentious, occasionally strayed from its central purpose, involving itself in unrelated subjects such as filmmaking and the military bureaucracy. Neither its advertising, which pronounced it a picture with something to offend everybody, nor its star-studded cast, almost as large as that of *It's a Mad, Mad, Mad, Mad World,* could sell the picture to the public.

Lovers and Other Strangers (1970), CIN. *Dir.* Cy Howard; *Sc.* Renee Taylor, Joseph Bologna, David Z. Goodman; with Gig Young, Bea Arthur, Bonnie Bedelia, Anne Jackson, Harry Guardino, Michael Brandon, Richard Castellano.

This domestic comedy, based on the short play by Bologna and Taylor, is a sort of early *Nashville* with a wedding background instead of a political rally. The plot cleverly brings together various couples and their romantic and sexual encounters during the wedding of Bonnie Bedelia and Michael Brandon. Comedienne Anne MEARA, the bride's older sister, is married to Harry Guardino, who pleads with her for the right to be boss of their family. Bob DISHY and Marian Hailey portray two singles perpetually on the brink of a farcical situation. As if frozen in time like a grotesque version of Keats' young romantics painted on his famous Grecian Urn, he continually tries to bed her while she keeps resisting. Gig YOUNG, parodying Spencer TRACY, is father of the bride who can't decide between his wife and his mistress. But the most fascinating couple in this comedy are the wonderful Bea ARTHUR and Richard CASTELLANO, the parents of the groom who sound like the Italian version of George BURNS and Gracie ALLEN. "Don't look for happiness," Arthur advises her second son, who is seeking a divorce from Diane KEATON, "it will only make you miserable." And to Keaton she confides about her own husband: "I tried to understand Frank—not that there's much to understand. That's why I was so hurt when he strayed. But you know me, I always try to look on the bright side. I said to myself, 'Well, at least she's the one who'll be nauseous now.'" Later, Arthur says of a foundering marriage: "I can understand her wanting to leave, but I can't understand her leaving." Meanwhile her pathetic husband wanders through the wedding repeating his now famous line: "What's the story?" When his son tells him that he and his wife are strangers, Castellano replies: "We're all strangers. After a while you get used to it. You become deeper strangers. That's a sort of love." The song, "For All We Know," won an Academy Award.

Lowe, Edmund (1892–1971), actor. Worked in stock and on Broadway before entering films in 1917. A versatile actor, he portrayed urbane romantic characters as well as coarse and wild ones, especially in a series of raucous adventure comedies during the early sound period. His most popular comedies were those in which he co-starred with Victor McLAGLEN, including the adaptation of the Laurence Stallings-Maxwell Anderson antiwar play, *What Price Glory.* The horseplay and buffoonery between Lowe, who played Sergeant Quirt, and his foil, Captain Flagg, led to sequels, including *The Cockeyed World* and *Women of All Nations.* Lowe appeared in dozens of films during a career that spanned five decades.

SELECTED FILMS: *The Spreading Dawn* (1917), *Vive la France!* (1918), *Peacock Alley* (1922), *Nellie, the Beautiful Cloak Model* (1924), *What Price Glory* (1926), *Is Zat So?, Publicity Madness* (1927), *The Cockeyed World* (1929), *Don't Bet on Women, Women of All Nations* (1931), *Misleading Lady* (1932), *Hot Pepper, Dinner at Eight* (1933), *No More Women, Gift of Gab* (1934), *Mad Holiday, Seven Sinners* (1936), *Every Day's a Holiday* (1938), *Honeymoon Deferred* (1940), *Double Date* (1941), *Good Sam* (1948), *Heller in Pink Tights* (1960). ∎

Lowery, Scooter, child actor. Appeared in several early silent "OUR GANG" comedy shorts for producer Hal ROACH.

SELECTED FILMS: Thundering Fleas, Shivering Spooks, The Fourth Alarm (1926). ■

Myrna Loy

Loy, Myrna (1905–), actress. Began her long film career with Cecil B. DeMille in 1923. Born Myrna Williams, she starred in many dramatic films during the 1920s and 1930s, often cast as an oriental seductress or a local vamp. Sound films, however, allowed her to develop a new screen personality, that of an elegant comedienne. Her more memorable roles were those in sophisticated comedies, especially as Nora Charles in the "THIN MAN" detective-comedy series. Together with co-star William POWELL as her carefree husband, Nick, she delighted the public with her wit and charm. In *The Thin Man*, the first in the series, Nick invites an odd assortment of guests, including police and criminals, to dinner in an attempt to solve a murder case. "Waiter, will you serve the nuts," she announces, and then attempts to correct herself. "I mean, will you serve the guests the nuts." She was voted Hollywood's number one female box-office attraction in 1936 and was among the Box Office Top Ten of screen personalities in 1937 and 1938. In her later years she worked at the United Nations and on Broadway.

SELECTED FILMS: Pretty Ladies (1925), The Cave Man, The Exquisite Sinner, So This Is Paris (1926), Ham and Eggs at the Front, If I Were Single, Simple Sis, A Sailor's Sweetheart (1927), Pay As You Enter, State Street Sadie (1928), Fancy Baggage, Hardboiled Rose (1929), Cock o' the Walk (1930), The Naughty Flirt (1931), The Wet Parade, Love Me Tonight, The Animal Kingdom (1932), When Ladies Meet (1933), The Thin Man (1934), Libeled Lady, After the Thin Man (1936), Double Wedding (1937), Too Hot to Handle (1938), Another Thin Man (1939), Love Crazy, Shadow of the Thin Man (1941), The Thin Man Goes Home (1944), The Senator Was Indiscreet, Song of the Thin Man (1947), Mr. Blandings Builds His Dream House (1948), Cheaper by the Dozen (1950), The April Fools (1969), The End (1978), Just Tell Me What You Want (1979). ■

Lubin, Arthur (1901–), director. Began his Hollywood career as an actor in silent films. By 1934 he was directing light films for Universal studios. He turned out melodramas and lowbrow comedies, many of which were pedestrian films. He was responsible for many ABBOTT AND COSTELLO entries as well as a handful of "FRANCIS" comedies.

SELECTED FILMS: A Successful Failure (1934), Honeymoon Limited (1935), Beloved Brat (1938), Mickey the Kid, Call a Messenger (1939), Meet the Wildcat (1940), Buck Privates, In the Navy, Hold That Ghost, Keep 'Em Flying (1941), Ride 'Em Cowboy (1942), Delightfully Dangerous (1945), Francis (1950), Queen for a Day, Francis Goes to the Races (1951), Francis Goes to West Point, It Grows on Trees (1952), Francis Covers the Big Town (1953), Francis Joins the Wacs (1954), Francis in the Navy (1955), The First Traveling Saleslady (1956), The Incredible Mr. Limpet (1964), Hold On! (1966), Rain for a Dusty Summer (1971). ■

Lubitsch, Ernst (1892–1947), director. Began his film career in 1909 in his native Germany as a minor actor. He then tried the theater but soon returned to films, writing, acting in, and directing a series of comedies about a character called Meyer, a Jewish merchant. By 1919 he was assigned to larger productions, generally historical romances. Warner Brothers took notice of his talents and, in the early 1920s, invited him to work in the United States. During the next few years he directed a group of exceptional sophisticated comedies that brought him international recognition for his ironic humor, verbal wit, and mastery of the film medium.

The sound era posed no problem for Lubitsch. He entered it with the same confidence and creativity he brought to the silents. He capitalized on the introduction of sound by integrating music and dialogue into his themes and stories. Eventually he became known for the "Lubitsch touch," a specific technique that combined visual humor with amoral comedy that initially was disturbing, but Lubitsch's wit and control mitigated any trace of prurience. Part of his genius lay in his economy of expression. He was able to distill characterization, or present his major themes, lust and greed, into a single shot or image. The ostensibly innocent glances of two strangers, closed doors, and uncovered windows suggested more than what appeared on the screen—all of which delighted the viewer and confounded the censors of the period. Sensuality and eroticism were transformed into caprice.

His contributions to the art of film comedy were many. His simple sets took on new meaning. The gaudy and cluttered look favored by many studios was replaced with more symbolic and relevant sets that underscored the themes and characters of his film. He was one of the first directors to use a mobile camera during the sound era. He employed sound creatively, using it to suggest rhythm and excluding it when the visual was to be emphasized.

Although his settings were often exotic lands or mythical kingdoms and his characters were foreign, these elements were clearly metaphors for America. His good-natured ridicule of our weaknesses influenced much of the work of other important directors, including Lewis Milestone and Wesley RUGGLES in the 1920s and Otto PREMINGER, Joseph MANKIEWICZ, and Billy WILDER during the sound period. The Academy of Motion Picture Arts and Sciences honored him in 1937 for his "25-year contribution to motion pictures." A study of the director's work, *The Lubitsch Touch*, by Herman Weinberg, was published in 1971.

SELECTED FILMS: *Rosita (1923), The Marriage Circle, Three Women, Forbidden Paradise (1924), Kiss Me Again, Lady Windermere's Fan (1925), So This Is Paris (1926), The Student Prince (1927), The Love Parade (1929), Monte Carlo (1930), The Smiling Lieutenant (1931), Trouble in Paradise (1932), Design for Living (1933), The Merry Widow (1934), Desire (1936), Angel (1937), Bluebeard's Eighth Wife (1938), Ninotchka (1939), The Shop Around the Corner (1940), That Uncertain Feeling (1941), To Be or Not to Be (1942), Heaven Can Wait (1943), Cluny Brown (1946), That Lady in Ermine (1948).* ■

Lucas, Wilfred (1871–1940), actor, director. Began his screen career in 1907 as an actor and appeared in films for various directors, including D. W. Griffith and Mack SENNETT. By 1913 he switched to directing comedy shorts for Sennett's KEYSTONE studios where he worked with some of the foremost comics of the period, including "Fatty" ARBUCKLE, Mabel NORMAND, and Minta DURFEE. In the early 1920s he returned to acting, playing leads and supporting roles for the next 20 years in a variety of genres, including comedies with LAUREL AND HARDY and WHEELER AND WOOLSEY.

It was with Stan and Ollie in *Pardon Us* that he gave one of his more memorable and thankless roles as the condescending warden and straight man to the boys. As they are about to be released after serving time as illegal brewers, he announces: "Begin life anew. Forget this. . . . Anything to help you where you stopped off, let me know. . . ." To which Stan responds: "Can we take your order for a couple of cases?"

SELECTED FILMS (as director): Get Rich Quick, Cohen's Outing, A Game of Pool, Fatty's Day Off, What Father Knew, Willie Minds the Dog, Billy Dodges Bills, Across the Alley, The Janitor (1913), A Misplaced Foot (1914), Her Sacrifice (1926).

SELECTED FILMS (as actor): The Barbarian (1908), Cohen's Outing (1913), The Westerners (1918), The Beautiful Liar (1921), The Barnstormer (1922), A Broadway Butterfly (1925), Just Imagine (1930), Pardon Us, Cracked Nuts (1931), Red Noses (1932), The Devil's Brother (1933), Modern Times (1936), The Baroness and the Butler, College Swing (1938), Zenobia (1939), A Chump at Oxford, Brother Orchid (1940), The Sea Wolf (1941). ∎

Ludwig, Edward (1899–), director. Appeared as an actor in silent films before turning to directing in the early sound period. Working for different studios, he turned out chiefly low-budget dramas and light films, which were often visually superior to those of other directors.

SELECTED FILMS: Steady Company (1932), They Just Had to Get Married (1933), Let's Be Ritzy, Friends of Mr. Sweeney (1934), Old Man Rhythm, Three Kids and a Queen (1935), Her Husband Lies (1937), That Certain Age (1938), Born to Sing (1942), Three Is a Family (1944), The Gun Hawk (1963). ∎

Ludwig, William (1912–), screenwriter. Wrote screenplays from the late 1930s to the early 1960s. Working alone and in collaboration, he turned out many of the "ANDY HARDY" films as well as other comedies and dramas. He and his

co-writer won an Oscar in 1955 for Interrupted Melody.

SELECTED FILMS: Love Finds Andy Hardy, Out West With the Hardys (1938), The Hardys Ride High (1939), Love Crazy (1941), Andy Hardy's Blonde Trouble (1944), Julia Misbehaves (1948), The Merry Widow (1952), Hit the Deck (1955), Ten Thousand Bedrooms (1957), Back Street (1961). ∎

Lufkin, Sam (1892–1952), actor. Worked in silent and sound comedy films as a supporting actor. He appeared chiefly in numerous LAUREL AND HARDY shorts and features through the 1930s. His screen career spanned the years 1924 through 1940.

SELECTED FILMS: Leave 'Em Laughing, The Finishing Touch, From Soup to Nuts, You're Darn Tootin', Their Purple Moment, Should Men Go Home?, Two Tars (1928), Liberty, Wrong Again, That's My Wife, Double Whoopee, They Go Boom, Bacon Grabbers (1929), Pardon Us, Beau Hunks (1931), Any Old Port, The Music Box, County Hospital, Scram! (1932), Sons of the Desert (1933), Going Bye Bye!, Them Thar Hills (1934), Our Relations (1936), Swiss Miss (1938), The Flying Deuces (1939). ∎

Luke, Keye (1904–), actor. Began his Hollywood career as a commercial artist. After working as technical adviser, he appeared in his first film in 1934. He played major and minor parts over the years in many films, but his most memorable role was as Charlie Chan's Number One Son in the mystery series. The Honolulu detective usually had to get his impetuous offspring out of hot water. His most bittersweet role was that of an educated attendant to James CAGNEY in Something to Sing About, retitled The Battling Hoofer. Luke plays a frustrated Chinese actor who must demean himself as an obsequious servant at a film studio.

SELECTED FILMS: The Painted Veil (1934), Here's to Romance, Charlie Chan in Paris (1935), Anything Goes, King of Burlesque, Charlie Chan at the Opera

(1936), *Something to Sing About* (1937), *The Gang's All Here, Let's Go Collegiate, Bowery Blitzkrieg* (1941), *Mexican Spitfire's Elephant* (1942), *Salute to the Marines* (1943), *Andy Hardy's Blonde Trouble* (1944), *How Do You Do?, Between Two Women* (1945), *Love Is a Many Splendored Thing* (1955), *Nobody's Perfect* (1968), *Won Ton Ton, the Dog Who Saved Hollywood* (1976). ∎

Lullaby. Fictional comic sidekick in the western series, "The Three Mesquiteers," produced by Republic studios. He was portrayed by comic actor and ventriloquist Max TERHUNE, who, with his dummy Elmer, enlivened more than 20 films in the series, including *The Trigger Trio* (1937), *Pals of the Saddle* (1938), and *Three Texas Steers* (1939).

Lum and Abner. A popular comedy team on radio during the late 1930s and 1940s. For more than 20 years Chester Lauck (1902–1980), an ex-bank teller, and Norris Goff (1906–1978), formerly in the grocery business, portrayed the folksy pair. Occasionally they brought their hillbilly humor to the screen in several routine films.

SELECTED FILMS: *Dreaming Out Loud* (1940), *Bashful Bachelors* (1942). ∎

Lund, John (1913–), actor. Worked in advertising, on Broadway in 1941, and on radio before making his film debut in 1946. A handsome actor, he appeared in dramas and comedies in leading and supporting roles but never rose to stardom. By the 1960s he was relegated to minor roles in pedestrian films.

In *A Foreign Affair* American Congresswoman Jean ARTHUR in postWorld War II Germany watches films of a suspected Nazi collaborator (Marlene DIETRICH) garbed in a low-cut, strapless gown. "I wonder what holds up that dress?" she questions. "It must be that German will power," Lund replies.

SELECTED FILMS: *To Each His Own* (1946), *The Perils of Pauline, Variety Girl* (1947), *A Foreign Affair, Miss Tatlock's Millions* (1948), *My Friend Irma* (1949), *No Man of Her Own, My Friend Irma Goes West* (1950), *The Mating Season, Darling, How Could You!* (1951), *Latin Lovers* (1953), *High Society* (1956), *Affair in Reno* (1957), *The Wackiest Ship in the Army* (1960), *If a Man Answers* (1962). ∎

Lydon, Jimmy (1923–), actor. Worked as a child actor on radio and Broadway before making his debut in films in 1939 at age 16. A popular teen-age actor, he starred in light films, including nine "HENRY ALDRICH" comedies. In his later career in front of the cameras he did not fare so well.

SELECTED FILMS: *Back Door to Heaven* (1939), *Bowery Boy* (1940), *Cadets on Parade* (1942), *My Best Gal, The Town Went Wild* (1944), *Twice Blessed* (1945), *The Affairs of Geraldine* (1946), *Life With Father* (1947), *When Willie Comes Marching Home* (1950), *Gasoline Alley* (1951), *Scandalous John* (1971), *Vigilante Force* (1976). ∎

Lynde, Paul (1926–1982), actor. Worked on Broadway, in nightclubs, in television, and in films. A pessimistic and sneering comic, he delivered his lines with a prissiness that enchanted his audiences. He appeared in light films and did the voice-over for various characters in animated features, including *Charlotte's Web* (1973). His screen work did nothing to further his career and attempts to star him in his own television show failed. He seemed to be successful only as a guest on others' shows and as a panelist on quiz programs.

In *Send Me No Flowers* he apprises would-be plot purchaser Rock HUDSON of an attractive feature. "All the monuments are four feet tall. As you see, it gives a wonderful impression of uniformity."

SELECTED FILMS: New Faces (1954), Son of Flubber, Bye, Bye Birdie, Under the Yum Yum Tree (1963), For Those Who Think Young, Send Me No Flowers (1964), Beach Blanket Bingo (1965), The Glass Bottom Boat (1966), How Sweet It Is (1968), The Villain (1978). ▪

Lynn, Diana (1926–1971), actress. Made her first appearance in films in 1939 at age 13. As a charming juvenile performer and ingenue, she scored highly in a string of above-average light films, enjoying a few years of popularity with the public. Her adult features met with less success, but she had a fruitful career in the theater and television until she succumbed to a stroke. Unfortunately, Hollywood never fully utilized the potential talents of this witty performer.

In The Miracle of Morgan's Creek she played Betty HUTTON'S 14-year-old sister. When well-meaning but simpleminded Eddie BRACKEN gets arrested after trying to help the pregnant Hutton out of her predicament, Lynn says disparagingly, "I told you what to expect from that pickle-face." "You mustn't talk about him that way," Hutton objects. "He was only trying to do his best." "Imagine if he hadn't been really trying," Lynn suggests.

SELECTED FILMS: They Shall Have Music (1939), The Major and the Minor (1942), Henry Aldrich Gets Glamour (1943), The Miracle of Morgan's Creek, And the Angels Sing, Our Hearts Were Young and Gay (1944), Out of This World, Duffy's Tavern (1945), The Bride Wore Boots (1946), Easy Come, Easy Go, Variety Girl (1947), Texas, Brooklyn and Heaven, Every Girl Should Be Married (1948), My Friend Irma (1949), Peggy (1950), Bedtime for Bonzo (1951), You're Never Too Young, The Kentuckian (1955). ▪

Lynn, Sharon E. (1904–1963), actress. Began her screen career in silent films in the 1920s playing bit parts. She appeared chiefly as a supporting player in dramas and light films. She also appeared on stage.

SELECTED FILMS: Aflame in the Sky, Clancy's Kosher Wedding, Jake the Plumber (1927), Give and Take (1928), Sunny Side Up, The One Woman Idea (1929), Crazy That Way, Man Trouble (1930), Too Many Crooks (1931), The Big Broadcast (1932), Big Executive (1933), Enter Madame, Go Into Your Dance (1935), Way Out West (1937), West Point Widow (1941). ▪

Lynn, William H. (1888–1952), actor. Worked in stock, in vaudeville, and on Broadway in the 1930s before joining Hollywood as a dependable character player. Short and bald, he played mature roles, often as genial senior citizens, in light films.

SELECTED FILMS: Harvey (1950), Mr. Belvedere Rings the Bell, Harvey, Katie Did It (1951), The Outcasts of Poker Flat (1952), The Twonky (1953). ▪

Lyon, Ben (1901–1979), actor. Appeared on stage before entering films during World War I. A handsome and likable performer, he became a star in silent and sound dramas and comedies. His most memorable role was that of a flyer in Hell's Angels (1930), featuring Jean HARLOW. He later moved to England with his wife, Bebe DANIELS, where they appeared on stage, on radio, and in films.

SELECTED FILMS: Open Your Eyes (1919), Potash and Perlmutter (1923), The Pace That Thrills, Bluebeard's Seven Wives (1925), The Perfect Sap, For the Love of Mike, High Hat (1927), Lummox, Alias French Gertie (1930), The Hot Heiress, Misbehaving Ladies (1931), Week Ends Only (1932), Dancing Feet (1936), He Loved an Actress (1938). ▪

Lyons, Eddie (1886–1926), actor. Made his film debut in 1911 in silent comedy shorts. As one of the stars in comedy producer Al CHRISTIE'S company, he appeared in many relatively high-quality two-reelers from 1915 to 1917 co-starring with Lee MORAN. The team proved a profitable venture for Universal studios. By 1920 he was producing, directing, and starring in his own shorts as well as producing films featuring other comics such as Bobby DUNN. He appeared also in dramatic roles during the silent era until his untimely death at age 40.

SELECTED FILMS: *Almost a Suicide, Making a Man of Her, Henpecked Ike (1912), Some Runner (1913), When the Mummy Cried for Help, All Aboard, Eddie's Little Nightmare, Eddie's Little Love Affair, Little Egypt, Some Fixer, Almost a Knockout, Love and a Savage, Some Chaperon (1915), Once a Plumber, Roman Romeos, A Shocking Night (1921), The Lodge in the Wilderness (1926).* ■

Lyons and Moran. See Eddie Lyons and Lee Moran.

Lytton, L. Rogers (1867–1924), actor. Entered early silent films in the 1910s. He appeared as a supporting player in dramas and light films.

SELECTED FILMS: *Off the Road, Papa Put One Over (1912), Three Girls and a Man (1913), Jerry's Uncle's Namesake (1914), My Official Wife (1916), A Regular Girl (1919), His Brother's Keeper (1921), Zaza (1923), A Sainted Devil (1924).* ■

M

"Ma and Pa Kettle" films. A popular comedy series about the misadventures of a hillbilly family based on characters created by Betty MacDonald in her novel *The Egg and I.* Marjorie MAIN and Percy KILBRIDE, who played the husband-and-wife team in the original film adaptation of the novel, scored a hit in the roles and launched the popular series which ran from 1949 through 1957. Main, as the uncontrollable wife, was hilarious, as was her vacillating foil of a husband. In 1955 Kilbride retired from the low-budget series. After nine films and an eight-year run, the series ended.

SELECTED FILMS: *Ma and Pa Kettle (1949), Ma and Pa Kettle Go to Town (1950), Ma and Pa Kettle Back on the Farm (1951), Ma and Pa Kettle at the Fair (1952), Ma and Pa Kettle on Vacation (1953), Ma and Pa Kettle at Home (1954), Ma and Pa Kettle at Waikiki (1955), The Kettles in the Ozarks (1956), The Kettles on Old MacDonald's Farm (1957).* ■

"Mabel's Strange Predicament." See Charlie Chaplin.

Mabley, Moms (1897–1975), comedienne, actress. Worked in vaudeville as a teenager, touring the black theater circuit, until the late 1920s when she came to New York. She was a feature attraction at Harlem's Apollo Theater. Although a popular entertainer with black audiences, she never played the major mainstream circuits or vaudeville houses during the 1920s and 1930s. It was not until the 1960s that she got national exposure through television. She then turned out hit comedy records. A toothless comic of irreverent and off-color jokes and stories, she finally gained the fame she deserved. Her screen appearances were rare, but she did appear in minor roles in a few films during the 1930s and had a major role in another in 1974, a year before her death.

SELECTED FILMS: *The Emperor Jones (1933), Killer Diller (1947), Amazing Grace (1974).* ■

MacArthur, Charles (1895–1956), screenwriter, playwright. Worked as a reporter before teaming with fellow journalist Ben HECHT to script a succession of popular plays, including *The Front Page,* which was made into a film in 1931. Organizing their own production company, they continued their collaboration during the early sound era in Hollywood, writing cynical and witty screenplays. The pair directed several of their own works during the 1930s at Paramount's Astoria studios in New York. During the mid-1930s and 1940s MacArthur continued to write screenplays, stories, and dialogue alone or with others. He was married to Helen Hayes and was the stepfather of television and screen actor James MacArthur.

SELECTED FILMS: *Way for a Sailor, Paid (1930), The New Adventures of Get-Rich-Quick Wallingford (1931), Crime Without Passion, Twentieth Century (1934), Barbary Coast, Once in a Blue Moon, The Scoundrel (1935), Soak* the Rich (1936), The Senator Was Indiscreet, Lulu Belle (1948). ∎

MacBride, Donald (1894–1957), actor. Appeared as a character player in early sound comedy shorts as well as features during the 1930s and 1940s. A New York-based actor, he appeared in some of George BURNS and Gracie ALLEN'S early comedy shorts made for Paramount at its Astoria, New York, studio. Often cast as a bungling detective or nervous, short-tempered employee on the verge of a nervous breakdown, he appeared in numerous light films. His forte seemed to be mystery and detective comedies to which he added comic relief with his tight-lipped sneers and wide-eyed annoyance. He was particularly memorable as the distraught hotel clerk in Room Service starring the MARX BROTHERS.

In Topper Returns he played the perennial bungling detective who is summoned to an old, spooky mansion to solve a murder. Frustrated and confused, he yells at one of the suspects, cabdriver Dennis O'Keefe. "Where's your taxi?" "Where do you think?" O'Keefe replies. "I'm not paid to think!" MacBride shouts, then continues. "I'm from City Hall!"

SELECTED FILMS: Room Service, Northwest Passage (1939), Private Detectives (1940), Here Comes Mr. Jordan, Topper Returns, Love Crazy (1941), They Got Me Covered, Two Yanks in Trinidad (1942), A Stranger in Town, Best Foot Forward (1943), The Thin Man Goes Home (1944), Abbott and Costello in Hollywood (1945), Good News (1947), Bowery Battalion, Texas Carnival (1951), The Seven Year Itch (1955). ∎

MacCall, Mary C., Jr., screenwriter. Wrote screenplays alone and in collaboration and stories for Hollywood films for more than two decades. She penned most of the scripts for the popular "MAISIE" series which starred Ann SOTHERN. Although specializing in comedy, she turned out entertaining dramas and westerns as well.

SELECTED FILMS: Street of Women (1932), A Midsummer Night's Dream (1935), It's All Yours (1937), Breaking the Ice (1938), Maisie (1939), Kathleen (1941), Keep Your Powder Dry (1945), Dancing in the Dark, Mr. Belvedere Goes to College (1949), Juke Box Rhythm (1959). ∎

McCarey, Leo (1898–1969), director. Began his film career in 1918 as assistant director and, later, as GAGMAN for producer Hal ROACH. He wrote and directed many of the Charley CHASE comedy shorts. He was instrumental in furthering the careers of several silent comics during the 1920s, including those of LAUREL AND HARDY. He directed some of their best two-reelers, such as "The Battle of the Century" (1927) and "Two Tars" (1928), films that reflected his expertise at developing sight gags.

The advent of sound did not hamper McCarey. In fact, he very comfortably continued to employ sight gags with efficacy in films like Duck Soup (the classic mirror scene in which Harpo attempts to imitate Groucho Marx) and The Milky Way (in which fight contender Harold Lloyd during training hurdles confidently over a hedge only to land in a stream). He turned out feature-length comedies starring some of the major comedians of the period, including Eddie CANTOR, W. C. FIELDS, Mae WEST, the MARX BROTHERS, and Harold LLOYD.

Although he specialized in comedy, he occasionally directed sentimental and dramatic films. Not unlike Frank CAPRA (who had a similar career), he was able to combine sentimentality and farce into winning films. This becomes evident in the highly successful Ruggles of Red Gap, a film that could have resulted in mawkishness under a lesser director. He won Academy Awards for The Awful Truth (1937) and Going My Way (1944).

SELECTED FILMS: All Wet (1924), Bad Boy (1925), Dog Shy, Be Your Age (1926), Liberty, Wrong Again, The Sophomore, Red Hot Rhythm (1929), Let's Go Native (1930), The Kid From Spain (1932), Duck Soup (1933), Six of a Kind, Belle of the Nineties (1934), Ruggles of Red Gap (1935), The Milky Way (1936), Love Affair (1939), Once Upon a Honeymoon (1942), Good Sam (1948), Rally 'Round the Flag, Boys! (1958), The Devil Never Sleeps (1962). ■

McCarey, Ray (1904–1948), director. Began his film career in the 1920s as a prop boy. Following stints as assistant director and screenwriter, he began directing comedies in the early sound era for producer Hal ROACH. He turned out two-reelers starring OUR GANG and LAUREL AND HARDY and eventually directed a handful of unspectacular light features. But even his low-budget films have moments, such as the skillfully handled and exciting ballgame scenes in It Happened in Flatbush (1942), a baseball comedy-drama starring Lloyd Nolan. He was the younger brother of director Leo McCAREY.

SELECTED FILMS: Scram!, Pack Up Your Troubles (1932), Millions in the Air (1935), Three Cheers for Love (1936), Oh, Doctor!, Let's Make a Million (1937), Goodbye, Broadway (1938), Torchy Runs for Mayor (1939), You Can't Fool Your Wife, Little Orvie (1940), The Perfect Snob (1941), It Happened in Flatbush (1942), So This Is Washington (1943), Atlantic City (1944), The Gay Intruders (1949). ■

McCarthy, Charlie. See Edgar Bergen.

McCarty, Mary (1924–1980), actress. Made her film debut in the 1930s as a child performer. She appeared opposite such stars as Shirley TEMPLE, Jane WITHERS, and Judy GARLAND but never attained their popularity. Cast chiefly as a supporting actress in come-

dies, she appeared in sentimental dramas as well as light films.

SELECTED FILMS: Babes in Toyland (1934), Keep Smiling, Rebecca of Sunnybrook Farm (1938), The Sullivans (1944), The French Line (1954), Babes in Toyland (1961), My Six Loves (1963). ■

McComas, Ralph, actor. Worked in early silent films as a leading man and supporting player, chiefly for Universal studios. He appeared in many one- and two-reel comedies with Eileen SEDGWICK during World War I.

SELECTED FILMS: It's Cheaper to Be Married, A Bare Living, Good Morning Nurse, A Woman in the Case, His Family Tree, The Thousand Dollar Drop, Swearing Off, Flat Harmony, Making Monkey Business, Not Too Thin to Fight (1917), Passing the Bomb, The Butler's Blunder, The Fickle Blacksmith (1918). ■

McCoy, Harry (1894–1937), actor. Began his film career in 1911 in early silent comedy shorts. As one of Mack SENNETT'S stock company, he appeared with some of the leading comics of the period, including Charlie CHAPLIN, Chester CONKLIN, and Mabel NORMAND. For a short time he teamed up with Max ASHER and played Jake in the comedy series, "Mike and Jake." Occasionally he starred in some of the one-reelers for Sennett. By the 1920s he seldom appeared before the camera. Instead, he turned his attention to writing comedy, including two features, The Chaser (1928) and Midnight Daddies (1930).

SELECTED FILMS: Mike and Jake at the Beach (1913), Mabel's Strange Predicament, Caught in a Cabaret, Mabel's Busy Day, The Property Man, The Masquerader, His New Profession, Those Love Pangs, Tillie's Punctured Romance, How Heroes Are Made (1914), A One Night Stand, For Better—But Worse, Merely a Married Man (1915), A Movie Star, Perils of the Park, The Great Pearl Tangle, His Last Laugh, Bubbles of Trouble, She Loved a Sailor (1916), High and

Dry (1917), False Roomers (1919), His Wife's Friend (1920), Skirts (1921), Dashing Thru, Heir-Loons (1925), Hearts of Men (1928), Meet the Wife (1931). ∎

McCrea, Joel (1905–), actor. Began his film career playing bit parts in silent films during the 1920s. By the end of the decade his roles increased, but he did not achieve full recognition until the mid-1930s. A tall, good-looking, versatile actor, he starred in Depression dramas, adventure films, and sophisticated comedies. He brought the qualities of strength, dignity, and reserve to his roles. By the 1950s he was appearing chiefly in westerns.

In *Ride the High Country* (1962) he portrayed a proud ex-lawman slightly down on his luck. He tries to explain away a hole in his boot: "Juan Fernandez made those boots for me in San Anton'— special order. I had a hell of a time getting him to put that hole in there. A fine craftsman, Juan, but he never did understand the principle of ventilation."

SELECTED FILMS: Penrod and Sam (1923), A Self-Made Failure (1924), So This Is College (1928), Girls About Town (1931), Business and Pleasure, The Sport Parade (1932), The Richest Girl in the World (1934), Woman Wanted (1935), Banjo on My Knee, Two in a Crowd (1936), Woman Chases Man (1937), Three Blind Mice (1938), He Married His Wife (1940), Sullivan's Travels (1941), The Great Man's Lady, The Palm Beach Story (1942), The More the Merrier (1943), Cry Blood, Apache (1970). ∎

McCullough, Paul. See Clark and McCullough.

McDaniel, Hattie (1895–1952), actress. Worked as a band vocalist before entering films, usually as a maid to the leading lady. She appeared in dozens of films during the 1930s and 1940s, often as comic relief, a role she played with gusto. She was the first black woman to sing on radio. She won an Oscar as Best Supporting Actress for her role in *Gone With the Wind* (1939).

In the tradition of Hollywood in the 1930s, she faced the same indignities as other stereotyped character players of minority groups. Her male counterpart, black actor Fred TOONES, was listed as "Snowflake" in several films, while the rather heavy-set McDaniel was addressed as "Tiny" by Jean HARLOW in *Libeled Lady*. One of her more memorable scenes was in the comedy *The Mad Miss Manton* (1938) where, under orders from her mistress (Barbara STANWYCK), she douses Henry FONDA in the face with a pitcher of ice water. She was also a popular singer and comedienne on radio and television, starring in her own show, "Beulah."

In *The Male Animal* she played Henry FONDA'S maid. Fonda, portraying a college professor, answers the telephone instead of having his maid do it. She cocks her head, eyes him askew, and asks: "You didn't think you was me, did you?"

SELECTED FILMS: The Golden West (1932), I'm No Angel (1933), Judge Priest (1934), The Little Colonel, Alice Adams (1935), Libeled Lady, Showboat (1936), Saratoga, Nothing Sacred, True Confession (1937), The Mad Miss Manton, Carefree (1938), Zenobia (1939), Affectionately Yours (1941), The Male Animal (1942), Margie, Song of the South (1946), Mr. Blandings Builds His Dream House, Family Honeymoon (1948), The Big Wheel (1949). ∎

McDonald, Frank (1899–), director. Worked in various capacities in the theater before settling in Hollywood in 1933. By 1935 he began his long career as director, turning out scores of routine films ranging in genre from comedy to melodrama.

SELECTED FILMS: Broadway Hostess (1935), Smart Blonde (1936), Her Husband's Secretary, The Adventurous Blonde (1937), Blondes at Work, Flirting With Fate (1938), Jeepers Creepers (1939), Barnyard Follies (1940), Country Fair (1941), Mountain Rhythm (1942),

Swing Your Partner (1943), One Body Too Many (1944), Sioux City Sue (1946), Linda Be Good (1947), French Leave (1948), The Big Sombrero (1949), Father Takes the Air (1951), Mara of the Wilderness (1965). ∎

MacDonald, J. Farrell (1875–1952), actor. Worked in the theater before appearing in early silent films. In 1911 he joined IMP studios and for the next few years appeared in many films. After a short stint at directing, he returned to acting full time, appearing in leads and then in character roles. He was often cast in ethnic roles, especially portraying Irishmen. He worked alongside some of the leading screen personalities of the period, including Betty GRABLE, Constance BENNETT, Gary COOPER, and Oliver HARDY. A versatile actor, he played in hundreds of dramas and light films during a career that extended over five decades.

In My Darling Clementine (1946) he played a bartender in whom Henry FONDA, as Wyatt Earp, confides. "Mac, you ever been in love?" "No," MacDonald replies, "I've been a bartender all my life."

SELECTED FILMS: The Last Egyptian (1914), Rags (1915), Come On Over (1922), The Shamrock Handicap (1926), Ankles Preferred, The Cradle Snatchers (1927), The Cohens and the Kellys in Paris, Bringing Up Father, Abie's Irish Rose, Riley the Cop (1928), Song o' My Heart (1930), The Brat (1931), Me and My Gal (1932), The Irish in Us (1935), Slim, Topper (1937), Zenobia (1939), The Miracle of Morgan's Creek (1940), The Beautiful Blonde From Bashful Bend (1949), Mr. Belvedere Rings the Bell, Elopement (1951). ∎

MacDonald, Jeanette (1901–1965), actress, singer. Appeared on the Broadway stage in the 1920s before entering films in 1929. She starred in sophisticated and light musical comedies in the early 1930s, finally teaming up with singer Nelson Eddy to form the most successful singing duo in film history. By the 1940s their type of film became unpopular at the box office. MacDonald retreated into minor film roles but continued to sing on stage. Her earlier films with Maurice CHEVALIER and those directed by Ernst LUBITSCH are still delightful and entertaining.

In The Merry Widow, for example, she played a rich widow whom Maurice CHEVALIER meets at the famous Maxim's in Paris. Not knowing her true identity, he attempts to seduce her by leading her to an upstairs private dining room where he turns the lights down low and embraces her. She gently maneuvers herself away and turns on the lights. Chevalier is frustrated. She points to a portrait of Napoleon on the wall. "A great man," she says. "His only trouble was he attacked too soon."

SELECTED FILMS: The Love Parade (1929), Monte Carlo, Let's Go Native, The Lottery Bride, Oh, for a Man! (1930), Don't Bet on Women, Annabelle's Affairs (1931), One Hour With You, Love Me Tonight (1932), The Merry Widow (1934), Naughty Marietta (1935), I Married an Angel (1942), Follow the Boys (1944), Three Daring Daughters (1948), The Sun Comes Up (1949). ∎

Jeanette MacDonald

MacDonald, Kenneth (–1972), actor. Worked as a supporting player in dramas and comedy shorts during the 1940s and 1950s. Adept at playing unsavory scoundrels and crooked politicians, he appeared chiefly with the THREE STOOGES in the two-reelers they made for Columbia Pictures.

SELECTED FILMS: Monkey Businessmen (1946), Hold That Lion (1947), Crime on Their Hands (1948), Punchy Cowpunchers, Studio Stoops (1950), Hula La-La (1951), Three Dark Horses (1952), Booty and the Beast, Loose Loot (1953), Of Cash and Hash, Hot Ice (1955), Scheming Schemers (1956). ∎

Mace, Fred (1879–1917), actor. Appeared in minor parts in stage musicals (where he had once worked with Mack SENNETT) before entering early silent comedies as lead comic or supporting player. He worked for Biograph studios in New York and for IMP, making comedy shorts. In 1911, when KEYSTONE awarded Sennett his own comedy film unit on the West Coast, he hired his old friend, along with several other players, and they all headed for California. A husky and balding comedian, Mace played supporting roles as well as leads for Sennett. In "Mabel's Stratagem" (1912) he portrayed a flirtatious employer who hires pretty Mabel NORMAND (the star comedienne of Sennett's "Fun Factory") but is caught in the act by his suspicious wife. He starred in some of Sennett's early productions, such as "One-Round O'Brien" (1912), a knockabout comedy that proved popular and raised Mace's status as a comic. Later Sennett joined him as co-star in a series of comedies about two bungling detectives. Mace made another series of comedies, this time with popular funnyman Ford STERLING. The "Cohen" films were part of the ethnic stereotypes that Sennett and other studios resorted to for laughs. The portly Mace also played Spanish and Italian stereotypes. Aware of his increasing box-office ap-

peal, he left Sennett and tried his fortune with other studios. The change proved unprofitable and he returned in 1916 only to leave again the next year. His career in comedy films ended abruptly with his death at age 38.

SELECTED FILMS: Cohen Collects a Debt, The Water Nymph, Riley and Schultz, The Beating He Needed, Pedro's Dilemma, Stolen Glory, Ambitious Butler, Mabel's Lovers, At It Again, The Deacon's Trouble, A Temperamental Husband, Mr. Fix-It, Pat's Day Off, A Family Mix-Up (1912), Saving Mabel's Dad, The Elite Ball, Just Brown's Luck, The Battle of Who Run, The Stolen Purse, Mabel's Heroes, The Professor's Daughter, The Cure That Failed, The Gangsters (1913), A Versatile Villain (1915). ∎

McEveety, Vincent, director. Turned out several light films during the 1970s, chiefly targeted at juvenile or family audiences.

SELECTED FILMS: Firecreek (1968), The Million Dollar Duck (1971), The Biscuit Eater (1972), Charley and the Angel (1973), Superdad, The Castaway Cowboy (1974), The Strangest Man in the World (1975), Gus (1976), Herbie Goes to Monte Carlo (1977), The Apple Dumpling Gang Rides Again (1979). ∎

MacFadden, Hamilton (1901–), director. Appeared on stage and worked as a theatrical director before entering films in 1930. He directed chiefly B films, working in several genres, including light comedies.

SELECTED FILMS: Oh, for a Man!, Harmony at Home, Crazy That Way (1930), Their Mad Moment (1931), Cheaters at Play (1932), Second Hand Wife, Trick for Trick, As Husbands Go (1933), Stand Up and Cheer, She Was a Lady, Hold That Girl (1934), It Can't Last Forever (1937), Inside the Law (1942). ∎

McFarland, Spanky (1928–), child actor. Posed for advertising as a baby before entering films at age three. Born

George Emmett McFarland, he replaced chubby Joe COBB in Hal ROACH'S successful "OUR GANG" series and was featured in virtually all the shorts through the 1930s and 1940s. The most popular member of the group, the pudgy tot soon became its leader, getting the others into and out of comical predicaments. He appeared as well in a handful of non-gang feature-length films and comedy shorts, including a 1934 two-reeler, "One Track Mind," with Thelma TODD and ZaSu PITTS. By the 1940s he left the screen to pursue other occupations. Like Shirley TEMPLE, he demonstrated a tremendous amount of a true actor's ability to "listen" visually and command attention.

SELECTED FILMS (features): Day of Reckoning (1933), Miss Fane's Baby Is Stolen, Kentucky Kernels (1934), O'Shaughnessy's Boy (1935), General Spanky (1936), Peck's Bad Boy With the Circus (1939), Johnny Doughboy (1943), The Woman in the Window (1944). ∎

MacFarlane, George, actor. Appeared in early sound films as a supporting actor. Although he played in relatively few features, many of them were comedies. He supported some of the leading personalities of the period, including James CAGNEY and the comedy teams of WHEELER AND WOOLSEY and SMITH AND DALE.

SELECTED FILMS: Nix on Dames, South Sea Rose (1929), Happy Days, Half Shot at Sunrise (1930), Rich Man's Folly (1931), Taxi, Union Depot, Fireman, Save My Child, The Heart of New York (1932). ∎

McGann, William (1895–1977), director. Began his film career before World War I as a second cameraman. When he returned from military service, he obtained a position as a director of photography, advancing to assistant director by 1923. He became a full-fledged director during the early sound period, grinding out numerous low-budget, but competent, features. He worked in various genres, including comedy, melodrama, and the western.

SELECTED FILMS: On the Border (1930), I Like Your Nerve (1931), Maybe It's Love, A Night at the Ritz (1935), Freshman Love, Brides Are Like That, Polo Joe (1936), Penrod and Sam, Marry the Girl, Sh! the Octopus (1937), Penrod and His Twin Brother (1938), Everybody's Hobby (1939), Wolf of New York (1940), We Go Fast (1941), Frontier Badman (1943). ∎

McGiver, John (1913–1975), actor. Began his Hollywood career as a character actor in the 1950s. He appeared in dramas and light films, often with a troubled expression. He worked with some of the leading personalities of the period, including James STEWART, Rock HUDSON, and Jerry LEWIS.

SELECTED FILMS: Love in the Afternoon (1957), Mr. Hobbs Takes a Vacation (1962), Who's Minding the Store? (1963), Man's Favorite Sport? (1964), Marriage on the Rocks (1965), Made in Paris (1966), The Spirit Is Willing (1967), The Apple Dumpling Gang (1975). ∎

McGowan, Hugh. See Hughie Mack.

McGowan, Robert (1901–), director. Worked for producer Hal ROACH'S Pathe studios in the 1920s, directing many of the comics of Roach's stock company. His most important directorial efforts were in shaping the "OUR GANG" two-reel comedies at Pathe. He was with the series from its inception, directing many of the silent entries from 1922 through 1928 for Pathe and then later for MGM.

SELECTED FILMS: One Terrible Day, Our Gang, A Quiet Street (1922), The Champeen, The Big Show, Dogs of War, Derby Days, Sunday Calm (1923), Tire Trouble, The Mysterious Mystery (1924), The Big Town, Circus Fever, Better Movies, One Wild Ride (1925), Good Cheer, Buried Treasure (1926), Ten Years Old,

Baby Brother (1927), The Smile Wins (1928).

McGuire, Kathryn (1897–1978), actress. Worked as a dancer before entering silent films in the early 1920s. She appeared in dramas and comedies, often accompanying some of the major comics of the period, including Lupino LANE and Buster KEATON.

One of her best roles occurred in Keaton's *The Navigator*, in which the two innocents are set adrift aboard an ocean liner. Her inappropriate intuitions cause Keaton endless problems on the abandoned ship. When they sight another ship, for instance, he searches desperately for the correct flag, but she suggests a more attractive one—it just happens to be the quarantine sign—which causes the rescue ship to turn in flight. When sound arrived, she abandoned her film career.

SELECTED FILMS: *Bucking the Line, Playing With Fire (1921), The Shriek of Araby, The Love Pirate (1923), Sherlock Jr., The Navigator (1924), Two-Fisted Jones (1925), Midnight Faces (1926), Naughty but Nice, The Girl in the Pullman (1927), Children of the Ritz, The Lost Zeppelin (1929).* ■

McGuire, Marcy, actress. Appeared as a supporting player in a string of comedies during the 1940s and 1950s. She worked with such screen personalities as Frank SINATRA and MARTIN AND LEWIS.

SELECTED FILMS: *Seven Days' Leave (1942), Around the World (1943), Higher and Higher, Seven Days Ashore (1944), It Happened in Brooklyn (1947), You Gotta Stay Happy (1948), Jumping Jacks (1952).* ■

McGuire, Mickey. See "Mickey McGuire" and Mickey Rooney.

McGuire, Paddy, actor. Worked in early silent films, especially comedy shorts. He appeared as a supporting player in some of Charlie CHAPLIN'S best shorts for ESSANAY studios. A versatile performer, he portrayed a gallery of characters, including sparring partners, waiters, farmhands, and villains.

SELECTED FILMS: *The Champion, The Jitney Elopement, The Tramp, Work, The Bank, Shanghaied, A Night in the Show (1915).* ■

Frank McHugh (left)

McHugh, Frank (1898–1981), actor. Appeared on stage at age ten in his parents' act and later on Broadway before entering films. As a supporting actor in more than 100 films, he often added comic relief (through the use of broad humor and his high-pitched voice) and a feeling of amiability to his films. He was especially effective in many of the Warner Brothers 1930s musicals, such as *Footlight Parade* (1933) and the "Gold Diggers" films.

In *All Through the Night* (1942) he played a Runyonesque character and friend to Humphrey Bogart. Bogart, as a big-time gambler, describes the way a murder victim had his hand raised just before he was killed. "He was trying to tell me something," Bogart muses. "Maybe he wanted to leave the room," McHugh suggests.

SELECTED FILMS: *The Dawn Patrol (1930), The Front Page (1931), High Pressure (1932), Elmer the Great (1933), The Irish in Us, A Midsummer Night's Dream (1935), Three Men on a Horse (1936), Ever Since Eve (1937), Swing Your Lady, Boy Meets Girl (1938), On Your Toes*

(1939), Her Cardboard Lover (1942), State Fair (1935), There's No Business Like Show Business (1954), Easy Come, Easy Go (1967). ▪

McHugh, Matt (–1971), actor. Appeared occasionally in film comedies as a supporting player. He played minor characters in several comedy shorts starring the THREE STOOGES. He was the brother of comic character actor Frank McHUGH.

SELECTED FILMS: Pardon My Clutch (1948), Wham! Bam! Slam! (1955). ▪

McIntyre, Christine (–1984), actress. Worked chiefly as a supporting player in comedy shorts during the 1940s and 1950s. An attractive blonde, she appeared during this period as the heroine or femme fatale in numerous two-reelers which starred, among others, the THREE STOOGES and Harry LANGDON.

SELECTED FILMS: Idle Roomers, No Dough, Boys (1944), Three Pests in a Mess, Micro Phonies (1945), The Three Troubledoers, Three Little Pirates (1946), Out West, Brideless Groom, All Gummed Up (1947), Squareheads of the Round Table, Crime on Their Hands (1948), Who Done It?, Feulin' Around (1949), Punchy Cowpunchers, Dopey Dicks, Love at First Bite, Three Hams on Rye (1950), The Awful Sleuth (1951), Knutzy Knights, Scotched in Scotland (1954), Of Cash and Hash, Hot Ice (1955), Husbands Beware, Hot Stuff (1956). ▪

Mack, Charles E. See Moran and Mack.

Mack, Helen (1913–1986), actress. Performed on Broadway as a child before entering film in the silent era. An attractive, dark-haired lead player, she continued into the sound period, appearing in dramas and light films although she specialized in melodramas. Perhaps her best line was in *Son of Kong* (1933), when she

loses her pet monkey. As Robert ARMSTRONG, who that same year starred in *King Kong*, searches for the creature, she asks: "Have you ever caught a monkey?"

SELECTED FILMS: The Little Red School House (1923), Pied Piper Malone (1924), Sweepings, Melody Cruise, Christopher Bean (1933), All of Me, Kiss and Make Up, The Lemon Drop Kid, College Rhythm (1934), The Milky Way (1936), Fit for a King (1937), His Girl Friday (1940), Strange Holiday (1945). ▪

Mack, Hughie (1884–1927), actor. Appeared in early silent comedy shorts as a supporting player or lead comedian. An obese figure, he began his film career with VITAGRAPH studios in 1913 under his real name, Hugh McGowan, and accompanied the legendary comic John BUNNY. For the next few years he starred in his own series for Vitagraph as well as other studios, including Mack SENNETT'S in 1919. A knockabout comic, he never achieved the fame that some of his contemporaries attained. Aside from his corpulence, he offered little in the way of natural comedy or acting ability. By the mid-1920s he was relegated to minor roles in serials and features.

SELECTED FILMS: John Tobin's Sweetheart, Roughing the Cub, The Hero (1913), The New Secretary, The Win(k)some Widow (1914), Trifling Women (1922), Going Up (1923), Reno (1924), A Woman's Faith, The Merry Widow (1925), Four Sons, The Wedding March (1928). ▪

Mack, James T. (1871–1948), actor. Entered silent films in the 1920s following a long stage career. He appeared as a supporting player in dramas and light films.

SELECTED FILMS: The Cruise of the Jasper B, Fools of Fashion (1926), Wild Geese, The First Night, Husband Hunters, Women's Wares, Swim, Girl, Swim (1927), The Home Towners (1928), Ain't It the Truth (1929), Hello Sister (1930), I Hate Women (1934), G-Men (1935). ▪

Mack, Lester (1906–1972), actor. Came to films late in life following a long stage career. He appeared as a character player in a handful of light films. He also worked as a supporting actor in television.

SELECTED FILMS: *Funny Girl, Star, The Night They Raided Minsky's, For Love of Ivy (1968).* ∎

Mack, Russell (1892–1972), director. Worked in the theater before entering films during the early sound period. He directed several light films in the 1930s. *Once in a Lifetime,* a funny satire on Hollywood and those who make movies, was his most notable work.

SELECTED FILMS: *Second Wife, Big Money (1930), Heaven on Earth, Mississippi (1931), The All American, Once in a Lifetime (1932), Private Jones (1933), The Meanest Gal in Town, The Band Plays On (1934).* ∎

Mack, Wilbur (1873–1964), actor. Worked as a blackface comic, in theater repertory, and in an act, "Mack and Walker," with his wife, Nella WALKER. When Hollywood converted to sound, he began his long screen career as a supporting player following several appearances in silent films. Dark and sinister-looking, he was often cast as a villain in westerns although he played in many light films as well. His screen appearances spanned three decades.

SELECTED FILMS: *Gold and Grit (1925), Honky Tonk, Slim Fingers, An Everyday Occurrence (1929), The Czar of Broadway, The Girl Said No (1930), Annabelle's Affairs (1931), The Loud Speaker (1934), Redheads on Parade, A Night at the Opera (1935), A Day at the Races (1937), Half a Sinner (1940), Dixie (1943), Atlantic City (1944), Ladies' Man (1947), Stage Struck (1948).* ∎

Mackaill, Dorothy (1903–), actress. Worked on stage in her native England and in the Ziegfeld Follies before entering films during the silent period. She appeared as leading ladies in dozens of comedy shorts and light feature films.

SELECTED FILMS: *Bits of Life (1921), The Streets of New York (1922), The Fighting Blade (1923), What Shall I Do? (1924), Chickee, Shore Leave, Joanna (1925), Subway Sadie (1926), Man Crazy (1927), Ladies' Night in a Turkish Bath, Lady Be Good, The Barker (1928), Children of the Ritz, His Captive Woman, Two Weeks Off (1929), Strictly Modern, The Flirting Widow, The Office Wife (1930), No Man of Her Own (1932), The Chief, Picture Brides (1933), Cheaters (1934).* ∎

MacKenna, Kenneth (1899–1962), actor. Appeared on stage before entering silent films as male lead. He continued into the sound period playing main roles and eventually character parts. Most of his early work was in light films. During the 1930s he directed several features.

SELECTED FILMS: *Miss Bluebeard, A Kiss in the Dark (1925), The American Venus (1926), Lunatic at Large (1927), Pleasure Crazed, Love, Live and Laugh, South Sea Rose (1929), Crazy That Way, Sin Takes a Holiday (1930), High Time (1960), 13 West Street (1962).* ∎

McLaglen, Victor (1886–1959), actor. Appeared in silent films in his native England before coming to Hollywood. His large frame and craggy face made him a natural for rugged but lovable character roles. He was featured in many silent and sound dramas and light films, occasionally starring in some.

One of his early successes in a comic role occurred in the silent version of *What Price Glory* (1926), which contained a fair share of horseplay between Captain Flagg (McLaglen) and Sergeant Quirt (Edmund LOWE) as well as spectacular battle sequences. The squabbling of the two men, usually over a female, became so popular that they continued their rows into the sound era in several sequels. McLaglen later appeared in several John FORD films, often as a tough sergeant and comic relief. It was under

Ford's direction that he won his only Oscar, for his portrayal of Gypo Nolan in *The Informer* (1935).

In *She Wore a Yellow Ribbon* (1949) he played a cavalry soldier who has recently been mustered out of the service. A detachment of soldiers arrives at the local tavern to take the hard-drinking, boisterous McLaglen into custody. When he is asked to go peacefully, he responds: "Laddie, I've never gone any place peacefully in my life."

SELECTED FILMS: *The Beloved Brute* (1924), *A Girl in Every Port* (1928), *The Cockeyed World, Hot for Paris* (1929), *On the Level, A Devil With Women* (1930), *Women of All Nations* (1931), *Hot Pepper, Laughing at Life* (1933), *No More Women, The Captain Hates the Sea* (1934), *Under Pressure* (1935), *Klondike Annie* (1936), *Wee Willie Winkie* (1937), *Gunga Din, Rio, The Big Guy* (1939), *Broadway Limited* (1941), *Call Out the Marines* (1942), *The Princess and the Pirate* (1944), *Rough, Tough and Ready* (1945), *The Quiet Man* (1952), *Lady Godiva* (1955), *The Abductors* (1957). ∎

MacLaine, Shirley (1934–), actress. Appeared on stage at the age of four as a dancer, in chorus lines on Broadway, and as a model before entering films in 1954. A versatile and talented actress, she was as at home in comedies and musicals as in dramas. Her rise to stardom was swift; within five years of appearing in her first feature, her salary skyrocketed from $6,000 to $250,000 per film. Uninhibited, sometimes kooky, she has always appeared warm and natural on screen. She is the brother of actor Warren Beatty.

In *The Yellow Rolls Royce* (1965), a film she made in England, she portrayed an American gangster's moll who is totally blase about the wonders of European architecture. Her view of the Tower of Pisa: "So it leans."

She has devoted a large part of her time to liberal causes, campaigning occasionally for liberal candidates. Her 1973 tour of China led to her documen-

tary, *The Other Half of the Sky: A China Memoir*, which she wrote, produced, and co-directed. Her more recent work, *Out on a Limb* (1983), describes her mystical experiences and was adapted as a television feature starring MacLaine. She was nominated four times for Oscars: *Some Came Running* (1959), *The Apartment* (1960), and *Irma La Douce* (1963), finally winning one for her performance in *Terms of Endearment* (1983). Her memoirs appear in *Don't Fall Off the Mountain*, published in 1970.

SELECTED FILMS: *The Trouble With Harry* (1954), *Artists and Models* (1955), *Around the World in 80 Days* (1956), *The Matchmaker* (1958), *Ask Any Girl* (1959), *Ocean's Eleven, Can-Can, My Geisha, Two for the Seesaw* (1962), *What a Way to Go!* (1964), *John Goldfarb, Please Come Home* (1965), *Gambit* (1966), *Sweet Charity* (1969), *Being There* (1979), *Loving Couples, A Change of Seasons* (1980), *Cannonball Run II* (1984). ∎

MacLane, Barton (1902–1969), actor. Worked on stage before entering films as a supporting player in the late 1920s. Known chiefly for his tough-guy roles in numerous gangster films and westerns, he also appeared in several light films. He co-starred as a cop with Glenda Farrell in the popular "Torchy Blane" action-comedy series produced in the late 1930s. In all, he appeared in approximately 200 films.

SELECTED FILMS: *The Quarterback* (1926), *Cocoanuts* (1929), *Tillie and Gus* (1933), *Ever Since Eve, The Adventurous Blonde* (1937), *Torchy Gets Her Man* (1938), *Melody Ranch* (1940), *Barnacle Bill* (1941), *All Through the Night* (1942), *Let's Dance* (1950), *The Geisha Boy* (1958), *Pocketful of Miracles* (1961), *Arizona Bushwackers* (1968). ∎

MacLean, Douglas (1890–1967), actor. Began his film career in early silent, light films. Handsome and well attired, he starred in breezy shorts and features throughout the 1920s. He was not a comic in the tradition of a CHAPLIN or a KEATON; like many other personalities of the 1920s, he was more an actor who depended heavily on scripts and plots. The humor came more frequently from title cards than from personal clowning. When sound came to Hollywood, he turned to producing, often turning out films with some of the leading comics of the period, including, among others, WHEELER AND WOOLSEY, W. C. FIELDS, and George BURNS and Gracie ALLEN.

SELECTED FILMS: As Ye Sow (1914), Johanna Enlists, Fuss and Feathers, Mirandy Smiles (1918), Captain Kidd, Jr., The Home Breaker, 23 1/2 Hours' Leave (1919), Mary's Ankle, The Jailbird, The Rookie's Return (1920), Chickens, The Home Stretch (1921), The Hottentot (1922), The Sunshine Trail (1923), That's My Baby (1926), Soft Cushions (1927), The Carnation Kid (1929). ∎

McLeod, Norman Z. (1898–1964), director. Began his film career after World War I as an animator. He then worked as a GAGMAN for comedy producer Al CHRISTIE. By 1928 he was directing films and continued in this capacity for four decades, turning out chiefly comedies starring some of the foremost comics of the period, including, among others, W. C. FIELDS, Bob HOPE, Danny KAYE, and the MARX BROTHERS. Although not especially innovative, he was a capable director who, when furnished with good material and talented performers, turned out well-constructed and highly entertaining features.

SELECTED FILMS: Taking a Chance (1928), Along Came Youth, Finn and Hattie, Monkey Business (1931), Horse Feathers, If I Had a Million (1932), Mama Loves Papa, Alice in Wonderland (1933), Melody in Spring, It's a Gift (1934), Redheads on Parade, Here Comes Cookie (1935), Early to Bed, Mind Your Own Business (1936), Topper (1937), Merrily We Live (1938), Topper Takes a Trip (1939), Lady Be Good (1941), Panama Hattie (1942), Swing Shift Maisie (1943), The Kid From Brooklyn (1946), The Secret Life of Walter Mitty, The Road to Rio (1947), The Paleface (1948), My Favorite Spy (1951), Never Wave at a WAC (1952), Casanova's Big Night (1954), Alias Jesse James (1959). ∎

MacMahon, Aline (1899–), actress. Appeared on stage before entering films during the early sound period. Although her sorrowful eyes and face worked in her favor in dramatic roles, she was equally comfortable in comedies. She was often cast as the experienced and cynical friend of the leading lady or ingenue. She starred in a series of low-budget mysteries during the 1930s, in which she played a nurse. She received an Academy Award nomination as Best Supporting Actress for her role in Dragon Seed (1944).

In Once in a Lifetime she played a former vaudevillian who decides to open an elocution school to help silent film stars make the transition to sound. When one of her dim-witted partners, Jack Oakie, says that he doesn't know anything about this field, she quips, "You don't know anything about anything, but if what they say about Hollywood is true, you'll go far."

SELECTED FILMS: Five Star Final (1931), The Heart of New York, Week End Marriage, Once in a Lifetime (1932), Gold Diggers of 1933 (1933), Big Hearted Herbert, Babbitt, The Merry Frinks (1934), Mary Jane's Pa, Ah, Wilderness! (1935), When You're in Love (1937), The Lady Is Willing (1942), The Mighty McGurk (1946), The Eddie Cantor Story (1953), I Could Go On Singing, All the Way Home (1963). ∎

McMahon, Horace (1906–1971), actor. A dark-haired, crooked-nosed Runyonesque character player who worked on both sides of the law. He played small-time hoodlums as well as frustrated detectives chiefly in urban dramas and light films. He scored a hit in the stage production and film version of *Detective Story* (1951).

SELECTED FILMS: *The Wrong Road, Navy Blues, A Girl With Ideas, Double Wedding* (1937), *Broadway Musketeers* (1938), *The Gracie Allen Murder Case, Laugh It Off, She Married a Cop, That's Right—You're Wrong* (1939), *Margie, My Favorite Wife* (1940), *Rookies on Parade, The Bride Wore Crutches, The Stork Pays Off* (1941), *Jail House Blues* (1942), *The Navy Way* (1944), *Abbott and Costello Go to Mars* (1953), *Susan Slept Here* (1954), *Beau James, The Delicate Delinquent* (1957), *The Detective* (1968). ∎

McMurphy, Charles, actor. Began his screen career in the 1920s. He worked as a supporting player in late silent and early sound comedy shorts and features, appearing chiefly in films starring LAUREL AND HARDY.

SELECTED FILMS: *Two Tars* (1928), *Night Owls, Below Zero, Hog Wild* (1930), *Scram!* (1932), *Me and My Pal* (1933), *The Spoilers* (1942). ∎

MacMurray, Fred (1908–), actor. Worked with bands and in a Broadway revue and a musical before entering films in the early 1930s. At first assigned various roles, he eventually settled comfortably into light films, often as the friendly leading man who gets the girl. Portraying characters that ranged from tough bodyguards to fretful baby specialists, he starred in numerous farces and sophisticated comedies over a career that spanned more than five decades. During the 1960s he starred in a series of comedies for the Walt Disney studios. Occasionally he appeared with equal adeptness in dramas.

In *Hands Across the Table* manicurist Carole LOMBARD twice draws blood while working on MacMurray's hands. "If you think I should have ether," he wryly suggests, "don't be afraid to say so."

SELECTED FILMS: *Friends of Mr. Sweeney* (1934), *The Gilded Lily, Alice Adams, Hands Across the Table, The Bride Comes Home* (1935), *The Princess Comes Across* (1936), *Champagne Waltz, True Confession* (1937), *Swing You Sinners* (1938), *Honeymoon in Bali* (1939), *Too Many Husbands* (1940), *One Night in Lisbon, New York Town* (1941), *The Lady Is Willing, Take a Letter, Darling* (1942), *No Time for Love* (1943), *Standing Room Only, And the Angels Sing* (1944), *Murder, He Says* (1945), *Pardon My Past* (1946), *The Egg and I* (1947), *On Our Merry Way* (1948), *Family Honeymoon, Father Was a Fullback* (1949), *Never a Dull Moment* (1950), *A Millionaire for Christy, Callaway Went Thataway* (1951), *The Shaggy Dog* (1959), *The Apartment* (1960), *The Absent-Minded Professor* (1961), *Bon Voyage!* (1962), *Son of Flubber* (1963), *Follow Me, Boys!* (1966), *The Happiest Millionaire* (1967), *The Swarm* (1978). ∎

McNear, Howard (1905–1969), actor. Appeared in comedy roles in light films during the 1950s and 1960s. He supported some of the leading comic actors of the period, including Jack LEMMON and Walter MATTHAU.

SELECTED FILMS: *The Long, Long Trailer* (1954), *Bundle of Joy* (1956), *Bell, Book and Candle* (1958), *The Big Circus* (1959), *Bachelor Flat, Follow That Dream* (1962), *Irma La Douce* (1963), *Kiss Me, Stupid* (1964), *The Fortune Cookie* (1966). ∎

McQueen, Butterfly (1911–), actress. Appeared in a Harlem theater group in 1914 at age three and on Broadway in 1937 before entering films in 1939. As a tear-shedding maid possessed of a high-pitched voice, she added comic relief to the few films in which she appeared. Her most memorable role remains that of Prissy in *Gone With the Wind*.

SELECTED FILMS: *Gone With the Wind* (1939), *Affectionately Yours* (1941), *Cabin in the Sky, I Dood It* (1943), *Since You Went Away* (1944), *Flame of the Barbary Coast, Mildred*

Pierce (1945), Duel in the Sun (1947), The Phynx (1970), Amazing Grace (1974). ■

McWade, Robert (–1938), actor. Appeared on stage before entering films during the silent period. He played character roles in more than one hundred dramas and light films, typically as judges, district attorneys, doctors, etc.

SELECTED FILMS: Second Youth (1924), The Home Towners (1928), Feet First (1930), Too Many Crooks, Girls About Town (1931), Movie Crazy (1932), Hard to Handle (1933), Hold That Girl, Let's Be Ritzy, The Lemon Drop Kid (1934), The County Chairman, Cappy Ricks Returns (1935), The Big Noise, Anything Goes (1936), We're on the Jury, Good Old Soak (1937), Of Human Hearts (1938). ■

Madcap comedy. See Screwball comedy.

Chill Wills and Marjorie Main

Main, Marjorie (1890–1975), actress. Worked in stock, in vaudeville, and, in 1916, on Broadway before entering films in the early 1930s. A strong character actress with a reputation as a scene stealer, she was often cast as a slum mother in a string of melodramas following her memorable role as the unforgiving mother of gangster Humphrey Bogart

in Dead End (1937), a part she also played in the original Broadway play.

Born Mary Tomlinson, she distinguished herself as a superb comedienne in the 1940s in a series of films co-starring with Wallace BEERY and in the 1950s in another popular comedy series, "MA AND PA KETTLE," in which she portrayed the rambunctious wife of co-star Percy KILBRIDE. She has also appeared with other notable comics of the period, including ABBOTT AND COSTELLO. She abandoned her film career in 1957.

In The Belle of New York (1952) she played the wealthy dowager-aunt of playboy Fred ASTAIRE. She warns her nephew's fiancee: "Charles has one trait, a characteristic he inherited from his uncle's side of the family." "What's that?" the young woman asks. "He's no good."

SELECTED FILMS: A House Divided (1931), Hot Saturday (1932), Take a Chance (1933), Too Hot to Handle (1938), Another Thin Man (1939), Turnabout, I Take This Woman (1940), Barnacle Bill (1941), The Bugle Sounds, We Were Dancing, Jackass Mail, Tish (1942), Gentle Annie, Meet Me in St. Louis (1944), Murder, He Says (1945), The Harvey Girls, Bad Bascomb (1946), The Egg and I, The Wistful Widow of Wagon Gap (1947), Big Jack, Ma and Pa Kettle (1949), Summer Stock (1950), The Long, Long Trailer (1954), Friendly Persuasion (1956). ■

"Maisie" comedies. A series of films starring Ann SOTHERN as an externally tough but soft-hearted showgirl. Produced by MGM, these low-budget comedies displayed Sothern's buoyant personality as she personified the new role of women in World War II. Occasionally a popular performer, such as Red SKELTON, would appear to help things along. Portraying a scatterbrained blonde gold-digger who perpetually gets herself into and out of comical scrapes, she managed to carry the series through ten entries from 1939 to 1947.

SELECTED FILMS: *Maisie (1939), Congo Maisie, Gold Rush Maisie (1940), Maisie Was a Lady, Ringside Maisie (1941), Maisie Gets Her Man (1942), Swing Shift Maisie (1943), Maisie Goes to Reno (1944), Up Goes Maisie (1946), Undercover Maisie (1947).* ∎

"Making a Living" (1914), KEY. *Dir.* Henry Lehrman; *Sc.* not listed; with Charlie Chaplin, Henry Lehrman, Virginia Kirtley, Alice Davenport, Minta Durfee, Chester Conklin.

This one-reel comedy was Charlie Chaplin's first film, an inauspicious beginning for the comic. Although he had been hired by producer Mack SENNETT to work in KEYSTONE comedies, he did not receive any assignment for weeks. Finally, the moment arrived. He plays an impoverished Englishman sporting a frock coat, monocle, and walrus mustache. His famous "tramp" character had not yet emerged, but his inventiveness and his subtlety can be seen, if only in brief glimpses. Seeking employment, he gets a job as a reporter. He steals a fellow news photographer's camera that contains a picture of a car accident and rushes back to his boss, claiming the photo as his own. Later, he is spotted by the photographer who chases him through the streets. Chaplin was disappointed in the final product, especially in the cuts that were made. Producer Mack Sennett and director Henry Lehrman imbued their Keystone comedies with broad farce and a rapid tempo; they were not interested in the nuances Charlie attempted to insert.

Malone, Molly (1895–1952), actress. Worked in vaudeville before entering early silent films. She began her screen career starring in comedy shorts for producer Al CHRISTIE and eventually played leads in feature-length dramas, serials, and light films through the 1920s.

SELECTED FILMS: *Straight Shooting, Bucking Broadway (1917), Wild Women,*

A Woman's Fool (1918), It's a Great Life (1920), Just Out of College, Made in Heaven, Sure Fire (1921), A Poor Relation, The Freshie (1922), Little Johnny Jones (1923), The Knockout Kid (1925), Daring Deeds (1927). ∎

Man Who Came to Dinner, The (1941), WB. *Dir.* William Keighley; *Sc.* Julius Epstein, Philip Epstein; with Monty Woolley, Bette Davis, Ann Sheridan, Billie Burke, Jimmy Durante.

The film version of the Broadway comedy by George S. Kaufman and Moss Hart, who were paid $250,000 for their work, turned out to be a witty and entertaining feature but not a classic comedy like *My Man Godfrey, His Girl Friday,* or *It Happened One Night.* Monty WOOLLEY plays Sheridan Whiteside, the arrogant critic and dinner guest who injures his leg and decides to stay on. Woolley had created the role on stage. Most of the sparkling dialogue emanates from the Whiteside character. "Would you take your clammy hand off my chair," he churlishly addresses his nurse. "You have the touch of a love-starved cobra." He says of his own relationship with his parents: "I left home at the age of four, and I haven't been back since. They can hear me on the radio, and that's enough for them." He entices hostess Billie BURKE'S cook and butler to enter his employ. "My cook and butler have been with me for 10 years," she protests. "I'm commuting their sentence," Woolley quips. Bette DAVIS portrays his secretary while cheering up newspaperman Richard Travis, who has dreams of marriage. "I suppose some poor girl could fall for you," she says, "if you came with a set of dishes." Whiteside supposedly was based on Alexander Woollcott. Other characters have their real-life counterparts as well: Jimmy DURANTE'S Banjo, Harpo MARX; Ann Sheridan's role, Gertrude Lawrence; and Reginald GARDINER'S character, Noel Coward. Billie Burke plays the mistress of the home that the pompous critic takes over.

Mander, Miles (1888–1946), actor. Appeared in and directed silent and sound films in his native England before settling in Hollywood during the mid-1930s as a character player. A stern figure with a neat mustache and a distinctive voice, he appeared chiefly in low-budget dramas and serials although he made several light films as well.

SELECTED FILMS: Here's to Romance (1935), Youth on Parade, Wake Up and Live (1937), The Mad Miss Manton (1938), The Three Musketeers, The Little Princess (1939), Road to Singapore (1940), To Be or Not to Be, You're Telling Me (1942), Four Jills in a Jeep (1944), Week-End at the Waldorf (1945), The Walls Came Tumbling Down, The Imperfect Lady (1946). ■

Manhattan. See Woody Allen.

Mankiewicz, Herman (1897–1953), screenwriter. Worked as an overseas reporter for the Chicago Tribune and as a Broadway drama critic before entering films in the 1920s as a screenwriter. He wrote the titles for silent films, adaptations, dialogue, and many screenplays alone and occasionally in collaboration. Although his work at times went uncredited, his writing talent in both dramas and light films entertained film audiences for more than four decades. His most memorable screenplay, which he co-wrote with Orson Welles, was for Citizen Kane (1941). Even his scripts for routine adventure films like The Spanish Main (1945) contained witty dialogue, particularly in the lines spoken by charming villain Walter Slezak.

SELECTED FILMS: The Road to Mandalay, Stranded in Paris (1926), Fashions for Women, The Gay Defender (1927), Abie's Irish Rose (1928), The Dummy (1929), Honey, Ladies Love Brutes, The Royal Family of Broadway, Ladies' Man (1931), Girl Crazy (1932), Dinner at Eight, Another Language (1933), The Show-Off (1934), After Office Hours (1935), My Dear Miss Aldrich (1937), It's a Wonderful World (1939), Rise and Shine (1941), Christmas Holiday (1944), The Pride of St. Louis (1952). ■

Mann, Delbert (1920–), director. Worked as a stage and television director before entering films. Although he directed a number of dramas, he specialized in romantic comedies and bedroom farces. He won an Oscar for Marty (1955), his first directorial effort.

SELECTED FILMS: The Bachelor Party (1957), Lover Come Back (1961), That Touch of Mink (1962), Dear Heart (1964), Quick Before It Melts (1965), Mister Buddwing (1966), Fitzwilly (1967), The Pink Jungle (1968), Birch Interval (1976). ■

Mann, Hank (1888–1971), actor. Worked as a trapeze acrobat before entering early silent films in 1912. Sporting a thick mustache, the large-framed comic who was born David W. Liebermann became a steady member of Mack SENNETT'S stock company, appearing in numerous comedy shorts, either as supporting player or lead comic. He was one of the original KEYSTONE KOPS. He appeared also in a few Charlie CHAPLIN one- and two-reelers while at Sennett's KEYSTONE studio. In 1917 he moved to Fox studios to star in and occasionally direct a series of two-reel comedies. He continued to act in films well into the sound era, his screen career spanning five decades. He was the prizefighter in Chaplin's City Lights.

Like his friend and co-comic Chester CONKLIN, he was a renowned scene stealer, but that was not enough to raise him to the top rung of comedians. He was never given the opportunity to develop his own screen character, whether under the guidance of Sennett, who rushed his pictures out to meet tight schedules, or other studios that exploited Mann's talents instead of nurturing them. He was to remain a second-string comic.

SELECTED FILMS: Algy on the Force, The Waiter's Picnic (1913), Mabel's Strange Predicament, Caught in a Cabaret, The Knockout, Tillie's Punctured Romance (1914), The Village Blacksmith, Hearts and Spars (1916), The Janitor (1919), Mystic Mush (1920), Quincy Adams Sawyer (1922), Don't Marry for Money (1923), Empty Hands (1924), The Sporting Venus (1925), The Boob (1926), The Ladybird, Paid to Love (1927), Spite Marriage (1929), Sinner's Holiday (1930), City Lights (1931), Million Dollar Legs (1932), Modern Times (1936), The Great Dictator (1940), The Perils of Pauline (1947), The Caddy (1953), Abbott and Costello Meet the Keystone Kops (1955), Daddy-O (1959). ■

Mansfield, Jayne (1933–1967), actress. Appeared occasionally in television and on Broadway before entering films in 1955. A well-proportioned blonde, she made several light films and quickly rose to fame as one of Hollywood's major sex symbols of the 1950s and 1960s. Her popularity, however, declined in the mid-1960s, and she found herself relegated to low-budget and foreign films. She died in an automobile accident at age 34.

In The Girl Can't Help It she played an aspiring buxom singer. Holding two milk bottles against her breasts, she complains: "Everybody thinks of me as a sexpot; nobody thinks of me as equipped for motherhood."

SELECTED FILMS: Pete Kelly's Blues (1955), Female Jungle, The Girl Can't Help It (1956), Will Success Spoil Rock Hunter?, Kiss Them for Me (1957), The Sheriff of Fractured Jaw (1958), It Happened in Athens (1962), Promises! Promises! (1963), The Fat Spy, Las Vegas Hillbillies (1966), A Guide for the Married Man (1967), Single Room Furnished (1968). ■

March, Fredric (1897–1975), actor. Started out in banking before switching to show business. Born Ernest Frederick McIntyre Bickel, he appeared on stage during the early 1920s, occasionally in films as a bit player, and on Broadway in 1926 before entering films on a full-time basis. An accomplished and versatile actor, he played a wide range of roles in a variety of genres. In dramas like Death Takes a Holiday (1934) and Mary of Scotland (1937) he personified integrity, often portraying intelligent, worldly characters. Along with other talented stars such as Carole LOMBARD, Claudette COLBERT, Irene DUNNE, and Cary GRANT, he pioneered in SOPHISTICATED COMEDY and SCREWBALL COMEDY, making these genres palatable to the general public. He was married to actress Florence Eldridge.

In Nothing Sacred (1937) March, a cynical reporter, describes his hard-nosed editor: "He's got a different quality of charm. He's sort of a cross between a ferris wheel and a werewolf—but with a lovable streak, if you care to blast for it." He won Academy Awards for Dr. Jekyll and Mr. Hyde (1932) and The Best Years of Our Lives (1946).

SELECTED FILMS: The Dummy, The Wild Party, Paris Bound, Footlights and Fools, The Marriage Playground (1929), Ladies Love Brutes, True to the Navy (1930), The Royal Family of Broadway, Honor Among Lovers (1931), Smilin' Through (1932), Design for Living (1933), All of Me, Good Dame (1934), Trade Winds (1939), Bedtime Story (1941), I Married a Witch (1942), The Iceman Cometh (1973). ■

March, Hal (1920–1970), actor, comic. Appeared in television before entering films as a comedian or comic relief character. His screen career, however, never blossomed, and he was relegated to routine films and minor roles.

SELECTED FILMS: The Gracie Allen Murder Case (1939), Ma and Pa Kettle Go to Town (1950), The Eddie Cantor Story (1953), The Atomic Kid, Yankee Pasha (1954), It's Always Fair Weather, My Sister Eileen (1955), Hear Me Good (1957), Send Me No Flowers (1964), A Guide for the Married Man (1967). ■

Marcus, James A. (1868–1937), actor. Entered early silent films in 1915 following a long stage career. He appeared as a supporting player in numerous dramas, historical works, and light films during a screen career that spanned three decades.

SELECTED FILMS: *Little Lord Fauntleroy* (1921), *Come On Over* (1922), *Beau Brummell* (1924), *The Goose Hangs High, All Around the Frying Pan, Lightnin'* (1925), *The Lily, The Traffic Cop, The Texas Streak* (1926), *The Bachelor's Baby, The Meddlin' Stranger, Beauty Shoppers* (1927), *Buck Privates* (1928), *In Holland* (1929), *Back Pay* (1930), *The Lonely Trail* (1936). ∎

Margolin, Janet (1943–), actress. Appeared on Broadway before entering films in 1962. She won a film festival award as best actress for her title role in *David and Lisa* (1962), her first film. She has played in dramas and light films, usually cast as an ingenue.

SELECTED FILMS: *David and Lisa* (1962), *Enter Laughing* (1967), *Buona Sera, Mrs. Campbell* (1968), *Take the Money and Run* (1969), *Your Three Minutes Are Up* (1973), *Annie Hall* (1977), *The Last Embrace* (1979). ∎

Marin, Edwin L. (1899–1951), director. Began his career in films immediately after World War I as an assistant cameraman. He held a variety of jobs in Hollywood before becoming a full-time director during the sound era. Turning out chiefly well-made minor films destined for the second half of a double bill, he worked in different genres, including westerns, dramas, and comedies.

SELECTED FILMS: *The Death Kiss, The Sweetheart of Sigma Chi* (1933), *Affairs of a Gentleman, Paris Interlude* (1934), *All American Chump* (1936), *Married Before Breakfast* (1937), *Everybody Sing, Hold That Kiss, Listen, Darling* (1938), *Fast and Loose, Maisie* (1939), *Henry Goes Arizona, Gold Rush Maisie, Hullabaloo* (1940), *Maisie Was a Lady, Ringside Maisie* (1941), *A Gentle-*

man After Dark, Miss Annie Rooney (1942), *Show Business* (1944), *Fort Worth* (1951). ∎

Marion, Edna (1908–1957), actress. Appeared in vaudeville, on stage, and as a supporting player in silent films. One of producer Hal ROACH'S more talented comediennes, she worked in silent comedy shorts with Charlie CHASE and LAUREL AND HARDY.

SELECTED FILMS: *The Desert's Price, Her Daily Dozen, My Baby Doll, Powdered Chickens, Putting on Airs, Puzzled by Crosswords, Dangerous Peach* (1925), *The Call of the Wilderness, Readin' 'Ritin' 'Rithmetic* (1926), *Sugar Daddies* (1927), *From Soup to Nuts, Should Married Men Go Home?* (1928), *Skinner Steps Out* (1929), *Romance of the West, Today* (1930). ∎

Marion, Frances (1887–1973), screenwriter. Worked in advertising, as a model, as a film actress, and as a reporter before turning to screenwriting, a career that was to span four decades. One of Hollywood's most popular writers during the silent and sound eras, she penned more than a hundred dramas, historical romances, and comedies alone and in collaboration. She was awarded Oscars for *The Big House* (1930) and *The Champ* (1931). During the 1920s she directed a handful of films.

SELECTED FILMS (as actress): *A Girl of Yesterday, The Jest of Jealousy* (1915), *Little Lord Fauntleroy* (1921), *New York Town* (1941).

SELECTED FILMS (as screenwriter): *Fanchon the Cricket, Little Pal* (1915), *All Man* (1916), *Poor Little Rich Girl, Rebecca of Sunnybrook Farm, The Little Princess* (1917), *M'Liss, He Comes Up Smiling* (1918), *Captain Kidd, Jr., A Regular Girl* (1919), *Pollyanna, The Flapper* (1920), *The Primitive Lover, Sonny* (1922), *Potash and Perlmutter* (1923), *The Lady, His Supreme Moment, Lazybones* (1925), *Partners Again* (1926), *The Callahans and the Murphys* (1927), *Bringing Up Father* (1928), *Let Us*

Be Gay, Good News, Min and Bill (1930), Dinner at Eight (1933), Green Hell (1940). ∎

Marion, George (1860–1945), actor. Worked in stock and minstrel shows and became a Broadway director in the 1910s. He entered silent films in 1915 and continued into the sound period playing character roles in dramas and light films. A mature figure with disheveled white hair and a sympathetic expression, he was best known for his role as Anna Christie's sea-captain father. In fact, he appeared in that capacity in the original play in 1921, the silent version in 1923, and in the sound adaptation starring Greta Garbo in 1930. He was the father of screenwriter George Marion, Jr.

SELECTED FILMS: Go Straight (1921), The Girl I Loved, A Million to Burn (1923), Bringin' Home the Bacon (1924), On the Go, Clothes Make the Pirate, Straight Through (1925), Rolling Home, The Wise Guy (1926), Loco Luck (1927), A Lady's Morals, Hook, Line and Sinker (1930), Man to Man (1931), Her First Mate (1933), Port of Lost Dreams (1935). ∎

Marion, Sid (1900–1965), actor. Worked on stage as well as in films from the early 1930s. He appeared chiefly as a supporting player in dramas and light features, continuing to perform in films until his death.

SELECTED FILMS: The Mighty Barnum (1934), Lady of Burlesque (1943), Oh, You Beautiful Doll, Jiggs and Maggie in Jackpot Jitters (1949), Love That Brute, Woman From Headquarters (1950), Call Me Madam (1953), The Outlaws Is Coming (1965). ∎

Markey, Gene (1895–1980), screenwriter, novelist, playwright. Settled in Hollywood as a screenwriter at the close of the silent period following the publication of several novels and short stories. He turned out a succession of light films and dramas alone and in collaboration

throughout the Depression years. He later became a producer.

SELECTED FILMS: The Battle of Paris, Lucky in Love, Mother's Boy (1929), The Floradora Girl (1930), The Great Lover, Inspiration (1931), Baby Face, Luxury Liner, Midnight Mary (1933), The Merry Frinks (1934), Let's Live Tonight (1935), On the Avenue (1937), You're the One (1941), Wonder Boy (1951). ∎

Marlowe, June (1903–1984), actress. Appeared in silent and sound films as a leading lady and supporting actress. Allegedly discovered by director Malcolm St. Clair while she was performing in a high school play, she played in his two-reel series of adventure films. By 1924 she was appearing in full-length features. She was signed by Warner Brothers to play alongside Rin-Tin-Tin, the famous dog. The studio billed her as "the most beautiful girl on the screen," giving her a series of ingenue roles.

A polite, sometimes shy person, she appeared in films with some of the leading comics of the period, including LAUREL AND HARDY, Harry LANGDON, and Charley CHASE. She is probably best remembered for her role as Miss Crabtree, the pretty teacher, who was featured in six of the "OUR GANG" comedies (1930–1932).

SELECTED FILMS: When a Man's a Man (1924), The Pleasure Buyers (1925), The Old Soak (1926), The Life of Riley, Alias the Deacon, Wild Beauty (1927), Free Lips (1928), Teacher's Pet, Fast Work, School's Out (1930), Love Business, Little Daddy, Pardon Us, Shiver My Timbers (1931), Readin' and Writin' (1932), Slave Girl (1947). ∎

Mars, Kenneth (1936–), actor. Played comedy character roles during the 1960s and 1970s, usually as eccentrics. Perhaps his most memorable role was that of the obsessed Naziphile-playwright whose play is adapted into a musical by Zero MOSTEL in *The Producers.*

SELECTED FILMS: The Producers (1967), Desperate Characters (1971), What's Up, Doc? (1972), Paper Moon (1973), Young Frankenstein (1974), Night Moves (1975). ■

Marsh, Betty, actress. Worked in early silent film shorts as part of Mack SENNETT'S KEYSTONE stock company. She appeared as a supporting player to some of the leading comics of the period, including, among others, Fred MACE, Hank MANN, and Mack SWAIN.

SELECTED FILMS: A Janitor's Wife's Temptation (1915), A Modern Enoch Arden, Gypsy Joe (1916). ■

Marsh, Joan (1913–), actress. As an infant, appeared on stage, then played child roles in the 1920s in films starring Mary PICKFORD. A chic blonde, she returned to the screen at the beginning of the sound era to play alluring leads and supporting roles in melodramas and light films.

SELECTED FILMS: Daddy Long Legs (1919), Pollyanna (1920), The King of Jazz, Little Accident (1930), Three Girls Lost, Shipmates, Maker of Men (1931), The Wet Parade, Bachelor's Affairs, That's My Boy (1932), It's Great to Be Alive, Three-Cornered Moon, Rainbow Over Broadway (1933), You're Telling Me, Many Happy Returns, We're Rich Again (1934), Dancing Feet, Life Begins in College, Hot Water (1937), The Lady Objects (1938), Idiot's Delight, Fast and Loose (1939), Road to Zanzibar (1941), Follow the Leader (1944). ■

Marsh, Mae (1895–1968), actress. Began her screen career in 1911 in early silent films for pioneer studios like Kalem and BIOGRAPH. At the latter, she worked under director D. W. Griffith playing delicate but determined heroines. She left films in the mid-1920s, returning during the sound period as a character actress. She displayed an exceptional talent for drama as well as comedy. She was the sister of actress Marguerite MARSH.

SELECTED FILMS: Fighting Blood (1911), Home Folks, The New York Hat (1912), The Primitive Man (1913), Hoodoo Ann, The Marriage of Molly-O, The Little Liar (1916), Polly of the Circus (1917), All Woman (1918), Spotlight Sadie (1919), Daddies (1924), Rebecca of Sunnybrook Farm, That's My Boy (1932), Great Guns (1941), Donovan's Reef (1963). ■

Marsh, Marguerite (1892–1925), actress. Entered films during the early silent period. Appeared as female leads and in supporting roles in numerous dramas and light films. She never reached the popular success of her sister, actress Mae MARSH.

SELECTED FILMS: The Mender of the Nets (1912), His Nobs, the Plumber (1913), Blue Blood and Red (1914), Casey at the Bat, Little Meena's Romance (1916), Our Little Wife (1918), Fair Enough (1919), Phantom Honeymoon, Wits vs. Wits (1920), Oh Mary Be Careful (1921), Boomerang Bill, The Lion's Mouse (1922). ■

Marshall, George (1891–1975), director. Appeared as an extra and in featured roles in silent films and wrote screenplays for comedy shorts before turning his attentions in 1916 to directing. Throughout the 1920s he turned out numerous comedy shorts and features for different studios. With the advent of sound, he directed many highly entertaining features starring some of the foremost comics of the period, including W. C. FIELDS, LAUREL AND HARDY, Bob HOPE, and Dean MARTIN and Jerry LEWIS. He also directed four comedy shorts of the ZaSu PITTS-Thelma TODD series in the early 1930s but with limited success.

SELECTED FILMS: Love's Lariat (1916), Why Trust Your Husband? (1921), Smiles Are Trumps (1922), Pack Up Your Troubles, Their First Mistake (1932), Ever Since Eve, She Learned

About Sailors (1934), Life Begins at Forty (1935), Can This Be Dixie? (1936), Hold That Co-Ed (1938), You Can't Cheat an Honest Man, Destry Rides Again (1939), The Ghost Breakers (1940), True to Life (1943), Murder, He Says, Hold That Blonde (1945), Monsieur Beaucaire (1946), My Friend Irma (1949), Fancy Pants, Never a Dull Moment (1950), Off Limits, Scared Stiff (1953), The Second Greatest Sex (1955), The Sad Sack (1957), The Mating Game (1959), Papa's Delicate Condition (1963), Boy, Did I Get a Wrong Number! (1966), Hook, Line and Sinker (1969). ∎

Marshall, Tully (1864–1943), actor. Worked on stage before entering silent films in 1914. One of the most prolific character actors, Marshall, born William Phillis, appeared in hundreds of silent and sound films of all genres. He portrayed a wide range of characters, from villains to old codgers. In Stand-In (1937) he scrutinizes the abundance of candles on his birthday cake and quips: "Looks like a forest fire." A variation on the gag was used by Clark GABLE in But Not for Me (1959).

SELECTED FILMS: Paid in Full (1914), The Countess Charming (1917), M'Liss (1918), Cheating Cheaters (1919), Too Much Business (1922), Her Temporary Husband (1923), Hold Your Breath (1924), Clothes Make the Pirate (1925), Twinkletoes (1926), She Couldn't Say No (1930), Cabin in the Cotton (1932), Laughing at Life (1933), Mr. Boggs Steps Out, She Asked for It (1937), College Swing (1938), Go West (1940), Ball of Fire (1941), Hitler's Madman (1943). ∎

Martin, Chris-Pin (1893–1953), actor. Appeared in dozens of action features, chiefly westerns, as a character player or comic relief character. A rotund actor born in Tucson, Arizona, of Mexican extraction, he played Pancho in the "Cisco Kid" westerns. His most memorable role was his portrayal of Chris, the stereotyped, but humorous, Mexican

way station attendant, in John FORD'S classic western, Stagecoach. When he complains about his only two objects of affection—his recalcitrant horse and his Apache wife who has abandoned him—and regrets that he should have beaten "her," a companion asks: "Who? Your wife?" "No," he replies, "my horse."

SELECTED FILMS: The Rescue (1929), The Cisco Kid (1931), Girl Crazy (1932), The Gay Desperado (1936), Stagecoach, The Return of the Cisco Kid (1939), Down Argentine Way, The Mark of Zorro (1940), Weekend in Havana (1941), Mexican Hayride (1948), The Beautiful Blonde From Bashful Bend (1949), A Millionaire for Christy (1951), Ride the Man Down (1952). ∎

Martin, Dean (1917–), actor, singer. Worked as a nightclub singer, as part of comedy team with Jerry LEWIS, and in television before entering films in 1949. Martin, born Paul Crocetti, was a minor entertainer before he met Lewis. He skyrocketed to fame, as did Jerry, through their partnership. Martin sang while the boyish Lewis clowned behind him, mimicking the singer. Together they made 16 comedies. When they split up, Dean continued to act in films. Displaying warmth and charm, as well as a laid-back attitude, he began a new career in dramatic and light films. In Kiss Me, Stupid he prepares to perambulate in Kim Novak's garden and says leeringly, "She can show me her parsley." For a list of films with Jerry Lewis, see MARTIN AND LEWIS.

SELECTED FILMS (without Lewis): Ten Thousand Bedrooms (1957), Who Was That Lady?, Bells Are Ringing (1960), All in a Night's Work (1961), Sergeants 3, Who's Got the Action? (1962), Who's Been Sleeping in My Bed? (1963), What a Way to Go!, Kiss Me, Stupid (1964), How to Save a Marriage—and Ruin Your Life, Five Card Stud (1968), The Wrecking Crew (1969), Something Big (1971), Mr. Rico (1975).

Martin, Dick. See Rowan and Martin.

Martin, Marion (1916–), actress. Appeared as a Broadway chorine before entering films in the early 1940s. A tall blonde, she played supporting roles in several big productions and leads chiefly in routine light films during the 1940s and 1950s, often with some of the leading comics of the period, including, among others, the MARX BROTHERS and Bob HOPE.

SELECTED FILMS: Sinners in Paradise, Youth Takes a Fling (1938), Boom Town (1940), Mexican Spitfire at Sea, The Big Store (1941), They Got Me Covered (1942), Swingtime Johnny (1943), Abbott and Costello in Hollywood (1945), Angel on My Shoulder (1946), Queen of Burlesque (1947), Oh, You Beautiful Doll (1950), Thunder in the Pines (1954), The Mikado (1967). ∎

Martin, Mary (1913–), actress. Began her film career in the late 1930s. She played leads and second leads in a string of light films. But she has achieved greater success on stage in several musical comedy hits.

In *Kiss the Boys Goodbye* she poses as a southern belle who has just arrived in the North. Noticing an equestrian statue, she asks theater director Don Ameche: "Who is that?" "General Sherman on a horse." "Who is that lady in front?" "That's 'Victory,' " he replies. "Isn't it just like a Yankee," she responds, "to let a lady walk."

SELECTED FILMS: The Rage of Paris (1938), Rhythm on the River, Love Thy Neighbor (1940), New York Town, Kiss the Boys Goodbye, Birth of the Blues (1941), Star Spangled Rhythm (1942), True to Life, Happy Go Lucky (1943), Main Street to Broadway (1953). ∎

Martin, Steve (1945–), comedian, actor. Worked in small clubs as a comic, wrote comedy material for television, starred in his own television show, and turned out several hit comedy records before entering films. A tall, good-looking, and likable comedian of the screw-

Steve Martin

ball school, he has starred chiefly in offbeat films, several of which have been below average. His most successful work has been with writer-director Carl REINER. His humor is a composite of shock material, the absurd, the bold sexual innuendo, the bizarre, and a bit of cynicism. One of his albums won a Grammy award.

In *All of Me*, a fantasy-comedy, he played a lawyer into whose body has entered the soul of a dead spinster (Lily TOMLIN). A sexy young woman who was supposed to receive the spirit into her body attempts to comfort the disconcerted Martin by helping him find the swami who will perform the transmigration. "If Miss Cutwater really is inside, he will help her leave your body and enter mine," she says. "I think I envy her," he says.

SELECTED FILMS: The Kids Are Alright, The Jerk (1979), Pennies From Heaven (1981), Dead Men Don't Wear Plaid (1982), The Man With Two Brains (1983), The Lonely Guy, All of Me (1984), Three Amigos!, Little Shop of Horrors (1986). ∎

Martin, Strother (1919–1980), actor. Began his film career as a bit player before specializing as a character actor in a variety of genres. Always entertaining, he added spice to any film in which he appeared. One of his more memorable roles was that of the sadistic and brutal warden of the chain gang camp in *Cool Hand Luke* (1967), in which he says repeatedly: "What we've got here is a failure to communicate." Perhaps his own line from the satirical western, *Butch Cassidy and the Sundance Kid* (1969), epitomizes his screen presence. "I'm what is known as a colorful character," he enlightens Paul NEWMAN and Robert REDFORD.

SELECTED FILMS: *The Asphalt Jungle* (1950), *Rhubarb* (1951), *The Shaggy Dog, The Horse Soldiers* (1959), *McLintock!* (1963), *The Flim Flam Man* (1967), *The Wild Bunch, True Grit* (1969), *Fool's Parade, Hannie Caulder* (1971), *Slap Shot* (1977), *Up in Smoke, The End* (1978), *Love and Bullets, The Champ* (1979), *Hotwire* (1980). ∎

Martin, Tony (1912–), singer, actor. Played in bands before entering films in the mid-1930s. He played leads and supporting roles in numerous light films. An attractive and personable singer, he continued appearing in person during his screen career.

SELECTED FILMS: *Follow the Fleet, Pigskin Parade, Banjo on My Knee* (1936), *You Can't Have Everything, Life Begins in College, Ali Baba Goes to Town* (1937), *Kentucky Moonshine* (1938), *Music in My Heart* (1940), *The Big Store* (1941), *Two Tickets to Broadway* (1951), *Easy to Love, Here Come the Girls* (1953), *Hit the Deck* (1955). ∎

Martin, Vivian, actress. Began her screen career in early silent films in the 1910s. An attractive performer with a flair for comedy, she appeared chiefly in lead roles in dramas and light films for Paramount studios.

SELECTED FILMS: *The Girl at Home, Giving Becky a Chance, A Kiss for Susie, Little Miss Optimist, Molly Entangled* (1917), *Jane Goes A-Wooing, Mirandy Smiles, A Petticoat Pilot* (1918), *Home Town Girl, The Third Kiss, You Never Saw Such a Girl* (1919). ∎

Dean Martin and Jerry Lewis

Martin and Lewis. A successful comedy team starring Dean MARTIN and Jerry LEWIS. They starred in 16 films between 1949 and 1956, with crooner Martin playing straight man to childlike Jerry's shenanigans. A zany and animated team, they had already had several years of experience in nightclubs and television. Lewis added most of the laughs; he was naturally funny, with his high-pitched voice and large mouth. The easy-going Martin, a perfect foil, usually chased and got the female lead while Lewis got into difficulties.

Under contract to Paramount, the duo had to contend with reworkings of old scripts for their comedy material and plots. But during their peak years, in the 1950s, it seemed that they could do no wrong. The studio converted *Lady Be Careful* (1936) and *The Fleet's In* (1942) into *Sailor Beware; Ghost Breakers* (1940) became *Scared Stiff;* and *Nothing Sacred* (1937) was adapted to *Living It Up.* Their routines at times seemed to emerge from vaudeville days. In *At War With the Army* Private Jerry Lewis is ordered about and harangued by his old friend, Sergeant Dean Martin. "You were the best man at my wedding," Jerry reminds him. "You're not kidding," Dean replies. And in *Sailor Beware* Jerry tries to emulate an experienced prize fighter. "What are you, a boxer?" Dean inquires. "What do I look like," Jerry counters, "a cocker spaniel? I was fighting Gene Tierney once—'' ''You mean Gene Tunney,'' Dean intervenes. ''You fight who you want,'' Jerry continues, ''I'll fight who I want.''

However, they relied more on visual gags than on dialogue. Although their films seemed to aim more at the youth market than at adults, they, or at least Jerry, gained a large following in Europe, especially France. By 1956, rumors about their splitting up came true. Allegedly, Martin was dissatisfied with the same roles, always filling in with a song while Lewis got all the major laughs. Lewis, on the other hand, was apparently taking himself too seriously as a master clown. The real causes of the break were never delineated publicly. However, both have moved on to successful individual careers while their greatness as a comedy team remains on film. For selected films of their individual careers, see Jerry LEWIS and Dean MARTIN.

SELECTED FILMS (as a team): My Friend Irma (1949), My Friend Irma Goes West, At War With the Army (1950), That's My Boy, Sailor Beware (1951), Jumping Jacks, Road to Bali (1952), The Stooge, Scared Stiff, The Caddy, Money From Home (1953), Living It Up, Three Ring Circus (1954), You're Never Too Young, Artists and Models (1955), Pardners, Hollywood or Bust (1956). ■

Marx Brothers, The. A popular movie comedy team composed of Groucho, Chico, Harpo, and occasionally Zeppo Marx. Chico (1886–1961), the oldest, was born Leonard and was nicknamed because he liked to chase girls, or ''chicks.'' Harpo (1888–1964), whose real name was Adolf, got his nickname because he played the harp. Groucho (1890–1977) was born Julius Henry and earned his nickname because of his irascibility. Gummo (1897–1977), born Milton, was named after the slang word for detective, ''gumshoe.'' Finally, Zeppo (1901–1979), who was originally named Herbert,

Chico, Zeppo, Groucho, and Harpo Marx

changed his nickname from Zippo to Zeppo.

Their mother, Minnie, started them off in show business by first giving them musical lessons and then pushing them into vaudeville as a team. When Gummo dropped out, Zeppo replaced him by the time the brothers appeared on Broadway. Beginning as a musical act, the group foundered until they finally emerged as comedians. After years in vaudeville and on Broadway, they perfected their unique style that film audiences are familiar with.

Fast-witted Groucho contributed the pun, insult, and wisecrack and developed his trademarks, his hunched-over walk, his outrageous mustache, and his startling glasses. In *A Day at the Races* a specialist questions veterinarian Groucho's diagnosis of Margaret Dumont. ''Her X-rays show nothing wrong with her.'' ''Who are you going to believe,'' Groucho asks, ''me or those crooked X-rays?''

Chico, with his pointed hat, contributed his Italian accent, awful puns, and piano-playing. In *The Cocoanuts* he confounds fast-talking Groucho, who is describing a map of expensive property: ''Here is a viaduct leading over to the mainland—'' ''Why a duck?'' Chico interjects. Groucho repeats himself, but to no avail. ''Why a duck? why-a-no-chicken?'' ''. . . You try to cross over there a chicken and you'll find out why a duck,'' Groucho explains. ''It's deep water, that's viaduct." "That's why-a-duck?" Chico persists.

Harpo, a talented harpist and mime, leered lecherously at females, and contributed general mayhem; he wore a top hat and a long white coat that contained everything from blowtorches to musical instruments. His only sane moments occurred when he played his beloved harp.

Zeppo remained aloof from his brothers' madcap misadventures, preferring to sing or romance the girls. He dropped out of the act after co-starring in five films.

While appearing in the stage play *Animal Crackers* on Broadway, the four brothers traveled to Paramount's Astoria studios in Long Island City to make their first film, *The Cocoanuts*, in 1929. Although the film emerged as quite stagy, the brothers were able to make their zany comedy work on screen. After starring in five films for Paramount, they moved to MGM where they made five films for that studio. Their last starring film was *Love Happy* (1949). They appeared in *The Story of Mankind* (1957) but had minor roles.

The Marx Brothers as a team gained even greater popularity years after they stopped making pictures. Their films constantly appear at revivals and at college festivals. Whereas other teams used either verbal or visual comedy, the brothers employed both. They went beyond LAUREL AND HARDY and ABBOTT AND COSTELLO in their zaniness, satire, and irreverence of the pompous; the team poked fun at everyone and everything. They excelled at timing, an essential element for successful comedy. Together they embodied the three most popular forms of humor—the gag (Groucho), dialect humor (Chico), and pantomime (Harpo). Their influence extends to current comics. Woody ALLEN borrows from each of the brothers (as well as from CHAPLIN and others), Bill MURRAY takes from the brothers as do others. The Marx Brothers were truly a unique and gifted comedy team. A study of their work, *The Marx Brothers:*

Their World of Comedy, by Allen Eyles, was published in 1966. Groucho's autobiography, *Groucho and Me*, was published in 1960, while Harpo's, *Harpo Speaks!*, written in collaboration with Rowland Barber, was published in 1961.

SELECTED FILMS: The Cocoanuts (1929), Animal Crackers (1930), Monkey Business (1931), Horse Feathers (1932), Duck Soup (1933), A Night at the Opera (1935), A Day at the Races (1937), Room Service, At the Circus (1939), Go West (1940), The Big Store (1941), A Night in Casablanca (1946), Love Happy (1949).

SELECTED FILMS (Groucho alone): Copacabana (1947), Mr. Music (1950), Double Dynamite (1951), A Girl in Every Port (1952), Will Success Spoil Rock Hunter? (1957), Skidoo (1968). ■

Elliott Gould in *M*A*S*H* (1970)

M*A*S*H (1970), TCF. *Dir.* Robert Altman; *Sc.* Ring Lardner, Jr.; with Donald Sutherland, Elliott Gould, Tom Skerritt, Sally Kellerman, Robert Duvall, Gary Burghoff.

Based on the novel *MASH* by Richard Hooker, the film centers around a Mobile Army Surgical Hospital in Korea during the war. The tone of the film is established early during a dispassionate conversation in a field operating room. "Is he an enlisted man or an officer?" "Enlisted man." "Okay, then make the stitches bigger." The conflict, aside from the stupidity of the war, revolves around the dedicated and religious Major Burns (Robert Duvall) and the pompous and equally dedicated Major O'Houlihan

(Sally KELLERMAN) in one corner and three young surgeons, Donald SUTHERLAND, Elliott GOULD, and Tom Skerritt, in the opposite corner. The young Turks declare war on the "straights," which leads to the sometimes cruel humor of the film. Memorable moments include the wiring and playback over the camp loudspeakers of the lovemaking between Duvall and Kellerman; the hilarious football game in which the opposing team is injected with a sense-dulling drug; and the "Last Supper" sequence to help the dentist, Painless Pole, overcome his fears of impotency. In an early scene the uptight nurse Kellerman, exasperated with the antics of surgeon Sutherland, wonders out loud "how a degenerate person like that ever reached a responsible position in the regular army corps." "He was drafted," a colleague answers. Altman's irreverent and witty look at the ironies of war and survival is filled with visual and sound techniques that have become his trademark. The film became a popular television series in the 1970s.

Mason, Marsha (1942–), actress. Appeared in television and on Broadway as well as in films. She has played in dramas in various media although she is best known for her comedy roles, especially those created by Neil SIMON. A talented performer, she has played a wide range of contemporary characters. from an abused woman to an alcoholic actress. She has accompanied such screen personalities as George Segal, Richard Dreyfuss, Jason Robards, and James Caan and has had starring roles (*Only When I Laugh*) as well.

SELECTED FILMS: Blume in Love (1973), The Goodbye Girl (1977), The Cheap Detective (1978), Chapter Two (1979), Only When I Laugh (1981), Max Dugan Returns (1983). ∎

Mason, Reginald (1882–1962), actor. Entered films during the silent era following a career on stage. He appeared as a supporting player in dramas and light films, continuing into the sound period.

SELECTED FILMS: Two Weeks (1920), The Highest Bidder (1921), A Bedtime Story, Topaze, Shanghai Madness, Brief Moment, The Big Brain, Baby Face (1933), Call It Luck, You Can't Buy Everything (1934), Suzy (1936). ∎

Mason, Shirley (1901–1979), actress. Worked on stage as a child performer before entering early silent films in 1914. She appeared in leading roles in both dramas and light films throughout the silent era, abandoning her screen career with the arrival of sound. She was the sister of silent screen star Viola Dana.

SELECTED FILMS: Vanity Fair (1915), Come On In, Goodbye, Bill (1918), Putting It Over, The Rescuing Angel, The Winning Girl (1919), Girl of My Heart (1920), Ever Since Eve, Jackie (1921), Little Miss Smiles (1922), Curly Top (1925), Sweet Rosie O'Grady, Don Juan's Three Nights (1926), Let It Rain, Sally in Our Alley (1927), The Show of Shows (1929). ∎

Mason, Sully P. (1906–1970), actor, musician. Worked as a saxophonist and band singer before entering films in the late 1930s. He appeared occasionally as a supporting player in light films. He later entered television.

SELECTED FILMS: That's Right, You're Wrong (1939), You'll Find Out (1940), Playmates (1941), Around the World (1943). ∎

Mason, William "Smiling Billy" (1888–1941), actor. Worked in vaudeville and on stage before entering early silent films in the 1910s. He played leads chiefly in comedy shorts. He starred in the "Baseball Bill" comedy shorts produced by Universal from 1916 to 1917. He helped Thomas Edison with the inventor's early film experiments.

SELECTED FILMS: Cupid's Quartet, A Corner in Whiskers, The Snare, Miss Simkins' Summer Boarder, Almost a

Man (1912), Dizzy Heights and Daring Hearts, Cinders of Love, A Dash of Courage (1916). ∎

Mather, Aubrey (1885–1958), actor. Appeared on stage and in films in his native England before settling in Hollywood in the early 1940s. A versatile performer, he played supporting roles in numerous dramas and light films, ranging from professors (Ball of Fire) to butlers or valets (The Hucksters). His wry sense of humor could enliven such dreary horror films as The Undying Monster (1942).

SELECTED FILMS: No, No, Nanette (1940), The Wife Takes a Flyer, Careful, Soft Shoulders, Ball of Fire (1942), Hello, Frisco, Hello, Heaven Can Wait (1943), The Mighty McGurk, It Happened in Brooklyn, For the Love of Rusty, The Hucksters (1947), Julia Misbehaves (1948), Everybody Does It (1949). ∎

Matheson, Tim (1949–), actor. Has appeared in television and chiefly in light films as a character actor. Beginning his screen career in the late 1960s with bit parts, he eventually got to play featured roles by the early 1980s. A talented comic actor, he has worked with many of the leading screen comics, including, among others, Bob HOPE, Lucille BALL, Dick VAN DYKE, John BELUSHI, and Mel BROOKS.

SELECTED FILMS: Divorce, American Style (1967), Yours, Mine and Ours (1968), How to Commit Marriage (1969), National Lampoon's Animal House (1978), The Apple Dumpling Gang Rides Again, 1941 (1979), A Little Sex (1982), To Be or Not to Be (1983), Up the Creek (1984), Fletch (1985). ∎

Matthau, Walter (1920–), actor. Worked in summer stock and on Broadway before entering films in the 1950s. Confined to supporting roles, often in westerns, he finally broke this cycle after his success in Neil Simon's Broadway

comedy The Odd Couple. Possessing an ungainly walk and delivering his lines from the side of his mouth, he starred in a string of film comedies that added to his popularity. Sometimes grouchy and irascible but always entertaining, he has developed into one of the foremost comedians of the screen. He won an Oscar for Best Supporting Actor as Jack LEMMON'S brother-in-law in The Fortune Cookie (1966) and was nominated for his roles in Kotch and The Sunshine Boys.

In the film version of The Odd Couple he complains about Jack Lemmon's compulsive cleanliness: "Two single men should not have a cleaner house than my mother."

SELECTED FILMS: The Kentuckian (1955), Bigger Than Life (1956), A Face in the Crowd (1957), Onionhead (1958), Who's Got the Action (1962), Island of Love, Charade (1963), Ensign Pulver, Goodbye Charlie (1964), A Guide for the Married Man (1967), The Secret Life of an American Wife (1968), Hello, Dolly!, Cactus Flower (1969), A New Leaf, Plaza Suite (1971), Pete 'n' Tillie (1972), The Front Page (1974), The Bad News Bears (1976), Casey's Shadow, House Calls, California Suite (1978), Little Miss Marker (1979), Hopscotch (1980), Buddy Buddy (1981), I Ought to Be in Pictures (1982), Movers & Shakers (1985). ∎

Maxey, Paul (1907–1963), actor. Appeared on stage, in television, and in films. Corpulent, round-faced, and mustached, he played executives, businessmen, and various promoters in numerous dramas and light films.

SELECTED FILMS: Below the Deadline (1946), Millie's Daughter (1947), Bride for Sale, A Dangerous Profession (1949), Curtain Call at Cactus Creek (1950), Casa Manana (1951), Here Come the Marines (1952). ∎

Maxwell, Edwin (1886–1948), actor. A character player from the late 1920s who appeared in numerous dramas and light films until the 1940s. A heavy-set, balding figure, he was often cast as suspicious characters.

SELECTED FILMS: The Jazz Singer (1927), The Taming of the Shrew (1929), Kiki, Daddy Long Legs, Ambassador Bill (1931), The Cohens and Kellys in Hollywood, You Said a Mouthful (1932), Dinner at Eight, Duck Soup (1933), Gift of Gab (1934), Thanks a Million (1935), Ninotchka (1939), His Girl Friday (1940), The Devil and Miss Jones (1941), The Great Moment (1944), The Vicious Circle (1948). ■

Maxwell, Elsa (1883–1963), columnist, actress. Stocky Hollywood gossip columnist who appeared occasionally as a light supporting player in a handful of films. She wrote several autobiographies, the last of which, Celebrity Circus, was published in 1961.

SELECTED FILMS: Hotel for Women (1939), Public Deb No. 1 (1940), Stage Door Canteen (1943). ■

Maxwell, Marilyn (1921–1972), actress, singer. Appeared on stage as a dancer at age three, worked as band vocalist, and radio singer before entering films in the early 1940s. An attractive blonde, she was cast in leading and supporting roles in both dramas and light films. Never an exceptionally talented actress, she did, however, give competent performances in many of her films. She worked with some of the leading comics of the period, including, among others, ABBOTT AND COSTELLO, Bob HOPE, and Jerry LEWIS.

SELECTED FILMS: Stand By for Action (1942), Presenting Lily Mars, Salute to the Marines, Thousands Cheer (1943), Swing Fever, Three Men in White, Lost in a Harem (1944), The Show-Off (1946), Summer Holiday (1948), Key to the City (1950), The Lemon Drop Kid (1951), Off Limits (1953), Forever, Darling (1956), Rock-a-bye Baby (1958), Critic's Choice (1963), The Lively Set (1964), The Phynx (1970). ■

May, Doris, actress. Began her screen career in early silent films in the 1910s. An attractive actress with a penchant for light comedy, she appeared in several films for Paramount studios.

SELECTED FILMS: 23 1/2 Hours' Leave (1919), Let's Be Fashionable, Mary's Ankle, What's Your Husband Doing? (1920), The Rookie's Return (1921). ■

May, Elaine (1932–), actress, director, screenwriter. Worked in radio and on stage in Chicago as part of the Compass Players with Mike NICHOLS before she became a star as part of a comedy act with Nichols. In 1961, when the act broke up, she wrote and directed stage plays. She transferred these talents to films in 1971.

SELECTED FILMS (as actress): Luv, Enter Laughing (1967), California Suite (1978).

SELECTED FILMS (as screenwriter): Such Good Friends (1971), Heaven Can Wait (1978).

SELECTED FILMS (as director): A New Leaf (1971), The Heartbreak Kid (1972), Mikey and Nicky (1976), Ishtar (1987). ■

Mayehoff, Eddie (1911–), actor. Worked as a band leader before entering films as a comedy character actor in the early 1950s. A somewhat beefy figure with a jutting jaw, he often played pompous but confused types.

SELECTED FILMS: That's My Boy (1951), Off Limits (1952), The Stooge (1953), Artists and Models (1955), How to Murder Your Wife (1965), Luv (1967). ■

Mayo, Archie (1891–1968), director. Appeared on stage, worked as an extra in silent films, and did a stint as a GAGMAN. He directed silent comedy shorts until 1926, when he started to turn out feature comedies, dramas, and adventures. A good craftsman and reliable contract director for Warner Brothers during the 1930s, he directed many fast-paced films but lacked the creativity to make many of his comedies come to life.

SELECTED FILMS: Money Talks, Christine of the Big Tops (1926), Johnny Get Your Hair Cut, Quarantined Rivals, Dearie, Slightly Used, The College Widow (1927), State Street Sadie (1928), The Sap, Is Everybody Happy? (1929), Oh, Sailor Behave! (1930), Under Eighteen, Night After Night (1932), Desirable (1934), Go Into Your Dance (1935), Give Me Your Heart (1936), Call It a Day (1937), Youth Takes a Fling (1938), Charley's Aunt (1941), Orchestra Wives (1942), Sweet and Low Down (1944), A Night in Casablanca, Angel on My Shoulder (1946). ∎

Mayo, Virginia (1920–), actress. Worked as a show girl before entering films in the early 1940s. An attractive and sexy blonde, she played supporting roles in a variety of films but is best known for her light films with comics Bob HOPE and Danny KAYE, for whom she was a perfect foil.

In South Sea Woman she played the title character who, testifying at the court martial of Burt Lancaster, tells the court that he is every inch a marine. "Why," she says, "he thinks when you go to heaven, you end up in the Halls of Montezuma."

SELECTED FILMS: Jack London (1943), Up in Arms, Seven Days Ashore, The Princess and the Pirate (1944), Wonder Man (1945), The Kid From Brooklyn (1946), The Secret Life of Walter Mitty (1947), A Song Is Born (1948), Always Leave Them Laughing (1949), Painting the Clouds With Sunshine (1951), She's Working Her Way Through College (1952), She's Back on Broadway (1953), Fort Utah (1947). ∎

Mazurki, Mike (1909–), actor. Worked as a professional athlete and wrestler before switching to playing toughs and sidekicks during the first half of his Hollywood career. Massive and mean-looking, he appeared in numerous dramas and light films, often portraying dumb hoodlums, doormen, and other Runyonesque characters. From the 1940s his image softened although he played

villains in comedies starring some of the leading comics of the period, including Bob HOPE, ABBOTT AND COSTELLO, Jack BENNY, and Jerry LEWIS.

SELECTED FILMS: Belle of the Nineties (1934), About Face (1942), Henry Aldrich Haunts a House, It Ain't Hay (1943), The Thin Man Comes Home, The Princess and the Pirate (1944), Abbott and Costello in Hollywood, The Horn Blows at Midnight (1945), Live Wires (1946), The Noose Hangs High (1948), My Favorite Spy (1951), Some Like It Hot (1959), The Errand Boy, Pocketful of Miracles (1961), All the Marbles (1981). ∎

Mazursky, Paul (1930–), director, screenwriter, actor. Began his film career in the 1950s as an actor playing minor roles in dramas. After some television writing and stage appearances, he returned to the film world and directed his first feature in 1969. He has turned out heart-warming dramas as well as light films, but his work has been uneven, ranging from Oscar-nominated entries (An Unmarried Woman, 1978) to superficial and sophomoric features.

SELECTED FILMS: Bob & Carol & Ted & Alice (1969), Alex in Wonderland (1970), Harry and Tonto (1974), Next Stop, Greenwich Village (1976), Willie and Phil (1979), Moscow on the Hudson (1984), Down and Out in Beverly Hills (1986). ∎

Meadows, Audrey (1924–), actress. A light character player with experience in television, on stage, and in films. She won an Emmy Award in 1954 for her portrayal of Ralph Kramden's long-suffering wife on "The Honeymooners." A gifted comedienne and actress, she has appeared only occasionally in films. She is the sister of film and television actress Jayne Meadows.

In That Touch of Mink she played a Horn and Hardart employee who provides free lunches to her friend by slipping the food through the automatic window slots. One day her supervisor catches her and says firmly: "Are you familiar with the company policy regarding giving away free food?" "No," she replies, "are we for or against it?"

SELECTED FILMS: That Touch of Mink (1962), Take Her, She's Mine (1963), Rosie! (1968). ∎

Meara, Anne (1929–), actress, comedienne. Worked on stage, in supper clubs, and in television as part of the comedy team of Stiller and Meara before making occasional appearances in films. The duo are famous for their sketches of ordinary people caught up in everyday problems and for their numerous witty commercials. An attractive redhead, she has carried her natural comedy over to her few screen roles although her film career has not brought her the same recognition that her stage work has. Her long-time partner and husband, Jerry STILLER, has also appeared separately in films.

SELECTED FILMS: The Out-of-Towners, Lovers and Other Strangers (1970), Nasty Habits (1976), Fame (1980). ∎

Donald Meek (right) and Frank Morgan

Meek, Donald (1880–1946), actor. Appeared on stage as well as in numerous films, usually as a character actor. A short, bald, and unimposing figure, Meek, who was born in Glasgow, Scotland, showed up chiefly in light films portraying fainthearted characters. One

of his most memorable roles was that of the timid whiskey drummer in John Ford's classic western, Stagecoach (1939). He worked with some of the foremost screen personalities and comedians of the period, including, among others, Jack BENNY, Shirley TEMPLE, Mae WEST, W. C. FIELDS, and Bob HOPE.

In Love on the Run (1936) he says to Clark GABLE: "We must hurry. You see, at 12 o'clock I turn into a pumpkin."

SELECTED FILMS: The Hole in the Wall (1929), The Merry Widow (1934), Accent on Youth, Top Hat (1935), The Toast of New York, Artists and Models (1937), Little Miss Broadway, You Can't Take It With You (1938), Hollywood Cavalcade (1939), My Little Chickadee (1940), Barnacle Bill (1941), Babes on Broadway (1942), They Got Me Covered (1943), Bathing Beauty (1944), State Fair (1945), Magic Town (1947). ∎

Meeker, George, actor. Appeared as a supporting player in numerous dramas and light films from the late 1920s to the 1940s. He worked with some of the brightest stars in Hollywood, including comics WHEELER AND WOOLSEY and Danny KAYE.

SELECTED FILMS: Four Sons (1928), Strictly Dishonorable (1931), Fireman, Save My Child, The Misleading Lady, Blessed Event (1932), Only Yesterday (1933), Hi, Nellie!, Hips, Hips, Hooray, Ever Since Eve (1934), Remember Last Night? (1935), Don't Get Personal, Walking on Air (1936), Four's a Crowd (1938), You're in the Army Now (1941), Up in Arms (1944), Her Sister's Secret (1947). ∎

Meighan, Thomas (1879–1936), actor. Appeared on Broadway before entering films where he became a popular leading man in early silent features. He played heroic roles through the 1920s and, with the advent of sound, continued to act in dramas and light films as a character actor.

SELECTED FILMS: Kindling (1915), M'Liss (1918), Male and Female (1919),

Why Change Your Wife? (1920), Cappy Ricks (1921), The Bachelor Daddy, Back Home and Broke (1922), The Ne'er-Do-Well, Woman-Proof (1923), Pied Piper Malone (1924), Irish Luck (1925), The Mating Call (1928), Cheaters at Play (1932), Peck's Bad Boy (1934). ■

Melton, Frank (1907–1951), actor. Came to films in the early 1930s as a supporting player. He appeared in numerous light films through the 1940s. He worked with some of the foremost comics of the period, including Will ROGERS and Bob HOPE.

SELECTED FILMS: Cavalcade, Mr. Skitch (1933), David Harum, Handy Andy, Judge Priest (1934), The County Chairman, The Daring Young Man, Welcome Home (1935), They Met in a Taxi (1936), Too Many Wives, Wild and Woolly (1937), Freshman Year, Marriage Forbidden (1938), The Cat and the Canary (1939), Second Chorus (1940), Pot o' Gold, Tanks a Million (1941), It's a Pleasure (1945), Do You Love Me? (1946). ■

Melville, Rose (1873–1946), actress. Worked in vaudeville and on stage before joining such pioneering film companies as Biograph and KEYSTONE during the early silent era. She appeared as a female lead or supporting player, frequently with her husband, Frank Minzey, in numerous comedy shorts.

SELECTED FILMS: She Came, She Saw, She Conquered, Leap Year Wooing, A Flock of Skeletons, When Things Go Wrong, Almost a Heroine, Romance and Riot, A Lunch Room Legacy, A Baby Grand, The Dumb Heiress, Her Great Invention, A Lucky Mistake, Setting the Fashion, The Wishing Ring, A Double Elopement (1916). ■

Menjou, Adolphe (1890–1963), actor. Studied engineering before choosing show business as a career. He appeared in vaudeville and on stage as well as in films. A dapper leading man in silent films, he achieved popularity in the 1920s portraying urbane characters, chiefly in comedies. During the sound era, when some studio executives considered his film career at an end, he continued to play worldly figures, either as the lead or supporting actor, in dramas and light films. He received an Academy Award nomination as Best Actor for his portrayal of the hard-nosed editor in the 1931 version of *The Front Page.* He appeared in well over 100 films during a screen career that spanned six decades.

In *State of the Union* he played a political party boss who asks wealthy backer Angela Lansbury: "What's your stake in all this?" "I want nothing," she replies. "People who want nothing worry me," he muses. "The price isn't right."

SELECTED FILMS: The Blue Envelope Mystery (1916), The Three Musketeers (1921), A Woman of Paris (1923), The Marriage Circle, The Fast Set (1924), The King of Main Street (1925), The Grand Duchess and the Waiter (1926), His Tiger Lady (1928), Bachelor's Affairs (1932), Little Miss Marker (1934), Broadway Gondolier (1935), One in a Million (1937), The Housekeeper's Daughter (1939), Turnabout (1940), Father Takes a Wife (1941), Roxie Hart (1942), Step Lively (1944), The Hucksters (1947), State of the Union (1948), To Please a Lady (1950), The Ambassador's Daughter (1956), Pollyanna (1960). ■

Merande, Doro (–1975), actress. Came to films in the early 1930s as a supporting player. She appeared in several dramas and light films during a screen career that spanned four decades. The bulk of her screen work consisted of her portrayals of matronly roles. She appeared also on stage and in television.

SELECTED FILMS: The Front Page (1931), The Seven Year Itch (1955), The Remarkable Mr. Pennypacker, The Gazebo (1959), Kiss Me, Stupid (1964), The Russians are Coming, the Russians Are Coming (1966), Skidoo (1968), Change of Habit (1969). ■

Mercer, Beryl (1882–1939), actress. Appeared on stage in her native England before entering Hollywood films in the early 1920s. She was the consummate screen mother (to Gary COOPER, Lew Ayres, James CAGNEY, etc.) in numerous dramas. She had featured roles in many light films during the silent and sound periods.

SELECTED FILMS: *Broken Chains (1922), Three Live Ghosts (1929), Seven Days' Leave, In Gay Madrid (1930), Merely Mary Ann (1931), Her Splendid Folly (1933), The Little Minister, The Richest Girl in the World (1934), Hitchhike Lady, Three Live Ghosts (1935), Call It a Day (1937), The Little Princess, A Woman Is the Judge (1939).* ■

Meredith, Burgess (1908–), actor. Appeared on stage from 1929 before entering films in 1936. A talented actor, he starred in numerous dramas and light films both in the United States and in Great Britain. He became a leading character actor in the 1970s, especially in his role of fight manager in the extremely popular *Rocky* films.

In *That Uncertain Feeling* he portrayed an eccentric concert pianist with whom Merle Oberon has become fascinated. He invites her to a modern art gallery where she is bewildered by the cubist and surrealist paintings. "Who painted it?" she asks about one artwork that he interprets for her. "A woman," he announces scornfully. "No man could be so malicious."

SELECTED FILMS: *Winterset (1936), There Goes the Groom (1937), Spring Madness (1938), Idiot's Delight (1939), Second Chorus, That Uncertain Feeling, Tom, Dick and Harry (1941), The Diary of a Chambermaid (1946), On Our Merry Way (1948), A Big Hand for the Little Lady (1966), Skidoo (1968), 92 in the Shade (1975), Rocky (1976), Foul Play (1978), The Day the World Ended (1979).* ■

Merkel, Una (1903–1986), actress. Worked for a short period in silent films in the 1920s. She switched to Broadway, but returned to the screen when sound arrived. After appearing in dramatic and historical films for D. W. Griffith and other directors, she moved to light films in which she often played the lead or the female lead's glib friend. In her later years she became an accomplished character actress on screen as well as on Broadway. During a career that spanned five decades, she appeared with some of the foremost comic performers of the period, including, among others, Jean HARLOW, Harold LLOYD, W. C. FIELDS, and Bob HOPE. One of her classic film moments occurred in *Destry Rides Again* when she and Marlene Dietrich engage in a hair-pulling battle over the pants of Mischa AUER.

Her comedic talents are amply displayed in *Born to Dance* (1936) in which she played sailor Sid SILVER'S wife. A diminutive figure with a large nose, he returns after a four-year absence but, having known each other for only a few days before they were married, she hardly recognizes him. "Aren't you glad to see me?" he asks. "I don't know yet." "But I'm your husband!" "Don't remind me of it," she exclaims. Later in the film she tells her three-year-old daughter that her father works for Uncle Sam. "What does Uncle Sam do for a living?" the child asks. "He's a collector," Merkel quips.

SELECTED FILMS: *The Fifth Horseman (1924), Don't Bet on Women, Daddy Long Legs (1931), She Wanted a Millionaire (1932), 42nd Street, Bombshell (1933), The Cat's Paw, The Merry Widow (1934), Biography of a Bachelor Girl, Baby Face Harrigan (1935), We Went to College (1936), Don't Tell the Wife, Good Old Soak (1937), Destry Rides Again (1939), The Bank Dick (1940), Road to Zanzibar, Cracked Nuts (1941), Twin Bed (1944), It's a Joke, Son (1947), The Bride Goes Wild (1948), Kill the Umpire (1950), I Love Melvin (1953), Bundle of Joy (1956), The Mating Game (1959), Spinout (1966).* ■

Merman, Ethel (1909–1984), actress, singer. Appeared on stage as a musical comedy star, in television, and in films. A dynamic entertainer, she possessed a vivacious personality and a strong voice that few could match when it came time to belt out a song. Merman, who was born Ethel Zimmerman, appeared chiefly in light films in lead or second lead roles.

In *Kid Millions* she and her boyfriend Warren HYMER scheme to swindle Eddie CANTOR out of an inheritance worth millions. Posing as Cantor's long-lost mother, she introduces dim-witted Hymer as his lost uncle. "Gee," Cantor wonders, "isn't Uncle Louie a funny duck?" "Oh, wait'll you get to know him," she answers. "He'll kill you."

SELECTED FILMS: *Follow the Leader (1930), We're Not Dressing, Kid Millions (1934), Anything Goes, Strike Me Pink (1936), Happy Landing, Straight, Place and Show (1938), Stage Door Canteen (1943), Call Me Madam (1953), There's No Business Like Show Business (1954), It's a Mad, Mad, Mad, Mad World (1963), Won Ton Ton, the Dog Who Saved Hollywood (1976).* ∎

Merrill, Dina (1925–), actress. Worked in stock, on Broadway, and in television before entering films in 1957. Born Nedema Hutton, she has appeared chiefly in light films, sometimes as the detached, uncaring female lead. She has co-starred with some of the leading comedians of the period, including Jerry LEWIS and Bob HOPE.

SELECTED FILMS: *Desk Set (1957), A Nice Little Bank That Should Be Robbed (1958), Don't Give Up the Ship, Operation Petticoat (1959), The Courtship of Eddie's Father (1963), I'll Take Sweden (1965), Running Wild (1973), The Greatest (1977), Just Tell Me What You Want (1979).* ∎

Merrily We Live (1938), MGM. *Dir.* Norman McLeod; *Sc.* Jack Jevne, E. Edward Moran; with Constance Bennett, Brian Aherne, Alan Mowbray, Billie Burke.

Another engaging SCREWBALL COMEDY about the rich, this film, coming almost in the wake of the successful *My Man Godfrey* (1936), has eccentric Billie BURKE hire sophisticated Brian AHERNE as the family servant to straighten out her bratty daughter, Constance BENNETT. Aherne, challenged by the frantic disorder of the household, attempts to introduce a semblance of order to each member's lifestyle while falling in love with the spoiled daughter. Other members of the cast add to the fun. Ann DVORAK plays the second daughter who falls for Aherne. Young Bonita Granville is as precocious as ever, while Patsy KELLY is her wisecracking self. Although the crazy shenanigans had all been done before in *Godfrey*, the film remains bright and entertaining. With this comedy, producer Hal ROACH made another bid at turning out feature-length films instead of his usual shorts. Screenwriters Jevne and Moran had worked with Roach on *Topper* the previous year, as had Bennett and Burke. She remained with Roach for two more entries in the fantasy series while the writers continued only for one sequel, *Topper Takes a Trip* (1939).

Mersereau, Violet, actress. Entered early silent films in the 1910s. A pretty actress with dark hair and eyes to match, she played female leads in a succession of dramas and light films, reaching the peak of her popularity during the World War I years.

SELECTED FILMS: *The Raggedy Queen, Susan's Gentleman, The Boy Girl, The Little Terror (1917).* ∎

Messinger, Gertrude, actress. Began her screen career in silent films in the early 1920s. A character player in both silent and early sound films, she appeared in several comedy shorts in "THE BOY FRIENDS" series of 1930–1932.

SELECTED FILMS: Penrod and Sam, The Barefoot Boy (1923), The Jazz Age, Two Weeks Off (1929), Doctor's Orders, Bigger and Better, Ladies Last (1930), Blood and Thunder, High Gear, Let's Do Things, Call a Cop, Mama Loves Papa (1931), Madame Racketeer (1932), Anne of Green Gables (1934), Adventurous Knights (1935). ■

"Mexican Spitfire" comedies. A series of slapstick comedies which ran from 1939 to 1943 and starred pretty Lupe VELEZ and rubber-legged Leon ERROL. Velez portrayed a hot-tempered female while Errol played a dual role: a roguish uncle and a drunken English lord. The entries, all of which were directed by Leslie GOODWINS, followed the conventions of mistaken identity and a frenetic conclusion. The series was based on the film The Girl From Mexico (1939).

SELECTED FILMS: Mexican Spitfire (1939), Mexican Spitfire Out West (1940), Mexican Spitfire's Baby (1941), Mexican Spitfire at Sea, Mexican Spitfire's Elephant, Mexican Spitfire Sees a Ghost (1942), Mexican Spitfire's Blessed Event (1943). ■

"Mickey McGuire" comedies. A series of comedy shorts produced in the late 1920s based on the popular comic strip created by cartoonist Fontaine Fox of "Toonerville Trolley" fame. The shorts starred a very young Mickey ROONEY, who, at this time, went under the name of Joe Yule, Jr., after his show-business father. He then adopted the name of the title character and, finally, in the early 1930s, acquired his current name. The series, directed by Al Herman and J.A. Duffy, depicted the humorous antics of a group of kids led by the tough little Mickey who sported a derby. The films attempted to emulate as well as compete with the more successful "OUR GANG" shorts produced by Hal ROACH.

SELECTED FILMS: Mickey's Movies, Mickey's Wild West, Mickey's Menagerie, Mickey's Great Idea, Mickey the Detective. ■

Middlemass, Robert (1885–1949), actor. Worked in stock and wrote stage plays before entering films in the 1930s. Grey-haired and distinguished-looking, he played military officers, executives, and professionals in dramas and light films through the 1940s. He is best remembered for writing the one-act play, The Valiant.

SELECTED FILMS: Cain and Mabel (1936), A Day at the Races (1937), Kentucky (1938), Little Old New York (1940), The Dolly Sisters (1945). ■

Middleton, Charles (1878–1949), actor. Worked in vaudeville and stock before entering films in the late 1920s. Tall and gaunt, he is best remembered for his fiendish roles, such as Ming the Merciless in the "Flash Gordon" serials. Although his forte was the melodrama, he appeared in many comedies, accompanying some of the leading comics of the period, including LAUREL AND HARDY in their two Foreign Legion films, Eddie CANTOR, and the MARX BROTHERS.

SELECTED FILMS: The Farmer's Daughter (1928), Way Out West (1930), Caught Plastered, Palmy Days (1931), Pack Up Your Troubles (1932), Duck Soup (1933), Behold My Wife!, David Harum (1934), Steamboat 'Round the Bend, The Virginia Judge (1935), We're on the Jury (1937), The Flying Deuces (1939), Wild Geese Calling (1941), The Town Went Wild (1944), How Do You Do? (1945), Spook Busters (1946), Road to Rio (1947), Jiggs and Maggie in Court (1947), Mr. Blandings Builds His Dream House (1948), The Last Bandit (1949). ■

Midler, Bette (1945–), actress, singer. Began her show business career in the early 1970s as a concert entertainer and recording artist. Known chiefly for her impudent, offbeat live performances, she made her film debut in 1978 in *The Rose*, a serious study of a tragic rock singer. She won an Oscar nomination as Best Actress for the role. Since then she has veered more toward comedy, scoring a hit in the very successful *Down and Out in Beverly Hills*, the film which established her as a formidable screen comedienne. A performer who can at times be abrasive and vulgar, she can also be hilarious and winning. James Spada's biography, *The Divine Bette Midler* (1984), contains numerous photographs.

SELECTED FILMS: The Rose (1978), Divine Madness (1980), Jinxed (1982), Down and Out in Beverly Hills (1986), Ruthless People (1986), Outrageous Fortune (1987). ∎

John Barrymore, Don Ameche, and Claudette Colbert in *Midnight* (1939)

Midnight (1939), PAR. *Dir*. Mitchell Leisen; *Sc*. Billy Wilder, Charles Brackett; with Claudette Colbert, Don Ameche, John Barrymore, Francis Lederer, Mary Astor, Monty Woolley.

Director Mitchell LEISEN styled this romantic farce after the earlier SCREW-BALL COMEDIES of the decade. A former art director, he embellished the production with lavish Parisian sets designed by Hans Dreier. The results added up to an opulent and hilarious comedy. Claudette COLBERT plays a penniless American singer stranded in Paris. Wealthy John BARRYMORE, who meets her at a private musicale that she has crashed, employs her to divert the attentions of his wife's lover. Meanwhile cabdriver Don AMECHE, who has fallen in love with Colbert, tracks her down to Barrymore's estate and poses as her husband. There is an abundance of witty dialogue, the forte of screenwriters WILDER and BRACKETT. Colbert, concerned about her multiple deceptions, is mollified by Barrymore. "My dear, it's amazing how little one has to explain to a man in love." "And when he stops being in love?" she asks. "Well," he replies, "that's when the alimony begins." A foppish guest at the luxurious home, studying the lavish display of food before him, is in a quandary about what to have for breakfast. "Wasn't there some animal who starved between two haystacks because he couldn't decide?" he asks. "Yes," host Barrymore confirms sarcastically, "Jackass." The entire cast is excellent, especially Barrymore in a hilarious telephone conversation, one of the highlights of the film. Leisen also directed the 1945 musical-comedy version titled *Masquerade in Mexico* starring Dorothy Lamour.

Midsummer Night's Sex Comedy, A. See Woody Allen.

Milestone, Lewis (1895–1980), director. Worked as a film cutter, assistant director, and screenwriter before advancing to full-fledged director in the mid-1920s. He turned out numerous dramas and light films during a career that spanned five decades. One of the major Hollywood directors, he was responsible for several works that have since become classics. However, much of his later output shows a decline in the high standards usually attributed to his earlier films. He won an Oscar as Best Comedy Director at the first Academy Awards ceremony for his silent comedy, *Two Arabian Knights*.

SELECTED FILMS: Seven Sinners (1925), Two Arabian Knights (1927), The Front Page (1931), Hallelujah, I'm a Bum

(1933), *The Captain Hates the Sea* (1934), *Paris in Spring* (1935), *Anything Goes* (1936), *My Life With Caroline* (1941), *No Minor Vices* (1948), *Kangaroo* (1952), *Ocean's Eleven* (1960), *Mutiny on the Bounty* (1962). ∎

Miljan, John (1892–1960), actor. Appeared on stage before entering silent films in 1923. Featured in more than 150 silent and sound features, he usually portrayed smooth villains. When he was not leading young women astray in melodramas, he had key character roles in a number of light films starring some of the foremost comedians of the period, including Mae WEST, Eddie CANTOR, and Fred ALLEN.

SELECTED FILMS: *Love Letters* (1923), *Footloose Widows*, *Almost a Lady* (1926), *The Clown*, *Sailor Izzy Murphy*, *Rough House Rosie* (1927), *The Little Snob*, *Lady Be Good* (1928), *Innocents of Paris*, *Hard-Boiled Rose* (1929), *His Night Out*, *Not So Dumb* (1930), *The Kid From Spain* (1932), *What! No Beer?* (1933), *Belle of the Nineties*, *The Ghost Walks* (1934), *Pardon Our Nerve* (1938), *Torchy Runs for Mayor* (1939), *The Cowboy and the Blonde* (1941), *Scattergood Survives a Murder* (1942), *The Merry Monahans* (1944), *It's in the Bag* (1945), *That's My Man* (1947), *Bonzo Goes to College* (1952), *The Lone Ranger and the City of Gold* (1958). ∎

Milland, Ray (1905–1986), actor. Appeared on stage and in films in his native England before journeying to Hollywood in 1930. The handsome and debonair Milland, who was born Reginald Truscott-Jones, played a variety of roles, including urbane characters in a string of romantic comedies. He also starred in costume dramas, westerns, and suspense films. He won an Oscar for his deft portrayal of an alcoholic in Billy WILDER'S *The Lost Weekend* (1945). During the 1950s he tried his skill at directing several films. He later appeared successfully on Broadway and in character roles in films. His autobiogra-

phy, *Wide-Eyed in Babylon*, was published in 1974.

SELECTED FILMS: *Way for a Sailor* (1930), *The Bachelor Father*, *Just a Gigolo*, *Blonde Crazy* (1931), *Polly of the Circus* (1932), *We're Not Dressing* (1934), *The Gilded Lily* (1935), *Next Time We Love*, *Three Smart Girls* (1936), *Easy Living* (1937), *Tropic Holiday*, *Say It in French* (1938), *The Doctor Takes a Wife* (1940), *Skylark* (1941), *The Lady Has Plans*, *The Major and the Minor* (1942), *Lady in the Dark* (1944), *Kitty*, *The Well Groomed Bride* (1946), *The Trouble With Women* (1947), *It Happens Every Spring* (1949), *Rhubarb* (1951), *Let's Do It Again* (1953), *Oliver's Story* (1978). ∎

Miller, Ann (1919–), singer, dancer, actress. Worked as a dancer before entering films in 1936. Her professional career may be divided into three phases: her appearances in routine musical comedies of the 1930s; her featured roles in MGM's big-budget musicals of the 1940s; and her triumph in Broadway musicals. She enlivened many minor films with her buoyant personality, her exceptional tap-dancing capabilities, and her beautiful legs. Her autobiography, *Miller's High Life*, was published in 1972.

SELECTED FILMS: *The Devil on Horseback* (1936), *Stage Door*, *The Life of the Party* (1937), *Having Wonderful Time*, *You Can't Take It With You*, *Room Service* (1938), *Too Many Girls*, *Melody Ranch* (1940), *Go West Young Lady* (1941), *True to the Army* (1942), *Reveille With Beverly*, *What's Buzzin', Cousin?* (1943), *Hey, Rookie*, *Carolina Blues* (1944), *Eve Knew Her Apples*, *Eadie Was a Lady* (1945), *The Kissing Bandit*, *Easter Parade* (1948), *On the Town* (1949), *Kiss Me Kate* (1953), *Hit the Deck* (1955), *The Opposite Sex*, *The Great American Pastime* (1956). ∎

Miller, Patsy Ruth (1905–), actress. Began her screen career at age 16 in silent films with Rudolph Valentino and Nazimova in the early 1920s. A talented performer, but never a star of the first rank, she appeared as the lead in dramas and light films into the early sound period. She abandoned her film career in the early 1930s.

SELECTED FILMS: Camille, The Sheik (1921), The Drivin' Fool (1923), Fools in the Dark, The Breath of Scandal (1924), Red Hot Tires, Hogan's Alley (1925), Oh, What a Nurse!, So This Is Paris, Private Izzy Murphy, King of the Turf (1926), Wolf's Clothing, Painting the Town, What Every Girl Should Know (1927), Hot Heels, Beautiful but Dumb (1928), The Fall of Eve, Twin Beds, The Hottentot, The Sap, So Long Letty (1929), Wide Open (1930), Night Beat (1931). ∎

Miller, Rube, actor. Worked as a supporting player in early silent comedy shorts for Mack SENNETT'S KEYSTONE studios. He appeared with some of the leading comics of the period, including, among others, Hank MANN, Ford STERLING, and "Fatty" ARBUCKLE. Within a short time he became a director for Sennett, and then moved on to other studios to turn out comedies. He directed several of Ben TURPIN'S shorts for Vogue studios.

SELECTED FILMS (as actor): In the Clutches of a Gang, Hard Cider, High Spots on Broadway, Hazel Met the Villain, When Reuben Fooled the Bandits, Our Country Cousin, A Gambling Rube (1914).

SELECTED FILMS (as director): For Ten Thousand Bucks, Some Liars, The Stolen Booking, Doctoring a Leak, Poultry a la Mode, Ducking a Discord, He Did and He Didn't, Picture Pirates, Shot in the Fracas, Jealous Jolts, The Wicked City (1916), A Circus Cyclone (1917). ∎

Millican, James (1910–1955), actor. Began his screen career in the early 1930s chiefly playing characters on the wrong side of the law. Thin, light-haired, and with a worried look, he never achieved major recognition although he became a familiar supporting actor of minor dramas, westerns, and light films during the 1940s and 1950s.

SELECTED FILMS: The Sign of the Cross (1932), Mr. Deeds Goes to Town (1936), You Can't Take It With You, Annabel Takes a Tour (1938), A Chump at Oxford (1940), Barnacle Bill, Love Crazy, Here Comes Mr. Jordan (1941), My Favorite Blonde (1942), Thousands Cheer (1943), Duffy's Tavern (1945), The Well-Groomed Bride (1946), Mister 880 (1950), Red Sundown (1956). ∎

Minciotti, Silvio (1882–1961), actor. Appeared on stage in his native Italy and on Broadway before entering films in the early 1950s. A well-attired, sincere-looking figure, he played character roles in dramas and light films, often as fatherly types.

SELECTED FILMS: Deported, Up Front, Strictly Dishonorable (1951), Francis Covers the Big Town (1953), Serenade (1956), Full of Life (1957). ∎

Mineau, Charlotte, actress. Worked in early silent films, especially as a supporting player in comedy shorts starring Charlie CHAPLIN. Tall and pretty, she portrayed a wide range of characters, including house detectives and mothers.

SELECTED FILMS: His New Job, A Night in the Show (1915), The Vagabond, The Count, Behind the Screen, The Rink (1916), Easy Street (1917), The Extra Girl (1924), Sparrows (1926). ∎

Minnelli, Vincente (1910–1986), director. Worked as an assistant stage manager and costume designer, director of Broadway musicals, and assistant film director before turning out his own films by the 1940s. He directed musicals, comedies, and dramas. Considered a stylist with an excellent sense of balance and proportion, especially in his lavish musical comedies, he used the camera creatively and employed production numbers to further the storyline. He remained with MGM studios for 26 years, directing several of the company's best musicals during the heyday of the genre—the 1940s and 1950s.

His later, non-musical films tended to permit style to dominate, leaving little in the way of substance, for which some American and foreign critics and fellow directors have taken him to task. But despite the criticism, he left a body of work that is highly individualistic and visually exciting. He won an Oscar for his direction of *Gigi* in 1958. He was married to Judy GARLAND and the father of Liza Minnelli. His autobiography, *I Remember It Well*, was published in 1972.

SELECTED FILMS: *Cabin in the Sky, I Dood It (1943), Meet Me in St. Louis (1944), Yolanda and the Thief (1945), The Pirate (1948), Father of the Bride (1950), Father's Little Dividend, An American in Paris (1951), The Band Wagon (1953), The Long Long Trailer (1954), Designing Woman (1957), Gigi, The Reluctant Debutante (1958), The Courtship of Eddie's Father (1963), Goodbye, Charlie (1964), A Matter of Time (1976).* ∎

Miracle of Morgan's Creek, The

(1944), PAR. *Dir.* Preston Sturges; *Sc.* Preston Sturges; with Betty Hutton, Eddie Bracken, William Demarest, Porter Hall.

Considered the director's best film, this hilarious comedy tells the story of a small-town girl, played by Betty HUTTON, who becomes pregnant after spending one night with a soldier who has been shipped overseas. Since she was smashed that fateful night, she barely recalls the events or the G.I.'s name. Fortunately for her, a local boob, played expertly by Eddie BRACKEN, who has always liked her, volunteers to marry her. The film has a surprise ending that was highly touted at the time the picture was released. The usual members of the director's stock company of character players are on hand to contribute to the zaniness, including William DEMAREST as Hutton's explosive father, Porter HALL, Brian DONLEVY, and Jimmy CONLIN. Diana LYNN plays Hutton's precocious 14-year-old sister.

STURGES was the wonder-boy director of the 1940s, turning out satirical comedies unmatched by his contemporaries. His wartime comedies gave audiences the escape they needed at a time when the country and much of the world were in the grips of a deadly conflict. But within the next few years his popularity as a major director declined almost as rapidly as it had risen.

Miranda, Carmen (1913–1955), singer, actress. Portuguese-born Brazilian singer who brightened a string of American light films during the 1940s. She sang on the radio and recorded songs in her native land and appeared in films in Brazil before coming to Hollywood. Dressed in lavish costumes and outlandish hats, she sang in her native tongue. When she wasn't performing, the "Brazilian Bombshell," as she was often listed, added comedy to a film by fracturing the English language.

Perhaps her most flamboyant moment occurred in *The Gang's All Here* in which her song, "The Lady With the Tutti Frutti Hat," is accompanied by dozens of chorines holding enormous bananas horizontally erect as she promenades down a corridor of strawberries while on her head rests a fruit-filled hat extending beyond the top of the screen. There is a museum in Rio dedicated to her.

In the above film she parries with Betty Grable. "Is that a diamond?" Miranda asks. "Yes," Grable says. "Does the size of it startle you?" "Yes," Miranda counters. "In Brazil we throw that kind away."

SELECTED FILMS: *Down Argentine Way (1940), That Night in Rio, Week-End in Havana (1941), Springtime in the Rockies (1942), The Gang's All Here (1943), Four Jills in a Jeep, Greenwich Village, Something for the Boys (1944), Doll Face, If I'm Lucky (1946), Copacabana (1947), A Date With Judy (1948), Nancy Goes to Reno (1950), Scared Stiff (1953).* ∎

Mitchell, Frank. See Mitchell and Durant.

Mitchell, Geneva (–1949), actress. Worked in films chiefly in the 1930s as a supporting player in comedy shorts. She appeared with some of the leading comics of the period, including, among others, the THREE STOOGES and Buster KEATON.

SELECTED FILMS: Restless Knights, Pop Goes the Easel (1935). ∎

Mitchell, Grant (1874–1957), actor. Appeared on stage in the early 1900s and, except for one isolated feature, did not come to films until the sound era. A former lawyer, he played character parts in more than 100 dramas and comedies and was often overwhelmed by demanding or eccentric screen wives.

SELECTED FILMS: Radio-Mania (1922), Week End Marriage (1932), He Learned About Women, Dinner at Eight (1933), The Show-Off, Twenty Million Sweethearts (1934), Traveling Saleslady, A Midsummer Night's Dream, It's in the Air (1935), First Lady (1937), The Headleys at Home (1938), It All Came True (1940), The Bride Wore Crutches, Nothing but the Truth (1941), My Sister Eileen (1942), Dixie (1943), See Here, Private Hargrove, Arsenic and Old Lace (1944), A Medal for Benny (1945), Easy to Wed (1946), Blondie's Holiday (1947), Who Killed Doc Robin? (1948). ∎

Mitchell, Millard (1900–1953), actor. Appeared on stage before entering films in the early 1940s. A slender, nasal-voiced character actor, he was adept in both tough and comedy roles in dramas and light films. His most memorable performance was that of an astute inmate in *My Six Convicts.*

SELECTED FILMS: Secrets of a Secretary (1931), Mr. and Mrs. Smith (1940), Get Hep to Love (1942), Slightly Dangerous (1943), A Foreign Affair (1948), Everybody Does It (1949), Mr. 880, USS

Teakettle (1950), My Six Convicts, Singin' in the Rain (1952), Here Come the Girls, The Naked Spur (1953). ∎

Mitchell and Durant. A popular comedy team during the 1920s and 1930s in burlesque and vaudeville. Frank Mitchell and Jack Durant began their careers in show business as acrobats. Their routines consisted chiefly of pratfalls and physical comedy, somewhat on the violent side and not unlike the comedy of the THREE STOOGES who were to follow them. Once their act became a little more sophisticated, they began to appear in Broadway revues. They were featured in several light films during the 1930s without much distinction. After the team split up in the late 1930s, Mitchell continued to appear in minor film roles while Durant returned to stage comedy.

SELECTED FILMS: She Learned About Sailors (1934), The Singing Kid (1936). ∎

Modern Times (1936), UA. Dir. Charlie Chaplin; Sc. Charlie Chaplin; with Charlie Chaplin, Paulette Goddard, Henry Bergman, Chester Conklin, Allan Garcia.

Made at a time when sound films were firmly entrenched and silents were finished, CHAPLIN'S silent comedy became as famous for its attacks on the machine age and its resulting dehumanization as for its comedic content. In one of the best scenes in the film, metaphorically and humorously, factory worker Charlie falls into the cogwheels of a massive machine. In another, he is placed in front of an automatic lunch machine designed to make the lunch break more efficient. But the device goes haywire, pummeling Charlie with soup, pie, and condiments. His skating scene while he is employed as a night watchman in a department store once again displays his balletic abilities. Like *City Lights* (1931), it is chiefly a silent film with a few incursions of sound, including some sound effects and his original musical score (which contains "Smile"). The final scene in which Charlie the tramp and Paulette GODDARD take to the open road as they start life anew is one of the most famous endings in the history of film.

Monroe, Marilyn (1926–1962), actress. Posed as a pin-up girl during World War II and worked as a model after the war before entering films. Her first screen appearances in the late 1940s were inauspicious ones. In fact, her first two studios, 20th Century-Fox and Columbia, did not renew her contract. But by the early 1950s, she was "discovered" by Hollywood and soon emerged as one of the most popular personalities in film history. There was something special about her. Her radiant smile instilled in us a sense of optimism; her vulnerability moved us; and her tragic life, beginning as a young girl raised in orphanages and foster homes after her mother was committed to a mental institution, affected us all. Whether Hollywood contributed to her destruction by mercilessly exploiting her or gave her empty and shattered life substance and meaning remains a much-debated controversy.

Often complaining that she had more talent than the sex-object image the studios projected of her, she began to add subtleties to the characters she portrayed and fought for and won the right to select her directors. The results of her efforts produced better films and won her respect as an accomplished actress. After her tragic death from an overdose of barbiturates, she gained even greater popularity with a sympathetic and adoring public. *Marilyn*, a biography by Gloria Steinem, was published in 1986.

She demonstrated a knack for comedy early in her short career. In *Monkey Business* (1952), for example, she plays Charles COBURN'S secretary. Chemist Cary GRANT notices her and observes, "My, you're here early this morning." "Mr. Oxie complained about my punctuation," she explains, "so I made sure I got here before nine."

SELECTED FILMS: *Scudda Hoo! Scudda Hay!* (1948), *Love Happy, All About Eve* (1950), *As Young As You Feel, Love Nest, Let's Make It Legal* (1951), *We're Not Married, O. Henry's Full House* (1952), *Gentlemen Prefer Blondes, How to Marry a Millionaire* (1953), *There's No Business Like Show Business* (1954), *The Seven Year Itch* (1955), *Bus Stop* (1956), *The Prince and the Showgirl* (1957), *Some Like It Hot* (1959), *Let's Make Love* (1960), *The Misfits* (1961). ∎

Monsieur Verdoux (1947), UA. Dir. Charlie Chaplin; Sc. Charlie Chaplin; with Charlie Chaplin, Mady Correll, Martha Raye, Allison Roddan.

In this early black comedy CHAPLIN portrayed the dual-natured loving husband and murderer of rich widows. Verdoux believes that he can earn more than a living doing individually what nations practice on a large scale. Success and profit are the important goals in our society. Chaplin plays a banker who is kind and loving to his wife and son, while at the same time engages in multiple murder. In none of his other works does he so savagely attack society, especially those who plunge countries into war solely for gain. When a journalist visits his prison cell and asks him to admit that crime does not pay, he replies: "Not on a small scale." Martha RAYE adds to the comedy as a rich widow who continually eludes Verdoux's attempts on her life. The film was picketed in many theaters, not because of its content but because of Chaplin's alleged political convictions at the time.

Montana, Bull (1887–1950), actor, athlete. A famous strong man who entered films in the early 1920s. He made a series of popular silent comedies for producer Hunt Stromberg, after which he continued to appear in films for other studios, occasionally playing heavies. With the advent of sound, he began to support other comics, including Buster KEATON.

SELECTED FILMS: *Brass Buttons (1919), Go and Get It (1920), Ladies' Man (1922), Painted People (1923), Good Morning, Judge, How to Handle Women (1928), The Show of Shows, Tiger Rose (1929), Palooka From Paduca (1935), When's Your Birthday? (1937).* ∎

Montgomery, Douglas (1908–1966), actor. Worked on stage and in television as well as in films beginning in the early 1930s. He appeared chiefly as a supporting player in dramas and light films. He also appeared in films as Douglas Kent.

SELECTED FILMS: *Waterloo Bridge, Five and Ten (1931), Music in the Air, Eight Girls in a Boat (1934), Lady Tubbs, Harmony Lane, Tropical Trouble (1935), Life Begins With Love (1937), The Cat and the Canary (1939), Woman to Woman (1946), When in Rome (1952).* ∎

Montgomery, Earl (1893–1966), actor. Began his film career in the 1910s in early silent comedies. He appeared in lead and supporting roles in silent and sound films.

SELECTED FILMS: *Bums and Boarders, Chumps and Cops, Farms and Fumbles (1918), Love and Leather, Damsels and Dandies, Zip and Zest, Harems and Hokum, Caves and Croquetts, Vamps and Variety (1919), Tea With a Kick (1923), Stop, Look and Listen (1926), Navy Born (1936).*

Montgomery, Peggy. See Baby Peggy.

Montgomery, Robert (1904–1981), actor. Worked at odd jobs following his father's death (which left his family penniless) before appearing successfully on Broadway at age 20. He entered films in 1929 and, two years and 14 features later, quickly advanced to a major player. Cast by MGM as an easy-going, light-hearted lead, he co-starred in a string of comedies with some of the foremost actresses of the period. Later in his career he portrayed more serious characters. He directed a few films without much critical excitement. During World War II he served in the United States Navy. He received two Oscar nominations as Best Actor: for *Night Must Fall* (1937) and *Here Comes Mr. Jordan* (1941).

In *Private Lives* (1931) he played the husband of Norma Shearer with whom he is always bickering. As his proposal for a peaceful marriage, he suggests: "Certain women should be struck regularly like gongs."

SELECTED FILMS: *The Single Standard, So This Is College, Three Live Ghosts, Their Own Desire (1929), Free and Easy, The Divorcee, Our Blushing Brides, Love in the Rough (1930), Inspiration, The Easiest Way, Strangers May Kiss, Shipmates (1931), Blondie of the Follies (1932), When Ladies Meet, Made on Broadway (1933), Biography of a Bachelor Girl, No More Ladies (1935), Petticoat Fever, Piccadilly Jim (1936), Ever Since Eve (1937), Three Loves Has Nancy (1938), Fast and Loose (1939), Here Comes Mr. Jordan (1941), June Bride (1948).* ∎

Moon Is Blue, The (1953), UA. Dir. Otto Preminger; Sc. F. Hugh Herbert; with William Holden, David Niven, Maggie McNamara, Tom Tully.

A landmark film in terms of its effect on the Production Code, this bedroom comedy today appears mild and leaves one wondering what all the fuss was about in the early 1950s. Director Otto PREMINGER challenged both the Code and the Legion of Decency by adapting F. Hugh HERBERT'S play almost exactly as it had been performed on Broadway. Words like "virgin," "mistress," and "seduction," normally banned from films up to that time, were not deleted. The subject matter, especially the frivolous way of discussing methods of seducing virgins, was regarded as particularly offensive. The Hollywood censors and other offended groups roared, but the publicity caused the box office to reply even more loudly. The studio moguls listened, and films were never the same.

Moore, Alvy (1925–), actor. Entered films in the early 1950s in aggressive, youthful roles. Thin and spirited, he appeared as a supporting player chiefly in light films before going into the production end of the film business.

SELECTED FILMS: Okinawa (1952), Susan Slept Here (1953), Designing Woman (1957), The Perfect Furlough (1958), The Wackiest Ship in the Army (1960), Everything's Ducky (1961), Move Over, Darling (1963), Three Nuts in Search of a Bolt (1964), The Gnome-Mobile (1966), Herbie Rides Again (1974). ■

Moore, Colleen (1900–), actress. Appeared in early silent films and gradually advanced to lead roles in dozens of light films. A popular star throughout the 1920s, Moore, who was born Kathleen Morrison, was often cast as a lively flapper. She was a natural comedienne whose wild antics and liberated attitude reflected the jazz age and helped set the fashions in American glamor. Her Dutchboy hair style became her trademark. Her autobiography, Silent Star, was published in 1968.

SELECTED FILMS: The Bad Boy, Hands Up! (1917), A Hoosier Romance (1918), Little Orphan Annie (1919), So Long Letty, Dinty (1920), His Nibs (1921), Come On Over, The Wall Flower (1922), Look Your Best, April Showers (1923), The Perfect Flapper (1924), Sally (1925), Irene, Ella Cinders, Twinkletoes (1926), Naughty but Nice (1927), Her Wild Oat, Oh, Kay! (1928), Smiling Irish Eyes, Footlights and Fools (1929), Social Register (1934). ■

Moore, Constance (1919–), actress. Worked as band vocalist, as radio singer, and on Broadway before migrating to Hollywood in the late 1930s. Gaining some popularity in the 1940s in lead and supporting roles, she appeared chiefly in B dramas and light films.

SELECTED FILMS: The Crime of Dr. Hallet, Swing That Cheer (1938), You Can't Cheat an Honest Man, Hawaiian Nights, Charlie McCarthy—Detective (1939), La Conga Nights, Argentine Nights, Ma, He's Making Eyes at Me (1940), Las Vegas Nights (1941), Take a Letter, Darling (1942), Show Business, Atlantic City (1944), Delightfully Dangerous (1945), Hit Parade of 1947, Hats Off to Rhythm (1947), Spree (1967). ■

Moore, Del (1917–1970), actor. Entered films in the early 1950s following a career on stage. He played leads and supporting roles in comedy shorts and light features, especially in the "JOE McDOAKES" series of one-reelers. He worked in several of Jerry LEWIS' comedies.

SELECTED FILMS: So You Want to Enjoy Life (1952), So You Want to Go to a Nightclub (1954), So You Want to Be a Gladiator, So You Want to Be a V.P. (1955), So You Think the Grass Is Greener (1956), The Errand Boy, It's Only Money (1962), The Nutty Professor (1963), The Patsy, The Disorderly Orderly (1964), The Big Mouth (1967), The Catalina Caper (1968). ■

Moore, Dickie (1925–), actor. Began his screen career as an infant in 1927. He soon became one of the most popular child actors during the 1930s. He appeared in dozens of "OUR GANG" comedy shorts and numerous features during a career that has spanned four decades. His popularity waned as he grew to adolescence.

SELECTED FILMS: The Beloved Rogue (1927), Husband's Holiday (1931), Manhattan Parade, The Expert, Million Dollar Legs (1932), Timothy's Quest, Star for a Night (1936), The Bride Wore Red (1937), The Arkansas Traveler (1938), The Under-Pup (1939), The Blue Bird (1940), Happy Land, Jive Junction (1943), The Member of the Wedding (1953). ∎

Dudley Moore

Moore, Dudley (1935–), actor. Worked on stage, as a cabaret pianist-comedian, and in films in his native England before appearing on the American screen. His diminutive size and English accent mark him as distinctive, while his madcap misadventures and shenanigans confirm him as a genuine comic, especially in his two most popular films, 10 and Arthur. He has scored the music for a number of films.

SELECTED FILMS: Foul Play (1978), 10 (1979), Wholly Moses! (1980), Arthur (1981), Lovesick, Romantic Comedy (1983), Best Defense, Micki and Maude, Unfaithfully Yours (1984). ∎

Moore, Ida (1883–1964), actress. Appeared on stage before entering films in the mid-1920s. For four decades she played a variety of roles in both dramas and comedies, with pleasant, matronly types predominating. She worked with a variety of popular comic actors and comedians of the period, including, among others, Maurice CHEVALIER, Bob HOPE, and Jerry LEWIS.

SELECTED FILMS: The Merry Widow, Thank You (1925), Once Upon a Time, She's a Soldier, Too (1944), Easy to Look At (1945), Easy Come, Easy Go, The Egg and I (1947), Good Sam (1948), Ma and Pa Kettle (1949), Fancy Pants, Harvey (1950), The Lemon Drop Kid (1951), The Desk Set (1957), Rock-a-Bye Baby (1958). ∎

Moore, Mary Tyler (1936–), actress. Worked as a dancer and television comedienne-actress from the late 1950s. She entered films in the early 1960s. But her career foundered until the late 1960s. Appearances on the Dick Van Dyke television show led to her being hired to star in her own television series, "The Mary Tyler Moore Show." She has won several Emmys. Her occasional forays on the large screen have not brought her the same success she experienced in television. She usually portrays saucy characters in light films although she has ventured into drama to critical acclaim.

In Thoroughly Modern Millie she played a 1920s flapper who is invited to a pretentious social event at which a talkative, boorish woman has dominated the conversation. "That diamond ring took my breath away," the officious guest comments at one point. "Not completely," Moore quips.

SELECTED FILMS: X-15 (1961), Thoroughly Modern Millie (1967), Don't Just Stand There!, What's So Bad About Feeling Good? (1968), Change of Habit (1969), Six Weeks (1982). ∎

Moore, Matt (1888–1960), actor. Entered films in 1913, at first playing leads in different genres. Although he specialized in romantic and heroic characters, he appeared in several entertaining light films as well. After 20 years of major roles in silent and early sound films, he was relegated to smaller parts for the remainder of his screen career, which, in all, spanned five decades. His brothers, Owen and Tom, were also popular screen actors.

SELECTED FILMS: *Traffic in Souls* (1913), *A Regular Girl* (1919), *Don't Ever Marry, Hairpins* (1920), *His Majesty, Bunker Bean* (1925), *Early to Wed, Summer Bachelors* (1926), *Tillie the Toiler* (1927), *Beware of Blondes, Dry Martini, Phyllis of the Follies* (1928), *Coquette* (1929), *The Front Page, Penrod and Sam* (1931), *Cock of the Air* (1932), *Anything Goes* (1936), *Good Sam* (1948), *Seven Brides for Seven Brothers* (1954), *An Affair to Remember* (1957). ■

Moore, Owen (1886–1939), actor. Appeared in BIOGRAPH films as early as 1908 and in silent comedy shorts. His screen career stretched over four decades. The Irish-born actor was married to Mary PICKFORD for a short time and played her male lead in several of her early films. He worked with some of the leading comics of the period, including Mabel NORMAND and Mae WEST. He was the brother of actors Matt and Tom Moore.

SELECTED FILMS: *The Valet's Wife* (1908), *Their First Misunderstanding* (1910), *The Battle of the Sexes* (1914), *Mabel Lost and Won* (1915), *Piccadilly Jim* (1920), *The Chicken in the Case* (1921), *Oh, Mabel Behave* (1922), *Her Temporary Husband* (1923), *Married?* (1926), *Tea for Three, Women Love Diamonds* (1927), *Husbands for Rent* (1928), *What a Widow!* (1930), *She Done Him Wrong* (1933), *A Star Is Born* (1937). ■

Moore, Terry (1929–), actress. Worked as a child model and in films as a youngster before developing into a sexually attractive actress. Born Helen Koford, she appeared in dramas and light films, receiving an Academy Award nomination for her role in *Come Back, Little Sheba* (1952).

SELECTED FILMS: *Maryland* (1940), *Safe at Home* (1941), *My Gal Sal* (1942), *The Great Rupert, He's a Cockeyed Wonder* (1950), *The Barefoot Mailman* (1951), *Daddy Long Legs* (1955), *Bernardine* (1957), *A Private's Affair* (1959), *Black Spurs* (1965). ■

Moore, Victor (1876–1962), actor, comedian. Worked as a comic in vaudeville and on stage before entering films in 1915. A short and plump character actor, he added humor to many light films and musicals. His biggest success was as the star of the Broadway musical, *Of Thee I Sing* (1932), in which he played a bumbling vice-president. He frequently portrayed confused and hesitant souls easily intimidated by bureaucrats and others. He continued to perform on stage between film assignments, appearing on the screen in more than 25 features.

In *Louisiana Purchase* (1941) he played an elderly United States senator on special assignment in New Orleans. He enters an exclusive French restaurant but, not understanding the exotic dishes on the menu, orders a ham sandwich. "We don't serve ham sandwiches!" the indignant owner states emphatically. "Oh, I understand," Moore replies, "this is a kosher restaurant."

SELECTED FILMS: *Snobs, Chimmie Fadden* (1915), *The Clown* (1916), *Heads Up, Dangerous Dan McGrew* (1930), *Gift of Gab* (1934), *Gold Diggers of 1937, Swing Time* (1936), *Meet the Missus* (1937), *This Marriage Business* (1938), *True to Life, The Heat's On* (1943), *Carolina Blues* (1944), *It's in the Bag, Duffy's Tavern* (1945), *Ziegfeld Follies* (1946), *It Happened on Fifth Avenue* (1947), *We're Not Married* (1952), *The Seven Year Itch* (1955). ■

Moorhead, Natalie, actress. Appeared as a second lead and supporting player in numerous films from the late 1920s until the 1940s. A sleek, attractive blonde, she played in melodramas and light films with some of the foremost stars of the period.

SELECTED FILMS: *Thru Different Eyes* (1929), *Runaway Bride, Hook, Line and Sinker* (1930), *Divorce Among Friends, Parlor, Bedroom and Bath, Strictly Dishonorable* (1931), *Three Wise Girls* (1932), *Only Yesterday* (1933), *The Thin Man* (1934), *The Adventurous Blonde* (1937), *Beloved Brat* (1938), *Flight Angels* (1940). ∎

Moran, George. See Moran and Mack.

Moran, Lee (1888–1961), actor. Appeared in early silent comedy shorts for various studios, including that of producer Al CHRISTY. In 1915 he was teamed up with comic Eddie LYONS. The duo made a highly popular series of comedies between 1915 and 1917 for Universal studios. Moran continued as a character actor after the team split up in 1920.

SELECTED FILMS: *Almost an Actress* (1913), *When the Mummy Cried for Help, All Aboard, Little Egypt Malone* (1915), *Ducks out of Water* (1917), *La La Lucille* (1920), *A Shocking Night* (1921), *The Fast Worker* (1924), *My Lady of Whims* (1925), *Her Big Night* (1926), *Wolf's Clothing* (1927), *Gold Diggers of Broadway* (1929), *Sweet Mama* (1930), *Uptown New York* (1932), *Goldie Gets Along* (1933), *The Circus Clown* (1934), *The Calling of Dan Matthews* (1936). ∎

Moran, Patsy (–1968), actress, comedienne. Began her film career in the 1930s as a comic character player. She appeared in several films, supporting some of the foremost comics of the period, including LAUREL AND HARDY. She also appeared on radio as a comedienne.

SELECTED FILMS: *Block-Heads* (1938). ∎

Moran, Peggy (1918–), actress. Worked on radio before appearing in numerous low-budget films during the 1930s and 1940s. A pretty female lead, she worked in various genres, including dramas and light films.

SELECTED FILMS: *Girls' School* (1938), *Little Accident, Ninotchka* (1939), *Oh, Johnny, How You Can Love, Spring Parade, Argentine Nights, Slightly Tempted, One Night in the Tropics* (1940), *Double Date* (1941), *Treat 'Em Rough, Seven Sweethearts* (1942), *King of the Cowboys* (1943). ∎

Moran, Polly (1884–1952), actress. Appeared in vaudeville before entering films in 1913. She worked for producer Mack SENNETT, turning out a string of comedy shorts. By 1920, after a brief return to the stage, she appeared in feature-length films. She continued in films until 1950. She co-starred with some of the foremost comics of the period, including, among others, Mae Busch, Charlie MURRAY, Ben TURPIN, Marie DRESSLER, and Eddie FOY.

SELECTED FILMS: *The Janitor* (1913), *Ambrose's Little Hatchet, Their Second Splash* (1915), *The Pullman Bride* (1917), *She Loved Him Plenty* (1918), *Skirts* (1921), *Luck* (1923), *Buttons* (1927), *Bringing Up Father* (1928), *So This Is College, Hot for Paris* (1929), *Way Out West* (1930), *Alice in Wonderland* (1933), *Down to Their Last Yacht* (1934), *Two Wise Maids* (1937), *Ladies in Distress* (1938), *Adam's Rib* (1949), *The Yellow Cab Man* (1950). ∎

Moran and Mack. A comedy team popular in the 1920s and 1930s. The team was made up of two former minstrel performers, George Moran and Charles E. Mack, who did their comedy act in blackface. They joined up in 1919, with Moran playing the straight man while Mack uttered the punchlines. After a few years in vaudeville, they appeared on Broadway in a series of successful shows. Their comedy records sold very well. In 1929 they signed with Paramount and were featured in *Why Bring That Up?* After the film, the team split up because of financial differences. When Moran left the act, Mack linked up with Bert SWOR, his old vaudeville partner, and the new team of Moran and Mack made another film, *Anybody's War* (1930). The film proved unprofitable and the studio canceled the duo's contract. On the road once again, Mack used several different partners in the declining act until Moran returned.

Mack SENNETT, the famous producer of silent slapstick comedies, who was facing his own crisis in sound films, approached them with an offer to appear in one more film, a musical comedy. *Hypnotized*, produced by a low-budget company, opened in 1932 to poor reviews. They continued in films, but turned out weak comedy shorts, such as "Two Black Crows in Africa," until Mack was killed in an automobile accident in 1934. Moran continued in vaudeville until his death in 1949. Known affectionately by their public as the "Two Black Crows," Moran and Mack may not have been as successful in films as they were on stage, but at least they gave the screen audiences a chance to see them in several of their famous routines.

Morante, Milburn (1887–1964), actor. Appeared in early silent comedy shorts from 1913. In the 1920s he made a series of one-reel comedies for Federated studios. He appeared in features of various genres, sometimes as a sidekick to the western hero. He also directed a handful of films during the 1920s.

SELECTED FILMS: *Rainbow Rangers* (1924), *Modern Youth* (1926), *The Swift Shadow* (1927), *The Little Buckaroo, The Fightin' Redhead* (1928), *The Freckled Rascal, The Little Savage* (1929), *Buzzy*

and the Phantom Pinto (1941), *Drifting Along* (1946), *Blazing Bullets* (1951). ■

Mantan Moreland (right)

Moreland, Mantan (1902–1973), actor. Worked in nightclubs and on stage before entering films in 1938. A popular comedian, he entertained at Harlem's famous Apollo Theater. He appeared in more than one hundred features during a career that spanned five decades. His most memorable role was that of Birmingham, Charlie Chan's stereotyped chauffeur in the popular detective series. As a comic-relief character, he would often be scared and get into scrapes with the detective's son.

Dark Alibi (1946) perhaps best represents the type of gags and comic relief he so aptly supplied. Chan's son (Benson Fong) berates him during an investigation. "You don't even know what a lawsuit is." "Sure I do," Moreland insists. "It's something that a police wears." Earlier in the film he says to Fong: "Why do you always have to hurry to a murder case? Why can't you just ooze on down to one?" Later, someone asks him: "Don't you ever do anything on time?" "Sure I do," he replies. "I bought a car once." "How?" "On time," he quips.

SELECTED FILMS: *Spirit of Youth* (1937), *Harlem on the Prairie* (1938), *One Dark Night* (1939), *Professor Creeps, Star Dust* (1940), *Cracked Nuts, It Started With Eve, Dressed to Kill* (1941), *A-Haunting We Will Go, Andy Hardy's*

Double Trouble, The Palm Beach Story (1942), *Hit the Ice, Cabin in the Sky* (1943), *Charlie Chan in the Secret Service, Bowery to Broadway* (1944), *The Spider, Captain Tugboat Annie* (1945), *Mantan Runs for Mayor* (1946), *The Chinese Ring* (1947), *Sky Dragon* (1949), *Rockin' the Blues* (1956), *Enter Laughing* (1967), *Watermelon Man* (1970), *The Young Nurses* (1970). ∎

Morgan, Dennis (1910–), actor, singer. Worked as a radio announcer and in opera before entering films in 1936. A handsome male lead, he appeared in numerous dramas and light films, chiefly for Warner Brothers. His specialty was musical comedy. He portrayed the Irish songwriter, Chauncey Olcott, in the biographical film, *My Wild Irish Rose.*

SELECTED FILMS: *Suzy, The Great Ziegfeld* (1936), *Three Cheers for the Irish* (1940), *Affectionately Yours* (1941), *Thank Your Lucky Stars* (1943), *The Very Thought of You* (1944), *Christmas in Connecticut* (1945), *Two Guys From Milwaukee, The Time, the Place and the Girl* (1946), *My Wild Irish Rose* (1947), *Two Guys From Texas* (1948), *It's a Great Feeling, The Lady Takes a Sailor* (1949), *Pretty Baby* (1950), *Uranium Boom* (1956). ∎

Morgan, Frank (1890–1949), actor. Worked at odd jobs before appearing in vaudeville and ultimately on Broadway in 1914. He entered silent films in 1916. It was not until the sound era that he became a full-time screen actor, chiefly as a major supporting player. He often portrayed confused and stammering, but likable, characters. His brother, Ralph, was a popular character actor in films.

In his most memorable role, the title character in *The Wizard of Oz* (1939), he looks on as the Wicked Witch fades away after Dorothy douses her with water. "She's been liquidated," he quips.

SELECTED FILMS: *The Suspect* (1916), *A Modern Cinderella* (1917), *Manhandled* (1924), *Laughter, Fast and Loose* (1930), *Hallelujah, I'm a Bum, The Nuisance, Bombshell* (1933), *The Cat and the Fiddle* (1934), *Naughty Marietta, The Perfect Gentleman* (1935), *Dancing Pirate, Dimples* (1936), *Saratoga* (1937), *Paradise for Three* (1938), *Henry Goes Arizona* (1939), *The Ghost Comes Home* (1940), *Thousands Cheer* (1943), *Casanova Brown* (1944), *The Cockeyed Miracle* (1946), *Summer Holiday* (1948), *Any Number Can Play* (1949), *Key to the City* (1950). ∎

Morris, Adrian (1907–1941), actor. Appeared in vaudeville before settling in Hollywood as a character player. Burly and round-faced, he played petty crooks, boisterous types, and sidekicks in dramas, light films, and serials. He came from a family of show people. His father, William Morris, was a famous stage and screen actor; his mother, Etta Hawkins, a comedienne; and his brother, Chester, a popular screen actor in the 1930s and 1940s.

SELECTED FILMS: *Me and My Gal* (1932), *Dr. Socrates* (1935), *There Goes the Groom* (1937), *The Grapes of Wrath* (1940). ∎

Morris, Chester (1901–1970), actor. Worked on Broadway at age 16 after appearing in several silent films as a child actor. He returned to the screen in 1929, scoring a big success. A lively actor with jet-black hair, he was quickly relegated to routine features as a tough guy after being featured in several major productions. Later, in the 1940s, he starred in a low-budget series of "Boston Blackie" mysteries. Frustrated with the lack of progress he was making in Hollywood, he returned to the stage. He later made a comeback in films and continued to appear on screen until his death. Although he was better known for his action films, he also made several light features.

SELECTED FILMS: *An Amateur Orphan* (1917), *Playing Around, The Divorcee* (1930), *Cock of the Air, Red*

Headed Woman (1932), Blondie Johnson, Tomorrow at Seven, King for a Night (1933), Let's Talk It Over, The Gay Bride (1934), Princess O'Hara (1935), They Met in a Taxi (1936), Girl From God's Country (1940), The Chance of a Lifetime (1943), One Way to Love (1945), The Great White Hope (1970). ∎

Morris, Howard (1919–), actor, director. Worked on stage and as a comedy writer and comic character player in television before entering films. His most memorable role was that of Sid CAESAR'S sidekick on the popular television revue, "Your Show of Shows." The diminutive comic began his screen career as an actor but soon switched to directing, chiefly comedy features.

SELECTED FILMS (as actor): Boys' Night Out (1962), Forty Pounds of Trouble, The Nutty Professor (1963), Way . . . Way Out (1966).

SELECTED FILMS (as director): Who's Minding the Mint? (1967), With Six You Get Egg Roll (1968), Don't Drink the Water (1969), Goin' Coconuts (1978). ∎

Morrison, Ernie "Sunshine Sammy" (–1975), child actor. Appeared in "Sunshine Sammy" silent comedies, in the early "OUR GANG" comedy series, and, later in his career, in a handful of "BOWERY BOYS" comedy features. He was at his most charming and most comical as a child performer, especially in the popular "Our Gang" two-reelers.

SELECTED FILMS: Haunted Spooks, Get Out and Get Under, Number Please (1920), Young Sherlocks (1922), The Champeen, The Cobbler, The Big Show, A Pleasant Journey, Lodge Night, July Days (1923), The Trouble, Big Business, The Buccaneers, Seein' Things, Cradle Robbers, It's a Bear (1924), Flying Wild, Spooks Run Wild (1941), Smart Alecks (1942). ∎

Morse, Robert (1931–), actor. Appeared on stage before entering films in 1956. A roguish comic with a boyish

innocence, he has plied his offbeat talents in varied genres, including comedies, musicals, and satires. After he appeared in a handful of light films and scored his biggest success in How to Succeed in Business Without Really Trying, his screen career faded. In A Guide for the Married Man he played Walter MATTHAU'S advisor on how to commit adultery. Matthau sets up a scheme using a steambath as an alleged place to spend evenings away from his wife, Ruth. "About the steambath," Morse counsels his friend, "there's one little improvement you can make. Tell Ruth that you're switching to a Finnish sauna where they hit you with tree branches while you're sweating it out." "Why is that better?" Matthau questions. "Well, you never know. Some day you may find yourself with a 'friend' who sort of gets carried away. The tree branches will explain the scratches on your back."

SELECTED FILMS: The Proud and the Profane (1956), The Matchmaker (1958), Honeymoon Hotel (1964), Quick Before It Melts, The Loved One (1965), How to Succeed in Business Without Really Trying, A Guide for the Married Man (1967), Where Were You When the Lights Went Out? (1968), The Boatniks (1970). ∎

Morton, James C. (–1942), actor. Worked chiefly in comedy shorts during the 1930s and 1940s as a supporting player. He appeared often as a heavy in many of the THREE STOOGES' films as well as those of other leading comics of the period, including LAUREL AND HARDY and Thelma TODD.

SELECTED FILMS: Sneak Easily (1933), Maid in Hollywood, One Horse Farmers (1934), Uncivil Warriors, Pardon My Scotch, The Fixer-Uppers, The Misses Stooge, Hoi Poloi (1935), The Bohemian Girl, Our Relations, Ants in the Pantry, Disorder in the Court, A Pain in the Pullman (1936), The Sitter-Downers (1937), Block-Heads, Healthy, Wealthy and Dumb, Three Missing Links

(1938), *Three Little Sew and Sews* (1939). ■

Moscovitch, Maurice (1871–1940), actor. Appeared on stage in his native Russia and in New York before entering films in the 1930s. He was a popular performer on the Yiddish stage in the 1920s. An affable, white-haired gentleman, he played character roles in dramas and light films, often as compassionate types and at other times rather impish sorts. Whatever the part, he enhanced each film with his warmth and charm.

SELECTED FILMS: *Susannah of the Mounties, Everything Happens at Night, Rio, Love Affair, In Name Only* (1939), *The Great Dictator* (1940). ■

Zero Mostel

Mostel, Zero (1915–1977), actor. Worked as a comic in nightclubs, on radio, and in vaudeville before entering films in 1943. Returning to his screen career following military service during World War II, he was plagued by the House Un-American Activities Committee and was finally blacklisted by the studios. In 1958 he returned to the stage where he achieved success in musical comedies. By 1966 he was back on the screen until his death. A heavy-set comedian with wild, bulging eyes containing a mischievous gleam, he provided a unique, offbeat flavor to his roles.

In *The Producers* he played a theater producer who schemes to keep a large sum of the backers' money by having his latest show bomb. When his plan backfires and the musical is a hit, he is dumbfounded. "I picked the wrong play, the wrong actors, the wrong director," he moans. "Where did I go right?"

SELECTED FILMS: *Du Barry Was a Lady* (1943), *The Guy Who Came Back, Mr. Belvedere Rings the Bell* (1951), *The Model and the Marriage Broker* (1952), *A Funny Thing Happened on the Way to the Forum* (1966), *The Producers* (1968), *The Great Bank Robbery* (1969), *The Angel Levine* (1970), *The Hot Rock* (1972), *Foreplay* (1975), *The Front* (1976). ■

Mowbray, Alan (1896–1969), actor. Appeared on stage before entering films in 1931. A talented and prolific character actor, he appeared in numerous dramas and light films, especially during the 1930s. He played an assortment of roles, often portraying pompous Englishmen and servants. He appeared in early television as well.

In *That Uncertain Feeling* he played a psychoanalyst who caters to Park Avenue wives. Merle Oberon reluctantly visits his office for the first time and says, "I'm sure there's absolutely nothing wrong with me." "I'm sure you'll feel differently after you leave this office," he replies. Later, after a battery of his questions, she admits that she has trouble sleeping while her husband sleeps very well. "Aha," Mowbray comments suggestively. "Are you trying to break up my marriage?" she questions. "No," he answers confidently, "only wake up your husband."

SELECTED FILMS: *God's Gift to Women* (1931), *Peg O' My Heart, Roman Scandals* (1933), *Night Life of the Gods* (1935), *My Man Godfrey* (1936), *On the Avenue, Topper* (1937), *Merrily We Live* (1938), *The Boys From Syracuse* (1940), *That Uncertain Feeling* (1941), *The Devil With Hitler* (1942), *His Brother's Sister* (1943), *Where Do We Go From*

Here? (1945), The Jackpot (1950), Androcles and the Lion (1953), The King and I (1956), A Majority of One (1962). ∎

"Mudville" comedies. A series of baseball films produced in 1917 by Selig studios. These light rural comedies starred Lee Morris and John Lancaster. The plots depended on such far-fetched gimmicks for laughs as hypnotism in *The Bush Leaguer* and female impersonation in *Baseball at Mudville*.

Muir, Esther (1895–), actress. Appeared chiefly as a comedienne in light films during the 1930s. She frequently portrayed feather-brained blondes in supporting roles. She played the foil to some of the leading comedians of the period, including the comedy teams of WHEELER AND WOOLSEY and the MARX BROTHERS. In *A Day at the Races*, for example, Chico and Harpo plaster her with wallpaper as she tries to snare Groucho.

SELECTED FILMS: A Dangerous Affair (1931), Sailor's Luck, So This Is Africa! (1933), Wine, Women and Song (1934), Racing Luck (1935), A Day at the Races, I'll Take Romance (1937), Romance in the Dark, Battle of Broadway (1938), Misbehaving Husbands (1940), Stolen Paradise (1941), X Marks the Spot (1942). ∎

Muir, Jean (1911–), actress. Appeared on stage before entering films. A tall, attractive blonde, she played female leads in light films during the 1930s and 1940s. She was blacklisted from films and television in the early 1950s, allegedly as a Communist sympathizer but later partially resumed her acting career on the stage and became a college instructor in drama.

SELECTED FILMS: The World Changes, Son of a Sailor (1933), Bedside, Female (1934), Orchids for You, A Midsummer Night's Dream (1935), Her Husband's Secretary, Dance, Charlie,

Dance (1937), And One Was Beautiful, The Lone Wolf Meets a Lady (1940), The Constant Nymph (1943). ∎

Mulhall, Jack (1887–1979), actor. Worked in stock and vaudeville and as a Gibson model before entering films in 1913. He made films for some of the pioneer studios in the New York area before embarking on a long Hollywood career that lasted for more than 40 years. A handsome actor with curly hair and a breezy style, he appeared in both silent and sound films, features and serials, often in lead roles. By the middle Depression years he began to play supporting roles. Although he appeared in different genres, he specialized in comedy. By the mid-1920s he teamed up with Dorothy MACKAILL to make a succession of popular films. He appeared with some of the leading personalities of the period, including Mabel NORMAND, Colleen MOORE, and Bebe DANIELS.

SELECTED FILMS: The House of Discord (1913), All for Business (1914), Mickey (1918), You Can Never Tell (1920), The Mad Whirl, Classified, Joanna (1925), Just Another Blonde, Subway Sadie (1926), The Poor Nut, Man Crazy (1927), Lady Be Good (1928), Children of the Ritz, Naughty Baby, Twin Beds (1929), Showgirl in Hollywood (1930), Lover Come Back (1931), The Old Fashioned Way (1934), 100 Men and a Girl (1937), Cheers for Miss Bishop, The Invisible Ghost (1941), Up in Smoke (1957), The Atomic Submarine (1959). ∎

Mulligan, Richard (1932–), actor. Worked in television a long time before he gained recognition as a talented comic actor. A tall figure with light hair, he began his film career with little fanfare in the mid-1960s, but has become a popular character player portraying eccentric, nervous types. One of his better film portrayals was as an escaped mental patient in *Teachers* who is accidentally hired as a substitute teacher in an inner-city high school. He quickly emerges as one of the few high-school instructors in the building who can motivate the students. As the men in white coats arrive to take him away, he announces with pride: "I'm a teacher."

SELECTED FILMS: *One Potato, Two Potato* (1964), *Little Big Man* (1970), *Scavenger Hunt* (1979), *S.O.B.* (1980), *Trail of the Pink Panther* (1982), *Teachers* (1984), *The Heavenly Kid, Micki and Maude, A Fine Mess* (1985). ∎

Mundin, Herbert (1898–1939), actor. Worked on stage and in films in his native England before coming to Hollywood. A short and portly figure, he appeared as a character actor, frequently playing comical pubkeepers or stewards, in more than 50 features, many of which were light films. He was often the comic relief in such dramas as *Mutiny on the Bounty* (1935) and adventure films as *Tarzan Escapes* (1936). One of his most memorable and humorous roles was that of the miller who was enamored of Una O'CONNOR in *The Adventures of Robin Hood* (1938).

SELECTED FILMS: *The Devil's Lottery, Almost Married, Bachelor's Affairs* (1932), *Pleasure Cruise, Adorable, Hoopla* (1933), *Ever Since Eve, Bottoms Up, Such Women Are Dangerous, Springtime for Henry* (1934), *Ladies Love Danger, The Perfect Gentleman* (1935), *Champagne Charlie* (1936), *You Can't Beat Love* (1937), *Lord Jeff* (1938), *Society Lawyer* (1939). ∎

Munshin, Jules (1915–1970), actor. Worked in vaudeville and on Broadway before entering films in 1948. A rubber-legged comedian with mournful eyes, he enhanced a string of 1940s musicals with his exuberance. He worked with some of the foremost screen personalities of the period, including, among others, Fred ASTAIRE, Frank SINATRA, and Gene KELLY.

In *On the Town* he played a sailor with 24 hours' shore leave. His pal, Frank SINATRA, obsessed with sightseeing,

announces: "I want to take in the beauties of New York." "And I want to take them out," Munshin adds.

SELECTED FILMS: *Easter Parade* (1948), *Take Me Out to the Ball Game, That Midnight Kiss, On the Town* (1949), *Monte Carlo Baby* (1954), *Ten Thousand Bedrooms, Silk Stockings* (1957), *Wild and Wonderful* (1964), *Monkeys, Go Home!* (1967). ∎

Munson, Ona (1903–1955), actress. Worked on stage and radio as well as in films from the late 1920s. She appeared as female leads and in supporting roles in dramas and light films. She was nominated for an Academy Award as Best Supporting Actress for her role in *Gone With the Wind* (1939).

SELECTED FILMS: *Head of the Family* (1928), *Going Wild, The Hot Heiress, The Collegiate Model, Broadminded* (1931), *His Exciting Night* (1938), *The Big Guy* (1940), *Lady From Louisiana, Wild Geese Calling* (1941), *The Cheaters* (1945), *The Magnificent Rogue* (1946), *The Red House* (1947). ∎

Murder, He Says (1945), PAR. Dir. George Marshall; Sc. Lou Breslow; with Fred MacMurray, Marjorie Main, Mabel Paige, Helen Walker, Jean Heather.

Fred MacMURRAY portrays an insurance investigator gathering statistics in this farcical black comedy. He accidentally blunders into the house of a clan of murdering hillbillies led by nasal-voiced Marjorie MAIN, who, like MacMurray, is hilarious in the film. Veteran character actor Porter HALL plays the senile father of this mad family which includes a pair of half-witted twins. The plot allows for plenty of visual comedy and good, clean slapstick. The highlight of this insanity is a dinner provided by Main, who has cooked up a poison that glows in the dark. So, naturally, the family continually turns off the lights as the table is spun around to place the poisoned dish in front of the appropriate guest. The film is reminiscent in some respects of the black comedy, *Arsenic and Old Lace,* starring Cary GRANT, which was released one year earlier.

Murfin, Jane (1893–1955), screenwriter, playwright. Wrote stage plays before coming to Hollywood in 1920. She contributed film stories and screenplays, some of which were written in collaboration, to the major studios. She specialized in romantic comedies and occasionally produced and directed.

SELECTED FILMS: *The Right to Lie* (1919), *Brawn of the North* (1922), *The Love Master, Flapper Wives* (1924), *Meet the Prince* (1926), *The Prince of Headwaiters* (1927), *Half Marriage* (1929), *Lawful Larceny, Leathernecking, The Runaway Bride* (1930), *Too Many Crooks, Friends and Lovers* (1931), *Rockabye* (1932), *Double Harness* (1933), *Spitfire* (1934), *Romance in Manhattan, Alice Adams* (1935), *I'll Take Romance* (1937), *Andy Hardy's Private Secretary* (1941), *Dragon Seed* (1944). ∎

Murphy, Eddie (1961–), actor. Worked as a stand-up comic in small clubs and comic performer in television before entering films in the early 1980s. With his built-in television following and his raffish style, he became an immediate success and a major screen personality. His raunchy comedy and winning personality have been able to convert weak comedies to record-breaking box-office grossers and have established him as one of the top film stars of the 1980s.

In *48 Hours* he played a convict whom detective Nick NOLTE springs from prison for two days to help him capture a murderous gang leader. "Now get this," Nolte announces, hammering out their relationship. "We're not partners, we're not brothers, we're not friends! I'm puttin' you down and keepin' you down until Ganz is locked up or dead, and if Ganz gets away, you're going to be sorry you ever met me!" "I'm sorry already," Murphy says.

SELECTED FILMS: *48 Hours* (1982), *Trading Places* (1983), *Best Defense, Beverly Hills Cop* (1984), *The Golden Child* (1986). ∎

Murphy, George (1902–), actor, dancer. Worked as a dancer in nightclubs and, with his partner and wife Julie Johnson, appeared on Broadway. He made his Hollywood debut in 1934 and for the next 20 years starred in a succession of musicals and romantic comedies. In his later films he turned to drama and in the early 1950s retired from the screen to enter politics. He was a United States senator (California) from 1967 to 1971. A handsome and dapper hoofer, he made numerous films with some of the leading stars and diversified personalities of the period such as Eddie CANTOR and Shirley TEMPLE. His autobiography, *Say, Didn't You Used to Be George Murphy?*, was published in 1970.

SELECTED FILMS: *Kid Millions* (1934), *I'll Always Love You, After the Dance* (1935), *Top of the Town* (1937), *Little Miss Broadway* (1938), *Risky Business* (1939), *Two Girls on Broadway, Little Nellie Kelly* (1940), *Tom, Dick and Harry, Ringside Maisie, Rise and Shine* (1941), *For Me and My Gal, This Is the Army* (1943), *Show Business* (1944), *Up Goes Maisie* (1946), *Tenth Avenue Angel* (1948), *Talk About a Stranger* (1952). ∎

Murphy, Joe (1877–1961), actor. Began his screen career in early silent films. He was one of Mack SENNETT'S original Keystone Kops. His most memorable role was that of the chinless Andy Gump in "The Gumps," a comedy series of two-reelers produced by Universal studios from 1923 to 1928. Murphy, a knockabout comedian, bore a striking resemblance to artist Sidney Smith's popular character. Although the films depended heavily on contrived plots and slapstick, Murphy was able to establish a plausible character, making the comedies successful.

Murphy, John Daly (1873–1934), actor. Worked on stage as well as in silent films during the 1920s. He appeared chiefly as a supporting player in light films.

SELECTED FILMS: Our Mrs. Chesney (1918), Thunderclap (1921), Polly of the Follies (1922), The Truth About Wives, You Can't Fool Your Wife (1923), Icebound (1924). ▪

Murphy, Ralph (1895–1967), director. Worked as a theatrical actor and director before migrating to Hollywood in the 1920s. After gaining experience as a dialogue director and screenwriter, he switched his interests to directing. He turned out dramas and light films from the early 1930s to the mid-1950s. Although he rarely was assigned to features designated as large productions, his films were often entertaining reflections of his craftsmanship.

SELECTED FILMS: The Big Shot (1931), Panama Flo (1932), Strictly Personal (1933), She Made Her Bed, The Great Flirtation (1934), One Hour Late (1935), Florida Special, Collegiate, Top of the Town (1936), Our Neighbors—the Carters (1939), Glamour Boy (1941), Mrs. Wiggs of the Cabbage Patch (1942), Rainbow Island, The Town Went Wild (1944), Sunbonnet Sue, How Do You Do? (1945), Mickey (1948), Captain Pirate (1952). ▪

Murphy, Robert "Bob" (1889–1948), actor. Entered films in the mid-1930s following a long career in vaudeville. He appeared chiefly as a character player in dramas and light films.

SELECTED FILMS: Broadway Gondolier (1935), Hideaway Girl, Two in a Crowd (1936), You're a Sweetheart (1937), Girl of the Golden West (1938), Shine On Harvest Moon (1944). ▪

Murray, Bill (1950–), actor, writer. Worked as a stage comic and writer, in television, and on radio before entering films in the late 1970s. He has specialized in low comedy, gross jokes, and generally offbeat humor. As his screen career progressed, however, he has refined his routines and style. Whether overbearingly sarcastic—as he is in much of his work—or boyishly conniving as he was in Ghostbusters, his comedic expertise and abundance of charm have propelled him into the ranks of the major film comedians.

In Stripes he played a taxi driver who loses his job, his car, his girlfriend, and is evicted from his living quarters. "I don't think I've ever been this happy," he concludes. Hoping to solve his problems, he enlists in the army where a recruiting sergeant asks him and his friend if they are homosexuals. "We're not," Murray replies, "but we're willing to learn." In Ghostbusters he hears a report of eggs leaping out of their shells and frying themselves and blinding lights emanating from the refrigerator. "Generally you don't get that kind of behavior in major appliances," he concludes after analyzing the situation.

SELECTED FILMS: Next Stop, Greenwich Village (1976), Meatballs (1979), Caddyshack, Where the Buffalo Roam (1980), Loose Shoes, Stripes (1981), Tootsie (1982), Ghostbusters, The Razor's Edge (1984), Little Shop of Horrors (1986). ▪

Murray, Charlie (1872–1941), actor. Worked with a circus, in vaudeville, and in stock before entering early silent films in 1911. He was one of the original comics of Mack SENNETT'S stock company at KEYSTONE, turning out numerous comedy shorts. He starred in various comedy series, including "Hogan" shorts and the "COHENS AND THE KELLYS" features co-starring George SIDNEY. A tireless and professional comic who never achieved the success that came to some of his colleagues, he nevertheless continued to make his audiences laugh for three decades.

SELECTED FILMS: A Disappointed Mama (1912), All Hail to the King (1913), A Fatal Flirtation, Tillie's Punctured Romance (1914), Hogan's Wild Oats (1915), His Wife's Friend (1918), Yankee Doodle in Berlin (1919), Home Talent (1921), Lilies of the Field (1924), The Wizard of Oz (1925), The Cohens and the Kellys (1926), McFadden's Flats, The Life of Riley (1927), Vamping Venus (1928), Caught Cheating (1930), Hypnotized (1932), Circus Girl (1937), Breaking the Ice, Road to Reno (1938). ■

Murray, Elizabeth M. (1871–1946), actress. Worked in vaudeville and on stage before entering silent films in the early 1920s. She appeared chiefly in light features, including several made during the sound period.

SELECTED FILMS: Little Old New York (1923), Lucky in Love (1929), The Bachelor Father (1931). ■

Murray, Jan (1917–), comedian, actor. Worked in nightclubs as a stand-up comic before World War II, on radio after he was discharged from the service, in musical comedy, and in television as an emcee of various shows. Although he is an accomplished comedian, his forte seems to be the ad lib. A tall, good-looking comic with dark hair, he has appeared occasionally as a comic character actor in films of little distinction.

SELECTED FILMS: Who Killed Teddy Bear? (1965), The Busy Body (1966), Tarzan and the Great River (1967). ■

Murray, John T. (–1957), actor. Appeared as a comic character player in sound comedy shorts in the 1930s and 1940s. A minor actor, he worked with some of the major comedians of the period, including, among others, Charlie CHASE and the THREE STOOGES.

SELECTED FILMS: The Wrong Miss Wright, Calling All Doctors, Man Bites Lovebug (1937), Chump Takes the Bump, Skinny the Moocher (1939). ■

Murray, Ken (1903–), actor. Worked in vaudeville before appearing occasionally in light films during the 1930s. His hobby of photographing Hollywood personalities over the years allowed him to accumulate interesting and entertaining "home movie" footage, which he showed from time to time to television audiences. A popular stage entertainer and personality, he never became a major screen comedian. His autobiography, Life on a Pogo Stick, was published in 1960.

SELECTED FILMS: Half Marriage (1929), Leathernecking (1930), Crooner (1932), You're a Sweetheart (1937), A Night at Earl Carroll's (1940), Juke Box Jennie (1942), Bill and Coo (1947), Son of Flubber (1963), Follow Me, Boys! (1966), The Power (1968). ■

Muse, Clarence (1889–1979), actor. Appeared in concerts, on radio, and in vaudeville before entering early sound films. A talented actor with a wide range of stock and stage experience, he was often cast in stereotyped black roles. He occasionally collaborated on film scripts and composed spirituals. He was "rediscovered" in the early 1970s. His screen career spanned five decades.

SELECTED FILMS: Hearts in Dixie (1929), A Royal Romance, Rain or Shine (1930), The Wet Parade, Cabin in the Cotton, Is My Face Red?, Washington Merry-Go-Round (1932), Flying Down to Rio (1933), The Personality Kid, Broadway Bill (1934), Harmony Lane (1935), Laughing Irish Eyes, Follow Your Heart (1936), The Toy Wife (1938), Way Down South (1939), Maryland, That Gang of Mine (1940), The Invisible Ghost (1941), Talk of the Town (1942), Honeymoon Lodge (1943), Jam Session (1944), Two Smart People (1947), Riding High (1950), She Couldn't Say No (1954), Buck and the Preacher (1972), The World's Greatest Athlete (1973), Car Wash (1976), Passing Through (1977). ■

"Music Box, The" (1932), MGM. *Dir.* James Parrott; *Sc.* Not listed; with Laurel and Hardy, Billy Gilbert, Charles Hall, William Gillespie.

Although by 1932 Laurel and Hardy were well established as a major film comedy team and did well at the box office, the critics remained cool to them. But this three-reel comedy converted many of them to fans of Stan and Ollie. The film won an Academy Award as the Best Short Subject of that year, the only formal recognition the boys received in their long screen career. The story centers on the duo's struggles to deliver a large piano to the top of a hill by way of a long, narrow staircase. Never able to perform even a simple task without great difficulty, the boys find this job particularly arduous and challenging as the piano goes bouncing down the staircase again and again. One of their problems is a short-tempered professor, played to the hilt by comedian Billy GILBERT. Stan and Ollie knock his hat off and it sails down the hill where a passing truck crushes it. Little do they realize that he is to be the recipient of the piano. Other humorous encounters include those with a nursemaid and a policeman. The comedy generally is sustained through the three reels, more so than in many other films of this length produced by Hal Roach. Most three-reelers look suspiciously padded; gags are repeated; and some of the comedy seems forced. "The Music Box" overcomes these shortcomings and emerges as one of the best works that Laurel and Hardy ever made.

Musical comedy. A film genre which emerged with the advent of sound with roots in similar stage productions. In the early and mid-1930s Warner Brothers dominated the field with its backstage stories, struggling young performers, run-down rooming houses, stage-door playboys, rich backers forever seeking to seduce one of the singers or dancers, and wisecracking dialogue. The films often contained an array of comic character actors; e.g., Guy KIBBEE, Ned SPARKS, Frank McHUGH, George E. STONE, Aline MacMAHON, Joan BLONDELL, ZaSu PITTS, Hugh HERBERT. Films like *42nd Street* (1933); the "Gold Diggers" series of 1929, 1933, 1935, and 1937; *Dames* (1934); and *Footlight Parade* (1933) set the standard that was then rigidly adhered to. Typical stars included Dick POWELL, Ruby Keeler, and James CAGNEY. The major production numbers usually had nothing to do with the plot of the film but were staged imaginatively by such talents as Busby Berkeley and Bobby Connolly. In the musical number "Shanghai Lil" from *Footlight Parade*, for example, American sailor James Cagney's search for Lil takes him to a waterfront dive frequented by an assortment of Orientals and Europeans including servicemen and prostitutes and to an opium den filled with drugged white women.

Paramount supplied its share of musical comedies during the early sound era. It had stars like Maurice CHEVALIER, who starred in the studio's first musical, *Innocents of Paris* (1929). A young Jeanette MacDONALD teamed up with the French entertainer to turn out such films as *The Love Parade* (1929), *The Smiling Lieutenant* (1931), and *One Hour With You* (1932). She also starred in *Monte Carlo* (1930) in which she sang "Beyond the Blue Horizon." The studio also specialized in revues which included a host of major screen personalities. In *Glorifying the American Girl*, released the same year as the above film, Eddie CANTOR, Rudy VALLEE, and Helen Morgan appeared. *Paramount on Parade* followed in 1930 and *The Big Broadcast* in 1932, starring Bing CROSBY, BURNS AND ALLEN, and Arthur Tracy, the streetsinger. Crosby became the studio's major musical figure during this period, starring in films like *College Humor*, *Too Much Harmony*, and *Going Hollywood*, all released in 1933.

Meanwhile, RKO came up with the most famous dance team of all time, Fred ASTAIRE and Ginger ROGERS, who together made a series of delightful musical comedies, including, among others, *Flying Down to Rio* (1933), *The Gay Divorcee* (1934), *Top Hat* (1935), *Swing Time* (1936), *Shall We Dance* (1937), and *Carefree* (1938). Character actors like Eric BLORE and Edward Everett HORTON added to the fun in these graceful and sophisticated films.

20th Century-Fox made its contributions with films starring Shirley TEMPLE, including *The Little Colonel* (1935) and *Little Miss Broadway* (1938); Alice Faye in *Music Is Magic* (1935), *Sing, Baby, Sing* (1936), and *On the Avenue* (1937); and Sonja Henie, the ice-skating champion, in films like *Thin Ice* (1937) and *My Lucky Star* (1938).

One of the largest studios, MGM, was a latecomer to musical comedy, with a few exceptions. *Broadway Melody* was released in 1929, but sequels did not begin until seven years later, with *Broadway Melody of 1936* and its two follow-ups in 1938 and 1940. Its Jeanette MacDonald-Nelson Eddy films did not begin to turn up until the mid-1930s with works like *Rose Marie* (1936), *Maytime* (1937), and *Sweethearts* (1938). And the "Babes" musicals starring Mickey ROONEY and Judy GARLAND were not produced until 1939 with *Babes in Arms*.

Many comedians and comedy teams whom the studios believed could not carry a film by themselves were featured in musicals. WHEELER AND WOOLSEY made *Rio Rita* (1929). BURNS AND ALLEN were in *The Big Broadcast* (1929) and its sequels, as well as in *College Humor* (1933) and *We're Not Dressing* (1934), all starring Bing Crosby. The RITZ BROTHERS showed up in *Sing, Baby, Sing* (1936), *One in a Million* (1937), and *The Goldwyn Follies* (1938). One musical comedy star of both the stage and screen was more than capable of carrying a film. Eddie Cantor, working for various studios, made *Whoopee!*

(1930), *The Kid From Spain* (1932), *Roman Scandals* (1933), and *Kid Millions* (1934), to mention only a few.

The next decade brought forth musical comedies with Donald O'CONNOR, Gloria JEAN, and Deanna DURBIN. By the mid-1940s MGM was producing major productions starring Gene KELLY, Judy GARLAND, Esther Williams, and Frank SINATRA. Films like *Meet Me in St. Louis* (1944), *Anchors Aweigh* (1945), *Ziegfeld Follies* (1946), *The Pirate* (1948), *Take Me Out to the Ball Game* (1949), and *On the Town* (1949) demonstrated what a studio could turn out with a large budget, color, and a gallery of top stars. At the same time 20th Century-Fox was producing costume musicals with stars like Betty Grable and comic-relief characters like Jack OAKIE, while Warner Brothers presented backstage musicals with Dennis MORGAN and comic character actors like Jack CARSON and S. Z. "Cuddles" SAKALL for comedy relief. Paramount, of course, had Bing Crosby and Bob HOPE. Danny KAYE rose to stardom in a succession of popular musical comedies beginning with *Up in Arms* in 1943.

MGM continued to dominate the genre in the 1950s with films like *An American in Paris* (1951), *Singin' in the Rain* (1952), *The Band Wagon* (1953), and *Seven Brides for Seven Brothers* (1954). Doris DAY sang her heart out for several Warner Brothers musicals before switching to straight comedy roles. Several studios turned to Broadway for material. Fox presented *Call Me Madam* in 1953, MGM produced *Guys and Dolls* in 1955, and Paramount offered *Li'l Abner* in 1959.

By the 1960s the genre was foundering. Studios were hesitant to sink large funds into films, especially musical comedies. Successful entries like *Mary Poppins* (1964) became the exceptions. By the 1970s the musical comedy, like the western, was practically dead, except for isolated entries such as *Little Shop of Horrors* (1986). The "golden age" of the musical comedy, the 1950s, presented some of Hollywood's brightest stars in some of the most lavish productions ever made.

Musicals from comedies. Aside from adapting stage musicals to the screen, Hollywood moguls through the years adapted many of their finest comedies into musicals, usually adding color, giving the new work a lavish production treatment, and employing popular contemporary performers and other creative personnel. If the film comedy was a hit as a straight black-and-white film in the 1930s or 1940s, why shouldn't it succeed at the box office in the 1940s or 1950s, especially with color, fresh stars, appealing costumes, and catchy tunes?

Almost no comedies from the silent era were transformed into musicals. But the Depression years offered a wide selection. In the cynical screwball comedy, *Nothing Sacred* (1937), Carole LOMBARD is a young woman from a small town who supposedly has only a few short weeks to live. Hard-nosed reporter Fredric MARCH takes her to the big city to show her a good time during her remaining weeks while exploiting her tragedy in his newspaper stories. In *Living It Up* (1954) Jerry LEWIS, in Lombard's role, has a sinus condition that is mistaken for a radiation disease, while Dean MARTIN plays his doctor. Janet LEIGH, in March's reporter role, brings Jerry to New York for publicity. *Room Service*, originally a stage farce, was converted into a film comedy in 1938 for the MARX BROTHERS. Ironically, one of their rare films without any musical interludes, it was remade as a musical comedy in 1944 and retitled *Step Lively*, starring Frank SINATRA, George MURPHY, and Adolphe MENJOU. The basic plot is kept intact as Murphy, a theatrical producer, manipulates to get his show in production. *Ninotchka*, the classic comedy of 1939, which starred Greta Garbo and Melvyn DOUGLAS, retained much of its charm in the 1957 musical remake, *Silk Stock-*

ings, with Cyd Charisse as the humorless Russian who comes to Paris and Fred ASTAIRE as the American who woos her. Both versions had top directors at the helm, Ernst LUBITSCH and Rouben Mamoulian, respectively. This was the latter's last film.

The 1940s proved to be an equally rich source for the studios. The sophisticated comedy *The Philadelphia Story* (1940), based on the hit stage production by Philip Barry, starred Cary GRANT, Katharine HEPBURN, and James STEWART, who won an Oscar for his role. The musical version, *High Society*, released in 1956, featured Bing CROSBY, Grace Kelly, and Frank Sinatra. Ernst Lubitsch's 1940 comedy, *The Shop Around the Corner*, starred James STEWART and Margaret Sullavan as two lonely people who work in the same establishment but don't know they are secret penpals. MGM gave the story a musical treatment in 1949 and retitled it *In the Good Old Summertime* with Van JOHNSON and Judy GARLAND in the chief roles. *Too Many Husbands*, a little-remembered film made in 1940, starred Jean ARTHUR, Fred MacMURRAY, and Melvyn DOUGLAS. In this comedy MacMurray, whom everyone thinks is dead, returns to find his wife, Arthur, married to Douglas. The mediocre musical remake, *Three for the Show* (1953), which 20th Century-Fox produced in the relatively new wide-screen process, Cinemascope, starred Betty GRABLE, Jack LEMMON, and Myron McCormick. The basis of the two films was Somerset Maugham's play, *Home and Beauty*. The weak comedy, *He Married His Wife* (1940), starring Joel McCREA and Nancy Kelly, was turned into a Betty Grable musical, *Meet Me After the Show*, in 1951. *Charley's Aunt*, a farcical stage comedy that was made into a film several times, the last version in 1941 with Jack BENNY playing the dual role of the student and the maiden aunt, was remade into a musical comedy in 1952 and retitled *Where's Charley?*, with Ray BOLGER in the lead role. Frank Loesser wrote the score which included the hit song "Once in Love With Amy." Another 1941 comedy, *Ball of Fire*, directed by Howard HAWKS, starred Barbara STANWYCK as a burlesque queen who helps a group of professors, led by Gary COOPER, with their slang dictionary. Danny KAYE and Virginia MAYO led the cast in the 1948 version, *A Song Is Born*, in which the research was concerned with jazz rather than slang. *Kismet* (1944), one of the few films to keep its original title in its musical transformation, starred Ronald COLMAN and Marlene Dietrich. The 1955 remake featured Howard Keel and Ann Blyth and the hit song, "Stranger in Paradise." *Anna and the King of Siam*, a successful film in 1946, starred Irene DUNNE as the English governess and Rex Harrison as the stubborn King. The story was adapted into a hit stage musical and then a lavish film, *The King and I* (1956), with Deborah Kerr and Yul Brynner in the lead roles.

Even the otherwise bland decade of the 1950s provided several comedies waiting to be converted into light musicals. Rosalind RUSSELL as *Auntie Mame* (1958), the free-spirited soul of this entertaining comedy, was a hard act for Lucille Ball to follow in the 1974 musical version, *Mame*. It failed with the critics and at the box office. *The Matchmaker* (1959), based on Thornton Wilder's stage comedy, starred Shirley BOOTH, Anthony Perkins, and Shirley MacLAINE. The story of a widower who plans to remarry and his dealings with a matchmaker was made into *Hello, Dolly!*, a musical stage comedy and finally a screen musical in 1969 with Barbra STREISAND and Walter MATTHAU. Gene Kelly directed.

The lesson to be learned from all these remakes is that as long as entertaining and successful comedies are made, other creative talents will always be thinking of ways to adapt them for another generation of audiences. After all, the thought of putting new wine in old bottles is not an entirely recent idea.

Mustin, Burt (1884–1977), actor. Appeared on radio as a singer and with a local theater group before coming to films in 1951 at age 67. He appeared as a comedy character player in several light films. He also worked in television.

SELECTED FILMS: *Detective Story* (1951), *The Big Country* (1957), *Rally 'Round the Flag, Boys* (1958), *Huckleberry Finn* (1961), *Son of Flubber, The Thrill of It All* (1963), *Cat Ballou* (1965), *Speedway* (1968), *The Love Bug* (1969), *Hail, Hero* (1970), *The Skin Game* (1971). ∎

My Favorite Wife (1940), RKO. Dir. Garson Kanin; Sc. Bella and Samuel Spewack; with Cary Grant, Irene Dunne, Gail Patrick, Randolph Scott, Donald MacBride.

Irene DUNNE, supposedly dead as the result of a shipwreck, returns seven years later on the day that her husband, Cary GRANT, is filing to declare his wife dead so that he can remarry. Complications arise when he learns that his wife had spent the years on an island with Randolph Scott, who plays a vegetarian scientist. Dunne, too, is incensed at Grant's "hasty" decision to marry another woman and follows the newlyweds on their honeymoon. Some highlights include two hilarious courtroom scenes and one at Yosemite National Park where Grant and Dunne reunite. The comedy is an updated version of Tennyson's *Enoch Arden*, which had been adapted for the screen several times, including 1908, 1911, and in 1963 as *Move Over, Darling*, starring Doris DAY and James GARNER.

My Favorite Year (1982). Dir. Richard Benjamin; Sc. Dennis Palumbo, Norman Steinberg; with Peter O'Toole, Mark Linn-Baker, Jessica Harper, Joseph Bologna.

This farcical comedy, set in the 1950s, becomes a showcase for the remarkably talented actor, Peter O'Toole. He gives a masterful performance as a perpetually inebriated film star. In his salad days he played Errol Flynn-type swashbuckling heroes. Mark Linn-Baker portrays a young television comedy writer who works for King Kaiser, the star of "The Comedy Cavalcade." He is assigned to chaperone O'Toole, keeping him sober and delivering him to rehearsals. The film is satiated with hilarious scenes, including one in which Linn-Baker takes O'Toole to his mother's apartment house in Brooklyn, another in which the drunken actor dangles from a roof, and those involving the proposed television show. Joseph BOLOGNA gives a particularly funny portrayal of Kaiser, the dictatorial comic, in this well-paced romp through the early days of television. The character of King Kaiser is allegedly a thinly disguised Sid Caesar while the young writer supposedly is Mel Brooks, who had worked for Caesar on his popular show in the 1950s.

ing FIELDS' enjoyment of marital bliss while she is romanced by the local stage-coach bandit. Later, she describes her encounter with the bandit: "It was a tight spot, but I managed to wiggle out of it." During a courtroom scene the judge admonishes her. "Are you trying to show contempt for this court?" he asks. "No," she replies, "I'm doing my best to hide it." She temporarily takes over a class of unruly students who have driven their teacher to resign. West studies the blackboard and reads: " 'I am a good boy. I am a good man. I am a good girl.' What is this, propaganda?" Fields contents himself with carousing at the bar, playing at sheriff, and telling tall tales of his more adventurous days on the frontier. A customer says to Fields as he is tending bar: "Squawk Mulligan tells me you buried your wife last year." "Yes, I had to," he replies. "She died." Old-timer Fuzzy KNIGHT, enticed into a card game with Fields, asks: "Is this a game of chance?" "Not the way I play it," is the reply.

W. C. Fields and Mae West in *My Little Chickadee* (1940)

My Little Chickadee (1940), U. *Dir.* Eddie Cline; *Sc.* Mae West and W. C. Fields; with Mae West, W. C. Fields, Joseph Calleia, Dick Foran, Donald Meek, Anna Nagel.

Although this is not the best vehicle for either of the two stars, it is interesting to see them work together. Mae WEST portrays Flower Belle Lee, a saloon singer, who marries Cuthbert J. Twillie, a conman drummer, to give her respectability in her next port of call, Greasewood City. West keeps postpon-

William Powell and Carole Lombard in *My Man Godfrey* (1936)

My Man Godfrey (1936), U. *Dir.* Gregory LaCava; *Sc.* Morrie Ryskind, Eric Hatch; with William Powell, Carole Lombard, Alice Brady, Eugene Pallette, Gail Patrick.

This SCREWBALL COMEDY, based on Eric Hatch's novel, exemplifies the genre that became popular in the 1930s.

It had the chief characteristics: the happy, carefree lives of the wealthy main characters; a household of zanies, an abundance of witty dialogue, and a quick tempo. Godfrey, a former playboy, played by William POWELL, sulks at a city dump where a group of partying rich find him during a scavenger hunt. They take him back and he is hired as a butler in the Bullock household, a collection of oddballs including Carole LOMBARD. By the film's end he manages to effect changes in each of the family members, while Lombard falls in love with him. He also converts part of the seedy waterfront into a nightclub, employing some of the down-and-outers he had met earlier. Powell was at the height of his popularity during this period, while Lombard was one of the foremost comediennes of the screen. Alice BRADY plays Mrs. Bullock while dependable Eugene PALLETTE portrayed her husband. Comic character players include, among others, Mischa AUER as a gigolo, Alan MOWBRAY, Grady SUTTON, and prissy Franklin PANGBORN. A weak 1957 remake starring David NIVEN and June ALLYSON did poorly at the box office.

Myers, Harry (1882–1938), actor. A tall, dignified leading man of silent and early sound films. He starred in the "Jonesy" series in 1908. He appeared in numerous dramas and light films, the most memorable of which was his portrayal of Charlie CHAPLIN'S rich but fickle friend in *City Lights* (1931) who only acknowledges Charlie the tramp when he (Myers) is drunk.

SELECTED FILMS: *Her Two Sons (1911), Baby (1915), Housekeeping (1916), A Connecticut Yankee in King Arthur's Court (1921), Handle With Care, Kisses (1922), Stephen Steps Out (1923), The Marriage Circle, Daddies (1925), The Beautiful Cheat, Up in Mabel's Room (1926), The First Night, Getting Gertie's Garter (1927), Wonder of Women (1929), Mississippi (1935), Damaged Lives (1937).* ∎

N

Nagel, Anne (1912–1966), actress. Appeared in numerous low-budget films during the 1930s and 1940s, either as lead or female lead's best friend. Born Ann Dolan, she worked in practically every genre, including comedies, westerns, serials, and horror films.

SELECTED FILMS: *I Loved You Wednesday* (1933), *Stand Up and Cheer* (1934), *Here Comes Carter* (1936), *Hoosier Schoolboy, Footloose Heiress, The Adventurous Blonde* (1937), *Unexpected Father, Should a Girl Marry?* (1939), *My Little Chickadee, Argentine Nights* (1940), *Meet the Chump, Never Give a Sucker an Even Break* (1941), *Prejudice* (1949). ∎

"Naggers, The." A series of comedy shorts produced from 1930 to 1932 about the trials and tribulations of a married couple. Former vaudeville and stage entertainer Jack NORWORTH and his second wife, Dorothy Norworth, played the leads in the popular comedies.

SELECTED FILMS: *The Naggers, The Naggers at Breakfast, The Naggers Go South* (1930), *The Naggers' Day of Rest, The Naggers Go Rooting, The Naggers Go Camping, The Naggers at the Dentist's, The Naggers in the Subway* (1931), *The Naggers at the Ringside, The Naggers Go Shopping, The Naggers at the Races, The Naggers' Housewarming* (1932). ∎

Naish, J. Carroll (1897–1973), actor. Appeared on stage before entering films in 1930. A versatile character player familiar with several languages, he frequently portrayed foreign types. His ex-

J. Carroll Naish (right) and Abner Biberman

pertise at makeup and dialect permitted him to impersonate Chinese (*The Hatchet Man*), Japanese (*Behind the Rising Sun*), Hispanics (*Ramona, Blood and Sand*), etc. He was equally convincing as a treacherous villain or sympathetic friend. Although the bulk of his acting involved dramatic roles, he was particularly effective and delightful in his comedy portrayals. He appeared in more than 150 dramas and light films, two of which brought him Oscar nominations—*Sahara* (1943) and *A Medal for Benny* (1945).

SELECTED FILMS: *Cheer Up and Smile* (1930), *Kick In, Tonight or Never, The Royal Bed* (1931), *The Kid From Spain* (1932), *Elmer the Great* (1933), *Sleepers East* (1934), *Her Jungle Love* (1938), *A Night at Earl Carroll's, Down Argentine Way* (1940), *That Night in Rio, Mr. Dynamite* (1941), *A Gentleman at Heart, Jackass Mail* (1942), *Good Morning, Judge* (1943), *Getting Gertie's Garter*

(1945), Bad Bascomb (1946), The Road to Rio (1947), That Midnight Kiss (1949), Annie Get Your Gun (1950), This Could Be the Night (1957), Dracula vs. Frankenstein (1973). ∎

Nash, Mary (1885–1976), actress. Worked on stage before entering films in 1934 in her mature years. She played mean matronly types and society women in dramas and light films for more than a decade before retiring from the screen in 1946.

SELECTED FILMS: Uncertain Lady (1934), The King and the Chorus Girl, Easy Living, Heidi (1937), The Little Princess (1939), Sailor's Lady, Gold Rush Maisie, The Philadelphia Story (1940), In the Meantime, Darling (1944), Yolanda and the Thief (1945), Monsieur Beaucaire, Swell Guy, Till the Clouds Roll By (1946). ∎

Nashville (1975), PAR. Dir. Robert Altman; Sc. Joan Tewkesbury; with Lily Tomlin, Keith Carradine, Shelley Duvall, Karen Black, Geraldine Chaplin, Ronee Blakely.

Altman's multi-charactered satirical comedy blends American politics with country music. Integrating the stories of more than 20 different characters whose paths cross during a highway accident at the beginning of the film, the director unfolds his devastating, and yet funny, epic vision of the United States. As in Coppola's *The Godfather* (1972), where the worlds of big business and organized crime are barely distinguishable, *Nashville* underscores the worlds of politics and popular music. Both have their self-serving and self-appointed leaders; both promote corruption and compromise; and both confuse reality and illusion. Lily TOMLIN, a gospel singer with a deaf son, has an affair with rock star Keith Carradine, whose song, "I'm Easy," received an Academy Award. Keenan WYNN plays a devoted and confused husband to a dying wife while his callous daughter pursues her musical ca-

reer. Geraldine Chaplin portrays a BBC commentator who takes her tape recorder to a junkyard of abandoned school buses as part of her oral documentary of the United States. Meanwhile, the town is preparing for a political rally for the presidential candidate of the Replacement party. He remains unseen throughout the film, but his voice continually emanates from a moving van, promising nebulous "replacements." Practically every song is satirical in this panoramic journey that hilariously examines some of the more bizarre elements of our society. New York film critics gave the film awards for Best Picture, Best Director, and Best Supporting Actress (Tomlin).

Natwick, Mildred (1908–), actress. Worked in stock and on Broadway before entering films in 1940. An offbeat character actress, she has appeared in dramas as well as light films.

In *Barefoot in the Park* she portrayed the mother of newlywed Jane FONDA. After climbing five flights of stairs to her daughter's apartment, she arrives exhausted. "I feel like we've died and gone to heaven," she pants, "only we had to climb up."

SELECTED FILMS: The Long Voyage Home (1940), Yolanda and the Thief (1945), The Late George Apley (1947), The Kissing Bandit (1948), Cheaper by the Dozen (1950), The Trouble With Harry (1955), The Court Jester (1956), Tammy and the Bachelor (1957), Barefoot in the Park (1967), If It's Tuesday, This Must Be Belgium, The Maltese Bippy (1969), At Long Last Love (1975). ∎

Navigator, The (1924), MGM. Dir. Buster Keaton, Donald Crisp; Sc. Clyde Bruckman, Joseph Mitchell, Jean Havez; with Buster Keaton, Kathryn McGuire.

The debate still continues among KEATON fans as to which of his features is his best, this one or *The General*. *The Navigator* was the most commercially popular of all his full-length films. Its uniqueness lies in its employment of basically only two characters, Keaton and Kathryn McGUIRE, who somehow manage to find themselves adrift aboard a deserted ocean liner. Keaton portrays a dimwitted millionaire and McGuire plays a socialite who is not only utterly useless to him but an impediment to any of his feeble attempts to rescue them. The sight gags are funny as well as clever, and the situations the inexperienced couple face are imaginative. Because the kitchen is set up to feed a large number of people, they prepare coffee by using six coffee beans in four gallons of water. They boil two eggs in a mammoth cauldron. When a Coast Guard ship is sighted, they seek help by raising a quarantine flag. Near the hilarious finale, they discover they are drifting toward an island of cannibals.

Nedell, Bernard (1898–1972), actor. Began his long screen career in early silent films in his native England. He settled in Hollywood in the late 1930s, playing character roles in dramas and light films until the early 1970s.

SELECTED FILMS: The Serpent (1916), Lucky Night, Some Like It Hot, They All Come Out (1939), Slightly Honorable (1940), Ship Ahoy (1942), Maisie Goes to Reno, One Body Too Many (1944), The Loves of Carmen (1948), Heller in Pink Tights (1970), Hickey and Boggs (1972). ■

Neilan, Marshall (1891–1958), actor, director. Worked in stock and on stage before entering films in 1911 at the suggestion of D. W. Griffith. At first playing only bit parts, he quickly advanced to lead roles. A suave, good-looking young man, he was a natural for the early silent films. He starred in a string of comedies for various studios, occasionally writing his own screen plays and directing key scenes.

By 1914 he turned to full-time directing at Kalem, a studio where he had earlier worked as an actor. In 1915 he returned temporarily to acting, starring in several vehicles with Mary PICKFORD. Once again he turned to directing, and in 1916 turned out his first feature-length film. By the mid-1920s his drinking problem interfered with his career, causing his reputation and the quality of his work to suffer. In the early 1930s he directed two-reel comedies for Mack SENNETT and Hal ROACH. He continued to direct sporadically until 1937, his films rarely rising above routine fare. His peak period occurred in the 1920s, when he turned out a succession of entertaining light films that starred some of the brightest talent of the period.

SELECTED FILMS (as actor): How Jim Proposed (1912), The Wedding Gown (1913), Men and Women (1914), May Blossoms (1915), Broadway Gold (1923), A Face in the Crowd (1957).

SELECTED FILMS (as director): The American Princess (1913), Ham the Piano Mover (1914), Freckles, Rebecca of Sunnybrook Farm, The Little Princess (1917), M'Liss, Hit-the-Trail Holliday (1918), Daddy Long Legs (1919), Dinty (1920), Penrod, Minnie (1922), The Sporting Venus (1925), Mike, Everybody's Acting (1926), Three Ring Marriage (1928), The Awful Truth, Tanned Legs (1929), Sweethearts on Parade (1930), The Lemon Drop Kid (1935), Swing It, Professor (1937). ■

Nellie Belle. The name of the jeep used by character actor Pat BRADY, who played the comic sidekick of Roy Rogers in the "King of the Cowboys"' numerous westerns.

Nelson, Gene (1920–), actor, director. Began his show business career on stage as a singer and dancer. Tall and good-looking, he played male leads in light musicals and comedies as well as dramas. He has directed several low-budget, light films, for which he has occasionally written the screenplays, and has appeared on Broadway and in television.

SELECTED FILMS (as actor): I Wonder Who's Kissing Her Now (1947), Apartment for Peggy (1948), The Daughter of Rosie O'Grady, Tea for Two (1950), She's Working Her Way Through College (1952), She's Back on Broadway, Three Sailors and a Girl (1953), So This Is Paris (1954), Thunder Island (1963).

SELECTED FILMS (as director): Hootenanny Hoot (1963), Kissin' Cousins, Your Cheatin' Heart (1964), Harum Scarum (1965), The Cool Ones (1967). ■

Neumann, Kurt (1906–1958), director. Emigrated from Germany and began his Hollywood career in 1925. After directing comedy shorts, he advanced to feature films, turning out numerous limited-budget films in several genres, including many entries in the "Tarzan" series. In addition to directing, he occasionally produced and wrote the screenplays for his films.

SELECTED FILMS: Fast Companions, My Pal the King (1932), King for a Night (1933), Let's Talk It Over, Half a Sinner (1934), The Affair of Susan (1935), Rainbow on the River (1936), Make a Wish (1937), Wide Open Faces (1938), Brooklyn Orchid, About Face (1942), Fall In, Taxi, Mister (1943), The Dude Goes West (1948), Reunion in Reno (1951), Counterplot (1959). ■

"New York Kiddie Troopers." A series of comedy shorts produced by Fox studios in the early 1930s. The films, possibly created to compete with the popular Hal ROACH "OUR GANG" shorts, featured children as the main characters and acted as a showcase for potential talent. One such child performer who appeared in six entries of the series was Eddie BRACKEN.

Newell, David, actor. Appeared as a supporting player in films from the late 1920s. He played chiefly in comedies during the 1930s.

SELECTED FILMS: Dangerous Curves, The Marriage Playground, The Kibitzer

(1929), Runaway Bride, Let's Go Native (1930), Woman Hungry (1931), New Morals for Old (1932), Made on Broadway (1933), Educating Father, Polo Joe (1936). ■

Newfield, Sam (1899–1964), director. Turned out innumerable comedy shorts and features from the early 1930s. Working for various low-budget studios, he directed largely routine dramas and light films, occasionally using pseudonyms to shroud his vast output.

SELECTED FILMS: Reform Girl (1933), Beggar's Holiday (1934), Racing Luck (1935), Harlem on the Prairie (1938), Danger! Women at Work (1943), Fuzzy Settles Down, Swing Hostess (1944), The Lady Confesses (1945), Blonde for a Day, Gas House Kids, Lady Chasers (1946), Three on a Ticket (1947), Skipalong Rosenbloom, Leave It to the Marines (1951), Wolf Dog (1958). ■

Newhart, Bob (1923–), actor, comedian. Worked as a stand-up, recording, and television comedian before entering films. He recorded his first album in the late 1950s, and it became an instant hit. By the mid-1970s he had his own television show that won Emmy and Peabody Awards. His roles in films have been chiefly those of comic relief. His comedy monologues consist usually of his telephone conversations or his speeches to imaginary audiences. In either situation he has proven to be bright, imaginative, and, most of all, very funny.

SELECTED FILMS: Hell Is for Heroes (1962), Hot Millions (1968), On a Clear Day You Can See Forever, Catch-22 (1970), Cold Turkey (1971), Little Miss Marker, First Family (1980). ■

"Newlyweds, The." A once-popular comic strip created in 1906 by George McManus (who also originated JIGGS AND MAGGIE). The strip was adapted into different comedy film versions. In 1913 it appeared as a series of cartoons under the title "Snookums." In 1927

Universal studios resurrected the characters in a series of two-reelers and kept the original title. "The Newlyweds" starred Ethlyne Clair and Syd SAYLOR as the inept parents and Sunny McKeen as Snookums. The comedy shorts were directed by Gus MEINS and others.

Newman, Paul (1925–), actor. Appeared in stock and on Broadway before entering films in 1955. A good-looking actor with attractive blue eyes, he soon became the foremost male performer on the American screen. Starring chiefly in dramas, he was nominated for several Oscars, winning for *The Color of Money* (1986). He has also turned out a number of successful light films, displaying a knack for comedy. Later in his career he began directing, also with some success.

In *Butch Cassidy and the Sundance Kid*, Newman, as Cassidy, returns to his gang's hideout in a desolate valley. "You know," he says to Sundance, his sidekick (Robert REDFORD), "everytime I see Hole-in-the-Wall again, it's like seeing it for the first time. And whenever that happens, I ask myself the same question: 'How can I be so darn stupid as to keep coming back here?' "

SELECTED FILMS: *The Silver Chalice* (1955), *Rally 'Round the Flag, Boys!* (1958), *What a Way to Go!* (1964), *Lady L* (1966), *The Secret War of Harry Frigg* (1968), *Butch Cassidy and the Sundance Kid* (1969), *The Sting* (1973), *Silent Movie* (1976), *Slap Shot* (1977), *Fort Apache, The Bronx* (1981), *Harry and Son* (1984). ■

Newmar, Julie (1935–), actress. Tall, blonde Broadway star who has been in television. She made her film debut in 1954 and has since appeared in several light films.

SELECTED FILMS: *Seven Brides for Seven Brothers* (1954), *Li'l Abner, The Rookie* (1959), *The Marriage-Go-Round* (1960), *For Love or Money* (1963), *The Maltese Bippy* (1969), *Up Your Teddy Bear* (1970). ■

Newmeyer, Fred C. (1888–), director. Began his long association with films as an extra in early silent films. By the 1920s, after some experience as an assistant director, he was turning out his own films. His most successful work during this period was the group of comedies he co-directed with Sam Taylor starring Harold LLOYD, including the bespectacled comic's classic, *Safety Last* (1923). He also directed W. C. FIELDS and Reginald DENNY. His films during the sound era were chiefly routine.

SELECTED FILMS: *Now or Never, I Do, Among Those Present, Never Weaken, A Sailor-Made Man* (1921), *Grandma's Boy* (1922), *Girl Shy, Hot Water* (1924), *The Freshman, The Perfect Clown* (1925), *The Lunatic at Large, The Potters, Too Many Crooks, On Your Toes* (1927), *That's My Daddy* (1928), *Sailor's Holiday* (1929), *Fast and Loose* (1930), *Subway Express* (1931), *The Big Race* (1934), *General Spanky* (1936). ■

Nichols, Barbara (1929–1976), actress. Worked as a model, stripper, chorus girl, and stage and television actress before entering films in 1956. A tall, blonde performer, she appeared in dramas as well as comedies, frequently portraying dumb blondes.

SELECTED FILMS: *River of No Return* (1954), *Miracle in the Rain* (1956), *The Pajama Game* (1957), *Who Was That Lady?, Where the Boys Are* (1960), *The Disorderly Orderly* (1964), *Dear Heart, The Loved One* (1965), *The Swinger* (1966), *Charley and the Angel* (1973), *Won Ton Ton, the Dog Who Saved Hollywood* (1976). ■

Nichols, Mike (1931–), comedy writer, comic, director. Worked in improvisational theater in Chicago before teaming up with Elaine MAY in the 1950s. They performed their comedy act in nightclubs and on television shows. They also cut some records. They decided to split up in the early 1960s, each moving into other areas of show business. Nichols began directing films and plays. As a comic, his material has depended heavily on satire and the domestic scene.

SELECTED FILMS (as director): Who's Afraid of Virginia Woolf? (1966), The Graduate (1967), Catch-22 (1970), Carnal Knowledge (1971). ∎

Nigh, William (1881–), director. Began his long association with Hollywood in 1911 as an actor. He soon switched to directing comedy shorts for Mack SENNETT but quickly moved to turning out features. His creative peak came in the 1920s in various genres. The quality of his work declined steadily during the sound period as he turned out low-budget films of routine interest.

SELECTED FILMS: The Stork's Nest (1915), Sunshine Alley (1918), Skinning Skinners (1921), The Little Giant (1926), Lord Byron of Broadway (1930), He Couldn't Take It (1933), Once to Every Bachelor, Two Heads on a Pillow (1934), Dizzy Dames, She Gets Her Man, His Night Out (1935), Don't Get Personal (1936), A Bride for Henry (1937), Zis Boom Bah (1941), Mr. Wise Guy (1942), The Ghost and the Guest (1943), I Wouldn't Be in Your Shoes, Stage Struck (1948). ∎

Groucho, Chico, Allan Jones, and Harpo in A Night at the Opera (1935)

Night at the Opera, A (1935), MGM. Dir. Sam Wood; Sc. George S. Kaufman, Morrie Ryskind; with Groucho, Harpo, Chico Marx, Allan Jones, Kitty Carlisle, Margaret Dumont.

One of the Marx Brothers' funniest films, A Night at the Opera contains their usual quota of puns, slapstick, insults, visual gags, and musical interludes. Margaret DUMONT'S imperious dignity is again under attack by the fast-talking Groucho. He arrives hours late for a dinner engagement with Dumont, takes one look at the check, and declares: "This is an outrage. If I were you I wouldn't pay it." And he quickly departs. Later, she reprimands him for not getting her into society. "You've done nothing but draw a very handsome salary," she says. In his reply, he addresses her as "my good woman." "I'm not your good woman!" she protests. "I don't care what your past has been," Groucho replies graciously. "To me, you'll always be my good woman." In the classic scene in which Groucho tries to explain the "sanity clause" to Chico, Groucho says: "That's what they call a sanity clause." "You can't fool me," Chico replies, smiling knowingly, "there ain't no Santy Claus." Sig RUMANN, playing a flustered impresario, comes in for his share of insults and abuse as the boys destroy his opera. Singer Allan JONES provides the romantic interest, thereby replacing Zeppo Marx, who never really had much to do in terms of the zany antics of his brothers. Kitty Carlisle is the girl Jones longs for. The famous crowded stateroom scene and the "sanity clause" bit retain their humor, as does much of the comedy which has made this film a minor classic.

Ninotchka (1939), MGM. Dir. Ernst Lubitsch; Sc. Charles Brackett, Billy Wilder, Walter Reisch; with Greta Garbo, Melvyn Douglas, Ina Claire, Bela Lugosi, Sig Rumann, Felix Bressart.

Ernst Lubitsch's satirical comedy was one of the few Hollywood films of the 1930s to touch upon the subject of Communism (Tovarich, released two years earlier, was another, with the same setting, Paris). Ninotchka, played magnificently by Greta Garbo, is a stern, robotlike Communist who falls under the spell of playboy Melvyn Douglas, who invokes the romantic City of Lights to help charm her. The film glistens with the magic of the two stars as well as with the director's subtleties and the screenwriters' wit. When the sullen Ninotchka arrives in Paris, she immediately asks a porter: "Why should you carry other people's bags?" "Well," he replies, "that's my business, madame." "That's no business," she corrects him, "that's social injustice." "That depends on the tip," he responds. Felix BRESSART, a fellow Russian, nervously greets her at the station. "How are things in Moscow?" "Very good," she replies. "The last mass trials were a great success. There are going to be fewer and better Russians." MGM in its advertising announced: "Garbo laughs!" And so did the critics and the audiences. The script became the basis of the Broadway musical, *Silk Stockings*, which, in turn, was adapted to the screen in 1957 starring Fred ASTAIRE and Cyd Charisse.

Niven, David (1909–1983), actor. Made his film debut as an inconspicuous extra in 1934. His sophisticated wit and charm soon brought him more important roles in romantic comedies until the advent of World War II. Of Scottish birth, he was one of the first Hollywood stars to enlist. After his service with the British Army, he returned to Hollywood to continue his film career. Although he was more widely known for his witty comedy portrayals, he won an Academy Award for his dramatic role in *Separate Tables* (1958). He authored two autobiographies, *The Moon's a Balloon* (1971) and *Bring on the Empty Horses* (1975).

SELECTED FILMS: *A Feather in Her Hat* (1935), *Palm Springs, Thank You, Jeeves* (1936), *Dinner at the Ritz* (1937), *Bluebeard's Eighth Wife* (1938), *Bachelor Mother* (1939), *Raffles* (1940), *The Perfect Marriage, The Bishop's Wife*

(1947), *The Moon Is Blue* (1953), *Around the World in 80 Days* (1956), *My Man Godfrey* (1957), *Ask Any Girl, Happy Anniversary* (1959), *The Pink Panther, Bedtime Story* (1964), *Murder by Death* (1976). ∎

Nixon, Marian (1904–), actress. Worked in vaudeville as a chorus girl before making her film debut in the early 1920s in silent comedy shorts. She quickly advanced to other genres and features, playing prim female leads. She abandoned her film career in 1936.

SELECTED FILMS: *Rosita, Big Dan, Cupid's Fireman* (1923), *Just Off Broadway* (1924), *I'll Show You the Town* (1925), *Spangles* (1926), *Out All Night* (1927), *How to Handle Women* (1928), *Geraldine, Say It With Songs, General Crack, Silks and Saddles* (1929), *Sweepstakes* (1931), *Amateur Daddy, Too Busy to Work* (1932), *Doctor Bull* (1933), *Strictly Dynamite, We're Rich Again, Embarrassing Moments* (1934), *Sweepstakes Annie* (1935), *Captain Calamity* (1936). ∎

Nobello, Arnold, clown, actor. Worked in circuses as a clown before he was hired in 1917 to star in a series of silent comedy shorts. Under the supervision of Hal ROACH, then employed by Rolin studios, Nobello, better known to his public as "Toto," appeared in a few films for the studio. His knockabout comedy consisted of his body being pulled and thrown about in such a fashion that it appeared as though it were without bones. He was ably assisted by veteran supporting comics, including Bud JAMISON. But he was unhappy with the world of movies and returned to the circus. His replacement at Rolin was a little-known English comedian, Stan LAUREL.

SELECTED FILMS: *The Movie Dummy, The One Night Stand* (1918). ∎

Nolan, Doris (1916–), actress. Worked as a model and on stage before entering films in 1936. She appeared as the female lead in a handful of films during the 1930s and 1940s, chiefly in light features. She retired from the screen in 1943, returning only to make one more film in England in 1975.

SELECTED FILMS: The Man I Marry (1936), Top of the Town, As Good As Married (1937), Holiday (1938), Irene, Moon Over Burma (1940), Follies Girl (1943), The Romantic Englishwoman (1975). ■

Nolan, Lloyd (1902–1986), actor. Appeared on stage before entering films in the mid-1930s. He played the male lead in many routine melodramas and light films for the first decade of his film career. His brittle delivery blended well with his personal charm and added conviction to his tough-guy roles.

In The Magnificent Fraud (1939) he played a self-seeking adventurer in a Latin-American country who hires actor Akim TAMIROFF to impersonate that country's president so that Nolan can pull off a multi-million-dollar deal. The actor detects a ray of light in the American. "You're not a very good crook," he says. "The fact is, you're quite a decent fellow." "That's right," Nolan replies indignantly, "insult me." From the 1940s he began getting meatier parts and demonstrated a facility for drama.

SELECTED FILMS: Stolen Harmony (1935), Big Brown Eyes (1936), Every Day's a Holiday (1938), The Magnificent Fraud (1939), Sleepers West, Mr. Dynamite (1941), It Happened in Flatbush, Just Off Broadway (1942), Two Smart People (1947), Easy Living (1949), The Lemon Drop Kid (1951), Never Too Late (1965), The Private Files of J. Edgar Hoover (1977). ■

Nolte, Nick (1941–), actor. Appeared in stock and television before making his film debut in 1977. A handsome, rugged actor with a strong screen presence and a raspy voice, he has appeared both in dramas and comedies. His burly appearance has helped him to give convincing performances in both football films (North Dallas Forty) and police comedy-dramas (48 Hours).

SELECTED FILMS: The Deep (1977), North Dallas Forty (1979), Cannery Row, 48 Hours (1982), Teachers (1984), Down and Out in Beverly Hills (1986). ■

Noonan, Tommy (1922–1968), actor. Worked as a comedy writer and live entertainer before entering films in 1945. A comic character actor into the 1960s, he occasionally produced and directed his own films.

SELECTED FILMS: George White's Scandals (1945), Gentlemen Prefer Blondes (1953), How to Be Very, Very Popular (1955), The Ambassador's Daughter, Bundle of Joy (1956), The Girl Most Likely (1958), The Rookie (1960), Swingin' Along (1962), Promises! Promises! (1963), Three Nuts in Search of a Bolt (1964), Cottonpickin' Chickenpickers (1967). ■

Mabel Normand

Normand, Mabel (1892–1930), actress. Worked as a model from age 13 before entering early silent films at age 16. She joined producer Mack SENNETT'S KEYSTONE company in

1912, remaining with him for many years. At first he employed her as a supporting player to other comics in his "Fun Factory" but was soon to star her in her own "Mabel" comedy shorts. He produced several full-length comedies starring Mabel, including *The Extra Girl.*

In "Mabel's Stratagem" (1912), a curious and perhaps daring film for the period, she played a personal secretary who is fired by the employer's jealous wife. Determined to regain her job, Mabel returns dressed as a male. This time the wife takes a romantic interest in Mabel, dates her, forces her onto her lap, and proceeds to fondle her! Considered the most talented comedienne of the silent screen, she starred in numerous comedy shorts, often directing or co-directing her own films and several starring Charlie CHAPLIN. In a short time she had her own unit devoted to feature-length films, the Mabel Normand Feature Film Company. In 1918 she joined the Goldwyn studios. But within a few years she was plagued by two scandals which hurt her blossoming career. Although she continued to appear in films, her popularity diminished. She returned to two-reel comedies produced by Hal ROACH. She married silent cowboy star Lew Cody in an effort to reconstruct her life, but it was too late. She succumbed to pneumonia and tuberculosis in 1930.

SELECTED FILMS: *The Diving Girl (1911), The Fatal Chocolate, Tomboy Bessie, Mabel's Adventures, Mabel's Stratagem, Barney Oldfield's Race for Life (1912), A Red Hot Romance, Her New Beau, Cohen Saves the Flag (1913), Mabel at the Wheel, Caught in a Cabaret (1914), Mabel's and Fatty's Wash Day, The Little Teacher, My Valet (1915), Fatty and Mabel Adrift, Bright Lights (1916), Mickey, The Venus Model, Peck's Bad Girl, Back to the Woods (1918), Sis Hopkins, Upstairs (1919), The Slim Princess (1920), Molly 'O (1921), Oh, Mabel Behave (1922), Suzanna, The Extra Girl (1923), One Hour Married, Raggedy Rose (1926).* ∎

North, Sheree (1933–), actress. Danced professionally as a child and worked as a model and entertainer in clubs and on Broadway before entering films in 1951. After some screen success her studio, 20th Century-Fox, groomed two other blondes, Jayne Mansfield and Mamie Van Doren, to fill the roles she would normally have gotten. She abandoned films and returned to the stage, returning to the screen once again in 1966. A talented blonde performer, she proved in her sporadic film career that she was not only a competent comedienne but a proficient dramatic actress as well.

SELECTED FILMS: *Excuse My Dust (1951), Here Come the Girls (1953), Living It Up (1954), How to Be Very, Very Popular (1955), The Lieutenant Wore Skirts, The Best Things in Life Are Free (1956), Mardi Gras (1958), The Trouble With Girls (1969), Telefon (1977).* ∎

Norton, Barry (1905–1956), actor. Began his screen career in the 1920s in silent films. For three decades he appeared as a supporting player in dramas and light films, including many Spanish-language versions made here.

SELECTED FILMS: *The Lily, What Price Glory (1926), Ankles Preferred (1927), Mother Knows Best (1928), The Exalted Flapper (1929), The Cocktail Hour, Only Yesterday, Lady for a Day (1933), I'll Take Romance (1937), Should Husbands Work? (1939), Around the World in 80 Days (1956).* ∎

Norton, Edgar, actor. Appeared as a character player in numerous silent and sound films. He played chiefly in light features, several of which were low-budget vehicles.

SELECTED FILMS: *Woman Proof (1923), The Fast Set (1924), A Regular Fellow (1925), Singed, The Student Prince (1927), Oh, Kay! (1928), The Love Parade (1929), Runaway Bride, One Romantic Night, Monte Carlo (1930), The Bachelor Father (1931), Love Me Tonight*

(1932), *A Lady's Profession* (1933), *Thirty Day Princess, The Richest Girl in the World* (1934), *When a Man's a Man* (1935), *Thunder in the Valley* (1947). ∎

Norton, Jack (1889–1958), actor. Worked in vaudeville before entering films in the early 1930s. Dapper in appearance and sporting a well-trimmed mustache, he specialized in playing drunks, chiefly in light roles. In real life, however, he was reported to have never touched the stuff. He was one of the most famous and easily recognizable character actors of the 1930s and 1940s, having appeared in more than 200 films.

SELECTED FILMS: *Cockeyed Cavaliers* (1934), *Don't Bet on Blondes* (1935), *Too Many Parents* (1936), *A Day at the Races* (1937), *Thanks for the Memory* (1938), *The Farmer's Daughter, The Bank Dick* (1940), *Road Show, Louisiana Purchase* (1941), *The Palm Beach Story, The Fleet's In* (1942), *Taxi, Mister* (1943), *Hail the Conquering Hero, The Big Noise* (1944), *Wonder Man, Her Highness and the Bellboy* (1945), *Bringing Up Father, The Kid From Brooklyn* (1946), *Mad Wednesday* (1947), *Variety Time* (1948). ∎

Norworth, Jack (1879–1959), actor, singer. Appeared in vaudeville and on stage before entering films in the late 1920s. He appeared in lead and supporting roles, chiefly in light features and numerous comedy shorts. He made a series of shorts, "The Naggers," with his second wife, Dorothy Norworth. His greatest success was as a singer with his first wife, Nora Bayes, with whom he made famous the song "Shine On, Harvest Moon." A musical biography of the team, *Shine On, Harvest Moon*, was released in 1944.

SELECTED FILMS: *Queen of the Night Clubs, Songs and Things, Odds and Ends* (1929), *The Naggers, The Naggers at Breakfast, The Naggers Go South* (1930), *The Naggers' Day of Rest, The Naggers Go Rooting, The Naggers Go Camping, The Naggers at the Dentist's,*

The Naggers in the Subway (1931), *The Naggers at the Ringside, The Naggers Go Shopping, The Naggers at the Races, The Naggers' Housewarming* (1932), *The Southerner* (1945). ∎

Nothing but the Truth (1941), PAR. *Dir.* Elliott Nugent; *Sc.* Ken Englund, Don Hartman; with Bob Hope, Paulette Goddard, Edward Arnold, Leif Erickson, Helen Vinson, Willie Best.

Frederic Isham's novel of a man who bets a large sum of money that he can tell the truth for 24 hours was transformed into a popular Broadway play in 1916. The premise proved so successful that three screen versions followed. The 1941 adaptation stars Bob HOPE as the shy stockbroker who makes the $10,000 wager. This embroils Hope in several embarrassing as well as humorous situations. An able supporting cast, including Glenn Anders, Willie BEST, and Rose Hobart, provides ample support in this farcical comedy. Taylor Holmes starred in the 1920 silent version, while Richard Dix was featured in the 1929 adaptation, both of which retained the original title.

Nothing Sacred (1937), UA. *Dir.* William Wellman; *Sc.* Ben Hecht; with Carole Lombard, Fredric March, Charles Winninger, Walter Connolly, Sig Rumann.

Another cynical yarn by Ben HECHT about the members of the Fourth Estate, this one is steeped in wit and humor as it reveals the story of Hazel Flagg, played by Carole LOMBARD, who allegedly has been inflicted with radium poisoning and has only a few weeks to live. Big city reporter Fredric MARCH and his hard-nosed editor, Walter CONNOLLY, see booming sales in the human-interest aspect of the tragedy. March goes to Flagg's small town to get the story and to make a national event of the victim. Later, her alcoholic doctor, played by Charles WINNINGER, discovers that she really is not ill. But Hazel, afraid of losing the chance of a lifetime to see the Big City, goes along with March's plans. The film excels in bright repartee, as did many of the 1930s comedies. March describes his editor as a "cross between a ferris wheel and a werewolf." Tired of the people feeling sorry for her, March says: "For good clean fun there's nothing like a wake." "Oh, please," Lombard interjects, "let's not talk shop." The old doctor says of members of the press: "The hand of God reaching down into the mire couldn't elevate one of 'em to the depths of degradation."

Novello, Jay (1904–1982), actor. Began his prolific screen career in the late 1930s. A dark character player with a neatly trimmed mustache, he appeared in dramas and light films in a variety of roles. He was equally at home on either side of the law.

SELECTED FILMS: Tenth Avenue Angel, Flirting With Fate (1938), The Girl From Havana (1939), Sleepytime Gal (1942), The Bullfighters (1945), Tell It to the Judge (1949), Ma and Pa Kettle on Vacation (1952), The Perfect Furlough (1958), Pocketful of Miracles (1961), The Man From the Diner's Club (1963), What Did You Do in the War, Daddy? (1966), The Comic (1969), The Domino Principle (1977). ■

Nugent, Elliott (1899–1980), actor, director. Worked in vaudeville and on Broadway and had some success as a playwright before appearing in silent films. His acting career continued into the sound era. In 1932 he began directing films, with comedy emerging as his strongest genre. Personal problems hindered his film career. He returned to Broadway where he continued to direct until the late 1950s. His autobiography, Events Leading Up to the Comedy, was published in 1965.

SELECTED FILMS (as actor): Headlines (1925), Wise Girls, So This Is College, Navy Blues (1929), Not So Dumb (1930), Stage Door Canteen (1943).

SELECTED FILMS (as director): The Mouthpiece (1932), Whistling in the Dark, Three-Cornered Moon (1933), Strictly Dynamite (1934), Enter Madame, Splendor (1935), And So They Were Married (1936), It's All Yours (1937), Professor Beware, Give Me a Sailor (1938), Nothing but the Truth (1941), The Male Animal (1942), The Crystal Ball (1943), Up in Arms (1944), My Favorite Brunette (1947), Mr. Belvedere Goes to College (1949), The Skipper Surprised His Wife (1950), Just for You (1952). ■

O

Jack Oakie

Oakie, Jack (1903–1978), actor. Worked in vaudeville and on Broadway before entering films in 1928. A stocky, round-faced comedian who played leads and supporting roles in dozens of films, he reached his peak of popularity in the 1930s in a series of light comedies. He portrayed good-natured, easy-going, simple-minded characters, especially in a succession of college comedies. Specializing in the surprise double-take, he mugged his way through numerous light films during the 1930s and 1940s. His most memorable role, that of a Mussolini-type ruler in Charlie CHAPLIN'S *The Great Dictator* (1940), won him an Academy Award nomination. He also appeared frequently on radio as a guest as well as the star of his own show.

In *Tomahawk* (1951) he played a frontier trader who is offered a job to scout for the United States Cavalry at five dollars a day. "Five dollars a day!" he exclaims. "It'll cost me more than that for whiskey to drown the boredom."

SELECTED FILMS: *Finders Keepers,* *The Fleet's In* (1928), *The Dummy,* *Sweetie* (1929), *Hit the Deck, The Sap From Syracuse, Let's Go Native* (1930), *Touchdown* (1931), *Million Dollar Legs, If I Had a Million* (1932), *Sailor Be Good, College Humor, Sitting Pretty* (1933), *Shoot the Works, College Rhythm* (1934), *Collegiate, Colleen* (1936), *Champagne Waltz* (1937), *Radio City Revels* (1938), *Tin Pan Alley* (1940), *Navy Blues, Rise and Shine* (1941), *Hello, Frisco, Hello* (1943), *The Merry Monahans, Bowery to Broadway* (1944), *That's the Spirit* (1945), *When My Baby Smiles at Me* (1948), *The Rat Race* (1960), *Lover Come Back* (1962). ∎

Oakland, Vivien (1895–1958), actress, child star. Began her long film career in silent comedy shorts in the 1920s following some vaudeville experience. A talented supporting player, she accompanied some of the leading comics of the period, including, among others, LAUREL AND HARDY and OLSEN AND JOHNSON, in both shorts and full-length features.

SELECTED FILMS: *Madonna of the Streets* (1924), *Tony Runs Wild* (1926), *Love 'Em and Weep* (1927), *The Time, the Place and the Girl, That's My Wife* (1929), *Personality, The Floradora Girl, The Matrimonial Bed, Below Zero, Oh, Sailor Behave* (1930), *Gold Dust Gertie* (1931), *The Tenderfoot, Scram!* (1932), *Only Yesterday* (1933), *The Bride Walks Out* (1936), *Way Out West* (1937), *A Chump at Oxford* (1940), *Bunco Squad* (1950). ∎

Ober, Philip (1902–1982), actor. Worked in advertising, on stage, and in television as well as in films. A character actor from the early 1950s, he appeared in dramas and light films until his retirement.

SELECTED FILMS: The Secret Fury (1950), Never a Dull Moment, The Clown (1954), Tammy and the Bachelor (1957), The High Cost of Loving (1958), The Mating Game (1959), The Facts of Life (1961), Assignment to Kill (1969). ∎

O'Brien, Dave (1912–1969), actor. Appeared on stage as song-and-dance man before entering films in the early 1930s. A versatile performer, he had many careers in Hollywood, including stuntman, cowboy star, comic actor in the "PETE SMITH" comedy shorts, and general performer. He had the dubious distinction of starring in the unintentionally funny Reefer Madness (1936), a cautionary tale about the effects of marijuana and considered by many to be one of the worst films ever made.

SELECTED FILMS: Jennie Gerhardt (1933), The Little Colonel, Welcome Home (1935), East Side Kids, The Ghost Creeps (1940), Spooks Run Wild, Flying Wild (1941), 'Neath Brooklyn Bridge (1943), Tahiti Nights (1944), Kiss Me, Kate (1953), The Desperadoes Are in Town (1956). ∎

O'Brien, Margaret (1937–), child actress. Worked as a model at age three before entering films one year later. Recognized as one of the most talented children to have appeared on the screen, she starred or co-starred in dramas and light films through the 1940s. Although she had a penchant for "crying" roles, she was equally adept at comedy, as in Bad Bascomb (1946), a western co-starring Wallace BEERY. Her film career suffered when she reached adolescence. She appeared in several South American films during the 1970s.

SELECTED FILMS: Babes on Broadway (1941), Thousands Cheer (1943),
The Canterville Ghost, Meet Me in St. Louis, Music for Millions (1944), Three Wise Fools (1946), Tenth Avenue Angel (1947), Big City (1948), Her First Romance (1951), Heller in Pink Tights (1960). ∎

O'Brien, Pat (1899–1983), actor. In stage musicals and dramas before entering films. Although he appeared sporadically in silent films, his screen career did not take off until the sound era. He played lead and supporting roles through the 1930s and 1940s in numerous crime films and comedies, chiefly for Warner Brothers. He portrayed fast-talking, tough reporters, cops, and priests, almost invariably representing the forces of good. His career slowed down during the 1950s. Remembered more for his tough-guy roles in gangster melodramas in which he co-starred with James CAGNEY, he also appeared in a handful of light films.

In Slightly Honorable (1940) he played an idealistic lawyer who is a pallbearer at the funeral of Clarence Buckman, a corrupt politician. "This is the first time Clarence has ever been on the level," he quips. His autobiography, Wind on My Back, was published in 1963.

SELECTED FILMS: Shadows of the West (1921), Honor Among Lovers, The Front Page, Personal Maid (1931), Bombshell (1933), 20 Million Sweethearts, Here Comes the Navy, Flirtation Walk, I Sell Anything (1934), The Irish in Us (1935), The Great O'Malley, Slim (1937), Women Are Like That, Boy Meets Girl (1938), The Torrid Zone (1940), Two Yanks in Trinidad (1942), His Butler's Sister (1943), Having Wonderful Crime (1945), Some Like It Hot (1959), The End (1978). ∎

O'Brien, Virginia (1921–), singer, actress. Worked on stage before entering films in the early 1940s. A talented comedienne, she sang with a refreshingly original frozen expression that delighted her audiences. Her unique singing style could not sustain her for more than about a dozen features, so she left films in the late 1940s, returning only once. At the height of her popularity, she worked with some of the leading comics of the period, including the MARX BROTHERS, Red SKELTON, and Ann SOTHERN.

SELECTED FILMS: Hullabaloo (1940), The Big Store, Ringside Maisie, Lady Be Good (1941), Ship Ahoy, Panama Hattie (1942), Du Barry Was a Lady, Thousands Cheer (1943), Two Girls and a Sailor, Meet the People (1944), The Harvey Girls (1945), The Show-Off, Till the Clouds Roll By (1946), Merton of the Movies (1947), Francis in the Navy (1955). ■

O'Connell, Arthur (1908–1981), actor. Worked in vaudeville and on stage before entering films in 1938. A versatile character player, he appeared in dramas and light films, usually as perplexed types. He received Academy Award nominations for his roles in Picnic (1956) and Anatomy of a Murder (1959).

He was particularly funny as a machinist aboard a damaged submarine in Operation Petticoat (1959). A confirmed woman-hater, he has to tolerate a group of nurses who are also temporarily aboard. When their major attempts to help him with the damaged machinery, he berates her. She finally reminds him that she is an officer. "Lady," he replies angrily, "Congress made you an officer, but God made you a woman! And a woman shouldn't mess around with a man's machinery!"

SELECTED FILMS: Freshman Year (1938), Blondie's Blessed Event (1942), It Happened Tomorrow (1944), One Touch of Venus, State of the Union (1948), Bus Stop, The Solid Gold Cadillac (1956), Operation Mad Ball (1957), Gidget (1959), Pocketful of Miracles (1961), Kissin' Cousins (1964), The Monkey's Uncle, The Great Race (1965), The Reluctant Astronaut (1967), If He Hollers, Let Him Go (1968), Suppose They Gave a War and Nobody Came? (1970), The Hiding Place (1975). ■

O'Connor, Carroll (1922–), actor. Worked on stage in Ireland before entering films in the United States in 1960. A pudgy supporting actor, he appeared in dramas and light films, often in minor roles, and was virtually unknown until he scored a success as Archie Bunker in television.

SELECTED FILMS: A Fever in the Blood (1960), What Did You Do in the War, Daddy?, Not With My Wife, You Don't! (1966), For Love of Ivy (1968), Kelly's Heroes (1970), Law and Disorder (1974). ■

O'Connor, Donald (1925–), actor. Worked in parents' vaudeville act before entering films at age 11. He appeared as a juvenile performer in a succession of light, chiefly routine, films in the late 1930s and 1940s. He reached the peak of his film career in the 1950s when he appeared in the popular "FRANCIS THE MULE" comedies and a handful of big-budget musical comedies. A highly talented, personable, and energetic entertainer, he has enlivened many of the films in which he appeared.

SELECTED FILMS: Melody for Two (1937), Sing, You Sinners (1938), Boy Trouble, Million Dollar Legs (1939), What's Cookin', Private Buckaroo (1942), It Comes Up Love, Strictly in the Groove (1943), This Is the Life, Bowery to Broadway, The Merry Monahans (1944), Patrick the Great (1945), Are You With It? (1948), Yes, Sir, That's My Baby (1949), Francis, The Milkman (1950), Singin' in the Rain (1952), Call Me Madam, I Love Melvin, Walkin' My Baby Back Home (1953), There's No Business Like Show Business (1954), Anything Goes (1956), The Buster Keaton Story (1957), That Funny Feeling (1965). ■

O'Connor, Robert Emmett (1885–1962), actor. Worked as a circus performer and in vaudeville before entering films in 1909. A supporting player, he often portrayed policemen or meddlesome characters. He worked with some of the leading comics of the period, including, among others, Eddie CANTOR, the MARX BROTHERS, and Red SKELTON.

SELECTED FILMS: *Tin Gods (1926), Smiling Irish Eyes (1929), In the Next Room, Alias French Gertie (1930), Reckless Living, Fanny Foley Herself, Public Enemy (1931), The Kid From Spain (1932), Don't Bet on Love (1933), Bottoms Up (1934), A Night at the Opera (1935), At Sea Ashore (1936), No Time for Comedy (1940), Tight Shoes (1941), Whistling in Brooklyn (1944), Boys' Ranch (1946).* ∎

O'Connor, Una (1880–1959), actress. Acted on stage in her native Ireland, England, and the United States before entering films. A versatile character player born Agnes McGlade, she portrayed haughty domestics and busybodies, frequently as comic relief, in light films and dramas. She gave two especially memorable performances: that of the shrieking housekeeper (which she eventually developed into an art) in *The Invisible Man* (1933) when she discovers the title character in his rented room; and, second, as the comical maid who flirts with Herbert MUNDIN in *The Adventures of Robin Hood* (1938).

SELECTED FILMS: *Cavalcade, Pleasure Cruise (1933), The Poor Rich (1934), The Perfect Gentleman (1935), Rose Marie, Suzy (1936), Call It a Day (1937), He Stayed for Breakfast (1940), Her First Beau (1941), Always in My Heart, My Favorite Spy (1942), Holy Matrimony (1943), The Canterville Ghost (1944), Christmas in Connecticut (1945), Cluny Brown (1946), The Corpse Came C.O.D., Ivy (1947), Adventures of Don Juan (1948), Witness for the Prosecution (1958).* ∎

O'Day, Molly (1911–), actress. Began her short screen career in silent films during the late 1920s. Born Molly Noonan, she appeared as female leads in dramas and light films, retiring from the screen in the mid-1930s.

SELECTED FILMS: *The Patent Leather Kid (1927), The Show of Shows (1929), Sob Sister (1931), Gigolettes of Paris (1933), Hired Wife, The Life of Vergie Winters (1934), Lawless Border (1935).* ∎

Walter Matthau and Jack Lemmon in *The Odd Couple* (1968)

Odd Couple, The (1968), PAR. *Dir.* Gene Saks; *Sc.* Neil Simon; with Jack Lemmon, Walter Matthau, Monica Evans, Carole Shelley, John Fiedler.

Based on Neil SIMON'S stage comedy, the film generally is faithful to the original plot about two divorced men who share an apartment. Problems soon arise over the domestic habits of each. Felix Unger, played by Jack LEMMON, is a hypochondriac and a stickler for cleanliness. Oscar Madison, portrayed by Walter MATTHAU, is a slob. Their friendship quickly deteriorates as Felix's obsession for neatness and spotlessness gets on Oscar's nerves. They argue like characters out of a marital comedy, with Oscar finally exploding and throwing a platter of spaghetti against the wall. "It's linguini," Felix corrects him. "Now it's garbage," his irate roommate replies. Oscar finally asks Felix to leave. "In other words, you're throwing me out." "Not other words!" Oscar fires back. "Those are the perfect words!" Felix finally moves out and Oscar resumes his poker games with his buddies. Simon's expertise in turning out funny dialogue remains unrivaled. His one-liners are often remembered long after the story is forgotten. "Two single men should not have a cleaner house than my mother," Oscar quips. At one point in the film Oscar is concerned that Felix may have committed suicide. "He'll kill himself just to spite me. Then his ghost will come back to haunt me—haunting and cleaning, haunting and cleaning, haunting and cleaning." This type of plot, basically set in one apartment, can be claustrophobic, but director Saks' moving camera avoids any sense of confinement. The film was one of the top box-office draws of the year.

O'Driscoll, Martha (1922–), actress. Began her film career as a juvenile performer in 1935. By the 1940s she was playing female leads in melodramas and light films, many of which were of routine quality. She appeared with some of the leading comics of the period, including Eddie CANTOR, OLSEN AND JOHNSON, and ABBOTT AND COSTELLO.

SELECTED FILMS: *Collegiate (1935), Champagne Waltz (1937), Mad About Music (1938), Judge Hardy and Son (1939), Forty Little Mothers, Li'l Abner (1940), The Lady Eve (1941), My Heart Belongs to Daddy (1942), Crazy House (1943), Follow the Boys, Ghost Catchers (1944), Here Come the Co-Eds, Her Lucky Night (1945), Carnegie Hall (1947).* ∎

O'Hanlon, George (1917–), actor. Worked on stage before entering films in the early 1940s as a comic performer. He appeared in comedy shorts and full-length dramas and light films. He was especially effective in the "JOE McDOAKES" single-reel comedies produced by Warner Brothers. The series ran from the late 1940s to 1956.

SELECTED FILMS: *The Great Awakening (1941), New Wine (1942), The Hucksters (1947), Are You With It?, June Bride (1948), Bop Girl (1957), The Rookie (1959), Charley and the Angel (1973).* ∎

O'Keefe, Dennis (1908–1968), actor. Had vaudeville experience before appearing in films in the mid-1930s. Working at first in minor parts under the name Bud Flanagan (he was born Edward Flanagan), he soon advanced to male lead roles in numerous dramas and light films, frequently playing spirited characters.

SELECTED FILMS: *Reaching for the Moon (1931), Gold Diggers of 1933, I'm No Angel, Duck Soup (1933), Mr. Deeds Goes to Town (1936), Hold That Kiss (1938), Unexpected Father (1939), La Conga Nights (1940), Topper Returns, Weekend for Three (1941), Tahiti Honey (1943), Abroad With Two Yanks (1944), Brewster's Millions, Getting Gertie's Garter, Doll Face (1945), The Company She Keeps (1950), The Lady Wants Mink (1953), All Hands on Deck (1961), The Naked Flame (1963).* ∎

Edna May Oliver and Frank Morgan

Oliver, Edna May (1883–1942), actress. Appeared on stage before entering silent films in the early 1920s. A stern-looking character player distinguished by her arched eyebrow and determined stare, she often portrayed waggish, sardonic old maids in melodramas and light films. Her sharp tongue added spice to numerous low-budget films through the 1930s and early 1940s. She co-starred with James GLEASON in a short-lived detective-comedy series as Hidlegarde

Withers, an amateur sleuth-teacher. She received an Academy Award nomination as Best Supporting Actress for her role in *Drums Along the Mohawk* (1939).

SELECTED FILMS: *Wife in Name Only* (1923), *Manhattan* (1924), *The Lucky Devil* (1925), *Let's Get Married* (1926), *Hook, Line and Sinker* (1930), *Cracked Nuts, Fanny Foley Herself* (1931), *Ladies of the Jury* (1932), *Only Yesterday, Alice in Wonderland* (1933), *The Poor Rich, We're Rich Again* (1934), *No More Ladies* (1935), *Little Miss Broadway* (1938), *Second Fiddle* (1939), *Pride and Prejudice* (1940), *Lydia* (1941). ▪

Olsen, Moroni (1889–1954), actor. Had extensive experience on stage before entering films in 1935. A character actor whose tall, stocky frame made him an imposing figure in more than 100 films, he often played earnest officials, rigid fathers, or historical figures. He was best known for his strong dramatic roles but made frequent forays into comedy.

SELECTED FILMS: *The Three Musketeers* (1935), *The Farmer in the Dell, M'Liss, Mummy's Boys* (1936), *Manhattan Merry-Go-Round* (1937), *Rose of Washington Square, The Three Musketeers, That's Right, You're Wrong* (1939), *Brother Rat and a Baby* (1940), *Life With Henry* (1941), *My Favorite Spy* (1942), *The Walls Came Tumbling Down* (1946), *Life With Father* (1947), *Father of the Bride* (1950), *Father's Little Dividend* (1951), *The Long, Long Trailer, Sign of the Pagan* (1954). ▪

Olsen and Johnson. A vaudeville and movie comedy team that critics frowned upon but audiences found funny. Ole Olsen (1892–1965), trained as a violinist, met Harold "Chic" Johnson (1891–1962), a ragtime pianist, in 1914, when the latter joined a musical quartet that Olsen had been playing with. Pooling their talents, they formed a musical act and toured the vaudeville circuit, gradually adding comedy to their routine. Within a few years their salary climbed from $250 a week to $2,500.

They became headliners by the early 1920s and organized their own traveling unit, including stooges, singers, and musicians.

When sound was added to films, the nationally known comedy team was invited to Hollywood by Warner Brothers. Their first film, *Oh Sailor Behave!* (1930), caused no great sensation. After several other attempts that did poorly at the box office, the duo returned to vaudeville. In 1933 they scored a hit on Broadway in *Take a Chance*, a musical revue. When the show completed its run, they traveled to the West Coast and appeared on radio. They also returned to the screen, making a few films for Republic studios.

By 1938 the team was back on Broadway in their own revue, *Hellzapoppin*. Despite the critics' attacks, it had an unprecedented run and established the comics as one of the foremost comedy teams in show business. The success of the revue led to another movie contract, this time with Universal. The boys tried to capture the revue on film, but the final results, although commercially successful, reflected little of the freshness and zaniness of the original. Other shows and films followed, with their last starring screen appearance in 1945. For the next decade they continued to tour theaters with their routines and made one unsuccessful attempt at a television series. Chic Johnson's death in 1962 ended the crazy antics of this unusual comedy team that brought laughter to its audiences for more than 40 years.

The richness and originality of Olsen and Johnson's comedy cannot be fully appreciated in their film efforts. Their offbeat humor depended heavily on wild sight gags, spontaneity, and the ability of the team to improvise from one performance to another. In many cases, the strictures of the film medium restrained their strongest qualities. Confined to conventional plots involving bland romances, the films were often written by minor writers and directed by second-string talents. A few critics have suggested that the team might have been better off turning out two-reelers instead of features. However, there are several golden moments in each film in which the comics reveal some of their comedy magic.

In *Ghost Catchers* Johnson, who unfortunately finds himself in a haunted house, announces: "Now don't get the idea that I'm afraid, because I don't believe in ghosts." Then, turning to the audience, he confides: "But then, I didn't believe in radio either."

SELECTED FILMS: *Oh Sailor Behave!* (1930), *Fifty Million Frenchmen, Gold Dust Gertie* (1931), *Country Gentlemen, All Over Town* (1937), *Hellzapoppin* (1941), *Crazy House* (1943), *Ghost Catchers* (1944), *See My Lawyer* (1945). ∎

O'Malley, Pat (1891–1966), actor. Began his long and prolific screen career in 1907 with Edison's film company. He appeared in a succession of melodramas and several comedies during the silent period as the male lead, then as supporting player in sound dramas and light films. His Hollywood career spanned more than five decades.

SELECTED FILMS: *The Papered Door* (1911), *Go and Get It* (1920), *The Game Chicken, My Wild Irish Rose* (1921), *Spangles, Watch Your Wife* (1926), *Pleasure Before Business* (1927), *Frisco Jenny* (1933), *The Man on the Flying Trapeze* (1935), *A Little Bit of Heaven* (1940), *Over My Dead Body* (1942), *Invasion of the Body Snatchers* (1956). ∎

Once in a Lifetime (1932), U. Dir. Russell Mack; *Sc.* Seton I. Miller; with Jack Oakie, Sidney Fox, Aline Mac-Mahon, Russell Hopton, ZaSu Pitts, Louise Fazenda, Gregory Ratoff.

Hollywood has produced numerous SATIRES about itself, warts and all. The silent era offered several, including *The Extra Girl* and *Merton of the Movies*, both released in 1924. Following *Lifetime* were such 1930s entries as *Bombshell* (1933) and *Boy Meets Girl* (1938).

Sullivan's Travels appeared in 1941, while one of the best of the lot, *Singin' in the Rain*, was produced in 1952. This 1932 better-than-average entry, adapted from the George S. Kaufman-Moss Hart Broadway play, is set during the transitional period between silents and talkies, a time when studios and producers were panicking to make the necessary adjustment. Sensing that a small fortune can be made out of this dilemma, three unemployed vaudevillians, Jack OAKIE, Sidney Fox, and Russell Hopton, board a train for Hollywood with the idea of opening a school of elocution for the former silent screen stars. Oakie, a half-witted buffoon, is mistaken by film producer Gregory RATOFF for an original genius and is immediately assigned to direct a picture. He mistakenly selects the wrong script, a mediocre piece of writing, and turns it into a hit film. The noise on the soundtrack, caused by Oakie's cracking nuts during the shooting of the picture, is judged as avant-garde filmmaking by the critics. Aline Mac-MAHON portrays a cynical voice coach, while ZaSu PITTS plays a bumbling studio receptionist. Earlier in the film Ratoff, who has a thick European accent, listens to the proposal for giving his stars speech lessons. "Of course we can't get them to talk as well as you—" explains one of the ex-vaudevillians. "Vell," Ratoff agrees understandably, "I don' expeck miracles." Although some of the more derisive material of the original play was omitted from Seton Miller's final script, the comedy retains most of the satirical flavor.

"One A.M." See Charlie Chaplin.

One, Two, Three (1961), UA. Dir. Billy Wilder; *Sc.* Billy Wilder, I.A.L. Diamond; with James Cagney, Arlene Francis, Horst Buchholz, Pamela Tiffin.

Probably director Billy Wilder's fastest-paced comedy, the film is set in contemporary West Berlin. James CAGNEY portrays a Coca-Cola representative who

James Cagney (second from left), Horst Buchholz, and Pamela Tiffin in *One, Two, Three* (1961)

explodes when he discovers that his boss's daughter (Pamela Tiffin) has married a Communist. "He's not a Communist," Tiffin insists. "He's a Republican. He comes from the Republic of East Germany." Cagney attempts to convert the groom (Horst Buchholz) into a dapper nobleman and executive and has only a few hours to perform the miracle. But the groom is less than cooperative. "I spit on your money! I spit on Fort Knox! I spit on Wall Street!" he exclaims. "Unsanitary little jerk, isn't he?" Cagney replies. His frantic performance as he overcomes one obstacle after another and blurts out orders in rapid-fire to a battery of underlings recalls his earlier dynamic roles while under contract to Warner Brothers. "The race that produced the Taj Mahal, William Shakespeare, and striped toothpaste can't be all bad," he states at one point. This was Cagney's last screen appearance for the next 20 years, when he made a brief return in *Ragtime* (1981). Wilder engaged in some risky business by adding political satire to his farce at a time when East-West relations were, at best, strained. However, the witty film, broadly adapted from a Molnar plot, was a critical and commercial success.

O'Neal, Ryan (1941–), actor. Worked as a lifeguard and television stuntman and actor before entering films in 1969. His co-starring role in *Love Story* (1970) brought him an Academy Award nomination and helped rocket him to stardom. He has appeared in dramas and comedies. He is the father of actress Tatum O'NEAL.

SELECTED FILMS: *The Big Bounce (1969), The Games (1970), What's Up, Doc? (1972), The Thief Who Came to Dinner, Paper Moon (1973), Nickelodeon (1976), The Main Event (1979), So Fine (1981), Partners (1982), Irreconcilable Differences (1984).* ■

O'Neal, Tatum (1963–), actress. Began her screen career as a child performer in *Paper Moon* and became an overnight star. By the ripe age of 14 she had two Hollywood "firsts" to her credit: the youngest performer to win an Academy Award as Best Supporting Actress (for the above film) and highest-paid child in the annals of films with her $350,000—9 percent of net—contract for *The Bad News Bears*. She is the daughter of actor Ryan O'NEAL and actress Joanna Moore.

SELECTED FILMS: *Paper Moon (1973), The Bad News Bears, Nickelodeon (1976), Little Darlings (1979), Circle of Two (1980).* ■

O'Neil, Sally (1908–1968), actress. Entered silent films in 1925, playing saucy female leads. Pretty and trim-figured, O'Neil, who was born Virginia Noonan, continued to appear chiefly in light films through the mid-1930s.

SELECTED FILMS: *Don't, Sally, Irene and Mary (1925), Battling Butler (1926), Slide, Kelly, Slide, Frisco Sally Levy, The Callahans and the Murphys (1927), Bachelor's Paradise, The Mad Hour, The Battle of the Sexes (1928), Broadway Fever, Hardboiled, On With the Show, The Sophomore (1929), Hold Everything (1930), The Brat (1931), Ladies Must Love (1933).* ■

O'Neill, Henry (1891–1961), actor. Worked on stage before entering films in the early 1930s. Tall and distinguished, he played a variety of roles, including professionals and fathers. He appeared in more than 150 dramas and light films during a career that spanned three decades.

SELECTED FILMS: *I Loved a Woman (1933), Flirtation Walk, Wonder Bar, Big-Hearted Herbert, Midnight (1934), Dinky, We're in the Money, The Big Noise (1936), The Great O'Malley (1937), Brother Rat (1938), Everybody's Hobby (1939), Whistling in the Dark (1941), Air Raid Wardens (1943), Keep Your Powder Dry (1945), Bad Bascomb (1946), Holiday Affair (1949), The Milkman (1950), The Wings of Eagles (1957).* ■

Operation Petticoat (1960), U. *Dir.* Blake Edwards; *Sc.* Stanley Shapiro, Maurice Richlin; with Cary Grant, Tony Curtis, Joan O'Brien, Dina Merrill, Arthur O'Connell.

This comedy, set during World War II in the Pacific, was one of Universal's biggest hits in 1960. The appropriate mixture of plot elements and stars helped to provide the many laughs. Cary GRANT, the captain of a damaged submarine, is determined to make it seaworthy once again so that it can do battle. He pleads with his superior officer to give the *Sea Tiger* another chance. "It's like a beautiful woman dying an old maid," he explains. This sets the sexual tone of the film. Tony CURTIS is his scheming junior officer whose wheeling and dealing provide the proper equipment and supplies as well as several complications for Grant. He writes in the vessel's log: "To paraphrase Churchill, never have so few stolen so much from so many." During a Japanese air attack on the base, Grant inquires as to the whereabouts of Curtis. "All Mr. Holden said was that in confusion there is profit," a sailor replies. When the sub is ready to leave, the engineer has trouble getting it started. To help things along, Curtis hires an island witch doctor to perform a religious ceremony. As Grant looks on in disbelief, the sub's engines begin to work successfully. On one of their stops at an island about to be overrun by the Japanese, they are forced to take aboard a handful of nurses,

creating further problems in the already tight quarters among the sex-starved crew. Curtis is quick to invite one of the female guests to his cabin, offering her some of his garments, to which she replies: "A girl just doesn't get into any man's pajamas." When he finally maneuvers her into a rubber raft, another officer warns the captain that they are missing. "When a girl's under 21," Grant explains to the concerned officer, "she's protected by the law; when she's over 65, she's protected by nature; anywhere in between, she's fair game." Machinist's mate Arthur O'CONNELL has his own difficulties with the chief nurse, an officer, who insists on aiding him with his engines. At first he resists, then succumbs to her mechanical skills and her charms, in that order. "You're different," he confesses to her in a soft voice. "You're not a woman. You're more than that. You're a mechanic." The film contains hilarious visual gags as well, making it one of the best war comedies to come out of Hollywood.

Oppenheimer, George, screenwriter. In Hollywood from the early 1930s writing screenplays alone and in collaboration. He turned out numerous hilarious scripts for some of the leading comedians of the period, including, among others, Eddie CANTOR and the MARX BROTHERS.

SELECTED FILMS: *Roman Scandals (1933), Libeled Lady (1936), A Day at the Races, I'll Take Romance, Married Before Breakfast (1937), Man-Proof, Paradise for Three, Three Loves Has Nancy (1938), I Love You Again (1940), The Feminine Touch, Two-Faced Woman (1941), The Youngest Profession (1943), Anything Can Happen (1952), Tonight We Sing (1953).* ■

Opperman, Frank, actor. Worked in early silent comedy shorts, chiefly for Mack SENNETT'S KEYSTONE studios. As a supporting player, he worked with some of the leading comics of the period,

including, among others, Ford STER-
LING, Polly MORAN, and Charlie
CHASE.

SELECTED FILMS: *Hash House Mash-
ers, The Rent Jumpers, My Valet (1915),
The Hunt, Better Late Than Never, A
Dash of Courage (1916), Her Fame and
Shame (1917).* ∎

Orth, Frank (1880–1962), actor.
Worked in vaudeville and on stage before making his screen debut in 1929. He
starred with his wife, Ann CODEE, in a
string of comedy shorts for several years
and finally switched to feature-length
dramas and light films in the mid-1930s.
As a character actor he portrayed various
roles, but that of bartender predominated.

SELECTED FILMS: *Welcome Stranger
(1935), Hot Money (1936), Footloose
Heiress (1937), His Girl Friday (1940),
My Gal Sal, The Magnificent Dope,
Springtime in the Rockies (1942), Hello,
Frisco, Hello, Coney Island, Sweet Rosie
O'Grady (1943), Greenwich Village
(1944), Mother Wore Tights (1947),
Cheaper by the Dozen, Father of the
Bride (1950), Here Come the Girls
(1953).* ∎

Osborne, Vivienne (1896–1961), actress. Entered films in 1920 after much
stage experience as a dancer. She left
Hollywood to star on Broadway after
appearing in several films but returned
to the screen in the 1930s. A pretty,
dark-haired actress, she had lead or featured roles in numerous dramas and
light films.

SELECTED FILMS: *Over the Hill to the
Poor House (1920), The Beloved Bache-
lor, Husband's Holiday (1931), The Dark
Horse, Week-End Marriage (1932), Lux-
ury Liner, Sailor Be Good (1933), No
More Ladies (1935), Let's Sing Again
(1936), Champagne Waltz (1937),
Dragonwyck (1946).* ∎

Osmond, Cliff (1937–), actor. Plump
character player of television and films.
He has appeared chiefly in comic roles
during the 1960s and 1970s, specializing
in characters of lesser intellect.

SELECTED FILMS: *Irma la Douce
(1963), Kiss Me, Stupid (1964), The Fortune Cookie (1967), The Front Page
(1974), Shark's Treasure (1975), The Apple Dumpling Gang Rides Again, The
North Avenue Irregulars (1979).* ∎

O'Sullivan, Maureen (1911–), actress.
Began her film career in 1930 with no
stage experience. Director Frank Borzage
noticed her in Dublin in 1930 and
brought her to Hollywood. Best remembered as Tarzan's mate during the early
1930s, she appeared as well in numerous
dramas and light films, often as the female lead. She left her screen career in
the early 1940s to devote more time to
her family but has occasionally returned
to films. She is the mother of actress Mia
FARROW.

SELECTED FILMS: *Song o' My Heart,
So This Is London, Just Imagine, The
Princess and the Plumber (1930), Sky-
line, The Big Shot (1931), The Cohens
and Kellys in Trouble, Tugboat Annie
(1933), The Thin Man (1934), The
Bishop Misbehaves (1935), A Day at the
Races, My Dear Miss Aldrich (1937),
Hold That Kiss, Spring Madness (1938),
Maisie Was a Lady (1941), Bonzo Goes to
College (1952), Never Too Late (1965),
The Phynx (1970).* ∎

O'Toole, Peter (1932–), actor. Worked
on stage and in films in England before
becoming an international movie star
after his appearance in *Lawrence of
Arabia* (1962). The suave, handsome,
Irish-born actor has turned to lighter
roles in recent years. One of his best light
roles was that of the charming, over-the-
hill swashbuckling matinee hero in *My
Favorite Year.* Constantly drunk, he is
hired to appear as a guest on a television
program hosted by a Sid Caesar-type
comic, resulting in a hilarious performance by O'Toole.

SELECTED FILMS: What's New, Pussycat? (1965), How to Steal a Million (1966), Casino Royale (1967), The Stunt Man (1980), My Favorite Year (1982). ∎

Ott, Fred (1860–1936), mechanic. Acted in the now historical few feet of film called "Fred Ott's Sneeze" or "Sneeze" (1893) while employed at Thomas Edison's studio in Orange, New Jersey. Not actually an actor, he was asked to pose while Edison photographed him in this short scene that lasts but a few seconds and that several film historians cite as the first American film comedy.

Ottiano, Rafaela (1894–1942), actress. Worked as an actress in her native Italy before migrating to Hollywood during the silent period. A character player with dark hair and large eyes, she continued to appear in dramas and light films in the sound era, often portraying untrustworthy domestics.

SELECTED FILMS: The Law and the Lady (1924), Washington Masquerade (1932), She Done Him Wrong (1933), The Last Gentleman (1934), Lottery Lover, Remember Last Night?, Curly Top (1935), Riffraff, That Girl From Paris, Mad Holiday (1936), I'll Give a Million (1938), Paris Honeymoon (1939), Topper Returns (1941), I Married an Angel (1942). ∎

"Our Gang." A long-running series of two-reel comedies created by producer Hal ROACH in 1922 and featuring a group of children as the major characters. The original "gang" included Mickey DANIELS, Jackie CONDON, Ernie "Sunshine Sammy" MORRISON (who had already been established in his own comedy series), and Peggy CARTWRIGHT. Chubby Joe COBB, Mary KORNMAN, Jackie DAVIS, and Allan "Farina" HOSKINS eventually joined the successful series, as did the dog, Pete.

Members of the gang who outgrew their roles were quickly replaced with new children. Overweight Joe Cobb was replaced by Norman "Chubby" CHANEY in 1928. Matthew "Stymie" BEARD replaced "Farina." Jean DARLING replaced Mary Kornman. Several of the gang members went on to stardom in feature films, including Jackie COOPER, Scotty BECKETT, Robert Blake, and Dickie MOORE. Others stayed with the gang for many years. Spanky McFARLAND, who became the group's leader, joined in 1932 and stayed for eleven years. Cute little Darla HOOD remained for six years. William Henry "Buckwheat" THOMAS served a ten-year stretch. The popular, freckle-faced Carl "Alfalfa" SWITZER joined in 1935 and during the next six years appeared in more than 60 entries.

Success for the series was attributed to several factors. The naturalness of the children was refreshing, especially when individual young superstars like Jackie COOGAN in silent films and Shirley TEMPLE in talkies at times evoked a sense of artificiality. Second, the realistic situations they got themselves into were familiar to both young and old audiences, who found it easy to identify with the youngsters and their antics. Also, the concept of a cast of unknown child actors as the main characters was basically original. Other child stars may have been more talented, but the gang children were less affected.

One of the many interesting aspects of the series was the treatment of the black members of the group. At a time when adult black performers were invariably reduced to playing stereotypes in all film genres, the series, which stretched across three decades, was more liberal in its treatment of the interaction between white children and black children. Both races were treated equally in the classroom, in the neighborhood, by other children, and at parties (which, it should be noted, were always held in white homes). However, certain racial subtleties are apparent. The black child actors, although quite popular with the public, rarely had major roles in the numerous entries; they never advanced above the white performers in the screen credits. Also, the black members of the gang appeared by their attire to be poorer or of a lower social class than their white counterparts.

Since the series had such a long life, it was only natural that it had different directors. Robert McGOWAN directed the bulk of the silent comedies, with Tom McNamara, Mark Haldane, Anthony Mack, and Charles Oelze turning out occasional entries.

Hal Roach sold the rights to "Our Gang" to MGM in 1938. The giant studio continued to turn out entries in the series; in fact, it made more than 50 shorts. As virtually all neighborhood movie houses began to convert to a schedule of two full-length features and perhaps a one-reeler, the "Our Gang" comedies became an anomaly. Perhaps their decline was caused by the slickness of the MGM product, by World War II, or by the changing times in general. Whatever the reasons, in 1944 the last short, "Dancing Romeo," was made. So ended a unique comedy series that brought laughter to several generations. Fortunately, the series was resurrected for television under the name "The Little Rascals," continually acquainting new audiences with the shenanigans of a group of lovable kids.

SELECTED FILMS: One Terrible Day, Our Gang (1922), The Champeen (1923), Tire Trouble (1924), The Big Town (1925), Good Cheer (1926), Bring Home the Turkey (1927), Playin' Hookey (1928), Election Day (1929), Teacher's Pet (1930), Love Business (1931), Readin' and Writin' (1932), Mush and Milk (1933), For Pete's Sake (1934), Beginner's Luck (1935), Bored of Education (1936). ∎

Our Hospitality. See Buster Keaton.

Overman, Lynne (1887–1943), actor. Worked in vaudeville and on stage before entering films in the late 1920s. A versatile character player and occasional male lead known for his dry wit, he spoke in a cracked, multi-pitched voice and often portrayed distrustful but amiable types in dramas and light films. He appeared in comedy shorts in the early 1930s before advancing to feature-length films where he gained great popularity for the next ten years.

In Little Miss Marker, for example, he played a cashier who is cynical about his boss, overly frugal bookmaker Sorrowful Jones (Adolphe MENJOU), who has just lost 20 dollars on a bettor he trusted. "Every time I get big-hearted—" Menjou begins. "When was the other time?" Overman interjects. Later in the film his boss plays straight man once again to his cashier's barbs. "Listen," he explains, "I've always been generous in a quiet way." "Practically silent," Overman adds.

SELECTED FILMS: Kisses (1929), Five Minutes From the Station (1930), Poor Fish (1933), Midnight, Little Miss Marker, Broadway Bill (1934), Enter Madame!, Paris in Spring (1935), Collegiate, Poppy, Three Married Men (1936), Blonde Trouble, Nobody's Baby, Don't Tell the Wife, Hotel Haywire, True Confession (1937), Caught in the Draft (1941), Roxie Hart, Star Spangled Rhythm (1942), Dixie (1943), The Desert Song (1944). ∎

Ovey, George (1870–1951), actor. Began his film career in early silent comedy shorts in 1915. A pint-sized comedian, he starred in his own series of shorts known as "Jerry" comedies. He later appeared as a comic-relief character in feature-length films during the 1920s and the early sound period.

SELECTED FILMS: Jerry and the Gunman, Jerry to the Rescue, Jerry's Revenge (1915), The Arizona Sweepstakes, The Sporting Lover (1926), Pals in Peril (1927), My Friend From India (1928), Hit the Deck (1930), Alice in Wonderland (1933). ■

Owen, Garry, actor. Began his screen career in early sound films. He appeared as a supporting player in dramas and light films, working with some of the most famous personalities of the period, including, among others, James CAGNEY, Spencer TRACY, Gary COOPER, and Cary GRANT.

SELECTED FILMS: Child of Manhattan, Hold Your Man, Son of a Sailor (1933), Little Miss Marker (1934), Hold 'Em Yale (1935), True Confession (1937), Arsenic and Old Lace (1944), The Admiral Was a Lady (1950), The Milkman (1950). ■

Owen, Reginald (1887–1972), actor. Worked on stage in his native England and on Broadway before settling in Hollywood in 1929. A versatile and prolific character player and occasional male lead, he appeared in well over 100 dramas and light films during a career that spanned almost 40 years, often playing British types.

In The Earl of Chicago (1940) he announces: "I've just been to Canada, Porcupine, Ontario. Sounds a very uncomfortable place, and it jolly well is."

SELECTED FILMS: The Letter (1929), Platinum Blonde (1931), Fashions of 1934, Music in the Air (1934), The Good Fairy (1935), Petticoat Fever, Love on the Run (1936), The Bride Wore Red (1937), Fast and Loose (1939), Charley's Aunt, Lady Be Good (1941), Woman of the Year, I Married an Angel (1942), The Canterville Ghost (1944), Monsieur Beaucaire (1946), Julia Misbehaves (1948), Red Garters (1954), The Thrill of It All (1963), Mary Poppins (1964), Rosie (1967). ■

P

Paige, Janis (1922–), actress. Began her film career in 1944 after having studied opera singing. A lively redhead, she appeared in light films during the 1940s and 1950s, usually playing second lead roles.

SELECTED FILMS: *Bathing Beauty, Hollywood Canteen* (1944), *Her Kind of Man, Two Guys From Milwaukee, The Time, the Place and the Girl* (1946), *Romance on the High Seas* (1948), *Two Gals and a Guy* (1951), *Silk Stockings* (1957), *Please Don't Eat the Daisies* (1960), *Bachelor in Paradise* (1961), *Follow the Boys* (1963), *Welcome to Hard Times* (1967). ∎

Paige, Mabel (1880–1954), actress. Appeared on stage as a child performer before entering early silent comedy shorts in 1915. Later in her career she turned to wisecracking character roles in sound features.

SELECTED FILMS: *Mixed Flats* (1915), *Lucky Jordan* (1942), *The Crystal Ball, Happy Go Lucky, True to Life* (1943), *Out of This World, Murder, He Says* (1945), *She Wouldn't Say Yes* (1946), *Beat the Band, Her Husband's Affairs* (1947), *If You Knew Susie, The Mating of Millie* (1948), *The Petty Girl* (1950), *Houdini* (1953). ∎

Paige, Robert (1910–), actor. Worked as a radio announcer before entering films in the early 1930s, chiefly in shorts. By the latter part of the decade he began playing leads in numerous low-budget dramas and light films. He reached the height of his screen career in the 1940s. He later switched to television.

SELECTED FILMS: *Annapolis Farewell* (1935), *Cain and Mabel* (1936), *There's Always a Woman* (1938), *Hellzapoppin* (1941), *Jail House Blues, What's Cookin', Almost Married, Pardon My Sarong, Get Hep to Love* (1942), *Hi' Ya Chum, Cowboy in Manhattan, Fired Wife* (1943), *Her Primitive Man, Can't Help Singing* (1944), *Shady Lady* (1945), *Marriage-Go-Round* (1961), *Bye Bye Birdie* (1963). ∎

Paiva, Nestor (1905–1966), actor. Appeared in more than 100 films as a character actor. Bald, moon-faced, and broad-chested, he usually played foreigners in dramas and comedies. He has accompanied some of the leading comics of the period, including, among others, ABBOTT AND COSTELLO, Bob HOPE, Danny KAYE, LAUREL AND HARDY, and the THREE STOOGES.

SELECTED FILMS: *Ride a Crooked Mile* (1938), *The Magnificent Fraud, Midnight* (1939), *Hold That Ghost* (1941), *The Road to Morocco* (1942), *The Dancing Masters* (1943), *Road to Utopia* (1945), *The Well-Groomed Bride* (1946), *Road to Rio* (1947), *Mr. Blandings Builds His Dream House, The Paleface* (1948), *The Inspector General* (1949), *The Lady Pays Off* (1951), *Call Me Madam* (1953), *Casanova's Big Night* (1954), *The Lady Takes a Flyer* (1958), *The Three Stooges in Orbit* (1962), *The Spirit Is Willing* (1967). ∎

Eugene Pallette (left) and Edward Everett Horton (right)

Bob Hope and Jane Russell in *The Paleface* (1948)

Paleface, The (1948), PAR. *Dir.* Norman Z. McLeod; *Sc.* Ed Hartmann, Jack Rose, Frank Tashlin; with Bob Hope, Jane Russell, Robert Armstrong, Iris Adrian.

This western-comedy is probably one of Bob Hope's best post-World War II vehicles. He portrays a gun-shy dentist who comes under the protection of shapely Jane RUSSELL, a gun-totin' government agent on the trail of a gang selling rifles to hostile Indians. She marries Hope as a ploy to capture the desperadoes. The film abounds in Hope's wisecracks. "Remember," Russell says, "you promised to love, honor and obey." "Yeah," Hope concurs, "let's do it in the order named." Mistaken as the hero who has just saved a group of women and children from ravaging Indians, he begins to make a speech. "Ladies and gentlemen. At this time I'd like to say a few words—" "Let's get out of here before the Redskins come back!" the wagonmaster interjects. "Those are the words," Hope adds. The Academy Award-winning tune, "Buttons and Bows," is one of the highlights. Russell displays a penchant for comedy in this western spoof which was remade in 1968 as *The Shakiest Gun in the West* starring Don KNOTTS. In 1952 the two stars teamed up again for a competent sequel, *Son of Paleface*, directed by Frank Tashlin, one of the screenwriters of the original.

Pallette, Eugene (1899–1954), actor. Appeared on stage before entering early silent films in 1910. He played leads in silent dramas and by the 1920s established himself as a character actor. A portly figure with a rough voice, he enlivened more than 150 silent and sound dramas and light films during a career that spanned four decades. His irascible characters were as comical as his more cheerful figures. He was especially memorable as Friar Tuck in the 1938 version of *The Adventures of Robin Hood*.

In the comedy *Hell Below* (1933) he played a sailor aboard a submarine who incurs the wrath of cook Jimmy DURANTE. "What's the matter with the ham? It's imported from the States," Durante argues. "They must have towed it all the way over. It's salty," Pallette protests. "That's the way you cure ham," Jimmy explains. "If that ham was cured, it had a relapse," Pallette cracks. Even in dramas he was adept at comic relief. In *Bordertown* (1935) he portrayed a nightclub owner who has had all his teeth removed by a dentist friend. When he returns to his club to boast about what he has done, an acquaintance asks, "Did it hurt? Did it give you any pain?" "Only when I got the bill," he jokingly replies.

SELECTED FILMS: *Birth of a Nation (1915), Sunshine Dad (1916), Madame Who (1918), Twin Beds (1920), His Private Life (1928), The Dummy (1929), Let's Go Native (1930), Girls About Town (1931), Made on Broadway (1933),*

Strictly Dynamite (1934), *The Ghost Goes West, My Man Godfrey* (1936), *Topper* (1937), *There Goes My Heart* (1938), *He Stayed for Breakfast* (1940), *The Lady Eve* (1941), *Almost Married* (1942), *It Ain't Hay* (1943), *Pin-Up Girl* (1944), *The Cheaters* (1945), *Silver River* (1948). ■

Palm Beach Story, The (1942), PAR. Dir. Preston Sturges; Sc. Preston Sturges; with Claudette Colbert, Joel McCrea, Rudy Vallee, Mary Astor, Sig Arno, William Demarest.

Preston STURGES has loaded this madcap comedy with witty dialogue, many eccentric characters, and hilarious scenes. Claudette COLBERT, impatient with her husband, Joel McCREA, who can't seem to make a living, heads for Florida to meet a rich man. Instead, she meets the wealthy but zany husband-hunting Mary ASTOR and her equally dizzy brother, millionaire Rudy VALLEE, who practically steals the movie from the two stars. Vallee, who is misled by Colbert, thinks her husband is a monster and promises to "thrash him within an inch of his life." Suddenly, he has second thoughts and muses: "That's one of the tragedies of this life. The men that are most in need of a beating up are always enormous." McCrea, of course, trails after his wife to try to set things right. "Men don't get smarter as they grow older," Colbert says to her husband, "they just lose their hair." Meanwhile, Astor, with five divorces to her credit, advocates "love at first sight and marriage the next day." "And divorce him the next month," her brother adds. "Nothing is permanent in this world," she returns, "except Roosevelt." One of the highlights of the film is the unforgettable "Ale and Quail Club," a group of middle-aged inebriated revelers, including the perennial drunk, Jack NORTON, who, while on board a train, charge through the cars with their rifles and a pack of hunting dogs.

Palma, Joe, actor. Worked chiefly in comedy shorts during the 1930s, 1940s, and 1950s as a supporting player. He appeared in many of the THREE STOOGES' films.

SELECTED FILMS: *Goofs and Saddles* (1937), *From Nurse to Worse* (1940), *If a Body Meets a Body* (1945), *Beer Barrel Polecats, Uncivil Warbirds, Three Loan Wolves, Three Little Pirates* (1946), *Fiddlers Three* (1948), *Malice in the Palace* (1949), *Hugs and Mugs, Studio Stoops, Slaphappy Sleuths* (1950), *Income Tax Sappy, Musty Musketeers, Knutzy Knights, Shot in the Frontier, Fling in the Ring* (1954), *Stone Age Romeos* (1955), *Rumpus in a Harem, Hot Stuff, Scheming Schemers* (1956), *Guns A-Poppin', Outer-Space Jitters* (1957). ■

Palmer, Patricia (1895–1964), actress. Worked on stage and in silent films from 1916. She appeared as a female lead and supporting player in dramas and light films, including several westerns.

SELECTED FILMS: *Island of Desire, Public Approval* (1916), *Local Color* (1917), *The Rose of Wolfville* (1918), *The Money Corporal* (1919), *Things Men Do* (1921), *The Cowboy and the Lady* (1922), *To the Ladies, Mr. Billings Spends His Dime* (1923), *Hold Your Breath, A Pair of Hellions* (1924), *The Part Time Wife, Who's Your Friend?* (1925), *Naughty Nanette* (1927), *The Little Savage* (1929). ■

Panama, Norman (1914–), director, screenwriter. Wrote and directed many popular light films during the 1950s and 1960s, especially in collaboration with Melvin FRANK. He occasionally produced his own works. He worked with several popular comics of the period, including Danny KAYE and Bob HOPE.

SELECTED FILMS: *The Reformer and the Redhead* (1950), *Strictly Dishonorable, Callaway Went Thataway* (1951), *Knock on Wood* (1954), *The Court Jester, That Certain Feeling* (1956), *The Road to Hong Kong* (1962), *Not With My Wife*

You Don't! (1966), How to Commit Marriage, The Maltese Bippy (1969), I Will, I Will . . . for Now (1976). ∎

Pangborn, Franklin (1893–1958), actor. Worked on stage before entering films in the mid-1920s. A prolific and easily recognizable character actor, he usually portrayed dapper fusspots who took their positions as clerks and managers too seriously. He appeared chiefly in light films during a career that stretched across four decades. He supported many of the leading comedians of the period, including, among others, WHEELER AND WOOLSEY, W. C. FIELDS, Jack BENNY, and OLSEN AND JOHNSON.

In *Hail the Conquering Hero* he played a prissy master of ceremonies at a homecoming for an alleged World War II hero. Trying to bring order to a collection of four bands and having to decide which band is to play what and when, he cries despairingly: "Oh, Death, where is thy sting?"

SELECTED FILMS: *Exit Smiling (1926), Getting Gertie's Garter (1927), A Blonde for a Night (1928), The Sap (1929), Not So Dumb (1930), International House, Only Yesterday, Design for Living (1933), Cockeyed Cavaliers (1934), My Man Godfrey (1936), Easy Living (1937), Bluebeard's Eighth Wife (1938), Topper Takes a Trip (1939), The Bank Dick (1940), Sullivan's Travels (1941), The Palm Beach Story (1942), Crazy House (1943), The Great Moment (1944), The Horn Blows at Midnight (1945), Mad Wednesday (1947), The Story of Mankind (1957).* ∎

Panzer, Paul (1872–1958), actor. Worked on stage in Europe before migrating to the United States, where he began his screen career with Vitagraph studios. A true pioneer in silent films, Panzer, born Paul Wolfgang Panzerbeiter, appeared on screen as early as 1904 and continued in featured and supporting roles in dramas, serials, and light films for four decades.

SELECTED FILMS: *Stolen by Gypsies (1904), The Cheapest Way (1913), When Knighthood Was in Flower (1922), Week-End Husbands (1924), Too Many Kisses, The Fool, The Best Bad Man, The Mad Marriage (1925), The Dixie Merchant, The High Flyer (1926), Sally in Our Alley (1927), Glorious Betsy, The Candy Kid, George Washington Cohen (1928), First Aid (1931), A Bedtime Story (1933), Cain and Mabel (1936), Penrod's Double Trouble (1938), The Perils of Pauline (1947).* ∎

Pape, Edward Lionel (1867–1944), actor. Came to Hollywood in the 1920s to work in silent films following a long career on stage. He appeared as a supporting player in dramas and light films for 25 years.

SELECTED FILMS: *Nobody (1921), The Man Who Broke the Bank at Monte Carlo (1935), The King and the Chorus Girl, Wee Willie Winkie (1937), The Big Broadcast of 1938, Bluebeard's Eighth Wife, The Young in Heart (1938), Love Affair, Midnight, Fifth Avenue Girl (1939), The Philadelphia Story, Congo Maisie (1940), Charley's Aunt (1941), Almost Married (1942).* ∎

Paris, Jerry (1925–1986), actor, director. Appeared as a character actor in several films during the 1950s before switching to directing chiefly light films beginning in the late 1960s. He worked continually in television as an actor and director.

SELECTED FILMS (as director): *Don't Raise the Bridge—Lower the River, Never a Dull Moment, How Sweet It Is! (1968), Viva Max! (1969), The Grasshopper (1970), Star Spangled Girl (1971).* ∎

Park comedies. One- or two-reel silent films whose plots chiefly unfold in a park setting and often involve a romantic male, his rival, a pretty young woman, and a policeman. It seems obligatory to have one or more characters fall or get pushed into a nearby lake. The humor is a composite of gags, slapstick, mistaken identity, and chases. The greatest practitioner of park comedies was Charlie CHAPLIN. The films were economical to make, requiring no sets, and the location, Westlake Park, was close to the Los Angeles film studios. Whatever the reasons for the emergence of this minor genre, the park films gave the early silent comedies a welcome feeling of openness and dimension in contrast to the flat, claustrophobic studio sets that often resembled the artificial "flats" of stage sets.

"Twenty Minutes of Love" (1914) was Chaplin's first work in this genre. While roaming in the park, Charlie observes a variety of couples and attempts to steal a girl away from her boyfriend. A watch is stolen by someone, a policeman is summoned, and some strollers get pushed into the lake. In "Caught in the Rain" (1914) the settings are a hotel and a park where Charlie meets a married woman who has become separated from her husband. In "The Fatal Mallet" (1914) mischievous Charlie interferes with a couple in a park. When another flirt enters the picture, he knocks both men unconscious and wins the girl. "Mabel's Married Life" (1914) finds Charlie married to Mabel NORMAND. As they stroll in a park, intruder Mack SWAIN begins flirting with Mabel. In "Recreation" (1914) Charlie meets a young woman and, as they are getting acquainted, her sailor beau enters the scene and a brick-throwing fight ensues, with one of the missiles striking a policeman. The film "Those Love Pangs" (1914) once again has most of its major scenes in a park in which Chaplin is considering suicide after being jilted. A policeman talks him out of jumping into the lake, and Charlie is able to take revenge on his competition by tossing him into the lake. In the film "His Trysting Place" (1914) only the second half takes place in a park setting with two couples, Charlie and Normand

again and Mack Swain and Phyllis ALLEN. "Getting Acquainted" (1914) once again involves two married couples, with difficulties arising as Mabel Normand flirts with Chaplin, who is married to Phyllis Allen. In "His Prehistoric Past" (1914) the park serves only as a frame for this flashback comedy in which Charlie dreams that he is living among cavemen. "In the Park" (1915) finds Chaplin involved with a couple, a thief, and a policeman. In "A Woman" (1915) Charlie competes with a married flirt for the affections of a pretty young woman and eventually disposes of his rival by dumping him into a nearby lake.

Other comics used park settings in their films. Harold LLOYD in "Just Nuts" (1915), one of a series of his park films featuring his character, "Willie Work," plays a Chaplinesque tramp who engages in knockabout comedy and brick-throwing. Few sound films made use of this type of setting as a basis for the entire plot. In *Hallelujah, I'm a Bum* (1933) Al JOLSON plays the "mayor" of the hoboes and drifters who have made Central Park their home in this Depression film.

Parker, Barnett (1890–1941), actor. Appeared as a character player in the 1930s and 1940s. He portrayed various minor roles, specializing in faultless butlers. He appeared chiefly in light comedies at MGM and other studios, supporting such stars as William POWELL, Myrna LOY, and the MARX BROTHERS.

SELECTED FILMS: *The President's Mystery* (1936), *Married Before Breakfast, Double Wedding, Espionage, Love Is a Headache, Navy Blue and Gold* (1937), *Listen, Darling, Hold That Kiss, The Girl Downstairs* (1938), *At the Circus, Babes in Arms* (1939), *He Married His Wife, Love Thy Neighbor, Hullabaloo* (1940), *Kisses for Breakfast, The Reluctant Dragon* (1941), *New Wine* (1942). ∎

Parker, Cecilia (1915–), actress. In films since 1931, often in action and western features, before settling in as a member of the "ANDY HARDY" family. She portrayed Marion, Mickey ROONEY'S older sister, in the long-running and popular series. She occasionally ventured into other routine films.

SELECTED FILMS: Women of All Nations (1931), Enter Madame, Naughty Marietta, Ah, Wilderness! (1935), Old Hutch, Three Live Ghosts (1936), A Family Affair, Girl Loves Boy (1937), Seven Sweethearts (1942), Andy Hardy Comes Home (1958). ■

Parker, Dorothy (1893–1967), screen-writer, poet, satirist. A famous wit who occasionally contributed her writing talents to Hollywood films. She wrote songs, stories, and screenplays alone and in collaboration. Her most successful work for the screen was A Star Is Born (1937).

SELECTED FILMS: One Hour Late (1935), Suzy, Three Married Men, Lady Be Careful (1936), Woman Chases Man (1937), Sweethearts (1938), Trade Winds (1939), Weekend for Three (1941), The Fan (1949). ■

Parker, Jean (1912–), actress. Began her film career in 1932, usually playing ingenues in dramas and light films. A pretty performer with plenty of charm, Parker, born Linsa Zelinska, captured the hearts of her audiences. Following a few years of popularity, she abandoned acting in the mid-1940s. She had been relegated to low-budget features, much to her dissatisfaction. She returned to the screen from time to time in minor roles. She appeared in several LAUREL AND HARDY films.

SELECTED FILMS: Divorce in the Family (1932), Made on Broadway, Lady for a Day (1933), Princess O'Hara, The Ghost Goes West (1935), The Arkansas Traveler (1938), Zenobia, The Flying Deuces (1939), Detective Kitty O'Day,

One Body Too Many (1944), Three Red-heads From Seattle (1953), Stigma (1972). ■

Parks, Larry (1914–1975), actor. Played bit parts in routine films in the early 1940s until he was selected to portray the celebrated blackface singer in The Jolson Story (1946). A handsome and personable actor, he began to play leads in costume dramas and light films. But his rapid rise to stardom ended just as quickly during the House Un-American Activities Committee hearings when he admitted his membership in the Communist party. His film contract was canceled and he found no film work for years.

SELECTED FILMS: Mystery Ship, You Belong to Me (1941), You Were Never Lovelier, The Boogie Man Will Get You (1942), Reveille With Beverly (1943), Hey, Rookie!, She's a Sweetheart (1944), Sergeant Mike (1945), Down to Earth (1947), Emergency Wedding (1950), Love Is Better Than Ever (1952), Freud (1962). ■

Parkyakarkus (1904–1958), comedian. Appeared on radio during the Depression years, especially on the "Eddie Cantor Show." Using a Greek accent, he occasionally showed up in light films as a comedy character player. Born Harry Einstein, he was the father of actor-director Albert BROOKS.

In Strike Me Pink he applies for a position as bodyguard to Eddie CANTOR. "Did you say you can tear a telephone book in half?" Cantor asks. "Yes, sir," the applicant affirms, and proceeds to tear one page at a time. "Wait a minute, wait a minute!" Cantor objects. "You're tearing one page at a time!" "I ain't in a hurry," comes the reply.

SELECTED FILMS: Strike Me Pink (1936), The Life of the Party (1937), Night Spot, She's Got Everything (1938), Glamour Boy (1941), The Yanks Are Coming (1942), Sweethearts of the USA

(1944), Earl Carroll's Vanities, Out of This World, Movie Pests, Badminton (1945). ■

Parnell, Emory (1894–1979), actor. In vaudeville before entering films in the late 1930s. A versatile character actor in more than 100 features, he appeared in melodramas and light films. He supported some of the leading comedians of the period, including, among others, ABBOTT AND COSTELLO and MARTIN AND LEWIS.

SELECTED FILMS: *Call of the Yukon, Dr. Rhythm (1938), I Married a Witch (1942), The Miracle of Morgan's Creek (1944), Abie's Irish Rose (1946), The Show-Off (1947), Mr. Blandings Builds His Dream House, Here Comes Trouble (1948), The Beautiful Blonde From Bashful Bend, Ma and Pa Kettle (1949), Lost in Alaska (1952), Sabrina (1954), Artists and Models (1955), The Two Little Bears (1961), The Andromeda Strain (1971).* ■

Parnell, James (1923–1961), actor. Began his screen career in the early 1950s. He appeared as a supporting player in dramas and light films. He was the son of actor Emory PARNELL.

SELECTED FILMS: *G.I. Jane (1951), No Room for the Groom (1952), White Christmas (1954), You're Never Too Young (1955), The Birds and the Bees (1956), The Clown and the Kid, Incident in an Alley (1962).* ■

Parody. In films, a humorous imitation of another work, such as a particular novel, play, poem, or another film. The use of parody may be found in early silent comedies, and parody was employed by some of the leading screen comics. As early as 1914 Charlie CHAPLIN directed and starred in "The Face on the Bar Room Floor," a one-reel parody based on Hugh d'Arcy's popular poem of the same name. Two years later, in 1916, he made "Carmen," or "Burlesque of Carmen," an alternative title.

Chaplin, as Darn Hosiery, uses the vehicle for several hilarious antics, including a duel, a wrestling match, and a deceptive death scene in which he displays a mock knife to the audience.

Stan LAUREL, before teaming up with HARDY, made a series of these films in the 1920s, including "When Knights Were Cold" and "Mud and Sand" (1922), the latter of which, a funny spoof on Valentino's *Blood and Sand*, found him as Rhubarb Vaselino, a Latin lover. "Under Two Jags" poked fun at the Foreign Legion story; "The Soilers" (1923), at Rex Beach's novel of the Yukon and its several film adaptations, especially the William Farnum-Tom Santchi version of *The Spoilers*, including the famous fight scene; "Rupert of Hee-Haw" (1924), at *The Prisoner of Zenda*; "Dr. Pyckle and Mr. Pryde" (1925), at Robert Louis Stevenson's famous tale; and "On the Front Page" (1926), at Ben HECHT and Charles MacARTHUR'S Broadway play about the Chicago newspaper world.

Will ROGERS, who had greater success during the sound era, starred in several silent parodies. In "Doubling for Romeo" (1921) he burlesqued Shakespeare's hero. The following year he starred in "The Headless Horseman," a parody of Washington Irving's tale. "Two Wagons, Both Covered" (1924) poked fun at the popular western *The Covered Wagon*, directed by James Cruze the previous year.

The internationally famous French film comedian, Max LINDER, was invited to Hollywood to star in several productions. One of these, perhaps his most successful in the United States, was *The Three-Must-Get-There's* (1922), a spoof of the Dumas novel and the films based on it, especially the Douglas FAIRBANKS version. In the comedy he plays Dart-in-Again, a Fairbanks-type character who engages in a variety of duels and swashbuckling misadventures.

Perhaps the best film parodies were those of the cross-eyed, mustached comic Ben TURPIN. The contrast between the heroic or romantic characters he imitated and his own homeliness was so stark that the humor was considerably heightened. In 1919 he starred in "East Lynne With Variations," based on the old stage melodrama, and "Uncle Tom Without the Cabin," from Harriet Beecher Stowe's nineteenth-century novel. His five-reel *The Shriek of Araby* (1923) pokes fun at Valentino and his 1921 film, *The Sheik.* Turpin is kidnapped and taken to North Africa, where he replaces a sheik. He meets a female artist and takes her prisoner, introducing her to the ways of love. In 1924 he made his version of *Romeo and Juliet,* resulting in some very funny moments.

Other films during the silent period borrowed only the titles of famous works, the comedies having little or nothing to do with the characters or plot of the original. Mack SENNETT'S 1924 football comedy, "The Half-Back of Notre Dame," is an example, as is Buster KEATON'S *Sherlock, Jr.* (1924). Keaton's *The Three Ages,* made a year earlier, contained more elements of parody of a particular work; in this instance, an imitation of D. W. Griffith's classic, *Intolerance.*

The talkies contributed relatively few parodies. Douglas FAIRBANKS starred in *Around the World in 80 Minutes* (1931), a spoof of Jules Verne's novel, with co-screenwriter Robert E. Sherwood lending a hand. The following year Fairbanks lent his acrobatic prowess to a spoof of Defoe's work in the part-silent, part-sound light film, *Mr. Robinson Crusoe.* The RITZ BROTHERS appeared as *The Three Musketeers* in the 1939 version, along with Don AMECHE. The classic detective yarn of 1941, *The Maltese Falcon,* had the distinction of being parodied twice, by comedians ROWAN AND MARTIN in *The Maltese Bippy* (1969) and in *The Black Bird* (1975), starring George SEGAL, both versions offering very few laughs. John Huston, who directed *The Maltese Falcon* (1941), parodied the mystery genre in such works as *Beat the Devil* (1954).

More recent parodies include those made by some of our major comics and directors. Mel BROOKS directed *Young Frankenstein* (1974) and *High Anxiety* (1977), which parodied much of Hitchcock's work. The late British comedian Marty Feldman directed and starred in *The Last Remake of Beau Geste* (1977), while Peter Sellers was featured in an unsuccessful spoof of *The Prisoner of Zenda* in 1979. Woody ALLEN'S *Love and Death* and *Stardust Memories* in part parody foreign directors.

Parrish, Helen (1922–1959), actress. Appeared in silent films as a child, in "OUR GANG" comedy shorts, and, in the 1940s, was graduated to female leads in low-budget films, chiefly comedies. She also appeared in the "Smithy" comedies of 1927–1929.

SELECTED FILMS: *Babe Comes Home* (1927), *Words and Music* (1929), *X Marks the Spot* (1931), *When a Feller Needs a Friend* (1932), *Make Way for a Lady* (1936), *Three Smart Girls Grow Up* (1939), *I'm Nobody's Sweetheart Now* (1940), *Six Lessons From Madam La Zonga, Too Many Blondes* (1941), *They All Kissed the Bride* (1942), *Cinderella Swings It* (1943), *Trouble Makers* (1948), *The Wolf Hunters* (1949). ∎

Parrott, Charles. See Charlie Chase.

Parrott, James (1892–1939), actor, director. Began his film career as a comic in a series of shorts during the early 1920s. He later switched his position to behind the camera, directing numerous comedies starring his brother, Charlie CHASE, as well as several LAUREL AND HARDY films. One of his shorts, "The Music Box" (1932), won an Academy Award as the best short film of the year.

SELECTED FILMS (as director): *Their Purple Moment, Two Tars* (1928), *The Perfect Day, The Hoosegow* (1929), *Night Owls, Blotto, Brats, The Laurel and Hardy Murder Case, Below Zero, An-*

other Fine Mess (1930), Pardon Us, Helpmates (1931), County Hospital (1932), Twice Two (1933). ■

Parsons, Louella (1881–1972), columnist, screenwriter, actress. She wrote one of the most famous Hollywood gossip columns when the movie capital was in its heyday. She also penned several screenplays and novels. She appeared in a handful of light films.

SELECTED FILMS (as actress): Hollywood Hotel (1937), Without Reservations (1946), Starlift (1951). ■

Parton, Dolly (1946–), actress, singer. Appeared in television and recorded hit songs before entering films in 1980. An attractive, busty comedienne, she has co-starred in comedies and musicals.

In her first feature, *9 to 5*, she portrayed the personal secretary of an oppressive boss who's been spreading stories about their relationship. She finally pins him down in his private office and threatens: "If you ever say another word about me or make another indecent proposal, I'm gonna get that gun of mine and change you from a rooster to a hen with one shot!"

SELECTED FILMS: 9 to 5 (1980), Best Little Whorehouse in Texas (1982), Rhinestone (1984). ■

Pasha, Kalla (1877–1933), actor. Began his screen career in early silent comedies working for producer Mack SWAIN. He worked as a supporting player in dramas and light films through the 1920s.

SELECTED FILMS: Home Talent, A Small Town Idol (1921), Thirty Days (1922), Breaking Into Society, Hollywood, A Million to Burn, Racing Hearts, Ruggles of Red Gap (1923), Heads Up (1925), Don Juan's Three Nights, Rose of the Tenements (1926), Tillie's Punctured Romance (1928), The Show of Shows (1929). ■

Patrick, Gail (1911–1980), actress. Began her film career in the early 1930s after entering a Paramount talent search contest—which she lost. An attractive brunette, she played female leads and secondary roles in dramas and light films through the Depression years and the 1940s. She often portrayed cold females not averse to running off with other women's husbands. She left films in the late 1940s.

SELECTED FILMS: If I Had a Million (1932), No More Ladies, Doubting Thomas (1935), My Man Godfrey (1936), Her Husband Lies, Artists and Models (1937), Mad About Music (1938), My Favorite Wife, The Doctor Takes a Wife (1940), Love Crazy (1941), We Were Dancing (1942), Up in Mabel's Room (1944), Brewster's Millions, Twice Blessed (1945), Inside Story (1948). ■

Patrick, John (1905–), screenwriter, playwright. Wrote many screenplays between the mid-1930s and 1968, while continuing an active career as a competent playwright. His films ranged from dramas to comedies, from major productions to routine second features.

SELECTED FILMS: Educating Father (1936), Time Out for Romance (1937), Battle of Broadway (1938), Three Coins in the Fountain (1954), Love Is a Many Splendored Thing (1955), The Teahouse of the August Moon, High Society (1956), Les Girls (1957), The World of Suzie Wong (1961), Gigot (1962), The Main Attraction (1963), The Shoes of the Fisherman (1968). ■

Patrick, Lee (1911–1982), actress. Appeared on stage before entering films in 1929. She usually played tough, wisecracking blondes as the lead or supporting actress in dramas and light films. She returned to films in 1975 after an eleven-year absence to recreate her role as Effie, Sam Spade's secretary, in *The Black Bird*. She appeared in more than 75 films.

SELECTED FILMS: Strange Cargo (1929), Music for Madame (1937), Maid's Night Out (1938), Ladies Must Live, Father Is a Prince (1940), The Maltese Falcon, Kisses for Breakfast (1941), George Washington Slept Here (1942), Jitterbugs (1943), Moon Over Las Vegas (1944), Keep Your Powder Dry (1945), The Walls Came Tumbling Down (1946), Mother Wore Tights (1947), The Fuller Brush Girl (1950), Take Me to Town (1953), Auntie Mame (1958), Pillow Talk (1959), A Visit to a Small Planet (1960), Wives and Lovers (1963). ■

Patterson, Elizabeth (1874–1966), actress. Appeared on stage before entering films as a spinster aunt and in other matronly roles. A slender, delicate character actress, she enlivened more than 100 films during a screen career that spanned five decades.

In Men Without Names (1935) she voices her suspicions of modern technology. "Fryer-less cookers!" she exclaims. "Seems like it's goin' against nature somehow."

SELECTED FILMS: The Boy Friend (1926), Words and Music (1929), Harmony at Home (1930), Penrod and Sam (1931), Miss Pinkerton (1932), Dinner at Eight (1933), Mississippi (1935), Go West, Young Man (1936), Hold 'Em Navy (1937), Bluebeard's Eighth Wife (1938), The Cat and the Canary (1939), Tobacco Road (1941), Almost Married (1942), The Sky's the Limit (1943), Hail the Conquering Hero (1945), Miss Tatlock's Millions (1948), Katie Did It (1951), Pal Joey (1957), Tall Story (1960). ■

"Pawnshop, The" (1916), MUT. Dir. Charlie Chaplin; Sc. Charlie Chaplin; with Charlie Chaplin, Henry Bergman, Edna Purviance, John Rand, Albert Austin.

This two-reel comedy, made for Mutual and part of Chaplin's famous "golden dozen" produced by the studio, contains the classic comedy scene in which he pulverizes an alarm clock in front of its owner and then, sweeping all the springs and other pieces into the customer's hat, rejects the clock as unworthy of pawning. The irate customer, played by reliable Albert AUSTIN, is quickly subdued by Charlie with a mallet to the head. Charlie portrays an unlikely pawnbroker's assistant who flirts with his employer's daughter and practically wrecks his shop. The film is rich in Chaplin's sight gags and acrobatics, especially in the scene outside the shop involving a ladder. The comedy also illustrates that aspect of the tramp's character that is mischievous and recalcitrant in an environment peopled by even less noble souls than himself.

Payson, Blanche (1881–1964), actress. Began her screen career with producer Mack SENNETT. She appeared as a character player, often in comedy shorts, during the 1930s and 1940s. She supported such comics as LAUREL AND HARDY and Thelma TODD.

SELECTED FILMS: Below Zero (1930), Our Wife (1931), Helpmates, Red Noses (1932), All Over Town (1937), Cookoo Cavaliers, From Nurse to Worse (1940), An Ache in Every Stake (1941). ■

Pearce, Alice (1913–1967), actress. Appeared on stage before entering films in the late 1940s as character player. A charming comedienne with brown hair and a receding chin, she enhanced many dramas, musicals and comedies during the 1950s and 1960s, often portraying officious types.

SELECTED FILMS: On the Town (1949), The Belle of New York (1952), How to Be Very Very Popular (1955), The Opposite Sex (1956), My Six Loves, Tammy and the Doctor, The Thrill of It All (1963), The Disorderly Orderly, Kiss Me, Stupid (1964), Dear Brigitte (1965), The Glass Bottom Boat (1966). ■

Peary, Harold (1909–1985), actor, comedian. Appeared on radio before entering films with his famous "Gildersleeve" character, which he introduced in 1937 on the "Fibber McGee and Molly" radio show. He appeared as well in other routine comedy features.

SELECTED FILMS: Comin' Round the Mountain (1940), Look Who's Laughing, Country Fair (1941), Here We Go Again, Seven Days' Leave, The Great Gildersleeve (1942), Gildersleeve's Bad Day, Gildersleeve on Broadway (1943), Gildersleeve's Ghost (1944), Clambake (1967). ∎

Nat Pendleton

Pendleton, Nat (1895–1967), actor. Former Olympic wrestler who turned professional, appeared on stage in minor roles, then entered films as comedy character actor. He often portrayed dumb Runyonesque characters who inhabited either side of the law. He occasionally played leads, as in Top Sergeant Mulligan (1941). During his 25-year screen career he appeared in more than 100 films.

In Swing Your Lady (1938) he expresses his difficulties with the King's English. "Aw, gee," he pleads with Humphrey BOGART, "talk United States, will ya?"

SELECTED FILMS: The Hoosier Schoolmaster (1924), Let's Get Married (1926), Blonde Crazy (1931), Horse Feathers (1932), Lady for a Day, I'm No Angel (1933), The Thin Man, The Gay Bride (1934), Life Begins in College (1937), Swing Your Lady (1938), It's a

Wonderful World, At the Circus (1939), Buck Privates (1941), Jail House Blues (1942), Swing Fever (1944), Buck Privates Come Home (1947), Death Valley (1949). ∎

Penner, Joe (1905–1941), comedian. Worked as a mind-reader's assistant before switching to comedy. He performed in burlesque, vaudeville, and on the New York stage. He starred in a series of film comedy shorts during the early sound era. But his screen career came and went without distinction. Throughout the 1930s he starred in his own radio show, making his own few phrases household words. His most famous gag line was "Wanna buy a duck?"

SELECTED FILMS: College Rhythm (1934), Collegiate (1936), New Faces of 1937, The Life of the Party (1937), Go Chase Yourself, I'm From the City, Mr. Doodle Kicks Off (1938), The Day the Bookies Wept (1939), Millionaire Playboy, The Boys from Syracuse (1940). ∎

Penrod. Fictional young boy created by writer Booth Tarkington and portrayed on screen several times. In 1922 Gordon GRIFFITH interpreted the role; Ben Alexander played the part in Penrod and Sam in 1923; Leon Janney was Penrod in the first sound version (1931) and Billy Mauch repeated the role in 1937. Billy and his twin brother Bobby then starred in Penrod's Double Trouble (1938) and Penrod and His Twin Brother, also 1938. In the 1950s the Tarkington tales of small town America were converted into musicals in which Doris DAY appeared: On Moonlight Bay (1951) and By the Light of the Silvery Moon (1953), with Billy Gray in the role of the young lad.

Percy, Eileen (1899–1973), actress. Appeared on stage at age eleven, worked as a model, and performed in the Ziegfeld Follies before entering films in 1917. She played the female lead in several early films starring Douglas

FAIRBANKS, after which she continued in less important dramas and light films.

SELECTED FILMS: Wild and Woolly, Down to Earth, Reaching for the Moon (1917), In Mizzoura (1919), Her Honor the Mayor (1920), The Blushing Bride, Hicksville to Broadway, Little Miss Hawkshaw, The Tomboy (1921), The Flirt (1922), Let's Go (1923), That Model From Paris (1926), Spring Fever (1927), The Broadway Hoofer (1929), The Cohens and Kellys in Hollywood (1932). ∎

Perelman, S.J. (1904–1979), screenwriter, humorist. Author of humorous books and occasional screenplays. A celebrated wit, he wrote film stories and scripts alone and in collaboration. His most memorable contributions were his two screenplays for the MARX BROTHERS. He blended slang and the elegance of the English language into an erudite, rich mixture uniquely his own. His specialties of parody and burlesque were successful in his writing but often too sophisticated for his stage and screen audiences. He won an Academy Award for the screenplay of *Around the World in 80 Days*. Dorothy Herrmann's biography, *S.J. Perelman: A Life*, was published in 1986.

SELECTED FILMS: Monkey Business (1931), Horse Feathers (1932), Sitting Pretty (1933), Early to Bed, Florida Special (1936), Boy Trouble (1939), The Golden Fleecing (1940), Around the World in 80 Days (1956). ∎

Perkins, Osgood (1892–1937), actor. Appeared as a character player in silent and sound films through the 1930s. Although he played in several dramas, he was more effective as a comic character actor in light films. He was the father of actor Anthony Perkins.

SELECTED FILMS: The Cradle Buster (1922), Wild, Wild Susan (1925), Love 'Em and Leave 'Em (1926), Knockout Reilly (1927), Mother's Boy (1929), Tarnished Lady (1931), Kansas City Princess (1934), I Dream Too Much (1935), Gold Diggers of 1937 (1936). ∎

"Pete Smith Specialties." See Pete Smith.

Philadelphia Story, The (1940), MGM. *Dir.* George Cukor; *Sc.* Donald Ogden Stewart; with Cary Grant, Katharine Hepburn, James Stewart, Ruth Hussey.

Philip Barry's Broadway comedy was the perfect vehicle for Katharine HEPBURN. After starring in the stage production for a year, she played the lead in the MGM version and re-established herself as a major film star. Her screen career had almost come to a halt in the late 1930s as exhibitors complained that her pictures had failed to bring in the audiences. She portrays the temperamental daughter of John HALLIDAY and Mary NASH, a wealthy couple who have been separated for years. Hepburn, divorced from Cary GRANT, is about to marry John HOWARD. A magazine writer, James STEWART, and his photographer assistant, Ruth Hussey, intrude upon the household as the family prepares for the wedding. Barry's script is filled with sparkling dialogue as Hepburn, at first self-centered and uncaring, changes to a warm and affectionate young woman. Grant is charming and mischievous as her ex-husband who still loves her, while Stewart turns in a plausible performance as an idealistic writer who falls in love with Hepburn. He won an Academy Award for his role, as did Donald Ogden Stewart for his screenplay of this entertaining SOPHISTICATED COMEDY.

Phillips, Dorothy (1892–), actress. Began her screen career in early silent films and rose to stardom in the 1920s. She appeared in dramas and light comedies, later had minor roles in sound features.

SELECTED FILMS: Her Friend's Wife, Fate's Funny Frolic (1911), Hurricane's Gal (1922), The Gay Deceiver (1926), The Cradle Snatchers, Women Love Diamonds (1927), Jazz Cinderella (1930), The Man Who Shot Liberty Valance (1962).

Phillips, Eddie (1899–1965), actor. Handsome supporting player and occasional second male lead of silent and sound features. He appeared chiefly in light comedies.

SELECTED FILMS: *The Beauty Prize, George Washington, Jr.* (1924), *The Fourflusher* (1928), *College Love, The Collegians, His Lucky Day* (1929), *Dancing Sweeties, Big Boy* (1930), *Cross-Fire* (1933). ∎

"Phunphilms." A series of single-reel comedies starring Harold LLOYD as the country bumpkin, "Lonesome Luke." The shorts, which ran from 1915 through 1917 and were produced by Hal ROACH for the Rolin Film Company, gave Lloyd the opportunity to star in his own films after a weak start at KEYSTONE. The Luke character, with his tight-fitting attire and small mustache, was a far cry from his later, and more famous, dapper figure with the famous glasses. At first, the entries were not especially funny, but after several films and an improvement in quality, they became more accepted by exhibitors and the general public. Supporting Lloyd were Bebe DANIELS and Snub POLLARD, two comics destined to achieve success within the next few years.

Pichel, Irving (1891–1954), actor, director. Began his film career in the MGM script department in the late 1920s following Harvard and some stage acting. He entered films as an actor in the early 1930s, but gravitated to directing during the second half of his career. On screen, he appeared generally as a character actor in dramas although he made occasional forays into comedy (*I'm No Angel* [1933] with Mae WEST and *Topper Takes a Trip* [1938] with Constance BENNETT and Roland YOUNG). His directorial efforts, however, were divided equally between dramas and light films, some of which received deserved praise. His comedies, which lacked an individual style, generally contained broad hu-

mor, little subtlety, and a fast pace. His most bitterly satirical film, *A Medal for Benny*, dealt with prejudice against Mexican-Americans.

SELECTED FILMS (as director): *The Gentleman From Louisiana, Beware of Ladies* (1936), *The Sheik Steps Out, The Duke Comes Back* (1937), *The Pied Piper, Life Begins at 8:30* (1942), *A Medal for Benny* (1945), *Colonel Effingham's Raid, The Bride Wore Boots* (1946), *Mr. Peabody and the Mermaid* (1948), *The Great Rupert* (1950), *Day of Triumph* (1954). ∎

Pickens, Slim (1919–1983), actor. Worked in rodeos as a juvenile and as a clown before settling in Hollywood in 1930. A tall, husky character actor, chiefly in westerns, he gave a memorable performance as Major "King" Kong, the jingoistic air force pilot in the black comedy, *Dr. Strangelove* (1964).

SELECTED FILMS: *Rocky Mountain* (1950), *The Story of Will Rogers* (1952), *The Sun Shines Bright* (1953), *The Boys From Oklahoma* (1954), *The Great Locomotive Chase* (1956), *The Chartroose Caboose* (1960), *The Flim-Flam Man, Rough Night in Jericho* (1967), *Never a Dull Moment* (1968), *The Honkers* (1972), *Blazing Saddles* (1974), *The Apple Dumpling Gang* (1975), *Hawmps* (1976), *Mr. Billion* (1977), *Pink Motel* (1982). ∎

Pickford, Mary (1893–1979), actress. Toured with different road companies as a child actress, appeared on Broadway for David Belasco at age fourteen and in silent films in 1909 at sixteen for D. W. Griffith. During her reigning years in films she was the country's biggest draw at the box office. Her films proved so popular that by 1912 she was earning $500 a week, by 1916 her salary reached $10,000 per week with a $300,000 starting bonus, and by the next year her price rose to an unprecedented $350,000 per film. To reach these salaries, the shrewd "Little Mary," as her early admirers called her, had to keep shifting studios, which included BIOGRAPH, IMP, Paramount, and First National. In 1919 she helped form United Artists with partners D. W. Griffith, Douglas FAIRBANKS (her second husband), and Charlie CHAPLIN, a move which led critics to comment that it was as though the inmates were taking over the asylum.

Adored not only in the United States, but internationally as well, she was preferred by audiences in her most typical role of a sweet innocent with blonde curls whose resourcefulness and pluck could ward off almost any peril, a part she played well into her twenties and for which she was called "America's Sweetheart." When in 1928 she cut her curls and restyled her hair, her popularity declined. If the sound era was not particularly damaging to her career, neither was it helpful. Although she won an Oscar for her role in *Coquette* (1929), her first talking picture, the film met with only moderate success. Following several sound films that failed to arouse any enthusiasm among audiences, including a version of *The Taming of the Shrew* (1929) with Fairbanks, she retired from the screen and returned briefly to the stage.

Her dramas and light films had more economic than social ramifications, especially for Hollywood. The wholesomeness of her films and the integrity of the characters she portrayed were her reply to those critics who found only immorality on the screen. Her films brought respectability and prosperity to a town that many suspected bred loose living and other forms of corruption. It was difficult for critics to condemn a medium that had brought forth a strong moral force like Mary Pickford. Her autobiography, *Sunshine and Shadow*, was published in 1955.

SELECTED FILMS: The Violin Maker of Cremona, Her First Biscuits, Sweet and Twenty, Their First Misunderstanding (1910), Artful Kate (1911), Lena and the Geese, The New York Hat (1912), A Good Little Devil, Caprice (1913), Such a Little Queen (1914), Cinderella, Little Pal, Rags (1915), Poor Little Peppina (1916), The Poor Little Rich Girl, The Little Princess (1917), M'Liss, Johanna Enlists (1918), Captain Kidd, Jr., Daddy Long Legs (1919), Pollyanna (1920), Little Lord Fauntleroy (1921), Little Annie Rooney (1926), Sparrows (1926), My Best Girl (1927), Coquette, The Taming of the Shrew (1929), Kiki (1931), Secrets (1933). ∎

Picon, Molly (1898–), actress. Starred in vaudeville, on the Yiddish stage, and on Broadway. A petite performer specializing in comedy, she appeared in Yiddish films in the 1930s and only occasionally in English-speaking features.

SELECTED FILMS: Come Blow Your Horn (1963), Fiddler on the Roof (1971), For Pete's Sake (1974), Cannonball Run (1981). ∎

Pidgeon, Walter (1897–1984), actor. Appeared on stage before journeying to Hollywood during the mid-1920s. Attractive and distinguished, he was assigned chiefly to routine light films during his early screen career. By the 1940s he had established himself as a strong leading actor capable of handling the important and more serious roles for which he became best known. His earlier light films, however, reveal a talented performer with an ample sense of humor.

SELECTED FILMS: Mannequin, Miss Nobody, Marriage License? (1926), The Girl From Rio (1927), Woman Wise, Clothes Make the Woman (1928), A Most Immoral Lady (1929), Sweet Kitty Bellairs (1930), Kiss Me Again, Going Wild, The Hot Heiress (1931), Rockabye (1932), Big Brown Eyes (1936), As Good As Married, My Dear Miss Aldrich, A Girl With Ideas (1937), Too Hot to Handle, Listen, Darling (1938), It's a Date (1940), The Youngest Profession (1943), Weekend at the Waldorf (1945), Holiday in Mexico (1946), Julia Misbehaves (1948), Million Dollar Mermaid (1952), Dream Wife (1953), Hit the Deck (1955), Funny Girl (1968), Sextette (1978). ∎

Pie throwing. First used as a comic device in early silent slapstick films. One of the first comedy shorts in which pie throwing occurred was a KEYSTONE one-reeler, "A Noise From the Deep" (1913), directed by Mack SENNETT and starring "Fatty" ARBUCKLE and Mabel NORMAND, with Mabel doing the hurling at her co-star. Producer Sennett was quick to see the gag as a dependable laugh-getter. Virtually every silent comic indulged in this comedy caper at one time or another. The "custard pie," as it is often called in these routines, is a misnomer. Because they had to hold together during flight, the pies were made either from a paste or from a blackberry base covered with whipped cream. The film that holds the record for the most pies tossed is "The Battle of the Century," a 1927 short starring LAUREL AND HARDY. Allegedly, this Hal ROACH comedy used 3,000 pies in its climactic sequence.

Pierce, Al (–1961), actor, comic. Appeared as comic character player in Hollywood films during the 1940s and 1950s. He usually worked in minor light films for second-string studios such as Republic.

Pierlot, Francis (1876–1955), actor. Appeared as a character player in dramas and light films beginning in the early 1930s. He usually played professional characters.

SELECTED FILMS: Night Angel (1931), Strike Up the Band, Always a Bride (1940), A Gentleman at Heart (1942), The Doughgirls (1944), Two Guys From Milwaukee (1946), The Senator Was Indiscreet (1947), That Wonderful Urge (1948), My Friend Irma (1949), The Lemon Drop Kid, That's My Boy (1951), The Prisoner of Zenda (1952). ∎

"Pilgrim, The." See Charlie Chaplin.

Doris Day and Rock Hudson in *Pillow Talk* (1959)

Pillow Talk (1959), U. *Dir.* Michael Gordon; *Sc.* Maurice Richlin, Stanley Shapiro; with Doris Day, Rock Hudson, Tony Randall, Thelma Ritter.

The late Oscar Levant once remarked that he knew Doris DAY before she became a virgin. He was undoubtedly referring to this film, one of the first in a succession of bedroom comedies in which Day epitomized American virginity. Rock HUDSON shares a party line with her, and this leads to a verbal battle. He pursues her, but she holds out for wedding bells. In one scene she lambasts his licentiousness. "This may come as a surprise to you, but there are some men who don't end every sentence with a proposition." Tony RANDALL is hilarious as Hudson's confidant. "The trouble with you is, you're prejudiced against me because I'm part of a minority group—millionaires," he grouses. "You outnumber us but you'll never get us. We'll fight for our rights to the bitter end. We've got the money to do it." Thelma RITTER, as usual, is excellent. From today's vantage point, the film is a harmless trifle, but in 1959 its premise and the continual flow of sexual innuendoes and double entendres were rather daring. Its success brought the stars together for two additional films, *Lover Come Back* (1962) and *Send Me No Flowers* (1964). During these years Day and Hudson were consistently among the top three or four box-office draws, according to several national polls.

Pink Panther, The (1964), UA. *Dir.* Blake Edwards; *Sc.* Blake Edwards, Maurice Richlin; with David Niven, Robert Wagner, Peter Sellers, Claudia Cardinale, Capucine.

This is the first in the highly popular series of "Panther" comedies with Peter Sellers playing the inept French Inspector Clouseau. The plot revolves around the rivalry between two jewel thieves, uncle David NIVEN and nephew Robert Wagner. The bungling inspector falls out of windows, cannot turn a doorknob properly, and, worst of all, is cuckolded by his philandering wife. The visual gags and slapstick are performed slickly, the pace is just right, and the Swiss scenery is splendid. In this first entry the main story focuses on the crime caper and the romantic aspects, not on Clouseau, but he proved to be such an engaging character that future films in the series made him the lead. The title here refers to a famous and coveted jewel; later it was to pertain to the master jewel thief and nemesis of the inspector. Other films in the series, also directed by Blake EDWARDS, include *A Shot in the Dark* (1964), *The Return of the Pink Panther* (1975), *The Pink Panther Strikes Again* (1976), *Revenge of the Pink Panther* (1978), *Trail of the Pink Panther* (1982), *Curse of the Pink Panther* (1983). Loaded with slapstick and inventive chases, the entries have been singled out for their scenic backgrounds, their tempo, their musical scores, and their creative animated titles. In 1968 an English film, *Inspector Clouseau*, was released and starred Alan ARKIN with Bud YORKIN as director, but it was not part of the series. The last two entries were made after the death of Sellers. *Trail of the Pink Panther* used scenes from earlier films while *Curse of the Pink Panther* employed a new actor, Ted Wass.

Pious, Minerva (1909–1979), comedienne. Appeared on radio in the early 1940s before entering films. Establishing herself as Mrs. Nussbaum, a character on comedian Fred ALLEN'S popular radio show, she repeated her role on screen and went on to play other light parts in a handful of films.

In *It's in the Bag* Fred ALLEN calls on her, but she does not permit him to enter her apartment. "Outside I am speaking," she announces. "Inside I am having company." "Oh," Allen muses, "company." "The phone company," she explains. "They're taking out my telephone." "If I can call later—" he begins. "You could call. Without a telephone I couldn't answer." "All I want is some information," Allen tries to explain. "To get information you are needing a telephone," she replies.

SELECTED FILMS: It's in the Bag (1945), The Ambassador's Daughter, Joe Macbeth (1956), Love in the Afternoon (1957), Pinocchio in Outer Space (voice only) (1965). ■

Piper, Oscar. The fictional police inspector in the 1930s series of detective comedies starring Edna May OLIVER as Hildegarde Withers, an amateur sleuth. Piper was portrayed by character actor James GLEASON.

Pirosh, Robert (1910–), director, screenwriter. Worked in advertising before turning to writing screenplays in 1937. His scripts range from war films to sophisticated comedies. He occasionally directed dramas and light films, including *The Girl Rush* (1955) and *Spring Reunion* (1957).

SELECTED FILMS (as screenwriter): The Winning Ticket (1935), A Day at the Races (1937), I Married a Witch (1942), Up in Arms (1944), What's So Bad About Feeling Good? (1968). ■

Pitts, ZaSu (1898–1963), actress. Entered early silent films in 1917 as a supporting player in dramas and comedies. She appeared in several films starring Mary PICKFORD. A talented character actress who frequently played a confused maid or friend of the female lead, she utilized her hands in a unique way to express her frustration.

With the advent of sound she was stereotyped by the studios as a comedienne in spite of her success in dramatic roles, especially her performances in two films directed by Erich von Stroheim. While continuing in features in comic-relief roles, she signed with producer Hal ROACH in 1931 to co-star with Thelma TODD in a series of comedy shorts. She appeared also with comic actor Slim SUMMERVILLE in several features. One of the most popular supporting comic players during the 1930s and 1940s, she appeared in scores of films during a career that spanned five decades.

SELECTED FILMS: The Little Princess (1917), Poor Relations (1919), Patsy (1921), Three Wise Fools (1923), Lazybones (1925), Early to Wed (1926), Casey at the Bat (1927), Buck Privates (1928), The Dummy (1929), Monte Carlo (1930), The Unexpected Father (1932), Her First Mate (1933), The Gay Bride (1934), Ruggles of Red Gap (1935), No, No, Nanette (1940), Broadway Limited (1941), Let's Face It (1943), Life With Father (1947), Francis (1950), This Could Be the Night (1957), It's a Mad, Mad, Mad, Mad World (1963). ∎

Platt, Edward C. (1916–1974), actor. Worked as a dance-band singer before entering films in the early 1950s. A thin-faced, well-groomed character player, he appeared in dramas and light films, usually in bland roles. He switched to television where he attained moderate success as Don ADAMS' chief in the "Get Smart" comedy series.

SELECTED FILMS: Stalag 17 (1953), The Private World of Major Benson, Sincerely Yours (1955), Serenade, The Unguarded Moment, The Lieutenant Wore Skirts, Rock, Pretty Baby (1956), The High Cost of Loving (1958), Pollyanna (1960), A Ticklish Affair (1963), Bullet for a Bad Man (1964). ∎

Play It Again, Sam (1972), PAR. Dir. Herbert Ross; Sc. Woody Allen; with Woody Allen, Diane Keaton, Tony Roberts, Jerry Lacy, Susan Anspach, Jennifer Salt.

In this romantic comedy, based on Woody Allen's Broadway play, movie buff Allan Felix (Allen) is obsessed with Humphrey Bogart as his sexual mentor. Divorced by his wife, Felix withdraws from the outside world. "No matter what I'll say," he ponders about a visit to an analyst, "he'll say it's a sexual problem. Isn't that ridiculous? We don't even have relations any more." Bogart, in one of their imaginary talks, encourages Allen, admitting that he himself has had his face slapped many times. "Yeah," the comic replies, "but your glasses don't go flying across the room." His friends Linda and Dick Christie (Diane KEATON and Tony ROBERTS) try to get him dates. After a few disastrous attempts, he falls in love with Linda and they have an affair. "What were you thinking about while you were doing it?" she asks. "Willie Mays," he replies. "You always think of baseball?" she continues. "Keeps me going," he says. "I was wondering why you kept shouting, 'Slide!'" When her husband learns of the affair, he wonders: "Why didn't I see it coming? Me, who had the foresight to buy Polaroid at 8 1/2." Eventually, Allen gets the opportunity to play out the famous Bogart-Bergman airport scene from Casablanca; he finally is able to shed the ghost of Bogart, at least superficially, as he walks down the lonely tarmac into the fog. Compared to Allen's other screenplays, this one is more conventional but equally entertaining.

Pleshette, Suzanne (1937–), actress. Attractive and popular actress of stage and screen who made her film debut in 1958. She has starred in dramas and light films, but her acting talents, for the most part, have not been fully utilized by the studios.

In *Rome Adventure* she played a librarian who becomes romantically involved with student architect Troy Donahue. "You mean we'll never meet again?" he asks. "There's never and there's never," she answers.

SELECTED FILMS: *The Geisha Boy (1958), Rome Adventure (1962), 40 Pounds of Trouble (1963), The Ugly Dachshund, Mister Buddwing (1966), If It's Tuesday, This Must Be Belgium, How to Make It (1969), Suppose They Gave a War and Nobody Came (1970), Support Your Local Gunfighter (1971), The Shaggy D.A. (1976), Oh, God! Book II (1980).* ■

Poitier, Sidney (1924–), actor, director. Appeared on Broadway in the mid-1940s following a stretch in the military service. He began his screen career in 1950 and quickly advanced to stardom, becoming the top black actor in American films. A dynamic performer with sensitivity and an abundance of personality, he starred chiefly in dramas. He was nominated for an Academy Award for his role in *The Defiant Ones* (1958), a film that brought him the best actor award at the 1958 Berlin Film Festival. He eventually won an Oscar as Best Actor for *Lilies of the Field* (1963). He was the second black actor to win an Oscar (Hattie McDANIEL had received one for *Gone With the Wind*). By the early 1970s he was directing his own features, mainly comedies.

SELECTED FILMS (as director): *Buck and the Preacher (1972), Uptown Saturday Night (1974), Let's Do It Again (1975), A Piece of the Action (1977), Stir Crazy (1980), Hanky Panky (1982).* ■

Pollard, Daphne (–1978), actress. Appeared in Hollywood comedy shorts, chiefly in the 1930s, as a supporting player. Short and plump, she worked for the three major comedy producers, Mack SENNETT, Al CHRISTIE, and Hal ROACH. She portrayed Oliver HARDY'S wife in two films.

SELECTED FILMS: *Thicker Than Water (1935), Our Relations (1936).* ■

Pollard, Harry (1883–1934), director. Appeared on stage before entering early silent films in 1912 as an actor. Eventually he switched to directing.

SELECTED FILMS: *The Peacock Feather Fan (1914), The Girl Who Couldn't Grow Up (1917), Sporting Youth (1924), Oh, Doctor!, I'll Show You the Town (1925), The Cohens and the Kellys, Poker Faces (1926), Shipmates (1931), When a Feller Needs a Friend, Fast Life (1932).* ■

Pollard, Michael J. (1939–), actor. Appeared on stage before entering films in the early 1960s. He gained recognition, and an Academy Award nomination for Best Supporting Actor, for his role as the youthful member of Clyde's gang in *Bonnie and Clyde* (1967). An offbeat character actor, he has appeared in lead roles in several light films but has not sustained his popularity.

SELECTED FILMS: *Hemingway's Adventures of a Young Man (1962), The Russians Are Coming, the Russians Are Coming (1966), Caprice, Enter Laughing (1967), Jigsaw (1968), Hannibal Brooks (1969), Little Fauss and Big Halsy (1970), Dirty Little Billy (1972), Sunday in the Country (1975), Between the Lines (1977), Melvin and Howard (1979), America (1986).* ■

Pollard, Snub Harry (1886–1962), actor. Appeared in light opera in his native Australia before entering early silent films in the United States. A short comic with a walrus-type mustache, Pollard, born Harold Frazer, joined producer Hal ROACH'S stock company of comedians in 1915, chiefly as a supporting player to Harold LLOYD. By 1922, and after more than 100 single-reel comedies, he was rewarded with a series of two-reelers of his own.

His earlier shorts were routine slapstick entries and, because of the limitations of the single reel and a tight schedule, provided little in the way of characterization. The double-reel films offered him the opportunity to develop character. An inventive comic, he created his best work during this period, rivaling the films of many of his contemporaries.

Because he had no definite screen personality, he had to rely heavily on sight gags, and in this area he excelled. In his classic 1923 comedy short, "It's a Gift," he portrayed an inventor who gets through everyday chores with some highly original gadgets. These help him prepare his breakfast, get dressed, and straighten out his room—all handled automatically through a series of highly complex strings and levers. Getting to work is no problem with his engineless compact car that runs by his directing a huge magnet at other vehicles in traffic.

His popularity, however, declined by the late 1920s. With the advent of sound, he was relegated to minor roles in full-length films or sometimes supporting other leading comedians, including the THREE STOOGES. Never one of the top-ranking silent-screen comics, he was nevertheless one of the best and funniest of the second-string comics.

SELECTED FILMS: *Great While It Lasted (1915), Luke Laughs Last (1916), The Flirt (1917), The Lamb (1918), His Royal Slyness, All at Sea, Tough Luck (1919), Red Hot Hottentots, The Dippy Dentist, Any Old Port, Insulting the Sultan (1920), The Morning After, His Best Girl, The Jail Bird, The Hustler, Corner Pocket (1921), 365 Days, The Old Sea Dog, Hook, Line and Sinker (1922), The Courtship of Miles Sandwich, It's a Gift, Join the Circus (1923), The Big Idea, Why Marry? (1924), Are Husbands Human? (1925), The Doughboy, All Wet (1926), The Bum's Rush (1927), Ex-Flame (1930), Cockeyed Cavaliers (1934), Arizona Days (1937), The Perils of Pauline (1947), Who Was That Lady? (1960), Pocketful of Miracles (1961).* ■

Porcasi, Paul (1880–1946), actor. Appeared as an opera singer in his native Italy before migrating to Hollywood in the 1920s. A squat, bald character player usually brandishing a cigar, he appeared in several silents and, during the sound era, numerous dramas and light films.

SELECTED FILMS: *Say It Again (1926), Born Reckless (1930), The Good Bad Girl, I Like Your Nerve (1931), The Passionate Plumber, The Kid From Spain (1932), Grand Slam (1933), Wake Up and Dream (1934), Enter Madame (1935), The Bride Wore Red (1937), Argentine Nights (1940), Hi Diddle Diddle (1943).* ■

Poston, Tom (1927–), actor. Has appeared in dramas and light films, with the latter his forte. An offbeat, talented comedian, he has frequently been given roles beneath his talents.

SELECTED FILMS: *The City That Never Sleeps (1953), Zotz! (1962), Cold Turkey (1970), The Happy Hooker (1975), Rabbit Test (1978), Up the Academy (1980), Carbon Copy (1981).* ■

Potash and Perlmutter. A popular comedy team that appeared in several silent films during the 1920s. The first film, called *Potash and Perlmutter* (1923), based on the play by Montague Glass and Jules Goodman, starred Barney Bernard and Alexander CARR as the title characters respectively. Abe Potash, a good-hearted soul, and his easily excitable business partner, Morris, engage in friendly arguments, become entangled in a variety of misadventures, and employ the usual stereotyped Jewish mannerisms of the period for their humor.

Following Bernard's untimely death, film comedian George SIDNEY took over the role of Potash in the second film, *In Hollywood With Potash and Perlmutter* (1924), sometimes listed simply as *In Hollywood*. This film was also based on a play, *Business Before Pleasure*, by the same authors. Another film adaptation of a play was released in 1926. *Partners Again*, the last in the short-lived series, involved the pair's catastrophic business venture in the automobile industry with predictable results.

During and after the Potash and Perlmutter film series, both George Sidney and Alexander Carr appeared separately in other comedies. Sidney became the more famous of the two comics, starring in other series and continuing his screen career well into the 1930s. The comedy team no doubt contributed heavily to the success of the series, and the pictures, comprised chiefly of low-comedy routines, were popular with their audiences.

Potel, Victor (1889–1947), actor. Began his screen career in 1910 in early silent films. He appeared as supporting player in silent screen star Eileen SEDGWICK'S early comedy shorts. By the 1930s he was playing comic relief characters in low-budget westerns. He continued to play minor character roles into the 1940s, including parts in *The Big Store* with the MARX BROTHERS and *Mad Wednesday* with Harold LLOYD. He was one of Mack SENNETT'S KEYSTONE KOPS.

SELECTED FILMS: *Hired, Tired and Fired, Some Heroes, I'll Get Her Yet, Ain't He Grand?, Room Rent and Romance* (1916), *The Gasoline Habit* (1917), *A Lost Lady, Below the Line* (1925), *Partners* (1932), *Song of the Saddle, Yellow Dust* (1936), *The Big Store* (1941), *Mad Wednesday* (1947). ■

Potter, H. C. (1904–1977), director. Worked as a stage and screen director for three decades. He began directing films in 1936, specializing in comedy.

SELECTED FILMS: *Beloved Enemy* (1936), *The Cowboy and the Lady* (1938), *Congo Maisie* (1940), *Hellzapoppin* (1941), *Mr. Lucky* (1943), *The Farmer's Daughter, A Likely Story* (1947), *Mr. Blandings Builds His Dream House, You Gotta Stay Happy, The Time of Your Life*

(1948), *Three for the Show* (1955), *Top Secret Affair* (1957). ■

Powell, Dick (1904–1963), actor, singer, director. Worked as a band vocalist before entering films in the early 1930s as lead player in numerous Warner Brothers musical comedies. A handsome actor with a pleasant voice and abundance of youthful charm, he portrayed struggling, clean-cut young performers waiting for their big break. He starred in three of the popular "Gold Diggers" musicals during the 1930s. He was listed in the Box Office Top Ten of screen favorites in 1935 and 1936. In the 1940s he starred in light comedies and, by the end of World War II, began a new career successfully playing tough characters in realistic dramas. He directed several films during the 1950s and then began a new career in television, chiefly as an executive producer. He was married to actress Joan BLONDELL and then June ALLYSON.

SELECTED FILMS: *Blessed Event, Too Busy to Work* (1932), *The King's Vacation, 42nd Street, Footlight Parade, College Coach* (1933), *Wonder Bar, Dames* (1934), *Page Miss Glory, Broadway Gondolier, Thanks a Million* (1935), *Colleen* (1936), *On the Avenue, The Singing Marine* (1937), *Cowboy From Brooklyn, Hard to Get, Going Places* (1938), *Naughty but Nice* (1939), *Christmas in July, I Want a Divorce* (1940), *In the Navy, Model Wife* (1941), *Happy Go Lucky, True to Life, Riding High* (1943), *It Happened Tomorrow* (1944), *The Reformer and the Redhead* (1950), *You Never Can Tell* (1951), *Susan Slept Here* (1954). ■

Powell, Eleanor (1912–1982), actress, dancer. Appeared as a dancer on Broadway before entering films in the mid-1930s. A popular entertainer, she starred in several musical comedies during the 1930s and 1940s. She appeared in a few of the "Broadway Melody" series. When tap-dancing lost its appeal at the box office, she retired from the screen, appearing occasionally, and successfully, on stage and in nightclubs. She hosted a religious television program in the 1950s that won five Emmy Awards. In 1928 the Dancing Masters of America honored her as "The World's Greatest Female Tap Dancer."

SELECTED FILMS: George White's Scandals, Broadway Melody of 1936 (1935), Born to Dance (1936), Rosalie (1937), Honolulu (1939), Lady Be Good (1941), Ship Ahoy! (1942), Thousands Cheer, I Dood It (1943), Sensations of 1945 (1944), Duchess of Idaho (1950). ■

Powell, Jane (1929–), actress, singer. Appeared on radio before entering films in the 1940s. Blessed with a rich singing voice, good looks, and a pleasant personality, she starred in a series of light films playing innocent adolescents. Following ten years of screen popularity, she abandoned films in the late 1950s when good roles became scarce. However, she has continued to perform on stage and in television.

SELECTED FILMS: Song of the Open Road (1944), Delightfully Dangerous (1945), Holiday in Mexico (1946), A Date With Judy, Luxury Liner (1948), Nancy Goes to Rio (1950), Royal Wedding, Rich, Young and Pretty (1951), Small Town Girl, Three Sailors and a Girl (1953), Seven Brides for Seven Brothers (1954), Hit the Deck (1955), The Girl Most Likely (1957), The Female Animal, Enchanted Island (1958). ■

Powell, William (1892–1984), actor. Appeared on stage before entering silent films in 1922, usually in suave, villainous roles. With the advent of sound, his screen image changed as he began playing urbane detectives and other types in light films. A dapper figure with pleasing and distinguished looks, he scored his biggest success in the "Thin Man" series, in which he portrayed the amateur sleuth, Nick Charles, with Myrna LOY as his rich wife, Nora. The detective-comedy films, based on characters created by Dashiell Hammett, propelled the two former silent screen performers to stardom.

In films like My Man Godfrey, in which he played a hobo who is employed as a butler by a wealthy but spoiled family, and Libeled Lady, in which he is hired by a newspaper to compromise the young and wealthy Myrna LOY, he demonstrated his charm as well as his ability to handle both SOPHISTICATED and SCREWBALL COMEDY.

But the "Thin Man" series allowed Powell the opportunity to display his full talents, giving a convincing performance as the humorously cynical, half-inebriated detective who continually jousts with his wife. In one scene Loy reminds him to be cautious, that he may be killed. "You wouldn't be a widow long," he replies. "You bet I wouldn't," she returns, teasingly. "Not with your money," he adds. He starred in a string of comedies from the 1930s through the 1950s, often to critical acclaim. Charles Francisco's biography, Gentleman: The William Powell Story (1985), contains many photographs and a filmography.

SELECTED FILMS: Sherlock Holmes, When Knighthood Was in Flower (1922), Too Many Kisses (1925), Special Delivery (1927), Feel My Pulse (1928), Pointed Heels (1929), Ladies' Man (1931), The Thin Man (1934), Reckless (1935), My Man Godfrey, Libeled Lady (1936), Double Wedding (1937), The Baroness and the Butler (1938), Love Crazy (1941), The Heavenly Body (1944), Life With Father (1947), The Senator Was Indiscreet, Mr. Peabody and the Mermaid (1948), The Girl Who Had Everything, How to Marry a Millionaire (1953), Mister Roberts (1955). ■

Preisser, June (1920–1984), actress, dancer. Appeared on stage before entering films in the late 1930s. She reached her peak in the 1940s playing lively, acrobatic roles in youth-oriented light films, several of which were low-budget productions.

SELECTED FILMS: Babes in Arms, Dancing Co-Ed, Judge Hardy and Son (1939), Strike Up the Band (1940), Henry Aldrich for President (1941), Sweater Girl (1942), Babes on Swing Street (1944), Let's Go Steady (1945), Freddie Steps Out, High School Hero, Junior Prom (1946), Sarge Goes to College, Vacation Days (1947), Smart Politics, Music Man (1948). ∎

Preminger, Otto (1906–1985), director. Worked as theatrical director and producer in his native Vienna before coming to the United States in 1935. He directed a Broadway play and moved on to Hollywood where he did some occasional directing of routine films with mediocre results. He returned to Broadway, but was back in the film capital in 1942—this time as actor. After a few roles, chiefly as Nazis, he was again given a chance to direct. More successful this time, he continued to turn out films in various genres through 1980, his most acclaimed being Laura (1944).

His success over the years has been mixed. Some of his films reflect moments of genius, while others are thoroughly disappointing. He gained notoriety for his controversial and landmark film, his first production as an independent, The Moon Is Blue (1953), a slight comedy that brought the wrath of censors down on him. Because of terms like "virgin" and "pregnant," words that were traditionally banned from Hollywood films up to that time, the picture was released without the usual Production Code Seal of Approval. Most of his best works fall into the realm of drama, but he has directed several entertaining light features.

SELECTED FILMS: Under Your Spell (1936), Danger—Love at Work (1937), Margin for Error (1943), In the Meantime, Darling (1944), A Royal Scandal (1945), Centennial Summer (1946), That Lady in Ermine (1948), The Fan (1949), Angel Face (1953), Bonjour Tristesse (1958), Skidoo! (1968), Such Good Friends (1971), The Human Factor (1980). ∎

Prentiss, Paula (1939–), actress. In films from the early 1960s, usually playing lead roles. She has appeared in dramas as well as in light comedies although the latter seem to be her forte. She is married to actor Richard BENJAMIN.

SELECTED FILMS: Where the Boys Are (1960), The Honeymoon Machine, Bachelor in Paradise (1961), The Horizontal Lieutenant (1962), Follow the Boys (1963), Man's Favorite Sport?, The World of Henry Orient (1964), What's New, Pussycat? (1965), Catch-22 (1970), Last of the Red Hot Lovers (1972), Buddy Buddy (1981). ∎

Pressman, Michael (1950–), director. Began turning out films in the late 1970s. Although he has concentrated on slapstick comedy, some of his films, at best uneven, have demonstrated his ability to handle characterization and comic ideas with subtlety.

SELECTED FILMS: The Great Texas Dynamite Chase, The Bad News Bears in Breaking Training (1977), Those Lips, Those Eyes (1980), Some Kind of Hero (1982), Doctor Detroit (1983). ∎

Preston, Robert (1918–1987), actor. Began his long screen career in 1938. A handsome figure with a trim mustache, he rarely got the girl and was often overshadowed by the male star of the film. He spent the first half of his film career chiefly playing second leads in dramatic roles. Later, he starred or was featured in light films, especially after his stage successes in The Music Man, for which he won a Tony Award and repeated his role in the film version, and Mack and Mabel, in which he played Mack SENNETT. When he was well into his sixties, he played a major role as a gay entertainer with surprising energy and nuance in Blake EDWARDS' comedy Victor/Victoria, for which he won an Oscar.

In *The Music Man* he portrayed Professor Harold Hill, a fast-talking drummer and con-man. Arriving in River City, Iowa, he meets an old crony, Buddy HACKETT, who is working for a living. "So, you've gone legitimate, eh?" Preston sadly notes. "I knew you'd come to no good."

SELECTED FILMS: *King of Alcatraz (1938), Moon Over Burma (1940), Star Spangled Rhythm (1942), Variety Girl (1947), The Lady Gambles (1949), The Music Man (1962), Island of Love (1963), Mame (1974), Semi-Tough (1977), Victor/ Victoria (1982), The Last Starfighter (1984).* ∎

Prevost, Marie (1898–1937), actress. Began her film career in 1917 with producer Mack SENNETT as one of his "Bathing Beauties." He soon promoted her to a lead comedienne and for the next four years she appeared in numerous comedy shorts. She then switched to Universal studios, and by the mid-1920s established herself as a major film star of romantic comedy. She continued her successful career into the sound era but was soon relegated to lesser roles such as gum-chewing soubrettes. However, a more serious problem haunted her—that of weight. Her excessive dieting led to her early death at age 39.

SELECTED FILMS: *Her Native Dance (1917), Sleuths, The Village Chestnut (1918), Love, Honor and Behave (1920), Nobody's Fool (1921), Her Night of Nights (1922), Brass (1923), The Marriage Circle, Three Women (1924), Kiss Me Again (1925), Up in Mabel's Room (1926), Getting Gertie's Garter (1927), On to Reno (1928), Divorce Made Easy (1929), Sweethearts on Parade (1930), Reckless Living (1931), Three Wise Girls, Slightly Married (1932), Only Yesterday (1933), Hands Across the Table (1935), 13 Hours by Air (1936).* ∎

Price, Kate (1872–1943), actress. Worked in vaudeville and on stage before entering early silent films in 1912. She appeared chiefly as a supporting player in dramas and light films during a screen career that spanned more than three decades.

SELECTED FILMS: *Stenographers Wanted (1912), The Waiter's Ball (1916), Dinty (1920), My Wife's Relations, Come On Over, The New Teacher, The Guttersnipe (1922), Good-By Girls!, The Near Lady (1923), The Way of a Girl, The Sporting Venus, The Perfect Clown, Sally, Irene and Mary (1925), Irene, The Cohens and the Kellys (1926), Frisco Sally Levy, Casey Jones, Orchids and Ermine (1927), Easy Living (1937).* ∎

Price, Stanley L. (1900–1955), actor. Worked on stage as well as in films, beginning with silent features, serials, and comedy shorts. He also wrote screenplays during a Hollywood career that spanned four decades.

SELECTED FILMS: *Your Best Friend (1922), It Happened One Day (1934), Okay Toots! (1935), Tom Sawyer, Detective (1938), Seventeen, Moon Over Burma (1940), Bride by Mistake (1944), Studio Stoops, Dopey Dicks (1950), The Ten Commandments (1956).* ∎

Private Benjamin (1980), WB. Dir. Howard Zieff; Sc. Nancy Meyers, Charles Shyer, Harvey Miller; with Goldie Hawn, Eileen Brennan, Armand Assante, Robert Webber.

Following in the boots of films like *Buck Privates, Caught in the Draft,* and *At War With the Army,* this engaging army comedy covers the same ground but enlists the charming services of Goldie HAWN. She is delightful as a Jewish-American Princess who joins the army only to discover it's not what she had expected. There are several comical scenes, including an early one involving her brief marriage to Albert BROOKS as well as those of the war games and calisthenics. Eileen Brennan displays her considerable comedic talents as Hawn's spit-and-polish officer. All the other supporting players are exceptionally good. The trio of screenwriters also wrote the story for a later Hawn film, *Protocol*, which was less successful.

Zero Mostel and Gene Wilder in *The Producers* (1968)

Producers, The (1968), AVCO. *Dir.* Mel Brooks; *Sc.* Mel Brooks; with Zero Mostel, Gene Wilder, Kenneth Mars, Dick Shawn, Christopher Hewett.

The film has grown in stature over the years and has since reached the pantheon of classic comedies, along with selected works of the MARX BROTHERS and W. C. FIELDS, and features like *Some Like It Hot*. The wild plot concerns a former Broadway producer, played by Zero MOSTEL, who is down on his luck. He is relegated to satisfying the sexual fantasies of old women. "Their last thrill on the way to the grave," he explains. They pay for his services with fat investments in his next big production which, of course, he has no plans for. Into this lucrative scam walks a shy accountant, portrayed by Gene WILDER, who is coaxed into assisting Mostel. Together they expand the fraud into selling several hundreds percent of a failing show. With his new partner, Mostel finds the perfect play, *Springtime for Hitler*, an egregiously reprehensible and tasteless musical written by a practicing Nazi (Kenneth Mars) who would like to clear the name of his hero, the Fuhrer. With the right vehicle for failure, he strengthens his position by hiring the worst director and an aging hippie (Dick

SHAWN) for the lead. But his scheme, not the play, fails when the audience finds the production hilarious. "I picked the wrong play, the wrong actors, the wrong director," Mostel moans. "Where did I go right?" He and Wilder are found guilty, go to prison, and, unrepentant, oversell shares in their new play, *Prisoners of Love*. Although this was BROOKS' first film, it established him as a major force in screen comedy. His knack for irreverent and tasteless humor, his craziness, and his wonderfully kooky characters have influenced numerous directors and films as well as the direction of present-day comedy.

Prouty, Jed (1879–1956), actor. Worked on stage before entering films in the early 1920s. He appeared chiefly as a character player in more than 100 silent and sound comedies, often as a rural type. He portrayed the often perplexed father in the popular "JONES FAMILY" comedy series.

SELECTED FILMS: The Great Adventure, Room and Board (1921), Kick In (1922), The Gold Diggers (1923), The Knockout (1925), Don Juan's Three Nights (1926), Orchids and Ermine (1927), Domestic Meddlers (1928), Fall of Eve (1929), The Floradora Girl (1930), Annabelle's Affairs (1931), Business and Pleasure (1932), The Big Bluff (1933), Hollywood Party (1934), Navy Wife (1935), Educating Father (1936), Big Business, Hot Water (1937), Safety in Numbers (1938), Too Busy to Work (1939), Young As You Feel (1940), Mug Town (1943), Guilty Bystander (1950). ■

Provine, Dorothy (1937–), actress. Began her film career in the late 1950s. A pretty and talented performer, she has played leads in melodramas and light films, specializing in the latter. She became popular in television.

SELECTED FILMS: Live Fast, Die Young (1958), The 30-Foot Bride of Candy Rock (1959), It's a Mad, Mad, Mad, Mad World (1963), Good Neighbor

Sam (1964), The Great Race, That Darn Cat (1965), One Spy Too Many, Who's Minding the Mint? (1967), Never a Dull Moment (1968). ∎

Pryor, Richard (1940–), actor, comedian. Began his show business career as a piano player at a small nightclub where he would occasionally tell a few jokes. Arriving in New York in the 1960s and almost broke, he performed at a small Greenwich Village coffee house where he was spotted by television executives. A few appearances on network shows were all he needed. He soon became a popular comedian of nightclubs, television, records, and films. He entered films in the late 1960s doing bit parts, but within a few years he was playing leads. Famous for his irreverent, street-wise, ghetto humor, he has been criticized by some critics for his raw, excessive language in his "concert" films. He won much notoriety following his near-fatal accident when he set himself on fire while "free-basing" cocaine. He received an Academy Award nomination as Best Supporting Actor for his role in *Lady Sings the Blues* (1972). He has written comedy material for several television shows, one of which, a Lily TOMLIN special, won him an Emmy Award.

SELECTED FILMS: The Busy Body (1968), Dynamite Chicken (1972), Some Call It Loving (1973), Uptown Saturday Night (1974), Adios, Amigo, The Bingo Long Traveling All-Stars and Motor Kings, Car Wash, Silver Streak (1976), Greased Lightning, Which Way Is Up? (1977), The Wiz, California Suite (1978), The Muppet Movie (1979), Wholly Moses, In God We Trust, Stir Crazy (1980), Bustin' Loose (1981), Some Kind of Hero, The Toy (1982), Brewster's Millions (1985), Critical Condition (1987). ∎

Pryor, Roger (1901–1975), actor. Worked in stock and on Broadway in the mid-1920s before entering films in the early 1930s. He played leads in numerous dramas and light films, many of which were second features. Although he gained some popularity in a string of low-budget crime dramas, he never attained major star status. In the late 1940s he achieved greater success on the radio. He also organized his own dance band at about this time.

SELECTED FILMS: Moonlight and Pretzels (1933), I Like It That Way, Belle of the Nineties, Wake Up and Dream, Lady by Choice (1934), Dinky, The Girl Friend (1935), Sitting on the Moon (1936), She Couldn't Say No, The Officer and the Lady (1941), The Kid Sister, Scared Stiff (1945). ∎

Punsley, Bernard, actor. Appeared in several of the early "BOWERY BOYS" comedies during the late 1930s and early 1940s. He portrayed the "fat kid" in the series and contributed his share of the mayhem. He retired from his screen career to go to medical school and eventually became an obstetrician.

SELECTED FILMS: Little Tough Guy (1938), You're Not So Tough, Give Us Wings (1940), Hit the Road, Mob Town (1941), Tough As They Come, Mug Town (1942). ∎

Purcell, Dick (1908–1944), actor. Worked on stage and in films from the mid-1930s. A handsome, rugged lead player and sometimes supporting actor chiefly in low-budget features, he specialized in action dramas but appeared in light films as well. His career was cut short by a fatal heart attack at age 36.

SELECTED FILMS: Ceiling Zero (1935), Brides Are Like That, Times Square Playboy, The Captain's Kid, Melody for Two, Broadway Playboy (1936), Public Wedding, Navy Blues, Wine, Women and Horses (1937), Accidents Will Happen, Penrod's Double Trouble, Broadway Musketeers (1938), Drunk Driving, Irish Luck, Streets of New York (1939), The Bank Dick (1940), Two in a Taxi (1941), Reveille With Beverly (1943), Timber Queen (1944). ∎

Purdy, Constance (1885–1960), actress. Began her screen career in her middle years. She played character roles chiefly in light films during the 1940s and 1950s.

SELECTED FILMS: White Savage (1943), Air Raid Wardens, Double Up (1943), The Shocking Miss Pilgrim (1947), Blonde Dynamite (1950). ∎

Purviance, Edna (1894–1958), actress. Had no stage or show business experience before Charlie CHAPLIN selected her in 1915 to play his leading lady. An attractive and talented comedienne, she appeared in nearly all his films through the early 1920s. She acted in only two sound films, both directed by and starring Chaplin and in both she had bit parts. A trust established for her by Chaplin paid her an annual salary until her death.

SELECTED FILMS: A Night Out, The Champion, The Tramp, The Bank (1915), Burlesque on Carmen, The Floorwalker, The Pawnshop, The Rink (1916), Easy Street, The Cure, The Immigrant (1917), A Dog's Life, Shoulder Arms (1918), Sunnyside, A Day's Pleasure (1919), The Kid, The Idle Class (1921), Pay Day (1922), The Pilgrim, A Woman of Paris (1923), A Woman of the Sea (1926), Monsieur Verdoux (1947), Limelight (1952). ∎

"Putting Pants on Philip" (1927), MGM. Dir. Clyde Bruckman; Sc. not listed; with Laurel and Hardy, Harvey Clark.

An early work starring LAUREL AND HARDY, this two-reeler, considered by several film historians to be their first "official" film in which they worked as a team, gives a different picture of the boys from what today's audiences would expect. The rapport between Stan and Ollie is missing; Stan portrays a womanizer who chases after every female he sees; and, a small point, Hardy wears a straw hat instead of his usual bowler. The story concerns Ollie's waiting at the dock for his nephew to arrive from Scotland. When the lad (Stan) arrives in his kilts and busies himself chasing young women, Ollie is embarrassed. Later, as they walk home and Stan tries to wrap his arm around Ollie's, the disconcerted Ollie walks ahead of his nephew. One of the more hilarious moments occurs when Stan, having already lost his shorts, has his kilts blow up as he passes over a grating, causing two female passersby to faint. Another is the sequence in which Ollie tries to get Stan measured for a pair of conventional trousers. The film was made earlier than some others already released but was held back until the team gained greater popularity. It may not be a typical Laurel and Hardy film, but it is well constructed and superbly edited.

Q

Quaid, Randy (1950–), actor. Has appeared on Broadway and in television as well as in films. He has played featured roles in dramas and light vehicles. An attractive and talented actor, he has been hampered by several weak scripts.

SELECTED FILMS: *The Last Picture Show* (1971), *What's Up, Doc?* (1972), *Paper Moon* (1973), *The Choirboys* (1977), *Foxes* (1980), *Heartbeeps* (1981), *National Lampoon's Vacation* (1983). ∎

Qualen, John (1899–), actor. Worked in stock and on Broadway before entering films in 1931. A slight, pathetic-looking figure, he often played foreigners, especially Swedes, or ended up as the fall guy in dramas and light films. One of his most memorable roles was that of Muley, the displaced and dazed sharecropper, in *The Grapes of Wrath* (1940). He appeared in over 100 features for various studios during a film career that spanned five decades.

SELECTED FILMS: *Street Scene* (1931), *He Was Her Man* (1934), *The Farmer Takes a Wife* (1935), *Ring Around the Moon* (1936), *Nothing Sacred* (1937), *Joy of Living, Five of a Kind* (1938), *Honeymoon in Bali* (1939), *His Girl Friday, Angels Over Broadway* (1940), *Model Wife* (1941), *Larceny, Inc., Arabian Nights* (1942), *Swing Shift Maisie* (1943), *The Jackpot* (1950), *Hans Christian Andersen* (1952), *A Big Hand for the Little Lady* (1966), *Hail, Hero!* (1969), *Frasier, the Sensuous Lion* (1973). ∎

Quigley, Charles (1906–1964), actor. Worked on stage and in films from the early 1930s. He appeared in dramas, serials, and light films, chiefly as a supporting player during a screen career that spanned three decades.

SELECTED FILMS: *Saddle Buster* (1932), *King of Burlesque* (1935), *Lady From Nowhere, Racing Luck* (1936), *Girls Can Play* (1937), *Mexican Spitfire Out West* (1940), *Playgirl, Footlight Fever* (1941), *A Yank at Eton* (1942), *The National Barn Dance* (1944), *Duffy's Tavern* (1945), *Larceny in Her Heart* (1946), *David Harding, Counterspy* (1950). ∎

Quillan, Eddie (1907–), actor. Worked in vaudeville before entering films in the mid-1920s as part of producer Mack SENNETT'S stock company of comics. After appearing in several comedy shorts, he moved into full-length features in the late 1920s. An attractive and vigorous actor, he played lead and supporting roles in dramas and light films. He is the son of vaudeville and screen actor Joseph F. Quillan.

SELECTED FILMS: *A Love Sundae, Her Actor Friend* (1926), *College Kiddo, Love in a Police Station* (1927), *Show Folks* (1928), *Noisy Neighbors, The Sophomore* (1929), *Girl Crazy* (1932), *Strictly Personal* (1933), *Margie* (1940), *Melody Parade* (1943), *This Is the Life* (1944), *Song of the Sarong* (1945), *Sideshow* (1950), *Promises! Promises!, Move Over, Darling* (1963), *The Ghost and Mr.*

Chicken (1966), Angel in My Pocket (1969), How to Frame a Figg (1971), The Strongest Man in the World (1975). ∎

Quimby, Margaret (–1965), actress. Worked as a supporting player in silent and sound films. She appeared in dramas as well as light films.

SELECTED FILMS: The Teaser (1925), What Happened to Jones, The Whole Town's Talking (1926), New York, The Tired Business Man, The World at Her Feet (1927), Sally of the Scandals (1928), Lucky Boy, Two Men and a Maid (1929), Ladies Love Brutes, Trailing Trouble (1930). ∎

Quine, Richard (1920–), actor, director. As a child, performed in vaudeville and on radio before entering films in the early 1930s. He played juvenile roles through the 1930s and continued in supporting parts until the late 1940s when he switched to directing. He turned out dramas and light films, several of which were quite successful and highly entertaining.

SELECTED FILMS (as director): Leather Gloves (1948), Sunny Side of the Street (1951), Sound Off, Rainbow 'Round My Shoulder (1952), All Ashore (1953), So This Is Paris, My Sister Eileen (1955), The Solid Gold Cadillac (1956), Full of Life, Operation Mad Ball (1957), Bell, Book and Candle (1958), It Happened to Jane (1959), The Notorious Landlady (1962), Paris When It Sizzles, Sex and the Single Girl (1964), How to Murder Your Wife (1965), A Talent for Loving (1969), The Prisoner of Zenda (1978). ∎

Quinn, James "Jimmie" (1885–1940), actor. Began his film career in 1919 in silent films, appearing in lead and supporting roles, chiefly in comedies. He co-starred in a series of racetrack comedy shorts with Billie Sullivan.

SELECTED FILMS: Afraid to Fight, Rags to Riches (1922), Mile-a-Minute

Romeo, Second Hand Love (1923), Red Hot Tires, The Dixie Handicap, Pretty Ladies, The Wife Who Wasn't Wanted, Soft Shoes (1925), The Imposter (1926), Ginsberg the Great (1928), Come and Get It (1929), Hold Everything (1930), I Hate Women (1934), The Gilded Lily (1935). ∎

Quirk, Billy (1881–1926), actor. Worked in early silent comedy shorts and dramas for various studios, including BIOGRAPH for D. W. Griffith, Solax, IMP, and Vitagraph. During his stay at Biograph, he appeared as a supporting player in Mary PICKFORD'S films and was featured in a series of comedies as a character called Muggsy. Often portraying a lighthearted and charming suitor, he starred in a series of one-reelers for Vitagraph from 1914 to 1916.

But his success in films was short-lived; his comedy style relied heavily on situation, not character. Unlike many of his contemporaries, he was unable to develop a distinctive style or character of his own. His unsuccessful attempt to recapture his former glory as a top film comic came in 1921. Under contract to Reelcraft, an independent company, he appeared in his last comedy series.

SELECTED FILMS: The Son's Return, A Sound Sleeper, They Would Elope, His Wife's Visitor (1909), The Woman From Mellon's, A Rich Revenge, The Two Brothers, Muggsy's First Sweetheart (1910), Canned Harmony, Hubby Does the Washing (1912), Billy Fools Dad, Billy's Troubles (1913), In Bridal Attire, Father's Timepiece, The Egyptian Mummy (1914), Billy's Wager, Billy, the Bear Tamer (1915), At the Stage Door (1921), My Old Kentucky Home (1922), Success, Salomy Jane, Broadway Broke (1923), The Dixie Handicap (1925). ∎

Quirt, Sergeant. Fictional World War I soldier based on the character from the Broadway play *What Price Glory?* by Maxwell Anderson and Laurence Stallings. The fast-talking Quirt, played by

Edmund LOWE, and the slow-witted Flagg (Victor McLAGLEN), two feuding buddies in the 1926 film version of the drama, continued their popular brawling comedy in *The Cockeyed World* (1929), *Women of All Nations* (1931), and *Hot Pepper* (1933).

R

Rackin, Martin (1918–1976), screen-writer. Worked as a reporter and feature writer before switching careers in the early 1940s when he decided to try screenwriting. He turned out dramas and comedies, alone and in collaboration, featuring some of the leading comics of the period, including LAUREL AND HARDY and MARTIN AND LEWIS. During the 1950s he began producing films.

SELECTED FILMS: *Air Raid Wardens (1943), Riffraff (1947), A Dangerous Profession (1949), Sailor Beware (1951), The Stooge, Loan Shark (1952), The Clown (1953), North to Alaska (1960).* ∎

Radner, Gilda, actress. Appeared on Broadway and in television before entering films in the early 1980s. An offbeat comedienne, she is one of the graduates of the famous television show, "Saturday Night Live." Her material is often sexually oriented.

SELECTED FILMS: *Gilda Live, First Family (1980), Hanky Panky, It Came From Hollywood (1982), The Woman in Red (1984), Movers & Shakers (1985).* ∎

Ragland, Rags (1905–1946), actor. Former boxer and burlesque performer. Born John Lee Morgan Beauregard Ragland, he came to Hollywood in 1941 and portrayed comedy character roles through the 1940s. He appeared in more than 20 films, the vast majority of which were comedies. He worked with comic Red SKELTON in the "Whistling" comedy series and with ABBOTT AND COSTELLO.

SELECTED FILMS: *Ringside Maisie, Whistling in the Dark (1941), Maisie Gets Her Man, Whistling in Dixie, Born to Sing, Panama Hattie (1942), Du Barry Was a Lady, Girl Crazy, Whistling in Brooklyn (1943), Meet the People, The Canterville Ghost (1944), Abbott and Costello in Hollywood, Her Highness and the Bellboy (1945), The Hoodlum Saint (1946).* ∎

Ralph, Jessie (1864–1944), actress. Worked on Broadway before entering films in the early 1920s, late in her career. A versatile, dark-haired character player, she appeared in silent and sound dramas and comedies until the early 1940s. She specialized in matronly roles, playing genial grandmothers, maids, and governesses with dignity.

SELECTED FILMS: *Such a Little Queen (1921), Elmer the Great, Cocktail Hour (1933), One Night of Love, We Live Again (1934), The Unguarded Hour, Walking on Air, After the Thin Man (1936), Double Wedding (1937), Love Is a Headache (1938), The Blue Bird, The Bank Dick (1940), They Met in Bombay (1941).* ∎

Ralston, Esther (1902–), actress. Appeared in vaudeville while still a child before entering films in 1916. A lovely blonde, she soon rose to stardom, gaining wide popularity during the 1920s. She starred in dramas and light films, continuing to appear in features into the early 1940s.

SELECTED FILMS: *Phantom Fortunes (1916), Blinky, The Wild Party (1923), The Marriage Circle (1924), Peter Pan, The Goose Hangs High, The Lucky Devil, A Kiss for Cinderella (1925), The Quarterback (1926), Love and Learn, Half a Bride (1928), Mr. Dynamite, Ladies Crave Excitement (1935), As Good As Married (1937), Tin Pan Alley (1940), San Francisco Docks (1941).* ■

Ralston, Jobyna (1902–1967), actress. Worked as a chorus girl before making her film debut in 1921. An attractive ingenue, she co-starred in several of Harold LLOYD'S comedies during the silent era. She also appeared in other silents.

SELECTED FILMS: *The Call of Home, The Three Must-Get-Theres (1922), Why Worry? (1923), Girl Shy, Hot Water (1924), The Freshman (1925), Sweet Daddies, Gigolo (1926), The Kid Brother, Special Delivery, A Racing Romeo (1927), The Big Hop, The Toilers (1928), The College Coquette (1929), Sheer Luck (1931).* ■

Rambeau, Marjorie (1889–1970), actress. Appeared on stage before entering early silent films. A lovely young actress during the first half of her film career, she quickly developed into a versatile character player during the sound era in which she portrayed low- and high-brow matrons in dramas and light films. She co-starred with Wallace BEERY in several comedies.

SELECTED FILMS: *The Dazzling Miss Davison (1916), Syncopating Sue (1926), Min and Bill (1930), Strangers May Kiss, Leftover Ladies (1931), Strictly Personal (1933), Palooka, A Modern Hero, Grand Canary (1934), Merrily We Live (1938), Twenty-Mule Team, Tugboat Annie Sails Again (1940), Tobacco Road (1941), Oh! What a Night! (1944), Forever Female (1954), Man of a Thousand Faces (1957).* ■

Ramis, Harold, actor, writer. Has worked as a comic actor in light films beginning in the 1980s. He has also collaborated on screenplays for film comedies and appeared with other screen comics, including Bill MURRAY and Dan AYKROYD.

SELECTED FILMS: *Stripes (1981), Ghostbusters (1984).* ■

Rand, John (1872–1940), actor. Worked in early silent films, especially as a supporting player in comedy shorts starring Charlie CHAPLIN. He portrayed various characters, including bandleaders, shop assistants, waiters, male nurses, and masseurs. Along with cameraman Roland Totheroh, female lead Edna PURVIANCE, and other supporting comics such as Leo WHITE, he became part of Chaplin's permanent stock company.

SELECTED FILMS: *The Bank, Shanghaied, A Night in the Show (1915), Carmen, Police!, The Fireman, The Vagabond, The Count, The Pawnshop, Behind the Screen, The Rink (1916), The Cure, The Immigrant, The Adventurer (1917), The Idle Class (1921), Pay Day (1922), The Circus (1928).* ■

Rand, Sally (1903–1979), actress, dancer. Had no previous training in show business before entering Hollywood silent films in the mid-1920s. She appeared in major roles in several light features but became one of the many victims of the sound revolution. A talented, attractive, and well-proportioned performer, she achieved notoriety for her "obscene" live performance at the Chicago World's Fair in the early 1930s. Once again she was in demand.

SELECTED FILMS: *The Dressmaker From Paris, The Texas Bearcat (1925), Bachelor Brides, Gigolo, Man Bait (1926), Galloping Fury, Getting Gertie's Garter, His Dog (1927), A Girl in Every Port, Golf Widows (1928), Bolero (1934).* ■

Randall, Tony (1920–), actor. Appeared on stage and in television before making his film debut in 1957. A slender, animated actor with a melancholy expression, he is an adept comic who often portrays businessmen, officials, or friends of male leads. Born Leonard Rosenberg, he found his perfect role as Felix in television's "The Odd Couple."

In *Lover Come Back* (1961) he played the president of an advertising agency who bemoans his lot: "Wealthy people are hated and resented. Look what's written on the Statue of Liberty. Does it say 'send me your rich'? No, it says 'Send me your poor.' We're not even welcome in our own country."

SELECTED FILMS: *Oh, Men! Oh, Women!, Will Success Spoil Rock Hunter?* (1957), *The Mating Game, Pillow Talk* (1959), *Let's Make Love* (1960), *Boys' Night Out* (1962), *Island of Love* (1963), *The Seven Faces of Dr. Lao, Send Me No Flowers* (1964), *Hello, Down There* (1969), *Foolin' Around, Scavenger Hunt* (1979), *The King of Comedy* (1983). ∎

Randolph, Isabel (1890–1973), actress. Worked on stage, on Broadway, on radio, and in television. In her middle years when she entered films, she played matrons, including pillars of society, in several light films. She also appeared in westerns starring Roy Rogers and Gene Autry.

SELECTED FILMS: *On Their Own, Yesterday's Heroes* (1940), *Look Who's Laughing* (1941), *Jamboree* (1944). ∎

Randolph, Jane (1919–), actress. Appeared on stage before entering films in 1941. Born Jane Roerner, she played leads and supporting roles in routine dramas and light films through the 1940s. She appeared in several entries of the "Falcon" detective series.

SELECTED FILMS: *Manpower* (1941), *The Male Animal* (1942), *In the Meantime, Darling* (1944), *A Sporting Chance* (1945), *Abbott and Costello Meet Frankenstein* (1948). ∎

Raphaelson, Samson (1896–1983), screenwriter, playwright. Worked as a reporter and dabbled in advertising before turning to screenwriting. He turned out several lively scripts, alone and in collaboration, especially during the 1930s. Some of his best screenplays, laced with his sophisticated dialogue, were those that Ernst LUBITSCH directed. He became Lubitsch's favorite writing partner. Several of his Broadway plays were turned into films, including *The Jazz Singer*, which was adapted for the screen three times, the first of which made film history as the first talking feature.

SELECTED FILMS: *Boudoir Diplomat* (1930), *The Magnificent Lie, The Smiling Lieutenant* (1931), *One Hour With You, Trouble in Paradise* (1932), *The Merry Widow, Servants' Entrance* (1934), *Dressed to Thrill, Ladies Love Danger, Runaway Queen* (1935), *Heaven Can Wait* (1943), *The Harvey Girls* (1946), *That Lady in Ermine* (1948), *In the Good Old Summertime* (1949), *Main Street to Broadway* (1953). ∎

Ratoff, Gregory (1897–1960), actor, director. Appeared on stage in his native Russia and in the United States before entering Hollywood films during the early sound era. He often portrayed foreign characters in dramas and light films. By the mid-1930s be began to direct, receiving some critical acclaim.

In *Once in a Lifetime* he played a movie mogul with a thick accent. A group of ex-vaudevillians with a scheme to open an elocution school offer to help his silent stars make the transition to sound. "Of course we can't get them to talk as well as you—" one admits with a hint of obsequiousness. "Vell," Ratoff interjects in his best foreign accent, "I don' expeck miracles."

SELECTED FILMS (*as actor*): *Symphony of Six Million, Once in a Lifetime* (1932), *Professional Sweetheart, I'm No*

Angel, Sitting Pretty (1933), *Remember Last Night?* (1935), *Sing, Baby, Sing* (1936), *Seventh Heaven, Top of the Town* (1937), *Sally, Irene and Mary* (1938), *All About Eve* (1950), *O. Henry's Full House* (1952), *Once More, With Feeling* (1960), *The Big Gamble* (1961). ▪

SELECTED FILMS (as director): *Wife, Husband and Friend, Rose of Washington Square, Day-Time Wife* (1939), *Public Deb No. 1* (1940), *The Men in Her Life* (1941), *Two Yanks in Trinidad, Footlight Serenade* (1942), *Something to Shout About, The Heat's On* (1943), *Irish Eyes Are Smiling* (1944), *Where Do We Go From Here?* (1945), *Do You Love Me?* (1946), *Taxi* (1953), *Oscar Wilde* (1960). ▪

Raye, Martha (1916–), actress, comedienne. Worked as a child performer in her parents' vaudeville act and as a band vocalist while in her teen years before entering films in the mid-1930s. A lively, rubber-mouthed entertainer, she added spark to numerous, otherwise routine, light films. She usually portrayed supporting characters or comic sidekicks. One of her more memorable parts was that of an uncooperative widow victim of Charlie CHAPLIN'S *Monsieur Verdoux* (1947). After her studio did not renew her contract, she switched to television, first as a guest on numerous shows and finally as star of her own series. She worked with some of the leading comics of the period, including, among others, Jack BENNY, OLSEN AND JOHNSON, and Jimmy DURANTE.

SELECTED FILMS: *Rhythm on the Range, Hideaway Girl, College Holiday* (1936), *Waikiki Wedding, Mountain Music, Artists and Models, Double or Nothing* (1937), *Give Me a Sailor, College Swing, Tropic Holiday* (1938), *Never Say Die* (1939), *The Farmer's Daughter, The Boys From Syracuse* (1940), *Navy Blues, Keep 'Em Flying, Hellzapoppin* (1941), *Four Jills in a Jeep, Pin Up Girl* (1944), *Jumbo* (1962), *Concorde* (1979). ▪

Raymond, Gene (1908–), actor. Worked in stock at age five, on Broadway at fifteen, and in films in the early 1930s at age twenty-three. A handsome blonde, blue-eyed lead and supporting player, he captured the hearts of his female audiences. His personal tours to different cities during the 1930s almost invariably brought out large crowds of young women. He appeared in numerous light films during the 1930s and 1940s, but never achieved major stardom.

SELECTED FILMS: *Personal Maid* (1931), *If I Had a Million* (1932), *Ex-Lady, Flying Down to Rio* (1933), *Coming-Out Party, Transatlantic Merry-Go-Round* (1934), *Behold My Wife, Hooray for Love* (1935), *Love on a Bet, The Bride Walks Out* (1936), *That Girl From Paris, She's Got Everything* (1937), *Mr. and Mrs. Smith* (1941), *Hit the Deck* (1955), *I'd Rather Be Rich* (1964). ▪

Reagan, Ronald (1911–), actor, politician, U. S. President. Worked on radio before entering films in the late 1930s. He appeared in dozens of routine dramas and light films chiefly for Warner Brothers. After 20 lackluster years in Hollywood he turned to television, which boosted his sagging career. He entered politics in California and served as governor for eight years. After gaining national attention as a conservative and a competent administrator, he won the presidency of the United States in 1980. His First Lady is actress Nancy Davis. His critics have rarely permitted him to live down his role in *Bedtime for Bonzo*. He was president of the Screen Actors Guild from 1947 to 1952.

Although many of the characters he portrayed on the screen were quite stolid, he managed to deliver some humorous lines in the war drama *Desperate Journey* (1942). He portrayed a downed American pilot behind German lines. He and other members of the crew overpower several Nazi soldiers and begin to don the enemy's uniforms. Reagan, however, has trouble removing a soldier's trousers. "I've never seen a man so attached to his uniform," he quips.

SELECTED FILMS: Love Is in the Air (1937), Sergeant Murphy, Accidents Will Happen, Cowboy From Brooklyn, Brother Rat, Going Places (1938), Naughty but Nice (1939), Brother Rat and a Baby, An Angel From Texas, Tugboat Annie Sails Again (1940), Million Dollar Baby (1941), This Is the Army (1943), The Voice of the Turtle (1947), The Girl From Jones Beach (1949), Bedtime for Bonzo (1951), She's Working Her Way Through College (1952), The Killers (1964). ■

Redford, Robert (1937–), actor. Appeared on stage and in television before turning his talents to Hollywood films. A handsome figure with blonde hair and blue eyes, he rapidly gained popularity with movie audiences and catapulted to stardom. He has starred in dramas and light films, often as a reticent personality playing opposite more dynamic characters. However, his strong physical screen presence keeps such characters from completely dominating each scene. He has received deserved critical acclaim for some of his dramatic work on screen, especially in The Candidate and as the loner of the title in Jeremiah Johnson (both 1972), and has won an Oscar nomination for his role in The Sting. He has occasionally directed.

In Butch Cassidy and the Sundance Kid he played the title role of the outlaw Sundance, who is questioned by a suspicious player during a poker game. "You haven't lost a hand since you got the deal," the man says. "What's the secret of your success?" "Prayer," Redford replies.

SELECTED FILMS: War Hunt (1962), Situation Hopeless—But Not Serious (1965), Barefoot in the Park (1967), Butch Cassidy and the Sundance Kid (1969), Little Fauss and Big Halsy (1970), The Hot Rock (1972), The Sting (1973), The Electric Horseman (1979), Legal Eagles (1986). ■

Reed, Luther (1888–1961), screenwriter, director. Worked on newspapers before turning his attentions to writing for Hollywood films in 1916. By the mid-1920s he was directing for Paramount. When sound was introduced, he turned out several competent vehicles, but his career soon declined. His comedic skills are best represented in his screenplays.

SELECTED FILMS (as screenwriter): Let's Be Fashionable (1920), Beau Revel, Enchantment, Get-Rich-Quick Wallingford (1921), Beauty's Worth, When Knighthood Was in Flower (1922), Adam and Eva, Little Old New York (1923), The Great White Way, Yolanda (1924), Lovers in Quarantine, Womanhandled (1925), Let's Get Married, Kid Boots (1926), The Sweetheart of Sigma Chi (1933). ■

Reed, Theodore (1887–1959), director. Worked as a film editor from 1918, chiefly for Douglas FAIRBANKS, before turning his attention to directing. He turned out his first directorial effort for Fairbanks in the early 1920s and did other work for the swashbuckler. He returned to directing during the sound period, in the mid-1930s. His films were conventional but pleasant vehicles. He turned out the first "Henry Aldrich" film.

SELECTED FILMS: The Nut (1921), Lady Be Careful (1936), Double or Nothing (1937), Tropic Holiday (1938), I'm From Missouri, What a Life! (1939), Those Were the Days (1940), Life With Henry, Her First Beau (1941). ■

Reicher, Frank (1875–1965), actor. Began his prolific Hollywood career as a silent film director before switching to acting in the early 1920s. A serious-looking character player with a high forehead and a small grey mustache, he appeared in numerous dramas and light films in a variety of roles ranging from victims to authoritative figures. He portrayed the captain of the vessel which travels to Skull Island in the original *King Kong* film of 1933.

SELECTED FILMS: *Behind Masks* (1921), *Her Man o' War* (1926), *His Captive Woman* (1929), *Hi, Nellie!, Let's Talk It Over* (1934), *Kind Lady* (1935), *Old Hutch* (1936), *Laughing at Trouble, The Great O'Malley, Fit for a King* (1937), *Torchy Gets Her Man* (1939), *Father Takes a Wife* (1941), *To Be or Not to Be, I Married an Angel* (1942), *Scattergood's Ghost* (1944), *The Secret Life of Walter Mitty* (1947), *The Lady and the Bandit* (1951). ∎

Reiner, Carl (1922–), actor, comic, writer, director. Appeared on stage and in television before entering films in the 1960s in many capacities. He worked as a comedy writer for Sid CAESAR'S popular television show, remaining with the show for nine years. He has teamed with comedy writer Mel BROOKS in several successful humorous recordings. His comedy material is uneven, ranging from hilarious to unfunny to irreverent. His son, Rob Reiner, has gained fame in the popular television show, "All in the Family," and as a film director. His autobiographical novel, *Enter Laughing* (1958), was adapted to the screen in 1967.

SELECTED FILMS (as actor): *Happy Anniversary* (1959), *The Gazebo* (1960), *Gidget Goes Hawaiian* (1961), *The Thrill of It All, It's a Mad, Mad, Mad, Mad World* (1963), *The Russians Are Coming, the Russians Are Coming* (1966), *A Guide for the Married Man* (1967), *The Comic, Generation* (1969), *Oh, God!* (1977), *The End* (1978), *Dead Men Don't Wear Plaid* (1982). ∎

SELECTED FILMS (as director): *Enter Laughing* (1967), *The Comic* (1969), *Where's Poppa?* (1970), *Oh, God!* (1977), *The Jerk* (1979), *Dead Men Don't Wear Plaid* (1982). ∎

Reinhold, Judge (1957–), actor. Worked in television before entering films in the late 1970s in supporting and lead roles. A tall, good-looking, brown-haired actor, reminiscent of the 1940s star Van JOHNSON, he has moved up rapidly in the mid-1980s as a major film personality. He usually plays bumbling but innocent characters and has appeared in political satires, romantic comedies, and action comedies. Most of his roles thus far have been in light films. His first leading role came in 1986 in *Head Office.*

In *Beverly Hills Cop* he played a young detective who, with his partner, is pinned down by bursts of gunfire from a gang of smugglers. "You remember *Butch Cassidy and the Sundance Kid* when Redford and Newman are surrounded by the Bolivian army?" he says excitedly to his nervous partner.

SELECTED FILMS: *Running Scared* (1979), *Stripes* (1981), *Fast Times at Ridgemont High* (1982), *Beverly Hills Cop* (1984), *Head Office, Off Beat, Ruthless People* (1986). ∎

Reisner, Charles F. "Chuck" (1887–1962), actor, director, screenwriter. Appeared in vaudeville and on stage before settling in Hollywood during the early silent period. He contributed to early comedies in different capacities. He participated as a comic in several shorts, was assistant director for some of Charlie CHAPLIN'S films, and wrote screenplays between assignments. By the mid-1920s he was an established director and, for the next 25 years, concentrated on comedy. He worked with some of the foremost comics of the period, including, among others, Buster KEATON, W. C. FIELDS, the MARX BROTHERS, and ABBOTT AND COSTELLO.

SELECTED FILMS: *The Man on the Box* (1925), *Oh, What a Nurse!, The Better 'Ole* (1926), *The Missing Link* (1927), *Steamboat Bill, Jr.* (1928), *Noisy Neighbors* (1929), *Caught Short* (1930), *Stepping Out, Flying High* (1931), *The Chief* (1933), *The Show-Off* (1934), *It's in the Air* (1935), *The Big Store* (1941), *This Time for Keeps* (1942), *Harrigan's Kid* (1943), *Lost in a Harem* (1944), *The Traveling Saleswoman* (1950). ∎

Reitman, Ivan (1947–), director, producer. Produced several horror exploitation films before turning to directing comedies. With a blend of sarcasm and sweetness, his heroes are different from those created by his contemporaries; he avoids main characters who are weak, neurotic, or born to lose. This approach was used more effectively by Douglas FAIRBANKS in his silent comedies that emphasized the optimistic, buoyant American. Although Reitman's heroes may be unsettling to those in the audience more accustomed to the conventional comic hero who is cowardly and klutzy, his characters offer some freshness and originality.

SELECTED FILMS: Meatballs, Stripes (1979), Ghostbusters (1984), Legal Eagles (1986). ∎

Burt Reynolds (right) and Dom De Luise

Reynolds, Burt (1936–), actor. Appeared in television and on stage before showing up in minor film roles in the early 1960s. He gained a good deal of recognition in 1972 by having the dubious distinction of being the first male to appear nude in the two-page centerfold of *Cosmopolitan* magazine. His good looks, charm, and sense of humor, combined with the above notoriety, have endeared him to female audiences who view him as a sex symbol, while his "tough guy" roles made him popular with males.

He has, at times, surprised his critics by giving poignant character portrayals

in several dramas (*Deliverance,* 1972, etc.). Although he has complained that the studios see him only as a light and comic actor, he accepts this type of role with regularity.

In *Smokey and the Bandit* runaway bride Sally Field asks bootlegger Reynolds: "Don't you ever take your hat off?" "I take my hat off for one thing and for one thing only," he replies.

SELECTED FILMS: Angel Baby (1961), Sam Whiskey (1969), Skullduggery (1970), Fuzz, Everything You Always Wanted to Know About Sex but Were Afraid to Ask (1972), The Man Who Loved Cat Dancing (1973), The Longest Yard (1974), Lucky Lady, Hustle (1975), Silent Movie, Gator, Nickelodeon (1976), Smokey and the Bandit, Semi-Tough (1977), The End (1978), Starting Over (1979), The Cannonball Run, Paternity (1981), Best Friends (1982), Stroker Ace, The Man Who Loved Women (1983), City Heat (1984). ∎

Reynolds, Craig (1907–1949), actor. Worked in stock and vaudeville before settling in Hollywood, chiefly as a supporting player in low-budget films. Suave and handsome with a neat mustache, he played a few romantic leads in dramas and light films. His screen career ended abruptly when he was killed in a car accident at age 42.

SELECTED FILMS: Stage Struck, Here Comes Carter! (1936), Penrod and Sam (1937), The Fatal Hour (1940), Divorce (1945), Queen of Burlesque (1946). ∎

Reynolds, Debbie (1932–), actress. Came to films in 1948 after winning a local beauty contest. Besides good looks, she brought charm and her buoyant personality to numerous light films, making her one of the major screen stars of the 1950s and 1960s. She excelled in musicals as well as in romantic comedies. In the 1970s, as her popularity started to decline, she scored a hit on Broadway. In

The Pleasure of His Company (1961) she played an ingenue who describes her fiance (Tab Hunter) to her debonair father (Fred Astaire): "He's very progressive. He has all sorts of ideas about artificial insemination and all that sort of thing. He breeds all over the world."

SELECTED FILMS: *June Bride* (1948), *The Daughter of Rosie O'Grady, Three Little Words* (1950), *Singin' in the Rain, Skirts Ahoy!* (1952), *I Love Melvin, The Affairs of Dobie Gillis* (1953), *Susan Slept Here* (1954), *The Tender Trap* (1955), *Bundle of Joy* (1956), *Tammy and the Bachelor* (1957), *The Mating Game* (1959), *The Rat Race* (1960), *The Second Time Around* (1962), *My Six Loves* (1963), *Divorce, American Style* (1967), *How Sweet It Is* (1968), *That's Entertainment* (1974). ∎

Reynolds, Lynn, director. Entered films in the 1910s and was soon turning out dramas and light films, many of which were westerns starring popular cowboy actor Hoot GIBSON.

SELECTED FILMS: *It Happened in Honolulu, Secret of the Swamp* (1916), *Fast Company* (1918), *Chip of the Flying U, The Texas Streak* (1926), *Hey! Hey! Cowboy* (1927). ∎

Reynolds, Marjorie (1921–), actress. Appeared in silent films as a child actress and during the early 1930s played minor roles. By the 1940s she played leading lady roles with such stars as Bing CROSBY. An attractive blonde, she worked in numerous B westerns and action features as well as light films. She worked with several top comics of the period, including Jack OAKIE, Bob HOPE and ABBOTT AND COSTELLO. She may be best remembered as the wife of the William BENDIX character in the 1950s television comedy series "The Life of Riley."

SELECTED FILMS: *The Broken Wing* (1923), *College Humor, Wine, Women and Song* (1933), *Collegiate, College Holiday* (1936), *Champagne Waltz* (1937),

Chasing Trouble (1940), *Tillie the Toiler, Top Sergeant Mulligan, Dude Cowboy* (1941), *Holiday Inn* (1942), *Dixie* (1943), *Up in Mabel's Room, Three Is a Family* (1944), *Bring On the Girls, Duffy's Tavern* (1945), *Meet Me on Broadway, The Time of Their Lives, Monsieur Beaucaire* (1946), *No Holds Barred* (1952), *The Silent Witness* (1962). ∎

Rhodes, Billie, actress. Appeared as a singer on stage before entering early silent films in 1911. By 1917 she was starring in a series of one-reel comedies released by Mutual studios. She made several comedy shorts for producer Al CHRISTIE before moving on to silent features. She abandoned her screen career in the mid-1920s.

SELECTED FILMS: *Perils of the Sea* (1913), *Almost a King, And the Best Man Won, Their Friend the Burglar, Father's Helping Hand* (1915), *Her Hero, Some Nurse, A Two-Cylinder Courtship* (1917), *Beware of Blondes* (1918), *His Pajama Girl, The Star Reporter* (1922), *Leave It to Gerry, Fires of Youth* (1924). ∎

Rhodes, Erik (1906–), actor. Worked on radio and on stage before bringing his comedy character roles to Hollywood films in the early 1930s. He appeared in numerous light musicals and comedies during the decade, sometimes affecting a foreign accent as an unsuccessful Italian suitor. By the end of the 1930s he returned to the stage.

In *The Gay Divorcee* he portrayed Tonetti, an Italian who is hired as a co-respondent by divorce lawyer Edward Everett HORTON, who warns him not to try anything. "With me, strictly business," he promises. "My slogan: Your wife is safe with Tonetti—he prefers spaghetti."

SELECTED FILMS: *The Gay Divorcee* (1934), *A Night at the Ritz, Nitwits, Old Man Rhythm, Top Hat* (1935), *Chatterbox, Second Wife* (1936), *Woman Chases Man, Music for Madame, Fight for Your Lady, Beg, Borrow or Steal*

(1937), Meet the Girls, Say It in French (1938), On Your Toes (1939). ■

Riano, Renie (–1971), actress. Appeared on stage and as a character player in films during the 1940s and 1950s. Her major claim to fame was as Maggie, the social-climbing, roller-pin-swinging wife of Jiggs in the "JIGGS AND MAGGIE" comedy series based on George McManus' celebrated comic strip, "Bringing Up Father." Her husband was played by veteran vaudeville performer Joe YULE, who in real life was Mickey ROONEY'S father. She switched to television roles in the 1950s and 1960s.

SELECTED FILMS: Bringing Up Father (1946), Jiggs and Maggie in Court, Jiggs and Maggie in Society (1948), Jiggs and Maggie in Jackpot Jitters (1949), Jiggs and Maggie Out West (1950). ■

Rice, Florence (1907–1974), actress. Appeared on Broadway before going into films in the early 1930s. She played female leads chiefly in routine dramas and light films through the 1940s.

SELECTED FILMS: Fugitive Lady (1934), Best Man Wins (1935), Pride of the Marines (1936), Married Before Breakfast, Double Wedding, Beg, Borrow or Steal (1937), Paradise for Three, Vacation From Love, Sweethearts (1938), Four Girls in White, At the Circus (1939), Father Takes a Wife, Blonde From Singapore (1941), Tramp, Tramp, Tramp (1942), The Ghost and the Guest (1943). ■

Rice, Jack (1893–1968), actor. Began his screen career as a comic character player in the 1930s. Often portraying annoying types, he worked with comedian Edgar KENNEDY in his series of comedy shorts and appeared in several "BLONDIE" entries.

SELECTED FILMS: Blondie's Big Moment (1947), Blondie's Secret (1948). ■

Rich, Irene (1891–), actress. Played leads chiefly in Hollywood dramas after appearing in a bit role in 1918. She was often cast as worldly females through the 1920s. During the early sound period she played in light films, several of which starred Will ROGERS. Following her retirement from films, she gained great popularity on radio and appeared occasionally on Broadway. In the late 1930s she returned to films in matronly roles.

SELECTED FILMS: Stella Maris (1918), Jes' Call Me Jim (1920), Boys Will Be Boys (1921), Don't Tell the Wife, Dearie (1927), They Had to See Paris (1929), So This Is London, On Your Back (1930), Strangers May Kiss, Five and Ten, The Mad Parade (1931), Down to Earth, Her Mad Night (1932), That Certain Age (1938), Keeping Company (1941), Joan of Arc (1948). ■

Richard, Viola, actress. Appeared as a supporting player in late silent comedy shorts, especially those produced by Hal ROACH. She worked with LAUREL AND HARDY in several of their shorts.

SELECTED FILMS: Sailors Beware!, Do Detectives Think?, Flying Elephants (1927), Should Married Men Go Home? (1928). ■

Richards, Addison (1887–1964), actor. Worked on the stage before coming to Hollywood in the early 1930s. A reliable character actor, he appeared in more than 150 dramas and light films, often as an honest professional. He portrayed Polly's father in several of the ANDY HARDY comedies.

SELECTED FILMS: Riot Squad (1933), Let's Be Ritzy (1934), Dinky, Freckles (1935), Colleen (1936), Ready, Willing and Able (1937), Accidents Will Happen (1938), Slightly Honorable, Andy Hardy Gets Spring Fever (1939), My Little Chickadee (1940), Our Wife (1941), My Favorite Wife (1942), Always a Bridesmaid (1943), Men in Her Diary (1945), Henry the Rainmaker (1949), High Society (1955), For Those Who Think Young (1964). ■

Rickles, Don (1926–), actor, comedian. Appeared in nightclubs and television in the 1950s before entering films in the latter part of the same decade. On stage he has become famous as the master of insult humor. Usually featured as a comic character actor, the bald, moon-faced comedian has added humor to the films in which he appeared. But his screen career has not blossomed. He appears regularly as a guest in television and as a stand-up comic in swank nightclubs.

SELECTED FILMS: Run Silent Run Deep (1958), The Rabbit Trap (1959), The Rat Race (1960), Enter Laughing (1967), The Money Jungle (1968), Where It's At (1969), Kelly's Heroes (1970). ∎

Ridgely, John (1909–1968), actor. Worked on stage before joining Warner Brothers studios in the late 1930s as a supporting player. Tall and dark-haired, he worked with Glenda FARRELL in her popular "TORCHY BLANE" comedy series. He appeared in scores of dramas and light films in his 15-year screen career that ended when he decided to return to the stage and to switch to television. He died of a heart attack at age 58.

SELECTED FILMS: Larger Than Life (1937), Torchy Gets Her Man (1938), The Kid From Kokomo, Naughty but Nice (1939), Father Is a Prince, No Time for Comedy (1940), The Man Who Came to Dinner (1941), Arsenic and Old Lace (1943), Two Guys From Milwaukee (1946), Trouble Makers (1948), Once More, My Darling (1949), Room for One More, Off Limits (1952). ∎

"Rink, The" (1916), MUT. Dir. Charlie Chaplin; Sc. Charlie Chaplin; with Charlie Chaplin, Edna Purviance, Eric Campbell, Henry Bergman.

"The Rink," a two-reel comedy and one of Chaplin's "golden dozen" made while he was at Mutual studios, displayed his expertise with roller skates. He plays a rather sloppy waiter who is attracted to pretty socialite Edna PURVIANCE. At a skating party for the elite, he protects Edna from a boorish suitor, played by Eric CAMPBELL. In a ballet-like sequence on roller skates, Charlie reduces Campbell to a figure of ridicule. The versatile comic character actor Henry BERGMAN portrays Campbell's "wife" at the rink as well as an irate customer at the restaurant where Charlie is employed. The film has become a popular selection at Chaplin festivals and revivals and is often included in his compilation films. The fast-paced comedy demonstrates his nimbleness and timing as well as his skill on skates and is filled with clever visual gags.

Ripley, Arthur (1895–1961), screenwriter. Worked at various jobs for different studios, including Mack SENNETT'S, during the early silent period. He reached the peak of his Hollywood career as screenwriter during the 1920s. Together with director Harry EDWARDS and GAGMAN Frank CAPRA, he helped to develop the screen image of Harry LANGDON by contributing some especially effective scripts and stories for several of the comic's films. During the sound era he directed a handful of features.

SELECTED FILMS: Life's Darn Funny (1921), A Lady of Quality (1924), The Strong Man (1926), His First Flame, Long Pants, Three's a Crowd (1927), Heart Trouble (1928), Barnum Was Right (1929), Waterfront (1939). ∎

Risdon, Elisabeth (1887–1958), actress. Appeared on stage and screen in her native England before migrating to the United States where she acted on Broadway. She made her Hollywood film debut in the mid-1930s, appearing in more than 100 dramas and light films. A reliable character actress, she often portrayed mothers, grandmothers, and aunts. She played in several of the "MEXICAN SPITFIRE" entries of the popular comedy series.

SELECTED FILMS: Guard That Girl (1935), The King Steps Out, Theodora Goes Wild (1936), Cowboy From Brooklyn (1938), The Great Man Votes, Mexican Spitfire (1939), Honeymoon Deferred (1940), Mr. Dynamite (1941), The Lady Is Willing (1942), Never a Dull Moment (1943), In the Meantime, Darling (1944), Mama Loves Papa (1945), The Egg and I, Life With Father (1947), The Bride Goes Wild (1948), Scaramouche (1952). ∎

Riskin, Robert (1897–1955), screenwriter. Wrote stage plays before migrating to Hollywood as a screenwriter in the early 1930s. He wrote dialogue and adaptations as well as original scripts, chiefly for light films. He was especially adept at social comedy during the Depression years. A populist writer, particularly in his films for Frank CAPRA (*Lady for a Day, Mr. Deeds Goes to Town, Meet John Doe*), he treated with sympathy a wide range of characters, including bankers, criminals, rustics, newspapermen, and Runyonesque guys and dolls.

SELECTED FILMS: Platinum Blonde, Men in Her Life (1931), American Madness, Virtue (1932), Lady for a Day (1933), It Happened One Night, Broadway Bill (1934), The Whole Town's Talking (1935), Mr. Deeds Goes to Town (1936), You Can't Take It With You (1938), Meet John Doe (1941), The Thin Man Goes Home (1944), Riding High (1950), Here Comes the Groom (1951). ∎

Ritchie, Billie (1877–1921), actor. Appeared on stage in his native England and in the United States before entering early silent comedy films in 1914 for American production companies. He had been with Fred KARNO'S troupe, a company of English comic performers that included Charlie CHAPLIN and Stan LAUREL. His screen character, a tramp, was similar to that of Chaplin, and he was labeled, along with others including Billy WEST, as an imitator. Ritchie, under contract to L-KO studios,

continually maintained that he had developed it first on stage. His blossoming screen career ended with his untimely death.

SELECTED FILMS: Love and Surgery, Partners in Crime (1914), Almost a Scandal, A Meeting for Cheating (1915). ∎

Ritter, Thelma (1905–1969), actress. Appeared on stage before migrating to films in 1947. A versatile character player, she received a half-dozen Oscar nominations for her different roles. She frequently played frank, sarcastic servants or friends of the main characters.

In *Pillow Talk* (1959), for example, she played Doris DAY'S maid. Her employer, who is single, parades her lifestyle before Ritter: "I have a good job, a lovely apartment. I go out with very nice men to the best places. What am I missing?" "When you have to ask," Ritter replies, "believe me, you're missing it."

SELECTED FILMS: Miracle on 34th Street (1947), A Letter to Three Wives, Father Was a Fullback (1949), All About Eve, I'll Get By (1950), The Mating Season, The Model and the Marriage Broker (1951), The Farmer Takes a Wife, Pickup on South Street (1953), Rear Window, Daddy Long Legs (1955), A Hole in the Head (1959), The Misfits, The Second Time Around (1961), Move Over, Darling (1963), Boeing Boeing (1965), What's So Bad About Feeling Good? (1968). ∎

Ritz Brothers, The. A popular comedy team of the 1930s and 1940s. Al (1901–1965), Jim (1903–1985), and Harry (1906–1986), who were actually brothers, starred in vaudeville, in nightclubs, and in the theater before entering early sound films. Fox studios put the trio under contract and showcased them in their first feature film, *Sing, Baby, Sing* (1936), a musical comedy. The film was a hit, giving the brothers a good start in their new endeavor. Unfortunately, after their first few films, they were featured in vehicles that had limited budgets, thereby

The Ritz Brothers and Bela Lugosi (second from left)

adversely affecting the final product. The brothers' dancing, clowning, and other old vaudeville routines were generally entertaining, but no one feature rises above its routine production.

Another disadvantage they had to face was the constant comparison to their contemporaries, the MARX BROTHERS. The latter team was more innovative, more skilled, better outfitted by its studios (at first, Paramount, then MGM), and most important of all, funnier. However, the indefatigable Ritz Brothers had a built-in audience from their many years in show business, and their films developed new fans who found the energetic team entertaining. In 1943, after starring in about 14 features and one two-reeler, the team abandoned their screen career.

Their insane, knockabout comedy was fast-paced and their dance routines were highly complicated. In *Hi' Ya Chum*, their next-to-the-last film, they performed a ballet parody that demonstrated their talent for blending song and dance with comedy. Their last feature, *Never a Dull Moment* (1943), probably their best comedy, provides them with a nightclub setting for their talents. They pose as Chicago gangsters working as a song-and-dance act called the "Three Funny Bunnies" and do many of their favorite routines.

They were true headliners in their day, both on stage and on screen, although most critics rarely found them amusing. On the other hand, many of their fellow comics considered their material hilari-

ous and singled out brother Harry as one of the greatest comedians of all time. Their career spanned more than five decades.

SELECTED FILMS: Hotel Anchovy (1934), Sing, Baby, Sing (1936), One in a Million, On the Avenue, You Can't Have Everything, Life Begins at College (1937), The Goldwyn Follies, Kentucky Moonshine, Straight, Place and Show (1938), The Three Musketeers, The Gorilla, Pack Up Your Troubles (1939), Argentine Nights (1940), Behind the Eight-Ball (1942), Hi' Ya Chum, Never a Dull Moment (1943). ■

Rivers, Joan (1935–), comedienne, actress. Has worked as an entertainer in small clubs, in television, and as a comic actress in a handful of films. Her appearances on different television programs, particularly those with host Johnny Carson, have brought her fame and, briefly, her own late night show, while her film roles have been without distinction. A gifted performer specializing in comic put-downs, including her self-deprecating gags, she is at her best in informal situations such as television shows.

SELECTED FILMS: The Swimmer (1968), Rabbit Test (1978), The Muppets Take Manhattan (1984). ■

Roach, Bert (1891–1971), actor. A portly character actor who began his screen career in the early 1920s. He supplied the comic relief for several features from such major studios as MGM, Universal, and Warner Brothers. Appearing in both dramas and light films, he reached the peak of his career in 1927 when he received critical acclaim for his role as the friend of James Murray, who played the lead in *The Crowd*.

SELECTED FILMS: The Millionaire, The Rowdy (1921), The Flirt (1922), Excuse Me (1924), Don't, Smouldering Fires (1925), Money Talks, A Certain Young Man (1926), Wickedness Preferred (1927), Telling the World (1928),

*So Long Letty, The Aviator (1929), Vien-
nese Nights (1931), Goin' to Town, Here
Comes the Band (1935), Mad About Music (1938), Hi Diddle Diddle (1943), The
Perils of Pauline (1947).* ■

Hal Roach (right)

Roach, Hal (1892–), producer, director. Worked at odd jobs before coming to
Hollywood as a minor actor in westerns.
In 1915 he teamed up with Harold
LLOYD, whom he had met at Universal
studios, and produced his first film. He
built his own studio in 1919 where he
turned out numerous silent comedy
shorts, including the "LONESOME
LUKE" series starring his friend Lloyd,
the famous "OUR GANG" comedies, and
many of the LAUREL AND HARDY
shorts.

He was the second largest and most
popular producer of comedies, surpassed only by the king of comedy, Mack
SENNETT. Roach's films differed from
those of his competitor, who concentrated on wild and zany slapstick, developed more individual star comedians,
and presented more unrealistic sight
gags. Roach, on the other hand, focused
on more plausible plots and more structured humor. Eventually, he built up his
own stock company of more than competent comics, including Charlie
CHASE, Snub POLLARD, and Will
ROGERS. He specialized in talented and
creative directors, such as Leo Mc-
CAREY and Fred NEWMEYER. He ventured into feature-length comedies,
while other companies continued to turn

out only two- or three-reelers. More in
tune with the growing sophistication of
movie audiences, he was able to hurdle
the problems of the sound era better than
many of his competitors. In fact, his
studio flourished in the early 1930s
while Sennett's output and popularity
declined.

The sound era proved a creative period for Roach. He introduced such comedy teams as Thelma TODD and ZaSu
PITTS in a series of comedy shorts; he
won two Academy Awards for his shorts,
"The Music Box" (1932) starring Laurel
and Hardy, and "Bored of Education"
(1936), an "Our Gang" entry. By the late
1930s he had stopped producing short
films and made only features. In the
1950s he switched to producing for television.

A pioneer and innovator in film comedy, he was instrumental in introducing
some of the leading funnymen and comedy teams to the public. His feature
films, like *Topper* (1937), have become
minor classics. Above all, he made his
audiences laugh.

*SELECTED FILMS: Just Nuts, Lone-
some Luke (1915), The Flirt (1917), His
Royal Slyness (1919), High and Dizzy
(1920), Our Gang (1922), The White
Sheik (1924), Bad Boy (1925), The Battle
of the Century (1927), Two Tars (1928),
Big Business (1929), Brats (1930), Pardon Us (1931), Pack Up Your Troubles
(1932), Sons of the Desert (1933), Babes
in Toyland (1934), Our Relations (1936),
Way Out West (1937), Merrily We Live,
Swiss Miss (1938), The Housekeeper's
Daughter, Zenobia (1939), Turnabout
(1940), Road Show, Topper Returns
(1941), The Devil With Hitler (1944).* ■

"Road" films. A series of comedies
starring Bing CROSBY, Bob HOPE, and
Dorothy LAMOUR produced during the
1940s and 1950s by Paramount studios.
Each entry followed a similar pattern.
Crosby and Hope played two con men or
vaudeville troupers down on their luck
who compete for the affections of
Lamour—with Hope usually losing out.

Crosby supplied the romance and love songs while Hope provided most of the comedy and some singing. They would get into some type of scrape whereby Bing would volunteer Bob's services as a method of extricating themselves.

The films incorporated various forms of comedy. The usual one-liners abounded. Insults between the boys became a staple. For instance, in *Road to Utopia* Bing worries that Bob's hiccuping will start an avalanche. "Scare me," Hope proposes. "I can't," Crosby returns. "I don't have a mirror." Repartee was omnipresent. In *Road to Rio* Hope is bamboozled into riding a bicycle on a high wire. "We're getting $200 for this," Crosby announces enthusiastically. "Let me hold it," Hope replies. "At least I won't die poor." There are also sight gags, such as a mountain in the background of a scene, causing the boys to pause in reverence and comment that it is their bread and butter (the Paramount logo). They often use "in" jokes—referring to Crosby's brother Bob, etc. There are allusions to contemporary radio shows like "Hobby Lobby" and international figures like Eleanor Roosevelt. The films employed zany humor from time to time—for example, talking camels. Running gags spilled over from one entry into the next. Two examples of such gags were the boys' popular "Patty Cake" routine and Hope's losing Lamour to Crosby. In *Road to Morocco* they plan to rescue Lamour from the hands of an Arab chieftain. "We have to storm the place," Crosby concludes. "You storm," Hope replies, "I'll stay here and drizzle." Finally, their song-and-dance routines are always good for a few laughs.

The Road to Bali was the only entry produced in color. *Road to Hong Kong*, the final entry, was made in England. Some of the films, of course, are funnier than others. Several of their routines are badly dated, but for the most part the Crosby-Hope-Lamour combination remains entertaining and it is not difficult to understand why these performers were so popular.

SELECTED FILMS: *Road to Singapore* (1940), *Road to Zanzibar* (1941), *Road to Morocco* (1942), *Road to Utopia* (1946), *Road to Rio* (1947), *The Road to Bali* (1952), *Road to Hong Kong* (1962). ∎

Robards, Jason (1892–1963), actor. Entered silent films in the early 1920s following a successful stage career. A dark-haired leading man in his early parts, he made a smooth transition to sound films, including dramas, serials, light features, and comedy shorts, as a character actor portraying distinguished and authoritarian types on either side of the law. He was the father of Jason ROBARDS, Jr.

SELECTED FILMS: *The Land of Hope, The Gilded Lily* (1921), *The Cohens and the Kellys* (1926), *Polly of the Movies* (1927), *Some Mother's Boy* (1929), *Crazy That Way* (1930), *Caught Plastered* (1931), *Slightly Married* (1932), *Broadway Bill* (1934), *Sweethearts of the Navy* (1937), *I Love You Again* (1940), *Joan of Ozark* (1942), *The Farmer's Daughter* (1947), *If You Knew Susie* (1948), *Wild in the Country* (1961). ∎

Robards, Jason, Jr. (1922–), actor. Appeared on stage, on radio, and in television before making his film debut in 1959. Chiefly a strong dramatic actor, he has occasionally starred in light films, showing a propensity toward comedy as well. He has won awards for his roles on stage and in films, including the New York Drama Critics Award in 1957 and two Oscars for his roles in *All the President's Men* (1976) and *Julia* (1977). He was the son of stage and screen actor Jason ROBARDS.

In *A Thousand Clowns* he played an anti-establishment dropout who is raising his teenage nephew, Nick. Eventually, social service catches up with Robards. Concerned about the boy's future, one social worker paints a very bleak picture during a home visit. "Who writes your material for you, Charles Dickens?" Robards quips. Later, another social worker, pretty Barbara Harris, falls in love with him and one day surprises him by straightening out his flat. "I've been attacked by the *Ladies' Home Journal*," he comments.

SELECTED FILMS: *The Journey (1959), A Thousand Clowns (1965), A Big Hand for the Little Lady, Any Wednesday (1966), Divorce, American Style (1967), The Night They Raided Minsky's (1968), Fools (1970), The War Between Men and Women (1972), Melvin and Howard (1980), Max Dugan Returns (1983).* ∎

Robbins, Gale (1924–1980), actress. Worked as a model and band vocalist before entering films in the mid-1940s. A red-haired female lead and featured player, she appeared in dramas and light films for two decades and then returned to her singing career.

SELECTED FILMS: *In the Meantime, Darling (1944), Mr. Hex (1946), My Girl Tisa (1948), My Dear Secretary, The Barkleys of Broadway, Oh, You Beautiful Doll (1949), Three Little Words (1950), Strictly Dishonorable (1951), The Belle of New York (1952), Calamity Jane (1953), The Girl in the Red Velvet Swing (1955), Stand Up and Be Counted (1972).* ∎

Roberti, Lyda (1906–1938), actress. Worked as a cafe singer and in the circus in her native Poland and in vaudeville in the United States as well as on Broadway. W. C. FIELDS was impressed with her performance on stage and asked his studio to hire her for his upcoming film, *Million Dollar Legs.* A blonde character actress with a foreign accent, she appeared in fewer than a dozen light films before succumbing to a heart attack at age 32. She co-starred with some of the top comedians of the period, including, among others, W. C. FIELDS, Eddie CANTOR, and Joe E. BROWN.

One of her funniest roles was in the above-mentioned film in which she plays a Mata Hari-type spy. In an attempt to encourage an athlete to do his best during an important event, she turns on her sexual charms, suggestively moving her body. "I done all I can do," she says, then continues after a brief pause, "een publeec."

In *Wide Open Faces* (1938) starring Joe E. Brown she played gangster Alan Baxter's not-too-bright moll. "Why should he be mixed up with a soda jerk?" Baxter wonders out loud about a captured bank robber. "Maybe he was thirsty," she suggests. Later, Baxter decides to pay a visit to the soda jerk's town to find the missing bank money. "Pack all your clothes in the trunk," he says to his girl. "And go out with nothing?" she complains. "It's too cold."

SELECTED FILMS: *Dancers in the Dark, Million Dollar Legs, The Kid From Spain (1932), Three-Cornered Moon (1933), College Rhythm (1934), George White's Scandals, The Big Broadcast of 1936 (1935), Nobody's Baby, Pick a Star (1937), Wide Open Faces (1938).* ∎

Roberts, Beverly (1914–), actress. Worked on stage before appearing in films in the mid-1930s. She played leads in action melodramas and light films, with an emphasis on the latter.

SELECTED FILMS: *The Singing Kid, Sons o' Guns, Hot Money (1936), Her Husband's Secretary, Expensive Husbands, The Perfect Specimen (1937), Tenth Avenue Kid, Flirting With Fate (1938), Main Street Lawyer (1939), Buried Alive (1940).* ∎

Roberts, Doris (1930–), actress. Worked on stage and in television before making her film debut in 1961. A supporting player, she has appeared in dramas and light films. She has worked with such comedy actors as George SEGAL and Walter MATTHAU.

SELECTED FILMS: *Something Wild (1961), No Way to Treat a Lady (1968), A New Leaf, Little Murders, Such Good Friends (1971), Once in Paris . . . , Rabbit Test (1978).* ∎

Roberts, Florence (1860–1940), actress. Appeared as a character player chiefly in the 1930s. Perhaps best remembered as Granny in the "JONES FAMILY" comedy series, she portrayed kindly old matrons in dramas as well as in light films.

SELECTED FILMS: Kept Husbands, Everything's Rosie, Too Many Crooks, Fanny Foley Herself (1931), Melody Cruise, Hoopla (1933), Babes in Toyland (1934), The Nut Farm, Your Uncle Dudley (1935), Every Saturday Night, Educating Father (1936), Off to the Races, Big Business (1937), A Trip to Paris, Safety in Numbers (1938), Young As You Feel (1940). ■

Roberts, Joe, actor. Appeared as a supporting player in silent comedy shorts in the 1920s. He worked in several of Buster KEATON'S early films.

SELECTED FILMS: One Week, The Scarecrow, Convict 13, Neighbors (1920), The Haunted House, Hard Luck, The Goat, The Play House (1921), The Paleface, Cops, The Blacksmith, The Frozen North, The Electric House, Day Dreams (1922), The Love Nest, Three Ages, Our Hospitality (1923). ■

Roberts, Stephen R. (1895–1936), director. Worked as a stunt flyer at fairs and as stuntman in Hollywood before turning his interests to directing films in the early 1920s. He turned out silent comedy shorts and, during the 1930s, full-length romantic comedies and other light features. The bulk of his work was pleasant if routine.

SELECTED FILMS: Sky Bride, Lady and Gent, If I Had a Million (1932), One Sunday Afternoon (1933), The Trumpet Blows, Romance in Manhattan (1934), The Man Who Broke the Bank at Monte Carlo (1935), The Lady Consents, The Ex-Mrs. Bradford (1936). ■

Roberts, Theodore (1861–1928), actor. Appeared on stage before entering early silent films. A versatile character player, sometimes referred to as the "grand old man of the silents," he was featured in various film genres and was often employed in director Cecil B. DeMILLE'S spectacles.

SELECTED FILMS: Uncle Tom (1910), The Ghost Breaker (1914), After Five (1915), Pudd'n Head Wilson (1916), The Little Princess (1917), M'Liss, Such a Little Pirate (1918), Don't Change Your Husband, You're Fired! (1919), Miss Lulu Bett (1921), Our Leading Citizen (1922), Grumpy, Stephen Steps Out, To the Ladies (1923), 40 Winks (1925), The Cat's Pajamas (1926), Noisy Neighbors, Ned McCobb's Daughter (1929). ■

Roberts, Tony (1939–), actor. Worked on stage before making his film debut in 1965. Whether playing leads or supporting roles, he gives strong performances. A tall, attractive figure with an affable personality, he has appeared in several Woody ALLEN films. His greatest success as an actor has been on Broadway.

In Play It Again, Sam he played a friend of the depressed Woody Allen whose wife has left him. Roberts and his wife try to console him and within a short time Woody has an affair with his friend's wife. When Roberts learns of the affair, he wonders: "Why didn't I see it coming? Me, who had the foresight to buy Polaroid at 8 1/2."

SELECTED FILMS: The Beach Girls and the Monster (1965), $1,000,000 Duck, Star Spangled Girl (1971), Play It Again, Sam (1972), Annie Hall (1977), Just Tell Me What You Want (1979), Stardust Memories (1980), A Midsummer Night's Sex Comedy (1982), Key Exchange (1985), Radio Days (1987). ■

Robinson, Dewey (1898–1950), actor. Rough-looking, easily recognizable character actor of the 1930s and 1940s. He appeared in numerous light comedies, including those that starred such popular comics as WHEELER AND WOOLSEY, Mae WEST, the MARX BROTHERS, and MARTIN AND LEWIS. He played bartenders, bouncers, and other tough-looking characters.

SELECTED FILMS: *Notorious but Nice, Diplomaniacs, She Done Him Wrong* (1933), *Goin' to Town* (1935), *Mummy's Boys* (1936), *New Faces of 1937, The Toast of New York* (1937), *Come Live With Me* (1940), *The Big Store* (1941), *Always Together, The Wistful Widow of Wagon Gap* (1947), *My Friend Irma* (1949), *At War With the Army* (1950). ∎

Robinson, Edward G. (1893–1973), actor. Studied law at Columbia before appearing in stock and on Broadway in 1915. Born Emmanuel Goldenberg in Bucharest, he made one minor appearance in a silent film but did not appear steadily on the screen until the early talkies in 1929. Within a few years he emerged as a major film personality of the 1930s. A compelling and dynamic performer, he became famous for his gangster roles while at Warner Brothers, appearing in dozens of crime dramas during the 1930s. By the end of the decade he gained recognition as a proficient dramatic actor, starring in biographies and comedies as well. Off screen he became famous for his rare-book and art collection.

In the late 1940s he was accused of Communist activities, but the House Un-American Activities Committee cleared him of all charges. He was awarded posthumously a special Oscar for his overall achievements in film. His several comedies underscore the range of his acting abilities in a screen career that stretched over five decades and 100 films.

In *Larceny, Inc.* he played a mobster recently released from prison who learns that his slot machines have been smashed by the police. "Why, that's criminal!" he rages. "Not the machines, but the wanton destruction of private property!" Later in the film he buys a luggage store next to a bank and orders one of his gang to get two pickaxes for the digging. "Wouldn't that look suspicious?" one of his cronies asks. "Tell them we're building good will," he replies.

SELECTED FILMS: *The Bright Shawl* (1923), *A Lady to Love* (1930), *The Little Giant, I Loved a Woman* (1933), *Kid Galahad* (1937), *A Slight Case of Murder* (1938), *Brother Orchid* (1940), *Larceny, Inc.* (1942), *Mr. Winkle Goes to War* (1944), *It's a Great Feeling* (1949), *Actors and Sin* (1952), *A Hole in the Head* (1959), *Pepe* (1960), *My Geisha* (1962), *Good Neighbor Sam, Robin and the Seven Hoods* (1964), *Never a Dull Moment* (1968), *Soylent Green* (1973). ∎

Robson, May (1858–1942), actress. Began her acting career after she became a widow at age 25. She appeared on stage and on Broadway before entering early silent films. She gained popularity during the 1930s playing sharp-tongued, rebellious, but kindly old matrons either as a character actress or as lead. She was nominated for an Academy Award for her portrayal of Apple Annie in CAPRA'S *Lady for a Day* (1933), which was followed by a sequel the following year, *Lady by Choice.*

SELECTED FILMS: *How Molly Made Good* (1915), *Pals in Paradise* (1926), *The Rejuvenation of Aunt Mary, The Angel of Broadway* (1927), *Mother's Millions* (1931), *If I Had a Million, Little Orphan Annie* (1932), *Dinner at Eight, Alice in Wonderland* (1933), *You Can't Buy Everything, Lady by Choice* (1934), *Grand Old Girl* (1935), *Wife Vs. Secretary* (1936), *Bringing Up Baby* (1938), *Granny Get Your Gun, Irene* (1940), *Playmates* (1941), *Joan of Paris* (1942). ∎

"Rochester." See Eddie Anderson.

Rodney, Earl (1891–1932), actor. Appeared in vaudeville, on stage, and in early silent comedy shorts produced by KEYSTONE, Mack SENNETT'S studios. A supporting actor and sometimes lead player, he worked with several of the leading comics of the period, including, among others, Marie PREVOST. He was also a screenwriter and director.

SELECTED FILMS: Crooked to the End (1915), An Oily Scoundrel (1916), The Nick of Time Baby, Secrets of a Beauty Parlor (1917). ■

Rogell, Albert S. (1901–), director. Began his Hollywood career as a cameraman before progressing to assistant director and finally becoming a full-fledged director during the silent era. He made a smooth transition into sound films, specializing in westerns and other action features, the same genres he worked in during the silent period. He did, however, turn out several comedies as well. Much of his output consisted of low-budget films.

SELECTED FILMS: The Greatest Menace (1923), The Snob Buster (1925), Carnival Boat (1932), Air Hostess (1933), No More Women (1934), Roaming Lady (1936), Start Cheering (1938), For Love or Money, Hawaiian Nights, Laugh It Off (1939), Private Affairs, Argentine Nights, Li'l Abner (1940), Tight Shoes (1941), Sleepytime Gal, Butch Minds the Baby (1942), Love, Honor and Goodbye (1945), The Magnificent Rogue (1947), The Admiral Was a Lady (1950). ■

Rogers, Charles "Buddy" (1904–), actor. Charming and affable lead of silent and early sound features. Dark-haired and dimpled, he began his screen career in silent films in the late 1920s. He starred chiefly in romantic comedies and other light films. He married Mary PICKFORD in the mid-1930s. Abandoning his acting career in the late 1930s, he worked for a time as a bandleader. Switching careers once more, he became a film producer.

SELECTED FILMS: Fascinating Youth, So's Your Old Man (1926), My Best Girl (1927), Abie's Irish Rose, Varsity (1928), Heads Up, Safety in Numbers, Along Came Youth (1930), Best of Enemies, Take a Chance (1933), Dance Band, Old Man Rhythm (1935), This Way, Please (1937), Let's Make a Night of It (1938), *Mexican Spitfire's Baby, Sing for Your Supper (1941), An Innocent Affair (1948), The Parson and the Outlaw (1957).* ■

Rogers, Dora, actress. Appeared in early silent comedy shorts for producer Mack SENNETT'S KEYSTONE studios. As a supporting player, she worked with some of the leading comedians of the period, including, among others, Charlie CHASE, Chester CONKLIN, and Mack SWAIN.

SELECTED FILMS: Love, Loot and Crash, The Battle of Ambrose and Walrus (1915), A Modern Enoch Arden, Gypsy Joe, A Love Riot, Bucking Society, Her First False Step (1916), Dodging His Doom, His Naughty Thought, His Precious Life (1917). ■

Rogers, Ginger (1911–), actress. Worked in vaudeville before entering films. Her first screen appearances were in musical comedy shorts in the late 1920s, but she quickly advanced to feature films after gaining recognition in two hit Broadway shows. Settling in Hollywood permanently in 1931, she worked for different studios playing female leads and supporting roles. When she switched to RKO and was teamed as Fred ASTAIRE'S dancing partner, her career skyrocketed. Together, they made ten romantic musical comedies that entertained audiences of the 1930s and are still popular in revivals. The next decade gave her a chance to star in dramas and light films, proving her versatility as an actress. In the 1960s she returned to Broadway and scored a huge success, as she did on the London stage a few years later. Her grace and charm in the 1930s musicals and the comedic abilities that she demonstrated in the 1940s have made her one of Hollywood's greatest stars. She received an Oscar for her role in *Kitty Foyle.*

In *Stage Door* she played an aspiring dancer who is rehearsing a number with her partner, Ann Miller. A disagreeable playboy ogles her and, trying to make conversation, asks: "Are you practicing a new show?" "No," she replies sarcastically, "we're just getting over the D.T.s"

SELECTED FILMS: Young Man of Manhattan, Queen High, The Sap From Syracuse, Follow the Leader (1930), The Tenderfoot, You Said a Mouthful (1932), 42nd Street, Gold Diggers of 1933, Sitting Pretty (1933), Rafter Romance (1934), Top Hat (1935), Follow the Fleet (1936), Stage Door (1937), Having Wonderful Time, Vivacious Lady, Carefree (1938), Bachelor Mother, Fifth Avenue Girl (1939), Tom, Dick and Harry (1941), Roxie Hart, The Major and the Minor, Once Upon a Honeymoon (1942), Weekend at the Waldorf (1945), The Groom Wore Spurs (1951), We're Not Married, Monkey Business (1952), The First Traveling Saleslady (1956), Oh, Men! Oh, Women! (1957), Harlow (1965). ■

Will Rogers

Rogers, Will (1879–1935), actor, humorist. Appeared in vaudeville and on Broadway before being invited to star in silent films in 1918. A warm and personable performer on stage, and a star of several Ziegfeld Follies, he found it difficult to adapt to the film medium. Perhaps because of his dependence on verbal wit, especially his political barbs, he was not as successful in silents as he was in sound films. By the early 1930s he became a popular screen comedian, radio personality, and columnist.

He soon became famous for his witticisms: "I never met a man I didn't like." "Rumor travels faster but it don't stay put as long as truth." "I'd rather be right than Republican." "We are continually buying something we never get from a man that never had it." "Outside of traffic, there is nothing that has held this country back as much as committees."

His silent films, which he made for producer Hal ROACH, were no comic match for those of the great screen comedians such as CHAPLIN, KEATON, LLOYD, or LANGDON. But on their own merits, they were pleasant little parodies and satires. More important, they brought out his abundant charm and hinted at the potential comic talents that were to emerge during the sound era. Films like "Big Moments From Little Pictures" (1924) satirized several of the leading screen personalities of the period, including Douglas FAIRBANKS and Rudolph Valentino.

Known and idolized for his rural, cracker-barrel humor and philosophy, he became politically influential. He died in an airplane accident at age 56. His son, Will Rogers, Jr., portrayed his father on the screen in The Story of Will Rogers (1952), a respectable, if unilluminating, biography.

SELECTED FILMS: Laughing Bill Hyde (1918), Almost a Husband, Jubilo (1919), Honest Hutch (1920), Doubling for Romeo (1921), Two Wagons, Both Covered (1924), They Had to See Paris (1929), Lightnin' (1930), A Connecticut Yankee, Ambassador Bill (1931), Business and Pleasure, Down to Earth, Too Busy to Work (1932), State Fair, Doctor Bull (1933), The County Chairman, Life Begins at 40, Doubting Thomas, Steamboat 'Round the Bend, In Old Kentucky (1935). ■

Roland, Ruth (1892–1937), actress. Appeared on stage as a child performer. She came to Hollywood in 1911 to work in silent comedy shorts for KALEM studios. She was featured in a series of western comedy shorts in 1912. By 1915 she found her true screen career—that of serial heroine. In this capacity her popularity was second only to that of Pearl White.

SELECTED FILMS: A Second Shot, Arizona Bill (1911), Hypnotic Nell, Ranch Girls on a Rampage, The Hoodoo Hat (1912), Absent-minded Abe, While Father Telephoned (1913), And the Villain Still Pursued Her, Ham the Lineman, Ham and the Villain Factory, Ham the Piano Mover (1914), Where the Worst Begins, Dollar Down (1925), Reno (1930), From Nine to Nine (1936). ■

Roman Scandals (1933), UA. Dir. Frank Tuttle; Sc. William Anthony McGuire, George Oppenheimer, Arthur Sheekman; with Eddie Cantor, Ruth Etting, Gloria Stuart, Alan Mowbray, Edward Arnold.

Eddie Cantor had already made a name for himself as a star in vaudeville, on stage in the "Ziegfeld Follies," in several silent comedies, and two musical comedy films before making Roman Scandals. His dynamic stage presence, his ability to put over a song, and his comedic talents combined to make him one of the highest paid and most popular entertainers of the period. In the film he plays a grocery messenger in the town of West Rome who dreams he is in ancient Rome. He gets involved in a slave auction, in court intrigue with emperor Edward Arnold, in a harem of beautiful women, and as food taster for the emperor, all of which scenes provide plenty of laughs. At the slave market he is placed on the auction block for various citizens to examine. "Lady," he says to a potential buyer, "please don't touch unless you're gonna buy." An ugly old woman takes an interest in him. "I'm weak, I can't do any work," Cantor explains in an attempt to discourage her. "I'm not buying you for work," she says suggestively. "That's what I was afraid of," he concludes. Part of the fun involves the anachronisms he introduces, as when he mentions Mickey and Minnie Mouse to the bewilderment of his listeners. The songs and final production number are lively and entertaining and the film moves quickly. Cantor's earlier sound comedies, Palmy Days (1931) and The Kid From Spain (1932), were satisfactory diversions but were more reminiscent of stage revues, especially the latter, than of film narrative comedy. They lacked the overall cohesive quality and brightness of Scandals. Generally, the early Cantor films helped to introduce a new style of film musical, which differed from the backstage plot where songs and production numbers seemed to be added artificially. His films were more refreshing and natural. He spent the remainder of his show business life concentrating chiefly on his successful radio show and eventually in the new medium, television, which made his burgeoning film career in the 1930s of secondary importance.

Romantic comedy. Films with light, breezy love stories often based on a triangle for plot complications in which the hero or heroine chooses love over wealth or position. Also, romantic comedy always ends with a marriage or the promise of marriage. The comedy derives from one or more of the following: mistaken identity, disguise, farce, witty dialogue, slapstick, and an assortment of offbeat supporting players. The heroes and heroines, whether from the working class or upper class, are more fully drawn than the chief characters of SCREWBALL COMEDY or the farce. However, screwball and romantic comedy are often synonymous.

Much of the comedy output of the silent period was left in the hands of producers like Mack SENNETT and Hal ROACH and their army of comedians who turned out numerous one- and two-reelers—films that by and large were clown comedies, not romantic comedies. The major studios concentrated on drama, romance, westerns, and adventure but produced relatively few comedies. The light films they did make were based on these same genres; e.g., comedy-dramas, western comedies, adventure comedies, etc. However, a few romantic comedies did appear each year. In 1916, films like *It Happened in Honolulu*, *The Madcap*, and *Miss George Washington* were released. *Polly Redhead*, *The Raggedy Queen*, *The Spindle of Life*, and *Susan's Gentleman* came out in 1917. The year 1918 saw *A Rich Man's Darling*, *Amarilly of Clothesline Alley*, *Eve's Daughter*, and *Flare-Up Sal*. And in 1919 the marquees displayed *The Weaker Vessel*, *Bill Henry*, *Boots*, and *Come Out of the Kitchen*. Some of the most popular screen stars of the period, including Billie BURKE, Violet MERSEREAU, Louise Lovely, and Marguerite CLARK, appeared in these early romantic comedies.

In the 1920s each studio produced its share of romantic comedies, but the number was small in relation to other genres. Although the following entries are all from Paramount, they are representative of the genre during the decade. *All of a Sudden Peggy* (1920) starred Marguerite Clark and Jack Mulhall. *April Folly*, released the same year, featured Marion DAVIES. Billie Burke starred in *Away Goes Prudence*, also made in 1920. In 1921 Fatty ARBUCKLE co-starred with Lila Lee in *Crazy to Marry*. In 1925 Leatrice JOY made *The Dressmaker From Paris*, while Florence VIDOR and Edward Everett HORTON co-starred in *Marry Me*, about a teacher and a hypochondriac.

The genre did not blossom until the advent of sound. One of the factors might have been the decline of the comedy short. As early as 1929, Marion Davies, a French maiden, was pursued by two American soldiers in *Marianne*. In *Going Hollywood* (1933) the reverse occurs. Davies pursues Bing CROSBY all the way to California. The young women in these films were constantly faced with the dilemma of having to make a choice between the men in their lives. In *Love Before Breakfast* (1936) Carole LOMBARD is perplexed by Preston Foster and Cesar ROMERO. Claudette COL-

BERT in *The Bride Comes Home* (1935) must choose between Robert YOUNG and Fred MacMURRAY. Carole Lombard, a manicurist in *Hands Across the Table* (1935), is torn between wealthy Ralph BELLAMY and poor MacMurray.

Sometimes the story is set in some romantic European city, with Paris the most popular choice of the writers and studios. In *I Met Him in Paris* (1937) Claudette Colbert has three, not two, desirable admirers from whom to select. As the locales change, the numbers seem to increase. In *Ladies in Love* (1936) four female leads, including Janet GAYNOR and Loretta YOUNG, while on vacation in Budapest, set their sights on their likely victims. Danielle Darrieux practices a little deception to win the rich Douglas FAIRBANKS, JR. in *The Rage of Paris* (1938).

Money and position play important roles in many romantic comedies. In *The Richest Girl in the World* (1934) wealthy Miriam HOPKINS becomes overly cautious about whom she falls in love with and wants to make sure that her beau is in love with her, not her fortune. Jean ARTHUR in *More Than a Secretary* (1936) falls for her boss, George Brent. Society-girl Merle Oberon falls hopelessly in love with rodeo cowboy Gary COOPER in *The Cowboy and the Lady* (1938).

The genre continued to flourish during the 1940s. The heroine's problem of selecting the proper husband spilled over into this decade. Ginger Rogers has to choose among Alan Marshal, Burgess Meredith, and George Murphy in *Tom, Dick and Harry* (1941). Other plots from the 1930s were repeated, such as in *The Lady Takes a Chance* (1943). This time city girl Jean Arthur falls in love with rugged rodeo star John Wayne. Commoner Robert CUMMINGS falls for royal Olivia de Havilland in *Princess O'Rourke* (1943). But some entries in the 1940s actually added new twists. In *Take a Letter, Darling* (1942) executive Rosalind Russell hires Fred MacMurray as her secretary, but the employer-employee relationship doesn't last long. Mother Kay Francis and daughter Diana Barrymore in *Between Us Girls* (1942) both get entangled in romantic complications. Ginger Rogers disguises herself as a 12-year-old girl to beat the train fare in *The Major and the Minor* (1942) and becomes romantically involved with Ray MILLAND. In *She Wouldn't Say Yes* (1945) Rosalind Russell is a psychiatrist who eventually falls in love with patient Lee Bowman, while Jennifer Jones, a plumber in wartime England, falls in love with refugee Charles Boyer in *Cluny Brown* (1946).

Few changes occurred in the genre during the 1950s. Color and on-location shooting enhance the films as studio reliables attempt to carry the time-worn plots. In *Here Comes the Groom* (1951) Bing Crosby needs a wife so that he can bring two war orphans to the States. He wins back his ex-fiancee from the arms of Franchot TONE. In *Anything Can Happen* (1952), starring Jose Ferrer and Kim Hunter, an immigrant boy falls in love with an all-American girl. That same year John Wayne returned to his Irish roots in *The Quiet Man*, romanced Maureen O'Hara and had problems with her brother Victor McLAGLEN over the dowry. In the Academy Award-winning *Roman Holiday* (1953) princess Audrey HEPBURN temporarily flees her royal life while visiting Rome and falls in love with Gregory Peck. In *Sabrina* (1954) Audrey Hepburn, a chauffeur's daughter at a large estate, is wooed by two rich brothers, William HOLDEN and Humphrey BOGART. Olivia de Havilland, deciding to take in all of romantic Paris, is wooed by John Forsythe in *The Ambassador's Daughter* (1956). Other films include *Love in the Afternoon* and *Desk Set*, both released in 1957.

Breakfast at Tiffany's (1961) with Audrey Hepburn and George Peppard, *Bedtime Story* (1964) starring Marlon Brando and Shirley Jones, *The April Fools* (1969) with Jack LEMMON and Catherine Deneuve, *Ginger in the Morn-*

ing (1973) starring Sissy Spacek, Oscar-winning *Annie Hall* (1977) with Woody Allen and Diane KEATON, and *The Goodbye Girl* (1977) with Richard Dreyfuss and Marsha Mason were some of the romantic comedies released in the following two decades.

By the 1980s the genre began to falter. Except for such talents as Neil SIMON, relatively few screenwriters were able to come up with fresh material. Even some of the most popular stars of the decade were unable to surmount the scripts. John BELUSHI and Blair Brown starred in *Continental Divide* (1981), but the film received poor reviews. Burt REYNOLDS and Goldie HAWN struggled through *Best Friends* (1982), and Dudley MOORE tried to save the ironically titled *Romantic Comedy* (1983).

The romantic comedy has outlasted other light genres such as musical, western, sophisticated, and screwball comedy. It was almost replaced in the 1960s by the sex comedy but it survived. And it seems, along with the crime comedy, the most likely of the group not only to be resurrected but also to flourish.

Romero, Cesar (1907–), actor. Worked as a dancer and actor on Broadway before entering films in the early 1930s. The epitome of tall, dark, and handsome, he appeared in numerous dramas and light films, especially romantic comedies in which he played smooth, urbane characters. He was popular as the Cisco Kid in the several entries he made for the series.

SELECTED FILMS: The Shadow Laughs (1933), *The Thin Man* (1934), *Hold 'Em, Yale* (1935), *Love Before Breakfast* (1936), *Happy Landing* (1938), *Wife, Husband and Friend* (1939), *He Married His Wife, Tall, Dark and Handsome* (1941), *Springtime in the Rockies* (1942), *Julia Misbehaves* (1948), *Love That Brute* (1950), *Around the World in 80 Days* (1956), *Ocean's Eleven* (1960), *Sergeant Deadhead* (1965), *The Com-*

puter Wore Tennis Shoes (1970), The Strongest Man in the World (1975). ∎

Ann Rutherford and Mickey Rooney

Rooney, Mickey (1920–), actor. Worked on stage as a child performer in his parents' act before entering silent films in 1926 as Mickey Yule. He starred in a series of two-reel silent comedies, "Mickey McGuire," which spilled over into the sound era. The title character, a tough little tot with a derby, was based on Fontaine Fox's comic strip. Yule adopted the name McGuire, changing it a few years later to Rooney when he began to get roles in feature films. One of the highlights of his film career occurred when he was chosen to play Puck in Shakespeare's *A Midsummer Night's Dream* (1935) for Warner Brothers. His most famous role, however, was as ANDY HARDY in the popular family series.

By the late 1930s he replaced Shirley TEMPLE as the most popular box-office attraction. His star continued to ascend into the 1940s until he entered the military service. After World War II his popularity declined. He made several routine films that did not help his image. Bouncing back in the 1950s, he made a handful of competent dramas that proved his acting abilities. In the late 1970s he starred in a smash Broadway play, *Sugar Babies*, which once again confirmed the resilience of the diminutive, dynamic performer. His autobiography, *I.E.*, was published in 1965. In *Love Finds Andy Hardy* (1938) young Andy (Rooney) confides to his father (Lewis STONE): "You don't have to worry. I'm never going to get married—ever." "That's a momentous decision," he father reminds him. "Not until I'm middleaged," the son explains, "twenty-five or twenty-six."

SELECTED FILMS: *Orchids and Ermine (1927), My Pal, the King (1932), Blind Date (1934), Ah, Wilderness! (1935), A Family Affair (1937), Hold That Kiss (1938), Babes in Arms (1939), Girl Crazy (1943), Summer Holiday, Words and Music (1948), The Atomic Kid (1954), Francis in the Haunted House (1956), Operation Madball (1957), It's a Mad, Mad, Mad, Mad World (1963), Skidoo (1968), The Comic (1969), Pete's Dragon (1977), Find the Lady (1979).* ∎

Rorke, Hayden (1910–), actor. Worked on stage and on Broadway before entering films as a character actor. He has appeared chiefly in light films. He has also been seen widely in different television shows.

SELECTED FILMS: *An American in Paris (1953), Pillow Talk (1959), The Thrill of It All (1963), The Unsinkable Molly Brown, A House Is Not a Home, I'd Rather Be Rich (1964), The Barefoot Executive (1971).* ∎

Rose, Jack (1911–), screenwriter. Worked as a comedy writer on radio before writing scripts for Hollywood films. Beginning in the late 1940s, he wrote screenplays alone or in collaboration for numerous comedies, several for some of the leading comics of the period, including Bob HOPE.

SELECTED FILMS: *Road to Rio, Ladies' Man, My Favorite Brunette (1947), The Great Lover, Sorrowful Jones, It's a Great Feeling, Always Leave Them Laughing (1949), The Daughter of Rosie O'Grady, Riding High (1950), Room for One More (1952), April in Paris, Trouble Along the Way (1953), Living It Up, The Seven Little Foys (1955), Houseboat (1958), The Five Pennies (1959), On the Double (1961), Papa's Delicate Condi-*

tion, *Who's Been Sleeping in My Bed?* (1963), *The Incredible Mr. Limpet* (1964), *A Touch of Class* (1973), *Lost and Found* (1979). ∎

Rose, William (1918–), screenwriter. Wrote comedies for British films during the 1940s and 1950s before returning to the United States. He continued his screenwriting career in Hollywood, turning out both broad and some sophisticated comedies. He won an Oscar for *Guess Who's Coming to Dinner.*

SELECTED FILMS: *It's a Mad, Mad, Mad, Mad World* (1963), *The Russians Are Coming, the Russians Are Coming* (1966), *The Flim-Flam Man, Guess Who's Coming to Dinner* (1967), *The Secret of Santa Vittoria* (1969). ∎

Rosenbloom, "Slapsie" Maxie (1903–1976), prizefighter, actor. A former boxer who had won the world championship in his class before entering films in 1933. Writer Damon Runyon indirectly influenced the fighter to try show business. After Runyon had witnessed several of his bouts, he named him "Slapsie Maxie." Rosenbloom then hit upon the idea of portraying brawny, dimwitted types. A likable character actor, he often portrayed slap-happy ex-fighters in a string of light comedies through the 1950s, often supporting some of the leading comics of the period, including Bob HOPE, ABBOTT AND COSTELLO, and MARTIN AND LEWIS.

In *Mr. Moto's Gamble* (1938) the Japanese detective catches him picking someone's pocket. "I can't help taking things that attract my eyes," he confesses. "He's a kleptomaniac," Moto's nephew explains. "Thanks, pal, thanks," Maxie says, thinking he has been exonerated.

SELECTED FILMS: *Mr. Broadway* (1933), *Muss 'Em Up, Kelly the Second* (1936), *Nothing Sacred* (1937), *The Kid Comes Back* (1938), *The Kid From Kokomo* (1939), *Ringside Maisie, Louisiana Purchase* (1941), *Smart Alecks*

(1942), *Irish Eyes Are Smiling* (1944), *Men in Her Diary* (1945), *Skipalong Rosenbloom* (1951), *Abbott and Costello Meet the Keystone Kops* (1955), *Hollywood or Bust* (1956), *Don't Worry, We'll Think of a Title* (1966). ∎

Ross, Herbert (1927–), director. Worked as an actor, dancer, and choreographer before switching to director. He had directed several Broadway shows before trying his hand at films in 1969. His efforts are entertaining and reflect the skills he has brought with him from his previous experiences.

SELECTED FILMS: *Goodbye, Mr. Chips* (1969), *The Owl and the Pussycat* (1970), *T.R. Baskin* (1971), *Play It Again, Sam* (1972), *The Last of Sheila* (1973), *Funny Lady, The Sunshine Boys* (1975), *The Goodbye Girl* (1977), *California Suite* (1978), *Pennies From Heaven* (1981), *I Ought to Be in Pictures* (1982), *Max Dugan Returns* (1983), *Protocol* (1984). ∎

Ross, Shirley (1911–1975), actress. Worked as a blues singer for Gus Arnheim's orchestra before entering films in 1933. A blonde, grey-eyed musical talent, she appeared in minor roles for a few years at MGM studios. By the late 1930s she switched to Paramount and soon gained popularity in a series of light films. She retired from the screen in 1945, a wealthy woman. During her film career she starred in stage plays that brought her even greater fame. She worked with several comic performers, including Jean HARLOW, Maurice CHEVALIER, and Bob HOPE.

SELECTED FILMS: *Bombshell* (1933), *The Girl From Missouri, Hollywood Party, The Merry Widow* (1934), *Calm Yourself* (1935), *Hideaway Girl, Waikiki Wedding, Blossoms on Broadway* (1937), *Thanks for the Memory* (1938), *Paris Honeymoon, Cafe Society, Some Like It Hot, Unexpected Father* (1939), *Sailors on Leave, Kisses for Breakfast* (1941). ∎

Roth, Gene (–1976), actor. Appeared as a supporting player during the 1940s and 1950s. He worked chiefly in comedy shorts starring the THREE STOOGES and, in the 1950s, in features.

SELECTED FILMS: See My Lawyer (1945), Dunked in the Deep (1949), The Farmer Takes a Wife (1953), Commotion on the Ocean (1956), Outer Space Jitters (1957), Quiz Whiz, Pies and Guys (1958). ▪

Roth, Lillian (1910–1980), actress, singer. Performed on stage as a child, eventually starring on Broadway and in films during the 1920s and 1930s. But by the late 1930s her career was ruined when alcoholism and a string of divorces took their toll. She made a slight show business comeback in the late 1950s. Her autobiography, I'll Cry Tomorrow, was published in 1954 and adapted into a film the following year.

SELECTED FILMS: Pershing's Crusaders (1918), The Love Parade (1929), The Vagabond King, Animal Crackers, Sea Legs, Honey (1930), Take a Chance (1933), Communion (1977). ▪

Rowan and Martin. A popular comedy team of the 1960s and 1970s. Dan Rowan, born in 1922, had been a used-car salesman and a minor comedy writer at Paramount studios before he met and teamed up with Dick Martin. Martin, born the same year, had been a bartender. He had made a few attempts at forming a comedy act with different partners, but they were unsuccessful—until he stumbled across Rowan in 1952. Together they played various clubs and bars, finally landing on television where they scored their biggest success. Their show, "Laugh-In," which won four Emmy Awards the first season, ran for five years. Their comedy material, reminiscent of vaudeville-like banter, rarely touched political, social, or other controversial issues. In this sense they resembled ABBOTT AND COSTELLO more than they did such contemporaries as the Smothers Brothers. The team made only two films, both routine comedies. Although they were scheduled to make several more, their audiences did not seem overly enthusiastic about their screen appearances. Rowan, semi-retired, resides in Florida, while Martin has occasionally directed and hosted television shows.

SELECTED FILMS: Once Upon a Horse (1958), The Maltese Bippy (1969). ▪

Rowland, Roy (1910–), director. Began his film career in the 1930s as an assistant director but soon began to direct short subjects. He turned out two comedy series, the "How to" two-reelers starring Robert BENCHLEY and the popular "Pete Smith Specialties." By the 1940s he was directing full-length features, few of which were light films.

SELECTED FILMS: How to Sleep (1935), How to Vote, How to Become a Detective (1936), How to Figure Income Tax (1938), Lost Angel (1943), Our Vines Have Tender Grapes (1945), Tenth Avenue Angel (1948), Excuse My Dust (1951), Hit the Deck (1955), These Wilder Years, Meet Me in Las Vegas (1956). ▪

Royle, Selena (1904–1983), actress. Worked for many years on the stage before entering films in the early 1930s. A light-haired supporting player, she appeared in dramas and light films, usually as mothers and matrons, for about a dozen years and then retired from her screen career to live in Mexico with her husband.

SELECTED FILMS: The Misleading Lady (1932), Stage Door Canteen, Paddy Rollers (1943), The Harvey Girls (1945), No Leave, No Love (1946), A Date With Judy (1948), My Dream Is Yours, You're My Everything (1949), Murder Is My Beat (1955). ▪

Rubin, Benny (1899–1986), actor. Worked in burlesque and vaudeville before entering films in the late 1920s. He appeared in lead and supporting roles in a string of light films during the early 1930s. He later performed only as a character actor. His long screen career spanned six decades.

SELECTED FILMS: Naughty Baby, It's a Great Life (1929), Lord Byron of Broadway, Hot Curves, Sunny Skies, Leathernecking (1930), Sunny, Here Comes Mr. Jordan (1941), Mr. Wise Guy (1942), A Hole in the Head (1959), Pocketful of Miracles, The Errand Boy (1961), The Patsy (1964), That Funny Feeling (1965), Thoroughly Modern Millie (1967), Which Way to the Front? (1970), Won Ton Ton, the Dog Who Saved Hollywood (1976). ■

Ruby, Harry (–1974), screenwriter, author, composer. Wrote scripts and stories, alone or in collaboration, for several comedies and musical films during the 1930s and 1940s. He penned material for some of the leading comics of the period, including the MARX BROTHERS and Eddie CANTOR.

SELECTED FILMS (as author): Animal Crackers (1930), Broad Minded (1931), Duck Soup (1933), Hips Hips Hooray, The Circus Clown (1934), Kentucky Kernels (1935), Maisie Goes to Reno (1944), Three Little Words (1950).

SELECTED FILMS (as screenwriter): Horse Feathers, Kid From Spain (1932), Kentucky Kernels (1935), Walking on Air (1936), The Life of the Party (1937), Lovely to Look At (1952). ■

Ruggles, Charles (1886–1970), actor. Veteran character player of Broadway stage and Hollywood films whose career stretched across six decades. He began appearing in early silent films before World War I, but his best work on screen occurred during the 1930s. A kindly and distinguished figure with a slight mustache, he often played timorous souls. He enlivened numerous films with his wit and comic antics. His brother, Wesley RUGGLES, was a successful director.

In No Time for Comedy (1940) he played a cuckold who does not want another divorce. "I don't want to lose Amanda," he says. "I don't want to have my tombstone cluttered up with the names of my formerly beloved wives. It would leave no room for the more important data."

SELECTED FILMS: Peer Gynt (1915), The Heart Raider (1923), The Lady Lies (1929), Queen High, Charley's Aunt (1930), The Girl Habit (1931), Trouble in Paradise, If I Had a Million (1932), Mama Loves Papa (1933), Six of a Kind (1934), Ruggles of Red Gap (1935), Early to Bed (1936), Mind Your Own Business (1937), Bringing Up Baby (1938), The Farmer's Daughter (1940), Model Wife (1941), Incendiary Blonde (1945), The Perfect Marriage (1947), Papa's Delicate Condition (1963), Follow Me, Boys! (1966). ■

Ruggles, Wesley (1889–1972), director. Appeared in stock before settling in Hollywood as a supporting actor in early silent comedy shorts. By 1918 he switched careers and began to direct films. He turned out features in different genres, ranging from melodramas to comedies. More than half his films were light comedies. Although he never achieved the stature of directors such as LUBITSCH and Billy WILDER, he was a proficient craftsman whose best films are quite entertaining. He retired in 1946. He was the brother of actor Charles RUGGLES.

SELECTED FILMS: The Blind Adventure (1918), Piccadilly Jim (1920), Wild Honey, If I Were Queen (1922), Slippery McGee, Mr. Billings Spends His Dime (1923), The Kick-Off (1926), Silk Stockings (1927), Finders Keepers (1928), Girl Overboard (1929), Honey (1930), College Humor, I'm No Angel (1933), Shoot the Works (1934), The Bride Comes Home (1935), I Met Him in Paris (1937), Too Many Husbands (1941), Slightly Dangerous (1943), See Here, Private Hargrove (1944). ■

Rumann, Sig (1884–1967), actor. Worked on stage in his native Germany and on Broadway before entering films in the late 1920s as a supporting player. A stocky figure with a pronounced accent, he played both comic and sinister characters but was more effective as the former. He occasionally played the foil to Groucho MARX. He was at his most humorous when, as a haughty dignitary or other representative of the establishment, he became confused or frustrated.

In *To Be or Not to Be* he played a Nazi officer in occupied Poland who pans a performance by an actor played by Jack BENNY. "What he did to Shakespeare, we are doing now to Poland."

SELECTED FILMS: *The Royal Box (1929), The Farmer Takes a Wife, A Night at the Opera (1935), The Princess Comes Across (1936), A Day at the Races, Nothing Sacred (1937), Ninotchka (1939), Love Crazy (1941), To Be or Not to Be (1942), It Happened Tomorrow (1944), A Royal Scandal (1945), A Night in Casablanca (1946), Mother Wore Tights (1947), The Fortune Cookie (1966).* ∎

Runt, The. Fictional comic sidekick of "Boston Blackie," the popular detective-comedy series of the 1940s starring Chester MORRIS. The Runt was portrayed by veteran character actor George E. STONE.

Rural comedy. A popular type of film humor dating back to the early silent era. Rural comedy can be set in small towns and villages, on farms, or in what Hollywood likes to label as "hillbilly" country. As early as 1911, after Edwin S. Porter and D. W. Griffith had already directed dozens of rural comedies, ES-SANAY studios produced its "SNAKE-VILLE" comedies, a series of one- and two-reelers set in the fictitious village of Snakeville. Other series eventually emerged, such as the "ALIBI IKE," "Mustang Pete," and "HANK AND LANK" comedies, the last of which

starred Victor POTEL and Augustus CARNEY. Other famous comics and directors got their experience in these slapstick affairs, including Ben TURPIN and E. Mason HOPPER. Harold LLOYD, before he rose to stardom, appeared as "LONESOME LUKE," a country bumpkin, in an early comedy series from 1915 to 1917. Other films during this decade include "Independence, B'Gosh" (1918), in which a middle-aged couple inherit 89 million dollars; "Skinnay's School and Scandal" (1919); and "Greased Lightning" (1919), starring Charles RAY, who specialized in this genre through the 1920s.

During the 1920s the genre flourished. Film comedienne Mary Miles MINTER starred in *Judy of Rogues Harbor* in 1920. In 1922 Thomas Meighan played the young son in *Back Home and Broke* who is shunned by his town when the citizens learn that his deceased father left him penniless. He leaves in despair, only to return a wealthy man and buy up half the town. The "EDGAR" comedies of 1920–1921, based on the writings of Booth Tarkington about the adventures of a young boy in a small town, included titles like *Edgar's Hamlet* and *Edgar's Little Saw.* Tarkington also created a more popular young character called Penrod, who went on to appear in silents as well as sound films during the 1930s. Mark Twain's novels were often the source for light films during the silent era as well as the sound period and included *Tom Sawyer* (1917), *Huck and Tom* (1918), and *Huckleberry Finn* (1920). Buster KEATON turned out a very funny film about feuding clans in *Our Hospitality* (1923), set in the Shenandoah Valley.

Rural comedies continued their popularity into the Depression years. Comic actors like Bob BURNS and Stuart ERWIN starred in light features with country backgrounds. Burns made, among others, *Mountain Music* (1937), *The Arkansas Traveler* (1938), and *I'm From Missouri* (1939), while Erwin turned out *Dude Ranch* (1931) and

Small Town Boy (1937). The hillbilly comedy of yodeling comedienne Judy CANOVA first came to the screen in the mid-1930s. Several comic character actors, including Sterling HOLLOWAY and Grady SUTTON, excelled in portraying slow-witted yokels in dozens of rural comedies now long forgotten. Some of the top comedy teams occasionally used rural settings for their vehicles. WHEELER AND WOOLSEY starred in *Kentucky Kernels* in 1934. They adopt "Spanky" McFARLAND, take him south to collect his inheritance, and get embroiled in a feud. In 1938 the RITZ BROTHERS were featured in *Kentucky Moonshine*, starring Tony Martin and Marjorie Weaver. The brothers stir up trouble between feuding hillbillies in this low-budget light film.

By the 1940s the genre began to parody itself. The folksy radio stars, LUM AND ABNER, brought their hillbilly humor to the screen in *Dreaming Out Loud* (1940) and *Bashful Bachelors* (1942). Guy KIBBEE starred in the "SCATTERGOOD BAINES" series of rural comedies in the early years of the decade. Martha RAYE starred as an entertainer playing the farm circuit in *The Farmer's Daughter* (1940). In the very funny *Murder, He Says* (1945), Fred MacMURRAY stumbles across Marjorie MAIN'S hillbilly clan of killers. He and Main appeared together again two years later in *The Egg and I*, based on Betty MacDonald's novel. The film co-starred Claudette COLBERT as a city dweller who marries MacMurray and tries to adjust to life on his chicken farm. Main teamed up with Percy KILBRIDE as "Ma and Pa Kettle" as a result of this comedy. "The KETTLES" series began in 1949 and continued through the 1950s. ABBOTT AND COSTELLO tried their hand at rural settings during the 1940s. In *The Wistful Widow of Wagon Gap* (1947) Lou mistakenly kills a man and, according to the law, must take care of his family and wife (Marjorie Main).

The next decade had its share of rural comedies. In the low-budget arena veteran comic character actor Raymond WALBURN starred in a series of "Henry" comedies in which he played a small-town citizen who perpetually gets into difficulties with other townspeople. *Father's Wild Game* (1950) and *Father Takes the Air* (1951) were some of the entries, while other character players like Roscoe ATES and Walter CATLETT lent their comic support. ABBOTT AND COSTELLO made *Comin' Round the Mountain* in 1951, mixing things up in hillbilly territory. One of the most successful rural comedies came at the end of the 1950s. In *The Mating Game* (1959), government tax agent Tony RANDALL falls in love with farmer Paul DOUGLAS' daughter, Debbie REYNOLDS. Douglas, an iconoclastic farmer who has never paid any income tax, is under investigation by the IRS but manages to squeeze out of the problem in this delightful comedy.

Rural comedy as a mainstay of Hollywood fell out of favor beginning in the 1960s, partly as a result of television embracing the genre and partly, perhaps, the result of the "global village" concept. That mythical land in time and space where yokels sit in the general store around a potbelly stove and play checkers, ready to cast a suspicious eye on city slickers, may no longer have any hold on the public's imagination. The "feuds" are no longer with each other but with government agencies, real estate developers, and decaying factories that continue to close. Occasionally the genre is revived, as in *Bootleggers* (1974), where the story is set in the 1930s, and in the "Smokey and the Bandit" series, but the excitement and fun seem to be gone. Contemporary rural films tend to be dramas like *Country* and *The River*, in which the characters are faced with the problems of daily survival rather than with what to wear to the Saturday night barn dance.

Russell, Jane (1921–), actress. Worked as a model before she was discovered by Howard Hughes, who was searching for a particular bustline for his western film, *The Outlaw* (1943). She received much unfavorable publicity as a result but survived the controversy and rose to stardom on her own merits. She co-starred with some of the leading screen personalities of the period in several dramatic and light films.

In *Gentlemen Prefer Blondes* she played Marilyn MONROE'S friend who listens to Marilyn explain how the lack of money can lead to a loveless marriage: "If a girl has to worry about all the money she doesn't have, how is she going to have time for love?" Giving her friend a quizzical look, Russell replies, "That baffles me."

SELECTED FILMS: *The Paleface* (1948), *Double Dynamite* (1951), *Son of Paleface, Road to Bali* (1952), *Gentlemen Prefer Blondes* (1953), *The French Line* (1954), *Gentlemen Marry Brunettes* (1955), *The Fuzzy Pink Nightgown* (1957), *Darker Than Amber* (1970). ■

Rosalind Russell (right)

Russell, Rosalind (1908–1976), actress. Appeared on stage before entering films in the early 1930s. An elegant and talented star, she alternated between dramatic and light roles during her long screen career. Her popularity, however,

emerged from her forays into comedy where she demonstrated her wit and charm, adding spice to numerous films for four decades. Much of her expertise as a comedienne derived from her ability to suggest that she could talk faster than anyone thought possible. She made a successful return to the stage in her later years. Her autobiography, *Life Is a Banquet*, was published in 1977.

In *Hired Wife* she portrayed Brian Aherne's secretary who regretfully informs confidant John Carroll that her boss only notices her with the coming of spring. "I put him in his place," she declares. "A good opening move," Carroll says. "No," she corrects him. "He stayed there."

SELECTED FILMS: *Evelyn Prentiss* (1934), *The Night Is Young, Reckless* (1935), *It Had to Happen, Trouble for Two* (1936), *Man-Proof, Four's a Crowd* (1938), *Fast and Loose* (1939), *His Girl Friday, Hired Wife, No Time for Comedy* (1940), *Design for Scandal* (1941), *Take a Letter, Darling, My Sister Eileen* (1942), *What a Woman* (1943), *She Wouldn't Say Yes* (1945), *Tell It to the Judge* (1949), *Never Wave at a WAC* (1953), *Auntie Mame* (1958), *A Majority of One* (1961), *Gypsy* (1962), *The Trouble With Angels* (1966), *Mrs. Pollifax—Spy* (1971). ■

Russell, William D. (1908–1968), director. Began his career as a director of Hollywood films in 1946. He turned out several entertaining light comedies before turning his attentions to television.

SELECTED FILMS: *Our Hearts Were Growing Up* (1946), *Ladies' Man, Dear Ruth* (1947), *The Sainted Sisters* (1948), *Bride for Sale* (1949), *Best of the Badmen* (1951). ■

Rutherford, Ann (1917–), actress. Appeared on stage as a child actress and later on radio before entering routine films in 1935. A personable and saucy performer, she attained recognition when she was selected for the role of Polly in the popular "ANDY HARDY" films starring Mickey ROONEY. In addition to a dozen entries in the series, she appeared in other light films as well as dramas. She abandoned her screen career in 1950, returning in the 1970s for one last film.

SELECTED FILMS: The Fighting Marines (1935), The Bride Wore Red, You're Only Young Once (1937), Judge Hardy's Children, Love Finds Andy Hardy (1938), These Glamour Girls (1939), The Ghost Comes Home (1940), Whistling in the Dark (1941), Whistling in Dixie (1942), Whistling in Brooklyn (1943), Bedside Manner (1945), The Secret Life of Walter Mitty (1947), Operation Haylift (1950), They Only Kill Their Masters (1972). ∎

Ryan, Frank (1907–1947), director. Worked as a magazine cartoonist and writer before entering films in 1942 as a director. He turned out several entertaining light films before his untimely death. He collaborated on some of the screenplays for the films he directed.

SELECTED FILMS: Call Out the Marines (1942), Hers to Hold (1943), Can't Help Singing (1944), Patrick the Great (1945), So Goes My Love (1946). ∎

Ryan, Irene (1903–1973), actress. Worked in vaudeville and on radio before entering films in the early 1940s. She appeared as a wisecracking, sardonic character actress chiefly in light features. She left films temporarily in the early 1960s but gained popularity in television as Granny in "The Beverly Hillbillies."

SELECTED FILMS: Melody for Three (1941), Sarong Girl (1943), Hot Rhythm, San Diego, I Love You (1944), That's the Spirit (1945), The Diary of a Chambermaid, Little Iodine (1946), My Dear Secretary (1948), Ricochet Romance (1954), Spring Reunion (1957), Don't Worry, We'll Think of a Title (1966). ∎

Ryan, Peggy (1924–), actress. Began her show business career as a child performer in vaudeville. She made her film

debut in 1937 at age 13 and continued to appear in light films. A talented comedienne and all-around entertainer, she often co-starred with Donald O'CONNOR in routine musical comedies.

SELECTED FILMS: Top of the Town (1937), The Flying Irishman (1939), What's Cookin', Miss Annie Rooney, Private Buckaroo, Get Hep to Love (1942), Mister Big, Top Man (1943), Chip off the Old Block, Follow the Boys, The Merry Monahans, Bowery to Broadway (1944), Here Come the Co-Eds, That's the Spirit, Men in Her Diary (1945), All Ashore (1953). ∎

Ryan, Tim (1899–1956), actor, screenwriter. Worked in vaudeville and on radio before entering films in the early 1940s. He appeared chiefly in light films. His wife, Irene RYAN, also appeared in films. He wrote screenplays for many films, including several of the "BOWERY BOYS" comedies.

SELECTED FILMS: Private Affairs (1940), Bedtime Story, Get Hep to Love (1942), Reveille With Beverly, Sarong Girl, Swingtime Johnny (1943), Rockin' in the Rockies (1945), Bringing Up Father (1946), The Petty Girl (1950), From Here to Eternity (1953). ∎

Ryskind, Morrie (1895–1985), screenwriter. Began his Hollywood writing career in 1929 with the MARX BROTHERS' first film. He specialized in light comedy, turning out screenplays alone or in collaboration. He wrote several popular Broadway shows with playwright George S. KAUFMAN, two of which he adapted for the screen (*The Cocoanuts* and *Animal Crackers* with Kaufman). Assessing his early comedic contributions is difficult because of the strong influence of his co-writer, Kaufman. Later, he collaborated with other writers. Ryskind's individual style, for better or worse, may be seen in his screenplay based on his original play, *Palmy Days,* starring Eddie Cantor.

SELECTED FILMS: The Cocoanuts (1929), Animal Crackers (1930), Palmy Days (1931), A Night at the Opera, Anything Goes (1935), My Man Godfrey (1936), Room Service (1938), Man About Town (1939), Penny Serenade (1941), Claudia (1943), Where Do We Go From Here? (1945). ∎

S

Safety Last (1923), PAT. *Dir.* Fred Newmeyer, Sam Taylor; *Sc.* Hal Roach, Sam Taylor, Tim Whelan; with Harold Lloyd, Mildred Davis, Bill Strothers, Noah Young.

Almost every compilation film and documentary on the subject of silent comedy alludes to the famous scene of Harold LLOYD dangling from a skyscraper as he clings precariously to one of the hands of a huge clock. In *Safety Last* he portrays a young hayseed who works as a clerk in a big city department store. Substituting for a professional climber and determined to succeed in his task, he makes his way up the facade of the building as a publicity stunt he concocted. The ascension scenes take up almost half the length of the film as Lloyd overcomes various obstacles such as inquisitive pigeons that land on his shoulder and a revolving wind gauge which eventually strikes him in the head. Lloyd hired Bill Strothers, a professional steel worker and climber whom he had seen plying his skills on a building in Los Angeles, to portray his friend in the film and to teach him some of his techniques. With this film Lloyd proved that he, too, was a master of this genre. But Lloyd developed the form into a fine art. His timing and use of suspense added immeasurably to the total effect. Ironically, the film made such a strong impression on the public that he became known for years as the master of daredevil comedy although he made only a few such comedies.

Sahl, Mort (1926–), actor, comedian. Has worked as a stand-up comic in nightclubs and television and on stage beginning in the 1950s. His trademark has been his informal attire (he wears a sweater and carries a newspaper under one arm). He has been successful in transferring his offbeat, political humor to recordings as well. His occasional appearances in films, chiefly as comic relief, have not been as rewarding. A trenchant social and political satirist, he has been more effective with live audiences. His material has occasionally embroiled him in controversy. In recent years he has appeared on stage and in television with less frequency.

SELECTED FILMS: *In Love and War* (1958), *All the Young Men* (1960), *Johnny Cool* (1963), *Doctor, You've Got to Be Kidding!*, *Don't Make Waves* (1967). ∎

St. Clair, Malcolm (1897–1952), director, cartoonist. Entered the film industry in 1915 as a minor actor and GAGMAN for producer Mack SENNETT. Within a few years he was directing comedy shorts. In the 1920s he turned out feature-length films for different studios and was recognized by critics and peers as one of the major and most stylish directors of the decade.

With the advent of sound, he was relegated to low-budget features. He specialized in light films, and the mid-1920s found him in his prime. His biggest success during this decade was *Are Parents People?* (1925). He directed some of the leading comics of the period, including Buster KEATON and LAUREL AND HARDY.

SELECTED FILMS: *Rip & Stitch, Tailors (1919), Don't Weaken, Young Man's Fancy (1920), Call a Cop (1921), Bright Eyes, Twin Husbands (1922), George Washington, Jr. (1924), Are Parents People? (1925), The Show-Off (1926), Knockout Reilly (1927), Gentlemen Prefer Blondes, The Fleet's In (1928), The Boudoir Diplomat (1930), Goldie Gets Along (1933), She Had to Eat (1937), A Trip to Paris, Everybody's Baby (1938).* ∎

St. John, Al (1893–1963), actor. Worked as an acrobat and juggler before entering films during the early silent period. He appeared as a supporting comic for producer Mack SENNETT'S KEYSTONE studios, working alongside such greats as "Fatty" ARBUCKLE and Charlie CHAPLIN. He eventually starred in his own series of comedy shorts for different studios and, by the mid-1920s, played character parts in feature-length films. He specialized in physical comedy and stunting, a skill requiring expert timing.

With the advent of sound, he returned temporarily to comedy shorts and then settled into sidekick roles in numerous westerns, where he was affectionately known as "Fuzzy." He abandoned his long screen career in 1950 after appearing in hundreds of films.

SELECTED FILMS: *Algy on the Force (1913), Mabel's Strange Predicament, The Knockout, Tillie's Punctured Romance (1914), Bright Lights (1916), The Butcher Boy (1917), The Bellboy (1918), Fast and Furious (1921), The City Chap (1922), Young and Dumb (1923), The Garden of Weeds (1924), Pink Elephants (1926), She Goes to War (1929), The Outcasts of Poker Flat (1937), Fuzzy Settles Down (1944), Outlaw Country (1949).* ∎

St. John, Howard (1905–1974), actor. Worked on stage in the 1920s before entering films in the 1940s. As a charac-ter player in numerous dramas and light films, he often portrayed executives or influential characters.

SELECTED FILMS: *The Undercover Man (1949), Mister 880, Born Yesterday (1950), Stop, You're Killing Me (1952), Li'l Abner (1959), One, Two, Three, Lover Come Back (1961), Sex and the Single Girl (1964), Strange Bedfellows (1965), Don't Drink the Water (1969).* ∎

St. John, Jill (1940–), actress. Worked as a child in radio. She began her screen career in the early 1950s but did not gain recognition until the 1960s, when she was often cast as a dumb redhead. A lively and attractive actress, she starred in many light films. She made several features in England during the late 1960s and early 1970s.

SELECTED FILMS: *Thunder in the East (1953), Summer Love (1958), The Remarkable Mr. Pennypacker (1959), The Roman Spring of Mrs. Stone (1961), Come Blow Your Horn, Who's Been Sleeping in My Bed? (1963), Honeymoon Hotel (1964), Banning (1967).* ∎

Sais, Marin (1888–1971), actress. Began her screen career in early silent films for some of the major pioneer studios, including Vitagraph and Kalem. She appeared in dramas, serials, and comedies, including the "HAM AND BUD" comedy series. During the sound era she switched to character parts and continued to appear in features until 1949.

SELECTED FILMS: *Twelfth Night (1910), Lotta Coin's Ghost (1915), The Vanity Pool (1918), The Fighting Redhead (1949).* ∎

Sakall, S.Z. "Cuddles" (1884–1955), actor. Worked as a comedian on stage and in films in his native Hungary before migrating to Hollywood. He became one of the most popular and lovable character players on the American screen. A chubby figure with hanging jowls and a fractured command of the English lan-

S. Z. "Cuddles" Sakall and Jack Oakie

guage, he enlivened numerous films. He often played flustered restaurant owners, waiters, businessmen, and sympathetic confidants to lovers.

In *Thank Your Lucky Stars* (1943) he and Edward Everett HORTON portrayed two theatrical producers who are overwhelmed by Eddie CANTOR'S plans for a spectacular show. "It's chaos, utter chaos," Horton exclaims. "He wants us to dress the dancing girls as boiled potatoes and have them dive into a tank of sour cream." "Ridiculous," Sakall concludes, "it would splash."

SELECTED FILMS: *It's a Date, Spring Parade* (1940), *The Devil and Miss Jones* (1941), *Ball of Fire, Yankee Doodle Dandy, Casablanca,* (1942), *The Human Comedy* (1943), *Wonder Man, Christmas in Connecticut* (1945), *The Time, the Place and the Girl* (1946), *April Showers* (1948), *In the Good Old Summertime* (1949), *Tea for Two* (1950), *Lullaby of Broadway* (1951), *It's a Big Country* (1952), *Small Town Girl* (1953), *The Student Prince* (1954). ■

Saks, Gene (1921–), director. Appeared as an actor on stage and in television before turning his attentions to directing. He entered films in 1967 and has specialized in directing versions of stage musicals and comedies. He has occasionally appeared on screen in acting roles. His big break came when Paramount selected him over Billy WILDER to direct Neil Simon's *The Odd Couple.*

SELECTED FILMS (as director): *Barefoot in the Park* (1967), *The Odd Couple* (1968), *Cactus Flower* (1969), *Last of the*

Red Hot Lovers (1972), *Mame* (1974), *Brighton Beach Memoirs* (1986). ■

SELECTED FILMS (as actor): *A Thousand Clowns* (1965), *The Prisoner of Second Avenue* (1975), *The One and Only* (1978), *Lovesick* (1983). ■

Sale, Charles "Chic" (1885–1936), actor. Worked in vaudeville and on Broadway in musical comedy beginning in 1917. A master of rural humor as early as 1906, he became popular in small towns and villages across America. His fame in these areas lasted for decades. In the early 1920s he entered silent films and later sound features, often as a comic character actor. He appeared in comedies for producer Al CHRISTIE in the early 1920s. During the 1930s he played old-timers.

SELECTED FILMS: *His Nibs* (1921), *Marching On* (1929), *The Expert, Men of America, When a Feller Needs a Friend* (1932), *The Chief, Lucky Dog* (1933), *Treasure Island* (1934), *Man Hunt, The Man I Marry* (1936), *You Only Live Once* (1937). ■

Sale, Richard (1911–), director, screenwriter. Began directing and writing comedy material for Hollywood in the 1940s. Much of his directorial work was for low-budget films although several of his comedy screenplays for 20th Century-Fox were above average.

SELECTED FILMS (as director): *Spoilers of the North* (1947), *Campus Honeymoon* (1948), *A Ticket to Tomahawk* (1950), *Let's Make It Legal* (1951), *My Wife's Best Friend* (1952), *The Girl Next Door* (1953), *Gentlemen Marry Brunettes* (1954).

SELECTED FILMS (as screenwriter): *Rendezvous With Annie* (1946), *The Dude Goes West* (1948), *Mother Is a Freshman, Mr. Belvedere Goes to College* (1949), *Let's Do It Again* (1951), *The French Line, Woman's World* (1954), *Around the World in 80 Days* (1956), *The White Buffalo* (1977). ■

Sales, Soupy (1926–), comedian, actor. Worked as a radio script writer, a stand-up comic in small clubs, a disc jockey, and by 1950 the star of his own local children's television show. After a decade of clowning, ad libbing, and slapstick, he cut a comedy album that increased his popularity. His fame brought him to New York where he performed at the Paramount Theater to huge crowds. A succession of guest appearances on television followed. Affable and charming, he has appeared sporadically in films without distinction. His comedy routines are a zany composite of old gags, pie-throwing, and some original material.

SELECTED FILMS: The Two Little Bears (1961), Critic's Choice (1963), Birds Do It (1966). ∎

Sampson, Teddy (1895–1970), actress. Worked in early silent films, beginning with the Triangle Film Company in 1916. She was married to famous film comic Ford STERLING.

SELECTED FILMS: Bits of Life (1921), The Chicken in the Case, Outcast (1922), The Bad Man (1923). ∎

Samuels, Andy, child actor. Appeared in several early silent entries of the "OUR GANG" series of comedy shorts for producer Hal ROACH.

SELECTED FILMS: The Champeen, The Big Show, Dogs of War, Lodge Night, No Noise, Stage Fright (1923), Big Business, The Buccaneers, Seein' Things (1924). ∎

San Juan, Olga (1927–), actress, comedienne, dancer. Starred on radio before entering films in the 1940s. A lively entertainer, she appeared in several light films.

SELECTED FILMS: Rainbow Island (1944), Variety Girl (1947), Are You With It?, One Touch of Venus (1948), The Beautiful Blonde From Bashful Bend (1949). ∎

Sandrich, Mark (1900–1945), director. Began his Hollywood career performing various studio tasks before trying his hand at directing. In the late 1920s he turned out comedy shorts starring Lupino LANE and then turned to directing feature-length films. He continued in this capacity until his untimely death at age 45. A competent director, he displayed a penchant for musical comedies. Later in his career, he began producing his own films.

SELECTED FILMS: Runaway Girls (1928), The Talk of Hollywood (1929), Melody Cruise, Aggie Appleby—Maker of Men (1933), Hips Hips Hooray, Cock-eyed Cavaliers, The Gay Divorcee (1934), Top Hat (1935), Follow the Fleet (1936), Carefree (1938), Man About Town (1939), Buck Benny Rides Again, Love Thy Neighbor (1940), Skylark (1941), Holiday Inn (1942), I Love a Soldier (1944). ∎

"Sandy" comedies. See Baby Sandy.

Sanford, Stanley J. "Tiny" (1894–1961), actor. Worked as a character actor in silent and sound comedy shorts and features. He accompanied some of the leading comics of the period, including, among others, LAUREL AND HARDY and Charlie CHAPLIN. One of his more memorable roles was that of the policeman who looks on and takes notes as James FINLAYSON and Stan and Ollie battle it out in the classic short, "Big Business."

SELECTED FILMS: The Immigrant (1917), The World's Champion (1922), Sailors Beware!, Flying Elephants, The Second Hundred Years (1927), From Soup to Nuts (1928), Big Business, Double Whoopie, The Hoosegow (1929), Blotto, Below Zero, The Laurel and Hardy Murder Case (1930), Pardon Us (1931), The Chimp (1932), The Devil's Brother, The Midnight Patrol, Busy Bodies, Fits in a Fiddle (1933), Babes in Toyland (1934), Our Relations, Mummy's Boys, Modern Times (1936). ∎

Santell, Alfred (1895–1981), director. Began his Hollywood career during the early silent period as a comedy writer and occasional actor. He performed other functions before turning to directing in 1915, chiefly turning out comedy shorts. By the 1920s he was directing feature-length films, continuing in this capacity into the 1940s. He made dramas as well as comedies. Much of his work, however, was with low-budget features.

SELECTED FILMS: *My Valet (1915), Out of the Bag (1917), Home, James (1918), Fools in the Dark (1924), The Marriage Whirl (1925), Sweet Daddies, Subway Sadie (1926), Orchids and Ermine, The Gorilla (1927), Twin Beds (1929), Daddy Long Legs (1931), A Feather in Her Hat (1935), Breakfast for Two (1937), Having Wonderful Time, The Arkansas Traveler (1938), Beyond the Blue Horizon (1942), That Brennan Girl (1946).* ∎

Santley, Joseph (1889–1971), director. Starred on stage and in silent films as a child. He turned to directing films during the early sound period and turned out comedy shorts starring some of the leading comedians of the period, including, among others, the MARX BROTHERS. His features, many of them light comedies, were conventional works. He left films in 1950 and began a new career in television.

SELECTED FILMS: *The Cocoanuts (1929), Swing High (1930), Million Dollar Baby (1935), We Went to College, Walking on Air (1936), Meet the Missus (1937), She's Got Everything (1938), Two Bright Boys (1939), Rookies on Parade (1941), Yokel Boy, Joan of Ozark (1942), Chatterbox, Here Comes Elmer (1943), Rosie the Riveter, Brazil (1944), When You're Smiling (1950).* ∎

Satire. Films that lightly ridicule a particular aspect of society. Hollywood has poked fun at social, political, and economic institutions from the early silent days of moviemaking. Some comedians such as Will ROGERS specialized in the genre, while several subjects, including marriage, the rich, and Hollywood itself, received more than their share of gentle ridicule. Satire, of course, differs from parody, which lampoons a specific work.

One of the most popular targets of satirical comedy is the movie world. As early as 1916, films like "Behind the Screen" starring Charlie CHAPLIN were poking fun at themselves. Other films quickly followed, including *Hollywood* (1923), *The Extra Girl* (1924), *Merton of the Movies* (1924), *The Way of a Girl* (1925) which focused on screenwriters, *Once in a Lifetime* (1932), *Bombshell* (1933), *Hollywood Hotel, Stand-In,* and *Something to Sing About* (all 1937), *Boy Meets Girl* (1938), *The Bank Dick* (1940), *Sullivan's Travels* (1941), *The Perils of Pauline* (1947), *Singin' in the Rain* (1952), and *S.O.B.* (1981), to mention a few.

Often a particular film genre was satirized, the western being the most targeted. The acrobatic Douglas FAIRBANKS made several silent comedies of this nature before 1920. Other popular films included "Romantic Redskins" (1910) starring comedienne Dot FARLEY, "Pearl of the Golden West" (1913), "The Paleface" (1920) with Buster KEATON, *Two Wagons, Both Covered* (1924) with Will Rogers, *Go West* (1925) again with Keaton, *Monty of the Mounted* (1927), *Along Came Jones* (1945) starring Gary COOPER, *Destry Rides Again* (1939) with Marlene Dietrich and James STEWART, *Buck Benny Rides Again* (1940) starring Jack BENNY, *Go West* (1940) with the MARX BROTHERS, *Ride 'Em Cowboy* (1942) with ABBOTT AND COSTELLO, *The Paleface* (1948) with Bob HOPE, *Butch Cassidy and the Sundance Kid* (1969) with Paul NEWMAN and Robert REDFORD, and *Blazing Saddles* (1974).

Satires of other genres included films like *The Night Club* (1925), which ribbed the melodrama; *Lady Killer* (1933), on gangster movies; LAUREL AND HARDY'S *Pardon Us* (1931), on prison films;

The Crimson Pirate (1952), on swash-bucklers; *The Big Bus* (1976), on disaster movies; and *Young Frankenstein* (1974), on the "mad scientist" films.

Marriage and divorce were satirized in films like *Let's Get a Divorce* (1918) starring Billie BURKE, *Dangerous Curves Ahead* (1921), *Is Matrimony a Failure?* (1922), *Virtuous Liars*, *The Goldfish*, *Married Flirts*, *So This Is Marriage* (all 1924), *Pleasure Cruise* (1933), *No More Ladies* (1935), *Three Smart Girls* (1937), *Father Takes a Wife* and *The Feminine Touch* (1941), *Turnabout* (1940), *Confidentially Connie* (1953), *Full of Life* (1956), *Critic's Choice* (1963), *Good Neighbor Sam* (1964), *Divorce, American Style* (1967), *Lovers and Other Strangers* (1970), *For Pete's Sake* (1974), and *California Suite* (1978).

The worlds of advertising, the radio, and television came in for their fair share of ridicule in the following comedies. In *Christmas in July* (1940) Dick POWELL believes he has won an advertising contest. In *The Hucksters* (1947) Clark GABLE is involved with soap advertising. *It Should Happen to You* (1954) starred Judy Holliday whose picture appears on billboards. *Lover Come Back* (1961) has advertising executives Doris DAY and Rock HUDSON competing with each other. *The Thrill of It All* (1963) focuses on commercials and television.

Other films provided satires on various aspects of society. *Our Hospitality* (1923), on feuds; *The Fighting Coward* (1924), on the Old South; *Girl Without a Room* (1933), on modern art; *Duck Soup* (1933), on war; *Million Dollar Baby* (1935), on the Shirley TEMPLE craze; *Ninotchka* (1939), on Communism; *Gone Are the Days* (1963), on the Old South; *The Graduate* (1967), on American values; *Don't Make Waves* (1967), on California; *Goodbye Columbus* (1969), on suburban family life; *Cold Turkey* (1971), on Americans and their ability to solve a problem; *Hospital* (1971), on medical care; *Smile* (1975), on American beauty contests; . . . *And Justice for All* (1979), on our legal system; *Being There* (1979), on politics in American life.

Saville, Ruth (1894–1985), actress. Worked on stage before entering films during the early silent period in 1913. She became Ben TURPIN'S leading lady in many of his comedy shorts. She later appeared on radio and in television.

SELECTED FILMS: Never Too Late (1965). ■

Savo, Jimmy (1896–1960), comedian, entertainer. Began his show business career at age fourteen as a singer on New York's Bowery. He moved to vaudeville with his pantomime-comedy-singing act in the 1910s and to Broadway musical comedies by the mid-1920s. His comedy act was a composite of comic interpretations of popular songs and pantomime skits. A short, roly-poly comic with a perpetual smile, he appeared only occasionally in films.

SELECTED FILMS: Merry-Go-Round of 1938 (1937). ■

Sawyer, Joe (1901–1982), actor. Ubiquitous comedy character actor who began his film career in the early 1930s. Tough-looking and brawny, he often portrayed police officers and army sergeants in comedies and dramas. He is sometimes billed as Joseph Sauers.

SELECTED FILMS: Forgotten Commandments, Huddle (1932), Son of a Sailor (1933), Looking for Trouble (1934), Broadway Gondolier, Little Big Shot (1935), Fish (1936), Great Guy, Slim (1937), Tanks a Million, You're in the Army Now (1941), Taxi, Mister, Fall In, Prairie Chickens, Let's Face It (1943), Brewster's Millions, The Naughty Nineties (1945), If You Knew Susie (1948), The Lucky Stiff (1949), North to Alaska (1960). ■

Saylor, Syd (1895–1962), actor. Worked on the stage before settling in Hollywood as a comic during the 1920s.

He made a series of comedy shorts and then switched to feature films as a character actor, often portraying stuttering comic sidekicks in a string of routine westerns well into the sound period.

SELECTED FILMS: Red Hot Leather (1926), Million Dollar Legs (1932), The Nuisance (1933), Young and Beautiful (1934), The Dude Ranger, Goin' to Town (1935), Kelly the Second (1936), Wild and Woolly (1937), Little Miss Broadway (1938), $1,000 a Touchdown (1939), Swingtime Johnny (1943), Bedside Manner, See My Lawyer (1945), Sitting Pretty (1948), Cheaper by the Dozen, The Jackpot (1950), Escort West (1959). ■

"Scattergood Baines." A comedy series of rural life starring Guy KIBBEE as the friendly busybody of the town. Based on the writings of Clarence Buddington Kelland, the six entries ran from 1941 through 1942 and were directed by Christy CABANNE. They never gained the popularity that other series did, and the idea was soon dropped. In fact, the last film had its title changed from Scattergood Swings It to Cinderella Swings It, but nothing could save the weak series.

SELECTED FILMS: Scattergood Baines, Scattergood Pulls the Strings, Scattergood Meets Broadway (1941), Scattergood Rides High, Scattergood Survives a Murder, Cinderella Swings It (1942). ■

Schade, Fritz, actor. Worked in early silent comedy shorts for producer Mack SENNETT'S KEYSTONE studios as a supporting player. He appeared with some of the leading comics of the period, including, among others, Charlie CHAPLIN and Charlie CHASE.

SELECTED FILMS: Laughing Gas, The Face on the Barroom Floor, The Masquerader, The Rounders, Dough and Dynamite, His Prehistoric Past (1914), Only a Farmer's Daughter, Hash House Mashers, The Rent Jumpers, Love, Loot and Cash, A Lucky Leap, A Rascal in Wolfish Ways, Peanuts and Bullets (1915), The Hunt, The Snow Cure (1916), Her Native Dance, Dangers of a Bride (1917). ■

Schafer, Natalie (1912–), actress. Worked in stock and on stage before entering films in the 1940s. A gifted comedienne, she has appeared as a character actress, often portraying society matrons, in dramas and light films while alternating between Hollywood and Broadway. In the late 1950s she began to take on television assignments.

SELECTED FILMS: Marriage Is a Private Affair (1944), Keep Your Powder Dry, Molly and Me, Wonder Man (1945), Dishonored Lady (1947), Callaway Went Thataway (1951), The Girl Next Door (1953), Bernardine, Oh, Men! Oh, Women! (1957), 40 Carats (1973), The Day of the Locust (1975). ■

Schertzinger, Victor (1880–1941), director, composer. A concert violinist and conductor of musical-comedy orchestras before turning to directing early silent films. For four decades he turned out numerous dramas and light films, including several Bob HOPE-Bing CROSBY "ROAD" films.

SELECTED FILMS: The Clodhopper (1917), String Beans (1918), Made in Heaven (1921), Frivolous Sal (1926), Manhattan Cocktail (1928), Nothing but the Truth (1929), Safety in Numbers, Heads Up (1930), One Night of Love (1934), Let's Live Tonight (1935), Something to Sing About (1937), Road to Singapore, Rhythm on the River (1940), Road to Zanzibar (1941), The Fleet's In (1942). ■

Schildkraut, Joseph (1895–1964), actor. Worked on stage and in films in Germany and his native Austria before migrating to Hollywood in the early 1920s. Dark-haired and handsome, he played lead roles during the silent era and, with the advent of sound, made a smooth transition to character roles. Although he was often cast as suave villains during the latter half of his screen career, he also appeared in lighter roles, proving his versatility as an actor. He was especially effective in *The Cheaters* (1945).

SELECTED FILMS: *Orphans of the Storm (1922), Young April (1926), His Dog (1927), Cock o' the Walk (1930), Lady Behave (1937), The Baroness and the Butler (1938), Idiot's Delight, The Three Musketeers, Pack Up Your Troubles (1939), Meet the Wildcat (1940), Monsieur Beaucaire, The Plainsman and the Lady (1946), The Greatest Story Ever Told (1965).* ∎

Schilling, Gus (1908–1957), actor. Worked as a comedian in burlesque and on stage before switching to films in the early 1940s. Developing into a talented character actor, he often played uneasy types. He worked in several comedy shorts with Richard LANE as a comedy team, Schilling and Lane.

SELECTED FILMS: *Mexican Spitfire Out West (1940), It Started With Eve, Appointment for Love (1941), Chatterbox, Hers to Hold (1943), It's a Pleasure, See My Lawyer, A Thousand and One Nights (1945), Calendar Girl (1947), Angel on the Amazon (1948), Our Very Own (1950), Bigger Than Life (1956).* ∎

Schindell, Cy (1907–1958), actor. Worked chiefly in comedy shorts during the 1930s, 1940s, and 1950s as a supporting player. He appeared in many of the THREE STOOGES' films.

SELECTED FILMS: *Grips, Grunts and Groans, Dizzy Doctors, Back to the Woods, Cash and Carry (1937), Three Little Sew and Sews, A-Ducking They Did Go, Calling All Curs (1939), From Nurse to Worse, Boobs in Arms (1940), What's the Matador?, Matri-Phony (1942), Uncivil Warbirds, Monkey Businessmen (1946), Fright Night, Sing a Song of Six Pants, All Gummed Up (1947), Fiddlers Three, A Crime on Their Hands (1948), Fling in the Ring, Stone Age Romeos (1955).* ∎

Schreiber, Avery (1935–), actor, comedian. Worked as stand-up comic and part of comedy team with Jack BURNS. He appeared on Broadway, in television, and finally in a handful of films. A short, fleshy figure with a large mustache, he has also written comedy material for television specials.

SELECTED FILMS: *Swashbuckler (1976), The Last Remake of Beau Geste (1977), Scavenger Hunt (1979), Loose Shoes (1980), Jimmy the Kid (1983).* ∎

Screen biographies. See Film biographies.

Screwball comedy. A film genre of the 1930s that blended witty, sophisticated dialogue with vigorous slapstick, while the male and female leads supplied both the comedy and romantic elements. Cinderella stories were sometimes introduced in which playboy sons of millionaires fell in love with working-class heroines. Female leads, who were often heiresses, appeared to be independent or self-sufficient, at least on the surface. Male leads invariably were eligible bachelors, and, if they ever worked at all, never seemed to have conventional jobs. Wealthy parents of the male or female leads tried in vain to control the frantic life-style of their offspring while frowning upon the younger generation. Settings included mansions, nightclubs, country estates, or hotel or executive suites. Attire often consisted chiefly of evening wear or sports outfits. The pace was highly accelerated. However, the most important characteristic that earned these films the description of "screwball," "madcap," or, as several British film critics prefer to label them, "crazy" was the completely uninhibited behavior of the main characters. Usually members of the upper classes, they often felt free to be absurd, outrageous, or unconventional. The heroes and heroines demonstrated a freedom from artificial restraint that was unique in film comedies of the period. Other comic elements frequently included mistaken identities, romantic complications, and a host of eccentric supporting players.

Screwball comedies were born during the early years of the Depression and died off by the end of the decade although there were isolated attempts to revive the genre. Somehow only the pre-war years could produce the light-headedness and zany antics of these escape films. Some film historians date the genre from *It Happened One Night* (1934), in which Clark GABLE portrayed a reporter hired by the father of a run-away heiress (Claudette COLBERT) to find his daughter. However, several earlier comedies contain major elements of the genre. For example, in *Holiday* (1930), based on Philip Barry's Broadway play about nonconformity, Ann Harding played Linda Seton, the unconventional daughter of a wealthy banking family who falls in love with Johnny Case, portrayed by Robert Ames, who wants to abandon his world of finance and go on an extended vacation, much to the chagrin of Linda's father. The film was remade in 1938, and this second version is more fondly remembered by the public. In another early example, *Three-Cornered Moon* (1933), a film that contains several elements of screwball comedy, matriarch Mary BOLAND has her hands full trying to control her zany family.

In *Twentieth Century* (1934) John BARRYMORE played a temperamental Broadway producer who catapults lowly Carole LOMBARD to stardom. When she eventually decides to flee his dictatorial control, he threatens to commit suicide. When that ploy fails, he follows her aboard the "Twentieth Century" train with hilarious results.

By the middle of the decade the style was set and the films became a Hollywood staple. *Libeled Lady* (1936) starred four top MGM stars, Jean HARLOW, William POWELL, Spencer TRACY, and Myrna LOY, in a wacky story concerning heiress Loy who presents newspaperman Tracy with a five-million-dollar li-

bel suit. That same year Universal released *My Man Godfrey*, in which William Powell played an ex-millionaire hired by the wealthy and spoiled Bullock family as a butler. Not only does he straighten out each member of the clan, but he marries the daughter, Carole Lombard. Another 1936 entry, *Theodora Goes Wild*, starred Irene DUNNE as a small-town writer who pens a controversial novel. Melvyn DOUGLAS co-starred as the suave New York artist who did the illustrations for her book.

Screwball comedies continued to appear in the late 1930s, with some of the same stars who made the genre so popular. Claudette Colbert starred in *I Met Him in Paris* (1937). During her travels through Europe, Melvyn Douglas, Robert YOUNG, and Lee BOWMAN vie for her affections. In the same year Paramount released *Easy Living*, starring Jean ARTHUR, Edward ARNOLD, and Ray MILLAND. While working girl Arthur is riding on the top deck of a Fifth Avenue bus, she is hit with a mink coat thrown from a window by Arnold, who is irate at the amount of money his wife spent on the garment. Milland, who plays his son, eventually falls in love with Arthur after some humorous misunderstandings. In *Nothing Sacred*, also made in 1937, cynical newspaperman Fredric MARCH exploits (and is exploited by) small-town girl Carole Lombard, who allegedly has only a short time to live. He brings her to the big city for one last fling while the readers of his paper soak up all the details of the tragic story—until she learns that her doctor made a mistake. Katharine HEPBURN made her share of screwball comedies. In *Bringing Up Baby* (1938) she played a zany heiress who travels with her pet named "Baby," which just happens to be a leopard. Cary GRANT played a staid paleontologist who gets mixed up with Hepburn and her pet. During the same year she starred again with Cary Grant in the remake of the 1930 comedy, *Holiday*. She had the role originally played by Ann Harding while Grant portrayed Johnny. The veteran character actor, Edward Everett HORTON, appeared as the professor friend of Johnny in both film versions. *Midnight* (1939), one of the last screwball comedies of the period, starred Claudette Colbert as an American stranded in Paris. Taxi-driver Don AMECHE falls in love with her and follows her to a country estate where she is the guest of John Barrymore, who is hilarious in the film.

Other screwball comedies of the 1930s include *True Confession* (1937), starring Carole Lombard and Fred MacMurray; *Double Wedding* (1937), starring William Powell and Myrna Loy; *The Awful Truth* (1937), starring Irene Dunne and Cary Grant; *It's Love I'm After* (1937), with Bette DAVIS and Leslie Howard; *The Mad Miss Manton* (1938), starring Barbara Stanwyck and Henry FONDA; *The Rage of Paris* (1938), with Danielle Darrieux and Douglas FAIRBANKS, JR.; and *Merrily We Live* (1938), starring Constance BENNETT and Brian AHERNE.

Over the following decades studios and directors attempted to resurrect the genre with mixed results. The 1950s offered *A Millionaire for Christy* (1951), *Monkey Business* (1952) starring Marilyn MONROE, *Forever Darling* (1956), and *This Could Be the Night* (1957), to mention a few. *What's Up, Doc?* (1972), a reworking of *Bringing Up Baby*, and *Seems Like Old Times*, released in 1980, captured some of the flavor of the old screwball comedies.

Searl, Jackie (1920–), actor. Appeared as a child on radio before becoming a popular young actor in films during the 1930s. He usually portrayed brats and other disagreeable youths in dramas and comedies.

SELECTED FILMS: Daughters of Desire (1929), Finn and Hattie, Skippy, Newly Rich (1931), Topaze, High Gear (1933), Peck's Bad Boy (1934), Ginger (1935), Gentle Julia (1936), Wild and Woolly (1937), That Certain Age, Little Tough Guys in Society (1938), My Little Chickadee, Military Academy (1940), Glamour Boy (1941), The Paleface (1948). ■

Seaton, George (1911–1979), director, screenwriter. Worked as a stage actor and producer before turning to films in the early 1930s as a screenwriter. By the 1940s, after writing screenplays for such comedies as *A Day at the Races* starring the MARX BROTHERS, he was directing and writing a string of entertaining, if conventional, films for major studios. He later began producing his own films. He won Oscars for two of his films.

SELECTED FILMS: Diamond Horseshoe, Junior Miss (1945), The Shocking Miss Pilgrim, Miracle on 34th Street (1947), Apartment for Peggy (1948), Chicken Every Sunday (1949), For Heaven's Sake (1950), Teacher's Pet (1958), The Pleasure of His Company (1961), What's So Bad About Feeling Good? (1968), Showdown (1973). ■

"Second Hundred Years, The" (1927), MGM. *Dir.* Fred Guiol; *Sc.* Leo McCarey; with Laurel and Hardy, James Finlayson, Eugene Pallette, Tiny Sanford.

One of the funniest and best-constructed of Laurel and Hardy's two-reelers, the film centers on the misadventures of the duo as convicts intent on crashing out of the Big House. Unfortunately, one of their attempts, a tunnel, lands them in the warden's office. They seize their next opportunity by disguising themselves as painters and nonchalantly paint their way out of the prison gates. Followed by a suspicious police officer, they smear everything in their view, including store fronts, windows, parked cars, and lampposts. At one point Laurel is distracted momentarily as he is painting a lamppost and accidentally paints the backside of a passing woman who pauses before crossing the street. They steal some clothes and, mistaken for the owners of the garments, are invited into a limousine. As fate would have it, they are driven back to their prison, this time as guests of the unsuspecting warden. The film is the first official film starring Stan and Ollie as a genuine team (although several film historians believe that "Putting Pants on Philip" was their first as a team). Their style and delivery demonstrate their comic talent. They had already made less than a dozen films together, but in this short they have deliberately slowed down the pace while simultaneously developing the situation. Stan's character as most audiences conceive him is already established here. He approaches a fellow convict and asks him when he'll be getting out. The tough prisoner says that he has 30 more years to go. Laurel smiles, hands the unfortunate soul a letter, and says, "Mail this for me when you get out."

Sedgwick, Edward (1892–1953), director. Performed in the circus and in vaudeville before trying his hand at film acting in 1915. After appearing in comedy shorts, he switched to directing in the early 1920s, turning out chiefly light films. He made a smooth transition into sound films but was soon relegated to low-budget features. He directed some of the leading comics of the period, including, among others, Buster KEATON, Joe E. BROWN, LAUREL AND HARDY, and Red SKELTON.

SELECTED FILMS: Fantomas, Live Wires (1921), Blinky, Out of Luck (1923), Broadway or Bust (1924), Slide, Kelly, Slide (1927), Circus Rookies, The Cameraman (1928), Spite Marriage (1929), Doughboys, Free and Easy (1930), A Dangerous Affair (1931), The Passionate Plumber, Speak Easily (1932), Horse Play (1933), Here Comes the Groom (1934), Mister Cinderella (1936), Pick a Star, Riding on Air (1937), The Gladiator (1938), Beware Spooks (1939), Air Raid Wardens (1943), A Southern Yankee (1948), Ma and Pa Kettle Back on the Farm (1951). ∎

Sedgwick, Eileen (1895–), actress. Toured in vaudeville with her family act before entering films in 1915. During her early years she turned out a series of one- and two-reel comedies for different studios, including Universal and IMP. She rapidly rose to stardom in the 1920s in a string of routine melodramas and serials. By the late 1920s, however, her popularity peaked and she was relegated to supporting roles.

SELECTED FILMS: The Eagle's Nest (1915), Hired, Tired and Fired, Some Heroes, I'll Get Her Yet, Ain't He Grand?, Kill the Umpire, Room Rent and Romance (1916), The Honeymoon Surprise, It's Cheaper to Be Married, The High Cost of Starving, A Bare Living, Good Morning, Nurse, The Gasoline Habit, His Family Tree (1917), A Kitchen Hero, The Butler's Blunder, Oh, Man!, Repeating the Honeymoon (1918), Dream Girl (1921), Tin Hats (1927), A Girl in Every Port, Beautiful but Dumb (1928). ∎

Seely, Sybil, actress. Worked in silent comedies in the 1920s, especially as the female lead in several of comedian Buster KEATON'S early short films.

SELECTED FILMS: One Week, Convict 13, The Scarecrow (1920), The Boat (1921). ∎

Seff, Manuel, (1895–1969) screenwriter. Wrote routine screenplays during the 1930s chiefly for light films. He was also the author of original stories adapted to the screen, the bulk of which were comedies.

SELECTED FILMS (as screenwriter): Footlight Parade (1933), Kansas City Princess (1934), Gold Diggers of 1935, Traveling Saleslady (1935), Trouble for Two (1936), Breaking the Ice (1938), Jam Session (1944).

SELECTED FILMS (as original author): Blessed Event (1932), College Coach (1933), Bedside (1934), Slightly Tempted (1940), Married Bachelor (1941), Walk Softly, Stranger (1950). ∎

George Segal and Jane Fonda

Segal, George (1934–), actor. Worked as a musician and stage actor before entering films in the early 1960s. He has played male leads in dramas and light films, adding his charm and eccentric style to his roles. The themes of his comedies often concern domestic life and male-female relationships with Segal portraying unusually vulnerable and sympathetic characters.

SELECTED FILMS: The Young Doctors (1961), Bye Bye Braverman, No Way to Treat a Lady (1968), Loving, The Owl and the Pussycat, Where's Poppa? (1970), The Hot Rock (1972), A Touch of Class (1973), Russian Roulette, The Black Bird (1975), Fun With Dick and Jane (1977), Who Is Killing the Great Chefs of Europe? (1978), Lost and Found (1979), The Last Married Couple in America (1980), Carbon Copy (1981). ∎

Seiler, Lewis (1891–1963), director. Worked as a GAGMAN and assistant director during the silent era before becoming a full-fledged director by the mid-1920s. During the next three decades he turned out numerous melodramas and comedies, the bulk of which were routine.

SELECTED FILMS: Darwin Was Right (1924), Girls Gone Wild (1929), Ginger, Paddy O'Day (1935), Here Comes Trouble (1936), He Couldn't Say No, Penrod's Double Trouble (1938), The Kid From Kokomo (1939), Tugboat Annie Sails Again (1940), Kisses for Breakfast, You're in the Army Now (1941), Something for the Boys (1944), Molly and Me (1945), If I'm Lucky (1946), The Story of Lynn Stuart (1958). ∎

Seiter, William A. (1892–1964), director. Began his long career in films as an actor in Mack SENNETT'S KEYSTONE comedy shorts. By 1918 he was directing films and continued in this capacity through the mid-1950s. He worked with some of the leading comics of the period, including, among others, WHEELER AND WOOLSEY, the MARX BROTHERS, and ABBOTT AND COSTELLO. A proficient director in several genres, he turned out numerous routine but entertaining features.

SELECTED FILMS: Tangled Threads (1919), The Foolish Age (1921), Boy Crazy (1922), Listen Lester (1924), Where Was I? (1925), Skinner's Dress Suit (1926), Out All Night (1927), Why Be Good? (1929), The Flirting Widow (1930), Caught Plastered (1931), Girl Crazy (1932), Diplomaniacs, Sons of the Desert (1933), Rafter Romance (1934), Roberta (1935), Stowaway (1936), Life Begins in College (1937), Room Service (1938), Four Jills in a Jeep (1944), Little Giant (1946), One Touch of Venus (1948), Dear Brat (1951), Make Haste to Live (1954). ∎

Seitz, George B. (1888–1944), director. Turned out numerous dramas and light films, especially in the 1930s, his most prolific period. Much of his work was with low-budget or second features, which included the popular "ANDY HARDY" comedy series produced by MGM. An efficient craftsman, he directed many entertaining films.

SELECTED FILMS: Sally of the Subway (1932), The Women in His Life (1933), Times Square Lady, Calm Yourself, Kind Lady (1935), Absolute Quiet, The Three Wise Guys, Mad Holiday (1936), A Family Affair, Mama Steps Out, My Dear Miss Aldrich (1937), Judge Hardy's Children, Love Finds Andy Hardy (1938), The Hardys Ride High (1939), Love Finds Andy Hardy (1941),

Andy Hardy's Double Life (1942), Andy Hardy's Blonde Trouble (1944). ∎

Semels, Harry (1887–1946), actor. A supporting player in numerous comedies from the 1920s through the 1940s. Although he made several feature-length films, he appeared chiefly in comedy shorts during the 1930s and 1940s. He worked with the THREE STOOGES as well as with other leading comics, including LAUREL AND HARDY.

SELECTED FILMS: Beware of Blondes (1928), Subway Express (1931), Three Little Beers (1935), The Gay Desperado, Movie Maniacs, Half-Shot Shooters, Disorder in the Court (1936), Swiss Miss, Wee, Wee, Monsieur (1938), Three Little Sew and Sews (1939), Dutiful but Dumb (1941), Back From the Front, Dizzy Pilots (1943). ∎

Semon, Larry (1889–1928), actor. Began his film career in 1916 as a comedy writer and director for Vitagraph studios. He appeared in his own comedy shorts in 1917 and, by the early 1920s, gained enough popularity with his audiences to rival the master comics of the period, including CHAPLIN and Harold LLOYD. A diminutive, natural clown with a rubbery mouth, he specialized in the outrageous—including mechanical gags and inventive chases as well as the conventional slapstick routines and pratfalls. He usually portrayed a simpleton with a foolish grin. His popularity, however, did not last long.

His creativity and financial success carried him through much of the 1920s, but his conflicts with Vitagraph over his ever-increasing budgets at a time when the company's profits were declining led to a split. By the late 1920s and following a few box-office flops, his star began to diminish and he quit films to work in vaudeville. Plagued by financial worries and thoughts of failure, he suffered a nervous breakdown. He died bankrupt in 1928.

He just missed joining the comic greats of the silent era. Several reasons are usually suggested for his failure to attain that elusive greatness. He seemed to lack that extra spark of genius that we find in a Chaplin or a Lloyd. Like so many of his contemporaries, he lacked a distinct screen personality with whom his audience could identify. Whereas Chaplin had his tramp character well defined by the 1920s and Lloyd had his sprightly, dapper go-getter, Semon depended upon external objects and wild routines that could not sustain him for long or catapult him into the top echelons of the great film clowns. He was too similar to a dozen other funnymen who used the same material. Also, he was too repetitive in his sight gags. He could not sustain his films with his own personality, and his reliance on old material simply made his later comedies boring.

SELECTED FILMS: Rough Toughs and Roof Tops, Boasts and Boldness, Spooks and Spasms (1917), Babes and Boobs, Spies and Spills (1918), Passing the Buck, The Simple Life (1919), The Stage Hand, The Suitor (1920), The Sportsman, The Fall Guy (1921), The Sawmill, The Show, The Sleuth (1922), No Wedding Bells, Midnight Cabaret (1923), The Girl in the Limousine (1924), The Perfect Clown, The Wizard of Oz (1925), Stop, Look and Listen (1926), Spuds, Underworld (1927). ∎

Sennett, Mack (1880–1960), producer, director, actor. Worked in burlesque and Broadway musicals before entering films in 1908 as an actor for Biograph studios in New York City where D. W. Griffith was directing. He played a variety of comic roles but generally hayseeds. Entranced by this new medium, Sennett, born Michael Sinnott, attempted to learn as much as he could about it. He became Griffith's "right arm" where comedy was concerned. By 1910 he was directing film shorts for the studio while concentrating on comedy. Two years later he joined KEYSTONE, a new film company, directing slapstick comedies. He had cajoled some of Biograph's comics, including Fred MACE, Mabel NORMAND, and Ford STERLING, to follow him to the new studio.

Under Sennett, the company flourished and was recognized as the leader and innovator of comedy shorts. Other comedians joined the troupe. Roscoe "Fatty" ARBUCKLE, Chester CONKLIN, Slim SUMMERVILLE, Al ST. JOHN, and Mack SWAIN brought their talents to the stock company. The neophyte comic, Charlie CHAPLIN, found a temporary home at Keystone for one year before moving on to other studios.

The comedy product produced by Sennett was crude, often improvised, and always chaotic and zany, but it sold well. He broadened the genre as the demand increased, adding the famous "Bathing Beauties" and children's comedies. New directors were hired to relieve him so that he could supervise the various units.

By 1915 he had larger facilities and an increased budget, allowing him to cut some of the cruder elements of his comedies. He relied more on editing and situation comedy and less on physical humor. Still not satisfied, he left the studio in 1917 and organized his own company, once again taking many of the stars with him. He continued to produce two-reelers, but occasionally attempted feature-length comedies. He also discovered Harry LANGDON at this time. He continued in this vein until the end of the silent period. Although he continued to make comedy shorts well into the 1930s, he did not command the attention given to him in his heyday. Demand for his type of films decreased and, by 1935, when he abandoned films, he was almost bankrupt. In 1937 he was honored with a special Academy Award for his contributions to film comedy. He has deservedly earned the title, "King of Comedy."

Sennett brought many innovations to the world of film comedy, not to mention his "KEYSTONE KOPS" and other series. He often had his cameramen undercrank the camera so that action was accelerated. He would use stock footage of an actual event and then construct a story around it. He introduced a surrealistic world of cars dangling from cliffs or riding up the sides of buildings, of a chain of inept police officers wrapped around telephone poles, of commonplace worlds turned upside down. Finally, he developed the art of slapstick, the chase, and parody to the point that much of the comedy we see on the screen today can be traced to the wealth of films he left behind. His autobiography, *King of Comedy*, was published in 1954.

SELECTED FILMS (as producer): Cohen Collects a Debt, The Ambitious Butler, Mabel's Lovers, Brown's Seance (1912), Double Wedding, Her New Beau, The Bangville Police, The Firebug (1913), Love and Dynamite, Tango Tangles, Mabel at the Wheel, The Knockout, Tillie's Punctured Romance (1914), Those College Girls (1915), A Modern Enoch Arden (1916), Teddy at the Throttle (1917), Mickey (1918), A Submarine Pirate (1919), Love, Honor and Behave (1920), Oh, Mabel Behave (1922), The Shreik of Araby, The Extra Girl (1923), Picking Peaches (1924), Saturday Afternoon (1926), The Goodbye Kiss (1928), Midnight Daddies (1930), I Surrender Dear (1931), The Dentist, Hypnotized (1932), The Fatal Glass of Beer (1933), Way Up Thar (1935). ∎

Sessions, Almira (1888–1974), actress. Appeared as a character player in dramas and light films during the 1940s. She often portrayed eccentric and feather-brained types.

SELECTED FILMS: Chad Hanna (1940), Little Nellie Kelly, She Knew All the Answers (1941), Sullivan's Travels (1942), My Kingdom for a Cook, The Heat's On (1943), The Miracle of Morgan's Creek (1944), She Wouldn't Say Yes, The Diary of a Chambermaid (1946), Apartment for Peggy (1948), Rosemary McCoy (1949). ∎

Sex comedy. Films whose risque humor often encompasses sophisticated allusions and situations, double entendres, and suggestive innuendoes that may be visual as well as verbal. Many of the scenes are laid in bedrooms or drawing rooms, decorated in a stylized realism that underscores the theme of seduction. The male lead, the symbol of bachelorhood and virility, is usually the aggressor, but it is the female, sometimes virginal, always wary, who wins the battle of the sexes. The chief characters are often high-salaried executives who have the time and money to pursue their sexual fantasies. These films are sometimes referred to as bedroom farces or Hollywood sex comedies.

The genre dates back to the early silent films. John BUNNY, a popular film comic before World War I, made a series of comedy shorts centering on his extramarital complications. In one such typical romp, "Stenographers Wanted" (1912), Bunny and his partner advertise for stenographers and soon their office is occupied by dozens of beautiful young women. The husbands are in ecstasy for a while, until their wives enter and make their own choices. Cecil B. DeMILLE, known later for his epics, directed several sex comedies early in his career, including *Don't Change Your Husband* (1919), starring Gloria SWANSON; *Male and Female* (1919), based on James Barrie's comedy, *The Admirable Crichton*; and *Why Change Your Wife?* (1920). Director Ernst LUBITSCH made his share of silent sex comedies, less lurid and more witty than DeMille's, which included *Forbidden Paradise* and *The Marriage Circle* (both 1924).

In the early 1930s Mae WEST dominated the genre, swinging her hips, delivering her suggestive songs, and tossing about enough innuendoes to make the Hollywood censors uneasy. In films like *Night After Night* (1932), *She Done Him Wrong*, and *I'm No Angel* (both 1933), she not only treated sex lightly but acted as though she enjoyed it. Her songs, "Easy Rider" and "I Like a Man

What Takes His Time," intimated as much. Her lines went even further. "It's not the men in my life, it's the life in my men." "Penny for your thoughts—do I make myself clear, boys?" "When I'm good, I'm very good, but when I'm bad, I'm even better." Satirizing conventional morality, she portrayed the uninhibited woman who uses her sexual charms for pleasure and profit.

Another sex symbol of the period was Jean HARLOW, whose lines like "Would you be shocked if I put on something more comfortable?" excited not only her lover, Ben Lyon, in *Hell's Angels* (1930) but many in the audience. She enters her bedroom, disrobes discreetly while baring her back and shoulder, and puts on something sexier. In *Red Dust* (1932), set on a rubber plantation, she is told of the difficulties of sleeping at night because of the heat, to which she replies: "I'm not used to sleeping nights anyway." With the crackdown in 1934 by the Hays Office, a self-governing censorship body of the film industry, the sex comedy was laid to rest for the remainder of the decade, while "safer" subjects such as westerns, mysteries, romances, and films based on classics dominated the screen.

During the next decade several writers and directors began to break out of the strictures of the Hollywood code. In the zany film *The Palm Beach Story* (1942), Claudette COLBERT abandons her almost penniless husband, Joel McCREA, to hunt for a millionaire, while Mary ASTOR, her companion, searches for any man. *The Miracle of Morgan's Creek* (1944) barely escaped the censor's scissors. Betty Hutton goes on an all-night spree at a bash for departing G.I.s, resulting in her pregnancy. Although she had gotten married sometime that night (a concession to the censors), she cannot remember what the father looked like or his name.

By the 1950s Hollywood had created enough sex symbols to keep the genre flowing for more than a decade. Marilyn MONROE, vulnerable and sensual, starred in *Let's Make It Legal* (1951), *Monkey Business* (1952), *We're Not Married* (1952), *Gentlemen Prefer Blondes* (1953), and *The Seven Year Itch* (1955), among other sex comedies. Jayne MANSFIELD, in comedies like *The Girl Can't Help It* (1956) and *Kiss Them for Me* (1957), contributed her charms and sexuality to films for two decades. Jane RUSSELL, whose debut in *The Outlaw* (1943) was postponed because of the censorship problems of that film, was another star of the 1950s who flaunted her physical attributes in comedies like *Road to Bali* (1952), *The French Line* (1954), and *The Fuzzy Pink Nightgown* (1957). The film that was most notorious for challenging the Production Code was Otto Preminger's *The Moon Is Blue* (1953). An otherwise innocuous comedy starring William HOLDEN, David NIVEN, and Maggie McNamara, it contained words like "virgin" and "mistress" for the first time on screen.

Sex comedy took another turn, beginning in the late 1950s, particularly with the Rock Hudson-Doris Day features. Although the films of this type, which continued into the 1970s, showed little on the screen, they suggested much. The talk and action dealt with sex and seduction, pursuit and submission, subterfuge and coyness. In *Pillow Talk* (1959) Day and Hudson share a party-line telephone that he dominates, conversing with all his girlfriends. When she objects, he questions her ability to attract men. In their next comedy, *Lover Come Back* (1961), they are rival ad executives. He employs women to attract his clients, while she uses conventional methods. "I don't use sex to win accounts," she frets. "When do you use it?" Hudson asks. "I don't!" she replies, realizing too late what she has said. Other screen stars participated in the genre. Cary GRANT portrays a millionaire who tries to bed Doris Day in *That Touch of Mink* (1962). Tony Curtis in *The Perfect Furlough* (1958) is one of a group of sex-starved servicemen who is selected to enjoy a

trip to Paris, accompanied by psychiatrist Janet LEIGH. The following year he posed as an impotent millionaire in *Some Like It Hot*, eliciting the sympathy of Marilyn MONROE, who is eager to restore his sexuality.

Other films of this sort included *Kiss Me, Stupid* (1964), starring Dean MARTIN, *Mary, Mary* (1963), starring Debbie REYNOLDS and Barry Nelson; *Sunday in New York* (1963), with Jane FONDA and Cliff Robertson; and *Sex and the Single Girl* (1964), with Natalie Wood and Tony Curtis. One unusual entry, *Bob & Carol & Ted & Alice* (1969), dealt with sexual freedom among married couples. Robert Culp, Natalie WOOD, Elliot GOULD, and Dyan Cannon starred.

The 1970s and 1980s presented variations of these themes. Elliott Gould in one of his weakest comedies, *Move* (1970), portrays a pornography writer, while Richard BENJAMIN plays the title character in the unsuccessful *Portnoy's Complaint* (1972), based on Philip Roth's novel about the love-hate relationship between a son and his mother. Other films included *The Single Girls* (1973), a low-budget comedy with plenty of violence, and *The Seniors* (1978), one of the first sex comedies dealing with a relatively younger generation. In the latter film, college students open an alleged sex clinic. Woody ALLEN took a different approach in *Everything You Always Wanted to Know About Sex (But Were Afraid to Ask)* (1972). He used individual episodes to explore the themes of Dr. David Reuben's book. Many of the sex comedies produced in the 1980s were aimed chiefly at a younger audience. These YOUTH EXPLOITATION COMEDIES took advantage of the new frankness and were generally little more than sophomoric attempts at titillation. Films like *The Last Married Couple in America* (1980), starring George SEGAL and Natalie Wood, and Woody Allen's *A Midsummer Night's Sex Comedy* (1982) were exceptions.

Seymour, Dan (1915–1982), actor. Worked as a nightclub entertainer before settling in Hollywood in the early 1940s as a character player. Dark and fleshy, he often portrayed callous villains who enjoyed administering pain. He also appeared in light films, usually as a self-parody, including several ABBOTT AND COSTELLO entries.

SELECTED FILMS: Cairo, Road to Morocco (1942), Tahiti Honey, Rhythm on the Islands, Klondike Kate (1943), It's in the Bag (1945), A Night in Casablanca (1946), Hard Boiled Mahoney (1947), Unfaithfully Yours (1948), Abbott and Costello in the Foreign Legion (1950), Abbott and Costello Meet the Mummy (1955), The Buster Keaton Story, The Sad Sack (1957), Escape to Witch Mountain (1974). ■

Shannon, Harry (1890–1964), actor. Worked on Broadway stage before entering films in the early 1930s. A dependable character actor, he appeared in dramas and light films into the 1960s, often playing fathers and other mature roles.

SELECTED FILMS: Heads Up (1930), Young Tom Edison (1940), The Lady Is Willing, Once Upon a Honeymoon (1942), The Farmer's Daughter (1947), Mr. Blandings Builds His Dream House (1948), Three Little Words (1950), Gypsy (1962). ■

Shapiro, Stanley (1925–), screenwriter. Wrote for radio and television before trying his hand at writing screenplays in the early 1950s. Specializing in bedroom or SEX COMEDIES, he penned a string of successful films in the 1960s. His Pillow Talk (1959) brought him an Oscar for Best Screenplay. In 1964 he started to produce his own works as well as those of others.

SELECTED FILMS: South Sea Woman (1953), The Perfect Furlough (1958), Operation Petticoat (1959), Come September (1961), That Touch of Mink (1962), Bedtime Story (1964), A Very Special Favor (1965), How to Save a Marriage—and Ruin Your Life (1968), For Pete's Sake (1974), Carbon Copy (1981). ■

Shaughnessy, Mickey (1920–1985), actor. Worked as a nightclub entertainer before entering films in the early 1950s. A stocky, tough-looking character player, he appeared chiefly in comic roles in dramas and light films until the 1970s, after which he switched to television.

SELECTED FILMS: The Marrying Kind (1952), Don't Go Near the Water (1956), Designing Woman (1957), A Nice Little Bank That Should Be Robbed (1958), Don't Give Up the Ship (1959), Dondi (1960), Pocketful of Miracles (1961), A Global Affair (1963), Never a Dull Moment (1967), The Boatniks (1970). ■

Shavelson, Melville (1917–), director, screenwriter. Worked as a writer for radio before turning his talents to films. He wrote screenplays for a series of light films until the 1950s when he began directing and producing films. He wrote several scripts for Bob HOPE. Much of his writing is bright and funny while his directorial efforts have been either routine or a notch above average.

SELECTED FILMS (as director): The Seven Little Foys (1955), The Five Pennies (1959), It Started in Naples (1960), On the Double (1961), The Pigeon That Took Rome (1962), Yours, Mine and Ours (1968), The War Between Men and Women (1972), Mixed Company (1974).

SELECTED FILMS (as screenwriter): The Princess and the Pirate (1944), Wonder Man (1945), The Kid From Brooklyn (1946), Where There's Life (1947), Sorrowful Jones, The Great Lover (1949), Double Dynamite (1951), April in Paris (1952), Trouble Along the Way (1953). ■

Shawlee, Joan (1929–1987), actress. Worked as a model and as a comedienne in nightclubs before entering films in the mid-1940s. A tall character player, she usually portrays light-headed characters. She has appeared in dramas and comedies.

SELECTED FILMS: *House of Horrors, Lover Come Back (1946), Buck Privates Come Home (1947), The Marrying Kind (1952), All Ashore (1953), Some Like It Hot (1959), The Apartment (1960), Live a Little, Love a Little (1968), One More Train to Rob (1971), Buddy Buddy (1981).* ∎

Shawn, Dick (1929–1987), actor. Worked in nightclubs and on stage before entering films in 1956. An offbeat comedian whose best work has been in broad comedy, he has enlivened many films and was unforgettable as a stoned, over-the-hill hippie in *The Producers.*

In the above film he is interviewed for a part in a musical based on the life of Hitler. His mind blown by drugs, he can barely remember his name. "Lorenzo Saint Dubois," he finally says. "My friends call me LSD." "And what have you done, LSD?" "About six months," Shawn answers. "What do you do best?" "I can't do that here," he admits. "That's why they put me away, babe."

In *Love at First Bite* he played a police detective who hesitates to break into Dracula's apartment where Richard Benjamin's sweetheart is held captive. "If we don't," Benjamin explains, "her immortal soul will be lost forever." "If we do," Shawn frets, "I'll lose my pension."

SELECTED FILMS: *The Opposite Sex (1956), Wake Me When It's Over (1960), It's a Mad, Mad, Mad, Mad World (1963), A Very Special Favor (1965), What Did You Do in the War, Daddy? (1966), The Producers (1968), The Happy Ending (1969), Looking Up (1977), Love at First Bite (1979).* ∎

She Done Him Wrong (1933), PAR. Dir. Lowell Sherman; Sc. John Bright, Harry Thew; with Mae West, Cary Grant, Gilbert Roland, Noah Beery.

Repeating her stage role as Diamond Lil, a saloon entertainer during the Gay Nineties, Mae WEST sashays about seductively, collecting diamonds and men; tosses out numerous one-liners; and says

Cary Grant and Mae West in *She Done Him Wrong* (1933)

to Cary GRANT: "Why don't you come up sometime and see me?" If these elements are not entertaining enough, her suggestive songs, "A Man What Takes His Time" and "Easy Rider," surely top off a very entertaining self-parody. In one of the final scenes, when Grant is about to handcuff West, she asks, "Is that necessary? I wasn't born with them." Grant says that a lot of men would have been safer if she had. "I don't know," West counters, "hands aren't everything." The film exemplifies the problems West and Paramount faced with the more conservative members of the public. The Hollywood Production Code, introduced the following year, has been attributed in part to this film.

Shean, Al. See Gallagher and Shean.

Sheekman, Arthur (1901–1978), screenwriter. Wrote columns and drama criticism for newspapers before turning to writing screenplays for Hollywood films in the early 1930s. Working alone and in collaboration, he specialized in comedy scripts. He contributed dialogue for the MARX BROTHERS films.

SELECTED FILMS: *Roman Scandals (1933), Kid Millions (1934), Dimples, Pigskin Parade, Stowaway (1936), The Gladiator (1938), Blue Skies (1946), Dear Ruth, The Trouble With Women (1947), Dear Wife (1949), Young Man With Ideas (1952), Call Me Madam (1953), Bundle of Joy (1956), Some Came Running (1958), Ada (1961).* ∎

Sheridan, Ann (1915–1969), actress. Appeared as a minor actress in routine films in the early 1930s. Within a few years and a change of studio to Warner Brothers, she established herself as a competent and popular leading lady. Although the bulk of her films were dramas, she appeared in several comedies as well.

Her flair for comedy was demonstrated even in her dramatic roles. In *They Drive by Night* (1942) she played a hard-boiled, independent dame who must ward off the advances of tough truck drivers. "Do you believe in love at first sight?" asks George Raft. "Well," she replies, "it saves a lot of time."

SELECTED FILMS: *Search for Beauty, Kiss and Make Up, Shoot the Works, Ladies Should Listen (1934), Enter Madame (1935), Behold My Wife, Mississippi (1936), The Great O'Malley, Wine, Women and Horses, The Footloose Heiress (1937), She Loved a Fireman, Cowboy From Brooklyn, Broadway Musketeers (1938), Naughty but Nice (1939), Honeymoon for Three (1941), The Man Who Came to Dinner, George Washington Slept Here (1942), Good Sam (1948), I Was a Male War Bride (1949), The Opposite Sex (1956).* ■

Kathryn McGuire and Buster Keaton in *Sherlock, Jr.* (1924)

Sherlock, Jr. (1924), MGM. *Dir.* Buster Keaton; *Sc.* Jean Havez, Clyde Bruckman, Joseph Mitchell; with Buster Keaton, Ward Crane.

More than simply a satire of mystery films, this Buster Keaton comedy is one of his most imaginative features as well as his shortest. He plays a movie projectionist who daydreams of becoming a detective. While asleep, he dreams that the girl he loves is in danger from a villain who resembles his real-life rival in the melodrama he is currently projecting. Keaton, whose alter-ego rises from his sleeping form, literally takes us into a film as he engages in special effects and some very funny gags. Some memorable scenes include his entering the image on the screen and getting tossed into the orchestra pit of the movie house, his game of pool in which he is unaware that one of the balls contains a deadly bomb, and his wildly hilarious and thrilling ride on the handlebars of a runaway motorcycle. The film, in which Keaton takes us into his private movie world and its special effects to cleverly blend reality and illusion, anticipates Woody ALLEN'S *The Purple Rose of Cairo* (1985).

Sherman, Lowell (1885–1934), actor, director. Starred on Broadway before entering early silent films as an actor. By the early 1930s he added directing to his film career, specializing in romantic comedies.

SELECTED FILMS (as actor): *Way Down East, Yes or No (1920), The Gilded Lily (1921), The Spitfire, The Truth About Women (1924), You Never Know Women (1926), The Girl From Gay Paree (1927), General Crack (1929), He Knew Women, Oh, Sailor Behave! (1930).*

SELECTED FILMS (as director): *Lawful Larceny (1930), The Greeks Had a Word for Them, Ladies of the Jury (1932), She Done Him Wrong, Broadway Thru a Keyhole (1933), Night Life of the Gods (1935).* ■

Shields, Arthur (1896–1970), actor. Worked on stage in his native Ireland before coming to Hollywood. A tall, bespectacled character actor, he appeared in dramas and light films, often portraying men of the cloth. He was the brother of Barry FITZGERALD with whom he is sometimes confused.

SELECTED FILMS: The Plough and the Stars (1937), Little Nellie Kelly (1940), Broadway (1942), Roughly Speaking, Too Young to Know (1945), Easy Come, Easy Go, The Shocking Miss Pilgrim (1947), The Barefoot Mailman (1951), The Quiet Man (1952), Main Street to Broadway (1953), Pride of the Blue Grass (1954), For the Love of Mike (1960), The Pigeon That Took Rome (1962). ■

Shirley, Anne (1918–), actress. Worked as an artist's model as an infant to help support her family before beginning her screen career in silent films at the age of five. As a charming and plucky young performer. she enlivened many dramas and light films during the 1930s. As she matured she played ingenues and other roles, all with equal competence. She was singled out for her excellent performance as Laurel, Barbara STANWYCK'S daughter, in Stella Dallas (1937). She retired from films in 1945.

SELECTED FILMS: Moonshine Valley (1922), The Fast Set (1924), The Callahans and the Murphys (1927), Mother Knows Best (1928), City Girl (1930), Young America (1932), Anne of Green Gables (1934), Steamboat 'Round the Bend (1935), Chatterbox, M'Liss, Make Way for a Lady (1936), Too Many Wives (1937), Mother Carey's Chickens (1938), The Powers Girl (1942), Lady Bodyguard (1943), Murder My Sweet (1944). ■

"Shoulder Arms" (1918), FN. Dir. Charlie Chaplin; Sc. Charlie Chaplin; with Charlie Chaplin, Edna Purviance, Sydney Chaplin, Jack Wilson, Henry Bergman.

A fantasy-comedy set during World War I and considered Chaplin's best film to date, this three-reeler contains much satire as well as comedy. It tells the story of one average doughboy's daily life in the trenches. But he simply doesn't make a very good soldier, he can't seem to get instructions straight. During guard duty he dreams of city night life and good times, shown in split-screen. Highlights include Charlie's camouflage inside a tree trunk and his capture of 13 German soldiers. When someone asks how he managed this feat, he replies: "I surrounded them." The film caused some controversy for its star. Several of his critics wanted to know why he didn't enlist in the service when war broke out, or why he didn't return to his native England to join up with his fellow countrymen. Aside from its strong antiwar sentiment, the film underlines the camaraderie that exists among the common soldiers.

Showalter, Max (1917–), actor. Began his screen career in the late 1940s. Light-haired and good-looking, he played leads and supporting roles in light films and dramas. He also wrote music scores for the stage and screen. He occasionally appeared under the name Casey Adams.

SELECTED FILMS: Always Leave Them Laughing (1949), My Wife's Best Friend (1952), Vicki (1953), Bus Stop (1956), Designing Woman (1957), The Female Animal (1958), It Happened to Jane (1959), The Music Man (1961), Bon Voyage! (1962), Move Over, Darling (1963), Sex and the Single Girl (1964), How to Murder Your Wife (1965), 10 (1979), Racing With the Moon (1984). ■

Shriek of Araby, The (1923), APA. Dir. F. Richard Jones; Sc. Not listed; with Ben Turpin, Kathryn McGuire.

Ben TURPIN had a difficult time becoming one of the top comedians of the silent period. Always given supporting roles, he continually moved from one studio to another, seeking his rightful place as a lead player. Finally, Mack SENNETT, for whom he had worked earlier, gave him a chance in a series of two reelers in which the cross-eyed clown parodied many of the film stars and stage productions of the period. In

The Shriek of Araby (1923), a five-reeler that parodied Rudolph Valentino's romantic films, he played a theater worker dressed in a sheik's costume designed to hype the current attraction. He is kidnapped and taken abroad where a sheik uses him as a substitute for himself. Turpin sees a beautiful young artist, played by Kathryn McGUIRE, in the middle of a desert and decides to take her prisoner. He proceeds to teach her the ways of love, Turpin style. Elaborate sets, many special effects, and the steady hand of director F. Richard JONES help make this one of the comic's most memorable efforts. Kathryn McGuire went on to co-star with Buster KEATON the following year in that comedian's classic film, *The Navigator*.

Sidekicks. Character or supporting players who are traveling companions of the hero or main character. They usually provide the comic relief but do not essentially influence the plot in westerns. There are several obligatory characteristics of a conventional sidekick. He is typically a foil to the hero, especially in looks and in intelligence. He must never be better looking than his companion or more clever in terms of resolving the plot complication. He may give advice on love, character, or general human behavior, and assist the hero in times of trouble, but must maintain his secondary role concerning theme, plot, and resolution. Like Sancho Panza, he may be more realistic; like Dr. Watson, he may have particular skills. But these qualities ultimately are designed to act as a contrast or an aid to the hero.

Sidekicks have become a staple in the history of American B westerns, with some performers, like the lovable and crusty George "Gabby" HAYES, having virtually made a career of the role. Some have worked with the same cowboy stars for years, while others have assisted different actors. Several, including Snub POLLARD, Al ST. JOHN, and Ben TURPIN, were former comedy stars in silent films but had fallen on hard times. Others were famous in different areas of show business. Cliff EDWARDS, for example, also known as "Ukulele Ike," was a popular singer and recording artist, with song hits like "Charley My Boy" to his credit. Max TERHUNE was an accomplished ventriloquist who utilized his dummy in his westerns. Mischa AUER and Walter BRENNAN, both of whom were talented actors, moved on to play important second leads and supporting roles in major Hollywood productions. The following list, arranged alphabetically by sidekick and the cowboy(s) he assisted, provides a fair sample of the most famous actors who have served in this capacity over the years.

Roscoe ATES: Eddie Dean

Mischa AUER: Tim McCoy

Buzz Barton: Rex Bell

Pat BRADY: Roy Rogers

Walter BRENNAN: Tim McCoy, John Wayne

Smiley BURNETTE: Gene Autry, Roy Rogers

Sammy Cohen: Tom Tyler

Rufe Davis: Bob Livingston

Andy DEVINE: Roy Rogers

Cliff EDWARDS: Tim Holt

Raymond HATTON: Buck Jones, Tim McCoy, Johnny Mack Brown, Roy Rogers

George "Gabby" HAYES: Richard Arlen, Bill Elliott, Bob Steele, William Boyd, John Wayne, Johnny Mack Brown

Fuzzy KNIGHT: Robert Stack, Johnny Mack Brown, Kirby Grant

Emmett Lynn: Eddie Dean

Chris-Pin MARTIN: Jack Hoxie

Horace Murphy: Tex Ritter, Johnny Mack Brown

Snub POLLARD: Tex Ritter

Skeeter Robbins: Hoot Gibson

Al ST. JOHN: Donald Barry, Bob Steele, Buster Crabbe, George Houston, Fred Scott, Lash LaRue, Johnny Mack Brown

Syd SAYLOR: Bob Steele, Tex Ritter

Dub TAYLOR: Jimmy Wakely

Max TERHUNE: Ray Corrigan, John Wayne, John King

Ben TURPIN: Bob Custer

Wally Vernon: Don Barry

Guy Wilkerson: Dave O'Brien, Tex Ritter

Guinn "Big Boy" WILLIAMS: Bob Livingston

Frank Yaconelli: Ken Maynard, Tom Keene, Jack Randall.

Sidney, George (1876–1945), actor. Worked as a comedian in vaudeville and on stage before entering silent films in 1926. A heavy-set character player, he appeared chiefly in low-brow comedy films in the late 1920s and early 1930s. He co-starred with Charles MURRAY in the "COHENS AND THE KELLYS" series, portraying Cohen. He also appeared in several of the "POTASH AND PERLMUTTER" comedies. His specialty was ETHNIC HUMOR.

SELECTED FILMS: In Hollywood With Potash and Perlmutter (1924), Classified (1925), Partners Again, The Cohens and the Kellys, Sweet Daddies, Millionaires (1926), The Auctioneer, Lost at the Front, For the Love of Mike, The Life of Riley, Clancy's Kosher Wedding (1927), The Latest From Paris, Flying Romeos, Give and Take (1928), Around the Corner (1930), The Heart of New York (1932), Manhattan Melodrama (1934), Diamond Jim (1935), Good Old Soak (1937). ∎

Sidney, George (1916–), director. Appeared briefly on stage and worked in different capacities at MGM before finally advancing to director. He turned out a few of the "Pete Smith Specialties" comedy shorts and many "OUR GANG" two-reelers. By the early 1940s he was directing features. Concentrating on the musical genre, he has often been criticized for his extravagant productions that have frequently bordered on bad taste. He won two Academy Awards for his short subjects.

SELECTED FILMS: Free and Easy (1941), Thousands Cheer (1943), Bathing Beauty (1944), The Harvey Girls (1946), Annie Get Your Gun (1950), Show Boat (1951), Pal Joey (1957), Who Was That Lady? (1960), Bye Bye Birdie, A Ticklish Affair (1963), Viva Las Vegas (1964), Half a Sixpence (1968). ∎

Silent Movie. See Mel Brooks.

Silvers, Phil (1912–1985), actor, comedian. Worked in vaudeville and burlesque since childhood, at first as a singer, then, when his voice changed at age fifteen, as a comedian. He finally made it to Broadway in 1938. He appeared in early sound shorts before entering feature films in 1940. Fast-talking and bespectacled, he often played comic-relief roles, spicing up numerous light films. In 1947 he achieved Broadway stardom in the musical, High Button Shoes. He gained greater popularity in television during the 1950s. His autobiography, The Laugh Is on Me, was published in 1973.

SELECTED FILMS: Hit Parade of 1941 (1940), Tom, Dick and Harry, Lady Be Good, You're in the Army Now (1941), All Through the Night, My Gal Sal, Just Off Broadway (1942), A Lady Takes a Chance (1943), Four Jills in a Jeep (1944), A Thousand and One Nights, Don Juan Quilligan (1945), If I'm Lucky (1950), Top Banana (1954), Forty Pounds of Trouble, It's a Mad, Mad, Mad, Mad World (1963), A Funny Thing Happened on the Way to the Forum (1966), The Boatniks (1970), The Chicken Chronicles (1977), The Cheap Detective (1978), Racquet (1979). ∎

Silvers, Sid, actor. Appeared in films during the 1930s as a comedy character actor. Short and wiry, he appeared in light films, usually in comic-relief roles. He also wrote stories and screenplays for comedy films.

In Born to Dance he played a sailor who's in a rush to get to shore to see his wife. "Who'd marry you?" someone asks. "A minister," he quips. Later, the captain gives him a letter to deliver somewhere in Brooklyn. "I understand you were born in Brooklyn. What part?" he inquires. "All of me," replies Silvers.

SELECTED FILMS (as actor): My Weakness (1933), Bottoms Up, Transatlantic Merry-Go-Round (1934), Broadway Melody of 1936 (1935), Born to Dance (1936), 52nd Street (1937), Mr. Ace (1946).

SELECTED FILMS (as screenwriter): Broadway Melody of 1936 (1935), Born to Dance (1936), The Gorilla (1939), The Fleet's In, For Me and My Gal (1942), Two Tickets to Broadway (1951). ∎

Simon, Neil (1927–), screenwriter, playwright. Wrote comedy material for stage and television performers before turning to playwriting in the early 1960s. Many of his comedies have been adapted for the screen. One of the most successful playwrights of the American theater, he has written original screenplays as well as adaptations of his own stage works.

His recurrent themes of the frustrations of marriage, divorce, and male relationships often concern urban souls of varying professions. Although some of his plots may resemble those of television sitcoms, his characters are often very realistically drawn and easy to identify with. In his later plays and films, particularly Brighton Beach Memoirs, he began to focus on his recollections of his childhood years during the Depression and World War II, giving us his personal vision of America as it once was.

SELECTED FILMS (as screenwriter): After the Fox (1966), Barefoot in the Park (1967), The Odd Couple (1968), The Out-of-Towners (1970), Plaza Suite (1971), Last of the Red Hot Lovers, The Heartbreak Kid (1972), The Prisoner of Second Avenue, The Sunshine Boys (1975), Murder by Death (1975), The Goodbye Girl (1977), The Cheap Detective, California Suite (1978), Chapter Two (1979), Seems Like Old Times (1980), Only When I Laugh (1981), I Ought to Be in Pictures (1982), Max Dugan Returns (1983), Brighton Beach Memoirs (1986).

Simon, S. Sylvan (1910–1951), director. Worked as a stage director from 1933 and two years later entered film directing by way of Warner Brothers. He specialized in light films, working with some of the leading comic performers of the period, including, among others, Red SKELTON, ABBOTT AND COSTELLO, and Wallace BEERY. He turned out the popular "Whistling" comedy series starring Red Skelton. He switched to producing in the late 1940s, just before his death. Films he produced include The Good Humor Man and Born Yesterday.

SELECTED FILMS (as director): A Girl With Ideas (1937), Nurse From Brooklyn, The Road to Reno, Spring Madness (1938), The Kid From Texas, These Glamour Girls (1939), Two Girls on Broadway (1940), Whistling in the Dark (1941), The Bugle Sounds, Rio Rita (1942), Whistling in Brooklyn (1943), Abbott and Costello in Hollywood (1945), The Cockeyed Miracle (1946), Her Husband's Affairs (1947), The Fuller Brush Man (1948). ∎

Sims, Milton, actor. Worked as a supporting player in early silent comedy shorts. He appeared with one of the popular serial queens of the period, Eileen SEDGWICK, before she moved on to stardom.

SELECTED FILMS: It's Cheaper to Be Married, a Bare Living, A Woman in the Case, His Family Tree, The Thousand Dollar Drop, Swearing Off, Flat Harmony, Making Monkey Business, Not Too Thin to Fight (1917), Passing the Bomb, The Butler's Blunder, Oh, Man! (1918). ∎

Sinatra, Frank (1915–), singer, actor. Appeared on radio, in nightclubs, and as a band vocalist before entering films in 1941. Although chiefly known as a singer, he has played dramatic and comedy roles as well in a string of films. He has starred in and produced several comedies with a group of his close friends, known as the "Rat Pack." A true superstar of several media, he has had his share of controversy. He has been charged with associating with underworld figures and with being hot-headed. But his star has remained fixed as one of the greatest entertainers of his time. In *The Tender Trap* (1955) Sinatra portrayed a theatrical agent who is visited by David Wayne. "Do all agents live like this?" the impressed Wayne asks, seeing the apartment for the first time. "How much money are you making?" Sinatra replies, "Almost as much as I'm spending."

SELECTED FILMS: *Las Vegas Nights (1941), Reveille With Beverly (1943), Step Lively (1944), It Happened in Brooklyn (1947), Double Dynamite (1951), The Joker Is Wild (1957), A Hole in the Head (1959), Ocean's Eleven, Pepe (1960), Sergeants Three (1962), Come Blow Your Horn, Four for Texas (1963), Robin and the Seven Hoods (1964), That's Entertainment (1974).* ∎

Singleton, Penny (1908–), actress. Appeared on stage as a child, in vaudeville, and on Broadway in 1927 before entering films in 1930. A dark-haired, comic supporting player during the first half of the 1930s, she performed under her real name, Dorothy McNulty, in several films, most of which were minor vehicles. She reached the height of her popularity as BLONDIE in the famous comedy series, launched in 1938, which co-starred Arthur LAKE as her husband, Dagwood Bumstead. When the film series ended in the 1950s she remained active in show business, appearing on Broadway and in nightclubs. See the "Blondie" entry for a list of films in that series.

In *Blondie*, the first entry in the series, she says to husband Arthur Lake: "Sometimes it's harder to raise a husband than a baby."

SELECTED FILMS: *Good News, Love in the Rough (1930), After the Thin Man (1936), Swing Your Lady, Boy Meets Girl, The Mad Miss Manton, Hard to Get, Blondie (1938), Go West Young Lady* (1941), *Footlight Glamour (1943), Young Widow (1946), The Best Man (1964).* ∎

Sitka, Emil, actor. Supporting player in comedy shorts, chiefly during the 1940s, often portraying elderly gentlemen. He appeared as a regular in 35 THREE STOOGES two-reelers between 1947 and 1958, often undergoing some physical punishment, including getting knocked down, kicked, smashed in the head with sundry items, etc. He can also be seen in all the feature-length films of the Stooges produced in the 1960s as well as in films with other comics. He played in hundreds of films during a career that covered four decades.

SELECTED FILMS: *Half-Wits Holiday, Hold That Lion, All Gummed Up (1947), Pardon My Clutch (1948), Feulin' Around (1949), Punchy Cowpunchers, Three Hams on Rye (1950), Scrambled Brains (1951), Listen, Judge (1952), Bubble Trouble (1953), Shot in the Frontier (1954), Husbands Beware (1955), Scheming Schemers (1956), Horsing Around (1957), Pies and Guys (1958), The Three Stooges in Orbit (1962).* ∎

Gloria De Haven and Red Skelton

Skelton, Red (1913–), actor. Worked in medicine shows from age ten, showboats, circuses, burlesque, vaudeville, and radio before entering films in the late 1930s. A talented pantomimist, he often employs pratfalls and other physical routines as well as monologues. He became a popular MGM comic actor, starring in a series of "Whistling" comedy features, while maintaining a top rating through the 1940s as a radio comedian.

Skelton became a major television star in the 1950s and 1960s, his show running for 18 seasons. His series lasted longer than that of any other comedian. His reputation in this medium, however, overshadowed his influence as a comic actor in films. His screen career may be divided into two phases: the films in which he starred and those in which he appeared as a supporting player. Combined, he made fewer films than his comic contemporaries such as ABBOTT AND COSTELLO and Bob HOPE, but those vehicles in which he played the lead were generally funnier and better films than those starring other comics. He was more ingratiating, capable of winning his audiences to his side almost immediately; he seemed more genuine and sincere in his characterizations, and he proved a better actor than many of his comic contemporaries. His one shortcoming was his inability to rise above poor material; his character, that of a shy but inept soul, could not carry a weak script. Indeed, not many comedians can. But his best work, as in *A Southern Yankee* and *The Fuller Brush Man*, attests to his gifted and creative talents.

In *Neptune's Daughter* (1949) he portrayed a masseur at an exclusive country club. Called for an assignment, he prefers to listen to the end of a radio quiz show. "This is an important program," he explains. "They give away a lot of prizes. Last week there was an old maid from Pomona and she won a two-week vacation in a Tibet monastery—with all expenses paid."

SELECTED FILMS: *Having Wonderful Time* (1938), *Whistling in the Dark, Lady Be Good* (1941), *Ship Ahoy, Maisie Gets Her Man, Panama Hattie, Whistling in Dixie* (1942), *Du Barry Was a Lady, I Dood It, Whistling in Brooklyn* (1943), *Bathing Beauty* (1944), *Ziegfeld Follies, The Show-Off* (1946), *Merton of the Movies* (1947), *The Fuller Brush Man, A*

Southern Yankee (1948), *Neptune's Daughter* (1949), *The Yellow Cab Man, Watch the Birdie* (1950), *Excuse My Dust* (1951), *Lovely to Look At* (1952), *The Clown, Half a Hero, The Great Diamond Robbery* (1953), *Susan Slept Here* (1954), *Public Pigeon No. 1* (1957), *Those Magnificent Men in Their Flying Machines* (1965). ∎

"Skippy." A popular comic strip created by Percy Crosby that furnished the characters for a successful motion picture in 1930. The film, starring Jackie COOPER, was a commercial and critical success, receiving two nominations for Oscars (Best Picture and Best Actor) and winning an Academy Award for its director, Norman TAUROG.

Skipworth, Alison (1863–1952), actress. Appeared on stage in her native England and on Broadway in 1895 before entering films in 1930. A character player throughout the 1930s, she portrayed society matrons in many comedies, working with some of the leading comic stars of the period, including, among others, W. C. FIELDS, Mae WEST, Joe E. BROWN, and BURNS AND ALLEN. She was born Alison Groom.

In *The Princess Comes Across* (1936) she played the chaperone of Carole LOMBARD who is falling in love with a concertina player. "A concertina—and very vulgar," the chaperone remarks in a deprecating tone as she hears it being played in the next cabin. "A symbol of the lower classes. Put the thing on the floor and it crawls."

SELECTED FILMS: *Raffles* (1930), *Virtuous Husband, The Night Angel* (1931), *Night After Night, If I Had a Million* (1932), *Tonight Is Ours, A Lady's Profession, Tillie and Gus, Alice in Wonderland* (1933), *Six of a Kind, The Captain Hates the Sea* (1934), *Doubting Thomas, Shanghai* (1935), *The Gorgeous Hussy* (1936), *Two Wise Maids* (1937), *Ladies in Distress, Wide Open Faces* (1938). ∎

Slapstick. In films, a type of physical comedy. The chase, the pratfall, the throwing of pies, as well as other forms of cruel humor and violence are all part of the stock and trade of slapstick comedians. The term allegedly derived from the stage when a prompter would slap a stick as a cue for the audience to laugh. Not all physical comedy is slapstick. The pantomime of entertainers like Tati may be considered physical but not slapstick. Slapstick, which requires expert timing, implies both the use of physical gags aimed against someone for laughs and a sense of unreality as a result of the broad gags and the improbability of the stunts.

The use of slapstick in film can be traced back to 1895 in France with the pioneering work of Lumière. In the United States one of the earliest practitioners of the form and the producer who made it famous was Mack SENNETT. Virtually all the great and minor silent comedies and comics of the 1910s employed slapstick. One- and two-reelers were filled with characters falling or being pushed into lakes, knocked down by someone being chased, hit by a flying brick, or suffering some physical abuse at the hands of others.

"Fatty" ARBUCKLE and most of the cast in "Fatty at Coney Island" (1917) get knocked into a lake. Ford STERLING and his KEYSTONE KOPS kept falling out of their patrol wagon each time it made a turn. Charlie CHAPLIN crushed Eric CAMPBELL'S bandaged leg in a revolving door in "The Cure" and sent him flying across the room in "The Rink." Charley CHASE, Mabel NORMAND, Charlie MURRAY, and dozens of other movie clowns not only incorporated slapstick into their routines but made it the dominant means of evoking laughter, at least in the early stages of their film careers.

By the 1920s knockabout comedy—a circus term—as slapstick was sometimes referred to, lost much of its luster and was generally frowned upon by film critics of the period. Several of the more creative comedians like Chaplin, Buster KEATON, Harold LLOYD, and Harry LANGDON felt encouraged to break away from the old forms. They began to depend less on physical humor and more on comedy that rose out of characterization and plot. However, such producers as Sennett, Hal ROACH, and Al CHRISTIE continued to turn out slapstick comedies right up until the end of the silent period, culminating in shorts like "The Battle of the Century" with its classic pie-throwing sequence.

With the advent of sound in the late 1920s, slapstick was relegated to secondary importance while fast-talking heroes and heroines and wise-cracking comic character players dominated the comedy films. By the mid-1930s witty, urbane dialogue was gaining a foothold in sophisticated and screwball comedies, two genres that were to dominate light films for the next few decades. Meanwhile, slapstick was placed into the hands of minor comics and comedy shorts. The comedy teams of OLSEN AND JOHNSON, WHEELER AND WOOLSEY, and the RITZ BROTHERS specialized in it. Much of the work of the MARX BROTHERS contains its share of slapstick. Comedy shorts of the 1930s, turned out chiefly by Educational and Columbia studios, were basically dependent upon slapstick. These two-reelers often featured former silent comics who had fallen on hard times. Harry Langdon and Buster Keaton made dozens of these mediocre comedies. But the team that turned slapstick into a ritual was the THREE STOOGES. For almost thirty years Larry, Moe, and Curly, and later Shemp, explored new ways to hit each other and found new articles to toss about as well as relying heavily on old routines.

Other comics in the following decades frequently reverted to slapstick for laughs when their verbal material ran dry, including LAUREL AND HARDY, ABBOTT AND COSTELLO, Bob HOPE, Red SKELTON, Danny KAYE, and MARTIN AND LEWIS. Comedy films without major clowns sometimes rely chiefly on physical humor for laughs. Of these, *National Lampoon's Animal House* (1978) is a prime example. Stanley Kramer's *It's a Mad, Mad, Mad, Mad World* (1963) pays homage to producers like Sennett and their stable of funny-men. Other directors and screenwriters have learned to use slapstick judiciously, thereby turning out some very funny films without a tiresome amount of physical comedy. Blake EDWARDS' "PINK PANTHER" series as well as his other features, Woody ALLEN'S self-mocking works, and writer Neil SIMON'S comedies exemplify this direction.

Sleeper (1973), UA. *Dir.* Woody Allen; *Sc.* Woody Allen; with Woody Allen, Diane Keaton, John Beck, Mary Gregory.

Woody ALLEN'S comedy, set in the future, satirizes such widely diversified topics as technology, sex, and Albert Shanker. Allen combines his verbal and visual skills in this winning film, almost unanimously praised by the critics. His hero, Miles Monroe (Woody), an owner of a health food store in the 1970s, is transported 200 years into the future. This gives Allen an opportunity to express his views on a variety of subjects, including his distrust in governments and politics. "Political situations don't work," he says to a dissident member of this future society. "It doesn't matter who's up there—they're all terrible." He informs the citizens of 2173 about several notables of the twentieth century. On Charles DeGaulle: "a famous French chef"; on Norman Mailer: "a great writer who left his ego to the Harvard Medical School." On the lighter side: "This is some girl burning a brassiere," he explains, showing a photograph from his time. "You can see it's a very small fire." He finds himself emotionally involved with Diane KEATON, who says: "It's hard to believe you haven't had sex for 200 years." "Two hundred and four," he corrects her, "if you count my marriage."

The film moves rapidly, is filled with visual gags, and is consistently funny.

Sleeper, Martha (1907–), actress. Appeared as female and second leads in silent comedy shorts and features as well as in sound films. She worked for comedy producer Hal ROACH. After abandoning her screen career in the late 1930s, she appeared with some degree of success on Broadway.

SELECTED FILMS: *The Mailman* (1923), *Skinner's Big Idea, Taxi 13* (1928), *Our Blushing Brides (1930), Girls Demand Excitement, A Tailor-Made Man (1931), Huddle (1932), Midnight Mary (1933), Spitfire (1934), Rhythm on the Range (1936), Four Days' Wonder (1937), The Bells of St. Mary's (1945).* ∎

Slezak, Walter (1902–1983), actor. Worked on stage and in films in Germany before settling in the United States in the 1930s as a film and stage actor. Portly and impish, the Viennese-born actor became a steady Hollywood character player from 1942, portraying colorful villains and other types in dramas and light films. He also had a reputation as a writer and humorist. He left the screen in 1972 and committed suicide in 1983.

In *The Inspector General* (1949) he says to Danny Kaye: "If I'm not telling you the truth, may I be a wandering gypsy." "But you are a wandering gypsy," Kaye reminds him. "That just proves my point," Slezak replies.

SELECTED FILMS: *Once Upon a Honeymoon (1942), Step Lively, The Princess and the Pirate (1944), The Pirate (1948), The Yellow Cab Man, Abbott and Costello in the Foreign Legion (1950), Bedtime for Bonzo (1951), Confidentially Connie, Call Me Madam (1953), Ten Thousand Bedrooms (1957), Treasure Island (1971).* ∎

Smally, Phillips (1875–1939), actor, director. Appeared on stage before entering early silent films as an actor. By 1912 he was directing films of various genres and by 1917 his short career behind the camera had come to an end. He continued to act in silent and sound films through the mid-1930s, most of his appearances as a character player.

SELECTED FILMS (as actor): The Armorer's Daughter (1910), Two Wise Wives (1921), Cameo Kirby (1923), Single Wives, Cheap Kisses (1924), Charley's Aunt, The Awful Truth, The Fate of a Flirt, Soul Mates (1925), Man Crazy, Tea for Three (1927), Broadway Daddies (1928), True Heaven (1929), Charley's Aunt (1930), The Greeks Had a Word for Them (1932), Cocktail Hour (1933), Madame Du Barry (1934), Night Life of the Gods, All the King's Horses, A Night at the Opera (1935). ∎

Smith, Charles (1920–), actor. Appeared chiefly as a character player in the 1940s. He played, among other friendly characters, Henry's pal, Dizzy, in the "HENRY ALDRICH" series.

SELECTED FILMS: The General (1927), Tom Brown's School Days (1940), Henry Aldrich for President (1941), The Major and the Minor (1942), Out of This World (1945), Three Little Girls in Blue (1946), The Trouble With Women (1947), Two Weeks With Love (1950). ∎

Smith, Joe. See Smith and Dale.

Smith, Noel Mason (1890–), director. Began his film career as an assistant director of silent comedy shorts. As a full-fledged director, he worked for several pioneer studios such as Mack SENNETT'S, turning out comedies. He later directed full-length action features. Much of his work was routine.

SELECTED FILMS: The Broadway Gallant, The Merry Cavalier (1926), One Chance in a Million (1927), The Bachelor's Club, The Heroic Lover (1929), Calling All Husbands, Ladies Must Live, Always a Bride, Father Is a Prince (1940), Cattle Town (1952). ∎

Smith, Pete (1892–1979), producer. Known for his humorous shorts that he began turning out and narrating for MGM in 1931. His most successful, the "Pete Smith Specialties," starring Dave O'BRIEN as the hapless lead, were begun in 1936 and won him two Oscars and several other nominations. In all, he produced more than 300 shorts. He was honored in 1955 with a special Academy Award for his "witty and pungent" films. He committed suicide at age 87.

SELECTED FILMS: Penny Wisdom (1937), Quicker'n a Wink (1940). ∎

Smith, Sid (1892–1928), actor. Appeared in silent comedy shorts during the early 1920s. He and George Monberg co-starred as Percy and Ferdy, two of the HALL ROOM BOYS, a series of comedies based on H. A. McGill's once-popular comic strip.

SELECTED FILMS: A Howling Success (1919), The Ne'er-Do-Well (1923). ∎

Smith and Dale. The longest lasting vaudeville comedy team in history. Charlie Dale (1881–1971) and Joe Smith (1884–1981) first performed as a team in 1898. In 1900 they became part of the Avon Comedy Four, appearing in vaudeville and burlesque. By 1919 they had become known as Smith and Dale, performing on Broadway and at the Palladium in London. They reached their peak as entertainers in the 1920s and 1930s. Their film career, however, was not as successful as their live shows. They starred in comedy shorts for Paramount and Warner Brothers studios in 1929 and made their first feature-length film in 1932. With the demise of vaudeville, the comic duo was soon forgotten but made a slight comeback in the 1950s with guest appearances on television. Playwright Neil SIMON based his stage comedy, The Sunshine Boys, on their career. The film version, starring George BURNS and Walter MATTHAU, was released in 1975.

SELECTED FILMS: *The False Alarm Fire Co., Knights in Venice, Anything but Ham, Where East Meets West (1929), La Schnapps, Inc., S.S. Malaria (1930), The Heart of New York, Manhattan Parade (1932), A Nag in the Bag, Mutiny on the Body (1939), Two Tickets to Broadway (1951).* ■

"Smitty." A once-popular comic strip created by cartoonist Walter Berndt and made into a series of silent comedy shorts in the 1920s. The entries starred Billy Bruce, Jackie Combs, Betty Jane Graham, and Donald Haines as a group of self-assertive tots who got themselves into and out of humorous difficulties.

Smothers, Tom (1937–), actor. Part of the Smothers Brothers comedy team, the other half being Dick (1939–). The pair were very successful on television, hosting their own show for several years from the mid-1960s. Tom, whose role in the comedy act was that of a childlike, mischievous buffoon, switched to films without his brother but could not find a suitable character to sustain his screen image. In the late 1970s the brothers teamed up once more to star in a Broadway musical comedy, *I Love My Wife,* which they eventually took on the road.

SELECTED FILMS: *Get to Know Your Rabbit (1973), Silver Bears (1978), The Kids Are Alright, There Goes the Bride (1979), Serial (1980).* ■

"Snakeville" comedies. A series of silent comedy shorts created in 1911 by ESSANAY studios. Snakeville was a fictitious village used as a setting for different comedians and comedy teams, including the "HANK AND LANK" comedies starring Victor POTEL and Augustus CARNEY, the "ALKALI IKE," and the "Mustang Pete" series, all popular in their time. Several famous directors, such as E. Mason HOPPER, got their start by turning out one- and two-reel comedies for the "Snakeville" series.

Comics like Ben TURPIN appeared in several of the films.

SELECTED FILMS: *Alkali Ike's Automobile, Mustang Pete's Love Affair, A Western Kimono, Snakeville's Hen Medic, Snakeville's Champion, Snakeville's Debutantes (1911).* ■

Snerd, Mortimer. A dummy created by ventriloquist Edgar BERGEN. The dimwitted Snerd was often used as a foil to the more popular Charlie McCarthy, another Bergen creation, and appeared only occasionally in films.

"Snowflake." An epithet for the black actor, Fred TOONES, who appeared in several Hollywood productions as a comic character player. The film credits insensitively listed him as "Snowflake." For film titles, see Fred Toones.

Social comedy. Films that combine realistic characters, settings, and events with comic elements for the purpose of effecting reforms of various social institutions. While most comedy films deal with exaggeration, romanticism, or some form of fantasy, few suggest any underlying intentions other than entertainment. The social comedy clearly aims at pointing out a fault in society, thus differing from SCREWBALL COMEDY. Social comedies reached their peak in the 1930s and 1940s with directors like Frank CAPRA but also flourished in the films of Charlie CHAPLIN.

During the early silent period of films, the domestic comedy, with its well-attired, upper-class heroes and heroines; its drawing room settings; and its themes of romance, marriage, and family complications, was mistakenly labeled "social comedy" to distinguish it from slapstick and physical comedy. But a definite distinction exists between this type of domestic comedy, the "comedy of manners," and social comedy.

Always socially conscious, Chaplin had a penchant for adding realistic settings to his post-SENNETT comedies that either reflected his own humble beginnings in the slums of London or depicted the actual backgrounds of the characters in his films. In "Police!" (1916), for example, he sets scenes in a flophouse inhabited by society's outcasts. This is one of the earliest examples of his interest in social comedy. "Easy Street" (1917), one of his best short films, focuses on a slum neighborhood and its miscreants and bullies. Charlie, hired as a policeman, has a difficult time taming a block of ruffians. But the images of poverty, drug addicts, and the daily struggle of the poor are as striking as the incidents are comical. During the same year his film "The Immigrant" was released. It told of the hardships that Europeans faced on their voyage to America and as outsiders in a new land. Charlie, one of the immigrants, is penniless and hungry in the streets of New York. Edna PURVIANCE, whom he had met aboard the ship, tells him her mother has died. Aside from its farcical situations, the film underscores the fact that America was not the paradise that many immigrants dreamed it to be. In "A Dog's Life" (1918) Chaplin lives in a vacant lot, his only companion a mangy dog. The comedy, with its scenes of miserable social conditions, equates the lives of some unfortunates and that of the dog. *The Kid* (1921), co-starring Jackie COOGAN, was the Tramp's strongest statement yet about society's underdogs as Chaplin tries to raise an abandoned child amid threats from various bureaucracies. Chaplin made *City Lights* (1931) during the sound era but kept it as a silent film accompanied by a music track. Again he returned to the city milieu. Combining sentiment and social realism, the film tells the story of a luckless tramp who falls in love with a blind flower girl. *Modern Times* (1936) returns to his theme of daily survival as well as showing the effects of the assembly line on the lives of factory workers.

His sound films, *The Great Dictator* (1940) and *Monsieur Verdoux* (1947), are savage attacks on fascism and the dark side of human nature respectively. Disillusioned by the direction of society during the 1930s and 1940s, Chaplin grew bitter and less funny over the years.

The Depression years produced some of the best social comedies. In *Our Betters* (1933), starring Constance BENNETT and Gilbert Roland, an English lord (Alan Mowbray) desires to wed rich American Bennett, but she learns that he is interested only in her money. The film, which exposes social hypocrisy, strays from many of the characteristics of social comedy. Frank Capra in *Mr. Deeds Goes to Town* (1936) shows what happens when naive Gary COOPER, who has inherited millions of dollars, wants to help the little people with the money. The forces of big-city greed and corruption almost overwhelm the small-town innocence of Cooper. In *You Can't Take It With You* (1938) Capra makes a plea for individualism as he depicts the eccentric Sycamore family, each member of which does his or her "own thing." The following year the director turned out *Mr. Smith Goes to Washington*. Idealistic James STEWART journeys to Washington, D.C., as a fledgling member of the United States Senate, only to discover a world of corruption.

The next decade produced several social comedies. *The Devil and Miss Jones* (1941), starring Robert CUMMINGS, Jean ARTHUR, and Charles COBURN, has millionaire store owner Coburn working incognito in his own establishment to learn about the working conditions of his employees. In *A Medal for Benny* (1945), starring J. Carroll NAISH, Naish's son, a war hero, is to be decorated posthumously until the politicians learn he was of Mexican-American descent and living in poverty. In *Magic Town* (1947), an attack on invasion of privacy and the effects of big business on small-town life, pollster James Stewart discovers a town that is perfectly "average," a boon for his business. But when the townspeople learn about the phenomenon, their honest opinions and attitudes change and the statistical figures go awry.

The following decades produced little in this genre. In *The Mating Season* (1951) struggling John Lund marries wealthy Gene Tierney, only to be embarrassed when his mother, Thelma RITTER, visits and is mistaken for a maid. In *Putney Swope* (1969) blacks gain control of a Madison Avenue advertising agency and initiate drastic changes. *Claudine* (1974), starring Diahann Carroll and James Earl Jones, depicts the story of a mother with six children struggling to survive in a ghetto and her romance with a sanitation man. In 1977 Jane FONDA co-starred with George SEGAL in *Fun With Dick and Jane*, in which Fonda and jobless Segal turn to crime to support their middle-class home and family.

The social comedy often comes too close to home for many moviegoers and producers. Perhaps with the right combination of major actors and actresses and top writers, producers will gamble on the genre more often. It would be refreshing to see comedies that are not only funny but have something to say about social conditions.

Sokoloff, Vladimir (1889–1962), actor. Worked on stage in his native Russia and in German and French films before migrating to Hollywood in 1937. A short character actor with shifty eyes and, often, a beard, he portrayed a gallery of sympathetic as well as villainous foreigners in numerous dramas and light films.

In *Comrade X* (1940), a satirical comedy set in Russia, he played the newly appointed chief of police. Clark Gable, an American reporter, has proof that Sokoloff assassinated the former chief. Sokoloff acknowledges his role in the elimination of the man he has replaced. "How quickly fortune changes," he quips, "when we help it a little."

SELECTED FILMS: *The Prisoner of Zenda, Tovarich, Beg, Borrow or Steal, Expensive Husbands* (1937), *Love Crazy* (1941), *Road to Morocco* (1942), *Mr. Lucky* (1943), *The Blonde From Brooklyn, A Royal Scandal* (1945), *A Scandal in Paris, Two Smart People* (1946), *Taras Bulba* (1962). ■

Tony Curtis, Jack Lemmon, and Marilyn Monroe in *Some Like It Hot* (1959)

Some Like It Hot (1959), UA. Dir. Billy Wilder; Sc. Billy Wilder, I.A.L. Diamond; with Marilyn Monroe, Tony Curtis, Jack Lemmon, George Raft, Pat O'Brien, Joe E. Brown.

The film has reached the proportions of a comedy classic. With its legendary director and stars, its Roaring 1920s setting, and its farcical premise of female impersonation, the film has more going for it than most other comedies. Tony CURTIS and Jack LEMMON, two musicians who accidentally witness a gangland massacre, dress up as females and hide out with an all-girl band heading for Florida. Here they meet voluptuous Sugar Kane, played engagingly by Marilyn MONROE. Once in Florida, millionaire Joe E. BROWN falls in love with the disguised Lemmon, while Curtis, planning to seduce Monroe, assumes the role of a wealthy playboy. Meanwhile, the mob shows up and madness ensues. The comedy, filled with clever routines, one-liners, visual gags, and sexual innuendoes, continues relentlessly to the famous closing line in which Brown proposes to Lemmon, who finally reveals his true identity. To which the undeterred Brown replies, "Well, nobody's perfect." The bandleader of the all-girl ensemble closes the evening show: "Well, that's all for tonight, folks. This is Sweet Sue reminding all you daddios out there that every girl in my band is a virtuoso, and I intend to keep it that way." Monroe gives one of the best performances of her career. Jack Lemmon received an Oscar nomination for his role. Curtis does a hilarious impersonation of Cary Grant while disguised as the playboy. Other members of the cast offer strong support to this classic satirical spoof of the Jazz Age.

Sons of the Desert (1934), MGM. *Dir.* William A. Seiter; *Sc.* Frank Craven, Byron Morgan; with Stan Laurel, Oliver Hardy, Charlie Chase, Mae Busch, Dorothy Christie, Lucien Littlefield.

Several film critics and historians consider this to be one of LAUREL AND HARDY'S best features. Relying less on slapstick and concentrating on character and situation for laughs, the comedy seems less strained and more natural. Stan and Ollie are obligated to attend their lodge's convention, but their wives object. While Ollie argues with his wife (Mae BUSCH), Stan nibbles on the wax fruit in a bowl. "So you're the one who's been eating all my fruit!" Busch complains. Ollie feigns illness and his physician recommends an ocean voyage with Stan to assist him. The plan works and the boys take off for their fraternal gathering. On the day they are to return, their wives learn that the ship they were supposed to be on has sunk. The wives, worried about the fate of their husbands, go to a movie theater to help pass the time. On the screen they see Stan and Ollie frolicking about in a newsreel that has covered the convention. Stan, returning home and intimidated by his wife, breaks down and tells her the truth. She cuddles him, accepting his apology. Ollie, on the other hand, is assaulted

without mercy by his spouse. Unfortunately, this was the only film that SEITER ever directed for the boys, for he seemed to understand them and their style. He handled the duo unobtrusively, while exploring the humor in their personalities and their close bond. "The strong must help the weak," a speaker at the convention proclaims. Hardy looks at his friend Laurel with an air of self-satisfaction. It is in these more subtle moments that a good director can make the boys seem so human, while simultaneously evoking smiles from the audience.

Sophisticated comedy. Films about members of the upper class and concerned with adult subjects, including philandering husbands and their mistresses, frustrated wives and their lovers, ingenues and their infatuations, and heroines seeking liberation, all of which are treated humorously and satirically. This type of wry comedy, similar to the "comedy of manners" of the late eighteenth century and as practiced more recently by Oscar Wilde, W. Somerset Maugham, and Noel Coward, often adheres to certain conventions and character types. For example, drawing rooms, country estates, and gardens dominate the settings. Suave men of the world, acid-tongued hostesses or dowagers, and sensible confidant(e)s are some of the chief players. The dialogue is often witty and sparkling.

Three early practitioners of the sophisticated comedy during the silent period were Cecil B. DeMILLE, Charlie CHAPLIN, and Ernst LUBITSCH. In 1919 and the early 1920s DeMille began to popularize this type of film. *Male and Female* (1919), based on James Barrie's play, *The Admirable Crichton*, told the often-filmed story of shipwrecked aristocrats who become dependent for their survival upon their butler. He followed this the next year with *Why Change Your Wife?*, a risqué comedy about a husband and wife and their romantic partners, most of which takes place in boudoirs and bedrooms. In 1921 he directed *What Every Woman Knows* and *The Affairs of Anatol*, the former concerning love, marriage, and ambition, and the latter about a wayward husband and his sexual complications among the very rich.

Chaplin, attempting to depart temporarily from his more familiar style of comedy, produced and directed *A Woman of Paris* in 1923. In this ironic comedy Edna PURVIANCE escapes from her small French village to live in Paris, as mistress to the amorous but amoral Adolphe MENJOU. When she meets her former beau, their love is resurrected. Chaplin, who did not appear in the film except for a minor walk-on role, enhanced his film with a style that De-Mille's comedies lacked.

The most influential director of sophisticated comedy was Lubitsch. Impressed with Chaplin's work, he made *The Marriage Circle* in 1924, embellishing it and his comedies to follow with his own European wit and style. For the next 25 years he remained famous for "the Lubitsch touch." His other silents in this genre included *Kiss Me Again* (1925), *Lady Windermere's Fan* (1925), and *So This Is Paris* (1926). His sense of humor, intelligent and creative use of sets, and his overall style influenced not only other directors of the period, but those still to make a name for themselves in the early sound era.

The sophisticated comedy flourished during the Depression years while several of its characteristics pervaded other light genres of the 1930s, such as the screwball, musical, and romantic comedy. In *The Love Parade* (1929), a delightful Lubitsch film, naive Jeanette MacDONALD, as Queen of Sylvania, falls in love with Maurice CHEVALIER, who has a reputation as a boudoir diplomat. Snobbish parents in *Fast and Loose* (1930) object to their son and daughter marrying a showgirl and a mechanic, respectively. Lowell SHERMAN, director and star of *Bachelor Apartment* (1931), has his misadventures as an am-

orous playboy trying to keep his women from meeting one another. That same year Mary Brian in *The Runaround* beguiles Geoffrey Kerr into marriage. In *Love Me Tonight* (1932), a Lubitsch-type film directed by Rouben Mamoulian, French tailor Maurice Chevalier falls in love with princess Jeanette MacDonald. In Lubitsch's charming *Trouble in Paradise* (1932) the love between two professional jewel thieves, Miriam HOPKINS and Herbert MARSHALL, is threatened when he makes advances toward Kay Francis, their next victim. The "THIN MAN" films, of course, provide more than their share of sophisticated comedy as the well-to-do couple, William POWELL and Myrna LOY, dabble in crime, tease each other, and drink heartily. They set a pattern for mystery-comedy that was widely imitated. In *Cafe Society* (1939) socialite Madeleine CARROLL, on a bet, sets her matrimonial sights on Fred MacMURRAY. To close the decade with a spectacular example of the genre, Lubitsch presented *Ninotchka* the same year, with Greta Garbo as a cold Russian agent on a business trip to Paris where she falls for the charms of debonair Melvyn DOUGLAS.

The next decade continued to offer sophisticated comedies, but the war years slowed down the pace. *The Man Who Came to Dinner* (1941) displayed the charm of Monty WOOLLEY, who takes over a household with his zany entourage when he is forced to remain there after an accident. In *The Male Animal* (1942) college professor Henry FONDA fights to defend his individualism while his wife, Olivia de Havilland, is pursued by Jack CARSON, her former boyfriend. *The Talk of the Town*, released the same year, has Cary GRANT, a fugitive from justice, seeking refuge in the home of professor Ronald COLMAN.

The genre, for whatever reasons, was not as well represented during the 1950s. Several of the old directors were gone, as were the sharp and witty screenwriters. In their places came filmmakers like Vincente MINNELLI. In his elegant comedy *Designing Woman* (1957), sportswriter Gregory Peck and fashion designer Lauren Bacall have their marital complications. Minnelli made another attempt at the genre the following year with *The Reluctant Debutante*, about an English couple troubled over presenting their American-influenced daughter to society.

Over the years others tried to resurrect the sophisticated comedy with mixed results. Bob HOPE and Lucille BALL starred in *The Facts of Life* (1960), a worthwhile example of the genre. *Sex and the Single Girl*, with Natalie WOOD, Tony CURTIS, Lauren Bacall, and Henry Fonda, and *Good Neighbor Sam* (both 1964), starring Jack LEMMON and Romy Schneider, also are notable specimens of sophisticated comedy.

Sorvino, Paul (1939–), actor. Has appeared on stage and in television before entering films in 1970. He may usually be seen as a character actor but has also played leads. A slightly pudgy actor more at home in urban settings, he has appeared in dramas as well as comedies. He played the loquacious and philosophical cabbie in *Lost and Found*.

SELECTED FILMS: Where's Poppa? (1970), Made for Each Other (1971), A Touch of Class (1973), I Will, I Will . . . for Now (1976), Oh, God! (1977), The Brink's Job (1978), Lost and Found (1979), Off the Wall (1982), Vasectomy (1986). ■

Sothern, Ann (1909–), actress. Began her screen career in early sound films in the late 1920s playing small roles, then turned to Broadway where she was soon given lead roles before returning to the screen in 1933. A vibrant blonde endowed with looks and personality, she played leads in numerous light second features, often as a scatterbrained, wisecracking heroine. At first she appeared as a supporting player in so many low-budget films that her screen career was almost in jeopardy. She starred in her own series as "MAISIE," an independent working girl who usually became entangled in humorous situations. She also appeared in musical comedies and dramas. Retiring from the screen in the 1950s, she became just as successful in her new endeavor, television.

SELECTED FILMS: The Show of Shows (1929), Doughboys (1930), Let's Fall in Love (1933), Blind Date, Kid Millions (1934), The Girl Friend (1935), Walking on Air (1936), There Goes the Groom, She's Got Everything (1937), Trade Winds, Maisie, Joe and Ethel Turp Call on the President (1939), Brother Orchid (1940), Lady Be Good (1941), Panama Hattie (1942), April Showers (1948), The Judge Steps Out (1949), Nancy Goes to Rio (1950), Golden Needles (1974), Crazy Mama (1975). ■

Soule, Olan (1909–), actor. Appeared in stock and on radio before settling in Hollywood in the 1940s as a character actor. A tireless performer, he played a variety of roles in more than 150 dramas and light films. He has also made scores of appearances in television.

SELECTED FILMS: Destination Big House (1950), Cuban Fireball (1951), Call Me Madam (1953). ■

Space, Arthur (1908–1983), actor. Worked at odd jobs before turning to acting in stock and eventually on Broadway in the 1930s. He traveled to Hollywood, taking a chance that he might get work there. He was soon hired for a minor role and remained to appear as a supporting player in over 100 dramas and light films. Thin and bespectacled with a neatly trimmed mustache, he played a variety of roles from employers to professionals.

SELECTED FILMS: Random Harvest, Tortilla Flat (1942), The Big Noise (1944), The Fuller Brush Man (1948), The Spirit of St. Louis (1957). ■

Sparks, Ned (1883–1957), actor. Worked on stage before entering films in the early 1920s. A gloomy-faced, cigar-chewing comic character player born Edward Sparkman, he reached the peak of his popularity during the 1930s. He delivered his cynical lines in his unique grating and crabby voice.

In *The Star Maker* (1939) he played a publicity agent for impresario Bing CROSBY, who asks if there were any callers. "Only some child actors," Sparks answers. "I threw them down the stairs, and it did my heart good to hear them bounce."

SELECTED FILMS: *A Wide-Open Town (1922), Bright Lights, Soul Mates (1925), Mike (1926), The Big Noise, The Magnificent Flirt (1928), Nothing but the Truth (1929), Leathernecking, Conspiracy (1930), Iron Man (1931), Big City Blues (1932), 42nd Street, Gold Diggers of 1933, Lady for a Day, Too Much Harmony (1933), Down to Their Last Yacht, Servants' Entrance (1934), Sweet Adeline (1935), Collegiate (1936), One in a Million (1937), Hawaii Calls (1938), Stage Door Canteen (1943), Magic Town (1947).* ■

Spewack, Samuel (1899–1971), screenwriter, playwright. Worked as a reporter before scripting Broadway comedies and Hollywood films. He collaborated with his wife, Bella, whom he married in 1922, and together they turned out a succession of successful screenplays.

SELECTED FILMS: *The Nuisance (1933), The Cat and the Fiddle (1934), Rendezvous (1935), Vogues of 1938 (1937), Boy Meets Girl, The Chaser, Three Loves Has Nancy (1938), My Favorite Wife (1940), Week-End at the Waldorf (1945), Move Over, Darling (1963).* ■

Stahl, John M. (1886–1950), director. Worked on the stage before entering films in 1913 as a minor player. One year later he was directing films, a career that extended into the late 1940s. Displaying a distinct talent for visual effects, which emerged fully in the early 1930s, he turned out numerous dramas as well as light films. His style, sometimes called audacious, blended with his sincerity to overcome the shoddy material he was expected to convert into successful second features. He produced several films that he directed.

SELECTED FILMS: *Wives of Men (1918), Women Men Forget, Woman in His House (1920), Suspicious Wives (1922), Fine Clothes (1925), Memory Lane, The Gay Deceiver (1926), In Old Kentucky (1927), The Naughty Duchess (1928), A Lady Surrenders (1930), Strictly Dishonorable (1931), Only Yesterday (1933), Letter of Introduction (1938), Our Wife (1941), Holy Matrimony (1943), The Walls of Jericho (1947), Oh, You Beautiful Doll (1949).* ■

Stander, Lionel (1908–), actor. Worked on stage before entering films in 1932. At first appearing in comedy shorts, he rapidly moved to features within a few years to become a popular character actor, especially in light films. Dour-faced and often cynical, he brightened many films playing reporters and publicity men, until he collided with the House Un-American Activities Committee in the early 1950s. As a result, he was blacklisted from Hollywood. He continued his film career in Europe, returning only occasionally to the American screen. In *Professor Beware* he yells at a steer in a cattle car: "Get off my foot! Get off my foot or I'll cut a steak out of you!"

SELECTED FILMS: *The Scoundrel, Page Miss Glory (1935), Soak the Rich, The Milky Way, Mr. Deeds Goes to Town, Meet Nero Wolfe (1936), Professor Beware (1938), What a Life (1939), The Bride Wore Crutches (1940), The Kid From Brooklyn (1946), Mad Wednesday (1947), Unfaithfully Yours (1948), St. Benny the Dip (1951), The Loved One (1965), The Gang That Couldn't Shoot Straight (1971), The Black Bird (1975), Matilda (1978).* ■

Stang, Arnold (1925–), actor. Worked in radio and on stage before entering films in the early 1940s. A puck-like, nasal-voiced comic character actor, he appeared in several dramas and light films. He reached the height of his popularity as a comic television performer during the 1950s.

SELECTED FILMS: Seven Days' Leave (1942), So This Is New York (1948), Dondi (1961), The Wonderful World of the Brothers Grimm (1962), It's a Mad, Mad, Mad, Mad World (1963), Second Fiddle to a Steel Guitar (1965), Skidoo (1968), Hello Down There! (1969), The Gang That Couldn't Shoot Straight (1971). ∎

Stanley, Louise (1915–1982), actress. Entered films in the mid-1930s with no previous acting experience after being spotted in a restaurant by director Lewis Milestone. An attractive, athletic performer, she played minor roles at Paramount and then switched to Warners and later to other studios. She specialized in westerns although she appeared in several light features and shorts as well, working with such stars as Bing CROSBY, Ethel MERMAN, Hugh HERBERT, Jimmy DURANTE, and Charley CHASE. Her screen career lasted only five years when she decided to retire from films in 1940 and try acting in stock. Her first husband was actor Dennis O'KEEFE.

SELECTED FILMS: Anything Goes, Lady Be Careful (1936), Once a Doctor, Marry the Girl, Gracie at the Bat (1937), Start Cheering, Time Out for Trouble, Personal Secretary (1938), Sky Bandits (1940). ∎

Stanwyck, Barbara (1907–), actress. Began her show business career as a dancer, then switched to acting on Broadway in the 1920s before entering films. Her first screen role was in a silent film, her only one, in 1927. From the start she proved to be a talented actress, capable of playing a variety of roles in both comedies and dramas. She was nominated for an Academy Award as Best Actress four times (Stella Dallas, Ball of Fire, Double Indemnity, and Sorry, Wrong Number), usually portraying tough, independent women. Beautiful and husky-voiced, she reached her peak in the 1940s, both critically as well as financially (in 1944 she was the highest-paid woman in the country). She was born Ruby Stevens.

SELECTED FILMS: Broadway Nights (1927), Mexicali Rose (1929), Ladies of Leisure (1930), Baby Face (1933), The Bride Walks Out, Banjo on My Knee (1936), Breakfast for Two (1937), The Mad Miss Manton (1938), Remember the Night (1940), The Lady Eve, Meet John Doe (1941), Ball of Fire, The Great Man's Lady, The Gay Sisters (1942), Hollywood Canteen (1944), The Bride Wore Boots (1946), The Lady Gambles (1949), To Please a Lady (1950), Roustabout, The Night Walker (1964). ∎

Stapleton, Jean (1923–), actress. Worked in stock and on Broadway before entering films in 1958. A charming character actress born Jeanne Murray, she has appeared sporadically in films. Her greater popularity, however, came in the 1970s from her portrayal of Edith, the wife of the bigoted Archie Bunker, in the highly successful television series, "All in the Family."

SELECTED FILMS: Damn Yankees (1958), Bells Are Ringing (1960), Something Wild (1961), Cold Turkey (1971), The Buddy System (1984). ∎

Stapleton, Maureen (1925–), actress. Appeared on Broadway from 1946 and made her film debut in 1959. A versatile performer, she has portrayed a variety of tragic and comic characters, in slovenly types. The exceptional talent and sensitivity that she brings to her roles have earned her four Academy Award nominations and one Oscar as Best Supporting Actress for her role in Reds (1981).

In *Lost and Found* she portrayed the eccentric mother of George SEGAL, who brings his betrothed home for the first time. Stapleton, the owner of a bookstore, tells of her past trysts with some famous authors of the past and concludes with the following philosophy: "I don't believe in marriage. . . A bed is the only place that offers a man and a woman equal opportunity."

SELECTED FILMS: *Lonelyhearts (1959), Bye Bye Birdie (1963), Plaza Suite (1971), The Runner Stumbles, Lost and Found (1979), Johnny Dangerously (1984), Cocoon (1985).* ■

Stardust Memories (1980), UA. Dir. Woody Allen; Sc. Woody Allen; with Woody Allen, Charlotte Rampling, Jessica Harper, Tony Roberts.

In this comedy-drama Woody ALLEN explores the life of a successful filmmaker who finds little personal satisfaction in his achievements and sees his retinue as grotesque sycophants. In this virtual parody of Fellini's 8 1/2, Allen visualizes himself as victim, surrounded by shallow, superficial fans who continue to misinterpret the meanings of his films. His audiences, naturally, felt insulted. Even lines like "I don't know much about classical music; for years I thought that the Goldberg Variations were something Mr. and Mrs. Goldberg tried on their wedding night," or Allen's reply to a movie executive who calls him an atheist: "To you I'm an atheist, to God I'm the loyal opposition," could not ingratiate the film to its viewers. The critics treated the film harshly.

State of the Union (1948), MGM. Dir. Frank Capra; Sc. Myles Connolly, Anthony Veiller; with Spencer Tracy, Katharine Hepburn, Angela Lansbury, Van Johnson.

Spencer TRACY and Katharine HEPBURN teamed up for their fifth film in this political satire of a hard-working, idealistic American who is persuaded to run for the Presidency. Seduced by newspaper publisher Angela Lansbury to become a candidate, Tracy, a self-made millionaire, discovers the intricate system of political corruption. Hepburn, as his wife, witnesses her husband's transformation as he compromises one ideal after another. She decides to take on the power structure and the aggressive Lansbury. Hepburn's role was originally to have gone to Claudette COLBERT, who quit the production because her contract did not include a 5:00 PM work-stoppage clause. The talented cast includes Adolphe MENJOU as a manipulating campaign manager. When Lansbury confides to him that Tracy is beginning to wonder if there is any difference between the two parties, Menjou retorts: "There's all the difference in the world. They're in and we're out." Margaret HAMILTON plays a maid who develops a crush on reporter Van JOHNSON. Other supporting players also help to speed this charming comedy to its rather didactic conclusion. The film, based on the Pulitzer Prize-winning play by Howard Lindsay and Russel Crouse, has two shortcomings: its preachy conclusion and its dated naivete for today's more cynical audiences. However, the witty dialogue and the magic of its two stars make this a very entertaining work.

Steamboat Bill, Jr. See Buster Keaton.

Stein, Paul L. (1892–1951), director. Worked as a stage manager and screenwriter in America, as an actor and film director in his native Germany, and as a film director in the United States in the 1920s and early 1930s. In 1932 he moved to England where he continued his directorial career. Specializing in romantic comedies and dramas, he turned out several interesting and entertaining films while in the United States.

SELECTED FILMS: *My Official Wife (1926), Don't Tell the Wife, The Climbers (1927), Man-Made Woman, Show Folks*

(1928), Her Private Affair (1929), One Romantic Night, The Lottery Bride (1930), A Woman Commands (1932). ∎

Stephenson, Henry (1871–1956), actor. Worked on stage in his native England and in the United States before settling in Hollywood in the early 1930s as a dependable character player in dramas and light films. Tall and distinguished, he portrayed aristocratic roles in several historical features.

SELECTED FILMS: The Spreading Dawn (1917), Wild, Wild Susan (1925), The Animal Kingdom (1932), Double Harness (1933), Thirty Day Princess, What Every Woman Knows (1934), The Perfect Gentleman (1935), Walking on Air (1936), Wise Girl (1937), The Baroness and the Butler (1938), Spring Parade, It's a Date, Down Argentine Way (1940), Rings on Her Fingers (1942), Two Girls and a Sailor (1944), Ivy (1947), Julia Misbehaves (1948), Challenge to Lassie (1949). ∎

Sterling, Ford (1893–1939), actor. Ran away from home to join the circus. Born George Ford Stitch, he worked in vaudeville and on stage before entering early silent films in 1911 as a comic performer for producer Mack SENNETT. One of the original members of Sennett's famous KEYSTONE comedies stock company, he appeared in a long string of shorts with some of the leading comics of the period, including, among others, Mabel NORMAND and "Fatty" ARBUCKLE. He was one of the original KEYSTONE KOPS. Later, he emerged as the top studio comic and won his own series, the Sterling Comedies. In the 1920s, after leaving Sennett, he appeared as a character actor in feature-length films for different studios. Although he was one of the masters of physical comedy, this style of slapstick was slowly being phased out. By the 1930s he found assignments difficult to come by. He was, by any measurement, a pioneer of and major contributor to early screen comedy.

SELECTED FILMS: Abe Gets Even With Father (1911), Cohen Collects a Debt (1912), On His Wedding Day (1913), Love and Dynamite, Tango Tangles (1914), Court House Crooks, The Hunt (1915), His Wild Oats (1916), Stars and Bars, His Torpedoed Love (1917), Her Screen Idol (1918), Yankee Doodle in Berlin (1919), Love, Honor and Behave (1920), An Unhappy Finish (1921), Oh, Mabel Behave (1922), The Spoilers (1923), He Who Gets Slapped, So Big (1924), Stage Struck (1925), The American Venus, The Show-Off (1926), Casey at the Bat (1927), Gentlemen Prefer Blondes (1928), The Fall of Eve, Sally (1929), Showgirl in Hollywood, Kismet (1930), Her Majesty Love (1931), Alice in Wonderland (1933), Black Sheep (1935). ∎

Stevens, Connie (1938–), actress, singer. Appeared as a female lead in romantic films and light comedies during the 1960s and 1970s. A spirited performer and talented singer, she has also appeared on Broadway and in television and turned out several successful recordings.

SELECTED FILMS: Young and Dangerous (1957), Rock-a-Bye Baby, The Party Crashers (1958), Palm Springs Weekend (1963), Never Too Late (1965), Way . . . Way Out (1966), The Grissom Gang (1971), Scorchy (1976), Grease 2 (1982). ∎

Stevens, George (1904–1975), director. Began his Hollywood career in 1921 as an assistant cameraman. He later worked for Hal ROACH, again behind the camera, cranking out several LAUREL AND HARDY shorts. By 1930 he was directing comedy shorts and three years later he began turning out low-budget feature-length comedies for RKO studios. He soon became a major director, working with many of the leading screen figures of the period, including, among others, Katharine HEPBURN and Cary GRANT. A slow and exacting director, he rarely permitted excessive emotion or sentimentality to dominate his films. He is probably best known for his dramatic films but has also given the public several entertaining light films. His son, George Stevens, Jr., recently compiled a documentary about his father.

SELECTED FILMS: *The Cohens and Kellys in Trouble (1933), Bachelor Bait, Kentucky Kernels (1934), The Nitwits, Alice Adams (1935), Swing Time (1936), A Damsel in Distress (1937), Vivacious Lady (1938), Woman of the Year (1942), The More the Merrier (1943), The Only Game in Town (1970).* ■

Stevens, Stella (1936–), actress. Made her film debut in 1959 and went on to portray a variety of roles in dramas and light films. An attractive blonde, she scored a hit in the film adaptation of the Broadway musical *Li'l Abner*. She has appeared regularly in television.

SELECTED FILMS: *Say One for Me, Li'l Abner (1959), The Courtship of Eddie's Father, The Nutty Professor (1963), Advance to the Rear (1964), How to Save a Marriage—and Ruin Your Life (1969), Las Vegas Lady, Nickelodeon (1976), Wacko (1981), Chained Heat (1983).* ■

Stevenson, Charles E. (1888–1943), actor. Appeared as a character player in silent comedy shorts and features during the 1920s. Often portraying a policeman, he particularly supported Harold LLOYD in many of his best films.

SELECTED FILMS: *Bumping Into Broadway (1919), Number Please, Never Weaken (1920), A Sailor-Made Man (1921), Grandma's Boy, Doctor Jack (1922), The Rustle of Silk, Garrison's Finish, Safety Last, Why Worry? (1923), Pied Piper Malone, Girl Shy, Hot Water (1924), The Insidious Dr. Fu Manchu (1929).* ■

Stewart, Donald Ogden (1894–1980), screenwriter, playwright. Wrote novels and plays before establishing himself as a full-time Hollywood screenwriter in the early 1930s. He is best known for his

urbane screenplays and witty dialogue. Blacklisted during the McCarthy era, he moved to England. His autobiography, *By a Stroke of Luck*, was published in 1974.

SELECTED FILMS: *Tarnished Lady (1931), Going Hollywood (1933), No More Ladies (1935), Holiday (1938), Love Affair, The Night of Nights (1939), Kitty Foyle, The Philadelphia Story (1940), That Uncertain Feeling (1941), Without Love (1945), Life With Father (1947), Edward My Son (1949).* ■

James Stewart (right)

Stewart, James (1908–), actor. Worked in stock and on Broadway before entering films in the mid-1930s. The shy, gangling young actor with sluggish speech hardly fitted into the traditional patterns of romantic and heroic leads that Hollywood studios came to expect, but eventually his individual style helped him become one of the screen's most popular figures. He starred in dramas and comedies, working with some of the major directors and film personalities of the period. He received several nominations as Best Actor prior to and following his winning an Oscar for his role in *The Philadelphia Story* (1940). He also won other awards, including two New York Film Critics' Awards and a special citation at a Venice Film Festival. For most of the 1950s he was in the Top Ten of box-office favorites, reaching Number One in 1955. His screen career has stretched over five decades. In the 1970s he became the star of his own television show. He was awarded the

USO's Gold Medal in 1984. *James Stewart*, a biography written by Allen Eyles, was published in 1984.

SELECTED FILMS: *The Murder Man (1935), Wife Vs. Secretary, The Gorgeous Hussy, After the Thin Man (1936), Vivacious Lady, You Can't Take It With You (1938), It's a Wonderful World, Mr. Smith Goes to Washington, Destry Rides Again (1939), No Time for Comedy, The Philadelphia Story (1940), Come Live With Me, Pot o' Gold (1941), It's a Wonderful Life, Magic Town (1947), On Our Merry Way (1948), The Jackpot, Harvey (1950), Bell, Book and Candle (1958), Mr. Hobbs Takes a Vacation (1962), Take Her, She's Mine (1963), Dear Brigitte (1965), The Cheyenne Social Club (1970), Fool's Parade (1971), That's Entertainment (1974), The Magic of Lassie (1978).* ■

Stockdale, Carl (1874–1953), actor. Worked in early silent films, especially as a supporting player in comedy shorts starring Charlie CHAPLIN. He later appeared as a character actor in silent and sound features.

SELECTED FILMS: *The Champion, The Jitney Elopement, By the Sea, The Bank (1915), Red Hot Romance (1922), The Darling of New York, The Extra Girl (1924), A Regular Fellow (1925), See You in Jail (1927), The Love Parade (1929), Rawhide (1938).* ■

Stoloff, Benjamin (1895–1960), director. Began directing silent short films and features in the late 1920s and continued to turn out full-length films into the late '40s. Specializing in routine B movies, he worked in various genres.

SELECTED FILMS: *The Canyon of Light (1926), The Gay Retreat (1927), Plastered in Paris (1928), Speakeasy (1929), Happy Days, Soup to Nuts (1930), Three Rogues, Not Exactly Gentlemen (1931), The Night Mayor (1932), Palooka, Transatlantic Merry-Go-Round (1934), To Beat the Band, Swell Head (1935), Fight for Your Lady (1937), Radio City Revels (1938), Three Sons o' Guns (1941), Take It or Leave It (1944), Johnny*

Comes Flying Home (1946), It's a Joke, Son (1947). ■

Stone, Fred (1873–1959), actor. Worked in vaudeville and on stage before entering early silent films. A character player who was often seen in fatherly roles, he appeared only sporadically on the screen but gave memorable performances.

SELECTED FILMS: *The Goat (1918), Under the Top (1919), The Duke of Chimney Butte (1921), Smiling Faces (1932), Alice Adams (1935), The Farmer in the Dell, My American Wife (1936), Life Begins in College (1937), The Westerner (1940).* ■

Stone, George E. (1903–1967), actor. Worked in vaudeville as a song-and-dance performer and on stage before entering early silent films. A short, mousy-looking figure born George Stein, he reached the peak of his popularity in the 1930s and 1940s playing character roles in action films and light comedies and musicals. He portrayed Chester Morris' comic sidekick in the "Boston Blackie" series. He was equally effective on both sides of the law.

In *42nd Street* (1933) he played a stage manager who drilled the chorus girls, some of whom he knew intimately. "Anytime Annie," he recalls. "Say, who can forget her? She only said 'no' once, and then she didn't hear the question."

SELECTED FILMS: *Children of the Feud (1916), Just Pals (1920), Jackie (1921), Tenderloin, State Street Sadie (1928), Melody Lane, Skin Deep (1929), The Front Page (1931), Taxi! (1932), The Big Brain, Penthouse (1933), Hold 'Em, Yale (1935), Rhythm on the Range (1936), The Night of Nights (1939), Confessions of Boston Blackie (1941), The Devil With Hitler (1942), Abie's Irish Rose (1946), Guys and Dolls (1955), Some Like It Hot (1959), Pocketful of Miracles (1961).* ■

Stone, Lewis (1879–1953), actor. A tall, distinguished actor with stage and silent screen experience. He played leading roles in the 1920s and early 1930s. He then turned to portraying character roles in dramas and light films. He gained fame as Judge Hardy, Mickey Rooney's father in the "ANDY HARDY" comedy series, appearing in 14 entries. A contract player for MGM since the late 1920s, he was featured in more than 150 films in a screen career that spanned five decades.

In *The Courtship of Andy Hardy* (1942) he advises his daughter (Cecilia Parker): "I think a newspaper article should be about as long as a lady's skirt—long enough to cover the subject, but short enough to be interesting."

SELECTED FILMS: *The Man Who Found Out* (1915), *You Can't Fool Your Wife* (1923), *Cheaper to Marry* (1925), *The Girl From Missouri* (1934), *Suzy* (1936), *You're Only Young Once* (1937), *Joe and Ethel Turp Call on the President* (1939), *Three Wise Fools* (1946), *State of the Union* (1948), *Grounds for Marriage* (1950), *Angels in the Outfield* (1951), *All the Brothers Were Valiant* (1953). ∎

Stone, Milburn (1904–1980), actor. Came to Hollywood in the mid-1930s. He played in serials, action pictures, and light films as a second lead, comic sidekick, or character actor. A rather squat, neat-looking performer with a mustache, he finally gained recognition late in his career as Doc Adams in the "Gunsmoke" television series.

SELECTED FILMS: *The Fighting Marines*, *Ladies Crave Excitement* (1935), *The Milky Way*, *The Princess Comes Across* (1936), *Swing It, Professor* (1937), *Charlie McCarthy, Detective* (1939), *An Angel From Texas* (1940), *Frisco Lil* (1942), *Hi, Good Looking* (1944), *The Beautiful Cheat* (1945), *Her Adventurous Night* (1946), *Buck Privates Come Home* (1947), *The Sun Shines Bright* (1953), *The Private War of Major Benson* (1955), *Drango* (1957). ∎

Storch, Larry (1925–), actor, comedian. Worked as a comic in small clubs and on stage before entering films with regularity in 1960. He has appeared chiefly in light films as a comic character actor while occasionally starring in various television series.

SELECTED FILMS: *The Prince Who Was a Thief* (1951), *Who Was That Lady?* (1960), *40 Pounds of Trouble*, *Captain Newman, MD* (1963), *Sex and the Single Girl*, *Wild and Wonderful* (1964), *That Funny Feeling* (1965), *The Monitors* (1969), *The Happy Hooker Goes to Washington* (1977). ∎

Strauss, Robert (1913–1975), actor. Appeared on Broadway before entering films in the early 1950s. A gruff comic character player, he was nominated for an Oscar for his role as Animal in *Stalag 17*. His screen career, however, rapidly declined following some poor roles and weak vehicles. He appeared in television as well as in dramas and light films.

In *Stalag 17* he played a prisoner-of-war in a German camp. During an air raid he and his pal Harvey LEMBECK are chewed out for always being the last two out of the barracks. "Oh, yeah," Lembeck replies, "you try jumping in those trenches first. Everyone jumps on top of you." To which Strauss adds: "How do you think I got this hernia?"

SELECTED FILMS: *Sailor Beware* (1951), *Jumping Jacks* (1952), *Stalag 17*, *Here Come the Girls* (1953), *Money From Home*, *The Atomic Kid* (1954), *The Seven Year Itch* (1955), *Li'l Abner* (1959), *Wake Me When It's Over* (1960), *The Last Time I Saw Archie* (1961), *Girls! Girls! Girls!* (1962), *The Thrill of It All* (1963), *The Family Jewels* (1965), *Dagmar's Hot Pants* (1971). ∎

Strayer, Frank (1891–1964), director. Worked as an assistant director and actor in early silent films before establishing himself as a full-fledged director in the mid-1920s. He turned out numerous routine dramas and light films, his fame resting on the "BLONDIE" entries he directed. He was also responsible for several of the "JONES FAMILY" episodes during the 1930s.

SELECTED FILMS: The Fate of a Flirt (1925), When the Wife's Away (1926), Pleasure Before Business, Rough House Rosie (1927), Just Married (1928), The Fall of Eve (1929), Let's Go Places (1930), Caught Cheating, Anybody's Blonde (1931), Twin Husbands (1934), Society Fever (1935), Off to the Races, Big Business, Hot Water, Borrowing Trouble (1937), Blondie (1938), Go West, Young Lady (1941), It's a Great Life (1943), Mama Loves Papa (1945), I Ring Doorbells (1946), The Sickle and the Cross (1951). ∎

Streisand, Barbra (1942–), singer, actress. Worked in nightclubs, on Broadway, and in television before entering films in 1968. A dynamic entertainer and vibrant singer, she has made numerous successful recordings. She brought her acting and singing talents to the screen and won an Academy Award. Some of the material she has had to work with was mediocre, but her personality has often carried these films. She was the top female film star of the 1970s.

SELECTED FILMS: Funny Girl (1968), Hello Dolly! (1969), On a Clear Day You Can See Forever, The Owl and the Pussycat (1970), What's Up, Doc?, Up the Sandbox (1972), The Way We Were (1973), For Pete's Sake (1974), Funny Lady (1975), The Main Event (1979), All Night Long (1981), Yentl (1983). ∎

Strong Man, The (1926), FN. Dir. Frank Capra; Sc. Frank Capra, Arthur Ripley; with Harry Langdon, Priscilla Bonner.

Considered by many to be Harry LANGDON'S best work, the comedy concerns a Belgian soldier who falls in love with an American girl who corresponds with him. After the war he comes to the United States as a "strong man's" assistant and proceeds to look for his Mary Brown, stopping girls in the street

Harry Langdon and Priscilla Bonner in The Strong Man (1926)

and comparing the photo he has carried with him throughout the war. When he does find her in a small town, he discovers that she is blind. Using pantomime, sight gags, and slapstick, director Frank CAPRA and Langdon add an abundance of comic moments to the simple story. One of the funniest scenes occurs on a crowded bus with Langdon giving himself a chest rub for his cold, accidentally using a piece of Limburger cheese. Another outstanding scene involves a gangster's moll who hides some stolen loot on Langdon and then lures him to her apartment to recover it. Langdon, who thinks he is being seduced, lays waste the apartment as he tries to avoid her roaming hands. Capra's handling of Langdon's discovering that the girl is blind is accomplished so expertly that the sequence transcends sentiment and enhances the entire film. It anticipates a similar situation in Chaplin's City Lights.

Stuart, Gloria (1910–), actress. Worked on stage before signing with Universal studios in 1932. A beautiful blonde performer who usually played wholesome characters, she was unfortunately relegated to low-budget dramas and light features at the studio. But she became a favorite with her audiences. She retired from the screen in the mid-1940s, after appearing in more than four dozen films, to pursue a professional career as an artist.

SELECTED FILMS: *Street of Women, The All-American (1932), Roman Scandals, Sweepings (1933), Gift of Gab, Here Comes the Navy, I'll Tell the World (1934), Laddie (1935), Poor Little Rich Girl, Girl on the Front Page (1936), Rebecca of Sunnybrook Farm, Keep Smiling (1938).* ■

Sturges, Preston (1898–1959), director, screenwriter. Was a successful playwright before moving to Hollywood in the early 1930s. At first he wrote only dialogue, but he soon advanced to screenwriting, turning out eloquent scripts. By 1940 he was directing his own material for Paramount and, for the next few years, became one of the most successful directors in Hollywood. His satirical comedies won critical acclaim and were commercially profitable. He gathered about him a group of offbeat character actors and he was responsible for a series of witty films that blended sparkling dialogue with hilarious slapstick.

The Great McGinty, his first in a series of comedies for Paramount, was a refreshing lampoon on politics. His next, *Christmas in July,* was a spoof on radio advertising contests. He followed this with *The Lady Eve,* a sophisticated romantic comedy that placed him among the major directors of the decade and set the tone for a string of successful comedies.

But his reign was short-lived. By the mid-1940s he fell out of favor, his films came to lack the pungency of his early work. However, he left behind a group of films that remain entertaining and influenced an entire generation of writer-directors, including Billy WILDER, Nunnally JOHNSON, Frank TASHLIN, and Blake EDWARDS, who tried to emulate his style and his success.

SELECTED FILMS: *The Great McGinty, Christmas in July (1940), The Lady Eve, Sullivan's Travels (1941), The Palm Beach Story (1942), The Miracle of Morgan's Creek, Hail the Conquering Hero, The Great Moment (1944), Mad Wednesday (1947), Unfaithfully Yours (1948), The Beautiful Blonde From Bashful Bend (1949), The French They Are a Funny Race (1955).* ■

Sullivan's Travels (1941), PAR. Dir. Preston Sturges; Sc. Preston Sturges; with Joel McCrea, Veronica Lake, Porter Hall, William Demarest, Franklin Pangborn.

This well-paced comedy-drama about movie people revolves around a director, played by Joel McCREA, who grows tired of making only light films and wants to do a serious one about the poor and unemployed, titled *Brother, Where Art Thou?* Disguised as a hobo, he travels among the downtrodden only to learn that people want and need laughter. STURGES captures the attention of his audience immediately with the striking opening sequence, which turns out to be a film-within-a-film, a device employed by several subsequent directors, including Truffaut in his Oscar-winning *Day for Night* (1973). The film begins at night atop a freight train where two men are slugging it out to the death. Suddenly someone calls "Cut!" and we discover the scene is only a stage set and we are in the midst of the making of a film. Petite Veronica LAKE portrays a down-and-out actress whom McCrea meets on his dark journey, while several members of the director's stock company of character actors make their usual valuable contributions. Sturges does not allow the serious moments to interfere with the general comic tone. Wit and slapstick are prevalent. If there were a film sub-genre called road comedy (*It Happened One Night, Harry and Tonto,* several Chaplin shorts, the Hope-Crosby features, etc.), *Sullivan's Travels* would be very near the head of the list.

Sully, Frank (1908–1975), actor. Appeared as a supporting player in comedy shorts from the 1940s through the 1950s. He worked with various comedians at Columbia studios, including the THREE STOOGES.

SELECTED FILMS: Pardon My Backfire (1953), Guns A-Poppin' (1957). ∎

Summers, Hope (1902–1979), actress. Worked in stock and on radio before moving to Hollywood in the mid-1950s. Dark-haired and wide-eyed, she has appeared as a character player in several dramas and light films, usually playing matrons.

SELECTED FILMS: Black Patch (1957), Parrish (1961), The Couch (1962), The Hallelujah Trail (1965), The Ghost and Mrs. Chicken (1966). ∎

Slim Summerville

Summerville, Slim (1892–1946), actor. Appeared in early silent comedy shorts for producer Mack SENNETT'S KEYSTONE studios. A tall, gangling comic performer, he was one of the original KEYSTONE KOPS before establishing himself as one of Sennett's top funnymen, often portraying slow-witted country yokels. During the 1920s he switched to directing comedy shorts for various studios. With the advent of sound, he returned to acting. He starred in a series

of comedies with ZaSu PITTS and continued as a character actor into the 1940s.

In All Quiet on the Western Front (1930) he portrayed a cynical, battle-weary soldier, one of his more memorable roles. A group of new recruits, fresh out of high school and eager to enter the fighting, arrive at Summerville's billet. "We haven't eaten since breakfast," the leader of the young innocents announces. "We thought maybe you could tell us what we could do about it." "Eat without further delay," Slim replies.

SELECTED FILMS: The Knockout, Mabel's Busy Day, Tillie's Punctured Romance (1914), Her Painted Hero (1915), Roping Her Romeo (1917), Skirts (1921), The Texas Streaks (1926), One Hysterical Night, Strong Boy (1929), See America Thirst (1930), The Front Page (1931), They Just Had to Get Married, Her First Mate (1933), Their Big Moment (1934), The Farmer Takes a Wife (1935), Captain January, Pepper (1936), Off to the Races (1937), Kentucky Moonshine (1938), Gold Rush Maisie (1940), Tobacco Road (1941), I'm From Arkansas (1944), The Hoodlum Saint (1946). ∎

Sundberg, Clinton (1906–), actor. Worked as a teacher before entering films in the mid-1940s. A dark-haired character player, he appeared in numerous light films, often cast as a fussbudget or troubled assistant.

SELECTED FILMS: The Mighty McGurk, Love Laughs at Andy Hardy (1946), Living in a Big Way, Undercover Maisie (1947), Good Sam, Mr. Peabody and the Mermaid, A Date With Judy (1948), The Barkleys of Broadway (1949), Father Is a Bachelor (1950), On the Riviera, The Fat Man, As Young As You Feel (1951), The Belle of New York (1952), The Caddy (1953), The Birds and the Bees (1956), Bachelor in Paradise (1961), Hotel (1968). ∎

"Sunnyside." See Charlie Chaplin.

Sutherland, A. Edward (1895–1974), director. Worked in vaudeville and on stage before turning his interests to films in 1914. Starting as a stuntman and minor actor, he soon joined producer Mack SENNETT'S stock company of comics and appeared in several KEYSTONE comedy shorts. By 1924, after assisting Charlie CHAPLIN on *A Woman of Affairs* the previous year, he began his career as director. Specializing in light films, he turned out several comedies starring W. C. FIELDS. He worked with more leading comedians of the period than almost any other director. He directed Eddie CANTOR, Douglas FAIRBANKS, George BURNS, Gracie ALLEN, LAUREL AND HARDY, ABBOTT AND COSTELLO, and, of course, Fields.

SELECTED FILMS: *Coming Through, Wild, Wild Susan* (1925), *Behind the Front, It's the Old Army Game* (1926), *Fireman, Save My Child* (1927), *Tillie's Punctured Romance, What a Night!* (1928), *Pointed Heels* (1929), *The Social Lion, The Sap From Syracuse* (1930), *Palmy Days* (1931), *Mr. Robinson Crusoe* (1932), *International House* (1933), *Poppy* (1936), *Champagne Waltz, Every Day's a Holiday* (1937), *The Flying Deuces* (1939), *One Night in the Tropics* (1940), *Sing Your Worries Away* (1942), *Dixie* (1943), *Having Wonderful Crime* (1945), *Abie's Irish Rose* (1946). ∎

Sutton, Grady (1908–), actor. A popular character player during the 1930s and 1940s. A fleshy figure, he portrayed comic characters, especially dimwitted rural types. He co-starred in the early 1930s in a comedy series, "The BOY FRIEND," with Gertrude MESSINGER and two former "OUR GANG" members, Mary KORNMAN and Mickey DANIELS. He appeared in several shorts and feature films with W. C. FIELDS, often as his foil.

SELECTED FILMS: *The Mad Whirl, The Freshman* (1925), *Pack Up Your Troubles* (1932), *College Humor* (1933), *Alice Adams* (1935), *My Man Godfrey, Pigskin Parade* (1936), *Vivacious Lady* (1938), *You Can't Cheat an Honest Man* (1939), *The Bank Dick* (1940), *Bedtime Story* (1941), *A Lady Takes a Chance* (1943), *A Royal Scandal* (1945), *Jumbo* (1962), *My Fair Lady* (1964), *Paradise, Hawaiian Style* (1966), *Support Your Local Gunfighter* (1971). ∎

Swain, Mack (1876–1935), actor. Worked in minstrel shows, in vaudeville, and on stage for more than 20 years before entering early silent comedy shorts in 1913 for producer Mack SENNETT'S KEYSTONE studios. A tall, broad-framed comic, he specialized in slapstick, as did many in Sennett's stock company. He worked with CHAPLIN in some of his best films. Swain starred in his own comedy series (1914–1915), known as the "AMBROSE" films. He later worked for other studios, but during the 1920s he slid from popularity until Chaplin employed him for a major role in *The Gold Rush*. He continued in character roles and lead parts until the early 1930s. A veteran comic with long experience on stage and screen, he appeared in numerous comedies, utilizing his physical attributes to good effect. In a class with such notables as "Fatty" ARBUCKLE, Mabel NORMAND, Ford STERLING, Edgar KENNEDY, and Al ST. JOHN, he was one of the great slapstick comedians of the silent screen.

SELECTED FILMS: *Caught in a Cabaret, Laughing Gas, Ambrose's First Falsehood* (1914), *Our Dare Devil Chef, The Battle of Ambrose and Walrus* (1915), *The Idle Class* (1921), *Pay Day* (1922), *The Pilgrim* (1923), *The Gold Rush* (1925), *Footloose Widows* (1926), *Finnegan's Ball, The Beloved Rogue* (1927), *Gentlemen Prefer Blondes* (1928), *The Cohens and Kellys in Atlantic City* (1929), *Finn and Hattie* (1931), *Midnight Patrol* (1932). ∎

Swanson, Gloria (1897–1983), actress. Began her long film career in 1913 at ESSANAY'S Chicago studios. Born Gloria Swenson, she later joined, with her husband Wallace BEERY, Mack

SENNETT'S KEYSTONE studios in Hollywood where she appeared in a series of comedy shorts with Bobby VERNON. She left Sennett to appear in dramatic films and then signed with Paramount to star in several of Cecil B. DeMILLE'S farces. A beautiful and glamorous screen personality, she reached the height of her popularity in the mid-1920s. She made a successful transition to sound films, but her films failed critically and commercially. She abandoned her screen career in the mid-1930s, appearing only sporadically in films thereafter. She starred in a minor comedy in 1941 and in *Sunset Boulevard* in 1950, which once again brought her critical acclaim and stardom in the role of Norma Desmond, a former silent screen star desperately seeking a comeback.

At her peak during the 1920s, she was the epitome of style and fashion, both on and off screen. Her screen image was that of a sophisticated, headstrong female whose arrogance challenged the men in the audience and inspired the women. She reigned in Hollywood as though she were a true queen. Rejecting a contract offer of one million dollars from movie mogul Adolph Zukor, she elected, unfortunately, to produce her own films. This was the beginning of her descent.

SELECTED FILMS: At the End of a Perfect Day, His New Job, Sweedie Goes to College (1915), A Social Cub, Love on Skates, Haystacks and Steeples (1916), Teddy at the Throttle, Baseball Madness, The Pullman Bride (1917), You Can't Believe Everything (1918), Don't Change Your Husband, Male and Female (1919), The Affairs of Anatol (1921), The Impossible Mrs. Bellew (1922), My American Wife, Bluebeard's Eighth Wife (1923), The Humming Bird (1924), The Untamed Lady, Fine Manners (1926), What a Widow! (1930), Music in the Air (1934), Father Takes a Wife (1941), Airport 1975 (1974). ∎

"Sweedie" comedies. A series of silent shorts starring Wallace BEERY impersonating a Swedish maid. The films,

produced by ESSANAY studios from 1914 to 1915, consisted chiefly of knockabout comedy. Gloria SWANSON, Beery's wife at the time, appeared in at least one of the entries, "Sweedie Goes to College."

SELECTED FILMS: Sweedie the Swatter, Sweedie Learns to Swim, Sweedie at the Fair (1914), Sweedie's Suicide, Sweedie and Her Dog, Sweedie's Hopeless Love, Sweedie Goes to College, Sweedie in Vaudeville (1915). ∎

Sweet, Harry (1901–1933), actor, director. Supervised silent comedy shorts for Fox studios, directed several CLARK AND McCULLOUGH comedies, and appeared occasionally in light films during the 1930s.

SELECTED FILMS (as actor): Fascinating Youth (1926), Homesick (1928), Hit the Deck, True to the Navy, Her Man (1930), Carnival Boat (1932).

SELECTED FILMS (as director): Waltzing Around, Beneath the Law, Music Fiends (1929). ∎

Swickard, Joseph (1866–1940), actor. Began in early silent comedy shorts as a supporting player for Mack SENNETT'S KEYSTONE studios. Here he worked with some of the top comics of the period, including Mack SWAIN. He later appeared as a character actor in silent and sound features.

SELECTED FILMS: A Rowboat Romance, Laughing Gas, The Plumber (1914), The Best of Enemies, Love, Loot and Crash (1915), Love Will Conquer, The Village Vampire, His Wild Oats, Haystacks and Steeples, Ambrose's Cup of Woe (1916), Maytime (1924), The Wizard of Oz, Fifth Avenue Models (1925), Senor Daredevil (1926), Senorita (1927), Mamba (1930), The Girl Said No (1937), You Can't Take It With You (1938), Mexicali Rose (1939). ∎

Swift, David (1919–), director, screenwriter. Worked as an animator for Walt Disney studios, wrote comedy material for radio shows, and directed television programs before he turned to directing films in the early 1960s. Specializing in comedy, he turned out several entertaining features and wrote screenplays for other light films as well as for some of those which he directed.

SELECTED FILMS: Pollyanna (1960), The Parent Trap (1961), Love Is a Ball, Under the Yum Yum Tree (1963), Good Neighbor Sam (1964), How to Succeed in Business Without Really Trying (1967). ∎

Switzer, Carl "Alfalfa" (1926–1959), actor. Popular member of the "OUR GANG" comedy shorts from 1935. A freckle-faced youngster sporting a cowlick, he appeared in numerous entries in the above series through 1942, when he moved up to feature films. His adult screen career, however, faltered, and he was reduced to minor roles. He was fatally shot over a debt in 1959.

He is best remembered for his role in the comedy shorts as the wide-eyed, squeaky-voiced member of the gang who usually had a crush on a local girl or the teacher.

SELECTED FILMS: Southern Exposure, Beginner's Luck, Teacher's Beau, Sprucin' Up, Little Papa, Little Sinner, Our Gang Follies of 1936 (1935), Too Many Parents, Easy to Take, General Spanky (1936), Wild and Woolly (1937), The War Against Mrs. Hadley (1942), Johnny Doughboy, The Human Comedy (1943), The Gas House Kids (1946), State of the Union (1948), Pat and Mike (1952), The Defiant Ones (1958). ∎

Swor, Bert (1878–1943), actor. Worked in minstrel shows, in vaudeville, and on stage before entering films in the late 1920s. He appeared in several light films and comedy shorts. He was "Moran" for a while in the vaudeville and film comedy team of MORAN AND MACK.

SELECTED FILMS: Ducks and Deducts, A Colorful Sermon (1928), Why Bring That Up?, The Golfers, A Hollywood Star, The New Halfback, Uppercut O'Brien (1929), Anybody's War (1930). ∎

Sylvester. Fictional comic sidekick to Red SKELTON in the comedian's "WHISTLING" mystery-comedy series for MGM. He was portrayed by comic character actor Rags RAGLAND in all three entries, Whistling in the Dark (1941), Whistling in Dixie (1942), and Whistling in Brooklyn (1943).

T

Woody Allen (left), Marcel Hillaire (center) in
Take the Money and Run (1969)

Take the Money and Run (1969),
CIN. *Dir.* Woody Allen; *Sc.* Woody Allen, Mickey Rose; with Woody Allen,
Janet Margolin, Marcel Hillaire, Jacquelyn Hyde.

Woody ALLEN'S first directorial effort
as well as his first success, the comedy
uses a semi-documentary approach to
unfold the life story of Virgil Starkwell
(Woody), a compulsive thief. Allen's
screenplay is filled with humorous sight
gags and funny one-liners. Virgil's
former cello teacher in an interview recalls the musical ineptness of his student: "Virgil had no conception of the
instrument. He would try to blow into
it." In one scene Virgil cuts a glass panel
out of a jewelry store window and escapes with—the pane of glass. He says of
the meals given to the convicts on a
chain gang: "The men got one hot meal a
day—a bowl of steam." Virgil tells his
psychoanalyst: "I once stole a pornographic book which was written in
braille; I used to rub the dirty parts."
Many of Allen's themes (marriage, relationships) are present, including some
new variations: fear of isolation and failure. Without regrets, Virgil/Allen admits
of his crime-ridden/show business life:
"The hours are good, you travel a lot,
meet interesting people." Although
many of the gags hit their target, the film
lacks the depth of characterization and
structure to be found in his later work.

Talbot, Lyle (1902–), actor. Worked as
a magician and an actor in stock before
entering films in 1932. A handsome and
personable actor born Lisle Henderson,
he appeared in numerous dramas and
light films, alternating between male
leads and villainous roles. At the height
of his popularity in the 1930s, he continued to appear on the screen into the
1960s, when he started a new career in
television.

SELECTED FILMS: *Love Is a Racket,
No More Orchids* (1932), *She Had to Say
Yes, Havana Widows* (1933), *One Night
of Love* (1934), *It Happened in New York*
(1935), *The Singing Kid, Go West, Young
Man* (1936), *Second Honeymoon* (1937),
One Wild Night, The Arkansas Traveler
(1938), *Up in Arms, One Body Too Many*
(1944), *Champagne for Caesar, The Jackpot* (1950), *There's No Business Like
Show Business* (1954), *She Shoulda Said
No* (1957), *Sunrise at Campobello*
(1960). ■

Talbot, Nita (1930–), actress. Appeared as a sharp, wise-cracking supporting player in films during the 1950s
and 1960s. A talented comedienne, she
appeared also in television shows of the
1960s and 1970s.

SELECTED FILMS: *Bundle of Joy (1956), Once Upon a Horse, I Married a Woman (1958), Who's Got the Action? (1962), Girl Happy, That Funny Feeling, A Very Special Favor (1965), The Cool Ones (1967), Buck and the Preacher (1971).* ■

Talmadge, Constance (1900–1973), actress. Began her screen career in 1914 in early silent comedy shorts. In 1916 she joined D. W. Griffith and soon rose to stardom. Possessed of an awkward, adolescent charm and a propensity toward comedy, she became the leading star of sophisticated comedy during the silent period. She abandoned her screen career in the late 1920s, when sound was introduced. Her sister, Norma, dominated silent film dramas during the 1920s, while another sister, Natalie TALMADGE, appeared in several silent comedies. Anita Loos wrote a biography of the sisters titled *The Talmadge Girls* (1978).

SELECTED FILMS: *The Maid From Sweden, Buddy's First Call, The Egyptian Mummy (1914), Billy's Wager, Captivating Mary Carstairs (1915), The Missing Link, Intolerance (1916), The Honeymoon, The Matrimaniac (1917), A Temperamental Wife, Happiness a la Mode (1919), Two Weeks, The Love Expert (1920), Mama's Affair, Wedding Bells, Woman's Place (1921), The Primitive Lover, Polly of the Follies (1922), Dulcy (1923), The Goldfish (1924), Her Sister From Paris (1925), The Duchess of Buffalo (1926), Venus of Venice, Breakfast at Sunrise (1927).* ■

Talmadge, Natalie (1898–1969), actress. Appeared in early silent comedies, especially those starring Buster KEATON, whom she married. She was the sister of Constance and Norma Talmadge, both of whom were silent screen stars during the 1920s. She retired from films after her marriage, never achieving the critical acclaim poured upon her sisters.

SELECTED FILMS: *The Isle of Conquest (1919), Our Hospitality (1923).* ■

Talmadge, Norma (1897–1957), actress. Began her screen career in 1910 as a minor player with VITAGRAPH studios. She appeared in numerous silent comedies and dramas, reaching her height of fame in the 1920s in a string of melodramas. Known chiefly for her roles as suffering heroines, she starred in many comedies earlier in her career, portraying bellhops, maids, suffragettes, and generally mischievous brats. She retired from the screen in the early 1930s after a few unsuccessful attempts in sound films. Her sisters, Constance and Natalie, both starred in silent films.

SELECTED FILMS: *The Household Pest (1910), Mrs. 'Emery 'Awkins (1911), Mr. Butler Butles, Captain Barnacle's Messmate, The Extension Table, O'Hara Helps Cupid (1912), Casey at the Bat, Plot and Counterplot, Lady and Her Maid, 'Arriet's Baby, Country Barber, The Tables Turned, His Silver Bachelorhood, Under the Daisies, His Little Page (1913), Cupid Versus Money, Miser Murphy's Wedding Present, The Hero (1914), Captivating Mary Carstairs (1915), The Social Secretary (1916), Kiki (1926), Du Barry, Woman of Passion (1930).* ■

Talmadge, Richard (1896–1981), actor. Emigrated from Munich to Hollywood in the 1910s and found work as a stuntman. By the 1920s Talmadge, born Ricardo Metezetti, was acting in comedies and dramas. Burdened by his German accent when sound came to films, he switched to directing action sequences, working continuously into the 1960s. He specialized in daredevil stunts, similar to the style of Douglas FAIRBANKS, for whom he had previously worked. But his later films were low-budget, routine second features and never equaled the wit and charm of the Fairbanks vehicles.

SELECTED FILMS: *The Unknown (1921), Taking Chances, Wildcat Jordan, Lucky Dan (1922), Let's Go (1923), American Manners, Stepping Lively, Hail the Hero, Laughing at Danger (1924), The Wall Street Whiz, The Prince of Pep*

(1925), *The Broadway Gallant, The Bet-ter Man, The Merry Cavalier* (1926), *The Cavalier* (1928), *The Bachelor's Club* (1929), *The Poor Millionaire* (1930), *Speed Madness* (1932).* ■

Tamiroff, Akim (1899–1972), actor. Worked on stage before entering films in 1933. Short and stocky in appearance, he had an imposing presence on screen. He was chiefly cast in eccentric supporting roles, although he occasionally played leads. The Russian-born versatile actor was as effective in comedies as he was in dramatic films and played every con-ceivable foreign nationality. He received two Academy Award nominations for his roles in *The General Died at Dawn* (1936) and *For Whom the Bell Tolls.* He was featured in several of director Preston STURGES' comedies of the 1940s.

In *The Great McGinty* Tamiroff, a crooked political boss, invites an under-ling (Brian DONLEVY) into his bullet-proof limousine and, in a nostalgic mood, begins to reminisce about his humble beginnings. "Where I come from is very poor, see—" "What makes this bus so quiet?" Donlevy interjects, im-pressed with the plush vehicle. "It's the armor," the boss answers, annoyed; he then continues: "All the richness is gone a long time ago—" "Armored for what?" Donlevy interrupts again. "So people shouldn't interrupt me!" Tamiroff ex-claims.

SELECTED FILMS: *Okay America* (1932), *Queen Christina* (1933), *The Great Flirtation* (1934), *Naughty Marietta, Go Into Your Dance, The Gay Deception* (1935), *High, Wide and Hand-some* (1937), *Paris Honeymoon, The Magnificent Fraud* (1939), *The Great McGinty* (1940), *His Butler's Sister* (1943), *The Miracle of Morgan's Creek, Can't Help Singing* (1944), *A Scandal in Paris* (1946), *Fiesta* (1947), *My Girl Tisa* (1948), *Me and the Colonel* (1958), *Ocean's Eleven* (1960), *Romanoff and Juliet* (1961), *The Great Bank Robbery* (1969).* ■

Tansey, Emma (1884–1942), actress. Appeared in early silent comedy shorts during the 1920s. She was cast chiefly as a supporting player. She occasionally worked in films during the sound pe-riod.

SELECTED FILMS: *Young Oldfield, A Ten Minute Egg, Jeffries, Jr., All Wet, The Poor Fish* (1924), *Okay Toots!* (1935).* ■

Tashlin, Frank (1913–1972), director, screenwriter. Began his film career as an animator for Paul Terry cartoons, then switched to GAGMAN for Hal ROACH, and then returned to cartooning before turning to screenwriting in the 1940s. Following a degree of success in writing scripts for some of the leading comics, he turned to directing his own material in the 1950s. Perhaps because of his early work as a cartoonist, he specialized in visual gags which contained more knockabout comedy than subtle humor. Several of his comedies evoke middle-aged males who seem ill at ease with sexy women. He worked with many of the leading comedians of the period, including Bob HOPE, Danny KAYE, Red SKELTON, and MARTIN AND LEWIS.

SELECTED FILMS (as screenwriter): *Variety Girl* (1947), *The Paleface, The Fuller Brush Man* (1948).

SELECTED FILMS (as director): *The Lemon Drop Kid* (1951), *The First Time, Son of Paleface* (1952), *Marry Me Again* (1953), *Susan Slept Here* (1954), *Artists and Models* (1955), *The Lieutenant Wore Skirts, Hollywood or Bust* (1956), *Rock-a-Bye Baby, The Geisha Boy* (1958), *Say One for Me* (1959), *Cinderfella* (1960), *Bachelor Flat, It's Only Money* (1962), *The Man From the Diner's Club, Who's Minding the Store?* (1963), *The Disor-derly Orderly* (1964), *The Private Navy of Sgt. O'Farrell* (1968).* ■

Tashman, Lilyan (1899–1934), ac-tress. Worked as a model and a Ziegfeld Girl before entering silent films in the early 1920s. Portraying worldly, cynical blondes, she played leads or supporting roles in romantic dramas and light films into the early sound period until her untimely death at age 35.

SELECTED FILMS: Experience (1921), A Broadway Butterfly, Pretty Ladies, Bright Lights (1925), For Alimony Only, So This Is Paris (1926), The Stolen Bride, French Dressing (1927), Manhattan Cocktail (1928), The Marriage Playground (1929), No, No, Nanette, Puttin' on the Ritz, On the Level, The Matrimonial Bed (1930), One Heavenly Night, Millie (1931), The Wiser Sex (1932), Too Much Harmony (1933), Wine, Women and Song, Riptide (1934). ■

Taurog, Norman (1899–1981), director. Appeared on stage and in films in 1913 as a child actor. Within a few years he was directing silent comedy shorts starring some of the leading comics of the period, including Larry SEMON and Lloyd HAMILTON. For the next five decades he turned out numerous features, chiefly light films. He worked with some of the leading screen personalities of the period, including Eddie CANTOR, BURNS AND ALLEN, Bing CROSBY, Frank SINATRA, and Elvis Presley. Although he never developed an individual style, he did, however, demonstrate his skill at directing entertaining films in all genres.

SELECTED FILMS: Lucky Boy (1929), Sunny Skies, Hot Curves (1930), Finn and Hattie, Skippy (1931), Hold 'Em Jail (1932), A Bedtime Story (1933), We're Not Dressing (1934), Strike Me Pink, Rhythm on the Range (1936), Little Nellie Kelly (1940), Design for Scandal (1941), Are Husbands Necessary? (1942), Girl Crazy (1943), The Bride Goes Wild, Words and Music (1948), That Midnight Kiss (1949), Room for One More, Jumping Jacks, The Stooge (1952), Bundle of Joy (1956), Visit to a Small Planet (1960), Blue Hawaii (1961), Double Trouble (1967), Live a Little, Love a Little (1968). ■

"Taxi Boys" comedies. A series of ten two-reel films, produced by Hal ROACH in the early 1930s, concerning the mis-

adventures of a pair of bungling cab drivers. Roach was to use different comics from his stock company, hoping to find the right combination so that the new team could develop into another successful "Laurel and Hardy" team. The first entry, "What Price Taxi," starred Clyde COOK and Franklin PANGBORN. Composed chiefly of slapstick and hectic routines, it was reminiscent of previous silent comedy shorts. In the second entry, "Thundering Taxis," Cook had a new partner, an obscure actor, and once again the film contained much slapstick, a frantic pace, and little dialogue.

The next entry, "Strange Innertube," introduced an entirely new team made up of Ben BLUE, portraying a completely incompetent cabbie, the venerable Edgar KENNEDY, and Charles Rogers. In the next film Rogers was dropped and the Taxi Boys once again was pared down to a duo. Heavy-set Billy GILBERT and "skinny" Blue continued in the remainder of the series, only physically approaching the famous Laurel and Hardy pair who evoked more sympathy, charm, and humanity. However, Roach kept trying to improve the series until 1933, when the "Taxi Boys" turned in their uniforms. Billy continued to appear and star in other comedy series and light features, while Ben became a comic character actor in feature films. The demise of the series was, in a sense, a tribute to the talents and genius of Stan and Ollie.

Taylor, Dub (1908–), actor. Worked as a musician before entering films in the late 1930s. Short and squat, he has portrayed happy-go-lucky characters in light films. He has also appeared as comic sidekicks to several cowboy stars or as general old-timers in numerous B westerns. He is sometimes listed as Walter Dub Taylor.

SELECTED FILMS: You Can't Take It With You (1938), Mr. Smith Goes to Washington (1939), What's Buzzin'

Cousin (1943), You Can't Run Away From It (1956), No Time for Sergeants (1958), A Hole in the Head (1959), Pocketful of Miracles (1961), Don't Make Waves, The Shakiest Gun in the West (1967), Support Your Local Gunfighter (1971), Gator (1976), They Went That-a-Way and That-a-Way (1978), 1941 (1979), Used Cars (1980), Cannonball Run II (1983). ■

Taylor, Renee (1945–), actress, screenwriter, playwright. Has written in collaboration with her husband Joseph BOLOGNA several screenplays and Broadway plays, one of which have been transformed into popular film comedies. She has also appeared as a supporting player in light films by fellow screenwriters Neil SIMON and Mel BROOKS. The husband-wife team gained recognition for their hilarious play and film, *Lovers and Other Strangers.*

SELECTED FILMS (as actress): *The Producers (1968), Lovers and Other Strangers (1970), A New Leaf, Made for Each Other (1971), The Last of the Red Hot Lovers (1972), Lovesick (1983)* ■

Taylor, Sam (1895–1958), director, screenwriter. Began his long career in Hollywood in 1916 as a GAGMAN for KALEM studios. By the 1920s he was well entrenched as a major director. He had written the stories for and co-directed with Fred NEWMEYER, one of his frequent collaborators, several of Harold LLOYD'S best silent comedies, and was considered by the bespectacled comedian as one of his most talented workers. He continued to direct dramas and light films through the sound era, several of which starred some of the leading personalities of the period, including Beatrice Lillie, Mary PICKFORD, Douglas FAIRBANKS, and LAUREL AND HARDY. He often wrote or collaborated on the screenplays and stories for his films.

SELECTED FILMS: *Now or Never, I Do, Among Those Present, Never Weaken (1921), Safety Last, Why Worry? (1923), Girl Shy, Hot Water (1924), The Freshman (1925), For Heaven's Sake, Exit Smiling (1926), My Best Girl (1927), Coquette, The Taming of the Shrew (1929), Kiki, Ambassador Bill (1931), Out All Night (1933), The Vagabond Lady (1935), Nothing but Trouble (1945).* ■

Taylor, Vaughn (1910–1983), actor. Worked on stage before turning to films in the early 1930s as a supporting actor. Lean and balding with a thin mustache, he played kindly as well as corrupt roles. He continued his stage career while acting on screen, retiring in the mid-1970s because of illness.

SELECTED FILMS: *Lawyer Man (1932), Up Front, Francis Goes to the Races (1951), Back at the Front (1952), It Should Happen to You (1953), This Could Be the Night (1957), Andy Hardy Comes Home (1958), The Unsinkable Molly Brown (1964), Zebra in the Kitchen (1965), The Russians Are Coming, the Russians Are Coming (1966), The Shakiest Gun in the West (1967), Million Dollar Duck (1971), The Gumball Rally (1976).* ■

Taylor, Walter Dub. See Dub Taylor.

Taylor, William Desmond (1877–1922), director. Worked on stage and in films as an actor before switching to directing films in 1915. He turned out several of Mary PICKFORD'S films, which brought him recognition as a major director. He continued to direct dramas and light films while expanding his social life among Hollywood celebrities. An urbane and good-looking bon vivant with a promising career, he was mysteriously murdered one night in 1922 at a mansion. The investigation of his shooting exposed the seamy side of Hollywood life after-hours, including the use of drugs and involving several major stars including Mary Miles MINTER and

Mabel NORMAND. The scandal led to citizens' groups demanding that the film community improve its image. This was followed by cries for national censorship, leading eventually to Hollywood's Hays Office.

Sidney D. Kirkpatrick's nonfiction work, *A Cast of Killers*, published in 1986, chronicles the entire case based on new information found in the recently discovered papers of film director King Vidor.

SELECTED FILMS: *The Beggar Child* (1914), *The American Beauty, He Fell in Love With His Wife, The Parson of Panamint* (1916), *Jack and Jill* (1917), *Up the Road With Sally, His Majesty Bunker Bean, Mile-a-Minute Kendall, How Could You, Jean?, Johanna Enlists* (1918), *Captain Kidd, Jr., Anne of Green Gables* (1919), *Jenny Be Good* (1920), *The Top of New York* (1922). ∎

Teasdale, Verree (1906–1987), actress. Worked on Broadway stage from the early 1920s before entering films in 1929. An attractive blonde, she appeared chiefly in comedy features as the female lead or a supporting player through the 1930s and 1940s. She worked with some of the leading screen stars of the period, including, among others, Eddie CANTOR and James STEWART.

In *I Take This Woman* she says to Rafael Storm: "Raoul, you have your qualities, but intelligence is not one of them."

SELECTED FILMS: *Syncopation* (1929), *The Sap From Syracuse* (1930), *Roman Scandals, They Just Had to Get Married* (1933), *A Modern Hero* (1934), *A Midsummer Night's Dream* (1935), *The Milky Way* (1936), *First Lady* (1937), *Topper Takes a Trip, Fifth Avenue Girl* (1939), *Turnabout, I Take This Woman, Love Thy Neighbor* (1940), *Come Live With Me* (1941). ∎

Temple, Shirley (1928–), actress. Began her film career at age four in comedy shorts featuring all-children casts. She then started to get small roles in features

Shirley Temple and Jimmy Durante

until she scored a hit in 1934 in *Stand Up and Cheer*. Within only a few months she became a screen star, winning a special Oscar that same year for her "outstanding contributions" to film entertainment. A blonde, dimpled natural actress with an overabundance of charm, she surpassed all the competition as the top box-office draw in 1938. Her popularity grew into a phenomenon. Parents curled their children's hair in imitation of the child star; Shirley Temple lookalike contests swept the nation; innumerable dolls of her likeness were sold each year.

In the early 1940s, following several unsuccessful films, she left Fox studios for MGM, but her fame began to decline. She continued to star in films as an adolescent, but the magic that once surrounded her was gone. In the late 1950s and 1960s she starred in her own shortlived television shows and later attempted unsuccessfully to enter Congress. Although her star burned brightly for only a few short years, she so dominated the screen world in the 1930s that she has become a true Hollywood legend. More than any other star she was able to upstage even the most experienced adult players. She was appointed the U.S. Representative to the United Nations by President Nixon and was a U.S. Ambassador to Ghana in the 1970s.

In *Rebecca of Sunnybrook Farm* (1938) she played an orphan who has been placed in a children's home. One of the directors, a stern matron, threatens to take away the child's pets, including her pet duck. Shirley, in an attempt to save the creature, praises its virtues. "My duck does wonderful tricks," she explains. "My duck can lay an egg." "And what's so wonderful about that?" the matron asks coldly. "Well," Shirley replies, "can you lay an egg?"

In *The Bachelor and the Bobby-Soxer* she played a teenager who likes her boyfriend, Hugo, but has also developed a crush on artist Cary GRANT. Confiding to Grant about her predicament, she says: "A few minutes ago I liked Hugo better, but now I like you better. It's funny how men change."

SELECTED FILMS: The Red-Haired Alibi (1932), Out All Night (1933), Little Miss Marker, Baby Take a Bow, Now and Forever, Bright Eyes (1934), The Little Colonel, Curly Top (1935), Dimples, Stowaway (1936), Heidi (1937), Little Miss Broadway (1938), The Little Princess (1939), Kathleen (1941), Kiss and Tell (1945), The Bachelor and the Bobby-Soxer (1947), Mr. Belvedere Goes to College, A Kiss for Corliss (1949). ■

Tenny. Fictional comic manservant to amateur sleuth Bulldog Drummond in the Paramount detective series of the late 1930s. He was portrayed by E. E. Clive in such films as *Bulldog Drummond Escapes, Bulldog Drummond's Revenge,* both 1937, *Bulldog Drummond's Peril* (1938), and *Bulldog Drummond's Bride* (1939).

Terhune, Max (1891–1973), actor. Worked in vaudeville as a comic, ventriloquist, and magician before entering films in the mid-1930s. He almost invariably played in B westerns as the comic sidekick of various cowboy stars. Accompanied by his dummy, he clowned his way through the 1930s and 1940s as a character called "Lullaby" or "Alibi,"

supporting such cowboys as Johnny Mack Brown and Ken Maynard. See also Sidekicks.

SELECTED FILMS: Ride Ranger Ride (1936), The Hit Parade (1937), Santa Fe Stampede (1938), Man of Conquest (1939), Trail Riders, Arizona Stagecoach, Boot Hill Bandits (1942), Two-Fisted Justice, Haunted Ranch, Land of the Wanted Men (1943), Harmony Trail (1944), Along the Oregon Trail (1947), Rawhide (1951), King and Four Queens, Giant (1956). ■

Myrna Loy and William Powell in *The Thin Man* (1934)

Thin Man, The (1934), MGM. Dir. W. S. Van Dyke; Sc. Frances Goodrich, Albert Hackett; with William Powell, Myrna Loy, Maureen O'Sullivan, Cesar Romero.

MGM set out to make a quick, inexpensive detective yarn, a popular genre of the period, perhaps to play as a second feature along with one of its big productions. Little did the studio heads realize the tremendous popularity that this mystery-comedy would achieve. Based on Dashiell Hammett's novel, the film stars William POWELL and Myrna LOY as Nick and Nora Charles, a sophisticated couple who really enjoy their married life. Nick, a retired detective, manages his wealthy wife's estate. They drink, tease each other, and toss about witticisms. "What were you doing on the night of October 5, 1902?'' he jokingly asks Nora. "I was just a gleam in my father's eye," she replies. When the police search the couple's bedroom, she remonstrates: "What's that man doing in my drawers?" To solve a murder case, they host a dinner for criminals and police alike. "Waiter," Loy calls out, "will you serve the nuts. I mean, will you serve the guests the nuts." The film was so successful that MGM released a series of sequels over the years. Powell portrayed detectives before and after this feature, but it remains his best work. The title originally alluded to the victim in the first entry, but in subsequent entries it came to refer to Nick Charles. Supposedly, director Van Dyke completed the film in 12 days.

"Thin Man Series, The." A group of sophisticated detective comedies based on the writings of Dashiell Hammett and starring William POWELL and Myrna LOY as Nick and Nora Charles. Produced by MGM, the six films spanned the 1930s and 1940s. Powell played the amateur sleuth while Loy, who was often kept in the dark concerning her husband's investigations, contributed her share of humor and sophistication. The series began with *The Thin Man* (1934), the title referring to the victim. But the name stuck and was applied to Nick. The unpretentious film so delighted its audiences that the surprised studio was practically forced to provide sequels.

From time to time, actors destined to become stars appeared in the films. James STEWART is one such example. Other supporting players were often excellent, running the gamut from Runyonesque characters like Ed BROPHY to old reliables like C. Aubrey Smith. The zany couple, who lived off Nora's inheritance, indulged in drinking bouts, parties, and travel. Film historians have noted that the domestic scenes in the initial entry were the first to depict realistically an amicable marriage on the American screen. Their dog, Asta, got

into his own scrapes and won the hearts of the public almost as much as his masters had. In *Another Thin Man* Nick Charles, Jr., was introduced into the series. Generally, the films offered wit, snappy dialogue, a juicy crime, and high production values.

SELECTED FILMS: After the Thin Man (1937), Another Thin Man (1938), Shadow of the Thin Man (1942), The Thin Man Goes Home (1944), Song of the Thin Man (1947). ∎

Thomas, Danny (1914–), actor, entertainer. Began his show business career in 1934 as a radio singer. Thomas, born Amos Muzyad Jacobs, switched to working as a comic in nightclubs in 1938 and entered films in the late 1940s. Although he was very popular and successful as a stand-up comic on stage, his screen career never took off. After appearing in a handful of light films, he once again switched media. It was in television ("Make Room for Daddy") that he achieved his greatest success. His daughter is actress and comedienne Marlo Thomas.

SELECTED FILMS: The Unfinished Dance (1947), Big City (1948), Call Me Mister, I'll See You in My Dreams (1951), The Jazz Singer (1953), Looking for Love (1964), Journey Back to Oz (1974). ∎

Thomas, Olive (1898–1920), actress. Worked as a model and a Ziegfeld Girl before entering silent films in 1916. Considered by many as "the world's most beautiful girl," she starred in a series of light films, demonstrating a penchant for comedy. By 1920 her meteoric rise in show business was over. She committed suicide in her hotel room in Paris.

SELECTED FILMS: Beatrice Fairfax (1916), Indiscreet Corrine, A Girl Like That, Madcap Madge, Betty Takes a Hand (1917), An Heiress for a Day, Limousine Life, The Follies Girl (1918), Prudence on Broadway, Out Yonder (1919), Footlights and Shadows, The Flapper (1920). ∎

Thompson, Al (1894–1966), actor. Worked chiefly in comedy shorts during the 1930s, 1940s, and 1950s as a supporting player. He appeared in many of the THREE STOOGES' films.

SELECTED FILMS: Restless Knights, Pop Goes the Easel, Pardon My Scotch (1935), Ants in the Pantry, Half-Shot Shooters, Disorder in the Court (1936), Grips, Grunts and Groans, Three Dumb Clucks (1937), Saved by the Belle (1939), You Nazty Spy, A-Plumbing We Will Go, From Nurse to Worse (1940), In the Sweet Pie and Pie (1941), Loco Boy Makes Good (1942), Back From the Front, Phony Express, A Gem of a Jam (1943), The Yoke's on Me (1944), Idiots DeLuxe, If a Body Meets a Body (1945), Beer Barrel Polecats, G.I. Wanna Go Home, Three Little Pirates (1946), Half-Wits' Holiday, All Gummed Up (1947), Fiddlers Three (1948), Love at First Bite (1950), Gypped in the Penthouse, Blunder Boys (1955). ■

Thomson, Kenneth (1899–1967), actor. Began his screen career in silent films, some of which were prestigious productions (The King of Kings). He later appeared as a supporting player in sound films, chiefly light features, through the mid-1930s.

SELECTED FILMS: Risky Business, Corporal Kate (1926), The Broadway Melody, The Girl From Havana (1929), A Notorious Affair, Sweet Mamma, Wild Company, Reno, Just Imagine (1930), Woman Hungry (1931), Movie Crazy, Her Mad Night (1932), The Little Giant, Son of a Sailor (1933), Many Happy Returns (1934), Behold My Wife (1935), Whispering Smith Speaks (1936). ■

Thornby, Robert, director. Worked in early silent comedy shorts for producer Mack SENNETT'S KEYSTONE studios. He directed the popular "Little Billy" comedies starring the young Paul JACOBS. He later moved to Universal studios where he turned out melodramas with such stars as Lon Chaney.

SELECTED FILMS: Little Billy's Triumph, Little Billy's Strategy, Little Billy's City Cousin, The Race (1914). ■

Thorpe, Richard (1896–), director. Worked in vaudeville and on stage before turning his sights on a film career in the early 1920s as an actor. By 1923 he was directing silent comedy shorts starring Charlie MURRAY. He soon began turning out feature-length films of different genres, many of which were of routine interest. Successfully making the transition to sound, he directed for MGM, moving up from low-budget to large-scale productions. A skilled craftsman and diligent worker, he directed numerous entertaining films for five decades, steadily turning out several films each year. Despite this large body of work, he was unable to develop an individual style.

SELECTED FILMS: Rough Ridin' (1924), College Days (1926), The First Night (1927), The Bachelor Girl (1929), Neck and Neck (1931), Slightly Married (1932), Notorious but Nice (1933), Cheating Cheaters (1934), Double Wedding (1937), Love Is a Headache (1938), Barnacle Bill (1941), Three Hearts for Julia (1943), Two Girls and a Sailor, The Thin Man Goes Home (1944), Her Highness and the Bellboy, What Next, Corporal Hargrove? (1945), This Time for Keeps (1947), A Date With Judy (1948), Ten Thousand Bedrooms (1957), The Honeymoon Machine (1961), The Horizontal Lieutenant (1962), Follow the Boys (1963), The Last Challenge (1967). ■

Three Must-Get-There's, The (1922), UA. Dir. Max Linder; Sc. Max Linder; with Max Linder, Frank Cooke, Caroline Rankin, Bull Montana, Jobyna Ralston.

The French film comedian Max LINDER was the leading comic of his country's cinema. He had appeared in minor stage roles in his native France before signing with Pathe films in 1905. Turning out a succession of comedy shorts, he soon developed his popular character, Max the dandy bachelor. By 1914 he had become an international celebrity. He made two trips to the United States, on the first of which, in 1916, he starred in several films for ESSANAY studios, and on the second and final one, in 1919, he made the above five-reeler for United Artists. His earlier work in America was not successful. In this affectionate parody of *The Three Musketeers* (1921), which had starred swashbuckler Douglas FAIRBANKS, Linder portrayed Dart-in-Again, the ingenuous youth who ends up insulting the famous musketeers when he arrives in Paris. The fight scenes and duels that follow display the unusual talents of the French comic. With agility and abandon he defeats the troops of the Court and the malevolent Cardinal Richelieu. Part of the good humor of the film lies in the modern contrivances that are introduced, such as motorcycles and telephones. Linder had a sense for the proper gags and inventive comedy, which has influenced the history of film comedy as well as other screen comics, including CHAPLIN, LAUREL AND HARDY, and the MARX BROTHERS. Chaplin, in fact, often acknowledged his debt to Linder. The Frenchman returned to Europe, made a film in Vienna in 1924, and returned to France. Faced with failing health, he committed suicide in 1925. He left behind a legacy of more than 300 films.

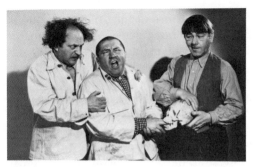

Larry, Curly, and Moe

Three Stooges, The. The famous trio, Moe and Jerry "Curly" HOWARD and Larry FINE, all former vaudevillians, who began their long partnership in 1928 as part of a comedy team known as "Ted Healy and His Stooges." Their first screen appearances came in 1933 and consisted of a series of mediocre shorts and several supporting roles in features (one of which was *Dancing Lady* starring Clark GABLE and Joan Crawford).

In 1934 Larry, Moe, and Curly switched from MGM studios to Columbia where they were featured in a few comedy shorts. Their third entry, "Men in Black," helped them to establish their pattern as a team, received an Oscar nomination, and won them a studio contract. They starred in almost 100 shorts over the next 14 years. In 1947 Curly, who had become ill, was replaced by an older brother, Shemp HOWARD, and the act continued with approximately 80 more two-reelers until 1955 when Shemp died. Joe PALMA filled in temporarily until Joe BESSER, a veteran comic, joined Moe and Larry. Later, Joe De Rita became part of the act. The Three Stooges were back in action once again—at least for another 16 shorts. In a move to phase out its short-subject department, Columbia did not renew the boys' contract in 1957. However, the studio had a backlog of the Stooges' shorts, and these were released through 1959. The team continued to appear in full-length features for various studios into the 1960s.

The titles of their films were frequently spoofs of contemporary feature films, songs, popular expressions, or simply puns, but seldom did the plots sustain any satirical intent. Among the different combinations of comics who made up the Three Stooges, the most popular was that of Moe, Larry, and Curly. Moe acted as the leader and meted out slaps, jabs, and other physical punishments at random. Curly, usually the recipient of the blows, was perhaps the most sympathetic as well as the funniest member. Larry was the intermediary between Moe and Curly but received his share of the physical abuse. Their best films were those of the 1930s and 1940s. Each of the boys occasionally appeared in films without the other members.

The Three Stooges lasted longer than any other comedy team. For more than 30 years and 200 shorts and features they continued to bring their brand of slapstick comedy to new generations. They have also won a permanent niche in television; hardly a season goes by without some stations reviving the series. Another unique aspect of the group was its unusual following despite the critics who continually attacked the crude knockabout comedy and the excessive violence. Somehow the Stooges survived their detractors. Their films were directed by Del LORD, Jules WHITE, and Charley CHASE.

SELECTED FILMS (shorts): Beer and Pretzels (1933), The Big Idea, Woman Haters (1934), Restless Knights (1935), Ants in the Pantry (1936), Dizzy Doctors (1937), Wee Wee Monsieur (1938), We Want Our Mummy (1939), You Nazty Spy (1940), I'll Never Heil Again (1941), Three Smart Saps (1942), Dizzy Detectives (1943), Idle Roomers (1944), Micro-Phonies (1945), Uncivil Warbirds (1946), Half-Wits' Holiday (1947).

SELECTED FILMS (features): Soup to Nuts (1930), Turn Back the Clock (1933), Myrt and Marge (1934), Start Cheering (1938), Time Out for Rhythm (1941), My Sister Eileen (1942), Rockin' in the Rockies (1945), Swing Parade of 1946 (1946), Gold Raiders (1951), Have Rocket, Will Travel (1959), Snow White and the Three Stooges (1961), The Three Stooges in Orbit (1962), It's a Mad, Mad, Mad, Mad World (1963), The Outlaws Is Coming (1965). ∎

Thrill comedy. A film genre that depends as much on suspense, excitement, speed, and special effects for laughs as on character, situation, and other conventional elements of humor. Mack SENNETT was an early practitioner and pioneer of this form of comedy. His "Teddy at the Throttle" (1917) has Gloria Swanson chained to railroad tracks by villain Wallace BEERY as a train comes bearing down on her. Many of his films depict flivvers going over cliffs, supported only by fragile ropes; main characters balancing themselves on girders atop unfinished skyscrapers; or heroes and heroines speeding or parked in autos across railroad tracks as locomotives bear down on them.

Other comedy producers, including Al CHRISTIE and Hal ROACH, followed suit. Almost all of the major comics, both in silent and sound films, starred in one or more thrill comedies. In "Her Torpedoed Love" (1917) comedienne Louise FAZENDA'S husband's ship is blasted out of the water. In "Barney Oldfield's Race for Life" (1913) the titular hero rushes to save heroine Mabel NORMAND, who has been tied to railroad tracks by Ford STERLING, somewhat of a parody of nineteenth-century stage melodrama. In another film, Al ST. JOHN hangs precariously from a protruding pole high over an amusement park. The acknowledged master of silent thrill comedies, Harold LLOYD, dangles from the hand of a clock high above a busy street, to the nervous delight of his audience in the 1923 classic "Safety Last." Charlie CHAPLIN employs elements of the thrill comedy in The Gold Rush (1925) when his Klondike cabin teeters upon a precipice. Buster KEATON in "The Balloonatic" (1923) is trapped on top of a hot-air balloon as it rises out of control into the wild blue; later, in the same film, he goes over a waterfall in a canoe. Reginald DENNY, who made a popular series of light action films in the 1920s, starred in several thrill comedies, including Sporting Youth in 1923. Eddie CANTOR hurtles down a rollercoaster in a runaway car in Strike Me Pink (1936). LAUREL AND HARDY board a biplane in Flying Deuces (1939) and have the scare of their lives. Even W. C. FIELDS, the king of the quip, engaged in this genre from time to time as he recklessly drives a limousine whose steering wheel, windshield, and axle come apart in The Bank Dick (1940).

Some critics and historians have attacked this genre for its deficiency of humor, noting that the works are in reality "thrill" films rather than true comedies. There seems to be more than some truth to this, especially upon viewing some of the above shorts or others like Monte Banks' "Safety First" (1928), where there are very few, if any, visual gags or routines; the excitement tends to be all, or at least the dominant factor.

Tillie's Punctured Romance (1914), KEY. *Dir.* Mack Sennett; *Sc.* Hampton Del Ruth; with Charlie Chaplin, Marie Dressler, Mabel Normand, Mack Swain.

This primitive comedy is a landmark film for several reasons: it was the first full-length comedy to come out of Hollywood; it launched the screen career of stage comedienne Marie DRESSLER; and it solidified Charlie CHAPLIN as a major film comic although he did not receive top billing. The plot concerns city slicker Chaplin who lures a rich farmer's daughter (Dressler) to the city where he intends to fleece her. His city girl friend (Mabel NORMAND) sees him with his new conquest and jealously follows them. Charlie learns even better news. It seems that Tillie's uncle has died and left her millions of dollars. But to Charlie's dismay, the uncle reappears at a most inopportune time. The remainder of the film relies on director Mack SENNETT'S usual bag of comedy techniques, including slapstick, visual gags, and a climactic chase in which nearly everyone plunges off a pier into the water. Both women in Charlie's life agree that he is a bounder and are happy when they see him dragged away by the police. Sennett used many members of his stable of screen comics, including Charlie CHASE, Charlie MURRAY, Edgar KENNEDY, Chester CONKLIN, Minta DURFEE, and Al ST. JOHN. A commercial success when it was released, the work is viewed today more for its historical importance than for its laughs. It is based on Edgar Smith's musical comedy, *Tillie's Nightmare* which

starred Dressler. A few other "Tillie" films followed with Dressler but without Chaplin. A 1928 remake, which starred W. C. FIELDS and Louise FAZENDA, failed at the box office.

Tincher, Fay, actress. Worked in early silent comedy shorts for various studios, including Majestic and MUTUAL. For the former, she had appeared in the popular "Billy" comedies, starring the child actor Paul JACOBS, in 1914. She was later hired by Mutual to star in her own series as Ethel, a stenographer.

SELECTED FILMS: The Two O'Clock Train, Bedelia's Bluff, Skirts, The French Milliner, The Lady Drummer, Laundry Liz (1916). ∎

Tinling, James (1889–1967), director. Began his film career in the 1920s doing odd jobs, including stunt work, around studios. After serving under Howard HAWKS, he started directing his own films in the late 1920s. He turned out chiefly low-budget melodramas and light films during a career that spanned four decades.

SELECTED FILMS: Very Confidential (1927), Soft Living, Don't Marry (1928), The Exalted Flapper, Words and Music (1929), One Mad Kiss (1930), Jimmy and Sally (1933), Three on a Honeymoon, Call It Luck (1934), Welcome Home (1935), Every Saturday Night, Champagne Charlie, Educating Father, Pepper, Back to Nature (1936), Sing and Be Happy (1937), Boy Friend (1939), Roses Are Red (1947), Trouble Preferred (1948), Tales of Robin Hood (1951). ∎

To Be or Not to Be (1942), UA. *Dir.* Ernst Lubitsch; *Sc.* Edwin Justus Mayer; with Jack Benny, Carole Lombard, Robert Stack, Lionel Atwill, Felix Bressart, Sig Rumann. With Mel BROOKS' 1983 adaptation of LUBITSCH'S black comedy available, it is interesting to take another look at the original. It was made during the early, bleak years of World War II, not the best occasion to release a

Carole Lombard and Jack Benny in *To Be or Not to Be* (1942)

Rita Hayworth, Dennis Morgan, George Tobias, James Gleason

farce about the fall of Poland. The film encountered another dark cloud. One of its stars, Carole LOMBARD, died before its release. The story concerns a troupe of Polish actors, led by Jack BENNY and his wife, Lombard, who are in Warsaw when the Nazis invade. When their theater is closed by the invaders, the players become involved in espionage and a final escape to freedom. Mayer's witty and tight script and Lubitsch's expert direction overcome minor criticisms of the film. Benny gives the finest performance of his film career and Lombard is as beautiful and sparkling as ever. The supporting actors contribute much to the dark humor. Sig RUMANN, as a Nazi officer, pans Benny's performance of *Hamlet*: "What he did to Shakespeare, we are doing now to Poland." Felix BRESSART is excellent as an old-time actor. Lubitsch was criticized for his insensitivity in making this film that may have seemed disturbing then but now appears no more than innocuous.

Tobias, George (1901–1980), actor. Worked on stage before appearing in films in the 1930s, frequently as a comic character actor. Stocky and round-faced, often with a bemused expression, he supported various Warner Brothers stars during the 1940s.

In *Ten Tall Men* he played a French Legionnaire who is guarding a captured desert princess. He observes the fiery daggers in her eyes, which are then translated into raging imprecations. "She hates with her tongue as well as her eyes," he says to his comrades. "She hates with everything. She is a real woman."

SELECTED FILMS: *Maisie, Ninotchka, They All Came Out* (1939), *Music in My Heart, Calling All Husbands* (1940), *The Bride Came C.O.D.* (1941), *Yankee Doodle Dandy, My Sister Eileen* (1942), *This Is the Army* (1943), *Make Your Own Bed* (1944), *Sinbad the Sailor, My Wild Irish Rose* (1947), *The Judge Steps Out* (1949), *Ten Tall Men* (1951), *The Seven Little Foys* (1955), *Silk Stockings* (1957), *A New Kind of Love* (1963), *The Glass Bottom Boat* (1966), *The Phynx* (1970). ■

Tobin, Dan (1909–1982), actor. Appeared as a character actor in dramas and light films. He began his film career in the 1930s and continued to play character roles into the 1970s. He has acted in television dramas as well.

SELECTED FILMS: *The Stadium Murders* (1938), *Woman of the Year* (1942), *The Bachelor and the Bobby-Soxer* (1947), *The Velvet Touch, Miss Tatlock's Millions* (1948), *Dream Wife* (1953), *The Catered Affair* (1956), *How to Succeed in Business Without Really Trying* (1967), *The Love Bug Rides Again* (1973). ■

Tobin, Genevieve (1901–), actress. Appeared on stage before entering films. She played in only one silent film, continuing her stage career until the sound era, when she returned to the screen. An attractive and energetic blonde, she played female leads and supporting roles in dramas and light films.

In *One Hour With You* she played the flirtatious wife of Roland YOUNG and the close friend of Jeanette Mac-DONALD, whom she visits. Interested in her romantic escapades, her friend asks: "And how's the composer you went with?" "He's gone," Tobin replies, "but he had such a wonderful touch."

SELECTED FILMS: *No Mother to Guide Her* (1923), *A Lady Surrenders, Free Love* (1930), *The Gay Diplomat* (1931), *One Hour With You* (1932), *Perfect Understanding, Pleasure Cruise, Goodbye Again* (1933), *Easy to Love, Kiss and Make Up* (1934), *The Goose and the Gander, Here's to Romance* (1935), *Snowed Under* (1936), *Zaza* (1939), *No Time for Comedy* (1940), *Queen of Crime* (1941). ∎

Todd, Thelma (1905–1935), actress. Worked as a model before making her film debut in 1926. A lively blonde, she appeared in many comedy shorts and features through the mid-1930s. She worked in films with popular comics Charley CHASE and Ed WYNN and soon starred in her own series. During the sound period she accompanied the MARX BROTHERS, WHEELER AND WOOLSEY, LAUREL AND HARDY, Harry LANGDON, and Jimmy DUR-ANTE. She was paired with Patsy KELLY and ZaSu PITTS in a series of comedy shorts. Her screen career as a bright comedienne was cut short when she was mysteriously found dead in her parked automobile.

SELECTED FILMS: *Fascinating Youth* (1926), *Rubber Heels, The Gay Defender* (1927), *Vamping Venus, The Haunted House* (1928), *Naughty Baby* (1929), *The Hot Heiress, Monkey Business* (1931), *This Is the Night, Horse Feathers, Speak Easily, Call Her Savage* (1932), *Cheating Blondes, The Devil's Brother, Son of a Sailor, Sitting Pretty* (1933), *Hips Hips Hooray, Palooka, Bottoms Up, Cockeyed Cavaliers* (1934), *The Bohemian Girl* (1935). ∎

Toler, Sidney (1874–1947), actor. Worked on stage before settling in Hollywood in the late 1920s to appear as a character player in sound films. Although more memorable for his portrayal of the Oriental sleuth, Charlie Chan, a role he took over in 1938 following the death of Warner Oland, he specialized in lighter films during the first half of his screen career. He worked with some of the leading comics of the period, including, among others, Jimmy DURANTE, Joe E. BROWN, LAUREL AND HARDY, and Fred ALLEN. His experience in comedy served him during the lighter moments in the detective series, especially in dealing with his impulsive number one son and the family chauffeur as well as with issuing his obligatory aphorisms.

In *Charlie Chan in City in Darkness* (1939) the detective learns that England's Chamberlain will confer with Hitler in Germany. "When spider send invitation to house," he comments, "fly better beware." Other similar gems from various entries in the series include: "Perfect case like perfect doughnut—has hole" and "Mind like parachute—only work when open."

SELECTED FILMS: *Madame X* (1929), *White Shoulders, Strictly Dishonorable* (1931), *Is My Face Red, Speak Easily, Blondie of the Follies, The Phantom President* (1932), *Spitfire, Here Comes the Groom* (1934), *Romance in Manhattan, The Daring Young Man, Orchids to You* (1935), *The Gorgeous Hussy, Our Relations* (1936), *Double Wedding* (1937), *Wide Open Faces, One Wild Night* (1938), *It's in the Bag* (1945). ∎

Tombes, Andrew (1889–), actor. Appeared in vaudeville and on stage before entering films during the Depression years. Bald and bespectacled, he appeared as a character player who, for twenty years, specialized in kindly roles, frequently portraying judges, undertakers, or physicians in dozens of dramas and light films.

SELECTED FILMS: The Bowery (1933), Moulin Rouge (1934), Doubting Thomas, Thanks a Million (1935), Easy Living (1937), Sally, Irene and Mary (1938), What a Life (1939), Louisiana Purchase (1941), Bedtime Story, Larceny, Inc., They All Kissed the Bride, Road to Morocco (1942), The Meanest Man in the World, Let's Face It (1943), Bring on the Girls (1945), The Jackpot (1950), How to Be Very Very Popular (1955). ∎

Tomlin, Lily (1939–), actress, comedienne. Worked as a waitress before appearing as a comic in small clubs and revues. After several spots on television, for which she won two Emmy awards, and a few hit comedy records, she was recognized as a talented and ingenious stand-up comic. Her hilarious character Ernestine, the nutty, obnoxious telephone operator, brought her national fame.

She made her film debut in 1975 in Nashville and won praise and an Oscar nomination for her poignant role as the frustrated mother of a deaf child. Her next film also brought her acclaim, but the films that followed were panned by the critics. However, she has eventually reestablished her position on stage and in films as one of America's major comics.

In 9 to 5 she played an agitated secretary who frets about losing her job. "I'm no fool," she confides to her co-workers. "I killed the boss. You think they're not going to fire me for a thing like that?"

SELECTED FILMS: Nashville (1975), The Late Show (1977), Moment by Moment (1978), 9 to 5 (1980), The Incredible Shrinking Woman (1981), All of Me (1984). ∎

Tomlin, Pinky (1907–), composer-singer, actor. Worked as a singer and songwriter ("Object of My Affection") before entering films in the 1930s. A unique song stylist, he appeared chiefly in light musicals, enlivening each film as well with his shy brand of comedy.

SELECTED FILMS: Times Square Lady, King Solomon of Broadway (1935), Paddy O'Day, Don't Get Personal (1936), Swing It, Professor (1937), Down in Arkansas (1938), Here Comes Elmer (1943). ∎

Tone, Franchot (1905–1968), actor. Worked in stock in the late 1920s and on Broadway before settling in Hollywood in the early 1930s. Handsome and sophisticated, he appeared in dramas and light films, often as a bon vivant, reaching the peak of his popularity in the late 1930s. He received an Oscar nomination for his role in Mutiny on the Bounty (1935). Between film assignments he would return to the stage, his first love. He continued to act in films during the next two decades, but the routine vehicles he appeared in periodically drove him back to the stage.

In Trail of the Vigilantes (1940) he played a cowboy whom a flirtatious 17 year old (Peggy Moran) has taken an interest in. "Walk behind me," he orders as they head back to a ranch. "Why?" she asks. "Because that's where you put temptation," he replies.

SELECTED FILMS: The Wiser Sex (1932), Midnight Mary, Bombshell, Dancing Lady (1933), The Girl From Missouri, Gentlemen Are Born (1934), Reckless, One New York Night, No More Ladies (1935), The King Steps Out, Suzy, The Gorgeous Hussy (1936), The Bride Wore Red (1937), Love Is a Headache (1938), The Girl Downstairs (1939), She Knew All the Answers (1941), The Wife Takes a Flyer (1942), True to Life (1943), Her Husband's Affairs (1947), Here Comes the Groom (1951), The High Commissioner (1968). ∎

Toones, Fred, actor. Appeared as a character actor chiefly in light films during the 1930s and 1940s. Notorious during this period for their insensitivity toward blacks and other racial groups, Hollywood studios sometimes listed him in the credits as "Snowflake." Huskily built and moon-faced, he portrayed the customary black porters, servants, and other domestics.

SELECTED FILMS: Twentieth Century, Lady by Choice (1934), Riddle Ranch (1935), Off to the Races (1937), Remember the Night, Seventeen, The Biscuit Eater (1940), The Palm Beach Story (1942). ■

Cary Grant, Roland Young, and Constance Bennett in *Topper* (1937)

Tootsie (1982), COL. *Dir.* Sydney Pollack; *Sc.* Larry Gelbart, Murray Schisgal; with Dustin Hoffman, Jessica Lange, Charles Durning, Teri Garr, Bill Murray, Dabney Coleman.

Dustin Hoffman, who had done some outstanding work in the past (*The Graduate* in 1967, *Little Big Man* in 1970), regained his standing as one of the finest contemporary actors when he slipped into drag in *Tootsie.* Hoffman portrays Michael, an unemployed, talented actor whose recalcitrance and fierce idealism have resulted in a lack of work. Determined to find an acting job, he disguises himself as a middle-aged actress, Dorothy Michaels, and auditions for a television soap opera role. "I'd like to make her a little more attractive," the director says to his cameraman about Hoffman/ Dorothy. "How far can you pull back?" "How do you feel about Cleveland?" the other quips. Dorothy wins the role and rapidly becomes a hit with the public. Meanwhile, Hoffman, as Dorothy, develops a close friendship with co-performer Jessica Lange and falls in love with her. Another complication occurs when Lange's father, a widower (Charles Durning), finds Dorothy more than just attractive. This comedy transcends farce. It is a sensitive, touching story of Dorothy, an eccentric character as created by Michael, who protests the sexist attitudes of the soap opera director (Dabney COLEMAN) and who emerges as a liberated voice defending what is right.

Topper (1937), MGM. *Dir.* Norman Z. McLeod; *Sc.* Jack Jevne, Eric Hatch, Eddie Moran; with Constance Bennett, Cary Grant, Roland Young, Billie Burke, Alan Mowbray.

By the 1930s, with short films rapidly being phased out, producer Hal ROACH sought material for feature comedies. Thorne Smith's light novel, *The Jovial Ghosts,* appeared just right. Here was a chance to blend sophisticated comedy with fantasy. Marion and George Kirby (Constance BENNETT and Cary GRANT), principal stockholders in Cosmo Topper's (Roland YOUNG) bank, are a fun-loving couple who, while joyriding one day in their sports car, meet with a fatal accident. But their fun-loving spirits cannot rest until they release conservative and henpecked Topper from his dull life of respectability. The Kirbys involve him in complications that upset his prim wife (Billie BURKE) but allow him to have a little fun in life. Possibly slightly dated today, this whimsical film has its charming and entertaining moments. Ghosts are fascinating screen subjects, especially humorous ghosts, and the special effects Hollywood can provide make them even more appealing. *Topper* was so popular that two sequels followed, *Topper Takes a Trip* (1939) and *Topper Returns* (1941), each of which only partially captured the spirit of the original. Roach turned to another Smith fantasy in 1940 when he made *Turnabout,* about a husband and wife switching personalities by means of a magical statuette.

"Torchy Blane" films. An action-comedy series of films starring Glenda FARRELL as a determined, wise-cracking reporter. Produced by Warner Brothers during the late 1930s, the entries co-starred Barton MacLane as a bemused policeman. Several of the entries were directed by William BEAUDINE. George Bricker and others wrote the screenplays.

SELECTED FILMS: *The Adventurous Blonde (1937), Torchy Blane in Panama, Torchy Gets Her Man (1938), Torchy Blane in Chinatown, Torchy Runs for Mayor, Torchy Plays With Dynamite (1939).* ■

Toto. See Arnold Nobello.

Tracy, Lee (1898–1968), actor. Appeared in stock and on Broadway in the early 1920s before entering films in the early sound era. He played leads and supporting roles in dramas and light films, often as a hard-nosed, cynical reporter and other urban types, reaching the peak of his popularity in the mid-1930s. Later in his acting career he appeared in television.

In *Bombshell* he played a ruthless publicity agent who exploits and manipulates the private and public life of a Hollywood film star (Jean HARLOW). When she protests about a series of scandalous stories he's been feeding the press, Tracy enlightens her on her importance. "Strong men take one look at your picture and go home and kiss their wives for the first time in ten years. You're an international tonic. You're a boon to repopulation in a world thinned out by war and famine!"

SELECTED FILMS: *Big Time (1929), She Got What She Wanted (1930), Love Is a Racket, Blessed Event, The Half-Naked Truth (1932), The Nuisance, Dinner at Eight, Bombshell (1933), The Lemon Drop Kid (1934), Crashing Hollywood (1938), Fixer Dugan (1939), The Best Man (1964).* ■

Spencer Tracy and Katharine Hepburn

Tracy, Spencer (1900–1967), actor. Appeared in stock and on Broadway in the late 1920s and early 1930s before entering films. Because of his rough exterior, he was typecast in tough-guy roles for a while. Within a few years he became one of the brightest stars in Hollywood. An apparently natural actor who could project earnestness and strength as well as good humor with little effort, he was acclaimed by the critics and embraced by the public. He won two Academy Awards and seven nominations for Oscars. He co-starred in nine light features with his close friend, Katharine HEPBURN. He starred in more than 75 dramas and comedies during an illustrious career that spanned four decades.

In *Father's Little Dividend* (1951) he played a father who is still skeptical about his daughter's marriage. "There's a fly in the ointment," he complains. "First he steals my daughter, then he makes a grandpa out of me." In *Pat and Mike* he portrayed a sports promoter who sees golf pro Katharine Hepburn for the first time and says appreciatively: "She's nicely packed. Not much meat on her, but what's there is cherce."

SELECTED FILMS: *Taxi Talks, The Strong Arm, The Hard Guy (1930), Six Cylinder Love, Goldie (1931), She Wanted a Millionaire (1932), The Show-Off, Bottoms Up (1934), Libeled Lady (1936), I Take This Woman (1940), Woman of the Year (1942), State of the Union (1948), Adam's Rib (1949), Father* of the Bride (1950), Pat and Mike (1952), Desk Set (1957), It's a Mad, Mad, Mad, Mad World (1963), Guess Who's Coming to Dinner (1967). ■

Tracy, William (1917–1967), actor. Appeared on Broadway before entering films in the late 1930s. A short, bouncy comic performer, he played chiefly in light films through the 1930s and 1940s, frequently as a dimwitted character.

In *The Shop Around the Corner* he played a messenger who tries to inflate the importance of his job. "I'm a contact man," he announces proudly to a local doctor. "I keep contact between Matuschek & Company and the customers— on a bicycle." "You mean an errand boy," the doctor remarks. "Doctor," Tracy persists, "did I call you a pill-peddler?"

SELECTED FILMS: *Brother Rat* (1938), *Million Dollar Legs* (1939), *Strike Up the Band* (1940), *Tobacco Road, Tanks a Million, Tillie the Toiler, She Knew All the Answers* (1941), *George Washington Slept Here, Hayfoot, About Face* (1942), *Fall In, Yanks Ahoy* (1943), *Here Comes Trouble* (1948), *As You Were* (1951), *Mr. Walkie Talkie* (1952), *Wings of Eagles* (1957). ■

"Tramp, The." See Charlie Chaplin.

Tramp, Tramp, Tramp (1926), FN. Dir. Harry Edwards; Sc. Frank Capra; with Harry Langdon, Joan Crawford.

This comedy was part of HARRY LANGDON'S trio of great films which were made before his tragic decline. *The Strong Man* (1926) and *Long Pants* (1927) were the other two. He was considered Charlie CHAPLIN'S major competitor as well as one of the top screen comics of the silent era. When a powerful shoe manufacturer and an unscrupulous landlord threaten Langdon and his father's small business that turns out handmade shoes, Langdon vows to save the firm. He enters a transcontinental walking race, sponsored by the rival shoe company, hoping to win the $25,000 prize. Meanwhile, he falls in love with the owner's daughter. The comic bits involve a series of obstacles he has to overcome before his faith and strong determination win out. He is hampered by a tornado as well as a brief incarceration. Another humorous bit involves his sharing a hotel room that he has decorated with innumerable pictures of his true love with a competitor in the race. Perhaps the best sequence occurs when Langdon, hampered with a ball and chain after escaping from a prison camp, doesn't notice that the chain has been cut by a moving train. Seeing his rival walker ahead of him, he unnecessarily picks up the heavy ball and continues in the race. Director Harry EDWARDS, who had worked on several of Langdon's earlier films, and writer Frank CAPRA, also associated with the comedian, add a comic cliff-hanging episode not unlike those which Harold LLOYD made famous.

Trask, Wayland (1887–1918), actor. Worked in stock before appearing in early silent comedy shorts for producer Mack SENNETT'S KEYSTONE studios as a supporting player. He usually portrayed the heroine's suitor who lost his love to the hero. A talented comedian, he accompanied some of the leading comics of the period, including, among others, Chester CONKLIN, "Fatty" ARBUCKLE, and Ford STERLING.

SELECTED FILMS: *The Great Vacuum Robbery, The Great Pearl Tangle* (1915), *Fatty and Mabel Adrift, His Hereafter, The Judge, A Love Riot, Her Marble Heart, Pills of Peril* (1916), *Dodging His Doom, A Maiden's Trust, Her Torpedoed Love, She Needed a Doctor, His Precious Life* (1917). ■

Travers, Henry (1874–1965), actor. On stage in England before migrating to the United States where he appeared on Broadway. Born Travers Heagery in Ireland, he entered Hollywood films in the early 1930s. An unobtrusive but likable character actor, he gave many winning performances in dramas and light films, most memorably as Clarence the timid angel in *It's a Wonderful Life* (1946). He was nominated for an Academy Award for his role in *Mrs. Miniver* (1942).

SELECTED FILMS: *Reunion in Vienna, Another Language* (1933), *Ready for Love* (1934), *Too Many Parents* (1936), *Anne of Windy Poplars* (1940), *Ball of Fire, A Girl, a Guy and a Gob* (1941), *The Very Thought of You* (1944), *The Naughty Nineties* (1945), *The Girl From Jones Beach* (1949). ▪

Travers, Vic (–1948), actor. Worked chiefly in comedy shorts during the 1930s and 1940s as a supporting player. He appeared in many of the THREE STOOGES' films.

SELECTED FILMS: *Tassels in the Air* (1938), *A-Ducking They Did Go, Oily to Bed, Oily to Rise, Three Sappy People* (1939), *In the Sweet Pie and Pie* (1941), *Loco Boy Makes Good, Three Smart Saps* (1942), *Phony Express* (1943), *Crash Goes the Hash, Busy Buddies, The Yoke's on Me* (1944), *Three Pests in a Mess* (1945), *Uncivil Warbirds, Three Troubledoers* (1946), *Half-Wits' Holiday, Hold That Lion, All Gummed Up* (1947), *Heavenly Daze* (1948). ▪

Treacher, Arthur (1894–1975), actor. Appeared on stage in his native England and on Broadway before entering films in the late 1920s. Tall and dour-looking, he soon found his niche in Hollywood portraying the definitive butler during the 1930s and 1940s. In the early 1960s he appeared in television. He supported some of the greatest stars in Hollywood.

SELECTED FILMS: *Battle of Paris* (1929), *Gambling Lady* (1934), *No More Ladies, Curly Top* (1935), *Anything Goes, Thank You, Jeeves, Under Your Spell, Stowaway* (1936), *Step Lively, Jeeves, Thin Ice* (1937), *Mad About Music, My Lucky Star, Always in Trouble* (1938), *The Little Princess* (1939), *Irene*

(1940), *Delightfully Dangerous* (1945), *That Midnight Kiss* (1949), *Love That Brute* (1950), *Mary Poppins* (1964). ▪

Treen, Mary (1907–), actress. Worked on stage before coming to Hollywood in the early 1930s. She appeared as a comic character player in numerous musicals and comedies, chiefly in working girl roles.

SELECTED FILMS: *Happiness Ahead* (1934), *Traveling Saleslady, Don't Bet on Blondes, A Night at the Ritz* (1935), *Colleen* (1936), *Ever Since Eve, Second Honeymoon* (1937), *Kentucky Moonshine* (1938), *Kitty Foyle* (1940), *They All Kissed the Bride* (1942), *They Got Me Covered* (1943), *It's a Wonderful Life* (1946), *Let's Live a Little* (1948), *Sailor Beware* (1952), *The Caddy* (1953), *The Sad Sack* (1957), *Who's Minding the Store?* (1963), *The Strongest Man in the World* (1975). ▪

Trimble, Laurence (1885–1954), director. Wrote short stories and worked as an actor and screenwriter for Vitagraph studios in 1910 before turning his interests to directing. He turned out several of the popular John BUNNY and Flora FINCH silent comedy shorts. After a short stay in England, where he produced his own films, he returned to the United States and continued to direct films through the 1920s.

SELECTED FILMS: *Saved by the Flag* (1910), *The Pickwick Papers, Sisters All, Checkmated, There's Music in the Hair* (1913), *The Love Master* (1924), *My Old Dutch* (1926). ▪

Trivers, Barry (–1981), screenwriter. Began writing screenplays in the mid-1930s and for two decades continued to turn out, alone and in collaboration, dozens of dramas and light films.

SELECTED FILMS: *Romance in the Rain* (1934), *Lady Tubbs, Manhattan Moon, Night Life of the Gods, Three Kids and a Queen* (1935), *Here Comes Trouble, Three Cheers for Love* (1936), *Army*

Girl (1938), Boy Friend (1939), Dreaming Out Loud (1940), The Men in Her Life (1941), There's Something About a Soldier, What a Woman! (1943), Intrigue (1947). ∎

Trotti, Lamar (1900–1952), screenwriter. Worked as a journalist before switching his career to writing screenplays for Fox studios. He wrote several of the studio's major films. Working alone and in collaboration, first with Dudley Nichols, he created dramas and light films, including numerous historical features.

SELECTED FILMS: *The Man Who Dared (1933), Bachelor of Arts, Call It Luck, Hold That Girl (1934), Steamboat 'Round the Bend (1935), Can This Be Dixie?, Pepper (1936), Wife, Doctor and Nurse (1937), The Baroness and the Butler, Kentucky (1938), Mother Wore Tights (1947), The Walls of Jericho, When My Baby Smiles at Me (1948), You're My Everything (1949), Cheaper by the Dozen (1950), As Young As You Feel (1951).* ∎

Trouble in Paradise (1932), PAR. Dir. Ernst Lubitsch; Sc. Grover Jones, Samson Raphaelson; with Miriam Hopkins, Kay Francis, Herbert Marshall, Charles Ruggles.

Offering sophisticated comedy at its best, this charming film concerns two jewel thieves, played by Miriam HOPKINS and Herbert MARSHALL, whose romance almost comes apart when he woos their next victim, portrayed by the attractive Kay Francis. To gain admittance to Francis' home and large fortune, Marshall returns her lost bag which he had stolen and is hired as her secretary. Later, Hopkins gets a job at the estate as a typist. Comic character actors Charles RUGGLES and Edward Everett HORTON portray suitors interested in Francis. Art director Hans Dreier's well-designed sets add to the richness of the production. LUBITSCH'S lustrous handling of each scene with wit and artistry lifts the work from its light

plot to an elegant and entertaining comedy.

Truex, Ernest (1890–1973), actor. Appeared on the stage before entering films in 1913. He began his screen career portraying mischievous characters, but with the arrival of sound, he played docile husbands and middle-aged men. A short, figure with a bald head and a little mustache, he appeared in more than 50 dramas and light films in a screen career that spanned six decades.

SELECTED FILMS: *Caprice (1913), A Good Little Devil (1914), Oh, You Women! (1919), The Night of the Pub (1920), Whistling in the Dark, The Warrior's Husband (1933), Mama Runs Wild (1938), It's a Wonderful World, Bachelor Mother (1939), His Girl Friday, Slightly Honorable, Christmas in July, Calling All Husbands (1940), Private Buckaroo (1942), True to Life (1943), Her Primitive Man (1944), A Night in Paradise (1946), Fluffy (1965).* ∎

Trunnelle, Mabel, actress. Worked in early silent films for Thomas Edison from 1909. A popular actress of the time, she starred in dramas and light films, continuing to appear on screen into the 1920s.

SELECTED FILMS: *The Prince and the Pauper (1909), Mary's Masquerade, How Mrs. Murray Saved the American Army, A Modern Cinderella (1911), Dogs, All for Jim (1912), The New Pupil (1913), The Blue Coyote Cherry Crop (1914), Olive's Other Self, Ranson's Folly (1915), Singed Wings (1922), The Love Trap (1923).* ∎

Tufts, Sonny (1911–1970), actor. Worked on stage and in nightclubs as a singer before entering films in 1939. A tall blonde, he played leads chiefly in routine films. His parts were friendly, good-natured characters in numerous light comedies. In more recent times he became the undeserved subject of derisive trivia questions.

SELECTED FILMS: *Ambush* (1939), *I Love a Soldier, Here Come the Waves, In the Meantime, Darling* (1944), *Duffy's Tavern, Bring on the Girls* (1945), *The Well-Groomed Bride, Cross My Heart* (1946), *Variety Girl, Easy Come, Easy Go* (1947), *Easy Living* (1949), *The Seven Year Itch* (1955), *Cottonpickin' Chickenpickers* (1967). ∎

"Tugboat Annie." A comedy series created by writer Norman Reilly Raine and initiated in the early 1930s about a tough, middle-aged skipper of the "Narcissus." Marie DRESSLER starred as the title character in the first entry, *Tugboat Annie* (1933), directed by Mervyn LeROY. Wallace BEERY played her unfortunate husband. Dressler had appeared with Beery a few years earlier in the box-office smash, *Min and Bill*, for which she won an Academy Award as Best Actress. The audiences enjoyed the chemistry between the two stars and MGM delighted in the financial rewards of the reunion. In the first sequel, *Tugboat Annie Sails Again* (1940), directed by Lewis SEILER, reliable Marjorie RAMBEAU took over the helm while her co-star, Alan HALE, provided some of the laughs. The third and last film in the series, *Captain Tugboat Annie* (1945), directed by Phil Rosen, introduced another Annie. This time she was played by Jane DARWELL, who had portrayed the stalwart matriarch Ma Joad in *The Grapes of Wrath*, with ample assistance from comic character actor Edgar KENNEDY.

Weak comedy situations, routine dialogue, and uninspiring plots caused the films to depend heavily on their stars to carry the humor. And that was exactly the strength of the series. An interesting procession of supporting players joined the crew from time to time, including Ronald REAGAN, Robert YOUNG, Maureen O'Sullivan, Jane Wyman, and Mantan MORELAND.

Tugend, Harry (1898–), screenwriter. Performed on radio and in vaudeville and wrote radio shows before settling in Hollywood in the mid-1930s as a screenwriter. He occasionally produced features as well. Specializing in light comedy, he wrote alone and in collaboration, turning out scripts for such famous comedians as Eddie CANTOR, Bob HOPE, and Red SKELTON.

SELECTED FILMS: *King of Burlesque, The Littlest Rebel, Thanks a Million* (1935), *Pigskin Parade, The Poor Little Rich Girl* (1936), *Ali Baba Goes to Town, Wake Up and Live* (1937), *Little Miss Broadway, Sally, Irene and Mary, Thanks for Everything* (1938), *Second Fiddle* (1939), *Caught in the Draft* (1941), *The Lady Has Plans* (1942), *Let's Face It, True to Life* (1943), *A Southern Yankee, A Song Is Born* (1948), *Take Me Out to the Ball Game* (1949), *Public Pigeon No. 1* (1957), *Pocketful of Miracles* (1961), *Who's Minding the Store?* (1963). ∎

Tully, Tom (1908–1982), actor. Worked as a reporter and as an actor in radio and on Broadway before settling in Hollywood during World War II as a character player. Thick-set and rough-looking, with a face more like that of a former pugilist than that of a reporter, he appeared in both dramas and light films. He was equally comfortable as Shirley TEMPLE'S father in two features or as a corrupt warden. He received an Academy Award nomination for his role as an easy-going captain in *The Caine Mutiny* (1954).

SELECTED FILMS: *Mission to Moscow* (1943), *The Town Went Wild* (1944), *Kiss and Tell* (1945), *June Bride* (1948), *A Kiss for Corliss, The Lady Takes a Sailor* (1949), *Texas Carnival* (1951), *Love Is Better Than Ever* (1952), *Trouble Along the Way, The Moon Is Blue* (1953), *The Wackiest Ship in the Army* (1960), *McHale's Navy Joins the Air Force* (1965), *Charley Varrick* (1973). ∎

Tunberg, Karl (1907–), screenwriter. Began his long Hollywood career in the late 1930s. He has written screenplays, alone and in collaboration, for several dramas and numerous light films.

SELECTED FILMS: *Life Begins in College (1937), Hold That Co-Ed (1938), Down Argentine Way, Public Deb No. 1 (1940), Tall, Dark and Handsome, Week-End in Havana (1941), My Gal Sal (1942), Dixie (1943), Standing Room Only (1944), Bring on the Girls, Kitty (1945), The Imperfect Lady (1947), Up in Central Park, You Gotta Stay Happy (1948), Love That Brute (1950), Count Your Blessings (1959), Where Were You When the Lights Went Out? (1968), How Do I Love Thee? (1970).* ■

Turner, Florence (1885–1946), actress. Appeared on stage as a child actress before entering films in 1906 for VITAGRAPH studios. She soon rose to stardom, gaining fame as the "Vitagraph Girl." After a brief stay in England where she made personal appearances on stage and starred in several films, she returned to the United States. She continued to act in silent dramas and comedies through the 1920s, but her popularity slowly declined. By the sound era she was under contract to MGM where she played minor roles.

SELECTED FILMS: *How to Cure a Cold (1907), The New Stenographer (1908), How Championships Are Won—and Lost (1910), The Show Girl (1911), Jean Intervenes, Aunty's Romance (1912), The House in Suburbia (1913), All Dolled Up (1921), The Mad Marriage (1925), College (1927), Jazzland (1928), The Kid's Clever (1929), Ridin' Fool (1931).* ■

Turner, Kathleen (1954–), actress. Has worked in television, on stage, and in films from the early 1980s. An attractive and highly talented actress, she is equally at home in drama or comedy and can be poignant and funny simultaneously. She received an Academy Award for her role in *Peggy Sue Got Married.*

SELECTED FILMS: *Body Heat (1981), The Man With Two Brains (1983), Romancing the Stone (1984), Prizzi's Honor (1985), Peggy Sue Got Married (1986).* ■

Ben Turpin

Turpin, Ben (1874–1940), actor. Worked in burlesque before entering silent film comedies for ESSANAY studios in 1907. The film company had a Chicago branch, and this was where the comic was performing his "Happy Hooligan" stage act. After a few years in films, he returned to burlesque and in 1914 rejoined the film company. Having never starred in a film at Essanay, he left the company in 1916 and signed with Vogue.

His status rose as a featured comic at his new home, but he was performing the same old routines at the same frantic slapstick pace. Dissatisfied with the direction in which his career was headed, he again switched studios. In 1917 he joined the King of Comedy, Mack SENNETT.

Under the supervision of Sennett, the odd-looking, cross-eyed comic finally reached stardom. When several of Sennett's top comics, including CHAPLIN and "Fatty" ARBUCKLE, left to sign with other studios, it was Turpin whom the producer depended on to bring in the large profits and to save his studio. But the dependence was mutual. It was

Sennett's tutelage that helped the little comedian refine his routines and develop into more than just another slapstick clown.

Employing broad pantomime and low comedy, Turpin starred in a string of successful comedies. He focused on parodies of stage plays and popular films, poking fun at the then current stars. He could play straight roles and get laughs. His strength lay in his bizarre appearance. In *The Shriek of Araby* (1923) he parodied the romantic films of Rudolph Valentino, while in his two-reel comedies like "Yukon Jake" he satirized the western genre. He continued to enjoy success during the entire silent era and developed into one of the best of the minor screen comics of the period. He appeared in only one important sound film, *Saps at Sea* (1940), starring LAUREL AND HARDY.

SELECTED FILMS: *Midnight Disturbance (1909), His New Job, A Night Out (1915), When Papa Died, His Blowout, Picture Pirates (1916), A Circus Cyclone, Caught in the End, A Clever Dummy, Roping Her Romeo (1917), Two Tough Tenderfeet (1918), East Lynne With Variations, Yankee Doodle in Berlin, Uncle Tom Without the Cabin, Salome vs. Shenendoah (1919), Down on the Farm (1920), A Small Town Idol (1921), The Shriek of Araby, Where's My Wandering Boy Tonight? (1923), Romeo and Juliet (1924), Raspberry Romance, The Marriage Circus (1925), When a Man's a Prince, A Harem Knight (1926), A Hollywood Hero, Daddy Boy (1927), Saps at Sea (1940).* ∎

Twelve Chairs, The. See Mel Brooks.

Twelvetrees, Helen (1907–1958), actress. Appeared on stage before entering films in the late 1920s. Born Helen Jurgens, she played lead roles in melodramas and comedies during the early sound era.

In *The Ghost Talks* she is asked if she always lisps. "No," she replies, "only when I speak."

SELECTED FILMS: *The Ghost Talks, Blue Skies, Words and Music (1929), Swing High (1930), Millie (1931), Panama Flo, Is My Face Red (1932), A Bedtime Story (1933), She Gets Her Man (1935), Unmarried (1939).* ∎

Ralph Forbes, Carole Lombard, and John Barrymore in *Twentieth Century* (1934)

Twentieth Century (1934), MGM. *Dir.* Howard Hawks; *Sc.* Ben Hecht, Charles MacArthur; with John Barrymore, Carole Lombard, Walter Connolly, Roscoe Karns.

One of the earliest and best of the SCREWBALL COMEDIES of the 1930s, this film demonstrated the comedic talents of its two leads. The legendary stage actor John BARRYMORE had been in films since 1913, but he had never starred in this genre. Film comedienne Carole LOMBARD had earned her stripes playing in silent comedies opposite some of the leading comics of the 1920s. Now they appeared together in this battle-of-the-sexes comedy, Barrymore as a famous, egomaniacal stage director and jealous lover, and Lombard as a talented actress who wants to be free of his suffocating influence and ego. The story begins in a theater during the rehearsal of a new play and ends on board the Twentieth Century train with Barrymore trying to convince his star to return to Broadway. The farcical situations are hilarious and the dialogue from the writers of *The Front Page* is witty. Barrymore during rehearsals gives his cast a heart-rending speech on how much he loves the theater and actors. But moments later, when he is forced to demonstrate a particular role, he mutters: "I never thought I should sink so low as to become an actor." When he threatens to slit his throat if Lombard leaves him, she quips: "If you did, grease paint would run out of it." He intimidates those around him with his one recurrent threat: "I close the iron door on you." Others in the cast add to the hilarity. Walter CONNOLLY plays the director's much-abused manager, while character actor Etienne GIRARDOT gives a memorable performance as a religious fanatic who wanders through the train pasting "Repent" stickers everywhere. The film is based on HECHT and MacARTHUR'S play, which was later transformed into a Broadway musical, *On the Twentieth Century.*

"Two Black Crows." See Moran and Mack.

Tyrell, John (1900–1949), actor. Worked chiefly in comedy shorts during the 1930s and 1940s as a supporting player. He appeared in many of the THREE STOOGES' films.

SELECTED FILMS: Three Little Sew and Sews, Three Sappy People (1939), You Nazty Spy, A-Plumbing We Will Go, Nutty but Nice, From Nurse to Worse, Boobs in Arms (1940), All the World's a Stooge, In the Sweet Pie and Pie, Some More of Samoa (1941), Loco Boy Makes Good, What's the Matador?, Three Smart Saps (1942), They Stooge to Conga, A Gem of a Jam (1943), Crash Goes the Hash, Busy Buddies, Gents With Cents, No Dough, Boys (1944), Three Pests in a Mess, Booby Dupes, Micro-Phonies (1945). ■

U

Ullman, Elwood (–1985), screenwriter. Wrote screenplays, alone and in collaboration, for many Hollywood comedies and action films during the 1950s and 1960s. He also turned out numerous comedy shorts for Columbia studios. He wrote scripts for the "BOWERY BOYS" series and for the THREE STOOGES. He also did film adaptations, including *Sailor Beware* (1951), a Dean MARTIN and Jerry LEWIS comedy. The bulk of his work resulted in routine, low-budget films.

SELECTED FILMS: *Gold Raiders (1951), The Bowery Boys Meet the Monster, Jungle Gents, Paris Playboys (1954), Bowery to Bagdad, Ma and Pa Kettle at Waikiki (1955), Dig That Uranium (1956), Spook Chasers (1957), In the Money (1958), Snow White and the Three Stooges (1961), The Three Stooges in Orbit (1962), The Outlaws Is Coming (1965), Ghost in the Invisible Bikini (1966).* ∎

Underwood, Loyal (1893–1966), actor. Worked in early silent films, especially as a supporting player in comedy shorts that starred Charlie CHAPLIN.

SELECTED FILMS: *The Count (1916), Easy Street, The Cure, The Immigrant, The Adventurer (1917), A Dog's Life, Shoulder Arms (1918), Sunnyside, A Day's Pleasure (1919), Pay Day (1922), The Pilgrim (1923), The Dixie Handicap (1924), The Star Boarder (1952).* ∎

Unfaithfully Yours (1948), TCF. *Dir.* Preston Sturges; *Sc.* Preston Sturges;

with Rex Harrison, Linda Darnell, Kurt Kreuger, Barbara Lawrence, Rudy Vallee.

Preston STURGES directed this black comedy at the twilight of his short career. After a string of successful satirical comedies, he turned out two box-office flops, *The Lost Moment* and *Mad Wednesday*. He moved to 20th Century-Fox for this, his next film, hoping, along with his sympathetic critics and loyal fans, to recapture some of his past greatness. But the film failed to generate any resurgence for the once-popular writer-director. Rex Harrison portrays a symphony conductor who, suspecting his wife of having an affair, concocts three plans of revenge: murder, renunciation, and suicide, each visualized in detail during different musical compositions. Although Sturges engages in an overabundance of slapstick, which weakens the film considerably, he manages to provide plenty of wit and sparkling dialogue. When Lionel STANDER is informed that Harrison's plane is stranded in the neighborhood of Nova Scotia, he remarks: "What a neighborhood!" Rudy VALLEE, who had played a millionaire in an earlier Sturges comedy, *The Palm Beach Story* (1942), has a similar role here. "There is one reassuring thing about airplanes," he philosophizes, "they always come down." Comic actor Edgar KENNEDY, in one of his better roles, plays a sympathetic private detective who is hired to follow Harrison's wife. He is also in awe of the great conductor. "Nobody handles Handel like you handle Handel! And your

594

Delius! Delirious!'' he exhorts. The first half of the comedy represents Sturges at his best. The film, however, marked the beginning of the end of his Hollywood career. A remake appeared in 1984 starring Dudley MOORE.

Urban comedy. A light film, either silent or sound, set in a big city, in which the character players are chiefly Runyonesque, the law is ineffectual, community life is practically nonexistent, the tempo is often accelerated, amorality flourishes, and good English is rarely spoken. Since the early days of silent comedies and melodramas, Hollywood has painted the big city larger than life, an almost mythical land that is both alluring and forbidding. A strong case can be made for either side of the question of whether Hollywood reflected the attitudes Americans already had of the city or whether the studios and their writers created this image of urban life. Since a large segment of movie audiences still lived in rural communities during the early decades of this century, the city remained for many an exotic world that was not only exciting and wonderful but a place to be treated with suspicion and caution. These attitudes made urban settings perfect for films dealing with drama as well as comedy. All Hollywood may have done was to exaggerate or reinforce these preconceived notions through repetition and the inherent power of film. Of course, another, more simple, explanation may be that early film studios like Biograph were located in the city proper, thereby making urban settings more economical and accessible. In urban comedies the city itself assumes the role of a major character. In CHAPLIN'S *City Lights* (1931), for example, the busy, frantic, uncaring streets act as foil to the little tramp whose pace is slower and whose sense of caring extends to a blind girl selling flowers or a drunk about to kill himself. The street urchins, who are not much better off than the tramp, have been influenced by the insensitivity of the city. They tug at Charlie's torn garments and harass him as he strolls along. Many of Chaplin's films fit into this genre, since he consciously provided social commentary in such comedies as ''Easy Street'' and ''A Dog's Life,'' which emphasized the harsh realities of urban existence.

Minor characters in these films are often grotesques: bookies, gamblers, small-time hoods, flashy gangsters, floozies, and gunmolls. However, they usually possess soft hearts and warmth. They inhabit a range of locales—newspaper offices, saloons, betting joints, streetcorners, pool halls, and restaurants. In *All Through the Night* (1942) gambler Humphrey Bogart and his Runyonesque cronies, who include Frank McHUGH, Phil SILVERS, Jackie GLEASON, and William DEMAREST, socialize in a local restaurant. In *Sorrowful Jones* (1949) Bob HOPE and his bevy of gamblers inhabit a betting parlor. The Bowery Boys have their own club room in an abandoned basement.

The law is frequently represented by some bungling detective who wears his derby indoors, puffs on a cigar, and pompously accuses the wrong people. He sometimes has an assistant who is even dumber than he is. Character players who excelled in this role include James GLEASON, Nat PENDLETON, Ed GARGAN, Sam LEVENE, and Donald MacBRIDE. Sometimes they played the half-witted underlings to a slightly more intelligent police chief, while at other times they handled, or more likely fumbled, the case on their own.

These comedies rarely establish family or community ties. Characters have no parents or children, belong to no church, support no civic causes except their own pockets. This contrasts sharply with rural comedy, in which villagers know each other, travel with their family, talk about Sundays at church, and look forward to the next local picnic. In the original *Little Miss Marker* (1934) as well as its three remakes, all based on a Damon Runyon story, the major characters, a group of gamblers and bookies, have no relatives. Perhaps that is why they take a liking to Shirley TEMPLE, who played the orphan they adopted. Early in the film she is the only one with a semblance of family—a weak father who gambles away everything and then commits suicide.

The pace of urban comedies is faster as if to catch up to the traffic. The characters talk fast and rush around as if they are running out of time. Again, this pace differs from that of rural films, which have a deliberately slower tempo. One of the best examples is Howard HAWKS' comedy, *His Girl Friday* (1940), starring Cary GRANT, Rosalind RUSSELL, and Ralph BELLAMY. Although the film contains almost no exterior shots, the viewer is left with the impression that city life is frantic as the actors rush through their speeches and step on each others' lines while events occur at a furious pace. City comedies consciously or unconsciously reflect a tone of amorality as gamblers and bookies, bar girls and streetwalkers, muggers and con men drift about with impunity. These types may supply plenty of laughs, but they underscore the loose values within a city. This characteristic is exemplified in the relatively recent comedy, *The Out-of-Towners* (1970). Jack LEMMON and Sandy Dennis portray tourists who come to New York City only to face every conceivable mishap. Their mugger goes free, they lose their luggage, and the city, including its officials, virtually ignores them. Fifteen years after the release of the above film, conditions have changed very little, according to the comedy *Crocodile Dundee* (1986), an Australian film shot partially in New York City. A good-natured and likable Australian from the outback is brought to Manhattan where he is confronted by muggers, streetwalkers, and thugs, all of whom roam the streets and alleys apparently with complete freedom.

Finally, the obligatory broken English of the character players, including law officers, editors, and storekeepers, gives the urban film its special flavor and adds to its humor. Performers like Ed BROPHY, Warren HYMER, James GLEASON, and Sam LEVENE specialized in fracturing the language. Urban comedies number in the hundreds, at least. The low-budget "BOWERY BOYS" series would fit into this category.

SELECTED FILMS: Coney Island Princess (1916), Mr. Fix-It (1918), Girls (1919), True as Steel, East of Broadway (1924), Oh, Doctor! (1925), Speedy (1928), Sidewalks of New York (1931), Tight Shoes (1939), New York Town (1941), The Big Street, The Magnificent Dope, My Sister Eileen (1942), Ladies' Man (1947), So This Is New York (1948), The Lemon Drop Kid, Love Nest, St. Benny the Dip (1951), Taxi! (1953), Pocketful of Miracles (1961), Robin and the Seven Hoods, The Troublemaker (1964), A Thousand Clowns (1965), The Producers (1968), The Lords of Flatbush (1974), So Fine, They All Laughed (1981). ∎

Urecal, Minerva (1896–1966), actress. Appeared as a character actress chiefly in low-budget dramas and light films. A dour, matronly figure, she began her screen career in the 1930s and continued into the 1960s portraying cruel types as well as comical characters. She supported such diverse comics as LAUREL AND HARDY, the THREE STOOGES, Jimmy DURANTE, ABBOTT AND COSTELLO, and the BOWERY BOYS.

SELECTED FILMS: Sadie McKee (1934), Bonnie Scotland (1935), Her Husband's Secretary, Oh, Doctor! (1937), Start Cheering (1938), The Ghost Creeps (1940), Six Lessons From Madame La Zonga (1941), Hit the Ice (1943), Men in Her Diary (1945), The Noose Hangs High, Good Sam (1948), The Traveling Saleswoman (1950), Lost in Alaska (1952), She's Back on Broadway (1953), Mr. Hobbs Takes a Vacation (1962). ∎

Usher, Guy (1875–1944), actor. Supporting player who appeared in dramas and light films during the 1930s and 1940s. He worked with some of the leading comedians of the period, including, among others, Eddie CANTOR and W. C. FIELDS.

SELECTED FILMS: *Face in the Sky, Fast Workers (1933), All of Me, Good Dame, The Hell Cat, Kid Millions (1934), It's a Gift, Hold 'Em Yale, Grand Exit, Make a Million (1935), Lady for a Night (1942).* ■

V

Vaccaro, Brenda (1939–), actress. Appeared in stock and on Broadway before entering films in the late 1960s. She has had featured roles in dramas and comedies, but with the exception of one Academy Award nomination for her role in *Once Is Not Enough* (1975), she has not received full recognition of her potential talent.

SELECTED FILMS: *Where It's At* (1969), *I Love My Wife* (1970), *Zorro, the Gay Blade* (1981), *Supergirl* (1984). ∎

Vague, Vera (1905–1974), actress. Worked on radio and stage before entering films in the early 1940s. A talented comedienne who also went under her real name, Barbara Jo Allen, she appeared chiefly in light B films.

SELECTED FILMS: *Melody and Moonlight, Village Barn Dance* (1940), *Kiss the Boys Goodbye, Ice Capades* (1941), *Mrs. Wiggs of the Cabbage Patch, Design for Scandal, Larceny, Inc.* (1942), *In Rosie's Room* (1944), *Snafu* (1945), *Square Dance Katy* (1950), *The Opposite Sex* (1956), *Born to Be Loved* (1959). ∎

Vallee, Rudy (1901–1986), singer, actor. Appeared on radio, in nightclubs, and on stage before entering films in 1929. Often holding his famous megaphone, he appeared in romantic and light films. Later in his film career he developed into an accomplished character actor.

In *The Palm Beach Story* he played an eccentric millionaire who meets runaway wife Claudette COLBERT. Under the impression that her husband is an unsavory character, he threatens to "thrash him within an inch of his life." He develops second thoughts, however. "That's one of the tragedies of this life," he muses. "The men that are most in need of a beating up are always enormous."

SELECTED FILMS: *The Vagabond Lover* (1929), *International House* (1933), *Gold Diggers in Paris* (1938), *Second Fiddle* (1939), *Too Many Blondes* (1941), *The Palm Beach Story* (1942), *Happy Go Lucky* (1943), *It's in the Bag* (1945), *People Are Funny, The Fabulous Suzanne* (1946), *The Bachelor and the Bobby-Soxer* (1947), *Mad Wednesday* (1947), *Mother Is a Freshman* (1949), *How to Succeed in Business Without Really Trying* (1967), *Sunburst* (1975). ∎

Van, Bobby (1930–1980), dancer, actor, singer. Entertained in nightclubs and on stage before entering films in the 1950s. Born Robert King, he was also a gifted choreographer. He appeared in a series of light films through the 1970s.

SELECTED FILMS: *Because You're Mine* (1952), *Small Town Girl, The Affairs of Dobie Gillis, Kiss Me Kate* (1953), *Lost Horizon* (1973). ∎

Van Dyke, Dick (1925–), actor. Worked in nightclubs and television and on Broadway in 1960, which led to a Hollywood contract in 1963. An angular, versatile performer possessing an abundance of charm, he quickly rose to fame in a series of light films. He won several

Emmy Awards for his successful television show. His comedy style is predominantly visual and includes slapstick.

In *Divorce, American Style* he played the unfortunate husband of Debbie Reynolds who, during a divorce proceeding and fighting none too cleanly, manages to obtain the house, the car, and the custody of two children. "The uranium mine to her," he grumbles, "and the shaft to me."

SELECTED FILMS: *Bye Bye Birdie (1963), What a Way to Go!, Mary Poppins (1964), The Art of Love (1965), Lt. Robinson Crusoe, USN (1966), Divorce, American Style, Fitzwilly (1967), Never a Dull Moment (1968), Some Kind of a Nut, The Comic (1969), Cold Turkey (1971), The Runner Stumbles (1979).* ■

Van Dyke, W.S. (1889–1943), director. Worked as a child performer in vaudeville and stock before entering silent films as an assistant to D. W. GRIFFITH. In 1917 he began directing his own films, a career that spanned four decades. He turned out features in every genre. An expert craftsman, he was responsible for many entertaining and successful films, but few were of any significance. He directed several of the "THIN MAN" entries.

SELECTED FILMS: *Gift o' Gab (1917), According to Hoyle (1922), Penthouse (1933), The Thin Man (1934), Naughty Marietta (1935), It's a Wonderful World, Andy Hardy Has Spring Fever (1939), I Take This Woman, I Love You Again (1940), The Feminine Touch (1941), I Married an Angel, Journey for Margaret (1942).* ■

Van Patten, Dick (1928–), actor. Appeared on Broadway as a child and in films on a regular basis in the early 1960s. As a supporting player, he appeared in dramas and light films. He has gained greater popularity in television than he has in films.

SELECTED FILMS: *Reg'lar Fellers (1941), Making It (1971), Superdad (1974), The Strongest Man in the World (1975), Gus, The Shaggy D.A. (1976), Freaky Friday, High Anxiety (1977).* ■

Van Patten, Joyce (1934–), actress. Appeared as a child on stage and worked on radio. She began to act in films on a regular basis in the late 1960s while working steadily in television. She is the sister of Dick VAN PATTEN.

SELECTED FILMS: *Reg'lar Fellers (1941), The Trouble With Girls (1969), Pussycat, Pussycat, I Love You (1970), Something Big (1971), Mame (1974), The Manchu Eagle Murder Caper Mystery (1975), The Bad News Bears, Mikey and Nicky (1976).* ■

Van Peebles, Melvin (1932–), director, writer. Worked at odd jobs, wrote novels, and directed and wrote his first film in France, *The Story of a Three-Day Pass* (1968). Returning to the United States, he turned out several light films that were generally poorly received by the critics. He in turn attacked the critics for their lack of understanding of his black-culture films. He collaborated on the screenplay for *Greased Lightning* (1977).

SELECTED FILMS: *Watermelon Man (1970), Sweet Sweetback's Baadasssss Song (1971).* ■

Van Pelt, Ernest, actor. Worked in early silent films, especially as a supporting player in comedy shorts starring Charlie CHAPLIN.

SELECTED FILMS: *In the Park, The Jitney Elopement, The Tramp (1915).* ■

Van Riper, Kay (–1948), screenwriter. Wrote screenplays during the 1930s and 1940s. She turned out, alone and in collaboration, light scripts, chiefly for the "ANDY HARDY" series at MGM studios.

SELECTED FILMS: A Family Affair (1937), Judge Hardy's Children, Out West With the Hardys, You're Only Young Once (1938), Babes in Arms, The Hardys Ride High (1939), Lady Be Good (1941). ■

Van Upp, Virginia (1902–1970), screenwriter, actress. Worked as a child actress in silent films, script girl, and at other assorted jobs before turning to writing screenplays for dramas and light films alone and in collaboration. By the 1940s she switched to producing films at Columbia.

SELECTED FILMS (as screenwriter): Pursuit of Happiness (1934), Easy to Take, My American Wife, Poppy, Too Many Parents (1936), Swing High, Swing Low (1937), Cafe Society, Honeymoon in Bali (1939), One Night in Lisbon (1941), The Crystal Ball, Young and Willing (1943), Cover Girl, Together Again (1944), She Wouldn't Say Yes (1945), Here Comes the Groom (1951). ■

Van Zandt, Phil (1904–1958), actor. Worked in stock and on Broadway in the 1920s before entering films in the late 1930s as a character player. Often portraying unsavory characters, he appeared in numerous comedy shorts and features during the 1940s and 1950s, especially in many two-reelers starring the THREE STOOGES. He committed suicide at age 54.

SELECTED FILMS: Those High Grey Walls (1939), Boobs in Arms (1940), Air Raid Wardens (1943), A Thousand and One Nights (1945), Squareheads of the Round Table, Mummy's Dummies (1948), Dopey Dicks (1950), Three Arabian Nuts (1951), Spooks (1953), Knutzy Knights, Scotched in Scotland, Knock on Wood (1954), Bedlam in Paradise (1955), Hot Stuff (1956), Outer Space Jitters (1957), Fifi Blows Her Top (1958). ■

Van Der Veer, Ellinor (–1976), actress. Began her screen career in silent films in the mid-1920s. A talented comedienne

and character player, she appeared in several comedy shorts starring LAUREL AND HARDY and the THREE STOOGES.

SELECTED FILMS: The Second Hundred Years, The Battle of the Century (1927), From Soup to Nuts (1928), The Hoosegow (1929), Going Bye Bye (1934), Pop Goes the Easel, Slightly Static (1935), No Census No Feeling (1940), Loco Boy Makes Good (1942). ■

Varconi, Victor (1896–1976), actor. Worked on stage in his native Hungary and in films in Europe before migrating to Hollywood during the silent period. After playing leads through the early 1930s, Varconi, born Mihaly Varkoniji, turned to character acting. He often appeared in sinister roles in dramas and light films, including several starring Bob HOPE.

SELECTED FILMS: Changing Husbands (1924), Angel of Broadway (1927), The Divine Lady (1929), Men in Her Life (1931), Mr. Dynamite, A Feather in Her Hat (1935), Dancing Pirate (1936), Big City (1937), My Favorite Blonde (1942), Where There's Life (1947), My Favorite Spy (1951), Atomic Submarine (1959). ■

Velez, Lupe (1908–1944), actress. Performed as a dancer in Mexican burlesque houses and on stage before entering films. A gifted comedienne who was born Maria Guadalupe Velez de Villalohos, she began her screen career in silent comedy shorts for producer Hal ROACH, and quickly moved up to feature films in stormy, temperamental roles. During her first few years in full-length films she was limited to dramatic roles. Exploiting her Hispanic accent, she shifted to lighter parts. In the 1940s she co-starred with Leon ERROL in the highly popular "MEXICAN SPITFIRE" comedy series. She worked with some of the leading film personalities of the period, including, among others, Charlie CHASE and Douglas FAIRBANKS. She committed suicide at age 36.

SELECTED FILMS: *Sailors Beware (1927), Tiger Rose (1929), Hot Pepper (1933), Palooka, Strictly Dynamite (1934), The Girl From Mexico (1939), Mexican Spitfire (1940), Six Lessons From Madame La Zonga, Playmates, Honolulu Lu (1941), Ladies' Day, Redhead From Manhattan (1943).* ■

Venable, Evelyn (1913–), actress. Appeared in stock before entering films in the early 1930s. A gifted and beautiful screen star who deserved better material than that assigned to her, she played in dramas and light films.

SELECTED FILMS: *Cradle Song (1933), The Country Chairman, The Little Colonel, Vagabond Lady, Alice Adams, Harmony Lane (1935), Star for a Night (1936), He Hired the Boss (1943).* ■

Verdon, Gwen (1925–), actress, singer. Performed on stage before entering films in the early 1950s. She appeared in several light films while continuing to star in Broadway musicals.

SELECTED FILMS: *On the Riviera, Meet Me After the Show (1951), The Farmer Takes a Wife (1953), Damn Yankees (1958).* ■

Vernon, Bobby (1897–1939), actor. Appeared on stage before entering films in 1913. A talented comic, he worked chiefly in early silent comedy shorts. He joined producer Mack SENNETT'S KEYSTONE studios for two years, then switched to Al CHRISTIE'S company where he continued to star in comedies. Although his screen career ended with the advent of sound, he continued to work in the film world as a comedy consultant.

SELECTED FILMS: *Almost an Actress, Mike and Jake at the Beach (1913), The Mystery of a Taxi Cab, Love and Graft, Love and Electricity (1914), Fickle Fatty's Fall, His Father's Footsteps, The Hunt (1915), His Pride and Shame, A Dash of Courage, Hearts and Sparks (1916), The Nick of Time, Baby, Teddy at the Throttle, The Sultan's Wife (1917), Second Childhood (1922), French Pastry (1925), Footloose Widows (1926), Ship a-Hooey (1932).* ■

Vernon, Wally (1904–1970), actor. Played supporting roles from the 1930s to the 1960s. He often appeared in light films, several of which were low-budget second features. He worked with some of the leading comics of the period, including the RITZ BROTHERS and Milton BERLE, as well as being a comic-relief character in westerns.

SELECTED FILMS: *Mountain Music, This Way Please (1937), Kentucky Moonshine, Meet the Girls, Sharpshooters (1938), The Gorilla (1939), Sailor's Lady (1940), Reveille With Beverly, Tahiti Honey, Pistol Packin' Mama, Canyon City (1943), Always Leave Them Laughing (1949), Bloodhounds of Broadway (1952), What a Way to Go! (1964).* ■

Vidor, Charles (1900–1959), director. In the United States since 1924 as an opera singer and assistant film director and writer. He began directing films in the early sound period and continued for three decades to turn out well-made and entertaining dramas and light features. His last film was completed by George CUKOR.

SELECTED FILMS: *The Bridge (1931), His Family Tree (1935), Muss 'Em Up (1936), She's No Lady (1937), The Lady in Question (1940), The Tuttles of Tahiti (1942), Cover Girl, Together Again (1944), Over 21 (1945), Hans Christian Andersen (1952), The Joker Is Wild (1957), Song Without End (1960).* ■

Vidor, Florence (1895–1977), actress. Began her film career in 1916 in silent films and gradually rose to stardom in the 1920s. A pretty and versatile actress, she starred in dramas and comedies. Her career came to an almost instant halt when she proved unable to make the transition to sound.

SELECTED FILMS: The Yellow Girl (1916), Poor Relations (1919), Beau Revel, Hail the Woman (1921), Skin Deep (1922), Alice Adams (1923), The Marriage Circle, Welcome Stranger (1924), Are Parents People?, Grounds for Divorce, Marry Me, The Trouble With Wives (1925), The Grand Duchess and the Waiter, You Never Know Women (1926), The World at Her Feet (1927), The Magnificent Flirt (1928), Chinatown Nights (1929). ■

Vidor, King (1894–1982), director. Worked in Hollywood at odd jobs until he won an opportunity in 1919 to direct his first feature. By the mid-1920s he was recognized as one of the major Hollywood directors. He was chosen by Marion DAVIES and William Randolph Hearst to direct Davies in two of her biggest silent comedy hits, *The Patsy* and *Show People*. In both the silent and sound periods he turned out several striking dramatic films, such as *The Big Parade* (1925), *The Crowd* (1928), and *Our Daily Bread* (1934), exceptional in their content as well as in their visual style. His comedies, however entertaining they may be, rarely reflect his genius as a director. *A Tree Is a Tree*, his autobiography, was published in 1953.

SELECTED FILMS: The Turn of the Road (1919), Conquering the Woman, Three Wise Fools (1923), Wild Oranges, His Hour (1924), The Patsy, Show People (1928), Not So Dumb (1930), The Champ (1931), Comrade X (1940), On Our Merry Way (1948), Solomon and Sheba (1959). ■

Vigoda, Abe (1921–), actor. Has had long careers in television and on stage. A tall figure with a prominent chin, he came to films late in his acting career but is a familiar face to the public because of his television shows. He has appeared sporadically in dramas and light films.

SELECTED FILMS: The Godfather (1972), The Cheap Detective (1978), Vasectomy (1986). ■

Virginia Judge, The. A comic character created by old-time vaudeville comedian Walter C. KELLY. The "judge" appeared in several films during the 1930s.

Vitagraph. A film production company established in 1896. Its founders, J. Stuart Blackton and Albert Smith, made their own newsreels or documentaries using locales around New York City, where the company was based. Their first work of fiction, *The Burglar on the Roof*, was made in 1897 on a rooftop. During the early 1900s Vitagraph emerged as the leader in comedy shorts which featured such popular stars as John BUNNY and Mr. and Mrs. Sidney DREW. The company did so well with its films that it was forced to expand, opening a studio in Brooklyn and one in California. Although Vitagraph thrived into the early 1920s with a succession of dramas and light vehicles, it was finally bought out by Warner Brothers in 1925.

W

Waggner, George (1894–1984), director, screenwriter. Appeared as an actor in silent films, wrote songs, turned to screenwriting in early sound films, and switched to directing in the 1940s. Most of his output, as screenwriter and director, has been in the realm of low-budget films. He wrote more comedy material, alone or in collaboration, than he directed.

SELECTED FILMS (as screenwriter): *Sweetheart of Sigma Chi* (1933), *Girl o' My Dreams, Once to Every Bachelor* (1934), *The Cowboy Millionaire, Cappy Ricks Returns, Champagne for Breakfast, Dizzy Dames, The Nut Farm, Spring Tonic* (1935), *Don't Get Personal* (1936), *Man From God's Country* (1958). ■

Walburn, Raymond (1887–1969), actor. Appeared in stock and on Broadway before entering films in 1929. A friendly character player with a walrus-like countenance, large eyes, and a mischievous spirit, he was featured in numerous dramas and light films. He played lead roles in several films, including his own comedy series in which he played Henry, a headstrong small-towner. See *Henry the Rainmaker.*

In *Born to Dance* (1936) he played the captain of a United States warship. "You sure do a lot of fishin', don't you?" a sailor asks. "Yes," Walburn replies, "I expect to run for President someday." Later, he invites the families and friends of the crew aboard to tour the vessel. "Can I visit the crow's nest?" a female visitor asks. "Certainly not," the captain objects. "This is the mating season."

SELECTED FILMS: *The Laughing Lady* (1929), *The Great Flirtation, Broadway Bill* (1930), *She Married Her Boss* (1935), *The King Steps Out* (1936), *Thin Ice* (1937), *Professor Beware* (1938), *The Under-Pup* (1939), *Christmas in July* (1940), *Louisiana Purchase* (1941), *Dixie, Let's Face It* (1943), *Hail the Conquering Hero* (1944), *Mad Wednesday* (1947), *State of the Union* (1948), *Leave It to Henry, Henry the Rainmaker* (1949), *Father Takes the Air* (1951), *The Spoilers* (1955). ■

Walker, Hal (1896–1972), director. Appeared on stage and worked as an assistant film director before emerging as a full-fledged director in the mid-1940s. A competent craftsman, he turned out chiefly light films starring such comedy teams as Bob HOPE and Bing CROSBY and MARTIN AND LEWIS before switching to television.

SELECTED FILMS: *Out of This World, Duffy's Tavern, The Stork Club* (1945), *Road to Utopia* (1946), *My Friend Irma Goes West* (1950), *At War With the Army, That's My Boy* (1951), *Sailor Beware* (1952), *Road to Bali* (1953). ■

Walker, Jimmie, comedian, actor. Appeared in television after a long stint in small nightclubs. Raised in a ghetto in the south Bronx, he bases much of his comedy on his experiences as well as on related topics, including politics, schools, and crime. He has appeared occasionally in films, but they did nothing to further his career. He has not been able to capture the popularity that he achieved in his hit television show, "Good Times."

SELECTED FILMS: Let's Do It Again (1975), Rabbit Test (1978), The Concorde—Airport '79 (1979). ∎

Walker, Johnnie (1894–1949), actor. Appeared on stage before entering silent films in lead roles. He played in dramas and light films into the early 1930s when his career foundered.

SELECTED FILMS: Over the Hill to the Poor House (1920), The Jolt (1921), The Spirit of the USA (1924), Transcontinental Limited, Lightning Reporter (1926), The Clown, Rose of the Bowery, Pretty Clothes (1927), Bare Knees, So This Is Love, The Matinee Idol (1928), The Melody Man, Ladies of Leisure, Ladies in Love (1930), Enemies of the Law (1931). ∎

Walker, Lillian (1887–1975), actress. Began her screen career in 1911 in silent comedies and dramas. A lively and personable blonde performer, she often co-starred in comedy shorts with the popular John BUNNY at VITAGRAPH studios. She established her own company in 1918 and continued to appear in films until the early 1920s, when she decided to abandon her screen career. She occasionally acted on stage in the late 1920s and early 1930s and appeared in several sound films.

SELECTED FILMS: The New Stenographer (1911), Alma's Champion (1912), Stenographers' Troubles, The Autocrat of Flapjack Junction (1913), Love, Luck and Gasoline (1914), A Model Wife (1915), The Princess of Park Row (1917), A Joyous Liar (1919), Love's Boomerang (1922), The Pusher-in-the-Face (1928), Enlighten Thy Daughter (1934). ∎

Walker, Nella (1886–1971), actress. Worked in vaudeville before entering films in the late 1920s. She developed into an accomplished character player who often portrayed congenial women of prominent social position in numerous comedies and dramas. She appeared with some of the leading comedians of the period, including ABBOTT AND COSTELLO, OLSEN AND JOHNSON, and Jimmy DURANTE.

In Buck Privates she played Lee Bowman's mother who protests what the Army has done to her boy. "How can they make a Yale man a private?"

SELECTED FILMS: The Vagabond Lover (1929), What a Widow! (1930), The Hot Heiress, Indiscreet (1931), Trouble in Paradise (1932), Reunion in Vienna (1933), All of Me (1934), McFadden's Flats, Captain January (1936), Three Smart Girls (1937), Three Smart Girls Grow Up (1939), I Love You Again (1940), Buck Privates, Hellzapoppin (1941), We Were Dancing (1942), Two Sisters From Boston (1946), Nancy Goes to Rio (1950), Sabrina (1954). ∎

Walker, Ray, actor. Appeared in lead roles in dramas and light films during the 1930s. Under contract to Monogram, a second-string studio, he starred in several musical comedies in the early 1930s. By the 1950s he was relegated to character roles.

SELECTED FILMS: Devil's Mate (1933), The Loud Speaker, Thirty Day Princess, Baby, Take a Bow (1934), Million Dollar Baby, The Girl Friend (1935), Laughing Irish Eyes (1936), Hideaway Girl, Angel's Holiday (1937), Hi Ya Chum, Crazy House (1943), Tars and Spars (1946), The Sainted Sisters (1948), The Blue Gardenia (1953). ∎

Walker, Robert (1918–1951), actor. Appeared in bit film parts and on radio before entering films in lead roles in the 1940s. He portrayed unaffected, boyish characters, chiefly in light films. Struggling with emotional and drinking problems, he had to be hospitalized for a period. Upon his release, he returned to films, giving an exceptional performance as the eccentric psychopath in Hitchcock's Strangers on a Train (1951). But his apparent recovery was short-lived; he died the same year.

SELECTED FILMS: Winter Carnival (1939), See Here, Private Hargrove (1944), Her Highness and the Bellboy, What Next, Corporal Hargrove? (1945), The Sailor Takes a Wife (1946), One Touch of Venus (1948), Please Believe Me, The Skipper Surprised His Wife (1950), My Son John (1952). ■

Walker, Walter "Wally" (1909–1975), actor. Entered silent films in the early 1920s as an extra. He appeared as a supporting player in several dramas and numerous light films, working in Hollywood through the mid-1940s. He accompanied some of the foremost comic performers of the period, including, among others, Joe E. BROWN, Eddie CANTOR, and Mae WEST.

SELECTED FILMS: The Chicken in the Case (1921), Reaching for the Moon, A Tailor-Made Man (1931), The Rich Are Always With Us, You Said a Mouthful, The Kid From Spain, Blessed Event (1932), I'm No Angel, Sitting Pretty (1933), Mrs. Wiggs of the Cabbage Patch, The Gay Bride (1934), Everybody's Old Man, Yours for the Asking (1936), The Cowboy and the Lady (1938), I Wouldn't Be in Your Shoes (1948). ■

Wallace, Jean (1923–), actress. Began her screen career in 1941. A vivacious blonde who was born Jean Wallasek, she has played leads in several comedies and dramas in the United States and England.

SELECTED FILMS: Louisiana Purchase (1941), You Can't Ration Love (1944), It Shouldn't Happen to a Dog (1946), When My Baby Smiles at Me (1948), The Good Humor Man (1950), Beach Red (1967). ■

Wallace, May (1877–1938), actress. Entered silent films in the early 1920s following a long career in vaudeville. She appeared as a supporting player in light features and numerous comedy shorts.

SELECTED FILMS: The Cup of Life, My Lady Friends (1921), Gimme (1923), Oh, You Tony! (1924), Painted Faces, Skirt Shy (1929), Love Business, Mama Loves Papa (1931), Readin' and Writin', Free Eats, Pooch, What's Your Racket?, Kid From Borneo (1933), The Chases of Pimple Street (1934), Beginner's Luck (1935), Arbor Day (1936), Roamin' Holiday (1937). ■

Wallace, Richard (1894–1951), director. Worked in the cutting room for producer Mack SENNETT and performed other miscellaneous tasks at various film studios before emerging as a director in the 1920s. Excellent at his craft, he turned out numerous effective dramas and entertaining light films, many of which proved profitable at the box office.

SELECTED FILMS: Syncopating Sue (1926), McFadden's Flats, The Poor Nut, American Beauty (1927), Lady Be Good, The Butter and Egg Man (1928), Innocents of Paris (1929), Seven Days' Leave, Anybody's War (1930), Eight Girls in a Boat, The Little Minister (1934), Wedding Present (1936), Blossoms on Broadway (1937), The Under-Pup (1939), She Knew All the Answers (1941), The Wife Takes a Flyer (1942), My Kingdom for a Cook (1943), It's in the Bag (1945), Let's Live a Little (1948), A Kiss for Corliss (1950). ■

Walsh, Knobby. Fictional comic relief character in the "Joe Palooka" films. Created by cartoonist Ham Fisher, Knobby was the fight manager and confidant of prizefighter Joe Palooka. He was portrayed in 1934 by Jimmy DURANTE in the feature Palooka, starring Stuart ERWIN in the title role, and by Leon ERROL in a low-budget series in the 1940s that featured newcomer Joe Kirkwood as the fighter. Finally, character player James GLEASON took over the role in the series following Errol's death.

Walsh, M. Emmet (1935–), actor. Came to Hollywood films in the late 1960s to play minor character roles. Heavy-set with light hair, he has played tough lawmen and officious bureaucrats in dramas and light films. By the mid-1980s his reputation as a sturdy character actor rose and he has gotten better roles since.

SELECTED FILMS: Stiletto (1969), Loving, Cold Turkey, Little Big Man (1970), They Might Be Giants (1971), What's Up, Doc? (1972), The Prisoner of Second Avenue (1975), Slap Shot (1977), The Jerk (1979), Cannery Row (1982), Fletch, The Best of Times (1985). ■

Walsh, Raoul (1887–1980), director. Acted on stage and in silent films in 1912 before turning in 1914 to directing. For the next five decades he turned out a succession of impressive films in different genres. He worked as assistant director to D. W. Griffith, who helped him do the first film on Pancho Villa with Christy Cabanne. A virile director chiefly of action and adventure features, he is almost always entertaining. His works have a finished look to them, reflecting his expertise in his craft.

His light films, like his dramas, are unpretentious and capture his sense of excitement and fun. Sailor's Luck, for example, about some sailors on shore leave, contains several hilarious scenes and a host of offbeat characters including Victor Jory as the corrupt landlord of a dance hall and comic character players Frank Moran and Sammy Cohen supplying their lowbrow gags. The final scene with its phallic suggestions has the hero and heroine (James Dunn and Sally Eilers) embracing in the back of a taxi where they slide down in the seat. The film then cuts to the guns of a warship firing away at the audience. The Horn Blows at Midnight, a fantasy-comedy starring Jack BENNY (the comedian considered this his worst film), has Benny as an angel who is assigned to destroy earth with Gabriel's horn. Again Walsh makes

effective use of character players, including Franklin PANGBORN, Allyn JOSLYN, Guy KIBBEE, Reginald GARDINER, and Margaret DUMONT. His autobiography, Each Man in His Time, was published in 1974.

SELECTED FILMS: The Life of General Villa (1914), Blue Blood and Red (1916), This Is the Life (1917), I'll Say So (1918), The Lucky Lady, The Lady of the Harem (1926), The Cock-Eyed World, Hot for Paris (1929), Women of All Nations (1931), Wild Girl, For Me and My Gal (1932), Sailor's Luck, The Bowery, Going Hollywood (1933), Every Night at Eight (1935), Klondike Annie (1936), Artists and Models (1937), College Swing (1938), The Horn Blows at Midnight (1945), A Private's Affair (1959), A Distant Trumpet (1964). ■

Walston, Ray (1918–), actor. Worked as a comic on the stage and in television before entering films in the late 1950s. A light-haired character actor of slight build, he has appeared in a string of light films. He has accompanied some of the top comic actors of the period, including, among others, Cary GRANT and Jack LEMMON.

SELECTED FILMS: Kiss Them for Me (1957), South Pacific, Damn Yankees (1958), Say One for Me (1959), Tall Story, The Apartment (1960), Wives and Lovers, Who's Minding the Store? (1963), Kiss Me, Stupid (1964), Caprice (1967), The Sting (1973), Silver Streak (1976), The Happy Hooker Goes to Washington (1977), Popeye (1980), Private School (1983), Johnny Dangerously (1984). ■

Walters, Charles (1911–1982), director. Worked as an actor, dancer, and film choreographer before switching to directing. He turned out lively and entertaining musicals and comedies for MGM during the 1940s and 1950s.

SELECTED FILMS: Good News (1947), Easter Parade (1948), The Barkleys of Broadway (1949), Three Guys Named Mike (1951), The Belle of New York (1952), Lili, Dangerous When Wet, Easy to Love (1953), The Glass Slipper, The Tender Trap (1955), High Society (1956), Don't Go Near the Water (1957), Ask Any Girl (1959), Please Don't Eat the Daisies (1960), Jumbo (1962), The Unsinkable Molly Brown (1964). ∎

Walters, Polly, actress. Appeared as a supporting player in early sound dramas and light films. She specialized in romantic comedies.

SELECTED FILMS: Smart Money, Expensive Women, Blonde Crazy, Manhattan Parade (1931), Taxi, Beauty and the Boss, Love Starved, Make Me a Star (1932), She Loves Me Not (1933). ∎

Walthall, Henry B. (1878–1936), actor. Appeared on Broadway before entering early silent films. A distinguished screen personality, he played leads in dramas during much of the silent period, switching to character roles in dramas and comedies during the 1930s. He was one of D. W. Griffith's repertory group at BIOGRAPH.

SELECTED FILMS: Pranks, Choosing a Husband (1909), A Splendid Hazard (1920), Dollar Down, Simon the Jester (1925), Everybody's Acting (1926), Me and My Gal, Cabin in the Cotton, Central Park (1932), 42nd Street, Laughing at Life (1933), Beggars in Ermine, Judge Priest, The Lemon Drop Kid (1934), China Clipper (1936). ∎

War humor. Comedy films with a wartime setting or which take place during battle, as distinguished from service or military comedy in which the characters are members of a branch of service during peacetime. War humor has always been a popular genre with the general movie audience. Almost every comedian and comedy team has made at least one of these films.

World War I set the stage and tone for this type of film. The hero was usually an inept soldier who, by either good luck or some brilliant stroke of genius, was able to redeem himself by performing a heroic deed. However, the war comedy was slow in coming during this conflict. Most of the product turned out by the studios was on the melodramatic side, including patriotic, propaganda, and atrocity films like D. W. Griffith's Hearts of the World, intended to stir the emotions of its audiences, not to evoke laughter. Eventually, major producers such as Mack SENNETT and such film stars as Charlie CHAPLIN began to turn their comedic talents toward war humor.

Chester CONKLIN in "An International Sneak" (1918), a spoof of the spy genre popular at the time, played an espionage agent. Chaplin made his now classic "Shoulder Arms" (1918), in which he plays a recruit who goes from training camp to the front lines, encountering tough sergeants, uninhabitable trenches, and hostile Germans. Producer Al CHRISTIE made "Shades of Shakespeare" (1918), which poked fun at the propaganda films of the period. "Kicking the Germ Out of Germany" (1918) starred Harold LLOYD as a spy and featured comedienne Bebe DANIELS as a nurse. Larry SEMON did his share in the war effort by capturing a spy in "Huns and Hyphens" (1918). Cross-eyed Ben TURPIN impersonated the Kaiser in "Yankee Doodle in Berlin" (1919), while Douglas MacLEAN was featured in "23 1/2 Hours Leave" the same year.

Other film personalities participated in the genre with equal fervor. Billie BURKE in "Arms and the Girl" (1917) played an impish American in France who rescues a fellow American from a German firing squad through the use of humorous pranks. On the home front Mr. and Mrs. Sidney DREW turned out a little comedy in 1917 titled "The Patriot," which dealt with conserving food. Director King VIDOR'S "Bud's Recruit" (1918) tells the story of a younger brother who tries to enlist in the service, thereby embarrassing his older brother into doing his duty.

The first half of the 1920s saw very few war films—comedies or dramas. Either Hollywood forgot about the Great War or the public was tired of the genre. But with the release of several blockbusters like *The Big Parade* and *What Price Glory?*, the war comedy returned with a vengeance. Harry LANGDON starred in *Soldier Boy* (1926) and *The Strong Man* (1927), the latter of which contained battle scenes only at the beginning. Wallace BEERY was teamed with Raymond HATTON in a series of war comedies, the first of which was titled *Behind the Front* (1926). Semon returned in *Spuds* (1927), comics Karl DANE and George K. ARTHUR starred in *Rookies* (1927), and George SIDNEY and Charlie MURRAY made *Lost at the Front* (1927). Even Broadway entertainer George JESSEL turned out two vehicles, *Private Izzy Murphy* and *Sailor Izzy Murphy*, both 1927. Comic Monty BANKS joined the flying corps in "Flying Luck" (1928).

Comedies set during World War I lingered on into the 1930s. MORAN AND MACK starred in *Anybody's War* (1930), Buster KEATON in *Dough Boys* (1930), and the comedy team of WHEELER AND WOOLSEY in *Half-Shot at Sunrise* (1930), about the boys' misadventures in Paris and at the front. LAUREL AND HARDY appeared in *Pack Up Your Troubles* in 1932, while wide-mouthed Joe E. BROWN made *Sons o' Guns* in 1936. The only film the MARX BROTHERS made that comes close to a war comedy was *Duck Soup* (1933), about a fictitious conflict between two mythical kingdoms. At the close of the decade the RITZ BROTHERS made their contribution to the genre in *Pack Up Your Troubles* (1939), and, like Stan and Ollie's war comedy of 1932, took the title from the popular World War I song.

World War II gave rise to a relatively new generation of comedians who turned to the conflict as a source for humor in the 1940s. But the decade started with Charlie Chaplin's *The Great Dictator* (1940), with its opening scenes taking place during a World War I battle. ABBOTT AND COSTELLO, the top comedy team of the decade, starred in *Buck Privates* (1941), *In the Navy* (1941), and

Buck Privates Come Home (1947). Bob HOPE made *Caught in the Draft* (1941), while the same year Jimmy DURANTE and Phil SILVERS were featured in *You're in the Army Now*. Danny KAYE, who portrayed a hypochondriac in *Up in Arms* (1944), nevertheless managed to snare a Japanese unit while he was on duty in the Pacific. Minor comic actors also participated in the steady stream of war comedies, including William TRACY in *About Face* (1942) and the young Robert WALKER in *See Here, Private Hargrove* (1944), an episodic story about a recruit's humorous misadventures in the army. In 1948 Red SKELTON made *A Southern Yankee*, a farce set during the Civil War, and not unlike Keaton's silent comedy, *The General* (1927).

Although the conflict had ended almost a decade earlier, the 1950s supplied several comedies about World War II. Dean MARTIN and Jerry LEWIS, the most popular comedy team of the 1950s, appeared in *At War With the Army* in 1950, their first starring film. The following year they made *Sailor Beware*. Lewis went on to star in one of his funniest films, *Don't Give Up the Ship* (1959), in which he misplaces a battleship during wartime. Bill Mauldin's wartime cartoon characters, Willie and Joe, were brought to the screen in *Up Front* (1951), starring David WAYNE and Tom EWELL, and in the sequel, *Back at the Front* (1952). Director John FORD launched *Mr. Roberts* in 1955, about life on a cargo ship during World War II, starring James CAGNEY as an oddball captain, Henry FONDA as an officer yearning to get into the action of the war, and Jack LEMMON as a scheming braggart. In 1957 Glenn Ford starred in the weak comedy, *Don't Go Near the Water*. Andy GRIFFITH repeated his Broadway role as the innocent hayseed in *No Time for Sergeants* (1958). One of the funniest post-war films, *Operation Petticoat* (1959), starred Cary GRANT as the skipper of a damaged submarine in the Pacific and Tony CURTIS as his resourceful officer. The

Korean conflict and the Vietnam War years offered few comedies, but one classic emerged in 1970, *M*A*S*H*, starring Elliott GOULD and Donald Sutherland as two offbeat surgeons who find their own methods to maintain their sanity at a field hospital in Korea.

Ward, Carrie (1862–1926), actress. Entered silent films in her middle years after long experience on stage. She appeared as a supporting player in dramas and light films until her death.

SELECTED FILMS: *Why Smith Left Home* (1919), *Old Lady 31* (1920), *One Wild Week, Her Winning Way* (1921), *The Top of New York, Penrod* (1922), *Breaking Into Society* (1923), *The Awful Truth, Who Cares, The Only Thing, The Golden Cocoon* (1925). ■

Ward, Fannie (1872–1952), actress. Worked in vaudeville and on stage before entering silent films in the 1910s. She appeared in lead and supporting roles in dramas and light films.

SELECTED FILMS: *The Cheat* (1915), *Each Hour a Pearl, Tennessee's Pardner* (1916), *The School for Husbands, Betty to the Rescue, Her Strange Wedding* (1917), *Our Better Selves* (1919), *The Hardest Way* (1922), *The Miracle Woman* (1929). ■

Ward, Lucille (1880–1952), actress. Began her screen career in silent films. She appeared as a supporting player in a handful of dramas and numerous light films during the 1920s and 1930s.

SELECTED FILMS: *High Gear Jeffrey, The Traveling Salesman* (1921), *Sixty Cents an Hour* (1923), *Sporting Youth* (1924), *Oh, Doctor!, His Majesty Bunker Bean, A Woman of the World* (1925), *What a Man!* (1930), *Little Miss Marker* (1934), *Old Sawbones* (1935), *Mother Carey's Chickens* (1938), *First Love* (1939), *Christmas in July* (1940), *Henry Aldrich's Little Secret* (1944). ■

Ward, Solly (1891–1942), actor. Entered films in the late 1920s following experience in burlesque and on stage. He appeared as a supporting player in dramas, light films, and numerous comedy shorts.

SELECTED FILMS: *At the Party* (1927), *Living on Love, She's Got Everything* (1937), *Everybody's Doing It, Maid's Night Out* (1938), *Conspiracy* (1939). ■

Warden, Jack (1920–), actor. Had careers as prizefighter and stage actor before entering films in 1951. Light-haired and energetic, he has appeared in leads and supporting roles as compelling characters. He received Academy Award nominations for his roles in *Shampoo* (1975) and *Heaven Can Wait* (1978). He has appeared often in television.

SELECTED FILMS: *You're in the Navy Now, USS Teakettle* (1951), *The Bachelor Party* (1957), *Wake Me When It's Over* (1960), *Bye Bye Braverman* (1968), . . . *And Justice for All, Being There* (1979), *Carbon Copy, So Fine* (1981). ■

Ware, Darrell (–1945), screenwriter. Began writing screenplays for Hollywood films in the 1930s. Working alone or in collaboration, usually with Karl TUNBERG, he turned out several entertaining scripts, chiefly for light films.

SELECTED FILMS: *Second Honeymoon, Wife, Doctor and Nurse* (1937), *Just Around the Corner* (1938), *Down Argentine Way, He Married His Wife, Public Deb No. 1* (1940), *Week-End in Havana* (1941), *My Gal Sal* (1942), *Dixie* (1943), *Standing Room Only* (1944), *Bring on the Girls, Kitty* (1945), *Love That Brute* (1950). ■

Warner, H.B. (1876–1958), actor. Appeared on stage in his native England and in the United States before entering early silent films in 1914. A distinguished character actor, he played sensible fathers, eminent officials, and historical figures in dramas and light films during a career that spanned five decades. He received an Oscar nomination for his supporting role in *Lost Horizon* (1937).

SELECTED FILMS: *The Ghost Breaker* (1914), *Zaza* (1913), *French Dressing* (1927), *Man-Made Women, The Naughty Duchess* (1928), *The Reckless Hour* (1931), *Mr. Deeds Goes to Town* (1936), *You Can't Take It With You* (1938), *The Gracie Allen Murder Case, Mr. Smith Goes to Washington* (1939), *Topper Returns* (1941), *It's a Wonderful Life* (1946), *The Judge Steps Out* (1949), *Here Comes the Groom* (1951), *The Ten Commandments* (1956). ▪

Warren, Fred H. (1880–1940), actor. Came to early silent films in the 1910s following experience in vaudeville. He appeared in dramas, light films, and a series of comedy shorts for MGM in 1938. His screen career spanned three decades.

SELECTED FILMS: *The Matrimaniac* (1916), *Her Official Fathers* (1917), *Sylvia on a Spree* (1918), *A Favor to a Friend, Turning the Tables* (1919), *Stephen Steps Out* (1923), *Her Husband's Secret* (1925), *Miss Nobody* (1926), *Three's a Crowd* (1927), *Kiki* (1931), *The Cat's Paw* (1934), *Ship Cafe* (1935). ▪

Warren, Ruth, actress. Appeared as a supporting actress, chiefly in the 1930s, in dramas and light films. Her film career extended into the late 1950s.

SELECTED FILMS: *Lightnin'* (1930), *Mr. Lemon of Orange, Six Cylinder Love, Annabelle's Affairs* (1931), *Mama Loves Papa* (1933), *Doubting Thomas* (1935), *45 Fathers* (1937), *He's a Cockeyed Wonder* (1950), *The Last Hurrah* (1958). ▪

Warwick, Robert (1878–1964), actor. Starred on Broadway before entering silent films in 1914. After military service in the World War, he returned to Hollywood to play leads through the silent era. He developed into a very competent character player when sound was intro-

duced to films. He appeared in more than 150 dramas and light vehicles in a career that stretched over five decades. He played judges, aristocrats, military officers, and other distinguished persons.

SELECTED FILMS: *The Man of the Hour* (1914), *In Mizzoura* (1919), *The Royal Bed* (1931), *Frisco Jenny* (1933), *The Awful Truth* (1937), *Going Places, The Magnificent Fraud* (1939), *Sullivan's Travels* (1941), *I Married a Witch, The Palm Beach Story* (1942), *Bowery to Broadway, The Princess and the Pirate* (1944), *Francis* (1950), *Lady Godiva* (1955), *It Started With a Kiss* (1959). ▪

Washburn, Alice (1861–1929), actress. Came to early silent films in her middle years after a long stage career. She appeared as a supporting player chiefly in light comedies.

SELECTED FILMS: *Aunt Miranda's Cat, Lazy Bill Hudson* (1911), *A Proposal Under Difficulties* (1912), *The Comedian's Downfall, Aunty and the Girls, With the Assistance of Shep* (1913), *The Sultan and the Roller Skates, On the Lazy Line* (1914), *His Dukeship, Mr. Jack, Kernel Nutt, the Janitor, Kernel Nutt Wins a Wife, Kernel Nutt the Footman, Kernel Nutt's Musical Shirt, Kernel Nutt and High Shoes* (1916). ▪

Washburn, Bryant (1889–1963), actor. Appeared on stage before entering early silent films in 1910. He rapidly rose to popularity playing romantic heroes in a succession of films. In the latter part of his career, which extended over four decades, he switched to character roles in dramas, serials, and light films, usually playing distinguished types.

SELECTED FILMS: *The New Manager* (1911), *One Wonderful Night* (1914), *Skinner's Dress Suit, Skinner's Baby* (1917), *The Poor Boob, It Pays to Advertise, Love Insurance, Why Smith Left Home* (1919), *An Amateur Devil, Burglar-Proof, A Full House, The Six Best Cellars, What Happened to Jones* (1920), *My Husband's Wives* (1924), *The Wizard of Oz (1925), Wet Paint (1926), Beware of Widows, Breakfast at Sunrise (1927), Skinner's Big Idea (1928), Swing High (1930), Sweet Genevieve (1947).* ∎

Watkin, Pierre (c.1894–1960), actor. Appeared as a character player in numerous films, chiefly during the 1930s and 1940s. He typically portrayed lawyers, doctors, and other professionals in dramas and light films.

SELECTED FILMS: *Dangerous (1935), It Had to Happen (1936), Bunker Bean, Swing Time (1936), Ever Since Eve, Breakfast for Two (1937), There's Always a Woman, Mr. Doodle Kicks Off (1938), There's That Woman Again (1939), I Love You Again, The Bank Dick (1940), Life With Henry, She Knew All the Answers, Great Guns (1941), Whistling in Dixie (1942), Swing Shift Maisie (1943), Over 21 (1945), Little Giant (1946), State of the Union (1948), The Maverick Queen (1956).* ∎

Watson, Bobby (1888–1965), actor. In vaudeville and on stage before entering silent films in the mid-1920s. A versatile player, he appeared in dramas and light films in a screen career that spanned four decades. His remarkable resemblance to Adolf Hitler led to his repeated portrayal of the dictator during World War II. He worked with some of the leading film comics of the period, including, among others, Bing CROSBY, Bob HOPE, and ABBOTT AND COSTELLO.

SELECTED FILMS: *That Royle Girl (1925), Follow the Leader (1930), Moonlight and Pretzels, Going Hollywood (1933), Wine, Women and Song (1934), The Adventurous Blonde (1937), Everything's on Ice (1939), Hit the Road (1941), The Devil With Hitler (1942), That Nazty Nuisance, The Miracle of Morgan's Creek (1943), Practically Yours (1944), Hold That Blonde (1945), The Paleface (1948), The Story of Mankind (1957).* ∎

Watson, Lucile (1979–1962), actress. On Broadway from the early 1900s before entering films during the early sound period. An accomplished character player, she emerged as a familiar face on the screen during the 1930s and 1940s, appearing in numerous dramas and comedies. She usually portrayed prominent society figures.

SELECTED FILMS: *What Every Woman Knows (1934), A Woman Rebels, Three Smart Girls (1936), The Young in Heart (1938), Model Wife (1941), The Thin Man Goes Home (1945), Julia Misbehaves, That Wonderful Urge (1948), Everybody Does It (1949), Let's Dance (1950), My Forbidden Past (1951).* ∎

Watson, Minor (1889–1965), actor. Began his screen career as a character player in early sound films. For more than three decades he portrayed professionals and genial fathers in numerous dramas and light films.

SELECTED FILMS: *24 Hours (1931), Our Betters, Another Language (1933), The Pursuit of Happiness (1934), Mr. Dynamite, Lady Tubbs (1935), When's Your Birthday? (1937), Love, Honor and Behave (1938), The Flying Irishman, The Hardys Ride Again, Maisie (1939), Moon Over Miami (1941), Woman of the Year (1942), Princess O'Rourke (1943), A Southern Yankee (1948), As Young As You Feel (1951), The Ambassador's Daughter (1956).* ∎

Way Out West (1937), MGM. Dir. James Horne; Sc. Jack Jevne, Charles Rogers, James Parrott, Felix Adler; with Stan Laurel, Oliver Hardy, Sharon Lynne, James Finlayson, Rosina Lawrence, Stanley Fields.

LAUREL AND HARDY'S entry into the Wild West afforded them the opportunity to make one of their funniest films. The boys have to deliver a deed for a mine to the daughter of a dead prospector. James FINLAYSON, a fixture in the duo's films, perfidiously diverts the deed into the hands of the wrong girl. Stan informs the impostor that her father is dead. "Is my poor daddy really dead?" she asks. "I hope so," he replies, "they buried him." Ollie turns over the deed to her. Eventually, they discover the real daughter and set things right, but not before several hilarious bits take place. One of the best moments in the film occurs when the phony heiress locks Stan in her bedroom and jumps on him to get the deed back. When she resorts to tickling, Laurel is utterly powerless as he screams hysterically. The sequence, photographed from various angles, is so effective that Stan's giggling and laughter become infectious. The film has no romantic sub-plot to interfere with the comedy, but the boys do engage in musical interludes. Stan and Ollie sing their comedy version of "In the Blue Ridge Mountains of Virginia" and do a surprisingly good soft shoe number outside a saloon. Even those who are not particularly fond of the pair could enjoy this western spoof.

Wayne, David (1916–), actor. On stage and on Broadway from the late 1930s before entering films in 1949. He has appeared in dramas and light films either as lead or character actor. A gifted performer, he has received greater acclaim for his stage roles than for his film portrayals.

SELECTED FILMS: *Portrait of Jennie, Adam's Rib (1949), The Reformer and the Redhead, My Blue Heaven (1950), Up Front, As Young As You Feel (1951), We're Not Married (1952), How to Marry a Millionaire (1953), The Tender Trap (1955), The Sad Sack (1957), The Front Page (1974), The Apple Dumpling Gang (1975).* ■

Weaver, Charlie. See Cliff Arquette.

Weaver, Doodles (1914–1983), actor. Appeared as a comic character player in features during the 1930s and 1940s, including several Andy CLYDE and THREE STOOGES shorts. He usually played hayseed characters because of his naturally rustic look. He worked with Spike JONES' band for several years. Realizing that his screen career was foundering, he became one of the first comics to enter the new medium, television, hosting his own show by the early 1950s. At age 69 he committed suicide.

SELECTED FILMS: *Behind the Headlines (1937), Li'l Abner (1940), A Girl, a Guy and a Gob (1941), The 30-Foot Bride of Candy Rock (1959), The Ladies' Man (1961), The Spirit Is Willing (1967).* ■

Weaver, Leon (Abner) (1882–1950), actor. Worked in vaudeville in the 1910s with his brother and sister-in-law in a musical comedy act, "The Arkansas Travelers," eventually advancing to Broadway. He did not appear in films until the late 1930s. He played comic roles, chiefly hillbillies, in a string of light films. His brother Frank appeared with Leon in these low-budget comedies.

SELECTED FILMS: *Swing Your Lady, Down in Arkansas (1938), Jeepers Creepers (1939), In Old Missouri, Grand Ole Opry, Friendly Neighbors (1940), Arkansas Judge, Tuxedo Junction (1941), Shepherd of the Ozarks, Mountain Rhythm (1942).* ■

Weaver, Marjorie (1913–), actress. Worked as a model, singer, and stage actress before settling in Hollywood in the mid-1930s. A spirited performer who appeared chiefly in second features, she played leads in dramas and light films.

SELECTED FILMS: *Transatlantic Merry-Go-Round (1934), Big Business, Hot Water, Second Honeymoon (1937), Sally, Irene and Mary, Kentucky Moonshine, Three Blind Mice, I'll Give a Million, Hold That Co-Ed (1938), The Honeymoon's Over (1939), Shooting High (1940), Just Off Broadway (1942), Let's Face It (1943), Fashion Model (1945), We're Not Married (1952).* ■

Weaver, Sigourney (1949–), actress. Appeared on stage, in films, and on Broadway by 1984. She was nominated for a Tony Award for her role in *Hurlyburly*. An attractive and spirited performer, she made her screen debut in 1979. In keeping with her philosophy that she discussed in a magazine interview about trying different genres and a variety of characters, she has starred in suspenseful science fiction and light comedies, working in the United States and in Europe. Her father is the former NBC executive, Pat Weaver.

SELECTED FILMS: *Alien (1979), Deal of the Century (1983), Ghostbusters (1984), One Woman or Two (1987).* ■

Clifton Webb

Webb, Clifton (1891–1966), actor. Performed on stage as a child, later turning to ballroom dancing, stage acting, and sporadic silent film appearances. After an absence of two decades, Webb, born Webb Parnallee Hollenbeck, returned to films in the 1940s portraying haughty, sardonic types in dramas and comedies. He emerged as the master conveyor of witty barbs. One of his most memorable parts was that of the droll babysitter, Mr. Belvedere, in the series of that name. He received Oscar nominations for his roles in *Laura* (1944) and *The Razor's Edge* (1946).

In *Sitting Pretty* he played a dapper gentleman who applies for a job as babysitter for Maureen O'Hara's three rambunctious children. "May I ask what is your profession?" O'Hara inquires. "Certainly," he replies. "I am a genius." In *Laura* he portrayed a cynical columnist who is interrupted by a sales representative who would like him to endorse a pen. "I don't use a pen," he states. "I use a goose quill dipped in venom." Later, in the same film, when detective Dana Andrews unceremoniously enters an apartment, Webb inquires: "Haven't you heard of science's newest triumph, the doorbell?" And finally, in *The Dark Corner* (1946) he comments: "How I detest the dawn! The grass looks like it's been left out all night."

SELECTED FILMS: *Polly With a Past (1920), New Toys (1925), Sitting Pretty (1948), Mr. Belvedere Goes to College (1949), Cheaper by the Dozen, For Heaven's Sake (1950), Mr. Belvedere Rings the Bell (1951), Dreamboat (1952), Mr. Scoutmaster (1953), The Remarkable Mr. Pennypacker, Holiday for Lovers (1959), Satan Never Sleeps (1962).* ■

Webber, Robert (1924–), actor. Has appeared in films and television in both dramas and comedies. He made his screen debut in 1950 and has since played supporting roles in numerous films. One of his better and rare comic performances occurred in *Private Benjamin*, an army comedy starring Goldie HAWN, in which he portrayed a tough, gung-ho paratroop commander who succumbs to his lust during war games. In one scene he alerts his soldiers: "There are mine fields up there. Most of the mines are inert. Some are ert."

SELECTED FILMS: *Highway 301 (1950), The Choirboys (1977), Casey's Shadow, Revenge of the Pink Panther (1978), Private Benjamin, Sunday Lovers (1980), S.O.B. (1981), Wrong Is Right (1982).* ■

Weber, Joe. See Weber and Fields.

Weber and Fields. A popular burlesque and vaudeville comedy team of
the 1920s and 1930s. The duo, Joe Weber
(1867–1942) and his partner Lew Fields
(1867–1941), appeared in a handful of
shorts and feature films in both the silent
and sound periods, but their screen work
never brought them the recognition they
had previously attained on stage. Fields
appeared in several films without his
partner.

SELECTED FILMS: Two of the Bravest,
The Best of Enemies, Fatty and the
Broadway Stars (1915), The Worst of
Friends (1916), The Corner Grocer
(1918), Friendly Enemies (1925), Mike
and Meyer (1927), Blossoms on Broadway (1937), Lillian Russell (1940). ∎

Weidler, Virginia (1927–1968), actress. Entered films at age three and
within a few years emerged as a popular
child star. Complete with freckles and
pigtails, she specialized in the roles
of little terrors and entertainingly met
the demand in a succession of light
films during the 1930s and 1940s. She
stole many a scene from the adult performers who were unfortunate enough to
appear with her. She began her stage
career at age six. As she matured, she
found film roles difficult to obtain. After
retiring from her screen career at age
sixteen, she starred in a Broadway show
at eighteen.

In The Philadelphia Story (1940) she
played Katharine HEPBURN'S precocious kid sister. Disappointed in her
sister's decision to marry John Howard,
she relishes every opportunity to belittle
him. In one scene at the local stables he
has trouble controlling his horse.
"What's the matter, Betsy," he says to
the animal, trying to calm it down, "you
act worried." "Maybe because his name
is Jack," Virginia explains.

SELECTED FILMS: Surrender (1931),
After Tonight (1933), Mrs. Wiggs of the
Cabbage Patch (1934), Laddie, Freckles
(1935), The Girl of the Ozarks, Trouble
for Two (1936), Mother Carey's Chick-
ens, Out West With the Hardys (1938),
The Great Man Votes, Fixer Dugan, The
Under-Pup, Bad Little Angel (1939),
Gold Rush Maisie (1940), Barnacle Bill
(1941), Babes on Broadway, Born to Sing
(1942), The Youngest Profession, Best
Foot Forward (1943). ∎

Weis, Don (1922–), director. Began
directing films in 1951 after working at
miscellaneous positions in Hollywood
studios. Often laboring with routine dramas and light films, he managed to lift
them slightly out of the mundane by
enhancing them with his individualistic
style.

SELECTED FILMS: Bannerline (1951),
Just This Once (1952), I Love Melvin,
Remains to Be Seen, A Slight Case of
Larceny, The Affairs of Dobie Gillis, Half
a Hero (1953), Critic's Choice (1963),
Pajama Party (1964), Billie (1965), The
Ghost in the Invisible Bikini (1966), Did
You Hear the One About the Traveling
Saleslady? (1968). ∎

Weld, Tuesday (1943–), actress. Appeared as a child actress in television
and low-budget films. Although numerous personal problems affected her
screen career, she was able to demonstrate her acting talents in several vehicles. Born Susan Weld, she has starred in
dramas and light films.

In Soldier in the Rain Jackie GLEA-
SON saves her from being roughed up
and she heartily thanks him. "You were
just like Randolph Scott on the late, late
movie," she says, adding, "a fat
Randolph Scott."

SELECTED FILMS: Rock Rock Rock
(1956), Rally 'Round the Flag, Boys!
(1958), The Five Pennies (1959), High
Time (1960), Bachelor Flat (1962), I'll
Take Sweden (1965), Lord Love a Duck
(1966), Serial (1979). ∎

Weldon, Ben (1901–), actor. Appeared
in films in England during the early
1930s before returning to his native

United States in 1936. Rather short and moon-faced, he portrayed small-time hoodlums and other minor characters in dramas and light films for the next 20 years, never achieving lead parts or any degree of stardom. He worked with some of the foremost screen personalities and comics of the period, including Shirley TEMPLE, Bing CROSBY, ABBOTT AND COSTELLO, Bob HOPE, Danny KAYE, and Dean MARTIN and Jerry LEWIS.

SELECTED FILMS: Kid Galahad, The King and the Chorus Girl, Back in Circulation (1937), Little Miss Broadway, Little Orphan Annie (1938), Hollywood Cavalcade, The Star Maker (1939), All Through the Night, Maisie Gets Her Man (1942), Here Comes Elmer (1943), It's in the Bag (1945), The Noose Hangs High, A Song Is Born (1948), Sorrowful Jones (1949), The Lemon Drop Kid (1951), Hollywood or Bust (1956), Spook Chasers (1957). ■

Wells, George (1909–), screenwriter. Wrote for radio before turning to Hollywood in 1946. Working alone and in collaboration, he penned many light screenplays for MGM. He occasionally tried his hand at producing.

SELECTED FILMS: Till the Clouds Roll By (1946), Merton of the Movies, The Show-Off (1947), Take Me Out to the Ball Game (1949), Summer Stock, The Toast of New Orleans (1950), Angels in the Outfield (1951), I Love Melvin (1953), Don't Go Near the Water, Designing Woman (1957), Ask Any Girl (1959), Where the Boys Are (1960), The Honeymoon Machine (1961), The Horizontal Lieutenant (1962), Penelope (1966), Three Bites of the Apple (1967), The Impossible Years (1968), Cover Me, Babe (1970). ■

Wesson, Dick (1919–1979), actor. Worked as a nightclub comic before entering films as a comic-relief character player in the late 1940s. He appeared in several dramas and light films, alternating with television appearances and live performances in clubs. He committed suicide at age 59.

SELECTED FILMS: Destination Moon (1949), Sunny Side of the Street (1951), About Face (1952), The Desert Song, Calamity Jane (1953), Paris Follies of 1956 (1955), The Errand Boy (1961), Rollercoaster (1977). ■

West, Billy (1893–1975), actor. Appeared in vaudeville before entering films in 1916. The most successful of the Charlie CHAPLIN imitators, West, born Roy B. Weissberg, starred in numerous comedy shorts assisted by such future comedians as Charlie CHASE and Oliver HARDY. His screen likeness to the Little Fellow was uncanny, although the little subtleties and much of the pathos, of course, were lacking. Eventually, he developed his own screen character, proving that he could be quite funny in his own right. He appeared in several features during the early sound era.

SELECTED FILMS: His Waiting Career (1916), His Day Out, Cupid's Rival, The Straight and the Narrow (1917), The Slave, The Rogue, Playmates, He's In Again (1918), A Wild Woman (1919), Sweethearts (1921), Don't Be Foolish (1923), Lucky Fool (1927), The Diamond Trail (1933), Motive for Revenge (1935). ■

West, Mae (1892–1980), actress. Appeared as a child actress on stage and worked in stock, burlesque, vaudeville, and on Broadway in the 1920s before entering films in the early sound era. She wrote, produced, and performed in plays on Broadway. Her first play was called *Sex*, and her second, *Drag*, was about homosexuality. A controversial performer on stage because of her sexual themes and innuendoes, she transported this contentious aspect of her act into her features. She kept the Hollywood censors busy with her double entendres, her songs, and her famous aphorisms. Her appearance on radio in the 1940s as a

Mae West (right) and Rochelle Hudson

guest of Edgar BERGEN and his dummy, Charlie McCarthy, caused a flurry of condemnation because of certain bits of dialogue that today seem harmless.

A buxom, slightly stocky blonde, she often parodied the sexual image that the prudish found so offensive. By the mid-1930s she had achieved the distinction of being the most highly paid woman in the United States. She usually wrote or collaborated on her screenplays, several of which were based on her own Broadway scripts. By the end of the decade her popularity declined. She attempted a slight comeback in 1970 at age 78, but the critics panned the film. A talented and gifted comedienne during her lifetime, she emerged as more than just another screen personality. During World War II, soldiers named a life-jacket after her.

Entertainers, writers, and others frequently quoted her one-liners. "There are two perfectly good men," a suitor says to her in *Klondike Annie*, "one dead and the other unborn." "Which one are you?" Mae retorts. "I wasn't always rich," she confides in *She Done Him Wrong*. "There was a time when I didn't know where my next husband was coming from." "For a long time I was ashamed of the way I lived," she confesses in *Goin' to Town*. "You reformed?" a lover queries. "No," she replies, "I got over being ashamed." In *Belle of the Nineties* her maid asks:

"Weren't you a little nervous when he gave you those jewels?" "No," Mae replies, "I was calm and collected." When her limousine breaks down in *Go West, Young Man*, handsome mechanic Randolph Scott is called to the scene. "I'm sorry," he says. "I don't carry spare parts." "Of course not," Mae replies, studying his well-built frame. "I wouldn't expect you to." And in *I'm No Angel*, when someone remarks that she was born in August, Mae replies: "Yeah, one of the hot months." Her autobiography, *Goodness Had Nothing to Do With It*, was published in 1959.

SELECTED FILMS: *Night After Night* (1932), *She Done Him Wrong*, *I'm No Angel* (1933), *Belle of the Nineties* (1934), *Goin' to Town* (1935), *Klondike Annie*, *Go West, Young Man* (1946), *Every Day's a Holiday* (1938), *My Little Chickadee* (1940), *The Heat's On* (1943), *Myra Breckinridge* (1970). ■

Westcott, Gordon (1903–1935), actor. Worked in early sound films, chiefly for Warner Brothers, as a supporting player until his untimely death. A handsome figure, he appeared in dramas as well as light films.

SELECTED FILMS: *Enemies of the Law* (1931), *Love Me Tonight* (1932), *He Learned About Women*, *The Working Man*, *Footlight Parade* (1933), *Call It Luck*, *Circus Clown*, *Kansas City Princess* (1934), *Go Into Your Dance*, *Going Highbrow*, *This Is the Life*, *Two Fisted* (1935). ■

Western comedies. Films in this genre fall into one of two general categories—comedies with a western background or the western spoof. One of the earliest western parodies was a short produced by Edison's film company titled "The Little Train Robbery." It was released a few years after Edwin S. Porter's "The Great Train Robbery" (1903) made its appearance.

Porter's film ushered in the western genre which soon proved not only popular but extremely lucrative. It was not unusual for a G. M. "Broncho Billy" Anderson western short, which cost $800 to produce, to earn $50,000. He produced, directed, and starred in more than 300 westerns between 1908 and 1915. The famous western star of silents and early sound films, Tom Mix, made more than 100 western shorts from 1911 to 1917, many of which emphasized his particular brand of casual humor. In the next few years his films specialized in action. Hoot GIBSON, who appeared as a supporting player and stuntman in the pre–World War I John Ford–Harry Carey westerns, carried on in the tradition of Tom Mix by starring in westerns with a comedy slant in the 1920s. Stage comedian Victor MOORE, who was to gain greater popularity decades later, made an early silent film appearance in 1915 in the western comedy *Chimmie Fadden Out West*.

Other screen actors began to appear in comedies utilizing western backdrops. One of the first was Franklyn FARNUM, who starred in such films as *A Stranger From Somewhere* (1916), *The Clean-Up* (1917), and *The Fighting Grin* (1918). Harry CAREY was featured in a series of comedy westerns directed by John FORD, including *Bucking Broadway* (1917), *A Woman's Fool* (1918), and *Roped* (1919). Ford would continue his relationship with the western for the next four decades, helping to establish it as a distinct American art form. The most popular screen personality of the period, Douglas FAIRBANKS, starred in a series of successful spoofs that glorified the western way of life. In films like *Manhattan Madness* (1916), *Wild and Woolly* (1917), and *Knickerbocker Buckaroo* (1919) he explored variations of this theme. In one he would have a western hero come east to teach the city slickers a thing or two, while in another film he would have an easterner travel west.

Producer Mack SENNETT and his zany group of clowns were quick to contribute their buffoonery and slapstick to the genre. In 1916 Mack SWAIN starred as a brave sheriff in "His Bitter Pill." His zeal for justice leads to a series of funny incidents. Charlie MURRAY starred in "His Hereafter" the same year, also playing a sheriff. In this comedy short he has problems with a local gambling hall.

By the 1920s western comedies began to concentrate on poking fun at the western genre and its hero. Roscoe "Fatty" ARBUCKLE appeared as a sheriff in *The Round-Up* in 1920. In 1921 Ben TURPIN made *A Small Town Idol*, produced by Sennett. He played a cowboy star who visits his home town. Ziegfeld Follies star Will ROGERS appeared in several western spoofs during the 1920s, including *Uncensored Movies* (1923) and "Two Wagons, Both Covered" (1924). In the former he burlesques western stars William S. Hart and Tom Mix, while the latter parodies director James Cruze's 1923 epic western, *The Covered Wagon*. Buster KEATON starred in *Go West* (1925) in which he portrayed Friendless, a character whose only pal is a cow named Brown Eyes.

Surprisingly, the 1930s, the decade which several film critics and historians call the "golden age of American films," offered little in the way of western comedies in relation to the large quantity of films produced. Eddie CANTOR repeated his Broadway role in the film version of *Whoopee!* (1930), playing a hypochondriac who travels west for his health in this "modern" western comedy. Some of Mae WEST'S films, such as *Klondike Annie* (1936), had elements of a western background, but they were not true westerns. *My Little Chickadee*, in which she co-starred with W. C. FIELDS, was released in 1940. LAUREL AND HARDY starred in *Way Out West* in 1937, one of their better feature-length comedies in which they do a few musical numbers as well as have a run-in with their perennial nemesis James FINLAYSON. Dramatic actors and actresses carried the genre, rather than comic players. In 1935 Charles LAUGHTON starred in *Ruggles of Red Gap*, in which he played an English butler whom American cattle baron Charles RUGGLES won from an English lord (Roland YOUNG) in a poker game. The satire contrasts the different lifestyles of the aspiring social climbers of western America with genteel English society. Mickey ROONEY and the HARDY clan brought their folksy humor to *Out West With the Hardys* (1938) when they spent their vacation at a western ranch. James STEWART and Marlene Dietrich starred in the satirical *Destry Rides Again* (1939), based on Max Brand's often-filmed novel. Stewart played a marshall who does not believe in carrying a gun, while Dietrich portrayed a saloon singer who falls in love with him. Weak as a western, the film gained from the dynamic personalities of its stars and an exceptional supporting cast, including such character players as Una MERKEL, Mischa AUER, Charles WINNINGER, and Billy GILBERT.

If the 1930s were the golden years of films, then the following decade can aptly be labeled the golden years of the western comedy. Almost every major screen comic and comedy team turned out at least one western. As mentioned above, Mae West and W. C. Fields started the decade off by teaming up in *My Little Chickadee* in 1940. Jack BENNY in the same year starred in the western spoof *Buck Benny Rides Again*, in which he attempts to persuade Ellen Drew that he is an authentic cowboy. *Go West,* another 1940 entry, starred the MARX BROTHERS in their zany antics including a wild climactic train ride. ABBOTT AND COSTELLO appeared in *Ride 'Em Cowboy* and *Rio Rita*, both released in 1942. In the latter, a remake of WHEELER AND WOOLSEY'S 1929 musical comedy, the boys work at a western ranch which is infested with Nazis. The RITZ BROTHERS made *Hi Ya, Chum* in 1943, a mediocre comedy in which they played restaurant owners in a California boom town. In 1946 Bing CROSBY and Bob HOPE co-starred in *Road to Utopia*, a better-than-average entry of their "ROAD" films. Two years later Hope teamed with Jane RUSSELL to make *The Paleface*, one of the most popular western spoofs of the decade. Even the THREE STOOGES participated in the genre with such shorts as "Three Troubledoers" (1946) and "Out West" (1947).

The number of western comedies decreased in the 1950s. In 1950 comedienne Joan DAVIS starred in *Traveling Saleswoman*, a mediocre comedy western co-starring Andy DEVINE. The following year Fred MacMURRAY starred in *Callaway Went Thataway*, a satire on the current popularity of Hopalong Cassidy. The new comedy team of MARTIN AND LEWIS appeared in *My Friend Irma Goes West* (1950) and starred in *Pardners* (1956), a disappointing comedy. The sluggish pace of the genre continued into the 1960s. Cowboy star John Wayne made the slapstick comedy *McLintock!* in 1963. Lee Marvin starred in a dual role in the western spoof, *Cat Ballou* (1965), for which he won an Oscar. He played a drunken gunslinger and an outlaw. That same year the Three Stooges made their last film, the feature-length *The Outlaws Is Coming*. A funny satire, it featured a large cast and some of their best routines. With the western itself fading from the American screen, western comedies became a rare breed. Actor James GARNER, who appeared for years on a western television show, starred in *Support Your Local Sheriff* in 1969 and a sequel, *Support Your Local Gunfighter*, two years later. The satirical *Butch Cassidy and the Sundance Kid* (1969), one of the best entries of the period, starred Paul NEWMAN and Robert REDFORD in the title roles.

In the following decades other western spoofs appeared sporadically. One of the most popular, Mel BROOKS' *Blazing Saddles* (1974), starred Cleavon Little as a black sheriff, Gene WILDER as a gunslinger, and Madeline KAHN as a saloon singer in the style of Marlene Dietrich.

This was Brooks' first hit film. Wilder made another attempt at the genre in *The Frisco Kid* in 1979, in which he portrays a Polish rabbi traveling west.

Some film critics and historians believe that the western has been replaced by the urban crime film with the local police officers and private detectives like Clint Eastwood substituting for the western heroes and sheriffs. Others think the genre has been superseded by the science fiction films or space operas like *Star Wars*. It may be too early to make a final judgment on the status of the western and its mythical icons. If we lose this genre, we lose an important part of our heritage as well as the western comedies and spoofs that usually follow in its wake.

Westley, Helen (1875–1942), actress. In vaudeville and stock and on Broadway before entering films in the early 1930s. She appeared as a character player in numerous dramas and light films, often playing crotchety, domineering but likable old dowagers.

SELECTED FILMS: *Moulin Rouge* (1934), *Show Boat, Dimples, Banjo on My Knee, Stowaway* (1936), *I'll Take Romance* (1937), *She Married an Artist, Keep Smiling, The Baroness and the Butler* (1938), *Zaza, Wife, Husband and Friend* (1939), *Lady With Red Hair* (1940), *Million Dollar Baby, The Smiling Ghost, Sunny* (1941), *Bedtime Story, My Favorite Spy* (1942). ∎

Westman, Nydia (1902–1970), actress. On stage as a child, later in stock and on Broadway before entering films in the early 1930s. A short, plump supporting player, she appeared in dramas and light films, often as spinsters in comic roles. She later was successful in television as well.

SELECTED FILMS: *Strange Justice* (1932), *One Night of Love, Ladies Should Listen* (1934), *Sweet Adeline, A Feather in Her Hat* (1935), *The Gorgeous Hussy* (1936), *Hullabaloo, 40 Little Mothers* (1940), *The Chocolate Soldier* (1941), *They All Kissed the Bride* (1942), *The Late George Apley* (1947), *The Velvet Touch* (1948), *The Horse in the Gray Flannel Suit* (1968), *Rabbit Run* (1970). ∎

Weston, Jack (1925–), actor. On Broadway and in television before settling in Hollywood in the late 1950s as a supporting or feature player. A portly figure with thinning hair, he has appeared in dramas and light films.

In *The Four Seasons* he played Rita Moreno's husband. "Do you have to say everything on your mind?" he says critically. "Do you think your thoughts should just fall down on your tongue like a gumball machine?"

SELECTED FILMS: *Stage Struck* (1958), *Please Don't Eat the Daisies* (1960), *All in a Night's Work, The Honeymoon Machine* (1961), *It's Only Money* (1962), *Palm Springs Weekend* (1963), *The Incredible Mr. Limpet* (1964), *The April Fools, Cactus Flower* (1969), *A New Leaf* (1971), *Fuzz* (1972), *Gator, The Ritz* (1976), *The Four Seasons* (1981), *High Road to China* (1983). ∎

What's Up, Tiger Lily? See Woody Allen.

Wheeler and Woolsey. Famous vaudeville and Broadway comedy team of the late 1920s who appeared in a series of comedy films during the 1930s. Bert Wheeler (1895–1968) and Robert Woolsey (1889–1937) teamed up in 1928 in a Ziegfeld show, *Rio Rita*. Before this, Wheeler had been a child performer with Gus Edwards' children's act and a vaudeville headliner in an act with his wife, Betty. He then joined Flo Ziegfeld for six years in the famous showman's Follies.

Robert Woolsey had been a jockey before he appeared in stock. In 1919 he was on Broadway and by 1921 he starred in a hit play. The bespectacled comedian with his perennial cigar enjoyed several further stage successes before Ziegfeld linked him with Wheeler.

Their first few films cast them as supporting players doing their old stage routines as comic relief within the settings of musical comedy. By 1930 they were given the opportunity to star in their own vehicle. The film, like those that were to follow, was panned by most critics but liked by the public. Their comedy relied heavily on their old material, on occasional patter songs, and on a host of puns and one-liners. If something worked well in an earlier film, it was repeated several times in later works. When Woolsey died in the late 1930s, Wheeler continued to appear in occasional films.

Today's audiences usually find the duo's pacing too slow, while the films in general are treated as oddities. However, enough good gags are scattered throughout each to hold one's attention. Never considered in the same league with the MARX BROTHERS or LAUREL AND HARDY, this minor team with its physical comedy and low humor nevertheless was able to entertain a generation of viewers. In *Half-Shot at Sunrise*, a World War I comedy, they disguise themselves as waiters. "I can't eat this duck," a customer complains. "Send for the manager." "It's no use," Woolsey confesses. "He won't eat it either." In *Caught Plastered* they played vaudevillians. "The manager said he didn't allow any profanity in his theater," Wheeler reminds his partner. "We didn't use any profanity," Woolsey insists. "No," Wheeler adds, "but the audience did." In *Peach O'Reno* Wheeler impersonated a woman. When someone remarks that he looks like a loose woman, Woolsey quips, "Don't worry, she'll be tight before the evening is over."

SELECTED FILMS: *Rio Rita* (1929), *The Cuckoos, Dixiana, Half Shot at Sunrise, Hook, Line and Sinker* (1930), *Cracked Nuts, Caught Plastered, Oh! Oh! Cleopatra, Peach O'Reno* (1931), *Girl Crazy, Hold 'Em Jail* (1932), *So This Is Africa, Diplomaniacs* (1933), *Hips Hips Hooray, Cockeyed Cavaliers, Kentucky Kernels* (1934), *The Nitwits* (1935), *Silly Billies, Mummy's Boys* (1936), *On Again, Off Again, High Flyers* (1937). ∎

Whelan, Tim (1893–1957), director, screenwriter. In theater as an actor and director before coming to Hollywood in 1920 to write screenplays. After working as a GAGWRITER for several Harold LLOYD comedies, he switched to directing films in the late 1920s. He turned out several competent but unstartling dramas and light films. He also directed films in England.

SELECTED FILMS: *The Perfect Gentleman* (1935), *Twin Beds, Seven Days' Leave* (1942), *Higher and Higher* (1943), *Swing Fever, Step Lively* (1944), *Texas Lady* (1955). ∎

Whistling in the Dark (1941), MGM. *Dir.* S. Sylvan Simon; *Sc.* Harry Clork, Albert Mannheimer, Robert MacGunigle; with Red Skelton, Ann Rutherford, Virginia Grey, Conrad Veidt, Rags Ragland, Eve Arden.

Not unlike fellow comedian Bob HOPE, who got his big film break playing the lead in a crime comedy, *The Cat and the Canary*, Red SKELTON owes much to his lead in *Whistling in the Dark*. Based on Lavinia Cross and Edward Carpenter's stage play about a mystery writer entangled in a real-life crime plot, the film has Skelton caught by villainous Conrad Veidt, who wants the writer to think up the perfect crime. The events are often hilarious as our hero attempts both to extricate himself from his dilemma and catch the crooks. The film was so successful at the box office that Skelton appeared in two sequels, *Whistling in Dixie* (1942) and *Whistling in Brooklyn* (1943). MGM had made an earlier version of the play in 1933 starring Ernest TRUEX as the thriller writer.

White, Alice (1907–), actress. Worked as a secretary and script girl before entering silent films in the late 1920s. A lively performer in light films as well as in dramas, she rapidly became a lead player, successfully making the transition into sound films. But as quickly as she rose, her film career soon plummeted and by the early 1940s she was assigned primarily to minor roles.

SELECTED FILMS: *The Sea Tiger, American Beauty, Breakfast at Sunrise (1927), The Big Noise, Gentlemen Prefer Blondes, The Mad Hour, Lingerie, Harold Teen, Show Girl (1928), Naughty Baby, Hot Stuff, Broadway Babies (1929), Playing Around, Sweet Mama, The Widow From Chicago, Sweethearts on Parade (1930), The Naughty Flirt (1931), Luxury Liner, King for a Night (1933), Gift of Gab (1934), Sweet Music (1935), Flamingo Road (1949).* ∎

White, Jesse (1919–), actor. In burlesque, vaudeville, stock, and on Broadway in the early 1940s before entering films in the 1950s. Stocky and moonfaced, he appeared as a character actor in numerous dramas and light films, often portraying humorous toughs.

SELECTED FILMS: *Kiss of Death (1947), Texas, Brooklyn and Heaven (1948), Harvey (1950), Bedtime for Bonzo (1951), Chimp for a Day (1953), The Girl Rush (1955), Designing Woman (1957), Three Blondes in His Life (1960), On the Double (1961), It's Only Money (1962), It's a Mad, Mad, Mad, Mad World (1963), The Ghost in the Invisible Bikini (1966), The Reluctant Astronaut (1967), The Cat From Outer Space (1978).* ∎

White, Jules (–1985), director, producer. Began in films working as a GAG-MAN for Mack SENNETT before turning to directing comedy shorts. He directed many films starring some of the foremost comics of the period. He is most noted for guiding the careers of the THREE STOOGES, hiring the trio for Columbia Pictures in 1934 and directing 104 of their two-reelers. His role in film comedy spanned five decades. He retired in the 1960s and was singled out by the Academy of Motion Picture Arts and Sciences for his contributions to film comedy.

SELECTED FILMS: *Three Missing Links (1938), Oily to Bed, Oily to Rise, Three Sappy People (1939), You Nazty Spy, A-Plumbing We Will Go (1940), I'll Never Heil Again, In the Sweet Pie and Pie (1941), Loco Boy Makes Good, What's the Matador? (1942), Dizzy Detectives, Back From the Front (1943), Crash Goes the Hash (1944), Idiots Deluxe (1945), Beer Barrel Polecats (1946), Half-Wits' Holiday (1947), I'm a Monkey's Uncle (1948), The Ghost Talks (1949), Love at First Bite (1950), Scrambled Brains (1951), A Missed Fortune (1952), Booty and the Beast (1953), Musty Musketeers (1954), Stone Age Romeos (1955), Creeps (1956), Rusty Romeos (1957), Sweet and Hot (1958), Sappy Bullfighters (1959).* ∎

White, Leo (1880–1948), actor. Worked in early silent films, especially as a supporting player in comedy shorts. He worked alongside some of the leading comedians of the period, including, among others, Charlie CHAPLIN and LAUREL AND HARDY. A versatile actor, he portrayed various characters, including German spies, elegant gentlemen, members of royalty, and gypsy women. His film career in comedies spanned four decades.

SELECTED FILMS: *His New Job, A Night Out, The Champion, In the Park, The Jitney Elopement, The Tramp, Work, A Woman, The Bank, Shanghaied, A Night in the Show (1915), Carmen, Police!, Triple Trouble, The Floorwalker, The Fireman, The Vagabond, The Count, Behind the Screen (1916), The Rustle of Silk (1923), The Ladybird (1927), Fra Diavolo (1933), The Great Dictator (1940).* ∎

White, Pearl (1889–1938), actress. Worked in a circus as a teenager and in stock before entering silent films in 1910. Although she attained her greatest popularity as a serial queen, beginning with *The Perils of Pauline* (1914), she earlier appeared in numerous one- and two-reel comedies for several studios. A pretty and charming performer, she actually had three screen careers before retiring from films in the mid-1920s. Her first consisted of the film shorts mentioned above, including westerns and dramas; the second, for which she is most famous, a string of serials; and finally several full-length dramas, the least successful of her endeavors. Her autobiography, *Just Me*, was published in 1919.

SELECTED FILMS: *The Life of Buffalo Bill, The Hoodoo, A Summer Flirtation, The Woman Hater (1910), Home Sweet Home (1911), Pals, Bella's Beau, Oh, Such a Night!, The Chorus Girl (1912), Heroic Harold, Pearl As a Detective, Accident Insurance, The Girl Reporter (1913), Lizzie and the Iceman, Willie's Disguise (1914).* ∎

Whitman, Phil, director. Turned out several silent comedy shorts in the 1920s. He worked chiefly with the popular comic Billy BEVAN, directing his "Tired Businessman" comedy series.

SELECTED FILMS: *Caught in the Kitchen, Motoring Mamas, Hubby's Latest Alibi, His New Steno (1928), Button My Back, Foolish Husbands, Pink Pajamas (1929).* ∎

Whoopee! (1930), UA. *Dir.* Thornton Freeland; *Sc.* William Counselman; with Eddie Cantor, Eleanor Hunt, Paul Gregory, John Rutherford.

In this film, based on the successful Broadway show produced by Flo Ziegfeld, which in turn was adapted from the stage comedy, *The Nervous Wreck* by Owen Davis, Eddie CANTOR recreates his role of a wisecracking hypochondriac who travels west for a quiet respite. At one point he remarks: "The doctor said if I have one more operation, he's going to put in a zipper." Inevitably, he finds himself entangled in a young couple's romance, involved with an Indian tribe, and pursued by a vindictive

sheriff and posse. The sheriff, looking for the culprit who ran off with his girl, questions the disguised Cantor. "Where are you from?" he asks. "We moved," Eddie replies. The gags generally hold up quite well, but some of the musical production numbers, staged by Busby Berkeley before he embarked for Warner Brothers, betray their stage origins. The film was one of the first musicals to be shot in two-color Technicolor (later, more refined Technicolor used a three-color process). The results are pleasing in a garish sort of way. Singer-comedian Cantor supplies several lively songs, including "Making Whoopee" and "My Baby Just Cares for Me," in this curious but entertaining relic. It was remade in 1944 as *Up in Arms* starring Danny Kaye.

Wickes, Mary (1916–), actress. Appeared in stock and on Broadway before settling in Hollywood in the early 1940s as a character player. An angular comedienne, she has often played comical meddlers or friends of the female leads in a succession of films.

SELECTED FILMS: *The Man Who Came to Dinner, Private Buckaroo, Who Done It? (1942), Higher and Higher (1943), June Bride (1948), The Petty Girl (1950), Young Man With Ideas (1952), Good Morning, Miss Dove (1955), Don't Go Near the Water (1957), It Happened to Jane (1959), The Music Man (1962), Dear Heart (1964), How to Murder Your Wife (1965), The Trouble With Angels (1966), Where Angels Go, Trouble Follows (1968), Snowball Express (1972).* ∎

Wild and Woolly (1917), Par. *Dir.* John Emerson; *Sc.* Anita Loos; with Douglas Fairbanks, Eileen Percy, Joseph Singleton, Forest Seabury, Charles Stevens.

At the time that Fairbanks made this action comedy, westerns had become very popular at the box office and were a staple of several Hollywood studios. For the most part, the cowboy stars of the period took the genre seriously. The granite-faced William S. Hart, for instance, who worked for the same studio as Fairbanks, portrayed a no-nonsense western hero of the strong, silent type who pursued injustice relentlessly. Fairbanks, on the other hand, treated the genre lightly. His bouncy enthusiasm and optimism dominated the plots and themes of his westerns, turning the films into good-natured and highly entertaining satires of the genre. In *Wild and Woolly* he played an eastern railroad clerk who yearned for the adventurous West. Arriving in Arizona, he finds that his dream has come true. Here is the true West he had read about and longed for. What he doesn't know is that the townspeople, learning that he is coming to evaluate the financial possibilities of the community, decide to "dress up" the town to his liking, complete with an old-fashioned saloon and dancehall, plenty of shooting (their guns containing blanks) and riding in the dusty streets, and a general atmosphere of the "old West." However, when some thieves decide to take advantage of the situation, Fairbanks springs into action and rounds up not only the gang but a band of hostile Indians as well, all to the townspeople's surprise and delight. Fairbanks made a series of lively westerns, including *Manhattan Madness* (1916) and *Knickerbocker Buckaroo* (1919), in which he kidded the genre as well as his own philosophy of the romantic easterner, bored with his job, who can find release only in the great outdoors. His first film, "The Lamb," made two years earlier, pitted him against a group of Indians whom he subdued without the use of weapons. He made more than 40 films between 1915 and 1931, employing his acrobatics to good advantage in costume dramas and films with contemporary settings.

Wilder, Billy (1906–), director, screenwriter. Worked as a screenwriter in Berlin before immigrating to the United States in the early 1930s. Arriving almost

penniless and with no knowledge of English, he joined Hollywood's immigrant community, which included such notable directors as Ernst LUBITSCH and Fritz Lang. After several sporadic collaborations on film scripts, he linked up in 1938 with fellow writer Charles BRACKETT. Together, they turned out a succession of classic screenplays, including, among others, *Ninotchka* and *Sunset Boulevard*. He continued to collaborate with other screenwriters, chiefly I. A. L. DIAMOND, while taking on directorial assignments as well.

His solo work, either as writer or director, has often reflected his more cynical side, that part of him which was usually softened by his more genteel collaborators. Except for an isolated dark allegory like *Ace in the Hole* (1951), his dramatic films often met with the same critical acclaim and commercial success as did his comedies. A disciple of Lubitsch, Wilder has tried to incorporate indirection, elegance, wit, and a fluid camera into most of his films. Critics, however, have occasionally objected to his use of exaggerated caricature, as in *One, Two, Three*; his inability to come to terms with serious themes, in works like *A Foreign Affair*; and his general departure from the Lubitsch style, exemplified by his last six or seven films. But as a body of work, his comedy films, aside from their high entertainment value, have helped to raise the level of maturity, sophistication, and intelligence of the typical Hollywood fare.

SELECTED FILMS (as screenwriter): *Music in the Air* (1934), *Luxury Liner* (1935), *Midnight, What a Life, Ninotchka* (1939), *Ball of Fire* (1942).

SELECTED FILMS (as director-screenwriter): *The Major and the Minor* (1942), *A Foreign Affair* (1948), *Sabrina* (1954), *The Seven Year Itch* (1955), *Some Like It Hot* (1959), *The Apartment* (1960), *One, Two, Three* (1961), *Irma la Douce* (1963), *Kiss Me, Stupid* (1964), *The Fortune Cookie* (1966), *Avanti!* (1972), *The Front Page* (1974), *Buddy Buddy* (1981). ∎

Gilda Radner and Gene Wilder

Wilder, Gene (1935–), actor. On stage and on Broadway before establishing himself as one of Hollywood's major comics. With his wide-eyed stare, he has played nervous, easily disconcerted characters. He has appeared in several Mel BROOKS comedies and has directed a few of his own films. He has written, directed, and starred in *The Adventure of Sherlock Holmes' Smarter Brother* (1975). He received an Academy Award nomination for his role as the emotionally unstable bookkeeper in *The Producers*.

In *Young Frankenstein* he played the title character who, at a train depot, asks a youngster: "Pardon me, boy! Is this the Transylvania Station?"

SELECTED FILMS: *Bonnie and Clyde* (1967), *The Producers* (1968), *Start the Revolution Without Me* (1970), *Willy Wonka and the Chocolate Factory* (1971), *Everything You Always Wanted to Know About Sex (but Were Afraid to Ask)* (1972), *Blazing Saddles, Young Frankenstein* (1974), *Silver Streak* (1976), *The World's Greatest Lover* (1977), *The Frisco Kid* (1979), *Stir Crazy* (1980), *Hanky Panky* (1982), *The Woman in Red* (1984). ■

Willes, Jean (1922–), actress. Began her screen career in the early 1940s. A tall, attractive blonde, she has appeared in dramas and light films, often portray-

ing loud prostitutes. Although she was given a few minor leads, she has never attained any degree of stardom.

SELECTED FILMS: *The Winner's Circle* (1948), *A Woman of Distinction* (1950), *Gobs and Gals* (1952), *All Ashore, Abbott and Costello Go to Mars* (1953), *Bowery to Bagdad* (1954), *The Lieutenant Wore Skirts* (1956), *No Time for Sergeants* (1958), *Ocean's 11* (1960), *Gypsy* (1962), *McHale's Navy* (1964), *Cheyenne Social Club* (1970), *Bite the Bullet* (1975). ■

Williams, Cara (1925–), actress. Began her Hollywood screen career in the early 1940s. She played supporting and lead roles in dramas and light films.

SELECTED FILMS: *Happy Land* (1943), *Something for the Boys, In the Meantime, Darling* (1944), *Don Juan Quilligan* (1945), *Sitting Pretty* (1948), *The Girl Next Door* (1953), *Monte Carlo Baby* (1954), *Meet Me in Las Vegas* (1956), *The Man From the Diner's Club* (1963), *The White Buffalo* (1977). ■

Williams, Esther (1923–), actress. Worked as a department store model and swimmer in Billy Rose's Aquacade before entering Hollywood films in the early 1940s. By 1944 MGM featured her in *Bathing Beauty*, and she rapidly advanced to stardom in musical comedies. A champion swimmer at age fifteen, she performed striking swimming feats in a succession of popular light films, all produced in Technicolor. Her screen career came to a sudden halt in the late 1950s when she attempted to become a dramatic actress. She abandoned films and went into business.

SELECTED FILMS: *Andy Hardy's Double Life* (1944), *Bathing Beauty* (1944), *Easy to Wed* (1946), *On an Island With You* (1948), *Take Me Out to the Ball Game, Neptune's Daughter* (1949), *Duchess of Idaho* (1950), *Callaway Went Thataway, Texas Carnival* (1951), *Skirts Ahoy!, Million Dollar Mermaid* (1952), *Dangerous When Wet, Easy to Love*

(1953), Jupiter's Darling (1955), The Big Show (1961). ∎

Williams, Guinn "Big Boy" (1899–1962), actor. Achieved some success as a professional baseball player before entering early silent films in 1919. After gaining experience in minor roles, he began to star in westerns through the 1920s and 1930s. In both decades he often switched to comic character roles, sometimes as the hero's dim-witted sidekick. A tall, burly figure, he appeared in numerous dramas and light films during a film career that spanned five decades.

In *Castle on the Hudson* (1940) he played a convict who enlightens fellow inmate John Garfield on the hazards of prison breaks. "I knew a guy who spent six months diggin' his way out of here and came up in the warden's office."

SELECTED FILMS: Almost a Husband (1919), The Freshie (1922), Slide, Kelly, Slide, Backstage, Babe Comes Home, The College Widow (1927), Ladies' Night at a Turkish Bath, Vamping Venus (1928), The Bachelor Father (1931), You Said a Mouthful (1932), Palooka (1934), Professor Beware, Hold That Co-Ed (1938), You'll Never Get Rich (1941), The Comancheros (1962). ∎

Williams, John (1903–1983), actor. Worked on stage and in films in his native England before settling in Hollywood as a minor character player. A tall, distinguished figure with a very English mustache, he appeared in dozens of dramas and light films. He was best known for his role as Inspector Hubbard in Hitchcock's *Dial M for Murder* (1954), a part he also played on stage.

SELECTED FILMS: Kind Lady (1950), The Student Prince, Sabrina (1954), The Solid Gold Cadillac (1956), Will Success Spoil Rock Hunter? (1957), Visit to a Small Planet (1960), Double Trouble, The Secret War of Harry Frigg (1967), No Deposit, No Return (1976), The Swarm (1978). ∎

Williams, Rhys (1897–1969), actor. Worked on the stage before settling in Hollywood in the early 1940s as a sturdy character player. Bald and portly with a Welsh accent, he appeared in dramas and light films, often cast as likable physicians, preachers, and other professional types.

SELECTED FILMS: How Green Was My Valley (1941), No Time for Love (1943), The Trouble With Women (1945), The Imperfect Lady (1946), The Farmer's Daughter (1947), The Inspector General (1949), Meet Me at the Fair (1952), There's No Business Like Show Business (1954), How to Be Very, Very Popular (1955), Merry Andrew (1958), Skullduggery (1969). ∎

Williams, Robin (1952–), actor, comedian. Appeared in small clubs and in television before entering films in 1980. A dynamic, hyperactive stand-up comic and gifted mimic, he has brought some of this energy and his manic charm to his screen portrayals. He has emerged as one of America's top comedians. His first cable special in 1978, for example, brought him $25,000, whereas his 1983 performance landed him $750,000.

SELECTED FILMS: Popeye (1980), The World According to Garp (1982), The Survivors (1983), Moscow on the Hudson (1984). ∎

Williamson, Robin (1889–1935), director. Entered film in the 1910s. He turned out early silent comedy shorts for independent studios. He directed several of Ben TURPIN'S films for Vogue before the comic moved to Mack SENNETT'S company.

SELECTED FILMS: The Music Marvels, The Butcher's Nightmare, His Bogus Boast, A Studio Stampede, Frightened Flirts, Why Ben Bolted, Masked Mirth, Bucking the Tiger, Caught in the End (1917). ∎

Willis, Leo (1890–1952), actor. Appeared as a supporting player during the 1920s and 1930s. He portrayed a variety of characters in numerous comedy shorts and features starring some of the leading comedians of the period, including LAUREL AND HARDY, Charlie CHASE, and the THREE STOOGES.

SELECTED FILMS: A Sailor-Made Man (1921), Powder and Smoke, Stolen Goods, A Ten Minute Egg, Jeffries, Jr. (1924), Big Red Riding Hood (1925), Flying Elephants, The Kid Brother (1927), The Hoosegow (1929), Below Zero (1930), Pardon Us, Bear Hunks, Monkey Business (1931), Seal Skins (1932), The Live Ghost, Six of a Kind (1934), Horses' Collars (1935), The Bohemian Girl (1936). ■

Wills, Chill (1903–1978), actor. Worked in tent shows, in vaudeville, and on stage before entering films in the mid-1930s with his singing group, Chill Wills and His Avalon Boys. He appeared as a character player in numerous westerns and other genres, often playing crusty but wise old-timers. He supplied the voice for the talking mule in the "FRANCIS" comedy series (except for the last entry).

SELECTED FILMS: Bar 20 Rides Again (1935), Sorority House (1939), Tugboat Annie Sails Again (1940), Her Cardboard Lover (1942), Best Foot Forward (1943), See Here, Private Hargrove (1944), What Next, Corporal Hargrove? (1945), Family Honeymoon (1948), Ricochet Romance (1954), Where the Boys Are (1961), The Steagle (1971), Mr. Billion, Poco (1977). ■

Wilson, Carey (1889–1962), screenwriter. Wrote stories and screenplays for various studios from the early 1920s. He turned out dramas and comedies, working occasionally in collaboration. By the late 1940s he turned to producing films on a full-time basis and was responsible for the popular "ANDY HARDY" comedy series at MGM studios.

SELECTED FILMS: Broken Chains (1922), The Masked Bride, Soul Mates (1925), Orchids and Ermine, Naughty but Nice, The Stolen Bride, American Beauty (1927), Oh, Kay! (1928), Why Be Good?, His Captive Woman (1929), The Flying Fool (1931), Judge Hardy and Son (1939). ■

Wilson, Dooley (1894–1953), actor, musician. Worked in vaudeville, stock, and nightclubs and on Broadway before entering films in the early 1940s. A minor supporting player for the most part, he became famous for his role as Sam in Casablanca (1942). He appeared in dramas and light films.

SELECTED FILMS: My Favorite Blonde, Night in New Orleans, Take a Letter, Darling (1942), Stormy Weather, Higher and Higher, Two Tickets to London (1943), Seven Days Ashore (1944), Triple Threat, Racing Luck (1948), Free for All, Come to the Stable (1949), Passage West (1951). ■

Wilson, Flip (1933–), comedian, actor. Worked as a comic in small clubs, struggling for about a decade before making several appearances in television in the mid-1960s. The national exposure changed his entire career. An animated performer with a unique, high-pitched voice, he has become a popular comic, starring in specials and his own series. His screen appearances have been rare.

SELECTED FILMS: Uptown Saturday Night (1974), Skatetown, USA, The Fish That Saved Pittsburgh (1979). ■

Wilson, Lois (1896–), actress. Entered films in 1916 following some stage experience and quickly moved up to playing female leads and, later, with the advent of sound, supporting roles. She co-starred with Bryant WASHBURN in several silent comedies, which almost made them a comedy team. She appeared in numerous dramas and light films during a screen career that spanned four decades. When she left films in the 1940s, she continued to act on stage and in television.

SELECTED FILMS: *The Dumb Girl of Portici (1916), It Pays to Advertise, Love Insurance, Why Smith Left Home (1919), Burglar-Proof (1920), Is Marriage a Failure?, Our Leading Citizen, The World's Champion (1922), Only 38, Ruggles of Red Gap (1923), Pied Piper Malone (1914), Irish Luck, Welcome Home (1925), The Show-Off (1926), French Dressing (1927), Lovin' the Ladies (1930), Wedding Present (1936), The Girl From Jones Beach (1949).* ∎

Charles Winninger

Wilson, Marie (1916–1972), actress. Began her screen career in the mid-1930s. She played supporting roles as well as leads in several dramas and many light films, often as the typical "dumb blonde."

SELECTED FILMS: *Babes in Toyland (1934), Stars Over Broadway (1935), Colleen (1936), Fools for Scandal, Boy Meets Girl, Broadway Musketeers (1938), The Sweepstakes Winner (1939), You Can't Ration Love (1944), No Leave No Love (1946), My Friend Irma (1949), My Friend Irma Goes West (1950), A Girl in Every Port (1952), Never Wave at a Wac, Marry Me Again (1953), Mr. Hobbs Takes a Vacation (1962).* ∎

Winkler, Henry (1946–), actor. Appeared in stock, on Broadway, and in television before making his film debut in 1974. A lightweight actor, he has starred in several film comedies, but has not been able to attain the success he had achieved in television.

In *The One and Only* he is quick to give advice. A girl confides to him: "I'm getting a degree in sociology. I don't know what to do with it." "Open up a sociology store," he suggests.

SELECTED FILMS: *Crazy Joe, The Lords of Flatbush (1974), Nickelodeon (1976), Heroes (1977), The One and Only (1978).* ∎

Winninger, Charles (1884–1969), actor. In vaudeville and on stage before entering early silent films to appear in comedy shorts in the mid-1910s. He played Cap'n Andy in the original production of *Show Boat* on Broadway. A portly, likable character actor, he played in feature-length dramas and light films beginning in the 1920s and continued into the 1950s. He portrayed the father of some of the leading screen juveniles, including Mickey ROONEY and Deanna DURBIN.

In *Nothing Sacred* (1937) he played an impish country doctor suspicious of members of the press. "I'll tell you what I think of newspapermen," he says to fast-talking city reporter Fredric MARCH. "The hand of God reaching down into the mire couldn't elevate one of them to the depths of degradation."

SELECTED FILMS: *The Doomed Groom (1915), Pied Piper Malone (1924), Summer Bachelors (1926), Soup to Nuts (1930), Flying High, God's Gift to Women (1931), Show Boat (1936), Three Smart Girls, Woman Chases Man, Every Day's a Holiday (1937), Hard to Get (1938), Destry Rides Again, Babes in Arms (1939), Little Nellie Kelly (1940), Friendly Enemies (1942), A Lady Takes a Chance (1943), She Wouldn't Say Yes (1945), Father Is a Bachelor (1950), Champ for a Day (1953), Raymie (1960).* ∎

Winslow, George "Foghorn" (1946–), child actor. Appeared in television before breaking into films in the 1950s. His one claim to fame was his bullfrog voice which enlivened a few features. He retired from his screen career in 1958 at age twelve.

SELECTED FILMS: *Room for One More, My Pal Gus, Monkey Business (1952), Gentlemen Prefer Blondes, Mr. Scoutmaster (1953), Artists and Models, Rock Pretty Baby (1956), Summer Love, Wild Heritage (1958).* ∎

Winters, Jonathan (1925–), comedian, actor. Appeared on radio, in small clubs as a stand-up comic, and in television before entering films in the early 1960s. His chameleon-like comedy style, although extremely creative, is difficult to describe. It ranges from offbeat to realistic, from sick humor to his invention of homespun characters. A portly, twinkle-eyed comedian with a bent for mischief, he has played character roles in several comedies.

SELECTED FILMS: *It's a Mad, Mad, Mad, Mad World (1963), The Loved One (1965), The Russians Are Coming, the Russians Are Coming, Penelope (1966), Eight on the Lam (1967), Viva Max! (1969), The Fish That Saved Pittsburgh (1979).* ∎

Winters, Linda. See Dorothy Comingore.

Winters, Roland (1904–), actor. Worked on stage and on radio before starring as the last Charlie Chan (1947–1949) in a series of low-budget detective films. But he was versatile enough to appear in other dramas and light films during his 25-year screen career. He later entered television.

SELECTED FILMS: *13 Rue Madeleine (1946), Once More, My Darling, Abbott and Costello Meet the Killer—Boris Karloff (1949), Captain Carey, U.S.A., To Please a Lady (1950), She's Working Her Way Through College (1952), Bigger Than Life (1956), Top Secret Affair (1957), Everything's Ducky, Blue Hawaii (1961), Follow That Dream (1962), Loving (1970).* ∎

Winters, Shelley (1922–), actress. Worked as a model and appeared in summer stock, in nightclubs as a chorus girl, and on Broadway in 1941. By 1943 she began appearing in films without much success. The turning point in her screen career occurred in 1948 with her role as a waitress in *A Double Life* starring Ronald COLMAN. In 1951 she was nominated for an Oscar for her role of a factory worker who was killed by Montgomery Clift in *A Place in the Sun* (1951). She won Academy Awards as Best Supporting Actress for her roles in *The Diary of Anne Frank* (1959) and *A Patch of Blue* (1965). She has appeared in several light films during her long career but has received few rewarding roles in recent years.

In *Buona Sera, Mrs. Campbell* she portrayed Phil SILVERS' wife, both of whom are visiting southern Italy. While in a hairdressing shop, Winters converses with other tourists. "You know what I'm really looking forward to?" she confides to the other customers. "That art treasure tour in Florence tomorrow. I hear you can pick up the most beautiful, marvelous bargains there." "Really?" interjects one of the listeners. "What are you interested in, painting or sculpture?" "Bedroom slippers," replies Winters.

SELECTED FILMS: *What a Woman! (1943), She's a Soldier, Too, Sailor's Holiday, Cover Girl (1944), Tonight and Every Night (1945), Living in a Big Way (1947), Behave Yourself (1951), Enter Laughing (1967), Buona Sera, Mrs. Campbell (1969), Flap (1970), Blume in Love (1973), Next Stop, Greenwich Village (1976), Pete's Dragon (1977), S.O.B. (1981), Over the Brooklyn Bridge (1984).* ∎

Withers, Grant (1904–1959), actor. Worked as a reporter before entering silent films in the mid-1920s. A handsome, versatile performer, he made a smooth transition to sound, starring in serials, westerns, melodramas, and light films, usually for minor studios. He appeared in more than 150 features in a screen career that spanned four decades, sometimes supporting major comics of the period, including Buster KEATON, W. C. FIELDS, and Mae WEST. He committed suicide at age 55.

SELECTED FILMS: The Gentle Cyclone (1926), College (1927), Bringing Up Father, Tillie's Punctured Romance (1928), Madonna of Avenue A, The Time, the Place and the Girl (1929), Dancing Sweeties (1930), Too Young to Marry (1931), Hold 'Em Yale, Goin' to Town (1935), Three Loves Has Nancy (1938), Mexican Spitfire Out West (1940), Woman of the Year (1942), A Lady Takes a Chance (1943), The Ghost Goes Wild (1947), Tropical Heat Wave (1952), Lady Godiva (1955), I, Mobster (1958). ■

Withers, Hildegarde. The fictional spinster schoolteacher and part-time amateur sleuth in a short-lived series of light detective-comedies produced in the early 1930s. She was portrayed by comic character actress Edna May OLIVER.

Withers, Jane (1926–), actress. Appeared as a child in vaudeville and on radio before entering films at age 6. Although she lacked the charm of other child performers like Shirley TEMPLE, she managed to win over her audiences with her own impish and energetic personality. She soon became one of the most popular young stars of the 1930s, appearing in a succession of light comedies for 20th Century-Fox. In 1938 she was listed among the Box Office Top Ten favorite film personalities. As she matured, her popularity declined and she left films in the late 1940s, appearing only occasionally in small roles.

SELECTED FILMS: Handle With Care (1932), Bright Eyes (1934), The Farmer Takes a Wife (1935), Paddy O'Day, Little Miss Nobody, Pepper (1936), The Holy Terror, Wild and Woolly, 45 Fathers (1937), Checkers, Rascals, Keep Smiling, Always in Trouble (1938), Pack Up Your Troubles, Boy Friend (1939), Shooting High, The Girl From Avenue A (1940), A Very Young Lady, Her First Beau (1941), My Best Gal (1944), The Affairs of Geraldine (1946), Captain Newman, M.D. (1964). ■

Witherspoon, Cora (1890–1957), actress. Performed on stage before settling in Hollywood as a character player in the early 1930s. She appeared in dramas and light films, often portraying overbearing wives and snobbish characters. She supported such popular comedians as WHEELER AND WOOLSEY, Harold LLOYD, and W. C. FIELDS.

SELECTED FILMS: Night Angel, Peach O'Reno (1931), Ladies of the Jury (1932), Midnight (1934), Piccadilly Jim, Libeled Lady (1936), Beg, Borrow or Steal, Personal Property (1937), Professor Beware (1938), The Bank Dick (1940), Over 21 (1945), The Mating Season (1951), Just for You (1952). ■

Wolfe, Bill, actor. Appeared as a supporting actor in the 1930s and 1940s, chiefly in light films. A tall, homely character player, he often worked with W. C. FIELDS.

SELECTED FILMS: Poppy (1936), You Can't Cheat an Honest Man (1939), My Little Chickadee, The Bank Dick (1940), Never Give a Sucker an Even Break (1941), Follow the Boys (1944), Sensations of 1945 (1945). ■

Wolfe, Ian (1896–), actor. Began his screen career in the mid-1930s playing mean and menacing types and continued in that capacity for decades. A lean, grim, balding minor character player with a dark mustache, he appeared in more than 100 dramas and light films, often playing uncaring landlords or other cold-hearted types.

SELECTED FILMS: *The Fountain (1934), The Firefly, Maytime (1937), Blondie, You Can't Take It With You (1938), Blondie Brings Up Baby (1939), Love Crazy (1941), We Were Dancing (1942), In Society (1944), Zombies on Broadway (1945), Without Reservations (1946), That Way With Women (1947), Mr. Blandings Builds His Dream House (1948), Here Comes the Groom (1951), Her Twelve Men (1954), Pollyanna (1960), The Frisco Kid (1979), Jinxed (1982).* ∎

Woman of the Year (1942), MGM. *Dir.* George Stevens; *Sc.* Ring Lardner, Jr., Michael Kanin; with Spencer Tracy, Katharine Hepburn, Fay Bainter, Reginald Owen.

In their first film together, Spencer TRACY and Katharine HEPBURN portray columnists working for the same newspaper. He is a sports reporter while she handles national and world events. Their paths cross and a conflict arises. To understand each other's work, they each agree to observe the other on assignment. This results in a funny scene as Tracy attempts to explain the rules of America's Favorite Pastime at Hepburn's first baseball game. Although they argue, they fall in love and marry. But the feuding between them plagues their marriage in this romantic comedy. Hepburn's busy schedule keeps her away from Tracy and their life together, adding to his hostility. Both are hilarious as they try to adjust to marital life. A classic scene occurs when Hepburn, trying to prove that she can be the perfect wife, engages in a losing battle with an array of kitchen appliances. On hand to assist in the fun are William BENDIX, Roscoe KARNS, and a host of other dependable supporting players. Lauren Bacall starred in a successful Broadway musical based on the film.

Wood, Natalie (1938–1982), actress. Began her screen career at age five in a minor role. She was later hired as a child player and rapidly became a young star. As she matured, her abundant charm and attractiveness helped her to maintain her popularity, and she emerged as a competent Hollywood star. She was thrice nominated for an Oscar (1955, 1961, 1963). She appeared in dramas and light films until her career ended suddenly with her tragic drowning.

In *Love With the Proper Stranger* (1963) she played Steve McQueen's lover who is carrying his child. "You want to hear me say 'I want to get married,'" he says, adding, "I want to get married." "Tell the truth," she responds. "If I said 'Okay,' your teeth would fall out of your mouth."

SELECTED FILMS: *Happy Land (1943), The Bride Wore Boots (1946), Miracle on 34th Street, The Ghost and Mrs. Muir (1947), Chicken Every Sunday, Father Was a Fullback (1949), Never a Dull Moment (1950), Dear Brat (1951), Gypsy (1962), Sex and the Single Girl (1964), The Great Race (1965), Penelope (1966), Bob & Carol & Ted & Alice (1969), The Last Married Couple in America (1979).* ∎

Wood, Peggy (1892–1978), actress. Appeared on Broadway at age 18 as a chorus girl. She continued her stage career in a variety of roles. Although her film debut came in 1919 in a silent film, she made only occasional appearances on the screen. A talented performer, she received an Academy Award nomination for her supporting role in *The Sound of Music*.

SELECTED FILMS: *Almost a Husband (1919), Wonder of Women (1929), Handy Andy (1934), Call It a Day (1937), The Housekeeper's Daughter (1939), The Bride Wore Boots, The Magnificent Doll (1946), Dream Girl (1948), The Sound of Music (1965).* ∎

Wood, Sam (1883–1949), director. Entered early Hollywood silent films as an actor, switched in 1915 to assistant director, and in 1919 became a full-fledged director. A competent director who worked in different genres, he turned out numerous dramas and light films during a career that spanned four decades. Although he has turned out a large body of work, much of which is entertaining, he has been generally neglected by film critics and historians, perhaps because of his deficiency in pictorial inventiveness or his lack of individual style.

SELECTED FILMS: Double Speed, Excuse My Dust, What's Your Hurry? (1920), The Snob, Peck's Bad Boy (1921), The Impossible Mrs. Bellew (1922), Bluebeard's Eighth Wife (1923), Rookies, The Fair Co-Ed (1927), The Latest From Paris (1928), So This Is College, It's a Great Life (1929), They Learned About Women, The Girl Said No, Way for a Sailor (1930), A Tailor-Made Man, Get-Rich-Quick Wallingford (1931), Hold Your Man (1933), A Night at the Opera (1935), A Day at the Races (1937), Stablemates (1938), The Devil and Miss Jones (1941), Casanova Brown (1944), Guest Wife (1945), Ivy (1947), Ambush (1950). ∎

Woodward, Guy (1858–1919), actor. Began his film career in early silent comedy shorts for producer Mack SENNETT'S KEYSTONE studios. A supporting player, he worked with some of the leading comics of the period, including "Fatty" ARBUCKLE and Chester CONKLIN.

SELECTED FILMS: The Best of Enemies, The Hunt, Fickle Fatty's Fall, His Father's Footsteps (1915), His Pride and Shame, A Dash of Courage, His Wild Oats, A Tugboat Romeo (1916), Dodging His Doom, A Shanghaied Jonah, Hula Hula Land (1917). ∎

Woolley, Monty (1888–1963), actor. Taught at Yale and appeared on Broadway in 1936 before entering films in 1937. Easily distinguished by his neatly trimmed beard and his loquacious manner, he portrayed astute characters chiefly in light films. Born Edgar Montillion Wooley, he received several Academy Award nominations. He portrayed the title character, his most memorable role, in both the stage and film versions of The Man Who Came to Dinner (1942).

In the above film he played a churlish radio personality who torments his much put-upon nurse: "Would you take your clammy hands off my chair! You have the touch of a love-starved cobra."

SELECTED FILMS: Live, Love and Learn, Nothing Sacred (1937), Everybody Sing, Artists and Models Abroad (1938), Midnight, Man About Town, Dancing Co-Ed (1939), The Pied Piper, Life Begins at Eight-Thirty (1942), Holy Matrimony (1943), Irish Eyes Are Smiling (1944), Molly and Me (1945), The Bishop's Wife (1947), Miss Tatlock's Millions (1948), As Young As You Feel (1951), Kismet (1955). ∎

Woolsey, Robert. See Wheeler and Woolsey.

Worthington, William, director. Worked in Hollywood directing silent dramas and light films during the period of the First World War. Much of his output was for Universal studios.

SELECTED FILMS: A Stranger From Somewhere (1916), Bringing Home Father, The Clean Up, The Man Who Took a Chance (1917). ∎

Wright, Will (1891–1962), actor. Entered films in 1936 and went on to appear in more than 100 films. A sturdy character player with sharp features, he often portrayed rural types and old-timers in dramas and light films.

SELECTED FILMS: China Clipper (1936), Blondie Plays Cupid (1940), Rookies on Parade (1941), Shut My Big Mouth (1942), Reveille With Beverly (1943), Eve Knew Her Apples (1945), Rendezvous With Annie (1946), Mother

Wore Tights (1947), Mr. Blandings Builds His Dream House (1948), Adam's Rib (1949), Excuse My Dust (1951), The 30-Foot Bride of Candy Rock (1959), Fail-Safe (1964). ■

Wyman, Jane (1914–), actress. Appeared on radio as a singer and in minor film roles in the 1930s as a comic-relief supporting player before emerging as a principal star in the mid-1940s. A versatile performer, she starred in dramas as well as light films, eventually winning an Academy Award for her role in Johnny Belinda (1948). She received several other Oscar nominations during a screen career that spanned four decades. She was the first wife of Ronald REAGAN.

SELECTED FILMS: Gold Diggers of 1937, My Man Godfrey (1936), Smart Blonde, The King and the Chorus Girl (1937), He Couldn't Say No, Wide Open Faces, Brother Rat (1938), Torchy Plays With Dynamite (1939), Tugboat Annie Sails Again (1940), Honeymoon for Three, You're in the Army Now (1941), Larceny, Inc., My Favorite Spy (1942), Princess O'Rourke (1943), Make Your Own Bed (1944), Magic Town (1947), The Lady Takes a Sailor (1949), Here Comes the Groom (1951), Let's Do It Again (1953), Bon Voyage! (1962), How to Commit Marriage (1969). ■

Wynn, Ed (1886–1966), actor. Appeared as a comic in vaudeville, in the Ziegfeld Follies, and on radio. His film career, although sporadic, was a successful one, especially during the latter part of his life when he began to play serious roles, one of which (The Diary of Anne Frank) brought him an Academy Award nomination. His son, Keenan WYNN, was a popular character actor.

In Stage Door Canteen he informs a group of soldiers: "In Washington, D.C. they have canteens where the Congressmen wait on the boys. These boys starve to death down there. You mark my words." "Why, Mr. Wynn?" one G.I. asks. "Well," he replies, "you know how long it takes a Congressman to pass anything."

SELECTED FILMS: Rubber Heels (1927), Follow the Leader (1930), The Chief (1933), Stage Door Canteen (1943), Cinderfella (1960), The Absent-Minded Professor, Babes in Toyland (1961), Son of Flubber (1963), The Patsy, Mary Poppins, Those Callaways (1964), Dear Brigitte, That Darn Cat (1965), The Gnome-Mobile (1967). ■

Wynn, Keenan (1916–1986), actor. Worked on radio, in stock, and on Broadway before entering films in the early 1940s. A resourceful character player, he appeared in many dramas and light films. He portrayed a range of characters, from con-men and servants in comedy-relief roles to unscrupulous figures in dramas. He was the son of actor-comedian Ed WYNN.

In Dr. Strangelove (1964) he played Colonel Guano, a dense but patriotic officer. During a critical moment at a nuclear base, officers who need some coins to call the President to stop an all-out, impending nuclear war want to break open a soda machine. But Guano will have none of this. "That's private property," the slow-witted colonel insists.

SELECTED FILMS: For Me and My Gal (1942), See Here, Private Hargrove (1944), Easy to Wed, The Thrill of Brazil (1946), Song of the Thin Man (1947), My Dear Secretary (1948), That Midnight Kiss (1949), Angels in the Outfield (1951), Kiss Me Kate (1953), Running Wild (1955), The Perfect Furlough (1959), The Absent-Minded Professor (1961), The Patsy (1964), The Great Race (1965), Cancel My Reservation (1972), The Shaggy D.A. (1976), Just Tell Me What You Want (1979), Best Friends (1982). ■

XYZ

Yarbrough, Jean (1900–1975), director. Began his Hollywood career in silent films working as a prop man for producer Hal ROACH. He became a director during the mid-1930s, following years of experience as an assistant director. Working for smaller studios, he turned out numerous second features, many of which were light films. He directed several ABBOTT AND COSTELLO comedies.

SELECTED FILMS: Rebellious Daughters (1938), The Gang's All Here, Father Steps Out, Let's Go Collegiate, To Sergeant Mulligan (1941), Freckles Comes Home, So's Your Aunt Emma!, She's in the Army (1942), Good Morning, Judge, Hi Ya, Sailor, So's Your Uncle (1943), Moon Over Las Vegas, In Society (1944), The Naughty Nineties (1945), Cuban Pete (1946), Henry the Rainmaker, Leave It to Henry, Master Minds (1949), Lost in Alaska (1952), Hot Shots (1956), Hillbillies in a Haunted House (1967). ∎

Yawitz, Paul (1905–1983), screenwriter. Worked as a publicist and Broadway columnist. He entered the film world in the 1930s as a writer, turning out, alone and in collaboration, numerous light films as well as dramas. He was responsible for many of the "Boston Blackie" detective features.

SELECTED FILMS: Breakfast for Two, They Wanted to Marry (1937), Affairs of Annabel, Crashing Hollywood, Go Chase Yourself, Blonde Cheat (1938), Fixer Dugan, Little Accident (1939), Honolulu Lu (1941), The Chance of a Lifetime, She Has What It Takes (1943), Louisiana Hayride (1944), Models, Inc. (1952). ∎

York, Dick (1928–), actor. Appeared on radio and stage before entering films in the 1950s. A tall, amiable performer, he made only a handful of films in which he usually portrayed naive, vulnerable second leads. When his screen career declined, he switched to television.

SELECTED FILMS: My Sister Eileen (1955), Operation Mad Ball (1957), Inherit the Wind (1960). ∎

York, Duke (1902–1952), actor. Worked chiefly in comedy shorts during the 1930s and 1940s as a supporting player. He appeared in many of the THREE STOOGES' films as well as those of other leading comics of the period, including W. C. FIELDS, BURNS AND ALLEN, and Thelma TODD.

SELECTED FILMS: The Old Fashioned Way (1934), All American Toothache, Here Comes Cookie (1935), Never Give a Sucker an Even Break, Some More of Samoa (1941), Pardon My Sarong, Who Done It? (1942), Three Little Twirps, Higher Than a Kite (1943), Idle Roomers (1944), Shivering Sherlocks (1948). ∎

Yorkin, Bud (1926–), director. Worked as a producer-director of television comedy shows in the 1950s before entering films in the 1960s as a director. He has turned out an entertaining series of light films, several of which he also produced.

SELECTED FILMS: Come Blow Your Horn (1963), Never Too Late (1965), Divorce, American Style (1967), Inspector Clouseau (1968), Start the Revolution Without Me (1970), The Thief Who Came to Dinner (1973). ∎

Yost, Dorothy, screenwriter. Began writing screenplays for Hollywood films in the early 1930s. Working alone and in collaboration, she wrote dramas and light films, specializing in the latter.

SELECTED FILMS: Hello Everybody (1933), The Gay Divorcee (1934), Alice Adams, Freckles, Laddie (1935), Bunker Bean, M'Liss, That Girl From Paris (1936), Racing Lady, There Goes the Groom, Too Many Wives (1937), Bad Little Angel (1939), Forty Little Mothers (1940), Saginaw Trail (1953). ∎

James Stewart and Edward Arnold in *You Can't Take It With You* (1938)

You Can't Take It With You (1938), COL. *Dir.* Frank Capra; *Sc.* Robert Riskin; with Jean Arthur, Lionel Barrymore, James Stewart, Edward Arnold.

Another representative Capra comedy, the film was adapted from the George S. KAUFMAN-Moss Hart Broadway play about the eccentric but happy Vanderhof family where each member does his or her own thing. James STEWART blunders into this frenetic household and falls for Jean ARTHUR, the granddaughter of patriarch Lionel BARRYMORE. Stewart is introduced to the family and boarders, including an aspiring play-

wright, an amateur fireworks maker, a xylophone player, and a would-be ballerina and her explosive Russian tutor, wonderfully played by Mischa AUER. The climactic meeting of the two patriarchs, the individualistic Barrymore and Stewart's tycoon father (Edward ARNOLD), is hilarious and pointed. The expert supporting cast, including Spring BYINGTON, Ann Miller, and especially Auer, add much to the hilarity of the film, which won Oscars for Best Direction and Best Picture.

Young, Alan (1919–), actor. Appeared on radio before making his film debut in the mid-1940s. Although endowed with a gift for comedy, he has been more successful in television than in films. He has appeared chiefly in light films. One of his better non-comedy roles was that of the friend of determined scientist Rod Taylor who travels into the future in *The Time Machine* (1960).

SELECTED FILMS: Margie (1946), Chicken Every Sunday, Mr. Belvedere Goes to College (1949), Aaron Slick From Punkin Crick (1952), Androcles and the Lion (1953), Gentlemen Marry Brunettes (1955), Tom Thumb (1958), The Cat From Outer Space (1978). ∎

Young, Bert, actor. Worked chiefly in comedy shorts during the 1930s and 1940s as a supporting player. He appeared in many of the THREE STOOGES' films.

SELECTED FILMS: Horses' Collars, Restless Knights (1935), Ants in the Pantry, Movie Maniacs, Half-Shot Shooters (1936), Dizzy Doctors, Back to the Woods, The Sitter-Downers (1937), Rockin' Through the Rockies, Nutty but Nice, No Census, No Feeling (1940), So Long, Mr. Chumps, Dutiful but Dumb, I'll Never Heil Again, In the Sweet Pie and Pie (1941), Loco Boy Makes Good, What's the Matador?, Even as I.O.U. (1942). ∎

Young, Bobby "Bonedust," child actor. Appeared in several silent comedy shorts featuring producer Hal ROACH'S famous "OUR GANG."

SELECTED FILMS: Better Movies (1925), Thundering Fleas, Shivering Spooks, The Fourth Alarm (1926). ∎

Young, Burt (1940–), actor. Began his screen career in the early 1970s following some stage experience in off-Broadway productions. A short, chubby figure, he has portrayed sympathetic characters in dramas and light films. He has occasionally written screenplays for several of his films. His most memorable role is that of Sylvester Stallone's brother-in-law in the Rocky films.

SELECTED FILMS: Carnival of Blood (1970), Born to Win, The Gang That Couldn't Shoot Straight (1971), Harry and Walter Go to New York (1976), The Choirboys (1977), All the Marbles (1981), Over the Brooklyn Bridge (1984), Rocky IV (1985). ∎

Young, Carleton (1907–1971), actor. Entered films in the mid-1930s as a character player. He often portrayed sophisticated characters in dramas and light films, occasionally playing leads. He appeared in several serials as well.

SELECTED FILMS: Happy Go Lucky (1936), Join the Marines (1937), Pride of the Bowery (1940), Buck Privates (1941), Take It or Leave It (1944), Thrill of a Romance (1945), The Kissing Bandit (1948), My Six Convicts (1952), Cheyenne Autumn (1964). ∎

Young, Clara Kimball (1890–1960), actress. Appeared on stage as a child and in vaudeville and stock before entering silent films in 1909. By 1914 she had risen in popularity and was considered one of the most well-liked screen stars of the period. By the early 1920s she fell out of favor with the public and returned to the stage. She re-entered films during the early sound period as a character

player chiefly in second features. She appeared in numerous dramas and several light films.

SELECTED FILMS: A Midsummer Night's Dream (1909), Lord Browning and Cinderella (1912), Beau Brummel, The Little Minister, Cupid Versus Women's Rights (1913), Happy Go Lucky, My Official Wife (1914), Cheating Cheaters (1919), Straight From Paris, Charge It (1921), Enter Madame (1922), She Married Her Boss, His Night Out (1935), The Roundup (1941). ∎

Young, Clifton (1917–1951), actor. Began his screen career as a child performer in the early silent "OUR GANG" comedy shorts of 1924. He appeared as a supporting player in light features, dramas, and a series of sound shorts, the "JOE McDOAKES" comedies, in the 1940s.

SELECTED FILMS: So You Want to Play the Horses (1946), My Wild Irish Rose, So You're Going on Vacation (1947), So You Want an Apartment, So You Want to Build a House, So You Want to Be a Detective, So You Want to Be in Politics (1948), A Woman of Distinction (1950). ∎

Young, Gig (1913–1978), actor. Worked in stock before entering films in 1940. Good-looking and charming, Young, who was born Byron Elsworth Barr, chiefly played second leads in comedies. After two nominations for Academy Awards, he won an Oscar for his role as the emcee in They Shoot Horses, Don't They? (1969). His career ended tragically in an apparent murder-suicide, the police finding his body and that of his wife lying next to him.

SELECTED FILMS: Misbehaving Husbands (1940), The Male Animal, The Gay Sisters (1942), Young at Heart (1955), Desk Set (1957), Teacher's Pet, The Tunnel of Love (1958), Ask Any Girl (1959), That Touch of Mink (1962), A Ticklish Affair (1963), Strange Bedfel-

lows (1965), Lovers and Other Strangers (1970), The Game of Death (1979). ∎

Young, Loretta (1913–), actress. Began her screen career as a child in silent films. With the advent of sound, she developed into a competent actress. At first she appeared chiefly in minor films, but was moved up to important features in the late 1930s, portraying major roles in dramas and light films. She received an Oscar for her role in *The Farmer's Daughter* (1947) and a nomination for her role in *Come to the Stable.* She left films in the 1950s to begin an entirely new and successful career in her own television show. She starred in dramas and light films. Her autobiography, *The Things I Had to Learn,* was published in 1961.

SELECTED FILMS: Naughty but Nice (1927), The Magnificent Flirt (1928), Loose Ankles (1930), Too Young to Marry, I Like Your Nerve, Platinum Blonde (1931), Taxi, Weekend Marriage (1932), Employees' Entrance, She Had to Say Yes (1933), The White Parade (1934), Ladies in Love (1936), Love Is News, Wife, Doctor and Nurse, Second Honeymoon (1937), Kentucky (1938), The Doctor Takes a Wife, He Stayed for Breakfast (1940), The Men in Her Life (1941), The Bishop's Wife (1947), Mother Is a Freshman, Come to the Stable (1949), It Happens Every Thursday (1953). ∎

Young, Noah (1887–1958), actor. Appeared as a supporting player in silent and sound comedy shorts and features. For more than two decades he worked with some of the leading comics of the period, including Harold LLOYD, LAUREL AND HARDY, Thelma TODD and Patsy KELLY, Charlie CHASE, and Snub POLLARD. He portrayed various characters, including bullies, counts, rowdies, and sheriffs.

SELECTED FILMS: Bumping Into Broadway (1919), His Royal Slyness, An Eastern Westerner (1920), I Do, A Sailor-Made Man, At the Ringside (1921), Grandma's Boy (1922), Safety Last (1923), Publicity Pays, Young Oldfield, Stolen Goods, A Ten Minute Egg, Too Many Mamas (1924), For Heaven's Sake (1926), Do Detectives Think?, Sugar Daddies (1927), Welcome Danger (1929), Feet First (1930), Movie Crazy (1932), Bum Voyage (1934), Bonnie Scotland (1935). ∎

Young, Robert (1907–), actor. Worked at odd jobs and in stock, appearing in dozens of productions, before entering films in the early 1930s. Handsome and debonair, he played likable characters in numerous films and appeared in both dramas and comedies, often as the male lead. But he sometimes lost the girl to other stars. After almost three decades of starring in more than 90 minor and major productions, he switched to television, where he scored another success in several shows, especially "Father Knows Best" and "Marcus Welby, M.D.," and won three Emmy Awards.

SELECTED FILMS: The Black Camel (1931), The Wet Parade, The Kid From Spain (1932), Tugboat Annie (1933), Carolina, Spitfire (1934), Calm Yourself, The Bride Comes Home (1935), The Bride Walks Out (1936), I Met Him in Paris, Married Before Breakfast, The Bride Wore Red (1937), Paradise for Three, The Toy Wife (1938), Honolulu, Maisie (1939), Lady Be Good, Married Bachelor (1941), Slightly Dangerous (1943), Claudia and David (1946), Sitting Pretty (1948), Bride for Sale, And Baby Makes Three (1951), Secret of the Incas (1954). ∎

Young, Roland (1887–1953), actor. Appeared on stage in his native England in 1908 and in the United States four years later. He made sporadic appearances in silent films, but it was during the sound era that he gained popularity. A comic character player, he had featured roles as dapper gentlemen in numerous light films, most memorably as the capricious Cosmo Topper in the series by that name. He was nominated for an Academy Award for the above role in the first film in the series.

In *One Hour With You*, Young, suspecting his wife of having an affair with another man, hires a detective to follow her. He looks up at a portrait of his wife as a blonde and confesses to the investigator: "When I married her she was a brunette. Now you can't believe a word she says."

SELECTED FILMS: *Sherlock Holmes* (1922), *New Moon* (1931), *One Hour With You*, *This Is the Night* (1932), *Pleasure Cruise* (1933), *His Double Life* (1934), *Ruggles of Red Gap* (1935), *The Unguarded Hour* (1936), *Topper*, *Ali Baba Goes to Town* (1937), *Topper Takes a Trip* (1938), *Yes, My Darling Daughter* (1939), *Private Affairs, No, No, Nanette, The Philadelphia Story* (1940), *Topper Returns, Two-Faced Woman* (1941), *The Lady Has Plans* (1942), *Standing Room Only* (1944), *The Great Lover* (1949), *That Man From Tangier* (1953). ∎

Young, Tammany (1887–1936), actor. Appeared as a supporting player in silent and early sound comedies. He worked with some of the leading comics of the period, including, among others, W. C. FIELDS and Mae WEST.

SELECTED FILMS: *Checkers, A Regular Girl* (1919), *Bits of Life, The Right Way* (1921), *A Bride for a Knight* (1923), *Sally of the Sawdust* (1925), *The Perfect Sap* (1927), *The Rube, Roadhouse Nights* (1930), *She Done Him Wrong* (1933), *Six of a Kind, You're Telling Me, The Old Fashioned Way, It's a Gift* (1934), *The Man on the Flying Trapeze* (1935), *Poppy* (1936). ∎

Young, Waldemar (1890–1938), screenwriter. Began his Hollywood career as a writer in 1917. He wrote dramatic and light screenplays alone and in collaboration for different studios. His career spanned three decades and included the silent and sound periods.

SELECTED FILMS: *The Fire Flingers* (1919), *Suds* (1920), *Our Leading Citizen* (1922), *You Can't Fool Your Wife,*

Salomy Jane (1923), *Women Love Diamonds* (1927), *Sally* (1929), *Penrod and Sam* (1931), *Love Me Tonight, Sinners in the Sun* (1932), *A Bedtime Story* (1933), *Poppy* (1936), *Man-Proof, Test Pilot* (1938). ∎

Teri Garr, Marty Feldman, Gene Wilder, and Peter Boyle in Young Frankenstein (1974)

Young Frankenstein (1974), TCF. Dir. Mel Brooks; Sc. Mel Brooks, Gene Wilder; with Gene Wilder, Peter Boyle, Marty Feldman, Teri Garr, Madeleine Kahn, Cloris Leachman.

Mel BROOKS' spoof of the mad-monster movies of the 1930s and 1940s became one of his most popular comedies among his many fans. He assembled several well-known screen stars, particularly those in the field of comedy. He shot the feature in black and white, using realistic sets and some of the equipment from the original thrillers. Gene WILDER, a third-generation Dr. Frankenstein, arrives in Europe to take over the family castle. "Pardon me, boy," he asks at the depot, "is this the Transylvania Station?" Standing in front of his father's castle and carrying his buxom assistant Teri GARR, Wilder says of the two huge appurtenances hanging from the door: "What a pair of knockers!" To which Garr replies: "Thank you." Once in his ancestor's lab, he becomes engrossed in the family experiments and attempts to breathe life into a monster (Peter Boyle). He is assisted by Igor (Marty FELDMAN), whose hump keeps shifting shoulders. Later, at a demonstration before a group of skeptical scientists, Wilder and his creation, dressed in a tuxedo, go into a dance routine to the tune of "Puttin' on the Ritz," one of the highlights of the work. Another glorious moment is the sequence with a blind man, a hilarious allusion to the original in *Bride of Frankenstein* (1935). The film was an unqualified success with both critics and audiences.

Youngman, Henny (1906–), comedian, actor. Worked in vaudeville and on stage before entering films in the 1940s. His screen appearances have been sporadic. A veteran stand-up comic, he has added comedy relief to light films.

SELECTED FILMS: *A Wave, a Wac and a Marine* (1944), *Nashville Rebel* (1966), *Won Ton Ton, the Dog Who Saved Hollywood, Silent Movie* (1976), *History of the World—Part I, National Lampoon Goes to the Movies* (1981). ■

Youngson, Robert (1917–1974), producer, compiler. Produced, wrote, and directed film shorts in the late 1940s and 1950s, two of which won Oscars. He later made a series of successful COMPILATION FILMS composed of excerpts from silent and sound comedies.

SELECTED FILMS: *50 Years Before Your Eyes* (1950), *The Golden Age of Comedy* (1957), *When Comedy Was King* (1960), *Days of Thrills and Laughter* (1961), *30 Years of Fun* (1963), *MGM's Big Parade of Comedy* (1964), *Laurel and Hardy's Laughing 1920s* (1965), *The Further Perils of Laurel and Hardy* (1968), *Four Clowns* (1970). ■

Youth sexploitation comedy. A film genre that focuses its visual and verbal gags on sexual teasing, embarrassment, and naivete. The films, invariably featuring young performers, one of whom is usually anxious to learn about sex, and a rock music sound track, gained popularity in the 1970s and 1980s. The settings often are high school or college campuses, where little learning occurs;

beaches, where bikinis are omnipresent; and resorts, where much of the slapstick comedy takes place.

SELECTED FILMS: *Guess What We Learned in School Today* (1970), *Cherry Hill High* (1972), *Hot Times* (1974), *Feelin' Up* (1976), *Seniors* (1978), *Incoming Freshmen* (1979), *Foolin' Around, Little Darlings* (1980), *Hot Bubblegum, Porky's, Private Lessons* (1981), *Beach Girls, Fast Times at Ridgemont High, Losin' It* (1982), *Private School, Risky Business, Screwballs, Spring Break* (1983), *Bachelor Party, Hardbodies, No Small Affair, Preppies, The Wild Life* (1984), *Private Resort* (1985). ■

Yule, Joe (1894–1950), actor. Worked in burlesque, vaudeville, and stock before entering films in 1939. A veteran comic, he appeared as a character player in several light films. He co-starred as Jiggs in the "JIGGS AND MAGGIE" comedy series of the late 1940s. His son, Mickey ROONEY, has continued the family tradition of performing comedy on both the stage and screen.

SELECTED FILMS: *Idiot's Delight, Sudden Money, Judge Hardy and Son* (1939), *Broadway Melody of 1940* (1940), *Kathleen* (1941), *Born to Sing, Jackass Mail* (1942), *Nothing but Trouble* (1944), *Bringing Up Father* (1946), *Jiggs and Maggie in Society* (1947), *Jiggs and Maggie Out West* (1950). ■

Zelig. See Woody Allen.

Zorina, Vera (1917–), actress, dancer. Appeared as a dancer on stage in her native Germany and in the United States before entering films in the late 1930s. She had featured roles in several entertaining films in which she danced and acted. By the late 1940s, as her screen career declined, she left Hollywood and returned to the stage.

In *Louisiana Purchase* she portrayed the owner of a posh New Orleans restaurant who has the dubious honor of joining Victor MOORE, as a United States senator, for lunch. Moore drinks only hot water with his meals. "Will you have some?" he offers. "Hot water?" she asks. "Yes." "No, thank you," she replies. "I've just had my bath."

SELECTED FILMS: The Goldwyn Follies (1938), On Your Toes (1939), Louisiana Purchase (1944), Star Spangled Rhythm (1942), Follow the Boys (1944), Lover Come Back (1946). ■